FEDERAL TAXATION OF PROPERTY TRANSACTIONS

LexisNexis GRADUATE TAX SERIES

FEDERAL TAXATION OF PROPERTY TRANSACTIONS

DAVID L. CAMERON

ELLIOTT MANNING

LexisNexis®

Casebook ISBN: 978-1-5934-5886-7
eBook ISBN: 978-0-3271-7690-9

Library of Congress Cataloging-in-Publication Data

Cameron, David L., 1957-
Federal taxation of property transactions / David L. Cameron, Elliott Manning
p. cm.
Includes index.
ISBN 978-1-5934-5886-7
1. Capital gains tax--Law and legislation--United States. 2. Property tax--Law and legislation--United States. 3. Income tax deductions for losses--United States. I. Manning, Elliott. II. Title.
KF6566.C36 2012
343.7305'245--dc23 2011048187

NOTE TO USERS
To ensure that you are using the latest materials available in this area, please be sure to periodically check the LexisNexis Law School web site for downloadable updates and supplements at www.lexisnexis.com/lawschool.

Editorial Offices
121 Chanlon Rd., New Providence, NJ 07974 (908) 464-6800
201 Mission St., San Francisco, CA 94105-1831 (415) 908-3200
www.lexisnexis.com

MATTHEW BENDER

(2012–Pub.3641)

PREFACE

The Lexis Graduate Tax Series grew out of the recognition that the goals of a graduate tax program are different from those of the tax curriculum at the J.D. level. J.D. tax courses are introductory in nature. Although many J.D. tax courses provide a good overview of their targeted areas of law, time rarely permits either an in-depth analysis of the more complicated provisions of the Code or Regulation or the application of those provisions to real-life problems. In essence, J.D. tax courses provide students a foundation in the core statutory and judicial concepts while a graduate tax program requires that students confront and apply the tax law that is applicable to sophisticated business transactions.

LL.M. programs build on, and significantly expand, students' knowledge of the Code, Regulations, and judicial doctrines, and enhance their Code and Regulations reading skills. LL.M. programs typically require students to concentrate on the primary sources of the law—the Code and Regulations. Students are expected to improve their ability to read, comprehend, and apply the Code and Regulations, and they do so by working on complex fact patterns that raise difficult legal issues.

At the same time, the regulatory construct has been in a state of considerable flux. Historically, matters were neatly divided between the SEC and the states. With its creation in 1934, the SEC was assigned the task of regulating corporate disclosure, particularly financial disclosure, while states continued to regulate the substantive standards of corporate governance. But in response to various corporate scandals and crises — most significantly, after the collapse of Enron and WorldCom in 2001 and 2002 — the post-Depression division of authority has shifted.

An important, but different, driving force behind the development of specially designed course materials for LL.M. programs is the dramatic expansion of the quantity and complexity of tax law over the past 40 to 50 years. The current commercially available versions of the Code and Regulations are roughly four times as large as their 1970 predecessors. Over that period, class time dedicated to tax has grown very little at the J.D. level. Covering much more material in the same period has led authors to write longer J.D. textbooks, many of which exceed one thousand pages. Such comprehensive coverage leads to extended textbook assignments. This both forces and permits students to bypass the assigned Code and Regulations provisions and spend their available time answering problems by reference solely to the author's explanation of the law in the textbook. Tax casebooks written primarily for the larger J.D. market that purport to be suitable for both J.D. and LL.M. tax courses also lean toward comprehensive explanations of the Code and Regulations, which tend to deflect students away from the primary sources.

Books in the Graduate Tax Series are designed to be read with, and complement, the study of the Code, Regulations, and underlying principles of the tax law. Although some chapters of the books in the Series provide a detailed explanation of a topic, more frequently the chapters provide a general, typically brief, overview of the topic together with more complete explanations of the applicable portions of the Code and Regulations that are particularly difficult to understand. Also, many of the problems are based on situations encountered in practice or found in decided cases. Although some of the questions either state or disclose the issues and even the applicable statutes, many of them require analysis of a given set of facts to first determine and then resolve the critical issues.

Students need to recognize that shifting the emphasis to primary sources and practice-based problems, which is made possible by reducing the time spent reading and analyzing cases and various secondary sources, increases the responsibility of the student for his or her education. It is harder to master a complex statute or regulation by studying it than it is to have someone explain it. It is also harder to identify the issues and applicable law from a group of facts than it is to answer short problems that identify the issue and the applicable law.

Students in an LL.M. program should be able to handle the higher level of personal responsibility. Furthermore, if one accepts the premise that students in an LL.M. program should develop the reading and comprehension skills necessary to interpret the Code and Regulations as well as master the core substantive concepts of the tax law, it is clear that students must dedicate a significant portion of their study time to the primary sources of the law. Like other books in the series, the focus of this book on the taxation of property transactions requires that students read, and grapple with, significant portions of the Code and Regulations.

In one sense, the taxation of property transactions is relatively straightforward. Tax practitioners typically think in terms of the taxpayer's investment in acquired property (i.e., the taxpayer's basis in that property), the possible recovery by the taxpayer of that investment while holding the property (i.e., depreciation or amortization), and the taxation of any gain or loss on a subsequent disposition of the property (i.e., gain or loss realization and recognition). But each of these areas involves considerable complexity, depending on the way in which the taxpayer acquired the property, whether the property was acquired separately or as part of an existing trade or business, the existence of any debt or other liability incurred in acquiring the property, the purpose for which the taxpayer holds the property, and the manner in which the property is disposed of. In addition, consideration must be given to the differences that exist between the treatment of tangible and intangible property, many of which are based on the historical evolution of the tax law and some of which reflect the increasing importance and value of intangible property as a business asset. At every step in this process, planning opportunities arise that permit tax practitioners to minimize the tax implications for their clients.

Two significant complications affect the taxation of property transactions. The first complication is the special treatment of capital gains and losses. Net capital gain in the hands of individuals is eligible for preferential rate rates while the deduction of capital losses is limited for both individual and corporate taxpayers. Transactions are frequently structured in an attempt to create net capital gain and avoid the characterization of losses as capital. Consequently, a thorough grounding in the characterization provisions of the Code and the effects of characterization on the taxpayer is essential to understand the application of the tax law. The second complication arises from the time value of money. Tax provisions that permit the generation of tax losses, in the form of interest and depreciation deductions, for example, may result in tax savings in early years even when these tax savings are offset by greater tax liability in later years. Taxpayers take these tax effects into account when evaluating different investments, and Congress has adopted a number of provisions to reduce the distortion of investment decisions that the tax law would otherwise create. This book aims to provide students with an appreciation for these two significant complexities through the descriptive materials and problems presented.

More specifically, Chapter 1 introduces the concepts of basis and realization that are fundamental to the taxation of all transactions involving property. Chapter 2 follows with the effects of taxing gains and losses from capital assets differently from ordinary gains and losses. Chapter 3 deals with liabilities, which are essentially the opposite of assets or property, so that they can be considered negative property. The tax effect of liabilities is, however, governed by different rules from those that relate to property. Although they affect the taxation of capital gains and losses, they are not similarly classified, so that relief from liability depends on the nature of the transaction giving rise to that relief. Chapter 4 covers the rules applicable to the capitalization of costs incurred in the creation or acquisition of property and the recovery of those costs through a variety of expensing, amortization, and depreciation provisions. Chapter 5 covers non-recognition transactions (other than transfers involving partnerships, corporations or trusts) in which gain or loss is not recognized on disposition but is deferred through the mechanism of substituted basis. Chapter 6 deals with deferred compensation issues and other special problems arising in executive compensation arrangement using employer stock or stock options that reflect the lure of capital gain treatment. Chapter 7 covers the complexities that arise from the cliché that property is a bundle of rights, particularly when the ownership and long-term right to possession is divided under a lease or similar arrangement. This chapter also includes issues involving transfers of partial interests in property, including life estates and remainders, and transfers of interests in intangible property represented by patents, copyrights, goodwill and similar intangible assets. Finally, Chapter 8 covers a number of special provisions that affect the deductibility of losses, including the wash sales rules, limitations on related party transactions, the at-risk and passive loss rules, and losses arising in certain leasing transactions.

In this course, students should focus on the assigned provisions of the Internal Revenue Code and Treasury Regulations, as well as the text and materials in the book, in analyzing the problems. The problems are designed to cover all of the core principles. Many of the problems include citations to cases or rulings, sometimes cases or rulings on which the problems are based. Students are encouraged to explore the cited cases and rulings in connection with working out the problems, although it is preferable that students try first to analyze them on their own. Students should also be aware that the law in many areas is uncertain and that practitioners (as well as the authors) do not necessarily agree with the analysis or results in some of the cited cases or rulings.

The material covered in a LL.M. course on the taxation of property transactions may also include some topics that are not addressed in this book, such as deferred payment sales, limitations on interest deductions, and the original issue discount rules. These topics are covered in another book in the Graduate Tax Series written by Professors Michael Lang, Elliott Manning, and Mona Hymel: Lang, Manning & Hymel, Federal Tax Accounting (Lexis/Nexis 2d ed., 2011). Their book, which also covers capitalization, amortization, and depreciation issues, is a useful complement to the material present here.

Although there is a vast literature on taxation of property transactions—principally in the form of articles in tax journals—most such articles focus on detailed aspects of the Code and Regulations. For students looking for additional discussion of the topics covered in this book, a helpful study guide is the last half of CHIRELSTEIN & ZELENAK, FEDERAL INCOME TAXATION (Foundation Press 12th ed., 2011). Students might also consider reading relevant portions of two excellent treatises for further coverage: BITTKER & LOKKEN, FEDERAL TAXATION OF INCOME, ESTATES AND GIFTS (WG & L 3d ed., 2005), and BITTKER, MCMAHON & ZELENAK, FEDERAL INCOME TAXATION OF INDIVIDUALS (WG &L 3d ed., 2002).

Portions of Chapter 2, Capital Gains and Losses, have been reprinted by permission of

CCH, a Wolters Kluwer business, from *Taxation of Capital Gains and Losses*, by John H. Birkeland and David Cameron.

Elliott Manning thanks his wife, Gail, for putting up with him during the writing process and otherwise. David Cameron thanks his spouse, Jane, for her support and encouragement during this and other taxing projects.

TABLE OF CONTENTS

Chapter 1 BASIS AND REALIZATION . . . 1

§ 1. INTRODUCTION . . . 1
§ 2. BASIS . . . 2
§ 2.01. In General . . . 2
Gladden v. Commissioner . . . 3
Notes and Comments . . . 7
Problems for Discussion . . . 8
§ 2.02. Tax Cost Basis . . . 9
§ 2.03. Basis of Gifts . . . 10
§ 2.04. Basis of Inherited Property . . . 12
§ 2.05. Substituted Basis . . . 13
§ 2.06. Basis of Property Received in a Taxable Exchange . . . 15
Philadelphia Park Amusement Co. v. United States . . . 15
Notes and Comments . . . 18
Problem for Discussion . . . 20
§ 2.07. Split Basis . . . 20
§ 2.08. Inclusion of Debt in Basis . . . 22
§ 2.09. Adjustments to Basis . . . 22
§ 3. REALIZATION OF GAIN OR LOSS . . . 23
§ 3.01. In General . . . 23
§ 3.02. Sale or Exchange . . . 24
Cottage Savings Association v. Commissioner . . . 25
Notes and Comments . . . 32
Problems for Discussion . . . 35
§ 3.03. Other Dispositions . . . 35
§ 3.03(a) Casualties and Abandonment . . . 35
§ 3.03(b) Transfer in Satisfaction of a Claim . . . 36
International Freighting Corporation, Inc. v. Commissioner . . . 37
Notes and Comments . . . 39
Problems for Discussion . . . 41
§ 3.03(c) Mortgaging Property as a Realization Event . . . 41
Woodsam Associates, Inc. v. Commissioner . . . 42
Notes and Comments . . . 44
§ 3.04. Part Sale/Part Gift . . . 44
Problem for Discussion . . . 45
§ 3.05. Inclusion of Debt in the Amount Realized . . . 46
§ 3.06. Recognition and Allowance . . . 46
§ 4. SALE OF A BUSINESS . . . 47

§ 4.01. Overview . . . 47
Williams v. McGowan . . . 47
Notes and Comments . . . 50
Problem for Discussion . . . 50
§ 4.02. § 1060 And the Residual Allocation Method . . . 50
Concord Control, Inc. v. Commissioner . . . 51
Notes and Comments . . . 54
Problem for Discussion . . . 56
§ 4.03. Contingent Payments and Liabilities . . . 56
Illinois Tool Works, Inc. v. Commissioner . . . 58
Notes and Comments . . . 66

Chapter 2 CAPITAL GAINS AND LOSSES . . . 69

§ 1. INTRODUCTION . . . 69
§ 2. MECHANICS OF DETERMINING NET CAPITAL GAIN . . . 73
§ 2.01 Non-Corporate Taxpayers . . . 73
(a) Applicable Tax Rates . . . 73
(b) Netting Capital Gains and Losses . . . 75
(c) Look-Through Rules Applicable to Pass-Through Entities . . . 80
(d) Capital Loss Limitations . . . 80
Problem for Discussion . . . 83
§ 2.02 Capital Gain and Loss Treatment for Corporate Taxpayers . . . 83
§ 3. DEFINITION OF A CAPITAL ASSET . . . 84
§ 3.01 Overview . . . 84
§ 3.02 Definition of "Property" . . . 85
Lattera v. Commissioner . . . 88
Problems for Discussion . . . 97
§ 3.03 Capital Asset Defined . . . 98
(a) Dealer Property . . . 100
Suburban Realty Company v. United States . . . 103
NOTES . . . 114
(b) Property Used in a Trade or Business . . . 124
(c) Intellectual and Artistic Property . . . 124
(d) Certain Notes and Accounts Receivable . . . 127
(e) Government Publications . . . 128
(f) Hedging Transactions . . . 129
(g) Commodities Derivative Financial Instruments . . . 132
(h) Trade or Business Supplies . . . 133
§ 4 SALE OR EXCHANGE . . . 133
§ 4.01 Overview . . . 133
§ 4.02 Judicial Interpretation . . . 135

Freeland v. Commissioner . . . 136
Notes . . . 140
Problems for Discussion . . . 141
§ 4.03 Extinguishment Doctrine . . . 141
Pounds v. United States . . . 143
§ 4.04 Statutory Sales . . . 145
(a) Worthless Securities and Nonbusiness Bad Debts . . . 146
(b) Loss on the Lapse of an Option . . . 146
(c) Amounts Received on the Cancellation of a Lease . . . 146
(d) Amounts Received on the Cancellation of Certain Property Rights . . 147
Problems for Discussion . . . 148
(e) Miscellaneous Statutory Sales . . . 149
§ 5. HOLDING PERIOD . . . 149
§ 5.01 Overview . . . 149
§ 5.02 Basic Rules for Determining Holding Period . . . 150
Problem for Discussion . . . 151
§ 5.03 Split Holding Periods . . . 151
§ 5.04 Holding Period for Inherited Property . . . 155
§ 5.05 Tacked Holding Periods . . . 155
(a) Tacking Permitted in Substituted Basis Transactions . . . 155
(b) Tacking Permitted in Carryover Basis Transactions . . . 157
(c) Miscellaneous Tacking Provisions . . . 158
Revenue Ruling 62-140 . . . 160
NOTE . . . 161
Problem for Discussion . . . 161
§ 6. SECTION 1231 GAINS AND LOSSES . . . 161
§ 6.01 Overview . . . 161
§ 6.02 The Mechanics of Section 1231 . . . 166
(a) Types of Property Included Under § 1231 . . . 166
(b) The Preliminary Hotchpot . . . 167
(c) The Primary Hotchpot . . . 169
(d) Non-Recaptured Net § 1231 Losses . . . 171
§ 6.03 Definition of Property Used in the Trade or Business . . . 173
(a) Property Used in the Trade or Business . . . 174
(b) The Inventory Exclusion . . . 175
(c) Miscellaneous Property Under § 1231 . . . 176
Problem for Discussion . . . 177

Chapter 3 LIABILITIES: DISCHARGE OF INDEBTEDNESS; MORTGAGED PROPERTY . . . 179

§ 1. WHAT IS A LIABILITY? . . . 180
§ 1.01. Conditions and Contingencies . . . 181
Milenbach v. Commissioner . . . 181
Milenbach v. Commissioner . . . 185
Notes and Comments . . . 186
Problems for Discussion . . . 187
§ 1.02. Obligations v. Liabilities . . . 188
Rev. Rul. 80-198, 1980-2 C.B. 113 . . . 188
Rev. Rul. 88-77, 1988-2 C.B. 129 . . . 190
Notes and Comments . . . 191
Albertson's, Inc. v. Commissioner . . . 191
Notes and Comments . . . 196
Problems for Discussion . . . 198
§ 2. DISCHARGE OF INDEBTEDNESS (DOI) . . . 199
§ 2.01. What Is DOI Income? . . . 199
United States v. Kirby Lumber Co. . . . 199
Notes and Comments . . . 200
Problems for Discussion . . . 202
§ 2.02. Medium of Payment . . . 203
United States v. Centennial Savings Bank FSB . . . 204
Notes and Comments . . . 207
Problems for Discussion . . . 209
§ 2.03. Disputed or Contingent Liability . . . 210
Zarin v. Commissioner . . . 210
Notes and Comments . . . 217
Problems for Discussion . . . 219
§ 3. MORTGAGED PROPERTY . . . 221
§ 3.01. In General . . . 221
§ 3.01(a). Basis . . . 221
Crane v. Commissioner . . . 222
Notes and Comments . . . 228
Problems for Discussion . . . 228
§ 3.01(b). Amount Realized . . . 229
Estate of Levine v. Commissioner . . . 229
Notes and Comments . . . 234
Problem for Discussion . . . 234
Commissioner v. Tufts . . . 235
Notes and Comments . . . 241
Problem for Discussion . . . 241

§ 3.02. Contingencies . . . 242
Mayerson v. Commissioner . . . 242
Notes and Comments . . . 247
Est. of Franklin v. Commissioner . . . 248
Notes and Comments . . . 251
Problems for Discussion . . . 251
§ 3.03. Speculative Security . . . 252
Brountas v. Commissioner . . . 252
Notes and Comments . . . 258
Problem for Discussion . . . 259
§ 3.04. *Tufts* and § 108(e)(5) . . . 260
Fulton Gold Corp. v. Commissioner . . . 261
Notes and Comments . . . 262
Rev. Rul. 91-31, 1991-1 C.B. 19 . . . 262
Notes and Comments . . . 263
Problems for Discussion . . . 265
§ 4. LIABILITY TRANSFER . . . 266
§ 4.01. Primary and Secondary Liability . . . 266
Lessinger v. Commissioner . . . 268
Notes and Comments . . . 274
Problems for Discussion . . . 276
§ 4.02. Deficiency . . . 278
Aizawa v. Commissioner . . . 278
Notes and Comments . . . 280
Problem for Discussion . . . 281
§ 4.03. Deductible Items . . . 281
Commercial Security Bank v. Commissioner . . . 281
Notes and Comments . . . 284
Problem for Discussion . . . 286
§ 5. DOI INCOME AND § 108 . . . 287
§ 5.01. Insolvency . . . 288
Carlson v. Commissioner . . . 288
Notes and Comments . . . 293
Merkel v. Commissioner . . . 293
Notes and Comments . . . 297
Rev. Rul. 90-16, 1990-1 C.B. 12 . . . 298
Notes and Comments . . . 299
Problem for Discussion . . . 299
§ 5.02. Attribute Reduction . . . 299
§ 5.03. Basis Reduction — § 1017 . . . 300
Problem for Discussion . . . 302

Chapter 4 CAPITALIZATION AND COST RECOVERY 305

§ 1. INTRODUCTION 305
§ 1.01. In General 305
§ 1.02. The Economics of Capitalization and Cost Recovery 306
§ 2. CAPITALIZATION 312
§ 2.01. In General 312
Indopco, Inc. v. Commissioner 316
Commissioner v. Idaho Power Co. 321
Encyclopaedia Britannica, Inc. v. Commissioner 328
Notes and Comments 331
§ 2.02. Uniform Capitalization Rules 332
Problem for Discussion 336
§ 2.03. Tangible Assets 337
Problem for Discussion 342
§ 2.04. Intangible Assets 342
Problems for Discussion 347
§ 2.05. Disputes and Litigation — Origin of the Claim 348
Woodward v. Commissioner 348
Problem for Discussion 351
§ 3. COST RECOVERY FOR TANGIBLE ASSETS 351
§ 3.01. In General 351
§ 3.02. Start-Up Expenditures 352
Revenue Ruling 99-23 354
Problem for Discussion 359
§ 3.03. Election to Expense Certain Business Assets 359
§ 3.04. Expensing of Certain Capital Expenditures 361
(a) Research and Experimental Expenses 361
Notes and Comments 363
(b) Environmental Remediation Costs 364
Revenue Ruling 94-38 365
Notes and Comments 368
Problem for Discussion 368
(c) Intangible Drilling Costs 369
(d) Mining Exploration and Development 371
§ 3.05. Bonus Depreciation 373
§ 3.06. Modified Accelerated Cost Recovery System 375
(a) General Principals 375
Simon v. Commissioner 376
Notes and Comments 387
(b) Mechanics of Depreciation 387
Revenue Procedure 87-56 392

Revenue Procedure 87-57 . . . 399
Notes and Comments . . . 418
(c) Special Provisions . . . 420
Problems for Discussion . . . 427
§ 3.07. Amortization of Intangible Assets . . . 428
(a) Section 197 Intangibles Assets . . . 429
(b) Non-Section 197 Intangible Assets . . . 432
Associated Patentees, Inc. v. Commissioner . . . 433
Revenue Ruling 60-358 . . . 435
Notes and Comments . . . 437
Problems for Discussion . . . 440
§ 3.08. Depletion . . . 441
§ 4. DEPRECIATION RECAPTURE . . . 444
§ 4.01. Personal Property . . . 445
§ 4.02. Real Property . . . 448
§ 4.03. Mining Interests and Timber . . . 449

Chapter 5 NONRECOGNITION TRANSACTIONS . . . 451

§ 1. LIKE-KIND EXCHANGES . . . 452
§ 1.01. Exchange . . . 453
Century Electric Co. v. Commissioner . . . 453
Jordan Marsh Co. v. Commissioner . . . 455
Notes and Comments . . . 459
Problems for Discussion . . . 461
§ 1.02. Boot, Liabilities and Basis . . . 462
§ 1.02(a). Liabilities . . . 464
Garcia v. Commissioner . . . 465
Rev. Rul. 79-44, 1979-1 C.B. 265 . . . 467
Notes and Comments . . . 468
Problem for Discussion . . . 469
§ 1.02(b). Boot and Installment Sales . . . 470
Installment Sales Revision Act of 1980 . . . 470
Notes and Comments . . . 472
Problem for Discussion . . . 474
§ 1.03. Multiparty Exchanges . . . 474
Rev. Rul. 75-291, 1975-2 C.B. 332 . . . 474
Rev. Rul. 77-297, 1977-2 C.B. 304 . . . 475
Barker v. Commissioner . . . 476
Notes and Comments . . . 479
Problem for Discussion . . . 481
§ 1.04. Deferred Exchanges . . . 483

Starker v. United States 483
Notes and Comments 491
Problem for Discussion 494
§ 1.05. Reverse *Starker* Exchanges 496
Rev. Proc. 2000-37, 2000-2 C.B. 308, *as modified by* Rev. Proc. 2004-51, 2004-2 C.B. 294 497
Notes and Comments 502
Problem for Discussion 504
§ 1.06. Like Kind 506
Rev. Rul. 82-96, 1982-1 C.B. 113 507
Rev. Rul. 82-166, 1982-2 C.B. 190 508
Notes and Comments 508
Problems for Discussion 515
§ 1.07. Held 516
Magneson v. Commissioner 516
Notes and Comments 521
Problems for Discussion 523
§ 1.08. Related Parties 524
Teruya Bros., Ltd. v. Commissioner 525
Notes and Comments 531
Problem for Discussion 532
§ 2. INVOLUNTARY CONVERSION 533
§ 2.01. Involuntary 534
Willamette Industries, Inc. v. Commissioner 535
Notes and Comments 541
Problem for Discussion 543
§ 2.02. Similar in Service or Use 544
Rev. Rul. 67-254, 1967-2 C.B. 269 544
Notes and Comments 545
Problem for Discussion 546
§ 2.03. Investor-Lessor 546
Rev. Rul. 64-237, 1964-2 C.B. 319 546
Notes and Comments 547
Problem for Discussion 548
§ 2.04. Like Kind Revisited 549
Rev. Rul. 67-255, 1967-2 C.B. 270 549
Notes and Comments 550
Problems for Discussion 552
§ 2.05. Proceeds 552
Buffalo Wire Works Co. Inc. v. Commissioner 553
Notes and Comments 560

Problems for Discussion 561
§ 3. OTHER NONRECOGNITION PROVISIONS 562
§ 3.01. Installment Sales and Repossessions 562
Greene v. Commissioner 563
Notes and Comments 567
Problems for Discussion 568
§ 3.02. Principal Residences 569
Rev. Proc. 2005-14, 2005-7 I.R.B. 528 571
Notes and Comments 576
Problem for Discussion 576
§ 3.03. Charitable Contributions 578
Haverly v. United States 578
Notes and Comments 580
Problem for Discussion 581

Chapter 6 EXECUTIVE COMPENSATION AND STOCK OPTIONS 583

§ 1. DEFERRED COMPENSATION 584
§ 1.01. Traditional Deferred Compensation Principles 584
Rev. Rul. 60-31, 1960-1 C.B. 174, *modified by* Rev. Rul. 64-279, 1964-2 C.B. 121 and Rev. Rul. 70-435, 1970-2 C.B. 100 584
Notes and Comments 589
Problem for Discussion 592
§ 1.02. 2004 Limitations — § 409A 593
Problem for Discussion 598
§ 2. RESTRICTED PROPERTY 599
§ 2.01. Stock Appreciation Rights (SARs) 599
Rev. Rul. 80-300, 1980-2 C.B. 165 599
Notes and Comments 600
Problem for Discussion 601
§ 2.02. Restricted Property — § 83 602
Alves v. Commissioner 607
Notes and Comments 610
Problems for Discussion 613
§ 2.03. Shareholder Grants 614
Rev. Rul. 80-76, 1980-1 C.B. 15 614
Notes and Comments 615
Problems for Discussion 615
§ 3. NONSTATUTORY STOCK OPTIONS (NSOs) 616
§ 3.01. Purchased Options 616
Rev. Rul. 78-182, 1978-1 C.B. 265 617

Notes and Comments 623
Problem for Discussion 624
§ 3.02. Grant, Exercise and Lapse of NSOs 624
Commissioner v. Lo Bue 625
Notes and Comments 628
Problems for Discussion 631
§ 3.03. Transfers of NSOs 632
Weigl v. Commissioner 632
Notes and Comments 642
Problems for Discussion 644
§ 3.04. Noncompensatory NSOs 645
§ 3.04(a). Determining Whether NSO Is Compensatory or Noncompensatory . 646
Centel Communications Co., Inc. v. Commissioner 647
Notes and Comments 655
Problem for Discussion 656
§ 3.04(b). Noncompensatory Options Taxed on Exercise 657
Sun Microsystems, Inc. v. Commissioner 657
Notes and Comments 662
Problems for Discussion 664
§ 3.05. Valuing NSOs 665
Problems for Discussion 666
§ 4. INCENTIVE STOCK OPTIONS (ISOs) 667
§ 4.01. ISO Requirements and Effects 667
Schumann v. Commissioner 670
Notes and Comments 672
Problems for Discussion 674
§ 4.02. Alternative Minimum Tax ("AMT") and ISOs 676
§ 4.02(a). Computing the AMT 676
Notes and Comments 678
Problem for Discussion 678
§ 4.02(b). The AMT and ISOs 679
Gresham v. Commissioner 679
Notes and Comments 682
Merlo v. Commissioner 682
Notes and Comments 686
Problem for Discussion 687
§ 4.02(c). Net Operating Loss ("NOL") Carryovers Under the AMT ("ATNOL") and ISOs 688
Spitz v. Commissioner 688
Notes and Comments 692

TABLE OF CONTENTS

Chapter 7 ADVANCED CHARACTERIZATION PROBLEMS 695

§ 1. REALITY OF SALE (SALE v. LEASE) 696
§ 1.01. Bootstrap Sales 697
Commissioner v. Brown 697
Notes and Comments 704
Problem for Discussion 705
§ 1.02. Natural Resource Interests 706
Wood v. United States 706
Rev. Rul. 69-352, 1969-1 C.B. 34 710
Notes and Comments 711
Problem for Discussion 712
§ 1.03. Retained Interest v. Amount Realized 713
Alstores Realty Corp. v. Commissioner 713
Notes and Comments 718
Problems for Discussion 719
§ 1.04. Lease versus Sale 721
Rev. Rul. 55-540, 1955-2 C.B. 39 722
Notes and Comments 726
Est. of Starr v. Commissioner 726
Notes and Comments 729
Problem for Discussion 729
§ 1.05. Leveraged Leasing 729
Frank Lyon Co. v. United States 731
Notes and Comments 742
Rev. Proc. 2001-28, 2001-1 C.B. 1156 744
Notes and Comments 751
Problems for Discussion 751
§ 2. TRANSFERS OF PARTIAL INTERESTS 752
§ 2.01. Gratuitous Transfers of Partial Interests 752
§ 2.01(a). Income from Services 753
Lucas v. Earl 753
Notes and Comments 754
Problems for Discussion 755
§ 2.01(b). Income from Property 756
Blair v. Commissioner 757
Helvering v. Horst 757
Harrison v. Schaffner 760
Notes and Comments 761
Problems for Discussion 762
§ 2.01(c). Appreciated Property versus Realized Income (How Ripe is the Fruit?) 762

Ferguson v. Commissioner 762
Notes and Comments 767
Problem for Discussion 768
§ 2.01(d). Escrows 769
Problems for Discussion 770
§ 2.02. Sales of Partial Interests — Ordinary Income Substitute 770
Hort v. Commissioner 771
McAllister v. Commissioner 773
Metropolitan Building Co. v. Commissioner 775
Commissioner v. P. G. Lake, Inc. 776
Notes and Comments 779
Problems for Discussion 781
§ 3. INTANGIBLES — CONTRACT RIGHTS, SELF-CREATED PROPERTY, AND GOODWILL (AND GOING CONCERN VALUE) 781
§ 3.01. Contract Rights 782
Commissioner v. Ferrer 782
Notes and Comments 789
Problem for Discussion 790
§ 3.02. Future Services versus Goodwill 791
Bisbee-Baldwin Corp. v. Tomlinson 791
Notes and Comments 796
Problems for Discussion 800
§ 3.03. Artists, Inventors, Franchises 801
§ 3.03(a). Copyrights 802
Rev. Rul. 54-409, 1954-2 C.B. 174 802
Rev. Rul. 54-599, 1954-2 C.B. 52 803
Notes and Comments 804
Problem for Discussion 805
§ 3.03(b). Patents 805
Kueneman v. Commissioner 806
Notes and Comments 808
Problem for Discussion 809
§ 3.03(c). Franchises and Trade Names 810
Stokely USA, Inc. v. Commissioner 810
Notes and Comments 817
Problem for Discussion 818
§ 4. RELATED TAXPAYERS 818
§ 4.01. § 482 — Applicability 818
Foglesong v. Commissioner 819
Foglesong v. Commissioner 825
Notes and Comments 829
Problem for Discussion 830

§ 4.02. § 482 — Applied . . . 831
Hamburgers York Road, Inc. v. Commissioner . . . 831
Notes and Comments . . . 839
Problems for Discussion . . . 840

Chapter 8 LIMITATIONS ON DEDUCTIONS AND LOSSES . . . 843

§ 1. INTRODUCTION . . . 843
§ 2. WASH SALES OF SECURITIES . . . 844
Estate of Estroff v. Commissioner . . . 847
Notes and Comments . . . 850
Problems for Discussion . . . 852
§ 3. LOSSES BETWEEN RELATED PARTIES . . . 852
Rev. Rul. 76-377, 1976-2 C.B. 89 . . . 855
Notes and Comments . . . 856
Problem for Discussion . . . 857
§ 4. AT-RISK RULES . . . 857
§ 4.01. In General . . . 858
Staff of the Joint Committee on Taxation . . . 862
Notes and Comments . . . 868
§ 4.02. At-Risk Amount . . . 872
Hubert Enterprises, Inc. v. Commissioner . . . 874
Notes and Comments . . . 879
§ 4.03. Stop Loss Agreements . . . 881
American Principals Leasing Corp. v. United States . . . 882
Notes and Comments . . . 891
§ 4.04. Qualified Nonrecourse Financing . . . 894
Problem for Discussion . . . 895
§ 5. PASSIVE LOSSES . . . 896
§ 5.01. In General . . . 896
S. Rep. No. 99-313, 99th Cong., 2d Sess. 713-718 (1986) . . . 897
§ 5.02. Passive, Non-Passive, and Investment Activities . . . 902
§ 5.03. Material and Significant Participation . . . 905
Thompson v. United States . . . 907
Notes and Comments . . . 917
§ 5.04. Rental Activities . . . 918
Bailey v. Commissioner . . . 920
§ 5.05. Self-Charged Items . . . 928
Hillman v. Internal Revenue Service . . . 929
§ 5.06. Disposition of a Passive Activity . . . 934
Problems for Discussion . . . 935
§ 6. LIMITATIONS ON LOSSES FROM LEASING TRANSACTIONS . . . 936

TABLE OF CONTENTS

U.S. TREASURY DEPARTMENT 937

H.R. Rep. No. 108-755, 108th Cong., 2d Sess. 654–663 (2004) 940

TABLE OF CASES TC-1

TABLE OF STATUTES TS-1

TABLE OF SECONDARY AUTHORITIES TA-1

INDEX I-1

Chapter 1

BASIS AND REALIZATION

§ 1. INTRODUCTION

An understanding of the concepts of basis and realization is fundamental to understanding the taxation of property transactions. Both concepts are relatively simple and straightforward on one level yet involve complexities on a deeper level that are central to the proper implementation of an income tax system. The concept of basis attempts to account for economic value that has already been subject to income taxation in order to prevent that value from being taxed twice. In addition, basis allows the tax system to account for economic value that was subject to tax but that may have subsequently been lost due to shifting economic conditions. Similarly, the concept of realization can be thought of simply as an issue of timing — a rule regarding when gain or loss should be accounted for for tax purposes. At a deeper level, however, the concept of realization has financial implications permitting the deferral of gain and the acceleration of loss to the taxpayer's benefit.

Under § 1001, gain or loss resulting from the "sale or other disposition" of property is equal to the difference between the "amount realized" and the "adjusted basis" of the property. Each of these terms is further defined by the Code and Regulations. The following sections of this chapter describe in detail each of these terms and the manner in which they have been applied by the Service and the courts. Section 2 begins this process by examining the concept of basis. As will become evident, the determination of the basis of an item of property is complicated by numerous special rules applicable when property is acquired in a variety of ways. However, Section 2 only begins the discussion of basis. Detailed discussions of such topics as the inclusion of debt in basis, basis adjustments resulting from capital improvements and depreciation, and limitations on deductions associated with basis are covered in subsequent chapters. Section 3 addresses the issues surrounding the concepts of realization and the amount realized. Although relatively straightforward when applied in the context of a simple sale of property, they become more complicated when more sophisticated transfers involving property are involved. These more sophisticated transactions force us to more closely examine exactly what we mean when we speak of realization and the amount realized.

§ 2. BASIS

§ 2.01. In General

§ 1001(a), 1011, 1012; Treas. Reg. § 1.61-6(a), 1.1012-1

Basis is perhaps the most fundamental concept in the study of taxation. Basis is used to determine the amount of any gain or loss on the disposition of property under § 1001 and as the starting point in calculating depreciation or amortization under §§ 167 and 197. Importantly, § 61(a)(3) includes only *gains*, not the proceeds, from dealings in property in gross income, which may be a requirement based on the definition of the term "income" under the Sixteenth Amendment. Basis is as important in describing a piece of property for tax purposes as its physical dimensions, color, or weight would be in describing the property for all other purposes. Property exists for tax purposes only if its basis can be determined, even if that basis happens to be zero.

Under § 1012, the basis of property is its cost. As stated in the Regulations, "[t]he cost is the amount paid for such property in cash or other property." Treas. Reg. § 1.1012-1(a). The cost of the property is frequently referred to as the original or unadjusted basis of the property in order to distinguish the cost basis from the adjusted basis of the property under § 1011. The adjusted basis of the property is its cost basis, increased or decreased as provided under § 1016.

The cost basis of property represents the taxpayer's original investment in the property for tax purposes. For example, if a taxpayer purchases a parcel of unimproved real property for $25,000 in cash, the taxpayer will take a basis in the property of $25,000. Upon a subsequent sale of the property for $35,000, the taxpayer will have $10,000 of gain. The taxpayer is permitted to recover his $25,000 investment in the property before any gain is attributed to him. Thus, basis ensures that the $25,000 previously paid for the property with after-tax dollars is not again subject to the income tax.

If the acquisition of the property is the result of an arm's-length transaction, the Code treats the basis of the property as the amount paid for the property. If the taxpayer happened to have obtained a bargain through, perhaps, his extraordinary negotiating ability, the additional value obtained will not be subject to tax until a subsequent sale of the property. If, however, the property is not acquired in an arm's-length transaction, as for instance between a corporation and its controlling shareholder or between an employer and employee, any excess of the fair market value of the property over the amount paid may be subject to tax. In such an instance, the basis of the property will be its fair market value rather than the amount paid. The burden is on the taxpayer to demonstrate that the acquisition of the property was the result of an arm's-length transaction.

When property is acquired asset by asset for an explicit price determined by the parties, the determination of the basis of each asset is straightforward. However, property is frequently acquired in groups, as for example the assets of an on-going trade or business, in which an allocation must be made of the consideration paid among the assets acquired. When the assets of a trade or business are involved, § 1060 requires that the residual method be used by the buyer to determine the basis of each asset. When the acquisition of a group of assets does not constitute the acquisition of a trade or business, the buyer must still allocate the consideration paid among the assets according to their fair market values based on valuations agreed upon between the buyer and seller or on valuations determined by appraisal.

Importantly, even the acquisition of a single parcel of property may involve a subsequent allocation of consideration if only a portion of the property is sold. Because both tangible and intangible property may be almost infinitely divided, the question arises regarding how the basis of only a portion of property should be determined. The Regulations recognize this problem and provide that the basis of the entire property must be "equitably apportioned" among its several parts. Treas. Reg. § 1.61-6(a). The following decision applies this regulatory provision in connection with the acquisition of real and intangible property.

GLADDEN v. COMMISSIONER

United States Court Of Appeals, Ninth Circuit
262 F.3d 851 (9th Cir. 2001)

W. Fletcher, Circuit Judge:

William and Nicole Gladden ("the Gladdens") appeal the Tax Court's ruling that they cannot allocate any of their cost basis in farmland to the sale of water rights appurtenant to the land. The Tax Court held that the Gladdens acquired the water rights in a "separate transaction" that occurred after the original land purchase, and that the cost basis of the rights was therefore zero. We reverse and remand.

I

The Gladdens are 50% partners in the Saddle Mountain Ranch partnership ("the partnership"), which farms 880 acres of land in the Harquahala Valley in Arizona. The partnership purchased the land in 1976 for $675,000. At the time of purchase, the land had no appurtenant water rights, but was within the boundaries of the Harquahala Valley Irrigation District ("HID"), an Arizona municipal corporation formed in 1964 to acquire water rights and distribute irrigation water in the area. In 1968, Congress had approved the Colorado River Basin Project Act, Pub. L. No. 90-537, which authorized construction of the Central Arizona Project ("CAP") to bring water from the Colorado River to, among other places, the Harquahala Valley. The Act provided that project water "shall not be made available directly or indirectly for the irrigation of lands not having a recent irrigation history as determined by the Secretary." . . . The partnership's land was eligible to receive CAP irrigation water because it had a "recent irrigation history" when it was purchased. In 1983, HID obtained the right to take Colorado River water for redistribution within its boundaries, and the partnership in turn obtained water rights from HID. Landowners within HID initially were not allowed to sell these water rights except as part of a sale of the land to which they were appurtenant. Ten years later, however, the federal government entered into an agreement with HID allowing these landowners to sell their water rights to the government without an accompanying sale of the land. The partnership took advantage of this agreement and sold its water rights for $1,088,132. The Gladdens' share of the sale price was $543,566. In their 1993 tax return, the Gladdens listed this amount as a capital gain. They offset this gain by the portion of the original purchase price for the land that they claimed was paid for the expectation of water rights. The Gladdens' calculation led to a reported taxable capital gain of $130,762.

The Commissioner disagreed with the Gladdens. She determined that the Gladdens' share of the sale of the water rights was properly characterized as a $543,566 receipt of ordinary income, with no offset for any price paid for an expectancy in the water rights. She issued the Gladdens a $110,809 notice of deficiency. The Gladdens petitioned for review in Tax Court. They contended that the water rights were a capital asset; that there had been a "sale or exchange" within the meaning of the Tax Code; that it was proper to allocate some portion of their tax basis in the land to the sale of the water rights; and that, because it was impossible to determine what portion of the basis should be allocated to the water rights, a capital gain from the sale of the water rights should not be recognized until all of the cost basis in the land had been recovered.

The Tax Court granted summary judgment to the Gladdens on the first two issues, holding that the water rights were a capital asset and that the rights had been sold or exchanged within the meaning of the Tax Code. However, it granted summary judgment to the Commissioner on the third issue, holding that the Gladdens could not apply any of their tax basis in the land to the sale of water rights because the partnership had purchased the land before acquiring those rights. Because of its holding on the third issue, the Tax Court found it unnecessary to reach the last issue.

. . . .

II

The controlling issue in this case is whether any of the cost basis in the land purchased by the partnership in 1976 can be allocated to water rights that were expected but not legally vested at the time of the land purchase. We begin our analysis with 26 C.F.R. § 1.61-6(a), which provides:

> When a part of a larger property is sold, the cost or other basis of the entire property shall be equitably apportioned among the several parts, and the gain realized or loss sustained on the part of the entire property sold is the difference between the selling price and the cost or other basis allocated to such part.

This regulation tells us that when property is acquired in a lump-sum purchase but then divided and sold off in parts, the cost basis of the property should generally be allocated over the several parts. For example, when a developer subdivides a large tract of land and sells the smaller parcels, he must allocate his cost basis in the overall property to the smaller parcels in order to calculate his gain or loss on the sales of those parcels. . . .

Section 1.61-6(a) would be easy to apply to this case if the water rights had already been vested when the partnership had purchased the land. If this had been true, the facts would closely resemble those of Inaja Land Co., Ltd. v. Comm'r, 9 T.C. 727 (1947), where the Tax Court applied the principle that was later codified in § 1.61-6(a). The city of Los Angeles had paid the taxpayer in Inaja Land $50,000 for a contract allowing the city to flood his land, and the taxpayer wished to assign some portion of the payment to recovery of his cost basis in the land. The Commissioner argued that he could not do so because the gain was ordinary income. The Tax Court disagreed, describing the transaction as the sale of an easement for a capital gain, and stating that "where property is acquired for a lump sum and subsequently disposed of a portion at a time, there must be an allocation of the cost or other basis over the several units and gain or loss computed on the disposition of each part." . . .

Section 1.61-6(a) would also be easy to apply if the partnership had purchased the property with no expectation that it would ever be able to acquire Colorado River water rights. If this were the case, we could be sure that none of the original cost of the land was attributable to the water rights, or to any expectancy of water rights. It would obviously be improper in such a case to allow the partnership to allocate any of the cost of their original land purchase to the sale of the later-acquired rights. See Plow Realty Co. v. Comm'r, 4 T.C. 600, 609 (1945) (where land was originally valued solely for cattle grazing qualities, subsequent sale of mineral rights had cost basis of zero); Rev. Rul. 66-58, 1966-1 C.B. 186 (taxpayer could not allocate cost basis in land to sale of cotton allotment acquired after land purchase and sold separately from land).

However, the Gladdens' case falls between the two easy cases. The water rights were not vested at the time the partnership purchased its land, but the purchase was made with a realistic expectation that water rights would eventually attach to the land. The Tax Court held that since the water rights were not vested when the land was purchased, they were acquired in a "separate transaction" from the land purchase for purposes of determining their tax basis. Because the water rights were acquired at no cost, the Gladdens therefore had zero cost basis in them. The Tax Court's theory would create a bright-line rule under which a taxpayer could never apportion any of his cost basis in land to the sale of an appurtenant water right that was not fully vested in the land at the time of purchase, even though in practical economic terms that expectation had a real economic value at the time of purchase.

The Tax Court's rule appears to us to be unsound. First, it would produce odd economic consequences. Where land is purchased at a premium based on the expectation of a future water right, separating the land and water rights for the purposes of allocating basis would cause the land to have an artificially high basis and the water rights to have an artificially non-existent basis. To illustrate, suppose Greenacre and Brownacre are two parcels of land that are identical except for the fact that Greenacre is almost certain to receive (but has not yet received) federally subsidized water rights, while Brownacre will almost certainly remain parched. As a result, Brownacre sells for $500 per acre, while Greenacre sells for $1000. Assume that each parcel is purchased by a separate taxpayer, and that both eventually receive water rights. Then both taxpayers sell their water rights for $500 in one year and their land for $500 a year later. Under the Tax Court's ruling, the owner of Brownacre would report a $500 capital gain in the first year and no gain or loss in the second, which reflects economic reality. But the owner of Greenacre would report a $500 capital gain the first year, and a $500 loss in the next, when in fact neither occurred.

Second, the Tax Court's rule may conflict with existing precedent. In Piper v. Comm'r, 5 T.C. 1104 (1945), a tax-payer had previously traded securities in one company for common stock and common stock subscription warrants in another company. When the taxpayer sold the common stock (including stock subsequently obtained by exercising the warrants), he was allowed to attribute some of his original basis to the warrants. In the words of the court, "it can not be said that the warrants had no value simply because they could not be exercised to immediate financial advantage at the time they were issued. . . . The fact that [the warrants] were highly speculative and entirely prospective is no basis . . . for denying to them any value." . . .

Finally, we draw support from Revenue Ruling 86-24, 1986-1 C.B. 80. There, a farmer purchased ten cows that had been artificially impregnated with transplanted embryos. The fair market value of the cows before their impregnation was "80x dollars" but the farmer paid "250x dollars" for them. After the cows gave birth, the farmer sold them (but kept their calves), this time for $80x. The IRS ruled that the farmer would not recognize any gain or loss on the sale of the cows; of the $250x purchase price, only $80x was properly allocated to basis in the cows themselves. According to the IRS, the remaining $170x that the farmer paid was the price of the embryos, and that amount was therefore properly treated as the farmer's basis in those embryos. This result mirrors the one we reach here; the farmer's basis in the calves was the premium he paid for the cows based on his expectation that they would give birth. . . .

For the foregoing reasons, we believe that the Gladdens may apportion some of their cost basis in the land to the later sale of water rights appurtenant to that land. More precisely, we hold that where a purchaser pays a premium for land based on a realistic expectation that water rights will attach to that land in the future, the purchaser may, upon sale of the later-acquired water rights, claim a cost basis equal to the premium paid.

The IRS has not cited any cases that contradict our holding. Its brief relies principally on Niagara Mohawk Power Corp. v. United States, 525 F.2d 1380 (Ct. Cl. 1975), where the Court of Claims held that a company that acquired water rights through a merger with another company could not use as its cost basis the fair market value of those rights at the time of acquisition. . . . Instead, the court determined that the proper basis for the rights was the cost of their acquisition, measured by the value of securities exchanged to obtain them. We believe that Niagara Mohawk is consistent, rather than inconsistent with our rule, for the value attached to the water rights in that case was the price actually paid for them. In the case before us, the IRS argues that the water rights came to the partnership at no cost, and that they therefore have a basis of zero. But this argument evades the question by assuming the answer. If the partnership paid a premium for its land, it did so because the land was expected to receive water rights, just as the cows in Rev. Rul. 86-24 were expected to produce calves. One expectation was less sure than the other, but both were reasonable.

III

Having determined that the Gladdens may apply some portion of the cost basis of the partnership's land purchase to the sale of its water rights, the question then becomes how much may be applied. Inaja Land guides us again. After determining that the taxpayer in that case was entitled to allocate some portion of the cost basis of the property to the sale of the easement, the Tax Court recognized the difficulty of determining the appropriate basis with precision. . . . Noting the general rule that taxpayers "should not be charged with gain on pure conjecture unsupported by any foundation of ascertainable fact," . . . the Tax Court held that where it is "impossible or impractical" to apportion basis among several portions of a property, a taxpayer need not recognize any capital gain until the entire cost basis of the property has been recovered. . . .

The Gladdens contend that, under Inaja Land, it is "impossible or impractical" to apportion a definite basis to the water rights, and that they are therefore entitled to recover their entire cost basis in the land before reporting any capital gain from the sale. . . . We are not so sure. For example, it may be possible to determine the premium price paid for the potential water rights by comparing the price of the land purchased by the partnership to prices of similar land without a "recent history of irrigation" and therefore without any expectation of water rights. The difference between these prices would be the premium paid for the expectation of future water rights.

However, because the Tax Court ruled against the Gladdens on summary judgment, the record is undeveloped. We cannot determine, based on the record now before us, either what portion of the cost of the land may have been a premium paid for the water rights later acquired by the partnership, or whether it is "impracticable or impossible" to determine what that premium may have been.

We therefore REVERSE and REMAND for further proceedings consistent with this opinion.

NOTES AND COMMENTS

1. As noted in the Ninth Circuit's opinion, the Tax Court in *Inaja Land Co. v. Commissioner*, 9 T.C. 727 (1947), determined that it was "impossible or impractical" to apportion the basis of the larger parcel of land to the interest transferred. *Inaja* involved a conveyance to the city of Los Angeles of a right of way and perpetual easements to discharge water upon and flood the taxpayer's land in connection with the water supply of the city. The taxpayer argued, and the court agreed, that

> it would be impracticable and impossible to apportion a definite basis to the easements here involved, since they could not be described by metes and bounds; that the flow of the water has changed and will change the course of the river; that the extent of the flood was and is not predictable; and that to date the city has not released the full measure of water to which it is entitled.

Id. at 735. As a result, the taxpayer's receipt of $50,000 in return for the conveyance was treated as a recovery of the taxpayer's basis in the land and taxable only to the extent that the proceeds exceeded that basis.

2. In Rev. Rul. 59-121, 1959-1 C.B. 212, and Rev. Rul. 68-291, 1968-1 C.B. 351, the Service concluded that where a taxpayer grants an easement that affects only a specific portion of an entire tract of land, only the basis properly allocable to the affected portion is reduced by the consideration received in determining the amount of gain realized, if any. For example, in Rev. Rul. 68-291, the taxpayer purchased a 600-acre farm for $60,000. Subsequently, an electric power company purchased an easement along the southern boundary of the farm for the construction and maintenance of a pole line. The taxpayer received $5,000 as consideration for granting the easement, which covered an area of approximately 20 acres. The Service noted that the allocable cost of the 20 acres affected by the easement was $2,000 ((20 acres/600 acres) x $60,000). As a result, the taxpayer realized $3,000 of gain ($5,000 payment - $2,000 basis) on the conveyance. *See also Beaver Dam Coal Co. v. United States*, 370 F.2d 414 (6th Cir. 1966) (where taxpayer paid premium to acquire entire farm to be able to strip mine coal for a portion, the total price paid is allocated disproportionately between coal bearing land and remainder in determining cost of coal land for purposes of depletion); *Fasken v. Commissioner*, 71 T.C. 650 (1979) (since oil and gas and other easements affected only a determinable portion of ranch land, allocation of basis to easements was feasible); Rev. Rul. 70-510, 1970-2 C.B. 159 (where amount paid for flooding easement computed as 20 percent of value of fee and flooding did not materially interfere with use of land, 20 percent of basis allocated to payment for easement).

PROBLEMS FOR DISCUSSION

Problem 1-1. As previously noted, the Regulations under § 61 provide that the basis of a single parcel of property must be "equitably apportioned" among its several parts if only a portion of the property is subsequently sold. Treas. Reg. § 1.61-6(a). What factors should be considered in determining whether or not the basis has been equitably apportioned?

Problem 1-2. Is the approach applied by the Service in Rev. Ruls. 59-121 and 68-291, discussed in Note 2 above, consistent with the approach adopted by the court in *Gladden*? Why might the Service have adopted the approach it did in these Rulings?

Problem 1-3. Is the result of the Tax Court's decision in *Inaja Land Co. v. Commissioner*, 9 T.C. 727 (1947), consistent with the Ninth Circuit's decision in *Gladden*? Of what relevance is the finding that the easement could not be described by metes and bounds or that its location might change over time?

Problem 1-4. In *Union Carbide Foreign Sales Corp. v. Commissioner*, 115 T.C. 423 (2000), the taxpayer entered into a 20-year lease of a ship used to transport liquid chemicals. Halfway through the lease term, the taxpayer realized that the lease was unduly burdensome and decided to acquire the ship and in doing so terminate its lease. The value of the ship without the lease was approximately $14 million while the value of the remaining term of the lease was approximately $94 million. The taxpayer acquired the ship for $108 million and argued that the acquisition price should be allocated between the ship and the lease. Because the taxpayer terminated the lease, it argued that it was entitled to a deduction of $94 million. Should the taxpayer prevail with its argument that it acquired two assets, the ship and the lease and then terminated the lease, or that should it be viewed as acquiring only one asset, the ship? *See* § 167(c)(2).

Problem 1-5. In *E. I. du Pont de Nemours & Co. v. United States*, 471 F.2d 1211 (Ct. Cl. 1973), the taxpayer contributed a royalty-free, non-exclusive license to certain foreign patents to its subsidiary in exchange for stock of the subsidiary. The Service argued that the transfer of the non-exclusive license was not eligible for nonrecognition treatment under § 351 of the Code. In support of its position, the Service noted that:

> if non-exclusive licenses are covered by 351, it will be extremely difficult to determine what portion of the transferor's basis for his patent should be carried over to a non-exclusive license, when the licensor retains the right to issue an indeterminate number of additional licenses. Generally, by section 362(a), the transferee's basis for the transferred property would be the "same as it would be in the hands of the transferor", increased by the amount of gain recognized by the transferor through the transfer.

Id. at 1219. Although the court acknowledged that "evaluation of non-exclusive licenses is complicated by the indefiniteness of the number of licenses that may be issued . . ." (*id.* at 1220), it did not find this concern sufficient to conclude that § 351 applied to the transfer involved. How should the basis of a non-exclusive license be determined in such a situation?

§ 2.02. Tax Cost Basis

Treas. Reg. § 1.61-2(d)

"Tax cost" is the phrase frequently used to describe the basis of property received in a taxable transaction. In such situations, the basis of the property received is equal to its fair market value. For example, assume that a taxpayer receives property with a fair market value of $10,000 from her employer for services rendered. The taxpayer must include $10,000 in gross income as compensation for services under § 61. Treas. Reg. § 1.61-2(d)(1) ("if services are paid for in property, the fair market value of the property must be included in income as compensation"). The basis in the taxpayer's hands is $10,000, the amount included in gross income. Treas. Reg. § 1.61-2(d)(2) ("[i]n computing the gain or loss from the subsequent sale of such property, its basis shall be the amount paid for the property increased by the amount of such difference included in gross income"). The taxpayer is treated in the same manner as if the employer had paid her $10,000 in cash, and the taxpayer subsequently purchased the property for its fair market value. *See also* § 301(d) (treating the basis of property received as a dividend as equal to the fair market value of the property).

An interesting question arises regarding the basis of property received when the value of the property is excluded from gross income. Assume for example that a taxpayer receives property with a fair market value of $200,000 in settlement of a claim involving a physical injury, the value of which is excluded under § 104(a)(2). If the basis of the property in the taxpayer's hands is zero, based on the fact that the taxpayer incurred no cost in acquiring the property for purposes of § 1012, then the taxpayer will realize $200,000 of gain on the subsequent sale of the property. In effect, the value of the settlement will not be excluded from gross income as directed by § 104(a)(2). The proper result is to treat the property as having a basis of $200,000 in the taxpayer's hands. On the subsequent sale of the property, the taxpayer will have neither gain nor loss and the value of the property received will be excluded from gross income as directed by § 104(a)(2).

§ 2.03. Basis of Gifts

§ 102, 1015, 7701(a)(43); Treas. Reg. § 1.1015-1, 1.1015-5

Section 102 provides that the donee of a gift does not have gross income as a result of the gift. Similarly, the donor is not generally treated as realizing a gain or loss on the transfer of property that constitutes a gift despite the fact that the fair market value of the property is greater than or less than the donor's basis in the property. In *Commissioner v. Duberstein*, 363 U.S. 278 (1960), the Supreme Court concluded that the existence of a gift is a question of fact dependent on whether the transfer is motivated by the "detached and disinterested generosity" of the donor.

> A gift in the statutory sense . . . proceeds from a "detached and disinterested generosity,"; "out of affection, respect, admiration, charity or like impulses." And in this regard, the most critical consideration . . . is the transferor's "intention." . . . "What controls is the intention with which payment, however voluntary, has been made."

Id. at 285–86 (citations omitted).

Assuming that a transfer of property constitutes a gift, the immediate question is the determination of the property's basis in the hands of the donor. Under § 1012, the donor could be viewed as having incurred no cost in acquiring the property and that the basis of the property should therefore be zero. On any subsequent sale of the property, the donee would realize gain equal to the full amount of the proceeds received. The problem with this result is that few, if any, gifts of property would be made; instead, the donor would typically sell the property and transfer the proceeds received to the donee. In this way, the basis of the property in the hands of the donor could be recovered without being treated as gain. However, the donor and donee may not wish to sell the property at the time of the gift but retain it in order to benefit from future appreciation in value.

Fortunately, § 1015 overrides § 1012 with respect to determining the basis of property received as a gift. As a general matter, § 1015 provides for a transferred basis of the property; the basis of the property in the hands of the donee is the same as the basis of the property in the hands of the donor. Such a basis is commonly referred to as a *carryover basis*. As a result, if the basis of the property in the hands of the donor is $70,000 and the property has a fair market value at the time of the gift of $100,000, the basis of the property in the hands of the donee will also be $70,000. In this way, if the donee subsequently sells the property for $100,000, the donee will realize $30,000 of gain, the same amount of gain that the donor would have realized if the donor rather than the donee had sold the property. If the property appreciates in value while held by the donee to $120,000 and the donee sells the property for that amount, the donee will realize $50,000 of gain, $30,000 of gain attributable to the period of time held by the donor and $20,000 attributable to the period of time held by the donee. In *Taft v. Bowers*, 278 U.S. 470 (1929), the Supreme Court held that taxing the donee with respect to the appreciation that arose while the property was held by the donor did not violate the Sixteenth Amendment.

Importantly, the general rule allows for the deferral of gain in connection with appreciation attributable to the period of time the property was held by the donor. In addition, the gain existing at the time of the gift can be transferred to the donee, who may be in a lower tax bracket than the donor.

The general rule is modified if, at the time of the gift, the fair market value of the property is less than the basis of the property in the donor's hands. In this situation, the basis of the property for gain purposes is the donor's basis in the property while the basis of the property for loss purposes is the property's fair market value. Assume for example that, at the time of the gift, the basis of the property in the donor's hands is $120,000 and that the fair market value of the property is only $100,000. If the donee sells the property for $130,000, the donee will realize a $10,000 gain equal to the $130,000 amount realized minus the $120,000 basis of the property for gain purposes. On the other hand, if the donee sells the property for only $90,000, the donee will realize a $10,000 loss equal to the $90,000 amount realized minus the $100,000 basis of the property for loss purposes. This rule prohibits the donor from transferring unrealized losses to the donee. The only loss that the donee may realize is the loss attributable to a decline in the value of the property while held by the donee. At the same time, the donee will not realize gain greater than the gain that would be realized if the donor had sold the property.

The use of one basis for gain purposes and another for loss purposes does create the possibility that on a subsequent sale of the property the donee will realize neither gain nor loss. Using the facts in the previous paragraph, if the donee sold the property for $115,000, the donee will realize neither gain nor loss. Using the $120,000 basis for gain purposes, the donee would realize a $5,000 loss. Using the $100,000 basis for loss purposes, the donee would realize a $15,000 gain. If the donee sells the property for any price between $100,000 and $120,000, the donee will realize neither gain nor loss.

The carryover basis of property received as a gift is increased by the portion of any gift tax paid that is attributable to appreciation in the property at the time of the gift. § 1015(d)(6). For example, assume that the donor transfers property to the donee with a fair market value of $36,000 and a basis of $24,000. The donor paid a gift tax of $18,000 on the full amount of the gift. Because the appreciation at the time of the gift is one-third of the value of the gift, the $24,000 carryover basis of the property is increased by $6,000 (one-third of the $18,000 gift tax paid). The basis of the property in the hands of the donee is thus $30,000. The calculation of the basis adjustment becomes more complicated if two or more gifts of property are made in any taxable period. *See* § 1015(d)(2); Treas. Reg. § 1.1015-5(b)(1)(ii).

The basis adjustment for a portion of the gift tax paid results in the donor being indifferent between selling the property and transferring the net proceeds to the donee or transferring the property to the donee as a gift and the donee selling the property thereafter. Using the facts of the preceding example, assume that the gift tax rate is 50 percent and the donee and donor are both taxable on any gain at a rate of 15 percent. As described above, the donor will pay a gift tax of $18,000 and, if the property is sold for $36,000, the donee will pay income tax of $900 (15 percent x ($36,000 amount realized - $30,000 basis). Alternatively, if the donee sold the property for $36,000, he would pay income tax of $1,800 (15 percent x ($36,000 amount realized - $24,000 basis). In addition, the donor would pay a gift tax of $17,100 (50 percent x ($36,000 - $1,800)). In both situations, the combined amount of gift and income taxes imposed on the donor and donee is $18,900.

The rules applicable to the determination of the basis of property acquired by gift require that the basis of the property in the hands of the donor be known. If the donee is unable to determine the basis of the property in the hands of the donor, the Service shall obtain such facts, if possible. § 1015(a). If it is impossible to obtain the information necessary to determine the basis of the property in the donor's hands, the basis shall be equal to the fair market value of the property as of the date the property was acquired by the donor.

§ 2.04. Basis of Inherited Property

§ 102, 1014; skim 1022; Treas. Reg. § 1.1014-1, 1.1014-4

Like the receipt of property acquired by gift, the receipt of property acquired by inheritance, bequest, or devise is not included in the recipient's gross income under § 102. Similarly, the decedent is not treated as realizing gain or loss on the transfer of property by inheritance, bequest, or devise despite the fact that the fair market value of the property is greater than or less than the decedent's basis in the property. Section 1014 provides that the basis of property acquired by inheritance, bequest, or devise in the hands of the recipient is the property's fair market value on the date of the decedent's death or on the optional valuation date under § 2032. § 1014(a).

The basis of property acquired by inheritance, bequest, or devise is typically referred to as receiving a "stepped-up basis" on the assumption that the fair market value of the property is greater than its basis in the hands of the decedent at the time of the decedent's death. In such a situation, any appreciation in the value of the property will become permanently excluded from taxation. However, if the basis of the property is greater than its fair market value at that time, the property will take a "stepped-down basis," again equal to the property's fair market value. In such a situation, neither the decedent nor the recipient will be able to realize the loss inherent in the property. As a result, an individual is encouraged to sell loss property in order to take advantage of the deduction of any loss before death but retain any gain property in order to avoid tax with respect to the appreciation.

Because of the potential for basis manipulation through transfers to individuals in anticipation of death, § 1014(e) provides that appreciated property transferred by gift and retransferred by inheritance, bequest, or devise to the donor or the donor's spouse will receive a carryover basis equal to the basis of the property in the decedent's hands immediately before death instead of a stepped-up basis if the date of the decedent's death is within one year of the gift. Presumably, the basis rules under § 1014 are sufficiently taxpayer favorable without providing taxpayers with additional planning opportunities. However, § 1014(e) applies only to retransfers by inheritance, bequest, or devise if the date of the decedent's death is within one year of the gift. Thus, opportunities for careful tax planning continue to exist with respect to gifts made more than one year prior to the decedent's death.

Under current law, the estate tax has been repealed for one year in 2010. Without further congressional action, the estate tax will return at the end of 2010. In anticipation of the one-year repeal, Congress also decided that the step-up or step-down of basis under § 1014 would no longer apply beginning at the end of 2009. § 1014(f). In lieu of the provisions under § 1014, § 1022 generally provides basis rules similar to, but not exactly the same as, the basis rules applicable to gifts under § 1015. Under these rules, the basis of property acquired from a decedent is equal to the lesser of the property's adjusted basis in the hands of the decedent or the fair market value of the property at the date of the decedent's death. § 1022(a). Consequently, like the gift situation, appreciation existing at the time of the decedent's death will be taxable to the recipient upon a subsequent sale of the property. Similarly, losses existing at the time of the decedent's death will disappear as the loss property will have a fair market value basis in the hands of the recipient.

However, Congress decided that a transferred or carryover basis would not be appropriate in all instances. The recipients of property from lesser valued estates that would have escaped the estate tax under prior law would suddenly find themselves without the benefit of the stepped-up basis rules of § 1014, resulting in higher income taxes. Consequently, § 1022 provides for two different increases in the basis of property acquired from a decedent. An aggregate basis increase of $1.3 million permitted for all of the decedent's property and an additional $3 million is permitted for qualified spousal property. §§ 1022(b) and 1022(c). These amounts are adjusted for inflation after 2010, presuming that Congressional action will extend the repeal of the estate tax and the application of § 1022 after the end of 2010. § 1022(d)(4). The statute provides detailed rules regarding the types of property to which the basis increases are applicable. §§ 1022(c) and 1022(d). In no instance, however, can the basis of property be increased above its fair market value. § 1022(d)(2). The basis increases are allocated among the property in the estate as determined by the executor. § 1022(d)(3). The degree to which the basis increases may be manipulated to increase the basis of depreciable property or property that is expected to be sold relatively quickly will be determined by Regulations that have yet to be promulgated.

§ 2.05. Substituted Basis

§§ 7701(a)(42), 7701(a)(43), and 7701(a)(44)

In addition to transfers by gift, the Code provides numerous instances in which the basis of property in the hands of the transferee is determined by reference to the basis of the property in the hands of the transferor. When the basis of property in the hands of the transferee is determined by reference to the basis of the property in the hands of the transferor, the basis is referred to as a "transferred basis." § 7701(a)(43). Such a basis is more commonly referred to as a *carryover basis*.

The most common transactions that give rise to a carryover basis are contributions of property by a shareholder to a corporation under § 351 or by a partner to a partnership under § 721 in exchange for stock in the corporation or an interest in the partnership. When the requirements of §§ 351 or 721 are satisfied, the transferor shareholder or partner recognizes neither gain nor loss, and the property receives a basis in the hands of the transferee corporation or partnership equal to the basis of the property in the hands of the transferor shareholder or partner immediately prior to the transfer. §§ 351(a), 362(a), 721(a), and 723. However, when, for example, a transferor shareholder receives boot as part of the exchange, gain is typically recognized and the basis of the property in the hands of the corporation is equal to the basis of the property in the hands of the shareholder increased by the amount of gain recognized. §§ 351(b) and 362(a).

Distributions of property from a partnership are also eligible for nonrecognition treatment under § 731(a)(1). As a result, the basis of the distributed property in the hands of the recipient partner is generally a carryover basis equal to the basis of the property in the hands of the partnership immediately before the distribution. § 732(a).

The Code provides that the basis of the property received in certain types of transactions will be equal to the basis of the property transferred. Such transactions are said to give rise to an *exchanged basis* for the property received. § 7701(a)(44). Typical examples of transactions that result in the property received having a substituted basis are, again, contributions of property by a shareholder to a corporation under § 351 or by a partner to a partnership under § 721 in exchange for stock in the corporation or an interest in the partnership. In these situations, the substituted basis property is the stock of the corporation or the partnership interest in the hands of the shareholder or partner. The basis of the stock or the basis of the partnership interest will be equal to the basis of the property contributed to the corporation or the partnership. §§ 358(a) and 722. Again, if a transferor shareholder receives boot as part of the exchange and gain is recognized as a result, the basis of the stock in the hands of the shareholder will be equal to the basis of the contributed property in the hands of the shareholder, increased by the amount of gain recognized and decreased by the amount of money or the fair market value of other property received in the exchange. §§ 351(b) and 358(a).

Another example of a transaction in which property receives an exchanged basis is property acquired in a like-kind exchange under § 1031. For example, if real property with a fair market value of $500,000 and a basis of $200,000 is exchanged for real property with a fair market value of $500,000, the so-called replacement property will have a basis equal to the basis of the relinquished property. The basis determination becomes somewhat more complicated if the taxpayer receives boot in addition to like-kind property, or if either the relinquished or the replacement property is subject to liabilities, in which case gain is recognized on the exchange. However, the property is still said to have an exchanged basis because the basis is determined in part by reference to the basis of the relinquished property. The treatment of like-kind exchanges under § 1031 is described in detail in § 1, *Like-*

Kind Exchanges, in Chapter 5, *Nonrecognition Transactions*.

§ 2.06. Basis of Property Received in a Taxable Exchange

As previously noted, basis represents the taxpayer's investment in the property for tax purposes. Under § 1012, basis is the taxpayer's cost of acquiring the property. Consequently, when property is acquired by purchase in an arm's-length transaction, the basis of the property is the amount paid by the taxpayer. However, when property is acquired in a taxable exchange, a question arises whether the basis of the property received should be equal to the fair market value of the property transferred or the fair market value of the property received. Of course, in exchanges between unrelated parties, the fair market values of the property transferred and received will typically be equal. But what if the values of the property are not equal? In such a situation, one might think that the taxpayer's cost for purposes of § 1012 is better represented by the fair market value of the property transferred. The Court of Claims considered this question in the following case.

PHILADELPHIA PARK AMUSEMENT CO. v. UNITED STATES

United States Court of Claims
126 F. Supp. 184 (Ct. Cl. 1954)

Laramore, Judge, delivered the opinion of the court:

The taxpayer corporation sues to recover $42,864.50, with interest thereon, representing alleged overpayment of income taxes for the calendar years 1944 and 1945. The taxpayer employed the accrual method of accounting and reported its income on a calendar year basis. The issue presented in this case is whether or not the taxpayer is entitled to include as a part of the cost of its franchise, for purposes of determining depreciation and loss due to abandonment, the undepreciated cost of a bridge exchanged for a 10-year extension of the franchise. The facts which have been stipulated by the parties may be summarized as follows: The taxpayer's predecessor was granted on July 6, 1889, by the City of Philadelphia, a franchise to construct, operate, and maintain for 50 years a passenger railway in Fairmount Park at its own cost and expense. . . .

Pursuant to the franchise the taxpayer's predecessor constructed the bridge in question, commonly known as Strawberry Bridge, over the Schuylkill River at a cost of $381,000. The bridge was 79½ feet wide and carried pedestrian and vehicular traffic in addition to taxpayer's streetcars. The taxpayer's principal business was the operation of an amusement park and the street railway was employed in the transportation of customers to the park. With the increase in automobile transportation the proportion of customers carried to the amusement park by the taxpayer's streetcars decreased over the years and during the latter years of its operation losses were sustained. Early in 1934 the City, in writing the taxpayer, pointed out that Strawberry Bridge was in need of extensive repairs, that it was taxpayer's obligation to make the repairs at taxpayer's expense, and threatened to close the bridge unless the repairs were made promptly. The taxpayer wrote the City explaining that its financial condition prevented the making of extensive repairs to the bridge and offered to transfer the ownership of the bridge to the City in exchange for a 10-year extension of the railway franchise. The City accepted the offer and on August 3, 1934, Strawberry Bridge was transferred to the City. The taxpayer reserved its right-of-way over the bridge for the duration of its franchise and agreed to maintain its facilities thereon. On November 14, 1934, the City amended the franchise and extended it from July 24, 1939, to July 24, 1949. The adjusted basis, i.e., the undepreciated or unrecovered cost of Strawberry Bridge at the time of the exchange was $228,852.74. The taxpayer's bookkeeper took depreciation on the bridge for the part of 1934 that taxpayer owned it and promptly wrote the asset off the books by a direct debit to surplus of $228,852.74, without reporting any gain or loss on the exchange or adding the undepreciated cost or fair market value of the bridge to the cost of the franchise. From that time until 1946 the taxpayer's bookkeeper did not record on the taxpayer's books or claim a deduction on its returns for the amortization of this cost. He also failed to take the undisputed deduction for the amortization of the undepreciated portion, $50,000, of the original cost of the franchise.

In 1946 the taxpayer arranged with a bus company to give passenger service to its amusement park, ceased operation of the railway, and abandoned its franchise. In its 1946 tax return the taxpayer claimed a loss due to abandonment of the railroad of $336,380.04, $74,445.89 of which was claimed to represent the undepreciated cost of the franchise. This produced a $128,897.97 net loss for the year 1946, and taxpayer claimed a net operating loss carry-back to 1944 and 1945 under section 122(b) of the Code.

On December 15, 1947, the taxpayer filed a claim for refund of 1944 taxes . . . based on a claimed depreciation deduction . . . founded upon the ground that the undepreciated cost of Strawberry Bridge . . . was the cost of the 10-year extension of its franchise and, therefore, should be amortized over the remaining life of the franchise. . . .

. . .

[W]e are only concerned with the cost basis, if any, of the 10-year extension of taxpayer's franchise and the tax consequences thereof for the years 1944, 1945, and 1946.

It is clear that the cost of this type franchise can be amortized over its life . . . . It is also clear that when a franchise is abandoned prior to the end of its term the owner is entitled to deduct, under section 23(f) [the predecessor of § 165(a)] of the Code, as a loss in the year of abandonment, the undepreciated cost of the franchise at that time. . . .

This brings us to the question of what is the cost basis of the 10-year extension of taxpayer's franchise. Although defendant contends that Strawberry Bridge was either worthless or not "exchanged" for the 10-year extension of the franchise, we believe that the bridge had some value, and that the contract under which the bridge was transferred to the City clearly indicates that the one was given in consideration of the other. The taxpayer, however, has failed to show that the exchange was one that falls within the nonrecognition provisions of section 112(b) of the Code and, therefore, it was a taxable exchange under section 112(a) [the predecessor of § 1001] of the Code.

The gain or loss, whichever the case may have been, should have been recognized, and the cost basis under section 113(a) [the predecessor of § 1012] of the Code, of the 10-year extension of the franchise was the cost to the taxpayer. The succinct statement in section 113(a) that "the basis of property shall be the cost of such property" although clear in principle, is frequently difficult in application. One view is that the cost basis of property received in a taxable exchange is the fair market value of the property *given* in the exchange. The other view is that the cost basis of property received in a taxable exchange is the fair market value of the property *received* in the exchange. As will be seen from the cases and some of the Commissioner's rulings the Commissioner's position has not been altogether consistent on this question. The view that "cost" is the fair market value of the property given is predicated on the theory that the cost to the taxpayer is the economic value relinquished. The view that "cost" is the fair market value of the property received is based upon the theory that the term "cost" is a tax concept and must be considered in the light of the designed interrelationship of sections 111, 112, 113, and 114, and the prime role that the basis of property plays in determining tax liability. We believe that when the question is considered in the latter context that the cost basis of the property received in a taxable exchange is the fair market value of the property *received* in the exchange.

When property is exchanged for property in a taxable exchange the taxpayer is taxed on the difference between the adjusted basis of the property given in exchange and the fair market value of the property received in exchange. For purposes of determining gain or loss the fair market value of the property received is treated as cash and taxed accordingly. To maintain harmony with the fundamental purpose of these sections, it is necessary to consider the fair market value of the property received as the cost basis to the taxpayer. The failure to do so would result in allowing the taxpayer a stepped-up basis, without paying a tax therefor, if the fair market value of the property received is less than the fair market value of the property given, and the taxpayer would be subjected to a double tax if the fair market value of the property received is more than the fair market value of the property given. By holding that the fair market value of the property received in a taxable exchange is the cost basis, the above discrepancy is avoided and the basis of the property received will equal the adjusted basis of the property given plus any gain recognized, or that should have been recognized, or minus any loss recognized, or that should have been recognized.

Therefore, the cost basis of the 10-year extension of the franchise was its fair market value on August 3, 1934, the date of the exchange. The determination of whether the cost basis of the property received is its fair market value or the fair market value of the property given in exchange therefor, although necessary to the decision of the case, is generally not of great practical significance because the value of the two properties exchanged in an arms-length transaction are either equal in fact, or are presumed to be equal. The record in this case indicates that the 1934 exchange was an arms-length transaction and, therefore, if the value of the extended franchise cannot be determined with reasonable accuracy, it would be reasonable and fair to assume that the value of Strawberry Bridge was equal to the 10-year extension of the franchise. The fair market value of the 10-year extension of the franchise should be established but, if that value cannot be determined with reasonable certainty, the fair market value of Strawberry Bridge should be established and that will be presumed to be the value of the extended franchise. This value cannot be determined from the facts now before us since the case was prosecuted on a different theory.

. . . If the value of the extended franchise or bridge cannot be ascertained with a reasonable degree of accuracy, the taxpayer is entitled to carry over the undepreciated cost of the bridge as the cost basis of the extended franchise. *Helvering v. Tex-Penn Oil Co.*, 300 U.S. 481, 499 [(1937)]; *Gould Securities Co. v. United States*, 96 F.2d 780 [(2d Cir. 1938)]. However, it is only in rare and extraordinary cases that the value of the property exchanged cannot be ascertained with reasonable accuracy. We are presently of the opinion that either the value of the extended franchise or the bridge can be determined with a reasonable degree of accuracy. Although the value of the extended franchise may be difficult or impossible to ascertain because of the nebulous and intangible characteristics inherent in such property, the value of the bridge is subject to more exact measurement. Consideration may be given to expert testimony on the value of comparable bridges, Strawberry Bridge's reproduction cost and its undepreciated cost, as well as other relevant factors.

. . .

We, therefore, conclude that the 1934 exchange was a taxable exchange and that the taxpayer is entitled to use as the cost basis of the 10-year extension of its franchise its fair market value on August 3, 1934, for purposes of determining depreciation and loss due to abandonment, as indicated in this opinion. . . .

NOTES AND COMMENTS

1. In *Philadelphia Park Amusement Co.*, the court concluded that the basis of property received in a taxable exchange is equal to the fair market value of the property received in the exchange. This is equivalent to saying that the basis of the property received in the exchange is equal to the basis of the property transferred plus any gain recognized on the exchange or minus any loss recognized on the exchange. In reaching this result, the court relies on the tax concept of cost, i.e., the value taken into account for tax purposes. The court deviated from the literal language of § 1012 in order "[t]o maintain harmony with the fundamental purpose" of the gain and basis provisions of the Code.

The court's analysis can probably best be understood through a simple example. Assume that T exchanges Blackacre for Greenacre. Blackacre has a fair market value of $100,000 and a basis of $60,000. Greenacre has a fair market value of $110,000. In such a situation, T will realize $50,000 of gain as a result of the exchange, equal to the fair market value of Greenacre minus the basis of Blackacre ($110,000 - $60,000). The Court concluded that T should have a basis in Greenacre of $110,000, its fair market value. This basis is also equal to T's basis in Blackacre increased by the gain realized in the exchange ($50,000 + $60,000). If T subsequently sells Greenacre for $110,000 in cash, he will realize neither gain nor loss on the sale ($110,000 - $110,000). This result puts T in the same position as if he sold Blackacre for $110,000 in cash and then purchased Greenacre for $110,000.

As the court noted, treating T as having a basis in Greenacre equal to the fair market value of Blackacre will subject T to a "double tax." Using the facts of the previous paragraph, T will again realize $50,000 of gain as a result of the exchange, equal to the fair market value of Greenacre minus the basis of Blackacre ($110,000 - $60,000). If T's basis is equal to $100,000, the fair market value of Blackacre, T will realize an additional $10,000 of gain on the subsequent sale of Greenacre for $110,000 in cash ($100,000 - $110,000). Thus, T is attributed with $60,000 of gain when T has benefited economically only to the extent of $50,000.

Alternatively, had the fair market value of Greenacre been less than the fair market value of Blackacre, T would have been undertaxed if the basis of Greenacre is equal to the fair market value of Blackacre. Assume the same facts as in the previous paragraph, except that the fair market value of Greenacre is only $90,000. In such a situation, T will realize $30,000 of gain as a result of the exchange, equal to the fair market value of Greenacre minus the basis of Blackacre ($90,000 - $60,000). If T's basis is equal to $100,000, the fair market value of Blackacre, T will realize a loss of $10,000 on the subsequent sale of Greenacre for $90,000 in cash ($90,000 - $100,000). Thus, T is attributed with net gain of only $20,000 ($30,000 - $10,000) when T has benefited economically to the extent of $30,000. This problem is avoided if the basis of Greenacre in T's hands is $90,000, its fair market value at the time of the exchange. In this situation, T will realize neither gain nor loss on the subsequent sale of Greenacre ($90,000 - $90,000).

2. In *Philadelphia Park Amusement Co.*, the court noted that the rule it adopted to determine the proper basis of the property received in a taxable exchange is usually not a significant issue because "the value of the properties exchanged in an arms-length transaction are either equal in fact, or are presumed to be equal." Because the exchange was characterized as being at arm's-length, the court concluded that, if the value of the ten-year extension of the franchise (i.e., property received) could not be determined, the basis of the franchise would be equal to the fair market value of the Strawberry Bridge (i.e., the property transferred). However, problems may arise in treating the properties as equal in value. In *Seas Shipping Co. v. Commissioner*, 371 F.2d 528 (2d Cir. 1967), *cert. denied*, 387 U.S. 943 (1967), part of the consideration for a sale of 10 ships was stock of the acquiring corporation. In valuing the stock, the court used what it called the "barter equation" method, which assigned a value to the shares in part by the value of the ships, even though the price was higher than the price at which the shares had ever sold.

Similarly, problems can arise when the values of the properties involved change between the time that the parties agree to exchange the properties and the actual exchange. Importantly, the taxable event is the date of the exchange, not the date that the agreement is reached. For example, in *Amerada Hess Corp. v. Commissioner*, 517 F.2d 75 (3d Cir. 1975), listed shares of the purchaser provided a significant portion of the consideration for a business acquisition. The price of the shares dropped by more than one-third from the value assigned in the negotiations by the time of closing. The court decided that the quoted price at closing controlled both the amount realized by the seller and the basis of the purchaser. It rejected the use of the negotiated value under the "barter equation" method on the ground that that method should be used only with difficult-to-value property. It distinguished *Seas Shipping Co.*, which had used the barter equation method in preference to quoted market price when the price of the stock involved vastly exceeded its normal trading price. It also noted that the barter equation method had the difficulty of there being no more reason to use one side of the barter than the other. The court then accepted the Service's concession that a blockage discount should be applied to reduce the quoted market price of the stock.

Both *Seas Shipping* and *Amerada Hess* implicitly reject the possibility that the values received by the two sides can be different. As Judge Friendly noted in a concurring opinion in *Seas Shipping*, the Service finds it intolerable that the seller use a low value in determining gain while the purchaser, which does not recognize gain on issue of its stock, uses a high value in determining basis. Nevertheless, under the principle of *Philadelphia Park*, this is the theoretically correct result. In *Seas Shipping*, the seller won. In *Amerada Hess*, it was the buyer. In his opinion, Judge Friendly implied that the parties had a duty to bargain over the values. The issue is now dealt with indirectly in § 1060, in which the parties are required to use the residual method in allocating consideration among the assets transferred on the sale of a trade or business. In addition, both parties are required to disclose their valuations to the Service. Although they are not required to agree regarding the valuations of the assets, as indicated by *Seas Shipping* and *Amerada Hess*, they can expect Service to object when they do not.

3. In *Philadelphia Park Amusement Co.*, the court noted that in the "rare and extraordinary" situation in which the values of neither the property received nor the property transferred could be determined, the basis of the property received would be equal to the basis of the property transferred. Such a carryover basis would only be appropriate, however, if neither gain nor loss was reported at the time of the exchange.

PROBLEM FOR DISCUSSION

Problem 1-6. Is *Philadelphia Park Amusement Co.* correct in suggesting that the proper measure of the basis of property received in an exchange is the value of what is received rather than what is given up? Does either *Seas Shipping* or *Amerada Hess* properly apply *Philadelphia Park Amusement Co.*? Are either *Seas Shipping* or *Amerada Hess* consistent with the decision of the Supreme Court in *United States v. Davis*, 370 U.S. 65 (1962), discussed in § 3.03(b)? In *Davis*, the Court held that a transfer of appreciated securities in a divorce in discharge of a wife's inchoate marital property rights resulted in gain.

§ 2.07. Split Basis

Although a particular piece of property typically has only one basis, it may have more than one basis if used for more than one purpose. For example, assume that a taxpayer acquires an automobile for $20,000 that he intends to use for both business and personal purposes. Assume that the automobile may be depreciated for business purposes over five years using the straight-line method. As a result, if the automobile is used solely for business purposes, the taxpayer would be entitled to $4,000 of depreciation each year. However, the taxpayer uses the automobile for business purposes only 80 percent of the time. Consequently, he is entitled to depreciation deductions of only $3,200 per year (80 percent of $4,000). At the end of five years, the taxpayer will have taken $16,000 of depreciation deductions reducing the basis of the automobile to $4,000.

What happens if, in year six, the taxpayer sells the automobile for $7,000? The question could be answered in two ways. The most obvious approach is simply to say that the taxpayer has a gain of $3,000 ($7,000 amount realized - $4,000 adjusted basis). Alternatively, the taxpayer could be thought to have acquired two assets, an automobile used for business purposes and an automobile used for personal purposes. Because 80 percent of the actual use of the automobile was for business purposes, 80 percent of the original acquisition cost of the automobile, $16,000, represented the cost of acquiring the automobile used for business purposes. The basis of this portion of the automobile has been completely recovered through depreciation deductions, with the result that this portion of the automobile has a zero basis. Because 20 percent of the actual use of the automobile was for personal purposes, 20 percent of the original acquisition cost of the automobile, $4,000, represented the cost of acquiring the automobile used for personal purposes. Because property used for personal purposes is not eligible for depreciation, the basis of this portion of the automobile remains $4,000. Under this alternative analysis, the sale of the automobile must be bifurcated into a business portion and a personal portion. Again, because 80 percent of the actual use of the automobile was for business purposes, $5,600, i.e., 80 percent of the proceeds received, is attributable to the business portion of the automobile. The remaining $1,400, i.e., 20 percent of the proceeds received, is attributable to the personal portion of the automobile. As a result, the taxpayer realizes the following gains and losses:

	Business Portion	Personal Portion
Amount Realized	$5,600	$1,400
Adjusted Basis	0	4,000
Gain (Loss) Realized	$5,600	($2,600)

Although the net result of this alternative approach is the same as the result of the original approach, i.e., $3,000 of gain, the two approaches are only the same if the loss on the personal portion of the automobile is deductible. However, such a loss is not deductible because only personal losses that result from a casualty or theft that satisfy certain requirements are deductible. § 165(c). Consequently, the difference between the two approaches is $3,000 of gain under the original approach or $5,600 of gain under the alternative approach.

The proper tax treatment in this situation is the alternative approach. *See Sharp v. United States*, 199 F. Supp. 743 (D. Del. 1961), *aff'd*, 303 F.2d 783 (3d Cir. 1962); Rev. Rul. 286, 1953-2 C.B. 20. To permit the taxpayer to realize only $3,000 of gain under the original approach is equivalent to allowing the taxpayer to deduct the $2,600 personal loss under the alternative approach. This example forces us to keep in mind that problems are often more complicated than they initially appear and that even the simplest of fact situations may be analyzed under more than one approach.

§ 2.08. Inclusion of Debt in Basis

In order to treat similarly situated taxpayers similarly, debt incurred in the acquisition of property is typically included in the basis of the property acquired. This approach provides a taxpayer who finances the acquisition of property with a loan from a third party with the same basis in the property as a taxpayer who acquires the property with cash from his own pocket. Thus, for example, a parcel of unimproved real property acquired by a taxpayer using $100,000 of his own cash will have a basis of $100,000 under § 1012. Similarly, a parcel of unimproved real property acquired by a taxpayer using $20,000 of his own cash and the proceeds of an $80,000 loan from a third-party lender will have a basis of $100,000 under § 1012. The manner in which the taxpayer finances the acquisition of property should not affect the basis of the property in the taxpayer's hands.

The reference in § 1012 to the "cost" of the property could be interpreted to permit a taxpayer to include in the basis of the property only those amounts that represent actual out-of-pocket investments in the property. Under such an interpretation, a parcel of unimproved real property acquired by a taxpayer using $20,000 of his own cash and the proceeds of an $80,000 loan from a third-party lender would have a basis of only $20,000 under § 1012. Only when the payments of principal are actually made under the loan would the taxpayer be permitted to include those amounts in basis. This approach to the treatment of debt might be viewed as appropriate because the loan proceeds were excluded from the taxpayer's income and, thus, have not been subject to tax. If the basis of property is intended to reflect the taxpayer's investment dollars that were previously subject to tax, the taxpayer should not be allowed to include in basis amounts that have not yet been subject to tax. However, the Service and the courts have consistently permitted taxpayers to include debt incurred in acquiring property in the property's basis on the assumption that the debt will be repaid with after-tax dollars. As described in § 3.03, this rule applies with respect to both recourse and nonrecourse debt. However, this rule also results in opportunities for tax shelter transactions that are the subject of the at-risk and passive loss rules of §§ 465 and 469. *See* §§ 3.04 and 8.03.

§ 2.09. Adjustments to Basis

§§ 1001(a), 1011, 1012, 1016; Treas. Reg. §§ 1.1001-1, 1.1011-1, 1.1012-1, 1.1016-1, 1.1016-3

In determining the amount of gain or loss under § 1001(a), a taxpayer is first permitted to recover the adjusted basis of the property. The amount realized in excess of the property's adjusted basis is treated as gain and the adjusted basis in excess of the amount realized is treated as a loss. Section 1011 provides that the adjusted basis for purposes of § 1001(a) is the cost basis of the property under § 1012 as adjusted under § 1016.

Section 1016 provides that the basis of property may be adjusted for "expenditures, receipts, losses, or other items properly chargeable to capital account, . . ." and for "exhaustion, wear and tear, obsolescence, amortization, and depletion . . ." § 1016(a). Thus, the cost of improvements made to property, such as the expansion of an existing building or the improvement of machinery, increase the basis of the property involved while deductible expenses, such as depreciation, cost recovery, and casualty losses, reduce the basis of the property involved. In addition, tax-free recoveries of basis, such as the payment received by the taxpayer in *Inaja Land Co. v. Commissioner*, 9 T.C. 727 (1947) (*see* § 2.01), will reduce the basis of property involved.

§ 3. REALIZATION OF GAIN OR LOSS

§ 3.01. In General

§§ 61(a)(3); 1001(a) and (b); Treas. Reg. §§ 1.61-6; 1.1001-1(a)

Section 1001(a) provides that the amount of gain is the excess of the amount realized over the adjusted basis of the property transferred. Similarly, the amount of loss is the excess of the adjusted basis of the property transferred over the amount realized. In other words, the transferor is entitled to recover the basis of the property before any gain is realized. If the amount realized is insufficient to allow the transfer to recover the basis of the property, a loss is realized equal to the unrecovered basis in the property.

Section 1001(b) provides that the amount realized is equal to the "sum of any money received plus the fair market value of the property (other than money) received." Consequently, the full economic benefit received by the transferor in return for the property must be considered, regardless of whether the benefit is received in the form of cash or property. If the transferor receives property other than cash, the fair market value of that property must be determined in order to properly compute the gain or loss realized on the transfer. Such valuation questions frequently involve disputes between taxpayers and the Service.

Importantly, § 1001(a) provides that gain or loss is realized only on the "sale or other disposition" of property. As a result, gain or loss arises only when a "realization event" is said to have occurred. The Regulations provide further guidance in this regard by stating that "gain or loss is realized from the conversion of property into cash, or from the exchange of property for other property differing materially either in kind or in extent. . . ." Treas. Reg. § 1.1001-1(a). However, sales and exchanges of property are not the only situations that are treated as realization events. The statute refers to the sale "or other disposition" of property. As described below, "other dispositions" can include the abandonment of property as well as the transfer of property in satisfaction of a claim.

Early Supreme Court decisions held that the realization requirement had constitutional dimensions under the Sixteenth Amendment's definition of income. For example, in *Eisner v. Macomber*, 252 U.S. 189 (1920), the Supreme Court held that the taxpayer's receipt of a stock dividend was not taxable because no realization event had occurred.

> The essential and controlling fact is that the stockholder has received nothing out of the company's assets for his separate use and benefit; on the contrary, every dollar of his original investment, together with whatever accretions and accumulations have resulted from employment of his money and that of the other stockholders in the business of the company, still remains the property of the company, and subject to business risks which may result in wiping out the entire investment. Having regard to the very truth of the matter, to substance and not to form, he has received nothing that answers the definition of income within the meaning of the Sixteenth Amendment.

Id. at 194–195. *See also Lynch v. Hornby*, 247 U.S. 339 (1918); *Towne v. Eisner*, 245 U.S. 418 (1918). However, in later cases the Supreme Court retreated from this position, stating that the realization requirement is "founded on administrative convenience." *Helvering v. Horst*, 311 U.S. 112, 116 (1940). *See also Helvering v. Bruun*, 309 U.S. 461 (1940) (concluding that the taxpayer was taxable on the increased value of leased property attributable to a building constructed by the tenant on the conclusion of the lease). *But see Commissioner v. Glenshaw Glass Co.*, 348 U.S. 426 (1955) (defining income as "undeniable accessions to wealth, *clearly realized*, and over which the taxpayers have complete dominion . . ." [emphasis added]).

Although no longer viewed as a constitutional imperative, the realization requirement has the advantage of avoiding the administrative burden of valuing assets that are not readily tradable like personal residences and interests in closely held businesses on an annual basis in order to properly determine the taxpayer's income. However, the administrative convenience of the realization requirement comes with a cost — the deferral of gain attributable to increases in the value of these assets, as well as gain attributable to increases in the value of assets, such as marketable securities, that could be easily valued on an annual basis. The benefits of deferral resulting from the realization requirement should not lightly be overlooked by tax practitioners who view realization as a structural aspect of the tax system. Indeed, the realization requirement has been modified by § 475, which requires securities dealers to "mark to market" their inventory of securities, and § 1256 which requires similar marking to market of specified types of derivatives, including futures, currency contracts, and some options. Furthermore, the Supreme Court's decision is *Macomber* has been modified by § 305, which taxes certain types of distributions involving stock dividends and other transactions that are considered the equivalent of such distributions.

§ 3.02. Sale or Exchange

Treas. Reg. § 1.1001-1(a)

As previously noted, the Regulations state that "gain or loss is realized from the conversion of property into cash, or from the exchange of property for other property differing materially either in kind or in extent. . . ." Treas. Reg. § 1.1001-1(a). Although little controversy regarding the existence of a realization event arises when property is transferred for cash, the same cannot be said when only exchanges of property are involved. The existence of a realization event on the exchange of property is clouded because of the materiality standard adopted by the Regulations. What does it mean that the properties exchanged must "differ[] materially either in kind or in extent . . ." in order for a realization event to occur? The following Supreme Court decision explored the realization requirement in the context of an exchange of properties and provided guidance regarding the materiality requirement.

COTTAGE SAVINGS ASSOCIATION v. COMMISSIONER

Supreme Court of the United States
499 U.S. 554 (1991)

MARSHALL, J., delivered the opinion of the Court.

The issue in this case is whether a financial institution realizes tax-deductible losses when it exchanges its interests in one group of residential mortgage loans for another lender's interests in a different group of residential mortgage loans. We hold that such a transaction does give rise to realized losses.

I

Petitioner Cottage Savings Association (Cottage Savings) is a savings and loan association (S & L) formerly regulated by the Federal Home Loan Bank Board (FHLBB). Like many S & L's, Cottage Savings held numerous long-term, low-interest mortgages that declined in value when interest rates surged in the late 1970's. These institutions would have benefited from selling their devalued mortgages in order to realize tax-deductible losses. However, they were deterred from doing so by FHLBB accounting regulations, which required them to record the losses on their books. Reporting these losses consistent with the then-effective FHLBB accounting regulations would have placed many S & L's at risk of closure by the FHLBB.

The FHLBB responded to this situation by relaxing its requirements for the reporting of losses. In a regulatory directive known as "Memorandum R-49," dated June 27, 1980, the FHLBB determined that S & L's need not report losses associated with mortgages that are exchanged for "substantially identical" mortgages held by other lenders.[1] The FHLBB's acknowledged purpose for Memorandum R-49 was to facilitate transactions that would generate tax losses but that

---

[1] [2] Memorandum R-49 listed 10 criteria for classifying mortgages as substantially identical.

"The loans involved must:

"1. involve single-family residential mortgages,

"2. be of similar type (e. g., conventionals for conventionals),

"3. have the same stated terms to maturity (e. g., 30 years),

"4. have identical stated interest rates,

"5. have similar seasoning (i. e., remaining terms to maturity),

"6. have aggregate principal amounts within the lesser of 2 1/2% or $100,000 (plus or minus) on both sides of the transaction, with any additional consideration being paid in cash,

"7. be sold without recourse,

would not substantially affect the economic position of the transacting S & L's.

This case involves a typical Memorandum R-49 transaction. On December 31, 1980, Cottage Savings sold "90% participation interests" in 252 mortgages to four S & L's. It simultaneously purchased "90% participation interests" in 305 held by these S & L's.[2] All of the loans involved in the transaction were secured by single-family homes, most in the Cincinnati area. The fair market value of the package of participation interests exchanged by each side was approximately $4.5 million. The face value of the participation interests Cottage Savings relinquished in the transaction was approximately $6.9 million.

On its 1980 federal income tax return, Cottage Savings claimed a deduction for $2,447,091, which represented the adjusted difference between the face value of the participation interests that it traded and the fair market value of the participation interests that it received. As permitted by Memorandum R-49, Cottage Savings did not report these losses to the FHLBB. After the Commissioner of Internal Revenue disallowed Cottage Savings' claimed deduction, Cottage Savings sought a redetermination in the Tax Court. The Tax Court held that the deduction was permissible. . . .

On appeal by the Commissioner, the Court of Appeals reversed. 890 F. 2d 848 (CA6 1989). . . .

Because of the importance of this issue to the S & L industry and the conflict among the Circuits over whether Memorandum R-49 exchanges produce deductible tax losses, we granted certiorari. . . . We now reverse.

II

Rather than assessing tax liability on the basis of annual fluctuations in the value of a taxpayer's property, the Internal Revenue Code defers the tax consequences of a gain or loss in property value until the taxpayer "realizes" the gain or loss. The realization requirement is implicit in § 1001(a) of the Code, . . . which defines "the gain [or loss] from the sale or other disposition of property" as the difference between "the amount realized" from the sale or disposition of the property and its "adjusted basis." As this Court has recognized, the concept of realization is "founded on administrative convenience." *Helvering v. Horst*, 311 U.S. 112, 116 (1940). Under an appreciation-based system of taxation, taxpayers and the Commissioner would have to undertake the "cumbersome, abrasive, and unpredictable administrative task" of valuing assets on an annual basis to determine whether the assets had appreciated or depreciated in value. . . . In contrast, "[a] change in the

---

"8. have similar fair market values,

"9. have similar loan-to-value ratios at the time of the reciprocal sale, and

"10. have all security properties for both sides of the transaction in the same state." . . .

[2] [3] By exchanging merely participation interests rather than the loans themselves, each party retained its relationship with the individual obligors. Consequently, each S & L continued to service the loans on which it had transferred the participation interests and made monthly payments to the participation-interest holders.

form or extent of an investment is easily detected by a taxpayer or an administrative officer." . . .

Section 1001(a)'s language provides a straightforward test for realization: to realize a gain or loss in the value of property, the taxpayer must engage in a "sale or other disposition of [the] property." The parties agree that the exchange of participation interests in this case cannot be characterized as a "sale" under § 1001(a); the issue before us is whether the transaction constitutes a "disposition of property." The Commissioner argues that an exchange of property can be treated as a "disposition" under § 1001(a) only if the properties exchanged are materially different. The Commissioner further submits that, because the underlying mortgages were essentially economic substitutes, the participation interests exchanged by Cottage Savings were not materially different from those received from the other S & L's. Cottage Savings, on the other hand, maintains that *any* exchange of property is a "disposition of property" under § 1001(a), regardless of whether the property exchanged is materially different. Alternatively, Cottage Savings contends that the participation interests exchanged were materially different because the underlying loans were secured by different properties.

We must therefore determine whether the realization principle in § 1001(a) incorporates a "material difference" requirement. If it does, we must further decide what that requirement amounts to and how it applies in this case. We consider these questions in turn.

A

Neither the language nor the history of the Code indicates whether and to what extent property exchanged must differ to count as a "disposition of property" under § 1001(a). Nonetheless, we readily agree with the Commissioner that an exchange of property gives rise to a realization event under § 1001(a) only if the properties exchanged are "materially different." The Commissioner himself has by regulation construed § 1001(a) to embody a material difference requirement:

> "Except as otherwise provided . . . the gain or loss realized from the conversion of property into cash, *or from the exchange of property for other property differing materially either in kind or in extent*, is treated as income or as loss sustained." Treas. Reg. § 1.1001-1, . . . (emphasis added).

Because Congress has delegated to the Commissioner the power to promulgate "all needful rules and regulations for the enforcement of [the Internal Revenue Code]," 26 U.S.C. § 7805(a), we must defer to his regulatory interpretations of the Code so long as they are reasonable, see *National Muffler Dealers Assn., Inc. v. United States*, 440 U.S. 472, 476-477 (1979).

We conclude that Treasury Regulation § 1.1001-1 *is* a reasonable interpretation of § 1001(a). Congress first employed the language that now comprises § 1001(a) of the Code in § 202(a) of the Revenue Act of 1924, . . .; that language has remained essentially unchanged through various reenactments. And since 1934, the Commissioner has construed the statutory term "disposition of property" to include a "material difference" requirement. As we have recognized, " 'Treasury regulations and interpretations long continued without substantial change, applying to unamended or substantially reenacted statutes, are deemed to have received congressional approval and have the effect of law.' " *United States v. Correll*, 389 U.S. 299, 305-306 (1967), quoting *Helvering v. Winmill*, 305 U.S. 79, 83 (1938).

Treasury Regulation § 1.001-1 is also consistent with our landmark precedents on realization. In a series of early decisions involving the tax effects of property exchanges, this Court made clear that a taxpayer realizes taxable income only if the properties exchanged are "materially" or "essentially" different. See *United States v. Phellis*, 257 U.S. 156, 173 (1921); *Weiss v. Stearn*, 265 U.S. 242, 253-254 (1924); *Marr v. United States*, 268 U.S. 536, 540-542 (1925); see also *Eisner v. Macomber*, 252 U.S. 189, 207-212 (1920) (recognizing realization requirement). Because these decisions were part of the "contemporary legal context" in which Congress enacted § 202(a) of the 1924 Act, see *Cannon v. University of Chicago*, 441 U.S. 677, 698-699 (1979), and because Congress has left undisturbed through subsequent reenactments of the Code the principles of realization established in these cases, we may presume that Congress intended to codify these principles in § 1001(a), see *Pierce v. Underwood*, 487 U.S. 552, 567 (1988); *Lorillard v. Pons*, 434 U.S. 575, 580-581 (1978). The Commissioner's construction of the statutory language to incorporate these principles certainly was reasonable.

B

Precisely what constitutes a "material difference" for purposes of § 1001(a) of the Code is a more complicated question. The Commissioner argues that properties are "materially different" only if they differ in economic substance. To determine whether the participation interests exchanged in this case were "materially different" in this sense, the Commissioner argues, we should look to the attitudes of the parties, the evaluation of the interests by the secondary mortgage market, and the views of the FHLBB. We conclude that § 1001(a) embodies a much less demanding and less complex test.

Unlike the question *whether* § 1001(a) contains a material difference requirement, the question of *what constitutes* a material difference is not one on which we can defer to the Commissioner. For the Commissioner has not issued an authoritative, prelitigation interpretation of what property exchanges satisfy this requirement. Thus, to give meaning to the material difference test, we must look to the case law from which the test derives and which we believe Congress intended to codify in enacting and reenacting the language that now comprises § 1001(a). . . .

We start with the classic treatment of realization in *Eisner v. Macomber, supra*. In *Macomber*, a taxpayer who owned 2,200 shares of stock in a company received another 1,100 shares from the company as part of a pro rata stock dividend meant to reflect the company's growth in value. At issue was whether the stock dividend constituted taxable income. We held that it did not, because no gain was realized. . . . We reasoned that the stock dividend merely reflected the increased worth of the taxpayer's stock, . . . and that a taxpayer realizes increased worth of property only by receiving "something of exchangeable value *proceeding from* the property," . . .

In three subsequent decisions — *United States v. Phellis, supra; Weiss v. Stearn, supra*; and *Marr v. United States, supra* — we refined *Macomber's* conception of realization in the context of property exchanges. In each case, the taxpayer owned stock that had appreciated in value since its acquisition. And in each case, the corporation in which the taxpayer held stock had reorganized into a new corporation, with the new corporation assuming the business of the old corporation. While the corporations in *Phellis* and *Marr* both changed from New Jersey to Delaware corporations, the original and successor corporations in *Weiss* both were incorporated in Ohio. In each case, following the reorganization, the stockholders of the old corporation received shares in the new corporation equal to their proportional interest in the old corporation.

The question in these cases was whether the taxpayers realized the accumulated gain in their shares in the old corporation when they received in return for those shares stock representing an equivalent proportional interest in the new corporations. In *Phellis* and *Marr*, we held that the transactions were realization events. We reasoned that because a company incorporated in one State has "different rights and powers" from one incorporated in a different State, the taxpayers in *Phellis* and *Marr* acquired through the transactions property that was "materially different" from what they previously had. *United States v. Phellis*, 257 U.S., at 169-173; see *Marr v. United States, supra*, at 540-542 (using phrase "essentially different"). In contrast, we held that no realization occurred in *Weiss*. By exchanging stock in the predecessor corporation for stock in the newly reorganized corporation, the taxpayer did not receive "a thing really different from what he therefore had." *Weiss v. Stearn, supra*, at 254. As we explained in *Marr*, our determination that the reorganized company in *Weiss* was not "really different" from its predecessor turned on the fact that both companies were incorporated in the same State. See *Marr v. United States, supra*, at 540-542 (outlining distinction between these cases).

Obviously, the distinction in *Phellis* and *Marr* that made the stock in the successor corporations materially different from the stock in the predecessors was minimal. Taken together, *Phellis, Marr*, and *Weiss* stand for the principle that properties are "different" in the sense that is "material" to the Internal Revenue Code so long as their respective possessors enjoy legal entitlements that are different in kind or extent. Thus, separate groups of stock are not materially different if they confer "the same proportional interest of the same character in the same corporation." *Marr v. United States*, 268 U.S., at 540. However, they *are* materially different if they are issued by different corporations, *id.*, at 541; *United States v. Phellis, supra*, at 173, or if they confer "different rights and powers" in the same corporation, *Marr v. United States, supra*, at 541. No more demanding a standard than this is necessary in order to satisfy the administrative purposes underlying the realization requirement in § 1001(a). See *Helvering v. Horst*, 311 U.S., at 116. For, as long as the property entitlements are not identical, their exchange will allow both the Commissioner and the transacting taxpayer easily to fix the appreciated or depreciated values of the property relative to their tax bases.

In contrast, we find no support for the Commissioner's "economic substitute" conception of material difference. According to the Commissioner, differences between properties are material for purposes of the Code only when it can be said that the parties, the relevant market (in this case the secondary mortgage market), and the relevant regulatory body (in this case the FHLBB) would consider them material. Nothing in *Phellis*, *Weiss*, and *Marr* suggests that exchanges of properties must satisfy such a subjective test to trigger realization of a gain or loss.

Moreover, the complexity of the Commissioner's approach ill serves the goal of administrative convenience that underlies the realization requirement. In order to apply the Commissioner's test in a principled fashion, the Commissioner and the taxpayer must identify the relevant market, establish whether there is a regulatory agency whose views should be taken into account, and then assess how the relevant market participants and the agency would view the transaction. The Commissioner's failure to explain how these inquiries should be conducted further calls into question the workability of his test.

Finally, the Commissioner's test is incompatible with the structure of the Code. Section 1001(c) of Title 26 provides that a gain or loss realized under § 1001(a) "shall be recognized" unless one of the Code's nonrecognition provisions applies. One such nonrecognition provision withholds recognition of a gain or loss realized from an exchange of properties that would appear to be economic substitutes under the Commissioner's material difference test. This provision, commonly known as the "like kind" exception, withholds recognition of a gain or loss realized "on the exchange of property held for productive use in a trade or business or for investment . . . for property of like kind which is to be held either for productive use in a trade or business or for investment." 26 U.S.C. § 1031(a)(1). If Congress had expected that exchanges of similar properties would *not* count as realization events under § 1001(a), it would have had no reason to bar recognition of a gain or loss realized from these transactions.

C

Under our interpretation of § 1001(a), an exchange of property gives rise to a realization event so long as the exchanged properties are "materially different" — that is, so long as they embody legally distinct entitlements. Cottage Savings' transactions at issue here easily satisfy this test. Because the participation interests exchanged by Cottage Savings and the other S & L's derived from loans that were made to different obligors and secured by different homes, the exchanged interests did embody legally distinct entitlements. Consequently, we conclude that Cottage Savings realized its losses at the point of the exchange.

The Commissioner contends that it is anomalous to treat mortgages deemed to be "substantially identical" by the FHLBB as "materially different." The anomaly, however, is merely semantic; mortgages can be substantially identical for Memorandum R-49 purposes and still exhibit "differences" that are "material" for purposes of the Internal Revenue Code. Because Cottage Savings received entitlements different from those it gave up, the exchange put both Cottage Savings and the Commissioner in a position to determine the change in the value of Cottage Savings' mortgages relative to their tax bases. Thus, there is no reason not to treat the exchange of these interests as a realization event, regardless of the status of the mortgages under the criteria of Memorandum R-49.

III

[The Court also determined that the Cottage Savings had sustained its losses within the meaning of § 165(a).]

IV

For the reasons set forth above, the judgment of the Court of Appeals is reversed, and the case is remanded for further proceedings consistent with this opinion.

So ordered.

JUSTICE BLACKMUN, with whom JUSTICE WHITE joins, concurring in part and dissenting in part. . . .

I dissent . . . from the Court's conclusions in these two cases that Centennial and Cottage Savings Association realized deductible losses for income tax purposes when each exchanged partial interests in one group of residential mortgage loans for partial interests in another like group of residential mortgage loans. I regard these losses as not recognizable for income tax purposes because the mortgage packages so exchanged were substantially identical and were not materially different.

The exchanges, as the Court acknowledges, were occasioned by the Federal Home Loan Bank Board's (FHLBB) Memorandum R-49 of June 27, 1980, and by that Memorandum's relaxation of theretofore-existing accounting regulations and requirements, a relaxation effected to avoid placement of "many S & L's at risk of closure by the FHLBB" without substantially affecting the "economic position of the transacting S & L's." . . . But the Memorandum, the Court notes, also had as a purpose "the facilit[ation of] transactions that would generate tax losses." . . . I find it somewhat surprising that an agency not responsible for tax matters would presume to dictate what is or is not a deductible loss for federal income tax purposes. I had thought that that was something within the exclusive province of the Internal Revenue Service, subject to administrative and judicial review. Certainly, the Bank Board's opinion in this respect is entitled to no deference whatsoever. . . . The Commissioner, of course, took the opposing position. See Rev. Rul. 85-125, 1985-2 Cum. Bull. 180; Rev. Rul. 81-204, 1981-2 Cum. Bull. 157.

It long has been established that gain or loss in the value of property is taken into account for income tax purposes only if and when the gain or loss is "realized," that is, when it is tied to a realization event, such as the sale, exchange, or other disposition of the property. Mere variation in value — the routine ups and downs of the marketplace — do not in themselves have income tax consequences. This is fundamental in income tax law.

In applying the realization requirement to an exchange, the properties involved must be materially different in kind or in extent. Treas. Reg. § 1.1001-1(a), . . . This has been the rule recognized administratively at least since 1935, . . . This makes economic as well as tax sense, for the parties obviously regard the exchanged properties as having equivalent values. In tax law, we should remember, substance rather than form determines tax consequences. . . . Thus, the resolution of the exchange issue in these cases turns on the "materially different" concept. The Court recognizes as much. . . .

That the mortgage participation partial interests exchanged in these cases were "different" is not in dispute. The materiality prong is the focus. A material difference is one that has the capacity to influence a decision. . . .

The application of this standard leads, it seems to me, to only one answer — that the mortgage participation partial interests released were not materially different from the mortgage participation partial interests received. Memorandum R-49, as the Court notes, . . . lists 10 factors that, when satisfied, as they were here, serve to classify the interests as "substantially identical." These factors assure practical identity; surely, they then also assure that any difference cannot be of consequence. Indeed, nonmateriality is the full purpose of the Memorandum's criteria. The "proof of the pudding" is in the fact of its complete accounting acceptability to the FHLBB. Indeed, as has been noted, it is difficult to reconcile substantial identity for financial accounting purposes with a material difference for tax accounting purposes. . . . Common sense so dictates.

This should suffice and be the end of the analysis. Other facts, however, solidify the conclusion: The retention by the transferor of 10% interests, enabling it to keep on servicing its loans; the transferor's continuing to collect the payments due from the borrowers so that, so far as the latter were concerned, it was business as usual, exactly as it had been; the obvious lack of concern or dependence of the transferor with the "differences" upon which the Court relies (as transferees, the taxpayers made no credit checks and no appraisals of collateral . . . ; the selection of the loans by computer programmed to match mortgages in accordance with the Memorandum R-49 criteria; the absence of even the names of the borrowers in the closing schedules attached to the agreements; Centennial's receipt of loan files only six years after its exchange, . . . ; the restriction of the interests exchanged to the same State; the identity of the respective face and fair market values; and the application by the parties of common discount factors to each side of the transaction — all reveal that any differences that might exist made no difference whatsoever and were not material. This demonstrates the real nature of the transactions, including nonmateriality of the claimed differences.

We should be dealing here with realities and not with superficial distinctions. As has been said many times, and as noted above, in income tax law we are to be concerned with substance and not with mere form. When we stray from that principle, the new precedent is likely to be a precarious beacon for the future.

I respectfully dissent on this issue.

NOTES AND COMMENTS

1. In deciding in the taxpayer's favor in *Cottage Savings*, the Supreme Court may have saved the government from future difficulty. The government in *Cottage Savings* argued that the taxpayer did not satisfy the materiality standard under the Regulations in order to prevent the taxpayer from deducting the economic losses

associated with the group of residential mortgages transferred. Had the government been successful before the Court, it would be interesting to see the government's reaction when a subsequent taxpayer asserted that no gain was realized in a similar transaction involving appreciated assets.

2. In Part II, B of its opinion, the Court noted that the Commissioner's position was incompatible with the structure of the Code, asserting that the like-kind exchange provisions of § 1031 would not be necessary if the Commissioner was correct regarding the materiality standard. The non-recognition of gain or loss under § 1031 is frequently justified on the grounds that the taxpayer's economic position with respect to the relinquished and replacement properties has not changed sufficiently to impose tax. *See* Treas. Reg. § 1.1002-1(c) (asserting that the differences between the properties exchanged "are more formal than substantial," and that the "new property is substantially a continuation of the investment still unliquidated"). However, how economically similar must the properties be to satisfy the like-kind requirement? Is the Commissioner's position in *Cottage Savings* so obviously incompatible with § 1031 as the Court states? The requirements of § 1031 are described in § 1, *Like-Kind Exchanges*, of Chapter 5, *Nonrecogntion Transactions*.

3. Most transfers of property, whether they take the form of a sale or an exchange, are obviously realization effects under the materiality standard of *Cottage Savings*. However, it is not difficult to hypothesize transfers that might not satisfy the standard. For example, assume that two individuals, A and B, hold a parcel of unimproved real property as tenants in common. A and B subdivide the property into two parcels, and A conveys his interest in Parcel 2 to B while B conveys his interest in Parcel 1 to A. As a result, A is the sole owner of Parcel 1 and B is the sole owner of Parcel 2. If the property prior to its subdivision had a fair market value of $100,000 and a basis of $40,000, did A and B each realize a gain of $15,000 when they conveyed their respective interests in the subdivided parcels to the other? As tenants in common, A could certainly have been viewed as owning a one-half interest in Parcel 2 with a fair market value of $25,000 and a basis of $10,000 (a one-half interest in one half of the property). The same could be said for B with respect to Parcel 1. Thus, when A and B conveyed their interests as co-tenants in Parcels 2 and 1, respectively, a realization event occurred, and A and B realized gain equal to the difference between the fair market values and the bases of their respective interests. Certainly, the legal relations that each had with respect to the parcels has changed from a tenancy in common to a sole owner of the fee.

In Rev. Rul. 73-476, 1973-2 C.B. 300, the Service concluded that if three tenants-in-common of three separate parcels rearrange their interests so that each party becomes the sole owner of one of the parcels, an exchange occurs so that gain or loss is realized under § 1001. *See also* Rev. Rul. 79-44, 1979-1 C.B. 265 (the transfer of interests in real property held by tenants in common that resulted in the conversion of two jointly owned parcels into two individually owned parcels is an exchange for purposes of § 1001). However, in Rev. Rul. 56-437, 1956-2 C.B. 507, the Service concluded that the conversion of a joint tenancy in corporate stock into a tenancy in common for the purpose of eliminating a survivorship feature was a nontaxable transaction for federal income tax purposes. How might these two rulings apply to the facts in the prior paragraph? *See* Priv. Ltr. Rul. 20-04-11-023 (concluding that Rev. Rul. 56-437 rather than Rev. Rul. 73-476 applies when a single parcel of property owned as tenants-in-common by three individuals is partitioned pursuant to an action under state law). Is the difference in these Rulings the result of the fact that Rev. Rul. 79-44 involved multiple parcels of property or that the legal change in Rev. Rul. 56-437 and Priv. Ltr. Rul. 200411023 occurred by operation of law rather than an exchange of interests?

4. The Service responded to the decision in *Cottage Savings* with the promulgation of Regulation § 1.1001-3, which defines the extent of the changes that the parties may make in connection with debt obligations that, when deemed significant, result in the realization of gain or loss under Regulation § 1.1001-1(a). More specifically, the Regulations provide that "a significant modification of a debt instrument, within the meaning of this section, results in an exchange of the original debt instrument for a modified instrument that differs materially either in kind or in extent." Treas. Reg. § 1.1001-3(b). A "modification" of a debt instrument is defined as:

> any alteration, including any deletion or addition, in whole or in part, of a legal right or obligation of the issuer or a holder of a debt instrument, whether the alteration is evidenced by an express agreement (oral or written), conduct of the parties, or otherwise.

Treas. Reg. § 1 1.1001-3(c)(1)(i). Changes or alterations in the legal rights of the parties are not generally modifications when they are pursuant to the terms of the instrument. Treas. Reg. § 1.1001-3(c)(1)(ii) and (d), examples (1), (2), (5), and (8). However, changes in the obligor, changes between recourse and nonrecourse, changes from debt to equity (other than the conversion of debt to equity under a conversion privilege), changes at the option of either party (other than the holder's unilateral, option that does not change a scheduled payment) are modifications even if pursuant to the original terms of the debt instrument. Treas. Reg. § 1.1001-3(c)(2) and (d), examples (4), (7), and (11). Modifications that are significant include: (i) changes in yield of more than one-quarter of a percentage point, or if greater more than five percent of the original yield, which would apply when the original yield was more than five percent; (ii) changing the time of payment by more than five percent of the original term or 50 percent of the original term if the term is less than five years; (iii) change in obligor of a recourse obligation, with exceptions for some reorganizations and other transactions; (iv) change in security or credit enhancement of a recourse obligation, or altering the security of a nonrecourse obligation; (v) changes from debt to equity if the change is a modification, including changes between recourse and nonrecourse (other than changing a secured debt to nonrecourse without changing payment expectations. Treas. Reg. §§ 1.1001-3(e) and 1.1001-3(g).

Prior to the promulgation of the Regulations under § 1.1001-3, the Service had ruled that the conversion of convertible debt obligations issued by a corporation that become a subsidiary of a holding company that assumed joint liability on the obligation and provided that the obligations become convertible into stock of the parent would not be taxable (Rev. Rul. 79-155, 1979-1 C.B. 153); that the mere extension of the maturity date of notes, accompanied by the agreement of some note holders to be the last to have their notes redeemed, is not a recognition transaction resulting in gain or loss, whether accomplished by notation on the original instrument or substitution of new instruments (Rev. Rul. 73-160, 1973-1 C.B. 365); and that the conversion of a convertible debenture into stock was not an exchange under § 1001 (Rev. Rul. 72-265, 1972-1 C.B. 222). On the other hand, it held that a modification of key person insurance where the policy provided an option to change the insured was a sufficiently fundamental or material change that the substance of the original contract is altered even though it was provided in the original contract (Rev. Rul. 90-109, 1990-2 C.B. 191); that changes in the terms of debt obligations of a corporation that became a subsidiary of a holding company to increase the interest rate and shorten the maturity was an exchange for purposes of § 1001, but for which nonrecognition treatment was available under the reorganization provisions (Rev. Rul. 79-155, 1979-1 C.B. 153); and that gain or loss was realized when the bonds of one corporation were converted into stock of another corporation pursuant to an option contained in the bonds (Rev. Rul. 69-135, 1969-1 C.B. 198).

PROBLEMS FOR DISCUSSION

Problem 1-7. How would the result in *Cottage Savings* change if the Regulations under § 1.1001-3 had applied? Does this change represent sound tax policy?

Problem 1-8. How do the Regulations under § 1.1001-3 affect the results in Rev. Rul. 79-155, 1979-1 C.B. 153 (conversion of convertible debt obligations issued of subsidiary of holding company that assumed joint liability on the obligation that become convertible into stock of the parent); Rev. Rul. 73-160, 1973-1 C.B. 365 (mere extension of the maturity date of notes, agreement of some note holders to be the last to have their notes redeemed. Rev. Rul. 72-265, 1972-1 C.B. 222 (conversion of convertible debenture into stock); Rev. Rul. 90-109, 1990-2 C.B. 191 (change of insured under key person insurance where the policy provided an option to change the insured); Rev. Rul. 79-155, 1979-1 C.B. 153 (increasing interest rate; shortening the maturity, and assumption of joint obligation by new parent of debt obligation of subsidiary acquired in a reorganization); and Rev. Rul. 69-135, 1969-1 C.B. 198 (conversion of bonds of one corporation into stock of another corporation pursuant to an option contained in the bonds)?

§ 3.03. Other Dispositions

§ 3.03(a) Casualties and Abandonment

A realization event for purposes of § 1001 may also occur when property is lost or destroyed as a result of a casualty or theft. Casualties typically involve the loss of property as a result of fire, storm, shipwreck, and similar events. *See* § 165(c)(2). A realization event may also occur as a result of theft, which the Regulations interpret to include larceny, embezzlement, and robbery. Treas. Reg. § 1.165-8(d). Realization events resulting from a casualty or theft may give rise to a loss equal to the unrecovered basis of the property involved. However, if the property is insured, any loss is reduced to the extent of the insurance proceeds received. Furthermore, gain may be realized as a result of a casualty or theft if the insurance proceeds exceed the basis of the property. Although any gain resulting from a casualty or theft is included in the taxpayer's gross income, the deduction by an individual of any loss resulting from a casualty or theft that is not connected to a trade or business or a transaction entered into for profit is limited under § 165(h).

In addition to casualties, a realization event may occur for purposes of § 1001 if the taxpayer abandons the property involved. In order to abandon tangible property, a taxpayer must intend "irrevocably to discard the asset so that it will neither be used again by him nor retrieved by him for sale, exchange, or other disposition.' Treas. Reg. § 1.167(a)-8(a)(4). Although intangible assets are not capable of physical abandonment, the courts have concluded that intangible assets may be abandoned when the taxpayer demonstrates an intention "to abandon the property, coupled with an act of abandonment, both of which must be ascertained from all of the surrounding facts and circumstances." *Massey-Ferguson, Inc. v. Commissioner*, 59 T.C. 220, 225 (1972), *acq.* (quoting from *Boston E. R. Co. v. Commissioner*, 16 T.C. 1084, 1108 (1951),*nonacq., aff'd*, 196 F.2d 923 (1st Cir. 1952)). Importantly, abandonment will not be found if the taxpayer intends to hold the property for possible future use or to realize potential future value from the property.

A realization event may also arise when property is rendered worthless. However, the courts have held that worthlessness must be evidenced by a "closed and completed transaction, fixed by identifiable events" establishing that the property is worthless in the taxable year for which the deduction is claimed. *Proesel v. Commissioner*, 77 T.C. 992 (1981); *Springfield Productions, Inc. v. Commissioner*, T.C. Mem. 1979-23, 38 T.C.M. 74. *See also* Treas. Reg. §§ 1.165-1(b) and 1.165-1(d)(1); Rev. Rul. 54-581, 1954-2 C.B. 112. Importantly, mere diminution in the value of an asset is not sufficient to establish worthlessness. Nevertheless, a taxpayer need not be an "incorrigible optimist" in determining when property becomes worthless. *See United States v. S.S. White Dental Mfg. Co.*, 274 U.S. 398 (1927).

In connection with property that is abandoned or rendered worthless, a loss is typically realized equal to the unrecovered basis of the property. However, if abandoned property is subject to a nonrecourse debt, the taxpayer will be treated as having an amount realized equal to the outstanding principal amount of the debt that will either reduce the amount of the loss realized or result in gain to the extent that the principal amount of the debt exceeds the taxpayer's basis in the property. *See Lockwood v. Commissioner*, 94 T.C. 252 (1990) (in which the abandonment of master musical recordings encumbered by purchase money nonrecourse debt was treated as an exchange and the loss calculated as equal to the difference between the amount of the debt and the taxpayer's adjusted basis in the property).

§ 3.03(b) Transfer in Satisfaction of a Claim

When property is transferred in satisfaction of a pre-existing claim or obligation of the taxpayer, gain or loss will result. For example, assume that a taxpayer borrowed $100,000 from a third-party lender. In order to satisfy the loan, the taxpayer transferred property to the lender with a fair market value of $100,000 and a basis of $65,000. As a result of the transfer, the taxpayer realizes gain of $35,000 ($100,000 amount realized - $65,000 basis). In this way, the taxpayer is treated as if he sold the property for $100,000 in cash, resulting in gain of $35,000, and transferred the cash to the lender in satisfaction of the loan. As the following decision explains, the transfer of property in satisfaction of a pre-existing claim can result in the realization of gain or loss in contexts other than that involving a debt.

INTERNATIONAL FREIGHTING CORPORATION, INC. v. COMMISSIONER

United States Court Of Appeals, Second Circuit
135 F.2d 310 (2d Cir. 1943)

During the years 1933 to 1935, inclusive, E. I. duPont deNemours and Company, Inc., owned all of taxpayer's stock and during the year 1936 it owned two-thirds of taxpayer's stock, the balance being owned by the General Motors Corporation. During the years 1933 to 1936, inclusive, taxpayer informally adopted the bonus plan of the duPont Company as its own bonus plan. Class A or class B bonus awards, or both, might be made to employees under that plan. Class B bonus awards (the only ones here involved) might be granted to those employees who, by their ability, efficiency and loyalty, had contributed most in a general way to the taxpayer's success, and were to be made from the portion of taxpayer's profits which its finance committee had set aside in the class B bonus fund. Only those employees were eligible for class B awards who on January first of the year in which the awards were made had been in the continuous employ of taxpayer at least two years. Recommendations for bonuses were to be made by the president or the heads of departments and were to be acted on by the executive committee or the board of directors. It was not incumbent on the executive committee or the board of directors to distribute the entire amount available in the fund. The taxpayer reserved the right at any time to discontinue the awarding of any bonuses.

Bonuses were in the form of common stock of the duPont Company or in the form of cash to be invested in such stock. Class B bonuses were to be awarded during February of each year "for services rendered during the preceding year." . . . [The] bonus custodian, appointed by the executive committee, was to manage all matters relating to bonus awards. When a class B bonus was awarded or invested in the common stock of duPont Company, a certificate for one-fourth of the shares, free from all restrictions, was to be delivered to the beneficiary immediately, and certificates for the balance were to be delivered to the bonus custodian who was to hold them for release to the beneficiary as follows: One-fourth of the total number of shares after the end of one year; one-fourth after the end of two years; and one-fourth after the end of three years. . . . An award in stock was to vest in the beneficiary all the rights of a stockholder in such stock, subject (1) to the right of the bonus custodian to possession of certificates evidencing the portion of the stock not immediately released; and (2) the right of the taxpayer, in case the beneficiary left taxpayer's service or was dismissed, to have that portion of the stock represented at the time by the debit balance of the beneficiary's account sold at the market value and the proceeds transferred to taxpayer. . . .

. . . During the calendar year 1936 taxpayer paid over and distributed to the beneficiaries of its class B bonus award, certificates representing 150 shares of the common stock of the duPont Company, whose cost to taxpayer at the date of delivery was $16,153.36 and whose market value was then $24,858.75. Each of the employees receiving those shares in 1936 paid a tax thereon, computing the market value at the time of delivery as taxable income.

Taxpayer took a deduction of $24,858.75 in its income tax return for 1936 on account of the 150 shares of stock distributed in that year to its employees. In a notice of deficiency the Commissioner reduced the deduction from $24,858.75 to $16,153.35, a difference of $8,705.39, determining that, as the bonus was paid in property, "the basis for calculation of the amount thereof is the cost of such property and not its market value as claimed on the return." This was the only adjustment which the Commissioner made to taxpayer's return and, as a result, the Commissioner determined a deficiency in the amount of $2,156.76, in taxpayer's tax liability for the year. Taxpayer filed a petition with the Tax Court for a redetermination of the deficiency thus determined. By an amended answer, the Commissioner, in the alternative, alleged that if it were held that taxpayer was entitled to a deduction in the amount of $24,858.75 on account of the payment of bonus in stock, then taxpayer realized a taxable profit of $8,705.39 on the disposition of the shares, and taxpayer's net taxable income otherwise determined should be increased accordingly.

The Tax Court held that taxpayer was entitled to a deduction for compensation paid in the year 1936 in the amount of $24,858.75. The Tax Court decided for the Commissioner, however, on the defense set forth in the Commissioner's amended answer, holding that taxpayer realized a gain of $8,705.39 in 1936 by paying the class B bonus in stock which had cost taxpayer $8,705.39 less than its market value when taxpayer transferred the stock to its employees. The deficiency resulting from this decision was $2,156.76. From that decision taxpayer seeks review.

FRANK, CIRCUIT JUDGE.

1. . . . We think the Tax Court correctly held that the market value at the time of delivery was properly deducted by the taxpayer as an ordinary expense of the business . . . because that delivery was an additional reasonable compensation for past services actually rendered. . . .

2. We turn to the question whether the transaction resulted in taxable gain to taxpayer. We think that the Tax Court correctly held that it did. The delivery of those shares was not a gift, . . . precisely because it was "compensation for services actually rendered," i.e., because the taxpayer received a full quid pro quo. Accordingly, cases holding that one is not liable for an income tax when he makes a gift of shares are not in point. . . .

3, 4. But, as the delivery of the shares here constituted a disposition for a valid consideration, it resulted in a closed transaction with a consequent realized gain. It is of no relevance that here the taxpayer had not been legally obligated to award any shares or pay any additional compensation to the employees; bonus payments by corporations are recognized as proper even if there was no previous obligation to make them; although then not obligatory, they are regarded as made for a sufficient consideration. Since the bonuses would be invalid to the extent that what was delivered to the employees exceeded what the services of the employees were worth, it follows that the consideration received by the taxpayer from the employees must be deemed to be equal at least to the value of the shares in 1936. Here then, as there was no gift but a disposition of shares for a valid consideration equal at least to the market value of the shares when delivered, there was a taxable gain equal to the difference between the cost of the shares and that market value.

For § 111(a) of the Revenue Act of 1936 [the predecessor to § 1001] . . . provides that the gain from "the sale or other disposition of property" shall be the excess of "the amount realized therefrom" over "the adjusted basis" provided in § 113(b) [the predecessor to § 1011] and § 113(b) — in the light of § 113(a) [the predecessor to § 1012], . . . — makes the "basis" the cost of such property. True, § 111(b) provides that "the amount realized" is the sum of "any money received plus the fair market value of the property (other than money) received." Literally, where there is a disposition of stock for services, no "property" or "money" is received by the person who thus disposes of the stock. But, in similar circumstances, it has been held that "money's worth" is received and that such a receipt comes within § 111(b). See Commissioner v. Mesta, 3 Cir., 123 F.2d 986, 988 . . . .[3]

The taxpayer properly asks us to treat this case "as if there had been no formal bonus plan" and as if taxpayer "had simply paid outright 150 shares of duPont stock to selected employees as additional compensation." On that basis, surely there was a taxable gain. For to shift the equation once more, the case supposed is the equivalent of one in which the taxpayer in the year 1936, without entering into a previous contract fixing the amount of compensation, had employed a transposition expert for one day and, when he completed his work, had paid him 5 shares of duPont stock having market value at that time of $500 but which it had bought in a previous year for $100. There can be no doubt that, from such a transaction, taxpayer would have a taxable gain. And so here.

The order of the Tax Court is affirmed.

NOTES AND COMMENTS

1. The principle that the disposition of property for services, and, by implication, any other deductible or nondeductible expenditure is a taxable disposition under § 1001, with the amount of the deduction or other allowance measuring the amount realized, has been applied to allow recognition of loss as well as gain. *See Montana Power Co. v. United States*, 171 F. Supp. 943 (Ct. Cl. 1959) (fair market value of stock transferred (with cash) to obtain release from burdensome contract deductible; excess of basis of stock over value is capital loss). The same principle applies even to gratuitous transfers subject to a liability or other obligation. *See Diedrich v. Commissioner*, 457 U.S. 191 (1982) (gain recognized on a net gift of property transferred subject to the gift tax to be paid by the donee).

Similarly, in *United States v. Davis*, 370 U.S. 65 (1962), the Court held that a transfer of appreciated securities in a divorce in discharge of a wife's inchoate

---

[3] [5] In these cases the taxpayer paid a money claim by delivering stock. What the taxpayer received was literally neither property nor money, yet it was held that there was a taxable transaction under § 111(b).

marital property rights resulted in gain. In answer to the problem that the rights could not be valued, the Court held that the value could be assumed to be equivalent to the value of the securities. Although the result in *Davis* has been modified as a result of the enactment of § 1041, which now treats the transfer as roughly equivalent to a gift, the principle should still apply in situations other than divorce. *See Farid-Es-Sultaneh v. Commissioner*, 160 F.2d 812 (2d Cir. 1947) (transfer of appreciated securities to prospective wife in anticipation of prospective marriage and subsequently executed pre-nuptial agreement in which she waived dower and other marital property rights was not a gift but a transfer for valuable consideration). One significant effect of § 1041 is to shift the inherent gain or loss in transferred property to the recipient spouse. *See Young v. Commissioner*, 240 F.3d 369 (4th Cir. 2001) (husband does not recognize gain on transfer of real property to satisfy a note on which husband subsequently defaulted given as part of a divorce settlement, even though wife sued and won judgment); *Yankwich v. Commissioner*, T.C. Mem. 2002-37 (agreement to make payments to wife equal to principal and interest received on a promissory note owned by husband, represented by husband's note with identical terms, treated as transfer of note so that wife taxable on interest, but not principal, when received); *Gibbs v. Commissioner*, T.C. Mem. 1997-196 (payments to divorced wife of her share of the value of the family business over ten years with interest at 9 percent was a nonrecognition transfer under § 1041 only to the extent of the principal).

On the other hand, transfers that separate interests in jointly owned property usually do not result in recognition of gain or loss. *See Beth W. Corp. v. United States*, 350 F. Supp. 1190 (S.D. Fla. 1972), *aff'd without a published opinion*, 481 F.2d 1401 (5th Cir. 1977) (conveyances by spouses to each other intended as equal division under a marital settlement agreement was partition for which no gain or loss was realized); Rev. Rul. 81-292, 1981-2 C.B. 158 (same result for an approximately equal division of the total value of jointly owned property in a state that is not a community property state, even though there is a transfer of some assets in their entirety to one spouse or the other); Rev. Rul. 74-347, 1974-2 C.B. 26 (husband realized gain on only to the extent that the wife received more than half of jointly-owned property to compensate for his retention of separately owned property; transaction treated as nontaxable division of jointly owned property with the husband's subsequent transfer of part of his share).

At one time, the Service took the position that § 1041 did not apply to assigned rights to income. *See Kochansky v. Commissioner*, 92 F.3d 957 (9th Cir. 1996) (lawyer husband taxed on full contingent fee even though obligated under divorce settlement to pay portion of fee to wife); Rev. Rul. 87-112, 1987-2 C.B. 207 (transferor taxable on accrued but unpaid interest on bond transferred to spouse in divorce). However, it has now concluded that § 1041 applies to nonstatutory stock options transferred in a divorce so that the recipient-spouse is taxed on the compensation when the option is exercised, but acknowledged that it will continue to apply assignment of income principles in cases like *Kochansky*, where the rights to the income are not vested at transfer. Rev. Rul. 2002-22, 2002-1 C.B. 849. On the other hand, the fact that the payments may be based on rights to income does not make the recipient spouse taxable on them. *See Balding v. Commissioner*, 98 T.C. 368 (1992) (amounts received by ex-wife in lieu of her uncertain claim to a share of her ex-husband's military pension were nontaxable under § 1041; although not stated (since the ex-husband was not a party), this presumably means he remains fully taxable on the pension).

2. Two Code provisions expressly provide for the transfer of the tax consequences when property is transferred to the recipient spouse. Section 453B(g) provides that the transferee spouse is taxed in connection with payments received under installment obligations transferred incident to divorce, and § 402(e)(1)(A) provides that the transferee spouse is taxable as an alternate payee for payments under a qualified domestic relations order authorized by § 401(a)(13) and defined in § 414(p).

PROBLEMS FOR DISCUSSION

Problem 1-9. Is the result in *Davis*, requiring the realization of gain or loss in connection with property transferred in a divorce, a necessary application of the result in *International Freighting* requiring the realization of gain or loss in connection with property transferred for the rendition of services?

Problem 1-10. Are the conclusions in Rev. Ruls. 74-347 (uneven division of joint property) and 81-292 (separation of joint property) and the holding in *Beth W. Corp.* (separation of tenancy by the entireties property) consistent with *United States v. Davis* (property transfer in divorce)? What are Mrs. Davis' tax consequences on receipt of the stock under *Davis*?

Problem 1-11. Does § 1041 overrule the result in *Davis*? What are the tax consequences to Mr. and Mrs. Davis under § 1041? What are the tax consequences to the taxpayers in Rev. Ruls. 74-347 and 81-292 and in *Beth W. Corp.* as a result of the enactment of § 1041?

Problem 1-12. Are the results in *Young* (no gain or loss recognized on the transfer of property to satisfy note given in divorce) and *Yankwich* (wife taxed on interest, but not principal of husband's mirror note) a proper application of § 1041? Is there any reason for a different result in *Farid-Es-Sultaneh* (gain or loss realized on the transfer of property in connection with prenuptial agreement)?

Problem 1-13. In light of the express provisions of §§ 453B(g) and 402(e)(1)(A) specifically dealing with the assignment of income between spouses and former spouses, was the Service justified in taxing the transferee spouse in Rev. Rul. 2002-22 in the absence of a similar provision? If so, is excluding cases like *Kochansky* justified as well? In light of these authorities, what would be the result in *Balding*, if Mrs. Balding established a right to a share of the military pension?

§ 3.03(c) Mortgaging Property as a Realization Event

When a taxpayer borrows money, the taxpayer is not considered to have gross income because of the corresponding obligation to repay the loan. The treatment of loans is described in greater detail in Chapter 3. Similarly, when a taxpayer borrows money secured by an interest in property, the situation is *not* treated as a realization event with an amount realized equal to the amount of the loan. The situation could be thought to be a bit murkier, however, if the loan is nonrecourse, rather than recourse. With a recourse loan, the taxpayer is personally liable for repayment of the loan. In other words, if the taxpayer defaults on the payment of the loan, the lender may foreclose on any property that secures the loan and may look to any other assets of the taxpayer to satisfy the loan. With a nonrecourse loan, the taxpayer is not personally liable for repayment of the loan. Consequently, if the taxpayer defaults on the payment of the loan, the lender may only foreclose on any property that secures the loan in order to satisfy the loan.

When a taxpayer borrows money on a recourse basis secured by an interest in property, the loan is not treated as a realization event on the assumption that the taxpayer will not default on the loan in order to protect the taxpayer's other assets. When a taxpayer borrows money on a nonrecourse basis secured by an interest in property, the taxpayer could be thought to have sold an interest in the property to the lender because it is the lender who bears the economic risk of loss if the value of the property drops below the amount of the loan. In this situation, the taxpayer can walk away from the property and the lender can only look to the property in satisfaction of the loan. Similarly, the taxpayer could be thought to have "locked in" any appreciation in value when the amount of the loan exceeds the basis of the property.

In the following opinion, the court considered whether a realization event occurred when the taxpayer borrowed money on a nonrecourse basis secured by an interest in property. Interestingly, the taxpayer was the one making this argument. Typically, one would think that the government would make such an argument in order to force the taxpayer to realize gain when the amount of the nonrecourse loan is in excess of the basis of the property. In this situation, the taxpayer made the argument that a realization event occurred on the earlier refinancing of a loan secured by the property because the taxpayer wanted to increase the basis of the property in order to reduce the amount of gain on a subsequent sale of the property.

WOODSAM ASSOCIATES, INC. v. COMMISSIONER

United States Court Of Appeals, Second Circuit
198 F.2d 357 (2d. Cir. 1952)

CHASE, CIRCUIT JUDGE

The petitioner paid its income . . . taxes for 1943 as computed upon returns it filed which included as part of its gross income $146,058.10 as gain realized upon the mortgage foreclosure sale in that year of improved real estate which it owned and which was bid in by the mortgagee for a nominal sum. It filed a timely claim for refund on the ground that its adjusted basis for the property had been understated and its taxable gain, therefore, was less than that reported. The refund claim was denied . . . . The decisive issue now presented is whether the basis for determining gain or loss upon the sale or other disposition of property is increased when, subsequent to the acquisition of the property, the owner receives a loan in an amount greater than his adjusted basis which is secured by a mortgage on the property upon which he is not personally liable. If so, it is agreed that part of the income taxes . . . taxes paid for 1943 should be refunded.

A comparatively brief statement of the admitted facts and their obvious, and conceded, tax consequences will suffice by way of introduction.

On December 29, 1934, Samuel J. Wood and his wife organized the petitioner and each transferred to it certain property in return for one-half of its capital stock. One piece of property so transferred by Mrs. Wood was the above mentioned parcel of improved real estate consisting of land in the City of New York and a brick building thereon divided into units suitable for use, and used, in retail business. The property was subject to a $400,000 mortgage on which Mrs. Wood was not personally liable and on which the petitioner never became personally liable. Having, thus, acquired the property in a tax free exchange, [under § 351] the petitioner took the basis of Mrs. Wood for tax purposes [under § 362]. Upon the final disposition of the property at the foreclosure sale there was still due upon the mortgage the principal amount of $381,000 and, as the petitioner concedes, the extent to which the amount of the mortgage exceeds its adjusted basis was income taxable to it even though it was not personally liable upon the mortgage. Crane v. C.I.R., 331 U.S. 1.

Turning now to the one item whose effect upon the calculation of the petitioner's adjusted basis is disputed, the following admitted facts need to be stated. Mrs. Wood bought the property on January 20, 1922 at a total cost of $296,400. She paid $101,400 in cash, took the title subject to an existing mortgage for $120,000 and gave a purchase money bond and second mortgage for $75,000. She had made payments on the first mortgage reducing it to $112,500, when, on December 30, 1925, both of the mortgages were assigned to the Title Guarantee and Trust Company. On January 4, 1926 Mrs. Wood borrowed $137,500 from the Title Guarantee & Trust Company and gave it a bond and mortgage for $325,000 on which she was personally liable, that being the amount of the two existing mortgages, which were consolidated into the new one, plus the amount of the cash borrowed. On June 9, 1931 this consolidated mortgage was assigned to the East River Savings Bank and, shortly thereafter, Mrs. Wood borrowed an additional $75,000 from that bank which she received upon the execution of a second consolidated mortgage for $400,000 comprising the principal amount due on the first consolidated mortgage plus the additional loan. However, this transaction was carried out through the use of a 'dummy' so that, under New York law, Mrs. Wood was not personally liable on this bond and mortgage. See In re Childs Co., 2 Cir., 163 F.2d 379. This was the mortgage, reduced as above stated, which was foreclosed.

The contention of the petitioner may now be stated quite simply. It is that, when the borrowings of Mrs. Wood subsequent to her acquisition of the property became charges solely upon the property itself, the cash she received for the repayment of which she was not personally liable was a gain then taxable to her as income to the extent that the mortgage indebtedness exceeded her adjusted basis in the property. That being so, it is argued that her tax basis was, under familiar principles of tax law, increased by the amount of such taxable gain and that this stepped up basis carried over to the petitioner in the tax free exchange by which it acquired the property.

While this conclusion would be sound if the premise on which it is based were correct, we cannot accept the premise. It is that the petitioner's transferor made a taxable disposition of the property, within the meaning of [§ 1001], when the second consolidated mortgage was executed, because she had, by then, dealt with it in such a way that she had received cash, in excess of her basis, which, at that time, she was freed from any personal obligation to repay. Nevertheless, whether or nor personally liable on the mortgage, 'The mortgagee is a creditor, and in effect nothing more than a preferred creditor, even though the mortgagor is not liable for the debt. He is not the less a creditor because he has recourse only to the land, unless we are to deny the term to one who may levy upon only a part of his debtor's assets.' C.I.R. v. Crane, 2 Cir., 153 F.2d 504, 506. Mrs. Wood merely augmented the existing mortgage indebtedness when she borrowed each time and, far from closing the venture, remained in a position to borrow more if and when circumstances permitted and she so desired. And so, she never 'disposed' of the property to create a taxable event which [§ 1001] makes a condition precedent to the taxation of gain. 'Disposition,' within the meaning of [§ 1001], is the "getting rid, or making over, of anything; relinquishment". . . . Nothing of that nature was done here by the mere execution of the second consolidated mortgage; Mrs. Wood was the owner of this property in the same sense after the execution of this mortgage that she was before. As was pointed out in our decision in the Crane case, supra, 153 F.2d at 505-506, ' * * * the lien of a mortgage does not make the mortgagee a cotenant; the mortgagor is the owner for all purposes; indeed that is why the 'gage' is 'mort,' as distinguished from a 'vivum vadium.' Kortright v. Cady, 21 N.Y. 343, 344. He has all the income from the property; he manages it; he may sell it; any increase in its value goes to him; any decrease falls on him, until the value goes below the amount of the lien.' Realization of gain was, therefore, postponed for taxation until there was a final disposition of the property at the time of the foreclosure sale. . . . Therefore, Mrs. Wood's borrowings did not change the basis for the computation of gain or loss.

Affirmed.

NOTES AND COMMENTS

As you will learn in Chapter 3, loans incurred in the acquisition of property are included in the basis of the property. Thus, for example, if a taxpayer purchases property with a fair market value of $100,000 for $20,000 of her own funds and $80,000 borrowed from a commercial lender, the property will have a basis of $100,000 in the taxpayer's hands. This rule applies in connection with nonrecourse as well as recourse loans. The Supreme Court's decision in *Crane v. Commissioner*, 331 U.S. 1 (1947), is frequently cited as authority for the treatment of nonrecourse loans in this manner. Similarly, the relief of any debt secured by the property sold is typically included as part of the amount realized under the Supreme Court's decision in *Commissioner v. Tufts*, 461 U.S. 300 (1983), and Treasury Regulation § 1.1001-2. The importance of the decision in *Woodsam Associates, Inc.*, lies in establishing the rule that a refinancing of debt secured by an interest in property does not affect the basis of the property.

§ 3.04. Part Sale/Part Gift

§ 1011(b); Treas. Reg. §§ 1.1001-1(e); 1.1011-2; 1.1015-4

Property may be transferred from one person to another for a price less than the fair market value of the property. If the transfer is motivated by the "detached and disinterested generosity" of the transferor, the transfer will be characterized in part as a gift of the property to the extent that its fair market value exceeds the price charged. For example, assume that Margaret owns stock with a fair market value of $20,000 that she sells to her son, Frederick, for $12,000. The stock has a basis in Margaret's hands of $10,000. The transfer is a realization event for Margaret. The only question is the extent of Margaret's gain.

The situation described above could be analyzed in two ways. Margaret could be thought to have sold the stock for $12,000, realizing $2,000 of gain ($12,000 amount realized - $10,000 basis). The basis of the stock in Frederick's hands would then be $12,000. If Frederick then sold the stock for $20,000, he would realize gain of $8,000. The $2,000 gain in Margaret's hands plus the $8,000 gain in Frederick's hands totals the $10,000 of gain that existed at the time Margaret transferred the stock to Frederick. Alternatively, Margaret could be thought to have sold 60 percent of the stock to Frederick for its full fair market value and made a gift of the remaining 40 percent of the stock. The basis of the stock sold would be $6,000 (60 percent of $10,000), resulting in gain of $6,000 ($12,000 amount realized - $6,000 basis). Frederick would take a cost basis in this portion of the stock of $12,000. With respect to the 40 percent of the stock transferred as a gift, Frederick would have a carryover basis of $4,000. If Frederick then sold the sold for $20,000, he would have gain of $4,000 — $0 gain with respect to the 60 percent of the stock purchased from his mother ($12,000 amount realized - $12,000 basis) and $4,000 with respect to the 40 percent of the stock transferred as a gift ($8,000 amount realized - $4,000 basis). Again, the $6,000 gain in Margaret's hands plus the $4,000 gain in Frederick's hands totals the $10,000 of gain that existed at the time Margaret transferred the stock to Frederick. The only difference between the two approaches is the amount and the timing of the gain.

The Regulations provide that the first approach is generally applicable. Treas. Reg. § 1.1001-1(e)(2), example (1). Presumably, the Regulations adopt this method as administratively easier because it avoids any need to determine the fair market value of the property transferred. However, if the transfer involves a bargain sale to a charitable organization, the second approach applies. § 1011(b); Treas. Reg. § 1.1011-2. The apparent justification for imposing the more complex approach in connection with a bargain sale to a charitable organization is attributable to the fact that a determination of the fair market value of the property will be necessary if the transferor intends to take a charitable contribution deduction and to the fact that any gain not realized at the time of the contribution will escape tax in the future as the property has been transferred to a tax exempt organization.

PROBLEM FOR DISCUSSION

Problem 1-14. Fred purchased stock five years ago for $10,000. The stock is now worth $25,000.

(a) What are the tax implications if he gives the stock to his daughter, Margaret, incurring a gift tax of $2,500, and she sells the stock one year later for $30,000?

(b) What are the tax implications if, at the time of the gift, the stock is worth $5,000, Fred incurs a gift tax of $500, and Margaret sells the stock one year later for $4,000? What if she sells the stock one year later for $7,000? For $12,000?

(c) What are the tax implications if Fred sells the stock to Margaret for $15,000? What if Fred gives the stock to Margaret and the stock secures a debt of $15,000, which Margaret agrees to pay?

§ 3.05. Inclusion of Debt in the Amount Realized

As described in greater detail in Chapter 3, the relief of any recourse or nonrecourse debt on the transfer of property is typically included in the amount realized on the transfer. Consequently, if a taxpayer transfers property for $20,000 in cash and the transferee agrees to pay an $80,000 loan secured by the property, the taxpayer's amount realized is $100,000 ($20,000 cash + $80,000 relief of the liability). If the basis of the property in the taxpayer's hands is $30,000, the taxpayer realizes gain of $70,000. For tax purposes, the taxpayer is treated in the same manner as if he had sold the property for $100,000 in cash. Of course, the buyer of the property would only be willing to pay the taxpayer $100,000 in cash for the property if the taxpayer uses $80,000 of the cash to pay off the $80,000 loan. Regardless of how the transaction is structured, the taxpayer walks away with gain of $70,000 and $20,000 of cash.

§ 3.06. Recognition and Allowance

§ 1001(c); skim §§ 165, 267(a)(1), 707(b)(1), 1091, and 1211; Treas. Reg. § 1.1001-2

To be included in the gross income of a taxpayer under § 61(a)(3), gains from dealings in property must be both realized and recognized. Importantly, § 1001(c) provides that all realized gains are recognized unless a "nonrecognition" provision applies. Nonrecognition provisions under §§ 1031 and 1033 involving like-kind exchanges and involuntary conversions are considered in Chapter 5. In addition, nonrecognition provisions applicable to transfers of property involving shareholders and corporations and partners and partnerships permeate Subchapters C and K of the Code. The gain that is realized but not recognized under these provisions is not permanently excluded from tax, however. Typically, the basis of the property in the hands of the transferor is carried over to the property in the hands of the transferee and/or the basis of the property received by the transferor is the same as the basis of the property transferred. As a result, the gain that was realized but not recognized is preserved to be realized and recognized in a later taxable transaction.

Like gain, losses from the sale or disposition of property must be both realized and recognized in order to be deductible. Again, § 1001(c) provides that all realized losses are recognized unless a "nonrecognition" provision applies. Taxpayers and their advisors typically structure transactions to take advantage of nonrecognition provisions in connection with transfers of property that give rise to gain and to avoid satisfying the requirements of nonrecognition provisions in connection with transfers of property that give rise to losses. Deferral of gain is generally beneficial from a taxpayer's perspective; deferral of losses is not. However, it is not always possible to avoid nonrecognition provisions when losses are involved.

To be deductible, losses must also be allowable. Section 165 is the general provision that limits the allowance of losses. In addition to § 165, numerous provisions disallow or limit the deductibility of losses, particularly when they arise between related parties. *See, e.g.*, §§ 267(a)(1), 707(b)(1), 1091, and 1211. Some of these provisions are described in Chapter 8. Thus, the realization of any loss is only the first step in determining whether that particular loss is deductible.

§ 4. SALE OF A BUSINESS

§ 4.01. Overview

As will be described in detail in Chapter 2, *Capital Gains and Losses*, the sale or exchange of certain types of assets may give rise to capital gain or loss. For individual taxpayers, net capital gain is subject to preferential tax rates under § 1(h). In addition, for both individual and corporate taxpayers, the deduction of capital losses may be limited. Thus, the identification of assets that may give rise to capital gain or losses is of importance in determining the tax consequences of any transaction. The basic definition of a capital asset is found in § 1221. A number of assets otherwise excluded from capital asset status under § 1221 may also be treated as capital assets under § 1231.

Obviously, the sale of a business involves the transfer of multiple assets, some of which may fall into the definition of a capital asset and others of which may not. The question, however, is whether the sale of a business itself should be conceptualized for tax purposes as the sale of a single asset or as the sale of multiple assets. The following seminal case explains why a sale of a business is not, itself, a sale of a single asset.

WILLIAMS v. MCGOWAN

United States Circuit Court of Appeals, Second Circuit
152 F.2d 570 (2d Cir. 1945)

L. Hand, Circuit Judge.

* * *

Williams, the taxpayer, and one, Reynolds, had for many years been engaged in the hardware business in the City of Corning, New York. On the 20th of January, 1926, they formed a partnership, of which Williams was entitled to two-thirds of the profits, and Reynolds, one-third. . . . The business was carried on through the firm's fiscal year, ending January 31, 1940, in accordance with this agreement, and thereafter until Reynolds' death on July 18th of that year. Williams settled with Reynolds' executrix on September 6th in an agreement by which he promised to pay her $12,187.90, and to assume all liabilities of the business; and he did pay her $2,187.98 in cash at once, and $10,000 on the 10th of the following October. On September 17th of the same year, Williams sold the business as a whole to the Corning Building Company for $63,926.28 — its agreed value as of February 1, 1940 — " plus an amount to be computed by multiplying the gross sales of the business from the first day of February, 1940 to the 28th day of September, 1940," by an agreed fraction. This value was made up of cash of about $8100, receivables of about $7000, fixtures of about $800, and a merchandise inventory of about $49,000, less some $1000 for bills payable. To this was added about $6,000 credited to Williams for profits under the language just quoted, making a total of nearly $70,000. Upon this sale Williams suffered a loss upon his original two-thirds of the business, but he made a small gain upon the one-third which he had bought from Reynolds' executrix; and in his income tax return he entered both as items of "ordinary income," and not as transactions in "capital assets." . . . The only question is whether the business was "capital assets" under [§ 1221] of the Internal Revenue Code . . .

It has been held that a partner's interest in a going firm is for tax purposes to be regarded as a "capital asset." . . . If a partner's interest in a going firm is "capital assets" perhaps a dead partner's interest is the same. . . . We need not say. When Williams bought out Reynolds' interest, he became the sole owner of the business, the firm had ended upon any theory, and the situation for tax purposes was no other than if Reynolds had never been a partner at all, except that to the extent of one-third of the "amount realized" on Williams' sale to the Corning Company, his "basis" was different. The judge thought that, because upon that sale both parties fixed the price at the liquidation value of the business while Reynolds was alive, "plus" its estimated earnings thereafter, it was as though Williams had sold his interest in the firm during its existence. But the method by which the parties agreed upon the price was irrelevant to the computation of Williams' income. The Treasury, if that served its interest, need not heed any fiction which the parties found it convenient to adopt; nor need Williams do the same in his dealings with the Treasury. We have to decide only whether upon the sale of a going business it is to be comminuted into its fragments, and these are to be separately matched against the definition in [§ 1221], or whether the whole business is to be treated as if it were a single piece of property.

Our law has been sparing in the creation of juristic entities; it has never, for example, taken over the Roman "universitas facti", and indeed for many years it fumbled uncertainly with the concept of a corporation. One might have supposed that partnership would have been an especially promising field in which to raise up an entity, particularly since merchants have always kept their accounts upon that basis. Yet there too our law resisted at the price of great and continuing confusion; and, even when it might be thought that a statute admitted, if it did not demand, recognition of the firm as an entity, the old concepts prevailed. . . . And so, even though we might agree that under the influence of the Uniform Partnership Act a partner's interest in the firm should be treated as indivisible, and for that reason a "capital asset" within [§ 1221], we should be chary about extending further so exotic a jural concept. Be that as it may, in this instance the section itself furnishes the answer. It starts in the broadest way by declaring that all "property" is "capital assets," and then makes three exceptions. The first is "stock in trade * * * or other property of a kind which would properly be included in the inventory"; next comes "property held * * * primarily for sale to customers"; and finally, property "used in the trade or business of a character which is subject to * * * allowance for depreciation." In the face of this language, although it may be true that a "stock in trade," taken by itself, should be treated as a "universitas facti," by no possibility can a whole business be so treated; and the same is true as to any property within the other exceptions. Congress plainly did mean to comminute the elements of a business; plainly it did not regard the whole as "capital assets."

As has already appeared, Williams transferred to the Corning Company "cash," "receivables," "fixtures" and a "merchandise inventory." "Fixtures" are not capital because they are subject to a depreciation allowance; the inventory, as we have just seen, is expressly excluded. So far as appears, no allowance was made for "good-will"; but, even if there had been, we held . . . that "good-will" was a depreciable intangible. It is true that the Supreme Court reversed that judgment . . . but it based its decision only upon the fact that there could be no allowance for the depreciation of "good-will" in a brewery, a business condemned by the Eighteenth Amendment. There can of course be no gain or loss in the transfer of cash; and, although Williams does appear to have made a gain of $1072.71 upon the "receivables," the point has not been argued that they are not subject to a depreciation allowance. That we leave open for decision by the district court, if the parties cannot agree. The gain or loss upon every other item should be computed as an item in ordinary income.

Judgment reversed.

Frank, Circuit Judge (dissenting in part).

I agree that it is irrelevant that the business was once owned by a partnership. For when the sale to the Corning Company occurred, the partnership was dead, had become merely a memory, a ghost. To say that the sale was of the partnership's assets would, then, be to indulge in animism. But I do not agree that we should ignore what the parties to the sale, Williams and the Corning Company, actually did. They did not arrange for a transfer to the buyer, as if in separate bundles, of the several ingredients of the business. They contracted for the sale of the entire business as a going concern. Here is what they said in their agreement: "The party of the first part agrees to sell and the party of the second part agrees to buy, all of the right, title and interest of the said party of the first part in and to the hardware business now being conducted by the said party of the first part, including cash on hand and on deposit in the First National Bank & Trust Company of Corning in the A. F. Williams Hardware Store account, in accounts receivable, bills receivable, notes receivable, merchandise and fixtures, including two G.M. trucks, good will and all other assets of every kind and description used in and about said business. * * * Said party of the first part agrees not to engage in the hardware business within a radius of twenty-five miles from the City of Corning, New York, for a period of ten years from the 1st day of October 1940."

To carve up this transaction into distinct sales — of cash, receivables, fixtures, trucks, merchandise, and good will — is to do violence to the realities. I do not think Congress intended any such artificial result. In the Senate Committee Report on the 1942 amendment to [§ 1221] said: "It is believed that this Senate amendment will be of material benefit to businesses which, due to depressed conditions, have been compelled to dispose of their plant or equipment at a loss. The bill defines property used in a trade or business as property used in the trade or business of a character which is subject to the allowance for depreciation, and real property held for more than six months which is not properly includible in the inventory of the taxpayer if on hand at the close of the taxable year or property held by the taxpayer primarily for sale to customers in the ordinary course of his trade or business. If a newspaper purchased the plant and equipment of a rival newspaper and later sold such plant and equipment at a loss, such plant and equipment, being subject to depreciation, would constitute property used in the trade or business within the meaning of this section." These remarks show that what Congress contemplated was not the sale of a going business but of its dismembered parts. Where a business is sold as a unit, the whole is greater than its parts. Businessmen so recognize; so, too, I think, did Congress. Interpretation of our complicated tax statutes is seldom aided by saying that taxation is an eminently practical matter (or the like). But this is one instance where, it seems to me, the practical aspects of the matter should guide our guess as to what Congress meant. I believe Congress had those aspects in mind and was not thinking of the nice distinctions between Roman and Anglo-American legal theories about legal entities.

NOTES AND COMMENTS

The result of the majority decision in *Williams v. McGowan*, which has clearly become the law, despite Judge Frank's vigorous dissent, is that it is the nature of the asset — not the nature of the transaction — that determines whether there is capital gain or loss. On one point, however, Judge Hand was wrong — goodwill is now recognized as a capital asset. The principle of *Williams v. McGowan* is now embodied in § 1060.

PROBLEM FOR DISCUSSION

Problem 1-15. Why isn't Judge Frank right in *Williams* in saying that what was sold was a business, not a group of individual assets? In particular, why does it make sense to treat a bulk sale of inventory outside the ordinary course of business as ordinary income?

§ 4.02. § 1060 And the Residual Allocation Method

§§ 1060, 197(a), (c)(1), and (d)(1)(A) and (B); Treas. Reg. §§ 1.1060-1(a)(1), 1.1060-1(b)(1) to (7), 1.1060-1(c)(1) to (4), 1.1060-1(d) Example 2, 1.1060-1(e), 1. 338-6(a) to (c)(2), 1.197-2(b)(1) and (2), 1.197-2(d)(1), and 1.197-2(e)(1)

The sale of a business may involve a number of tangible and intangible assets. Certainly, a number of types of real and personal tangible property may be involved, as well as intangible assets in the form of contract rights, such as accounts receivable. Goodwill and going concern value are two of the most common intangible assets. Goodwill is generally defined for tax purposes as "the value of a trade or business attributable to the expectancy of continued customer patronage." Treas. Reg. § 1.197-2(b)(1). *See Newark Morning Ledger Co. v. United States*, 507 U.S. 546 (1993) (adopting the shorthand description of goodwill as "the expectancy of continued patronage"). A business may also include going concern value generally defined as "the additional value that attaches to property by reason of its existence as an integral part of an ongoing business activity." Treas. Reg. § 1.197-2(b)(2). Moreover, a business may include such intangible assets as workforce in place, information base, and know-how. *See* Treas. Reg. §§ 1.197-2(b)(3)-(5). The existence of any of these assets in a transaction must be determined on a case-by-case basis.

Both the seller and the purchaser of a business are interested in the allocation of consideration among the various assets that make up the business. The seller is interested in the allocation of consideration received among the assets because of the characterization of gain or loss on each of the assets. Sellers typically prefer to allocate consideration to assets that will generate capital gain. Buyers are interested in the allocation of consideration paid among the assets in order to maximize the depreciation or amortization deductions that they will enjoy in the future. The details of depreciation and amortization are described in detail in § 3, *Cost Recovery*, of Chapter 4, *Capitalization and Cost Recovery*. In many instances, sellers and buyers have adverse tax interests so that the allocations to which they agree will generally be respected for tax purposes. However, as described in greater detail below, sellers and buyers are not obligated to agree as between themselves on an allocation of consideration among the assets transferred.

The following case considers the allocation issue from the perspective of the buyer. At the time of the transaction involved, neither goodwill nor going concern value was depreciable for tax purposes. Thus, the buyer was tempted to allocate as much consideration as possible to depreciable assets rather than to goodwill or going concern value. Although the current approach for the allocation of consideration among the assets of a businesses is the so-called residual method under § 1060 — in which goodwill and going concern value are allocated consideration equal to the excess of the purchase price over the value of all other tangible and intangible assets — an alternative at the time of the decision was to use a formula or other method to determine the value of goodwill. The following case is now obsolete on its facts, but it is still valid for estate tax and other valuations when there is no sales price to set the overall value of the business, including gifts, charitable contributions, and nonrecognition transactions in which basis must be allocated in proportion to value.

CONCORD CONTROL, INC. v. COMMISSIONER

United States Court of Appeals, Sixth Circuit
615 F.2d 1153 (6th Cir. 1980)

* * *

This case concerns the determination of the basis of taxpayer's tangible and intangible assets for purposes of depreciation. In 1959, K-D Lamp Division was a division of Automatic Burner Company, which was a subsidiary of Northeast Capital. Northeast Capital was controlled by four persons: Johnson, Fierman, Kaelin, and Hedden. In 1959, Duplan Corporation, which was controlled by the same four persons, bought K-D Lamp Division from Northeast Capital. In 1964, Duplan sold K-D Lamp Division to Interim Lamp Company, controlled by Stone. Stone immediately changed the name of the company to K-D Lamp Company. In 1966, Stone acquired the stock of Concord Control and merged K-D Lamp

Company into Concord Control. Our tax problem concerns the 1964 sale by Duplan to the Interim Lamp Company.

The 1964 contract of sale was negotiated between Johnson and Stone. . . . Stone obtained the services of an appraiser to determine the fair market value of the company's assets. . . . On the basis of the appraiser's report, Stone paid the fair market value less a discount for cash payment. The sales contract listed the price of each group of assets separately. The sales price for all intangible assets, such as goodwill, was $1.00. The parties believed that the company had no existing goodwill, because of some existing business problems and because it was in a very competitive market. The negotiations for a sales price did not discuss the sale of goodwill. The sales contract also included a price for "going concern value" in the $1.00 for intangible assets.

Concord Control calculated its depreciation losses for its tax reports using the listed sales prices of the tangible assets. The Commissioner determined, after his own appraisal, that the sales contract overly allocated the prices to depreciable tangible assets and covered up the prices for the nondepreciable intangible assets of goodwill and going concern value. . . .

The Tax Court found for Concord Control that the 1964 sale of the company did not include goodwill. The Tax Court found first that the sales contract was the result of arms-length bargaining, reflected the true intentions of the parties and was based on a bona fide appraisal. . . . As a supporting ground, the Tax Court found that the company could not expect continued patronage or competitive advantage and therefore possessed no goodwill that could have been sold.

The Tax Court held against Concord Control by finding that the purchase price did include substantial going concern value. Its reasoning was:

> [Concord Control] clearly did acquire an ongoing business that was earning money, had a trained staff of employees, had a product line presently ready for sale and equipment ready for immediate use. Simply stated, the purchase price paid by petitioner for the various assets acquired in 1964 included substantial going concern value which, as distinguished from goodwill, is the increase in the value of assets due to their existence as an integral part of an ongoing business. . . .

The Tax Court then had to determine the portion of the purchase price for each asset attributable to going concern value.

The Tax Court stated:

> The record is not entirely clear on this issue and contains no satisfactory formula for dividing the price paid for each asset between the base price of that asset and its going concern value. However, an allocation is required. Based upon a careful consideration of the record, we think we are justified in making the following allocations . . .

It allocated a percentage of the purchase price to going concern value, citing *Cohan v. Commissioner of Internal Revenue*, 39 F.2d 540 (2d Cir. 1930), as authority for making the allocations.

* * *

Concord Control argues on appeal that the Tax Court committed an error of law by automatically finding the existence of going concern value in the 1964 purchase price. We do not read the Tax Court's opinion as using such a per se rule and find the argument unmeritorious.

Concord Control contends that the Tax Court was clearly erroneous in finding the existence of going concern value. The burden of proof rests on the taxpayer in challenging the Commissioner's deficiency notice. We are convinced that the Tax Court properly defined the intangible assets and that its finding of going concern value is not clearly erroneous. We do not believe that the Tax Court decided inconsistently by finding an absence of goodwill and the existence of going concern value. These two intangible assets are separate and distinct. Also, the Tax Court did not make a finding that the total value of the tangible assets equaled the total 1964 contract price.

* * *

The Commissioner argues that the Tax Court erred in finding that no goodwill was purchased in 1964. The Commissioner contends that the Tax Court committed an error of law by requiring an expectancy of continued customer patronage or competitive advantage in addition to excess earnings over the normal industry average to establish the existence of goodwill. No Court has adopted the Commissioner's position and there is ample authority to the contrary. . . .

* * *

Though the Tax Court properly found the existence of going concern value, we believe a remand is necessary for the Tax Court to explain its method of calculating the amount of going concern value. We are unable to discern from the Tax Court's opinion the method it used to calculate the going concern value or why it chose that method. The Tax Court determined apparently that ten percent of the purchase price of realty was going concern value and that twenty percent of the purchase price of all other property was going concern value. The difference between real property and other property for the purpose of calculating going concern value is not explained. It is also not explained how the Tax Court chose those particular percentages.

The *Cohan* rule cannot save the Tax Court from explaining its calculation of going concern value. . . . We have never accepted or rejected the *Cohan* rule and decline to do either now. . . . The *Cohan* rule was developed to spare the taxpayer when the taxpayer establishes his entitlement to a deduction or to business expenses, but cannot substantiate the exact amount because of no recordkeeping. In our case, Concord Control, or its predecessors, possessed numerous relevant records and presented, or could have presented, much evidence to the Tax Court on the amount of going concern value or conversely the value of the tangible assets. Though we realize that there are few guidelines for the Tax Court to follow in assessing the amount of going concern value and that the Tax Court may be compelled to make broad estimates, it must at least explain its method of valuation and its reasons for choosing that method. . . .

* * *

NOTES AND COMMENTS

On remand, in *Concord Control, Inc. v. Commissioner*, 78 T.C. 742 (1982), the Tax Court refused to respect the contract terms on the ground that the parties had no real adverse tax interests in the allocation. It also refused to use the residual method on the ground that the value of the tangible assets could not be determined with reasonable accuracy because of conflicting appraisals. It then used a capitalization of earnings method of valuing the business as a whole. It determined that the value of the tangible assets was considerably more than the purchase price and treated "excess" earnings as reflecting going concern value. It then determined that the appraisal used in the contract represented the estimated fair market value of each asset as part of the going business. It then reduced the appraised value of each asset by a pro rata portion of the going concern value to determine the depreciable basis of each asset.

As indicated, § 1060 now mandates that the residual method be used in allocating basis to goodwill and going concern value in all purchases of a going business, among other reasons, to avoid difficult and uncertain assumptions that are demanded by the application of the formula method. Thus, under § 1060, for any "applicable asset acquisition," both the seller and the buyer must use the residual method to allocate the purchase price. Treas. Reg. § 1.1060-1(a). An applicable asset acquisition is any transfer of assets constituting a business in which the transferee's basis is determined wholly by reference to the purchase price paid for the assets, including a nonrecognition exchange under § 1031. Treas. Reg. § 1.1060-1(b)(1). Interestingly, a trade or business is any group of assets to which goodwill or going concern value can attach. Treas. Reg. § 1.1060-1(b)(2). In addition, a trade or business includes any active business under § 355 relating to corporate divisions, although it is difficult to image an active business under § 355 that would not have goodwill. The parties are also required to report certain transactions involving transfers of interests in business entities if an employment contract or covenant not to compete is entered into with major owners. § 1060(e).

Both the seller and the buyer are required to report the allocation to the Service, but they are not required to agree on the allocation. Treas. Reg. § 1.1060-1(e). If they do agree, as a practical matter they are bound to the terms of their agreement, but the Service is not. Treas. Reg. § 1.1060-1(c)(4). When they do not agree, in theory, the Service has the information to prevent whipsaw and to adjust either or both parties' reporting on audit. A whipsaw exists when each party reports an allocation of the purchase price that is most beneficial to itself by minimizing the tax liability confronted by each party. Whether or not the parties agree to a specific allocation, the amounts reported for goodwill and going concern value by the parties will differ because the selling price is reduced by the seller's transaction costs while the purchaser's is increased by its similar costs. Treas. Reg. § 1.1060-1(c)(3).

Sales of businesses, particularly those of closely-held businesses, frequently include covenants not to compete by employee shareholders. Prior to the enactment of § 197, when goodwill and going concern value were nonamortizable, but payments for covenants not to compete were deductible as the payments were made, purchasers had an incentive to allocate the "premium" paid for business assets to such covenants. However, because payments under a covenant not to compete are ordinary income to the recipient seller, sellers preferred payments for goodwill or going concern value that would generate capital gain. *See, e.g., General Ins. Agency, Inc. v. Commissioner*, 401 F.2d 324 (4th Cir. 1968) (no separate bargaining for covenant, sale proceeds all capital gain to seller and nondeductible goodwill for purchaser); *Hamlin's Trust v. Commissioner*, 209 F.2d 761 (1954) (covenant was a separately bargained element of sale; allocable proceeds are ordinary income); Rev. Rul. 69-643, 1969-2 C.B. 10 (amounts received for covenant are ordinary income, unless the covenant is merely an adjunct designed to secure to the purchaser the benefit of the goodwill, and does not reflect a genuine likelihood of competition). Buyers would often increase the payments under such covenants to compensate for the fact that such payments are ordinary income to the recipient, as long as the increase did not exceed the tax savings from the current deduction. Because § 197(d)(1)(E) now classifies both acquired goodwill and covenants not to compete as amortizable § 197 intangible assets, amortizable over 15 years, purchasers no longer confront these incentives. *See* § 3.06, *Amortization of Intangible Assets*, of Chapter 4, *Capitalization and Cost Recovery*. Moreover, recipients continue to benefit from allocations of the purchase price to goodwill or going concern value, which may result in capital gain rather than from allocations to covenants not to compete, which result in ordinary income.

The regulations under § 1060 specify that the seller is to allocate the purchase price among the assets using the residual method under Treas. Reg. §§ 1.338-6 and 1.338-7 substituting consideration for the aggregate deemed sales price ("ADSP"). Similarly, the buyer is to allocate the purchase price among the assets using the residual method under Treas. Reg. §§ 1.338-6 and 1.338-7 substituting consideration for the adjusted grossed-up basis ("AGUB"). Treas. Reg. § 1.1060-1(c)(2). In applying the residual method, the assets are divided into seven classes: Class I — cash and equivalents; Class II — actively traded personal property including CDs and foreign currency, but not stock of seller affiliates; Class III — assets marked to market and debt instruments with some exceptions; Class IV — inventory and property held for sale to customers; Class V — all other assets except those in Classes VI and VII; Class VI — § 197 intangible assets other than goodwill and going concern value; and Class VII — goodwill and going concern value. Treas. Reg. § 1.338-6(b). The purchase price allocated to each class in order, in an amount not to exceed the fair market value of that class. Treas. Reg. § 1.338-6(b)(1) and (2). The amount allocated to goodwill or going concern value is the excess of the purchase price over the identifiable value of the other classes. If the amount allocated to a class is less than the fair market value of the assets in that class, it is allocated pro rata among the assets, in proportion to fair market value.

When the class structure of § 1060 was initially established, goodwill and going concern value were nonamortizable. They are now amortizable over 15 years under § 197. Interestingly, Class V includes real property with a potential depreciable life of 39 years to the purchaser. This creates an incentive to minimize the value allocated to real property in Class V in order to leave larger allocations to Class VII. However, the seller may well have adverse tax interests. To the extent that the goodwill or going concern value were amortizable § 197 intangible assets in the hands of the seller, the seller has an incentive to resist such an allocation because the seller will have ordinary income to the extent of any depreciation recapture. In addition, the seller would prefer larger allocations of the purchase price to real property in Class V because any gain attributable to depreciation deductions taken with respect to the real property will not be taxable as ordinary income, but as unrecaptured § 1250 gain subject to a maximum tax rate of 25 percent under § 1(h)(1)(D). On the other hand, if the goodwill or going concern value were not amortizable § 197 intangible assets in the hands of the seller, the seller will be entitled to capital gain treatment. In this situation, the seller has no adverse interest to the purchaser's desire to minimize the allocation of the purchase price to any real property acquired in the transaction.

PROBLEM FOR DISCUSSION

Problem 1-16. Tarr Inc. transferred all of its investment management business to Ack, Inc. in consideration of $1,000,000. The assets transferred included its contracts with clients, which entitled Tarr to receive an annual commission of one percent of the value of the portfolio plus one percent of the income received by the clients. The contracts were cancelable by the customers or Tarr on 30 days notice, and were, by their terms, assignable. The transfer included the right to the name Tarr, all of the records of the company, its furniture and equipment, its staff of investment analysts, and its clerical staff. Under the terms of the contract, Tarr and its principal shareholder, Exec, were both required to sign a covenant not to compete for five years. What are the tax consequences of this sale to Tarr, Ack, and Exec? What difference would it make if instead Exec sold the stock of Tarr?

§ 4.03. Contingent Payments and Liabilities

Sales of businesses frequently involve contingent payments and contingent liabilities. Contingent payments often take the form of payments to be made by the buyer in the future based on the gross or net revenue of the business. Parties typically include such payments when they have differing opinions regarding the future profitability of the business. The seller may believe that the business commands a high purchase price because of its future profit potential, while the buyer may not believe that that profit potential will actually be realized. By including contingent payments as part of the purchase price, the seller will receive additional payments if the future profit is actually realized, and the buyer can avoid the risk of having paid a high purchase price if the future profit is not realized.

From a tax perspective, the problem with contingent payments is that the full purchase price will not be known at the time of the sale in order to determine the amount of the seller's gain on the assets sold or the buyer's basis in the assets acquired. If an election is made not to report gain under the installment method of § 453, the fair market value of the contingent payments must be determined and included as part of the amount realized on the sale. Treas. Reg. § 1.1001-1(g)(2). If the seller reports gain on the sale under the installment method, the Regulations specify how the bases of the assets sold will be recovered as the contingent payments are actually received. Treas. Reg. § 15A.453-1(c). Whether the gain on the sale is reported under the installment method, a portion of each deferred payment represents the time value of money and must properly be accounted for as ordinary income in determining the character of any gain realized by the seller. Treas. Reg. § 1.1275-4(c). From the seller's perspective, contingent payments are dealt with under § 453, which allows the seller to report gain under the installment method, and § 1274 or § 1275, which require that the seller account for any original issue discount ("OID") in the determination of gain or loss. *See* §§ 2.01(c), *Contingent Payment Obligations*, and 2.02(a), *Contingent Payment Installment Sales*, in Chapters 5 and 6, respectively, of Lang, Manning & Willis, FEDERAL TAX ACCOUNTING (LexisNexis, Graduate Tax Series, 2006).

From the buyer's perspective, the basis of an asset includes liabilities incurred in the acquisition of the asset. *See* Chapter 3, *Liabilities*. The most common type of liability is debt incurred by the buyer in order to finance the acquisition of the asset. This debt may be a liability from the buyer to the seller or from the buyer to a third party. As described above, the buyer may also incur an obligation to make contingent payments in the future to the seller. In addition, the buyer may assume certain types of liabilities of the seller, such as obligations to make future payments under existing employment contracts, to compensate third parties for existing environmental damage, or to compensate plaintiffs in pending or threatened litigation. Although the precise amount of these liabilities may be known at the time of the sale of the business, in many instances these amounts can only be estimated. The seller and the buyer presumably negotiate any up-front purchase price of the business based on estimates of the liabilities that the buyer will or will not be assuming.

From the buyer's perspective, the question that arises is when these contingent liabilities may be included in the basis of the acquired assets. Generally, a contingent liability cannot be included in basis until the contingency has been resolved. For example, in *Albany Car Wheel Co. v. Commissioner*, 40 T.C. 831 (1964), *aff'd per curium*, 333 F.2d 653 (2d Cir. 1964), the purchaser of a business assumed the seller's obligations for severance pay to the employees of a plant under a union contract. In connection with the purchase, the purchaser renegotiated the obligation to one that could be avoided by providing adequate notice of closing. When the plant subsequently closed, the purchaser fully discharged its obligations by providing notice of closing. The acquiring corporation attempted to include an amount on account of the severance pay obligation as part of its purchase price in determining the basis of the assets acquired. The court denied any basis adjustment attributable to the severance pay obligation because the obligation under the new contract was so contingent that it could not be considered part of the cost of the assets that the corporation acquired. The court concluded that any payments actually made under the contract would properly be taken into account only at that later time. *See also Denver & R. G. W. R. Co. v. United States*, 505 F.2d 1266 (Ct. Cl. 1974); *Pacific Transport Co. v. Commissioner*, 483 F.2d 209 (9th Cir.1973); *Meredith Corp. v. Commissioner*, 102 T.C. 406 (1997). If the contingency is resolved after the asset has been fully depreciated, the payment may be deductible when incurred. *Meredith Corp. v. Commissioner*, 108 T.C. 89 (1997). In addition, and like the seller, the buyer must properly account for that portion of each deferred payment that represents the time value of money as

OID. Treas. Reg. § 1.1275-4(c). *See* § 2.02(b), *Contingent Payment Installment Sales*, in Chapter 6, respectively, of Lang, Manning, & Willis, FEDERAL TAX ACCOUNTING (LexisNexis, Graduate Tax Series, 2006).

The regulations under § 338 provide special rules applying the residual method when there is a redetermination of the amount of consideration paid for a business as a result of contingent payments or contingent liabilities. In such a situation, the redetermined consideration is allocated using the residual method under Treas. Reg. § 1.338-6. Treas. Reg. § 1.338-7(b)(1). If, in the original application of the residual method, all of the assets other than those in Class VII (goodwill and going concern value) were allocated consideration equal to their fair market values, the increased consideration will be allocated solely to the Class VII assets. If, on the other hand, the consideration allocated in the original application of the residual method was insufficient to provide allocations equal to the fair market values of the assets in Classes I through VI, the bases of the assets in these other classes will also be affected. *See* Treas. Reg. § 1.338-7(e) Example 1. In either event, a basis redetermination will result, which, for depreciable assets, will require that depreciation deductions be redetermined in future years. *See Improvements and Basis Redeterminations* in § 3.06(c), *Special Provisions*, of Chapter 4, *Capitalization and Cost Recovery*. If an asset that was previously acquired has been disposed of or fully depreciated or amortized, "the increased amount otherwise allocable to such asset is taken into account under general principles of tax law . . . ." Treas. Reg. § 1.338-7(d)(1). Presumably, this means that, if the asset was disposed of, the additional amount may be treated as a loss in the year of the redetermination, the character of which would relate back to the character of the gain or loss realized on the disposition. Treas. Reg. § 1.338-7(e) Example 1 (referring to the decision in *Arrowsmith v. Commissioner*, 344 U.S. 6 (1952)). Similarly, if the asset has been fully depreciated or amortized, the additional amount may be deducted in the year of the redetermination.

The following opinion describes the tax treatment of a contingent liability assumed in the acquisition of the assets of a business. Although the eventual amount of the liability greatly exceeded its estimate at the time of the acquisition, the court required that the full amount of the liability be included in the basis of the acquired assets.

ILLINOIS TOOL WORKS, INC. v. COMMISSIONER

United States Court of Appeals, Seventh Circuit
355 F.3d 997 (7th Cir. 2004)

KANNE, *CIRCUIT JUDGE*.

Illinois Tool Works Inc. and its subsidiaries ("ITW") appeal from the tax court's determination that $6,956,590 of a more than $17 million court judgment paid by ITW should be capitalized as a cost of acquiring certain assets of the DeVilbiss Co. rather than deducted as an ordinary business expense. The judgment at issue was the result of a jury verdict in a patent infringement suit filed against DeVilbiss's former owner, Champion Spark Plug, Inc. ITW assumed the pending lawsuit, and its defense, upon its acquisition of DeVilbiss in 1990. ITW acknowledges that at least a portion of the judgment should be capitalized as a cost of acquisition, but disputes the amount. We agree with the determination of the tax court and affirm.

I. History

The facts are not in dispute. DeVilbiss was a division of Champion in the 1970s. In 1975, Jerome H. Lemelson, an inventor and engineer, wrote DeVilbiss and offered to license it certain of his patents, including the " '431 patent." DeVilbiss, fatefully, did not take Lemelson up on the offer.

Instead, in 1978, DeVilbiss acquired a license from a Norwegian company named Trallfa to sell its computer-controlled paint-spray robots. Attorneys for Lemelson contacted DeVilbiss in 1979, notifying it that certain of its products in the robot and manipulator field might be infringing on Lemelson's patents, including the '431 patent. DeVilbiss's director of robotic operations replied, summarily denying any infringement. Thereafter, in 1980, DeVilbiss and Trallfa entered a new license agreement whereby DeVilbiss gained the right to manufacture, as well as to sell, Trallfa robots.

The first of two relevant patent infringement suits brought by Lemelson followed in 1981. Lemelson launched that suit in the U.S. Court of Claims ("Court of Claims lawsuit") against the United States, alleging that its purchase and use of certain robots, including the Trallfa robot, infringed his patents. Champion, owner of DeVilbiss, entered as a third-party defendant. The government ultimately settled that suit for $5000 and sought indemnification from Champion. Notably, the presiding judge in that action told the parties prior to settlement that based on his view of the merits, Lemelson was unlikely to succeed.

Lemelson filed the second patent infringement suit in 1985 against Champion directly ("Lemelson lawsuit"), alleging as he had before that the Trallfa robot infringed on several of his patents, including the '431 patent. He sought damages relating to the sale of Trallfa robots prior to 1986. That case was stayed shortly after filing, pending the resolution of the 1981 Court of Claims lawsuit.

DeVilbiss retained counsel to represent it in the Lemelson lawsuit. That attorney, Mark C. Schaffer, specialized in intellectual property law. In his estimation the case was meritless, and he communicated the same to DeVilbiss. Larry Becker, division counsel and secretary of DeVilbiss at the time the Lemelson lawsuit was filed, also evaluated the case and came to the same conclusion. But, he set a range of exposure between $25,000 and $500,000 for internal purposes. In 1989, before ITW purchased DeVilbiss, Lemelson offered to settle for $500,000. DeVilbiss rejected the offer, countering with $25,000. Although not clear from the record, settlement discussions apparently stalled, and, in any event, no settlement was reached at that time.

ITW acquired DeVilbiss in 1990. In the purchase agreement, ITW agreed to assume certain liabilities of the seller, which included the pending Lemelson lawsuit. ITW became aware of the Lemelson lawsuit prior to closing, during the due diligence phase of the sale, which ITW conducted over a ten-to-fourteen-day period. As part of the due diligence review, DeVilbiss disclosed all of its pending litigation, including the Lemelson lawsuit. Although the damages claimed by Lemelson were described as "open" on the schedule provided to ITW, Becker reiterated his opinion that the lawsuit was meritless. ITW representatives, including its director of audits, vice president of patents and technology, and group technology counsel (the latter two patent attorneys), reviewed the Lemelson case and agreed with Becker. They ascribed a 98-to-99 percent chance of prevailing at trial, with a worst case scenario exposure of $1 million to $3 million. They also negotiated a $350,000 cash reserve to cover the attorneys' fees expected to be incurred in defending the suit. Except for the accountants, Arthur Andersen, and Schaffer, the outside counsel retained by DeVilbiss, the record reveals no other outside analysts brought in to examine the risk represented by the Lemelson lawsuit.

As a result of ITW's due diligence findings, the agreed purchase price for DeVilbiss was lowered from $126.5 million to $125.5 million. The Lemelson lawsuit was not a factor in this decision.

After the deal closed, the Lemelson lawsuit was reopened, and ITW assumed the defense as the real party in interest, although Champion remained named in the caption. ITW continued to employ Schaffer, the outside counsel initially hired by DeVilbiss, to represent it. At various points prior to and during trial, Lemelson offered to settle the case. The last offer, for more than $1 million, came after most of the evidence had been heard and at the urging of the trial court. ITW rejected the settlement offer and did not counter.

In January 1991, a jury returned a verdict in favor of Lemelson. It awarded $4,647,905 for patent infringement and $6,295,167 in prejudgment interest. The district court doubled the patent infringement award because the jury found that not only had the '431 patent been infringed, it had been willfully infringed. The willfulness finding was based in part on Champion's failure to secure an authoritative opinion on whether the Trallfa robot infringed the '431 patent until two months before trial. ITW was, to say the least, stunned by the $15,590,977 verdict.

ITW appealed and lost. It finally paid the judgment in 1992, which, with accumulated interest, totaled $17,067,339. On its 1992 tax return, it capitalized $1 million of the judgment as a cost of acquiring DeVilbiss and deducted the remaining $16 million as an ordinary business expense. The reason for the bifurcation, as explained in ITW's Form 8275-R Disclosure Statement that accompanied its 1992 return, was that since it could have settled the Lemelson lawsuit for $1 million, the remaining $16 million liability resulted from the post-acquisition business decision to reject the settlement offer and chance it in court. In essence, ITW contended that its gamble on a jury trial caused it to incur significant additional expenditures over $1 million (the perceived worth of the lawsuit based on the last settlement offer) — not the acquisition of DeVilbiss and its contingent liability in the form of the Lemelson suit. As such, ITW reasoned that the amount of the judgment attributable to its bad decisions should be deducted as an ordinary business expense rather than capitalized as a cost of acquisition. The Commissioner of Internal Revenue and the tax court rejected this novel *mea culpa* argument and so do we.[4]

---

[4] [2] Only $6,956,590 of the $17 million judgment is at issue on appeal because (a) ITW capitalized $1 million in its tax return, (b) the Commissioner conceded an allowance of $2,154,160 for post acquisition interest and expenses, and (c) the Commissioner conceded a reduction of $6,956,589 due to the sale of certain DeVilbiss assets acquired in the 1990 purchase.

II. Analysis

This case revolves around the difference between capital and ordinary business expenses as expressed in the Internal Revenue Code. The Code allows the immediate deduction of "all ordinary and necessary expenses paid or incurred during the taxable year in carrying on any trade or business." 26 U.S.C. § 162(a); *INDOPCO v. Commissioner*, 503 U.S. 79, 83 (1992). The opposite is true of capital expenses, which the Code defines as "an amount paid out for new buildings or for permanent improvements or betterments made to increase the value of any property or estate." 26 U.S.C. § 263(a)(1); *INDOPCO*, 503 U.S. at 83. Ordinary business expenses, then, are generally incurred to meet a taxpayer's immediate or *current* business needs within the present taxable year. *See id.* at 85. Capital expenses are generally incurred for the taxpayer's *future* benefit. *Id.* at 90 (noting that generally an expense is characterized as capital when "the purpose for which the expenditure is made has to do with the corporation's operations and betterment . . . for the duration of its existence or for the indefinite future or for a time somewhat longer than the current taxable year." (quotations omitted)).

The practical result of labeling an expense "ordinary" or "capital" is that generally a taxpayer can take an immediate, full deduction for ordinary business expenses and realize an immediate corresponding reduction in taxable income, while capital expenses generally result in smaller yearly deductions over time through amortization and depreciation. As summarized by the Supreme Court:

> The primary effect of characterizing a payment as either a business expense or a capital expenditure concerns the timing of the taxpayer's cost recovery: While business expenses are currently deductible, a capital expenditure usually is amortized and depreciated over the life of the relevant asset, or, where no specific asset or useful life can be ascertained, is deducted upon dissolution of the enterprise. See U.S.C. §§ 167(a) and 336(a); Treas. Reg. § 1.167(a), 26 C.F.R. § 1.167(a). Through provisions such as these, the Code endeavors to match expenses with the revenues of the taxable period to which they are properly attributable, thereby resulting in a more accurate calculation of net income for tax purposes.

INDOPCO, 503 U.S. at 83-84.

"Whether a taxpayer is required to capitalize particular expenses is a question of law, and our review is therefore de novo." *U.S. Freightways Corp. v. Commissioner*, 270 F.3d 1137, 1139 (7th Cir. 2001); *see also Wells Fargo & Co. v. Commissioner*, 224 F.3d 874, 880 (8th Cir. 2000). We note that ITW, who argues that the majority of the Lemelson judgment should be labeled ordinary business expenses, hence fully and immediately deductible, bears the burden of proving entitlement to the claimed deduction. *U.S. Freightways*, 270 F.3d at 1145. This is because income tax deductions are a matter of legislative grace and the exception to the norm of capitalization. *Id.; INDOPCO*, 503 U.S. at 84.

ITW's burden is particularly heavy because, as recognized by the tax court, our prior precedent states that there is a "well-settled general rule that when an obligation is assumed in connection with the purchase of capital assets, payments satisfying the obligation are non-deductible capital expenditures." *David R. Webb*

Co., Inc. v. Commissioner, 708 F.2d 1254, 1256 (7th Cir. 1983). ITW acknowledged the force of this rule when it capitalized a portion of the Lemelson judgment as attributable to the obligation (in the form of the pending lawsuit) assumed upon acquiring DeVilbiss.

Relying on *A.E. Staley Mfg. Co. v. Commissioner*, 119 F.3d 482 (7th Cir. 1997), though, ITW argues that the tax court erred by applying the rule articulated in *Webb* inflexibly and eschewing the pragmatic, "real life" inquiry advanced in *Staley*. Had it approached ITW's challenge properly, ITW posits, the tax court would have found that except for ITW's mishandling of the lawsuit after acquisition, the value of the Lemelson lawsuit would have been "capped" at $1 million. Thus, anything above $1 million should be attributable to decisions made in the course of defending the litigation and deducted as an ordinary business expense. *See, e.g., Commissioner v. Tellier*, 383 U.S. 687 (1966) (legal expenses incurred in defending against securities fraud charges deductible under § 162(a)); *Commissioner v. Heininger*, 320 U.S. 467 (1943) (legal expenses incurred in disputing adverse postal designation deductible as ordinary and necessary business expenses). We find fault with ITW's argument on several levels.

A. ITW misreads the tax court's approach to *Webb*.

First, the tax court did not apply *Webb* inflexibly. ITW reads the tax court's opinion to state that "any payment in satisfaction of a contingent liability acquired in a capital transaction is *always* a capital expenditure." (Appellants' Opening Br. at 19). We do not read the tax court's opinion so restrictively. Rather, we note the opinion accurately cites *Webb* for the proposition that "*generally*, the payment of a liability of a preceding owner of property by the person acquiring such property, whether or not such liability was fixed or contingent at the time such property was acquired, is not an ordinary and necessary business expense." *Illinois Tool Works, Inc. v. Commissioner*, 117 T.C. 39, 44-45 (2001) (emphasis added). The tax court's language analyzing ITW's case in light of the above general principle does not foreclose in every circumstance an outcome different than the one reached; rather, it simply notes that ITW's arguments for treating all but $1 million of the judgment as an ordinary business expense are not persuasive in "the present case." *Id.* at 47.

B. *Webb* controls

Next, we agree with the tax court that the facts of this straightforward case do not dictate a departure from *Webb*. In *Webb*, the taxpayer acquired a wood veneer company that many years ago agreed to pay an employee's widow, Mrs. Grunwald, a lifetime pension of $12,700 annually. 708 F.2d at 1255. The taxpayer knowingly assumed the liability to Mrs. Grunwald as part of the purchase agreement. *Id.* In tax years thereafter it attempted to deduct, as an ordinary and necessary business expense, the $12,700 paid to Mrs. Grunwald. The Commissioner determined that the $12,700 was not an ordinary business expense, but a capital one, which the tax court upheld. *Id.* at 1255-56.

We affirmed, observing that because the taxpayer agreed to assume the pension payments as part of its purchase agreement for the wood veneer business, the payments were more properly attributed to that capital investment, not its current business operations. *Id.* at 1256. In essence, the agreement to pay the debt to the widow served as part of the purchase price for the business. *Id.* ("Assumption of the obligation to make pension payments to Mrs. Grunwald was in theory and in fact, part of the cost of acquiring the assets of the wood veneer business from the taxpayer's predecessor.") Because the purchase of the wood veneer business was meant to enhance the taxpayer's operations into the future, the expenses to acquire it — which included the discharge of the annual debt to Mrs. Grunwald — had to be capitalized. *Id.* (stating that generally "when an obligation is assumed in connection with the purchase of capital assets, payments satisfying the obligation are non-deductible capital expenditures").

Similarly, ITW knowingly assumed the Lemelson lawsuit as part of the purchase agreement for the DeVilbiss assets. Because ITW agreed to pay that contingent liability in exchange for DeVilbiss, that contingent liability formed part of the purchase price. Because the DeVilbiss acquisition was meant to benefit ITW into the future, the expenses to acquire it — including the Lemelson lawsuit, once assigned a value through the judgment — must be capitalized.

ITW attempts to distinguish *Webb* based on the parties' expectation of the ultimate value of the Lemelson lawsuit and on ITW's alleged ability, post-acquisition, to negatively impact the liability amount. In *Webb*, the acquiring company knew that it owed an annual liability of $12,700 and that it would end when Mrs. Grunwald passed. Therefore, ITW argues, the parties in *Webb* had a complete understanding of the scope of the contingent liability at stake in the deal, unlike in the case before us where the parties to the transaction failed to grasp the risk represented by the Lemelson lawsuit. ITW also urges that since the taxpayer in *Webb* could do nothing to affect the amount of the liability, unlike here where the failure to accept a settlement offer increased the debt exponentially, *Webb* should be ignored.

ITW's attempts to distance itself from *Webb* are unavailing. ITW agreed to assume the Lemelson defense and pay any judgment, whatever it may be. Although we have no doubt the parties earnestly believed the case was meritless, ITW cannot dispute that it acknowledged some risk, albeit minimal, and did not take steps to mitigate that risk. It could have lowered the purchase price or inserted an indemnification clause in the purchase agreement to recoup any losses not anticipated by the parties. That a contingent liability, once fixed, exceeded the parties' expectations does not render it any less a part of the purchase price. *See Pacific Transport Co. v. Commissioner*, 483 F.2d 209, 213 (9th Cir. 1973) (noting that a taxpayer's failure to realize the substance or amount of a contingent liability assumed when acquiring property does not change its tax treatment — the payment must be capitalized); *but see Nahey v. Commissioner*, 196 F.3d 866, 870 (7th Cir. 1999) (criticizing *Pacific Transport* in *dicta*). In this case, protection from an aberrant jury verdict needed to be sought during contract formation, not after the fact in the form of an immediate tax deduction.

Moreover, ITW's entire premise that its actions after assuming the liability should be examined for the effect it had on increasing the amount of the ultimate indebtedness strays from the inescapable fact that, like the taxpayer in *Webb*, it accepted the indebtedness in order to acquire what it perceived to be a future benefit — DeVilbiss. Part of ITW's process of valuing the DeVilbiss assets and arriving at the purchase price included evaluating the Lemelson lawsuit. In that due diligence phase, ITW assessed a value to the suit based on how it foresaw the litigation unfolding once it took control of the defense. Its ability to affect the outcome of the Lemelson lawsuit was therefore already factored in. That things did not go according to plan, and that, in retrospect, it should have paid far less for DeVilbiss to account for size of the judgment assigned, does not change the tax character of the judgment in this case.

C. *Staley*'s Application

Finally, *Staley* does not warrant a different outcome, as ITW insists. In *Staley*, this Court reversed the tax court's determination that fees paid to investment bankers to unsuccessfully ward off a hostile takeover had to be capitalized by the defending company, rather than deducted as an ordinary business expense. 119 F.3d at 483. The tax court, in determining that these incidental fees were part of the capital transaction ultimately resulting in the taxpayer's hostile acquisition by a corporate raider, purported to follow the Supreme Court's decision in *INDOPCO v. Commissioner*, 503 U.S. 79 (1992). *Id.* at 485. The *INDOPCO* case also involved investment banking fees, but in the context of a friendly, as opposed to hostile, takeover of National Starch by Unilever. There the Court found that the money paid to the investment bankers by National Starch was for the purpose of facilitating a favorable merger with Unilever, thus changing the corporate structure for the benefit of future operations — a capital expense. *INDOPCO*, 503 U.S. at 88-90.

In disagreeing with the tax court's application of *INDOPCO*, we found it significant that the majority of the fees paid in *Staley* were for the purpose of defending against what the company perceived to be an unfavorable, hostile takeover. *Staley*, 119 F.3d at 491. Because defending a company against attack is considered a necessary and ordinary business expense, designed to benefit current operations, *id.* at 487, we remanded the case to the tax court. We asked it to allocate the fees paid between those activities that were considered in defense of the company, an ordinary expense immediately deductible, and those that facilitated the ultimate merger, a capital expense meant to benefit the company into the future. *Id.* at 492-493.

Our analysis in *Staley* was based on the recognition that distinguishing between ordinary expenses and those that must be capitalized can sometimes be difficult. *Id.* at 487 ("As the Supreme Court has noted, 'the cases sometimes appear difficult to harmonize,' and 'each case turns on its special facts.' " (quoting *INDOPCO*, 503 U.S. at 86)). When faced with this challenge, we observed that "distinguishing between ordinary and capital costs often requires a rather pragmatic approach." *Id. Staley* was such a case, with its factual similarities to the *INDOPCO* decision and turning on incidental, rather than direct, costs of an acquisition. Therefore, we specifically applied a "pragmatic assessment" to the underlying facts in order to decipher whether the fees incident to the hostile takeover were for current defense of the company or for an ultimate corporate change with benefits lasting into the future. *See id.* at 487-92.

Our task here is easier than in *Staley*. The taxpayer points us to no decision in conflict with *Webb*, where payments made to satisfy an obligation directly assumed as part of a bargained-for acquisition have not been capitalized as part of the purchase price of the asset. Regardless, applying the pragmatic approach called for in *Staley* results in the same outcome, and is implicit, if not explicit, in the tax court's opinion. The record consists of three sets of stipulated facts with dozens of attendant exhibits and a day-long trial transcript in which ITW presents seven witnesses. The tax court's opinion coalesced that testimony and documentary evidence into findings of fact, which ITW, by its own admission, embraces. From those facts and the arguments advanced by the parties, the tax court deduced that this was not a case in which the general rule articulated in *Webb* would not apply.

Looking at the facts, we agree. The ultimate goal of the pragmatic assessment advanced by *Staley* is to decode whether an expenditure is ordinary or capital in nature. Although ITW argues that paying $16 million more than the Lemelson lawsuit was allegedly worth could have no positive impact on the future of the company, it loses sight of the fact that what it got in exchange for its obligation to pay the judgment was the DeVilbiss assets. In this way, the Lemelson judgment was " 'incurred for the purpose of changing the corporate structure for the benefit of future operations' " and must be capitalized. *Staley*, 119 F.3d at 489 (quoting *INDOPCO*, 503 U.S. at 89). As stated by the court in *United States v. Smith*, observing that the substance, not the form of the transaction governs when determining tax treatment of a settlement paid to a former employee:

> If the corporation at its inception assumed a contingent obligation to pay [the employee], it is that assumption of liability which obligated the corporation and not any subsequent legitimate business purpose. In other words, the corporation did not have to pay because of the unfavorable judgment or because its directors deemed payment advisable but rather the corporation paid because it assumed the obligation when it became incorporated.

418 F.2d 589, 596 (5th Cir. 1969); *see also Staley*, 119 F.3d at 491 (noting that "the substance of the transaction, not its form, is controlling" (citing *Clark Oil & Refining Corp. v. United States*, 473 F.2d 1217, 1220-21 (7th Cir. 1973)). So too here it was not ITW's failure to accept the settlement offer that obligated it to pay the jury award, but its assumption of the lawsuit in order to acquire DeVilbiss.

If we examine the events post-acquisition, as ITW urges, the result is still the same. ITW focuses our attention primarily on its missed opportunity to settle the case, contending that had it only taken Lemelson up on his final $1 million offer, instead of staunchly placing its faith in its own valuation of the case, then the liability it acquired along with the DeVilbiss assets would not have increased exponentially. It states, "thus, a 'pragmatic,' 'real-life' assessment of the facts demonstrates that ITW's decision, made in the ordinary course of its business, to reject Lemelson's settlement offers was the proximate cause of the amount ultimately owed to Lemelson." (Appellant's Opening Br. at 32.) Yet, the patent suit claimed damages for infringing robots sold from 1979 to 1985, years before ITW acquired DeVilbiss. ITW's predecessor failed to accept Lemelson's $500,000 settlement offer in 1989. And, as noted by the patent trial court in upholding the jury's finding of willfulness: "Defendant's entire course of conduct from its total disregard of Plaintiff's 1975 letter to its unexplained failure to secure an authoritative opinion until two months before trial, demonstrates an utter lack of concern over Plaintiff's patent rights." (Tr. Ex. 19-J P 23.) A pragmatic assessment of this case leads to the conclusion that the Lemelson lawsuit was mishandled from the outset, arriving in ITW's hands fully formed. ITW's mistakes and missed opportunities had little to do with the ultimate valuation placed on the matter by the jury.

III. Conclusion

For the foregoing reasons, the decision of the tax court is AFFIRMED.

NOTES AND COMMENTS

The court in *Illinois Tools Works* cited the decision in *Nahey v. Commissioner*, 196 F.3d 866 (7th Cir. 1999). In some ways, *Nahey* represents the flip side of the situation in *Illinois Tool Works*. In *Nahey*, Wehr Corporation, a manufacturer of industrial equipment, sued Xerox Corporation for breach of contract, intentional fraud and misrepresentation, and negligent misrepresentation. The taxpayer, Nahey, subsequently acquired all of Wehr's assets, including the lawsuit, for $100 million in a leveraged buyout. In allocating the $100 million purchase price among the acquired assets, an accounting firm hired by Nahey assigned no value to the suit against Xerox, regarding it as too speculative to be valued. Six years later, Xerox settled the lawsuit by paying approximately $6 million, and the taxpayer reported the settlement proceeds as capital gain.

The Tax Court concluded that the proceeds constituted ordinary income and not capital gain because the settlement did not involve the sale or exchange of property or property rights, despite the fact that the taxpayer had acquired the right to prosecute the action as one of the assets of Wehr Corporation. The Seventh Circuit, in a decision by Judge Posner, affirmed the Tax Court's decision. The court reasoned, and Nahey conceded, that if Wehr had not been sold and had settled the lawsuit against Xerox on the same terms that Nahey did, the settlement would have been taxable to Wehr as ordinary income rather than as a capital gain because the amount received in the settlement would have replaced ordinary income of which Xerox had deprived Wehr. The court could find no reason that the tax treatment of the settlement should change "merely because of an intervening change in ownership."

In a concurring opinion by Judge Cudahy, he wondered whether the treatment of contingent liabilities and the fact that such liabilities must be capitalized in the basis of the acquired assets should serve as any guidance in this case, citing the decision in *Pacific Transport Co. v. Commissioner*, 483 F.2d 209 (9th Cir.1973). According to Judge Cudahy, "*Pacific Transport* is on all fours with the present case except that it involves the expense side rather than the income side."

> At oral argument, the panel asked questions of government counsel reflecting its concern that the government, after successfully arguing for capital treatment in cases like *Pacific Transport* involving the characterization of *expenses*, would continue to fight for ordinary income treatment

> when the issue involved the characterization of *income.* To no one's surprise, government counsel refused to represent that in the future the government would accept ordinary expense treatment when the shoe was on the other foot. . . . But this Court has, in related contexts in the past, aspired to treat settlement expenses and settlement income symmetrically.

Unfortunately, Judge Cudahy missed the mark in assuming that some type of symmetry should exist between the capitalization of certain expenditures and the characterization of gain. But Judge Cudahy was on the right track in his search for symmetry. If contingent liabilities assumed in the acquisition of business assets like those in *Pacific Transport* or *Illinois Tools Works* must be treated as an increase in the purchase price of the business and capitalized as part of the basis of the acquired assets, then the settlement proceeds in *Nahey* should properly be viewed as a reduction in the purchase price of the business, reducing the basis of the acquired assets. From the taxpayer's perspective in *Nahey*, the settlement proceeds would have been neither capital gain nor ordinary income, but a recovery of the taxpayer's basis in the acquired assets. Certainly, the regulations under § 338 in the application of the residual method recognize that a redetermined purchase price can result in either an increase or a decrease in the basis of the acquired assets. *See* Treas. Reg. § 1.338-7(e) Example 2 (illustrating a purchase price reduction as a result of a settlement of a claim alleging fraud by the buyer against the seller). Unfortunately, the taxpayer's attorney in *Nahey* seems not to have raised this argument.

Chapter 2

CAPITAL GAINS AND LOSSES

§ 1. INTRODUCTION

Gain and losses from the sale or exchange of capital assets are taxed differently than ordinary gains and losses under the Internal Revenue Code. Gains from the sale or exchange of capital assets are taxed at preferential rates for non-corporate taxpayers, while the deduction of losses from the sale or exchange of capital assets is limited for both corporate and non-corporate taxpayers. Consequently, taxpayers typically desire to have any property that they are disposing of treated as a capital asset when the disposition results in a gain but to avoid having any property that they are disposing of treated as a capital asset when the disposition results in a loss. Of course, the converse generally applies from the government's perspective.

In general terms, a "capital asset" includes most types of property held by a taxpayer for investment appreciation rather than for resale. I.R.C. § 1221. The Supreme Court has stated that the purpose of the preferential tax treatment of capital gains is to distinguish income from the typical operations of a business from one-time sales of property and to alleviate the burden that taxpayers would confront if the appreciation in the value of property accumulated over time were taxed all in the year of disposition.

> Congress intended that profits and losses arising from the everyday operation of a business be considered as ordinary income or loss rather than capital gain or loss. The preferential treatment provided by [the capital gain sections] applies to transactions in property which are not the normal source of business income. It was intended "to relieve the taxpayer from . . . excessive tax burdens on gains resulting from a conversion of capital investments, and to remove the deterrent effect of those burdens on such conversions."

Corn Prods. Refining Co. v. Commissioner, 350 U.S. 46, 52 (1955) (quoting *Burnet v. Harmel*, 287 U.S. 103, 106 (1932)). The burden on taxpayers that would exist in the absence of preferential rates for capital gains is often referred to as the "lock-in effect." The lock-in effect is actually the result of the realization requirement under § 1001 which, as previously described in Chapter 1, defers the inclusion in gross income of appreciation in the value of property until the taxpayer engages in a sale or other disposition of the property. Thus, the expected return of an alternative investment must be that much greater than the expected return of an existing investment in order to compensate the taxpayer for the tax liability imposed in shifting from one investment to another. According to this view, this tax burden creates a disincentive for taxpayers to sell appreciated property, thus reducing the mobility of investment capital in the economy.

A problem related to the lock-in effect is the so-called "bunching effect" in which, again as a result of the realization requirement, the accumulated gain from the appreciation in the value of property is all realized in the year of disposition. Consequently, a taxpayer may be forced into a higher marginal tax bracket in the year of disposition than if the appreciation had been taxed as it accrued. A preferential tax rate applicable to capital gains prevents the gain from being taxed at the higher marginal rate. Of course, the bunching effect does not arise to the extent that the amount of capital gain is insufficient to bump the taxpayer into a higher tax bracket or to the extent that the taxpayer's income was subject to tax in the highest marginal tax rate while the appreciation accrued. Because historically the tax rates under § 1 applicable to ordinary income were substantially higher than the rates under current law and the rates created many more and narrower tax brackets than under current law, the concerns regarding the bunching effect may no longer be as significant. Finally, and assuming these concerns remain relevant, the bunching effect would not justify taxing capital gains at a rate less than the taxpayer's usual marginal tax rate as is often the case under current law. Because the realization requirement under § 1001 effectively defers tax on interim appreciation, the possibility of a higher rate as a result of the bunching effect may be a reasonable price for the benefits of deferral. Presumably, taxpayers concerned about the bunching effect could arrange interim realization of gains, assuming reasonable transactions costs in doing so.

The preferential tax rates applicable to capital gain have also been justified on the basis that the realized "gain" does not necessarily represent an increase in any real purchasing power by the taxpayer when the gain is due in part to inflation in the price of goods generally. However, the current one-year holding period hardly seems to justify a significant tax rate reduction. If concerns regarding inflation were the justification for the preferential rates applicable to capital gains, lower rates depending on the length of time that the taxpayer has held the asset would presumably make greater sense from a policy perspective. Moreover, if the treatment of capital assets is based on a concern over the effects of inflation, it is surprising that the Code does not take inflation into account with respect to other types of assets. For example, inflation affects assets other than capital assets, such as depreciable real estate. However, the Code does not permit basis adjustments to correct the effects of inflation in connection with depreciable real estate when determining the amount of current depreciation. In addition, the absence of provisions in the Code to correct for the effects of inflation may mean that no correction is necessary with respect to capital assets. For example, because the Code does not provide an adjustment for the effect of inflation on liabilities, no net inflation adjustment should be necessary for assets acquired with borrowed funds. Indeed, because the deductible interest includes an inflation adjustment, the taxpayer, in effect, receives an unjustified deduction for the charge imposed by the lender for the fact that the borrowing is repaid in deflated funds.

In more recent years, Congress has increasingly relied on the need to increase savings and investment as a justification for the reduced tax rates applicable to capital. *See generally* Staff of the Joint Committee on Taxation, General Explanation of Tax Legislation Enacted in the 105th Congress 48 (1997) (referring to the economic goal of increased output and worker productivity through business investment). However, there is no substantial evidence that the special capital gain rate encourages savings or investment, although there is evidence that lowering the capital gains rate temporarily encourages rollover of investments. In any event, this justification may help to explain why different tax rates are applicable to the gain generated by different types of capital assets.

To implement the congressional intent that the preferential treatment of capital gains only be available in connection with appreciation in the value of property that has accrued over time, a statutory holding-period requirement is also imposed. Although the length of the holding period has varied, preferential tax treatment is currently available only in connection with gains from the sale or exchange of a capital asset that has been held for more than one year. I.R.C. § 1222. Gains from the sale or exchange of such assets are referred to as long-term capital gains. I.R.C. § 1222(3). Similarly, a taxpayer may realize losses from the sale or exchange of capital assets held for more than one year, which are referred to as "long-term capital losses," gains from the sale or exchange of capital assets held for not more than one year which are referred to as "short-term capital gains," and losses from the sale or exchange of capital assets held for not more than one year which are referred to as "short-term capital losses." I.R.C. §§ 1222(4), 1222(1), and 1222(2), respectively.

If a taxpayer has both capital gains and losses in a given tax year, the gains and losses must be netted under very specific rules set forth in the Code and Regulations in an ordering scheme that takes into account the holding period of the capital asset sold or exchanged. The favorable tax treatment of capital gains is technically available only to "net capital gain," which is defined as long-term capital gains in excess of: (1) long-term capital losses and (2) short-term capital losses in excess of short-term capital gains. I.R.C. §§ 1(h)(1) and 1222(11).

The maximum capital gain tax rate applicable to most forms of net capital gain is 15 percent as compared to the maximum ordinary income tax rate of 35 percent. I.R.C. § 1(h)(1)(C). Nevertheless, gain from the sale or exchange of certain types of capital assets such as "collectibles" and § 1202 stock (referred to as "28-percent rate gain") is taxed at a top marginal tax rate of 28 percent and gain resulting from the depreciation of improved real property (referred to as "unrecaptured § 1250 gain") is taxed at a top marginal tax rate of 25 percent. I.R.C. § 1(h)(1)(D) and 1(h)(1)(E). The 15 percent capital gain tax rate is reduced even further to five percent for low-income taxpayers whose taxable income would otherwise be taxed at a rate below 25 percent. I.R.C. § 1(h)(1)(B). This tax rate will be further reduced to zero for taxable years beginning after 2007.

The favorable tax treatment applicable to capital gains is passed through to the shareholders of corporations under Subchapter S as well as to the owners of other "pass through" entities under Subchapter K. I.R.C. §§ 1(h)(9), 1(h)(10), 702, and 1366; Treas. Reg. § 1.1(h)-1. Corporations other than S corporations, however, are not afforded the favorable tax rate and pay tax on capital gains at regular corporate income tax rates. I.R.C. § 11.

As previously mentioned, the deductibility of losses from the sale or exchange of capital assets is more limited than other types of business or investment losses, which are often fully deductible against a taxpayer's ordinary income. I.R.C. § 165(a), (c), and (f). In the case of losses from the sale or exchange of a capital asset, non-corporate taxpayers are permitted to deduct such losses only to the extent of capital gains plus "the excess of such losses over such gains" with a maximum of $3,000. I.R.C. § 1211(b). Consequently, capital losses can reduce a maximum of only $3,000 of ordinary income, and only to the extent that capital losses exceed capital gains for the year. Any nondeductible capital loss for the current taxable year is carried over to the next succeeding tax year. I.R.C. § 1212(b). Corporate taxpayers may deduct capital losses *only* to the extent of capital gain in the same year. I.R.C. § 1211(a). Any nondeductible capital loss may be carried back for three years and forward for five years and offset against other corporate income. I.R.C. § 1212(a)(1). These limitations prevent abuse by taxpayers who would otherwise face incentives to realize capital losses, deductible against ordinary income taxable at their top marginal tax rates, while continuing to hold appreciated capital assets taxable when the appreciation is realized at preferential rates.

Because of the significant rate differential between the taxation of ordinary income and the taxation of net capital gain, taxpayers attempt to structure transactions to obtain capital gain treatment when appreciated assets are sold or exchanged. Conversely, because of the severe limitations on the deductibility of capital losses, taxpayers attempt to avoid the impact of the limitations on the deductibility of capital losses, by either offsetting capital losses with capital gain or ensuring that the loss is not capital in nature and, therefore, potentially deductible under other provisions of the Code.

The remainder of this Chapter provides a detailed description of the principal concepts that arise in the taxation of capital gains and losses. This chapter will serve to illustrate the significant tax benefits that can be achieved by a non-corporate taxpayer with net capital gain in a given taxable year. These benefits must be contrasted, however, with the limitations that apply to both corporate and non-corporate taxpayers on the deductibility of capital losses incurred in a given taxable year.

After a description of the tax rates and limitations applicable to capital gains and losses realized by both non-corporate and corporate taxpayers in section 2, section 3 examines the statutory definition of a capital asset and discusses the extraordinary amount of judicial effort that has been devoted to applying this definition to actual cases. Section 4 then describes the sale or exchange requirement, including the various provisions of the Code that provide for sale or exchange treatment in specific situations. Section 5 then describes the rules and requirements applicable in determining the holding period of a capital asset. Finally, section 6 considers the relatively strange realm created by § 1231 under which the gains realized from the disposition of certain assets used in a trade or businesses, which, by definition, are not capital assets, may nevertheless be entitled to the preferential capital gain tax rates described in this chapter while avoiding the limitations generally applicable to deduction of losses arising from the sale or exchange of capital assets.

§ 2. MECHANICS OF DETERMINING NET CAPITAL GAIN

§ 2.01 Non-Corporate Taxpayers

(a) Applicable Tax Rates

I.R.C. § 1(h)

The following paragraphs describe the various tax rates that apply to net capital gain in the hands of a non-corporate taxpayer. As will be seen, the rate of tax can vary widely depending on the type of asset from which the gain is realized. While the tax rate applicable to net capital gain under § 1(h) is typically 15 percent, this rate can actually vary from a low of five percent to a high of 28 percent depending upon the type of asset generating the gain and the marginal tax rate applicable to the taxpayer's ordinary income. Importantly, the taxpayer's tax liability is determined first under the general provisions of § 1 given the taxpayer's filing status and without application of the preferential tax rates of § 1(h). I.R.C. § 1(h)(1)(A). Only then is the taxpayer's net capital gain effectively segregated from the taxpayer's remaining taxable income and the taxpayer's tax liability determined using the general provisions of § 1 and the preferential tax rates under § 1(h). Thus, the benefit of the lower 10 percent and 15 percent tax brackets is preserved with respect to any net capital gain that would otherwise fall within those brackets.

Section 1(h) of the Code defines three categories of net capital gain that are subject to varying degrees of preference with respect to the applicable tax rate — 28 percent rate gain, unrecaptured § 1250 gain, and adjusted net capital gain. Each of these types of net capital gain is described below.

28-Percent Rate Gain

28-percent rate gain is comprised of the gain from the sale or exchange of two types of assets — collectibles and § 1202 stock. I.R.C. § 1(h)(4). As the label states, gain from the sale or exchange of collectibles or § 1202 stock is subject to a maximum tax rate of 28 percent rather than the more preferential tax rate of 15 percent generally applicable to net capital gain. I.R.C. § 1(h)(1)(E).

The definition of "collectibles" includes any work of art, any rug or antique, any metal or gem, any stamp or coin, any alcoholic beverage, or any other tangible personal property specified in the Regulations. I.R.C. § 1(h)(5)(A) (cross referencing § 408(m)). Presumably, the congressional justification for not extending the more preferred 15 percent tax rate to gain from the sale of collectibles lies in the fact that tax benefits from the sale or exchange of such assets cannot provide an incentive for the creation of such assets. For gain from the sale or exchange of collectibles to qualify for the 28-percent rate, the collectible must be a capital asset, which means that gain from collectibles in the hands of a dealer in such property would not qualify for the reduced rate and would, instead, be taxed at ordinary tax rates.

A maximum tax rate of 28 percent also applies to a non-corporate taxpayer who sells or exchanges "qualified small business stock" as defined in § 1202 that has been held by the taxpayer for more than five years. I.R.C. §§ 1(h)(1)(E) and 1(h)(7). If the stock satisfies the definition of qualified small business stock, 50 percent of any gain on the sale or exchange of the stock is excluded from income.[1] I.R.C. § 1202(a)(1). The amount of the exclusion is increased to 75 percent of any gain on the sale or exchange of qualified small business stock acquired after February 17, 2009, and before September 28, 2010, and increased further to 100 percent of any gain on the sale or exchange of qualified small business stock acquired after September 27, 2010, and before January 1, 2011.[2] I.R.C. §§ 1202(a)(3) and 1202(a)(4).

Provided the qualified small business stock is a capital asset in the taxpayer's hands, the remaining gain is taxed at a maximum rate of 28 percent.[3] Thus, the effective tax rate on the sale of qualifying small business stock held for more than five years is generally 14 percent.[4] This benefit is minimal when compared to the 15-percent rate applicable to adjusted net capital gain as described below.

Unrecaptured § 1250 Gain

Section 1250 generally requires that any gain on the disposition of real property be treated as ordinary income to the extent of any "additional depreciation" taken with respect to the property. I.R.C. § 1250(a)(1)(A). Additional depreciation is defined as that portion of the depreciation previously claimed in excess of the depreciation that would have been available had the property been depreciated using the straight-line method.[5] I.R.C. § 1250(b)(1). Although any remaining gain on the disposition of real property may be treated as net capital gain if the property is treated as a capital asset in the hands of the taxpayer, § 1(h) provides that the portion of the remaining gain attributable to depreciation deductions is taxable at a maximum tax rate of 25 percent rather than the more favorable 15-percent tax rate.[6] I.R.C. §§ 1(h)(1)(D) and 1(h)(6).

---

[1] Provided the stock is acquired after December 21, 2000, and held for more than five years, 60 percent, rather than only 50 percent, of the gain from the sale or exchange of qualified small business stock in a corporation that is a qualified business entity (as defined in § 1397C(b)) may be excluded. I.R.C. § 1202(a)(2)(A).

[2] February 17, 2009, is the effective date of the American Recovery and Reinvestment Tax Act of 2009, Pub. L. No. 111-5, 123 Stat. 115 (2010), and September 27, 2010, is the effective date of the Small Business Jobs Act of 2010, Pub. L. No. 111-240, 124 Stat. 2504 (2010).

[3] Section 1202 gain is defined as the gain that would be excluded from gross income under § 1202(a) but for the 50-percent limitation in excess of the gain excluded from gross income under § 1202. I.R.C. § 1(h)(7). Because the percentage limitation under § 1202(a) is 50 percent, the amount excluded and the amount included is typically, but not always, the same. *See* I.R.C. § 1202(b)(1) (limiting the amount of gain that may be excluded under § 1202(a)).

[4] However, a portion of the amount excluded is a tax preference item for purposes of the alternative minimum tax. I.R.C. § 57(a)(7). *But see* I.R.C. § 1202(a)(4)(C) (providing that § 57(a)(7) does not apply to the gain excluded under § 1202(a) for qualified small business stock acquired after September 27, 2010, and before January 1, 2011).

[5] Because real property has been depreciable under § 168 using only the straight-line method since 1986, the relevance of depreciation recapture under § 1250 has declined considerably.

[6] The 25 percent tax rate also applies for purposes of the alternative minimum tax. I.R.C. § 55(b)(3)(D).

Adjusted Net Capital Gain

Adjusted net capital gain is equal to the amount of net capital gain in excess of the 28-percent rate gain and the unrecaptured § 1250 gain.[7] I.R.C. § 1(h)(3). Adjusted net capital gain is subject to a maximum tax rate of 15 percent.[8] I.R.C. § 1(h)(1)(C). However, for taxpayers in the 10 and 15 percent tax brackets, the adjusted net capital gain may be subject to an even lower tax rate. Section 1(h) provides that, if the adjusted net capital gain would be taxable at a rate below 25 percent because the taxpayer's taxable income (including the adjusted net capital gain) does not exceed the upper limit of the 15 percent tax bracket, the adjusted net capital gain is taxable at a maximum tax rate of five percent.[9] I.R.C. § 1(h)(1)(B). The five percent tax rate drops to zero percent for taxable years beginning after 2007.

(b) Netting Capital Gains and Losses

I.R.C. § 1222

A taxpayer may have more than one transaction that gives rise to a capital gain or loss in a given tax year. The taxpayer may also have capital losses that are carried forward from a prior year. In addition, the capital gains and losses, whether characterized in the current tax year or carried forward from a prior tax year, may be subject to different rates as discussed above. This section discusses the very intricate and important rules regarding how capital gains and losses are netted against one another in order to determine the taxpayer's net capital gain and the components of net capital gain — 28-percent rate gain, unrecaptured § 1250 gain, and adjusted net capital gain.

The Determination of Net Capital Gain

In a given tax year, a taxpayer may have *both* gains and losses from the sale or exchange of capital assets.[10] Moreover, such gains and losses may be either short-term or long-term depending upon whether the asset disposed of was held for more than one year, in which case the gain or loss will be long term, or for one year or less, in which case the gain or loss will be short term. I.R.C. § 1222(1)–(4). Regardless of the holding period involved, all capital gains will be included in the taxpayer's gross income under § 61, and all capital losses, unless the limitation under § 1211 applies, will be deductible in determining the taxpayer's adjusted gross income under § 62. I.R.C. §§ 61(a)(3) and 62(a)(3). If the taxpayer has net capital gain for the taxable year, the taxpayer's tax liability is determined first

---

[7] Adjusted net capital gain also includes "qualified dividend income" as defined under § 1(h)(11)(A). I.R.C. § 1(h)(3). However, qualified dividend income is not a form of capital gain but is included in the definition of adjusted net capital gain in order to ensure that it is subject to a maximum tax rate of 15 percent.

[8] The 15 percent tax rate also applies for purposes of the alternative minimum tax. I.R.C. § 55(b)(3)(C).

[9] The five and zero percent tax rates also apply for purposes of the alternative minimum tax. I.R.C. § 55(b)(3)(B).

[10] This discussion applies to gains and losses that are characterized as capital gain and losses under § 1231 as well as to gains and losses from the sale or exchange of capital assets under § 1221.

under the general provisions of § 1 given the taxpayer's filing status and without application of the preferential tax rates of § 1(h). I.R.C. § 1(h)(1)(A). Only then is the taxpayer's net capital gain effectively segregated from the taxpayer's remaining taxable income and the taxpayer's tax liability determined using the general provisions of § 1 and the preferential tax rates under § 1(h).

In order to determine the amount of net capital gain, the various types of gains and losses must be netted. The aggregate amount of long-term capital gains, long-term capital losses, short-term capital gains, and short-term capital losses is first determined. Long-term capital gains are then reduced by long-term capital losses to determine the amount of the taxpayer's net long-term capital gain or net long-term capital loss. I.R.C. § 1222(7) and (8). If the taxpayer has no net long-term capital gain, the taxpayer will have no net capital gain, and the preferential tax rates under § 1(h) will not be applicable. Short-term capital gains are then reduced by short-term capital losses to determine the amount of the taxpayer's net short-term capital gain or net short-term capital loss. I.R.C. § 1222(5) and (6). Finally, net capital gain is determined by reducing the net long-term capital gain by the net short-term capital loss.[11] I.R.C. § 1222(11). If the taxpayer has net short-term capital gain, the amount of net capital gain will equal the net long-term capital gain. If the taxpayer's net short-term capital loss exceeds the taxpayer's net long-term capital gain, the taxpayer will have no net capital gain, and the preferential tax rates under § 1(h) will not be applicable.

EXAMPLE 1:

T sold a number of assets in her investment portfolio over the course of the taxable year. These transactions generated $125,000 of long-term capital gain, $45,000 of long-term capital loss, $60,000 of short-term capital gain, and $20,000 of short-term capital loss. T also had $100,000 of income from compensation for services. Consequently, T has $285,000 of gross income, equal to the $100,000 compensation for services plus the $185,000 of capital gain. T may deduct the $65,000 of capital losses as a § 62 deduction in determining her adjusted gross income. Ignoring the effect of any itemized deductions or personal exemptions, T will have taxable income of $220,000. The netting of capital gains and losses will result in net capital gain of $80,000.

LTCG	$125,000	STCG	$60,000
LTCL	45,000	STCL	20,000
NLTCG	$80,000	NSTCG	$40,000

Net Capital Gain = NLTCG − NSTCL
= $80,000 − $0

In determining T's tax liability, the net capital gain of $80,000 will be segregated from her taxable income of $220,000 and the preferential tax rates available under § 1(h) will be applied to the $80,000 net capital gain

[11] Net capital gain is also reduced (but not below zero) by the amount that the taxpayer takes into account as investment income under § 163(d)(4)(B)(iii). I.R.C. § 1(h)(2).

and the general provisions of § 1 will be applied to the remaining taxable income of $140,000.

EXAMPLE 2:

In Example 1, assume that instead of $20,000 short-term capital loss, T had a $75,000 short-term capital loss. T again has $285,000 of gross income, equal to the $100,000 compensation for services plus the $185,000 of capital gain. T may deduct the $120,000 of capital losses as a § 62 deduction in determining her adjusted gross income. Ignoring the effect of any itemized deductions or personal exemptions, T will have taxable income of $165,000. The netting of capital gains and losses will result in net capital gain of $65,000.

LTCG	$125,000	STCG	$60,000
LTCL	45,000	STCL	75,000
NLTCG	$80,000	NSTCL	$15,000

Net Capital Gain = NLTCG B NSTCL
= $80,000 – $15,000
= $65,000

In determining T's tax liability, the net capital gain of $65,000 will be segregated from her taxable income of $165,000 and the preferential tax rates available under § 1(h) will be applied to the $65,000 net capital gain and the general provisions of § 1 will be applied to the remaining taxable income of $100,000.

The purpose of the netting rules applicable to capital gains and losses is to ensure that short-term capital gains do not receive the preferential tax rates available under § 1(h). In addition, the netting rules ensure that short-term capital losses are first used to reduce short-term capital gains and, if the taxpayer has net short-term capital losses, such losses are used to reduce net long-term capital gain. Effectively, short-term capital losses reduce short-term capital gains that would otherwise be taxable at ordinary income tax rates, and any net short-term capital losses reduce long-term capital gains (after reduction by any long-term capital losses) that would otherwise be taxable at the preferential tax rates under § 1(h). Thus, taxpayers are limited in their ability to deduct short-term or long-term capital losses against ordinary income that is taxable at the higher ordinary income tax rates.

Provided a taxpayer has net capital gain to which the preferential tax rates under § 1(h) are applicable, a determination must be made regarding the type of net capital gain in order to apply the proper tax rate. As described above, net capital gain is comprised of three types of gain — 28-percent rate gain, unrecaptured § 1250 gain, and adjusted net capital gain. 28-percent rate gain is taxable at a maximum tax rate of 28 percent, unrecaptured § 1250 gain is taxable at a maximum tax rate of 25 percent, and adjusted net capital gain is taxable at a maximum tax rate of 15 percent.

The individual gains that make up each of the three types of gain — 28-percent rate gain, unrecaptured § 1250 gain, and adjusted net capital gain — will have been included in the determination of the taxpayer's long-term capital gain. The question to be addressed is the order in which any long-term capital losses and any net short-term capital loss reduce each type of gain. Presumably, taxpayer's would prefer that such losses first reduce any 28-percent rate gain (which is taxed at the highest rate), followed by any unrecaptured § 1250 gain, and any adjusted net capital gain. In this way, taxpayers could reduce their tax liability. The Code imposes a number of additional netting rules to prevent taxpayer manipulation in this regard. The fundamental rule in this area is that gains and losses in each separate tax rate group are first netted against each other in order to determine a net gain or loss for the year in that particular group. Following this initial process, the taxpayer then determines whether any net losses exist in a given category that may be used to offset gains in another category.

Determining 28-Percent Rate Gain

Twenty-eight-percent rate gain is determined first by aggregating the taxpayer's gain from the sale or exchange of any collectibles and qualified small business stock. This gain is then reduced by any long-term capital loss resulting from the sale or exchange of any collectible, any net short-term capital loss, and any long-term capital loss that the taxpayer is carrying forward from a prior taxable year.[12] I.R.C. § 1(h)(4). The Code adopts a pro-taxpayer policy in this regard by allowing net short-term capital losses and any long-term capital loss carryforward to offset the net capital gain taxed at the highest tax rate. In addition, by allowing long-term capital loss carryforwards to offset 28-percent rate gain, the Code does not require that taxpayers keep track of the type of loss generating any long-term capital loss carryforward for proper application of the loss carryforward in future years.

Determining Unrecaptured § 1250 Gain

Unrecaptured § 1250 gain is determined first by aggregating that portion of the taxpayer's long-term capital gain that satisfies the definition of unrecaptured § 1250 gain from all transactions over the taxable year. I.R.C. § 1(h)(6)(A)(i). This aggregate gain is then reduced by any net loss that may have resulted in the determination of 28-percent rate gain as described above. I.R.C. § 1(h)(6)(A)(ii). Consequently, to the extent that any long-term capital loss resulting from the sale or exchange of any collectible, any net short-term capital loss, and any long-term capital loss that the taxpayer is carrying forward from a prior taxable year exceeds the taxpayer's gain from the sale or exchange of any collectibles and qualified small business stock that would otherwise be taxable at a maximum rate of 28 percent, the net loss will reduce the amount of any unrecaptured § 1250 gain that would otherwise be taxable at a maximum rate of 25 percent.

[12] The Code does not allow for the reduction of any 28-percent rate gain by any loss from the sale or exchange of any qualified small business stock held for more than five years. Such a loss would be a long-term capital loss and would reduce any long-term capital gains taxable at the 15-percent tax rate as adjusted net capital gain.

Determining Adjusted Net Capital Gain

Finally, § 1(h) requires the determination of adjusted net capital gain which is taxable at a maximum tax rate of 15 percent. Adjusted net capital gain is equal to the taxpayer's net capital gain reduced by any 28-percent rate gain and any unrecaptured § 1250 gain. I.R.C. § 1(h)(3). Adjusted net capital gain also includes "qualified dividend income" as defined under § 1(h)(11). However, qualified dividend income is not a form of capital gain but is included in the definition of adjusted net capital gain in order to ensure that it is subject to a maximum tax rate of 15 percent.

Utilization of Capital Losses

Another way to view the netting rules applicable to the determination of net capital gain and the components of net capital gain is to consider the order in which different types of capital losses that a taxpayer may realize will reduce the amount of capital gains that the taxpayer must include in gross income. Based on the statutory language and the description provided above, a taxpayer with short-term capital losses may use those losses to reduce capital gains in the following order:

- Short-term capital gains (subject to a 35-percent maximum tax rate);
- 28-percent rate gain (subject to a 28-percent maximum tax rate);
- Unrecaptured § 1250 gain (subject to a 25-percent maximum tax rate); and
- Adjusted net capital gain (subject to a 15-percent maximum tax rate).

Thus, short-term capital losses are utilized first to reduce the highest tax rate gains, leaving the lower tax rate gains subject to tax only if they remain after the netting process.

A taxpayer who has long-term capital losses from the sale or exchange of collectibles or a long-term capital loss carryforward offsets those losses against gains in the following order:

- 28-percent rate gain (subject to a 28-percent maximum tax rate);
- Unrecaptured § 1250 gain (subject to a 25-percent maximum tax rate);
- Adjusted net capital gain (subject to a 15-percent maximum tax rate); and
- Short-term capital gain (subject to a 35-percent maximum tax rate).

Thus, losses from the sale or exchange of collectibles or a long-term capital loss carryforward are not as valuable as short-term capital losses as they serve to reduce short-term capital gains taxed at a 35-percent maximum rate only if they exceed the taxpayer's net capital gain.

Finally, a taxpayer who has long-term capital losses in a year in which she also has capital gains offsets those gains in the following order:

- Adjusted net capital gain (subject to a 15-percent maximum tax rate);
- 28-percent rate gain (subject to a 28-percent maximum tax rate);
- Unrecaptured § 1250 gain (subject to a 25-percent maximum tax rate); and

- Short-term capital gain (subject to a 35-percent maximum tax rate).

The rules applicable to long-term capital losses are even less favorable than those applicable to losses from the sale or exchange of collectibles or long-term capital loss carryforwards as long-term capital losses must first offset adjusted net capital gain before they may be used to offset capital gains taxed at a higher marginal tax rate.

(c) Look-Through Rules Applicable to Pass-Through Entities

I.R.C. § 1(h)(5)(B), (9), and (10)

Treas. Reg. § 1.1(h)-1

Special "look-through" rules are applicable to taxpayers who claim capital gain treatment on the sale of a partnership interest, stock in an S-corporation, or interest in a trust. I.R.C. § 1(h)(5)(B), (9), and (10); Treas. Reg. § 1.1(h)-1. A selling partner, S-corporation shareholder, or trust beneficiary recognizes the amount of collectibles gain that would have been allocated to the partner, shareholder, or beneficiary had the *entity* sold all its collectibles in a fully taxable transaction immediately before the sale of the interest in the entity. Treas. Reg. § 1.1(h)-1(b)(2)(ii). In tiered entities, a partnership, S corporation, or trust is treated as owning its proportionate share of the collectibles of any partnership, S corporation, or trust in which it owns an interest either directly or indirectly through a chain of such entities. Treas. Reg. § 1.1(h)-1(d). Similarly, a selling partner recognizes the amount of any unrecaptured § 1250 gain that would have been allocated to the partner had the partnership sold all of its § 1250 property in a fully taxable transaction.[13] Treas. Reg. § 1.1(h)-1(b)(3)(ii). Again, in tiered entities, a partnership is treated as owning its proportionate share of any § 1250 property of any partnership in which it owns an interest either directly or indirectly through a chain of partnerships. Treas. Reg. § 1.1(h)-1(d). These "look through" rules are similar to those applicable to the sale of partnership interests in partnerships holding unrealized receivables or inventory items under § 751(a).[14]

(d) Capital Loss Limitations

I.R.C. §§ 1211, 1212

Although long-term capital gains are eligible for preferential treatment under the Code, capital losses are not. In an effort to prevent non-corporate taxpayers from manipulating the timing of capital losses to achieve tax benefits if no restrictions on deductibility otherwise applied, the Code applies significant limitations to the deductibility of capital losses. These limitations are tempered, however,

---

[13] Gain from the sale of a partnership interest that constitutes unrecaptured § 1250 gain is not treated as § 1231 gain even if § 1231 could otherwise apply to the sale of property by the partnership. Treas. Reg. § 1.1(h)-1(b)(3)(iii).

[14] I.R.C. § 1(h)(5)(B). Notification rules similar to those under § 751(a) apply in the case of sales or exchanges of interests in a partnership, S corporation, or trust to which this provision applies. Treas. Reg. § 1.1(h)-1(e).

by the ability of non-corporate taxpayers to carry nondeductible capital losses forward to future taxable years.

If a non-corporate taxpayer has losses from the sale or exchange of capital assets in a particular taxable year, such losses are deductible to the extent of capital gains plus the lesser of (1) $3,000 or (2) the excess of such losses over such gains.[15] I.R.C. § 1211(b). Consequently, capital losses in excess of capital gains are deductible against ordinary income only to the extent of $3,000. This limitation on the deductibility of capital losses applies regardless of whether the capital losses are short-term or long-term. Capital losses that are not deductible because of this limitation are referred to as a net capital loss. I.R.C. § 1222(10) (defining as net capital loss the "excess of the losses from sales or exchanges of capital assets over the sum allowed under section 1211").

Any net capital loss may be carried forward into future years without limitation until exhausted. I.R.C. § 1212(b)(1). Such losses are frequently referred to as capital loss carryforwards. Because the distinction between long-term and short-term capital losses is relevant to the netting process previously described, a net capital loss that is carried forward to a future taxable year must preserve the character of the losses that make up the net capital loss as either long-term or short-term. The preservation of the holding period of the losses that make up the net capital loss is accomplished through another set of netting rules. I.R.C. § 1212(b). Under these rules, the excess of any net short-term capital loss over any net long-term capital gain is treated as a short-term capital loss in the succeeding taxable year. I.R.C. § 1212(b)(1)(A). Similarly, the excess of any net long-term capital loss over any net short-term capital gain is treated as a long-term capital loss in the succeeding taxable year. I.R.C. § 1212(b)(1)(B). Before applying the netting rules, however, the amount of capital losses in excess of capital gains that was allowable as a deduction against the taxpayer's ordinary income under the limitation described above is treated as short-term capital gain.[16] I.R.C. § 1212(b)(2)(A).

EXAMPLE 3:

T has the following types of capital gains and losses for the taxable year: $25,000 of long-term capital gain, $45,000 of long-term capital loss, $18,000 of short-term capital gain, and $30,000 of short-term capital loss. T must include the $43,000 of capital gain in gross income and can deduct $46,000 (the amount of capital gains plus $3,000) of the $75,000 in capital losses as a § 62 deduction in determining his adjusted gross income. As a result, T has a net capital loss of $29,000 that he can carry forward to the succeeding

[15] The $3,000 amount is reduced to $1,500 in the case of a married individual filing a separate return.

[16] The amount that is treated as a short-term capital loss is actually the lesser of the (1) the amount of capital losses in excess of capital gains that was allowable as a deduction against the taxpayer's ordinary income under § 1211(b) or (2) the taxpayer's adjusted taxable income for the taxable year. I.R.C. § 1212(b)(2)(A). "Adjusted taxable income" is defined as the taxpayer's taxable income increased by (1) the amount of capital losses in excess of capital gains that was allowable as a deduction against the taxpayer's ordinary income under § 1211(b) and (2) the deduction for personal exemptions under § 151. I.R.C. § 1212(b)(2)(B). The purpose of this provision is to allow taxpayers to use ordinary deductions other than personal exemptions to reduce taxable income before deducting any capital losses in excess of capital gains against ordinary income. This allows the preservation of capital losses that may be carried forward to future taxable years.

taxable year. This net capital loss will be comprised of a $20,000 long-term capital loss and a $9,000 short-term capital loss determined as follows. First, and solely for purposes of determining the type of capital losses being carried forward, T is treated as having a $3,000 of short-term capital gain (the amount equal to the capital losses in excess of capital gains that was allowable as a deduction) in addition to the $18,000 of short-term capital gain that he actually realized. Consequently, T is treated a having the following net long-term capital loss and net short-term capital loss:

LTCG	$25,000	STCG	$21,000
LTCL	45,000	STCL	30,000
NLTCL	$20,000	NSTCL	$9,000

Second, T applies the netting rules described above. The excess of any net long-term capital loss ($20,000) over any net short-term capital gain ($0) is treated as a long-term capital loss in the succeeding taxable year ($20,000). Similarly, the excess of any net short-term capital loss ($9,000) over any net long-term capital gain ($0) is treated as a short-term capital loss in the succeeding taxable year ($9,000).

EXAMPLE 4:

In Example 3, assume that, instead of $18,000 in short-term capital gain, T has $35,000 in short-term capital gain. T must include the $60,000 of capital gain in gross income and can deduct $63,000 (the amount of capital gains plus $3,000) of the $75,000 in capital losses as a § 62 deduction in determining his adjusted gross income. As a result, T has a net capital loss of $12,000 that he can carry forward to the succeeding taxable year. This net capital loss will be comprised entirely of a $12,000 long-term capital loss determined as follows. First, and solely for purposes of determining the type of capital losses being carried forward, T is treated as having $3,000 of short-term capital gain (the amount equal to the capital losses in excess of capital gains that was allowable as a deduction) in addition to the $35,000 of short-term capital gain that he actually realized. Consequently, T is treated a having the following net long-term capital loss and net short-term capital gain:

LTCG	$25,000	STCG	$38,000
LTCL	45,000	STCL	30,000
NLTCL	$20,000	NSTCG	$8,000

Second, T applies the netting rules described above. The excess of any net long-term capital loss ($20,000) over any net short-term capital gain ($8,000) is treated as a long-term capital loss in the succeeding taxable year ($12,000). Similarly, the excess of any net short-term capital loss ($0) over any net long-term capital gain ($0) is treated as a short-term capital loss in the succeeding taxable year ($0).

As a result of the operation of these netting rules, the amount of capital losses in excess of capital gains that is allowed to be deducted against the ordinary income of a non-corporate taxpayer, subject to the $3,000 limitation, is, first, from any net short-term capital losses and only then from any net long-term capital losses.

PROBLEM FOR DISCUSSION

Problem 2-1. In the following situations, assume that the taxpayer had sufficient income from other sources that the taxpayer is in the top marginal tax bracket. How much gain is included in gross income, to what extent are the losses deductible, and what are the applicable tax rates?

Situation A

Summer home purchased seven years ago for $150,000 and sold this year for $250,000?

A sculpture purchased ten years ago for $50,000 and sold this year for $100,000?

ABC stock purchased eight months ago for $60,000 and sold for $70,000?

Situation B

Same as Situation A except that the sculpture is § 1202 stock.

Situation C

Same as Situation A except that, in addition, stock purchased ten months ago for $150,000 is sold for $90,000.

Situation D

Same as Situation A except that, in addition, stock purchased three years ago for $150,000 is sold for $90,000.

Situation E

Same as Situation A except that, in addition, the taxpayer sells stock resulting in a short-term capital loss of $170,000 and other stock resulting in a long-term capital loss of $10,000.

§ 2.02 Capital Gain and Loss Treatment for Corporate Taxpayers

I.R.C. §§ 11, 1201, 1211, 1212

Corporate taxpayers are not entitled to the benefit of the preferential tax rates afforded net capital gain in the hands of non-corporate taxpayers. The preferential tax rates under § 1(h) apply only to individuals otherwise taxable under § 1. The tax rates applicable to corporations are provided in § 11 of the Code. Although § 1201 limits the tax rate applicable to net capital gain in the hands of a corporate taxpayer to 35 percent, this provision currently provides no benefit because the top corporate marginal tax rate is currently 35 percent under § 11.[17] Consequently, the

[17] The effective corporate marginal tax rate can exceed 35 percent because § 11 provides for the phase-out of the lower marginal tax rates of 15 percent on taxable income less than $50,000, 25 percent on taxable income between $50,000 and $75,000, and 34 percent on taxable income between $75,000 and $10,000,000. I.R.C. § 11(b)(1)(A), (B), and (C) (flush language). Nevertheless, the limitation on the tax rate applicable to net capital gain under § 1201 does not apply if the effective marginal tax rate on net

tax rates applicable to both long-term and short-term capital gains are the regular corporate income tax rates otherwise applicable.

The absence of any preferential treatment for net capital gain does not make corporate taxpayers indifferent to the characterization of any gains and losses as capital, however. Indeed, the limitations on the deductibility of capital losses applicable to corporate taxpayers are even more restrictive than those applicable to non-corporate taxpayers. In the hands of a corporation, capital losses are deductible only to the extent of capital gains.[18] I.R.C. § 1211(a). Consequently, corporations are not entitled to deduct capital losses in excess of capital gains of up to $3,000 per year against ordinary income as are non-corporate taxpayers.

Any capital loss that is nondeductible because of this limitation may be carried back to each of the three taxable years preceding the loss year. I.R.C. § 1212(a)(1)(A). A net capital loss is carried back to the earliest of the taxable years to which it may be applicable. I.R.C. § 1212(a)(1) (flush language). However, the loss carryback may not cause an increase in a net operating loss in any carryback year. I.R.C. § 1212(a)(1)(A)(ii). That is, if the capital loss is carried back to a prior year, it must be offset against capital gain in that carryback year, but it cannot be so applied if the elimination of such capital gain would increase a net operating loss in the carryback year rather than simply reduce income in such carryback year. Any excess may be carried forward five years following the loss year. I.R.C. § 1212(a)(1)(B).

In the case of corporate taxpayers, any capital loss carryback or carryover is treated as a short-term capital loss for the year to which it is carried. I.R.C. § 1212(a)(1) (flush language). As such, it is grouped with any other capital losses for the year in which carried and is used to offset any capital gains. Any undeducted loss remaining after the three-year carryback and five-year carryforward is not deductible.

§ 3. DEFINITION OF A CAPITAL ASSET

§ 3.01 Overview

Sections 1221, 1222, and 1223 are the basic provisions that apply in the determination of capital treatment in connection with either gains or losses.[19] Under § 1222, capital gains and losses arise from the "sale or exchange" of a

---

capital gain is higher than 35 percent merely as a result of this phase-out. I.R.C. § 1201(a) (disregarding the last two sentences of § 11(b)(1) in determining if the tax rate exceeds 35 percent).

[18] The capital loss limitations under § 1211(a) do not apply to S corporations that pass through capital gains and losses to their shareholders as separately stated items to be reported on the shareholders' individual returns. *See* I.R.C. § 1366(a)(1).

[19] In addition to §§ 1221, 1222, and 1223, several other sections of the Code may be relevant to the determination of capital asset treatment in a particular situation. *See, e.g.*, §§ 1234(a) (providing capital gain and loss treatment on the sale or exchange of a an option if the property that is the subject of the option would be a capital asset in the holder's hands), 1234(b) (providing capital gain and loss treatment on the sale or exchange of a an option if the property that is the subject of the option would be a capital asset in the holder's hands), and 1235 (providing capital treatment on the transfer of a patent by a

"capital asset." I.R.C. § 1222(1)–(4). Therefore, the initial question in determining whether a transaction gave rise to capital gain or loss is whether the transaction at issue involved a capital asset. Section 1221 provides the definition of a capital asset, albeit in a negative fashion. Under § 1221, a "capital asset" is defined as "property held by the taxpayer (whether or not connected with its trade or business) . . . ." I.R.C. § 1221(a). Section 1221 then goes on to list eight specific asset classes that are excluded from the definition of a capital asset. Thus, if a transaction does not involve "property" held by the taxpayer, or involves "property" that falls within one of the eight exceptions set forth in § 1221, the special provisions of the Code applicable to capital gains and losses are generally inapplicable. This section provides a detailed discussion of the definition of a capital asset under § 1221.

§ 3.02 Definition of "Property"

I.R.C. § 1221

Treas. Reg. § 1.1221-1(a)

The definition of the term "capital asset" under § 1221(a) sets forth the requirement that only *property* held by the taxpayer can constitute a capital asset. In addition, the first sentence of the Regulations interpreting § 1221 states that "the term capital assets includes all classes of *property* not specifically excluded by Section 1221." Treas. Reg. § 1.1221-1(a) (emphasis added). However, neither the Code nor the Regulations defines the term "property" for the purposes of its application in the context of this provision. Consequently, the definition of the term "property" for purposes of the definition of a capital asset has been the subject of considerable judicial interpretation, including numerous pronouncements by the Supreme Court.

The general focus of these decisions has been to interpret the term in accordance with the underlying rationale that gives rise to special tax treatment of capital gains and losses in the first place. While the underlying rationale for favorable capital gain treatment is not crystal clear, the most commonly cited policy justifications are: (1) because the gain inherent in a capital asset held for a long time has accrued over that period, it would not be fair to tax the income at ordinary income tax rates in the year in which the gain is realized, and (2) it is economically beneficial to encourage the sale of assets with accrued appreciation through lower tax rates in order to ensure the mobility of investment capital. As the Supreme Court has stated:

> While a capital asset is defined in 117(a)(1) [of the Internal Revenue Code of 1939] as "property held by the taxpayer," it is evident that not everything which can be called property in the ordinary sense and which is outside the statutory exclusions qualifies as a capital asset. This Court has long held that the term "capital asset" is to be construed narrowly in accordance with the purpose of Congress to afford capital-gains treatment only in situations

---

holder). One of the most important provisions in this regard is § 1231 which allows capital asset treatment in connection with assets excluded from the definition of a capital asset under § 1221(a)(2).

> typically involving the realization of appreciation in value accrued over a substantial period of time, and thus to ameliorate the hardship of taxation of the entire gain in one year.

Commissioner v. Gillette Motor Transport, Inc., 364 U.S. 130, 134 (1960). The policy analysis underlying the definition of a capital asset has led the courts to adopt a more restrictive definition of the term "property" than would result from an application of state law property concepts, thereby limiting the application of the preferential long-term capital gain tax rates. *See* G.C.M. 39606 (concluding that state or local law is not controlling in determining whether an item constitutes property for federal tax purposes and that, under § 1221, property is entirely a creature of federal law).

The judicial interpretation of the term "property" as part of the definition of a capital asset has been designed to prevent the conversion of ordinary income into capital gain through the packaging of an ordinary income-producing asset in a form meeting the state law definition of property. *See, e.g., Commissioner v. Ferrer*, 304 F.2d 125, 129 (2d Cir. 1962) (stating that "it has long been settled that a taxpayer does not bring himself within the capital gains provision merely by fulfilling the simple syllogism that a contract normally constitutes "property," that he held a contract, and that his contract does not fall within a specified exclusion"). Perhaps the seminal decision in this regard is *Hort v. Commissioner*, 313 U.S. 28 (1941), in which the Supreme Court concluded that a lease termination payment paid by the lessee to the lessor was "merely a substitute for the rent reserved in the lease" and, thus, was taxable as ordinary income.[20] The fact that the lease could be considered as a form of property for state law purposes did not persuade the Court.

> Where, as in this case, the disputed amount was essentially a substitute for rental payments which [the former version of § 61(a)] expressly characterizes as gross income, it must be regarded as ordinary income, and it is immaterial that for some purposes the contract creating the right to such payments may be treated as "property" or "capital."

Hort v. Commissioner, 313 U.S. at 31. *See also United States v. Midland-Ross Corp.*, 381 U.S. 54 (1965) (stating that "this Court has consistently construed 'capital asset' to exclude property representing income items or accretions to the value of a capital asset themselves properly attributable to income"); *Holt v. Commissioner*, 303 F.2d 687 (9th Cir. 1962) (a lump sum payment in consideration for the right to receive income in the future treated as ordinary income); *Wiseman v. Halliburton Oil Well Cementing Co.*, 301 F.2d 654 (1962) (payments received under a contract terminating an exclusive license to use and to grant sub-licenses for the use of a patented process in exchange for a non-exclusive license and one-third of the royalties received from third-party licensees treated as a substitute for ordinary income); *Gladden v. Commissioner*, 112 T.C. 209 (1999), *rev'd and remanded on other issues*, 262 F.3d 851 (9th Cir. 2001) ("Where a taxpayer merely '[substitutes]

---

[20] Nevertheless, a payment by a lessor to a lessee for the termination of a below market lease will give rise to capital gain in the hands of the lessee. Commissioner v. McCue Bros. & Drummond, Inc., 210 F.2d 752 (2d Cir. 1954); Commissioner v. Golonsky, 200 F.2d 72 (3rd Cir. 1952). *See* Commissioner v. Ray, 210 F.2d 390 (5th Cir. 1954) (payments received by a lessee from a lessor for the release of a restrictive covenant treated as capital gain).

the right to receive ordinary income from one source for the right to receive ordinary income from another [source],' the rights transferred will not be considered a capital asset.").

Similarly, in *Commissioner v. P.G. Lake, Inc.*, 356 U.S. 260 (1958), the Court concluded that the transfer of an oil payment right did not represent the sale or exchange of a capital asset despite the fact that an oil payment right was an interest in real property for state law purposes. Instead, the Court simply concluded that the payment received in exchange for the right was "essentially a substitute for what would otherwise be received at a future time as ordinary income" and, thus, taxable as ordinary income. *Id.* at 265. The Court also stated:

> The substance of what was assigned was the right to receive future income. The substance of what was received was the present value of income which the recipient would otherwise obtain in the future. In short, consideration was paid for the right to receive future income, not for an increase in the value of the income-producing property.

Id. at 266. Likewise, in *Commissioner v. Gillette Motor Transport, Inc.*, 364 U.S. 130 (1960), the Court concluded that proceeds received for the temporary taking of the taxpayer's business facilities during World War II did not result in capital gain treatment despite the fact that the taxpayer received the proceeds as compensation under the Fifth Amendment for a taking of property.

Unfortunately, the position of the Court that property for purposes of § 1221 does not include a substitute for future payments that would be taxable as ordinary income is not as conceptually coherent as one might desire. As the Tax Court stated in *Foy v. Commissioner*, 84 T.C. 50, 65 (1985), "No single definitive explanation is available of what types of property qualify as capital assets under section 1221." The value of most types of property that are undoubtedly capital assets is based on the present value of future income streams that, when received, would otherwise be taxable as ordinary income. In *United States v. Dresser Industries, Inc.*, 324 F.2d 56 (5th Cir. 1963), the court recognized this problem:

> Another panel of this Court, in the case of United States v. Eidson, [310 F.2d 111 (5th Cir. 1962)] accepted literally the Supreme Court's generalization in *Lake*, . . . : "The substance of what was assigned was the right to receive future income. The substance of what was received was the present value of income which the recipient would otherwise obtain in the future. In short, consideration was paid for the right to receive future income, not for an increase in the value of the income-producing property.", to mean that any money paid which represents the present value of future income to be earned is always taxed as ordinary gains. As a legal or economic position, this cannot be so. The only commercial value of any property is the present worth of future earnings or usefulness. If the expectation of earnings of stock rises, the market value of the stock may rise; at least a part of this increase in price is attributable to the expectation of increased income. The value of a vending machine, as metal and plastic, is almost nil; its value arises from the fact that it will produce income.

Id. at 58–59. The court rationalized the decisions in this regard by distinguishing "the present sale of the future right to *earn* income and the present sale of the future right to *earned* income." *Id.* at 59 (emphasis added). Perhaps the courts' decisions can best be justified simply as an attempted pragmatic implementation of the asserted policy justifications for capital asset treatment.

The continuing validity of the Supreme Court's decisions in *Hort* and *P. G. Lake* has recently been recognized in decisions involving the treatment of payments for the assignment of future state lottery payments. For example, in *Davis v. Commissioner*, 119 T.C. 1 (2002), the taxpayer argued that the lump-sum proceeds received on the assignment of the right to a portion of the annual payments that the taxpayer would receive for having won the state lottery were taxable as long-term capital gain.[21] He maintained that the Supreme Court's decision in *Arkansas Best Corp. v. Commissioner*, 485 U.S. 212 (1988), had effectively overruled the Court's earlier decisions in *Hort* and *P. G. Lake* by adopting a more literal approach to the interpretation of § 1221. The Tax Court, however, disagreed with the taxpayer and relied on a footnote in the *Arkansas Best* opinion in which the Court distinguished the facts of the case before it from those in *Hort* and *P. G. Lake*. The Tax Court interpreted this footnote as a continued endorsement by the Supreme Court of its decisions in these earlier cases. The Ninth Circuit followed the Tax Court's analysis in *United States v. Maginnis*, 356 F.3d 1179 (9th Cir. 2004). The following decision by the Third Circuit attempts to make sense of the various precedents in this area.

LATTERA v. COMMISSIONER

United States Court of Appeals, Third Circuit
437 F.3d 399 (2006)

AMBRO, CIRCUIT JUDGE

Lottery winners, after receiving several annual installments of their lottery prize, sold for a lump sum the right to their remaining payments. They reported their sale proceeds as capital gains on their tax return, but the Internal Revenue Service (IRS) classified those proceeds as ordinary income. The substitute-for-ordinary-income doctrine holds that lump-sum consideration substituting for something that would otherwise be received at a future time as ordinary income should be taxed the same way. We agree with the Commissioner of the IRS that the lump-sum consideration paid for the right to lottery payments is ordinary income.

I. Factual Background and Procedural History

In June 1991 George and Angeline Lattera turned a one-dollar lottery ticket into $9,595,326 in the Pennsylvania Lottery. They did not then have the option to take the prize in a single lump-sum payment, so they were entitled to 26 annual installments of $369,051.

---

[21] *See also* Simpson v. Commissioner, T.C. Memo 2003-155, 85 T.C.M. (CCH) 1421; Johns v. Commissioner, T.C. Memo 2003-140, 85 T.C.M. (CCH) 1318; Boehme v. Commissioner, T.C. Memo 2003-81, 85 T.C.M. (CCH) 1039; United States v. Maginnis, 2002-2 U.S.T.C. (CCH) (50,494 (D. Ore. 2002).

In September 1999 the Latteras sold their rights to the 17 remaining lottery payments to Singer Asset Finance Co., LLC for $3,372,342. Under Pennsylvania law, the Latteras had to obtain court approval before they could transfer their rights to future lottery payments, and they did so in August 1999.

On their joint tax return, the Latteras reported this sale as the sale of a capital asset held for more than one year. They reported a sale price of $3,372,342, a cost or other basis of zero, and a long-term capital gain of the full sale price. The Commissioner determined that this sale price was ordinary income. In December 2002 the Latteras were sent a notice of deficiency of $660,784.

In March 2003 the Latteras petitioned the Tax Court for a redetermination of the deficiency. The Court held in favor of the Commissioner. The Latteras now appeal to our Court. . . .

III. Discussion

The lottery payments the Latteras had a right to receive were gambling winnings, and the parties agree that the annual payments were ordinary income. . . . But the Latteras argue that when they sold the right to their remaining lottery payments, that sale gave rise to a long-term capital gain.

Whether the sale of a right to lottery payments by a lottery winner can be treated as a capital gain under the Internal Revenue Code is one of first impression in our Circuit. But it is not a new question. Both the Tax Court and the Ninth Circuit Court of Appeals have held that such sales deserve ordinary-income treatment. *United States v. Maginnis*, 356 F.3d 1179, 1181 (9th Cir. 2004) ("Fundamental principles of tax law lead us to conclude that [the] assignment of [a] lottery right produced ordinary income."); *Davis v. Comm'r*, 119 T.C. 1, 1 (2002); *see also Watkins v. Comm'r*, T.C. Mem. 2004-244, 88 T.C.M. (CCH) 390, 393 (2004); *Clopton v. Comm'r*, T.C. Mem. 2004-95, 87 T.C.M. (CCH) 1217, 1217 (2004); *Boehme v. Comm'r*, T.C. Mem. 2003-81, 85 T.C.M. (CCH) 1039, 1041 (2003).

The Ninth Circuit's reasoning has drawn significant criticism, however. *See* Matthew S. Levine, Case Comment, *Lottery Winnings as Capital Gains*, 114 Yale L.J. 195, 197-202 (2004); Thomas G. Sinclair, Comment, *Limiting the Substitute-for-Ordinary Income Doctrine: An Analysis Through Its Most Recent Application Involving the Sale of Future Lottery Rights*, 56 S.C. L. Rev. 387, 421-22 (2004). In this context, we propose a different approach. We begin with a discussion of basic concepts that underlie our reasoning.

A. Definition of a capital asset

A long-term capital gain (or loss) is created by the "sale or exchange of a capital asset held for more than 1 year." I.R.C. § 1222(3). Section 1221 of the Internal Revenue Code defines a capital asset as "property held by the taxpayer (whether or not connected with his trade or business)." This provision excludes from the definition certain property categories, none of which is applicable here.

A 1960 Supreme Court decision suggested that this definition can be construed too broadly, stating that "it is evident that not everything which can be called property in the ordinary sense and which is outside the statutory exclusions qualifies as a capital asset." *Comm'r v. Gillette Motor Transp., Inc.*, 364 U.S. 130, 134 (1960). The Court noted that it had "long held that the term 'capital asset' is to be construed narrowly in accordance with the purpose of Congress to afford capital-gains treatment only in situations typically involving the realization of appreciation in value accrued over a substantial period of time, and thus to ameliorate the hardship of taxation of the entire gain in one year." *Id.* But the Supreme Court's decision in *Arkansas Best Corp. v. Commissioner*, 485 U.S. 212 (1988), at least at first blush, seems to have reversed that narrow reading. *Arkansas Best* suggests instead that the capital-asset definition is to be broadly construed. *See id.* at 218 ("The body of § 1221 establishes a general definition of the term 'capital asset,' and the phrase 'does not include' takes out of that broad definition only the classes of property that are specifically mentioned.").

B. The substitute-for-ordinary-income doctrine

The problem with an overly broad definition for capital assets is that it could "encompass some things Congress did not intend to be taxed as capital gains." *Maginnis*, 356 F.3d at 1181. An overly broad definition, linked with favorable capital-gains tax treatment, would encourage transactions designed to convert ordinary income into capital gains. . . . For example, a salary is taxed as ordinary income, and the right to be paid for work is a person's property. But it is hard to conceive that Congress intends for taxpayers to get capital-gains treatment if they were to sell their rights (*i.e.*, "property held by the taxpayer") to their future paychecks. . . . To get around this problem, courts have created the substitute-for-ordinary-income doctrine. This doctrine says, in effect, that " 'lump sum consideration [that] seems essentially a substitute for what would otherwise be received at a future time as ordinary income' may not be taxed as a capital gain." *Maginnis*, 356 F.3d at 1182 (quoting *Commissioner v. P. G. Lake, Inc.*, 356 U.S. 260, 265 (1958)) (alteration in original).

The seminal substitute-for-ordinary-income case is the 1941 Supreme Court decision in *Hort v. Commissioner*, 313 U.S. 28 (1941). Hort had inherited a building from his father, and one of the building's tenants canceled its lease, paying Hort a cancellation fee of $140,000. *Id.* at 29. Hort argued that the cancellation fee was capital gain, but the Court disagreed, holding that the cancellation fee was ordinary income because the "cancellation of the lease involved nothing more than relinquishment of the right to future rental payments in return for a present substitute payment and possession of the leased premises." *Id.* at 32.

The Supreme Court bolstered the doctrine in *Lake*. P.G. Lake, Inc. was an oil-and-gas-producing company with a working interest in two oil and gas leases. 356 U.S. at 261-62. It assigned an oil payment right "payable out of 25 percent of the oil attributable to [Lake's] working interest in the two leases." *Id.* at 262. Lake reported this assignment as a sale of property taxable as capital gain. *Id.* But the Court disagreed, holding that the consideration received was taxable as ordinary income. *Id.* at 264. The Court's reasoning gave full voice to the substitute-for-ordinary-income doctrine: "The lump sum consideration seems essentially a substitute for what would otherwise be received at a future time as ordinary income." *Id.* at 265.

* * *

The Latteras argue that the substitute-for-ordinary-income doctrine, which takes "property held by the taxpayer" outside the statutory capital-asset definition, did not survive *Arkansas Best*. But although *Arkansas Best* ostensibly cabined the exceptions to the statutory definition, it made clear that the *Hort-Lake* "line of cases, based on the premise that § 1221 'property' does not include claims or rights to ordinary income, had no application in the present context." *Arkansas Best*, 485 U.S. at 217 n.5. The Tax Court has several times confirmed that *Arkansas Best* "in no way affected the viability of the principle established in the [*Hort-Lake*] line of cases." *Davis*, 119 T.C. at 6 (citing cases). And the Ninth Circuit agrees. *Maginnis*, 356 F.3d at 1185. We follow suit, holding that the substitute-for-ordinary-income doctrine remains viable in the wake of *Arkansas Best*.

But there is a tension in the doctrine: in theory, all capital assets are substitutes for ordinary income. *See, e.g.*, William A. Klein *et al.*, *Federal Income Taxation* 786 (12th ed. 2000) ("A fundamental principle of economics is that the value of an asset is equal to the present discounted value of all the expected net receipts from that asset over its life."); *see also Lake*, 356 U.S. at 266 (noting that the lump-sum consideration — held to be ordinary income — paid for an asset was "the present value of income which the recipient would otherwise obtain in the future"). For example, a stock's value is the present discounted value of the company's future profits. *See, e.g., Maginnis*, 356 F.3d at 1182; *cf. United States v. Dresser Indus., Inc.*, 324 F.2d 56, 59 (5th Cir. 1963) (applying this concept to the value of land). "Read literally, the [substitute-for-ordinary-income] doctrine would completely swallow the concept of capital gains." Levine, *supra*, at 196 . . . . Also, an "overbroad 'substitute for ordinary income' doctrine, besides being analytically unsatisfactory, would create the potential for the abuse of treating capital losses as ordinary." Levine, *supra*, at 197. The doctrine must therefore be limited so as not to err on either side.

C. The lottery cases

Even before the Ninth Circuit decided *Maginnis*, the Tax Court had correctly answered the question of whether sales of lottery winnings were capital gains. In *Davis v. Commissioner*, lottery winners had sold their rights to 11 of their total 14 future lottery payments for a lump sum. . . . The Tax Court found that the lump-sum payment to the lottery winners was the "discounted value . . . of certain ordinary income which they otherwise would have received during the years 1997 through 2007." *Id.* at 7. The Court held, therefore, that (1) the purchaser of the lottery payment rights paid money for "the right to receive . . . future ordinary income, and not for an increase in the value of income-producing property"; (2) the lottery winners' right to their future lottery payments was not a capital asset; and (3) the lump-sum payment was to be taxed as ordinary income. *Id.*; *see also Watkins*, 88 T.C.M. (CCH) at 393 (following *Davis*, in a post-*Maginnis* decision); *Clopton*, 87 T.C.M. (CCH) at 1219 (citing Tax Court cases following *Davis*).

In 2004 the Ninth Circuit decided *Maginnis*, the first (and so far only) appellate opinion to deal with this question. Maginnis won $9 million in a lottery and, after receiving five of his lottery payments, assigned all of his remaining future lottery payments to a third party for a lump-sum payment of $3,950,000. *Maginnis*, 356 F.3d at 1180. The Ninth Circuit held that Maginnis's right to future lottery payments was not a capital asset and that the lump-sum payment was to be taxed as ordinary income. *Id.* at 1182.

The Court relied on the substitute-for-ordinary-income doctrine, but it was concerned about taking an "approach that could potentially convert all capital gains into ordinary income [or] one that could convert all ordinary income into capital gains." *Id.* The Court opted instead for "case-by-case judgments as to whether the conversion of income rights into lump-sum payments reflects the sale of a capital asset that produces a capital gain, or whether it produces ordinary income." *Id.* It set out two factors, which it characterized as "crucial to [its] conclusion," but not "dispositive in all cases": "Maginnis (1) did not make any underlying investment of capital in return for the receipt of his lottery right, and (2) the sale of his right did not reflect an accretion in value over cost to any underlying asset Maginnis held." *Id.* at 1183.

But two commentators have criticized the analysis in *Maginnis*, especially the two factors. *See* Levine, *supra*, at 197-202; Sinclair, *supra*, at 421-22. The first factor — underlying investment of capital — would theoretically subject all inherited and gifted property (which involves no investment at all) to ordinary-income treatment. *See* Levine, *supra*, at 198. It also does not explain the result in *Lake*, where the company presumably made an investment in its working interest in oil and gas leases, yet the Supreme Court applied ordinary-income treatment. *Id.* The second factor also presents analytical problems. Not all capital assets experience an accretion in value over cost. For example, cars typically depreciate, but they are often capital assets. *See* Sinclair, *supra*, at 421. Levine criticizes the second factor for "attempting to determine the character of a gain from its amount." Levine, *supra*, at 199. The *Maginnis* Court held that there was no accretion of value over cost in lottery winnings because there was no cost, as "Maginnis did not make any capital investment in exchange for his lottery right." 356 F.3d at 1184. But if Maginnis's purchase of a lottery ticket had been a capital investment, would the second factor automatically have been satisfied? (That is, the "cost" in that scenario would have been $1, and the increase would have been $3,949,999.) Our first instinct is no. Moreover, the second factor does not seem to predict correctly the result in both *Hort* (where a building was inherited for no "cost") and *Lake* (where the working interest in the oil lease presumably had a "cost"), in both of which the taxpayer got ordinary-income treatment.

Thus, while we agree with *Maginnis*'s result, we do not simply adopt its reasoning. And it is both unsatisfying and unhelpful to future litigants to declare that we know this to be ordinary income when we see it. The problem is that, "unless and until Congress establishes an arbitrary line on the otherwise seamless spectrum between *Hort-Lake* transactions and conventional capital gain transactions, the courts must locate the boundary case by case, a process that can yield few useful generalizations because there are so many relevant but imponderable criteria." 2 Bittker & Lokken, [*Federal Taxation of Income, Estates and Gifts* P47.9.5 (3d ed. 2000) (footnote omitted)].

We therefore proceed to our case-by-case analysis, but in doing so we set out a method for analysis that guides our result. At the same time, however, we recognize that any rule we create could not account for every contemplated transactional variation.

D. Substitute-for-ordinary-income analysis

In our attempt to craft a rubric, we find helpful a Second Circuit securities case and a recent student comment. The Second Circuit dealt with a similarly "seamless spectrum" in 1976 when it needed to decide whether a note was a security for purposes of section 10(b) of the 1934 Securities and Exchange Act. *See Exch. Nat'l Bank of Chi. v. Touche Ross & Co.*, 544 F.2d 1126, 1138 (2d Cir. 1976). The Court created a "family resemblance" test, (1) presuming that notes of more than nine months' maturity were securities, (2) listing various types of those notes that it did not consider securities, and (3) declaring that a note with maturity exceeding nine months that "does not bear a strong family resemblance to these examples" was a security. *Id.* at 1138, 1137-38. The Supreme Court, adopting this test in 1990, added four factors to guide the "resemblance" analysis: the motivations of the buyers and sellers, the plan of distribution, the public's reasonable expectations, and applicable risk-reducing regulatory schemes. *Reves v. Ernst & Young*, 494 U.S. 56, 65-67 (1990).

We adopt an analogous analysis. Several types of assets we know to be capital: stocks, bonds, options, and currency contracts, for example. *See, e.g., Arkansas Best*, 485 U.S. at 222-23 (holding — even though, as noted above, the value of a stock is really the present discounted value of the company's future profits — that "stock is most naturally viewed as a capital asset"); *see also id.* at 217 n.5 (distinguishing "capital stock" from "a claim to ordinary income"); *Simpson v. Comm'r*, T.C. Mem. 2003-155, 85 T.C.M. (CCH) 1421, 1423 n.7 (2003) (distinguishing "currency contracts, stocks, bonds, and options" from a right to receive lottery payments). We could also include in this category physical assets like land and automobiles.

Similarly, there are several types of rights that we know to be ordinary income, *e.g.*, rental income and interest income. In *Gillette Motor*, the Supreme Court held that ordinary-income treatment was indicated for the right to use another's property — rent, in other words. *See* 364 U.S. at 135. Similarly, in *Midland-Ross*, the Supreme Court held that earned original issue discount should be taxed as ordinary income. *See United States v. Midland-Ross Corp.*, 381 U.S. 54, 58 (1965). There, the taxpayer purchased non-interest-bearing notes at a discount from the face amount and sold them for more than their issue price (but still less than the face amount). *Id.* at 55. This gain was conceded to be equivalent to interest, and the Court held it taxable as ordinary income. *Id.* at 55-56, 58.

For the "family resemblance" test, we can set those two categories at the opposite poles of our analysis. For example, we presume that stock, and things that look and act like stock, will receive capital-gains treatment. For the in-between transactions that do not bear a family resemblance to the items in either category, like contracts and payment rights, we use two factors to assist in our analysis: (1) type of "carve-out" and (2) character of asset.

1. *Type of carve-out*

The notion of the carve-out, or partial sale, has significant explanatory power in the context of the *Hort-Lake* line of cases. As Marvin Chirelstein writes, the " 'substitute' language, in the view of most commentators, was merely a short-hand way of asserting that carved-out interests do not qualify as capital assets." Marvin A. Chirelstein, *Federal Income Taxation* P17.03, at 369-70 (9th ed. 2002).

There are two ways of carving out interests from property: horizontally and vertically. A horizontal carve-out is one in which "temporal divisions [are made] in a property interest in which the person owning the interest disposes of part of his interest but also retains a portion of it." Sinclair, *supra*, at 401. In lottery terms, this is what happened in *Davis, Boehme*, and *Clopton* — the lottery winners sold some of their future lottery payment rights (*e.g.*, their 2006 and 2007 payments) but retained the rights to payments further in the future (*e.g.*, their 2008 and 2009 payments). *See Clopton*, 87 T.C.M. (CCH) at 1217-18 (finding that the lottery winner sold only some of his remaining lottery payments); *Boehme*, 85 T.C.M. (CCH) at 1040 (same); *Davis*, 119 T.C. at 3 (same). This is also what happened in *Hort* and *Lake*; portions of the total interest (a term of years carved out from a fee simple and a three-year payment right from a working interest in an oil lease, respectively) were carved out from the whole.

A vertical carve-out is one in which "a complete disposition of a person's interest in property" is made. Sinclair, *supra*, at 401. In lottery terms, this is what happened in *Watkins* and *Maginnis* — the lottery winners sold the rights to all their remaining lottery payments. *See Maginnis*, 356 F.3d at 1181 (noting that the lottery winner assigned his right to receive all his remaining lottery payments); *Watkins*, 88 T.C.M. (CCH) at 391 (same).

Horizontal carve-outs typically lead to ordinary-income treatment. *See, e.g., Maginnis*, 356 F.3d at 1185-86 ("Maginnis is correct that transactions in which a taxpayer transfers an income right without transferring his entire interest in an underlying asset will often be occasions for applying the substitute for ordinary income doctrine."). This was also the result reached in *Hort* and *Lake*. *Lake*, 356 U.S. at 264; *Hort*, 313 U.S. at 32.

Vertical carve-outs are different. In *Dresser Industries*, for example, the Fifth Circuit distinguished *Lake* because the taxpayer in *Dresser* had "cut[] off a 'vertical slice' of its rights, rather than carved out an interest from the totality of its rights." *Dresser Indus.*, 324 F.2d at 58. But as the results in *Maginnis* and *Watkins* demonstrate, a vertical carve-out does not necessarily mean that the transaction receives capital-gains treatment. *See, e.g., Maginnis*, 356 F.3d at 1185 (holding "that a transaction in which a taxpayer sells his entire interest in an underlying asset without retaining any property right does not *automatically* prevent application of the substitute for ordinary income doctrine" (emphasis in original)); *see also id.* at 1186.

Because a vertical carve-out could signal either capital-gains or ordinary-income treatment, we must make another determination to conclude with certainty which treatment should apply. Therefore, when we see a vertical carve-out, we proceed to the second factor — character of the asset — to determine whether the sale proceeds should be taxed as ordinary income or capital gain.

2. *Character of the asset*

The Fifth Circuit in *Dresser Industries* noted that "there is, in law and fact, a vast difference between the present sale of the future right to *earn* income and the present sale of the future right to *earned* income." *Dresser Indus.*, 324 F.2d at 59 (emphasis in original). The taxpayer in *Dresser Industries* had assigned its right to an exclusive patent license back to the patent holder in exchange for a share of the licensing fees from third-party licensees. *Id.* at 57. The Court used this "right to earn income"/"right to earned income" distinction to hold that capital-gains treatment was applicable. It noted that the asset sold was not a "right to earned incomc, to be paid in the future," but was "a property which would produce income." *Id.* at 59. Further, it disregarded the ordinary nature of the income generated by the asset; because "all income-producing property" produces ordinary income, the sale of such property does not result in ordinary-income treatment. *Id.* (This can be seen in the sale of stocks or bonds, both of which produce ordinary income, but the sale of which is treated as capital gain.)

Sinclair explains the concept in this way: "Earned income conveys the concept that the income has already been earned and the holder of the right to this income only has to collect it. In other words, the owner of the right to earned income is entitled to the income merely by virtue of owning the property." Sinclair, *supra*, at 406. He gives as examples of this concept rental income, stock dividends, and rights to future lottery payments. *Id.*; *see also Rhodes' Estate v. Comm'r*, 131 F.2d 50, 50 (6th Cir. 1942) (*per curiam*) (holding that a sale of dividend rights is taxable as ordinary income). For the right to earn income, on the other hand, "the holder of such right must do something further to earn the income. . . . [because] mere ownership of the right to earn income does not entitle the owner to income." Sinclair, *supra*, at 406. Following *Dresser Industries*, Sinclair gives a patent as an example of this concept. *Id.* Assets that constitute a right to earn income merit capital-gains treatment, while those that are a right to earned income merit ordinary-income treatment. Our Court implicitly made this distinction in *Tunnell v. United States*, 259 F.2d 916 (3d Cir. 1958). Tunnell withdrew from a law partnership, and he assigned his rights in the law firm in exchange for $27,500. *Id.* at 917. When he withdrew, the partnership had over $21,000 in uncollected accounts receivable from work that had already been done. *Id.* We agreed with the District Court that "the sale of a partnership is treated as the sale of a capital asset." *Id.* The sale of a partnership does not, in and of itself, confer income on the buyer; the buyer must continue to provide legal services, so it is a sale of the right to *earn* income. Consequently, as we held, the sale of a partnership receives capital-gains treatment. The accounts receivable, on the other hand, had already been earned; the buyer of the partnership only had to remain a partner to collect that income, so the sale of accounts receivable is the sale of the right to *earned* income. Thus, we held that the portion of the purchase price that reflected the sale of the accounts receivable was taxable as ordinary income. *Id.* at 919.

Similarly, when an erstwhile employee is paid a termination fee for a personal-services contract, that employee still possesses the asset (the right to provide certain personal services) and the money (the termination fee) has already been "earned" and will simply be paid. The employee no longer has to perform any more services in exchange for the fee, so this is not like *Dresser Industries*' "right to earn income." These termination fees are therefore rights to earned income and should be treated as ordinary income. *See, e.g., Elliott v. United States*, 431 F.2d 1149, 1154 (10th Cir. 1970); *Holt v. Comm'r*, 303 F.2d 687, 690 (9th Cir. 1962); *see also* Chirelstein, *supra*, P17.03, at 376-77 (noting that "courts have held consistently that payments made to an employee for the surrender of his employment contract are ordinary").

The factor also explains, for example, the Second Circuit's complex decision in *Commissioner v. Ferrer*, 304 F.2d 125 (2d Cir. 1962). The actor Jose Ferrer had contracted for the rights to mount a stage production based on the novel *Moulin Rouge. Id.* at 126. In the contract, Ferrer obtained two rights relevant here: (1) the exclusive right to "produce and present" a stage production of the book and, if the play was produced, (2) a share in the proceeds from any motion-picture rights that stemmed from the book. *Id.* at 127. After a movie studio planned to make *Moulin Rouge* into a movie — and agreed that it would feature Ferrer — he sold these, along with other, rights. *Id.* at 128-29. Right (1) would have required Ferrer to have produced and presented the play to get income, so it was a right to earn income — thus, capital-gains treatment was indicated. Right (2), once it matured (*i.e.*, once Ferrer had produced the play), would have continued to pay income simply by virtue of Ferrer's holding the right, so it would have become a right to earned income — thus, ordinary-income treatment was indicated. The Second Circuit held as such, dictating capital-gains treatment for right (1) and ordinary-income treatment for right (2). *Id.* at 131, 134.[22]

---

[22] [5] One well-known result that these factors do not predict is the Second Circuit's 1946 opinion in *McAllister v. Commissioner*, 157 F.2d 235 (2d Cir. 1946). In that case, a widow was forced to sell her life estate in a trust to the remainderman. *Id.* at 235. Thus, she received a lump-sum payment in exchange for her right to all future payments from the trust. Although this was a vertical carve-out, susceptible to both types of treatment, she gave up her right to *earned* income, because she would have continued receiving payments simply by holding the life estate. Thus, the sale proceeds should have received ordinary-income treatment. The Court held instead that capital-gains treatment was indicated. *Id.* at 236.

But the result in *McAllister* has been roundly criticized. The Tax Court in that case had held that ordinary-income treatment was proper, *id.* at 235, and Judge Frank entered a strong dissent, *id.* at 237-41 (Frank, J., dissenting). The *McAllister* Court relied on a case that did not even discuss the capital-asset statute. *Id.* at 237 (majority opinion). Chirelstein writes that the "decision in *McAllister* almost certainly was wrong." Chirelstein, *supra*, P17.03, at 373. And a 2004 Tax Court opinion did not even bother to distinguish *McAllister*, stating simply that it was "decided before relevant Supreme Court decisions applying the substitute for ordinary income doctrine" (referring, *inter alia*, to *Lake*). *Clopton*, 87 T.C.M. (CCH) at 1219.

We consider *McAllister* to be an aberration, and we do not find it persuasive in our decision in this case.

E. Application of the "family resemblance" test

Applied to this case, the "family resemblance" test draws out as follows. First, we try to determine whether an asset is like either the "capital asset" category of assets (*e.g.*, stocks, bonds, or land) or like the "income items" category (*e.g.*, rental income or interest income). If the asset does not bear a family resemblance to items in either of those categories, we move to the following factors.

We look at the nature of the sale. If the sale or assignment constitutes a horizontal carve-out, then ordinary-income treatment presumably applies. If, on the other hand, it constitutes a vertical carve-out, then we look to the character-of-the-asset factor. There, if the sale is a lump-sum payment for a future right to *earned* income, we apply ordinary-income treatment, but if it is a lump-sum payment for a future right to *earn* income, we apply capital-gains treatment.

Turning back to the Latteras, the right to receive annual lottery payments does not bear a strong family resemblance to either the "capital assets" or the "income items" listed at the polar ends of the analytical spectrum. The Latteras sold their right to all their remaining lottery payments, so this is a vertical carve-out, which could indicate either capital-gains or ordinary-income treatment. But because a right to lottery payments is a right to earned income (*i.e.*, the payments will keep arriving due simply to ownership of the asset), the lump-sum payment received by the Latteras should receive ordinary-income treatment.

This result comports with *Davis* and *Maginnis*. It also ensures that the Latteras do not "receive a tax advantage as compared to those taxpayers who would simply choose originally to accept their lottery winning in the form of a lump sum payment," something that was also important to the *Maginnis* Court. *Maginnis*, 356 F.3d at 1184.[23]

IV. Conclusion

The lump-sum consideration paid to the Latteras in exchange for the right to their future lottery payments is ordinary income.[24] We therefore affirm.

PROBLEMS FOR DISCUSSION

Problem 2-2. T, an experienced life insurance agent, developed a special type of life insurance policy and entered into an employment agreement with an insurance company that will underwrite such policies, under which he promotes the policy

---

[23] [6] We do not decide whether Singer, who purchased the right to lottery payments from the Latteras, would receive ordinary income or capital gain if it later decided to sell that right to another third party. *See Maginnis*, 356 F.3d at 1183 n.4. Such a determination would need to be made on the specific facts of the transaction. For example, if Singer bought and sold such rights as part of its business, the lottery payment rights could theoretically fall under the inventory exclusion to the capital-asset definition. *Cf. Arkansas Best*, 485 U.S. at 222 (suggesting that if Arkansas Best had been a dealer in securities, its bank stock might have fallen within § 1221's inventory exclusion).

[24] [7] The Latteras appear to argue that their lottery ticket was itself a capital asset. We do not need to address this issue, as we note that the Latteras did not sell their winning ticket to Singer. Instead, they relinquished it in 1991 to the Pennsylvania State Lottery so they could claim their prize. They sold Singer eight years later not the physical lottery ticket but their right to the annual lottery payments.

and recruits and trains agents to sell the policy. Under the agreement, T receives as a commission a share of the first year's premiums on the policies and a share of any renewal commissions from premiums paid on the policies after the first year. The agreement also provides that after termination of his relationship with the insurance company, T will continue to receive commissions for policies entered into prior to the date of termination. After several years, T terminates his relationship with the insurance company and continues to receive commissions in accordance with the agreement. The insurance company subsequently pays T $45,000 in termination of his rights under the agreement, an amount equal to the present value of the anticipated commissions due on the policies entered into before the date of termination. Is T entitled to capital gain treatment with respect to the $45,000 payment? *See Vaaler v. United States*, 454 F.2d 1120 (8th Cir. 1972); *Luna v. Commissioner*, 42 T.C. 1067 (1964).

Problem 2-3. T holds a patent that is a capital asset in his hands. T transfers the right to exploit the patent to others in various parts of the world for terms co-extensive with the remaining legal life of the patent. The proceeds received for these transfers is equal to the present value of the royalty payments that T would have received if he had entered into exclusive license arrangements for similar terms. Is T entitled to capital gain treatment?

Problem 2-4. T holds a life estate in a trust, the payments from which are taxable as ordinary income. T transfers her life estate to the remainderman for a lump sum payment of $55,000. Is T entitled to capital gain treatment with respect to the $45,000 payment? *See McAllister v. Commissioner*, 157 F.2d 235 (2d Cir. 1946).

§ 3.03 Capital Asset Defined

Once it is established that a taxpayer has engaged in a transaction that involves property for purposes of § 1221, the next step in determining whether the special tax rules relating to capital gains and losses are applicable is to determine whether the property sold or exchanged by the taxpayer satisfies the definition of a "capital asset." As described above, § 1221(a) initially adopts a very expansive approach to this determination by providing that the term "capital asset" includes any "[p]roperty held by the taxpayer (whether or not connected with his trade or business) . . . ." Nevertheless, § 1221(a) then provides a list of eight separate categories of property that are exceptions to this broad definition of a capital asset. Consequently, only the property of the taxpayer that does not fall within one of those eight exceptions is, by definition, a capital asset.

In considering the statutory language under § 1221, the Supreme Court has been guided by the policy justifications underlying the preferential treatment of net capital gain. As the Court stated in *Corn Products Refining Company v. Commissioner*:

> [T]he capital-asset provision of § 177 [the predecessor to § 1221] must not be so broadly applied as to defeat rather than further the purpose of Congress. . . . Since this section is an exception from the normal tax requirements of the Internal Revenue Code, the definition of a capital asset

> must be narrowly applied and its exclusions interpreted broadly. This is necessary to effectuate the basic congressional purpose.

350 U.S. 46, 52 (1955). Consequently, the Supreme Court and numerous lower courts have all echoed this language and, at the very least, have indicated that the exceptions from the definition of a capital asset must be broadly applied in order that capital asset treatment does not become the norm. Although the Court might have been focusing on the preferential treatment accorded net capital gain with an eye to protecting government revenues, capital asset treatment is a two-edged sword. A narrow definition of capital assets will limit the ability of taxpayers to obtain preferential treatment with respect to net capital gain but will allow taxpayers greater tax benefits in connection with the deduction of losses by avoiding the limitation on the deduction of capital losses under § 1211. Conversely, a broader definition of capital assets will provide taxpayers with greater access to the preferential treatment afforded net capital gain but will also limit taxpayers with respect to the deduction of capital losses. Which approach is more protective of tax revenues will depend on economic conditions at any given time.

Regardless of their precise scope, the eight exceptions to the definition of a capital asset are:

(1) stock in trade, inventory, or property held primarily for sale to customers in the ordinary course of business — "dealer property" — under § 1221(a)(1);

(2) depreciable property or real property used in the taxpayer's trade or business — "business property" — under § 1221(a)(2);

(3) certain copyrights, literary, musical, or artistic compositions or a letter or memorandum — "certain artistic or intellectual property" — under § 1221(a)(3);

(4) accounts receivable from the sale of dealer property or resulting from services rendered — "accounts receivable" — under § 1221(a)(4);

(5) certain government publications acquired for less than their offered purchase price — "government publications" — under § 1221(a)(5);

(6) certain commodities derivatives and financial instruments held by commodities derivative dealers — "commodities derivatives" — under § 1221(a)(6);

(7) certain hedging transactions — "hedging transactions" — under § 1221(a)(7); and

(8) supplies regularly used or consumed by the taxpayer in the ordinary course of his business — "business supplies" under § 1221(a)(8).

Each of these eight exceptions from the definition of a capital asset is described below.

(a) Dealer Property

I.R.C. § 1221(a)(1)

Definitional Issues

The first exception to the definition of a capital asset under § 1221 applies to stock in trade of the taxpayer, inventory, and property held by the taxpayer primarily for sale to customers in the ordinary course of the taxpayer's trade or business under § 1221(a)(1). More specifically, § 1221(a)(1) applies to "stock in trade of the taxpayer or other property of a kind that would properly be included in the inventory of the taxpayer if on hand at the close of the taxable year, or property held by the taxpayer primarily for sale to customers in the ordinary course of his trade or business." Such property is frequently referred to as "dealer property." The purpose behind this exception follows directly from the asserted policy justification for capital gain treatment, which is to provide relief where the disposition of property involves the realization of appreciation in value that has accrued over a substantial period. As the Supreme Court has stated:

> Congress intended that profits and losses arising from the everyday operation of a business be considered as ordinary income or loss rather than capital gain or loss. The preferential treatment provided by [the capital gain sections] applies to transactions in property which are not the normal source of business income.

Corn Prods. Refining Co. v. Comm'r, 350 U.S. 46, 52 (1955). Certainly, transactions involving stock in trade of the taxpayer, inventory, and property held by the taxpayer primarily for sale to customers in the ordinary course of the taxpayer's trade or business are precisely the types of transactions for which capital treatment is unwarranted. This rationale applies to the gains from such transactions for non-corporate taxpayers as well as the losses from such transactions for both corporate and non-corporate taxpayers.

The application of the exception under § 1221(a)(1) is relatively clear in the case of merchants and manufacturers who maintain "stock in trade" or "inventory." *See, e.g., Levine v. Commissioner*, T.C. Mem. 1962-68. Although § 1221(a)(1) does not define the term "inventory," the courts have looked to the definition in the Regulations under § 471:

> Inventory should include all finished or partly finished goods and, in the case of raw materials and supplies, only those which have been acquired for sale or which will physically become a part of merchandise intended for sale. . . . Merchandise should be included in the inventory only if title thereto is vested in the taxpayer.

Cenex, Inc. v. United States, 156 F.3d 1377, 1379 (Fed. Cir. 1998) (quoting Treas. Reg. § 1.471-1). An automobile manufacturer who sells his cars to customers or dealers recognizes ordinary income because the asset sold is inventory. Similarly, the clothier who sells clothing to customers reports ordinary income even though the inventory sold may have been held for more than one year at the time of sale.

In each case, ordinary income results because the asset sold is inventory or stock in trade and, therefore, excluded from the definition of a capital asset under § 1221(a)(1). Ordinary income or loss treatment is appropriate because the value of inventory and stock in trade is reflective of the merchant's or manufacturer's efforts in creating and marketing the property and not from appreciation in value that has accrued over a substantial period. Even a bulk sale of inventory to a single purchaser will not produce capital gain. *Grace Bros., Inc. v. Commissioner*, 173 F.2d 170 (9th Cir. 1949). However, "a final liquidation of inventory, although accepted and predictable, would normally be eligible for capital gains treatment." *International Shoe Machine Corp. v. United States*, 491 F.2d 157, 160 (1st Cir. 1974).

There are, however, many business and investment situations that involve the sale of property in which its characterization as "stock in trade," "inventory," or "property held by the taxpayer primarily for sale to customers in the ordinary course of his trade or business" is less clear. This is particularly true in the context of sales or exchanges of real estate, and it is in this arena that many of the conflicts between the Service and taxpayers have arisen. *See, e.g., Suburban Realty Co. v. United States*, 615 F.2d 171 (5th Cir. 1980) (frequent and substantial sales made without developing property and without sales activity constitute ordinary gain); *Biedenharn Realty Co. v. United States*, 526 F.2d 409 (5th Cir. 1976) (en banc) (frequency and substantiality of sales is the most important factor in determining the nature of real estate sales, but the extent of improvements and sales activity should also be considered); *United States v. Winthrop*, 417 F.2d 905 (5th Cir. 1969) (primarily for sale in the ordinary course of business does not mean a formal business, but can include sales over time to customers even without sales activity); *Daugherty v. Commissioner*, 78 T.C. 623 (1982) (gain received from condemnation is ordinary income if the property was held primarily for sale to customers in the ordinary course of business prior to the condemnation). Unlike many types of "inventory" or "stock in trade," the value of real estate may reflect appreciation in value that has accrued over a substantial period for which capital treatment may be deemed appropriate as well as the efforts of the taxpayer in developing or marketing the property for which capital treatment is not appropriate. Although some type of allocation of the gain may appear appropriate in such a situation, § 1221 requires that the property either be deemed a capital asset or not. No allocation or bifurcation of the gain is permissible.

If the "inventory" or "stock in trade" aspects of § 1221(a)(1) do not readily apply, the capital gain issue turns on whether the property involved is "held by the taxpayer primarily for sale to customers in the ordinary course of his trade or business." I.R.C. § 1221(a)(1). Questions have arisen over virtually every clause of this phrase. One of the first questions concerned the interpretation of the word "primarily," which the Supreme Court addressed in *Malat v. Riddell*, 383 U.S. 569 (1966). *Malat* involved partners in a joint venture who held property with the dual purpose of development and sale. The Service argued that a purpose of holding property may be "primary" if it is a substantial purpose. With little analysis, the Court rejected this argument and held that, under a literal reading of the statutory provision, the word "primarily" means "of first importance" or "principally." *Id.* at 572. *See also International Shoe Machine Corp. v. United States*, 491 F.2d 157 (1st Cir. 1974) ("primarily" refers to the contrast "between sales made in the ordinary course of business and non-routine sales made as a liquidation of inventory" and not the "contrast between sales and leases"); *Scheuber v. Commissioner*, 371 F.2d 996 (7th Cir. 1967) ("primarily" allows for a "dual purpose," i.e., taxpayers can be in the business of selling real estate, but can hold certain properties for investment not in the ordinary course of business). As a result, if the possibility of sale is merely an incidental or secondary motive for the taxpayer's holding of property, the "primarily for sale" test will not be satisfied, and the property will qualify as a capital asset. *See Kirby Lumber Corp. v. Phinney*, 412 F.2d 598, 604 (5th Cir. 1969) (taxpayer not in the business of buying timber for resale could not be holding it "primarily for sale").

Cases concerning whether property is held primarily for sale to customers in the ordinary course of the taxpayer's trade or business have also focused on the question of whether the transfer involved "customers" and whether the transfer occurred in the "ordinary course" of the taxpayer's trade or business. In addressing the first issue, the courts have concluded that investors and traders in stocks and securities who are not securities dealers are not affected by the exception under § 1221(a)(1) because they do not have "customers" because they are selling to unknown and unrelated third parties. In addressing this second issue, the courts have first examined whether the taxpayers' activities rise to the level of a trade or business. *See, e.g., Farley v. Commissioner*, 7 T.C. 198 (1946), *acq.* (despite the frequency and continuity of real estate sales, taxpayer's activities did not constitute a trade or business). If a trade or business is found, the courts inquire whether the property was sold or exchanged in the "ordinary course" of that trade or business. Such a situation typically arises when the property is sold under extraordinary circumstances outside the normal course of the trade or business. *See, e.g., Estate of Ferber v. Commissioner*, 22 T.C. 261 (1954), *acq.* (auction and bulk sales of furs made by executors of retail fur dealer were of capital assets and produced capital gains).

Finally, a line of "rental-obsolescence" decisions exist in which gains from the sale of rental equipment, no longer useful for renting, may be taxable at capital gains rates. *See Hillard v. Commissioner*, 281 F.2d 279 (5th Cir. 1960); *Philber Equipment Corp. v. Commissioner*, 237 F.2d 129 (3d Cir. 1956); *Davidson v. Tomlinson*, 165 F. Supp. 455 (S.D. Fla. 1958); Rev. Rul. 75-544, 1975-2 C.B. 343. However, gains from sales of rental equipment may be treated as ordinary income if the equipment still retains rental income potential. *See International Shoe Machine Corp. v. United States*, 491 F.2d 157 (1st Cir. 1974); *Continental Can Co. v. United States*, 422 F.2d 405 (Ct. Cl. 1970); *Recordak Corp. v. United States*, 325 F.2d 460 (Ct. Cl. 1963). If a taxpayer is successful in avoiding the application of § 1221(a)(2), then the sale or exchange of the property in question will yield a capital gain or loss unless the property happens to fall within one of the other seven exceptions set forth in § 1221.

Judicial Interpretation

Numerous court battles have focused on application of § 1221(a)(1) and whether an asset falls within the definition of "dealer property." The judicial decisions in this regard are not always consistent in either result or method of analysis. In *Biedenharn Realty Co. v. United States*, 526 F.2d 409 (5th Cir. 1976), the Fifth Circuit recognized the difficulty that an ad-hoc application of various factors created for taxpayers, the Service, and the courts:

> Over the past 40 years, this case by case approach with its concentration on the facts of each suit has resulted in a collection of decisions not always reconcilable. Recognizing the situation, we have warned that efforts to distinguish and thereby make consistent the Court's previous holdings must necessarily be "foreboding and unrewarding." . . . Litigants are cautioned that "each case must be decided on its own peculiar facts. . . . Specific factors, or combinations of them are not necessarily controlling." . . . Nor are these factors the equivalent of the philosopher's stone, separating "sellers garlanded with capital gains from those beflowered in the garden of ordinary income."

Id. at 414–415 (citing *United States v. Winthrop*, 417 F.2d 905 (5th Cir. 1969); *Williams v. United States*, 329 F.2d 430 (5th Cir. 1964); *Thompson v. Commissioner*, 322 F.2d 122 (5th Cir. 1963); *Wood v. Commissioner*, 276 F.2d 586 (5th Cir. 1960); *Smith v. Commissioner*, 232 F.2d 142 (5th Cir. 1956)). Indeed, some uncertainty exists over whether the determination of "dealer property" is a question of law or a question of fact. *Compare United States v. Winthrop*, 417 F.2d 905, 910 (5th Cir. 1969) ("Though it has factual underpinnings this ultimate issue is inherently a question of law.") *with Mathews v. Commissioner*, 315 F.2d 101, 107 (6th Cir. 1963) ("the question whether property sold by a taxpayer at a profit was property held by the taxpayer primarily for sale to customers in the ordinary course of his trade or business, within the meaning of the statute, is essentially a question of fact") *and Sovereign v. Commissioner*, 281 F.2d 830 (7th Cir. 1960) (" 'Whether property sold or disposed of by a taxpayer was held for sale to customers in the ordinary course of his trade or business within the meaning of Section 117(a) is essentially a question of fact. . . .") For courts that treat the issue as a question of fact, the factual issues involved may be either objective (i.e., frequency of sales, improvements to the property in question, etc.) or subjective (i.e., the purpose of the taxpayer in acquiring, holding, and selling the property).

The following case illustrates the difficulties that the courts have confronted in attempting to apply § 1221(a)(1) in the context of a holder of a large tract of land on the outskirts of a major metropolitan area.

SUBURBAN REALTY COMPANY v. UNITED STATES

United States Court of Appeals, Fifth Circuit
615 F.2d 171 (5th Cir. 1980)

GOLDBERG, CIRCUIT JUDGE:

We must today answer the riddle at once adumbrated and apparently foreclosed by the false dichotomy created by the United States Supreme Court in *Malat v. Riddell*, 383 U.S. 569 . . . (1966) (*per curiam*): when profits have "aris(en) from the (ordinary) operation of a business" on the one hand and are also "the realization of appreciation in value over a substantial period of time" on the other, are these profits treated as ordinary income or capital gain? Lacking any clear guidance but the language of the capital asset statute itself, we turn to that language for the answer. Before we can arrive at this interesting and important question, however, we must once again tramp along (but not trample on) that time- and precedent-worn path which separates capital gains from ordinary income. By the time we emerge into the light at the far edge of the forest, we will find that the *Riddell* riddle has seemingly answered itself, and all that will remain will be a brief reassessment of our answer. In our peregrinations, we of necessity wander into virgin territory. We hope that we shed new light onto this murky terrain; at the least, we think we have neither riddled the cases nor muddled the issues.

I.

Suburban Realty Company was formed in November, 1937 to acquire an undivided one-fourth interest in 1,742.6 acres of land located in Harris County, Texas ("the property"). Suburban received its interest[25] in the property in exchange for all of its stock from four individuals who had themselves acquired the property in a foreclosure proceeding brought against the property as a result of a default in the payment of certain bonds, the payment of which was secured by the property. Suburban's corporate charter states that it was formed to erect or repair any building or improvement, and to accumulate and lend money for such purposes, and to purchase, sell, and subdivide real property, and to accumulate and lend money for that purpose.

The five transactions whose characterization is in dispute here concern six tracts of unimproved real estate sold from the property by Suburban between 1968 and 1971. . . .

The parties' legal contentions are closely bound to the facts. It is undisputed that, at the time of sale, the tracts at issue here were subject to a grass lease which apparently covered much of the property. Except for this grass lease, the six tracts, as well as much of the rest of the property, were never put to any substantial use. However, certain other portions of the property were the subject of greater activity. . . . We will first discuss Suburban's overall activities with respect to the entire property, and then turn to those portions of the property singled out by the parties as being the subject of greater activity.

A. Overall activities.

1. *Total Sales Activity From the Property.* Between 1939 and 1971, Suburban made at least 244 individual sales of real estate out of the property. Of these, approximately 95 sales were unplatted and unimproved property legally suitable for commercial development for any other purpose, and at least 149 sales were from platted property restricted to residential development.[26] In each of these 33 years, Suburban concluded at least one sale; in most years, there were four or more sales. Suburban's total proceeds from real estate sales over this period were $2,353,935. Proceeds from all other sources of income amounted to $474,845. Thus, eighty-three

---

[25] [2] The remaining three-fourths undivided interest was held by two individuals who acquired their interest at the same time that Suburban's shareholders acquired their interest. . . .

[26] [7] See Appendix, *infra*.

percent of Suburban's proceeds emanated from real estate sales; only seventeen percent flowed from all other sources.

2. *North Loop Freeway.* In 1957, the Texas Highway Department proposed that the limited access superhighway now known as the North Loop would be located from east to west across the property. In 1959 and 1960, Suburban sold at least two parcels out of the property to the Texas Highway Department for the purpose of constructing this highway. The location of the highway had a dramatic effect on the price of land in the area. Land which had been selling for between three and five thousand dollars per acre prior to announcement of the highway rose in value to between seven and twelve thousand dollars per acre.

3. *Corporate Discussions and Investments.* Starting not later than 1959, Suburban's officers, directors and stockholders began discussing liquidation of the corporation. Many of these discussions occurred after 1961, when Rice University became a stockholder of Suburban and the Treasurer of Rice University became a member of the board of directors. Because Rice University desired investments in income-producing assets rather than raw land, discussions concerning liquidation of Suburban's real estate holdings and the possibility of a partition of its holding among its stockholders were common. Starting in 1966, Suburban made substantial investments in stocks and bonds and began receiving substantial income from these investments.

B. Specific portions.

1. *Houston Gardens.* In 1938, Suburban and the other owners of the property formed a separate corporation, Houston Gardens Annex, Inc. ("Houston Gardens"), to plat and sell a parcel in the northeast quadrant of the property. The stock ownership in Houston Gardens was in the same proportion as ownership interests in the property — i.e., Suburban and Mrs. Talbot each owned one-quarter of the stock of Houston Gardens; Mr. Hamman owned one-half of the stock. Houston Gardens owned approximately 200 or 250 lots, which were generally sold in bulk to builders. These sales covered as many as 20, 30, or even 50 lots at a time. By 1961, Houston Gardens had sold all but two of its lots, and it was then liquidated. Houston Gardens never engaged in advertising, used brokers or real estate agents, or employed a sales organization at any time during its existence.

2. *Homestead Addition.* Certain portions of the property, located near its center, were designated as Homestead Addition Sections One, Two, Three, and Four. Little was done with Homestead Addition Section One except for platting it and running a few utility lines up to it.

Homestead Addition Section Two, however, was the primary subject of Suburban's activities. In July, 1948, Suburban acquired 100 percent ownership of Homestead Addition Section Two by exchanging cash and other land for the other owners' interests. Immediately thereafter, Suburban commenced development of Homestead Addition Section Two. . . . Suburban also built a lumberyard in Section Two. At the instance of one of the individuals whom Suburban hired to collect water bills and notes on houses and to manage the lumberyard, Suburban also built eleven houses in Section Two in the early 1950's. The last was built by 1955, and none was sold later than 1958. Between 1948 and 1966, Suburban sold 252 subdivided lots out of Section Two. About half of these lots were sold in bulk to builders — 10, 15, or 20 lots at a time. Homestead Addition Sections Three and Four were platted for residential use by Suburban in 1951. This area was never developed by Suburban, however. In 1961 the plats were withdrawn and cancelled. This had the effect of eliminating restrictions which prevented commercial use of the land. Subsequently, the real estate within Sections Three and Four was sold to commercial and industrial users.

3. *Other Parcels*. The remainder of the property appears to have been treated as one undifferentiated bulk by Suburban. It is from this undifferentiated, undeveloped remainder that the sales at issue here were made. There are no specific findings by the trial court, and there appears to be no evidence of record from which we could ourselves make findings, concerning the number and frequency of sales of real estate from other parts of the property. Rather, the evidence concerning annual sales groups all sales made by Suburban, including sales from the Homestead Addition Sections, together. However, it is clear that throughout the period 1939-1971, sales were being made from the remainder of the property.

II.

Our analysis of this case must begin with *Biedenharn Realty Co. v. United States*, 526 F.2d 409 (5th Cir. 1966)(en banc), *cert. denied*, 429 U.S. 819, . . . (1976). *Biedenharn* is this Court's latest (and only) *en banc* pronouncement concerning the characterization of profits of a real estate business as ordinary income or capital gain. The decision answers the characterization question by evaluating certain "factors" often present in cases of this ilk.[27] *Biedenharn* attempts to guide the analysis in this area by assigning different levels of importance to various of the "factors." Substantiality and frequency of sales is called the most important factor. . . . Improvements to the land, solicitation and advertising efforts, and brokerage activities also play an important part in the *Biedenharn* analysis.

The question before us today, put into the *Biedenharn* framework, can be stated as follows: when a taxpayer engages in frequent and substantial sales over a period of years, but undertakes no development activity with respect to parts of a parcel of land, and engages in no solicitation or advertising efforts or brokerage activities, under what circumstances is income derived from sales of undeveloped parts of the parcel ordinary income?

The *Biedenharn* framework allows us to ask the question, but gives us little guidance in answering it. In the principal recent cases, there has always been a

---

[27] [16] In the *United States v. Winthrop*, 417 F.2d 905 (5th Cir. 1969), the following factors were enumerated:

> (1) the nature and purpose of the acquisition of the property and the duration of the ownership; (2) the extent and nature of the taxpayer's efforts to sell the property; (3) the number, extent, continuity and substantiality of the sales; (4) the extent of subdividing, developing, and advertising to increase sales; (5) the use of a business office for the sale of the property; (6) the character and degree of supervision or control exercised by the taxpayer over any representative selling the property; and (7) the time and effort the taxpayer habitually devoted to the sales.

conjunction of frequent and substantial sales with development activity relating to the properties in dispute. . . . The conjunction of these two factors "will usually conclude the capital gains issue against (the) taxpayer." . . .

Today, we must go into territory as yet unmapped in this Circuit. Suburban's case is at once more favorable to the taxpayer than *Biedenharn*'s and less so. It is more favorable because, *with respect to the particular parcels of land here at issue*, it is undisputed that Suburban undertook no development or subdivision activity. It is less favorable because *Biedenharn* was continually engaged in business activities other than real estate sales, whereas Suburban was for many years doing little else. Following the *Biedenharn* framework alone, we would be left with yet another essentially *ad hoc* decision to be made. We could justify a decision for either party, yet remain confident that we were being fully consistent with the analysis in *Biedenharn*. However, although there will always remain a certain irreducible *ad hoc*-ishness in this area, we are now firmly convinced that the uncertainty can be substantially reduced by turning to the divining rod of capital gains versus ordinary income — the statute itself.

III.

The jurisprudence of the "real estate capital gains-ordinary income issue" in this Circuit has at times been cast somewhat loose of its statutory mooring. The ultimate inquiry in cases of this nature is whether the property at issue was "property held by the taxpayer primarily for sale to customers in the ordinary course of his trade or business." . . . In our focus on the "tests" developed to resolve this question, we have on occasion almost lost sight entirely of the statutory framework. The "tests" or "factors," . . . have seemingly acquired an independent meaning of their own, only loosely tied to their statutory pier. . . .

The tendency to overemphasize the independent meaning of the "factors" has been accompanied by, perhaps even caused by, a tendency to view the statutory language as posing only one question: whether the property was held by the taxpayer "primarily for sale to customers in the ordinary course of his trade or business." This determination was correctly seen as equivalent to the question whether the gain was to be treated as ordinary or capital. However, probably because the question "is the gain ordinary" is a single question which demands an answer of yes or no, the courts have on occasion lost sight of the fact that the statutory language requires the court to make not one determination, but several separate determinations. In statutory construction cases, our most important task is to ask the proper questions. In the context of cases like the one before us, the principal inquiries demanded by the statute are:

1) was taxpayer engaged in a trade or business, and, if so, what business?

2) was taxpayer holding the property primarily for sale in that business?

3) were the sales contemplated by taxpayer "ordinary" in the course of that business?[28]

[28] [19] In other types of cases, or even in real estate cases with different factual patterns, other

* * *

. . . [O]nce the inquiry is redirected towards the statutory inquiries, the ultimate relevance of the *Biedenharn* factors becomes apparent. It will remain true that the frequency and substantiality of sales will be the most important factor. But the reason for the importance of this factor is now clear: the presence of frequent and substantial sales is highly relevant to each of the principal statutory inquiries listed above. A taxpayer who engages in frequent and substantial sales is almost inevitably engaged in the real estate business. The frequency and substantiality of sales are highly probative on the issue of holding purpose because the presence of frequent sales ordinarily belies the contention that property is being held "for investment" rather than "for sale." And the frequency of sales may often be a key factor in determining the "ordinariness" question.

The extent of development activity and improvements is highly relevant to the question of whether taxpayer is a real estate developer . . . but, standing alone, some degree of development activity is not inconsistent with holding property for purposes other than sale. The extent of development activity also seems to be only peripherally relevant to the "ordinariness" question. Thus, under the statutory framework, as under *Biedenharn*, the extent of development activity and improvements, although an important factor, is less conclusive than the substantiality and frequency of sales.

Solicitation and advertising efforts are quite relevant both to the existence of a trade or business and to taxpayer's holding purpose. . . . However, in cases like *Biedenharn*, their absence is not conclusive on either of these statutory questions for, as we noted there, "even one inarguably in the real estate business need not engage in promotional exertions in the face of a favorable market." . . .

We need not comment individually on each of the other *Biedenharn-Winthrop* factors. It should be apparent that each factor is relevant, to a greater or lesser extent, to one or more of the questions posed by the statute along the path to the ultimate conclusion.[29]

---

questions may be crucial. For example, whether the contemplated purchasers were "customers" of the taxpayers, or whether business activity is to be imputed to taxpayer so as to be considered "taxpayer's business," could be an important inquiry. Yet other inquiries may be demanded by the statutory language in other contexts. . . .

[29] [24] We will here attempt to clear up some of the confusion relating to the relevance of the percentage of taxpayer's average annual income attributable to real estate sales. This percentage has often been mentioned in the real estate cases; its significance has never been clear. . . . Rather, these decisions have referred to the percentage, often compared it to the comparable percentage in another case, and perhaps noted that the percentage in the case being decided was like or unlike the percentage in another case. Once the percentage is related to the statutory inquiries, it can easily be seen that the percentage may or may not be relevant depending on the facts of the case and the taxpayer's claims. Two examples are appropriate here.

First, a taxpayer who has made only a few sales involving fairly modest dollar amounts may argue that he is not in the real estate business. The taxpayer's claim to capital gain treatment is likely to be weaker if he can point to no other business activities; i.e., if close to 100 percent of his income is derived from sales of real estate. Conversely, if the taxpayer is also engaged in extensive activities other than real estate sales, the presence of another trade or business may make it less likely that he will be found to be in the real estate business. However, frequent real estate sales activity substantial in dollar amount will likely conclude the "trade or business" question against taxpayer. He will be held to be engaged in

IV.

Having laid the framework for the requisite analysis, we must now apply that framework to the facts here. . . .

* * *

A. Was Suburban in the real estate business?

This is a relatively simple issue. The question is whether taxpayer has engaged in a sufficient quantum of focused activity to be considered to be engaged in a trade or business. The precise quantum necessary will be difficult to establish, and cases close to the line on this issue will arise.

Happily, we need not here define that line. It is clear to us that Suburban engaged in a sufficient quantity of activity to be in the business of selling real estate. Suburban's sales were continuous and substantial. It completed at least 244 sales transactions over the 33-year period 1939-1971. This averages to over 7 transactions per year. Proceeds from these sales exceeded 2.3 million dollars.

* * *

Suburban relies heavily on the insignificance of its subdivision and development activity and the total absence of any advertising or sales solicitation activity on its part. However, the first two absences do not concern us at all. We need not decide whether its subdivision and development activities were sufficient to compel the conclusion that Suburban was in the real estate development business. We rely solely on Suburban's real estate sales business.

---

both the real estate business and his other business. . . .

The taxpayer's next argument will likely be that the property is held "primarily" for use in his other business (e. g., farming) rather than "for sale." If a large percentage of his income derived from the land in dispute is earned other than by sale, his claim that his primary holding purpose is for use in his other business is buttressed. This would clearly be the case if a few small tracts of land were sold from a large active farm. Conversely, if most of the income derived from the land in dispute is earned from real estate sales, it is more likely that the taxpayer's primary holding purpose is "for sale."

In *Biedenharn*, the percentage offered was real estate sales as compared to total income. The fact that this percentage was low (11.1%), . . . demonstrated that Biedenharn was engaged in businesses other than real estate (*e.g.*, securities investments). These other businesses did not relate to the property in dispute. Thus, the percentage offered was not relevant to *Biedenharn*'s holding purpose. The relevant percentage would have been real estate sales profits compared to total income from the land (which would include, *e. g.*, income from farming or leasing the land).

A second situation in which a percentage is relevant involves a taxpayer attempting to demonstrate that certain parcels of land were held for purposes other than for sale. This taxpayer could concede that he was in the real estate development business, but would argue that certain specific parcels of land were not held "primarily for sale." . . . These specific properties, he would argue, were held for other purposes. In this situation, a relevant percentage would be profits from (or number of) sales from property held primarily for sale as compared to profits from (or number of) all sales. If many of taxpayer's sales, or much of his profit, emanated from properties he claimed to hold for purposes other than "for sale," the taxpayer would be highly unlikely to establish capital gain treatment. Conversely, if a taxpayer who engaged in a high volume subdivision business sold one clearly segregated tract in bulk, he might well prevail in his claim to capital gain treatment on the segregated tract.

* * *

Suburban also seeks solace from the fact that it never purchased any additional real estate to replenish acreage it sold. As is the case with the presence of sales activity, the presence of such purchases tends to demonstrate that a taxpayer is engaged in a real estate business, but their absence is not conclusive. . . .

* * *

B. What was Suburban's primary purpose for holding the properties whose characterization is here in dispute?

Put into the framework being used here, Suburban's contention concerning holding purpose is two-fold. Principally, it argues that, at the time of the sales in dispute, the properties were not being held for sale. Alternatively, it contends that it "originally acquired its property as an investment . . . , and it continued to hold it for investment purposes." . . .

We reject Suburban's statement of the legal principle upon which its first argument is premised. It simply cannot be true that "the decisive question is the purpose for which (the property) 'primarily' was held when sold." . . . At the very moment of sale, the property is certainly being held "for sale." The appropriate question certainly must be the taxpayer's primary holding purpose at some point before he decided to make the sale in dispute.

* * *

The "holding purpose" inquiry may appropriately be conducted by attempting to trace the taxpayer's primary holding purpose over the entire course of his ownership of the property. See *Malat* . . .[30] Thus, the inquiry should start at the time the property is acquired. We seek to divine the taxpayer's primary purpose for acquiring the property. In this case, we are willing to assume, as Suburban argues, that the property was acquired principally as an investment. We then seek evidence of a change in taxpayer's primary holding purpose. Here, such evidence is plentiful and convincing.

The property was acquired in December, 1937. Houston Gardens Annex, Inc. was formed in 1938 to plat and sell a portion of the property. Sales commenced by 1939, and sales were transacted in each year thereafter. From 1946 through 1956,

---

[30] [36] It is not clear to us from the *Malat* decision whether "primarily" means "predominates at a certain point of time" or "predominates over the life of taxpayer's ownership of the asset." This could be critical if, for example, a taxpayer held a piece of property primarily for sale over many years, but then, shortly but not immediately before sale, switched his primary holding purpose to one of investment. If the appropriate measure of "primarily" is at a fixed instant of time, this taxpayer would be entitled to capital gain treatment if the other requirements of § 1221 are met. However, taxpayer's "primary holding purpose" over the length of his ownership of the asset would still be "for sale," and, if this is the proper test, ordinary income treatment would be mandated.

We express no opinion on the resolution of this issue, for it is unnecessary to our decision. We find Suburban's primary holding purpose to be "for sale" both at the relevant moment of time, if the first proposed test is appropriate, and over most of the period of Suburban's ownership of the property, if the second proposed test is appropriate. See ensuing discussion in text.

approximately 17 sales per year occurred. Proceeds from sales exceeded $8,500 each year, and were as high as $69,000 (in 1952). Also during this period, the development activity pertaining to Homestead Addition Two was occurring. . . . This development activity clearly contemplated, and was accompanied by, sales.

All of these factors convince us that, by the mid-1940's at the latest, and probably much earlier, Suburban's primary holding purpose was "for sale." . . .

With its primary holding purpose through the 1940's and 1950's fixed at "for sale," Suburban is then entitled to show that its primary purpose changed to, or back to, "for investment." Suburban claims that this shift occurred either in 1959, when its officers and directors discussed liquidation; in 1961, when Rice University became a stockholder of Suburban, further liquidation discussions were held, and the plats were withdrawn; or, at the latest, in 1966, when further liquidation discussions were held and Suburban began investing in securities.

We view this determination to be a closer call than any of the others in this case. The frequency of sales did drop off after the late 1950's. Suburban had discontinued its development activities.[31] Also, 1961 was the year the plats for Homestead Additions Three and Four were withdrawn.

This withdrawal of plats could be quite significant. Unlike liquidation discussions, which were apparently a dime a dozen for Suburban, withdrawal of the plats was an action taken by Suburban which may evince a different relationship to its land. The critical question is whether this withdrawal indicated that henceforth the land was being held principally as an investment or simply showed that Suburban was attempting to maximize sales profits by selling to commercial users.

The continuing sales activity is strong evidence that the latter interpretation is the correct one. Moreover, the trial court found that the withdrawal evinced "an attempt to maximize profits from the sale of real estate and to capitalize on the new North Loop Freeway which would cross (Suburban's) property." Thus, we conclude that Suburban's primary purpose for holding the property remained "for sale" at the time of the transactions here disputed.[32]

* * *

---

[31] [38] These two factors are probative of a changed holding purpose, as they tend to demonstrate a different corporate attitude towards the real estate. They are not conclusive of this issue, however. . . .

[32] [42] Some of our skepticism over Suburban's claim to have changed its holding purpose stems from the fact that it points to so many separate times when its purpose may have changed. This leads us to believe that Suburban was merely gradually shifting its strategies as market conditions changed in an effort to maximize sales profits. We do not reject outright the possibility that a sequence of events separate in time may indicate a gradual change in holding purpose from "for sale" to "for investment." However, we would be more likely to find a "change of purpose" argument convincing if a discrete event were followed by a string of zero's in the annual sales column figures, especially if this were followed by a sale of the remainder of taxpayer's property in a small number of transactions.

C. Were the sales contemplated by Suburban "ordinary" in the course of Suburban's business?

We need say no more on this question than quote from the discussion of this issue in *Winthrop* . . . :

> The concept of normalcy requires for its application a chronology and a history to determine if the sales of lots to customers were the usual or a departure from the norm. History and chronology here combine to demonstrate that (taxpayer) did not sell his lots as an abnormal or unexpected event. (Taxpayer) began selling shortly after he acquired the land; he never used the land for any other purpose; and he continued this course of conduct over a number of years. Thus, the sales were . . . ordinary.

. . . The same is true here.

V.

Having relied on the language of § 1221 itself to determine that the assets here at issue were not capital assets, we must return for a moment to the query posed at the outset. In this case, as we have demonstrated, sales of the type here in dispute were precisely what Suburban's business was directed towards. In other words, the profits garnered from these sales arose from the ordinary operation of Suburban's business.

At the same time, however, these profits did not arise principally from the efforts of Suburban. Rather, they arose from the same historical, demographic, and market forces that have caused the City of Houston to grow enormously during the years Suburban held the land. Shrewdly, Suburban held on to much of its land. It only sold relatively small portions year by year. Thus, by 1968, market forces and the location of the North Loop Freeway had driven up the value of Suburban's land. We must decide whether the policies motivating lower tax rates on capital gains and the controlling precedents expressing those policies require that we ignore the plain language of § 1221 and hold for Suburban.

The key cases we must explore here number three. First is *Malat*. . . . It lends us no aid. As we have previously stated, it suggests that profits cannot arise from both "the (ordinary) operation of a business" and "appreciation in value accrued over a substantial period of time." Yet here we have profits which fall squarely into both categories.

We thus turn to the two cases from which the *Malat* court quotations are taken, *Commissioner v. Gillette* . . . and *Corn Products*. . . . In *Gillette*, the Supreme Court said:

> This Court has long held that the term "capital asset" is to be construed narrowly in accordance with the purpose of Congress to afford capital-gains treatment only in situations typically involving the realization of appreciation in value accrued over a substantial period of time, and thus to ameliorate the hardship of taxation and the entire gain in one year.

. . . We note that the quoted language does not state that all gains emanating from appreciation in value over a substantial period of time are to be treated as capital gains. Rather, it states the logical converse of that proposition; i.e., that capital gain treatment will be proper only if the gain emanates from appreciation in value. Instances of gain emanating from appreciation being treated as ordinary income are not inconsistent with this proposition.

We also note the Supreme Court's recognition of the attempt by Congress to avoid taxing income earned over a period of years in one year. In Suburban's case, although it is true that with respect to each individual parcel of land there is a "bunching" effect, taxation of the overall gains from the property as a whole has been spread over a long period of years. Thus, the "bunching" effect has been minimized. Last, we note the Supreme Court's admonition to construe the term "capital asset" narrowly. . . .

Further support for a narrow construction of the term "capital asset" and a broad interpretation of its exclusions comes from *Corn Products*, the third key case in this area. . . . More importantly, the Supreme Court in *Corn Products* squarely stated:

> Congress intended that profits and losses arising from the everyday operation of a business be considered as ordinary income or loss rather than capital gain or loss.

It is this type of profit that is before us today.

We thus conclude that § 1221(1) should be construed in accord with its plain meaning, and that, if the other requirements of § 1221(1) are met, when the ordinary business of a business is to make profits from appreciation in value caused by market forces, those profits are to be treated as ordinary income. Such is the case here.

VI.

Our journey over, we have nothing more to add. The decision of the district court dismissing Suburban's complaint is AFFIRMED.

APPENDIX

Date	Number Commercial Sales	Number Residential Sales	Total Number Sales
1939	4	0	4
1940	3	?*	3+*
1941	1	?	1+
1942	2	?	2+
1943	1	?	1+
1944	3	?	3+
1945	5	?	5+

* Records incomplete for 1940-45.

1946	11	6	17
1947	3	12	15
1948	0	21	21
1949	3	6	9
1950	6	46	52
1951	1	6	7
1952	4	14	18
1953	2	6	8
1954	0	5	5
1955	1	16	17
1956	1	6	7
1957	1	1	2
1958	1	3	4
1959	3	1	4
1960	1	0	2
1961	2	0	2
1963	4	0	3
1964	6	0	4
1965	4	0	6
1966	7	0	5
1967	4	0	4
1968	1	0	3
1969	4	0	3
1970	1	0	1
1971	4	0	4
TOTAL	95	149+	244+

NOTES

1. From the diverse judicial decisions that have considered the application of § 1221(a)(1), various factors can be identified that the courts have examined in arriving at their decisions although different courts will consider different combinations of the factors described below and may exclude consideration of some of the factors altogether. In addition, different courts may afford different weight to the various factors in reaching their decisions. Thus, the application of the factors set forth below is more an art than a science. However, it is helpful to review the following factors in analyzing a given factual situation:

(1) *The purpose of the taxpayer in holding the property at the time of the sale or exchange.* If the taxpayer intends to sell a given property to customers in the ordinary course of his trade or business, the capital gain exclusion of § 1221(a)(1) should apply. Such a purpose may also exist even if the taxpayer originally acquired the property with the purpose of holding it for investment and not for sale in the ordinary course of his trade or business. Because this factor is subjective, it often must be proved by other objective factors.

(2) *The number and frequency of sales made by the taxpayer.* A taxpayer involved in numerous sales in a given tax year, or over a period of tax years, is more likely to be treated as a dealer than one who seldom or rarely makes such sales or exchanges. This factor has been cited as the most important of all the factors. Although substantial and frequent sales activity standing alone has never been held to be automatically sufficient to trigger ordinary income treatment, the conjunction of frequent and substantial sales and development activity will usually conclude the capital gains issue against the taxpayer.

(3) *The extent of the taxpayer's activity in developing or improving the property.* If the value of the property is attributable to improvements made by the taxpayer, the property is less likely to be treated as a capital asset. In the case of real property, such improvements could include zoning and subdivision approvals, grading, installation of off-site or on-site improvements, and similar activities. Some courts have denied capital asset status on the ground that the increase in the value of the property has been a result of the "personal efforts" of the taxpayer rather than the mere passage of time. This "personal efforts" rationale is not, however, universally accepted.

(4) *Marketing, soliciting and advertising efforts in connection with the sale of the property.* Some, but not all, courts view an active marketing program as an indication that the taxpayer is in the trade or business of selling to customers the property marketed. Although the absence of advertising and marketing activities may be a favorable factor to the taxpayer in achieving capital asset status, it is not necessarily conclusive. As stated by one court, "even one inarguably in the real estate business need not engage in promotional exertions in the face of a favorable market." *Biedenharn Realty Co. v. United States*, 526 F.2d 409, 418 (5th Cir. 1976).

(5) *The amount of gain obtained on the sale, particularly in relation to the taxpayer's other sources of income.* If a large gain arises from a property held for a relatively short period, or if the gain from potential dealer sales is large in proportion to the taxpayer's total income, then the gain is more likely to be treated as ordinary income. The courts generally look more favorably on gain that is accumulated over a long period, given the policy justifications for capital gain treatment. If the gain from the sale of the property is an insignificant portion of the taxpayer's total income, it is less likely to be treated as arising from the taxpayer's "trade or business."

(6) *The absence of special circumstances.* If there are special circumstances surrounding the sale of the property, the sale may be more likely to generate capital gain. For instance, if the property: was recently acquired by inheritance, involves the liquidation through multiple sales of a property held for a long period, or the sale is the result of unexpected economic conditions, then the courts may view such sale as not being "in the ordinary course of business." These situations are more fully discussed in the next subsection.

Importantly, however, in *Suburban Realty Co. v. United States*, 615 F.2d 171 (5th Cir. 1980), the court recognized that the factors themselves are not the focus of the analysis.

Subdivision of Investor Property Under § 1237

I.R.C. § 1237

Treas. Reg. § 1.1237-1

Because of the significant amount of controversy surrounding the application of the exception under § 1221(a)(1) to the sale of real estate, Congress enacted § 1237 to provide a "safe harbor" guaranteeing capital gain treatment in connection with the sale of parcels or lots from a larger tract of land if the requirements of the section are satisfied. Although § 1237 would initially appear to be an attractive tax planning tool in the real estate area, its practical application is extremely limited because of its many requirements and the numerous exceptions to its application. The unusual taxpayer who is able to satisfy all the requirements of the section would very likely not have invoked the exception under § 1221(a)(1) as an initial matter. Consequently, § 1237 provides few practical planning benefits.

When its requirements have been satisfied, § 1237 provides that the activities of the taxpayer in subdividing and selling real property will be disregarded in determining whether the taxpayer is a dealer in real property. Consequently, if there is no evidence, other than the permitted subdivision and selling activities, that the taxpayer is a dealer and the other requirements of § 1237 are satisfied, the sales will not fall within the § 1221(a)(1) exception as dealer property, and the assets sold will be deemed capital assets. I.R.C. § 1237(a); Treas. Reg. § 1.1237-1(a)(2). The permitted subdivision and selling activities include the actual subdivision itself as well as advertising, promotion, and selling activities, including the use of sales agents in connection with the sale of lots in the subdivision. Treas. Reg. § 1.1237-1(a)(2).

In order to qualify for special treatment under § 1237, the taxpayer cannot be a C corporation and must satisfy the following additional requirements:

(1) The subdivided tract cannot have been held by the taxpayer for sale to customers in the ordinary course of business at any time prior to the sale. I.R.C. § 1237(a)(1); Treas. Reg. §§ 1.1237-1(a)(5) and 1.1237-1(b)(1).

(2) In the year of sale, the taxpayer selling the subdivided property cannot hold any other property for sale to customers in the ordinary course of business. I.R.C. § 1237(a)(1); Treas. Reg. §§ 1.1237-1(a)(5) and 1.1237-1(b)(1). A taxpayer is considered to hold property that he owns individually, jointly, or as a member of a partnership. Treas. Reg. § 1.1237-1(b)(3).

(3) The taxpayer cannot have made substantial improvements that substantially enhance the value of the lot or parcel prior to its sale. I.R.C. § 1237(a)(2); Treas. Reg. §§ 1.1237-1(a)(5) and 1.1237-1(c)(1). Nor may an improvement be made pursuant to a contract of sale entered into between the taxpayer and the buyer. I.R.C. § 1237(a)(2). Although the determination whether improvements substantially enhance the value of the lot or

parcel depends on the circumstances of each case, improvements that increase the value of a lot by 10 percent or less will not be considered substantial while improvements that increase the value of a lot by more than 10 percent will be considered along with all other relevant factors. Treas. Reg. § 1.1237-1(c)(3)(ii).

(4) Except in the case of property acquired by inheritance or devise, the property must have been held for at least five years although the holding period of a prior owner may be "tacked" in accordance with the general rules of § 1223. I.R.C. § 1237(a)(3); Treas. Reg. §§ 1.1237-1(a)(5) and 1.1237-1(d).

Provided that the requirements of § 1237 have been satisfied, sales of the property will generally yield capital gain to the seller only with respect to the first five lots sold. I.R.C. § 1237(b)(1); Treas. Reg. §§ 1.1237-1(a)(5) and 1.1237-1(e)(2)(i). In the first taxable year that a sixth lot is sold, a portion of the gain from all of the sales in that year, and from all of the sales in subsequent years, will be treated as ordinary income in an amount equal to five percent of the selling price of each lot. I.R.C. § 1237(b)(1); Treas. Reg. §§ 1.1237-1(a)(5) and 1.1237-1(e)(2)(ii). Expenditures incurred in connection with the sale of the property are deductible first from the amount treated as ordinary income and the remainder, if any, reduce the amount realized on the sale or exchange. I.R.C. § 1237(b)(2); Treas. Reg. § 1.1237-1(e)(2)(ii) examples (1) and (2).

The difficulty in relying on § 1237 is that its criteria are not entirely objective. Even if the quantitative requirements of § 1237 are satisfied, the Service could still argue that the section is inapplicable because the property was held primarily for sale to customers in the ordinary course of business, because the statute specifically excludes such property from its application. Although the Service could not claim that such a property falls within § 1221(a)(1) as dealer property because of the subdivision itself or because of the taxpayer's marketing activities, it could certainly argue that other aspects of the taxpayer's relationship with the property (i.e., the taxpayer's intent in acquiring the property, the frequency of sales, off-site improvements, etc.) bring the property within § 1221(a)(1). Thus, this "safe harbor" provision is of extremely limited practical utility.

The Liquidation of Investment Theory

There is a line of cases that seems to overlay the "dealer" analysis, particularly in the real estate area, whereby a taxpayer who may have engaged in numerous sales of heavily marketed property to customers is nevertheless entitled to capital gain treatment on the ground that such sales were simply the most profitable method of liquidating his investment. *See, e.g., Heller Trust v. Commissioner*, 382 F.2d 675 (9th Cir. 1967) ("where the facts clearly demonstrate that a taxpayer held certain property as an investment, and further show that this purpose continued until shortly before the time of a sale, and that the sale is prompted by a liquidation intent, the taxpayer should not lose the benefits provided for by the capital gain provisions"); *Alabama Mineral Land Co. v. Commissioner*, 250 F.2d 870 (5th Cir. 1957) ("in the course of gradual and passive liquidation, . . . sales made in following such a course are sales of capital assets"); *Farley v. Commissioner*, 7 T.C. 198 (1946)

("Where . . . the active elements of development and sales activities are absent, the fact of liquidation is not, in our opinion, to be disregarded"). However, to successfully invoke the liquidation of investment theory, taxpayers must generally satisfy the following requirements:

(1) The taxpayer must have originally held the property for investment rather than sale;

(2) The decision to liquidate the investment must be driven by an unexpected change in the circumstance of either the taxpayer or the property; and

(2) A bulk sale of the property must either be impractical or be projected to yield a substantially smaller return to the investor than multiple sales.

Courts have concluded that the poor health of the taxpayer or a decline in the value of the investment because of a bad real estate market are examples of unexpected circumstances. *See, e.g., Curtis Co. v. Commissioner*, 232 F.2d 167 (3d Cir. 1956) (taxpayer acquired property for rental purposes, but sold it when restrictions on sales price were lifted); *Goldberg v. Commissioner*, 223 F.2d 709 (5th Cir. 1955) (taxpayers' sale of property after rental business became unprofitable was considered a capital gain); *Estate of Barrios v. Commissioner*, 265 F.2d 517 (5th Cir. 1959) (terminal illness of the taxpayer's husband and drainage problems causing farming use to be discontinued considered a change in circumstances). In *Biedenharn Realty Co. v. United States*, 526 F.2d 409, 421 (5th Cir. 1976), the court noted that "Acts of God, condemnation of part of one's property, new and unfavorable zoning regulations, or other events forcing alteration of taxpayer's plans create situations making possible subdivision and improvement as a part of a capital gains disposition." In the cases in which these requirements were satisfied, the taxpayers obtained capital asset treatment on the liquidation of their investments even though the liquidation involved a relatively large number of sales.

Related Party Transactions

The analysis of whether a given sale or exchange will result in capital gain for the seller becomes more complex when related parties are involved. There are two fundamental issues that arise when a taxpayer selling or exchanging property owns an interest in the purchaser or is involved with other entities that conduct the same or similar activities to the seller. The first issue is whether the activities and attributes of the related entities will be attributed to the seller and, therefore, aggregated with the seller's activities in applying § 1221(a)(1), as described above. The second issue is whether certain statutory provisions that override the capital asset determination under § 1221 and impose ordinary income treatment on the seller will apply under the facts at hand.

It is not entirely clear when the activities of a related entity will be attributed to a taxpayer in determining whether that taxpayer is engaged in a trade or business for purposes of § 1221(a)(1). If a taxpayer is involved in multiple sales of property through separate single-member limited liability companies, in which the taxpayer is the sole member, the activities of each limited liability company will be directly attributed to the taxpayer because a single-member limited liability company is a "disregarded entity" for federal tax purposes. Treas. Reg. § 301.7701-3(b)(1)(ii) and (b)(2)(C). Although the activities of a closely-held corporation are generally not attributable to a taxpayer/shareholder, the courts have concluded that activities of such a corporation may be relevant to this question. For example, in *Tibbals v. United States*, 362 F.2d 266 (Ct. Cl. 1966), the taxpayer sold subdivided tracts of land to his wholly owned corporation for subsequent development. The court concluded that the activities of the corporation were attributable to the taxpayer/shareholder.

> It is established that, in determining the trade or business of an individual taxpayer, the business activities of his closely-held corporation will not be attributed to him, but it is also true that a taxpayer may be individually in the same business as his corporation, may make that business his own, or may utilize the company in his own business. It is therefore appropriate, in circumstances such as these, to see whether the taxpayer uses his controlled company — for instance, as agent, co-participant, or joint venture — to implement or further his own personal business, as he easily can. That type of inquiry has often been made by the courts, including this one, in cases testing (under § 117(a) of the 1939 Code or § 1221 of the 1954 Code) whether profit from a sale of property was ordinary income or capital gain.

Id. at 272. Attributing the development activities of the corporation to the taxpayer/shareholder prevented the taxpayer/shareholder from obtaining capital gain treatment on sales of the undeveloped property. The precise import of the decision in *Tibbals* is unclear, however, because the taxpayer had previously been personally involved in the development of other property for his own account and had taken certain steps to have the county install water, sewer, and street improvements at the tract prior to the time of the transfer to the development corporation. As such, the taxpayer could have been deemed to be engaged in the trade or business of selling land even in the absence of attribution of the corporate activities. The court, however, found the facts in the case substantially similar to those in *Browne v. United States*, 356 F.2d 546 (Ct. Cl. 1966), in which the taxpayer had been engaged in substantial personal developmental activities, made use of a controlled corporation to continue the development activities in connection with the specific parcel at issue, and had been engaged in comparable purchases of other real estate for development. In both cases the court concluded that, because the taxpayer was engaged in the trade or business of selling real property, the gain realized on the sale of the property should be treated as ordinary income. *But see Gordy v. Commissioner*, 36 T.C. 855 (1961) (capital gain permitted in connection with sales of property to a controlled corporation when there was no showing of personal activities by the taxpayer-stockholder equivalent to the platting, subdividing, installation of streets, and utility arrangements).

However, in *Bramblett v. Commissioner*, 960 F.2d 526 (5th Cir. 1992) a partnership sold land to a corporation that in turn sold the land to unrelated third parties. The partnership and the corporation were owned by the same four people, and each person possessed the same ownership interest in the partnership and the corporation. The purpose of the arrangement was to secure capital gain treatment on the sale of the property by the partnership to the corporation while the corporation, as the developer of the property, received ordinary income treatment on the sale of the property to unrelated third parties. The goal was to develop the property in order to maximize its value but to bifurcate the gain into ordinary and capital gain through the use of the related corporation. The government argued that the activities of the corporation should be attributed to the partnership and the gain realized by the partnership on the sale of the property to the corporation should be taxed as ordinary income. The Fifth Circuit rejected this argument, concluding that the partnership was not directly engaged in the selling of land for purposes of § 1221(a)(1), that the corporation was not the agent of the partnership, and that the activities of the corporation could not be attributed to the partnership under a substance over form analysis. The court also recognized that there existed a business purpose to the arrangement beyond tax benefits: "there was clearly at least one major independent business reason to form the corporation and have it develop the land and sell it — that reason being to insulate the partnership and the partners from unlimited liability from a multitude of sources." *Id.* at 533. In addition, the court found no substantial evidence that the transactions between the partnership and the corporation were not at arm's length or that all business and legal formalities had not been observed.

Based on the decision in *Blamblett*, a partnership that has held appreciated real property for a significant period and would like to maximize its value by undertaking certain development activities should consider selling the property to a controlled S corporation on an installment sale basis. Provided the partnership is not engaged in the business of selling real property such that § 1221(a)(1) would apply, the partnership should realize capital gain on the sale. The S corporation could then develop the property and, although it would realize ordinary income on the subdivision and sale of the property, the gain would be limited to the excess of the sale proceeds from the subdivision and sale of the property over the increased basis resulting from the acquisition of the property. If the above structure is honored, the holders of the property will have achieved capital gain treatment to the extent of the pre-development appreciation of the property and ordinary income treatment on any appreciation in the property resulting from the development activities. From a tax policy standpoint, this bifurcated treatment of the gain in the hands of the partnership and the S corporation may be the most equitable in a situation in which a portion of the gain on property is due to market conditions and the passage of time and a portion is due to development and sales activity.

The Corn Products *Doctrine*

Volumes have been written by commentators concerning the so-called *Corn Products* doctrine since the Supreme Court's decision in *Corn Prods. Refining Co. v. Commissioner*, 350 U.S. 46 (1955). Although the *Corn Products* doctrine at its zenith appeared to establish a judicially created exception to the definition of a capital asset for purposes of § 1221, the Court's 1988 decision in *Arkansas Best Corp. v. Commissioner*, 485 U.S. 212 (1988), substantially limited the scope of the doctrine. With the enactment of § 1221(a)(7) and the promulgation of Regulations thereunder, which provide the exclusive treatment of hedging transactions, the *Corn Products* doctrine has become little more than a historical footnote. Nevertheless, because of the numerous judicial decisions and administrative pronouncements that gave application and context to the *Corn Products* doctrine over its slightly more than 33-year life, a limited discussion of it is warranted.

In *Corn Products Refining Company v. Commissioner*, the taxpayer was a manufacturer of corn starch, syrup, sugar, oils and feeds. In order to limit the risk it confronted in obtaining a supply of raw corn sufficient to satisfy its manufacturing needs at a price that would allow it to compete successfully with cane and beet sugar, the taxpayer began a program of acquiring a long position in corn futures.

> At harvest time each year it would buy futures when the price appeared favorable. It would take delivery on such contracts as it found necessary to its manufacturing operations and sell the remainder in early summer if no shortage was imminent. If shortages appeared, however, it sold futures only as it bought spot corn for grinding. In this manner it reached a balanced position with reference to any increase in spot corn prices. It made no effort to protect itself against a decline in prices.

Corn Products Refining Company, 350 U.S. at 48–49 (footnote omitted). The taxpayer incurred both gains and losses in connection with the disposition of the corn futures and, for the years at issue, the taxpayer had realized a net gain. Although it had originally reported the gains and losses as ordinary, the taxpayer subsequently contended that the corn futures were capital assets giving rise to capital gains and losses.

The Supreme Court concluded that the activities of the taxpayer in acquiring and disposing of the corn futures were integrally related to its manufacturing activities and, as such, should give rise to ordinary income and loss. According to the Court:

> We find nothing in this record to support the contention that Corn Products' futures activity was separate and apart from its manufacturing operation. On the contrary, it appears that the transactions were vitally important to the company's business as a form of insurance against increases in the price of raw corn. Not only were the purchases initiated for just this reason, but the petitioner's sales policy, selling in the future at a fixed price or less, continued to leave it exceedingly vulnerable to rises in the price of corn. Further, the purchase of corn futures assured the company a source of supply which was admittedly cheaper than constructing additional storage facilities for raw corn. Under these facts it is difficult to imagine a program more closely geared to a company's manufacturing enterprise or more important to its successful operation.

Id. at 50. The Court recognized, however, that the corn futures did not fall within the literal provisions of any one of the statutory exceptions from the definition of a capital asset. Nevertheless, the Court concluded that policy justifications required that the corn futures not be treated as capital assets.

Although the decision in *Corn Products* was a victory for the government, taxpayers soon learned that a narrow definition of capital assets was a benefit when losses, rather than gains, were involved. At the insistence of taxpayers, the courts began to distinguish between assets held for an investment purpose from those held for a business purpose. Assets held for an investment purpose were capital assets while those held for a business purpose were not, under the developing *Corn Products* doctrine. For example, in *Mansfield Journal Co. v. Commissioner*, 274

F.2d 284 (6th Cir. 1960), the taxpayer was a newspaper publisher who entered into a ten-year contract with a newsprint supplier to ensure a ready supply of newsprint at a reasonable cost. When it did not have a need for the delivery of newsprint under the contract, the taxpayer transferred its right to receive newsprint to third parties for consideration. The court concluded that the proceeds received by the taxpayer were ordinary income under the *Corn Products* doctrine.

More significantly, the courts extended the *Corn Products* doctrine to the transfer of corporate stock where the taxpayer could demonstrate that the stock had been held for a business purpose. Some courts applied a "business purpose/ investment purpose" test under which they considered whether the taxpayer held the stock for a business purpose or an investment purpose, allowing ordinary treatment in the former situation and requiring capital treatment in the latter situation. Other courts applied a "substantial investment" test under which they considered whether the taxpayer held the stock for a substantial investment purposes. If so, capital treatment applied despite the existence of a business purpose; if not, ordinary treatment applied. The problem with tests that depended on the motives or intent of the taxpayer was their susceptibility to taxpayer manipulation. If gain resulted from the disposition of the stock, the taxpayer would have little difficulty maintaining that the stock had been held for an investment purpose if, indeed, the transaction was even identified as involving a noncapital asset by the government. Alternatively, if loss resulted from the disposition of the stock, the taxpayer could argue that the stock had been held for a business purpose. Nevertheless, the *Corn Products* doctrine received general acceptance by taxpayers, the Service, the courts, and presumably Congress.

The Supreme Court revisited the *Corn Products* doctrine in 1988 when it decided *Arkansas Best Corp. v. Commissioner*, 485 U.S. 212 (1988). The taxpayer in *Arkansas Best* was a diversified holding company that acquired a significant percentage of the stock in National Bank of Commerce (Bank) in 1968. In 1972, Bank began to suffer financial difficulties. The taxpayer acquired additional shares of Bank stock after 1972 in an effort to improve its financial condition. The taxpayer subsequently sold the majority of its interest in Bank in 1975 realizing a significant loss. The taxpayer contended that the loss was an ordinary loss under the *Corn Products* doctrine.

The Supreme Court began by considering the statutory language of § 1221. It found that the consideration of the taxpayer's investment or business purpose in holding the asset was in direct conflict with the definition of a capital asset as "property held by the taxpayer (whether or not connected with his trade or business) . . . ." According to the Court, "[t]he broad definition of the term 'capital asset' explicitly makes irrelevant any consideration of the property's connection with the taxpayer's business, whereas petitioner's rule would make this factor dispositive." *Id.* at 217. It also concluded that the exceptions from the definition of a capital asset contained in § 1221 were exclusive, and not illustrative, thus foreclosing the courts from fashioning any nonstatutory exceptions.

The Court did not overrule its earlier decision in *Corn Products*, however. Instead, it viewed the decision as an application of the inventory exception under § 1221(a)(1). According to the Court, the corn futures in that case were "surrogates" for the raw corn itself which would have fallen under § 1221(a)(1) as inventory.

> [A]lthough the corn futures were not "actual inventory," their use as an integral part of the taxpayer's inventory-purchase system led the Court to treat them as substitutes for the corn inventory such that they came within a broad reading of "property of a kind which would properly be included in the inventory of the taxpayer" in § 1221.

Id. at 221. The Court maintained that the business purpose inquiry was not relevant in the general question whether the property involved was a capital asset as an initial matter but only in determining the applicability of the inventory exception.

> The close connection between the futures transactions and the taxpayer's business in Corn Products was crucial to whether the corn futures could be considered surrogates for the stored inventory of raw corn. For if the futures dealings were not part of the company's inventory-purchase system, and instead amounted simply to speculation in corn futures, they could not be considered substitutes for the company's corn inventory, and would fall outside even a broad reading of the inventory exclusion. We conclude that Corn Products is properly interpreted as standing for the narrow proposition that hedging transactions that are an integral part of a business' inventory-purchase system fall within the inventory exclusion of § 1221.

Id. at 221–222. Because the stock in *Arkansas Best* was not a surrogate for the taxpayer's inventory, the Court determined that the *Corn Products* doctrine was irrelevant to the resolution of the case. As such, the stock was properly viewed as a capital asset giving rise to a capital loss.

As a result of the decision in *Arkansas Best,* the *Corn Products* doctrine was largely limited to the characterization of hedging transactions involving the taxpayer's inventory, including any direct substitutes for the taxpayer's inventory. *See, e.g., Cenex, Inc. v. United States*, 156 F.3d 1377, 1381 (Fed. Cir. 1998) ("The ECI stock transaction, in contrast, is not closely related to Cenex's inventory-purchase system and cannot fairly be considered an inventory surrogate."); *Pike v. United States*, 88 F.3d 54, 55 (1st Cir. 1996) ("there must be some objectively demonstrable nexus to an 'inventory-purchase system' " in order to fall within the *Corn Products* doctrine after *Arkansas Best*); *Federal Nat'l Mortgage Ass'n v. Commissioner*, 100 T.C. 541 (1993) (allowing ordinary loss treatment on hedging transactions that were an integral part of the system by which Fannie Mae purchased and held mortgages under *Arkansas Best*); *Dial v. Commissioner*, 968 F.2d 898 (9th Cir. 1992) (denying ordinary loss treatment with respect to Treasury bill futures contracts because the contracts were purchased and sold primarily for the purpose of making profits from the trading and not to assure the taxpayer a supply of raw materials necessary to the functioning of his business). However, even this remnant of the *Corn Products* doctrine has been supplanted by the enactment of § 1221(a)(7). Consistent with the legislative history to § 1221(a)(7), the Regulations provide that, except as otherwise provided therein, gain or loss from a hedging transaction is not made ordinary "on the grounds that property involved in the transaction is a surrogate for a noncapital asset, that the transaction serves as insurance against a business risk, that the transaction serves a hedging function, or that the transaction serves a similar purpose or function." Treas. Reg. § 1.1221-2(a)(3). In addition, the legislative history explicitly provides that § 1221(a)(7) is "the exclusive means through which the gains or losses with respect to a hedging transaction are treated as ordinary." S. Rep. No. 201, 106th Cong., 1st Sess. 25 (1999). Consequently, the Supreme Court's decision in *Corn Products* has been relegated to little more than a historical footnote.

(b) Property Used in a Trade or Business

I.R.C. § 1221(a)(2)

Treas. Reg. § 1.1221-1(b)

The second exception to the definition of a capital asset under § 1221 applies to depreciable property and real property used in the taxpayer's trade or business under § 1221(a)(2). I.R.C. § 1221(a)(2); Treas. Reg. § 1.1221-1(b). For purposes of § 1221(a)(2), depreciable property is any property "of a character which is subject to the allowance for depreciation provided in section 167." Importantly, this exception does not apply to all depreciable property or to all real property. If the property is held for investment purposes rather than trade or business purposes, the exception is inapplicable. Treas. Reg. § 1.1221-1(b) (providing that "[p]roperty held for the production of income, but not used in a trade or business of the taxpayer, is not excluded from the term "capital assets" even though depreciation may have been allowed with respect to such property . . ."). Consequently, an apartment building held for investment purposes by the taxpayer is a capital asset despite the fact that the building is depreciable under §§ 167 and 168. Although depreciable property and real property held for investment purposes are capital assets, some or all of the gain realized on the sale or exchange of such property may be treated as ordinary income under the depreciation recapture provisions of §§ 1245 and 1250. Sections 1245 and 1250 are further described in § 6, below.

The exception under § 1221(a)(2) is not the last word on the characterization of depreciable property and real property used in the taxpayer's trade or business, however. Section 1231 will apply to such property if the taxpayer has held the property for more than one year. I.R.C. § 1231b)(1). Under § 1231, gains or losses from such property may be treated as capital gains or losses, in which case the general rules otherwise applicable to capital gains and losses will apply. Section 1231 is also further described in § 6, below.

(c) Intellectual and Artistic Property

I.R.C. § 1221(a)(3)

Treas. Reg. § 1.1221-1(c)

The third exception to the definition of a capital asset under § 1221 applies to certain types of intellectual and artistic properties under § 1221(a)(3). The primary purpose of this exception is to deny capital gain treatment on the sale or exchange of artistic or literary property by the individual whose personal efforts resulted in the creation of the property. In addition, the exception prevents artists and writers from obtaining a charitable contribution deduction for their works equal to the fair market value of the property contributed. A charitable contribution deduction in an amount equal to the fair market value of appreciated property donated to a qualifying charitable organization is available only if the contributed property would give rise to long-term capital gain if sold or exchanged. I.R.C. § 170(e)(1)(A). If the property contributed to a charitable organization falls within the exception under § 1221(a)(3), the deduction is limited to the taxpayer's adjusted basis in the contributed property, which is usually insignificant.

Specifically, § 1221(a)(3) excludes from the definition of a capital asset (1) a copyright, (2) a literary musical or artistic composition, and (3) a letter or memorandum, or (4) similar property in the hands of the taxpayer whose personal efforts created such property.[33] I.R.C. § 1221(a)(3)(A); Treas. Reg. § 1.1221-1(c)(1) and (2). The exception from capital asset treatment also applies to all of these types of property if the basis of the property in the hands of an individual who did not create the property is determined in whole or in part by reference to the basis of the property in the hands of the person who did create the property. I.R.C. § 1221(a)(3)(C); Treas. Reg. § 1.1221-1(c)(1) and (2). Finally, with respect to a letter, memorandum, or similar property, the exception also applies if the property is held by the person for whom the property was prepared or produced. I.R.C. § 1221(a)(3)(B); Treas. Reg. § 1.1221-1(c)(2).

The provisions of this exception clearly apply to the author of a book, the writer of a song, the creator of a theatrical production, radio or television show who sells the property to a third party. In many such cases, however, capital asset treatment would not be available because the sale would be made to customers in the ordinary course of the individual's trade or business under § 1221(a)(1) even if the exception for literary and intellectual property did not exist. *See, e.g., Fields v. Commissioner*, 14 T.C. 1202 (1950), *acq., aff'd*, 189 F.2d 950 (2d Cir. 1951) (denying playwright capital gain treatment for proceeds from the sale of motion picture rights prior to the enactment of § 1221(a)(1) because the copyright was property held for sale to customers in the ordinary course of the taxpayer's business); *Rider v. Commissioner*, 16 T.C. 1456 (1951), *aff'd*, 200 F.2d 524 (8th Cir. 1952) (taxpayer engaged in the trade or business of being a professor as well as a writer; manuscripts treated as property held for sale to customers in the ordinary course of the taxpayer's business); Rev. Rul. 62-141, 1962-2 C.B. 182 (taxpayers who produced and leased television and movie films and tapes treated as holding such property for sale to customers in the ordinary course of their trade or business). The exception under § 1221(a)(3) makes it clear, however, that the creators of artistic and literary works will recognize ordinary income on the sale of such works even though their activities in this regard have not yet risen to the level of a "trade or business."

---

[33] Section 1221(b) was recently amended to provide that, at the election of the taxpayer, §§ 1221(a)(1) and 1221(a)(3) do not apply to the sale or exchange of musical compositions or copyrights in musical works by a taxpayer described in § 1221(a)(3). I.R.C. § 1221(b)(3). The Ways and Means Committee simply stated that "it is appropriate to allow taxpayers to treat as capital gain the income from a sale or exchange of musical compositions or copyrights in musical works the taxpayer created." H.R. Rep. No. 109-304, 109th Cong., 1st Sess. 57 (2005). The provision does not change the prior law's treatment of charitable contributions of such compositions or copyrights, however. I.R.C. § 170(e)(1)(A).

Some dispute has developed over the scope of the term "similar property" for purposes of the exception under § 1221(a)(3). The Regulations make it clear that the term "similar property" includes "a theatrical production, a radio program, a newspaper cartoon strip, or other property eligible for copyright protection (whether under statute or common law). . . ." Treas. Reg. § 1.1221-1(c)(1). With respect to the scope of the term "similar property" in connection with letters and memoranda, the Regulations make it clear that the term includes:

> a draft of a speech, a manuscript, a research paper, an oral recording of any type, a transcript of an oral recording, a transcript of an oral interview or of dictation, a personal or business diary, a log or journal, a corporate archive including a corporate charter, office correspondence, a financial record, a drawing, a photograph, or a dispatch.

Treas. Reg. § 1.221-1(c)(2). *See Chronicle Publishing Co. v. Internal Revenue*, 97 T.C. 445 (1991) (publisher's clippings library characterized as corporate archive); *Glen v. Commissioner*, 79 T.C. 208 (1982) (tape-recordings of interviews with noted scientists qualified as similar property); *Morrison v. Commissioner*, 71 T.C. 683 (1979), *aff'd per curiam*, 611 F.2d 98 (5th Cir. 1980) (correspondence, memoranda, and files relating to congressional activities and constituent matters deemed similar property). As an example of similar property, the Service concluded that a newspaper morgue file constituted a corporate archive for purposes of the Regulations, rejecting the taxpayer's argument that a corporate archive must "chronicle the business activities and decisions" of the taxpayer. Tech. Adv. Mem. 90-37-001. Nevertheless, § 1221(a)(3) does not apply to "a corporate archive, office correspondence, or a financial record" that is disposed of as part of the sale of an ongoing business if the property has no significant value separate and apart from its use in the business. Treas. Reg. § 1.1221-1(c)(2).

In addition to questions concerning similar property, questions have arisen under § 1221(a)(3) concerning the situations in which "personal efforts" of the taxpayer have been expended in creating property. The Regulations provide that a taxpayer expends personal efforts if the taxpayer "performs literary, theatrical, musical, artistic, or other creative or productive work which affirmatively contributes to the creation of the property, or if such taxpayer directs and guides others in the performance of such work." Treas. Reg. § 1.1221-1(c)(3). Consequently, if a literary, musical or artistic composition is the subject of either individual or collaborative effort, the individual or individuals involved will each be treated as having created the product with his or her personal efforts. If, on the other hand, the taxpayer "merely has administrative control over writers, actors, artists, or personnel and . . . does not substantially engage in the direction and guidance of such persons in the performance of their work," the property is not deemed to have been created as a result of the taxpayer's personal efforts. Treas. Reg. § 1.1221-1(c)(3). Nevertheless, letters, memoranda, or similar property prepared by personnel who are under the administrative control of a taxpayer, such as a corporate executive, are deemed to have been prepared by the taxpayer whether or not the property is actually reviewed by the taxpayer. *Id.*

The question whether a taxpayer's personal efforts have resulted in the creation of property raise an interesting issue when the taxpayer is a business entity and the property is created by its employees. In Rev. Rul. 55-706, 1955-2 C.B. 300, *superseded in part by* Rev. Rul. 62-141, 1962-2 C.B. 182, the Service concluded that films produced by a publicly owned motion picture company were not covered by § 1221(a)(3):

> Many corporations, including some whose stock is widely held and traded on established stock exchanges, create copyrights as well as other property described in paragraph (3) of section 1221. The property created by these corporations is not considered to be created by the personal efforts of a taxpayer where all of the costs and expenses are paid for by the corporation at the current going rate for the services rendered. The production of each of the films in the instant case involved a multiplicity of skills and abilities, the combined efforts of numerous individuals of various backgrounds and trades, and the use of substantial amounts of capital. Thus, no single individual may be said to have created by his personal efforts the films in question or a property in the films.

Rev. Rul. 55-706, 1955-2 C.B. 300, 301–302. *See also Commissioner v. Ferrer*, 304 F.2d 125 (2d Cir. 1962).

Finally, the application of the exception under § 1221(a)(3) has also raised questions whether certain interests that the taxpayer is transferring that are in the nature of literary or artistic rights rise to the level of "property" for purposes of § 1221(a) in the first instance. The courts have held that an "idea" or "concept" may constitute "property" for the purposes of this capital gain exclusion particularly if such idea or concept is ultimately reduced to writing. This issue is explored in greater depth in § 3 of Chapter 7.

As previously noted, the exception under § 1221(a)(3) applies not only to taxpayers whose personal efforts resulted in the creation of the literary or artistic property, but also to those in whose hands the basis is determined, in whole or in part, by reference to the basis of the property in the hands of the person whose efforts created the property. I.R.C. § 1221(a)(3)(C); Treas. Reg. § 1.1221-1(c)(1) and (2). The carryover basis generally derives from property received by gift but may also flow from property contributed to entities such as partnerships or corporations in certain situations. I.R.C. §§ 361, 723, and 1015. If the basis of the property in the hands of the donee or transferee is determined in whole or in part with reference to the basis of the property in the hands of the person whose efforts created the property, then the exception under § 1221(a)(3) will be applicable. Under current law, property inherited from a taxpayer generally does not receive a carryover basis in the hands of the transferee. I.R.C. § 1014. However, beginning in 2010, property acquired from a decedent is treated as if transferred by a gift. I.R.C. § 1022. Nevertheless, § 1221(a)(3)(C) specifically provides that, despite the potential carryover basis occurring from such transfers, property received by reason of bequest or devise will be treated as a capital asset for estates of decedents dying after 2009.

(d) Certain Notes and Accounts Receivable

I.R.C. § 1221(a)(4)

Treas. Reg. § 1.1221-1(d)

Section 1221(a)(4) excludes from the definition of a capital asset accounts or notes receivable that are acquired in the ordinary course of a trade or business for either: (1) the performance of services rendered by the taxpayer or (2) the sale of property under § 1221(a)(1) (i.e., inventory, stock in trade, or property held primarily for sale to customers in the ordinary course of business). Consequently, the sale or exchange of such a note or account receivable will generate ordinary income. This is a logical result, particularly if the amount of the note or account receivable was not taken into income by the taxpayer at the time received, because the satisfaction of the note or account receivable is merely a deferred payment that would have been ordinary income if the initial payment had been made in cash. In the case of taxpayers selling inventory or stock in trade, however, use of the accrual method of accounting is generally required. I.R.C. § 471. Therefore, the face amount of the note or account receivable is reported as ordinary income at the time it comes into existence. Nevertheless, a note or account receivable accrued as income at its face value and subsequently sold at a profit yields ordinary income under § 1221(a)(4). More importantly, a note or account receivable accrued as ordinary income and subsequently discounted or sold at a loss will yield an ordinary rather than capital loss. Treas. Reg. § 1.1221-1(d). *See Burbank Liquidating Corp. v. Commissioner*, 39 T.C. 999 (1963), *acq., aff'd in part and rev'd in part,* 335 F.2d 125 (9th Cir. 1964) (mortgage loans made in the ordinary course of the taxpayer's business are "notes receivable acquired . . . for services rendered" and, thus, are ordinary rather than capital assets under § 1221(a)(4)).

Notes or accounts receivable that are not acquired by a taxpayer for services or for property described in § 1221(a)(1) are capital assets unless the taxpayer is a dealer in such notes or accounts receivable, in which case they are excluded from definition of a capital asset under § 1221(a)(1). *See Lehr v. Commissioner*, 18 T.C. 373 (1952) (note sold at a discount treated as a capital loss where note not held for sale to customers in the ordinary course of the taxpayer's trade or business). As a result of these rules, in situations in which a note and account receivable is sold at a loss or discounted and the exception under § 1221(a)(1) is unavailable, a taxpayer will seek to categorize the note or receivable either as having been received for services rendered by the taxpayer in the ordinary course of his trade or business or, in the alternative, as having been received in exchange for property described in § 1221(a)(1). On the other hand, if a note or account receivable is sold at a gain (as could be the case for those notes bearing particularly high rates of interest from a creditworthy debtor), the taxpayer will attempt to avoid the exceptions under §§ 1221(a)(1) and 1221(a)(4) in order to obtain capital gain treatment.

(e) Government Publications

I.R.C. § 1221(a)(5)

Another exception, with very limited application, from the definition of a capital asset applies with respect to certain publications of the United States government. As described below, this exception was enacted largely to limit the availability of charitable contribution deductions in connection with such property, typically by government officials and employees.

This exception applies to any publication of the United States government (including the Congressional Record) that is: (1) received from the United States government or any agency thereof for a price less than the public sale price of such publication and (2) held by a taxpayer who received the publication or a taxpayer who holds a carryover basis in the publication from the taxpayer who received the publication. I.R.C. § 1221(a)(5). Thus, if a taxpayer obtains a United States government publication at a reduced cost or at no cost from the government, any subsequent sale of the publication will yield ordinary income. The same rule applies to any taxpayer who receives such publication as a gift from the original recipient.

The broader application of this exception, however, does not relate to sales or exchanges. Rather, it relates to the tax treatment of charitable contributions of such government publications to a charitable organization made by taxpayers with the objective of obtaining a charitable contribution deduction under § 170 in an amount equal to the fair market value of the publications. The treatment of United States government publications as a non-capital asset limits the charitable deduction to the taxpayer's cost basis in the property contributed. I.R.C. § 170(e)(1)(A). The enactment of this exclusion from capital asset status resulted from the perceived inequity of allowing a member of Congress or a government employee to receive a tax benefit from the contribution of a United States government publication to a charitable organization when the publication was originally obtained at a discount or at no cost whatsoever.

Importantly, this exclusion from the definition of a capital asset applies only to publications of the United States government or any agency thereof. Consequently, it does not apply to publications of foreign governments, state governments, or those of other political subdivisions. Although the term "publication" is not defined in the statute or Regulations, the inference from the language of § 1221(a)(5) is that it applies to those publications of the United States government or an agency thereof that are offered for sale to the public. Thus, other United States government documents may, by implication, be excluded from the provisions of this section. *See* Priv. Ltr. Rul. 82-40-009 (concluding that the original military strike orders for the flight missions that dropped atomic bombs on Japan during World War II were not excluded from capital asset status under § 1221(a)(5)).

(f) Hedging Transactions

I.R.C. § 1221(a)(7)

Treas. Reg. § 1.1221-2

The exceptions from the definition of a capital asset for hedging transactions, commodity derivatives, and business supplies were added to the Code in 1999. As described above, the treatment of hedging transactions under § 1221 had a tortuous evolution beginning with the Supreme Court's 1955 decision in *Corn Prods. Refining Co. v. Comm'r*, 350 U.S. 46 (1955), which spawned an additional, judicially created, exception to the definition of a capital asset for certain types of trade or business-related property. Although the Supreme Court retreated from the so-called *Corn Products* doctrine 33 years later in its 1988 decision in *Arkansas Best Corp. v. Commissioner*, 485 U.S. 212 (1988), its earlier decision in *Corn Products* continued to apply to certain types of common hedging transactions.

Section 1221(a)(7) excludes from the definition of a capital asset any hedging transaction that is clearly identified by the taxpayer as such before the close of the day on which it was acquired, originated, or entered into. I.R.C. § 1221(a)(7); Treas. Reg. § 1.1221-2(a)(1). A "hedging transaction" is defined as any transaction entered into by the taxpayer in the normal course of his trade or business primarily to *manage:* (1) the risk of price changes or currency fluctuations with respect to ordinary property held by the taxpayer or (2) the risk of interest rate changes, price changes, or currency fluctuations with respect to borrowings made or ordinary obligations incurred by the taxpayer. I.R.C. § 1221(b)(2)(A)(i) and (ii); Treas. Reg. § 1.1221-2(b)(1) and (2). Consequently, gain or loss incurred in connection with an identified hedging transaction will be treated as an ordinary gain or loss and not as a capital gain or loss. As a result, taxpayers will presumably desire to avoid having a transaction characterized as a hedging transaction when they realize a gain so that they can obtain the preferential treatment applicable to net capital gain under § 1(h) and to have a transaction characterized as a hedging transaction when they realize a loss so that they can deduct the loss without regard to the limitations applicable to capital losses under § 1211. Although the identification requirement will prevent significant manipulation in this regard, the Code gives the Treasury Department explicit regulatory authority to properly characterize unidentified hedging transactions as such and improperly identified transactions as not being hedging transactions. I.R.C. § 1221(b)(2)(B).

Regulations under § 1221 have expanded on the statutory language of the exception under § 1221(a)(7). A hedging transaction is entered into in the "normal course" of the taxpayer's trade or business if the transaction is entered into "in furtherance of" the trade or business. Treas. Reg. § 1.1221-2(c)(1). According to the Regulations, "[t]his rule includes managing risks relating to the expansion of an existing business or the acquisition of a new trade or business." Property constitutes "ordinary property" if a sale or exchange of the property would not produce capital gain or loss under any circumstances. Treas. Reg. § 1.1221-2(c)(2). Similarly, an obligation constitutes an ordinary obligation if the performance or termination of the obligation by the taxpayer could not produce capital gain or loss. Treas. Reg. § 1.1221-2(c)(2). With respect to the question whether a hedging transaction is entered into "primarily to manage risk," the Regulations adopt a "facts and circumstances" standard, taking into account the taxpayer's business and the specific transaction involved. Treas. Reg. § 1.1221-1(c)(4)(i). "A taxpayer's hedging strategies and policies as reflected in the taxpayer's minutes or other records are evidence of whether particular transactions were entered into primarily to manage the taxpayer's risk." Treas. Reg. § 1.1221-1(c)(4)(i). Finally, the determination whether a hedging transaction is entered into primarily to manage risk may be made on a business unit by business unit basis, looking at particular groups of activities and the assets and liabilities attributable to those activities as separate business units. Treas. Reg. § 1.1221-1(c)(4)(i).

Because of the potential breadth of the managing risk standard, the Regulations provide specific examples of transactions that manage risk and state that a transaction not otherwise described therein or in published guidance or by private letter ruling does not manage risk. Treas. Reg. § 1.1221-1(c)(4)(ii). Transactions that serve to reduce a taxpayer's risk are deemed to manage the taxpayer's risk. Treas. Reg. § 1.1221-1(d)(1)(i). Under this definition of managing risk, written options and fixed-to-floating price hedges that reduce risk will be deemed to manage the taxpayer's risk. Treas. Reg. § 1.1221-1(d)(1)(iii) and (iv). Although risk reduction is generally determined only after all of the taxpayer's operations are considered, a hedge of a particular asset or liability will be respected if it reduces the risk attributable to that asset or liability and the hedge is reasonably expected to reduce the overall risk of the taxpayer's operations. Treas. Reg. § 1.1221-1(d)(1)(ii). In addition, interest rate conversions, transactions that counteract hedging transactions, and the recycling of hedging transactions all manage risk. Treas. Reg. § 1.1221-1(d)(2), (3), and (4). As the only example of a transaction that is not entered into primarily to manage risk, the Regulations describe the purchase or sale of a debt instrument, equity security, or annuity contract even if the transaction limits or reduces the taxpayer's risk with respect to ordinary property, borrowings, or ordinary obligations. Treas. Reg. § 1.1221-1(d)(5)(i). *See also* Treas. Reg. § 1.1221-1(d)(5)(ii) example (1) (in which the taxpayer borrows money and purchases debt instruments both with comparable floating interest rates), example (2) (in which the taxpayer purchases shares in a mutual fund after agreeing to pay compensation in the future based on the return of the fund), and example (3) (in which the taxpayer invests funds in variable annuity contracts after agreeing to provide a nonqualified retirement plan to its employees with returns based on the returns available under the annuity contracts).

Special rules apply to consolidated groups in the context of whether the risk of one of the members of the group may be considered the risk of all members of the group. Treas. Reg. § 1.1221-2(e). The Regulations provide that, unless the taxpayer elects otherwise, the consolidated group is treated as a single entity and the risks of one member thereof are considered the risks of the entire entity as if all of the members of the group were divisions of a single corporation. Treas. Reg. § 1.1221-2(e)(1). Consequently, inter-company transactions do not constitute hedging transactions because they do not serve to manage the risks of the entity. Nevertheless, a consolidated group may elect separate-entity treatment under which the risk of one member is not treated as the risk of the other members. Treas. Reg. § 1.1221-2(e)(2). Under this election, inter-company transactions may be treated as hedging transactions. Treas. Reg. § 1.1221-2(e)(2)(ii) and (iii).

The Regulations also expand on the statutory requirement that a taxpayer entering into a hedging transaction must clearly identify it as a hedging transaction before the close of the day upon which the taxpayer acquires, originates or enters into the transaction. Treas. Reg. § 1.1221-2(f)(1). The taxpayer must make a "substantially contemporaneous" identification of the item, items, or risk being hedged. Treas. Reg. § 1.1221-2(f)(2). A valid identification requires that the taxpayer identify the transaction that creates risk and the type of risk that the transaction creates. Treas. Reg. § 1.1221-2(f)(2)(i).

> For example, if a taxpayer is hedging the price risk with respect to its June purchase of corn inventory, the transaction being hedged is the June purchase of corn and the risk is price movements in the market where the taxpayer buys its corn.

Treas. Reg. § 1.1221-2(f)(2)(i). The Regulations provide that an identification is not "substantially contemporaneous" if it is made more than 35 days after entering into the hedging transaction. Treas. Reg. § 1.1221-2(f)(2)(ii). The Regulations also provide specific rules regarding how a taxpayer must record the identification on his or its particular books and records. Treas. Reg. § 1.1221-2(f)(4). Importantly, the identification requirements may not be manipulated to a taxpayer's benefit. That is, a non-hedging transaction may not be identified as a hedging transaction in order to obtain ordinary loss treatment, and a taxpayer may not avoid identifying a hedging transaction in order to obtain capital gain treatment. I.R.C. § 1221(b)(2)(B); Treas. Reg. § 1.1221-2(g).

(g) Commodities Derivative Financial Instruments

I.R.C. § 1221(a)(6)

An additional exception from capital asset status applies to any commodities derivative financial instrument held by a commodities derivative dealer. I.R.C. § 1221(a)(6). A commodities derivative dealer is defined as "a person which regularly offers to enter into, assume, offset, assign, or terminate positions in commodities derivative financial instruments with customers in the ordinary course of a trade or business." I.R.C. § 1221(b)(1)(A). The purpose of this provision was to resolve any uncertainties concerning the potential treatment of commodities derivative financial instruments as capital assets. Congress believed that, because commodities derivative financial instruments are integrally related to the ordinary course of the trade or business of commodities derivative dealers, such instruments should give rise to ordinary income or loss. This rule is similar to the provision applicable to dealers in other types of securities contained in § 1236.

The definition of a "commodities derivative financial instrument" is "any contract or financial instrument with respect to commodities . . . the value or settlement price of which is calculated by or determined by reference to a specified index." I.R.C. § 1221(b)(1)(B)(i). A "specified index" is defined as any one or more, or any combination of, a fixed or variable rate, price, or amount, that is based on "any current, objectively determinable financial or economic information with respect to commodities that is not within the control of any of the parties to the contract and is not unique to any of the parties' circumstances." I.R.C. § 1221(b)(1)(B)(ii). As a result, commodities derivative financial instruments include swaps, caps, floors, options, futures contracts, forward contracts, and similar financial instruments. S. Rep. No. 120, 106th Cong., 1st Sess. 196 (1999). Nevertheless, this provision does not apply to any financial instrument held by a commodities derivative dealer that is not connected to the activities of the dealer in his capacity as a dealer and that is identified upon acquisition as not being dealer property in the dealer's records. I.R.C. §§ 1221(a)(6)(A) and 1221(a)(6)(B). The instrument must be identified as not connected to the activities of the dealer as a dealer before the close of the day on which the instrument is acquired, originated, or entered into. I.R.C. §§ 1221(a)(6)(B).

This provision is obviously of extremely limited application and is directed at dealers in commodities derivatives who might otherwise argue that the commodities derivative financial instruments with which they are involved are not within the purview of § 1221(a)(1) and, thus, are capital assets when gains are realized but are within the purview of § 1221(a)(1) and, thus, are not capital assets when losses are realized.

(h) Trade or Business Supplies

I.R.C. § 1221(a)(8)

The final exception to capital asset treatment relates to property that is "supplies of a type regularly used or consumed by the taxpayer in the ordinary course of a trade or business of the taxpayer." I.R.C. § 1221(a)(8). This provision was enacted to resolve any question under the inventory exception of § 1221(a)(1) that sales of business supplies, the cost of which may have been expensed in the year of acquisition, would not receive capital treatment if subsequently sold or exchanged. For example, in *Osteopathic Med. Oncology & Hematology, P.C., v. Commissioner*, 113 T.C. 376 (1999), the Tax Court had concluded that supplies consumed by the consumer in the course of providing services were not inventory for purposes of the accounting method rules of § 471. This holding raised the concern that such supplies would not be considered inventory for purposes of § 1221(a)(1) as well. Section 1221(a)(8) was also intended to complement the exclusion under § 1221(a)(7) to ensure that hedging transactions with respect to business supplies would receive ordinary income treatment. There are currently no administrative, judicial, or regulatory interpretations of this provision.

§ 4 SALE OR EXCHANGE

§ 4.01 Overview

The special tax treatment of capital gains and losses applies only in connection with the "sale or exchange of a capital asset. . . ." I.R.C. § 1222. As a result, not all dispositions of capital assets for which gain or loss is realized under § 1001 will give rise to capital gain or loss under § 1222.[34] Unfortunately, there is no specific statutory or regulatory definition of the terms "sale" or "exchange." Consequently, there has been considerable judicial interpretation in the area. In addition, Congress has acted in this regard by passing specific statutory provisions directing that a particular type of transaction not otherwise constituting a sale or exchange according to the judicial definition of the phrase be treated as a sale or exchange for tax purposes. These provisions are sometimes referred to as "statutory sales."

---

[34] This result is frequently attributed to the difference between the language of § 1001(a), referring to "sale or other disposition of property" and that of § 1222, referring to "the sale or exchange of a capital asset." Such a result may have been unintended by Congress, however, if the language of § 1001(c) is considered. Section 1001(c) requires that, unless otherwise provided, the gain or loss realized on "the sale or exchange of property" is to be recognized. No court has suggested that, by adopting the more limited sale or exchange language under § 1001(c), Congress intended that any gain or loss realized under § 1001(a) on an "other disposition" of property that does not constitute a sale or exchange is not recognized under § 1001(c). Presumably, Congress intended that the "sale or exchange" language of § 1001(c) be co-extensive with the (sale or other disposition" language of § 1001(a).

As an example of both judicial action and Congressional response in defining the sale or exchange requirement, the early Supreme Court decision in *Helvering v. William Flaccus Oak Leather Co.*, 313 U.S. 247 (1941), is instructive. In this case, the buildings, machinery, and equipment used in the taxpayer's business were destroyed by fire. The taxpayer realized a gain on the receipt of insurance proceeds covering the property because the property had been fully depreciated. The taxpayer claimed that the gain realized was a capital gain and attempted to deduct capital losses that it had also realized to the extent of the capital gain. The Service argued that the gain on the conversion of the business property was ordinary income because the conversion was not the result of a sale or exchange and, thus, reduced the amount of the taxpayer's capital losses that were deductible. The Court agreed with the Service, concluding that an involuntary conversion of property is neither a sale nor an exchange.

> Neither term is appropriate to characterize the demolition of property and subsequent compensation for its loss by an insurance company. Plainly that pair of events was not a sale. Nor can they be regarded as an exchange, for "exchange," as used in [the predecessor to § 1222] implies reciprocal transfers of capital assets, not a single transfer to compensate for the destruction of the transferee's asset.

Id. at 249. Despite the Supreme Court's decision in this case, Congress subsequently enacted the predecessor to § 1231, which currently allows capital gain or loss treatment on an involuntary conversion of assets used in a taxpayer's trade or business in certain situations.

The decision in *William Flaccus Oak Leather Company* also illustrates the motivation behind both taxpayer and Service attempts to craft a narrow or expanded scope to the sale or exchange requirement. When a gain is involved, a taxpayer will normally assert that a sale or exchange occurred and that the asset sold or exchanged was a capital asset, thereby yielding favorable tax treatment. In the *William Flaccus Oak Leather Company* case, the taxpayer was also looking for capital gain treatment in order to increase the amount of capital losses that were deductible. However, when a loss is involved, a taxpayer will normally assert that no sale or exchange has occurred or that the asset sold or exchanged was not a capital asset, thereby yielding an ordinary loss. The Service has the opposite incentive in order to create ordinary income in the gain situation and capital loss in the loss situation. However, the successful assertion by the Service of a limited scope to the sale or exchange requirement when gain is involved may redound to the taxpayer's benefit when losses are involved.

As previously noted, there are numerous provisions in the Internal Revenue Code which dictate that a sale or exchange be deemed to occur for tax purposes. Most of these statutes have arisen from cases in which the existence of a sale or exchange was uncertain and subject to judicial interpretation. For example, in *Fairbanks v. United States*, 306 U.S. 436 (1939), the Supreme Court concluded that gain realized on the redemption of bonds before their maturity was not entitled to capital gain treatment because the redemption did not satisfy the sale or exchange requirement. The result in the case was overturned by the enactment of the predecessor to § 1271(a). Before considering these so-called statutory sales, the following discussion examines those situations in which the judicial definition of the sale or exchange requirement remains relevant.

§ 4.02 Judicial Interpretation

As previously noted, the courts have interpreted the "sale or exchange" language under § 1222 more narrowly than the "sale or other disposition" language of § 1001. This approach is consistent with the traditional view on the part of the courts that the definition of a capital asset must be narrowly applied in order not to afford capital gain treatment in situations not otherwise intended by the asserted policy justifications for such treatment.

In applying the statutory language, the courts have consistently found the sale or exchange requirement satisfied when taxpayers have voluntarily transferred the property involved. In addition, the Tax Court has stated that the distinguishing characteristic of a sale or exchange is the receipt of consideration:

> The touchstone for sale or exchange treatment is consideration. If, in return for assets, any consideration is received, even if nominal in amount, the transaction will be classified as a sale or exchange.

La Rue v. Commissioner, 90 T.C. 465, 483 (1988). Although the receipt of consideration may be a necessary condition to the sale or exchange requirement, it is not a sufficient condition. The factual determination that a sale has occurred can only be made after eliminating the possibility that the transfer constitutes only a lease or license of the property involved. If the transfer constitutes a lease or license of the property, no basis recovery is permitted, and the taxpayer must report the entire proceeds received as ordinary income. *See Commissioner v. Gillette Motor Transport, Inc.*, 364 U.S. 130 (1960) (if only the use of property is taken in a condemnation action, the compensation received is a substitute for rent taxable as ordinary income and not as capital gain). This determination may be particularly difficult when the transfer involves contingent payments or when the transferor reserves certain rights with respect to the transferred property. Some of these difficulties have been resolved through specific statutory provisions. For example, § 1235 permits capital gain on the transfer of a patent by a holder despite the receipt of payments contingent on the "productivity, use, or disposition" of the patent while § 1253 prohibits capital gain treatment when the transferor retains any "significant power, right, or continuing interest" in connection with the transfer of a trademark, trade name, or franchise. These two sections are discussed in greater detail in § 3 of Chapter 7.

Despite the possible interpretation that a "sale or exchange" applies only in connection with a voluntary transaction, the courts have not been so limiting. In *Helvering v. Hammel*, 311 U.S. 504 (1941), the Supreme Court concluded that the sale or exchange requirement was satisfied by a foreclosure sale. *See also Helvering v. Nebraska Bridge Supply & Lumber Co.*, 312 U.S. 666 (1941) (reversing the judgment of the Eighth Circuit that the sale or exchange requirement did not extend to a tax sale of real property). Similarly, the courts have found the sale or exchange requirement satisfied in connection with gain or loss realized on the condemnation of property. *Hawaiian Gas Products, Ltd. v. Commissioner*, 126 F.2d

4 (9th Cir. 1942). However, under the Supreme Court's decision in *William Flaccus Oak Leather Co.*, the involuntary conversion of property by fire or other casualty does not constitute a sale or exchange.

The sale or exchange requirement has also been considered in the context of the worthlessness, forfeiture, and abandonment of property. The unrecovered basis of worthless property may give rise to a loss deduction if the loss is allowed under § 165. Because no sale or exchange of the property is involved, the loss is an ordinary loss rather than a capital loss. *But see* §§ 165(g) and 166(d)(1)(B) (treating the worthlessness of certain securities and debts as the sale or exchange of a capital asset). This result is unaffected if the taxpayer abandons the property. *Citron v. Commissioner of Internal Revenue*, 97 T.C. 200 (1991); *Hutcheson v. Commissioner*, 17 T.C. 14 (1951); *Gannon v. Commissioner*, 16 T.C. 1134 (1951). However, as the following decision makes clear, if the taxpayer is relieved of a liability, even one for which the taxpayer is not personally liable, the courts have found that the sale or exchange requirement is satisfied.[35]

FREELAND v. COMMISSIONER

United States Tax Court
74 T.C. 970 (1980)

* * *

Petitioner purchased real estate in California in 1968 for $50,000, paying the vendor $9,000 cash and giving a purchase money deed of trust (hereinafter mortgage) for the balance of $41,000. By 1975, when the balance due on the purchase price was still $41,000, certain conditions existed which reduced the fair market value of the property to $27,000. Since under California law petitioner was not personally liable on the note secured by the purchase money mortgage petitioner decided to terminate his interest in the property, which he accomplished by reconveying the property to the vendor-mortgagee by quitclaim deed dated October 27, 1975, for no monetary consideration. Petitioner claims an ordinary loss in the amount of $9,182 for 1975 as a result of the transaction. The amount of the loss is not in dispute, but respondent determined that the loss is deductible only as a loss on the sale or exchange of a capital asset subject to the limitations provided in sections 1211 and 1212.

Section 165(a) and (c)(2) allows a deduction from ordinary income for losses incurred in transactions entered into for profit. The above sections, however, are limited by section 165(f) which provides that losses from sales or exchanges of capital assets shall be allowed only to the extent allowed in sections 1211 and 1212. That petitioner's interest in the mortgage property was a capital asset is not in

---

[35] The amount of any nonrecourse liability must be included in the taxpayer's amount realized on the transfer of the property in determining the amount of any gain or loss. Treas. Reg. §§ 1.1001-2(a)(1) and 1.1001-2(a)(4)(i). *See Commissioner v. Tufts*, 461 U.S. 300 (1983). With respect to any recourse liability, the taxpayer's amount realized includes the amount of the liability only the extent of the fair market value of the property. Treas. Reg. §§ 1.1001-2(a)(1), 1.1001-2(a)(2), and 1.1001-2(a)(4)(ii). *See Lockwood v. Commissioner*, 94 T.C. 252 (1990) (treating the abandonment of depreciable property subject to a nonrecourse liability as an exchange and determining the amount of the loss equal to the property's basis in excess of the liability).

dispute. The issue is whether petitioner's transfer of the property to the mortgagee was a "sale or exchange" within the meaning of those sections.

The parties have framed the issue in terms of abandonment, both parties implicitly agreeing that a loss sustained on abandonment is an ordinary one. Petitioner states that the issue to be decided is whether a disposition by abandonment constitutes a sale or exchange. Respondent concedes that an abandonment of property is not a disposition by sale or exchange, but argues that this disposition was the equivalent of a foreclosure sale rather than an abandonment.

It appears that by reconveying the property to the seller, petitioner accomplished an abandonment under California law. . . . But regardless of whether petitioner's intent and overt act of reconveyance qualified the reconveyance as an abandonment under California law, we are concerned here with whether the voluntary reconveyance *per se* constituted a sale or exchange within the meaning of section 1211(b)(1) of the Internal Revenue Code. . . .

That a disposition, causing gain or loss to be recognized under section 1001, occurs upon a reconveyance of property in satisfaction of a mortgage obligation is well settled. . . .

The question whether a reconveyance of property to a seller-mortgagee by various means and under various circumstances constitutes a sale or exchange for Federal tax purposes has been before the courts in numerous cases over an extended period of time, with the conclusions being at times inconsistent and confusing. Factors that have been given consideration include (1) whether the transfer was voluntary or involuntary, (2) whether the mortgage debt was released or not, and whether the transferor received any additional (even minimal) consideration or boot, (3) whether the transferor-mortgagor was personally liable on the mortgage debt, (4) whether the transferor-mortgagor received any tax benefits from including the mortgage debt in his basis while he held the property, and (5) whether the fair market value of the property at the time of the reconveyance exceeded or was less than the unpaid balance due on the mortgage debt. . . .

It has been well established that where a taxpayer transfers property to his mortgagee in settlement of a mortgage obligation for which he is personally liable, any loss sustained by him will be deemed to have resulted from a sale or exchange on the ground that the taxpayer received consideration in return for transferring this property, the consideration being his release from liability. . . .

. . . In *Helvering v. Hammel*, . . . the Supreme Court concluded that a foreclosure sale (or involuntary sale) constituted a sale or exchange resulting in a capital loss, the rationale being that there was no intent on the part of Congress to differentiate between a forced sale and a voluntary one. In that case there was an actual sale, albeit involuntary, and a deficiency judgment was taken against the debtor. However, in the course of its opinion the Court reviewed the legislative history of the capital gains and losses provisions and noted that in 1934 Congress amended those provisions to close a loophole which permitted a taxpayer to sell property within 2 years and take an ordinary loss (because it was not a capital asset unless held 2 years) or hold onto it for 2 years and then sell it for a capital gain, if a gain was realized. It also noted that Congress enlarged the scope of the provisions relating to losses from sale of capital assets by including therein losses upon dispositions of property by methods other than sale and without reference to the voluntary actions of the taxpayer (such as losses on redemptions, etc.). The Court concluded that Congress intended a broad meaning for the words "sales or exchanges" as used in the capital gain and loss provisions, and clearly Congress did not intend to permit deduction in full of losses resulting from forced sales of capital assets while taxing only a fraction of the gains resulting from the sales of similar assets.

Shortly after the *Hammel* case, the Supreme Court decided *Helvering v. Nebraska Bridge & Lumber Co.* . . . In that case the taxpayer's land was bid in by the State at a tax sale and taxpayer decided not to redeem it because his plans for use of the land had not materialized. Both the Board of Tax Appeals and the Eighth Circuit Court of Appeals had held that the forfeiture was not a sale within the meaning of the capital gains and loss provisions. The Court of Appeals said that in enacting then section 117(d), Revenue Act of 1934 (the predecessor of section 1211(a)), Congress was dealing with losses from transfers of property where the transferor received some equivalent for the property parted with; however, in the case before them, the transfer of title to the State was not only involuntary but was without any consideration moving to the transferor and no debt of his was either paid or reduced. Hence, the proceeding merely resulted in the extinguishment of the owner's title and was not a sale. The Supreme Court reversed per curiam on the authority of *Hammel,* suggesting that a transaction could be both involuntary and without consideration passing to the transferor and still be a sale within the capital gain and loss provisions.

Hammel has also been relied on as authority for the proposition that a foreclosure sale constitutes a sale regardless of whether the taxpayer is personally liable for the mortgage indebtedness. . . .

In late 1947, the Supreme Court decided *Crane v. Commissioner* . . .

We do not overlook footnote 37 to the *Crane* opinion wherein it is said:

> Obviously, if the value of the property is less than the amount of the mortgage, a mortgagor who is not personally liable cannot realize a benefit equal to the mortgage. Consequently a different problem might be encountered where a mortgagor abandoned the property or transferred it subject to the mortgage without receiving boot. That is not this case.

While the above-quoted footnote 37 to the *Crane* opinion was clearly dictum it has created further uncertainty in this area. Petitioner relies on it, in this case, pointing out that he had no personal obligation on the note, that the fair market value of the property at the time of the reconveyance was less than the unpaid balance on the note, and that he received no boot on the reconveyance. . . .

* * *

Here of course, we are concerned with whether there was a sale. Although indirectly related to that issue, *Crane* and the cases that followed it were primarily related to how much gain or loss was realized. We will first direct our attention to the issue here involved.

Hammel clearly establishes that Congress intended the words "sale or exchange" to have a broad meaning, not to be limited to the standard transfer of property by one person to another in exchange for a stated consideration in money or money's worth. Here, there was a voluntary transfer of the property by petitioner to the mortgagee which event fixed the amount of petitioner's loss. Had petitioner held on to the property until the mortgagee foreclosed there would undoubtedly have been a sale under *Hammel*. We see no reason why an involuntary transfer should qualify as a sale anymore than should a voluntary reconveyance to the mortgagee in lieu of foreclosure. And for the same reasons stated in *Hammel* we do not believe Congress intended to permit a taxpayer to take an ordinary loss by voluntarily reconveying the property to the mortgagee and to take a possible capital gain by forcing the mortgagee to foreclose. The reconveyance to the mortgagee effectively terminated petitioner's interest in the property but the mortgagee received property having a value — it was not simply an extinguishment of petitioner's title, it was a transfer of that title to the mortgagee. We do not know whether the mortgage debt was cancelled — it simply became uncollectible.

Nor do we believe Congress intended that the character of the transaction be determined by whether the transferor received boot, even though minimal. . . . According to petitioner's argument he could have converted what he claims to be an ordinary loss into a capital loss by accepting $5 boot from the mortgagee. In short, we believe that under the rationale of *Hammel* a reconveyance by the mortgagor to the mortgagee constitutes a sale even though the mortgagor had no personal liability on the debt. As noted below, the rationale of *Crane* supplies the consideration.

It has been held that where there is a sale consideration is not necessary. As heretofore noted this would appear to be the conclusion reached by the Supreme Court in *Helvering v. Nebraska Bridge Supply & Lumber Co.* . . .

Nevertheless in the older cases dealing with whether a transaction was a sale for capital gain and loss purposes so much emphasis was put on whether the transferor and/or the transferee received a benefit, or consideration, that we will address the question here. Under *Hammel*, a foreclosure sale is considered to be a sale for purposes of sections 1211 and 1212 and under *Crane* the full amount of the indebtedness is includable in the amount realized. *Tufts* and the other cases cited hold that the amount realized is not limited to the fair market value of the security property even though there is no personal liability on the note. We do not understand why there should be any difference between a foreclosure sale of the security property or a voluntary reconveyance of the property to the mortgagee. In either event the mortgagor's interest in the property is terminated and title is transferred to someone else and the mortgagor receives nothing out of the transaction. In both instances the mortgagor is relieved of property which has a lien on it, and is also relieved of the obligation to pay taxes and assessments against the property. There is no forgiveness of indebtedness in either case, although there is a change in the mortgagor's balance sheet or net worth. He no longer has the liability to account for, nor does he have the assets. . . . We believe the holdings of *Crane* and subsequent cases decided in the light of *Crane* mandate the conclusion that relief from indebtedness, even though there is no personal liability, is sufficient to support a sale or exchange. . . .

Furthermore, if the full amount of the indebtedness is included in computing gain or loss on the transaction, we see no reason why its elimination should not also support a sale. And as heretofore noted, even if the amount realized was limited to the fair market value of the property that would involve only the amount of the gain or loss, not whether there was consideration to support a sale, if such is necessary. The fact that the property is worth less than the face amount of the debt may be a reason for reconveying the property to the mortgagee, but it should not change the character of the transaction. Nor should the fact that petitioner realized no tax benefits in the form of depreciation deductions which he held the property determine the characterization. The transaction is a capital transaction involving a capital asset and should be, and we think was intended to be, governed by the capital gain and loss provisions.

* * *

In conclusion we hold that petitioner's voluntary reconveyance of the property to the mortgagee for no monetary consideration ("boot") was a sale within the meaning of sections 1211 and 1212 of the Code, even though petitioner had no personal obligation on the mortgage debt, the fair market value of the property at the time of the reconveyance was less than the unpaid balance due on the mortgage debt, and petitioner had received no tax benefits in the form of depreciation deductions with respect to the property while he held it. Consequently, petitioner's loss was a capital loss subject to the limitations of section 1211(b).

Decision will be entered for the respondent.

NOTES

1. As indicated in *Freeland*, the Supreme Court in *Helvering v. Hammel*, 311 U.S. 504 (1941), held that the forced nature of a foreclosure did not allow the loss on a foreclosure to be treated as an ordinary loss, treating the foreclosure as a sale or exchange to require foreclosure losses on capital assets to be offset against capital gains and otherwise subject to capital loss limitations. Other cases have reached the same result as *Freeland. See Yarbro v. Commissioner*, 737 F.2d 479 (5th Cir. 1984) (abandonment of property subject to nonrecourse mortgage); *Middleton v. Commissioner*, 77 T.C. 310 (1981), *aff'd per curiam*, 693 F.2d 124 (11th Cir. 1982) (same).

2. The decision in *Freeland* raises the possibility that the abandonment of a partnership interest could give rise to capital gain or loss. In *Citron v. Commissioner of Internal Revenue*, 97 T.C. 200 (1991), limited partners in a partnership created to produce a movie became involved in a dispute over the negative produced by a third party, decided not to pursue litigation to obtain the negative, and renounced any interest in the partnership or the negative, which was the partnership's only asset. The partnership had no liabilities because the producer of the negative was responsible for all costs. The loss was ordinary under the principle that an abandonment is not a sale or exchange. However, in Rev. Rul. 93-80, 1993-2 C.B. 239, the Service considered the abandonment of a partnership interest in two situations — one in which the abandoning partner shared partnership liabilities, and one in which he did not. The Service determined that the loss is capital when

the partner shares in liabilities because there is a deemed distribution on account of the relief from the liability even if the liability is nonrecourse. On the other hand, the loss is ordinary when the partner does not share partnership liabilities because there is no sale or exchange, noting that even a de minimis deemed distribution would make the entire loss capital. The results in each situation would be the same if the partnership interest was found to be worthless.

PROBLEMS FOR DISCUSSION

Problem 2-5. Is the distinction made in Rev. Rul. 93-80 and *Citron* based on the absence of partnership liabilities sound? What, if anything, is the relationship between these cases and *International Freighting* and *Davis* in Chapter 1?

§ 4.03 Extinguishment Doctrine

The courts have also considered the sale or exchange requirement in the context of payments received for the cancellation or termination of certain contract rights, including leases. In general, the courts have concluded that no sale or exchange occurs when contract rights are cancelled or terminated because the property does not survive the transaction under the so-called "extinguishment doctrine." The extinguishment doctrine is based on the decisions by the Second Circuit in *Commissioner v. Starr Bros., Inc.*, 204 F.2d 673 (2d Cir. 1953); *General Artists Corp. v. Commissioner*, 205 F.2d 360 (2d Cir. 1953); and *Commissioner v. Pittston Co.*, 252 F.2d 344 (2d Cir. 1958). *See also* S. Rep. No. 33, 105th Cong., 1st Sess. 133 (1997) (referring to the extinguishment doctrine and intending to limit its scope through the enactment of § 1234A). Because the property did not survive the transfer, no sale or exchange for purposes of § 1222 was deemed to have occurred.

Despite its involvement in the creation of the extinguishment doctrine, the Second Circuit questioned the justification for distinguishing between a transfer of contract rights to a third party under which the contract rights are not extinguished and the release of contract rights to one of the original contracting parties that results in the extinguishment of the rights. In *Commissioner v. Ferrer*, 304 F.2d 125 (2d Cir. 1962), the court considered a situation in which the taxpayer, the actor Jose Ferrer, released certain theatrical and movie rights that he had previously acquired from the author Pierre LaMure to the novel "Moulin Rouge" in return for consideration from the production company, Moulin Productions, inc., owned by the movie director, John Huston. Ferrer had acquired three interests from LaMure: (1) a lease of the exclusive right to present a play based on the novel, (2) the power to prevent LaMure's transfer of the motion picture rights until the play had run for a specified period, and (3) a percentage of the author's proceeds from the transfer of the motion picture rights if Ferrer consented to the transfer. Their agreement provided that LaMure retained the full legal and equitable title to the copyright, subject to Ferrer's interests. Subsequently, when Huston acquired the motion picture rights from LaMure, Ferrer agreed to release of all of the rights previously acquired in return for a percentage interest in the net profits of the movie. Ferrer claimed that he was entitled to capital gain treatment with respect to the payments received. Despite its precedents concerning the extinguishment doctrine, the court found the doctrine of little assistance.

> In the instant case we can see no sensible business basis for drawing a line between a release of Ferrer's rights to LaMure for a consideration paid by Moulin, and a sale of them, with LaMure's consent, to Moulin or to a stranger who would then release them. . . . Tax law is concerned with the substance, here the voluntary passing of "property" rights allegedly constituting "capital assets," not with whether they are passed to a stranger or to a person already having a larger "estate."

Id. at 131. The Court concluded that its decisions in *Starr Bros.*, *General Artists*, and *Pittston* were better justified on the basis that the property involved represented only the right to receive periodic income that was not a capital asset. Following the decision in *Ferrer*, several courts concluded that the Second Circuit had repudiated the extinguishment doctrine. *Turzillo v. Commissioner*, 346 F.2d 884 (6th Cir. 1965); *United States v. Dresser Industries, Inc.*, 324 F.2d 56 (5th Cir. 1963). Nevertheless, the Service and courts, including the Second Circuit, have applied the extinguishment doctrine since *Ferrer*. *See Wolff v. Commissioner*, 148 F.3d 186 (2d Cir. 1998); *Stoller v. Commissioner*, 994 F.2d 855 (D.C. Cir. 1993); *Billy Rose's Diamond Horseshoe, Inc. v. United States*, 448 F.2d 549 (2d Cir. 1971); *Nahey v. Commissioner*, 111 T.C. 256 (1998), *aff'd*, 196 F.3d 866 (7th Cir. 1999); Rev. Rul. 75-527, 1975-2 C.B. 30. *See also* Priv. Ltr. Rul. 2004-27-025 (applying the extinguishment doctrine to the termination of a long-term power purchase agreement).

However, in applying the extinguishment doctrine, the courts have distinguished between simple contract rights and more substantial "property" interests. Thus, payments from a lessor to a lessee to cancel or terminate the remaining term of a lease have been held to give rise to capital gain. *Commissioner v. Ray*, 210 F.2d 390 (5th Cir. 1954); *Commissioner v. Golonsky*, 200 F.2d 72 (3d Cir. 1952). *See also McAllister v. Commissioner*, 157 F.2d 235 (2d Cir. 1946) (payment to life tenant for transfer of life interest in trust to remainderman was capital gain). The court in *Commissioner v. McCue Bros. & Drummond, Inc.*, 210 F.2d 752 (2d Cir. 1954), distinguished the earlier decisions applying the extinguishment doctrine by noting that, in those cases, "the contractual right was not transferred, but was released and merely vanished. However, we think the right of possession under a lease or otherwise, is a more substantial property right which does not lose its existence when it is transferred." *Id.* at 753. The Service recognized the distinction between leases and general contract rights and acquiesced in *McCue*. Rev. Rul. 56-531, 1956-2 C.B. 983, clarified by Rev. Rul. 75-527, 1975-2 C.B. 30. The holding of Revenue Ruling 56-531 also applied to the release of a lease covenant restricting the lessee's use of the leased premises. However, the Service made clear that it "will continue to regard the relinquishment of simple contract rights as not involving the sale or exchange of a capital asset . . . and will treat amounts received in consideration of such relinquishment as constituting ordinary income. . . ." As described in § 4.03, the judicial disapproval of the extinguishment doctrine with respect to lease terminations has been codified under § 1241. In addition, the extinguishment doctrine has been significantly narrowed as the result of amendments to § 1234A.

POUNDS v. UNITED STATES

United States Court of Appeals, Fifth Circuit
372 F.2d 342 (5th Cir. 1967)

WISDOM, CIRCUIT JUDGE:

* * *

. . . The taxpayer, Horace Pounds, now deceased, was a real estate broker and expert appraiser in Houston, Texas. During the year 1954, the American National Insurance Company, Galveston, Texas, owned a 16 acre tract of land in Houston listed for sale with Jim Elrod, a real estate broker. Pounds did not have a listing on this land. He knew, however, that O.J. Gilson was interested in investing in real estate. Pounds, working through Elrod, arranged for the sale of the 16 acres to Gilson. Neither Gilson nor American National paid any commissions to the two brokers; but in return for their services, Gilson agreed to pay each of them 121/2 per cent of any net profits he might make on the land. The day the deal was closed, Pounds purchased Elrod's rights to the possible future profits for $2500.00.

The same day, January 20, 1954, Gilson delivered to Pounds a letter evidencing his obligation under the previous oral agreements. The letter in part provided:

> In accordance with our verbal agreement, this letter confirms your interest in the net profits anticipated, if and when they develop, from the property owned by me, as follows: [Property described by metes and bounds.] It is specifically understood and agreed that you do not hold any title interest in the above mentioned properties. It is further agreed that at such time as this property is sold and the total investment has been recovered, including taxes and other expenses which may develop in the interim from its purchase date to the date of sale, such excess as develops to be net profit which shall [sic.] divided, first 25% of the actual net profits shall be remitted as appreciation and remuneration for your efforts in working out all of the details necessary in the consummation of this deal.

In 1958 and 1959, Gilson sold most of the property to the Harris County Flood Control District and the State of Texas. In accordance with the terms of the contract, he paid Pounds $14,481.41, one fourth of the net profits. . . .

There are essential differences between the rights Pounds acquired for the services he rendered and the rights he purchased from Elrod. . . .

We discuss first the 12½ per cent interest in the profits that Pounds received in place of the usual agent's commission.

a. We start with the fact that this interest was compensation for Pounds' personal service as a real estate agent. . . .

Compensation for services rendered constitutes ordinary income under Section 61(a) of the Code. . . . A real estate agent's ordinary income derived from compensation for personal services in selling land cannot be transmuted into capital gain by measuring its value in terms of possible profits from the sale of the land. Pounds simply had an open transaction involving his commission. The fact that the transaction was not closed until the property was sold in 1958-59 cannot change the character of the transaction. . . .

B. The express language of the letter contract negatives any inference that Pounds acquired an interest in the land that could be considered a capital asset. . . . Pounds had only an expectancy to share in anticipated net profits from a future sale "*if and when* they [developed]". (Emphasis added.)

* * *

C. We note, in passing, that Pounds, a cash basis taxpayer, made no pretense of treating his contract right/commission as income in 1954; he did not report the actual or constructive receipt of the commission in 1954. We note too that a serious valuation problem would arise in determining the 1954 value of a right to future profits on real estate under the control of a third person, and that undervaluation would allow income clearly taxable at ordinary rates to be treated improperly as capital appreciation.

* * *

These problems of defining a capital asset do not exist with regard to the 12½ per cent interest in the profits which Pounds purchased from Elrod. His "basis" in the property is fixed by the $2500 purchase price. . . . And unlike the other 121/2 per cent interest Pounds held, this interest can in no way be considered compensation for services. It makes no difference that Elrod, the original owner of these rights, acquired them as compensation for services. Once the rights passed from his hands, they lost their character as compensation and became instead an investment by Pounds. The Treasury has recognized this change in the character of a right to receive income as it changes hands. GCM 24849 states:

> Once such rights to income from property or for services are separated from the earner by his act of assignment, they become property rights owned by the purchaser or assignee with a basis in his hands measured by the consideration paid. . . .

* * *

B. Even if we should assume that the interest Pounds purchased from Elrod was a capital asset, we should be forced to conclude that the amount Pounds realized when Gilson performed his contractual obligation must be taxed as ordinary income. Section 1222 of the Code defines a long term capital gain as "gain from the sale or exchange of a capital asset held for more than 6 months * * *". (Emphasis added.) Congress, however, has never defined the term "sale or exchange". . . .

. . . If there was a sale or exchange, it must have been between Pounds and Gilson, and its subject must have been Pounds' contract claim against Gilson.

Before the transaction took place, Pounds had an enforceable claim against Gilson, since there had in fact been a profit on the sale of the land. Gilson had $14,481.14. After the transaction, Pounds had the $14,481.14, but Gilson had nothing. In ordinary terms, Gilson fulfilled his contractual obligation to Pounds, thereby extinguishing Pounds' claim against him. The Supreme Court has said that the terms "sale" and "exchange" are to be given their ordinary meaning. . . . And the courts have universally recognized that mere collection of an obligation, purchased or not, does not fit the ordinary meaning of "sale or exchange".

* * *

Congress has clarified the treatment to be accorded many of these ambiguous transactions having some of the characteristics of a sale or exchange but which do not fall clearly within those terms. For example, section 1241 provides that "Amounts received by a lessee for the cancellation of a lease, or by a distributor of goods for the cancellation of a distributor's agreement * * * shall be considered as amounts received in exchange for such lease or agreement." (Emphasis added.) Section [1272(a)(1)] directs that amounts received on the retirement of certain bonds or other evidences of indebtedness be treated as having been received in exchange for the bonds. . . .

. . . [T]he Court considered the involuntary conversion of depreciated real property into cash insurance proceeds. After examining the various "sale or exchange" provisions of the 1939 Code, the Court concluded:

> These sections demonstrate that Congress has expressly specified the ambiguous transactions which are to be regarded as sales or exchanges for income tax purposes. They are convincing evidence that the involuntary conversion of respondent's property, which bears far less resemblance to a sale or exchange than the transactions embraced in [§§ 331 and 1271(a)(1)] is not to be placed in one or the other of those categories by implication. . . .

C. If Pounds' interest were considered a capital asset and if it had been sold to a third party shortly before Gilson disposed of the real estate, the income realized from the sale should be taxable at capital gains rates. . . . If such a sale should give rise to capital treatment, the result we reach in this case may seem formalistic. There is substance, however, in the distinction between this case and one in which the contract right is sold to a third party. One of the reasons for according special tax treatment to capital transactions is to facilitate the disposal of appreciated property. . . . In light of this consideration, our distinction becomes meaningful. Until Gilson sold the real estate, Pounds had complete control over the timing of the realization of income from his interest. Taxation at capital gains rates might have minimized the tax considerations which would have gone into a decision to liquidate his interest or to change the form of his investment. Such taxation might have encouraged him to sell or exchange his contract interest. But once Gilson sold the land, special tax treatment was no longer necessary or even relevant. Pounds had lost control over the timing of his income realization. . . .

§ 4.04 Statutory Sales

Because of the uncertainty surrounding the precise contours of the judicial interpretation of the sale or exchange requirement, Congress has enacted a number of statutory provisions explicitly providing that transfers will satisfy the sale or exchange requirement. The following discussion describes several of these provisions.

(a) Worthless Securities and Nonbusiness Bad Debts

I.R.C. §§ 165(g) and 166(d)

Losses resulting from worthless securities and nonbusiness bad debts are treated as losses from the sale or exchange of a capital asset even though such assets may never be conveyed to a third party. I.R.C. §§ 165(g) and 166(d). Consequently, such losses are potentially subject to the restrictive capital loss limitations of § 1211.

(b) Loss on the Lapse of an Option

I.R.C. § 1234

Treas. Reg. § 1.1234-1

Section 1234 provides that gain or loss on the sale or exchange of an option is to be considered as gain or loss from the sale or exchange of property with the same character as the property to which the option relates would have in the hands of the taxpayer if the property had been acquired. I.R.C. § 1234(a)(1). As a result, the sale of an option to acquire property that would be a capital asset in the taxpayer's hands will give rise to capital gain or loss. The period for which the taxpayer has held the option determines whether the capital gain or loss is short-term or long-term. Treas. Reg. § 1.1234-1(a)(1). In addition, § 1234 provides that a loss attributable to the failure to exercise an option is to be treated as though the option were sold or exchanged on the date it expires. I.R.C. §§ 1234(a)(1) and 1234(a)(2). Thus, the lapse of an option to acquire property that would be a capital asset in the taxpayer's hands will give rise to a capital loss. Treas. Reg. § 1.1234-1(b). The loss on the lapse of an option under § 1234 is not deductible, however, unless it is allowed under § 165. Treas. Reg. §§ 1.1234-1(f) and 1.1234-1(g) example (2). This latter aspect of § 1234 prevents a taxpayer from obtaining ordinary loss treatment simply by allowing the option to lapse rather than transferring the option for no consideration. In the absence of § 1234, ordinary loss treatment would result on the lapse of such an option because the sale or exchange requirement of § 1222 would not otherwise be satisfied.

The grantor of an option typically is treated as receiving ordinary income in an amount equal to the premium paid for the option if the option lapses without exercise. Treas. Reg. § 1.1234-1(b). The premium is included in the grantor's gross income when the option lapses rather than when the premium is received. Section 1234 modifies the character of the income attributable to the grantor and provides that, in certain circumstances, the premium received is treated as short-term capital gain on the lapse of an option to purchase property. I.R.C. § 1234(b)(1). Property for this purpose is limited, however, to stock and securities, commodities, and commodity futures. I.R.C. § 1234(b)(2)(B).

(c) Amounts Received on the Cancellation of a Lease

I.R.C. § 1241

Under § 1241, amounts received by a lessee for the cancellation of a lease are considered amounts received in exchange for the lease. I.R.C. § 1241. Thus, § 1241 represents a codification of the judicial decisions that had held that the extinguishment doctrine did not apply to amounts received by a lessee for the cancellation of a lease. *See Commissioner v. McCue Bros. & Drummond, Inc.*, 210 F.2d 752 (2d Cir. 1954); *Commissioner v. Ray*, 210 F.2d 390 (5th Cir. 1954); *Commissioner v. Golonsky*, 200 F.2d 72 (3d Cir. 1952). Such amounts are subject to favorable capital gain treatment assuming that the lease is a capital asset in the taxpayer's hands and the taxpayer has held the lease for more than one year. Importantly, § 1241 applies to leases of both real and personal property. Treas. Reg. § 1.1241-1(a). In addition, a payment for the partial cancellation of a lease falls within § 1241 "if the cancellation relates to a severable economic unit, such as a portion of the premises covered by a lease, [or] a reduction in the unexpired term of a lease . . . ." Treas. Reg. § 1.1241-1(b). However, payments received for other modifications of leases are not treated as amounts received for cancellation of a lease under § 1241. Finally, § 1241 has no application in determining whether the lease is a capital asset in the taxpayer's hands even though its cancellation qualifies as an exchange. Treas. Reg. § 1.1241-1(a).

Example:

T leases office space from his landlord, L, for a term of 10 years at $100,000 per year. Although the grant of the leasehold interest by L to T is the transfer of a property interest under state law, the lease is not deemed to be the sale or exchange of a capital asset and the rental payments due to L are ordinary income to L. Five years into the lease, L approaches T and tells him that he has a prospective tenant who will pay $200,000 per year for the leasehold space. Consequently, L will pay T the sum of $150,000 for the cancellation of his lease. The $150,000 is treated as an amount received in exchange for the lease agreement under § 1241. Because T has held the lease for more than one year and assuming that the lease is a capital asset in T's hands, the amounts received are long-term capital gain.

Section 1241 also applies to any amounts received by a distributor of goods on the cancellation of the distributor's agreement if the distributor had a substantial capital investment in the distributorship. A distributorship agreement under § 1241 applies only to the marketing or marketing and servicing of goods. Treas. Reg. § 1.1241-1(c). It does not apply to agreements for selling intangible property or for rendering personal services. A substantial capital investment in a distributorship must be reflected in physical assets such as inventories of tangible goods, equipment, machinery, storage facilities, or similar property. An investment is not considered substantial unless it consists of a significant fraction or more of the facilities for storing, transporting, processing, or otherwise dealing with the goods distributed, or consists of a substantial inventory of such goods. Id.

(d) Amounts Received on the Cancellation of Certain Property Rights

I.R.C. § 1234A

Section 1234A provides that gain or loss attributable to the cancellation, lapse, expiration or other termination of a right or obligation with respect to property that is, or would be upon acquisition, a capital asset in the hands of the taxpayer will be treated as gain or loss from the sale of a capital asset. The purpose of this provision is to prohibit the application of the extinguishment doctrine in certain transactions, thus eliminating an election on the part of taxpayers to obtain capital gain or ordinary loss treatment depending on whether the taxpayer sold the property or allowed the right to lapse. As stated in the legislative history:

> The Committee believes that some transactions, such as settlements of contracts to deliver a capital asset, are economically equivalent to a sale or exchange of such contracts since the value of any asset is the present value of the future income that such asset will produce. In addition, to the extent that present law treats modifications of property rights as not being a sale or exchange, present law effectively provides, in many cases, taxpayers with an election to treat the transaction as giving rise to capital gain, subject to more favorable rates than ordinary income, or an ordinary loss that can offset higher-taxed ordinary income and not be subject to limitations on use of capital losses. The effect of an election can be achieved by selling the property right if the resulting transaction results in a gain or providing for the extinguishment of the property right if the resulting transaction results in a loss.

H.R. Rep. No. 148, 105th Cong., 1st Sess. 453 (1997). The provision also eliminated the uncertainty surrounding the application of the extinguishment doctrine in connection with the modification of property rights.

Like § 1241, § 1234A applies to leases of both real and personal property but has broader application. For example, and according to the legislative history, amounts received by a lessor from a lessee to release the lessee from a requirement that the premise be restored on termination of the lease would give rise to capital gain treatment if the lease represented a capital asset in the hands of the lessor. H.R. Rep. No. 148, 105th Cong., 1st Sess. 454 (1997) (citing *Billy Rose's Diamond Horseshoe, Inc. v. United States*, 448 F.2d 549 (2d Cir. 1971), and *Sirbo Holdings, Inc. v. Commissioner*, 509 F.2d 1220 (2d Cir. 1975), as situations in which capital gain treatment was denied because there was no sale or exchange). The legislative history also noted that § 1234A would apply to the forfeiture of a down payment under a contract to purchase stock. *Id.* (citing *United States Freight Co. v. United States*, 422 F.2d 887 (Ct. Cl. 1970) (holding that such a forfeiture was an ordinary loss)). Similarly, if the lease is an asset held by the lessor in the lessor's trade or business, the transaction will be treated as the sale of § 1231 property that may give rise to capital gain treatment. As these examples of the application of § 1234A illustrate, § 1234A applies to lessors as well as lessees and applies to modifications of a lease that would not give rise to a partial termination or cancellation under § 1241.

PROBLEMS FOR DISCUSSION

Problem 2-6. How would *Pounds* come out under § 1234A?

Problem 2-7. Does § 1234A make the disappearing asset issue irrelevant? If so, why enact § 1234A instead of changing "sale or exchange" in § 1222 to "disposition?" If not, what is left?

(e) Miscellaneous Statutory Sales

Other statutory provisions also provide for sale or exchange treatment in situations that might not otherwise rise to the level of a sale or exchange. Such provisions include the following:

1. Certain distributions of property from a corporation to its shareholders are deemed to be sales or exchanges, thereby giving rise to capital gain or loss. For example, the distribution of property from a corporation that has no earnings and profits to its shareholders in excess of the shareholder's basis will be treated as gain from the sale or exchange of those shares. I.R.C. § 301(c)(3).

2. Gain or loss on the distribution of property by a partnership to a partner in certain circumstances is treated as gain or loss from the sale or exchange of the partnership interest of the distributee partner. I.R.C. § 731(a).

3. The transfer of all substantial rights in a patent by a holder of that patent is treated as the sale or exchange of a capital asset despite the fact that the payments received are contingent on the "productivity, use, or disposition" of the patent. I.R.C. § 1235(a)(2). For a discussion of § 1235, see § 3 of Chapter 7.

4. Amounts received by the holder on retirement of certain debt instruments are treated as having been received in exchange for that instrument. I.R.C. § 1271. Thus, the holder of a debt instrument with a basis less than its face may recognize capital gain upon the payment of the debt instrument.

5. In addition, several provisions of the Code specify that certain transactions are not to be treated as a sale or exchange. For example, the transfer of a franchise, trademark, or trade name is not treated as a sale or exchange of a capital asset if the taxpayer retains significant power, right, or continuing interest with respect to the property transferred. I.R.C. § 1253(a). For a discussion of § 1253, *see* § 3 of Chapter 7.

§ 5. HOLDING PERIOD

I.R.C. § 1223

Treas. Reg. §§ 1.1223-1(a), (b), and (f)

§ 5.01 Overview

The preferential income tax rates applicable to net capital gain for a noncorporate taxpayer are available only in connection with gain from the sale or exchange of capital assets held by the taxpayer for more than one year. This requirement is the result of the rather convoluted definitional provisions of § 1222.

Specifically, long-term capital gain is defined as "gain from the sale or exchange of a capital asset held for more than 1 year, . . ." I.R.C. § 1222(3). Similarly, long-term capital loss is defined as "loss from the sale or exchange of a capital asset held for more than 1 year, ..." I.R.C. § 1222(4). Net capital gain, the amount for which the preferential tax rates are available, is defined as the excess of net long-term capital gain over net short-term capital loss. I.R.C. § 1222(11). Net capital gain can only result if the taxpayer has realized long-term capital gain in excess of both any long-term capital loss and any net short-term capital loss. Thus, the availability of the preferential tax rates requires the existence of gain from the sale or exchange of a capital asset held for more than one year. Because long-term capital gain is potentially taxed at preferential rates, it is virtually always the taxpayer, rather than the government, who is seeking to prove that a holding period of more than one year has been met at the time that a capital asset is sold or exchanged.

The length of the required holding period to achieve the favorable capital gain tax treatment has varied over the years from a low of six months to a high of two years. Given the reasons for granting favorable tax treatment to long-term capital gains, one year would appear to be the minimum appropriate holding period. The most commonly cited theory for providing favorable capital gain treatment is that the selling taxpayer is recognizing income that has accrued over a period of time but that must be reported in one year and is, therefore, unfairly "bunched" into one year and subject to higher taxes under the progressive rate system. A holding period of more than one year ensures that at least two taxable years are involved in the appreciation of the asset upon which the taxable gain is reported. *See* H.R. Rep. No. 658, 94th Cong., 2d Sess. 342 (1976) (six month holding period cannot be justified by any unfairness resulting from the bunching problem since the tax liability for all other types of income is determined on an annual basis). A more rational approach, given the underlying "bunching of income" theory, would be to gradually decrease the tax rate based upon the number of years an asset is held prior to sale. Such an approach has periodically been considered by Congress but discarded in favor of administrative simplicity represented by the bright-line test of "more than one year."

§ 5.02 Basic Rules for Determining Holding Period

Whether a capital asset has been held for more than one year at the time of a sale or exchange would appear to invite a straightforward determination of the date of acquisition compared to the date of sale. In many cases it is that simple. However, there are a myriad of special rules, regulatory and administrative interpretations, and statutory rules and exceptions that must be superimposed upon the basic calculation. Once the interplay of these various rules is in focus, there may be significant planning opportunities allowing a taxpayer to take advantage of a given rule or exception with a view toward ultimately achieving long-term capital gain.

The fundamental rule relating to the holding period of a capital asset is that the holding period is computed by excluding the day upon which the taxpayer acquires the property, but including the day upon which the taxpayer disposes of the property. Rev. Rul. 70-598, 1970-2 C.B. 168 (stating that "in computing a period of 'years' or 'months' prescribed, in a contract or statute, >from' or >after' a designated day, date, act, or other event, the day thus designated is excluded and the last day of the prescribed period is included, unless a different intent is definitely evidenced"); Rev. Rul. 66-7, 1966-1 C.B. 188 (same).

Example 1:

> T acquired a vacant lot as an investment on June 5, 2002, with the closing of the acquisition taking place at 10:00 a.m. On June 5, 2003, T sells the property at a gain, and the closing of the sale takes place at 4:00 p.m. in the afternoon. Although T has technically held the property for 365 (assuming no leap year) days and six hours, he would not be entitled to long-term capital gain. He is treated as acquiring the property on June 6, 2002 and selling it June 5, 2003. Thus, he has not held the asset for more than one year under the applicable rules.

See Frederick v. United States, 68-1 U.S.T.C. & 9195 (1968) (stock acquired on April 10, 1963 at approximately 10 a.m. and sold on October 10, 1963 at 11:20 a.m. not held for more than six months). *See Caspe v. United States*, 694 F.2d 1116 (8th Cir. 1982) (securities purchased on November 30, 1972, and sold on May 31, 1973, not held for more than six months); *Fogel v. Commissioner*, 203 F.2d 347 (5th Cir. 1953) (property purchased on June 19, 1945, and sold on December 19, 1945, not held for more than six months).

For transactions executed over a stock exchange, the trade date rather than the settlement date controls the determination of the holding period. Rev. Rul. 70-598, 1970-2 C.B. 168. Consequently, the holding period begins the day after the purchase order is executed and ends on the day that the sale order is executed, regardless of the settlement date for the acquisition or sale. Interestingly, the holding period may end prior to the time that gain is realized on the sale by a cash method taxpayer.

PROBLEM FOR DISCUSSION

Problem 2-8. In Rev. Ruls. 66-7 and 70-598, what sense does it make to measure holding periods by months so that a six-month period from January 1 to July 1 is only 181 days while one from July 1 to January 1 is 184 days?

§ 5.03 Split Holding Periods

Treas. Reg. § 1.1223-3

Complications arise in determining the holding period of a capital asset when the asset was acquired gradually or in several stages. For example, when a newly constructed building is sold, the selling taxpayer may have held the underlying land for more than one year, but the building for less than one year. In addition, construction of a portion of a new building may have been completed more than one year ago and, therefore, held for more than one year. Similarly, if a partnership interest is gradually acquired over time, but sold in its entirety, a portion of the interest sold may have been held for more than one year and a portion for one year or less. Likewise, a taxpayer's position in a given marketable security may have been gradually acquired so that a portion of the block sold has been held for more than one year, a portion not.

In the case of property recently constructed, or under construction, at the time of its sale, the rule is that the asset may be bifurcated with the portion of the asset held for more than one year yielding long-term capital gain and that held for one year or less yielding short-term capital gain. Thus, the portion of the sale price allocated to the land beneath a constructed building, the land having been held for more than one year, and any portion of the building completed more than one year prior to sale, would qualify for long-term capital gain treatment. For example in Rev. Rul. 75-524, 1975-2 C.B. 342, the Service considered a situation in which a newly constructed building with a cost basis of $100x was sold on December 20, 1972. A portion of the building had been completed as of June 19, 1972, and that portion of the building had a cost basis of $30x. The Service concluded that a portion of the building, with a cost basis of $30x, had been held for more than six months and, therefore, the gain allocable to that portion of the building was characterized as long-term capital gain. *See also Paul v. Commissioner*, 206 F.2d 763 (3d Cir. 1953) (concluding that the portion of the gain properly allocable to that part of the building that was erected more than six months before the sale may be given long-term capital gain treatment); *Russo v. Commissioner*, 68 T.C. 135 (1977) (although allocation of gain is permissible, taxpayer must prove with accuracy the cost of the completed portion of the building); *Aagaard v. Commissioner*, 56 T.C. 191 (1971), *acq.* (where 40 percent of a newly constructed building was completed six months prior to its sale, 60 percent of the capital gain attributable to the sale of the building was short-term); *Draper v. Commissioner*, 32 T.C. 545 (1959) (adopting the allocation approach provided for by the Third Circuit in *Paul v. Commissioner* and overturning its earlier decision in *Paul v. Commissioner*, 18 T.C. 601 (1952)), *acq.* on another issue.

The rules relating to the sale of a partnership interest are complex. The sale or exchange of a partnership interest may give rise to ordinary income, capital gain, or a combination of both, pursuant to the rules of §§ 741 and 751. To the extent that capital gain is recognized, such gain may either be short-term or long-term depending upon the holding period of the partnership interest. If the partnership interest was acquired over a period of time, so that some portion of the interest was held for more than one year, and some for one year or less, then the gain or loss realized on the sale of all or a part of the partnership interest is bifurcated into long-term and short-term gain or loss, based upon the portion of the partnership interest held, respectively, for more than one year and that held for less than one year. Treas. Reg. § 1.1223-3(c). This allocation is based on the fair market value of the partnership interest. According to the Regulations,

> The portion of a partnership interest to which a holding period relates shall be determined by reference to a fraction, the numerator of which is the fair market value of the portion of the partnership interest received in the transaction to which the holding period relates, and the denominator of which is the fair market value of the entire partnership interest (determined immediately after the transaction).

Treas. Reg. § 1.1223-3(b)(1). As described below, the determination of the holding period of a partnership interest is made somewhat more complex as a result of the tacking of holding periods under § 1223(1).

In a great many partnerships or limited liability companies that are taxed as partnerships, the interests of the partners or members may shift, or "flip-flop." For example, a "money partner" and a "service partner" may share partnership profits on a 50/50 basis until the money partner receives a distribution of his capital, plus a specified rate of return, at which time the profit ratio "flip-flops" so that the money partner receives only 25 percent of any additional profit and the promoter or service partner receives 75 percent. If the partnership interests of the service partner were sold less than one year following the "flip-flop," the Service could theoretically argue that the 25 percent increase was held for less than one year and, therefore, the portion of the sale price attributable to that increase is short-term, rather than long-term, capital gain. The taxpayer's response is that the interest was held from the outset and merely matured at the time that the money partner achieved "payout." The Regulations resolve the issue favorably for the taxpayer by providing that a change in partnership percentage interests resulting from a "flip-flop" or from a disproportionate distribution to one partner does not affect the holding period of the partners in their partnership interests. Treas. Reg. § 1.1223-3(f) example (7).

A similar problem arises in the sale of a group of securities that were acquired at different times. In such a situation, the gain or loss realized on the sale of the group must be allocated among the individual securities in determining the long-term or short-term character thereof. Where a taxpayer is unable to identify the acquisition date of the individual securities sold, the securities sold are deemed to be the first acquired. Treas. Reg. § 1.1223-1(i) (referring to Treas. Reg. § 1.1012-1(c)).

Example 2:

T acquires 100 shares of General Motors stock on May 1, 2001 and an additional 100 shares on June 1, 2001. The shares are physically retained by T's broker. On May 15, 2002, T tells his broker to sell 150 of his shares, without designating to the broker which particular shares are to be transferred. All 150 shares are sold at a gain. The gain on 100 of the shares sold will be long-term capital gain in the amount by which the net proceeds attributable to such 100 shares exceeds the amount paid for the 100 shares acquired on May 1, 2001. The gain on the remaining 50 shares will constitute short-term capital gain to the extent that the amount of proceeds attributable to the sale of such 50 shares exceeds the basis of one-half of the shares acquired on June 1, 2001.

Finally, determining the holding period of property that is or has been subject to an option to purchase prior to its acquisition is also complicated. It is clear that the period during which a taxpayer holds an option prior to its exercise cannot be added to the holding period of the property acquired. *Helvering v. San Joaquin Fruit & Inv. Co.*, 297 U.S. 496 (1936) (land is acquired when the option to purchase is exercised, not when the option is purchased); *Becker v. Commissioner*, 378 F.2d 767 (3d Cir. 1967) (period during which option for stock held not included in the holding period of the stock itself); *Commissioner v. Cummings*, 77 F.2d 670 (5th Cir. 1935) (stock acquired upon exercise of option is considered "new property" acquired on the date of exercise); *Weir v. Commissioner*, 10 T.C. 996 (1948), *aff'd per curiam*, 173 F.2d 222 (3d Cir. 1949) ("the time during which an option to purchase is held unexercised is not to be included within the holding period of the property acquired by use of such option"). *See also Hoven v. Commissioner*, 56 T.C. 50 (1971), *acq.* (property not acquired until contract of sale executed and taxpayer acquired benefits and burdens of ownership). The holding period for property acquired through the exercise of an option begins when the taxpayer actually exercises the option and acquires the property and not when the option itself is granted. An exception may apply, however, if it is clear at the time the option is granted that the option will be exercised and the burdens and benefits of the underlying property are effectively passed to the option holder on the date that the option is granted. *Merrill v. Commissioner*, 40 T.C. 66 (1963), *aff'd*, 336 F.2d 771 (9th Cir. 1964) (property considered acquired when buyer took possession and began paying taxes and seller had no further obligations even though legal title had not yet passed); Rev. Rul. 75-563, 1975-2 C.B. 199 (the granting of the irrevocable written option treated as a sale of property).

Conversely, the holding period of property does not terminate by a grant of an option to acquire the property. However, a property owner seeking to extend his holding period to more than one year by granting the prospective purchaser an option to purchase (rather than an immediate outright sale) may have his holding period truncated if the option holder effectively owns the property during the option period. *Martin v. Commissioner*, 379 F.2d 282 (6th Cir. 1967) (lease with option to purchase was considered an installment sales contract when its terms were specifically designed to provide the taxpayer with long-term capital gain treatment).

Example 3:

> T owns a parcel of unimproved real estate that he has held for six months. T is approached by a developer desirous of acquiring the property for the purposes of developing it into a residential project. Rather than sell the property outright, T enters into a lease of the property for six months and two days, at the end of which term the developer has the right to purchase the property at a fixed price. T requires that 50 percent of the fixed purchase price be paid to him as non-refundable option money, that will be forfeited if the sale does not close, but be applied to the purchase price if it does. During the lease term, the developer must pay all insurance and taxes relating to the property and the developer is permitted to begin the construction of infrastructure, which will serve the residential community, including the installation of water, sewer, and roads. Six months and two days following the grant of the option, the developer purchases the property, receiving credit for the 50 percent option payment. Although T technically held title to the property for more than one year prior to his sale, the burdens and benefits of ownership passed to the developer at the time the option was granted. It was clear at the time the option was granted that the developer would exercise the option because of the extraordinarily large option payment that would otherwise have been forfeited and because of his investment in the infrastructure costs for the property.

§ 5.04 Holding Period for Inherited Property

I.R.C. § 1223(9)

Property acquired from a decedent generally qualifies for long-term capital gain treatment even if it is sold within one year following the date of death. I.R.C. § 1223(9)(B). This rule applies only if the property is included in the decedent's estate and takes as its basis the fair market value of the property at the time of the decedent's death. I.R.C. § 1223(9)(A). Although such property may be subject to federal estate tax, any pre-death appreciation in value is eliminated for federal income tax purposes by the receipt of a fair market value basis in the hands of the grantee. In addition, any appreciation in the value of the inherited property following the decedent's death may then be realized and recognized as long-term capital gain even though the sale of such property takes place less than one year following the death of the decedent. These rules do not apply, however, to property that represents income in respect of a decedent. I.R.C. § 1014(c).

§ 5.05 Tacked Holding Periods

In determining whether a taxpayer has met the one-year holding period that may give rise to the preferential capital gain tax rates, there are numerous situations in which the taxpayer may add to his actual holding period the holding period of a prior owner of the property sold or exchanged of the holding period of property exchanged for the property subsequently sold. The ability to include the holding period of a prior owner or of other property is called "tacking."

(a) Tacking Permitted in Substituted Basis Transactions

I.R.C. § 1223(1)

Section 1223 sets forth 16 specific instances in which a taxpayer's actual holding period may be increased to include that of a prior owner or other property. The most important of these are the first two. Section 1223(1) provides that if a taxpayer receives property in an exchange, and the basis of such property is determined in whole or in part by reference to the property relinquished in the exchange, then the property received will include the holding period of the property relinquished.[36] In simpler terms, if the property received in an exchange has, in whole or in part, a "substituted basis," the holding period of the relinquished property can be added to that of the replacement property.

Importantly, this provision applies only if the relinquished property was a capital asset or § 1231 property. This provision prevents taxpayers from obtaining capital gain treatment by selling the stock of a newly created corporation to which a noncapital asset was contributed in anticipation of its sale. *See Commissioner v. Gracey*, 159 F.2d 324 (5th Cir. 1947) (permitting tacking of the holding period of a

---

[36] Section 1223(1) specifically provides that an involuntary conversion described in § 1033 is considered an exchange of the property converted for the property acquired to replace it. I.R.C. § 1223(1)(A). *See* Rev. Rul. 72-451, 1972-2 C.B. 480 (allowing the tacking of holding periods for replacement property following a casualty under § 1223(1)(A)). Distributions of stock or securities under § 355 are also treated as an exchange for purposes of § 1223(1). I.R.C. § 1223(1)(B).

noncapital asset to that of stock received in exchange for the contribution of the property to a corporation; resulting gain on sale of stock characterized as long-term capital gain).

Section 1223(1) applies to tax-free exchanges of property under §§ 351, 721, and 1031. For example, if property is transferred to a partnership in exchange for a partnership interest, no gain or loss is recognized on the transfer, and the partner typically receives a basis in his partnership interest equal to the basis of the property transferred. I.R.C. §§ 721 and 722. Provided that the property contributed to the partnership was a capital asset or § 1231 property, the holding period of the contributed property will be tacked to the holding period of the partnership interest under § 1223(1) because the basis of the partnership interest is itself based on the basis of the contributed property. When both cash and property are contributed to a partnership in exchange for a partnership interest, the basis of the partnership interest must be bifurcated to properly account for the different holding periods involved.

Example 4:

> T contributes cash of $5,000 and a capital asset with a fair market value of $10,000 but with a basis of only $5,000 to Partnership TUV in return for a 50 percent interest in TUV. T held the capital asset for two years prior to its contribution to the partnership. After the exchange, the basis of T's partnership interest is $10,000 and the fair market value of the partnership interest is $15,000. Because T received one-third of her interest in exchange for the $5,000 cash contribution, the holding period of one-third of her partnership interest starts the day after the contribution. Because T received two-thirds of her partnership interest in exchange for the contribution of the capital asset, the holding period of two-thirds of her partnership interest is two years under § 1223(1).

See Treas. Reg. § 1.1223-3(f) Example (1).

In the corporate context, a shareholder who receives stock of a corporation in a corporate formation or a corporate reorganization that is not taxable pursuant to § 351 or § 354 takes a basis in his shares equal to the basis of the property conveyed to the corporation in exchange for the stock received pursuant to § 358. Thus, the holding period of the shares received includes that of the property transferred to the corporation issuing the shares in the formation or reorganization under § 1223(1).

Section 1223(1) also applies in connection with a distribution of property in liquidation of a partner's interest in a partnership under § 731(a). Because property received in liquidation of a partner's interest in a partnership takes the basis of the distributee partner's partnership interest under § 732(b), the holding period of the partnership interest may be tacked to the holding period of the distributed property under § 1223(1).

It is important to note that in order for the holding period of the relinquished property to be tacked to that of the replacement property, the basis of the replacement property must be determined only "in whole or in part" by reference to the relinquished property. I.R.C. § 1223(1). Thus, for example, if boot is received in a like-kind exchange so that the basis of the relinquished property is increased by the amount of boot recognized pursuant to § 1031(d), the holding period of the relinquished property is still tacked to that of the replacement property because the basis of the replacement property is determined "in part" by reference to the basis of the relinquished property.

Example 5:

T owns a parcel of real estate that is a capital asset and has a basis of $40,000 and a value of $100,000. He exchanges the property for like-kind replacement property with a value of $75,000 and receives $25,000 in cash. Under § 1031(b), T must recognize $25,000 of the $60,000 of gain realized on the exchange as a result of the receipt of "boot." Under § 1031(d), the basis of the replacement property is the basis in the relinquished property ($40,000) decreased by the amount of cash received ($25,000) and increased by the amount of "boot" recognized in the transaction ($25,000). Thus, the basis of the replacement property is $40,000. The holding period for the replacement property includes that of the relinquished property because the basis of the replacement property is determined "in part" by reference to that of the relinquished property.

(b) Tacking Permitted in Carryover Basis Transactions

I.R.C. § 1223(2)

Section 1223(2) provides that when a taxpayer takes a "carryover" basis from a prior owner, then the subject property includes the holding period of such prior owner. Specifically, the statute provides that the holding period includes "[t]he period for which such property was held by any other person, if . . . such property has, for the purpose of determining gain or loss from the sale or exchange, the same basis in whole or in part in his hands as it would have in the hands of such other person." I.R.C. § 1223(2). The Regulations provide an example involving the most obvious case of a carryover basis, that of property received as a gift which has a value in excess of the donor's basis at the time of its receipt by the donee. Treas. Reg. § 1.1223-1(b). In such a situation, § 1015 provides that the basis of the gift in the donee's hands is equal to the donor's basis. I.R.C. § 1015(a). Because the basis of the property in the hands of the donee is determined by the basis of the property in the hands of the donor, the donor's holding period may be tacked onto that of the donee.

Example 6:

T made a gift to her son, S, of marketable securities with a value of $40,000. Her basis in the shares was $20,000. T paid a federal gift tax on the gift of $8,000. Pursuant to §§ 1015(a) and 1015(d), S receives a basis in the shares equal to that of his mother ($20,000) increased by that portion of the gift tax paid that bears the same ratio to the gift tax paid as the appreciation in the property bears to the fair market value of the property ($4,000). Because his $24,000 basis in the shares is determined "in part" by reference to the basis of the shares in the hands of his mother, he can tack his mother's holding period for the shares to his own holding period under

§ 1223(2). If, for example, his mother's holding period was more than one year, S could sell the shares on the date of the gift, and his gain of $16,000 would be characterized as long-term capital gain.

Section 1015 also provides, however, that if the donor's basis in the property exceeds its fair market value at the time of the gift, the basis for determining loss is the fair market value of the property at the time of the gift rather than the donor's basis. Because the donee's basis would not be determined in whole or in part by reference to the basis of the property in the hands of the donor, the tacking provisions of § 1223(2) would not apply. Nevertheless, tacking has been allowed in connection with property acquired in a part sale/part gift even when the basis in the hands of the donee is the price paid rather than the donor's basis. *Citizen's Nat'l Bank v. United States*, 417 F.2d 675 (5th Cir. 1969). *See also Turner v. Commissioner*, 49 T.C. 356 (1968), *aff'd per curiam*, 410 F.2d 752 (6th Cir. 1969).

There are many other situations, aside from property transferred by gift, in which the basis of the transferor in a given property is "carried over" to the transferee. Property transferred to a corporation in a tax-free formation or reorganization is carried over from the shareholder to the corporation. I.R.C. § 362. If the corporation is a C corporation, the holding period may be largely irrelevant because the benefit of favorable long-term capital gain tax rates is not available to C corporations. For S corporations, however, the long-term capital gain recognized by a corporation is taxable to its shareholders as such. Consequently, the holding period of property contributed by its shareholders is relevant to an S corporation and § 1223(2) allows the S corporation to tack the shareholder's holding period to that of the corporation.

Section 1223(2) also applies in the context of property distributed from a subsidiary corporation to its parent. Because the basis of property distributed from a subsidiary to its parent carries over to the parent under § 334(b), the holding period of the subsidiary in such property is tacked to that of the parent. Once again, this may well be irrelevant as it relates to C corporations because of the inapplicability of the favorable capital gain rates. In addition, a qualified S corporation subsidiary is treated as a division of its parent, and no intercorporate transfers are deemed to occur for tax purposes.

In the case of partnerships, the basis of property contributed to a partnership in exchange for a partnership interest is carried over from the transferring partner to the partnership. I.R.C. § 723. Consequently, the holding period of the property in the hands of the partner is tacked to that of the partnership. Conversely, a nonliquidating distribution of property other than money from a partnership to a partner results in a basis carryover from the partnership to the distributee partner. I.R.C. § 732(a). Once again, the carryover basis results in a tacking of the partnership's holding period to that of the partner with respect to the property distributed.

(c) Miscellaneous Tacking Provisions

The other subsections of § 1223 cover specific situations permitting or denying tacking of holding periods, some of which are relatively narrow in scope and some of which are broad. The most important of these are as follows:

(1) Section 1091 prohibits the deduction of any loss on the sale of stock or securities when substantially identical stock or securities are purchased within a period 30 days prior or 30 days after the date of the sale. In such case, the basis of the purchased shares must be adjusted to account for the disallowed loss. Under § 1223, the holding period of the replacement stock or securities includes that of the stock or securities the loss from the sale of which was not deductible. I.R.C. § 1223(3).

(2) The holding period of stock acquired via a nontaxable stock dividend includes the period during which the taxpayer held the stock with respect to which the stock dividend was issued. I.R.C. § 1223(4).

(3) The holding period of stock or securities acquired by exercise of stock rights or options held by the taxpayer does not include the time during which such rights or options were held. The holding period of such stock or securities begins only on the date of exercise of such rights or options. I.R.C. § 1223(5). However, a taxpayer who takes delivery of a commodity pursuant to a commodity futures contract may include in his holding period for the commodity the time during which the futures contract was held so long as the futures contract was a capital asset in his hands. I.R.C. § 1223(7). The same tacking rule applies to a securities futures contract. I.R.C. § 1223(14).

(4) Real property sold by a seller who provides financing and receives a note from the purchaser may ultimately be reacquired by the seller as a result of foreclosure of the mortgage or deed of trust securing such note. In such a situation, § 1038 provides the seller tax relief on the foreclosure of the property and the cancellation of the note. In such cases, the period during which the seller held the property prior to the sale to the defaulting debtor is tacked to the holding period beginning with the date of reacquisition by the seller. Treas. Reg. § 1.1038-1(g)(3). The holding period in the hands of the reacquiring seller does not, however, include the period during which it was held by the defaulting buyer.

Example 7:

T sells his ranch to S for $1,000,000. The purchase price is paid $250,000 down and $750,000 in the form of S's promissory note, which is secured by a first mortgage on the property. At the time of the sale, T has held the property for eight months. After successfully making her first annual payment on the note, S defaults on the payment due on the second anniversary of the note. T forecloses and reacquires title 30 months following the original sale date. He holds the property for an additional six months and sells it to a separate buyer, X, for cash. T's holding period for the property at the time of his sale to X is 14 months (the eight months he originally held the property plus the six months he held it after foreclosure, but not including the 30 months during which S held title to the property). Consequently, the sale to X would qualify for long-term capital gain treatment.

REVENUE RULING 62-140

1962-2 C.B. 181

In November 1960, a taxpayer purchased, for $1 each, rights issued by a corporation entitling him, upon payment of $99, to subscribe to a debenture to be issued by such corporation. On December 1, 1960, the taxpayer subscribed for such debenture which was issued on December 10, 1960. The debenture contained a clause providing that its holder might receive one share of common stock of the issuing corporation upon surrender of the debenture, accompanied by payment of $50. The taxpayer presented the debenture, accompanied by payment of $50 and received one share of common stock. Held, (a) No gain or loss was realized upon the surrender of the debenture and payment of $50 for a share of common stock in accordance with the terms contained in the debenture. (b) Each share of stock acquired has a split holding period for purposes of determining long-term or short-term capital gain or loss, that part of the taxpayer's property in each share of stock which is attributable to his ownership of the debenture to be treated as held beginning with and including the date on which the right to acquire the debenture was exercised, section 1223(6) of the Internal Revenue Code of 1954 and section 1.1223-1 (f) of the Income Tax Regulations, and, and that part of the taxpayer's property in each share of stock which is attributable to the additional cash investment required for the acquisition of the stock to be treated as held beginning with the date following the date of acquisition. . . .

It will be necessary to determine the portion of the taxpayer's property in the stock which is attributable to each component of the investment where the stock is disposed of at a time when, in accordance with holding (b) above, there may be both long-term and short-term capital gain or loss from disposition. For example, assume that the fair market value of one share of stock on the date of conversion is $200. Of the taxpayer's $150 basis for each share of stock, $100 is his basis for that portion attributable to his ownership of the debenture and $50 is his basis for that portion attributable to the additional cash investment. Since the market value of the stock was $200 on the date of conversion, it may fairly be said that the portion of such value attributable to his ownership of the debenture was $150. . . . Thus, 150/200 of the taxpayer's property in the stock is attributable to his ownership of the debenture and 50/200 of the taxpayer's property in the stock is attributable to his additional cash investment. . . . The following table illustrates the manner of computing the gain or loss attributable to the taxpayer's ownership of the debenture (long-term) and his gain or loss attributable to the additional cash investment (short-term) . . . :

1. Total amount realized from disposition of stock	200	240	180	150	120	80
2. Portion of amount realized attributable to taxpayer's ownership of debenture. [150/200 of amount shown on line 1]	150	180	135	112.50	90	60

3. Gain (or loss) attributable to debenture, *i.e.*, long-term gain (or loss) realized from disposition. [Amount shown on line 2 less $100, the portion of the tax-payer's basis in stock attributable to the debenture]	50	80	35	12.50	(10)	(40)
4. Portion of amount realized attributable to taxpayer's additional cash investment. [50/200 of amount shown on line 1]	50	60	45	37.50	30	20
5. Gain (or loss) attributable to additional cash investment, *i.e.*, short-term gain (or loss) realized from disposition. [Amount shown on line 4 less $50, the portion of taxpayer's basis for the stock attributable to additional cash investment]	0	10	(5.)	(12.50)	(20)	(30)

NOTE

Although the stock received by exercise of the conversion privilege receives a "tacked" holding period so that the entire appreciation attributable is long-term capital gain when combined, the holding period of the bond and stock exceeds one year, there is no tacking for the holding period of the option, either for the price paid for the option or for the appreciation attributable to that investment. Thus the stock acquired has a split holding period, measured in part by the conversion portion and in part by the option portion.

PROBLEM FOR DISCUSSION

Problem 2-9. In Rev. Rul. 62-140, is tacking the holding period for the conversion part consistent with not tacking for the warrant part? Is the allocation method consistent with the tacking holding? Under the principles of the Supreme Court's decision in *Cottage Savings*, why is there no realization on conversion?

§ 6. SECTION 1231 GAINS AND LOSSES

§ 6.01 Overview

I.R.C. §§ 1221(a)(2), 1231, 1245, 1250

As previously described, the definition of a capital asset under § 1221 excludes depreciable property used in a taxpayer's trade or business as well as real property used in a taxpayer's trade or business. I.R.C. § 1221(a)(2). If no other section of the Code applied to modify this definition, all gain or loss realized with respect to such property would result in ordinary income or ordinary loss. However, the realization of gain with respect to such property, particularly any real property, may be the result of appreciation over time. Consequently, the policy justifications for capital gain treatment might be thought to properly extend to any gain reflecting long-term appreciation in value.

Section 1231 modifies the application of § 1221 and extends capital gain or loss treatment to depreciable and real property used in a taxpayer's trade or business under certain circumstances. If such property has been held for more than one year at the time of its sale or exchange, the gain may be treated as though it resulted from a sale or exchange of a capital asset, resulting in long-term capital gain potentially afforded preferential tax treatment as net capital gain. I.R.C. § 1231(a)(1); Treas. Reg. §§ 1.1231-1(a) and 1.1231-1(b). As a result, such property is sometimes referred to as a "quasi-capital asset." In addition, if such property is held for more than one year and is sold at a loss, the loss may well retain its character as an ordinary, rather than a capital, loss and, therefore, be deductible against the ordinary income of the taxpayer. I.R.C. § 1231(a)(2); Treas. Reg. §§ 1.1231-1(a) and 1.1231-1(b). This potential for the same asset to yield capital gain if it has appreciated in value but an ordinary loss if has depreciated in value would appear to be very pro-taxpayer. In many situations, however, taxpayers must be aware of the exceptions, netting requirements and recapture provisions within § 1231 itself, as well as the application of other provisions of the Code, before being able to take advantage of the benefits available under § 1231.

In order to understand the application of § 1231, an examination of the historical development of this unusual provision provides insight into its current application. During the depression of the 1930s, the definition of a capital asset included property used in a taxpayer's trade or business. As a result, business owners at that time were reluctant to replace worn-out manufacturing equipment because the deductibility of losses on the sale or exchange of such equipment were limited by the capital loss disallowance provisions. Congress responded to this situation in 1938 by enacting the predecessor to § 1221(a)(2), which excluded business property from the definition of a capital asset. This exclusion was beneficial to taxpayers because it allowed business owners to deduct the losses on the sale or exchange of such property from their ordinary income. The government, thus, provided an economic incentive to replace worn-out equipment.

By 1942, however, the economic climate of the country had changed with the onset of World War II. Business assets, particularly those used in the shipping industry, were being condemned by the government and converted to wartime use. In addition, many privately owned vessels were sunk or destroyed, creating losses for their owners that were not covered by insurance. Congress enacted the predecessor to § 1231 in that year and permitted taxpayers to characterize gain on the condemnation of business property transferred to the government as capital gain and allowing taxpayers to characterize as ordinary any losses on the involuntary conversion or destruction of such property. The language of the statute, however, extended capital gain treatment not only to involuntary conversions of property by the government but also any sale or exchange of appreciated business property. When the war ended, the underlying rationale for allowing capital gain on the sale or exchange of business property largely disappeared. Nevertheless, capital gain and ordinary loss treatment remain available in connection with property falling within the scope of § 1231.

From 1942 through 1962, virtually all of the gain realized on the sale of § 1231 property was characterized as capital gain. Starting in 1962, the benefits of § 1231 have slowly been eroded. Currently, very little of the gain realized from the sale or exchange of such property is treated as capital gain and taxed at the most preferential tax rate available to non-corporate taxpayers under § 1(h).

The application of § 1231 was first significantly limited, particularly with respect to personal property, by the enactment of § 1245 in 1962. Section 1245 generally applies to personal property, regardless of whether the property is tangible or intangible. I.R.C. § 1245(a)(3). Section 1245 trumps § 1231 and requires that gain resulting from basis reductions attributable to depreciation deductions in prior years be "recaptured" and treated as ordinary income regardless of the provisions of § 1231.[37] Section 1245 achieves this result by requiring the taxpayer to treat as ordinary income the amount by which the lower of the recomputed basis of the property or the amount realized exceeds the adjusted basis of the property. I.R.C. § 1245(a)(1). The recomputed basis of the property is equal to its adjusted basis plus all deductions previously allowed for amortization of depreciation, including deductions under §§ 179, 179A, 190, and 193. I.R.C. §§ 1245(a)(2)(A) and 1245(a)(2)(C). Thus, only if personal property is sold or exchanged, typically for an amount in excess of its original cost basis, will that portion of the gain reflecting an increase in the value of the property over its original cost be eligible for capital gain treatment under § 1231. This result is in keeping with the policy justification for capital gain treatment as "typically involving the realization of appreciation in value accrued over a substantial period of time." *Commissioner v. Gillette Motor Transport, Inc.*, 364 U.S. 130, 134 (1960). However, § 1245 also applies to recovery as ordinary income any gain attributable to basis reductions under §§ 108(b) and 1017(b) due to discharge of indebtedness, income excluded from gross income under § 108(a). I.R.C. § 1017(d). In addition, if the basis of any property that is neither § 1245 nor § 1250 property is adjusted under §§ 108(b) and 1017(b), such property is to be treated as § 1245 property and the basis adjustments treated as a depreciation deductions potentially recaptured as ordinary income on any subsequent disposition.

The interplay of §§ 1231 and 1245 became considerably broadened with the enactment of § 197 in 1993. Section 197 permits taxpayers to amortize a number of acquired and self-created intangible assets over a period of 15 years but further provides that any intangible asset amortizable under § 197 is to be treated as property that is of a character subject to depreciation under § 167. I.R.C. § 197(f)(7); Treas. Reg. § 1.197-2(g)(8). Consequently, the sale of any amortizable § 197 intangible asset used in a taxpayer's trade or business and held for more than one year is governed by § 1231 but, because of § 1245, will yield capital gain only if the asset is sold at a price in excess of its original cost, with any gain attributable to basis reductions reflecting amortization deductions being recaptured as ordinary income.

---

[37] Importantly, if the gain on property is reported under the installment sale rules of § 453, all of the depreciation recapture is required to be recognized by the seller in the year of the sale rather than under the installment method. I.R.C. § 453(i).

Section 1245 also contains an interesting provision applicable only to § 197 intangible assets. Under this provision, if more than one § 197 intangible asset is sold as part of a transaction or a series of related transactions, the amount of depreciation recapture is determined as if all of the § 197 intangible assets were a single asset. I.R.C. § 1245(b)(8)(A). This rule prevents taxpayers from manipulating the amount of consideration among the § 197 intangible assets so as to reduce the amount of gain characterized as ordinary income. The legislative history provides the following example:

> In year 1, a taxpayer acquires two section 197 intangible assets for a total of $45. Asset A is assigned a cost basis of $15 and asset B is assigned a cost basis of $30. The allocation is irrelevant for amortization purposes, as the taxpayer will be entitled to a total of $3 per year ($45 divided by 15 years).
>
> In year 6, the basis of A is $10 and the basis of B is $20. Taxpayer sells the assets for an aggregate sale price of $45, resulting in gain of $15. The character of this gain depends on the recapture amount, which depends in turn on the relative sales prices of the individual assets. Taxpayer has claimed $5 of amortization, and therefore has $5 of recapture potential, with respect to A. Taxpayer has claimed $10 of amortization, and therefore has $10 of recapture potential, with respect to B.
>
> Under present law, if the sale proceeds are allocated $15 to A and $30 to B, the gain on assets A and B will be $5 and $10, respectively. These amounts match the recapture potential for each asset so the full amount of the gain will be recaptured as ordinary income. However, if the sale proceeds instead are allocated $25 to A and $20 to B, the full $15 will be recognized with respect to A, and only $5 (full recapture potential with respect to A) will be recaptured as ordinary income. The remaining $10 of gain attributable to A will be treated as capital gain. No gain (and thus no recapture) will be recognized with respect to Asset B, and only $5 of the $15 recapture potential is recognized.
>
> Under the Act, the taxpayer calculates recapture as if assets A and B were a single asset. For purposes of the calculation, the proceeds are $45 and the gain is $15. Because a total of $15 of amortization has been claimed with respect to assets A and B, the full $15 gain is recaptured as ordinary income.

Staff of the Joint Committee on Taxation, Description and Technical Explanation of the Conference Agreement of H.R. 6, Title XIII, The "Energy Tax Incentives Act of 2005," 80–81 (JCX-60-05).

Although the example suggests otherwise, this provision applies to the disposition of more than one § 197 intangible asset in the same or related transactions regardless of whether or not the assets were actually acquired in the same transaction. Thus, § 197 intangible assets acquired at different times and in different transactions, as well as self-created intangible assets amortizable under § 197, will be treated as a single asset for purposes of § 1245 if disposed of in the same or related transactions. Importantly, this rule does not apply to the disposition of any amortizable § 197 intangible asset if its basis is greater than its fair market value. I.R.C. § 1245(b)(8)(B). Presumably, this exception ensures that the taxpayer recognizes the maximum amount of depreciation recapture and that any loss on the disposition of any § 197 intangible asset is potentially treated as a capital loss rather than as a reduction in the amount of depreciation recapture.

Section 1250, which generally applies to the recapture of depreciation relating to real property, was enacted in 1969, but differs from § 1245 by treating as ordinary income only the gain realized on the disposition of the property attributable to depreciation deductions in excess of straight-line depreciation. I.R.C. §§ 1250(a)(1) and 1250(b)(1). Under current law, residential rental property and nonresidential real property are depreciable only under the straight-line method. I.R.C. § 168(b)(3). Consequently, § 1250 is generally inapplicable to characterize as ordinary income any portion of the gain realized when a building used in a trade or business is sold.[38] However, § 1250 may still apply to recover as ordinary income any gain attributable to basis reductions under §§ 108(b) and 1017(b) due to discharge of indebtedness income excluded from gross income under § 108(a). I.R.C. § 1017(d). Although all of the gain on the sale or exchange of real property used in a trade or business will generally fall under § 1231, not all of that gain characterized under § 1231 as capital gain is taxed at the most preferential tax rate applicable to net capital under. § 1(h). That portion of any gain on the sale or exchange of real property that is attributable to depreciation deductions, including depreciation calculated using the straight-line method, is taxed at a maximum rate of 25 percent rather than the more preferential tax rate of 15 percent. I.R.C. §§ 1(h)(1)(D) and 1(h)(6) (referring to the gain taxed at a maximum rate of 25 percent as "unrecaptured section 1250 gain"). Typically, only the gain in excess of the original cost basis of the property is taxed at the lower 15 percent rate.

Importantly, §§ 1245 and 1250 state that the gain to be treated as ordinary income on a disposition of property is to be "recognized notwithstanding any other provision of this subtitle." I.R.C. §§ 1245(a)(1) (flush language) and 1250(a)(1)(B)(ii) (flush language). However, both sections contain provisions limiting their application in the case of transfers by gift, inheritance, and certain nonrecognition transactions such as those under §§ 351, 721 and 1031. I.R.C. §§ 1245(b)(1)–(5) and 1250(d)(1)–(5). Nevertheless, on any subsequent disposition of the transferred property by the transferee, the transferee must apply §§ 1245 and 1250 by taking into account all depreciation deductions taken by both the original transferor and the transferee if the transferee took a substituted basis in the property. *See* I.R.C. § 1245(a)(2)(A) (defining the recomputed basis as the property's adjusted basis plus "all adjustments reflected in such adjusted basis on account of deductions . . . allowed or allowable *to the taxpayer or to any other person* for depreciation or amortization" (emphasis added)). Thus, the transferee may have ordinary income attributable to depreciation recapture even if the property is not depreciable in his hands.

The interplay of the depreciation recapture provisions with § 1231 and the multiple rate structure for capital gain from the sale or exchange of real property

---

[38] For corporate taxpayers, § 291(a)(1) requires that 20 percent of the gain not treated as depreciation recapture under § 1250 but that would be depreciation recapture if the depreciable real property fell under § 1245 also be treated as ordinary income.

used in a taxpayer's trade or business is not the only factor limiting the usefulness of § 1231. Section 1231 involves a complicated netting process that requires not only the gains and losses from the sale or exchange of business property but also the gains and losses from certain other property which is destroyed or involuntarily converted be combined and netted before the ultimate application of § 1231 is made. I.R.C. §§ 1231(a)(1), 1231(a)(2), and 1231(a)(4)(C). In addition, if a taxpayer has deducted ordinary losses pursuant to § 1231 in the prior five-year period, then gain that would otherwise be treated as capital gain is converted to ordinary income. I.R.C. § 1231(c). This provision was enacted in 1984 to prevent taxpayers from intentionally timing gains or losses to recognize ordinary losses in one year and capital gain in the next.

§ 6.02 The Mechanics of Section 1231

Calculating the gains and losses that are characterized as capital or ordinary under § 1231 can involve a complicated matching and netting of various transactions which occur during a given tax year. For many business taxpayers, however, the full ambit of the statutory scheme does not come into play because the business will not experience all of the various types of transactions contemplated by § 1231 in any one particular year. For many small businesses, § 1231 transactions are relatively rare and the taxation of the few transactions that do occur is relatively straightforward. In larger businesses, however, where the transactions covered by § 1231 are more frequent, the entire netting process may very well occur on an annual basis.

(a) Types of Property Included Under § 1231

Before examining the details of the characterization process under § 1231, the definition of "property used in the trade or business," which is the principal type of property that falls within the scope of § 1231, must be appreciated. Such property is defined as "property used in the trade or business, of a character which is subject to the allowance for depreciation provided in section 167, held for more than 1 year, and real property used in the trade or business, held for more than 1 year." I.R.C. § 1231(b)(1); Treas. Reg. § 1.1231-1(c)(1). Property used in the trade or business thus follows the exclusion from the definition of a capital asset under § 1221(a)(2) but is limited to only that property held for more than one year. The requirement that property for purposes of § 1231 be held for more than one year means that the gains and losses characterized as capital gains and losses under § 1231will be treated as long-term capital gains and losses. As described below, § 1231 also applies to other types of property, most importantly capital assets held by the taxpayer for more than one year in connection with a trade or business or a transaction entered into for profit that are involuntarily converted. I.R.C. §§ 1231(a)(4)(B)(ii) and 1231(a)(4)(C)(ii); Treas. Reg. §§ 1.1231-1(a) and 1.1231-1(c)(2). Without the application of § 1231, the involuntary conversion of such assets would not result in capital gain or loss treatment because of the failure to satisfy the sale or exchange requirement of § 1222. Property that falls within the scope of § 1231 will be referred to collectively as § 1231 property.

The hypothetical cauldron in which the various gains and losses from § 1231 transactions are matched and netted is referred to in tax parlance as the "hotchpot." The hotchpot is comprised of gains and losses from three specific types of transactions set forth in the statutory scheme. The three types of transactions are:

(1) Gains and losses arising from the involuntary conversion of (a) property used in the taxpayer's trade or business or (b) any capital asset that is held for more than one year in connection with the taxpayer's trade or business or a transaction entered into for profit and that is involuntarily converted as a result of fire, storm, shipwreck, theft, or other casualty. I.R.C. § 1231(a)(4)(B); Treas. Reg. § 1.1231-1(e)(3).

(2) The second category of § 1231 transactions includes gains and losses from a compulsory conversion resulting from "seizure, or an exercise of the power of requisition or condemnation or the threat or imminence thereof" of (a) property used in the taxpayer's trade or business, or (b) any capital asset that is held for more than one year in connection with the taxpayer's trade or business or a transaction entered into for profit by the taxpayer. I.R.C. §§ 1231(a)(3)(A)(ii) and 1231(a)(3)(B); Treas. Reg. § 1.1231-1(e)(1).

(3) The third category of § 1231 transactions includes gains and losses from the sale or exchange of property used in the taxpayer's trade or business and held for more than one year. I.R.C. §§ 1231(a)(3)(A)(i) and 1231(a)(3)(B); Treas. Reg. § 1.1231-1(a).

Importantly, gains are included in the § 1231 process only if, and to the extent that, they are included in computing the taxpayer's gross income, and losses are included in the § 1231 process only if, and to the extent that, they are included in computing the taxpayer's taxable income. I.R.C. § 1231(a)(4)(A); Treas. Reg. § 1.1231-1(d). Consequently, the gains and losses must be recognized under § 1001(c) and the losses allowed under § 165. In addition, if property falling within § 1231 is sold at a gain and such gain is reported by the selling taxpayer under the installment sale rules of § 453, only the portion of gain reported in a given year under the installment sale rules is included in the § 1231 calculation for that year. Consequently, the gain on the sale of such property may be characterized as ordinary income in one year and capital gain in the next depending on the other § 1231 gains and losses that the taxpayer incurs in each taxable year.

In order to characterize the gains and losses resulting from casualties, condemnation, and sales or exchanges of § 1231 property, § 1231 adopted a two tier process in which the gains and losses included in each tier are compared. Based on a determination whether the aggregate gains exceed the aggregate losses or the aggregate losses exceed the aggregate gains, the individual gains and losses are characterized as either ordinary or capital gains and losses. The two-tier § 1231 characterization process is discussed more fully below.

(b) The Preliminary Hotchpot

The first step in the § 1231 characterization process is to compare the gains and losses resulting from the involuntary conversion of property used in the taxpayer's trade or business and of any capital asset held by the taxpayer for more than one year in connection with a trade or business or a transaction entered into for profit.[39] Involuntary conversions for this purpose are limited to fire, storm, shipwreck, or other casualty, or from theft, and do not include condemnation or requisition. I.R.C. § 1231(a)(4)(C); Treas. Reg. § 1.1231-1(e)(3). This comparison of gains and losses is known as the "preliminary hotchpot" or "firepot." Gains arise in the firepot if insurance proceeds received as a result of a designated casualty exceed the adjusted basis of the property destroyed or damaged. A loss would obviously occur if the qualifying casualty were not covered by the taxpayer's insurance or if the insurance proceeds were less than the adjusted basis of the property involuntarily converted.

If the aggregate losses in the preliminary hotchpot exceed the aggregate gains, then both the gains and losses are excluded from the § 1231 characterization process and are characterized under other sections of the Code. In most cases, when the losses exceed the gains in the preliminary hotchpot, the gains and losses will be ordinary. Thus, the exclusion of gains and losses included in the preliminary hotchpot from further inclusion in the § 1231 characterization process is favorable to the taxpayer since the losses may simply be deducted by the taxpayer as ordinary losses without regard to other § 1231 gains. I.R.C. § 165(c)(1).

Example 1:

T operates a commercial fishing fleet. The business is organized as a single-member limited liability company with T as the only member. In 2007, one of his fishing boats is destroyed by a terrorist act that is considered by the insurance company as an act of war — not covered by the insurance policy. The adjusted basis of the boat at the time of its destruction is $1,000,000. Assuming that there are no other gains or losses from involuntary conversions (i.e., fire, storm, shipwreck, theft, or other casualty) during 2003, the aggregate losses included in the preliminary hotchpot will exceed the aggregate gains. As a result, the $1,000,000 loss is no longer included in the § 1231 characterization process and is deductible by the taxpayer as an ordinary loss incurred in his trade or business.

If the aggregate gains in the preliminary hotchpot exceed the aggregate losses, then both the gains and the losses are included in the primary hotchpot to be subsequently compared with the gains and losses from the other § 1231 transactions. The result is that gains and losses included in the preliminary hotchpot are provided with a second opportunity to be treated as capital gains and losses depending on the results of other § 1231 transactions that occurred during the taxpayer's taxable year.

---

[39] Importantly, the gains and losses from involuntary conversions that are included in this first step in the § 1231 characterization process do not include losses arising from the involuntary conversion of assets that are neither part of the taxpayer's trade or business nor held by him for investment. Casualty losses with respect to personal use assets may nevertheless be deductible by an individual taxpayer under § 165(c)(3) to the extent allowed and as characterized under § 165(h).

(c) The Primary Hotchpot

If the aggregate gains exceed the aggregate losses in the preliminary hotchpot, then those gains and losses are included in a second comparison of aggregate gains and aggregate losses known as the "primary hotchpot." The primary hotchpot includes, in addition to the preliminary hotchpot gains and losses: (i) compulsory conversions (i.e., condemnations) of property used in a trade or business and capital assets held for more than one year held in connection with a trade or business or a transaction entered into for profit and (ii) gains or losses from the sale or exchange of property used in a trade or business, as described above. I.R.C. §§ 1231(a)(3)(A)(ii) and 1231(a)(3)(A)(i). The comparison of gains and losses in the primary hotchpot is made by simply totaling the gains from these three types of property on the one hand, and the losses therefrom on the other. If the aggregate gains exceed the aggregate losses, the individual gains and losses in the hotchpot are characterized as long-term capital gains and losses. I.R.C. § 1231(a)(1). If the aggregate losses equal or exceed the aggregate gains, all individual gains and losses are characterized as ordinary gains and losses. I.R.C. § 1231(a)(2).

Example 2:

T operates a commercial fishing fleet. The business is organized as a single-member limited liability company with T as the only member. In late 2007, one of his warehouses burns to the ground. The building had been depreciated on a straight-line basis from its original cost of $1,000,000 to an adjusted basis of $500,000. T received insurance proceeds in the amount of $1,500,000, the replacement value of the warehouse. He elects not to rebuild or replace the warehouse but simply to pocket the proceeds. With respect to the characterization of the $1,000,000 gain that he realized as a result of the casualty, no portion of the gain will be treated as ordinary income under § 1250 because no portion of the gain is the result of depreciation deductions in excess of straight-line depreciation. Assuming that T had no other gains or losses as a result of an involuntary conversion (i.e., as a result of fire, storm, shipwreck, theft, or other casualty) or condemnation, had no other gains or losses from the sale or exchange of property used in his trade or business, the $1,000,000 gain will be treated as long-term capital gain under § 1231. The $1,000,000 of gain is included in the preliminary hotchpot, and, because the gains exceed the losses, they are included in the primary hotchpot. Again, because the aggregate gains exceed the aggregate losses in the primary hotchpot, the gain is treated as a long-term capital gain. Assuming that T is not required to recapture any of this gain as ordinary income under § 1231(c) because he had no net § 1231 losses during the prior five years, the $1,000,000 long-term capital gain will be included on his tax return along with any other capital gains and losses in determining the amount of net capital gain subject to the preferential tax rates under § 1(h). Assuming that he has no other capital gains or losses, $500,000 of the $1,000,0000 of net capital gain will be treated as unrecaptured § 1250 gain and taxed at a maximum tax rate of 25 percent and the remaining $500,000 of the $1,000,0000 of net capital gain will be treated as adjusted net capital gain and taxed at a maximum tax rate of 15 percent.

It should be emphasized that there is no actual "netting" of gains and losses involved in either the preliminary hotchpot or the primary hotchpot. Instead, the individual gains and losses, as characterized under § 1231, are included on the taxpayer's return and treated just as any other gains and losses from the sale or exchange of a capital asset.

Example 3:

T owns a small business that manufactures teddy bears. The business is operated in the form of a single-member LLC, of which T is the sole member. During the 2007 tax year, the following transactions involving § 1231 property occur:

(1) One of her delivery trucks is stolen. Because of the negligence of the driver of the truck in leaving the keys in the unattended truck, insurance coverage is denied. The adjusted basis of the truck at the time of its theft is $10,000.

(2) Due to a widening of the highway adjacent to T's manufacturing plant, a portion of the real property on which her plant is located is condemned. She receives condemnation proceeds of $100,000, which she does not intend to reinvest. The adjusted basis of the property taken was $20,000.

(3) T sells one of the industrial sewing machines used in the teddy bear manufacturing process that has been owned by the business for more than one year. The original cost of the sewing machine was $50,000 and its adjusted basis at the time of sale is $25,000. The sale price of the sewing machine is $40,000.

(4) The business has a license to manufacture souvenir bears for the local professional baseball team. T originally paid $75,000 for the license. The original license cost has been amortized under § 197 for five years and has a current adjusted basis of $50,000. T, with the consent of the licensor, sells the licensing rights to a competitor for $100,000.

T's business has not claimed any ordinary losses pursuant to § 1231 over the last five years.

The transactions described above result in the following gains and losses:

Loss from the theft of the Truck	$10,000
Gain from Land Condemnation	80,000
Gain from Sale of Sewing Machine	15,000
Gain from Sale of Souvenir Franchise	50,000

Before considering the application of the § 1231 characterization process, any depreciation recapture under either § 1245 or § 1250 must be identified and characterized as ordinary income. The entire $15,000 of gain realized on the sale of the sewing machine is the result of depreciation deductions previously taken which reduced the basis of the sewing machine below its fair market value. As a result, the gain is characterized under § 1245 as ordinary income and is not included in the § 1231 characterization process. In addition, $25,000 of the gain on the sale of the souvenir franchise is characterized as ordinary income under § 1245 and is also excluded from the § 1231 characterization process. The gains and losses included in § 1231 are, thus, limited to the following:

Loss from the theft of the Truck	$10,000
Gain from Land Condemnation	80,000
Gain from Sale of Sewing Machine	15,000

The first step in the § 1231 characterization process is to identify the gains and losses included in the preliminary hotchpot. The sole transaction for this purpose is the theft of the truck which resulted in a $10,000 loss. Because the losses in the preliminary hotchpot exceed gains, the $10,000 loss is excluded from further consideration in the § 1231 characterization process and may be deducted as an ordinary loss under § 165(c)(1).

The $25,000 of gain on the franchise and the $80,000 gain on the condemnation of the land used in the trade or business is included in the primary hotchpot. Because the aggregate gains ($105,000) exceed the aggregate losses ($0), the individual gains are characterized as capital gains. Thus, $80,000 gain on the condemnation of the land and the $25,000 gain from the sale of the franchise are treated as long-term capital gains and are included along with all of T's other capital gains and losses in the determination of her net capital gain for the taxable year. If she has no other capital gains or losses, she will have $105,000 of net capital gain that will be treated under § 1(h) as adjusted net capital gain subject to a maximum tax rate of 15 percent.

(d) Non-Recaptured Net § 1231 Losses

Despite the application of the § 1231 characterization process to determine whether gains and losses attributable to § 1231 property will be treated as capital gains or losses, such gains and losses may be recharacterized in whole or in part as ordinary gain or loss if the taxpayer has had § 1231 gains and losses treated as ordinary gains and losses within the five previous taxable years. The reason for this recharacterization under § 1231(c) is to prevent taxpayers from manipulating the timing of gains and losses under § 1231 so as to obtain ordinary losses in one taxable year and capital gains in the next taxable year.

Example 4:

T operates a trade or business with assets that constitute § 1231 property. The sale or exchange of one of these assets will result in a loss of $40,000 while the other will result in a gain of $60,000. T can sell either of these assets in the current taxable year, Year 1, or the following taxable year, Year 2. If he sells both of the assets in Year 1, the gains and losses will be characterized under § 1231 as long-term capital gains and losses. If T has no other capital gains or losses, he will have $20,000 of net capital gain that will be taxed at a maximum tax rate of 15 percent for a tax liability of $3,000.

However, the tax results are different if T sells the loss asset in Year 1 and the gain asset in Year 2. Assuming that he has no other transactions involving § 1231 property in either taxable year, the $40,000 loss in Year 1 will be characterized as an ordinary loss under § 1231, and the $60,000 gain in Year 2 will be characterized as a capital gain. Assuming that T is in the 35 percent tax bracket, the $40,000 ordinary loss in Year 1 will save him $14,000 in tax liability and the $60,000 capital gain in Year 2 will result in a tax liability of $9,000. Together, the tax savings in the current taxable year and the tax liability in the subsequent taxable year result in a net tax savings of $5,000.

T would clearly prefer the second approach in which he sells the loss asset in Year 1 and the gain asset in Year 2. Instead of a tax liability on $3,000 if he sold the two assets in the same year, he has a net tax savings of $5,000 by selling the two assets in different years. This $8,000 difference results from the fact that the $40,000 loss in Year 1 offsets ordinary income taxed at 35 percent while the additional $40,000 of net capital gain in Year 2 is taxed at 15 percent. The 20 percentage point difference in tax rates saves T $8,000 in tax liability when the $40,000 loss is used to offset ordinary income rather than long-term capital gain.

Section 1231(c) prevents taxpayers from manipulating the timing of their gains and losses under § 1231 to generate a tax benefit by introducing the concept of non-recaptured net § 1231 losses. Non-recaptured net § 1231 losses are equal to the aggregate of the net § 1231 losses for the five most recent preceding taxable years in excess of the net § 1231 losses that have not yet been recaptured. I.R.C. § 1231(c)(2). A net § 1231 loss is the excess of the § 1231 losses over the § 1231 gains. I.R.C. § 1231(c)(4). Similarly, a net § 1231 gain is the excess of the § 1231 gains over the § 1231 losses. I.R.C. § 1231(c)(3). If a taxpayer has non-recaptured net § 1231 losses, and in the current year has a net § 1231 gain, the net section § 1231 gain must be treated as ordinary income to the extent of the net § 1231 loss. I.R.C. § 1231(c)(1).

Example 5:

Returning to the facts of Example 4 in which T sells the loss property in Year 1 and the gain property in Year 2, § 1231(c) will not affect the characterization of the loss in Year 1. However, in Year 2, T will have non-recaptured § 1231 losses of $40,000 because he had $40,000 of § 1231 losses in excess of § 1231 gains in the preceding five years, none of which has been recaptured. Although the $60,000 gain in Year 2 will be characterized as a capital gain as a result of the primary hotchpot, § 1231(c) will require that T treat $40,000 of the $60,000 capital gain as ordinary income, and only the remaining $20,000 will be treated as capital gain. Consequently, in Year 2, he will have a tax liability of $17,000 ($40,000 of ordinary income taxed at 35 percent plus $20,000 of capital gain taxed a 15 percent).

Together, the tax savings in Year 1 of $14,000 and the tax liability in Year 2 of $17,000 results in a net tax liability of $3,000. This is the same tax liability that T would have experienced if he had sold both assets in Year 1 as described in the first part of Example 4.

Despite the existence of § 1231(c), T could have achieved his tax minimization objective in the second part of Example 4 if he had sold the gain asset in Year 1 and the loss asset in Year 2. In this situation, he would not have any non-recaptured net § 1231 loss that would require any portion of the gain realized in Year 1 to be recharacterized as ordinary income. In addition, the loss in Year 2 would have been characterized as an ordinary loss under the general characterization provisions of § 1231. However, the net § 1231 loss created in Year 2 would result in non-recaptured § 1231 losses of $40,000 that would require the recharacterization of any net § 1231 gain subsequently realized in Years 3 through 7.

When § 1231(c) requires the recharacterization of any net § 1231 gain as ordinary income, an issue arises regarding which of the types of net capital gain under § 1(h) (i.e., 28 percent rate gain, unrecaptured § 1250 gain, or adjusted net capital gain) that might otherwise result from the § 1231 characterization process must be recharacterized as ordinary income. The Code itself provides only that the recharacterized ordinary income is to be allocated among the types of net capital gain in accordance with Regulations to be issued by the Secretary. I.R.C. § 1(h)(8). Although no Regulations have yet been promulgated, the Service has issued a notice in which any 28 percent rate gain resulting from the § 1231 characterization process is first recharacterized as ordinary income followed by any unrecaptured § 1250 gain, and then any adjusted net capital gain. 1997-2 C.B. 309, Notice 97-59. This result is generally favorable to taxpayers as it first recharacterizes as ordinary income the capital gain that would be taxed at the highest maximum capital gain rate before it recharacterizes capital gain that would be taxed at more preferential tax rates.

§ 6.03 Definition of Property Used in the Trade or Business

A previously described, § 1221(a)(2) excludes from the definition of a capital asset any property held by a taxpayer that is used in a trade or business and is of a character subject to the allowance for depreciation under § 167 or any real property used in a trade or business. Without the application of § 1231, any gains or losses resulting from the sale or exchange of such property would not result in capital gains or losses. However, the definition of "property used in the trade or business" for purposes of § 1231 includes the very types of property excluded by § 1221(a)(2) provided such property is held by the taxpayer for more than one year. I.R.C. § 1231(b)(1); Treas. Reg. § 1.1231-1(c)(1). These two categories of property encompass the vast majority of all business assets that qualify for § 1231 treatment. Thus, property used in the trade or business is eligible for capital gain and loss treatment depending on the outcome of the § 1231 characterization process. Section 1231 also includes three other types of property: (i) timber, coal and iron ore to which § 631 applies; (ii) certain livestock other than poultry; and (iii) certain unharvested crops. I.R.C. §§ 1231(b)(2), (3), and (4); Treas. Reg. §§ 1.1231-1(c)(3), (4), and (5). Nevertheless, property used in that trade or business does not include inventory-type property, copyrights and certain types of related intangible property if held by the taxpayer who created such property, and government publications. I.R.C. §§ 1231(b)(1)(A), (B), (C), and (D); Treas. Reg. §§ 1.1231-1(c)(1)(i) and (ii). These types of property are also excluded from the definition of a capital asset. I.R.C. §§ 1221(a)(1), (3), and (5).

The following materials discuss in greater detail the types of property that are included and excluded from the scope of § 1231.

(a) Property Used in the Trade or Business

Section 1231 applies to property held by a taxpayer that is used in a trade or business and is of a character subject to the allowance for depreciation under § 167 or any real property used in a trade or business, provided such property is held for more than one year. I.R.C. § 1231(b)(1); Treas. Reg. § 1.1231-1(c)(1). Consequently, to be included in the § 1231 characterization process, personal property must have been used in that taxpayer's trade or business of the taxpayer and must have been subject to allowance for depreciation. Importantly, intangible assets used in the taxpayer's trade or business that are amortizable under either § 167 or § 197 fall within § 1231 except for certain types of copyrights and other related intangible assets that are otherwise excluded from § 1231. *See* I.R.C. § 197(f)(7).

Real property, on the other hand, must only have been used in the taxpayer's trade or business regardless of whether the property is itself depreciable. For purposes of § 1231, real property includes improvements constructed on land, leasehold interests, and easements. *See* Rev. Rul. 72-85, 1972-1 C.B. 234. To fall within § 1231, however, all property used in the trade or business must have been held for more than one year.

The inclusion under § 1231 of real property used in a taxpayer's trade or business and held for more than one year raises the issue whether a taxpayer holding real property is engaged in a trade or business or whether the property is held merely for investment. If the real property is held for investment and not in a trade or business, it is not excluded from the definition of a capital asset under § 1221(a)(1) and is not included in the § 1231 characterization process. Consequently, gain or loss realized with respect to such an asset is capital gain or loss. Real property used in a trade or business, on the other hand, is excluded from the definition of a capital asset under § 1221(a)(2) but, if held for more than one year, will generate a gain or loss on disposition that will be included in the 1231 calculation.

A taxpayer holding a single rental property to which he provides little or no services may not be treated as engaged in a trade or business. For example, in *Grier v. United States*, 120 F. Supp. 395 (D. Conn. 1954), *aff'd per curiam*, 218 F.2d 603 (2d Cir. 1955), a taxpayer inherited a house that he rented to the same individual for a number of years. The court concluded that the taxpayer's activities with respect to the house were so minimal that the property was not used in the taxpayer's trade or business and that, therefore, the resulting loss on the sale of the property was a capital loss. However, other courts have held to the contrary and the law with regard the proper treatment of a taxpayer holding a single rental asset is not entirely clear. *See Alvary v. United States*, 302 F.2d 790 (2d Cir. 1962); *Fackler v. Commissioner*, 133 F.2d 509 (6th Cir. 1943); *Crawford v. Commissioner*, 16 T.C. 678

(1951), *acq.* Nevertheless, a taxpayer holding one or two rental properties subject to triple net leases, where minimal services are provided and where the taxpayer carries on an independent unrelated trade or business would have a viable argument that the properties are held for investment and, although depreciable, constitute capital assets such that any gain from the disposition of such properties is not properly included in the § 1231 characterization process.

(b) The Inventory Exclusion

Inventory and property held primarily for sale to customers in the ordinary course of the taxpayer's trade or business are explicitly excluded from the § 1231 characterization process. I.R.C. §§ 1231(b)(1)(A) and (B). Even without these specific statutory exclusions, personal property falling within these categories would fail to fall within the definition of property used in the trade or business under § 1231 because such property is not "of a character which is subject to the allowance for depreciation." Real property, on the other hand, need not be depreciable in order to qualify for tax treatment under § 1231. I.R.C. § 1231(b)(1). Consequently, the statutory exclusion would appear to apply only to unimproved real property held as inventory or primarily for sale to customers in the ordinary course of the taxpayer's trade or business. *But see* Rev. Rul. 86-149, 1986-2 C.B. 67 (concluding that a real estate developer could not use the LIFO method of inventory accounting under § 471 because real property was not inventory and relying on the decisions in *Homes by Ayres v. Commissioner*, 795 F.2d 832 (9th Cir. 1986), and *W. C. & A. N. Miller Dev. Co. v. Commissioner*, 81 T.C. 619 (1983)). In order to determine whether the gain or loss from the sale of unimproved real estate will be included in the § 1231 characterization process or excluded under this provision, the taxpayer's other real estate activities must be carefully examined to determine whether the taxpayer is engage in a trade or business involving real property and, thus, a "dealer" in such property. This is the same question that arises with respect to the exclusion from the definition of a capital asset under § 1221(a)(1) in connection with property held primarily for sale to customers in the ordinary course of the taxpayer's trade or business. If the taxpayer is determined to be a dealer, then the gain or loss from the sale or exchange of real property is not eligible for capital gain treatment because such property is excluded from the definition of capital asset by § 1221(a)(1) and excluded from the definition of property used in the trade or business for purposes of § 1231 as well.

As previously noted, personal property of a character which is subject to the allowance for depreciation provided in § 167 would, by definition, appear to exclude inventory. However, certain judicial decisions have treated depreciable personal property as inventory, thus excluded from the § 1231 characterization process. For example, in *Hollywood Baseball Asso. v. Commissioner*, 423 F.2d 494 (9th Cir. 1970). the Ninth Circuit held that depreciable minor league baseball player contracts generated ordinary income when sold at a profit because they were "integrally related" to the business of the taxpayer. The Ninth Circuit held that, although the minor league contracts were not held primarily for sale to customers in the ordinary course of business, they were sold with sufficient frequency and constituted such an integral part of the business of the baseball team that the gain or loss was ordinary because it was part of the business's day-to-day operations.

Similarly, in *International Shoe Machine Corp. v. United States*, 491 F.2d 157 (1st Cir. 1974), depreciable shoe manufacturing equipment sold by the taxpayer was deemed to be part of the day-to-day operations of the business of the taxpayer and, therefore, resulted in ordinary income.

Both of these decisions were rendered at the height of the application of the Supreme Court's decision in *Corn Prods. Refining Co. v. Comm'r*, 350 U.S. 46 (1955), which sought to broaden the exception to capital asset treatment beyond the five (at that time) statutory exceptions set forth in § 1221(a). In both *Hollywood Baseball* and *International Shoe*, the assets sold were held to be neither capital assets under § 1221 nor assets qualifying for § 1231 treatment under the *Corn Products* doctrine. Nevertheless, the Supreme Court severely constricted the *Corn Products* doctrine in *Arkansas Best Corp. v. Commissioner*, 485 U.S. 212 (1988), which held that the decision in *Corn Products* should be limited to certain inventory hedging transactions as falling within the definition of "inventory" under § 1221(a)(1), and should not be viewed as creating a broad additional exception to the definition of capital asset. Congress subsequently enacted § 1221(a)(7) to ensure that various types of hedging transactions were, in fact, excluded from the definition of capital asset. Consequently, the *Corn Products* doctrine should be of no continuing relevance to the characterization of property under § 1221 as a capital asset.

In the wake of *Arkansas Best* and the enactment of § 1221(a)(7), it would appear that the decisions in *Hollywood Baseball* and *International Shoe*, which did not involve inventory hedging transactions, would lack any continuing viability. Unless the Service can place the sale or exchange of the personal property squarely within the definition of "inventory" or "property held primarily for sale to customers in the ordinary course of business," which typically means that the property should not have been subject to the allowance for depreciation in the first place, depreciable personal property should be included within the § 1231 characterization process as property used in the trade or business in the post-*Arkansas Best* environment.

(c) Miscellaneous Property Under § 1231

Included in the § 1231 characterization process are three specific types of assets: timber, coal and iron ore with respect to which an election under § 631 is made, livestock, and growing crops. I.R.C. §§ 1231(b)(2), (3), and (4). The primary purpose of including these types of property within the scope of § 1231 is to permit farmers to obtain ordinary losses (rather than restricted capital losses) when these types of assets are transferred or destroyed. For example, if a farmer cuts timber that has been held for more than one year, he may elect to have the cutting of the timber treated as a sale or exchange of the timber. I.R.C. § 631(a). The gain or loss is then subject to the § 1231 characterization process regardless of the nature of the taxpayer's trade or business or the purpose for which the timber is held. Similarly, when coal or domestic iron ore held for one year is disposed of, the gain or loss may be included in the § 1231 characterization process. I.R.C. § 631(c).

Livestock falling within the scope of § 1231 includes (a) cattle and horses regardless of age, held by a taxpayer for 24 months or more for draft, breeding, dairy, or sporting purposes and (b) other livestock regardless of age, held by the taxpayer for 12 months or more for draft, breeding, dairy, or sporting purposes, but not including poultry. I.R.C. § 1231(b)(3)(B). *See* Treas. Reg. § 1.1231-2(a)(3). Whether the livestock is held for by the taxpayer for draft, breeding, dairy, or sporting purposes depends on the facts and circumstances in each case. Treas. Reg. § 1.1231-2(b)(1). As a result of the inclusion of livestock within the scope of § 1231, a farmer may realize capital gain on the sale or exchange of such property. On the other hand, if such livestock is destroyed by disease or sold on account of drought, such involuntary conversions may give rise to ordinary loss. *See* Rev. Rul. 61-216, 1961-2 C.B. 134.

Finally, gains and losses realized in connection with unharvested crops on land used in a taxpayer's trade or business and held for more than one year are also included in the § 1231 characterization process if the crop and land are sold or exchanged or compulsorily or involuntarily converted at the same time to the same person. I.R.C. § 1231(b)(4). Section 1231 does not apply, however, if the taxpayer retains any right or option to reacquire the land that the unharvested crop is on. Treas. Reg. § 1.1231-1(f).

PROBLEM FOR DISCUSSION

Problem 2-10. T is the sole proprietor of a small business. In the current year, she had gains and losses from the sale of the following assets:

	Sale Price	Adjusted Basis	Original Basis
A painting purchased in 1998	$10,000	$6,000	$6,000
Tech, Inc., stock purchased in 2003 and satisfying the requirements of § 1202	40,000	20,000	20,000
ACME stock purchased in 2007		15,000	15,000
Extel stock purchased earlier in the year	15,000	20,000	15,000
Depreciable real property used in her business and purchased in 1990 and depreciated using the straight-line method	75,000	35,000	65,000
Depreciable personal property A used in her business and purchased in 2005	5,000	7,500	20,000
Depreciable personal property B used in her business and purchased in 2007	15,000	5,500	10,000

Depreciable personal property C used in her business, purchased in 2006, and fully expensed under § 179	7,500	0	12,000
Depreciable personal property D used in her business, purchased in 2007 and destroyed in a flood but insured for its full fair market value	17,000	3,000	12,000
Depreciable personal property E in her business, purchased in 2000 and stolen; no insurance coverage	0	4,000	9,000
A sailboat used for personal purposes purchased in 1998	20,000	30,000	30,000

a. Characterize the gains and losses and determine (without actually calculating) the tax treatment under § 1(h).

b. What differences would have resulted if T had not sold the depreciable real property and had sold property A for only $1,000?

c. What if T had had a non-recaptured net section 1231 loss of $5,000 from a prior year? What is the purpose behind § 1231(c)?

Chapter 3

LIABILITIES: DISCHARGE OF INDEBTEDNESS; MORTGAGED PROPERTY

Liabilities are, essentially, the opposite of assets or property — a liability is considered by economists as a negative asset. Among the most common liabilities are those incurred for borrowed money or for seller-financed purchases of property. Although in a sense the liability offsets the money or property, it is treated separately for financial accounting, tax, and other purposes. Accordingly, a liability is a negative asset. When viewed in this manner, transactions involving the transfer of liabilities to another obligor, or relief from liabilities, can have the same economic consequences as the payment or receipt of money. Thus, being relieved from, or transferring a liability to, another person can represent receipt of payment of income, the consideration for an acquisition of an asset, receipt of a gift or a charitable contribution or, for the party granting the relief or accepting the transfer of the liability, payment of an expense, payment of consideration for property acquired, or payment of a personal or other expenditure that is neither capitalizable nor deductible. The transfer of a liability in connection with the transfer of property is likely to be part of the consideration for the transfer of the property, whether or not the liability is actually secured by the property involved.

Section 1 provides a definition of a liability for tax purposes by reference to the regulations under § 752, which contain detailed rules regarding the allocation of partnership liabilities among the partners. Although not specifically applicable to situations outside of the partnership context, the regulatory definition of a liability for purposes of § 752 provides a conceptual definition of a liability that will assist in understanding the treatment of liabilities for tax purposes more generally. Section 2 discusses the concept of discharge of indebtedness income ("DOI"). DOI arises when a taxpayer has previously received the proceeds of a loan that were not included in gross income, acquired an asset with borrowed funds that were included in determining depreciable or amortizable basis, and is relieved of the obligation to pay without making full payment. Transactions involving mortgaged property, including the determination of the basis of property when acquired through the use of debt and of the amount realized on the disposition of such property are examined in section 3. This section considers when the distinction between recourse and nonrecourse debt is important. Section 4 continues this discussion and describes the tax implications on the transfer of property subject to a liability. Section 5 describes the exclusion of DOI income under § 108 under certain circumstances. Even though § 108 does not typically result in a permanent exclusion of DOI income, because most taxpayers will be required to reduce certain "tax attributes" that will have the effect of increasing their tax liability in the future, it still provides a major timing advantage.

§ 1. WHAT IS A LIABILITY?

Treas. Reg. § 1.752-1(a)(4)

The Code provides no definition of the term "liability" or of the related term "indebtedness." The following regulation under § 752 relating specifically to partnership liabilities, however, contains a definition that provides not only a good working definition for partnership tax purposes, but also for all federal tax purposes. Indeed, as indicated by the materials later in this section, it has been applied to nonrecognition transactions to corporations, option payments, and disallowing tax shelters, but without explicitly defining the terms liability or indebtedness. Section 1.01 *Conditions or Contingencies* develops the definition in the context of contingent obligations, while § 1.02 *Obligations v. Liabilities* does so for even fixed obligations that have not been taken into account for tax purposes.

§ 1.752-1. Treatment of Partnership Liabilities.

(a) Definitions. . . .

* * *

(4) *Liability defined* — (i) *In general.* An obligation is a liability for purposes of section 752 and the regulations thereunder, only if and to the extent that incurring the obligation —

(A) Creates or increases the basis of any of the obligor's assets (including cash);

(B) Gives rise to an immediate deduction to the obligor; or

(C) Gives rise to an expense that is not deductible in computing the obligor's taxable income and is not properly chargeable to capital.

(ii) *Obligation.* For purposes of this paragraph . . . , an obligation is any fixed or contingent obligation to make payment without regard to whether the obligation is otherwise taken into account for purposes of the Internal Revenue Code. Obligations include, but are not limited to, debt obligations, environmental obligations, tort obligations, contract obligations, pension obligations, obligations under a short sale, and obligations under derivative financial instruments such as options, forward contracts, and futures contracts.

* * *

As the definition indicates, a liability requires an underlying obligation. As stated in the regulation, an obligation is "any fixed or contingent obligation to make a payment . . ." and includes a number of common types of obligations such as debt, tort, and contract obligations. However, not all obligations are liabilities for tax purposes. In order to be a liability, the obligation must have created or increased the basis of any of the obligor's assets, resulted in an immediate deduction for the obligor, or given rise to a nondeductible and noncapitalized expense of the obligor. Thus, a liability arises when the obligor receives borrowed money, acquires property financed by the obligation to pay — usually, but not always — secured by the acquired property, or is incurred to pay a gift, a personal expense, or another expenditure that is neither deductible nor capitalizable, such as a fine. If the obligation has not had one of these effects — for example, an account payable of a cash-method taxpayer that is not deductible until paid — it is not a liability for tax purposes. On the other hand, income received in advance that is included in income gives rise to an obligation to provide the required services or other performance, but because the inclusion in income accounts for the receipt of cash, the performance obligation is not a liability.

The following materials develop and apply the concepts of this partnership regulation as a general working definition of liability for other contexts as well.

§ 1.01. Conditions and Contingencies

The first part of the definition of a liability under Treas. Reg. § 1.752-1(a)(4)(i)(A) covers two types of transactions — those that create or increase the basis of an asset. The reference to the basis of an asset is a convoluted way of saying that obligations incurred to acquire property are liabilities. This aspect of the definition of a liability is considered in detail in § 3, *Mortgaged Property*. The parenthetical "including cash" is a convoluted way of saying that the obligation to repay a loan is also a liability. Although, as a general principle, all receipts of cash or property are included in gross income, unless an exemption applies, it is well recognized that the proceeds of a borrowing are not included in gross income when there is a corresponding acknowledged debt or loan obligation, even though no Code or regulations provision says so.

Most loan or debt obligations are relatively straightforward and require that the obligor repay the lender a fixed amount plus interest in the future. When there are contingencies that may affect the obligation to repay, however, it is not clear whether the receipt of cash or property should be excluded from the recipient's gross income because of an offsetting debt or loan obligation, as illustrated by the following case, which highlights the effect of state law in determining whether there is a "fixed or contingent obligation to make payment."

MILENBACH v. COMMISSIONER

United States Tax Court
106 T.C. 184 (1996)

* * *

. . . Sheldon R. Milenbach was a limited partner of the Los Angeles Raiders (the Raiders) during 1980 through 1982. . . .

The Raiders own and operate a professional football club and hold a franchise in and are a member of the National Football League (NFL). During the years in issue, the Raiders' principal places of business were Oakland, California, and Los Angeles, California, respectively. For many years prior to 1980, the Raiders played their professional football games at the Oakland-Alameda County Coliseum (Oakland Coliseum) in Oakland, California. The Raiders' lease of the Oakland Coliseum expired at the close of the 1979 NFL season.

Los Angeles Colesium Agreement

* * *

On July 5, 1982, the Raiders entered into a memorandum of agreement (1982 MOA) with the LAMCC. The 1982 MOA provided that the Raiders would begin playing their home games at the LA Coliseum in 1982 and that the LAMCC would loan the Raiders $6.7 million, at 10-percent interest, to be advanced as follows: $675,000 per year for the first 4 years and $4 million no more than 5 years from July 5, 1982. . . .

Beginning with the 1982 NFL season and throughout the years in issue, the Raiders played their home games at the LA Coliseum. The Raiders and the LAMCC did not enter into a formal lease (1984 lease) until December 8, 1984. The 1984 lease was made effective, however, as of the beginning of the 1982 NFL season. The 1984 lease included provisions for the $6.7-million loan to the Raiders on essentially the same terms as the 1982 MOA and contained a repayment provision that was essentially the same as the 1982 MOA repayment provision, *i.e.*, 12 percent of net revenues from operations of suites to be constructed by the Raiders. All physical improvements to the LA Coliseum and the surrounding premises, *i.e.*, the practice facilities, were to revert to the LAMCC upon the termination of the lease. As to the construction of the suites, the 1984 lease provided:

> 7.05 Construction of the Suites and the Press Box Improvements shall commence as soon as practicable *as determined by the Lessee [Raiders] in its reasonable discretion,* having in mind pending and potential litigation involving the parties hereto, or either of them, financial considerations, and *other considerations reasonably deemed important or significant to the Lessee.* Lessee shall use its best efforts to begin and complete Suite construction as soon as possible and upon completion subject to the terms hereof, to use its best efforts to rent, lease, license, grant or otherwise deal with the same so as to maximize their use and obtain the reasonable rental value thereof. The plans and specification for the Press Box Improvements and Suites and the timing and manner of all construction at the Stadium must be approved by Lessor, which approval will not be unreasonably withheld or delayed. * * * [Emphasis added.]

The 1980 MOA, the 1982 MOA, and the 1984 lease were the result of arm's-length bargaining between the Raiders and the LAMCC.

The $6.7-million loan was represented by a promissory note dated November 30, 1984, the terms of which were as provided in the 1982 MOA and the 1984 lease. The Raiders were to commence repayment of the $6.7-million loan 3 years after the completion of construction of the suites. The loan was nonrecourse against the Raiders, secured solely by the improvements to be made. The $6.7-million loan was funded with a $4-million advance in 1984 and by . . . credits against the rent due from the Raiders . . . .

The Raiders took corresponding deductions for their rent expense.

Due to the concern of the Los Angeles Olympic Committee over the timing of construction, plans to construct the suites prior to the 1984 Summer Olympics were abandoned. In 1985 and 1986, the Raiders worked with architects and contractors on the design and planning of the suites. The construction of the suites began in early 1987 but was halted on or about February 18, 1987. Construction was stopped due to a dispute between the Raiders and the LAMCC over the obligations of the LAMCC to perform certain improvements to the LA Coliseum.

The Raiders made no payments on the LAMCC loan. The Raiders did not construct the suites at the LA Coliseum.

The LAMCC did not seek repayment of the $6.7 million until after the Raiders signed a memorandum of agreement with the City of Irwindale (Irwindale MOA) . . . . The LAMCC filed a lawsuit against the Raiders on September 30, 1987, claiming that the Raiders were in breach of their lease and demanding repayment of the $6.7 million. In the Raiders' answer to the LAMCC complaint, the Raiders alleged:

> That Raiders has not constructed the suites or the press box improvements referred to in the lease agreement because, by reason of considerations reasonably deemed important and significant to Raiders, including plaintiff's [LAMCC's] breach of its commitment to modernize and reconfigure the stadium as hereinafter alleged, Raiders *was never under any obligation to construct the suites or press box improvements*, and, Raiders has not obtained a building permit or the surety bonds referred to in the lease agreement * * * [Emphasis added.]

The lawsuit was settled on September 11, 1990, with the parties entering into a mutual release.

Respondent, in the notice of deficiency for 1982 and in the FPAA's for 1983, 1984, 1985, and 1986, disallowed the Raiders' rent deductions because the rent was not currently payable and was considered part of the "loan" from the LAMCC. In the alternative, if the rent deductions were allowed, respondent determined that the amount advanced under the "loan" was includable in gross income. For 1984, respondent determined that the additional $4-million advance was includable in the Raiders' gross income.

* * *

OPINION

Los Angeles Coliseum Agreement

Gross income, as used in the Internal Revenue Code, includes all income from whatever source derived, sec. 61(a), encompassing all "accessions to wealth, clearly realized, and over which the taxpayers have complete dominion." *Commissioner v. Glenshaw Glass Co.*, 348 U.S. 426, 431 (1955). Generally, proceeds of a loan do not constitute income to a borrower because the benefit is offset by an obligation to repay. . . . Whether a particular transaction actually constitutes a loan, however, is to be determined upon consideration of all of the facts. . . .

Petitioners argue that the $6.7 million received from the LAMCC was a loan and, therefore, not taxable income. Respondent contends that the Raiders did not have an unconditional obligation to repay the $6.7 million, and, thus, the Raiders had taxable income upon receipt of the funds.

* * *

The Raiders had the discretion to determine if and when the suites would be constructed, as demonstrated by the terms of the 1982 MOA and the 1984 lease. Although both documents limited the Raiders' discretion by a standard of reasonableness, the agreements gave the Raiders great latitude in the timing of construction.

Where the performance of a party's obligations under a contract is subject to such party's unlimited discretion, the duties ostensibly imposed upon that party are illusory for income tax purposes. . . . While the Raiders may well have intended to construct the suites, in the context of the agreement, any obligation to construct the suites was illusory.

Petitioners point out that the Raiders, under the terms of the agreement, were to "begin and complete * * * construction as soon as possible"; the timing of construction, however, was still to be determined by the Raiders, in their reasonable discretion. Planning for the suites was undertaken in 1985 and 1986 and actual construction began and was halted in February 1987. While construction was stopped due to a dispute between the Raiders and the LAMCC, the Raiders at this time were contemplating their move to Irwindale, which was represented by a formal agreement in August 1987.

Repayment of the $6.7 million was to commence 3 years after the construction of the suites, and repayment was to be solely from the net revenues from suite operations. If the Raiders did not construct the suites, which was the case, there would be no suite revenues to use for repayment. No default or alternative payment provision was included in the 1982 MOA, the 1984 lease, or the promissory note. The nonrecourse promissory note was secured only by the improvements, *i.e.*, the suites. When the Raiders did not construct the suites, the LAMCC was without a source for repayment.

* * *

No evidence was presented to indicate that the LAMCC sought to enforce the Raiders' agreement to build the suites prior to the Raiders' announcement of their intention to move to Irwindale in late 1987. Petitioners presented testimony of representatives of both the Raiders and the LAMCC, purportedly to show the intent to repay and to enforce repayment. The testimony is ambiguous and is contradicted in many respects by documentary exhibits. The objective manifestations of intent in this instance are more persuasive to us.

Due to the contingent nature of the Raiders' obligation, an unconditional and enforceable debt did not exist for tax purposes at the times that the $4 million advance and the rent credits were received by the Raiders from the LAMCC. Thus, we sustain respondent's determination that the Raiders had income in 1982, 1983, 1984, 1985, and 1986 equal to the amount of the rent credits, and that, in 1984, the Raiders had an additional $4 million in income from the advance made in 1984.

* * *

MILENBACH v. COMMISSIONER

United States Court of Appeals, Ninth Circuit
318 F.3d 924 (9th Cir. 2003)

* * *

A loan is generally not taxable income because the receipt of the loan is offset by the obligation to repay the loan. *Comm'r v. Tufts*, 461 U.S. 300, 307 (1983). For this rule to apply, however, the loan must be an "existing, unconditional, and legally enforceable obligation for the payment of a principal sum. . . .

Whether a transaction is a loan for federal income tax purposes is ultimately a question of federal law. . . . Initially, however, state law determines the rights and obligations of the parties to a transaction. . . . But once an obligation is created by local law, it is subject to the federal definition of taxability. . . . Here, the dispositive question is whether the LAMCC Agreement was sufficient, under California law, to subject the Raiders to a non-illusory and enforceable obligation to repay the LAMCC advances. If the Raiders were subject to an "existing, unconditional, and legally enforceable obligation" to repay the LAMCC advances, the advances are properly treated as loans for federal income tax purposes. . . .

Contrary to the Tax Court's conclusion, the Raiders' broad discretion in the timing of the construction of the suites did not make the contract illusory. Under California law, an obligation under a contract is not illusory if the obligated party's discretion must be exercised with reasonableness or good faith. *See Storek & Storek, Inc. v. Citicorp Real Estate, Inc.*, . . . (holding that a promise to pay only if satisfied is not illusory if the ability to claim dissatisfaction is limited by the standard of reasonableness) . . . .

Here, the Raiders were required to exercise their discretion reasonably and nothing in the LAMCC Agreement indicates that construction of the suites was optional. Both the 1982 MOA and the Lease state that the suites "shall be" constructed and both require the Raiders to use their "reasonable" discretion in deciding the exact timing in the construction of the suites. The Lease also required the Raiders to use their "best efforts" both to construct the suites as soon as possible and to operate them in such a way as to maximize the profits to be derived from them. At no point were the Raiders free to ignore their obligation to construct the suites. They could only delay the construction for a reasonable time and were required to use their best efforts to complete the suites and begin repayment of the loan. These limitations on the Raiders' discretion were sufficient to create a non-illusory obligation both to construct the suites and to repay the loan that would have been enforceable under California law. The fact that the obligations were later extinguished by the settlement of the 1987 lawsuit does not indicate that the obligation was illusory at the time the contract was made. Accordingly, we conclude that the Tax Court erred in holding that the LAMCC Agreement was illusory.

Because the Raiders had a non-illusory, unconditional obligation to repay the LAMCC loan, the payments were properly treated as loans and were excludable from income in the year in which they were received.

* * *

NOTES AND COMMENTS

In *Milenbach*, there was no question that the Raiders received cash and incurred duties under the LAMCC Agreement. In terms of Treas. Reg. § 1.752-1(a)(4)(ii) and its definition of a liability, the issue was whether those duties amounted to a "fixed or contingent obligation to make payment," so as to be an "obligation." Of course, the issue was not framed in terms of the partnership regulations but it might have been clearer if it had. In keeping with these terms, had the duties constituted an obligation, the receipt of cash would have been excludable from the Raiders' gross income because of the offsetting liability.

The Tax Court determined that the Raiders' duties were not obligations because the Raiders did not have to construct the suites. The Court of Appeals decided, applying state law, that the Raiders did have to make reasonable efforts to construct the suites. On this point, the case also illustrates the complex interplay between federal and state law in tax matters. As stated, state law determines the legal rights and obligations of the taxpayer, but the Code in its broadest sense — including all interpretative material — determines the tax consequences of those rights and obligations. In *Milenbach*, the issue was not the federal tax law characterization, but whether state law imposed a legal duty on the Raiders. The Tax Court said no, but the Court of Appeals said yes. Unfortunately, the case does not deal with the tax consequences of the settlement that let the Raiders completely off the hook. We return to that issue in § 2.1 *In General* dealing with discharge of indebtedness.

There are a number of other situations that are not loans, but that involve receipt of cash that is not included in income on receipt because there are offsetting obligations that create liabilities under the Treas. Reg. § 1.752-1(a)(4)(A) definition. Thus, receipt of payment in a short sale of securities creates a liability because of the receipt of the payment, even though the ultimate outcome of the short sale transaction is not known at the time of receipt, and may result in gain or loss on the securities sold short. *See* Rev. Rul. 95-26, 1995-1 C.B. 131 (partnership obligation to lender of stock used to close a short sale is a liability); Rev. Rul. 95-45, 1995-1 C.B. 53 (same for short sale obligation assumed in § 351 transaction); *Salina Partnership L.P. v. Commissioner*, T.C. Memo. 2000-352 (tax shelter case rejecting claim that the uncertainty about the value of the securities to be delivered prevented the treatment of the consideration as a liability in a partnership short sale). Similarly, receipt of payment as consideration for grant of an option to purchase property from, or to sell property to, is not income. Because the tax treatment of the payment is uncertain until the option is exercised — in which case the payment is consideration for the property sold or an offset against the basis of the property purchased — or, if the option is not exercised, the payment is treated as gross income when the option lapses. *See* Rev. Rul. 78-182, 1978-1 C.B. 265 (premiums on CBOE options not income on receipt); *Virginia Iron Coal & Coke Co. v. Commissioner*, 37 B.T.A. 195, *aff'd*, 99 F.2d 919 (4th Cir. 1938), *cert. denied*, 307 U.S. 630 (1939) (payment received for option to purchase stock of a subsidiary not taxed in year of receipt, because not clear whether it would be part of purchase price if option exercised; income when option lapsed); *Commissioner v. Dill Co.*, 294 F.2d 291 (3d Cir. 1961) (payment for renewal of license of trademark plus an option to purchase the zero-basis trademark was not income in year of receipt, because could not tell if it would be applied to purchase price). Similarly, receipt of consideration for a short sale of securities creates a liability in the amount of the cash received, even though the value of the securities at the time of the closing of the short sale may be more or less than the amount of the consideration received.

Milenbach is one of a vast number of cases in which the issue is whether a duty to repay gives rise to a bona fide liability, or true debt. Many of these cases involve questions whether investments in corporations and other business entities are classified as debt obligations or are really disguised equity investments. These issues are considered in courses on corporate or business entity taxation. Similar issues arise in determining whether transactions among related parties represent loans, gifts, or other types of transfers. *See, e.g., Geftman v. Commissioner*, 154 F.3d 61 (3d Cir. 1998) (transfers by trusts that had received distributions from an estate back to the estate to provide it with funds to settle estate liabilities did not create bona fide indebtedness); *Frierdich v. Commissioner*, 925 F.2d 180 (7th Cir. 1991) (taxpayer had current income loan from executrix of estate payable out of fees from estate at below market interest rate; not arm's-length transaction); Tech. Adv. Mem. 2000-40-004 (loan to new employees linked to bonus agreement providing bonuses equal to loan payments and term forgiving balance on termination of employment other than for cause or quitting was immediate income). Because the obligor has no personal liability on a nonrecourse liability, as discussed in § 3.03 *Speculative Security*, there is a question of whether the nonrecourse liability is a fixed or contingent obligation to pay money when the encumbered property is of uncertain value. There are similar issues in determining whether a cancelled obligation was an indebtedness that are considered in § 2, *Discharge of Indebtedness*.

PROBLEMS FOR DISCUSSION

Problem 3-1. As indicated in the quoted portion of the *Milenbach* Tax Court opinion, the Raiders entered a similar deal with the City of Irwindale. The Irwindale MOA provided that Irwindale would loan the Raiders $115 million to be used in the construction of a stadium in Irwindale where the Raiders would play their home games beginning with the 1992 NFL season. Irwindale advanced the Raiders $10 million against the $115-million loan. The $10 million was to be repaid solely from the revenues of the stadium to be built. In addition to the $10 million advance, the Irwindale MOA required an additional $10 million to be placed in an escrow interest-bearing account within seven (7) days, but Irwindale never made the escrow deposit. Under the Irwindale MOA, if contemplated obstacles imposed by third parities interfered, the parties' legal obligations would be excused only to the extent of any injunctions, but this provision did not excuse the failure to make the escrow deposit. There were third-party lawsuits and other obstacles that prevented the building of the stadium. As a result, Irwindale acknowledged in the third-party lawsuit that "regardless of what happens, the Raiders are permitted to keep the $10,000,000." Nevertheless, in a portion of the opinion not quoted, the Tax Court held that the $10,000,000 was a bona fide loan. On what basis, if any, is the

Irwindale situation distinguishable from the LAMCC situation?

Problem 3-2. Team made up-front payments to Player, for which Player signed a note, payable (with interest) over five years. At the same time, Team agreed to pay annual bonuses at least equal to the annual principal and interest payments on the note. The bonuses were to be applied automatically to the notes, with any excess paid to Player. The principal of the note is accelerated if Player is cut from the roster, but is payable only out of any amounts still owed to Player. If the Player is traded, Team will apply a portion of the consideration it receives from the trade to payment of the note. (i) Under the Tax Court opinion in *Milenbach* is the note a bona fide obligation? (ii) Under the Court of Appeals opinion? *See* Rev. Rul. 78-182, (premiums on CBOE options); *Geftman* (transfers from trusts back to estate); *Frierdich* (loan to estate's lawyer); Tech. Adv. Mem. 2000-40-004 (loan for signing bonus).

§ 1.02. Obligations v. Liabilities

I.R.C. § 357(c)(3); § 358(h); § 704(c)(3)

Treas. Reg. § 1.752-1(a)(4)(i)(B) includes as a liability incurring an obligation that "[g]ives rise to an immediate deduction to the obligor." This provision recognizes that accounts payable and similar obligations of accrual-method taxpayers become liabilities when the deduction is allowed. However, fixed obligations to make deductible payments, for example, payables of cash-method taxpayers, are not liabilities because no deduction is allowed until payment. Thus, there must be an obligation for there to be a tax liability, but not every obligation is a liability for tax purposes.

A number of Code provisions, including § 357(c)(3), relating to nonrecognition transfers to corporations, and § 704(c)(3), relating to similar contributions to partnerships, adopt the principle that accounts payable by a cash-method taxpayer are not liabilities. The following rulings, which predate the partnership regulations, explain this position, and indicate that it applies more broadly than the specific statutory provisions.

Rev. Rul. 80-198, 1980-2 C.B. 113

* * *

Individual *A* conducted a medical practice as a sole proprietorship, the income of which was reported on the cash receipts and disbursements method of accounting. *A* transferred to a newly organized corporation all of the operating assets of the sole proprietorship in exchange for all of the stock of the corporation, plus the assumption by the corporation of all of the liabilities of the sole proprietorship. The purpose of the incorporation was to provide a form of business organization that would be more conducive to the planned expansion of the medical services to be made available by the business enterprise.

The assets transferred were tangible assets having a fair market value of $40,000 and an adjusted basis of $30,000 and unrealized trade accounts receivable having a face amount of $20,000 and an adjusted basis of zero. The liabilities assumed by the corporation consisted of trade accounts payable in the face amount of $10,000. The liabilities assumed by the corporation also included a mortgage liability, related to the tangible property transferred, of $10,000. *A* had neither accumulated the accounts receivable nor prepaid any of the liabilities of the sole proprietorship in a manner inconsistent with normal business practices in anticipation of the incorporation. If *A* had paid the trade accounts payable liabilities, the amounts paid would have been deductible by *A* as ordinary and necessary business expenses under section 162 of the Code. The new corporation continued to utilize the cash receipts and disbursements method of accounting.

* * *

In *Hempt Bros., Inc. v. United States*, 490 F.2d 1172 (3d Cir. 1974), *cert. denied*, 419 U.S. 826 (1974), the United States Court of Appeals for the Third Circuit held, as the Internal Revenue Service contended, that a cash basis transferee corporation was taxable on the monies it collected on accounts receivable that had been transferred to it by a cash basis partnership in a transaction described in section 351(a) of the Code. The corporate taxpayer contended that it was not obligated to include the accounts receivable in income; rather the transferor partnership should have been taxed on the stock the partnership received under the assignment of income doctrine . . .

The court in *Hempt Bros.* solved the conflict between the assignment of income doctrine and the statutory non-recognition provisions of section 351 of the Code by reasoning that if the cash basis transferor were taxed on the transfer of the accounts receivable, the specific congressional intent reflected in section 351(a) that the incorporation of an ongoing business should be facilitated by making the incorporation tax free would be frustrated.

The facts of the instant case are similar to those in *Hempt Bros.* in that there was a valid business purpose for the transfer of the accounts receivable along with all of the assets and liabilities of *A*'s proprietorship to a corporate transferee that would continue the business of the transferor. Further, *A* had neither accumulated the accounts receivable nor prepaid any of the account payable liabilities of the sole proprietorship in anticipation of the incorporation, which is an indication that, under the facts and circumstances of the case, the transaction was not designed for tax avoidance.

HOLDING

The transfer by *A* of the operating assets of the sole proprietorship (including unrealized accounts receivable) to the corporation in exchange solely for the common stock of the corporation and the assumption by the corporation of the proprietorship liabilities (including accounts payable) is an exchange within the meaning of section 351(a) of the Code. Therefore, no gain or loss is recognized to *A* with respect to the property transferred, including the accounts receivable. For transfers occurring on or after . . . (the effective date of . . . sections 357(c)(3) and 358(d)(2) of the Code) the assumption of the trade accounts payable that would give rise to a deduction if *A* had paid them is not, pursuant to section 357(c)(3), considered as an assumption of a liability for purposes of sections 357(c)(1) and 358(d). . . .

A's basis in the stock received in the exchange of property for stock under section 358(a)(1) of the Code is $20,000 which is calculated by decreasing *A*'s $30,000 basis in the assets transferred by the $10,000 mortgage liability under sections 358(a)(1)(A) (ii) and 358(d)(1). No adjustment to such basis is made under section 358(a)(1)(A)(ii) because of the assumption by the corporation of the $10,000 in accounts payable inasmuch as the general rule of section 358(d) (1), which requires the basis in the stock received to be decreased by the liabilities assumed, does not apply by reason of section 358(d)(2), which provides that section 358(d)(1) does not apply to the amount of any liabilities defined in section 357(c)(3) such as accounts payable that would have been deductible by *A* as ordinary and necessary business expenses under section 162 in the taxable year paid if *A* had paid these liabilities prior to the exchange. See Rev. Rul. 80-199, with respect to transfers which have occurred before . . . the enactment of the Revenue Act of 1978.

* * *

Rev. Rul. 88-77, 1988-2 C.B. 129

* * *

A is a partner in *P* partnership. *P* files returns on a calendar year basis and uses the cash receipts and disbursements method of accounting. At the close of the taxable year at issue, *P*'s accrued expenses and accounts payable consisted of 100x dollars for interest expense and accounts payable of 200x dollars for services received.

* * *

Rev. Rul. 60-345, 1960-2 C.B. 311, holds that, for purposes of section 752 of the Code, the term 'liabilities' includes a cash basis partnership's obligations for the payment of outstanding trade accounts, notes, and accrued expenses.

The present issue is similar to that arising under section 357(c) of the Code when property and liabilities are contributed to a controlled corporation in exchange for stock. For purposes of determining the basis of the stock received in the exchange under section 358 and any gain that must be recognized on the exchange under section 357(c), section 357(c)(3) provides that the term "liabilities" shall not include obligations the payment of which would give rise to a deduction or that would constitute a guaranteed payment under section 736(a). This rule is subject to an exception found in section 357(c)(3)(B) for liabilities the incurrence of which resulted in the creation of, or an increase in, the basis of any property. . . .

The legislative history accompanying the amendment to section 704(c) made by the Tax Reform Act of 1984 explicitly rejected the conclusion reached in Revenue Ruling 60-345 in favor of an interpretation of section 752 that is consistent with section 357(c). . . .

Under *P*'s method of accounting, *P*'s obligations to pay amounts incurred for interest and services are not deductible until paid. For purposes of section 752 of the Code, the terms 'liabilities of a partnership' and 'partnership liabilities' include an obligation only if and to the extent that incurring the liability creates or increases the basis to the partnership of any of the partnership's assets (including cash attributable to borrowings), gives rise to an immediate deduction to the partnership, or, under section 705(a)(2)(B), currently decreases a partner's basis in the partner's partnership interest. The preceding sentence uses the term 'assets' to include capitalized items that are properly allocable to future periods, such as organizational expenses and construction period expenses.

The liabilities incurred by *P* for interest expense and services do not create or increase the basis of a partnership asset or give rise to a deduction when incurred. Therefore, for purposes of computing *A*'s adjusted basis in *P*, *A* may not treat P's accrued expenses and accounts payable as a liability of the partnership.

* * *

NOTES AND COMMENTS

In Rev. Rul. 80-199, 1980-2 C.B. 122, the Service ruled that it would apply the principle of § 357(c)(3) that deductible obligations are not liabilities for purposes of § 351 to transfers before the effective date of the enactment of § 357(c)(3). It did so, relying on *Focht v. Commissioner*, 68 T.C. 223 (1977), *acq.*, which had reached the same conclusion prior to the enactment of § 357(c)(3), but limited its conclusion to §§ 357 and 358(d). Rev. Rul. 88-77 indicates that the limitation no longer applies.

Under the definition of "liability" implicit in Rev. Ruls. 80-198, 88-77 and 80-199, a deferred compensation obligation is not a liability. The following case does not directly address the definitional issue, but deals with the implications of increases in such obligations to reflect the time value of money, in quite different terms in reaching a result consistent with treating the deferred compensation obligation as not being a liability on which interest can accrue.

ALBERTSON'S, INC. v. COMMISSIONER

United States Court of Appeals, Ninth Circuit
42 F.3d 537 (9th Cir. 1994)

* * *

> [Prior to 1982, Albertson's entered into deferred compensation agreements ("DCAs") with certain employees and independent contractors ("DCA participants") providing for deferral of specified bonuses and other compensation ("basic amounts") for an agreed period of time. The DCAs provided that the DCA participants would receive an additional amount for the time value of the deferred payments (computed at an agreed rate) that accumulated on the basic amounts ("additional amount") when they became entitled to payment of the basic amount. The arrangement allowed Albertson's to use the basic and additional amounts as a source of working capital. The Service initially granted Albertson's request to deduct the additional amounts (but not the basic amounts) as they accrued, but changed its policy, contending that all amounts provided for in the deferred

compensation agreements (*i.e.*, both the basic and the additional amounts) were deductible only when received by Albertson's employees. A divided Tax Court found that the additional amounts represented compensation, not interest, and were therefore not deductible until the end of the deferral period under § 404(a)(5) & (d). A nine-member majority held that the additional amount was not currently deductible because it was not interest. A four-member concurrence argued that the additional amount was interest, but that § 404's timing restrictions applied to both compensation and interest. A five-member dissent argued that the additional amount was interest and that § 404's timing restrictions applied *only* to compensation. One judge did not participate, and one judge voted in favor of the majority *and* the concurrence. Thus, twelve judges agreed that the additional amounts were not deductible interest under § 404. The 9th Circuit first held that the additional amounts constituted interest within the definition of § 163(a) and that interest payments were not governed by the timing restrictions of § 404, but on rehearing, reversed itself and held against the deduction, stating:]

. . . The question is not an easy one, however. . . . This is simply one of those cases — and there are more of them than judges generally like to admit — in which the answer is far from clear and in which there are conflicting rules and principles that we are forced to try to apply simultaneously. Such accommodation sometimes proves to be impossible. In some cases, as here, convincing arguments can be made for both possible results, and the court's decision will depend on which of the two competing legal principles it chooses to give greater weight to in the particular circumstance. Law, even statutory construction, is not a science. It is merely an effort by human beings, albeit judges, to do their best with imperfect tools to arrive at a correct result.

* * *

In its petition for rehearing, the government, far more forcefully and clearly than it did originally, has articulated the purpose of the timing restrictions outlined in I.R.C. § 404: to encourage employers to invest in qualified compensation plans by requiring inclusions and deductions of income and expense to be "matched" for nonqualified plans. . . . The matching principle, widely recognized to be the key to I.R.C. § 404, provides significant tax incentives for employers to invest in qualified deferred compensation plans, which are nondiscriminatory and ensure that employees receive the compensation promised to them. . . . As the Commissioner forcefully argues, our original interpretation of I.R.C. § 404 undercut the essential purpose of that provision by violating the matching principle and creating a taxation scheme that favors the type of plan that Congress intended to discourage. *See infra* . . . . For this reason, we granted the Commissioner's petition for rehearing. . . .

* * *

An examination of the differences between qualified and nonqualified plans is essential to an understanding of the purpose of the congressional scheme governing deferred compensation agreements. Congress has imposed few restrictions upon nonqualified deferred compensation plans. An employer may limit participation in a nonqualified plan to highly paid executives, and it need not guarantee equal benefits for all participants. In addition, the employer is not required to set aside any funds or provide any guarantees (beyond the initial contractual promise) that its employees will receive the compensation. Thus, promised benefits for unfunded, nonqualified plans are subject to the claims of the employer's general creditors.

Under a qualified plan, in contrast, an employer may not discriminate in favor of officers, shareholders, or highly compensated employees. I.R.C. § 401(a)(4) & (a)(5). In addition, a qualified plan must satisfy minimum participation and coverage standards concerning eligibility and actual rates of participation. I.R.C. § 401(a)(2) & (a)(26), 410. The amounts which an employer may contribute to qualified plans and the benefits which qualified plans may provide are also restricted. I.R.C. §§ 401(a)(17), 415.

A qualified plan also provides significant guarantees that employees will receive the compensation promised to them. It generally must be funded through a trust. I.R.C. § 401(a). Neither the corpus nor the income of the trust may be diverted for any purpose; they can only be used for the exclusive benefit of the participants. I.R.C. § 401(a)(2). . . .

It is clear that few employers would adopt a qualified deferred compensation plan, with all of its burdensome requirements, if the taxation scheme favored nonqualified plans or treated nonqualified and qualified plans similarly. Although qualified plans provide significant benefits to employees, they allow employers little flexibility in structuring a plan, require them to provide extensive coverage, prevent them from discriminating in favor of highly compensated employees, and involve a significant initial outlay of funds. . . .

The most significant difference between the two types of plans, for purposes of tax deductibility, is that under a qualified plan the employer must turn over annually to a third party the basic amounts that are deferred and may not use those amounts for the employer's own benefit. Thus, the employer, in effect, is required to make the deferred payments at the time the employee is earning the compensation. It is only the employee's right to receive the funds that is delayed. In contrast, an employer with a nonqualified plan is not required to turn any funds over to anyone until the end of the deferred compensation period. Such an employer may use those funds for its own purposes for a period of many years. In a nonqualified plan, it is not only the employee's right to receive the funds that is deferred; the employer's obligation to part with the funds is deferred as well. . . .

* * *

. . . In [deferring deduction of nonqualified deferred compensation when accrued], Congress forced employers who chose to retain their funds for their own use to wait until the *end* of the deferral period, when these amounts were includible in plan participants' taxable income, before they could take deductions for deferred compensation payments. However, employers who maintained a "qualified" plan that met the rigorous requirements of the Internal Revenue Code (and now ERISA), including turning over the sums involved to a trust fund (or purchasing an annuity), were allowed to continue to take the annual deductions even though their employees would not receive the deferred compensation until a later year . . .

* * *

Commentators have widely agreed that this "matching principle" is the key to section 404. As Boris Bittker and Lawrence Lokken have observed, "[t]he most consistent feature for the rules for nonqualified plans is that the employer is ordinarily allowed no deduction for contribution, payments or benefits until they are taxed to the employee." . . .

* * *

Albertson's maintains that section 404 only requires that the basic amounts of compensation be matched; it argues that all additional amounts paid to compensate an employee for the time value of money represent "interest" payments for which an employer may take an immediate deduction. In light of the clear purpose underlying section 404 — to encourage employers to create qualified plans for their employees — we decline to ascribe such an intention to Congress.

. . . In order to adopt Albertson's proposal and allow employers to take current deductions for additional "interest" payments, we would be required to conclude that Congress created a system in which employers could deduct a substantial portion of the nonqualified deferred compensation package long before its employees had received any of those funds. For example, when the additional amounts are calculated for a compensation package deferred over a fifteen-year period using an interest rate similar to that used by Albertson's, an employer can classify more than seventy percent of the deferred compensation package as "interest payments." . . . Moreover, we note that, under Albertson's deferred compensation agreement, participants have the option of deferring payment of the total sum available to them upon retirement for an additional period of up to fifteen years. *All* payments during that additional period would also constitute "interest," and the deductible portion of the final compensation package would thus increase exponentially.

Albertson's has been unable to explain why Congress, in designing a taxation scheme to encourage the creation of qualified plans, would require an employer that maintains a nonqualified plan to defer taking a deduction on the basic amounts of a promised compensation package but nevertheless allow that employer to take current deductions on amounts that constitute a substantial portion of the compensation package, merely because that portion is classified as "interest." Given that the interest payments will often constitute the bulk of the total compensation package that an employee under a nonqualified plan ultimately receives, it would make little sense to impose a matching requirement upon "basic" payments but not upon "interest" payments. Albertson's interpretation of section 404 would seriously undermine the incentive structure designed by Congress to encourage employers to establish qualified plans.

* * *

Albertson's has not been able to refute the argument that its interpretation of section 404 undercuts the provision's central purpose. Equally important, it offers us no reason why Congress would have wanted to treat the "interest" part of the deferred compensation package differently from the basic amounts for tax purposes.

Instead, Albertson's rests its argument upon its contention that, because the plain language of § 404 only refers to "compensation" rather than "interest," the employers have a statutory right to deduct the additional amounts as interest under § 163. In this connection, Albertson's points out that section 404 prohibits deduction under sections 162 and 212 but not under section 163, and it is the latter section that governs the deduction of interest. Albertson's argument as to the plain language of the statute is a strong one. We certainly agree that the additional payments resemble "interest" and that, under a literal reading of the statutory language, the deduction of interest is not affected by section 404. However, holding such payments to be deductible "interest" under section 404 would lead to an anomalous result: a taxation scheme designed to make nonqualified plans less attractive would in many cases provide incentives for adopting such plans, and a provision intended to apply the matching principle to nonqualified deferred compensation agreements would exempt substantial portions of DCA payments from its application.

In the end we are forced, therefore, to reject Albertson's approach. We may not adopt a plain language interpretation of a statutory provision that directly undercuts the clear purpose of the statute. . . .

. . . In *Bob Jones University*, the Supreme Court addressed the question of whether I.R.C. § 501(c)(3) — which provides that "corporations . . . organized and operated exclusively for religious, charitable . . . or educational purposes" are entitled to tax exemption — included educational institutions with racially discriminatory policies. Even though Congress had explicitly outlined eight categories of exempt organizations in section 501(c)(3) without making any mention of additional requirements beyond those outlined in the statute, the Supreme Court interpreted the statute to include an additional requirement: the organization in question must serve a valid charitable purpose. . . . Thus, the Court was willing to read additional language into the text of the statute because an alternative interpretation would undermine the fundamental purpose of the legislation. As the Court itself noted, "[i]t is a well-established canon of statutory construction that a court should go beyond the literal language of a statute if reliance on that language would defeat the plain purpose of the statute." . . .

In rejecting Albertson's appeal, we take heed of the Supreme Court's instructions concerning the proper interpretation of the Internal Revenue Code when the plain language of the provision leads to an unreasonable result and directly contradicts its underlying purpose: the provision "*must* be analyzed and construed within the framework of the Internal Revenue Code and against the background of the congressional purposes." *Id.* (emphasis added). . . .

* * *

. . . Whether or not the additional amounts constitute interest, allowing Albertson's to deduct them prior to their receipt by their employees would contravene the clear purpose of the taxation scheme governing deferred compensation agreements. Accordingly, we vacate the portion of our original opinion dealing with deferred compensation agreements and affirm the Tax Court's holding that Albertson's may not currently deduct the additional amounts.

* * *

NOTES AND COMMENTS

The partnership regulations' definition of liability, and their exclusion of obligations that will give rise to a deduction but have not yet become deductible emphasizes that, for tax purposes, the relevant amount of a liability is the amount that has been taken into account for tax purposes in connection with incurring the liability, without regard to the amount of the legal obligation to pay under state law. This tax amount is the rough analogue of the concept of the basis of an asset. The Code and regulations do not, however, contain provisions analogous to the general basis provisions of §§ 1011 to 1023 or the more specific provisions, primarily relating to nonrecognition exchanges in §§ 358 and 362 for corporations, 722-23, 732-34 and 742-43 for partnerships, and 1031(d) for nonrecognition exchanges. Similarly, there is no consistent terminology for determining the relevant amount of a liability in the Code or Regulations. Section 357(c) refers to the "amount" of a liability; § 108(b) also refers to the "amount" of indebtedness excluded from gross income; § 171(b) refers to the "amount payable at maturity;" and §§ 1273(b) and 1272(a)(4) of the original issue discount rules refer to the "issue price" and "adjusted issue price" (the latter term being the equivalent of adjusted basis — that is, the issue price after taking into account amortization of discount). For convenience, this Chapter uses the term "tax amount" to refer to the equivalent of the basis/adjusted basis for liabilities. In addition, the concept that obligations with a zero tax amount has been extended from deductible obligations to contingent ones, even those for capitalizable expenditures, and presumably for nondeductible, noncapital expenditures, which, as a result, are taken into account for tax purposes when paid, or when the contingency lapses or is satisfied. *See* Rev. Rul. 95-74, 1995-2 C.B. 36 (contingent obligation for environmental clean-up costs transferred in § 351 transactions are not liabilities; such obligations are taken into account by the transferee corporation when paid); Priv. Ltr. Rul. 2000-13-044 (deferred compensation obligations of a branch of a foreign corporation that are paid by a domestic successor are deductible by the successor when paid); *cf.* Rev. Rul. 2005-42, 2005-2 C.B. 67 (cost of environmental cleanup attributable to production activities is inventory cost in year incurred under Treas. Reg. §§ 1.263A-1(c)(1) and 1.263A-1(c)(2), so that it is capitalized into the then-current year's production, even if not related to current year's production).

Under the tax amount concept implicit in Treas. Reg. § 1.752-1(a)(4)(i)(B), the tax amount of the deferred compensation obligation in *Albertson's* should be, of course, zero. This raises the question whether adjustments to such obligations to reflect the time value of money have independent status or are simply additions to the underlying obligation. The implicit answer in the *Albertson's* opinion is that they lay somewhere in between. The express holding is that the additional amounts are interest, but subject to the timing rules of § 404(a)(5), with the result that the additional amounts/interest are treated as part of the underlying obligation. Because there is no Code or Regulations definition, two classic definitions of interest for tax purposes are from the Supreme Court cases of *Old Colony R. Co. v. Commissioner*, 284 U.S. 552, 560 (1932): interest is "the amount one has contracted to pay for the use of borrowed money," and *Deputy v. Du Pont*, 308 U.S. 488, 498 (1940): that interest is "compensation for the use or forbearance of money." In *Old Colony*, the Court refused to treat bond premiums received before the adoption of the Sixteenth Amendment as a reduction in the deduction for interest paid after adoption, on the ground that the premium was income when the bond was issued, which was before the effective date of the Sixteenth Amendment. In *du Pont*, the Court refused to treat as deductible interest amounts paid by a major shareholder to the owner of the borrowed stock equivalent to the dividends paid on the shares in a transaction involving, in effect, the short sale of the stock to key employees when it had also held that the amounts did not qualify as business expenses (before the enactment of what is now § 212). Although the results of these cases no longer apply, they illustrate the difficulty of defining "interest." Nevertheless, under either definition, the additional amounts in *Albertson's* are not interest. The basic deferred compensation amounts are not liabilities, although they are obligations owed to the employees. Accordingly, the amount owned is not "borrowed money." The *du Pont* definition comes closer, but still there is nothing borrowed from the employees equivalent to stock in a short sale. *See also* Rev. Rul. 83-22, 1983-1 C.B. 17 (dividends on restricted stock that is not vested under Treas. Reg. § 1.83-1(a) are compensation, not dividends); Chief. Couns. Adv. 2008-36-025 (amounts paid as prejudgment interest are not deductible as interest because there is no liability until the judgment is final, but they may be deductible as part of the judgment; reviews authorities). The authors suggest that adopting the express view that the "additional amounts" are not interest, but additional deferred compensation, is more appropriate as being consistent with the definition of a liability exemplified by the partnership regulations.

Although the exclusion of obligations that have not been taken into account for tax purposes from the definition of a liability when applying most provisions of the Code that deal with the tax consequences of transfers and other dispositions of liabilities makes sound tax sense, like all sensible tax concepts, it is subject to abuse. For example, one form of recent corporate tax shelter involved the transfer of assets with a basis roughly equal to their fair market values to a corporation along with the transfer of obligations that were not liabilities to the corporation in an amount equal to the value of the assets. The contribution of assets and obligations was followed by a sale of the stock of the transferee corporation. Although the obligations reduced the value of the transferee corporation's stock in the transferor's hands, the obligations did not reduce the basis of the stock, allowing the stock to be sold at a large loss, in effect accelerating the deduction of the transferred obligations. Section 358(h) was subsequently enacted to limit this type of abuse for corporate transfers. *See* 2001-1 C.B. 730, Notice 2001-17 (describing and attacking two versions of this device under § 358(h) for transactions after its effective date; relies on anti-tax-shelter arguments for those before); *Coltec Indus. v. United States*, 62 Fed. Cl. 716 (Cl. Ct. 2004)(allowing the loss on such a transaction prior to the effective date of § 358(h) and finding adequate business purpose despite acknowledged tax-shelter aspects)*vacated by and remanded by,* 454 F.3d 1340 (Fed. Cir. 2006) (transaction disregarded and loss disallowed because it lacked economic substance, even though acknowledged that the loss was technically allowable prior to the enactment of § 358(h)); *Black & Decker Corp. v. United States*, 2004 U.S. Dist. LEXIS 17351, 2004-2 U.S.T.C. ¶ 50,390, 94 A.F.T.R.2d (RIA) 5620, *modified by* 340 F. Supp. 2d 621 (D. Md. 2004) (granting summary judgment for taxpayer on similar transaction); *aff'd, rev'd and rem'd*, 436 F.3d 431 (4th Cir. 2006) (affirmance on denial of summary judgment to

Service; reversal on grant of summary judgment to taxpayer; remand to apply sham transaction doctrine). Treas. Reg. § 1.752-1(a)(4) containing the definition of a liability that begins this Section was promulgated as part of regulatory modifications containing principles applicable to transfers in the partnership context similar to those applicable in the corporate context under § 358(h). A nonstatutory approach to achieving the correct approach would be determine that the obligation was not a liability in determining the tax consequences of the nonrecognition transaction, but that it became a liability when the stock was transferred, reducing basis at that time.

PROBLEMS FOR DISCUSSION

Problem 3-3. Chemco has operated a manufacturing plant for many years on Site. It transferred the plant to Venco, a corporation organized as a joint venture with another manufacturing company, in a nonrecognition transaction under § 351. An inspection in connection with the formation of the joint venture determined that the plant's prior manufacturing operation had resulted in pollution that will have to be cleaned up if the expansion planned for the manufacturing plant by the joint venture is to receive required regulatory approvals. Some of the clean-up expenditures will be deductible when paid, some relate to pollution caused in producing products that were sold by Chemco before the transfer, and some will have to be capitalized. The joint venture partner has agreed to have Venco make the expenditures. Which, if any, of the environmental clean-up costs are liabilities transferred? *See* Rev. Rul. 2005-42 (cleaning up own environmental mess is inventory cost); Rev. Rul. 95-74 (contingent obligations in nonrecognition transfer under § 351); Rev. Rul. 80-198 (deductible obligations); Rev. Rul. 80-199 (deductible corporate obligations before § 357(c)); Rev. Rul. 88-77 (deductible partnership obligations); Priv. Ltr. Rul. 2000-13-044 (deductible obligations of foreign predecessor).

Problem 3-4. Ceeco had nonqualified deferred compensation obligations to officers, directors, and senior managers of $10,000,000 that will not be payable for an average of 10 years, in connection with Div, a trade or business that it proposes to sell. The net basis of Div's assets is $11,000,000, reflecting assets with an adjusted basis of $16,000,000 and liabilities (not including the deferred compensation obligations) of $5,000,000. Nevertheless, the net worth of Div is only $1,000,000, because the deferred compensation obligations, although not liabilities, nevertheless reduce the value of Div. The deferred compensation obligations are worth $10,000,000 even though they are not payable for many years, because the deferred compensation agreement provides that the amounts increase each year by a factor equal to the prime rate. If Ceeco transfers Div to Newco, which assumes the deferred compensation obligations, and sells the Newco stock for $1,000,000, is it entitled to a $10,000,000 loss, because the basis of the Newco shares is $11,000,000 because, under § 358(d)(2) the transferred deferred compensation obligation does not reduce basis? *See* § 358(h); Notice 2001-17 (attack on devices); *Coltec Indus. v. United States* (allows similar transaction); *Black & Decker Corp. v. United States* (same).

Problem 3-5. How, if at all, would the policy-based analysis of *Albertson's* affect the authorities listed in the Notes and Comments and the results in Problems 3-3 and 3-4?

§ 2. DISCHARGE OF INDEBTEDNESS (DOI)

The concept that a liability is an amount that has been taken into account for tax purposes means that there must be an appropriate accounting of the liability for tax purposes when it is transferred or otherwise terminated. When a taxpayer is relieved of a liability without providing adequate consideration, the reduction or elimination of the liability results in discharge of indebtedness income (DOI). Many authors refer to DOI income as COD income, an acronym for Cancellation of Debt, but, because the statutory phrase is "discharge of indebtedness," this Chapter uses the term DOI. This section deals with the tax consequences of DOI income, including distinguishing situations in which the relief from the liability actually represents DOI income, and those in which the relief from the liability is merely a medium of payment.

Section 2.01 provides a detailed discussion of DOI income by focusing on the Supreme Court's decision in *United States v. Kirby Lumber Co.*, 284 U.S. 1 (1931). When the property is transferred to satisfy a liability or obligation, or a liability is transferred in connection with the transfer of property, the transfer is usually part of the amount realized from the sale of the property. This and related issues for encumbered property are discussed in § 2.02 *Medium of Payment*, and in § 3 *Mortgaged Property*. The transfer or other relief from a liability can also be medium of payment for compensation, a gift, or anything else that can be paid for with money or property. When this is the case, the tax consequences are determined by the nature of the transaction. Section 2.03 *Disputed or Contingent Liability*, addresses the contentious issue when a dispute of contingency relating to an obligation means that the taxpayer's relief from the obligation is not DOI.

§ 2.01. What Is DOI Income?

I.R.C. § 61(a)(12); Treas. Reg. § 1.61-12(a), I.R.C. § 108; Treas. Reg. § 1.108(a)-1; I.R.C. § 1017, Treas. Reg. § 1.1017-1(a) to (d).

Section 61(a)(12) explicitly provides that gross income includes income from DOI, but does not otherwise define the term. Nor do the regulations provide any significant additional guidance, stating only that "[t]he discharge of indebtedness, in whole or in part, may result in the realization of income." Treas. Reg. § 1.61-12(a). The following seminal case provides a theory for including DOI in gross income.

UNITED STATES v. KIRBY LUMBER CO.
Supreme Court of the United States
284 U.S. 1 (1931)

Mr. Justice Holmes delivered the opinion of the Court.

In July, 1923, the plaintiff, the Kirby Lumber Company, issued its own bonds for $12,126,800 for which it received their par value. Later in the same year it purchased in the open market some of the same bonds at less than par, the difference of price being $137,521.30. The question is whether this difference is a taxable gain or income of the plaintiff for the year 1923. By the Revenue Act of . . . 1921, . . . gross income includes "gains or profits and income derived from any source whatever," and by the Treasury Regulations authorized by § 1303, that have been in force through repeated reenactments, "If the corporation purchases and retires any of such bonds at a price less than the issuing price or face value, the excess of the issuing price or face value over the purchase price is gain or income for the taxable year." Article 545 (1) (c) of Regulations 62, under Revenue Act of 1921. . . . We see no reason why the Regulations should not be accepted as a correct statement of the law.

In *Bowers v. Kerbaugh-Empire Co.*, 271 U.S. 170, the defendant in error owned the stock of another company that had borrowed money repayable in marks or their equivalent for an enterprise that failed. At the time of payment the marks had fallen in value, which so far as it went was a gain for the defendant in error, and it was contended by the plaintiff in error that the gain was taxable income. But the transaction as a whole was a loss, and the contention was denied. Here there was no shrinkage of assets and the taxpayer made a clear gain. As a result of its dealings it made available $137,521.30 assets previously offset by the obligation of bonds now extinct. We see nothing to be gained by the discussion of judicial definitions. The defendant in error has realized within the year an accession to income, if we take words in their plain popular meaning, as they should be taken here. *Burnet v. Sanford & Brooks Co.*, 282 U.S. 359, 364.

Judgment reversed.

NOTES AND COMMENTS

In his opinion in *Kirby Lumber*, Justice Holmes emphasized the freeing of assets as the basis for including DOI in gross income. Under the freeing of assets approach, the consideration received for incurring the liability, i.e., the tax amount of the obligation, is not relevant, because the amount of the assets freed is the amount of the legal obligation in excess of any consideration paid. Because, on the facts of *Kirby Lumber*, there was no difference between the principal amount of the legal obligation and the tax amount of the obligation, Justice Holmes did not have to consider whether the result would be different if, for example, a $1,000 obligation was originally issued at a discount price of $900. Under the approach that the relevant amount for DOI income is the tax amount of the obligation in excess of the consideration paid — the amount of DOI in this example would be based on the consideration received for incurring the obligation, $900, rather than the $1,000 legal obligation. Thus, if the obligation is cancelled in consideration of a payment of $850, the DOI income is $50. Because the discount is usually amortized over the life of the obligation, the tax amount of the obligation should also be adjusted for any amortized discount. Thus, if the obligation is cancelled in consideration of a payment of $850 when $10 of the discount had been amortized, the DOI income should be $60 — the difference between the $910 tax amount of the obligation and the $850 of consideration paid. This principle is explicitly recognized in § 108(e)(3), which provides adjustments for unamortized premium and discounts. Section 108(e)(2) adopts a similar tax amount approach by excluding from DOI income amounts that would be deductible when paid.

The determination of the amount of DOI income becomes more complex, and confused, when the debt obligation is issued in a nonrecognition or other exchange transaction. The courts have held that a corporation that issued debt obligations as a dividend does not have DOI income when it retires the obligation for less than the principal amount. Thus, in *Commissioner v. Rail Joint Co.*, 61 F.2d 751 (2d Cir. 1932), the court held that there was no DOI income even though the dividend had been accounted for at the principal amount of bonds, because the issuer did not receive consideration. The result is questionable because the debt obligation issued by the corporation to its shareholders was treated as a dividend to the same extent as if they had parted with assets for both the shareholders and the corporation in adjusting its earnings and profits. Similarly, in *Fashion Park, Inc. v. Commissioner*, 21 T.C. 600 (1954) *nonacq.*, the court held that there was no DOI income on retirement of $50 face value bonds exchanged for $50 par preferred stock issued for $5 a share at a price less than the $50 face value but more than the $5 issue price of the preferred, because the issuer did not increase its assets on the exchange, again ignoring the fact that the recipients had the equivalent of $50 claim on corporate assets, even though some distant predecessors may have paid only $5 for the preferred stock. These cases seem to be applying what may be considered a tax benefit approach in measuring the DOI by the amount received by the corporation rather than either a freeing of assets approach, which would result in DOI income, because, at the time of the retirement, the holders had a claim on corporate assets based on the principal amount of the debt obligations. Other cases have similarly used the historical amount received for stock to determine the issue price of debt obligations exchanged for the stock. *See Commissioner v. National Alfalfa Dehydrating & Milling Co.*, 417 U.S. 134 (1974) (amount originally received for preferred stock exchanged for bonds determines issue price for purposes of DOI, even if bonds worth significantly less than the amount originally received for the preferred stock when exchanged); *United States Steel Corp. v. United States*, 848 F.2d 1232 (Fed. Cir. 1988) (no DOI income when bonds redeemed for less than their principal amount and value when exchanged for stock, because amount paid on redemption exceeded consideration originally received for stock); Rev. Rul. 77-437, 1977-2 C.B. 28 (DOI income when bonds with principal amount lower than principal amount and higher interest rate issued to retire bonds with higher principal and with lower interest rate; implicitly rejects treating original consideration as creating bond premium on the newly issued bonds). Although these cases can be considered to reflect a tax amount approach, it is questionable whether the tax amount should be measured by the historical consideration received by the corporation instead of the amount of the claim resulting from intervening exchanges; although when the exchange is a nonrecognition exchange, the historical approach may be consistent with the substituted basis that results from such an exchange.

A similar historical consideration approach seems to be applied when a taxpayer guarantees the debt obligation of a third party. Generally, a settlement of a guarantee or similar obligation does not result in DOI income to the guarantor. Thus, in *Payne v. Commissioner*, T.C. Memo. 1998-227, *rev'd on other issues* 224

F.3d 415 (5th Cir. 2000), the court held that there was no DOI income on settlement of the guaranty obligation for approximately half of the principal balance of the guaranteed loan, because guaranteed loan provided the guarantor with no increase in net worth. The court noted that borrower may have had DOI income on release. *See Bradford v. Commissioner*, 233 F.2d 935 (6th Cir. 1956) (similar result and reasoning when taxpayer's note given as substitute for husband's note was released for payment of half of the principal; court notes it does not consider effect on husband, or any gift tax liability). Although a strict freeing of assets approach would seem to result in DOI income, the courts have relied more on a tax benefit approach in finding no DOI income for the guarantor, while instructing the Service that it pursued the wrong legal theories or the wrong taxpayer. *See also Friedland v. Commissioner*, T.C. Memo. 2001-236 (father did not recognize gain on transfer of appreciated securities to satisfy guaranty of son's liability, which was, of course reduced by value of shares; effect of transaction on son not discussed); Chief Couns. Adv. 2004-02-004 (Nov. 26, 2003) (no DOI on release of restitution judgment for overcharges by controlled corporation that indirectly benefited taxpayer; controlled corporation was similar to guarantor), in which case, the DOI income (or gain in *Friedland*) would tax the wrong person, There would be no DOI under a tax amount approach in any of the cases because the guarantee obligation is not a liability for a cash-method taxpayer, because, even if the guarantee payment is deductible, there is no deduction until payment, so that the guarantor has no deduction or other tax effect for unpaid amounts. Even if, as suggested by the courts in *Payne* and *Bradford*, (and as implicit in *Friedland*), there is economic benefit to the borrower, the benefit is a gift by the guarantor that should not be considered a nondeductible noncapital expenditure. In short, the seemingly unsatisfactory results in most of these cases reflect the fact that the cases do not deal with all aspects of the transactions or all taxpayers involved.

PROBLEMS FOR DISCUSSION

Problem 3-6. What is the effect in *Milenbach* of the settlement between the Raiders and LAMCC under *Kirby Lumber* and § 108? The Irwindale settlement? *See* Problem 3-1.

Problem 3-7. Senior pledged 200 shares of Pubco stock with a basis of $1,000 and a value of $2,500,000 as security for a loan of $2,000,000 by Countribanc to Devco, a corporation in which Junior, Senior's son, was the majority, but not sole, shareholder, as security for Countribanc's $500,000 loaned to Junior for his contribution to capital of Devco, and as security for Junior's guaranty of the $2,000,000 loan by Countribanc to Devco for a development project known as Fantastic, which was secured by a mortgage on Devco's development project. Senior did not guarantee the loan to Devco, nor did he join in or otherwise guarantee Junior's guarantee. His sole role was providing the shares as collateral. Prior to the transaction for which Senior provided collateral, Devco and Junior had successfully developed a number of projects. Unfortunately, the Fantastic project was not successful. Countribanc foreclosed on Fantastic and, when it became clear that it would not realize more than $1,000,000 on the foreclosure sale of Fantastic, Contribanc also foreclosed on the Pubco stock, which was then worth only $1,000,000, for a total realization of $2,000,000, Notwithstanding the unpaid balance of $500,000 on Junior's guarantee, Contribanc released Junior from personal liability, in part because Senior was still immensely wealthy and a good customer. What are the tax consequences to Senior, Junior, Devco, and Countribanc of these transactions? *See* § 108(e)(2); *Payne* (no DOI on release from guarantee); *Bradford* (discounted payment of note substituted for that of husband); *Friedland* (appreciated property transferred to settle guarantee); Chief Couns. Adv. 2004-02-004 (release from restitution obligation): Rev. Rul. 95-74 (contingent obligations in nonrecognition transfer under § 351); Rev. Rul. 80-198 (deductible obligation transferred); Rev. Rul. 80-199; Rev. Rul. 88-77 (deductible partnership obligation); Priv. Ltr. Rul. 2000-13-044 (deductible obligations of foreign predecessor); Rev. Rul. 95-26 (short sale obligation); Rev. Rul. 95-45 (short sale obligation).

Problem 3-8. Ceeco issued $1,000,000 principal amount of its 10½% notes due in 25 years for $900,000 (which represented an effective interest rate of about 12%) to a syndicate of institutional lenders. The notes now have an adjusted issue price (tax amount of $930,000 as a result of amortization of a portion of the original issue discount. At a current effective interest rate of approximately 13¾%, the notes are now worth about $800,000. (a) Ceeco proposes to issue in exchange $850,000 principal amount of 14 percent debentures, due in 25 years, that have a slightly higher yield of 13.9 percent. (i) What are the tax consequences to Ceeco and the syndicate (the holders)? (ii) How would the results differ if Ceeco issued its own common stock with a value of $850,000 in exchange for the 10½% notes? (iv) How would the results differ if Ceeco discharges the obligation by distributing real property with an adjusted basis of $400,000, fair market value of $850,000? (iv) How, if at all, would the results differ if new notes had an interest rate of 15 percent and a fair market value of $900 for each $850 principal amount, representing a yield of about 14 percent? *See* § 108(e)(8) and (10); § 1272(a)(4); § 1273(b)(2) and (4); Treas. Reg. § 1.1273-2(d); *National Alfalfa* (bonds exchanged for preferred stock); *United States Steel Corp.* (redemption of bonds exchanged for stock); *Rail Joint* (debt obligations issued as dividend); *Fashion Park* (redemption of bonds exchanged for stock); Rev. Rul. 77-437 (lower principal bonds exchanged for higher principal bonds).

§ 2.02. Medium of Payment

Relief from a liability, including transfer of the liability to another person, is a medium of payment that can serve any tax function that can be served by a transfer of cash or property. As illustrated in the decision in *United States v. Centennial Savings Bank FSB*, which follows, it can be difficult to differentiate when the cancellation or reduction of a liability is a medium of payment and when it is DOI. Although the stated facts of the case do not make it clear, accrual-method banks are entitled to accrue interest on certificates of deposit at the stated interest rate, even though it is possible that the holder will withdraw the funds before the full term and collect interest at the lower rate for the period the certificate was outstanding. *See* Rev. Rul. 76-308, 1976-2 C.B. 133, *amplifying* Rev. Rul. 71-63, 1971-1 C.B. 143. Accordingly, Centennial Savings Bank paid the holders cashing in certificates of deposit early an amount less that the amount of interest it had accrued by the amount referred to as the early withdrawal penalty. As a result, under the liability definition in the partnership regulations, the accrued interest had become a liability. The bank claimed that the difference was DOI income while the Service claimed it was gross income from receipt of an early withdrawal penalty. The importance of the distinction resides in the fact that DOI income may be excludable from gross income under § 108 under certain circumstances. Section 108 is described in detail in § 5 *DOI Income and § 108* of this Chapter.

UNITED STATES v. CENTENNIAL SAVINGS BANK FSB

Supreme Court of the United States

499 U.S. 573 (1991)

* * *

Justice Marshall delivered the opinion of the Court.

* * *

Centennial is a mutual savings and loan institution (S & L) formerly regulated by the Federal Home Loan Bank Board (FHLBB). . . .

* * *

The second set of transactions was Centennial's collection of early withdrawal penalties from customers who prematurely terminated their CD accounts. Each CD agreement established a fixed-term, fixed-interest account. . . . Consistent with federal regulations, each agreement also provided that the depositor would be required to pay a penalty to Centennial should the depositor withdraw the principal before maturity. . . . Thus, in the event of premature withdrawal, the depositor was entitled under the CD agreement to the principal and accrued interest, minus the applicable penalty. . . .

Centennial collected $258,019 in early withdrawal penalties in 1981. In its tax return for that year, Centennial treated the penalties as income from the discharge of indebtedness. Pursuant to 26 U.S.C. §§ 108 and 1017 (1982 ed.), Centennial excluded the $258,019 from its income and reduced the basis of its depreciable property by that amount.

On audit, the Internal Revenue Service . . . determined that Centennial should have declared as income the early withdrawal penalties collected that year. . . .

* * *

The Court of Appeals affirmed the District Court's conclusion that Centennial was entitled to treat the early withdrawal penalties as income from the discharge of indebtedness under § 108. The court reasoned that "the characterization of income as income from the discharge of indebtedness depends purely on the spread between the amount received by the debtor and the amount paid by him to satisfy his obligation." . . . Under this test, the early withdrawal penalties constituted income from the discharge of indebtedness, the court concluded, because the penalties reduced the size of Centennial's obligation to its depositors. . . . The court rejected the United States' characterization of the penalties as merely a "medium of payment" for Centennial's performance of its "separate obligation" to release the deposits prior to maturity. . . .

* * *

We next consider the question whether the early withdrawal penalties collected by Centennial constituted "income by reason of the discharge . . . of indebtedness" excludable from income under 26 U.S.C. § 108(a)(1) (1982 ed.). We conclude that the penalties were not subject to exclusion under § 108 because the depositors who paid these penalties did not "discharge" Centennial from any repayment obligation.

The version of § 108 in effect for the 1981 tax year states:

> "Gross income does not include any amount which (but for this subsection) would be includible in gross income by reason of the discharge (in whole or in part) of indebtedness of the taxpayer if —
>
> . . . .
>
> "(C) the indebtedness discharged is qualified business indebtedness." 26 U.S.C. § 108(a)(1) (1982 ed.).

"Qualified business indebtedness" includes "indebtedness . . . incurred or assumed . . . by a corporation." . . . Income from the discharge of qualified business indebtedness can be excluded from gross income under § 108 only if the taxpayer elects to reduce the basis of his depreciable property by an amount equal to the income excluded. . . . Thus, the effect of § 108 is not genuinely to exempt such income from taxation, but rather to defer the payment of the tax by reducing the taxpayer's annual depreciation deductions or by increasing the size of taxable gains upon ultimate disposition of the reduced-basis property.

In characterizing early withdrawal penalties as discharge-of-indebtedness income, Centennial, like the Court of Appeals, focuses purely on the "spread" between the debt that Centennial assumed upon the opening of each CD account and the amount that it actually paid each depositor upon the closing of the account. . . . When a depositor opens a CD account, Centennial notes, the bank becomes indebted to the depositor for the principal of the deposit plus accrued interest. By virtue of its collection of an early withdrawal penalty, however, the bank satisfies the debt for less than that amount should the depositor withdraw the principal before maturity. The end result, in Centennial's view, is no different from what it would have been had the bank and depositor (freed from the restraints of bank regulatory law) formed no agreement on an early withdrawal penalty at the outset but rather negotiated a forgiveness of that amount at the time of withdrawal.

We reject this analysis because it fails to make sense of § 108's use of the term "discharge." As used in § 108, the term "discharge . . . of indebtedness" conveys *forgiveness of*, or *release from*, an obligation to repay. A depositor who prematurely closes his account and pays the early withdrawal penalty does not forgive or release any repayment obligation on the part of the financial institution. The CD agreement itself provides that the depositor will be entitled only to the principal and accrued interest, less the applicable penalty, should the depositor prematurely withdraw the principal. Through this formula, the depositor and the bank have determined in advance precisely how much the depositor will be entitled to receive should the depositor close the account on any day up to the maturity date. Thus, the depositor does not "discharge" the bank from an obligation when it accepts an amount equal to the principal and accrued interest minus the penalty, for this is exactly what the bank is obligated to pay under the terms of the CD agreement.

Because § 108 presupposes the "discharge" of an obligation to repay, we disagree with Centennial and the Court of Appeals' conclusion that the "spread" between the debt assumed by Centennial and the amount paid by Centennial upon the closing of the account is sufficient to trigger § 108. The existence of such a spread is sufficient to demonstrate that Centennial enjoyed an accession to income equal in size to the amount of the penalty. But because this income was not the product of the release of any obligation assumed by Centennial at the outset of the bank-depositor relationship, it does not constitute income "by reason of [a] discharge." In sum, to determine whether the debtor has realized "income by reason of the discharge . . . of indebtedness," it is necessary to look at *both* the end result of the transaction *and* the repayment terms agreed to by the parties at the outset of the debtor-creditor relationship.

This common-sense reading of the statutory language best comports with the purpose underlying § 108. The tax-deferral mechanism in § 108 is designed to mitigate the effect of treating the discharge of indebtedness as *income*. See 26 U.S.C. § 61(a)(12) (1982 ed.) ("gross income . . . includes . . . income from discharge of indebtedness"). Borrowed funds are excluded from income in the first instance because the taxpayer's obligation to repay the funds offsets any increase in the taxpayer's assets; if the taxpayer is thereafter released from his obligation to repay, the taxpayer enjoys a net increase in assets equal to the forgiven portion of the debt, and the basis for the original exclusion thus evaporates. See *United States v. Kirby Lumber Co., 284 U.S. 1, 3 (1931); Commissioner v. Jacobson, 336 U.S. 28, 38 (1949);* see also *Commissioner v. Tufts, 461 U.S. 300, 307, 310-311, n. 11 (1983).* But while the cancellation of the obligation to repay increases the taxpayer's assets, it does not necessarily generate cash with which the taxpayer can pay the resulting income tax. Congress established the tax-deferral mechanism in § 108 so that the prospect of immediate tax liability would not discourage businesses from taking advantage of opportunities to repurchase or liquidate their debts at less than face value. See H. R. Rep. No. 855, 76th Cong., 1st Sess., 5 (1939); S. Rep. No. 1631, 77th Cong., 2d Sess., 77-78 (1942). See generally Wright, *Realization of Income Through Cancellations, Modifications, and Bargain Purchases of Indebtedness: I*, 49 Mich. L. Rev. 459, 477, 492 (1951).

This rationale is squarely implicated only when the debtor is seeking forgiveness or cancellation of a pre-existing repayment obligation. A debtor who negotiates in advance the circumstances in which he will liquidate the debt for less than its face value is in a position to anticipate his need for cash with which to pay the resulting income tax and can negotiate the terms of the anticipated liquidation accordingly. Moreover, insofar as the CD agreements at issue in this case committed Centennial to releasing the deposits at the sole election of the depositors, Centennial abandoned any control whatsoever over whether and when these particular debt obligations would be liquidated. Consequently, unlike a debtor considering the negotiation of an adjustment of the terms of his duty to repay, Centennial had no discretion to take the tax effects of the transaction into account before liquidating its debt obligations at less than face value.

It is true, as Centennial points out, that construing § 108 to apply only to debt reductions stemming from a negotiated forgiveness of a duty to repay withholds a tax incentive to include "anticipatory discharge" terms in the credit agreement at the outset. But we read the statutory language as embodying a legislative choice not to extend the benefits of § 108's deferral mechanism that far. For the reasons that we have stated, Congress could easily have concluded that only debtors seeking a release from a pre-existing repayment obligation need or deserve the tax break conferred by § 108. Consistent with the rule that tax-exemption and -deferral provisions are to be construed narrowly, *Commissioner v. Jacobson, supra,*; . . . , we conclude that Congress did not intend to extend the benefits of § 108 beyond the setting in which a creditor agrees to release a debtor from an obligation assumed at the outset of the relationship.

* * *

NOTES AND COMMENTS

Although the specific portion of § 108 at issue in *Centennial Savings* has been repealed, the basic conclusion that not every relief from a liability is DOI income is clearly sound. Centennial Savings' obligation to the holders of its CDs was clearly a liability because it was allowed to accrue the stipulated interest currently under Rev. Rul. 71-160. The Court determined that the reduction for early withdrawal was a permissible penalty, not a gratuitous discharge of the liability by the holder. Even though both DOI income and collection of a penalty, or reduction in an interest accrual, another alternate interpretation, are all ordinary income, characterization of the income as DOI would have permitted Centennial to defer the income by electing to reduce the basis of its property under § 108 as then in effect, even though the reduction was not an adjustment of purchase price. A similar result treating the adjustment of accrued interest as ordinary income would be to treat the interest adjustment as a correction of an accrual made that was reasonable when the exact amount determined in a later year is different, which, under the regulations, is taken into income in the later year and not as an adjustment to the earlier accrual. Treas. Reg. § 1.461-1(a)(3) (last sentence). The current, much more limited, provision for basis adjustment for certain DOI income is discussed in § 5.03 *Basis Adjustment — § 1017*.

Thus, reduction or cancellation of a liability can be a reduction in purchase price or payment of damages. In *Spartan Petroleum Co. v. United States*, 437 F. Supp. 733 (D.S.C. 1977), cancellation of a liability for funds borrowed by distributor from the producer of the distributor's products, in connection with termination of a distribution contract was determined to be part of damages for termination, not DOI income. Similarly, Rev. Rul. 2004-37, 2004-1 C.B. 583, determined that reduction in the principal amount of a note given as the exercise price of a stock option to reflect the reduced value of the stock is compensation under Treas. Reg. § 1.83-4(c), not DOI income. And in Rev. Rul. 84-176, 1984-2 C.B. 34, reduction in the liability of customer who refused to pay for goods received when the seller defaulted under the contract was characterized as contract damages, not DOI income, when the customer settled its claim for breach and the seller's claim for payment of the goods delivered by paying one-half of the amount owed for the goods originally received.

Similarly, when an obligation is incurred in a foreign currency that was considered a liability incurred by the U.S. company at the then exchange rate, it results in income when the same amount of the foreign currency is repaid but at a time when the exchange rate was lower so that it represented a reduction in the liability as measured at the time of incurrence. *See Philip Morris Inc. v. Commissioner*, 71 F.3d 1040 (2d Cir.), *aff'g* 104 T.C. 61 (1995) (determines that such income was not DOI, but court did not state what it was), *but see Kentucky & I. T. R. Co. v. United States*, 330 F.2d 520 (6th Cir. 1964) (such income was DOI but the decision rendered before that in *Centennial Savings*). Section 108(e)(5) treats reduction in an obligation incurred to purchase property as a reduction in the purchase price of the property, so that it is not discharge of indebtedness income. This is discussed in § 3.04 Tufts *and § 108(e)(5).*

A number of statutory provisions allow the compromise of tax or other liabilities to the government for less than the amount owed. Although treating the liability reduction as DOI income generally seems inconsistent with the grant of the statutory privilege, not all cases agree. In *Cook v. United States*, 95-2 U.S.T.C. ¶ 50,396 (M.D. Fla. 1995), a retired civil servant who had erroneously received both a military disability pension and a civil service pension that credited the military service had DOI income, not a gift, when the government waived collection of the overpayment pursuant to a statutory provision that allowed such waivers when collection would be inequitable, apparently taking into account the retiree's poor financial condition. The court determined that neither the government's recognition of a moral or legal duty to waive, nor a waiver because of collection difficulties avoided DOI income. There is inconsistent authority on whether reduction in tax liabilities under statutory provisions for an offer in compromise creates DOI income. In *Eagle Asbestos & Packing Co. v. United States*, 348 F.2d 528 (Ct. Cl. 1965), a lump sum settlement under an offer in compromise for prior tax liability plus interest was held not to be taxable even to the extent of the portion of interest previously properly deducted by accrual-method taxpayer. In *Yale Ave. Corp. v. Commissioner*, 58 T.C. 1062 (1972), on the other hand, the taxpayer conceded that compromise of tax liability was DOI income, and unsuccessfully argued insolvency to avoid being taxable. *Denman Tire & Rubber Co. v. Commissioner*, 192 F.2d 261 (6th Cir. 1951) determined that the discounted purchase of note given in compromise of taxes was not a gift but DOI income. On the other hand, the Service seems to have decided not to try to collect tax on any such DOI income. Serv. Cent. Adv. 1998-039 states that the Service should not send Form 1099-C for tax cancelled under offer-in-compromise; citing *Eagle Asbestos*, but not *Yale Avenue* or *Denham Tire. See* Richard C. E. Beck, *Is Compromise of a Tax Liability Itself Taxable? A Problem of Circularity in the Logic of Taxation*, 14 VA. TAX REV. 153 (1994).

The gratuitous discharge of a liability can be a gift, although, outside the family context, such gifts should be rare. *Compare Helvering v. American Dental Co.*, 318 U.S. 322 (1943), finding gratuitous cancellation of accrued, and deducted, interest owed by a corporation to be a gift, even in the absence of evidence of donative intent, with the later case of *Commissioner v. Jacobson*, 336 U.S. 28 (1949) finding a similar discounted purchase was not a gift, because the creditor accepted best price available. *See Plotinsky v. Commissioner*, T.C. Memo. 2008-244 (student whose federal student loan balance was reduced when he made 36 consecutive on-time payments pursuant to an inducement to consolidate college and law school student loans with a lender, had DOI income for the reduction; the reduction was not a gift).

When the liability is owed by a business entity to an owner of an interest in the business entity it may be a contribution to capital, *see* Rev. Rul. 78-330, 1978-2 C.B. 147 (contribution of debt to subsidiary immediately prior to reorganization to avoid excess of liabilities over basis recognized, had significance because subsidiary remained alive); *but see* Rev. Rul. 68-602, 1968-2 C.B. 135 (similar contribution of capital immediately prior to liquidation to make subsidiary solvent so that liquidation would be a nonrecognition transaction was not recognized); *see also* Tech. Adv. Mem. 98-22-005 (Jan. 16, 1998) (transfer of account payable by subsidiary for inventory purchased from parent to subsidiary was nonrecognition contribution to capital so that subsidiary did not recognize DOI or reduce price of inventory).

PROBLEMS FOR DISCUSSION

Problem 3-9. CountriSavings, a cash-method S&L, issued CDs identical to those issued by Centennial Savings, but, of course, could not deduct the unpaid interest. It paid $21,175,000 to holders of its CDs in the principal amount $20,000,000, on which interest of $1,200,000 had accrued at the stated rate to the date of withdrawal. What is the tax treatment of the $25,000 difference for CountriSavings? Would the result have been different if *Centennial Savings* had been decided in favor of Centennial? *See* § 108(e)(2); Treas. Reg. § 1.461-1(c)(3) (last sentence).

Problems 3-10. Terry, who owed $100,000 in taxes and $25,000 in accrued interest had the liability reduced to $75,000 pursuant to an offer in compromise under § 7122. What is the tax consequence to Terry of the $50,000 reduction in liability? *See* Cook (release of liability to repay excess pension); *Yale Avenue* (compromise of tax liability); *Eagle Asbestos* (lump sum offer-in-compromise including accrued interest); *Denham Tire* (compromise of note given in compromise of tax); Serv. Cent. Adv. 1998-039 (no Form 1099-C for tax cancelled under offer-in-compromise).

Problem 3-11. Propp operated a retail store. He had a long-term contract with Supp to purchase men's shirts at $30 a shirt. After delivering 5,000 shirts in 20X1, Supp failed to deliver the rest and Propp had to scramble to find substitutes at $50 a shirt, even though they were of lower quality and customer appeal. Propp refused to pay for the 5,000 shirts. Supp sued and Propp counterclaimed. The lawsuit was settled in 20X3 with Propp paying $100,000 (equal to $20 per shirt) for the shirts h had received and agreeing to release Supp from the long-term supply oblig By the time of the settlement, Propp had, of course, sold the 5,000 shirts reported his taxable income based on a price of $30 per shirt. What is th the settlement? *See Spartan Petroleum* (termination of distributorshi Reg. § 1.461–1(a)(3) (adjustment of earlier accrual); Rev. Rul. 84-176 dispute); *Centennial Savings Bank* (early withdrawal penalty). Rev. Rul. 2004-37 (reduction in note used to exercise stock option); Rev. Rul. 84-176 (settlement of contract dispute); Tech. Adv. Mem. 98-22-005 (parent contribution of account payable from subsidiary to it).

Problem 3-12. Multinat borrowed €1,000,000 when each Euro was worth $1.30 for use by its European branches. It repaid 1,000,000 with funds from its European operations when the Euro was worth only $1.20. Does it have DOI income? If not, what is the tax consequence of the approximately $100,000 difference? *See Philip Morris Inc.* (paying foreign currency debt in depreciated currency was not DOI; court did not state what it was); *Kentucky & Indiana Terminal R.R* (paying foreign currency debt in depreciated currency was DOI income; before *Centennial Savings*); *Kirby Lumber* (discount redemption of bonds); *Centennial Savings* (early withdrawal penalty).

§ 2.03. Disputed or Contingent Liability

As the volume of litigation attests, it is not uncommon for disputes to arise about liabilities to pay for goods or services. If the dispute arises before the obligation is taken into account for tax purposes — that is, before it has become a liability — there should be no DOI income. If the dispute involves an obligation to pay for property, any reduction in the liability should be a purchase price adjustment under § 108(e)(5), as described in greater detail in § 5 *DOI Income and § 108*. In other cases, particularly those relating to the third category of liability under Treas. Reg. § 1.752-1(a)(4)(i) — nondeductible, noncapital expenditures — the proper treatment of a reduction in the liability or obligation is less clear, as illustrated by the following controversial case.

ZARIN v. COMMISSIONER

United States Court of Appeals, Third Circuit
916 F.2d 110 (3d Cir. 1990)

* * *

Zarin was a professional engineer who participated in the development, construction, and management of various housing projects. A resident of Atlantic City, New Jersey, Zarin occasionally gambled, both in his hometown and in other places where gambling was legalized. To facilitate his gaming activities in Atlantic City, Zarin applied to Resorts International Hotel ("Resorts") for a credit line in June, 1978. Following a credit check, Resorts granted Zarin $10,000 of credit. Pursuant to this credit arrangement with Resorts, Zarin could write a check, called a marker,[2] and in return receive chips, which could then be used to gamble at the casino's tables.

Before long, Zarin developed a reputation as an extravagant "high roller" who routinely bet the house maximum while playing craps, his game of choice. Considered a "valued gaming patron" by Resorts, Zarin had his credit limit increased at regular intervals without any further credit checks, and was provided

[2] A "marker" is a negotiable draft payable to Resorts and drawn on the maker's bank.

a number of complimentary services and privileges. By November, 1979, Zarin's permanent line of credit had been raised to $200,000. Between June, 1978, and December, 1979, Zarin lost $2,500,000 at the craps table, losses he paid in full.

Responding to allegations of credit abuses, the New Jersey Division of Gaming Enforcement filed with the New Jersey Casino Control Commission a complaint against Resorts. Among the 809 violations of casino regulations alleged in the complaint of October, 1979, were 100 pertaining to Zarin. Subsequently, a Casino Control Commissioner issued an Emergency Order, the effect of which was to make further extensions of credit to Zarin illegal.

Nevertheless, Resorts continued to extend Zarin's credit limit through the use of two different practices: "considered cleared" credit and "this trip only" credit. Both methods effectively ignored the Emergency Order and were later found to be illegal.

By January, 1980, Zarin was gambling compulsively and uncontrollably at Resorts, spending as many as sixteen hours a day at the craps table. During April, 1980, Resorts again increased Zarin's credit line without further inquiries. That same month, Zarin delivered personal checks and counterchecks to Resorts which were returned as having been drawn against insufficient funds. Those dishonored checks totaled $3,435,000. In late April, Resorts cut off Zarin's credit.

Although Zarin indicated that he would repay those obligations, Resorts filed a New Jersey state court action against Zarin in November, 1980, to collect the $3,435,000. Zarin denied liability on grounds that Resort's claim was unenforceable under New Jersey regulations intended to protect compulsive gamblers. Ten months later, in September, 1981, Resorts and Zarin settled their dispute for a total of $500,000.

The Commissioner of Internal Revenue ("Commissioner") subsequently determined deficiencies in Zarin's federal income taxes for 1980 and 1981, arguing that Zarin recognized $3,435,000 of income in 1980 from larceny by trick and deception. After Zarin challenged that claim by filing a Tax Court petition, the Commissioner abandoned his 1980 claim, and argued instead that Zarin had recognized $2,935,000 of income in 1981 from the cancellation of indebtedness which resulted from the settlement with Resorts.

Agreeing with the Commissioner, the Tax Court decided, eleven judges to eight, that Zarin had indeed recognized $2,935,000 of income from the discharge of indebtedness, namely the difference between the original $3,435,000 "debt" and the $500,000 settlement. *Zarin v. Commissioner*, 92 T.C. 1084 (1989). Since he was in the seventy percent tax bracket, Zarin's deficiency for 1981 was calculated to be $2,047,245. With interest to April 5, 1990, Zarin allegedly owes the Internal Revenue Service $5,209,033.96 in additional taxes. Zarin appeals the order of the Tax Court.

* * *

The sole issue before this Court is whether the Tax Court correctly held that Zarin had income from discharge of indebtedness. Section 108 and section 61(a)(12) of the Code set forth "the general rule that gross income includes income from the discharge of indebtedness." I.R.C. § 108(e)(1). The Commissioner argues, and the

Tax Court agreed, that pursuant to the Code, Zarin did indeed recognize income from discharge of gambling indebtedness.

Under the Commissioner's logic, Resorts advanced Zarin $3,435,000 worth of chips, chips being the functional equivalent of cash. At that time, the chips were not treated as income, since Zarin recognized an obligation of repayment. In other words, Resorts made Zarin a tax-free loan. However, a taxpayer does recognize income if a loan owed to another party is cancelled, in whole or in part. I.R.C. §§ 61(a)(12), 108(e). The settlement between Zarin and Resorts, claims the Commissioner, fits neatly into the cancellation of indebtedness provisions in the Code. Zarin owed $3,435,000, paid $500,000, with the difference constituting income. Although initially persuasive, the Commissioner's position is nonetheless flawed for two reasons.

* * *

Initially, we find that sections 108 and 61(a)(12) are inapplicable to the Zarin/Resorts transaction. Section 61 does not define indebtedness. On the other hand, section 108(d)(1), which repeats and further elaborates on the rule in section 61(a)(12), defines the term as any indebtedness "(A) for which the taxpayer is liable, or (B) subject to which the taxpayer holds property." . . . In order to come within the sweep of the discharge of indebtedness rules, then, the taxpayer must satisfy one of the two prongs in the section 108(d)(1) test. Zarin satisfies neither.

Because the debt Zarin owed to Resorts was unenforceable as a matter of New Jersey state law,[7] it is clearly not a debt "for which the taxpayer is liable." I.R.C. § 108(d)(1)(A). Liability implies a legally enforceable obligation to repay, and under New Jersey law, Zarin would have no such obligation.

Moreover, Zarin did not have a debt subject to which he held property as required by section 108(d)(1)(B). Zarin's indebtedness arose out of his acquisition of gambling chips. The Tax Court held that gambling chips were not property, but rather, "a medium of exchange within the Resorts casino" and a "substitute for cash." Alternatively, the Tax Court viewed the chips as nothing more than "the opportunity to gamble and incidental services . . ." . . . We agree with the gist of these characterizations, and hold that gambling chips are merely an accounting mechanism to evidence debt.

Gaming chips in New Jersey during 1980 were regarded "solely as evidence of a debt owed to their custodian by the casino licensee and shall be considered at no time the property of anyone other than the casino licensee issuing them." . . . Thus, under New Jersey state law, gambling chips were Resorts' property until transferred to Zarin in exchange for the markers, at which point the chips became "evidence" of indebtedness (and not the property of Zarin).

Even were there no relevant legislative pronouncement on which to rely, simple common sense would lead to the conclusion that chips were not property in Zarin's hands. Zarin could not do with the chips as he pleased, nor did the chips have any

---

[7] The Tax Court held that the Commissioner had not met its burden of proving that the debt owed Resorts was enforceable as a matter of state law. . . . There was ample evidence to support that finding. . . .

Blackacre. Basis: $100,000.

Sail → Perch. Price: { $200,000. / $80,000 × 10. } = 1000,000.

installment method:

Sail's gain: 1000,000 − 100,000 = 900,000.

900,000 / 100,0000 = 90%.

↓

§453. { 90% of each payment → gain
10% of each payment → recovery of basis. }

↓

{ $200,000 → 180,000 gain.
$80,000 × 10 → 72,000 × 10. gain. }
900,000.

{ $200,000 → 20,000 recovery of basis
$80,000×10 → 8,000×10. recovery of basis }
100,000.

boot: 200,000 − 180,000 = 20,000

independent economic value beyond the casino. The chips themselves were of little use to Zarin, other than as a means of facilitating gambling. They could not have been used outside the casino. They could have been used to purchase services and privileges within the casino, including food, drink, entertainment, and lodging, but Zarin would not have utilized them as such, since he received those services from Resorts on a complimentary basis. In short, the chips had no economic substance.

Although the Tax Court found that theoretically, Zarin could have redeemed the chips he received on credit for cash and walked out of the casino, . . . reality of the situation was quite different. Realistically, before cashing in his chips, Zarin would have been required to pay his outstanding IOUs. New Jersey state law requires casinos to "request patrons to apply any chips or plaques in their possession in reduction of personal checks or Counter Checks exchanged for purposes of gaming prior to exchanging such chips or plaques for cash or prior to departing from the casino area." . . . Since his debt at all times equaled or exceeded the number of chips he possessed, redemption would have left Zarin with no chips, no cash, and certainly nothing which could have been characterized as property.

Not only were the chips non-property in Zarin's hands, but upon transfer to Zarin, the chips also ceased to be the property of Resorts. Since the chips were in the possession of another party, Resorts could no longer do with the chips as it pleased, and could no longer control the chips' use. Generally, at the time of a transfer, the party in possession of the chips can gamble with them, use them for services, cash them in, or walk out of the casino with them as an Atlantic City souvenir. The chips therefore become nothing more than an accounting mechanism, or evidence of a debt, designed to facilitate gambling in casinos where the use of actual money was forbidden. Thus, the chips which Zarin held were not property within the meaning of I.R.C. § 108(d)(1)(B).

In short, because Zarin was not liable on the debt he allegedly owed Resorts, and because Zarin did not hold "property" subject to that debt, the cancellation of indebtedness provisions of the Code do not apply to the settlement between Resorts and Zarin. As such, Zarin cannot have income from the discharge of his debt.

* * *

Instead of analyzing the transaction at issue as cancelled debt, we believe the proper approach is to view it as disputed debt or contested liability. Under the contested liability doctrine, if a taxpayer, in good faith, disputed the amount of a debt, a subsequent settlement of the dispute would be treated as the amount of debt cognizable for tax purposes. The excess of the original debt over the amount determined to have been due is disregarded for both loss and debt accounting purposes. Thus, if a taxpayer took out a loan for $10,000, refused in good faith to pay the full $10,000 back, and then reached an agreement with the lender that he would pay back only $7000 in full satisfaction of the debt, the transaction would be treated as if the initial loan was $7000. When the taxpayer tenders the $7000 payment, he will have been deemed to have paid the full amount of the initially disputed debt. Accordingly, there is no tax consequence to the taxpayer upon payment.

The seminal "contested liability" case is *N. Sobel, Inc. v. Commissioner*, 40 B.T.A. 1263 (1939). In *Sobel*, the taxpayer exchanged a $21,700 note for 100 shares of stock from a bank. In the following year, the taxpayer sued the bank for rescission, arguing that the bank loan was violative of state law, and moreover, that the bank had failed to perform certain promises. The parties eventually settled the case in 1935, with the taxpayer agreeing to pay half of the face amount of the note. In the year of the settlement, the taxpayer claimed the amount paid as a loss. The Commissioner denied the loss because it had been sustained five years earlier, and further asserted that the taxpayer recognized income from the discharge of half of his indebtedness.

The Board of Tax Appeals held that since the loss was not fixed until the dispute was settled, the loss was recognized in 1935, the year of the settlement, and the deduction was appropriately taken in that year. Additionally, the Board held that the portion of the note forgiven by the bank "was not the occasion for a freeing of assets and that there was no gain . . . " . . . Therefore, the taxpayer did not have any income from cancellation of indebtedness.

There is little difference between the present case and *Sobel*. Zarin incurred a $3,435,000 debt while gambling at Resorts, but in court, disputed liability on the basis of unenforceability. A settlement of $500,000 was eventually agreed upon. It follows from *Sobel* that the settlement served only to fix the amount of debt. No income was realized or recognized. When Zarin paid the $500,000, any tax consequence dissolved.[10]

Only one other court has addressed a case factually similar to the one before us. In *United States v. Hall*, 307 F.2d 238 (10th Cir. 1962), the taxpayer owed an unenforceable gambling debt alleged to be $225,000. Subsequently, the taxpayer and the creditor settled for $150,000. The taxpayer then transferred cattle valued at $148,110 to his creditor in satisfaction of the settlement agreement. A jury held that the parties fixed the debt at $150,000, and that the taxpayer recognized income from cancellation of indebtedness equal to the difference between the $150,000 and the $148,110 value affixed to the cattle. Arguing that the taxpayer recognized income equal to the difference between $225,000 and $148,000, the Commissioner appealed.

The Tenth Circuit rejected the idea that the taxpayer had any income from cancellation of indebtedness. Noting that the gambling debt was unenforceable, the Tenth Circuit said, "The cold fact is that taxpayer suffered a substantial loss from gambling, the amount of which was determined by the transfer." . . . In effect, the Court held that because the debt was unenforceable, the amount of the loss and resulting debt cognizable for tax purposes were fixed by the settlement at $148,110. Thus, the Tenth Circuit lent its endorsement to the contested liability doctrine in a factual situation strikingly similar to the one at issue.

The Commissioner argues that *Sobel* and the contested liability doctrine only apply when there is an unliquidated debt; that is, a debt for which the amount cannot be determined. . . . Since Zarin contested his liability based on the unenforceability of the entire debt, and did not dispute the amount of the debt, the Commissioner would have us adopt the reasoning of the Tax Court, which found

[10] Had Zarin not paid the $500,000 dollar settlement, it would be likely that he would have had income from cancellation of indebtedness. The debt at that point would have been fixed, and Zarin would have been legally obligated to pay it.

that Zarin's debt was liquidated, therefore barring the application of *Sobel* and the contested liability doctrine. . . .

We reject the Tax Court's rationale. When a debt is unenforceable, it follows that the amount of the debt, and not just the liability thereon, is in dispute. Although a debt may be unenforceable, there still could be some value attached to its worth. This is especially so with regards to gambling debts. In most states, gambling debts are unenforceable, and have "but slight potential . . ." *United States v. Hall*, 307 F.2d 238, 241 (10th Cir. 1962). Nevertheless, they are often collected, at least in part. For example, Resorts is not a charity; it would not have extended illegal credit to Zarin and others if it did not have some hope of collecting debts incurred pursuant to the grant of credit.

Moreover, the debt is frequently incurred to acquire gambling chips, and not money. Although casinos attach a dollar value to each chip, that value, unlike money's, is not beyond dispute, particularly given the illegality of gambling debts in the first place. This proposition is supported by the facts of the present case. Resorts gave Zarin $3.4 million dollars of chips in exchange for markers evidencing Zarin's debt. If indeed the only issue was the enforceability of the entire debt, there would have been no settlement. Zarin would have owed all or nothing. Instead, the parties attached a value to the debt considerably lower than its face value. In other words, the parties agreed that given the circumstances surrounding Zarin's gambling spree, the chips he acquired might not have been worth $3.4 million dollars, but were worth something. Such a debt cannot be called liquidated, since its exact amount was not fixed until settlement.

To summarize, the transaction between Zarin and Resorts can best be characterized as a disputed debt, or contested liability. Zarin owed an unenforceable debt of $3,435,000 to Resorts. After Zarin in good faith disputed his obligation to repay the debt, the parties settled for $500,000, which Zarin paid. That $500,000 settlement fixed the amount of loss and the amount of debt cognizable for tax purposes. Since Zarin was deemed to have owed $500,000, and since he paid Resorts $500,000, no adverse tax consequences attached to Zarin as a result.[12]

* * *

In conclusion, we hold that Zarin did not have any income from cancellation of indebtedness for two reasons. First, the Code provisions covering discharge of debt are inapplicable since the definitional requirement in I.R.C. section 108(d)(1) was not met. Second, the settlement of Zarin's gambling debts was a contested liability. We reverse the decision of the Tax Court and remand with instructions to enter judgment that Zarin realized no income by reason of his settlement with Resorts.

---

[12] The Commissioner argues in the alternative that Zarin recognized $3,435,000 of income in 1980. This claim has no merit. Recognition of income would depend upon a finding that Zarin did not have cancellation of indebtedness income solely because his debt was unenforceable. We do not so hold. Although unenforceability is a factor in our analysis, our decision ultimately hinges upon the determination that the "disputed debt" rule applied, or alternatively, that chips are not property within the meaning of I.R.C. section 108.

STAPLETON, CIRCUIT JUDGE, dissenting.

* * *

Resorts sells for cash the exhilaration and the potential for profit inherent in games of chance. It does so by selling for cash chips that entitle the holder to gamble at its casino. Zarin, like thousands of others, wished to purchase what Resorts was offering in the marketplace. He chose to make this purchase on credit and executed notes evidencing his obligation to repay the funds that were advanced to him by Resorts. As in most purchase money transactions, Resorts skipped the step of giving Zarin cash that he would only return to it in order to pay for the opportunity to gamble. Resorts provided him instead with chips that entitled him to participate in Resorts' games of chance on the same basis as others who had paid cash for that privilege.[1] Whether viewed as a one or two-step transaction, however, Zarin received either $3.4 million in cash or an entitlement for which others would have had to pay $3.4 million.

Despite the fact that Zarin received in 1980 cash or an entitlement worth $3.4 million, he correctly reported in that year no income from his dealings with Resorts. He did so *solely* because he recognized, as evidenced by his notes, an offsetting obligation to repay Resorts $3.4 million in cash. *See, e.g., Vukasovich, Inc. v. Commissioner*, 790 F.2d 1409 (9th Cir. 1986) . . . . In 1981, with the delivery of Zarin's promise to pay Resorts $500,000 and the execution of a release by Resorts, Resorts surrendered its claim to repayment of the remaining $2.9 million of the money Zarin had borrowed. As of that time, Zarin's assets were freed of his potential liability for that amount and he recognized gross income in that amount. . . . *Tufts* . . . ; . . . . *Kirby Lumber* . . . ; *Vukasovich* . . . . *But see United States v. Hall*, 307 F.2d 238 (10th Cir. 1962).[2]

The only alternatives I see to this conclusion are to hold either (1) that Zarin realized $3.4 million in income in 1980 at a time when both parties to the transaction thought there was an offsetting obligation to repay or (2) that the $3.4 million benefit sought and received by Zarin is not taxable at all. I find the latter alternative unacceptable as inconsistent with the fundamental principle of the Code that anything of commercial value received by a taxpayer is taxable unless expressly excluded from gross income. *Commissioner v. Glenshaw Glass Co.*, 348 U.S. 426 . . . (1955); *United States v. Kirby Lumber Co., supra.* I find the former alternative

[1] I view as irrelevant the facts that Resorts advanced credit to Zarin solely to enable him to patronize its casino and that the chips could not be used elsewhere or for other purposes. When one buys a sofa from the furniture store on credit, the fact that the proprietor would not have advanced the credit for a different purpose does not entitle one to a tax-free gain in the event the debt to the store is extinguished for some reason.

[2] This is not a case in which parties agree subsequent to a purchase money transaction that the property purchased has a value less than thought at the time of the transaction. In such cases, the purchase price adjustment rule is applied and the agreed-upon value is accepted as the value of the benefit received by the purchaser; *see e.g., Commissioner v. Sherman*, 135 F.2d 68 (6th Cir. 1943); *N. Sobel, Inc. v. Commissioner, 40 B.T.A. 1263 (1939)*. Nor is this a case in which the taxpayer is entitled to rescind an entire purchase money transaction, thereby to restore itself to the position it occupied before receiving anything of commercial value. In this case, the illegality was in the extension of credit by Resorts and whether one views the benefit received by Zarin as cash or the opportunity to gamble, he is no longer in a position to return that benefit.

unacceptable as impracticable. In 1980, neither party was maintaining that the debt was unenforceable and, because of the settlement, its unenforceability was not even established in the litigation over the debt in 1981. It was not until 1989 in this litigation over the tax consequences of the transaction that the unenforceability was first judicially declared. Rather than require such tax litigation to resolve the correct treatment of a debt transaction, I regard it as far preferable to have the tax consequences turn on the manner in which the debt is treated by the parties. For present purposes, it will suffice to say that where something that would otherwise be includable in gross income is received on credit in a purchase money transaction, there should be no recognition of income so long as the debtor continues to recognize an obligation to repay the debt. On the other hand, income, if not earlier recognized, should be recognized when the debtor no longer recognizes an obligation to repay and the creditor has released the debt or acknowledged its unenforceability.[4]

In this view, it makes no difference whether the extinguishment of the creditor's claim comes as a part of a compromise. Resorts settled for 14 cents on the dollar presumably because it viewed such a settlement as reflective of the odds that the debt would be held to be enforceable. While Zarin should be given credit for the fact that he had to pay 14 cents for a release, I see no reason why he should not realize gain in the same manner as he would have if Resorts had concluded on its own that the debt was legally unenforceable and had written it off as uncollectible.[5]

I would affirm the judgment of the Tax Court.

NOTES AND COMMENTS

Gallons of ink have been spilled, and reams of paper consumed, in analyzing and criticizing the decision in *Zarin*. In addition to the theories in the dissent, commentators have suggested that the reduction in Zarin's liability to Resorts is better characterized as compensation for services in attracting bettors, or a purchase price reduction for the chips. Given the popularity of gambling in all of its forms, similar controversies are likely to continue to arise.

Turning back to the partnership regulations' definition of liability, one question is whether "indebtedness" for purposes of §§ 61(a)(12) and 108 necessarily has the same meaning as "liability." Section 108 uses the term liability apparently synonymously with indebtedness in two provisions, § 108(d)(3) and (e)(2), although, as noted above, the use in § 108(e)(2) refers to an obligation for a deductible item as a liability. Particularly, given § 108(e)(2), excluding from DOI income amounts that would be deductible when paid, it is difficult to see any reason not to use the same definition, at least as a working definition. If so, *Zarin* highlights an issue not

---

[4] *Cf. Bear Manufacturing Co. v. United States*, 430 F.2d 152 (7th Cir. 1970) (termination of a liability for tax purposes turns not on running of applicable statute of limitations, but on conduct of the parties), *cert. denied*, 400 U.S. 1021 . . . (1971).

[5] A different situation exists where there is a bona fide dispute over the amount of a debt and the dispute is compromised. Rather than require tax litigation to determine the amount of income received, the Commission treats the compromise figure as representing the amount of the obligation. I find this sensible and consistent with the pragmatic approach I would take.

addressed in the partnership regulations — *when* an obligation "gives rise to an expense that is not deductible in computing the obligor's taxable income and is not properly chargeable to capital." Given the breadth of the definition of "obligation," there is no doubt that Zarin had an obligation to pay Resorts. The partnership regulations do not, however, provide *when* an obligation gives rise to an expenditure that is neither deductible nor capitalizable under Treas. Reg. § 1.752-1(a)(4(i)(C). Basis is generally increased when the obligation to pay for the property becomes fixed, without regard to the taxpayer's method of accounting, while the timing of a deduction is generally determined by the taxpayer's method of accounting (subject to deferral under the economic-performance provisions that generally require that the obligor defer the deduction until the recipient takes it into income. Because nondeductible, noncapital expenditures tend to be expenses that are denied deduction on tax policy grounds, like federal income taxes or fines and penalties, or that are personal items that are similar to expenses, they probably should be deemed incurred when they would be deductible under the taxpayer's method of accounting if they were deductible or would be included in basis if they would otherwise be capitalized. Thus, if Zarin's gambling losses were deductible, there would be no liability until the losses were paid, assuming Zarin is a cash-method taxpayer (curiously neither the Tax Court nor the court of appeals considered his method of accounting sufficiently relevant to state), he would not have a deductible loss until payment, and it is unlikely that his "marker" was payment. Under this reasoning § 108(e)(2) would provide that there was no DOI income. In *United States v. Hall*, 307 F.2d 238 (10th Cir. 1962), there was no DOI income on settlement of a gambling debt by transfer of cattle, because amount of gambling loss and unenforceable debt were fixed only on transfer of the cattle, but the taxpayer still recognized gain for any excess of value of cattle transferred over basis. Of course, if Zarin (or Hall) was an accrual-method taxpayer his hypothetically deductible loss would be deductible, at least up to his gambling winnings, with any excess a nondeductible noncapital expenditure, so that they would become a liability when incurred. On the other hand, if Zarin's obligation was incurred to buy chips, his method of accounting would be irrelevant, and his marker would be a liability. One reason Resorts extended credit to Zarin was that he apparently inspired others to gamble. Casinos, apparently, are willing to make favorable arrangements to attract such customers. *See* Chief Couns. Adv. 2000-39-037, which determined that foreign gamblers with similar significant gambling histories, who made advance arrangements to pay their markers in full when they won, but to discount their markers to 50 percent when they lost, over a gambling spree, received a purchase price adjustment, and not DOI income. On the other hand, when the funds borrowed to gamble are legally required to be repaid, failure to do so results in income. *See Collins v. Commissioner*, 3 F.3d 625 (2d Cir. 1993) (compulsive gambler who, despite the policy of his employer, New York's off-track-betting agency, placed bets on horse races and did not pay for them; collected winnings when he won, but confessed his violation when he couldn't cover, which resulted in liability to OTB's theft insurer, which covered the embezzlement obtained a judgment against him that he did not pay, had income).

When the transaction does not involve gambling, taxpayers have greater difficulty avoiding DOI income. In *Preslar v. Commissioner*, 167 F.3d 1323 (10th Cir. 1999), the taxpayer purchased a ranch in foreclosure to develop it as a sportsman's resort. The purchase was financed by the foreclosing lender that had informally agreed to accept installment contracts of purchasers of lots in the resort as payment. He had DOI income when he settled the loan for less than the amount borrowed, when FSLIC, which had taken over the original lender that had gone bankrupt, refused to honor the informal agreement. The court held that dispute as to method of payment did not convert fixed amount of borrowing into a disputed claim; and refused to follow *Zarin*. Similarly, in *Vukasovich, Inc. v. Commissioner*, 790 F.2d 1409 (9th Cir. 1986), a taxpayer, who settled his obligation with guarantor of a loan used to purchase cattle in tax shelter for less than the amount borrowed, had DOI income, even though the cattle venture operated by the guarantor resulted in overall loss; because the tax shelter loss and the guarantee were separable transactions in different tax years.

Although an arrangement that substitutes a new obligation for the old does not give rise to DOI income at least if the amount of the new obligation is not less than the old, the same rule does not apply if the new obligation is conditional or contingent. Thus, in *Jelle v. Commissioner*, 116 T.C. 63 (2001), farmers had DOI income when they were allowed to retain property by paying an amount equal to value of the property, even though the agreement required them to recapture the difference between that amount and loan principal by payments to the lender if they sold the property within 10 years for more than they paid to retain the property, because the contingent repayment obligation did not keep the original obligation in effect. The opinion did not deal with the effect of any repayment on a sale within 10 years that could be characterized as additional basis, or as repayment of the DOI income. In *Zappo v. Commissioner*, 81 T.C. 77 (1983), a similar contingent obligation under a guarantee by a seller that the purchaser of property would realize specified profits did not offset the liabilities transferred with the property in determining the gain on the transaction, because a guaranty was an inchoate obligation at the time of its making, so that there was no real continuation of indebtedness when a highly contingent obligation is substituted for a true debt. Again there is no consideration of the effect of any future payment.

PROBLEMS FOR DISCUSSION

Problem 3-13. Niraz, like Zarin, a "high roller" who attracted a following at casinos, but was no more successful than Zarin, lost $1,000,000. He then discovered the existence of deals like that in Chief Couns. Adv. 2000-39-037 after he had lost $1,000,000, and made a similar arrangement with Big Casino, under which he would pay his markers in full when he won, but was only required to pay half if he lost. He arranged to apply the deal to the $1,000,000 markers and paid $500,000 in complete settlement. He subsequently lost an additional $2,000,000, so that he was only required to pay $1,000,000. Niraz, however, cheated, by having a confederate cash his chips when he won $500,000, letting his ally keep $50,000, so that he showed losses of $2,500,000, and received a $1,250,000 discount when he was only entitled to a $1,000,000 discount. What is the tax consequence of the $500,000 discount for the markers incurred before the deal was made? Of the $1,000,000 agreed discount under the deal? Of the $250,000 extra "discount"? *See Collins* (OTB employee); *Vukasovich* (settlement of obligation to guarantor-operator of cattle tax shelter); *Hall* (cattle transferred to settle gambling loss); Rev. Rul. 95-74 (contingent obligations in nonrecognition transfer under § 351); Rev. Rul. 80-198 (deductible obligation after § 357(c)(3)); Rev. Rul. 80-199 (deductible obligation before § 357(c)(3); Rev. Rul. 88-77 (deductible partnership obligation); Chief Couns. Adv. 2000-39-037 (foreign gamblers); Priv. Ltr. Rul. 2000-13-044 (deductible obligations of foreign predecessor); Rev. Rul. 95-26 (partnership short sale); Rev. Rul. 95-45 (short-sale obligation contributed in § 351 transaction).

Problem 3-14. Invest, a cash-method taxpayer, was involved in a serious automobile accident while driving under the influence on a purely personal trip. Vic sued and recovered a tort judgment for $500,000 in excess of all available insurance, which was upheld on appeal. Invest persuaded Vic to accept $300,000, by a combination of claims of poverty and the threat that he had his assets so well protected that Vic would never collect. If he had been on business when the accident occurred, he would not have been able to deduct the $300,000 damages until paid under § 461(h)(2)(C) Does Invest have DOI for the $200,000? *Vukasovich* (settlement of obligation to guarantor-operator of cattle tax shelter); *Hall* (cattle transferred to settle gambling loss); Rev. Rul. 95-74 (contingent obligations in nonrecognition transfer under § 351); Rev. Rul. 80-198 (deductible obligation after § 357(c)(3)); Rev. Rul. 80-199 (deductible obligation before § 357(c)(3); Rev. Rul. 88-77 (deductible partnership obligation); Chief Couns. Adv. 2000-39-037 (foreign gamblers); Priv. Ltr. Rul. 2000-13-044 (deductible obligations of foreign predecessor); Rev. Rul. 95-26 (partnership short sale); Rev. Rul. 95-45 (short-sale obligation contributed in § 351 transaction).

Problem 3-15. Dev purchased Blackacre as the site to subdivide for a residential development, from Sail for $1,000,000. At the time of the purchase Sail was in default on the mortgage payments. Countribanc held the defaulted mortgage, but had held off foreclosure to delay, if not avoid, showing a loss on the mortgage, because it was in financial difficulties itself. Accordingly, it was willing to give Dev favorable terms. It loaned Dev 100 percent of the purchase price with interest at 10 percent, and agreed to accept the 20-year 14 percent installment notes of purchasers of lots and homes in the residential development for 90 percent of the stated principal. When it had accepted such installment notes for $300,000 of the mortgage payments, bank regulators insisted that Countribanc could not credit such notes for regulatory purposes, and that it would have to insist on cash for the remaining payments. Because the installment notes did not provide Dev with cash, and could not be financed with other lenders for more than 50 percent of face, Dev negotiated with Countribanc and the regulators to settle the mortgage for a payment of $400,000, which he financed with another bank on the security of the Blackacre installment notes and other assets. He further agreed that if he realized more than $1,000,000 on the remaining installment notes or on other disposition of the remaining portions of Blackacre within 10 years, he would pay 50 percent of the excess Countribanc up to $300,000 plus interest at 10 percent until payment, but would not have to make any payments after end of 10 years. Does he have DOI of $300,000? *See* § 108(e)(5); *Preslar* (settlement of loan on ranch with dispute over method of payment); *Zarin* (settlement of gambling debt); *Hall* (cattle transferred to settle gambling loss); *Jelle* (retain farm by paying value to terminate mortgage, but subject to recapture); *Zappo* (contingent obligation under a guarantee that the purchaser of property would realize specified profits did not offset the liabilities transferred with the property in determining the gain on the transaction).

§ 3. MORTGAGED PROPERTY

§ 3.01. In General

As indicated above, by the inclusion in Treas. Reg. § 1.752-1(a)(4)(A) of an amount that "[c]reates or increases the basis of an obligor's assets . . ." any purchase money obligation, whether recourse or nonrecourse, that is included in basis is a liability. Section 3.01(a) *Basis* applies this principle. The obvious implication that a similar amount representing the liability must be included in the amount realized when the encumbered property is disposed of is discussed in § 3.01(b) *Amount Realized.*

§ 3.01(a). Basis

I.R.C. § 1012; Treas. Reg. § 1.1012-1(a)

Section 1012 provides that the basis of property is the cost of such property. Consequently, if Perch purchases Blackacre from Sail for $50,000 in cash from Perch's own pocket, Perch's basis in Blackacre is $50,000. Perch's basis in Blackacre represents Perch's investment in Blackacre for tax purposes. Moreover, the cash that Perch paid to acquire Blackacre was after-tax dollars; thus, by giving Perch a basis in Blackacre of $50,000, the Code ensures that these dollars will not be subject to tax in the future.

Many taxpayers do not acquire property solely with cash from their own pockets, however. Taxpayers typically acquire property though financing the acquisition with money borrowed, either from a third party or from the seller. The question then arises regarding the proper determination of the taxpayer's basis in the property when acquired with borrowed funds. For example, if Perch purchases Blackacre from Sail for $50,000 in cash, $10,000 from Perch's own pocket and $40,000 that Perch borrows from a commercial lender, should Perch's basis in Blackacre be $50,000, the same as when the $50,000 had come from Perch's own pocket, or should it be $10,000 and thereafter increased as Perch makes the principal payments on the loan? Because the $40,000 proceeds of the loan were not taxable when received by Perch because of the offsetting obligation to repay the loan, giving Perch a basis in Blackacre of $50,000 is to effectively include in basis untaxed dollars. Nevertheless, tax law generally allows the taxpayer to include in the basis of property any debt incurred in the acquisition of that property on the assumption that the debt will be repaid in the future with after-tax dollars. In addition, this approach treats taxpayers who are able to acquire property without financing the same as taxpayers who use financing and avoids the difficulties that would be encountered if the basis of the property were increased as principal payments were made on the loan, particularly if the property is depreciable.

There are two types of debt that are commonly available for the acquisition of property, recourse and nonrecourse debt. Typically, lenders will require that both types of debt be secured by the property being acquired through a recorded mortgage in the case of real property, or a perfected security interest in the case of personal property. The difference between recourse and nonrecourse debt lies in the lender's remedies in the case of the borrower's default. In the case of recourse debt, the lender may look to the borrower's other assets for satisfaction of the debt if the value of the property securing the debt is inadequate to repay the debt. In the case of nonrecourse debt, however, the lender may look only to the property securing the debt for repayment of the debt. This means that the borrower is not personally liable for the debt if the property declines in value below the amount of the debt. Thus, one of the traditional attributes of ownership — risk of loss — has been wholly or partially shifted from the borrower to the lender. The degree of risk shifted to the lender depends on the amount of the investment by the borrower in the property in addition to the borrowed funds. Obviously, the lender is at greatest risk when it provides 100 percent financing of the acquisition cost of the property and lenders frequently impose higher interest rates for nonrecourse debt than for recourse debt.

Despite the split in risk when nonrecourse debt is involved, the tax law usually assumes that the borrower is the owner of the property and has all of the tax attributes of the owner, while the lender has only the status of a creditor. As a result, the full amount of both recourse and nonrecourse debt incurred in connection with the acquisition of any property will be included in the basis of that property. Of course, there is always the complexity that arises if the debt is not a bona fide liability, a risk that is greater for nonrecourse than recourse debt, particularly nonrecourse debt provided by the seller. Some of these issues are considered in § 3.02 *Contingencies*, § 3.03 *Speculative Security*, and § 3.04 *Scope of* Franklin.

When property is acquired subject to an existing recourse, or nonrecourse, liability that the acquirer does not assume, there is no direct borrowing, but because the obligation to pay the liability is a condition of retaining the property, the transferred liability serves the same function in representing the purchase price. The following seminal case involves a taxpayer who sought to avoid some of the adverse consequences of this principle.

CRANE v. COMMISSIONER

Supreme Court of the United States
331 U.S. 1 (1947)

Mr. Chief Justice Vinson delivered the opinion of the Court.

The question here is how a taxpayer who acquires depreciable property subject to an unassumed mortgage, holds it for a period, and finally sells it still so encumbered, must compute her taxable gain.

Petitioner was the sole beneficiary and the executrix of the will of her husband, who died January 11, 1932. He then owned an apartment building and lot subject to a mortgage, which secured a principal debt of $255,000.00 and interest in default of $7,042.50. As of that date, the property was appraised for federal estate tax purposes at a value exactly equal to the total amount of this encumbrance. Shortly after her husband's death, petitioner entered into an agreement with the mortgagee whereby she was to continue to operate the property — collecting the rents, paying for necessary repairs, labor, and other operating expenses, and reserving $200.00 monthly for taxes — and was to remit the net rentals to the mortgagee. This plan was followed for nearly seven years, during which period petitioner reported the gross rentals as income, and claimed and was allowed deductions for taxes and operating expenses paid on the property, for interest paid on the mortgage, and for the physical exhaustion of the building. Meanwhile, the arrearage of interest increased to $15,857.71. On November 29, 1938, with the mortgagee threatening foreclosure, petitioner sold to a third party for $3,000.00 cash, subject to the mortgage, and paid $500.00 expenses of sale.

Petitioner reported a taxable gain of $1,250.00. Her theory was that the "property" which she had acquired in 1932 and sold in 1938 was only the equity, or the excess in the value of the apartment building and lot over the amount of the mortgage. This equity was of zero value when she acquired it. No depreciation could be taken on a zero value.[2] Neither she nor her vendee ever assumed the mortgage, so, when she sold the equity, the amount she realized on the sale was the net cash received, or $2,500.00. This sum less the zero basis constituted her gain, of which she reported half as taxable on the assumption that the entire property was a "capital asset."

The Commissioner, however, determined that petitioner realized a net taxable gain of $23,767.03. His theory was that the "property" acquired and sold was not the equity, as petitioner claimed, but rather the physical property itself, or the owner's rights to possess, use, and dispose of it, undiminished by the mortgage. The original basis thereof was $262,042.50, its appraised value in 1932. Of this value $55,000.00 was allocable to land and $207,042.50 to building. During the period that petitioner held the property, there was an allowable depreciation of $28,045.10 on the building, so that the adjusted basis of the building at the time of sale was $178,997.40. The amount realized on the sale was said to include not only the $2,500.00 net cash receipts, but also the principal amount[6] of the mortgage subject to which the property was sold, both totaling $257,500.00. The selling price was allocable in the proportion, $54,471.15 to the land and $203,028.85 to the building. The Commissioner agreed that the land was a "capital asset," but thought that the building was not. Thus, he determined that petitioner sustained a capital loss of $528.85 on the land, of which 50% or $264.42 was taken into account, and an ordinary gain of $24,031.45 on the building, or a net taxable gain as indicated.

* * *

The 1938 Act, § 111(a) [equivalent to § 1001(a)], defines the gain from "the sale or other disposition of property" as "the excess of the amount realized therefrom over the adjusted basis provided in section [§ 1011] . . ." It proceeds, [§ 1001(b)], to

[2] This position is, of course, inconsistent with her practice in claiming such deductions in each of the years the property was held. The deductions so claimed and allowed by the Commissioner were in the total amount of $25,500.00.

[6] The Commissioner explains that only the principal amount, rather than the total present debt secured by the mortgage, was deemed to be a measure of the amount realized, because the difference was attributable to interest due, a deductible item.

define "the amount realized from the sale or other disposition of property" as "the sum of any money received plus the fair market value of the property (other than money) received." Further, in [§ 1016], the "adjusted basis for determining the gain or loss from the sale or other disposition of property" is declared to be "the basis determined under subsection (a), adjusted . . . [(a)(2)] . . . for exhaustion, wear and tear, obsolescence, amortization . . . to the extent allowed (but not less than the amount allowable) . . ." The basis under subsection (a) "if the property was acquired by . . . devise . . . or by the decedent's estate from the decedent," [§ 1014], is "the fair market value of such property at the time of such acquisition."

Logically, the first step under this scheme is to determine the unadjusted basis of the property, under [§ 1014], and the dispute in this case is as to the construction to be given the term "property." If "property," as used in that provision, means the same thing as "equity," it would necessarily follow that the basis of petitioner's property was zero, as she contends. If, on the contrary, it means the land and building themselves, or the owner's legal rights in them, undiminished by the mortgage, the basis was $262,042.50.

We think that the reasons for favoring one of the latter constructions are of overwhelming weight. In the first place, the words of statutes — including revenue acts — should be interpreted where possible in their ordinary, everyday senses. The only relevant definitions of "property" to be found in the principal standard dictionaries are the two favored by the Commissioner, *i.e.*, either that "property" is the physical thing which is a subject of ownership, or that it is the aggregate of the owner's rights to control and dispose of that thing. "Equity" is not given as a synonym, nor do either of the foregoing definitions suggest that it could be correctly so used. Indeed, "equity" is defined as "the value of a property . . . above the total of the liens. . . ." The contradistinction could hardly be more pointed. Strong countervailing considerations would be required to support a contention that Congress, in using the word "property," meant "equity," or that we should impute to it the intent to convey that meaning.

In the second place, the Commissioner's position has the approval of the administrative construction of [§ 1014]. With respect to the valuation of property under that section, Reg. 101, Art. 113(a) . . . promulgated under the 1938 Act, provided that "the value of property as of the date of the death of the decedent as appraised for the purpose of the Federal estate tax . . . shall be deemed to be its fair market value . . ." The land and building here involved were so appraised in 1932, and their appraised value — $262,042.50 — was reported by petitioner as part of the gross estate. This was in accordance with the estate tax law and regulations, which had always required that the value of decedent's property, undiminished by liens, be so appraised and returned, and that mortgages be separately deducted in computing the net estate. As the quoted provision of the Regulations has been in effect since 1918, and as the relevant statutory provision has been repeatedly reenacted since then in substantially the same form, the former may itself now be considered to have the force of law.

Moreover, in the many instances in other parts of the Act in which Congress has used the word "property," or expressed the idea of "property" or "equity," we find no instances of a misuse of either word or of a confusion of the ideas. In some parts of the Act other than the gain and loss sections, we find "property" where it is unmistakably used in its ordinary sense. On the other hand, where either Congress or the Treasury intended to convey the meaning of "equity," it did so by the use of appropriate language.

A further reason why the word "property" in [§ 1011(a)] should not be construed to mean "equity" is the bearing such construction would have on the allowance of deductions for depreciation and on the collateral adjustments of basis.

Section [167] permits deduction from gross income of "a reasonable allowance for the exhaustion, wear and tear of property . . ." Section [167(c)] . . . declare[s] that the "basis upon which exhaustion, wear and tear . . . are to be allowed" is the basis "provided in section [§ 1011] for the purpose of determining the gain upon the sale" of the property, which is the [§ 1011] basis "adjusted . . . for exhaustion, wear and tear . . . to the extent allowed (but not less than the amount allowable) . . ."

Under these provisions, if the mortgagor's equity were the [§ 1011] basis, it would also be the original basis from which depreciation allowances are deducted. If it is, and if the amount of the annual allowances were to be computed on that value, as would then seem to be required, they will represent only a fraction of the cost of the corresponding physical exhaustion, and any recoupment by the mortgagor of the remainder of that cost can be effected only by the reduction of his taxable gain in the year of sale. If, however, the amount of the annual allowances were to be computed on the value of the property, and then deducted from an equity basis, we would in some instances have to accept deductions from a minus basis or deny deductions altogether. The Commissioner also argues that taking the mortgagor's equity as the [§ 1011] basis would require the basis to be changed with each payment on the mortgage, and that the attendant problem of repeatedly recomputing basis and annual allowances would be a tremendous accounting burden on both the Commissioner and the taxpayer. Moreover, the mortgagor would acquire control over the timing of his depreciation allowances.

Thus it appears that the applicable provisions of the Act expressly preclude an equity basis, and the use of it is contrary to certain implicit principles of income tax depreciation, and entails very great administrative difficulties. It may be added that the Treasury has never furnished a guide through the maze of problems that arise in connection with depreciating an equity basis, but, on the contrary, has consistently permitted the amount of depreciation allowances to be computed on the full value of the property, and subtracted from it as a basis. Surely, Congress' long-continued acceptance of this situation gives it full legislative endorsement.

We conclude that the proper basis under [§ 1014] is the value of the property, undiminished by mortgages thereon, and that the correct basis here was $262,042.50. The next step is to ascertain what adjustments are required under § [1016]. As the depreciation rate was stipulated, the only question at this point is whether the Commissioner was warranted in making any depreciation adjustments whatsoever.

Section [1016] provides that "proper adjustment in respect of the property *shall in all cases be made* . . . for exhaustion, wear and tear . . . to the extent allowed (but not less than the amount allowable) . . ." (Italics supplied.) The Tax Court found on adequate evidence that the apartment house was property of a kind subject to physical exhaustion, that it was used in taxpayer's trade or business, and consequently that the taxpayer would have been entitled to a depreciation allowance under [§ 167], except that, in the opinion of that Court, the basis of the property was zero, and it was thought that depreciation could not be taken on a zero basis. As we have just decided that the correct basis of the property was not zero, but $262,042.50, we avoid this difficulty, and conclude that an adjustment should be made as the Commissioner determined.

Petitioner urges to the contrary that she was not entitled to depreciation deductions, whatever the basis of the property, because the law allows them only to one who actually bears the capital loss, and here the loss was not hers but the mortgagee's. We do not see, however, that she has established her factual premise. There was no finding of the Tax Court to that effect, nor to the effect that the value of the property was ever less than the amount of the lien. Nor was there evidence in the record, or any indication that petitioner could produce evidence, that this was so. The facts that the value of the property was only equal to the lien in 1932 and that during the next six and one-half years the physical condition of the building deteriorated and the amount of the lien increased, are entirely inconclusive, particularly in the light of the buyer's willingness in 1938 to take subject to the increased lien and pay a substantial amount of cash to boot. Whatever may be the rule as to allowing depreciation to a mortgagor on property in his possession which is subject to an unassumed mortgage and clearly worth less than the lien, we are not faced with that problem and see no reason to decide it now.

At last we come to the problem of determining the "amount realized" on the 1938 sale. Section [1001(b)], it will be recalled, defines the "amount realized" from "the sale . . . of property" as "the sum of any money received plus the fair market value of the property (other than money) received," and [§ 1001(a)] defines the gain on "the sale . . . of property" as the excess of the amount realized over the basis. Quite obviously, the word "property," used here with reference to a sale, must mean "property" in the same ordinary sense intended by the use of the word with reference to acquisition and depreciation in [§ 1011], both for certain of the reasons stated heretofore in discussing its meaning in [§ 1011], and also because the functional relation of the two sections requires that the word mean the same in one section that it does in the other. If the "property" to be valued on the date of acquisition is the property free of liens, the "property" to be priced on a subsequent sale must be the same thing.

Starting from this point, we could not accept petitioner's contention that the $2,500.00 net cash was all she realized on the sale except on the absurdity that she sold a quarter-of-a-million dollar property for roughly one per cent of its value, and took a 99 per cent loss. Actually, petitioner does not urge this. She argues, conversely, that because only $2,500.00 was realized on the sale, the "property" sold must have been the equity only, and that consequently we are forced to accept her contention as to the meaning of "property" in [§ 1001]. We adhere, however, to what we have already said on the meaning of "property," and we find that the absurdity is avoided by our conclusion that the amount of the mortgage is properly included in the "amount realized" on the sale.

Petitioner concedes that if she had been personally liable on the mortgage and the purchaser had either paid or assumed it, the amount so paid or assumed would be considered a part of the "amount realized" within the meaning of [§ 1001(b)]. The cases so deciding have already repudiated the notion that there must be an actual receipt by the seller himself of "money" or "other property," in their narrowest senses. It was thought to be decisive that one section of the Act must be construed so as not to defeat the intention of another or to frustrate the Act as a whole, and that the taxpayer was the "beneficiary" of the payment in "as real and substantial [a sense] as if the money had been paid it and then paid over by it to its creditors.

Both these points apply to this case. The first has been mentioned already. As for the second, we think that a mortgagor, not personally liable on the debt, who sells the property subject to the mortgage and for additional consideration, realizes a benefit in the amount of the mortgage as well as the boot.[37] If a purchaser pays boot, it is immaterial as to our problem whether the mortgagor is also to receive money from the purchaser to discharge the mortgage prior to sale, or whether he is merely to transfer subject to the mortgage — it may make a difference to the purchaser and to the mortgagee, but not to the mortgagor. Or put in another way, we are no more concerned with whether the mortgagor is, strictly speaking, a debtor on the mortgage, than we are with whether the benefit to him is, strictly speaking, a receipt of money or property. We are rather concerned with the reality that an owner of property, mortgaged at a figure less than that at which the property will sell, must and will treat the conditions of the mortgage exactly as if they were his personal obligations. If he transfers subject to the mortgage, the benefit to him is as real and substantial as if the mortgage were discharged, or as if a personal debt in an equal amount had been assumed by another.

Therefore we conclude that the Commissioner was right in determining that petitioner realized $257,500.00 on the sale of this property.

* * *

Petitioner contends that the result we have reached taxes her on what is not income within the meaning of the Sixteenth Amendment. If this is because only the direct receipt of cash is thought to be income in the constitutional sense, her contention is wholly without merit. If it is because the entire transaction is thought to have been "by all dictates of common sense . . . a ruinous disaster," as it was termed in her brief, we disagree with her premise. She was entitled to depreciation deductions for a period of nearly seven years, and she actually took them in almost the allowable amount. The crux of this case, really, is whether the law permits her to exclude allowable deductions from consideration in computing gain. We have already showed that, if it does, the taxpayer can enjoy a double deduction, in effect, on the same loss of assets. The Sixteenth Amendment does not require that result any more than does the Act itself.

Affirmed.

---

[37] Obviously, if the value of the property is less than the amount of the mortgage, a mortgagor who is not personally liable cannot realize a benefit equal to the mortgage. Consequently, a different problem might be encountered where a mortgagor abandoned the property or transferred it subject to the mortgage without receiving boot. That is not this case.

* * *

NOTES AND COMMENTS

During the period she owned the property Ms. Crane claimed depreciation of approximately $28,000, which is, of course, inconsistent with the position she took that the property she inherited was only the "equity." It is, however, consistent with the fact that the property was apparently valued for estate tax purposes at approximately $262,000. The approximately $23,500 net gain determined by the Service essentially represents the amount of the depreciation, plus the $2,500 net proceeds of the sale ($3,000 proceeds - $500 expenses of sale) or $30,500, reduced by the $7,000 accrued interest at the time of Mr. Crane's death, as noted in footnote 6. The propriety of that adjustment is discussed in the *Levine* case in § 3.01(b) *Amount Realized.* The numbers in the case are further confused by the fact that Ms. Crane reported half of the net proceeds as capital gain, reflecting a 50 percent deduction for capital gains at the time of the case, while the Service determined an approximately $500 capital loss on the land with a similar 50 percent deduction, but an approximately $24,000 gain on the building as ordinary income, apparently as a kind of recapture of the depreciation net of the $7,000 interest accrued at Mr. Crane's death. Leaving aside the adjustment for the accrued interest, taxing Ms. Crane on the depreciation she had claimed and been allowed hardly seems a harsh result. *See Parker v. Delaney*, 186 F.2d 455 (1st Cir. 1950) (Magruder concurring and suggesting that the same result could have been reached even with an original basis of zero by reducing a zero basis by the amount of depreciation "allowed" as provided the equivalent of § 1016(a)(2)).

The Court accepts the coincidence that the value of the property at the date of Mr. Crane's death equaled exactly the amount of the $255,000 mortgage, plus approximately $7,000 of accrued interest, which strains belief. The acceptance of that value in the opinion avoids the issue of the effect of a nonrecourse liability in excess of the value of the property at the time of acquisition. Section 3.03 *Speculative Security* addresses the issue. The Court similarly avoids the issue of whether the amount of the mortgage exceeded the value at the time Mrs. Crane disposed of the property, by considering that apparently nominal $3,000 payment as indicating that it did not. In doing so, the Court appended what may be the most famous footnote in tax history, footnote 37. The issues raised by footnote 37 are considered in § 3.01(b)(2) *Liability in Excess of Value (Overmortgaged Property).*

PROBLEMS FOR DISCUSSION

Problem 3-16. Invest purchased Blackacre for $300,000 from Sail, paying $100,000 in cash, with the balance paid by a recourse purchase money note and mortgage to Sail of $200,000. When the mortgage had been reduced to $150,000, she refinanced with a new $400,000 nonrecourse mortgage from Countribanc, using $150,000 to pay Sail, receiving the $250,000 in cash, which she used for purposes unrelated to Blackacre. What is the effect on her basis in Blackacre of receipt of the $250,000 proceeds? What is the effect of her disposition of Blackacre subject to the nonrecourse mortgage for $50,000 cash? For $50,000 worth of stock in a nonrecognition transaction? *See Woodsam Associates, Inc. v. Commissioner*, discussed in § 3.03(c) *Mortgaging Property as a Realization Event* in Chapter 1; § 357(c)(1)

§ 3.01(b). Amount Realized

Treas. Reg. § 1.1001-2

The clear holding of *Crane* is that not only is the nonrecourse mortgage taken into account in determining basis, but that it is also part of the amount realized. This must, of course, be extended to treating any liability transferred with property as part of the amount realized, at least up to the amount of the value of the property. This is now provided explicitly by Treas. Reg. § 1.1001-2(a). In general, this principle applies equally to recourse and nonrecourse liabilities. Section 3.01(b)(1) *Liability in Excess of Basis* discusses why this principle applies for nonrecourse liabilities in excess of basis, even in otherwise nonrecognition transactions, *see* Treas. Reg. § 1.1001-2(a)(4)(iii); while § 3.01(b)(2) *Liability in Excess of Value (Overmortgaged Property* extends it even to liabilities in excess of value at the time of disposition, at least for nonrecourse liabilities, *see* Treas. Reg. § 1.1001-2(a)(4)(i). Section 4.01 *Primary and Secondary Liability* considers the contrasting effect when recourse liabilities transferred or cancelled exceed value. *See* Treas. Reg. § 1.1001-2(a)(2)

§ 3.01(b)(1) Liability in Excess of Basis

Although there is no controversy that nonrecourse liabilities are part of the amount realized when property is sold subject to such liabilities, some taxpayers claimed that the same result did not apply to the transfer of property as a gift. The following case explains why this position is unsound.

ESTATE OF LEVINE v. COMMISSIONER

United States Court of Appeals, Second Circuit
634 F.2d 12 (2d Cir. 1980)

FRIENDLY, CIRCUIT JUDGE:

The estate of Aaron Levine and his widow Anna appeal from a part of a decision of the Tax Court . . . which found a deficiency of $130,428.42 in Aaron Levine's 1970 income tax. The deficiency resulted from a determination by the Commissioner that the taxpayer had realized gain upon his gift, on January 1, 1970, of income producing property consisting of land and a building at 20-24 Vesey Street in New York City (the property) to a previously created trust for the benefit of three grandchildren.

The property was originally purchased on November 1, 1944, by a corporation wholly owned by Levine. On August 22, 1957, the corporation, which was in the course of dissolution, made a liquidating distribution of the property to the taxpayer. Thereafter Levine obtained two non-recourse mortgages secured by the property. One of these, for $500,000, was obtained on March 17, 1966, from the Bowery Savings Bank and represented the consolidation of numerous earlier mortgages. The other, for $300,000, was obtained from the Commercial Trading

Company on November 21, 1968; this was later amortized to $280,000.

Levine filed a gift tax return for 1970 reporting the transaction as follows:

20-24 Vesey Street, City, County and State of New York — Appraisal value	$925,000.00
Mortgages	
Bowery Savings Bank	$500,000.00
Interest accrued 12/1/69 to 12/31/69	2,291.67
Commercial Trading*	280,000.00
Interest accrued 12/1/69 to 12/31/69	3,616.67
	$785,908.34

Expenses incurred by donor in 1969 and assumed and paid by donee:

Improvements	$117,716.53
Supplies	387.83
Repairs	1,253.93
Paint	63.60
Electricity	1,827.56
Steam	3,324.13
Total expenses	124,573.58
Total mortgages, interest and expenses	910,481.92
Equity	$14,518.08

and paid a gift tax on the equity of $14,518.08. The propriety of this was not challenged. However, the Commissioner assessed a deficiency in income tax on the ground that Levine had realized a gain in the amount of the excess of the total mortgages, interest and expenses aggregating $910,481.34, all of which were assumed by the donee, over Levine's adjusted basis, which, as increased by stipulation between the parties, was $485,429.55. The result was an excess of $425,051.79 and, upon application of capital gains rates, a deficiency of $130,428.42 in income tax. . . .

At first blush the layman and even the lawyer or judge not conditioned by exposure to tax law would find it difficult to understand how a taxpayer can realize $910,484.91 in gain by giving away property in which he possessed an equity of $14,518.08. Doubtless Mrs. Crane experienced a similar difficulty when she was held to have realized $275,500 (for a net taxable gain of $23,031.45), after she netted a mere $2,500 on the sale of an apartment building that she had inherited subject to a $255,000 mortgage and $7,042.50 in overdue interest payments, and had sold, under threat of foreclosure, subject to the same mortgage principal and $15,857.71 in defaulted interest payments. However, as stated in the ironic dictum of a distinguished tax practitioner's imaginary Supreme Court opinion, "[everyday] meanings are only of secondary importance when construing the words of a tax statute and are very seldom given any weight when a more abstruse and technical

* Between November 1968 and January 1970, $20,000 of the $300,000 principal was amortized.

meaning is available." In any event, *Crane* binds us whatever the yearnings of our untutored intuitions may be. What is more, few scholars quarrel with the wisdom of its holding, as distinguished from some of its language including the famous note 37, . . . of which more hereafter.

* * *

Taxpayer argues that, be all this as it may *Crane* is inapplicable because the transaction here was a gift and not a sale.

Apart from the general incongruity in finding that a gift yields a realized gain to the donor, petitioner argues that it is by no means clear how the Code's gross income, realization and recognition provisions apply to a donor's "gain" realized as incidental to a gift. Section 61(a)(3) defines gross income to include "[gains] derived from dealings in property" — a term seemingly broad enough to include gains from gifts. The same is true with respect to § 1001(a), which provides that "[the] gain from *the sale or other disposition of property* shall be the excess of the amount realized therefrom over the adjusted basis provided in section 1011 for determining gain. . . .' (emphasis supplied). Apparent difficult is encountered, however, when we come to the critical provision, § 1001(c), entitled "[recognition] of gain or loss", which states that "[except] as otherwise provided in this subtitle, the entire amount of the gain or loss, determined under this section, on *the sale or exchange* of property shall be recognized." (emphasis supplied).

Taxpayer suggests that the change in language from "other disposition of property" in § 1001(a), which seems broad enough to encompass a gift, but see *United States v. Davis*, . . . to "sale or exchange" in § 1001(c), which would appear not to be so, postpones recognition of any "gain" realized in the instant transaction. This, he argues, is appropriate because while a sale or exchange results in the transferee's acquisition of a new basis, see § 1012, a gift ordinarily transfers the donor's basis plus any gift tax paid to the donee, § 1015, and tax on any gain can thus fairly be postponed until the donee engages in a taxable disposition. However, this argument overlooks

> [the] general rule . . . that when property is sold or otherwise disposed of, any gain realized must also be recognized, absent an appropriate nonrecognition provision in the Internal Revenue Code.

. . . A comparison of the present § 1001(c) with its pre-1976 predecessors, which, of course, are here controlling, suggests that § 1001(c) merely limits nonrecognition to certain transactions described in detail elsewhere in the Code and does not confer it on all dispositions other than sales or exchanges. However, we need not decide this question in view of our disposition of the case.

Levine relies also on the established principle that a gift of appreciated unmortgaged property does not give rise to a gain, even when deductions have been taken for business expenses which were necessary to the appreciation of the property. . . . However, the transaction here in question was not a "pure" gift. The donee assumed not only the $785,908.34 in mortgages and accrued interest for which Levine was not personally liable but also the $124,573.58 of 1969 expenses, not constituting a lien, for which he was. If the donee had paid the latter sum directly to Levine, this case would clearly be governed by *Crane* since the donor would have received "boot". However, the assumption of another's legal obligation or debt is considered income under *Old Colony Trust Co.* . . . We can thus see no sound reason for reaching a result differing from that in *Crane* on the facts of this case.[8] We need not decide what the result should be if Levine had merely donated the property subject to non-recourse mortgages without an explicit "sale" element — in this case, the donee's assumption of his 1969 personal liabilities. . . .

* * *

. . . It is comforting to note, however, that an analysis of Levine's tax returns indicates his successful conversion of the appreciated value of the Vesey Street property into "benefits" at least as tangible as those in *Crane*. The calculation of Levine's taxable gain, as found by the Tax Court, may be presented as follows:

(1) Amount realized		
(a) Expenses assumed by donee		$124,573.00
(b) Mortgages		780,000.00
(c) Interest payments assumed by donee		5,908.34
(d) Total		$910,481.34
(2) Less: Adjusted basis		
(a) Unadjusted basis[11]	$385,485.02	
(b) Plus: Capital Improvements	334,542.00	
(c) Improvements paid for by donee	117,716.53	
(d) Subtotal	837,743.55	
(e) Less: Depreciation	352,314.00	
(f) Adjusted basis		$485,429.55
(3) Gain		$425,051.79

Of the total taxable gain of $425,051.59, the sum of $124,573.00 may be allocated directly to the 1969 expenses which Levine shifted to the donee-trust. As was previously noted, these expenses are closely akin to the "boot" of $2,500 received by Mrs. Crane. In addition Levine's mortgage schedule . . . indicates that of the $780,000 in mortgages on the Vesey Street property at the time of its transfer, at least $235,044.22 derived from an outstanding mortgage which Levine acquired with the property in 1957, while the remaining $564,955.77 represents the net non-

[8] No difficulty is caused by the famous footnote 37 in *Crane*, . . . Here the value of the property exceeded the amount of the mortgage. As developed in the text, the assumption of the $124,573.78 in indebtedness is equivalent to "boot" — if indeed a "boot" requirement survives. See *Parker v. Delaney* . . . (applying *Crane* where the mortgagor abandoned property to the mortgagee and received nothing). In any event we read the *Crane* footnote's emphasis on "boot" as simply evidentiary; the receipt of boot was thought to show that the property was worth more than the amount of the mortgages, see, *Parker v. Delaney*, . . . ("Boot served to show [an excess of value over the mortgages] in the *Crane* case, but the payment of boot is of course not the only means of showing whether or not value is equal to or more than the liens on the property disposed of.")

[11] The record does not indicate Levine's unadjusted basis, but this can readily be calculated by subtracting capital improvements from, and adding depreciation deductions to, the stipulated adjusted basis of $485,429.55.

recourse indebtedness incurred during the period of Levine's ownership. As the table above indicates $334,452 of the later amount was reinvested in capital improvements. Since the original mortgage of $235,044.22 must be assumed to have contributed toward Levine's unadjusted basis in the property,[12] and the subsequent capital improvements adjusted Levine's basis upward by the extent of their value, $569,496.23 (or $235,044.22 + $334,452.00) in basis credit derives solely from the non-recourse mortgages. Yet, upon disposition of the property in 1970 Levine's stipulated basis was merely $485,429.55. The shortfall between this and the aggregate contribution of the non-recourse mortgages, *i.e.*, $84,066.68, can only be explained by depreciation deductions that Levine could not have taken but for the mortgages. Finally, there are two additional sources of "benefit" in this case with no analogue in *Crane*. One is the sum of $210,503.77 out of Levine's net borrowings of $544,955.77, . . . which was apparently not reinvested in capital improvements on the property, and which the taxpayer may thus be considered to have "pocketed". The second is the $5,908.34 in interest payments owed by the taxpayer but assumed by the donee.[13] Together, these four varieties of "benefit" sum exactly to what was found to be the taxpayer's total taxable income:

(a) expenses assumed by donee	$124,573.58
(b) depreciation resulting from nonrecourse mortgages	84,066.68
(c) pocketed mortgage funds	210,503.77
(d) interest assumed by donee	5,908.34
Total	$425,051.79

To tax these "benefits" upon a disposition, at capital gains rates and without interest, is scarcely harsh. Failure to do so would mean, so far as we can see, that the $210,503.77 which the taxpayer obtained for his personal use by non-recourse loans against the appreciation of the property would never be taxed either as ordinary income or as gain (although, unless paid off by the donee, it would diminish any realization on the property), and that the benefits obtained by the depreciation deductions would remain untaxed unless and until the donee sold the property, when they would operate as a reduction of the donee's adjusted basis which was passed on to the donee. In light of the seeming equity of the result reached, an otherwise similar case lacking the element of personal debt assumed by the donee might lead us to look with sympathy on the scant case-law suggesting that the *Crane* principle may apply even to "pure" gifts, . . . even though a taxpayer could avoid application of *Crane* by withholding his beneficence until death. For reasons we have indicated, we simply do not find it necessary to decide that broader question on the facts here before us.

The judgment of the Tax Court is affirmed.

---

[12] Levine acquired his encumbered property at a basis equal to its market value, I.R.C. § 334(a). Since any subsequent payments on the principal of the original mortgage would not have increased Levine's basis, . . . this mortgage must be deemed to be included in the original basis of the property.

[13] The Commissioner in *Crane* did not include a similar sum of $15,857.71 in interest payments assumed by the buyer of the mortgaged property, . . . apparently because interest due was a deductible item. This issue has not been raised before us.

NOTES AND COMMENTS

Although Judge Friendly's tax-benefit analysis is not essential to his opinion, it elegantly explains the necessity of taxing the transferor on the transfer of the nonrecourse liabilities, even in gratuitous transfers. Thus, in *Madorin v. Commissioner*, 84 T.C. 667 (1985), the grantor of a grantor trust who was treated as the owner of the trust's assets realized gain on conversion of the trust to nongrantor trust in which he was no longer treated as owner of the assets, to the extent that the trust assets included a partnership interest subject to liabilities in excess of basis. *See* Rev. Rul. 77-402, 1977-2 C.B. 222 (same). In Rev. Rul. 81-163, 1981-1 C.B. 433, the same principle was applied to a transfer to a charity of property encumbered by a nonrecourse mortgage in the context of the allocation of basis under § 1011(b), resulting in gain recognized by the donor, even though the liability was less than the total basis of the property transferred to the charity. Of course, it had long been recognized that a transfer of business or investment property subject to a nonrecourse liability was a sale or exchange when the property was transferred to the nonrecourse lender. Thus, in *Freeland v. Commissioner*, 74 T.C. 970 (1980), the surrender of mortgaged property subject to a nonrecourse mortgage to the lender was a sale or exchange resulting in gain recognition. The same result was reached in *Yarbro v. Commissioner of IRS*, 737 F.2d 479 (5th Cir. 1984), treating the abandonment of property subject to nonrecourse mortgage as a sale or exchange. On the other hand, in *Citron v. Commissioner of Internal Revenue*, 97 T.C. 200 (1991), there was no sale or exchange on surrender of partnership interest that was not subject to any liabilities. Rev. Rul. 93-80, 1993-2 C.B. 239, follows *Citron*, but finds sale or exchange of a partnership interest subject to allocable share of partnership liabilities. All of these authorities are discussed in § 4.02 *Judicial Interpretation* in Chapter 2, *Capital Gains and Losses.*

The opinion is also interesting for highlighting, but not deciding, because the issue was raised too late, the effect the transfer of deductible obligations that had not given rise to a tax benefit. As indicated by a less famous footnote, n. 6, the issue was also present in *Crane*, but not decided because the Service did not include the accrued interest in the amount realized. The effect of the transfer of property subject to deductible obligations is covered in § 4.03, *Deductible Items.*

PROBLEM FOR DISCUSSION

Problem 3-17. Invest purchased Blackacre, which was improved with a commercial office building some years ago for $1,000,000, paying $100,000 down, and financing the balance with a $900,000 nonrecourse balloon note and mortgage from Countribanc. After depreciation, the adjusted basis of the property is now $700,000, which is also its value. She would like to dispose of the property without recognizing the $200,000 excess of the mortgage over the adjusted basis. Advise her as to the tax consequences if she: (i) quit claims it to the mortgagee, (ii) abandons it; (iii) gives it to her favorite charity; (iv) had placed it in a grantor trust and now renounces the powers that made it a grantor trust, without any disposition by the trust; or (v) any other proposal you can suggest with better results. Invest wants to dispose of it without paying tax on the transfer. *See* § 1011(b); Treas. Reg. § 1.1001-2(e) example 5; *Yarbro* (abandonment of property subject to nonrecourse mortgage as sale or exchange); *Madorin* (conversion of grantor trust with encumbered property); *Freeland* (surrender of mortgaged property to lender as sale or exchange); Rev. Rul. 81-163 (charitable contribution of encumbered property); Rev. Rul. 77-402 (conversion of grantor trust with encumbered property).

§ 3.01(b)(2) Liability in Excess of Value (Overmortgaged Property)

I.R.C. § 7701(g), Treas. Reg. § 1.1001-2(a)(4)(i)

Footnote 37 in *Crane* implied that when the value of the property is less the amount of a nonrecourse mortgage, a different problem might be encountered than that involved in *Crane*. The implications of that footnote resulted in reams of discussion and thousands of tax shelters. The following case sets out the result, one that seems inevitable, at least in retrospect, when the issue finally returned to the Supreme Court 35 years later.

COMMISSIONER v. TUFTS

Supreme Court of the United States
461 U.S. 300 (1983)

Justice Blackmun delivered the opinion of the Court.

* * *

Over 35 years ago, in *Crane v. Commissioner*, 331 U.S. 331 (1947), this Court ruled that a taxpayer, who sold property encumbered by a nonrecourse mortgage (the amount of the mortgage being less than the property's value), must include the unpaid balance of the mortgage in the computation of the amount the taxpayer realized on the sale. The case now before us presents the question whether the same rule applies when the unpaid amount of the nonrecourse mortgage exceeds the fair market value of the property sold.

* * *

Section 752(d) of the Internal Revenue Code . . . , specifically provides that liabilities involved in the sale or exchange of a partnership interest are to "be treated in the same manner as liabilities in connection with the sale or exchange of property not associated with partnerships." Section 1001 governs the determination of gains and losses on the disposition of property. Under § 1001(a), the gain or loss from a sale or other disposition of property is defined as the difference between "the amount realized" on the disposition and the property's adjusted basis. Subsection (b) of § 1001 defines "amount realized": "The amount realized from the sale or other disposition of property shall be the sum of any money received plus the fair market value of the property (other than money) received." At issue is the application of the latter provision to the disposition of property encumbered by a nonrecourse mortgage of an amount in excess of the property's fair market value.

* * *

On August 1, 1970, respondent Clark Pelt, a builder, and his wholly owned corporation, respondent Clark, Inc., formed a general partnership. The purpose of the partnership was to construct a 120-unit apartment complex in Duncanville, Tex., a Dallas suburb. Neither Pelt nor Clark, Inc., made any capital contribution to the partnership. Six days later, the partnership entered into a mortgage loan agreement with the Farm & Home Savings Association (F&H). Under the agreement, F&H was committed for a $1,851,500 loan for the complex. In return, the partnership executed a note and a deed of trust in favor of F&H. The partnership obtained the loan on a nonrecourse basis: neither the partnership nor its partners assumed any personal liability for repayment of the loan. Pelt later admitted four friends and relatives, respondents Tufts, Steger, Stephens, and Austin, as general partners. None of them contributed capital upon entering the partnership.

The construction of the complex was completed in August 1971. During 1971, each partner made small capital contributions to the partnership; in 1972, however, only Pelt made a contribution. The total of the partners' capital contributions was $44,212. In each tax year, all partners claimed as income tax deductions their allocable shares of ordinary losses and depreciation. The deductions taken by the partners in 1971 and 1972 totaled $439,972. Due to these contributions and deductions, the partnership's adjusted basis in the property in August 1972 was $1,455,740.

In 1971 and 1972, major employers in the Duncanville area laid off significant numbers of workers. As a result, the partnership's rental income was less than expected, and it was unable to make the payments due on the mortgage. Each partner, on August 28, 1972, sold his partnership interest to an unrelated third party, Fred Bayles. As consideration, Bayles agreed to reimburse each partner's sale expenses up to $250; he also assumed the nonrecourse mortgage.

On the date of transfer, the fair market value of the property did not exceed $1,400,000. Each partner reported the sale on his federal income tax return and indicated that a partnership loss of $55,740 had been sustained.[1] The Commissioner of Internal Revenue, on audit, determined that the sale resulted in a partnership capital gain of approximately $400,000. His theory was that the partnership had realized the full amount of the nonrecourse obligation.[2]

* * *

This case presents that unresolved issue [footnote 37 in *Crane*]. We are disinclined to overrule *Crane*, and we conclude that the same rule applies when the unpaid amount of the nonrecourse mortgage exceeds the value of the property transferred. *Crane* ultimately does not rest on its limited theory of economic

---

[1] The loss was the difference between the adjusted basis, $1,455,740, and the fair market value of the property, $1,400,000. On their individual tax returns, the partners did not claim deductions for their respective shares of this loss. In their petitions to the Tax Court, however, the partners did claim the loss.

[2] The Commissioner determined the partnership's gain on the sale by subtracting the adjusted basis, $1,455,740, from the liability assumed by Bayles, $1,851,500. Of the resulting figure, $395,760, the Commissioner treated $348,661 as capital gain, pursuant to § 741 . . . and $47,099 as ordinary gain under the recapture provisions of § 1250 of the Code. The application of § 1250 in determining the character of the gain is not at issue here.

benefit; instead, we read *Crane* to have approved the Commissioner's decision to treat a nonrecourse mortgage in this context as a true loan. This approval underlies *Crane*'s holdings that the amount of the nonrecourse liability is to be included in calculating both the basis and the amount realized on disposition. That the amount of the loan exceeds the fair market value of the property thus becomes irrelevant.

When a taxpayer receives a loan, he incurs an obligation to repay that loan at some future date. Because of this obligation, the loan proceeds do not qualify as income to the taxpayer. When he fulfills the obligation, the repayment of the loan likewise has no effect on his tax liability.

Another consequence to the taxpayer from this obligation occurs when the taxpayer applies the loan proceeds to the purchase price of property used to secure the loan. Because of the obligation to repay, the taxpayer is entitled to include the amount of the loan in computing his basis in the property; the loan, under § 1012, is part of the taxpayer's cost of the property. Although a different approach might have been taken with respect to a nonrecourse mortgage loan,[5] the Commissioner has chosen to accord it the same treatment he gives to a recourse mortgage loan. The Court approved that choice in *Crane*, and the respondents do not challenge it here. The choice and its resultant benefits to the taxpayer are predicated on the assumption that the mortgage will be repaid in full. When encumbered property is sold or otherwise disposed of and the purchaser assumes the mortgage, the associated extinguishment of the mortgagor's obligation to repay is accounted for in the computation of the amount realized.[6] . . . Because no difference between recourse and nonrecourse obligations is recognized in calculating basis,[7] *Crane* teaches that the Commissioner may ignore the nonrecourse nature of the obligation in determining the amount realized upon disposition of the encumbered property. He thus may include in the amount realized the amount of the nonrecourse mortgage assumed by the purchaser. The rationale for this treatment is that the original inclusion of the amount of the mortgage in basis rested on the assumption that the mortgagor incurred an obligation to repay. Moreover, this treatment balances the fact that the mortgagor originally received the proceeds of the

---

[5] The Commissioner might have adopted the theory, implicit in *Crane*'s contentions, that a nonrecourse mortgage is not true debt, but, instead, is a form of joint investment by the mortgagor and the mortgagee. On this approach, nonrecourse debt would be considered a contingent liability, under which the mortgagor's payments on the debt gradually increase his interest in the property while decreasing that of the mortgagee. . . . Because the taxpayer's investment in the property would not include the nonrecourse debt, the taxpayer would not be permitted to include that debt in basis. . . .

[6] In this case, respondents received the face value of their note as loan proceeds. If respondents initially had given their note at a discount, the amount realized on the sale of the securing property might be limited to the funds actually received. *See Commissioner v. Rail Joint Co.*, 61 F.2d 751, 752 (CA2 1932) (cancellation of indebtedness); *Fashion Park, Inc. v. Commissioner*, 21 T.C. 600, 606 (1954) (same). *See generally* J. Sneed, The Configurations of Gross Income 319 (1967) ("[It] appears settled that the reacquisition of bonds at a discount by the obligor results in gain only to the extent the issue price, where this is less than par, exceeds the cost of reacquisition").

[7] The Commissioner's choice in *Crane* "laid the foundation stone of most tax shelters," Bittker, *Tax Shelters, Nonrecourse Debt, and the Crane Case*, 33 Tax L. Rev. 277, 283 (1978), by permitting taxpayers who bear no risk to take deductions on depreciable property. Congress recently has acted to curb this avoidance device by forbidding a taxpayer to take depreciation deductions in excess of amounts he has at risk in the investment. . . . § 465(a) . . . .

nonrecourse loan tax-free on the same assumption. Unless the outstanding amount of the mortgage is deemed to be realized, the mortgagor effectively will have received untaxed income at the time the loan was extended and will have received an unwarranted increase in the basis of his property.[8] The Commissioner's interpretation of § 1001(b) in this fashion cannot be said to be unreasonable.

The Commissioner in fact has applied this rule even when the fair market value of the property falls below the amount of the nonrecourse obligation. Treas. Reg. § 1.1001-2(b) . . . Because the theory on which the rule is based applies equally in this situation, . . . , we have no reason, after *Crane*, to question this treatment.[11]

Respondents received a mortgage loan with the concomitant obligation to repay by the year 2012. The only difference between that mortgage and one on which the borrower is personally liable is that the mortgagee's remedy is limited to foreclosing on the securing property. This difference does not alter the nature of the obligation; its only effect is to shift from the borrower to the lender any potential loss caused by devaluation of the property. If the fair market value of the property falls below

---

[8] Although the *Crane* rule has some affinity with the tax benefit rule, see Bittker, *supra*, at 282; Del Cotto, *Sales and Other Dispositions of Property Under Section 1001: The Taxable Event, Amount Realized and Related Problems of Basis*, 26 BUFFALO L. REV. 219, 323-324 (1977), the analysis we adopt is different. Our analysis applies even in the situation in which no deductions are taken. It focuses on the obligation to repay and its subsequent extinguishment, not on the taking and recovery of deductions. *See generally* Note, 82 COLUM. L. REV., at 1526-1529.

[11] Professor Wayne G. Barnett, as *amicus* in the present case, argues that the liability and property portions of the transaction should be accounted for separately. Under his view, there was a transfer of the property for $1.4 million, and there was a cancellation of the $1.85 million obligation for a payment of $1.4 million. The former resulted in a capital loss of $50,000, and the latter in the realization of $450,000 of ordinary income. Taxation of the ordinary income might be deferred under § 108 by a reduction of respondents' bases in their partnership interests.

Although this indeed could be a justifiable mode of analysis, it has not been adopted by the Commissioner. Nor is there anything to indicate that the Code requires the Commissioner to adopt it. We note that Professor Barnett's approach does assume that recourse and nonrecourse debt may be treated identically.

The Commissioner also has chosen not to characterize the transaction as cancellation of indebtedness. We are not presented with and do not decide the contours of the cancellation-of-indebtedness doctrine. We note only that our approach does not fall within certain prior interpretations of that doctrine. In one view, the doctrine rests on the same initial premise as our analysis here — an obligation to repay — but the doctrine relies on a freeing-of-assets theory to attribute ordinary income to the debtor upon cancellation. *See United States v. Kirby Lumber Co.*, 284 U.S. 1, 3 (1931). According to that view, when nonrecourse debt is forgiven, the debtor's basis in the securing property is reduced by the amount of debt canceled, and realization of income is deferred until the sale of the property. *See Fulton Gold Corp. v. Commissioner*, 31 B.T.A. 519, 520 (1934). Because that interpretation attributes income only when assets are freed, however, an insolvent debtor realizes income just to the extent his assets exceed his liabilities after the cancellation. *Lakeland Grocery Co. v. Commissioner*, 36 B.T.A. 289, 292 (1937). Similarly, if the nonrecourse indebtedness exceeds the value of the securing property, the taxpayer never realizes the full amount of the obligation canceled because the tax law has not recognized negative basis.

Although the economic benefit prong of *Crane* also relies on a freeing-of-assets theory, that theory is irrelevant to our broader approach. In the context of a sale or disposition of property under § 1001, the extinguishment of the obligation to repay is not ordinary income; instead, the amount of the canceled debt is included in the amount realized, and enters into the computation of gain or loss on the disposition of property. According to *Crane*, this treatment is no different when the obligation is nonrecourse: the basis is not reduced as in the cancellation-of-indebtedness context, and the full value of the outstanding liability is included in the amount realized. Thus, the problem of negative basis is avoided.

the amount of the outstanding obligation, the mortgagee's ability to protect its interests is impaired, for the mortgagor is free to abandon the property to the mortgagee and be relieved of his obligation.

This, however, does not erase the fact that the mortgagor received the loan proceeds tax-free and included them in his basis on the understanding that he had an obligation to repay the full amount. . . . When the obligation is canceled, the mortgagor is relieved of his responsibility to repay the sum he originally received and thus realizes value to that extent within the meaning of § 1001(b). From the mortgagor's point of view, when his obligation is assumed by a third party who purchases the encumbered property, it is as if the mortgagor first had been paid with cash borrowed by the third party from the mortgagee on a nonrecourse basis, and then had used the cash to satisfy his obligation to the mortgagee.

Moreover, this approach avoids the absurdity the Court recognized in *Crane*. Because of the remedy accompanying the mortgage in the nonrecourse situation, the depreciation in the fair market value of the property is relevant economically only to the mortgagee, who by lending on a nonrecourse basis remains at risk. To permit the taxpayer to limit his realization to the fair market value of the property would be to recognize a tax loss for which he has suffered no corresponding economic loss. Such a result would be to construe "one section of the Act . . . so as . . . to defeat the intention of another or to frustrate the Act as a whole."

In the specific circumstances of *Crane*, the economic benefit theory did support the Commissioner's treatment of the nonrecourse mortgage as a personal obligation. The footnote in *Crane* acknowledged the limitations of that theory when applied to a different set of facts. *Crane* also stands for the broader proposition, however, that a nonrecourse loan should be treated as a true loan. We therefore hold that a taxpayer must account for the proceeds of obligations he has received tax-free and included in basis. Nothing in either § 1001(b) or in the Court's prior decisions requires the Commissioner to permit a taxpayer to treat a sale of encumbered property asymmetrically, by including the proceeds of the nonrecourse obligation in basis but not accounting for the proceeds upon transfer of the encumbered property. *See Estate of Levine v. Commissioner* . . . .

* * *

When a taxpayer sells or disposes of property encumbered by a nonrecourse obligation, the Commissioner properly requires him to include among the assets realized the outstanding amount of the obligation. The fair market value of the property is irrelevant to his calculation. We find this interpretation to be consistent with *Crane* . . . and to implement the statutory mandate in a reasonable manner. . . .

* * *

JUSTICE O'CONNOR, concurring.

I concur in the opinion of the Court, accepting the view of the Commissioner. I do not, however, endorse the Commissioner's view. Indeed, were we writing on a slate clean except for the decision in *Crane* . . . , I would take quite a different approach — that urged upon us by Professor Barnett as *amicus*.

Crane established that a taxpayer could treat property as entirely his own, in spite of the "coinvestment" provided by his mortgagee in the form of a nonrecourse loan. That is, the full basis of the property, with all its tax consequences, belongs to the mortgagor. That rule alone, though, does not in any way tie nonrecourse debt to the cost of property or to the proceeds upon disposition. I see no reason to treat the purchase, ownership, and eventual disposition of property differently because the taxpayer also takes out a mortgage, an independent transaction. In this case, the taxpayer purchased property, using nonrecourse financing, and sold it after it declined in value to a buyer who assumed the mortgage. There is no economic difference between the events in this case and a case in which the taxpayer buys property with cash; later obtains a nonrecourse loan by pledging the property as security; still later, using cash on hand, buys off the mortgage for the market value of the devalued property; and finally sells the property to a third party for its market value.

The logical way to treat both this case and the hypothesized case is to separate the two aspects of these events and to consider, first, the ownership and sale of the property, and, second, the arrangement and retirement of the loan. Under *Crane*, the fair market value of the property on the date of acquisition — the purchase price — represents the taxpayer's basis in the property, and the fair market value on the date of disposition represents the proceeds on sale. The benefit received by the taxpayer in return for the property is the cancellation of a mortgage that is worth no more than the fair market value of the property, for that is all the mortgagee can expect to collect on the mortgage. His gain or loss on the disposition of the property equals the difference between the proceeds and the cost of acquisition. Thus, the taxation of the transaction *in property* reflects the economic fate of the *property*. If the property has declined in value, as was the case here, the taxpayer recognizes a loss on the disposition of the property. The new purchaser then takes as his basis the fair market value as of the date of the sale. . . .

In the separate borrowing transaction, the taxpayer acquires cash from the mortgagee. He need not recognize income at that time, of course, because he also incurs an obligation to repay the money. Later, though, when he is able to satisfy the debt by surrendering property that is worth less than the face amount of the debt, we have a classic situation of cancellation of indebtedness, requiring the taxpayer to recognize income in the amount of the difference between the proceeds of the loan and the amount for which he is able to satisfy his creditor. 26 U.S.C. § 61(a)(12). The taxation of the financing transaction then reflects the economic fate of the loan.

The reason that separation of the two aspects of the events in this case is important is, of course, that the Code treats different sorts of income differently. A gain on the sale of the property may qualify for capital gains treatment, §§ 1202, 1221 . . . while the cancellation of indebtedness is ordinary income, but income that the taxpayer may be able to defer. §§ 108, 1017 . . . Not only does Professor Barnett's theory permit us to accord appropriate treatment to each of the two types of income or loss present in these sorts of transactions, it also restores continuity to the system by making the taxpayer-seller's proceeds on the disposition of property equal to the purchaser's basis in the property. Further, and most important, it allows us to tax the events in this case in the same way that we tax the economically identical hypothesized transaction.

Persuaded though I am by the logical coherence and internal consistency of this approach, I agree with the Court's decision not to adopt it judicially. We do not write on a slate marked only by *Crane*. The Commissioner's long-standing position . . . is now reflected in the regulations. Treas. Reg. § 1.1001-2 . . . In the light of the numerous cases in the lower courts including the amount of the unrepaid proceeds of the mortgage in the proceeds on sale or disposition . . . it is difficult to conclude that the Commissioner's interpretation of the statute exceeds the bounds of his discretion. As the Court's opinion demonstrates, his interpretation is defensible. One can reasonably read § 1001(b)'s reference to "the amount realized from the sale or other disposition of property" (emphasis added) to permit the Commissioner to collapse the two aspects of the transaction. As long as his view is a reasonable reading of § 1001(b), we should defer to the regulations promulgated by the agency charged with interpretation of the statute. . . . Accordingly, I concur.

NOTES AND COMMENTS

Thus, *Tufts* effectively eliminates *Crane*'s footnote 37 in a manner foreshadowed by *Levine*, and other authorities that had reached the same result, including Treas. Reg. § 1.1001-2(a)(4)(i) and (c) Example 2, but in a manner that, in rejecting Prof. Barnett's suggestion in his *amicus* brief, abandons the equating of recourse and nonrecourse debt that was one of the cornerstones of *Crane*. As indicated under Treas. Reg. § 1.1001-2(a)(2) and (c) Example 8, Tufts and his partners would have realized some DOI income if the mortgage was recourse. Although not highlighted in the discussion of Prof. Barnett's brief, including the entire nonrecourse liability in the amount realized without regard to the value of the property is not always advantageous to the taxpayer. This issue is discussed in § 5 *DOI Income and § 108*.

Section 7701(g), enacted in 1984, codifies the result in *Tufts*, by providing that in determining gain or loss for all purposes of the Code the fair market value of property subject to a nonrecourse liability shall be treated as not less than the amount of the nonrecourse liability. Although cited from time to time in regulations, including some making determinations without regard to § 77701(g), there are no regulations under the provision itself more than a quarter of a century later.

PROBLEM FOR DISCUSSION

Problem 3-18. On the basis of *Crane, Levine, Tufts*, Treas. Reg. § 1.1001-2, and other authorities cited in this § 3.01 what is Fred Bayles' basis in the property acquired from the Tufts et al. partnership? *See* also *Philadelphia Park, Seas Shipping*, and *Amerada Hess*, discussed in Chapter 1 § 2.06. Note: We will return to this issue after considering additional authorities in § 3.02 *Contingencies*.

§ 3.02. Contingencies

Notwithstanding the decision in *Crane*, which allowed basis equal to the amount of the liability that was nonrecourse to Ms. Crane, there is obvious potential for abuse when property is acquired subject to a nonrecourse purchase-money liability in the amount of the full stated purchase price. It makes sense to allow a Perch a basis of $50,000 in Blackacre when Perch pays $10,000 in cash and $40,000 borrowed from a commercial bank, even on a nonrecourse basis, because the bank's business interest is reasonably assumed to assure that the property is worth the full amount of the purchase price. The same should be true if the nonrecourse loan is the balance of the purchase price from Sail, the seller of Blackacre, because Perch is not likely to agree to a price in excess of value because of the risk of loss of the cash payment. On the other hand, when the entire $50,000 purchase price is represented by a nonrecourse mortgage, Perch no longer has any risk of loss, so that Perch's position is not that different from a holder of an option. If Blackacre is depreciable property, Perch may have an incentive to agree to a price of $60,000 or $100,000 for Blackacre (even though it is only worth $50,000), if the value of the depreciation or the other benefits of owning Blackacre for the period until significant payments become due are great enough.

Accordingly, the Service frequently resists granting basis equal to the amount of the mortgage, arguing that the nonrecourse aspect makes the liability contingent, and that *Crane* was limited to acquiring property subject to an existing mortgage. The following is one of its more notable defeats. As you read it, see what factors lead to treating the sale as bona fide so as to distinguish it from the abusive case above. The following case illustrates what the court determined was a nonabusive situation.

MAYERSON v. COMMISSIONER

United States Tax Court
47 T.C. 340 (1966)

* * *

> [The taxpayer, a licensed real estate broker and active investor, who had successfully developed shopping centers and motel and apartment projects, remodeling older structures when necessary, was interested in a "fixer-upper" property known as the 8th and Walnut Building that had many building violations. He acquired it on December 31, 1959, from the Balch Estate. for no cash and a nonrecourse purchase-money note in the face amount of $332,500 secured by a long-term mortgage. If the purchase-money obligation was paid off within the first year, or the 2 succeeding years, the price would be reduced to $275,000 or $298,750, respectively. Thereafter, the price would increase to the face amount of the mortgage note, a maximum of $332,500. He received a valid warranty deed.]

* * *

Following the transfer of title, petitioner contacted architects and had engineering surveys made of the property. Costs of conversion were explored with several independent contractors. . . .

The outstanding building orders were reduced from 72 to 25 by March 4, 1960, and were further reduced to 6 by December 16, 1964. This was done by petitioner at his expense in order to keep the building open and also to comply with the requirements of the purchase-money mortgage. . . .

In addition to repairs required by the building orders and normal maintenance, petitioner has made several major improvements. Garage entrances were widened, the building was rewired, the lobbies were reconditioned with the installation of new ceilings and fronts. Several thousands of dollars were spent to create offices on the second floor of the building as part of an experiment to test the potential for renting office space at highly competitive rates. . . .

Following the transfer of title in 1959, petitioner executed leases with tenants and paid utilities, insurance, and real estate tax bills. In late December of 1964, petitioner learned that the owner of a nearby building was contemplating another area for a garage. After discussions with the owner of this building, petitioner convinced him to lease the entire 8th and Walnut Building. By using this lease as collateral, petitioner was for the first time able to get a conventional mortgage loan from a financial institution. After securing this loan, petitioner negotiated with the Balch Estate and in January of 1965 the parties agreed to a settlement to discharge the note and purchase-money mortgage by the payment of the flat sum of $200,000. Petitioner made no payment of principal with respect to the purchase-money mortgage from the time of the initial $10,000 down payments until the negotiated settlement resulting in payment of $200,000 to discharge this lien.

* * *

Respondent determined that petitioner's claimed deduction for depreciation of the 8th and Walnut Building was excessive and not allowable under section 167 during the years in question. A depreciation deduction is allowed for property used in a trade or business or held for the production of income. Section 167[c] of the Code provides that the basis for the depreciation deduction is the adjusted basis provided in section 1011 for the purpose of determining the gain on the sale or other disposition of such property. Generally, the adjusted basis for determining gain or loss from the sale of property is the amount paid for such property in cash or other property. Sec. 1.1012-1, Income Tax Reg. Thus, in a situation of outright purchase, the amount paid for the property constitutes the depreciable basis. Moreover, it is well accepted that a purchase-money debt obligation for part of the price will be included in basis. This is necessary in order to equate a purchase-money mortgage situation with the situation in which the buyer borrows the full amount of the purchase price from a third party and pays the seller in cash. It is clear that the depreciable basis should be the same in both instances.

Respondent's position is essentially that the purchase-money mortgage involved in this case was a nullity and that a capital investment in the subject property had not occurred. The $10,000 cash downpayment was treated . . . as the cost of obtaining a 99-year lease, thus qualifying for amortization deductions over the term of the lease. This treatment gives rise to the inference that respondent determined that the transaction actually resulted in the creation of a long-term lease. On brief, respondent adds the additional contention that in effect all petitioner acquired was an option to purchase at any time during the alleged lease.

Respondent's position apparently results from his objections to certain features of the purchase-money mortgage. Petitioner was not personally liable on the mortgage, and the only recourse available to the mortgagee in case of default was foreclosure against the property; the property was the only security under the mortgage agreement. Respondent argues that when there is no enforceable and binding personal obligation with respect to the purchase price, no debt is created.

The absence of a debt is also indicated by the indefinite amount of the alleged obligation, according to respondent. This is evidently a reference to the fact that petitioner could pay off the mortgage in the first or 2 succeeding years with an amount stipulated in the purchase-money mortgage which was less than the face amount due after the expiration of 3 years. Thus, the amount due on the mortgage could fluctuate between three different sums depending upon whether payment occurred within the first year, the second, or third year, or years thereafter.

Respondent also emphasizes the fact that after two initial payments of $5,000 each, no portion of the principal of the purchase-money mortgage was due on or before 99 years from the date of the obligation. Petitioner did have the option, however, to make payments of principal at any time during the term of the mortgage. Petitioner was obligated to pay a fixed sum of $18,000 per year, designated as interest, in monthly installments. If the principal due on the mortgage was reduced below $300,000, then interest was payable at the rate of 6 percent per year on the unpaid balance.

It is undisputed that petitioner became the owner of legal title to the 8th and Walnut Building. There is no hint of a sham transaction in the transfer of title to the building and respondent makes no contention that the transaction was a sham or rigged to appear to be a sale and mortgage back when it was in fact something else. We are concerned with an arm's-length transaction entered into between knowledgeable strangers for business motives. It is well accepted, however, that depreciation is not predicated upon ownership of property but rather upon an investment in property. . . . It therefore follows that the benefit of the depreciation deduction should inure to those who would suffer an economic loss caused by wear and exhaustion of the business property. . . .

* * *

We must first decide whether the absence of personal liability with respect to the purchase-money mortgage precludes the inclusion of any amount attributable to the mortgage in the depreciable basis of the property. If this is true, depreciation based on the purchase-money mortgage should be denied regardless of the existence of a bona fide debt obligation for the mortgage. An analysis of this question must begin with the Supreme Court's landmark decision in *Crane* . . .

The relevance of the *Crane* case to the issue of depreciable basis arises due to section 167([c]) which states that the basis for depreciation shall be the same as the basis for gain or loss on a sale or exchange under section 1011. Thus, the *Crane* case constitutes strong authority for the proposition that the basis used for depreciation as well as the computation of gain or loss would include the amount of an unassumed mortgage on the property.

* * *

The respondent argues that the *Crane* case should not apply in a purchase situation since the basis in that case started with fair market value and not cost, as in the case of a purchase. The reasoning of the *Crane* case, however, seems equally applicable to a purchase situation and indeed was so applied in . . . and *Parker v. Delaney* . . . . It should also be applied here.

The element of the lack of personal liability has little real significance due to common business practices. As we have indicated in our findings it is not at all unusual in current mortgage financing of income-producing properties to limit liability to the property involved Taxpayers who are not personally liable for encumbrances on property should be allowed depreciation deductions affording competitive equality with taxpayers who are personally liable for encumbrances or taxpayers who own unencumbered property. The effect of such a policy is to give the taxpayer an advance credit for the amount of the mortgage. This appears to be reasonable since it can be assumed that a capital investment in the amount of the mortgage will eventually occur despite the absence of personal liability. The respondent has not suggested any rationale that would reasonably require a contrary conclusion. The lien created by the purchase-money mortgage . . . should be included in basis for the purpose of computing depreciation.

Having determined that the absence of personal liability with respect to a purchase-money mortgage does not preclude the inclusion of the mortgage in the depreciable basis of the property, we must decide whether the purchase-money mortgage involved in this case should be considered a bona fide debt obligation. Respondent argues that even if the usual purchase-money mortgage should be included in depreciable basis, this doctrine would be inapplicable in a situation where the alleged debt instrument does not create any obligation to pay the purchase price.

The bases for respondent's contention that no debt obligation was created are the absence of personal liability on the mortgage and the fact that the principal of the mortgage was not due for 99 years. We have already discussed the relative unimportance of personal liability in modern business transactions. We hold that this does not affect the validity of the mortgage debt. Therefore, if we are to conclude that there was no debt it must be because of the 99-year term for maturity. Although this term does seem unusually long, after viewing the totality of the circumstances and all the evidence of record we have found and hold that a valid debt obligation was created by the purchase-money mortgage in question.

Contrary to respondent's asserted position, we do not believe that this transaction was in reality or substance a lease with an option to purchase. The uncontroverted testimony of petitioner and a representative of the Balch Estate was that a sale was intended with an understanding that there would be a conversion to institutional mortgage financing as soon as possible. These witnesses were forthright, impressive, and entirely believable. It is clear that the 99-year term was never expected to run its course, but even absent this factor, it should be realized that a definite contractual obligation was created which would have had to be fulfilled by or before a definite date in the future. The sales transaction was normal in every other way, and the actions of the parties to the transaction certainly support our conclusions that a bona fide sale occurred and a valid debt obligation for most of the purchase price was created. Petitioner invested in improvements for the building and undertook the usual duties of a property owner. He worked diligently to find the highest and best use for the property so that he could obtain conventional financing. Within a few years he succeeded and retired the mortgage as the parties understood and hoped.

As we view the evidence before us, we do not have a substance versus form situation here because substance and form coincide. Although it can be argued that the economic realities of the transaction would be the same whether the transaction was characterized as a sale with a purchase-money mortgage or a long-term lease with an option to purchase at any time, the evidence is convincing that the parties to the transaction intended a sale and mortgage and the form was consistent with this intent. We therefore hold that the transaction was in substance as well as form an effective sale and purchase-money mortgage for income tax purposes.

Respondent's final argument for denial of the depreciation deductions on the 8th and Walnut Building is based on the proposition that even though the purchase-money mortgage imposed an obligation on petitioner, the obligation cannot be considered as part of the depreciable basis since the cost of property for the purpose of determining basis for depreciation does not include any amount with respect to obligations which are contingent and indefinite in nature. *Columbus & Greenville Railway Co.*, 42 T.C. 834 (1965); *Albany Car Wheel Co.*, 40 T.C. 831 (1963), *affirmed per curiam*, 333 F.2d 653 (C.A. 2, 1964); *Lloyd H. Redford*, 28 T.C. 773 (1957). An example of the type of contingency referred to in the preceding proposition was present in the *Albany Car Wheel Co.* case. In that case we found that the purchaser-taxpayer's obligation under the purchase agreement to procure a release of the predecessor's liability under a union contract for severance pay was of such a contingent nature that it could not be considered a part of the cost of the assets acquired. Whether it would ever be necessary to satisfy any severance pay obligations was unknown at the time of the sale.

* * *

We hold that the doctrine supported by the foregoing cases is inapplicable to the subject purchase-money mortgage. Respondent contends that the amount of the obligation was indefinite because of the varying amounts due under the terms of the instrument and the fact that the purchase-money mortgage was eventually settled for the negotiated price of $200,000, a substantial reduction from the amount due under the instrument.

There were only two variables in the overall purchase price of the property, and they were specified in dollar amounts. The price depended then upon whether the purchase-money mortgage was paid within the first year, the second year, or years thereafter. We would classify such a price reduction for early payment as a bonus discount. The presence of such optional discounts does not make the purchase price indefinite. It merely provided an incentive for very early retirement of the mortgage which did not occur. The cost basis at the time of purchase should be the nondiscount price; the entire principal of the note and mortgage was due unless the discounted sums were paid in the first 2 years. It was not prepaid so as to provide for the application of the discount provisions and hence no adjustment in basis is required during the years before us. It is evident from the record that if the lien on the property provided by the mortgage were to be discharged at any time prior to its due date, the then fixed amount would necessarily have to be paid. There was nothing contingent or indefinite about the obligation here.

The subsequent settlement of the purchase-money mortgage for less than the amount due under the terms of the instrument should not affect the allowable depreciation in taxable years prior to the settlement. . . . Here we are concerned with an arm's-length business transaction and there is no logical basis for disregarding the purchase price provided for in the purchase-money mortgage.

* * *

NOTES AND COMMENTS

The Service's grudging acquiescence to *Mayerson* in Rev. Rul. 69-77, 1969-1 C.B. 59, stated that it would follow *Mayerson* only "in situations where it is clear that the property has been acquired at its fair market value in an arm's-length transaction creating a bona fide purchase and a bona fide debt obligation," apparently conceding that this was the case in *Mayerson*. It did not provide any other useful guidance. Nevertheless, in *Bolger v. Commissioner*, 59 T.C. 760 (1973), nonrecourse liabilities were recognized as valid when a real estate entrepreneur arranged to buy commercial properties through separate finance corporations that borrowed the purchase price from commercial lenders secured by the properties, net leased them to a user under a "hell or high water" lease under which the user agreed to pay the rent regardless of destruction and other events that would normally terminate a lease. The corporations distributed the properties subject to the respective leases and mortgages, but the shareholders did not assume personal liability. Because the fair market value of the property equaled the purchase price, the mortgages were included in the shareholders' basis.

The Service's argument in *Mayerson* that a contingent liability is not included in basis was supported by *Albany Car Wheel Co. v. Commissioner*, 40 T.C. 831 (1963), *aff'd per curiam*, 333 F.2d 653 (2d Cir. 1964) (cited in *Mayerson*), in which a corporate purchaser of a plant in a business rapidly becoming obsolete assumed the seller's obligations for "severance pay" under a union contract. In connection with the purchase, the acquiring corporation renegotiated the obligation to one that could be avoided by providing adequate notice of closing. When the plant closed, it fully discharged its obligations by rehiring certain laid-off employees and deducting their wages. The acquiring corporation attempted to include an amount on account of the severance pay obligation as part of its purchase price in determining the basis of the assets. The court denied any basis adjustment attributable to the severance pay obligation, because the obligation under the new contract was so contingent that it could not be considered part of the cost of the assets that the corporation acquired. The court concluded that any payments actually made under the contract would properly be taken into account only at that time. The principle that contingent liabilities are not included in basis until fixed is reflected in Treas. Reg. § 1.1012-1(g); and Treas. Reg. § 1.1275-4(c).

One distinction between *Mayerson* and *Albany Car Wheel,* of course, was that the contingencies in *Albany Car Wheel* were based on a contingency specified in the contract, not the factual risk of nonpayment because of decline in value. The Service was more successful in the following case, where there was no contingency specified in the contract, but where the risk of overstated basis was significant. Although the liability for the purchase price was not recognized, the ground for nonrecognition was that it was "contingent."

EST. OF FRANKLIN v. COMMISSIONER

United States Court of Appeals, Ninth Circuit
544 F.2d 1045 (9th Cir. 1976)

SNEED, CIRCUIT JUDGE:

This case involves another effort on the part of the Commissioner to curb the use of real estate tax shelters.[1] In this instance he seeks to disallow deductions for the taxpayers' distributive share of losses reported by a limited partnership with respect to its acquisition of a motel and related property. These "losses" have their origin in deductions for depreciation and interest claimed with respect to the motel and related property. . . . The Tax Court held that the transaction constituted an option exercisable in 1979 and disallowed the taxpayers' deductions. . . . We affirm this disallowance although our approach differs somewhat from that of the Tax Court.

The interest and depreciation deductions were taken by Twenty-Fourth Property Associates (hereinafter referred to as Associates), a California limited partnership of which Charles T. Franklin and seven other doctors were the limited partners. The deductions flowed from the purported "purchase" by Associates of the Thunderbird Inn, an Arizona motel, from Wayne L. Romney and Joan E. Romney (hereinafter referred to as the Romneys) on November 15, 1968.

Under a document entitled "Sales Agreement," the Romneys agreed to "sell" the Thunderbird Inn to Associates for $1,224,000. The property would be paid for over a period of ten years, with interest on any unpaid balance of seven and one-half percent per annum. "Prepaid interest" in the amount of $75,000 was payable immediately; monthly principal and interest installments of $9,045.36 would be paid for approximately the first ten years, with Associates required to make a balloon

---

[1] An early skirmish in this particular effort appears in *Manuel D. Mayerson,* 47 T.C. 340 (1966) which the Commissioner lost. The Commissioner attacked the substance of a nonrecourse sale, but based his attack on the nonrecourse and long-term nature of the purchase money note, without focusing on whether the sale was made at an unrealistically high price. In his acquiescence to *Mayerson,* 1969-2 CUM. BULL. xxiv, the Commissioner recognized that the fundamental issue in these cases generally will be whether the property has been "acquired" at an artificially high price, having little relation to its fair market value. "The Service emphasizes that its acquiescence in *Mayerson* is based on the particular facts in the case and will not be relied upon in the disposition of other cases except where it is clear that the property has been acquired at its fair market value in an arm's length transaction creating a bona fide purchase and a bona fide debt obligation." Rev. Rul. 69-77, 1969-1 CUM BULL. 69.

payment at the end of the ten years of the difference between the remaining purchase price, forecast as $975,000, and any mortgages then outstanding against the property.

The purchase obligation of Associates to the Romneys was nonrecourse; the Romneys' only remedy in the event of default would be forfeiture of the partnership's interest. The sales agreement was recorded in the local county. A warranty deed was placed in an escrow account, along with a quitclaim deed from Associates to the Romneys, both documents to be delivered either to Associates upon full payment of the purchase price, or to the Romneys upon default.

The sale was combined with a leaseback of the property by Associates to the Romneys; Associates therefore never took physical possession. The lease payments were designed to approximate closely the principal and interest payments with the consequence that with the exception of the $75,000 prepaid interest payment no cash would cross between Associates and Romneys until the balloon payment. The lease was on a net basis; thus, the Romneys were responsible for all of the typical expenses of owning the motel property including all utility costs, taxes, assessments, rents, charges, and levies of "every name, nature and kind whatsoever." The Romneys also were to continue to be responsible for the first and second mortgages until the final purchase installment was made; the Romneys could, and indeed did, place additional mortgages on the property without the permission of Associates. Finally, the Romneys were allowed to propose new capital improvements which Associates would be required to either build themselves or allow the Romneys to construct with compensating modifications in rent or purchase price.

In holding that the transaction between Associates and the Romneys more nearly resembled an option than a sale, the Tax Court emphasized that Associates had the power at the end of ten years to walk away from the transaction and merely lose its $75,000 "prepaid interest payment." It also pointed out that a deed was never recorded and that the "benefits and burdens of ownership" appeared to remain with the Romneys. Thus, the sale was combined with a leaseback in which no cash would pass; the Romneys remained responsible under the mortgages, which they could increase; and the Romneys could make capital improvements.[2] The Tax Court further justified its "option" characterization by reference to the nonrecourse nature of the purchase money debt and the nice balance between the rental and purchase money payments.

Our emphasis is different from that of the Tax Court. We believe the characteristics set out above can exist in a situation in which the sale imposes upon the purchaser a genuine indebtedness within the meaning of section 167(a), Internal Revenue Code of 1954, which will support both interest and depreciation deductions. They substantially so existed in *Hudspeth v. Commissioner*, 509 F.2d 1224 (9th Cir. 1975) in which parents entered into sale-leaseback transactions with their children. The children paid for the property by executing nonnegotiable notes and mortgages equal to the fair market value of the property; state law proscribed

---

[2] There was evidence that not all of the benefits and burdens of ownership remained with the Romneys. Thus, for example, the leaseback agreement appears to provide that any condemnation award will go to Associates. . . .

deficiency judgments in case of default, limiting the parents' remedy to foreclosure of the property. The children had no funds with which to make mortgage payments; instead, the payments were offset in part by the rental payments, with the difference met by gifts from the parents to their children. Despite these characteristics this court held that there was a bona fide indebtedness on which the children, to the extent of the rental payments, could base interest deductions. . . .

In none of these cases, however, did the taxpayer fail to demonstrate that the purchase price was at least approximately equivalent to the fair market value of the property. Just such a failure occurred here. The Tax Court explicitly found that on the basis of the facts before it the value of the property could not be estimated. . . . In our view this defect in the taxpayer's proof is fatal.

Reason supports our perception. An acquisition such as that of Associates if at a price approximately equal to the fair market value of the property under ordinary circumstances would rather quickly yield an equity in the property which the purchaser could not prudently abandon. This is the stuff of substance. It meshes with the form of the transaction and constitutes a sale.

No such meshing occurs when the purchase price exceeds a demonstrably reasonable estimate of the fair market value. Payments on the principal of the purchase price yield no equity so long as the unpaid balance of the purchase price exceeds the then existing fair market value. Under these circumstances the purchaser by abandoning the transaction can lose no more than a mere chance to acquire an equity in the future should the value of the acquired property increase. While this chance undoubtedly influenced the Tax Court's determination that the transaction before us constitutes an option, we need only point out that its existence fails to supply the substance necessary to justify treating the transaction as a sale *ab initio*. It is not necessary to the disposition of this case to decide the tax consequences of a transaction such as that before us if in a subsequent year the fair market value of the property increases to an extent that permits the purchaser to acquire an equity.

Authority also supports our perception. It is fundamental that "depreciation is not predicated upon ownership of property but rather upon an investment in property . . . *Mayerson* . . . . No such investment exists when payments of the purchase price in accordance with the design of the parties yield no equity to the purchaser. . . . In the transaction before us and during the taxable years in question the purchase price payments by Associates have not been shown to constitute an investment in the property. Depreciation was properly disallowed. Only the Romneys had an investment in the property.

Authority also supports disallowance of the interest deductions. This is said even though it has long been recognized that the absence of personal liability for the purchase money debt secured by a mortgage on the acquired property does not deprive the debt of its character as a bona fide debt obligation able to support an interest deduction. . . . However, this is no longer true when it appears that the debt has economic significance only if the property substantially appreciates in value prior to the date at which a very large portion of the purchase price is to be discharged. . . . Prior to the date at which the balloon payment on the purchase price is required, and assuming no substantial increase in the fair market value of the property, the absence of personal liability on the debt reduces the transaction in economic terms to a mere chance that a genuine debt obligation may arise. This is not enough to justify an interest deduction. To justify the deduction the debt must exist; potential existence will not do. For debt to exist, the purchaser, in the absence of personal liability, must confront a situation in which it is presently reasonable from an economic point of view for him to make a capital investment in the amount of the unpaid purchase price. . . .

Our focus on the relationship of the fair market value of the property to the unpaid purchase price should not be read as premised upon the belief that a sale is not a sale if the purchaser pays too much. Bad bargains from the buyer's point of view — as well as sensible bargains from buyer's, but exceptionally good from the seller's point of view — do not thereby cease to be sales. *See Commissioner v. Brown*, 280 U.S. 543 . . . (1965) . . . . We intend our holding and explanation thereof to be understood as limited to transactions substantially similar to that now before us.

AFFIRMED.

NOTES AND COMMENTS

Thus, we have two extremes for the treatment of nonrecourse debt in determining the basis of acquired property — the full amount of the nonrecourse debt included in basis under *Crane* and *Mayerson*, and no portion of the nonrecourse debt included in basis under *Franklin*. A third possibility — the inclusion of the nonrecourse debt in basis in an amount equal to the fair market value of the property — was adopted in *Pleasant Summit Land Corp. v. Commissioner*, 863 F.2d 263 (3d Cir. 1988), *cert. denied sub nom., Commissioner v. Prussin*, 493 U.S. 901 (1989), *on remand, Prussin v. Commissioner*, T.C. Memo. 1990-287, *aff'd without opinion*, 947 F.2d 936 (3d Cir. 1991). In *Pleasant Summit*, the court determined that, even though the mortgage exceeded the fair market value of the property, so that the then-mortgagor had no incentive to pay it in full, the creditor would have an incentive to adjust the mortgage to fair market value, so that a basis equal to value was appropriate. On remand, the Tax Court determined the fair market value of the property and also concluded that the interest deductions should be limited to interest at a reasonable rate on that reduced value. In Action on Decision 1991-09, the Service announced it would not follow *Pleasant Summit/Prussin*, and would continue to litigate this issue based on the rationale of *Franklin*, arguing that even at the time of default the borrower would still have no equity in the property to protect, so it could just as prudently abandon the property.

PROBLEMS FOR DISCUSSION

Problem 3-19. Reconsider Problem 3-18 in light of *Franklin* (excessive nonrecourse liability not included in basis), *Mayerson* (nonrecourse liability included in basis), *Pleasant Summit/Prussin* (nonrecourse liability included at FMV of encumbered property) and *Bolger* (nonrecourse liability included in basis). (i) What should be Bayles' basis in the property? (ii) Does Bayles own the property during the mortgage period, or is his interest only an option, a remainder, or something else? (iii) If any basis less than the full amount of the mortgage is appropriate, how should any mortgage payments be allocated: (a) between principal and interest under the amortization schedule in the original note? (b) between principal under a hypothetical amortization schedule on the adjusted debt over the remaining term of the mortgage? or (c) between principal and interest under some other schedule? (iv) If (b), should any excess payment over the hypothetical amortization of principal be treated as additional basis, or additional interest, or what?

Problem 3-20. Sail sold Blackacre, which had a basis of $600,000 and was subject to a recourse mortgage of $1,000,000, to Perch. Blackacre was subject to pollution that required cleanup if it was to be used as Perch planned. Although the cleanup was clearly necessary, the amount that would be required was unknown. Perch's engineer estimated that the cost would be $400,000, while Sail's claimed that it could be done for $100,000. Perch agreed to assume the $1,000,000 recourse mortgage, and to make the next payments until she had discharged her share, but only until the clean-up costs were determined. To the extent that the cleanup costs were more than $100,000, Sail would then be required to make additional mortgage payments until the principal had been reduced by an amount equal to the excess of the cost over $100,000. The cleanup took more than two years and cost $275,000. As a result, Sail made the next mortgage payments until the principal had been reduced by $175,000. (i) What is Sail's amount realized and Perch's basis in Blackacre? (ii) What are the tax consequences to Perch and Sail of the payments until Sail had completed her share of the payments? *See Pleasant/Prussin* (fair market value basis for purchaser of property subject to a liability in excess of value); *Albany Car Wheel* (no basis for contingent severance payment until paid); Rev. Rul. 95-74 (contingent obligations in nonrecognition transfer under § 351).

§ 3.03. Speculative Security

Many tax shelter transactions involved speculative security of types that make the real estate shelter in *Franklin* look like blue chip stocks. Whatever it was worth, the Thunderbird Inn was an operating motel that clearly had significant value, albeit one that was almost certainly significantly less than the stated purchase price. The following case involves one such arrangement, involving wildcat drilling that is of interest in part because of a peculiar issue of statutory construction. To deal with the ABC deal described by then-Judge Breyer, Congress had decreed that a production payment was treated as a liability. Judge Breyer explains why that provision does not prevent application of the *Franklin* principle, providing a useful warning against a too-literal interpretation of Code provisions.

BROUNTAS v. COMMISSIONER

United States Court of Appeals, First Circuit
692 F.2d 152 (1st Cir. 1982)

BREYER, CIRCUIT JUDGE. In this "tax shelter" case, we are asked to determine the propriety of certain deductions taken by a limited partner in an oil-and-gas drilling partnership. There is little question that subsequent changes in the law have made deductions similar to those at issue here improper for individual taxpayers. See . . .

§ 465 . . . (the "at risk" provisions). But, under the law as it stood when the deductions were taken, which is the law we must apply, the propriety of the deductions is a complicated and unsettled question. . . .

I

This case arises out of the activities of a Texas limited partnership known as "Coral I." The partnership was organized in 1972, and was set up to explore and develop "oil and gas" property. The case involves two investors in Coral I. One is CRC Corp., which was both a limited and general partner. The other is Paul Brountas, one of several limited partners in Coral I. Brountas contributed $10,000 in 1972 and $1,000 in 1973. . . .

The Coral I partnership worked in essentially the following manner: At the outset, partners would contribute money (as Brountas did in the amount of $10,000). This money would then be used to buy participations in what looked like promising "oil and gas" ventures. These ventures were invariably set up by CRC officials, and then sold in fractional interests to various CRC-managed partnerships (such as Coral I) and the CRC on its own account. In each case, a venture encompassed a package of several (typically three) oil and gas leasehold interests, or "prospects." These prospects (leaseholds) were owned by an "operator" — an entrepreneur unrelated to CRC who wanted to develop the prospects but lacked the money to do so. The investors had the money at a time when it was apparently difficult to obtain in the oil and gas industry; they were in a position to strike advantageous bargains.

The bargains followed a uniform pattern. The operator would agree to convey to the investors a set of "oil and gas" leaseholds and would agree to drill a test well on each. The test well was often an expensive undertaking because CRC officials insisted that the operator agree to complete the well no matter how difficult this proved to be. In return, the investors agreed to pay the operator a "total" contract price. This price consisted of a "lease purchase price" and a "drilling contract price," corresponding to the two parts of the operator's agreement. Each of these component prices was apparently negotiated separately with the operator by someone on CRC's behalf. The Tax Court found, and the government does not contest, that the two prices were each the result of arms-length bargaining and represented reasonable charges for the leaseholds and obligations in question.

The investors, however, did not pay the total price in cash. Rather, they paid the contract price with what the Tax Court found amounted to 40 percent in cash and 60 percent in a "nonrecourse" note. The "nonrecourse" note bore interest and was payable "on demand" after a certain time (usually about five years). It was "secured" by a percentage of oil and gas production from the underlying prospects, by a percentage of the leaseholds themselves, and by some of the equipment used. . . . [I]t was quite clear to all concerned that neither principal nor interest on a note would ever be paid if the prospects in a given venture all proved to be nonproducers. The investors were not personally liable on the notes . . . .

The agreement between the investors and the operator provided the operator with one further potential source of compensation for drilling the test wells — a "development option." If a well proved successful, the agreement allowed the operator to gain an "equity" interest in its production by entering into a "completion joint venture" with the investors. . . . The operator and investors would then share all future costs and production in a specified ratio (subject to certain additional restrictions and conditions not relevant here).

The limited partners believed they had invested in a leveraged "tax shelter." This type of shelter provides an investor with tax deductions greater in amount than the cash that he initially provides for the investment. These extra deductions can be subtracted from the investor's ordinary income, thus "sheltering" some of his ordinary income from tax. Of course, these extra deductions may someday be offset when the investor must recognize "income" though he receives no payment. But this day of reckoning is in the future, and in the meantime the government has provided the investor at least with what is effectively an interest-free loan of the dollars that it otherwise would have taxed away. . . .

We can illustrate how the promoters and investors thought this shelter would work by using the facts of this case in simplified form. Assume the operator conveys a package of prospects to investors for $250,000 and agrees to drill test wells on each prospect for another $750,000. The investors, in turn, agree to pay the "total contract price" of $1,000,000 with $400,000 in cash and $600,000 in a nonrecourse note payable out of production and secured (as indicated above) by production, leaseholds, and equipment. The operator and the investors further agree to allocate $100,000 of the cash and $150,000 of the note to the "purchase price" of the prospects, and $300,000 of the cash and $450,000 of the note to the "drilling contract price." In short, they agree that the same note/cash ratio as applies to the total price shall also apply to the two component prices. For simplicity, assume that there is only one investor, a partnership called Coral I, and that a (hypothetical) limited partner called Brountas has contributed cash equal to one percent, or $4,000, of the partnership's initial cash capital. Assuming these numbers, Brountas' argument amounts to a claim that he is entitled to deduct $7,500 as expenses. This figure — $7,500 — equals one percent (Brountas' share) of the total "drilling contract" price.

Brountas' argument begins with the fact that the cost of drilling an oil well is an immediately deductible expense. This is so because the Internal Revenue Code allows taxpayers (who make the proper election) to deduct all "intangible drilling and development costs" (or IDC's) in the year incurred. . . . § 263(c) . . . ; Treas. Reg. § 1.612-4(a) (1965). The Code treats other expenses less favorably. The cost of machinery and equipment must be capitalized and depreciated. The cost of acquiring leaseholds is not immediately deductible, but instead becomes part of the investor's tax "basis" and must be recovered gradually through the depletion allowance or on final disposition of the property as an offset against "amount realized." But unlike these costs, the "intangible" costs of drilling and developing a well, such as "wages, fuel, repairs, hauling, supplies . . . [and] the cost to [the investors here] of any drilling or development work . . . done for them by contractors under any form of contract," Treas. Reg. § 1.612-4(a) (1965) are immediately deductible.

Brountas thus claims that the partnership incurred what (in our example) amounts to $750,000 in IDC's in its first year. This expense consists of its payment to the operator (in return for a promise to drill) of $300,000 cash and $450,000 in nonrecourse notes. Brountas believes that the partnership, an accrual base taxpayer, can accrue as an expense in 1972 the future obligation to pay money that the notes represent. And, as a one percent partner, Brountas seeks to deduct one percent of the partnership's total IDC expense, or $7,500.

Brountas is aware that he must first demonstrate that he has a "basis" in the partnership of at least $7,500. The Internal Revenue Code limits the share of partnership losses that a partner may deduct to the extent of the partner's "basis" in the partnership. . . . § 704(d) (1976). This basis includes the money or other property that the partner has contributed to the partnership. . . . §§ 705 & 722 (1976). But, in our example, that amounted only to $4,000. How then can Brountas deduct $7,500? Brountas points to § 752(a), which states that "[a]ny increase in a partner's share of the liabilities of a partnership . . . shall be considered as a contribution of money. . . . "The nonrecourse notes, he explains, are liabilities of the partnership. Hence, his basis increases by his share of the notes, or $6,000, and thus § 704 does not limit his right to deduct his proportionate share of the IDC expense.

* * *

Brountas, the taxpayer, can prevail only if 1) his partnership basis increased sufficiently to allow him to deduct his full proportionate share of partnership expenses, and 2) the partnership's accrual for tax purposes — and hence the partners' deduction — of the total (cash plus noncash) "cost" of the drilling contract were proper. We shall address each of these issues in turn.

* * *

. . . [W]here no partner is personally liable on a partnership liability (*e.g.*, nonrecourse indebtedness), the regulations provide that "all partners, including limited partners, shall be considered as sharing such liability . . . in the same proportion as they share the profits." . . . The question before us here is whether the nonrecourse indebtedness in this case amounts to "liability" for purposes of § 752(a). We believe that it does not.

* * *

. . . The liabilities that investors typically are allowed to include in basis are relatively definite liabilities such as those upon which a lender might rely when he advances money to a borrower. . . .

When, however, an obligation to pay is both nonrecourse and not secured by property of at least equivalent value, courts have been reluctant to consider it a liability that increases an investor's basis. Thus, cases subsequent to *Crane* have found it proper to include nonrecourse debt in basis only insofar as the value of property securing the debt is equal to or greater than the face amount of the debt. See, *e.g.*, *Estate of Franklin* . . .

These decisions are consistent, for payment of a nonrecourse obligation is unlikely to be speculative to the extent that it is secured by property with a determinable value. Moreover, these decisions cannot be based upon a belief that the value of a nonrecourse note is limited to the value of the property that secures it, for a $1 million nonrecourse note secured by a $200,000 building is, other things being equal, considerably more valuable than a $200,000 note secured by the same building. (The note's value will reflect the fact that the building's value might rise, in which case the holder of the first note will receive more money than the holder of the second.) Therefore, these decisions must reflect an administrative fact — namely, the fact that it is simpler, when faced with obligations to pay that are highly uncertain, to wait and see if the contingency occurs. If it does not occur, the obligations need never enter basis, for they do not represent any obligation to pay. If it does occur, the extent of the monetary obligation will be reasonably capable of calculation, and any change in basis (where appropriate) can then be determined.

* * *

We now turn to the question of whether § 636 requires a different result. That section states in subsection (a) that a "production payment that is carved out of a mineral property shall be treated . . . as if it were a purchase money mortgage loan and shall not qualify as an economic interest in the mineral property." See also . . . § 636(b) (1976) (retained production payment). Brountas and the Tax Court reasoned as follows: 1) The nonrecourse obligations here amounted to "production payments." 2) Under § 636 production payments are to be treated like "loans." 3) True loans involve a lender who expects the borrower's obligation to be paid and are typically treated as a liability that increases partnership basis. 4) Hence, the obligations here should be added to Brountas' basis.

To understand the flaw in this reasoning, one must understand both what a production payment is and the purpose underlying § 636. Essentially, a production payment is a limited right to receive revenue from the production of mineral in place. The right may be limited by a dollar amount, by an amount of the mineral, and by a period of time. . . . But a right that is not so limited — a right to receive revenue in perpetuity or until the mineral is exhausted — would be a "royalty," not a "production payment."

* * *

Next, it is important to understand the purpose of § 636. When it enacted § 636, Congress feared that by creating "production payments," owners of oil wells could secure certain unjustified tax advantages. The precise way in which production payments achieved these advantages varied, depending, for example, on whether the payment was "carved out" by the property owner and transferred to one who in return provided services, money, etc., or whether it was "retained" by the seller when he sold the property. But, one can intuitively grasp the sort of problem that Congress saw by considering the following:

Suppose that Smith assigns to Jones the butcher (in return for meat) a "right" to $20 worth of Smith's future income. That income, when received by Smith, despite the 'assignment', is first taxed as Smith's income and then again as Jones'. Suppose that Smith assigns $100,000 of future rents in Smith's apartment house to Jones in return for services. Again, the $100,000 rent is taxed as Smith's income first. Suppose Jones has sold the apartment house to Smith for $1 million taking $900,000 in cash and the remainder in the form of a 'right' to the first $100,000 of rent. Again, the rent is taxed as Smith's income, for Jones is considered to have loaned Smith the extra $100,000 needed to pay the full $1 million and Smith is considered to be paying back this loan out of the apartment house rent. . . . These examples would have worked out differently, however, before § 636 if we were dealing with oil, rather than apartment houses, for an assignment of what might have looked like future income (or rents) or a retained right to that income — if properly characterized as a "production payment" — was considered to be the income only of the person who received (or retained) the payment. That person was considered to possess an "economic interest" in the producing property; the income that it produced (that went to him) would be considered his income alone, not that of others who might possess "economic interests" in the property. Hence, if Smith paid Jones for services with an oil "production payment" (rather than a right to a share of apartment house rents) the payments, as they flowed in, would not be considered part of Smith's income. And, if Jones sold Smith for $1 million an oil property (rather than an apartment house), retaining a $100,000 production payment (instead of a right to $100,000 of rents), the $100,000 as it flowed in would not be considered Smith's income; that is to say, it would not be treated as if Jones had loaned Smith $100,000 which was being paid back out of income that went to Smith.

These examples illustrate the essence of what Congress felt was wrong. Congress felt that the oil property owner or buyer should be treated basically like the apartment house owner or buyer. He should not be allowed to pay for services or pay for his property (by creating a production payment) with what Congress viewed as "pre-tax" dollars. . . .

The way Congress dealt with this problem in § 636 was to require that some (but not all) production payments be treated like "loans." . . . (carved-out exploration or development production payment not treated as a loan). . . . As the Tax Court explained in this case:

> When a production payment is treated as a loan, it is treated "as if" the recipient (holder) of the production payment loaned money, equipment, or services to the creator of the production payment, in return for which the recipient received rights under the production payment. When production is realized and the holder of the production payment is paid, the payments are treated as repayment of the liability created by the loans.

. . . Thus, after § 636, the transferor of the production payment or buyer of the property (Smith in our examples) will normally be charged with the income used to satisfy the production payment.

Congress, then, was concerned with the special "income attribution" effect of production payments. It changed that effect in § 636 so that, for example, the buyer of the oil property would be treated like the buyer of the apartment house. This was its object in saying that a "production payment" should be treated as a "mortgage loan" (§ 636(a)) or a "purchase money mortgage loan" (§ 636(b)).

Given this background, the Tax Court and Brountas cannot draw from 1) § 636's use of the word "loan" and 2) the fact that loan repayment obligations are normally not highly contingent or speculative, the conclusion that § 636 prohibits treating any production payments for basis purposes as highly contingent or speculative. . . .

[T]reating highly speculative or contingent payment obligations in the presence of § 636 just as they would be treated in its absence would not, as far as we know, interfere with any of § 636's stated purposes.

. . . [O]ne can consider the notes — the payment obligations — at issue here as if they were "loan repayment" obligations (for income attributive purposes) and at the same time consider them as highly speculative or contingent payment obligations (for basis purposes). . . .

* * *

Finally, the single argument that gives us pause consists of the claim that where production payments are at issue, highly contingent or speculative repayment obligations should not be distinguished from others because production payments are always speculative. One can never be certain whether there is sufficient oil to meet the payment. We do not consider this argument determinative, however, because one can still distinguish among degrees of uncertainty; a right to collect funds from a property where oil has not yet been found would seem far more speculative than rights secured by the production of existing wells. . . .

In sum, we do not believe that § 636 changes the tax basis treatment that Brountas' nonrecourse notes would receive without it. . . .

* * *

. . . [T]he same facts that make the nonrecourse notes too speculative or contingent to enter Brountas' basis in the partnership make it improper for the partnership to accrue the expense that it claims transfer of the notes to the operator represented. That is to say, because Coral I's note would effectively be paid only from the proceeds of any oil and gas delivered, "all the events" necessary to determine the fact and amount of liability had not yet occurred. . . .

The fact that the Tax Court found that the notes had economic substance, . . . does not change our result. A note may have economic substance yet be so contingent as not to warrant its accrual as a present expense. . . .

* * *

NOTES AND COMMENTS

As indicated in the *Notes and Comments* in § 1.01 *Conditions and Contingencies*, there is the omnipresent issue in all liability transactions, particularly those involving nonrecourse liabilities, whether the liability is bona fide. Nevertheless, determining the tax status of any payments made on the nonrecourse liability, and of the ownership of any encumbered property, is necessary for the proper determination of the tax consequences to the parties. Thus, in *Franklin*, the Tax Court characterized the transaction as an option, while Judge Sneed simply concluded that the nonrecourse obligation did not represent an investment in the property sufficient to justify depreciation, and that the debt was not real enough to support an interest deduction. In Rev. Rul. 78-29, 1978-1 C.B. 62, a nonrecourse note to purchase a patent, secured by a patent and its proceeds was determined not to be debt when the taxpayer did not prove that the value of the patent approximated the amount of the debt. Rev. Rul. 77-110, 1977-1 C.B. 58, reached a similar result for a nonrecourse note given as purchase price of movie, when the value not proved. Then-Judge, now Justice, Breyer in *Brountas* took a slightly different tack by concluding that the notes were too contingent to be liabilities, in effect, that they had not given rise to an expenditure in the terms of the partnership regulations. *See* Rev. Rul. 80-235, 1980-2 C.B. 229 (nonrecourse note to purchase an untested technology involving converting coal into oil payable only out of cash flow on the process was a contingent obligation that does not provide basis).

In some other transactions, the claimed nonrecourse liability based on speculative security was determined to be an equity investment in the venture, particularly when it was made by a party who had an interest in the project in success of the project that provided it with a profit potential much greater than its interest on its purported loan, so that the lender was really a partner, in effect, although not always expressly, making the "lender" a "partner. Thus, in *Carnegie Productions, Inc. v. Commissioner*, 59 T.C. 642 (1973) funds provided by a major studio distributor to a partnership that was to be the producer of a motion picture and that was to contribute the services of Paddy Chayefsky, who would write the screenplay and act as "associate producer" of the picture was determined to be a joint venture, even though the producer partnership had the legal right to make all decisions with respect to the filming and content of the picture, when the actual disbursement of the funds was subject to the joint control of the partnership and the distributor-lender. Similarly, in *Saviano v. Commissioner*, 765 F.2d 643 (7th Cir. 1985), a nonrecourse loan from a tax shelter promoter to pay deductible mining development expenses, with loan secured only by production from the mine, was determined to be an investment in the project in the nature of a joint venture and not a loan that allowed the other investors to deduct mining expenses; and the proceeds of option to purchase gold produced from a similar mine was not a true option allowing deferral of the payment by the venture, but was income in the year of receipt. *See* Rev. Rul. 77-125, 1977-1 C.B. 130 (nonrecourse loan from a bank guaranteed by film producer for services in producing movie is not a true loan; expenditures of proceeds are expenses of producer, not of the claimed service provider); Rev. Rul. 72-350, 1972-2 C.B. 394 (nonrecourse "loan" to an otherwise unrelated wildcat oil and gas exploration limited partnership secured by unproven leases and expensive but virtually unsalvageable oil and gas well installations, convertible into a 25 percent interest in the partnership's profits was capital investment).

PROBLEM FOR DISCUSSION

Problem 3-21. Invest purchased a 10 percent interest for $50,000 in a partnership that purchased a patent for a black box that is supposed to do wondrous things. The purchase price is $2,000,000, of which the tax shelter partnership will pay $10,000 in cash out of the capital contributions of Invest and the other partners, with the remaining capital contributions spent for fees and expenses of the promoter-manager. The patent holder provided a market study that indicated a potential market for $40,000,000 of patented products over a five-year period. This would produce profits of $10,000,000 at the estimated manufacturing cost of 50 percent per unit, or would produce royalties of $4,000,000 if licensed at a reasonable royalty rate of 10 percent. The remaining $1,990,000 will be financed by selling nonrecourse convertible debentures to a venture capital firm that will receive 75 percent of the proceeds of any licenses, and will have the option to convert $1,000,000 of the debentures into a 50 percent interest in the tax shelter entity. What is Invest's 10 percent share of the basis of the patent? *See Brountas*; *Saviano* (nonrecourse debt to develop gold mine); *Carnegie Productions* (nonrecourse loan for movie production costs from distributor); Rev. Rul. 80-235 (nonrecourse loan for coal conversion technology); Rev. Rul. 78-29 (nonrecourse loan for untested technology); Rev. Rul. 78-125 (nonrecourse loan as purchase price of movie negative); Rev. Rul. 77-110 (nonrecourse loan for movie production services); Rev. Rul. 72-350 (convertible nonrecourse loan on wildcat oil properties).

§ 3.04. *Tufts* and § 108(e)(5)

Treating the entire amount of a nonrecourse liability encumbering property transferred as an amount realized under *Tufts* and Treas. Reg. § 1.1001-2(a)(4)(i) means that there is no DOI income, even when the value of the property is less than the amount of nonrecourse liability. On the other hand, the reduction of a nonrecourse liability while the property is retained does not involve an amount realized or a sale or exchange, so that it may result in DOI income, unless the reduction is treated as a purchase price adjustment. In *Hirsch v. Commissioner*, 115 F.2d 656 (7th Cir. 1940), the payment of a mortgage assumed on the purchase of property for less than the amount owed was determined to be a purchase price adjustment, not DOI income. Similarly, in *Allen v. Courts*, 127 F.2d 127 (5th Cir. 1942), the compromise of subordinated third-party loan to purchase a New York Stock Exchange Seat (during the Depression) for less than amount owed was purchase price adjustment, not DOI income. Section 108(e)(5) provides that a reduction in the debt obligation to the seller of property for a solvent taxpayer is a purchase price adjustment and not DOI income. This provision does not, however, allow a reduction in third-party financing that was obtained to finance a purchase of property to be treated as purchase price adjustment, so that any such adjustment for a solvent taxpayer is DOI income. Reflecting the subprime mortgage crisis, § 108(a)(1)(E) and 108(h), in effect, provide such a purchase price adjustment for qualified principal residence mortgage indebtedness discharged after Jan. 1, 2007, and before Jan. 1, 2013. *See* § 5.03 *Basis Reduction — § 1017*, for a further discussion of the application of § 108(h). DOI income was realized on adjustments of lender-financed personal residence mortgage before the enactment of § 108(a)(1)(E) and (h), and, presumably will be after its expiration, unless it is made permanent by subsequent legislation. Thus, in *Sutphin v. United States*, 14 Cl. Ct. 545 (1988) (reduced payment that reflects interest rate below current market to discharge mortgage obtained to purchase residence was not purchase price adjustment (prior to enactment of § 108(a)(1)(E) and (h)), the opinion distinguishes *Hirsch* as applying only to reductions to reflect value of the property below the amount of the debt. *See* Rev. Rul. 82-202, 1982-2 C.B. 35 (same). Rev. Rul. 92-99, 1992-2 C.B. 35 (write-down of nonrecourse mortgage obtained to purchase property is not purchase price adjustment); Tech. Adv. Mem. 85-47-001 (lender deduction for write-down of mortgage with rate below current market, even though borrower obtained new second mortgage at higher rate).

The following case finds such a purchase price adjustment for a reduction in a nonrecourse liability that encumbered the property when acquired before the enactment of § 108(e)(5): Whether the result is still sound is a matter of dispute.

FULTON GOLD CORP. v. COMMISSIONER

United States Board of Tax Appeals
31 B.T.A. 519 (1934)

Seawell: The petitioner, a corporation, in 1920 purchased from the Hopkinson Bergen Co. a piece of improved real estate in New York City for $600,000. There was an outstanding mortgage on the property for $450,000 and petitioner received the property subject to the mortgage, payment of which, however, it did not assume. In consideration of the payment of the mortgage before maturity the holder agreed to accept less than the face amount of the mortgage in satisfaction thereof. Accordingly, in May 1922 the petitioner paid the sum of $407,853 in full settlement of the mortgage and legal expenses and other charges incurred in the transaction.

In 1929 the petitioner sold the property for $652,166.67, and in its return for that year reported taxable gain of $46,781.57 resulting from the sale, based upon a cost of $600,000. In determining a deficiency of $10,635.50 in income tax against the petitioner for 1929 the respondent reduced the cost basis used by the petitioner by $42,147, representing the difference between the face amount of the mortgage and the sum paid in full settlement thereof, including legal expenses and other charges. The petitioner questions only this basis of cost.

* * *

In *American Seating Co.*, . . . the taxpayer acquired assets subject to an outstanding mortgage securing bonds issued by the seller. Subsequently the buyer purchased the bonds then outstanding in the hands of the public for less than par and the mortgage was satisfied. Our holding was that the payment represented a part of the cost of the assets and did not result in taxable income in the year it was made.

The *Kirby Lumber Co.* case . . . do[es] not appear to be opposed to such ruling. The basis for the Court's holding[s] is, as we read the decisions, that the purchases released assets offset by personal obligations under the bonds, resulting in a corresponding accession to income.

Here the petitioner, instead of assuming the mortgage, bought the property subject to it, and by making the purchase on such terms incurred no personal liability for the debt. Accordingly, payment of the mortgage did not result in the liquidation of a personal debt. By it the petitioner merely satisfied an encumbrance on property in which it had an equity and there was no release of assets "previously offset by the obligation" of the notes or bonds evidencing the debt secured by the mortgage. . . .

. . . [I]t does not appear that the real property was at any time after 1920 worth less than $600,000, and, if so, the petitioner's equity therein was never, in fact, at stake. . . . [W]e do not think it or the *Kirby Lumber Co.* case governs the question here. We think the correct result was reached by us in *American Seating Co.* . . .

Reviewed by the Board.

Decision will be entered for the respondent.

* * *

NOTES AND COMMENTS

Although cryptic in its explanation, the court treated the reduction in the nonrecourse debt as a purchase price adjustment, not as DOI income. Other cases before the enactment of § 108, including the *Hirsch* and *Allen* cases discussed above, treated the adjustment of third-party lending to finance a purchase as a purchase price adjustment. The decision in *Fulton Gold* was cited approvingly on this point in n. 11 in *Tufts*, but the Service has taken the position that *Tufts* overruled *Fulton Gold*, as shown in the following ruling:

Rev. Rul. 91-31, 1991-1 C.B. 19

* * *

In 1988, individual *A* borrowed $1,000,000 from *C* and signed a note payable to *C* for $1,000,000 that bore interest at a fixed market rate payable annually. *A* had no personal liability with respect to the note, which was secured by an office building valued at $1,000,000 that *A* acquired from *B* with the proceeds of the nonrecourse financing. In 1989, when the value of the office building was $800,000 and the outstanding principal on the note was $1,000,000, *C* agreed to modify the terms of the note by reducing the note's principal amount to $800,000. The modified note bore adequate stated interest within the meaning of section 1274(c)(2).

The facts here do not involve the bankruptcy, insolvency, or qualified farm indebtedness of the taxpayer. Thus, the specific exclusions provided by section 108(a) do not apply.

* * *

In *Gershkowitz v. Commissioner*, 88 T.C. 984 (1987), the Tax Court, in a reviewed opinion, concluded, in part, that the settlement of a nonrecourse debt of $250,000 for a $40,000 cash payment (rather than surrender of the $2,500 collateral) resulted in $210,000 of discharge of indebtedness income. The court, following the *Tufts* holding that income results when a taxpayer is discharged from liability for an undersecured nonrecourse obligation upon the disposition of the collateral, held that the discharge from a portion of the liability for an undersecured nonrecourse obligation through a cash settlement must also result in income.

The Service will follow the holding in *Gershkowitz* where a taxpayer is discharged from all or a portion of a nonrecourse liability when there is no disposition of the collateral. Thus, in the present case, *A* realizes $200,000 of discharge of indebtedness income in 1989 as a result of the modification of *A*'s note payable to *C*.

In an earlier Board of Tax Appeals decision, *Fulton Gold* . . . a taxpayer purchased property without assuming an outstanding mortgage and subsequently satisfied the mortgage for less than its face amount. In a decision based on unclear facts, the Board of Tax Appeals, for purposes of determining the taxpayer's gain or loss upon the sale of the property in a later year, held that the taxpayer's basis in the property should have been reduced by the amount of the mortgage debt forgiven in the earlier year.

The *Tufts* and *Gershkowitz* decisions implicitly reject any interpretation of *Fulton Gold* that a reduction in the amount of a nonrecourse liability by the holder of the debt who was not the seller of the property securing the liability results in a reduction of the basis in that property, rather than discharge of indebtedness income for the year of the reduction. *Fulton Gold,* interpreted in this manner, is inconsistent with *Tufts* and *Gershkowitz.* Therefore, that interpretation is rejected and will not be followed.

* * *

NOTES AND COMMENTS

In Rev. Rul. 92-99, 1992-2 C.B. 35 the Service held that reduction of a nonrecourse note that arose out of the purchase of property resulted in DOI income and stated that only debt obligations to the seller of the property may be treated as purchase price reductions, explicitly refusing to follow *Hirsch* and *Allen.* Although Rev. Rul. 91-31 does not note it, the nonrecourse loans cancelled in *Gershkowitz,* although made by a party that had various roles in the tax-shelter deal involved in that case, were not loans incurred to acquire the property secured by them. Accordingly, the issue of purchase price adjustment was not involved in *Gershkowitz,* so that it is difficult to see how the *Gershkowitz* decision implicitly rejects the purchase price adjustment holding of *Fulton Gold.* Although not involved in *Gershkowitz,* which dealt with transactions before its enactment, the more interesting issue is the effect of § 108(e)(5), which was enacted in 1980 but is not cited in Rev. Rul. 91-31. Indeed, it is not clear why either *Gershkowitz* or *Fulton Gold* are referred to at all in Rev. Rul. 91-31, which is stated to be amplifying Rev. Rul. 82-202, 1982-2 C.B. 35, which determined that DOI income is realized on a discounted prepayment of a bank mortgage obtained to purchase a residence, because, even though the bank mortgage was obtained to purchase the residence, it was not obtained from the seller of the residence. Because the facts in Rev. Rul. 91-31 do not differ in any significant way from those in Rev. Rul. 82-202, the apparent purpose of Rev. Rul. 91-31 is to create an opportunity for the Service to declare that it believes that *Fulton Gold* has no continuing validity. In doing so, it adds nothing to the language of § 108(e)(5), and it does not address the fact that unlike the nonrecourse borrowing in Rev. Ruls. 82-202 and 91-31, the nonrecourse liability in *Fulton Gold* did not represent any borrowed funds, but it was incurred as part of the purchase price when the seller transferred the property to Fulton Gold as purchaser, subject to the liability. Accordingly, a reasonable argument can be made that there should be a purchase price adjustment in the very narrow *Fulton Gold* and *Hirsch* situations, in which the nonrecourse liability reduced or cancelled was incurred by taking the property subject to a liability that was not assumed. Unlike the liability in Rev. Rul. 91-31 that was incurred to finance the purchase of property, like the liability in *Crane*, the nonrecourse borrowing in *Fulton Gold* was part of the purchase price because the liability was transferred by Fulton Gold's seller to it.

The result in *Pleasant Summit/Prussin* — treating a similar liability as part of the purchase price to the extent of the value of the property — is consistent with this approach. It is interesting to note that the lender's modification of the amount of the liability in Rev. Rul. 91-31 is the type of adjustment — a reduction of a nonrecourse liability to the value of the property — that the Service claimed in Action on Decision, 1991-09 (Mar. 29, 1991), would not occur because the lender had no incentive to agree to such an adjustment as a basis for not following *Pleasant Summit/Prussin*. Rev. Rul. 91-31 was issued approximately two months after AOD 1991-09.

Preslar v. Commissioner, 167 F.3d 1323 (10th Cir. 1999), treating a purchaser of a ranch in foreclosure, to be developed as a sportsman's resort, even though "assisted by the original lender," had DOI income when he settled the loan for less than the amount borrowed, is not inconsistent because the purchase was from the owner in default, which used the proceeds to pay the lending bank, which used them to clear prior liens. The original lender that had informally agreed to accept installment contracts of purchasers of lots in the resort as payment, but the FSLIC, which had taken over the original lender that had gone bankrupt, refused to honor informal agreement. The claim that the dispute as to method of payment converted the fixed amount of borrowing into a disputed claim was rejected by the court, which refused to follow *Zarin*. In *2925 Briarpark, Ltd. v. Commissioner*, 163 F.3d 313 (5th Cir. 1999), *aff'g* 73 T.C.M. (CCH) 3218 (1997) the amount realized on sale to a third party of property subject to a nonrecourse mortgage in excess of the value of the property was held to include, as part of the amount realized, an amount of the mortgage released by the bank as part of deal. In effect, the transaction was treated as surrender to the bank rather than sale to third party. An earlier conversion of the undersecured loan from recourse to nonrecourse did not result in discharge of indebtedness because the lender made a simultaneous build-out loan indicating expectation of increase in value from improvements. In a broad sense, *2925 Briarpark* is *Pleasant Summit/Prussin* with a markdown by the lender as part of the purchase.

In short, although a significant argument can be made that § 108(e)(5) is the exclusive means of obtaining a purchase price adjustment for a reduction in a liability owed to one not the seller of the property, in the author's opinion, Rev. Rul. 91-31 does not do so satisfactorily. In any event, the holding of Rev. Rul. 91-31 has been significantly modified by the enactment of § 108(a)(1)(D) and (c), which provide for an exclusion from DOI and a basis adjustment when qualified real property business indebtedness is cancelled or reduced. These provisions are discussed in § 5 *DOI Income and § 108*.

PROBLEMS FOR DISCUSSION

Problem 3-22. During a period of high interest rates, Own accepted the "generous" offer of Countribanc to pay 80 percent the remaining principal balance of the Countribanc loan he had used to purchase his residence, which was approximately equal to the discounted value of the remaining payments at then-current interest rates on home mortgage loans. Although the loan was recourse, under state law, Own would not have been liable for a deficiency on foreclosure of the mortgage on his residence that secured the loan. Own was happy to do so because the loan had reached the stage when most of the payments were nondeductible principal payments. Countribanc wanted the funds so that it could invest them at then current high rates, since its borrowing costs were at a rate higher than the interest rate on Own's loan. Indeed, Countribanc loaned Own part of the amount needed to pay off the old loan under a home equity loan, at the higher rates, the payments of which will provide him with large interest deductions. What are the tax consequences to Own and Countribanc of the payment under *Kirby Lumber*, § 108, or otherwise? *See* § 108(e)(5) and (h); *Hirsch* (purchase price adjustment); *Allen* (same); *Fulton Gold* (reduction in nonrecourse obligation on property at time of purchase was reduction in purchase price); Rev. Rul. 91-31 (reduction in nonrecourse purchase obligation is DOI income); *Sutphin* (discounted payment of mortgage to purchase residence); Rev. Rul. 82-202 (same); Rev. Rul. 92-99 (write-down of nonrecourse mortgage to value of encumbered property); Tech. Adv. Mem. 85-47-001 (lender deduction).

Problem 3-23. Invest, an individual, purchased Blackacre in 20X1 for $1,000,000 from Sail, for $100,000 in cash and a $900,000 nonrecourse balloon loan from Countribanc. In 20X3, when Blackacre's value had declined to $800,000 and the balloon loan came due, she surrendered Blackacre to Countribanc in lieu of foreclosure. (i) What are the tax consequences to Invest? (ii) If Invest purchased Blackacre from Countribanc for $800,000, financed by a new $800,000 nonrecourse balloon loan from Countribanc the day after she surrendered Blackacre to Countribanc, what are the tax consequences to Invest? (iii) How is the result different if, instead, the existing balloon mortgage is reduced to $800,000 and extended? *See* § 108(a)(1)(D) and (c); *Crane* (nonrecourse liability included in basis and amount realized); *Mayerson* (nonrecourse liability for 100% of purchase price recognized); *Tufts* (nonrecourse liability in excess of value is amount realized); *Fulton Gold* (modification of liability encumbering property at acquisition is purchase price adjustment); Rev. Rul. 91-31 (modification of nonrecourse liability is DOI); *Gershkowitz* (same); *Preslar.* (same for foreclosure); 2925 *Briarpark* (liability reduction on sale of property is amount realized, not DOI).

§ 4. LIABILITY TRANSFER

I.R.C. §§ 357(a)(1), 357(c), and 358(d) and 752(c); Treas. Reg. §§ 1.752-1(d) and (e) and 1.1031-1(d); Treas. Reg. § 1.1001-2 (a)(1) and (2).

Although much of the preceding material has involved transfer of liabilities, those materials have not involved any controversy as to whether and when a liability is transferred. This section fills that gap. As with the term "liability," discussed in § 1 *What is a Liability?* there is no definition, or consistent terminology, in the Code or Regulations for when a liability is transferred. A number of Code and regulation provisions refer, usually in connection with the transfer of property, to "liabilities assumed" or "liabilities to which the property is subject," *See e.g.*, §§ 357(a)(1) ("assumes"), 357(c), ("assume") and 358(d) ("assume" or "assumed"); Treas. Reg. § 1.752-1(d) ("assumption"); 1.752-1(e) (transfer of property subject to a liability as "assumption"); and 1.1031(d)-2 ("assumption" or "subject to"). A 1999 amendment deleted references in §§ 357 and 358 to taking property "subject to" a liability. Other statutory and regulatory provisions refer to the "discharge" of a liability or of indebtedness. *See* Treas. Reg. § 1.1001-2 ("discharge of liabilities"); *cf.*, § 108 ("discharge of indebtedness").

The most general regulation provision dealing with liability transfer is Treas. Reg. § 1.1001-2, somewhat misleadingly titled "Discharge of liabilities." The basic focus of Treas. Reg. § 1.1001-2 is the transfer of a liability as part of the consideration for the transfer of property. Treas. Reg. § 1.1001-2(a)(1) states the unsurprising general principle that the transfer of a liability is part of the amount realized, while Treas. Reg. § 1.1001-2(a)(2) treats as income from discharge of indebtedness any excess of the amount of a *recourse* liability over the fair market value of the property used to satisfy it. Because a transferor generally remains at least secondarily liable for a recourse mortgage encumbering transferred property, § 4.01 *Primary and Secondary Liability*, explores when the liability should be considered transferred. Similarly, § 4.02 *Deficiency* discusses the effect of a deficiency judgment in a foreclosure proceeding. Finally, § 4.03 *Deductible Items* discusses the consequences of transfer of property encumbered by obligations that are not liabilities.

§ 4.01. Primary and Secondary Liability

Treas. Reg. § 1.1001-2; Treas. Reg. § 1.752-1(d) and (e); I.R.C. § 357(d).

As indicated in *Commissioner v. Tufts*, discussed in § 3.01(b)(2) *Liability in Excess of Value (Overmortgaged Property)*, a nonrecourse liability is automatically transferred with the encumbered property, because the property is the only thing the lender can look to for payment. Treas. Reg. § 1.1001-2(a)(4)(i) expresses this result. Thus, the full amount of any nonrecourse liability is included in the transferor's amount realized, regardless of the value of the encumbered property. The transfer of a recourse liability is more complex, because the original obligor remains liable under state law to the creditor, even when a transferee or another third party expressly assumes the liability unless the creditor expressly agrees to release the original obligor. Except in the rare case of a release of the seller by the creditor, the assuming party becomes primarily liable, while the original obligor is secondarily liable, and, if required to pay the creditor, will have a right to try to collect from the assuming party. Accordingly, despite the transferor's continuing liability under state law, Treas. Reg. § 1.1001-2(a)(4)(ii) provides that a recourse liability is transferred in full when the transferee assumes it. Thus, if Sail transfers Blackacre to Perch when it is subject to a $1,000,000 liability secured by a mortgage on Blackacre that Perch expressly assumes, the entire $1,000,000 liability is included in Sail's amount realized from the transfer of Blackacre and in Perch's basis in Blackacre.

When property is transferred subject to a recourse liability that the transferee does not assume, although the transferee has an incentive to pay the liability in order to keep the property, the transferor remains personally liable to the creditor and, if required to pay, will have the right to foreclose on the property. Thus, the full amount of any recourse liability is included in the transferor's amount realized. In the preceding example, if Perch did not assume the liability and mortgage, Perch's strong incentive to make the required payments on the property are generally sufficient to reach the same result. If, however, the value of transferred property is less than the amount of any indebtedness, the treatment of recourse and nonrecourse liabilities diverge. Although as held by the Court in *Tufts*, the full amount of any nonrecourse liability is included in the transferor's amount realized, when property encumbered by a recourse liability is transferred, Treas. Reg. § 1.1001-2(a)(2) treats the transferor's amount realized as limited to the value of the property, with any excess of the liability discharged over the value of the property transferred treated as DOI income. Although Treas. Reg. § 1.1001-2(b) provides that the fair market value of any property that secures a liability is not to be considered in determining the extent to which the transferor is treated as discharged of those liabilities, it makes a specific exception in Treas. Reg. § 1.1001-2(a)(2), and provides that DOI income is realized to the extent that a recourse liability in excess of the fair market value of the encumbered property is discharged.

Literally, Treas. Reg. § 1.1001-2(b) could also be read to require that the transferor's amount realized be limited to the fair market value of the property securing the recourse liability with any excess liability treated as DOI income when property is transferred subject to a recourse liability in excess of its value that the transferee does not assume, so that the transferor remains subject to a secondary liability that is far from theoretical. When the creditor retains the right to collect the excess, because Treas. Reg. § 1.1001-2(a)(4)(ii) only treats the transferor as discharged when another person assumes the liability, there should be no DOI income. Unless the transfer is ignored under a principle like *Franklin*, treating the entire $1,000,000 liability as transferred under Treas. Reg. § 1.1001-2(b) when Blackacre is only worth $750,000, so that Sail's amount realized and Perch's basis are both $1,000,000 seems improper. The appropriate result appears to be that expressed in § 752(c) and Treas. Reg. § 1.752-1(e), relating to partnerships, limiting the transfer of the liability to the $750,000 value of Blackacre, which implicitly leaves Perch with the liability to the extent of the $250,000 excess of value. Under this approach, Sail's amount realized and Perch's basis are both $750,000, leaving the accounting for the remaining $250,000 until it is paid, with additional amount realized for Sail and additional basis for Perch if she pays, but no further tax consequence if Sail pays. If neither pays and the creditor, in effect, discharges the balance, Sail should have DOI income at that time.

Finally, Treas. Reg. § 1.1001-2(a)(3), in effect, spells out the consequences of *Est. of Franklin* discussed in § 3.02 *Contingencies*, by providing that an acquisition liability that was not included in determining basis is not included in amount realized. This is, of course, also consistent with the partnership regulations' definition of liability, because the obligation is not a liability under that definition.

To add to the confusion, it is possible for a transferor of property subject to a recourse mortgage to expressly agree to continue make the payments on the recourse mortgage as they come due, usually in the form of a "wrap-around" mortgage. In a wraparound mortgage the transferor sells the property for a price, usually involving deferred payments, in an amount equal to the gross value of the property, without reducing the price for the amount of the liability encumbering the property, and agrees with the transferee to continue servicing the underlying mortgage. Such arrangements can serve various business purposes, including preserving for the transferor the benefit of an old loan that has an interest rate well below current rates, or giving the purchaser the advantage of higher interest deductions, or avoiding high, possibly usurious interest rates on the second mortgage that would apply to the excess of the deferred payments over the amount of the underlying mortgage. Such arrangements were expressly sanctioned in *Professional Equities v. Commissioner*, 89 T.C. 165 (1987), *acq.* Although not a wrap-around mortgage, in the following controversial case involving a nonrecognition transfer to a controlled corporation under § 351, when the liabilities transferred exceeded the basis of the assets transferred, the contributing shareholder issued his own, not in the amount of the excess, to avoid recognizing gain on the excess.

LESSINGER v. COMMISSIONER

United States Court of Appeals, Second Circuit
872 F.2d 519 (2d Cir. 1989)

* * *

Sol Lessinger operated a proprietorship under the name "Universal Screw and Bolt Co." . . . [H]e was also the sole shareholder and chief executive officer of Universal Screw & Bolt Co., Inc. Both businesses were engaged in the wholesale distribution of metal fasteners . . . .

In 1976, the factor that had provided working capital to the proprietorship refused to continue lending funds to it as a noncorporate entity because under New York law one can charge higher interest rates of a corporation. . . . The Universal proprietorship was then consolidated into the Universal corporation in 1977. The Tax Court found that the taxpayer was not informed of the details of the transaction.

The proprietorship's unaudited balance sheet dated December 31, 1976, shows that the business had a negative net worth.

A summary of the balance sheet, with amounts rounded to thousands, reads as follows:

Assets		
Cash, accounts receivable, and inventory		1,314
Marketable securities and mutual funds		267
Fixed assets (net of depreciation)		106
Other (good will, prepaid expenses, etc.)		46
Total assets		approx. 1,733
Liabilities and Capital		
Trade accounts payable		416
Notes payable due within one year		991
(Breakdown: Chemical Bank	203	
Trade	464	
Auto loan & ins.	9	
Trefoil (factor)	315)	
Misc. (due to broker, taxes, loans, and exchanges)		12
Accrued expenses		162
Notes payable due after one year		342
(Breakdown: Chemical Bank	338	
Trade	4)	
Sol Lessinger — capital		(190.)
Total liabilities and capital		approx. 1,733

The consolidation of the proprietorship into the corporation was conducted in a most casual manner, the transfer transaction being naked in its simplicity. The taxpayer already owned all of the corporation's stock, and no new stock was issued. There were no written agreements documenting the transfer. On January 1, 1977, the proprietorship's bank account was closed, and the corporation took over the proprietorship's operating assets. Only two items of any significance were not transferred: The taxpayer had borrowed funds from Chemical Bank to purchase mutual fund shares, and the shares secured the loan. These items appear on the balance sheet above as the mutual fund shares and the Chemical Bank loan. The taxpayer retained the shares and sold them to pay the loan himself later in January 1977.

The corporation expressly assumed the other proprietorship liabilities except accounts payable. All notes payable were changed to show that the corporation was the maker of the notes, and the debt to the factor was expressly assumed. While the corporation did not expressly assume liability for the proprietorship's accounts payable, it did pay those accounts during the first six months of 1977.

On June 1, 1977, journal entries were made to the corporation's books to reflect the consolidation. Various corporate asset accounts were debited (*i.e.*, increased) to show the addition of the proprietorship's assets, and corporate liability accounts were credited (*i.e.*, increased) by the amount of the proprietorship's liabilities. Total proprietorship liabilities exceeded total proprietorship assets by $255,499.37, and that amount was debited to a corporate asset account in an entry entitled "Loan Receivable — SL." A ledger sheet entitled "Sol Lessinger" showed the debit with the description "[m]erger of company" as well as a $3,500 debit for a personal debt the corporation paid for Sol.

* * *

The taxpayer's personal wealth, however, was not limited to that of the corporation (or the mutual fund shares which he sold in 1977). He also owned a realty corporation called "87-89 Chambers Street Corporation" ("Chambers") that, at the time of the consolidation, held about $41,000 in cash equivalents and a long-term leasehold of the premises the corporation occupied. The taxpayer introduced into evidence an appraisal of the property which was conducted in 1980 and which valued the leasehold at $230,000 as of January 1, 1977. . . .

* * *

The taxpayer's principal argument, broadly stated, is that section 357 is inapplicable to him because in neither an accounting nor an economic sense did he realize a gain. He "merely exchanged creditors" from trade creditors to Universal, and his gain, therefore, was a "phantom" which Congress did not intend to tax.

* * *

Having determined that the proprietorship's accounts payable should be included in the category of liabilities assumed, we must determine whether the taxpayer's purported debt to his corporation would offset those liabilities and prevent a net excess of liabilities over assets.

A journal entry of the corporation showed $255,499.37 as a loan receivable from the taxpayer, which in turn was posted on a general ledger sheet as a debit to the taxpayer's account. That account was credited with a $62,209.35 adjustment resulting from the sale of the taxpayer's mutual funds and the paydown of the Chemical Bank loan. . . . [T]he debit balance of $196,790 in the taxpayer's account after the adjustment was never paid down; instead it increased to the sum of $237,044 in 1982. Marine Midland Bank required the open account to be formalized in 1981 in a note which collateralized the bank's loan to the corporation.

The Tax Court refused to count the debt as "property" transferred in the transaction, although its reasoning is not explicit. First, the opinion says that the corporate accounting entry entitled "Loan receivable — [Sol Lessinger]" "merely represents the excess of the liabilities over the adjusted basis," noting that the debt was not at first represented by a promissory note and that Lessinger paid no interest on it. . . . The Tax Court opinion concludes that "[e]ven if [Lessinger] had executed a note, it would have a zero basis in the hands of the corporation." . . . The Tax Court thus apparently believed there were two independently sufficient reasons to ignore the debt: first, that it was artificial, and, second, that it would have had a zero basis.

We are unpersuaded by the argument that the obligation was artificial. The Commissioner argues:

> This open account was not so much a debt as it was an accommodation by the corporation to its president and sole shareholder, who was having liquidity problems. In effect, he caused the corporation to apply its assets

> to satisfy his personal obligations, including those owed to trade creditors which were shortly to fall due, intending to pay the money back only as and when he found it convenient to do so.

. . . The Commissioner points out that the receivable lacked a due date, interest, security, or "other accepted features of true debt," but this analysis begs the question we have before us. . . . We believe that the receivable was an enforceable demand obligation. The decisions that the Commissioner cites for the definition of "true debt" concern the advance of funds to a close corporation by its shareholders. . . . A taxpayer in that setting may seek to mischaracterize a capital contribution as debt in order for the corporation to be able to treat the obligation in a way that would disguise nondeductible dividends as deductible interest payments. In that context, the courts have defined "classic debt" narrowly as "an unqualified obligation to pay a sum certain at a reasonably close fixed maturity date along with a fixed percentage in interest," although the essential factor is a "binding obligation." . . .

We believe, however, that a due date, interest, and security are not necessary to characterize Lessinger's obligation to his corporation as debt, and that his obligation was binding. The promissory note he signed in 1981, which the corporation endorsed to Marine Midland as collateral for a loan, is significant because it shows that Marine Midland depended on his personal responsibility. . . . Lessinger received consideration when he gave his promise to the corporation, and we have no doubt that any court would enforce that promise to protect the corporate creditors if the corporation failed . . . .

We now turn to the Tax Court's second reason for ignoring the debt. The Tax Court quoted *Alderman*, . . . which, like our case, involved the incorporation of an accrual basis proprietorship with a negative net worth. In *Alderman*, the Tax Court disregarded the taxpayers' personal promissory note to their corporation because

> [t]he Aldermans incurred no cost in making the note, so its basis to them was zero. The basis to the corporation was the same as in the hands of the transferor, *i.e.*, zero. Consequently, the application of section 357(c) is undisturbed by the creation and transfer of the personal note to the corporation.

. . . Section 357(c) does support the *Alderman* court's reliance on the concept of basis, but the statutory language is not addressed to a transaction such as Lessinger's, where the transferor's obligation has a value to the transferee corporation. The *Alderman* court did not consider the value of the obligation to the transferee.

* * *

"Basis," as used in tax law, refers to assets, not liabilities. . . . Liabilities by definition have no "basis" in tax law generally or in section 1012 terms specifically. The concept of "basis" prevents double taxation of income by identifying amounts that have already been taxed or are exempt from tax. . . . The taxpayer could, of course, have no "basis" in his own promise to pay the corporation $255,000, because that item is a liability for him. We would add parenthetically that to this extent *Alderman* was correct in describing the taxpayers' note there. But the corporation should have a basis in its obligation from Lessinger, because it incurred a cost in the transaction involving the transfer of the obligation by taking on the liabilities of the proprietorship that exceeded its assets, and because it would have to recognize income upon Lessinger's payment of the debt if it had no basis in the obligation.[4] Assets transferred under section 351 are taken by the corporation at the transferor's basis, to which is added any gain recognized in the transfer. . . . Consideration of "adjusted basis" in section 357(c) therefore normally does not require determining whether the section refers to the "adjusted basis" in the hands of the transferor-shareholder or the transferee-corporation, because the basis does not change. But here, the "basis" in the hands of the corporation should be the face amount of the taxpayer's obligation.[5] We now hold that in the situation presented here, where the transferor undertakes genuine personal liability to the transferee, "adjusted basis" in section 357(c) refers to the transferee's basis in the obligation, which is its face amount.[6]

Yet the Commissioner says that to reverse the Tax Court would . . . "effectively eliminate section 357(c) from the Internal Revenue Code." Would it? The question of substance is whether the taxpayer in fact realized a gain from the transaction. He certainly did not do so by a cancellation of his indebtedness. If there was any cancellation, it was illusory: While his trade creditors at the time of the incorporation may have been paid off (or their accounts rolled over as a result of sales and payments by the corporation and further advances of credit by the trade creditors), the taxpayer's indebtedness to the corporation itself continued (except to the extent he paid it off). If Lessinger had a "gain" from the incorporation, it did not show up in his personal balance sheet, let alone by way of economic benefit in his pocket.

The purpose of section 357(c) is to provide a limited exception to section 351's nonrecognition treatment that operates, as the Commissioner reminds us here, "where the transferor realized economic benefit which, if not recognized, would otherwise go untaxed." . . . Section 351 was intended to allow changes in business form without requiring the recognition of income. . . . The transferor-shareholder recognizes income only to the extent that he receives boot in the form of money or other property. . . . In 1938, the Supreme Court held that under the predecessor of section 351, . . . any assumption of liability by the transferee would be

[4] Our approach requires acceptance of the fact that section 362(a), which requires a carryover basis for "property" transferred in nonrecognition transactions under section 351, cannot be applied to the corporation's valuation of its receivable from the taxpayer. The purpose of the predecessor to section 362 was to avoid allowing the corporation a new, stepped-up basis from which to deduct depreciation expenses. . . . Another purpose of transferred bases generally is to defer recognition of gain or loss. . . . In Lessinger's transaction, there simply were no gains or losses to be deferred. The excess of liabilities over assets (which Lessinger's promise to the corporation remedied) was caused by the proprietorship's insolvency — the excess of current payables over current receivables — rather than by unrecognized gain in any asset's basis.

[5] The Commissioner does not suggest that the obligation was so worthless as to warrant reduction of its face amount. We note as well that we do not here address the problem of an obligation whose present value is significantly lower than its face amount.

[6] Curiously, the Commissioner does not actually make *Alderman*'s zero-basis argument. The taxpayer, on the other hand, attempts to convince us that, as an accrual basis taxpayer, he had a "basis" in his personal obligations to the corporation. We note, however, that the fact that he would have had a liability on his books does not require the conclusion that he had a "basis" in it for tax purposes.

considered a payment of money or property to the transferor, causing the transferor to recognize income. . . . Congress reacted immediately by enacting . . . the predecessor of section 357(a), which provided that the assumption of a liability should not be considered the payment of property or money and should not provoke the recognition of gain. . . .

Congress did not add section 357(c), which requires the recognition of gain when liabilities exceed assets, until 1954, when a House committee referred to the section as an "additional safeguard[] against tax avoidance not found in existing law." . . . Some provision was necessary to ensure that manipulations of credit and depreciation were not used to realize tax-free gains. . . . The House and Senate committees that approved section 357(c) both cited a single example of a transaction that the section was intended to govern: If a taxpayer transfers property with an adjusted basis of $20,000 subject to a $50,000 mortgage, he should recognize $30,000 gain. . . . While some have argued that section 357(c) was designed to avoid a negative basis, its application in the Congress's example is also quite reasonable. The transferor, who has already benefited by depreciating the property or holding it while its value appreciates, has income because he will never have to pay the mortgage. Forcing the taxpayer in our case to recognize a gain, however, would be contrary to Congress's intent because it would tax a truly phantom gain, because his liability to the corporation, as we have said, was real, continuing, and indirectly, at least, enforceable by the corporation's creditors.

* * *

Section 357(c) was amended in 1978 to solve a problem that had forced the courts to fashion delicate constructions of the section's language in order to conform with legislative intent. A cash basis transferor has no basis in accounts receivable. The Tax Court originally held that such a transferor would have to recognize gain if, after counting her accounts payable as transferred liabilities, liabilities exceeded assets. . . . This analysis meant that the owner of almost any ongoing business transferred liabilities exceeding assets when incorporating. The Tax Court later developed an approach that excluded accounts payable from liabilities . . . Congress added section 357(c)(3) in 1978, and it now excludes from subsection (c)(1) "a liability the payment of which . . . would give rise to a deduction." This history, while not directly relevant to Lessinger,[8] is instructive. In *Bongiovanni*, "a too literal reading of the words of the statute [would have] produce[d] an inequitable result which cannot be allowed to stand," . . . and "Congress certainly could not have intended such an inequitable result especially in light of its expressed purposes in enacting Sections 351 and 357(c)," . . . We find those words equally applicable here.

We conclude that our holding will not "effectively eliminate section 357(c)." Lessinger experienced no enrichment and had no unrecognized gains whose recognition was appropriate at the time of the consolidation. Any logic that would tax him would certainly represent a "trap for the unwary." . . . Lessinger could

---

[8] Section 357(c)(3) is inapplicable because Lessinger's proprietorship was on the accrual basis. None of the liabilities would have produced deductions if paid by the transferor because those expenses had been previously deducted when they were entered in the proprietorship's records. . . .

have achieved incorporation without taxation under the Commissioner's theory by borrowing $260,000 cash, transferring the cash to the corporation (or paying some of the trade accounts payable personally), and later causing the corporation to buy his promissory note from the lender (or pay it off in consideration of his new promise to pay the corporation). If taxpayers who transfer liabilities exceeding assets to controlled corporations are willing to undertake genuine personal liability for the excess, we see no reason to require recognition of a gain, and we do not believe that Congress intended for any gain to be recognized.

* * *

NOTES AND COMMENTS

The practical effect of this decision is the same as if Lessinger had expressly retained responsibility for the accounts payable and other liabilities. Of course, by following the course he did, he avoided having to expend the cash when the liabilities came due; at the cost, however, of having to account for his obligation to the corporation someday. On a technical level, because Lessinger issued his note in the offsetting amount, a major argument made by the Service was that the note had a zero basis, which amounts, in substance, to an argument that the note should be treated as a promise to pay that has no current tax effect. *See* Rev. Rul. 74-503, 1974-2 C.B. 117, which similarly found that a subsidiary had zero basis in parent stock received under § 351, so that it recognized gain on disposition of the stock). Rev. Rul. 74-503 was ambiguously revoked by Rev. Rul. 2006-2, 2006-1 C.B. 261, which states that the remaining conclusions of the ruling were under study. The results of any such study have not been published.

The zero basis argument, if carried to its logical conclusion, means that when the note is paid, the corporation has gain on collection and, if the corporation is an S corporation, would mean that Lessinger would have gain from paying his own note. Underlying this position, presumably, is a concern, in a related party situation, as to whether Lessinger will ever be called upon by the corporation he controls to pay. Under this approach, the note is not considered a current transfer of property, but a promise to make a future contribution to the corporation. This deferral approach, at least, avoids the silliness of taxing the payment. On the other hand, the fact that the note, when formally issued later, was pledged to Marine-Midland Bank gives the obligation additional reality. The risk of bankruptcy or other financial distress of the corporation, as making the note a real economic investment, was the equivalent of borrowing from a third party, and was not a sham. This argument was the basis of a similar result in *Peracchi v. Commissioner*, 143 F.3d 487 (9th Cir. 1998). If the note is not recognized as valid under the principle of *Franklin*, so that the obligation is treated as a promise of future contribution, there is no tax effect when it is transferred or discharged. *See* Treas. Reg. § 1.1001-2(a)(3); *Hudson v. Commissioner*, 103 T.C. 90 (1994) (no discharge of indebtedness income on termination of liability under a tax-shelter note not recognized as valid). Although Treas. Reg. § 1.1001-2(a)(4)(ii) includes a recourse liability assumed by the transferee as part of the amount realized, some courts delay the gain until the liability is paid. In *Estate of Weeden v. Commissioner*, 685 F.2d 1160 (9th Cir. 1982), the court determined that the donor did not recognize gain on a net gift of property, subject to the obligation of the donees to pay the gift tax, until they paid it in the next year, because the donor remained statutorily liable until then); *Maher v. Commissioner*, 469 F.2d 225 (8th Cir. 1972), a shareholder who transferred property subject to a liability that the corporation assumed, was held to realize dividend income when the corporation paid liability, not when the liability was assumed, because the transferor shareholder remained secondarily liable until the corporation paid. On the other hand, when the transferor expressly retains primary liability as in *Professional Equities* discussed above, the transfer of encumbered property subject to the liability does not cause the liability to be included in amount realized. In *Zappo v. Commissioner*, 81 T.C. 77 (1983) a contingent obligation under a guarantee that the purchaser of property would realize specified profits did not offset the liabilities transferred with the property in determining the gain on the transaction, because a guaranty is an inchoate obligation at the time of its making, so that there is no real continuation of indebtedness when a highly contingent obligation is substituted for a true debt.

In *Jackson v. Commissioner*, 708 F.2d 1402 (9th Cir. 1983), the court found that a liability was not transferred when the taxpayer transferred a partnership interest, subject to a partnership recourse liability in excess of the basis of the partnership interest on which the corporate transferee did not assume primary liability, so that transferor remained personally, although apparently only secondarily, liable for the partnership liability, which originally had been incurred by the transferor individually. The court noted that the reduction in the shareholder's basis in his stock in corporate stock for partnership losses would increase the taxable gain or reduce the loss realized when the stock was sold. In a later decision in the same circuit, *Owen v. Commissioner*, 881 F.2d 832 (9th Cir. 1989), the court found that a partnership recognized gain under section 357(c) on a § 351 transfer to a wholly-owned corporation of property subject to liabilities in excess of basis, and that the liability transferred was not reduced for transferor guarantees and a liability retention agreement that was not executed until six months after the transfer. The language of the opinion apparently limits or overrules *Jackson* as: (i) having been decided without the benefit of the *Tufts* case and (ii) having involved transfer of partnership interest not directly encumbered by partnership's liabilities, but the opinion ignores the crucial fact of the delayed date of the retention agreement. In Tech. Adv. Mem. 96-40-001, the Service ruled that when a shareholder who had taken out several loans cross-collateralized by all of the taxpayer's real property transferred one of the properties to an S corporation in a § 351 transaction, the basis of the shares of the S corporation is zero because the entire amount of the liabilities is deemed transferred and that amount exceeds the basis of the property transferred; it is irrelevant that the taxpayer remained fully liable for the note; but the memo does not state the relation between the total amount of the liabilities and the fair market value of the property transferred, not how much gain the taxpayer presumably recognized on the transfer; it relies on *Owen*).

These authorities, particularly Tech. Adv. Mem. 96-40-001, created opportunities for abuse by enhancing the basis of property transferred subject to liabilities that were not expected to be paid by the transferee. As a result, Congress eliminated "acquires property subject to" from § 357(a), so that only a liability "assumed" is considered transferred, and to the adoption of § 357(d), which defines assumption of a liability for purposes of nonrecognition corporate transfers, with authority for regulations to extend the definition to other parts of the Code. Assumption of recourse liabilities requires that the transferee agree to, and be expected to, satisfy the liability. Nonrecourse liabilities are considered transferred with the encumbered property, except to the extent of the lesser of (i) the excess over any assets subject to the same nonrecourse liability that are retained by the transferor who has agreed to satisfy the nonrecourse liability or (ii) the fair market value of any retained assets determined without regard to § 7701(g), which creates a general principle that the value of property transferred subject to a nonrecourse liability is not less than the amount of the liability. This provision, particularly if extended by regulation, may significantly affect when a liability is transferred. Section 357(d), as amended in 1999, defines assumptions of nonrecourse liabilities specifically, and narrowly, as those that the transferee has agreed to, and is expected to satisfy. It also has a special rule for the transfer of a nonrecourse liability that is also secured by property retained by the transferor. The Service is considering such regulations. *See* REG 100818-01 *Advance Notice of Proposed Rulemaking, Liabilities Assumed in Certain Transactions*, 68 Fed. Reg. 23,931 (May 6, 2003), and Announcement 2003-37, 2003-1 C.B. 1025. Both focus on assumption of nonrecourse liabilities, with a major focus on giving effect of agreements and understandings as to the degree to which the transferor and transferee will satisfy the liability with a default rule of allocating in proportion to fair market value of the encumbered property in the absence of an agreement. They do not deal directly with recourse liabilities except to provide that a transferee's agreement to be personally liable for a recourse mortgage is enough to transfer it without any agreement with the lender, and say that there is no assumption without such an agreement. Nevertheless, a significant agreement can be made that in the absence of an agreement the encumbering liability is transferred to the extent, and only to the extent, of the fair market value of the underlying property, so that the excess should not be included in the amount realized or as DOI income. There has been no further action on the proposed regulations nearly ten years later, and such proposed regulations are not in the 2009-10 Priority Guidance Plan. *See* 2009 TNT 225-28.

PROBLEMS FOR DISCUSSION

Problem 3-24. What are the tax consequences to Lessinger and Universal Screw & Bolt Co., Inc., if Marine Midland demands payment from Lessinger on his note after a default by Universal and Lessinger pays? What if Lessinger also defaults? *See Kirby Lumber* (discharge of indebtedness income on retirement of liability). What would have been the tax consequence if the Service had won its case? *See* Treas. Reg. § 1.1001-2(a)(3); *Hudson* (tax-shelter note not valid).

Problem 3-25. Invest purchased Blackacre for $300,000, paying $100,000 in cash, with the balance by a recourse purchase money mortgage of $200,000. When the mortgage had been reduced to $150,000, she refinanced with a new $400,000 recourse note and mortgage from Countribanc, receiving the $250,000 in cash, which she used for purposes unrelated to Blackacre. In 20X1, she sold Blackacre to Perch, subject to the recourse mortgage, for deferred payments of $300,000 payable over 10 years with adequate stated interest, but Perch did not assume the mortgage. What is Invest's amount realized? *See* Treas. Reg. § 1.1001-2(a); *Levine* (gain recognized on gift subject to liability in excess of basis); *Weeden* (donees agree to pay gift tax); Rev. Rul. 81-163 (charitable contribution of encumbered property?

Problem 3-26. How, if at all, would the result in Problem 3-25 change if the mortgage on Blackacre was nonrecourse and the sale to Perch was under a wrap-around mortgage in which Perch agreed to pay $700,000 over 10 years and Invest agreed with Perch to make the debt service payments on the underlying nonrecourse mortgage, but expressly stated that the obligation was for the benefit of Perch only, and not for the benefit of Countribanc, and that Perch's sole recourse against Invest would be to offset any default against future payments due from Perch to Invest? The schedule of the payments on the deferred payment obligation was such that the unpaid amount would always be adequate to cover any such default. *See* Treas. Reg. § 1.1001-2(a)(4)(i); *Tufts* (transfer subject to nonrecourse liability in excess of basis and value); *Professional Equities* (transfer of encumbered property under wrap-around mortgage); *Lessinger* (transferor's note in § 351 transfer of property subject to liabilities in excess of basis of other property); *Peracchi* (same); *Zappo* (guaranty of profits does not offset liabilities transferred); *Jelle* (retain farm by paying value to terminate mortgage, but subject to recapture).

Problem 3-27. How, if at all, would the result in Problem 3-25 change if, in 20X1, Invest transferred Blackacre to Newco, a corporation in which she had the largest interest, but not a majority, in a nonrecognition transaction under § 351, subject to the recourse mortgage, for Newco shares worth $300,000. (i) What is Invest's amount realized? § 357(c)(1). (ii) How would the result differ if Newco did not assume the mortgage liability, although all parties expected Newco to pay it when it came due? *See* § 357(d); *Jackson* (recourse liability not transferred on § 351 contribution of partnership interest); *Owen* (recourse liability is automatically transferred even if not assumed); Tech. Adv. Mem. 96-40-001 (entire amount of cross-collateralized liability transferred with transfer of each encumbered property); *Professional Equities* (transfer of encumbered property under wrap-around mortgage); *Maher v. Commissioner*, 469 F.2d 225 (8th Cir. 1972); *Pleasant/Prussin* (fair market value basis for purchaser of property subject to nonrecourse liability in excess of value); REG 100818-01 *Advance Notice of Proposed Rulemaking, Liabilities Assumed in Certain Transactions*, 68 Fed. Reg. 23,931 (May 6, 2003), and Announcement 2003-37, 2003-1 C.B. 1025. (iii) If Ceeco assumed the mortgage, but Invest expressly guaranteed the assumption to Countribanc? *See Zappo* (guaranty of profits does not offset liabilities transferred); *Jelle* (retain farm by paying value to terminate mortgage, but subject to recapture).

Problem 3-28. Perch in Problem 3-25 used Blackacre for a real estate development that proved to be a disaster. In 20X3, Countribanc foreclosed, but was only able to realize $200,000 on the foreclosure sale and collected the then-deficiency of $100,000 from Invest, but she was, of course, unable to collect from Perch. What is the tax consequence to Invest of the default, foreclosure, and inability to collect from Perch? *See Jackson* (recourse liability not transferred on § 351 contribution of partnership interest); *Owen* (recourse liability is automatically transferred even if not assumed); § 357(d); *Maher* (transfer of stock to corporation that assumes liability and pays in a later year); *Weeden* (donees agree to pay gift tax).

§ 4.02. Deficiency

When the borrower defaults under a recourse mortgage and the lender forecloses, the property is sold, and, if the proceeds are not sufficient to discharge the amount owed to the lender, the borrower is subject to a judgment for the deficiency. Frequently, however, the borrower's ability to pay the deficiency is questionable. The following case deals with how the amount realized on a foreclosure is determined, treating the foreclosure price, not the full amount of the mortgage liability, as the amount realized, so that the taxpayer was allowed a deductible loss on the foreclosure.

AIZAWA v. COMMISSIONER

United States Tax Court

99 T.C. 197 (1992), *aff'd without pub. op.*, 29 F.3d 630 (9th Cir. 1994)

TANNENWALD, JUDGE.

* * *

Petitioners owned rental property which they purchased in 1981 for $120,000 plus $433 in closing costs. At the time of purchase, they gave the sellers a $90,000 recourse mortgage note with interest only payable at the rate of $750 monthly, and the entire principal due and payable in June 1985. They made their last payment of interest in February 1985. Petitioners did not make any payment on the principal when due.

In 1987, the sellers obtained a judgment of $133,506.91 against petitioners in a foreclosure action, consisting of $90,000.00 mortgage principal, $18,000.00 accrued and unpaid interest, $25,000.00 in attorney's fees and $500.00 in court costs. Also in 1987, the property was sold to the sellers at a foreclosure sale for $72,700.00 which was applied to petitioners' obligation under such judgment, leaving a deficiency judgment of $60,806.91.

There is no dispute between the parties that the foreclosure sale constituted a sale for tax purposes, . . . that petitioners suffered a loss thereon in 1987, and that petitioners' basis in the property at the time of the foreclosure sale was $100,091.38. Their dispute is with respect to the calculation of the "amount realized" on the foreclosure sale. . . .

Surprisingly, as far as we can determine, this is the first time a court has confronted this issue directly. Petitioners contend that the deficiency judgment should be deducted from the unpaid mortgage principal and that the difference of $29,193.09 ($90,000.00 minus $60,806.91) constitutes the amount realized on the foreclosure sale which, when deducted from their basis, produces a loss of $70,898.29 ($100,091.38 minus $29,193.09). Respondent counters that the $90,000.00 unpaid mortgage principal constitutes the amount realized on the foreclosure sale which, when deducted from petitioners' basis, produces a loss of $10,091.38 ($100,091.38 minus $90,000.00).[4]

Petitioners' position suffers from the infirmity that it calculates the amount realized by offsetting against only the unpaid principal balance of the mortgage the total amount of the deficiency judgment, which includes not only such unpaid balance but also the amounts representing accrued interest, attorney's fees, and court costs, amounts which petitioners, who are cash-basis taxpayers, have not yet paid. A proper calculation along the lines of petitioners' position, at the very least, would have added such latter amounts to the unpaid mortgage principal before making the indicated subtraction or alternatively omitted them from the calculation of the deficiency judgment. Such equalizing would produce the result that the "amount realized" under section 1001(a) would be an amount represented by the proceeds of the foreclosure sale, a result we reach but by a different path. . . .

Petitioners' reliance on *R. O'Dell & Sons* . . . is misplaced. That case involved the question whether the taxpayer's loss should be recognized in the year of discharge of the deficiency judgment or the year of the foreclosure sale. Because of the close proximity of the sale and the discharge, the Court resolved the question in favor of the latter point in time. . . .

Turning to respondent's position, we think it does not present an acceptable resolution of the issue before us. It requires petitioners to treat as money received an amount of their unpaid mortgage principal obligation from which they have not yet been discharged, leaving to the future the tax consequences of any subsequent payments or settlement of the deficiency judgment for less than the unpaid amount. *Cf. Arrowsmith* . . . . Such treatment presents an obvious complication in that, if petitioners are thereafter relieved, either in whole or in part, of their obligation for the unpaid mortgage principal subsumed in the deficiency judgment, the usual rules as to income from discharge of an indebtedness will be difficult to apply. Those rules rest on the premise that taxpayers should not be permitted to retain the economic benefit of money received (or alternatively the freeing of assets which would otherwise have to be used to repay the indebtedness) in respect of which they have not previously paid a tax, see . . . *Tufts* . . . . By hypothesis, this situation will not obtain because petitioners will have already in effect paid the tax on their obligation for the amount of the unpaid mortgage principal.

The key to the resolution of the issue before us lies in the recognition that, in this case, there is a clear separation between the foreclosure sale and the unpaid recourse liability for mortgage principal which survives as part of a deficiency judgment. In the decided cases, the courts concluded that such survival did not exist and that the discharge of the recourse liability was closely related to, and should be considered an integral part of, the foreclosure sale. . . .

Where, as in this case, such separateness exists, the significance of the amount of the proceeds of the foreclosure sale becomes apparent. It cannot be gainsaid that the property was sold for $72,700 (an amount which we have no reason to conclude did not represent the fair market value of the property) and that petitioners

[4] Respondent does not contend that the accrued and unpaid interest or attorney's fees or court costs of the foreclosure should be so included. *Cf. Allan* . . . .

received, by way of a reduction in the judgment of foreclosure, that amount and nothing more. That is the "amount realized" under section 1001(a) which is subtracted from petitioners' basis in order to determine the amount of their loss.

We are aware of the fact that this approach enables petitioners to increase their loss by $17,300 ($90,000 less $72,700) representing borrowed funds which they might not repay and on which they have not yet paid a tax. But this is nothing more than the logical consequence of *Crane* . . . , which has been treated as sanctioning the right of a cash-basis taxpayer to include the amount of an unpaid mortgage liability in his or her basis. . . . To the extent that this presents a problem, it involves only a question of timing since subsequent events will eliminate any benefit petitioners may have obtained. They will not be entitled to deduct, as additional losses, any future payment against such unpaid principal, since the amount of such payment has already in effect been deducted. Additionally, they will be required to account for any benefit which they may obtain by way of a subsequent discharge, in whole or in part, of the amount of their indebtedness represented by the borrowed funds that have not been repaid.

Nothing in . . . *Tufts* . . . requires the rejection of the proceeds of the foreclosure sale, which represent fair market value of the property, as the amount realized for the purpose of determining petitioners' loss. The language of the Supreme Court, which suggests that fair market value is irrelevant where that value is less than the amount of the unpaid mortgage principal . . . was directed to the situation where that mortgage obligation was discharged — a situation which does not obtain herein. . . .

* * *

In sum, we conclude that the $72,700.00 proceeds of the foreclosure sale constitute the "amount realized" under section 1001(a) and that consequently petitioners' loss was $27,391.38 (petitioners' basis of $100,091.38 less the foreclosure sale proceeds of $72,700.00).

* * *

NOTES AND COMMENTS

The *Aizawa case* is strange in that the Service position, in effect, treated the recourse liability as a nonrecourse liability, so that the entire amount was realized on the sale. This is, of course, inconsistent with Treas. Reg. § 1.1001-2(a)(2), which treats the excess of the liability over value as discharge of indebtedness income. Because that provision is not referred to in the opinion, apparently neither the Service nor Aizawa's lawyer referred to it, even though it had been adopted in 1980. Perhaps the Service was unwilling to allow a current loss with DOI income deferred until the default judgment is terminated. As a practical matter, this means that the DOI income does not arise until the lender sends a Form 1099-C Cancellation of debt statement to the debtor and the Service. Note that even though the deficiency judgment included accrued interest, attorney's fees, and court costs, the Service did not include these presumably deductible amounts in its determination of the amount realized. This is, of course, consistent with the partnership regulations' definition of "liability" as including only amounts that have resulted in a deduction. In *Johnson v. Commissioner*, T.C. Memo. 1999-162, the amount of unpaid deductible mortgage interest at the time of foreclosure was not included in the amount realized on foreclosure when the fair market value of property was less than the principal of the mortgage.

Because the amount of outstanding debt represents money already expended by the lender, a lender may bid any amount up to the amount of the loan without out-of-pocket cost. Thus, a lender's bid is not necessarily indicative of the value of the property. *See Frazier v. Commissioner*, 111 T.C. 243 (1998) (debtor's amount realized determined by the value of the property, not the higher amount of the lender's bid); Treas. Reg. § 1.1001-2(a)(1) and (c) Example 8.

PROBLEM FOR DISCUSSION

Problem 3-29. Invest, a cash-method taxpayer, purchased Blackacre in 20X1 for $300,000, with $60,000 in cash, and $240,000 borrowed from Countribanc, under a balloon, interest only, recourse note and mortgage. In 20X3, Invest defaulted on the mortgage, when there was $20,000 unpaid interest on the mortgage. Even though Countribanc expected to sell Blackacre for $200,000, it bid in at the foreclosure sale for the full $260,000 mortgage principal balance and unpaid interest, foregoing a doubtfully collectible deficiency judgment to delay showing a loss on the transaction. Countribanc sold Blackacre to Vulture in 20X1 for $190,000. (i) How would you advise Invest to report the foreclosure? (ii) What, if any risks, do you need to advise him about if he follows your advice? *See* § 108(e)(2); Treas. Reg. § 1.1001-2(a)(1) and (c) Example 8; *Frazier* (fair market value, not bid price, determines amount realized); *Johnson* (unpaid interest not included in amount realized).

§ 4.03. Deductible Items

Treas. Reg. § 1.461-4(d)(5) and (g)(1)(C); Treas. Reg. §§ 1.1001-1(g); 1.1012-1(g)

Liabilities transferred are included in the seller's amount realized under *Crane*, *Tufts*, Treas. Reg. § 1.1001-2(a)(a), and other authorities too numerous to mention, and are included in the purchaser's basis under *Crane*, *Mayerson*, and other authorities also too numerous to mention. But what about deductible items that are not liabilities, and that are excluded for DOI under § 108(e)(2)? The following case answers this question.

COMMERCIAL SECURITY BANK v. COMMISSIONER

United States Tax Court
77 T.C. 145 (1981)

* * *

TANNENWALD, CHIEF JUDGE.

* * *

Orem was a Utah corporation with its principal place of business in Orem, Utah. Orem filed its Federal income tax returns on a calendar year basis using the cash receipts and disbursements method of accounting. Orem's last taxable year ended on June 14, 1974, because it ceased to exist as of that date. See sections 443(a)(2) and 441(b)(3).

Orem's complete liquidation met the requirements of section 337(a). Within a 12-month period after adopting its plan of liquidation, Orem sold its assets to petitioner in consideration of the payment of $1,175,000 in cash and the assumption by petitioner of all of Orem's existing obligations and liabilities (including any Federal or state income taxes of Orem due by reason of the transaction). Petitioner determined the price it was willing to pay for Orem's assets on the basis of estimating all of Orem's items of income and expense as if Orem were on the accrual basis at the time of closing of the sale. Among the "accruable" items were [accrued interest receivable and accrued business liabilities]:

Orem's final tax return included the "accrued interest receivables" in income and deducted the "accrued business liabilities." Respondent accepted Orem's inclusion in income of the items of "accrued interest receivables" but disallowed the deduction of the "accrued business liabilities." Those liabilities appear to represent items of a character which would have been deductible by Orem when paid under sections 162 and 163, and respondent has not contended otherwise.

Petitioner's primary position accepts the inclusion of the "accrued interest receivables" in Orem's income but disputes the denial of the deduction of the "accrued business liabilities." It contends that its assumption of those liabilities should be treated as the receipt of an equivalent amount of cash to Orem and the payment of those liabilities by Orem, with the result that the deductions therefor were properly taken by Orem in its final return. Alternatively, petitioner argues that Orem was at least entitled to offset a portion of the liabilities representing accrued interest payable against the "accrued interest receivables." Respondent asserts (1) that, under all circumstances, the inclusion of "accrued interest receivables" in Orem's income was proper, (2) that, by claiming a deduction for the "accrued business liabilities," Orem changed its method of accounting without obtaining respondent's prior consent, see section 446(e), and (3) that Orem is under no circumstances entitled to deduct any of those liabilities, because it remained a cash basis taxpayer and did not pay them. For reasons which are hereinafter set forth, we agree with petitioner's primary position that the "accrued business liabilities" are deductible in full.

At the outset, we note that there can be no question but that the "accrued interest receivables" were properly includible in Orem's income for its last taxable year, and petitioner does not contend otherwise. . . . It is also beyond question (and petitioner does not argue otherwise) that the amount of the "accrued business liabilities" would, but for the impact of section 337, have been taken into account in computing Orem's gain or loss from the sale. . . . But it does not necessarily follow that those liabilities are deductible. That, as we see it, is a separate issue.

Orem seeks to deduct only those liabilities which had accrued on the date of sale. It is clear that had Orem simply sold all its assets and retained its liabilities, the deductions now being contested would have been deductible only as the liabilities were actually paid. . . . It is equally clear, however, that if Orem had retained those liabilities, the amount of cash it would have received would have been correspondingly increased. Indeed, this is the foundation of petitioner's argument that, by accepting less cash for its assets in exchange for the assumption of its liabilities, Orem effectively paid the accrued liabilities at the time of the sale. We agree.

We recognize that Orem itself did not actually satisfy the accrued liabilities by direct payment to, or unrestricted crediting of the accounts of, the ultimate obligees. . . . But in substance, by accepting less cash than it otherwise would have received, it made an actual payment to petitioner which was sufficient to justify the deductions. . . . We emphasize that we are not holding that Orem was making a constructive payment of the liabilities in question — an approach which sometimes presents considerable difficulty where a cash basis taxpayer is involved, particularly with respect to the relationship (or, more properly, the absence of a relationship) between constructive receipt and constructive payment. *Vander Poel, Francis & Co.* . . . Consequently, respondent's arguments based upon sections 1.446-1(c)(1)(i) and 1.461-1(a)(1), Income Tax Reg., limiting deductions to those "actually made" are beside the point.

Respondent's reliance on *Arcade Restaurant* . . . is misplaced. In that case, we held that the assumption of a corporation's liabilities by its shareholders as part of the corporation's complete liquidation was not a "payment" sufficient to support a deduction of those liabilities on the corporation's final income tax return. Aside from any question as to the "antiqueness" of the case, the fact is that there was no sale or other exchange of value; rather, the shareholders took whatever assets and liabilities the corporation had. In the instant case, however, the amount of cash which Orem received for its assets was diminished by the amount of its liabilities, and it is that diminution which permits a finding of actual payment distinguishing the instant case from *Arcade* . . .

Respondent argues that to allow Orem the deduction claimed herein will permit a situation akin to a double deduction, because the amount of the liabilities deemed paid by their assumption increases the basis of the assets acquired by petitioner, with a resulting potential tax benefit to petitioner upon the ultimate disposition of those assets, *i.e.*, decreased gain or loss.[8] There is no question but that an increase in basis occurs. *Crane* . . . Nevertheless, we think that respondent's argument misses the mark.

Because the purchase price which petitioner paid was equal to the value of Orem's assets less the value of its liabilities, allowing petitioner to increase its basis by the amount of the liabilities assumed simply brings its basis back to the full value of the assets, value paid in part to Orem and in part to the obligees of the accrued liabilities in dispute. . . . Petitioner's basis is precisely what it would have been had Orem retained its accounts payable and paid them itself, and in such case, the

---

[8] It is clear that petitioner may not deduct any of the accrued liabilities in the year of purchase or at any other time. . . .

deductions would clearly have materialized. . . . Thus, petitioner's basis in the purchased assets is perfectly consistent with allowing Orem the disputed deductions.[9]

Respondent contends that allowing Orem to deduct the accrued liabilities in this case will have the effect of permitting Orem to change its method of accounting without respondent's prior approval. Yet, as we have made clear above, that is not the case; by receiving less for its assets, Orem discharged its liabilities and can be considered as having effectively paid them. Moreover, by requiring Orem to include "accrued interest receivables" in income, respondent has in effect put Orem on an accrual basis as to those items, and we think his reliance on a highly technical reading of his regulations to say that similar treatment should not be accorded to the "accrued business liabilities" is questionable. This observation is, we think, particularly applicable in the instant situation, where the items in question are, as far as this record reveals, not only of a character otherwise qualifying for deduction under sections 162 and 163 . . . but also appear to have been intimately related to the items of "accrued interest receivables."

Respondent admits that his position in this respect produces a "harsh" result. We note that respondent himself, utilizing his authority under section 446, to require a taxpayer to change from a completed contract to a percentage of completion method of accounting, has avoided such a "harsh" result in the area of sales of assets in the course of liquidation by cash basis corporate taxpayers using the completed contract method of reporting income, by allocating not only the income earned from long-term contracts prior to the sale but also a proportionate part of the costs incurred. . . . And this Court has been sufficiently flexible to suggest that a cash basis taxpayer be allowed to deduct unpaid items related to income allocated to the taxpayer although not yet received by him. . . .

Decision will be entered under Rule 155.

NOTES AND COMMENTS

Thus, *Commercial Security* confirms the unremarkable principle that when assets are transferred subject to deductible items, the assets constitute payment of the deductible items, allowing a cash-method taxpayer to deduct them. Stated another way, the transfer converts obligations into liabilities. To the extent that the assets transferred produce capital or section 1231 gain, while the deduction is ordinary, this is advantageous to the taxpayer. Thus, the Service was not being generous in *Crane*, when, as indicated in footnote 6, it did not treat the accrued interest as part of the amount realized. Similarly, if his lawyers had been as alert as those in *Commercial Security*, which was involved a transaction only four years

---

[9] Had Orem retained its liabilities and then satisfied them itself, it is possible that some of the deductions would not have ripened until Orem's next taxable year (we are assuming that Orem would not have dissolved until after it had paid its debts) because only then would some of the accrued liabilities have become due. Thus, our holding allows some acceleration of deductions. However, because we are faced with liabilities which have already accrued (i.e., would already be deductible in full had Orem been on the accrual basis), the amount of the acceleration is minimal and no more than the usual by-product of accrual accounting. See section 1.446-1(c)(1)(ii), Income Tax Reg. Liabilities of a transferor which do not accrue until after the transfer are, of course, deductible by the transferee when paid or accrued. . . .

later, Levine should have been allowed the deductions referred to in footnote 13.

Because deductions can be deferred for reasons other than the cash-method, including §§ 83(f) and 404(a)(5) for deferred compensation, and § 461(h) for lack of economic performance, or because they are too contingent to be deducted by even accrual-method taxpayers under the "all events" test, the question is whether the *Commercial Security* principle extends to these obligations. Treas. Reg. § 1.461-4(d)(5) and (g)(1)(C) extend the principle to deductions deferred under the economic performance provisions, but only for obligations transferred as part of a transfer of a trade or business. When the purchaser pays the deferred compensation or similar obligation, so that the employee recognizes income immediately, the purchaser who pays does not get the deduction, because the payment is part of the purchase price. Thus, in Tech. Adv. Mem. 89-39-002, the seller of a business was entitled to deduct deferred compensation that had been earned but not deducted because it had not been paid, even though they would be paid by the purchaser. The ruling cites *Commercial Security*. A similar result was reached in Tech. Adv. Mem. 94-38-001, allowing the seller deductions for amounts paid by the purchaser to holders of the seller's outstanding incentive stock options, nonstatutory stock options, and stock appreciation rights that were paid by the purchaser.

Contingent liabilities should be considered deferred payments under the installment method when it applies, and otherwise may have to be included in amount realized under Treas. Reg. § 1.1001-1(g)(3). The corollary is that the obligation transferred is not deductible when paid by the purchaser, but is part of the purchaser's basis. Thus, in *Ill. Tool Works, Inc. v. Commissioner*, 117 T.C. 39 (2001), *aff'd*, 355 F.3d 997 (7th Cir. 2004), the purchaser was required to treat as purchase price the entire amount of a patent liability it assumed in acquiring a business, even though the judgment was many times the amount estimated at time of the acquisition. The *Illinois Tool* case is discussed in § 4.03 *Contingent Payments and Liabilities*, in Chapter 1 *Basis and Realization*. Similarly, in *David R. Webb Co. v. Commissioner*, 708 F.2d 1254 (7th Cir. 1983), discussed in *Illinois Tool Works*, deferred compensation obligations assumed as part of the acquisition of a business are part of the purchase price, capitalized when paid. The purchaser cannot include contingent obligations in basis until paid. Treas. Reg. § 1.1012-1(g)(1). Although not discussed in these cases, the seller should be entitled to the deduction for these items when the payments are included in the amount realized.

On the other hand, if the payment is considered to be made on account of a purchaser obligation, the payment is not part of the purchase price, but is deductible by the purchaser when made and, of course, not by the seller. Accordingly, in Tech. Adv. Mem. 97-21-002, severance payment obligations to employees of the acquired target resulting from a downsizing immediately after acquisition were treated as a deductible expense of the purchaser, not a liability of the old target because the severance payments did not become due until the downsizing even though the risk of downsizing existed at the time of the sale. Similarly, in Tech. Adv. Mem. 97-31-001, increased severance payment obligations negotiated as part of stock acquisition to provide protection to continuing employees was not required to be capitalized as purchase price, because, although negotiated at the time of the sale, they did not affect the price. The same principle was applied in Field Serv. Adv. 2000-48-006, which held that the deemed purchaser in a § 338(h)(10) transaction (a sale of stock treated as a sale of corporate assets) was not allowed to deduct corporate franchise tax and pre-closing interest for franchise taxes for periods prior to the sale that was being disputed at the time of the closing and that were paid directly by the seller under an indemnification agreement, but it was allowed to deduct post-closing interest also paid by the seller. The franchise tax and pre-closing interest were to be capitalized by the purchaser when they became fixed and the post-closing interest was deductible when fixed; but the seller's payments of all three items reduced basis when paid by the seller, which was later than when they were fixed, so that the basis increases for the tax and pre-closing interest were offset by the seller's payments, there was a time difference; post-closing interest provided a deduction offset by a basis reduction, with a timing difference as well.

Commercial Security does not, however, change the result of Rev. Rul. 80-198, 1980-2 C.B. 113; Rev. Rul. 80-199, 1980-2 C.B. 122; Rev. Rul. 88-77, 1988-2 C.B. 129; and Rev. Rul. 95-74, 1995-2 C.B. 36, excluding deductible items from the status of liabilities when transferred in nonrecognition transactions, and providing that the inherent deduction is allowed, when realized, by the transferee. In nonrecognition transactions with a transferred basis, the amount realized is irrelevant except to the extent of boot, including liabilities in excess of basis, and tax attributes related to assets and liabilities transferred are carried over to the transferee.

PROBLEM FOR DISCUSSION

Problem 3-30. Invest has owned and operated a commercial building for many years. In 20X1, in the course of a robbery on the premises, several people were severely injured and one person was killed. The person injured and the heirs of the person killed claimed that Invest was negligent in not providing adequate security. Although Invest believes she will ultimately prevail, and that in any event her exposure over and above insurance coverage (of $1,500,000) is not in excess of $500,000, she is tired of litigation. In 20X4, she sold the property to the Perch for $1,000,000, over the $3,000,000 recourse mortgage liability encumbering the building, on condition that Perch assume the recourse mortgage liability and full responsibility for further conduct of the litigation (to the extent not handled by the insurance company), as well as for any ultimate damages in excess of the insurance. The property is clearly worth $1,500,000 over the mortgage, but no more than $2,000,000 over the mortgage. (i) What are Invest's amount realized, and any deduction, and Perch's basis immediately after the sale? *See* Treas. Reg. §§ 1.1001-1(g) and 1.1012-1(g); *David R. Webb Co.* (deferred compensation obligation capitalized by purchaser); (ii) What is the result for Invest and Perch of a settlement or final judgment of $250,000 above the insurance? *See* Tech. Adv. Mem. 89-39-002 (earned but unpaid compensation paid by purchaser and assumed deferred compensation); Tech. Adv. Mem. 94-38-001 (amounts paid by purchaser for incentive stock options, nonstatutory stock options, and stock appreciation rights granted by a target corporation); Tech. Adv. Mem. 97-21-002 (severance payments by purchaser); Tech. Adv. Mem. 97-31-001 (increased severance payments by purchaser); Field Serv. Adv. 2000-48-006 (indemnified disputed franchise tax liabilities). (iii) What is the result for Invest and Perch if unexpectedly the final judgment is $5,000,000 above the insurance? *See Illinois Tool Works* (judgment in patent litigation assumed on acquisition as purchase price).

§ 5. DOI INCOME AND § 108

I.R.C. §§ 108 and 1017

Section 108(a) provides a general exclusion from DOI income for taxpayers in bankruptcy and for taxpayers who are insolvent but not in bankruptcy. § 108(a)(1)(A and (B) and (a)(2)(A). The meaning of insolvency is discussed in § 5.01 *Insolvency*. There is a similar exclusion for qualified farm indebtedness that does not require insolvency. § 108(a)(1)(C), (a)(2)(B) and (g). Similarly, § 108(a)(1)(D) and (c) provide an exclusion for discharge of qualified real property business indebtedness for noncorporate taxpayers who elect; and as a reflection of the sub-prime mortgage crisis, § 108(a)(1)(E) and (h) provide one for qualified principal residence, except that the personal residence exclusions takes priority over the bankruptcy and insolvency ones unless the taxpayer elects otherwise. § 108(a)(2).

The exclusion is primarily a deferral because § 108(b) provides for reduction of tax attributes — net operating loss, certain credit and capital loss carryovers, and the basis of the taxpayer's property. Although § 108(b)(2) prescribes a specific order for attribute reduction, § 108(b)(5) allows taxpayers to elect to apply the attribute reduction first to depreciable property held at the beginning of the next year. The reduction in carryovers, of course, substitutes reductions in items that would otherwise provide a future tax benefit for current income. The reduction in attributes other than basis is discussed in § 5.02 *Attribute Reduction*.

As a general rule, reducing the basis of depreciable property provides a longer deferral, because the effect is spread over the remaining depreciable life of the property, particularly because it is applied first to depreciable real property. § 1017(b)(1); Treas. Reg. § 1.1017-1(a)(1). Although the basis reduction for qualified personal residence is applied to the residence, the one for qualified real property indebtedness is applied to depreciable property in general and is not traced to the property acquired with the indebtedness. Because all of the basis adjustments are governed by § 1017, they are discussed in § 5.03 *Basis Reduction*. Because the purchase price adjustment under section 108(e)(5) discussed in § 3.04 *Tufts* and § 108(e)(5), eliminates DOI income, the conditions and limitations of § 1017 do not apply to purchase price adjustments. On the other hand, § 108(a)(2) and § 1017 apparently may apply to a seller reduction of a purchase obligation for a bankrupt or insolvent taxpayer.

Section 108(d) provides definitions and special rules for partnerships and S corporations. Section 108(e) contains a miscellany of special rules and limitations that mostly represent reactions to specific issues or problems, including § 108(e)(2) and § 108(e)(5), both of which have been discussed earlier. Section 108(e)(4) treats acquisition by a related party as acquisition by the debtor, with any applicable DOI if the acquisition price is less than the tax amount of the indebtedness. Corporate and partnership debt adjustments are covered in § 108(e)(6), (8) and (10). Section 108(e)(7) provided regulatory authority for extending these adjustments to partnerships, S corporations, and other pass-through entities, but no such regulations have been issued. Section 108(f) provides relief for students who earn discharge of student loans by working in public benefit positions. *See* Rev. Rul. 2008-34, 2008-28 I. R. B. 76 (student loans refinanced by law school under a loan repayment assistance program that discharged all or part of the refinanced loan when the student worked in a law-related public service position for, or under the director of a charitable or government organization for a specified period of time qualified under § 108(f) so that the discharge was not DOI income).

Section § 6050P and Treas. Reg. § 1.6050P-1 and 2 require financial institutions and Government (apparently meaning Federal Government) agencies to report any indebtedness discharged during the year on a Form 1099-C sent to the taxpayer. Although Treas. Reg. § 1.6050P refers to §§ 61 and 108, it does not define discharge of indebtedness by reference to either provision. The return is required to be filed only when there is an identifiable event, including bankruptcy and insolvency proceeds, expiration of the statute of limitations, and a decision to discontinue collection. A taxpayer who receives a Form 1099-C that reports a relief from a liability or obligation that is not discharge of indebtedness income, presumably needs to attach a copy of the Form 1099-C to the return for the year it is received, and explain why it is improper. *See Hahn v. Commissioner*, T.C. Memo. 2007-75 (refuses to grant summary judgment for amounts taxpayer claimed were improperly reported by FDIC on Form 1099-C because accrued interest, late charges, attorney's fees, and other costs were not indebtedness).

§ 5.01. Insolvency

Bankruptcy is easily defined as involving a case under Title 11, the Bankruptcy Code. Insolvency outside bankruptcy is determined by the excess of the tax amount of liabilities over the value of assets, § 108(d)(3), what is informally called the bankruptcy test. This definition is consistent with the "freeing of assets" or improvement of net worth approach of *United States v. Kirby Lumber Co.*, 284 U.S. 1 (1931), discussed in § 2.01 *What is DOI?* The definition, of course, requires determining what assets and what liabilities are relevant. The following case determines that the tax definition includes assets that are exempt from creditors' claims, while the one that follows determines that contingent obligations are not liabilities for purposes of the definition.

CARLSON v. COMMISSIONER

United States Tax Court

116 T.C. 87 (2001)

[Carlson was a commercial fisherman who owned a fishing vessel, the Yantari, that was financed by a bank loan. The taxpayer became delinquent when the loan balance was $137,142, and the bank foreclosed. The Yantari was sold at foreclosure for $95,000 resulting a capital gain to Carlson of $28,621, with DOI income for the remaining $42,142 of the bank loan. The taxpayer's assets immediately before the foreclosure sale were $875,251, including an Alaska limited entry fishing permit valued at $393,400 (and the Yantari), and liabilities of $515,930 (including the bank loan).

* * *

The parties' general dispute here is whether, pursuant to section 108(a)(1)(B), petitioners may exclude from gross income for the year at issue $42,142 of DOI income resulting from the foreclosure sale on February 8, 1993. The parties agree that resolution of that issue depends on whether, immediately before that foreclosure sale, petitioners were insolvent within the meaning of section 108(d)(3). The parties' specific dispute here concerns the meaning of the word "assets" as used in section 108(d)(3).

It is petitioners' position that the word "assets" as used in section 108(d)(3) does not include assets that are exempt from the claims of creditors under applicable State law. In support of that argument, petitioners rely principally on *Cole v. Commissioner*, 42 B.T.A. 1110 (1940) . . . . According to petitioners, petitioners' fishing permit, which had a fair market value of $393,400 immediately preceding the foreclosure sale on February 8, 1993, is an asset exempt from the claims of creditors under the law of the State of Alaska. . . . If the Court were to sustain petitioners' position, the parties agree that petitioners would be insolvent within the meaning of section 108(d)(3) and that the insolvency exception of section 108(a)(1)(B) would exclude from their gross income for the year at issue $42,142 of DOI income resulting from the foreclosure sale on February 8, 1993.

* * *

Congress enacted section 108(a)(1)(B) and related provisions (*i.e.*, section 108(a)(3), (d)(3), and (e)(1)) into the Code in 1980 as part of the Bankruptcy Tax Act of 1980 . . . . The stated purpose of the 1980 Bankruptcy Tax Act was to "accommodate bankruptcy policy and tax policy." . . . . . .

The committee reports . . . describe in pertinent part the tax law governing DOI income that was extant at the time Congress passed the 1980 Bankruptcy Tax Act, as follows:

> Under present law, income is realized when indebtedness is forgiven or in other ways cancelled (sec. 61(a)(12) . . .).
>
> There are several exceptions to the general rule of income realization. Under a judicially developed "insolvency exception," no income arises from discharge of indebtedness if the debtor is insolvent both before and after the transaction; and if the transaction leaves the debtor with assets whose value exceeds remaining liabilities, income is realized only to the extent of the excess. . . .

* * *

. . . [In] *Dallas Transfer & Terminal Warehouse Co. v. Commissioner*, 70 F.2d 95 (5th Cir. 1934), . . . the taxpayer was relieved of indebtedness as the lessee of certain real property with respect to unpaid rent and other bills totaling $107,881 when it conveyed to the lessor of that property certain real property of lesser value (*i.e.*, $42,507) in which the taxpayer's equity at the time of conveyance was $17,507. . . . The Court of Appeals held that the taxpayer did not realize income as a result of that transaction. . . . In so holding, the Court of Appeals stated:

> In effect the transaction was similar to what occurs in an insolvency or bankruptcy proceeding when, upon a debtor surrendering, for the benefit of his creditors, property insufficient in value to pay his debts, he is discharged from liability for his debts. This does not result in the debtor acquiring something of exchangeable value in addition to what he had before. There is a reduction or extinguishment of liabilities without any increase of assets. There is an absence of such a gain or profit as is required to come within the accepted definition of income. * * * It hardly would be contended that a discharged insolvent or bankrupt receives taxable income in the amount by which his provable debts exceed the value of his surrendered assets. * * *

* * *

In *Lakeland Grocery Co. v. Commissioner*, 36 B.T.A. 289 (1937), . . . the taxpayer entered into a so-called composition settlement under which the taxpayer paid its creditors $15,473 in consideration of being relieved of its indebtedness to those creditors in the amount of $104,710. Prior to entering into the composition settlement, the taxpayer was insolvent. After that settlement, the taxpayer had net assets of $39,597, which, as noted by the Board, "were freed from the claims of creditors as a result of the * * * [discharge of indebtedness]." . . . . The Board held that the taxpayer realized gain to the extent of the value of the assets freed from the claims of its creditors, *i.e.*, to the extent it had assets (*i.e.*, $39,597) which ceased to be offset by any liability. . . .

* * *

We explained in *Merkel* that Congress

> codified the net assets test in section 108(a)(1)(B), (a)(3), and (d)(3) as a means of determining an exclusion from gross income of an item of income derived from the discharge of indebtedness. . . . That framework requires an examination of the debtor's assets and liabilities for the purpose of determining whether the debtor's net worth turns positive (assets exceed liabilities), *i.e.*, whether assets are freed, as a result of the debtor's being discharged of indebtedness.

* * *

> From our examination of the statutory language, the legislative history, and the relevant cases cited in the committee reports, we conclude that the analytical framework of the insolvency exclusion and its related provisions [in section 108] is based on the freeing-of-assets theory. * * *
>
> A solvent debtor is capable of meeting his financial obligations because his assets equal or exceed his liabilities. That excess (if any) is not increased when an obligation that offsets assets is paid in full because the reduction in liabilities is equal to the reduction in assets. If the reduction in liabilities exceeds the reduction in assets, then, under the freeing-of-assets theory, the solvent debtor has realized a gain to the extent of that excess. * * * Pursuant to the freeing-of-assets theory, a debtor does not realize income when discharged of a particular indebtedness, however, if his postdischarge

> liabilities equal or exceed his postdischarge assets (if any); *i.e.*, under the net assets test, the debtor's liabilities equal or exceed his assets after the discharge (or, the statutory insolvency calculation shows that the debtor is insolvent by an amount greater than or equal to the discharge of indebtedness income * * *

. . .

With the foregoing in mind, we shall now consider petitioners' argument that we follow *Cole* . . . , in defining the word "assets" as used in the definition of the term "insolvent" in section 108(d)(3). In *Cole*, the Board began its analysis by acknowledging that . . . the taxpayer, a resident of New York, would realize income upon the discharge of his indebtedness "to the extent of the excess of total assets over total liabilities immediately after * * * [discharge]." . . . In determining whether there was such an excess, the Board stated:

> In determining the amount in [*sic*] which petitioner's net assets were increased as a result of the cancellation of petitioner's indebtedness by his creditor, *i.e.*, the amount of petitioner's assets which ceased to be offset by claims of creditors, there should be, and has been, omitted from the value of petitioner's assets the value of his equity in ten life insurance policies. * * * . . .

The Board explained in *Cole* that it excluded the value of the taxpayer's equity in certain life insurance policies from its determination of the value of the taxpayer's assets because "Under the applicable law of New York * * * such equity in insurance was free from claims of creditors." . . .

We reject petitioners' argument that we apply *Cole* in this case. When Congress enacted the insolvency exception into the Code as section 108(a)(1)(B), one of the related provisions it also enacted is section 108(e)(1). Section 108(e)(1) provides that, for purposes of title 26 of the United States Code (*i.e.*, the Internal Revenue Code, including section 61(a)(12)), "there shall be no insolvency exception from the general rule that gross income includes income from the discharge of indebtedness" except as provided in section 108(a)(1)(B). . . . :

* * *

We conclude that section 108(e)(1) precludes in this case (or in any other case involving the insolvency exception in section 108(a)(1)(B)) the application of *Cole* . . . , and any other judicially developed insolvency exception to the general rule of section 61(a)(12) that gross income includes income from the discharge of indebtedness. . . .

. . . One of the stated policies of the 1978 Bankruptcy Reform Act was "to provide a fresh start", . . . for debtors coming out of bankruptcy. The principal mechanism adopted by Congress in the 1978 Bankruptcy Reform Act for providing such a "fresh start" in the Federal bankruptcy laws is through the discharge of debts. . . .

Congress also adopted another method in the 1978 Bankruptcy Reform Act for providing a "fresh start" to debtors coming out of bankruptcy, namely, allowing debtors in bankruptcy to retain after bankruptcy certain property classified as exempt property. . . . In determining whether a debtor in bankruptcy is insolvent for purposes of title 11, the debtor's title 11 exempt property, which includes property exempt from the claims of creditors under applicable State law, is excluded from the property he otherwise owns. . . .

. . . when Congress enacted into the Code the insolvency exception in section 108(a)(1)(B) and the definition of "insolvent" in section 108(d)(3), it knew that it had decided to, and did, define the term "insolvent" in section 101(26) of the 1978 Bankruptcy Reform Act, . . . to exclude specifically title 11 exempt property of a debtor in bankruptcy, including property exempt from the claims of creditors under applicable State law, in determining whether that debtor is insolvent for purposes of the Federal bankruptcy laws. . . . However, Congress decided to, and did, adopt a different definition of the term "insolvent" in section 108(d)(3) for purposes of section 108. . . . [t]he definition of that term which Congress adopted for purposes of section 108 does not specifically exclude assets of a debtor that are exempt from the claims of creditors under applicable State law or any other title 11 exempt property in determining whether the debtor is insolvent. We conclude . . . that Congress did not intend to exclude assets exempt from the claims of creditors under applicable State law from a taxpayer's assets for purposes of determining whether the taxpayer is insolvent within the meaning of section 108(d)(3). . . .

* * *

. . . As we explained in *Merkel . . . at 475.*

> Congress' indicated purpose of not burdening an insolvent debtor outside of bankruptcy with an immediate tax liability, * * *, together with the operation of the insolvency exclusion [section 108(a)(1)(B)] and its limitation under section 108(a)(3), in accordance with the statutory insolvency calculation [section 108(d)(3)], suggest that Congress intended to make a debtor's ability to pay an immediate tax on income from discharge of indebtedness the controlling factor in determining whether a tax burden is imposed. * * *

* * *

Although an asset of a debtor may be exempt from the claims of creditors under applicable State law, if that asset and the debtor's other assets exceed the debtor's liabilities, the debtor has the ability to pay an immediate tax on income from discharged indebtedness. In the instant case, immediately preceding the foreclosure sale on February 8, 1993, the aggregate fair market value of petitioners' assets was $875,251, which included petitioners' fishing permit valued at $393,400 that they claim is exempt from the claims of creditors under the law of the State of Alaska. At that time, petitioners' liabilities totaled $515,930. On the record before us, we find that petitioners had the "ability to pay an immediate tax on", . . . the $42,142 of DOI income resulting from the foreclosure sale in question. . . .

* * *

NOTES AND COMMENTS

The *Merkel* case referred to in *Carlson* dealt with the other part of the insolvency equation, the obligations to be taken into account as liabilities in determining whether the taxpayer is insolvent. It concluded that a contingent obligation under a guarantee should not be taken into account unless the taxpayers proved that the contingency was likely to occur, which they could not on the facts of the case, because by the time of the case, the guarantee had expired without requiring any payment by the taxpayer. In reading the case, try to determine how the issue should be determined when the outcome of the contingency is still open.

* * *

MERKEL v. COMMISSIONER

United States Court of Appeals, Ninth Circuit
192 F.3d 844 (9th Cir. 1999)

* * *

This case calls upon us to decide the standard for determining when a contingent obligation to pay is a "liability" for purposes of determining insolvency under . . . § 108(d)(3).

. . . The Tax Court found that Appellants failed to prove that as of the measurement date it was likely they "would be called upon to pay" a claimed liability, and thus Appellants' total liabilities did not exceed the fair market value of their assets. Accordingly, the Tax Court found that Appellants were not insolvent under § 108(d)(3) and therefore could not exclude discharge of indebtedness income under the insolvency exclusion set forth in . . . § 108(a)(1)(B). . . .

* * *

For the most part, the facts of this case are undisputed. During the taxable year 1991, Appellants were general partners in HMH Partners ("HMH"). The Merkels and Hepburns each owned twenty-five percent of HMH, and a third party owned the remaining fifty percent. On September 1, 1991, Great Western Bank granted forgiveness to HMH on a $1,439,000 nonrecourse note. As a result, as twenty-five percent partners, the Merkels and Hepburns each received $359,721 of discharge of indebtedness as distributable income. Appellants reported this debt discharge in their 1991 income tax returns. They excluded it from income, however, under 26 U.S.C. § 108(a)(1)(B) based upon their claimed insolvency.

* * *

The parties stipulated that the issue before the Tax Court was whether Appellants were insolvent within the meaning of 26 U.S.C. § 108(d)(3) immediately before the forgiveness of the note by Great Western Bank on September 1, 1991. Section 108(d)(3) defines "insolvent" as "the excess of liabilities over the fair market value of assets." To determine whether Appellants were insolvent under the statute, the Tax Court had to decide whether Appellants' guaranty on a loan was a § 108(d)(3) "liability" as of August 31, 1991. If the guaranty was a liability,

Appellants were insolvent and the debt discharge was properly excludable from gross income under 108(a)(1)(B).

Appellants personally had guaranteed a loan made in 1986 by Security Pacific Bank (the "Bank") to Systems Leasing Corporation ("SLC"), a computer leasing business of which the Merkels and Hepburns each owned half. SLC was the sole maker of the note evidencing the debt to the Bank. Appellants personally guaranteed the SLC note pursuant to a document entitled "Continuing Guaranty (and Security Agreement)" (the "Guaranty"). As of April 16, 1991, the unpaid balance of the SLC note exceeded $3,100,000, and SLC was in default of its note obligations. At no time did the Bank make any formal written demand for payment from Appellants pursuant to the Guaranty.

On May 31, 1991, SLC, the Bank and Appellants, as guarantors, entered into a structured workout agreement (the "Letter Agreement") concerning the repayment of the indebtedness to the Bank. Under the Letter Agreement: (1) SLC agreed to pay the Bank $1,100,000 (the "payoff") on or before August 2, 1991 (the "settlement date"); (2) the Bank agreed to release its security interests in the remaining collateral upon payment of the payoff by the settlement date; and (3) after payment of the payoff by the settlement date, the Bank would refrain from exercising any remedies under the SLC note or the Guaranty if bankruptcy were not filed by or for SLC or the Merkels or Hepburns, among others, voluntarily or involuntarily, within 400 days after the settlement date (a "bankruptcy event").

SLC paid $1,100,000 to the Bank by the settlement date as called for under the Letter Agreement, and the Bank thereafter released its security interests in the remaining collateral of SLC. No bankruptcy petition was filed with respect to SLC, the Merkels or Hepburns, or any other persons or entities relevant to the Letter Agreement as of August 31, 1991.[6]

The Commissioner argued before the Tax Court that Appellants' obligation under the Guaranty was not a liability for purposes of calculating insolvency under § 108(d)(3) because the term "liabilities" encompasses only obligations to pay that are ripe and in existence immediately before the discharge of indebtedness. In sustaining the Commissioner's determinations of income tax deficiency, the Tax Court took a different tack, holding that Appellants failed to prove by a preponderance of the evidence that as of August 31, 1991 (the measurement date), they "would be called upon to pay" their obligation under the Guaranty, and that therefore, the obligation was not a liability for purposes of calculating insolvency under § 108(d)(3). Accordingly, the Tax Court found that Appellants' total liabilities so proved did not exceed the fair market value of their assets and held that the discharge of indebtedness income could not be excluded under § 108(a)(1)(B). This appeal followed.

* * *

The parties agree that the determinative issue in this case is whether on August

[6] In fact, no bankruptcy event occurred during the 400-day period, and at the expiration of the 400-day period, the Bank released SLC from its liability as the maker of the SLC note and Appellants from the Guaranty.

31, 1991, Appellants' Guaranty was a "liability" for purposes of determining insolvency under § 108(d)(3). In resolving this issue, we must take into account that under the Letter Agreement, Appellants' obligation to pay pursuant to the Guaranty was contingent upon the occurrence of a bankruptcy event.

* * *

In determining whether the Guaranty, as modified by the Letter Agreement, was a liability under § 108(d)(3), we find little guidance from the text and structure of the statute. The term "liabilities" is not defined in the Internal Revenue Code or in any Treasury Regulation. Moreover, § 108(d)(3) does not indicate how likely the occurrence of a contingency must be in order to count the obligation as a liability.

Black's Law Dictionary defines "liability" as a "broad legal term . . . including almost every character of hazard or responsibility, absolute, contingent, or likely." . . . Under this definition, the Guaranty could be considered a liability because it is a "responsibility" that is "contingent." But, it is not clear from the statute whether Congress intended for all contingent liabilities to be considered in the insolvency calculation under § 108(d)(3). . . .

Appellants concede that such a broad construction of the statute is unwarranted. Moreover, we are compelled to construe exclusions from income narrowly. See Centennial Savs. Bank, 499 U.S. at 583-84. Accordingly, because the plain language of the statute does not limit which contingent liabilities, if any, may be counted in calculating insolvency under § 108(d)(3), we are compelled to examine the legislative history of the insolvency exclusion to ascertain Congress' intent. . . .

* * *

The origins of § 108(a)(1)(B) demonstrate that Congress intended for only those liabilities in the amount that actually offset assets to be considered in calculating insolvency for purposes of the income tax exclusion. We agree with the Tax Court's conclusion that "an indiscriminate inclusion of obligations to pay . . . in the statutory insolvency calculation[], without any consideration of how speculative those obligations may be, would render meaningless any inquiry into whether assets are freed upon the discharge of indebtedness." We also agree, based on Congress' purpose of not burdening an insolvent debtor with an immediate tax liability, that Congress considered a debtor's ability to pay an immediate tax on discharge of indebtedness income the "controlling factor" in determining whether the § 108(a)(1)(B) exception applies. Accordingly, a taxpayer claiming to be insolvent for purposes of § 108(a)(1)(B) and challenging the Commissioner's determination of deficiency must prove by a preponderance of the evidence that he or she will be called upon to pay an obligation claimed to be a liability and that the total amount of liabilities so proved exceed the fair market value of his or her assets.

The dissent urges instead that we adopt a construction of § 108(a)(1)(B) and § 108(d)(3) which would define "liability" as including all liabilities discounted by the probability of their occurrence. We agree with the dissent that as a general proposition " 'discounting a contingent liability by the probability of its occurrence is good economics and therefore good law.' " . . . (quoting *Covey v. Commercial Nat'l Bank*, 960 F.2d 657, 660 (7th Cir. 1992) (construing 11 U.S.C. § 101(32)(A), which defines insolvency for purposes of bankruptcy). As sound as the economic policy outlined by the dissent may be, however, it is not the law Congress enacted when it sought to "accommodate" bankruptcy policy with tax policy. See S. Rep. No. 96-1035. Unlike the statutory provision at issue in *Covey*, the definition of insolvency in the Internal Revenue Code expressly requires a fair market valuation of assets only and not liabilities. See 26 U.S.C. § 108(d)(3).

The issue in *Covey* was whether a firm was "insolvent" as defined in the Bankruptcy Code. Under the Bankruptcy Code, " 'insolvent' means . . . with reference to an entity other than a partnership and a municipality, financial condition such that the sum of such entity's debts is greater than all of such entity's property, at a fair valuation." . . . [T]he Seventh Circuit held: "To decide whether a firm is insolvent . . . a court should ask: What would a buyer be willing to pay for the entire package of assets and liabilities? If the price is positive, the firm is solvent; if negative, insolvent." . . . The Seventh Circuit's analysis is supported by the plain language of 11 U.S.C. § 101(32)(A), as the phrase "at a fair valuation" may be read to modify both "debts" and "property," and the definition of insolvency encompasses both, as so modified. By contrast, § 108(d)(3) defines insolvency as "the excess of liabilities over the fair market value of assets." Unlike 11 U.S.C. § 101(32)(A), the phrase "fair market value" in § 108(d)(3) modifies "assets" but not "liabilities." That Congress explicitly stated that "assets" under § 108(d)(3) were to be valued at fair market value, and did not state the same as to liabilities, suggests that it did not intend liabilities to be valued at fair market value. Moreover, that Congress explicitly provided under 11 U.S.C. § 101(32)(A) that both "debts" and "property" were to be valued "at a fair valuation" suggests that it knows how to provide for comparable treatment of liabilities and assets when that is what intends to do.

Thus, it is the dissent that departs from the plain meaning of the statute by imbuing it with an economic analysis neither express in the statutory language nor supported by an examination of congressional intent. Indeed, in seeking to import a valuation mechanism in reliance upon five cases from other circuits decided exclusively in the "bankruptcy context," . . . the dissent fails to recognize, as Congress clearly did, that tax policy is distinct from bankruptcy policy. . . .

Having determined that a taxpayer claiming to be insolvent for purposes of § 108(a)(1)(B) and challenging the Commissioner's determination of deficiency must prove by a preponderance of the evidence that he or she will be called upon to pay an obligation claimed to be a liability and that the total amount of liabilities so proved exceed the fair market value of his or her assets, we now address whether the Tax Court correctly sustained the Commissioner's determination of deficiency in this case.

* * *

The Tax Court found that Appellants failed to prove that a bankruptcy event was likely to occur. Appellants do not contest this finding on appeal. Because Appellants failed to prove that a bankruptcy event was likely to occur and therefore failed to prove that, as of August 31, 1991, they would be called upon to pay any amount to the Bank, the Tax Court correctly found that Appellants were not insolvent on August 31, 1991. The Tax Court's decision sustaining the Commissioner's determinations of income tax deficiency is affirmed.

NOTES AND COMMENTS

Thus, the effect of these decisions is a narrow definition of insolvency in which all assets are taken into account, but not all nontax claims are. The IRS had reached similar results in Rev. Rul. 92-53, 1992-2 C.B. 48, dealing with the effect of nonrecourse liabilities in determining insolvency. It held that an excess of the value of other assets over recourse liabilities, which, by definition, are not available to the holder of the nonrecourse liability, are taken into account only to the extent of the value of the encumbered property. On the other hand, the excess of a nonrecourse liability over the value of the encumbered property is not taken into account in determining solvency when a recourse obligation is reduced or eliminated, on the ground that the excess does not affect the taxpayer's ability to pay recourse debt. Applying these principles, when a nonrecourse liability exceeds the value of the mortgaged property but the debtor has other assets in excess of his recourse liabilities, the write-down of the nonrecourse mortgage results in DOI to the extent of the excess of the other assets over recourse debt. As in *Carlson*, the result is to count assets that the taxpayer has available to pay the tax on the DOI income.

The refusal in *Merkel* to consider the contingent obligation as a liability is, of course, consistent with the definition of liability under the partnership regulations, because, by definition, the contingent obligation has not been taken into in account in basis, as a deduction, or as an expenditure. *See Zappo v. Commissioner*, 81 T.C. 77 (1983) (contingent obligation under a guarantee that the purchaser of property would realize specified profits did not offset the liabilities transferred with the property in determining the gain on the transaction, because a guaranty is an inchoate obligation at the time of its making, so that there is no real continuation of indebtedness when a highly contingent obligation is substituted for a true debt). On the other hand, the risk of having to make payment on the obligation does affect ability to pay. On the facts in *Merkel*, the potential payment obligation was eliminated long before the audit of the tax return and, in view of the shortness of the contingency period, was resolved before the filing of the return for the year of the discharge if the taxpayers obtained an extension of time to file. One does not have to be much of cynic to suspect that 20/20 hindsight, the only perfect vision, influenced the courts' findings that the taxpayers did not carry the burden of proving they would be called on to pay the obligation when, in fact, they had not made any payment. The suggestion of the dissenting judge that the obligation should be taken into account based on discounting the probability of its occurrence may make theoretical sense in view of the statutory determination of insolvency at the time of discharge, but is certain to result in the wrong amount being taken into account — too much if nothing is paid and too little if the full amount is paid. Although the error can be corrected by requiring reporting additional income in the year of resolution when nothing is paid, or allowing a deduction for the excess when the full amount is paid, the practical effect of using hindsight probably covers most cases. *See Jelle v. Commissioner*, 116 T.C. 63 (2001) (farmers had DOI when allowed to retain property by paying amount equal to value of the property, even though the agreement required them to recapture difference between that amount and loan principal by payments to lender if they sold the property within 10 years for more than they paid to retain the property; contingent repayment obligation did not keep original obligation in effect).

In the *Carlson* case, Carlson recognized a capital gain on the foreclosure sale of the Yantari. This result is explained in the following ruling.

Rev. Rul. 90-16, 1990-1 C.B. 12

* * *

X was the owner and developer of a residential subdivision. To finance the development of the subdivision, *X* obtained a loan from an unrelated bank. *X* was unconditionally liable for repayment of the debt. The debt was secured by a mortgage on the subdivision.

X became insolvent (within the meaning of section 108(d)(3) of the Code) and defaulted on the debt. *X* negotiated an agreement with the bank whereby the subdivision was transferred to the bank and the bank released *X* from all liability for the amounts due on the debt. When the subdivision was transferred pursuant to the agreement, its fair market value was 10,000x dollars, *X*'s adjusted basis in the subdivision was 8,000x dollars, and the amount due on the debt was 12,000x dollars, which did not represent any accrued but unpaid interest. After the transaction *X* was still insolvent.

* * *

Section 1.1001-2(a)(1) of the regulations provides that . . . the amount realized from a sale or other disposition of property includes the amount of liabilities from which the transferor is discharged as a result of the sale or disposition. Section 1.1001-2(a)(2) provides that the amount realized on a sale or other disposition of property that secures a recourse liability does not include amounts that are (or would be if realized and recognized) income from the discharge of indebtedness. . . .

In the present situation, *X* transferred the subdivision to the bank in satisfaction of the 12,000x dollar debt. To the extent of the fair market value of the property transferred to the creditor, the transfer of the subdivision is treated as a sale or disposition upon which gain is recognized under section 1001(c) of the Code. To the extent the fair market value of the subdivision, 10,000x dollars, exceeds its adjusted basis, 8,000x dollars, *X* realizes and recognizes gain on the transfer. *X* thus recognizes 2,000x dollars of gain.

To the extent the amount of debt, 12,000x dollars, exceeds the fair market value of the subdivision, 10,000x dollars, *X* realizes income from the discharge of indebtedness. However, under section 108(a)(1)(B) of the Code, the full amount of *X*'s discharge of indebtedness income is excluded from gross income . . . .

If the subdivision had been transferred to the bank as a result of a foreclosure proceeding in which the outstanding balance of the debt was discharged (rather than having been transferred pursuant to the settlement agreement), the result would be the same. A mortgage foreclosure, like a voluntary sale, is a 'disposition' within the scope of the gain or loss provision of section 1001 of the Code. . . .

* * *

NOTES AND COMMENTS

Thus, Rev. Rul. 90-16 emphasizes that a foreclosure or similar disposition of property subject to a recourse liability by an insolvent taxpayer results in DOI income only to the extent that the amount of liability discharged exceeds the value of the property, and that insolvency does not eliminate gain (or loss) on the taxable foreclosure sale. This result is now embodied in Treas. Reg. § 1.1001-2(a)(2) and (c) Ex. 8. The result for an insolvent taxpayer is a bad news/good news situation. The bad news is that, despite the insolvency, gain on the disposition of the property is recognized immediately equal to the excess of the value of the property over its basis, with the limited good news that the gain is capital or section 1231 gain to the extent that the property qualifies, and that the DOI income is eligible for deferral under the insolvency exclusion. The entire amount of any nonrecourse liability is amount realized, so that no amount is deferrable or excludible DOI income. Thus, an insolvent taxpayer is worse off in a situation involving nonrecourse debt than one involving recourse debt.

PROBLEM FOR DISCUSSION

Problem 3-31. The facts are the same as in *Merkel* except that SLC filed for bankruptcy within the 400-day period, and the Merkels and Hepburns settled their liability on the guarantees by paying $50,000 each in 1992. What are the tax consequences for 1991 an 1992 of these events? *See Zappo* (guaranty of profits does not offset liabilities transferred); *Jelle* (retain farm by paying value to terminate mortgage subject to recapture); *Friedland* (appreciated property transferred to settle guarantee); *Payne* (no DOI on release from guarantee).

§ 5.02. Attribute Reduction

Treas. Reg. §§ 1.108-4 and -7

When no election is made to reduce basis first as described in § 5.03 *Basis Adjustment — § 1017*, or when the basis of property is less than the amount of the DOI income, specified tax attributes are reduced. This implicitly recognizes that some of the losses sustained by the taxpayer were financed by the discharged debt. Within broad limits the effect is the same as if the DOI income were realized in the year of discharge and applied against the carryover attributes, but treating the DOI income as excluded results in somewhat awkward computations.

The excluded DOI income is applied first dollar-for-dollar against any net operating loss ("NOL") for the year of discharge, and then against NOL carryovers for that year. § 108(b)(2)(A) and (3)(A); Treas. Reg. § 1.108-7(a)(1)(i), (b) and Examples 1 and 2. This computation reflects that the excluded DOI income was not taken into account in determining the NOL for the year of discharge. When there is taxable income for the year of the discharge the income is determined, and NOL (and capital loss) carryovers to that year are applied against income from the year, before the DOI income is applied against the carryovers, in the order in which they are carried over to the year. § 108(b)(4)(A) and (B). This has the effect of using carryovers first as if the DOI income had not been realized.

To the extent that the DOI income has not been absorbed by the NOL for the year, and by NOL carryovers to the year, it is next applied against the general business credit (a combination of more than 30 credits), and the minimum tax credit. These credits are reduced at 33⅓ percent to the dollar, reflecting that they are applied against tax, not gross income, with a rate that is below the top corporate rate, but above the current top individual rate. § 108(b)(3)(B). As with the NOL, they are reduced after the tax for the year of the discharge is determined. § 108(b)(4)(A). After reduction, any basis reduction (assuming the election to reduce basis first has not been made), the passive activity loss and credit carryovers and foreign credit carryovers are reduced under the same principles.

In the unlikely case that the DOI income exceeds all of the above attributes, including basis reduction, the exclusion means that there are no tax consequences from the remaining DOI income. Because borrowing for business or investment purposes almost always results in expenses or losses or basis of assets, this costless DOI income presumably applies to borrowing for personal purposes, including expenditures that are neither capital nor deductible.

§ 5.03. Basis Reduction — § 1017

I.R.C. § 108; Treas. Reg. §§ 1.108-4, -5 and -6; I.R.C. § 1017; Treas. Reg. § 1.1017

Basis reduction is the first attribute reduction when an election under § 108(b)(5) is made, the fifth when no election is made, for bankrupt or insolvent taxpayers, or for reduction in qualified farm indebtedness, and the only attribute reduction when an election is made by solvent noncorporate taxpayers for qualified real property business indebtedness or qualified personal residence indebtedness The basis reduction is made under § 1017 and applies generally to property held at the beginning of the year after the year of the DOI income.

When the basis reduction is fifth attribute reduction, it is applied to: (i) real property used in trade or business or for investment other than real property held for sale to customers that is secured by the discharged indebtedness, (ii) business or investment personal property not held for sale, (iii) other capital or § 1231 property, (iv) noncapital assets under § 1231, and (v) property that is not business or investment property. § 1017(a) and (b)(1); Treas. Reg. § 1.1017-1(a) and (b)(1) and (2). The reduction is limited to the excess of the basis of the listed properties over the taxpayer's aggregate remaining liabilities, in effect leaving adequate basis for subsequent DOI income. § 1017(b)(2); Treas. Reg. § 1.1017-1(b)(3).

When the basis reduction is made under the § 108(b)(5) election to reduce basis first, the reduction is applied only to depreciable or amortizable property, but is limited to the basis of such property at the beginning of the year *after* the year in which the DOI income is recognized. § 1017(b)(3)(A) and (B); Treas. Reg. § 1.1017-1(c)(1) and (e). The reduction is applied in the same order as described in the preceding paragraph, with the addition of real property held for sale to customers, if the taxpayer so elects, and for partnership interests, if the partnership consents, as it must, at the request of the partner, but the complexities of the partnership adjustment will not be discussed further here. § 1017(b)(3)(B), (C) and (D); Treas.

Reg. § 1.1017-1(e) and (f). If there is not enough basis in the depreciable assets to absorb all of the DOI income, the attribute reduction proceeds as described in § 5.02 *Attribute Reduction*, with the basis as the fifth attribute limited to remaining property. Treas. Reg. § 1.1017-1(c)(2) and (3).

The basis reduction for qualified farm indebtedness of a solvent farmer is essentially the same as for bankrupt or insolvent taxpayers, except that it is limited to qualified property, which is any trade or business property, not only farm property, but also not including investment or personal use property. § 108(g)(3)(C). The exclusion is limited to the sum of the qualified property and the adjusted tax attributes, which are the tax attributes (other than basis) discussed in § 5.02 *Attribute Reduction*, with the credit attributes multiplied by three so that they can be compared with the discharged indebtedness. § 108(g)(3)(B). Qualified farm indebtedness must have been incurred in the taxpayer's trade or business of farming, and must have been incurred by one who has received 50 percent or more of the gross receipts from the trade or business of farming, effectively excluding weekend farmers or others for who farming is a sideline. In addition, the discharged debt must have been owed to qualified person, who must be either one regularly engaged in the business of lending money or a government or governmental agency, who is not related to the farmer and not the one who sold the property.

The basis reduction for DOI for qualified real property business indebtedness applies only to depreciable real property. § 108(c)(1); § 1017(b)(3)(F); Treas. Reg. § 1.1017-1(c). There is no basis reduction for other property, and there is no other attribute reduction if there is insufficient basis in depreciable real property to absorb the DOI income. The amount of the basis reduction is limited to the excess of the amount of the liability over the fair market value of the real property secured by the discharged indebtedness, and to the aggregate basis of depreciable real property held by the taxpayer at the time of the discharge. The basis of the qualifying secured real property is reduced before that of other depreciable real property. Treas. Reg. § 1.1017-1(c)(1). For example, if Terry owns an apartment building subject to a loan secured by a mortgage on the apartment building in the principal amount of $10,000,000 that is reduced to $4,000,000 when the current value of the building, the entire $6,000,000 can be applied as a basis reduction. If the adjusted basis of the building (excluding land) is $6,000,000 or more, the entire $6,000,000 of the DOI income from the reduction is applies to the building portion. If, on the other hand, the adjusted basis is $7,000,000 with $2,000,000 allocated to the land), only $5,000,000 applies to the apartment building and the $1,000,000 is applied as a basis reduction to other depreciable business real property. Unlike the basis reduction for insolvency, the basis reduction for qualified real property business indebtedness is made at the time of the reduction in the indebtedness and the realization of DOI income.

Qualified real property business indebtedness is indebtedness incurred in connection with real estate used in trade or business and secured by the real property but, if incurred after December 31, 1992, it must be incurred or assumed to acquire, construct or substantially improve the property. § 108(c)(3) and (4). Thus, it covers most commercial real estate acquired after the effective date. Technically the election to make the basis reduction is an election to have the indebtedness treated as qualified real property business indebtedness. There does not seem to be any reason that farm indebtedness that is not qualified farm indebtedness, but that meets the definition of qualified real property business indebtedness, should not be eligible for exclusion and basis reduction under that provision.

The basis reduction for qualified personal residence indebtedness discharged after Jan. 1, 2007, and before Jan. 1, 2013, is applied solely to the personal residence, so that it is not made under § 1017. § 108(h)(1). *See* § 3.04, *Tufts* and § 108(e)(5), for a further discussion of § 108(h). Qualified personal residence indebtedness is the same as acquisition indebtedness for which the taxpayer can receive an interest deduction as qualified residence interest under § 108(h)(2), except that the eligible amounts are doubled. When only part of the indebtedness is qualified personal residence indebtedness, the discharge is applied first to the qualified portion. § 108(h)(4). There is also an exception when the discharge is related to services rendered or any other factor not related to the taxpayer's financial condition. § 108(h)(3). Under general tax principles, it would appear that a similar exception would apply to all other discharges, because, to the extent that consideration is supplied, there is no DOI income. A principal residence is one eligible for the exclusion of gain on sale under § 121. § 108(h)(5).

A basis reduction under § 1017 is not a disposition resulting in gain or loss, § 1017(c)(2), but it is treated as depreciation subject to recapture on disposition under the principles discussed in § 6.01 *Overview* in Chapter 2 *Capital Gains and Losses*. § 1017(d). When the basis reduction applies to property that is not § 1245 or § 1250 property, the property is treated as § 1245 property, although, to the extent that the other property is ordinary income property, the characterization should not matter except for exchanges that are otherwise nonrecognition exchanges, but subject to recapture, including like-kind exchanges under § 1031. This treatment prevents adding conversion of ordinary income into capital gain to the deferral benefit of the basis reduction. Because § 1250 recapture for real property applies only to the excess over straight-line depreciation, and because § 1017(d)(2) provides that straight-line depreciation is computed without regard to the § 1017 basis reduction, ordinary income recapture is amortized over the remaining depreciable life of the property. Although it is not completely clear, the amortized portion of the reduction for real property that is § 1250 property should be unrecaptured § 1250 gain subject to the 25 percent rate.

PROBLEM FOR DISCUSSION

Problem 3-32. In 20X1, Propp acquired an office building for $1,200,000, in part with the proceeds of a $1,000,000 nonrecourse note from Countribanc, with adequate stated interest, that was secured by the office building. In 20X3, when the value of the office building was $800,000 and the outstanding principal on the note was $950,000, Countribanc agreed to modify the terms of the note by reducing the note's principal amount to $800,000, with adequate interest. In 20X2, Propp had acquired a shopping center financed by a nonrecourse note and mortgage in the amount of $1,000,000 from Countribanc, with adequate stated interest, which was secured by the shopping center. In 20X3, Propp was also the owner and developer of a residential subdivision. The land had been acquired in 20X2 for $300,000 from

Invest, who had acquired the land many years earlier on the edge of the metropolitan area in the correct belief that it would be worth a bundle one day, and who accepted a nonrecourse note in the full amount of the purchase price, to be paid out of proceeds from the sale of the land, or from a portion of the proceeds of sales of the subdivision. To finance the development of the subdivision, Propp obtained a $1,500,000 recourse loan also from Countribanc, secured by a first lien on the subdivision. Invest agreed to subordinate the nonrecourse purchase money note and mortgage for the land to the Countribanc development loan on the belief that the development would enhance payment of sale price of the land because a portion of the sale price of each house was required to be paid on the nonrecourse note and mortgage. The terms of the Countribanc note and mortgage permitted the required payments to Invest.

At the time of the modification, Propp's other assets had an aggregate fair market value of $100,000, and Propp was personally liable to Cred on other indebtedness in the amount of $150,000. Cred agreed to accept assets from Propp with a fair market value of $100,000 and basis to Propp of $40,000 in settlement of Propp's $150,000 recourse indebtedness. Propp has $75,000 in net operating loss carryovers to 20X3 and $50,000 taxable income in 20X3. These facts may be summarized as follows:

Asset	**Cost**	**Liability**	**Balance**	**FMV 20X3**	**DOI**
Office Building	$1,200,000	$1,000,000 (nonrecourse)	$950,000	$800,000	$150,000
Shopping Center	$1,000,000	$1,000,000 (recourse)	$1,000,000	$1,000.000	
Subdivision Land	$300,000	$300,000 (nonrecourse)	$300,000	$300,000	
Subdivision Dev.	$1,500,000	$1,500,000 (recourse)	$1,500,000	$1,500,000	
Other	$40,000			$100,000	
Other Liab.		$150,000			$50,000
Total	$4,040,000	$3,950,000	$3,750,000	$3,700,000	$200,000
NOL Carryforward	$75,000				

What are the tax consequences if the liability reductions for the Office Building and the liability to Cred occur: (i) In bankruptcy? *See* §§ 108 and 1017; Treas. Reg. § 1.1017-1; *Fulton Gold* (modification of liability encumbering property at acquisition is purchase price adjustment); *Hirsch* (purchase price adjustment); *Allen* (same), *Sutphin* (discounted payment of mortgage to purchase residence); Rev. Rul. 82-202 (same); Rev. Rul. 92-99 (write-down of nonrecourse mortgage to value of encumbered property); Rev. Rul. 91-31 (modification of nonrecourse liability is DOI); *Gershkowitz* (same); *Preslar* (same for foreclosure); Rev. Rul. 90-16 (gain recognized by insolvent taxpayer on foreclosure sale. (ii) If outside of bankruptcy, when Propp is insolvent? *See Merkel* (contingent liabilities not included in determining solvency); Rev. Rul. 92-53 (effect of recourse and nonrecourse liabilities in determining solvency and DOI). (iii) If Propp has $200,000 of other assets, including $75,000 of exempt assets? *See Carlson* (exempt assets included in determining solvency). (iv) If, instead of the office building, the reduced obligation to Countribanc is qualified farm indebtedness, and Propp is a qualified farmer?

Chapter 4

CAPITALIZATION AND COST RECOVERY

§ 1. INTRODUCTION

§ 1.01. In General

Capitalization is the concept under which the costs incurred by a taxpayer in acquiring or maintaining property must be aggregated and treated as the basis of the property rather than currently deducted. As you saw in Chapter 1, § 1012 treats as the basis of property the cost of that property. Of course, taxpayers are entitled to deduct the expenses of a trade or business or an activity engaged in for profit under §§ 162 and 212 respectively. But expenses under §§ 162 and 212 are only deductible if the expenses need not be capitalized under § 263 or § 263A. Drawing the line between deductible expenses under §§ 162 and 212 and those that must be capitalized under § 263 or § 263A has led to considerable controversy between taxpayers and the Service. Numerous judicial decisions can be found that address the capitalization question in a multitude of situations. The Service has attempted in recent years to provide taxpayers with guidance in this regard through the promulgation of regulations under § 263 in connection with both tangible and intangible property. Section 2 of this chapter provides a detailed review of the principal cases that have informed the treatment of capital expenditures as well as a discussion of the voluminous regulations that have attempted to provide greater clarity in this area.

Taxpayers could be limited to recovering their investment in property only on the ultimate sale or exchange of the property involved through the determination of gain or loss under § 1001. If, on a subsequent sale or exchange, the fair market value of the property had increased above its original cost basis, only the amount realized in excess of the property's basis would be treated as gain. Thus, the taxpayer would recover his investment in the property tax free. Similarly, if on a subsequent sale or exchange, the fair market value of the property had fallen below its original cost basis, the taxpayer would realize a loss equal to the difference between the amount realized and the property's basis. This loss might then be available to reduce the taxpayer's other income, again allowing the taxpayer to recover his investment in the property tax free.

However, for certain types of property used in a taxpayer's trade or business or an activity conducted for profit, taxpayers are allowed to recover the cost of the property prior to a sale or exchange through depreciation or amortization deductions under § 167. Methods of depreciation and amortization determine the portion of the property basis that may be deducted annually. Conceptually, depreciation and amortization serve the same function. Depreciation is frequently the term used in connection with tangible property while amortization is the term used in connection with intangible property. Because depreciation and amortization deductions reduce the taxpayer's income, the taxpayer's investment in the property is again recovered tax free. In addition, depreciation and amortization deductions reduce the property's basis in order to properly reflect the fact that the taxpayer has recovered a portion of the taxpayer's investment for tax purposes.

The Code recognizes various methods of depreciation and amortization, some of which are statutorily prescribed and others of which may be used at the taxpayer's election. Section 3 of this chapter provides a detailed discussion of the types of property for which depreciation and amortization are available and methods that taxpayer's may employ. Importantly, § 168 provides the methods of depreciation applicable to tangible property while §§ 167 and 197 provide the methods of amortization applicable to intangible property. Section 3 also describes a number of special statutory provisions that Congress has enacted that allow taxpayers to deduct the costs of acquiring or maintaining property, thereby avoiding the capitalization requirements of §§ 263 and 263A, or that allow taxpayers to deduct all or a portion of the basis of acquired property, thereby avoiding in whole or in part the necessity of determining future depreciation or amortization deductions.

Finally, § 4 describes the concept of recapture. Because depreciation and amortization deductions reduce the basis of property, gain realized on an eventual sale or exchange may be attributable, in whole or in part, to such deductions. When taken, such deductions reduced the taxpayer's ordinary income that would otherwise have been taxed at the taxpayer's highest marginal tax rate. Upon sale or exchange of the property, however, the gain might be entitled to capital treatment under § 1221 or § 1231. To prevent taxpayers from benefiting from the preferential tax rates applicable to capital gains under such circumstances, §§ 1(h), 1245, and 1250 require taxpayers to "recapture" the gain attributable to depreciation and amortization deductions on the sale of such property as ordinary income in the case of personal property or as "unrecaptured § 1250 gain" taxable at a top marginal tax rate of 25 percent rather than the more favorable 15 percent rate applicable to adjusted net capital gain in the case of real property.

§ 1.02. The Economics of Capitalization and Cost Recovery

Before embarking on a discussion of the legal requirements surrounding the concepts of capitalization and cost recovery, the economic implications of capitalization and cost recovery require exploration. After a moment's reflection, it is easy to see that a taxpayer would prefer to avoid the capitalization requirement and simply deduct immediately the cost of acquiring or maintaining property. If capitalization is required, the recovery of the taxpayer's investment must be postponed. If the property involved is used in the taxpayer's trade or business or in an activity for the production of income, the taxpayer may be entitled to recover his investment over some period through either depreciation or amortization deductions in later years. Alternatively, if the property is not subject to depreciation or amortization, the taxpayer's investment may only be recovered on ultimate disposition. Either situation is less advantageous from the taxpayer's perspective due to the time value of money.

But how important is the time value of money from the taxpayer's perspective? Perhaps this question can most easily be answered through an illustration. Assume that T is considering purchasing a widget maker. This widget maker, once turned on, will produce widgets for six years without any further investment by T. Assume that at the end of Year 6 the widget maker is worthless. T expects that the widget maker will produce widgets generating $10,000 annually. The first question is what will T pay for the widget maker? To properly answer this question, we would have to know the return that T could expect to make from any alternative investments that he could make, adjusted for the level of risk inherent in the widget business as compared to the other possible business investments. Let's assume that T is looking for a pre-tax return from the widget maker of 10 percent. If his expected return is any less than 10 percent, he would invest his money in an alternative investment. At a 10 percent return, T would be willing to pay $43,553.

Let's assume that T pays $43,553 for the widget maker at the end of Year 0 and starts making widgets on January 1, Year 1. What are the economic implications for T if T is permitted to deduct the entire purchase price of the widget maker in Year 0 when it is purchased? As Table 1 shows, T would have tax savings of $15,243 in Year 0 as a result of the $43,553 deduction, but would pay taxes of $3,500 in Years 1 through 6 on the $10,000 of income earned by the widget maker each year. Thus, T would pay net taxes of $5,757 during the ownership of the widget maker. But this analysis compares Year 1 dollars with Year 6 dollars without taking into account the time value of money. Let's look at things in present value terms as of the end of Year 0, assuming a discount rate of 10 percent. In this case, the sum of T's tax liability in Years 1 through 6 exactly equals T's tax savings in Year 0. In other words, the immediate expensing of the cost of an asset producing income in future years is equivalent to the imposition of a 0 percent effective tax rate on the income produced by the asset. Not only is the immediate expensing of the cost of such an asset preferable, it results in tax-free income! Perhaps this analysis explains why the Supreme Court has noted that "deductions are exceptions to the norm of capitalization." *INDOPCO, Inc. v. Commissioner*, 503 U.S. 79, 84 (1992).

Table 4.1

	Year							
	0	**1**	**2**	**3**	**4**	**5**	**6**	**Total**
Gross Income	0	10,000	10,000	10,000	10,000	10,000	10,000	60,000
Cost Recovery	43,553	0	0	0	0	0	0	43,553
Taxable Income	-43,553	10,000	10,000	10,000	10,000	10,000	10,000	16,447
Tax Liability @ 35%	-15,243	3,500	3,500	3,500	3,500	3,500	3,500	5,757
Present Value of Tax Liability	-15,243	3,182	2,893	2,630	2,391	2,173	1,976	0
Pre-Tax Income	-43,553	10,000	10,000	10,000	10,000	10,000	10,000	
IRR	10.00%							
After-Tax Income	-28,309	6,500	6,500	6,500	6,500	6,500	6,500	
IRR	10.00%							

Another way to see the effect of the immediate expensing of the cost of an income-producing asset is to compare the rate of return on the cash flow generated by the asset before and after taxes. From a pre-tax perspective, T will invest $43,553 in the widget maker to generate $10,000 annually for six years. This results in an internal rate of return on the $43,553 investment of 10 percent. From an after-tax perspective, T invests $43,553 in acquiring the widget maker, but the $43,553 deduction of the acquisition cost in Year 0 saves T $15,243 in taxes. Thus, T actually invests only $28,309. Because he must pay taxes of $3,500 on the $10,000 of income generated by the widget maker each year, the after-tax cash flow is only $6,500. With an initial investment of $28,309 in Year 0 and an annual cash flow of $6,500 in Years 1 through 6, T's internal rate of return is also 10 percent. Taxes have not reduced T's pre-tax rate of return. This is equivalent to the imposition of a 0 percent effective tax rate.[1] Although it appears that T is paying taxes each year of $3,500, that tax liability is exactly offset by tax savings in Year 0 from a present value perspective.

This same analysis could be applied to determine the implications if T were only allowed to recover his investment in the widget maker for tax purposes in Year 6, the year that the widget maker is rendered worthless. Table 4.2 shows the results of this analysis. As in the previous situation, T's pre-tax return is 10 percent on his $43,553 investment. However, from an after-tax perspective, taxes have reduced his return to five percent. This occurs because T's tax savings from the recovery of his investment in the widget maker is deferred from Year 0 in the previous situation to Year 6 in this situation. Although he is paying the same net amount in taxes in both situations, $5,757, his tax savings from the recovery of his investment in Year 6 will not offset the tax liability in Years 1 through 6 from a present value perspective.

[1] The effective tax rate using a particular cost recovery method is related to the after-tax internal rate of return for that method and the pre-tax internal rate of return according to the following formula: 1 – (after-tax IRR for the particular cost recovery method / pre-tax IRR). Thus, the effective tax rate is 0 percent using immediate expensing because the after-tax internal rate of return for that method and the pre-tax internal rate of return are equal (i.e., 1 – (10%/10%)).

Indeed, from a present value perspective, T will be paying $6,639 in taxes over the life of the widget maker. Again, T's effective tax rate differs from the nominal tax rate. T's effective tax rate is 45.2 percent as compared to the nominal tax rate of only 35 percent.

Table 4.2

	Year							
	0	**1**	**2**	**3**	**4**	**5**	**6**	**Total**
Gross Income	0	10,000	10,000	10,000	10,000	10,000	10,000	60,000
Cost Recovery	0	0	0	0	0	0	43,553	43,553
Taxable Income	0	10,000	10,000	10,000	10,000	10,000	-33,553	16,447
Tax Liability @ 35%	0	3,500	3,500	3,500	3,500	3,500	-11,743	5,757
Present Value of Tax Liability	0	3,182	2,893	2,630	2,391	2,173	-6,629	6,639
Pre-Tax Income	-43,553	10,000	10,000	10,000	10,000	10,000	10,000	
IRR	10.00%							
After-Tax Income	-43,553	6,500	6,500	6,500	6,500	6,500	21,743	
IRR	5.48%							

The discussion thus far raises the question whether there exists a "proper" method of cost recovery. One might have expected that a 35 percent tax rate would have reduced T's pre-tax return by 35 percent — from 10 percent to 6.5 percent. So-called "economic depreciation" produces such a result. Economic depreciation measures the annual decline in the value of an asset as measured by the present value of the expected return from the asset. Returning to the facts of the previous illustration, assume that T invests $43,553 in a widget maker that will return $10,000 per year for six years. T is willing to make such an investment because, at the beginning of Year 1, the present value of $10,000 per year for six years discounted at 10 percent is $43,553, as shown in Table 4.3. At the beginning of Year 2, however, the value of the widget maker has declined because T has only five more years of income that will be generated by the widget maker. At the beginning of Year 2, the present value of $10,000 per year for five years discounted at 10 percent is $37,908. This represents a decline in value of $5,645 from the beginning of Year 1 to the beginning of Year 2 due solely to the passage of time. The same approach can be taken to determine the decline in value between each of the following years. At the beginning of Year 6, the value of the widget maker is $9,091 while at the end of the year the widget maker will be worthless. Thus, the decline in value over the course of Year 6 is $9,091. Of course, we have no idea how the fair market value of the widget maker will actually fluctuate over this six-year period. It may increase in value if widgets become scarce and the value of widgets themselves increases above the expected value at the beginning of Year 1. Alternatively, the widget maker may decline in value if widgets become plentiful and the value of widgets themselves declines below the expected value at the beginning of Year 1.

Table 4.3

	Year							
	1	**2**	**3**	**4**	**5**	**6**	**Total**	**Decline**
Gross Income	10,000	10,000	10,000	10,000	10,000	10,000		
PV of Gross Income								
Beg. Year 1	9,091	8,264	7,513	6,830	6,209	5,645	43,553	5,645
Beg. Year 2		9,091	8,264	7,513	6,830	6,209	37,908	6,209
Beg. Year 3			9,091	8,264	7,513	6,830	31,699	6,830
Beg. Year 4				9,091	8,264	7,513	24,869	7,513
Beg. Year 5					9,091	8,264	17,355	8,264
Beg. Year 6						9,091	9,091	9,091

It is important to note that under the assumptions made in this illustration, the decline in the value of the widget maker, i.e., the economic depreciation, is decelerated — smaller declines in value in early years and larger declines in value in later years. Economic depreciation that follows this pattern is frequently referred to as "sinking-fund" depreciation. Economic depreciation is not, however, always decelerated. Economic depreciation in this illustration is decelerated because the income stream generated by the widget maker is assumed to be constant over the life of the asset. Assets in the real world do not generally generate constant income streams over their lives. Depending on when the income generated by the asset arises, economic depreciation can be decelerated, pro rata (i.e., straight-line), or even accelerated. The problem, of course, in the real world in the determination of economic depreciation is in estimating when the income from the asset will be generated.

This economic depreciation can now be used to determine the amount of depreciation that is permitted for tax purposes as shown in Table 4.4. As in Tables 4.1 and 4.2, the total amount of gross income, cost recovery deductions, and net tax liability results. The only difference is the timing of the cost recovery deductions. As in Tables 4.1 and 4.2, T's pre-tax return is 10 percent on his $43,553 investment. Using economic depreciation, however, T's after-tax return is reduced from 10 percent to 6.5 percent, which would be expected after applying a nominal tax rate of 35 percent. Thus, from a present value perspective, economic depreciation results in an effective tax rate equal to the nominal tax rate. If T were permitted cost recovery deductions at a rate greater than allowed using economic depreciation, T's effective tax rate would be reduced below the nominal tax rate of 35 percent. As we saw in Table 4.1, immediate deduction of the cost of acquiring the widget maker would reduce T's effective tax rate to 0. Alternatively, if T were permitted cost recovery deductions at a rate less than allowed using economic depreciation, T's effective tax rate would be increased above the nominal tax rate of 35 percent. As we saw in Table 4.2, deferring T's recovery of his investment until Year 6 increased T's effective tax rate to 45.2 percent.

Table 4.4

	Year							
	0	1	2	3	4	5	6	Total
Gross Income		10,000	10,000	10,000	10,000	10,000	10,000	60,000
Cost Recovery		5,645	6,209	6,830	7,513	8,264	9,091	43,553
Taxable Income		4,355	3,791	3,170	2,487	1,736	909	16,447
Tax Liability @ 35%		1,524	1,327	1,109	870	607	318	5,757
Present Value of Tax Liability		1,386	1,097	834	594	377	180	4,467
Pre-Tax Income	-43,553	10,000	10,000	10,000	10,000	10,000	10,000	
IRR	10.00%							
After-Tax Income	-43,553	8,476	8,673	8,891	9,130	9,393	9,682	
IRR	6.50%							

Finally, consider the situation in which T is permitted to recover the cost of the widget maker pro rata over the six-year life of the asset. This situation is shown in Table 4.5. Again, the total amount of gross income, cost recovery deductions, and net tax liability are the same as in the previous situation. Because the cost recovery deductions are accelerated as compared to economic depreciation, we would expect that the after-tax internal rate of return would be greater than the 6.5 percent result when using economic depreciation. Indeed, the internal rate of return is 6.66 percent, slightly, but not significantly, greater than that involving economic depreciation. This is equivalent to a drop in the effective tax rate from 35 percent to 33.4 percent.

Table 4.5

	Year							
	0	1	2	3	4	5	6	Total
Gross Income		10,000	10,000	10,000	10,000	10,000	10,000	60,000
Cost Recovery		7,259	7,259	7,259	7,259	7,259	7,259	43,553
Taxable Income		2,741	2,741	2,741	2,741	2,741	2,741	16,447
Tax Liability @ 35%		959	959	959	959	959	959	5,757
Present Value of Tax Liability		872	793	721	655	596	542	4,179
Pre-Tax Income	-43,553	10,000	10,000	10,000	10,000	10,000	10,000	
IRR	10.00%							
After-Tax Income	-43,553	9,041	9,041	9,041	9,041	9,041	9,041	
IRR	6.66%							

The concept of economic depreciation is important because it serves as a baseline from which to compare the economic implications of different cost recovery methods that are actually permitted under the Code. As described in § 3, various methods are available under the Code that permit cost recovery deductions in excess of those allowed using economic depreciation. In such situations, the effective tax rate applicable to the income generated by the assets depreciated using such methods may be less than that nominally imposed. Congress is, of course, aware of this economic reality and frequently provides for the use of such methods in order to create incentives for greater business investment in order to stimulate the economy.

§ 2. CAPITALIZATION

§ 2.01. In General

I.R.C. § 162(a); 212; 263

Treas. Reg. §§ 162-1(a); 162-4; 1.212-1(a), 1.212-1(k), 1.212-1(n); 1.263(a)-1; 1.263(a)-2

Section 263 is the most important provision in the Code requiring the capitalization of the costs of acquiring and improving property. Unfortunately, the language of § 263, which prohibits the deduction of "[a]ny amount paid out for new buildings or for permanent improvements or betterments made to increase the value of any property or estate" is not particularly helpful in distinguishing those expenditures that may be deducted under § 162 or § 212 and those that must be capitalized. Until recently, the Regulations provided little additional guidance except to the extent of providing certain "catchphrases" that could be used in formulating arguments for or against capitalization. For example, the Regulations provide that a capital expenditure includes "[t]he cost of acquisition, construction, or erection of buildings, machinery and equipment, furniture and fixtures, and similar property having a useful life substantially beyond the taxable year." Reg. § 1.263(a)-2(a). Similarly, the Regulations under § 162 note that "[t]he cost of incidental repairs which neither materially add to the value of the property nor appreciably prolong its life . . . may be deducted as an expense. . . . Repairs in the nature of replacements, to the extent that they arrest deterioration and appreciably prolong the life of the property shall . . . be capitalized. . . . " Reg. § 1.162-4.

Because of the lack of clear statutory or regulatory guidance, the courts were frequently asked to resolve disputes between taxpayers and the Service regarding capitalization. In doing so, the courts developed four conceptual approaches through which to discuss the issue. The first approach addressed the question whether the expenditures involved created "a separate and discrete asset." The most well-known decision applying this framework was *Commissioner v. Lincoln Sav. & Loan Ass'n*, 403 U.S. 345 (1971), which is discussed in the *INDOPCO* decision provided below. In *Lincoln Savings & Loan*, the Court concluded that, if the expenditures create a separate and discrete asset, they must be capitalized. This approach is not without its difficulties in practice because almost any expenditure could be viewed as creating some type of tangible or intangible asset. For example, a portion of employee salaries otherwise deductible under § 162 could be thought to generate goodwill, an intangible asset in the employer's hands.

The second framework addressed the question whether the expenditures involved resulted in benefits to be realized beyond the current taxable year. This so-called "future benefits test" was most authoritatively articulated in *INDOPCO, Inc. v. Commissioner*, 503 U.S. 79 (1992). Again, this framework was difficult to apply in practice because at least a portion of almost any expenditure can be viewed as giving rise to potential future benefits. For example, advertising expenses frequently generate both short-term and long-term benefits in the form of name recognition. Nevertheless, the Regulations have long treated advertising expenses as deductible under § 162. *See* Reg. § 1.162-20(a)(2). Concerns that the Service would challenge taxpayer deductions by asserting the existence of future benefits following the *INDOPCO* decision forced the Service to clarify its position in this regard through a number of Revenue Rulings. *See, e.g.*, Rev. Rul. 95-32, 1995-1 C.B. 8 (allowing a utility to currently deduct expenditures incurred in implementing energy conservation and load management programs); Rev. Rul. 94-77, 1994-2 C.B. 19 (allowing an employer to currently deduct severance payments made to employees); Rev. Rul. 94-38, 1994-1 C.B. 35 (allowing the current deduction of certain environmental remediation costs); Rev. Rul. 94-12, 1994-1 C.B. 36 (allowing the current deduction of incidental repair costs); Rev. Rul. 92-80, 1992-2 C.B. 57 (allowing the current deduction of advertising expenses).

The third approach addressed the question whether the expenditure was more properly characterized as a repair or an improvement. This approach was based directly on the language of the Regulations under §§ 162 and 263. Improvements or replacements were typically characterized as either materially increasing the property's value or materially prolonging the property's useful life. The application of this approach required an intensive factual inquiry into the expenditures involved and the resulting impact on the value and/or useful life of property in question. *See, e.g.*, *Ingram Indus. Inc. v. Commissioner*, T.C. Memo. 2000-323 (permitting the deduction of expenditures incurred in maintaining the taxpayer's towboat engines because the expenditures did not appreciably prolong the life or materially add to the value of the boats); *Plainfield-Union Water Co. v. Commissioner*, 39 T.C. 333 (1962) (permitting as a repair the deduction of expenditures incurred in cleaning and lining with cement a system of water mains and pipes used in providing water to customers in various towns); *Midland Empire Packing Co. v. Commissioner*, 14 T.C. 635 (1950) (permitting the deduction of expenditures to oilproof the basement of a plant used for the curing of hams and bacon and the storage of meat and hides by adding a concrete lining to the walls and floor); *Mt. Morris Drive-in Theater Co. v. Commissioner*, 25 T.C. 272 (1955), *aff'd per curiam*, 238 F.2d 85 (6th Cir. 1956) (requiring the capitalization of expenditures incurred to acquire and construct a drainage system in connection with its drive-in theater). In attempting to provide additional guidance in this area, some courts adopted a "put versus keep" distinction under which expenditures incurred to "put" a particular asset in efficient operating condition would be capitalized as improvements while expenditures incurred that merely "keep" an asset in efficient operating condition were deductible as repairs. *See, e.g.*, *Dominion Resources, Inc. v. United States*, 48 F. Supp. 2d 527 (E.D. Va. 1999), *aff'd*, 219 F.3d 359 (4th Cir. 2000); *Estate of Walling v. Commissioner*, 373 F.2d 190 (3d Cir. 1967); *Jones v. Commissioner*, 242 F.2d 616 (5th Cir. 1957).

A major problem in applying the repair versus improvement approach concerned identifying the proper unit of property to consider. An expenditure to repair a leaking roof may result in a longer useful life for the roof itself but not for the entire building. Thus, looking at the roof as opposed to the building could produce a difference in result. For example, *Fedex Corp. v. United States*, 2003-1 U.S.T.C. ¶ 50,405 (W.D. Tenn. 2003), the taxpayer argued that the costs incurred in its "off-wing maintenance program" were deductible under § 162 as a cost of repair when the entire aircraft was viewed as the appropriate unit of property in applying the regulatory provisions. On the other hand, the government asserted that the costs were appropriately capitalized under § 263 because the aircraft engines and auxiliary power units, not the entire aircraft, were the appropriate unit of property for analysis. In an initial ruling, the district court concluded that the question could not be answered through a summary judgment motion because the determination of the appropriate unit of property was a question of fact involving an inquiry into the "functional interdependence" of the engines, auxiliary power units, and the frames of the aircraft. In a subsequent decision, the court agreed with the taxpayer and permitted the deduction of the costs incurred. *FedEx Corp. v. United States*, 291 F. Supp. 2d 699 (W.D. Tenn. 2003), *aff'd*, 412 F.3d 617 (6th Cir. 2005). With respect to the question regarding the appropriate unit of property, the court identified four factors that must be considered: (1) how the property is treated within the industry for regulatory, market, management, or accounting purposes; (2) whether the economic useful lives of the component part and the larger unit of property are coextensive; (3) whether the larger unit of property and the component part can function without each other; and (4) whether the component part can be and is maintained while affixed to the larger unit of property. *See also Smith v. Commissioner*, 300 F.3d 1023 (9th Cir. 2002) (concluding that an aluminum reduction cell, rather than entire cell line, was the appropriate unit of property); *Ingram Indus. Inc. v. Commissioner*, T.C. Memo. 2000-323 (concluding that a towboat, and not the towboat engine, was the appropriate unit of property); *La Salle Trucking Co. v. Commissioner*, T.C. Memo. 1963-274 (concluding that truck engines, tanks, and cabs were each separate units of property).

Under the repair versus improvement approach, the courts also developed a doctrine under which repair expenditures had to be capitalized if they were incurred as part of a plan to rehabilitate or improve the property. Under this doctrine, an expenditure made as part of a general plan of rehabilitation, modernization, and improvement of the property must be capitalized, even though, standing alone, the expenditure might have been classified as one of repair or maintenance. *See, e.g., Moss v. Commissioner*, 831 F.2d 833 (9th Cir. 1987); *United States v. Wehrli*, 400 F.2d 686 (10th Cir. 1968); *Stoeltzing v. Commissioner*, 266 F.2d 374, 376 (3d Cir. 1959); *California Casket Co. v. Commissioner*, 19 T.C. 32 (1952), *acq.* However, the plan of rehabilitation doctrine did not apply to situations in which the plan did not include substantial capital improvements and repairs to the same asset, the plan primarily involved repair and maintenance items, or the work was performed merely to keep the property in an ordinarily efficient operating condition. *Schroeder v. Commissioner*, T.C. Memo. 1996-336; Rev. Rul. 88-57, 1988-2 C.B. 36; Rev. Rul. 70-392, 1970-2 C.B. 33. In Rev. Rul. 2001-4, 2001-1 C.B. 295, the Service considered three situations involving a maintenance program by a commercial airline and concluded that expenditures incurred in conjunction with so-called "heavy maintenance visits" had to be capitalized to the extent the expenditures materially added to the value of, substantially prolonged the useful life of, or adapted the airframe to a new or different use, as well as any expenditures incurred as part of a plan of rehabilitate, modernize, or improve the aircraft. The plan of rehabilitation doctrine was particularly controversial in connection with expenditures incurred to remediate environmental contamination of buildings resulting from asbestos. *See Cinergy Corp. v. United States*, 55 Fed. Cl. 489 (2003) (permitted the taxpayer to deduct the costs of removing and encapsulating asbestos fireproofing in its building under § 162); *Norwest Corp. v. Commissioner*, 108 TC 265 (1997) (rejected the taxpayer's claim that the cost of removing asbestos as part of the renovation of a building was currently deductible); Tech. Adv. Mem. 94-11-002 (permitted the deduction of costs incurred for the encapsulation of asbestos-containing insulation reasoning that the expenditures did not increase the value or prolong the useful life of the taxpayer's property).

The final approach addressed whether capitalization (and presumably some type of depreciation or amortization) or immediate expensing would more properly match the cost of the expenditure with the income that the expenditure would generate — a central objective of capitalization. Although each of the other frameworks could be viewed as a means of addressing the question of matching, the courts found an explicit matching inquiry a more expedient means of resolving controversies in certain situations. However, pressed too far, a matching requirement could impose administrative burdens on taxpayers without any significant benefit for the government. For example, in *United States Freightways Corp. v. Commissioner*, 270 F.3d 1137 (7th Cir. 2001), the Seventh Circuit addressed the question whether recurring expenditures incurred in the acquisition of assets with useful lives of one year or less, but whose lives extended beyond the current taxable year, must be capitalized. Although acknowledging the importance of the matching principle, the court noted that "perfection is a lot to ask for, even in the administration of the tax laws. . . ." *Id.* at 1146. Based on the administrative burden that a strict matching rule would impose on the taxpayer as well as several other factors, the court concluded that capitalization was not necessary. The administrative burden of a strict matching requirement is also discussed by the Seventh Circuit in its decision in *Encyclopaedia Britannica, Inc. v. Commissioner*, 685 F.2d 212 (1982), which follows.

Another significant question that arose in the capitalization inquiry is the extent to which otherwise deductible costs, such as managerial expenses, overhead, and other indirect costs must be capitalized when the direct costs or acquiring or improving property must be capitalized. Again, administrative burdens arise if some type of apportionment of indirect costs must be made by taxpayers. The Supreme Court's decision in *Commissioner v. Idaho Power Co.*, 418 U.S. 1 (1974), which follows, addresses this issue.

INDOPCO, INC. v. COMMISSIONER

Supreme Court of the United States
503 U.S. 79 (1992)

JUSTICE BLACKMUN delivered the opinion of the Court.

In this case we must decide whether certain professional expenses incurred by a target corporation in the course of a friendly takeover are deductible by that corporation as "ordinary and necessary" business expenses under § 162(a) of the Internal Revenue Code.

I

Most of the relevant facts are stipulated. . . . Petitioner INDOPCO, Inc., formerly named National Starch and Chemical Corporation and hereinafter referred to as National Starch, is a Delaware corporation that manufactures and sells adhesives, starches, and specialty chemical products. In October 1977, representatives of Unilever United States, Inc., also a Delaware corporation (Unilever), expressed interest in acquiring National Starch, which was one of its suppliers, through a friendly transaction. National Starch at the time had outstanding over 6,563,000 common shares held by approximately 3,700 shareholders. The stock was listed on the New York Stock Exchange. Frank and Anna Greenwall were the corporation's largest shareholders and owned approximately 14.5% of the common. The Greenwalls, getting along in years and concerned about their estate plans, indicated that they would transfer their shares to Unilever only if a transaction tax free for them could be arranged.

Lawyers representing both sides devised a "reverse subsidiary cash merger" that they felt would satisfy the Greenwalls' concerns. Two new entities would be created — National Starch and Chemical Holding Corp. (Holding), a subsidiary of Unilever, and NSC Merger, Inc., a subsidiary of Holding that would have only a transitory existence. In an exchange specifically designed to be tax free under § 351 of the Internal Revenue Code, 26 U.S.C. § 351, Holding would exchange one share of its nonvoting preferred stock for each share of National Starch common that it received from National Starch shareholders. Any National Starch common that was not so exchanged would be converted into cash in a merger of NSC Merger, Inc., into National Starch.

In November 1977, National Starch's directors were formally advised of Unilever's interest and the proposed transaction. At that time, Debevoise, Plimpton, Lyons & Gates, National Starch's counsel, told the directors that under Delaware law they had a fiduciary duty to ensure that the proposed transaction would be fair to the shareholders. National Starch thereupon engaged the investment banking firm of Morgan Stanley & Co., Inc., to evaluate its shares, to render a fairness opinion, and generally to assist in the event of the emergence of a hostile tender offer.

Although Unilever originally had suggested a price between $65 and $70 per share, negotiations resulted in a final offer of $73.50 per share, a figure Morgan

Stanley found to be fair. Following approval by National Starch's board and the issuance of a favorable private ruling from the Internal Revenue Service that the transaction would be tax free under § 351 for those National Starch shareholders who exchanged their stock for Holding preferred, the transaction was consummated in August 1978.[1]

Morgan Stanley charged National Starch a fee of $2,200,000, along with $7,586 for out-of-pocket expenses and $18,000 for legal fees. The Debevoise firm charged National Starch $490,000, along with $15,069 for out-of-pocket expenses. National Starch also incurred expenses aggregating $150,962 for miscellaneous items — such as accounting, printing, proxy solicitation, and Securities and Exchange Commission fees — in connection with the transaction. No issue is raised as to the propriety or reasonableness of these charges.

On its federal income tax return for its short taxable year ended August 15, 1978, National Starch claimed a deduction for the $2,225,586 paid to Morgan Stanley, but did not deduct the $505,069 paid to Debevoise or the other expenses. Upon audit, the Commissioner of Internal Revenue disallowed the claimed deduction and issued a notice of deficiency. Petitioner sought redetermination in the United States Tax Court, asserting, however, not only the right to deduct the investment banking fees and expenses but, as well, the legal and miscellaneous expenses incurred.

The Tax Court, in an unreviewed decision, ruled that the expenditures were capital in nature and therefore not deductible under § 162(a) in the 1978 return as "ordinary and necessary expenses." *National Starch and Chemical Corp. v. Commissioner*, 93 T.C. 67 (1989). The court based its holding primarily on the long-term benefits that accrued to National Starch from the Unilever acquisition. *Id.*, at 75. The United States Court of Appeals for the Third Circuit affirmed, upholding the Tax Court's findings that "both Unilever's enormous resources and the possibility of synergy arising from the transaction served the long-term betterment of National Starch." *National Starch & Chemical Corp. v. Commissioner*, 918 F.2d 426, 432-433 (1990). In so doing, the Court of Appeals rejected National Starch's contention that, because the disputed expenses did not "create or enhance . . . a separate and distinct additional asset," see *Commissioner v. Lincoln Savings & Loan Assn.*, 403 U.S. 345, 354 (1971), they could not be capitalized and therefore were deductible under § 162(a). 918 F.2d at 428-431. We granted certiorari to resolve a perceived conflict on the issue among the Courts of Appeals. . . .[1]

---

[1] [2] Approximately 21% of National Starch common was exchanged for Holding preferred. The remaining 79% was exchanged for cash. . . .

[1] [3] Compare the Third Circuit's opinion, 918 F.2d at 430, with *NCNB Corp.* v. *United States*, 684 F.2d 285, 293-294 (CA4 1982) (bank expenditures for expansion-related planning reports, feasibility studies, and regulatory applications did not "create or enhance separate and identifiable assets," and therefore were ordinary and necessary expenses under § 162(a)), and *Briarcliff Candy Corp.* v. *Commissioner*, 475 F.2d 775, 782 (CA2 1973) (suggesting that *Lincoln Savings* "brought about a radical shift in emphasis," making capitalization dependent on whether the expenditure creates or enhances a separate and distinct additional asset). See also *Central Texas Savings & Loan Assn.* v. *United States*, 731 F.2d 1181, 1184 (CA5 1984) (inquiring whether establishment of new branches "creates a separate and distinct additional asset" so that capitalization is the proper tax treatment).

II

Section 162(a) of the Internal Revenue Code allows the deduction of "all the ordinary and necessary expenses paid or incurred during the taxable year in carrying on any trade or business." 26 U.S.C. § 162(a). In contrast, § 263 of the Code allows no deduction for a capital expenditure — an "amount paid out for new buildings or for permanent improvements or betterments made to increase the value of any property or estate." § 263(a)(1). The primary effect of characterizing a payment as either a business expense or a capital expenditure concerns the timing of the taxpayer's cost recovery: While business expenses are currently deductible, a capital expenditure usually is amortized and depreciated over the life of the relevant asset, or, where no specific asset or useful life can be ascertained, is deducted upon dissolution of the enterprise. See 26 U.S.C. §§ 167(a) and 336(a); Treas. Reg. § 1.167(a) . . . (1991). Through provisions such as these, the Code endeavors to match expenses with the revenues of the taxable period to which they are properly attributable, thereby resulting in a more accurate calculation of net income for tax purposes. See, *e. g.*, *Commissioner v. Idaho Power Co.*, 418 U.S. 1, 16 (1974); . . .

In exploring the relationship between deductions and capital expenditures, this Court has noted the "familiar rule" that "an income tax deduction is a matter of legislative grace and that the burden of clearly showing the right to the claimed deduction is on the taxpayer." *Interstate Transit Lines v. Commissioner*, 319 U.S. 590, 593 (1943); *Deputy v. Du Pont*, 308 U.S. 488, 493 (1940); *New Colonial Ice Co. v. Helvering*, 292 U.S. 435, 440 (1934). The notion that deductions are exceptions to the norm of capitalization finds support in various aspects of the Code. Deductions are specifically enumerated and thus are subject to disallowance in favor of capitalization. See §§ 161 and 261. Nondeductible capital expenditures, by contrast, are not exhaustively enumerated in the Code; rather than providing a "complete list of nondeductible expenditures," *Lincoln Savings*, 403 U.S. at 358, § 263 serves as a general means of distinguishing capital expenditures from current expenses. See *Commissioner v. Idaho Power Co.*, 418 U.S. at 16. For these reasons, deductions are strictly construed and allowed only "as there is a clear provision therefor." *New Colonial Ice Co. v. Helvering*, 292 U.S. at 440; *Deputy v. Du Pont*, 308 U.S. at 493.

The Court also has examined the interrelationship between the Code's business expense and capital expenditure provisions. In so doing, it has had occasion to parse § 162(a) and explore certain of its requirements. For example, in *Lincoln Savings*, we determined that, to qualify for deduction under § 162(a), "an item must (1) be 'paid or incurred during the taxable year,' (2) be for 'carrying on any trade or business,' (3) be an 'expense,' (4) be a 'necessary' expense, and (5) be an 'ordinary' expense." 403 U.S. at 352. See also *Commissioner v. Tellier*, 383 U.S. 687, 689 (1966) (the term "necessary" imposes "only the minimal requirement that the expense be 'appropriate and helpful' for 'the development of the [taxpayer's] business,' " quoting *Welch v. Helvering*, 290 U.S. 111 (1933)); *Deputy v. Du Pont*, 308 U.S. at 495 (to qualify as "ordinary," the expense must relate to a transaction "of common or frequent occurrence in the type of business involved"). The Court has recognized, however, that the "decisive distinctions" between current expenses and capital expenditures "are those of degree and not of kind," *Welch v. Helvering*, 290 U.S. at 114, and that because each case "turns on its special facts," *Deputy v. Du Pont*, 308

U.S. at 496, the cases sometimes appear difficult to harmonize. . . .

National Starch contends that the decision in *Lincoln Savings* changed these familiar backdrops and announced an exclusive test for identifying capital expenditures, a test in which "creation or enhancement of an asset" is a prerequisite to capitalization, and deductibility under § 162(a) is the rule rather than the exception. . . . We do not agree, for we conclude that National Starch has overread *Lincoln Savings*.

In *Lincoln Savings*, we were asked to decide whether certain premiums, required by federal statute to be paid by a savings and loan association to the Federal Savings and Loan Insurance Corporation (FSLIC), were ordinary and necessary expenses under § 162(a), as Lincoln Savings argued and the Court of Appeals had held, or capital expenditures under § 263, as the Commissioner contended. We found that the "additional" premiums, the purpose of which was to provide FSLIC with a secondary reserve fund in which each insured institution retained a pro rata interest recoverable in certain situations, "serve to create or enhance for Lincoln what is essentially a separate and distinct additional asset." 403 U.S. at 354. "As an inevitable consequence," we concluded, "the payment is capital in nature and not an expense, let alone an ordinary expense, deductible under § 162(a)." *Ibid.*

Lincoln Savings stands for the simple proposition that a taxpayer's expenditure that "serves to create or enhance . . . a separate and distinct" asset should be capitalized under § 263. It by no means follows, however, that *only* expenditures that create or enhance separate and distinct assets are to be capitalized under § 263. We had no occasion in *Lincoln Savings* to consider the tax treatment of expenditures that, unlike the additional premiums at issue there, did not create or enhance a specific asset, and thus the case cannot be read to preclude capitalization in other circumstances. In short, *Lincoln Savings* holds that the creation of a separate and distinct asset well may be a sufficient, but not a necessary, condition to classification as a capital expenditure. . . .

Nor does our statement in *Lincoln Savings*, 403 U.S. at 354, that "the presence of an ensuing benefit that may have some future aspect is not controlling" prohibit reliance on future benefit as a means of distinguishing an ordinary business expense from a capital expenditure.[6] Although the mere presence of an incidental future benefit — "*some* future aspect" — may not warrant capitalization, a taxpayer's realization of benefits beyond the year in which the expenditure is incurred is undeniably important in determining whether the appropriate tax treatment is immediate deduction or capitalization. See *United States v. Mississippi Chemical Corp.*, 405 U.S. 298, 310 (1972) (expense that "is of value in more than one taxable year" is a nondeductible capital expenditure); *Central Texas Savings & Loan Assn. v. United States*, 731 F.2d 1181, 1183 (CA5 1984) ("While the period of the benefits may not be controlling in all cases, it nonetheless remains a prominent, if not

[6] [6] Petitioner contends that, absent a separate-and-distinct-asset requirement for capitalization, a taxpayer will have no "principled basis" upon which to differentiate business expenses from capital expenditures. . . . We note, however, that grounding tax status on the existence of an asset would be unlikely to produce the bright-line rule that petitioner desires, given that the notion of an "asset" is itself flexible and amorphous. . . .

predominant, characteristic of a capital item"). Indeed, the text of the Code's capitalization provision, § 263(a)(1), which refers to "permanent improvements or betterments," itself envisions an inquiry into the duration and extent of the benefits realized by the taxpayer.

III

In applying the foregoing principles to the specific expenditures at issue in this case, we conclude that National Starch has not demonstrated that the investment banking, legal, and other costs it incurred in connection with Unilever's acquisition of its shares are deductible as ordinary and necessary business expenses under § 162(a).

Although petitioner attempts to dismiss the benefits that accrued to National Starch from the Unilever acquisition as "entirely speculative" or "merely incidental," . . . the Tax Court's and the Court of Appeals' findings that the transaction produced significant benefits to National Starch that extended beyond the tax year in question are amply supported by the record. For example, in commenting on the merger with Unilever, National Starch's 1978 "Progress Report" observed that the company would "benefit greatly from the availability of Unilever's enormous resources, especially in the area of basic technology." . . . Morgan Stanley's report to the National Starch board concerning the fairness to shareholders of a possible business combination with Unilever noted that National Starch management "feels that some synergy may exist with the Unilever organization given a) the nature of the Unilever chemical, paper, plastics and packaging operations . . . and b) the strong consumer products orientation of Unilever United States, Inc." . . .

In addition to these anticipated resource-related benefits, National Starch obtained benefits through its transformation from a publicly held, freestanding corporation into a wholly owned subsidiary of Unilever. The Court of Appeals noted that National Starch management viewed the transaction as " 'swapping approximately 3500 shareholders for one.' " . . . Following Unilever's acquisition of National Starch's outstanding shares, National Starch was no longer subject to what even it terms the "substantial" shareholder-relations expenses a publicly traded corporation incurs, including reporting and disclosure obligations, proxy battles, and derivative suits. . . . The acquisition also allowed National Starch, in the interests of administrative convenience and simplicity, to eliminate previously authorized but unissued shares of preferred and to reduce the total number of authorized shares of common from 8,000,000 to 1,000. . . .

Courts long have recognized that expenses such as these, " 'incurred for the purpose of changing the corporate structure for the benefit of future operations are not ordinary and necessary business expenses.' " *General Bancshares Corp. v. Commissioner*, 326 F.2d at 715 . . . . Deductions for professional expenses thus have been disallowed in a wide variety of cases concerning changes in corporate structure. Although support for these decisions can be found in the specific terms of § 162(a), which require that deductible expenses be "ordinary and necessary" and incurred "in carrying on any trade or business," courts more frequently have characterized an expenditure as capital in nature because "the purpose for which the expenditure is made has to do with the corporation's operations and betterment, sometimes with a continuing capital asset, for the duration of its existence or for the indefinite future or for a time somewhat longer than the current taxable year." *General Bancshares Corp. v. Commissioner*, 326 F.2d at 715. The rationale behind these decisions applies equally to the professional charges at issue in this case.

IV

The expenses that National Starch incurred in Unilever's friendly takeover do not qualify for deduction as "ordinary and necessary" business expenses under § 162(a). The fact that the expenditures do not create or enhance a separate and distinct additional asset is not controlling; the acquisition-related expenses bear the indicia of capital expenditures and are to be treated as such.

The judgment of the Court of Appeals is affirmed.

COMMISSIONER v. IDAHO POWER CO.

Supreme Court of the United States
418 U.S. 1 (1974)

MR. JUSTICE BLACKMUN delivered the opinion of the Court.

This case presents the sole issue whether, for federal income tax purposes, a taxpayer is entitled to a deduction from gross income, under § 167 (a) of the Internal Revenue Code of 1954, 26 U.S.C. § 167 (a), for depreciation on equipment the taxpayer owns and uses in the construction of its own capital facilities, or whether the capitalization provision of § 263 (a)(1) of the Code, 26 U.S.C. § 263 (a)(1), bars the deduction. . . .

I

Nearly all the relevant facts are stipulated. The taxpayer-respondent, Idaho Power Company, is a Maine corporation organized in 1915, with its principal place of business at Boise, Idaho. It is a public utility engaged in the production, transmission, distribution, and sale of electric energy. The taxpayer keeps its books and files its federal income tax returns on the calendar year accrual basis. The tax years at issue are 1962 and 1963.

For many years, the taxpayer has used its own equipment and employees in the construction of improvements and additions to its capital facilities. The major work has consisted of transmission lines, transmission switching stations, distribution lines, distribution stations, and connecting facilities.

During 1962 and 1963, the tax years in question, taxpayer owned and used in its business a wide variety of automotive transportation equipment, including passenger cars, trucks of all descriptions, power-operated equipment, and trailers. Radio communication devices were affixed to the equipment and were used in its daily operations. The transportation equipment was used in part for operation and maintenance and in part for the construction of capital facilities having a useful life of more than one year.

On its books, the taxpayer used various methods of charging costs incurred in connection with its transportation equipment either to current expense or to capital accounts. To the extent the equipment was used in construction, the taxpayer charged depreciation of the equipment, as well as all operating and maintenance costs (other than pension contributions and social security and motor vehicle taxes) to the capital assets so constructed. This was done either directly or through clearing accounts in accordance with procedures prescribed by the Federal Power Commission and adopted by the Idaho Public Utilities Commission.

For federal income tax purposes, however, the taxpayer treated the depreciation on transportation equipment differently. It claimed as a deduction from gross income *all* the year's depreciation on such equipment, including that portion attributable to its use in constructing capital facilities. The depreciation was computed on a composite life of 10 years and under straight-line and declining-balance methods. The other operating and maintenance costs the taxpayer had charged on its books to capital were not claimed as current expenses and were not deducted. . . .

Upon audit, the Commissioner of Internal Revenue disallowed the deduction for the construction-related depreciation. He ruled that that depreciation was a nondeductible capital expenditure to which § 263 (a)(1) had application. He added the amount of the depreciation so disallowed to the taxpayer's adjusted basis in its capital facilities, and then allowed a deduction for an appropriate amount of depreciation on the addition, computed over the useful life (30 years or more) of the property constructed. A deduction for depreciation of the transportation equipment to the extent of its use in day-to-day operation and maintenance was also allowed. . . .

The taxpayer asserts that its transportation equipment is used in its "trade or business" and that depreciation thereon is therefore deductible under § 167 (a)(1) of the Code. The Commissioner concedes that § 167 may be said to have a literal application to depreciation on equipment used in capital construction, . . . but contends that the provision must be read in light of § 263(a)(1) which specifically disallows any deduction for an amount "paid out for new buildings or for permanent improvements or betterments." He argues that § 263 takes precedence over § 167 by virtue of what he calls the "priority-ordering" terms (and what the taxpayer describes as "housekeeping" provisions) of § 161 of the Code, 26 U.S.C. § 161, and that sound principles of accounting and taxation mandate the capitalization of this depreciation.

It is worth noting the various items that are not at issue here. The mathematics, as such, is not in dispute. The taxpayer has capitalized, as part of its cost of acquisition of capital assets, the operating and maintenance costs (other than depreciation, pension contributions, and social security and motor vehicle taxes) of the transportation equipment attributable to construction. This is not contested. The Commissioner does not dispute that the portion of the transportation equipment's depreciation allocable to operation and maintenance of facilities, in contrast with construction thereof, qualifies as a deduction from gross income. There is no disagreement as to the allocation of depreciation between construction and maintenance. The issue, thus comes down primarily to a question of timing, . . .

that is, whether the construction-related depreciation is to be amortized and deducted over the *shorter* life of the equipment or, instead, is to be amortized and deducted over the *longer* life of the capital facilities constructed.

II

Our primary concern is with the necessity to treat construction-related depreciation in a manner that comports with accounting and taxation realities. Over a period of time a capital asset is consumed and, correspondingly over that period, its theoretical value and utility are thereby reduced. Depreciation is an accounting device which recognizes that the physical consumption of a capital asset is a true cost, since the asset is being depleted.[5] As the process of consumption continues, and depreciation is claimed and allowed, the asset's adjusted income tax basis is reduced to reflect the distribution of its cost over the accounting periods affected. The Court stated in *Hertz Corp.* v. *United States*, 364 U.S. 122, 126 (1960): "[The] purpose of depreciation accounting is to allocate the expense of using an asset to the various periods which are benefited by that asset." . . . When the asset is used to further the taxpayer's day-to-day business operations, the periods of benefit usually correlate with the production of income. Thus, to the extent that equipment is used in such operations, a current depreciation deduction is an appropriate offset to gross income currently produced. It is clear, however, that different principles are implicated when the consumption of the asset takes place in the construction of other assets that, in the future, will produce income themselves. In this latter situation, the cost represented by depreciation does not correlate with production of current income. Rather, the cost, although certainly presently incurred, is related to the future and is appropriately allocated as part of the cost of acquiring an income-producing capital asset.

The Court of Appeals opined that the purpose of the depreciation allowance under the Code was to provide a means of cost recovery, *Knoxville v. Knoxville Water Co.*, 212 U.S. 1, 13-14 (1909), and that this Court's decisions, *e. g., Detroit Edison Co.* v. *Commissioner*, 319 U.S. 98, 101 (1943), endorse a theory of replacement through "a fund to restore the property." 477 F.2d, at 691. Although tax-free replacement of a depreciating investment is one purpose of depreciation accounting, it alone does not require the result claimed by the taxpayer here. Only last Term, in *United States v. Chicago, B.&Q.R. Co.*, 412 U.S. 401 (1973), we rejected replacement as the strict and sole purpose of depreciation:

> "Whatever may be the desirability of creating a depreciation reserve under these circumstances, as a matter of good business and accounting practice,

---

[5] [7] The Committee on Terminology of the American Institute of Certified Public Accountants has discussed various definitions of depreciation and concluded that:

> "These definitions view depreciation, broadly speaking, as describing not downward changes of value regardless of their causes but a money cost incident to exhaustion of usefulness. The term is sometimes applied to the exhaustion itself, but the committee considers it desirable to emphasize the cost concept as the primary if not the sole accounting meaning of the term: thus, *depreciation* means the cost of such exhaustion, as *wages* means the cost of labor."

2 APB Accounting Principles, Accounting Terminology Bulletin No. 1 — Review and Resume para. 48, p. 9512 (1973) (emphasis in original).

> the answer is . . . [depreciation] reflects the cost of an existing capital asset, not the cost of a potential replacement.' " *Id.*, at 415.

Even were we to look to replacement, it is the replacement of the constructed facilities, not the equipment used to build them, with which we would be concerned. If the taxpayer now were to decide not to construct any more capital facilities with its own equipment and employees, it, in theory, would have no occasion to replace its equipment to the extent that it was consumed in prior construction.

Accepted accounting practice and established tax principles require the capitalization of the cost of acquiring a capital asset. In *Woodward v. Commissioner*, 397 U.S. 572, 575 (1970), the Court observed: "It has long been recognized, as a general matter, that costs incurred in the acquisition . . . of a capital asset are to be treated as capital expenditures." This principle has obvious application to the acquisition of a capital asset by purchase, but it has been applied, as well, to the costs incurred in a taxpayer's construction of capital facilities. . . .

There can be little question that other construction-related expense items, such as tools, materials, and wages paid construction workers, are to be treated as part of the cost of acquisition of a capital asset. The taxpayer does not dispute this. Of course, reasonable wages paid in the carrying on of a trade or business qualify as a deduction from gross income. § 162(a)(1) of the 1954 Code, 26 U.S.C. § 162 (a)(1). But when wages are paid in connection with the construction or acquisition of a capital asset, they must be capitalized and are then entitled to be amortized over the life of the capital asset so acquired. . . .

Construction-related depreciation is not unlike expenditures for wages for construction workers. The significant fact is that the exhaustion of construction equipment does not represent the final disposition of the taxpayer's investment in that equipment; rather, the investment in the equipment is assimilated into the cost of the capital asset constructed. Construction-related depreciation on the equipment is not an expense to the taxpayer of its day-to-day business. It is, however, appropriately recognized as a part of the taxpayer's cost or investment in the capital asset. The taxpayer's own accounting procedure reflects this treatment, for on its books the construction-related depreciation was capitalized by a credit to the equipment account and a debit to the capital facility account. By the same token, this capitalization prevents the distortion of income that would otherwise occur if depreciation properly allocable to asset acquisition were deducted from gross income currently realized. . . .

An additional pertinent factor is that capitalization of construction-related depreciation by the taxpayer who does its own construction work maintains tax parity with the taxpayer who has its construction work done by an independent contractor. The depreciation on the contractor's equipment incurred during the performance of the job will be an element of cost charged by the contractor for his construction services, and the entire cost, of course, must be capitalized by the taxpayer having the construction work performed. The Court of Appeals' holding would lead to disparate treatment among taxpayers because it would allow the firm with sufficient resources to construct its own facilities and to obtain a current deduction, whereas another firm without such resources would be required to capitalize its entire cost including depreciation charged to it by the contractor.

Some, although not controlling, weight must be given to the fact that the Federal Power Commission and the Idaho Public Utilities Commission required the taxpayer to use accounting procedures that capitalized construction-related depreciation. Although agency-imposed compulsory accounting practices do not necessarily dictate tax consequences, *Old Colony R. Co.* v. *Commissioner*, 284 U.S. 552, 562 (1932), they are not irrelevant and may be accorded some significance. *Commissioner v. Lincoln Savings & Loan Assn.*, 403 U.S. 345, 355-356 (1971). The opinions in *American Automobile Assn.* v. *United States*, 367 U.S. 687 (1961), and *Schlude v. Commissioner*, 372 U.S. 128 (1963), urged upon us by the taxpayer here, are not to the contrary. In the former case it was observed that merely because the method of accounting a taxpayer employs is in accordance with generally accepted accounting procedures, this "is not to hold that for income tax purposes it so clearly reflects income as to be binding on the Treasury." 367 U.S., at 693. . . . Nonetheless, where a taxpayer's generally accepted method of accounting is made compulsory by the regulatory agency *and* that method clearly reflects income, it is almost presumptively controlling of federal income tax consequences.

The presence of § 263(a)(1) in the Code is of significance. Its literal language denies a deduction for "[any] amount paid out" for construction or permanent improvement of facilities. The taxpayer contends, and the Court of Appeals held, that depreciation of construction equipment represents merely a decrease in value and is not an amount "paid out," within the meaning of § 263(a)(1). We disagree.

The purpose of § 263 is to reflect the basic principle that a capital expenditure may not be deducted from current income. It serves to prevent a taxpayer from utilizing currently a deduction properly attributable, through amortization, to later tax years when the capital asset becomes income producing. The regulations state that the capital expenditures to which § 263(a) extends include the "cost of acquisition, construction, or erection of buildings." Treas. Reg. § 1.263 (a)-2 (a). This manifests an administrative understanding that for purposes of § 263(a)(1), "amount paid out" equates with "cost incurred." The Internal Revenue Service for some time has taken the position that construction-related depreciation is to be capitalized. Rev. Rul. 59-380, 1959-2 Cum. Bull. 87; Rev. Rul. 55-252, 1955-1 Cum. Bull. 319.

There is no question that the cost of the transportation equipment was "paid out" in the same manner as the cost of supplies, materials, and other equipment, and the wages of construction workers. The taxpayer does not question the capitalization of these other items as elements of the cost of acquiring a capital asset. We see no reason to treat construction-related depreciation differently. In acquiring the transportation equipment, taxpayer "paid out" the equipment's purchase price; depreciation is simply the means of allocating the payment over the various accounting periods affected. As the Tax Court stated in *Brooks v. Commissioner*, 50 T.C., at 935, "depreciation — inasmuch as it represents a using up of capital — is as much an 'expenditure' as the using up of labor or other items of direct cost."

Finally, the priority-ordering directive of § 161 — or, for that matter, § 261 of the Code, 26 U. S. C. § 261 — requires that the capitalization provision of § 263(a) take precedence, on the facts here, over § 167(a). Section 161 provides that deductions specified in Part VI of Subchapter B of the Income Tax Subtitle of the Code are "subject to the exceptions provided in part IX." Part VI includes § 167 and Part IX includes § 263. The clear import of § 161 is that, with stated exceptions set forth either in § 263 itself or provided for elsewhere (as, for example, in § 404 relating to pension contributions), none of which is applicable here, an expenditure incurred in acquiring capital assets must be capitalized even when the expenditure otherwise might be deemed deductible under Part VI.

The Court of Appeals concluded, without reference to § 161, that § 263 did not apply to a deduction, such as that for depreciation of property used in a trade or business, allowed by the Code even though incurred in the construction of capital assets. We think that the court erred in espousing so absolute a rule, and it obviously overlooked the contrary direction of § 161. To the extent that reliance was placed on the congressional intent, in the evolvement of the 1954 Code, to provide for "liberalization of depreciation," H. R. Rep. No. 1337, 83d Cong., 2d Sess., 22 (1954), that reliance is misplaced. The House Report also states that the depreciation provisions would "give the economy added stimulus and resilience without departing from realistic standards of depreciation accounting." *Id.*, at 24. To be sure, the 1954 Code provided for new and accelerated methods for depreciation, resulting in the greater depreciation deductions currently available. These changes, however, relate primarily to computation of depreciation. Congress certainly did not intend that provisions for accelerated depreciation should be construed as enlarging the class of depreciable assets to which § 167(a) has application or as lessening the reach of § 263(a). . . .

We hold that the equipment depreciation allocable to taxpayer's construction of capital facilities is to be capitalized.

The judgment of the Court of Appeals is reversed.

It is so ordered.

MR. JUSTICE DOUGLAS, dissenting.

This Court has, to many, seemed particularly ill-equipped to resolve income tax disputes between the Commissioner and the taxpayers. The reasons are (1) that the field has become increasingly technical and complicated due to the expansions of the Code and the proliferation of decisions, and (2) that we seldom see enough of them to develop any expertise in the area. Indeed, we are called upon mostly to resolve conflicts between the circuits which more providently should go to the standing committee of the Congress for resolution.

That was the sentiment behind *Dobson v. Commissioner*, 320 U.S. 489, written by Mr. Justice Jackson and enthusiastically promoted by Mr. Justice Black, Mr. Justice Frankfurter, and myself. *Dobson*, save for egregious error and constitutional questions, would have left picayune cases such as the present one largely to the Tax Court, whose expertise is well recognized. But *Dobson* was short-lived, as Congress made clear its purpose that we were to continue on our leaden-footed pursuit of law and justice in this field. Internal Revenue Code of 1939, § 1141, as amended, 62 Stat. 991.

Now that we are on our own I disagree with the Court in disallowing the present claim for depreciation. A company truck has, let us say, a life of 10 years. If it cost $10,000, one would expect that "a reasonable allowance for the exhaustion, wear and tear" of the truck would be $1,000 a year within the meaning of 26 U.S.C. § 167(a). That was the provision in the House Report of the 1954 Code when it said that it provided for "a liberalization of depreciation with respect to both the estimate of useful life of property and the method of allocating the depreciable cost over the years of service." H. R. Rep. No. 1337, 83d Cong., 2d Sess., 22.

Not so, says the Government. Since the truck was used to build a plant for the taxpayer and the plant has a useful life of 40 years, a lower rate of depreciation must be used — a rate that would spread out the life of the truck for 40 years even though it would not last more than 10. Section 167(a) provides for a depreciation deduction with respect to property "used in the (taxpayer's) trade or business" or "held for the production of income" by the taxpayer. There is no intimation that § 167(a) is not satisfied. The argument is rested upon § 161 which allows the deductions specified in § 167(a) "subject to the exceptions" in § 263 (a) which provides:

> "No deduction shall be allowed for —
>
> "(1) Any amount paid out for new buildings or for permanent improvements or for betterments made to increase the value of any property or estate . . . ."

I agree with the Court of Appeals that depreciation claimed on a truck whose useful life is 10 years is not an amount "paid out" within the meaning of § 263 (a)(1). If "payment" in the setting of § 263(a)(1) is to be read as including depreciation, Congress — not the courts — should make the decision.

I suspect that if the life of the vehicle were 40 years and the life of the building were 10 years the Internal Revenue Service would be here arguing persuasively that depreciation of the vehicle should be taken over a 40-year period. That is not to impugn the integrity of the IRS. It is only an illustration of the capricious character of how law is construed to get from the taxpayer the greatest possible return that is permissible under the Code. . . .

The IRS, however, has ruled that depreciation on construction equipment owned by a taxpayer and used in its construction work must be capitalized. That Revenue Ruling, as the Court of Appeals held, is a legal opinion within the agency, not a Regulation or Treasury decision. It is without force when it conflicts with an Act of Congress.

If the test under § 263(a)(1) were the cost of capital improvements, the result would be different. But, as noted, the test is "any amount paid out," which certainly does not describe depreciation deductions unless words are to acquire esoteric meanings merely to accommodate the IRS. Congress is the lawmaker; and taking the law from it, we should affirm the Court of Appeals.

ENCYCLOPAEDIA BRITANNICA, INC. v. COMMISSIONER

United States Court of APPEALS, Seventh Circuit
685 F.2d 212 (1982)

POSNER, CIRCUIT JUDGE.

Section 162(a) of the Internal Revenue Code of 1954, 26 U.S.C. § 162(a), allows the deduction of "all the ordinary and necessary expenses paid or incurred during the taxable year in carrying on any trade or business . . . ," but this is qualified (see 26 U.S.C. § 161) by section 263(a) of the Code, which forbids the immediate deduction of "capital expenditures" even if they are ordinary and necessary business expenses. We must decide in this case whether certain expenditures made by Encyclopaedia Britannica, Inc. to acquire a manuscript were capital expenditures.

Encyclopaedia Britannica decided to publish a book to be called The Dictionary of Natural Sciences. Ordinarily it would have prepared the book in-house, but being temporarily short-handed it hired David-Stewart Publishing Company "to do all necessary research work and to prepare, edit and arrange the manuscript and all illustrative and other material for" the book. Under the contract David-Stewart agreed "to work closely with" Encyclopaedia Britannica's editorial board "so that the content and arrangement of the Work (and any revisions thereof) will conform to the idea and desires of [Encyclopaedia Britannica] and be acceptable to it"; but it was contemplated that David-Stewart would turn over a complete manuscript that Encyclopaedia Britannica would copyright, publish, and sell, and in exchange would receive advances against the royalties that Encyclopaedia Britannica expected to earn from the book.

Encyclopaedia Britannica treated these advances as ordinary and necessary business expenses deductible in the years when they were paid, though it had not yet obtained any royalties. The Internal Revenue Service disallowed the deductions and assessed deficiencies. Encyclopaedia Britannica petitioned the Tax Court for a redetermination of its tax liability, and prevailed. The Tax Court held that the expenditures were for "services" rather than for the acquisition of an asset and concluded that therefore they were deductible immediately rather than being, as the Service had ruled, capital expenditures. "The agreement provided for substantial editorial supervision by [Encyclopaedia Britannica]. Indeed, David-Stewart's work product was to be the embodiment of [Encyclopaedia Britannica's] ideas and desires. David-Stewart was just the vehicle selected by [Encyclopaedia Britannica] to assist . . . with the editorial phase of the Work." Encyclopaedia Britannica was "the owner of the Work at all stages of completion" and "the dominating force associated with the Work." . . .

As an original matter we would have no doubt that the payments to David-Stewart were capital expenditures regardless of who was the "dominating force" in the creation of The Dictionary of Natural Sciences. The work was intended to yield Encyclopaedia Britannica income over a period of years. The object of sections 162 and 263 of the Code, read together, is to match up expenditures with the income they generate. Where the income is generated over a period of years the expenditures should be classified as capital, contrary to what the Tax Court did here. From the publisher's standpoint a book is just another rental property; and just as the expenditures in putting a building into shape to be rented must be capitalized, so, logically at least, must the expenditures used to create a book. It would make no difference under this view whether Encyclopaedia Britannica hired David-Stewart as a mere consultant to its editorial board, which is the Tax Court's conception of what happened, or bought outright from David-Stewart the right to a book that David-Stewart had already published. If you hire a carpenter to build a tree house that you plan to rent out, his wage is a capital expenditure to you. See Commissioner of Internal Revenue v. Idaho Power Co., 418 U.S. 1, 13 (1974).

We are not impressed by Encyclopaedia Britannica's efforts to conjure up practical difficulties in matching expenditures on a book to the income from it. What, it asks, would have been the result if it had scrapped a portion of the manuscript it received from David-Stewart? Would that be treated as the partial destruction of a capital asset, entitling it to an immediate deduction? We think not. The proper analogy is to loss or breakage in the construction of our hypothetical tree house. The effect would be to increase the costs of construction, which are deductible over the useful life of the asset. If the scrapped portion of the manuscript was replaced, the analogy would be perfect. If it was not replaced, the tax consequence would be indirect: an increase or decrease in the publisher's taxable income from the published book.

What does give us pause, however, is a series of decisions in which authors of books have been allowed to treat their expenses as ordinary and necessary business expenses that are deductible immediately even though they were incurred in the creation of long-lived assets — the books the authors were writing. The leading case is Faura v. Commissioner, 73 T.C. 849 (1980); it was discussed with approval just recently by a panel of the Tenth Circuit in Snyder v. United States, 674 F.2d 1359, 1365 (10th Cir. 1982), and was relied on heavily by the Tax Court in the present case.

We can think of a practical reason for allowing authors to deduct their expenses immediately, one applicable as well to publishers though not in the circumstances of the present case. If you are in the business of producing a series of assets that will yield income over a period of years — which is the situation of most authors and all publishers — identifying particular expenditures with particular books, a necessary step for proper capitalization because the useful lives of the books will not be the same, may be very difficult, since the expenditures of an author or publisher (more clearly the latter) tend to be joint among several books. Moreover, allocating these expenditures among the different books is not always necessary to produce the temporal matching of income and expenditures that the Code desiderates, because the taxable income of the author or publisher who is in a steady state (that is, whose output is neither increasing nor decreasing) will be at least approximately the same whether his costs are expensed or capitalized. Not the same on any given book — on each book expenses and receipts will be systematically mismatched — but the same on average. Under these conditions the benefits of capitalization are unlikely to exceed the accounting and other administrative costs entailed in capitalization.

Yet we hesitate to endorse the *Faura* line of cases: not only because of the evident tension between them and *Idaho Power*, supra, where the Supreme Court said that expenses, whatever their character, must be capitalized if they are incurred in creating a capital asset, but also because *Faura*, and cases following it such as *Snyder*, fail in our view to articulate a persuasive rationale for their result. *Faura* relied on cases holding that the normal expenses of authors and other artists are deductible business expenses rather than nondeductible personal expenses, and on congressional evidence of dissatisfaction with the Internal Revenue Service's insistence that such expenses be capitalized. See 73 T.C. at 852-61. But most of the cases in question (including all those at the court of appeals level), such as Doggett v. Burnet, 65 F.2d 191 (D.C. Cir. 1933), are inapposite, because they consider only whether the author's expenditures are deductible at all — not whether, if they are deductible, they must first be capitalized. . . .

Yet despite all this we need not decide whether *Faura* is good law, and we are naturally reluctant to precipitate a conflict with the Tenth Circuit. The Tax Court interpreted *Faura* too broadly in this case. As we interpret *Faura* its principle comes into play only when the taxpayer is in the business of producing a series of assets that yield the taxpayer income over a period of years, so that a complex allocation would be necessary if the taxpayer had to capitalize all his expenses of producing them. This is not such a case. The expenditures at issue are unambiguously identified with The Dictionary of Natural Sciences. We need not consider the proper tax treatment of any other expenses that Encyclopaedia Britannica may have incurred on the project — editorial expenses, for example — as they are not involved in this case. Those expenses would be analogous to author Faura's office and travel expenses; they are the normal, recurrent expenses of operating a business that happens to produce capital assets. This case is like *Idaho Power*, supra. The expenditure there was on transportation equipment used in constructing capital facilities that Idaho Power employed in its business of producing and distributing electricity, and was thus unambiguously identified with specific capital assets, just as Encyclopaedia Britannica's payment to David-Stewart for the manuscript of The Dictionary of Natural Sciences was unambiguously identified with a specific capital asset.

It is also relevant that the commissioning of the manuscript from David-Stewart was somewhat out of the ordinary for Encyclopaedia Britannica. Now the word "ordinary" in section 162 of the Internal Revenue Code has two different uses: to prevent the deduction of certain expenses that are not normally incurred in the type of business in which the taxpayer is engaged ("ordinary" in this sense blends imperceptibly into "necessary"), Deputy v. du Pont, 308 U.S. 488, 495 (1940); Trustees of Graceland Cemetery Improvement Fund v. United States, 515 F.2d 763, 778 (Ct. Cl. 1975), and to clarify the distinction between expenses that are immediately deductible and expenses that must first be capitalized, Commissioner v. Tellier, 383 U.S. 687, 689-90 (1966). (A merging of these two distinct senses of the word is a possible explanation for the result in *Faura*.) Most of the "ordinary," in the sense of recurring, expenses of a business are noncapital in nature and most of its capital expenditures are extraordinary in the sense of nonrecurring. Here, as arguably in *Idaho Power* as well — for Idaho Power's business was the production and distribution of electricity, rather than the construction of buildings — the taxpayer stepped out of its normal method of doing business. In this particular project Encyclopaedia Britannica was operating like a conventional publisher, which obtains a complete manuscript from an author or in this case a compiler. The conventional publisher may make a considerable contribution to the work both at the idea stage and at the editorial stage but the deal is for a manuscript, not for services in assisting the publisher to prepare the manuscript itself. Yet we need not consider whether a conventional publisher should be permitted to deduct royalty advances made to its authors as current operating expenses, merely because those advances are for it recurring business expenses because its business is producing capital assets. *Idaho Power*, though factually distinguishable, implies one answer to this question (no), [and] *Faura* another (yes) . . . . But the principle of *Faura*, whatever its soundness, comes into play only when the expenditure sought to be immediately deducted is a normal and recurrent expense of the business, as it was not here. . . .

There is another point to be noted about the distinction between recurring and nonrecurring expenses and its bearing on the issue in this case. If one really takes seriously the concept of a capital expenditure as anything that yields income, actual or imputed, beyond the period (conventionally one year, United States v. Wehrli, 400 F.2d 686, 689 (10th Cir. 1968)) in which the expenditure is made, the result will be to force the capitalization of virtually every business expense. It is a result courts naturally shy away from. . . . It would require capitalizing every salesman's salary, since his selling activities create goodwill for the company and goodwill is an asset yielding income beyond the year in which the salary expense is incurred. The administrative costs of conceptual rigor are too great. The distinction between recurring and nonrecurring business expenses provides a very crude but perhaps serviceable demarcation between those capital expenditures that can feasibly be capitalized and those that cannot be. Whether the distinction breaks down where, as in the case of the conventional publisher, the firm's entire business is the production of capital assets, so that it is literally true that all of its business expenses are capital in nature, is happily not a question we have to decide here, for it is clear that Encyclopaedia Britannica's payments to David-Stewart were of a nonnormal, nonrecurrent nature.

In light of all that we have said, the contention that really what David-Stewart did here was to render consulting services to Encyclopaedia Britannica no different from the services of a consultant whom Encyclopaedia Britannica might have hired on one of its in-house projects, which if true would make the payments more "ordinary" in the *Faura* sense, is of doubtful relevance. . . . This was a turnkey project, remote from what is ordinarily understood by editorial consultation. While maybe some creators or buyers of capital goods — some authors and publishers — may deduct as current expenses what realistically are capital expenditures, they may not do so . . . when the expense is tied to producing or acquiring a specific capital asset. . . .

REVERSED AND REMANDED.

NOTES AND COMMENTS

The decisions in *INDOPCO*, *Idaho Power*, and *Encyclopaedia Britannica* provide a context for the issues that arise in determining whether an expenditure is properly capitalized or deducted. Of course, taxpayers prefer a result in which capitalization can be avoided. Perhaps because of the tremendous amount of controversy and uncertainty in this area under such general standards, as well as the lack of uniformity that can result in the treatment of taxpayers, both Congress and the Service have attempted to provide greater guidance through statutory and regulatory means. In 1986, Congress took the first step by enacting § 263A which, along with its implementing Regulations, was intended to provide a consistent, uniform, and comprehensive set of rules applicable to capitalization of costs incurred in the acquisition, production, holding, and disposition of tangible property. More recently, the Service has promulgated Regulations under § 263 providing detailed guidance concerning the capitalization of costs incurred to acquire or create intangible assets (Reg. §§ 1.263(a)-4) and Proposed Regulations concerning the capitalization of amounts paid to acquire, produce, or improve real or personal property (Prop. Reg. §§ 1.263(a)-2 and 1.263(a)-3). To a large degree, the judicial decisions that previously served as the primary guidance concerning capitalization have been rendered irrelevant as a result of these statutory and regulatory developments.

§ 2.02. Uniform Capitalization Rules

I.R.C. § 263A

Treas. Reg. §§ 1.263A-1(a)(1), (a)(3), (b)(1), (b)(5), (b)(9), (b)(11), (c), (e), (f), and (g); 1.263A-2(a)(1)(i), (a)(2), and (a)(3)

Section 263A requires the capitalization of a wide variety of costs attributable to property produced by the taxpayer or acquired for resale in a trade or business or an activity conducted for profit. Allocable costs include the direct costs of producing or acquiring such property and the property's share of any indirect costs. For example, manufacturers are subject to § 263A, and the direct and indirect costs incurred are included in the cost of goods sold of the inventory held by the manufacturer. For taxpayers who produce property for their own use, the direct and indirect costs are included in the basis of the property produced. According to the legislative history to § 263A, the purpose behind its enactment was to provide a consistent, uniform, and comprehensive set of rules applicable to capitalization of costs incurred in the acquisition, production, holding, and disposition of property. H.R. Rep. No. 426, 99th Cong., 2d Sess. 615–638 (1986); S. Rep. No. 313, 99th Cong., 2d Sess. 133–152 (1986).

Specifically, § 263A defines "property" as real or tangible personal property produced by the taxpayer and real and personal property acquired by the taxpayer for resale to customers. I.R.C. § 263A(b); Reg. § 1.263A-1(a)(3). Nevertheless, tangible personal property for purposes of § 263A also includes films, sound recordings, videotapes, books, and other "similar" forms of property that are intended to be produced on a tangible medium and mass distributed in a form that is not substantially altered. I.R.C. § 263A(b); Reg. § 1.263A-2(a)(2) Thus, the costs of authoring a book, including the costs of producing a manuscript and procuring a copyright or license for the project, must be capitalized. It should be noted that a taxpayer must distinguish between the production of property and the provision of services because § 263A does not apply to the provision of services by a bona-fide service provider. Reg. § 1.263A-1(b)(11). Examples of service providers include taxpayers performing services in the fields of health, law, engineering, architecture, accounting, actuarial science, performing arts, and consulting. In addition, § 263A may not be applicable, even where the provision of services results in the production of tangible personal property. Reg. §§ 1.263A-1(b)(11). For example, § 263A does not require capitalization of expenditures incurred in an attorney's production of a will or an architect's production of blueprints because the production of property is incidental to the services rendered. Reg. § 1.263A-2(a)(2)(ii)(*B*)(*2*).

The Regulations under § 263A describe the types of costs that must be capitalized. Taxpayers must capitalize all direct, and certain indirect, costs allocable to the production of property. Direct costs include both direct material costs and direct labor costs. "Direct material costs" are defined as "the costs of those materials that become an integral part of specific property produced and those materials that are consumed in the ordinary course of production and that can be identified or associated with particular units or groups of units of property produced." Reg. § 1.263A-1(e)(2)(i)(*A*). Similarly, "direct labor costs" are defined as "costs of labor that can be identified or associated with particular units or groups of units of specific property produced." Reg. § 1.263A-1(e)(2)(i)(*B*).

Indirect costs that must be capitalized include all costs other than direct costs. Indirect costs are properly allocable to property when the costs "directly benefit or are incurred by reason of the performance of production or resale activities." Reg. § 1.263A-1(e)(3)(i). Examples of indirect costs include the following:

1. Indirect labor costs, officers' compensation, pension and other related costs, and employee benefit expenses;
2. Indirect material costs, purchasing costs, handling costs, and storage costs;
3. Cost recovery, including depreciation, amortization, and depletion;
4. Rent, taxes, insurance, utilities, repair and maintenance;
5. Engineering and design costs, spoilage, tools and equipment, and quality control;
6. Bidding costs, licensing and franchise costs, interest, and capitalizable service costs.

Reg. § 1.263A-1(e)(3)(ii). For example, in *Plastic Eng'g & Tech. Servs., Inc. v. Commissioner*, T.C. Memo. 2001-324, the court required the capitalization of royalty payments incurred by a patent licensee as indirect costs under § 263A to be recovered over time through the taxpayer's cost of goods sold. The Regulations specify a number of methods by which such costs may be allocated among property produced by the taxpayer. Reg. §§ 1.263A-1(f) and 1.263A-1(g)(3). Despite the general language of the Regulations, the capitalization of certain costs, such as licensing and franchise costs, will depend on the manner in which the payment of such costs is structured. In *Robinson Knife Mfg. Co. v. Commissioner*, 600 F.3d 121 (2d Cir. 2010), the Second Circuit addressed the deductibility of trademark royalty payments paid to third-party licensors and concluded that royalty payments: (1) calculated as a percentage of sales revenue from certain inventory and (2) incurred only upon sale of such inventory are not capitalizable under

§ 263A. The decision does not apply, however, to non-sales-based royalties such as manufacturing-based or minimum royalties.

Despite this seemingly comprehensive list of indirect costs, the Regulations specify a number of types of indirect costs that are *not* capitalized. Reg. §§ 1.263A-1(e)(3)(iii). These noncapitalizable costs include marketing, selling, advertising, and distribution costs, as well as general management and administrative costs that are not incurred by reason of the performance of production or resale activities of the taxpayer.

As noted above, § 263A also requires the capitalization of costs incurred in connection with property acquired for resale. Under § 263A(b)(2), property acquired for resale includes real or personal property described in § 1221(1) and, thus, includes stock in trade, inventory, and property held primarily for sale to customers in the ordinary course of a trade or business. Unlike § 263A(b)(1), which applies to "real or tangible personal property" produced by the taxpayer, § 263A(b)(2) applies to "real and personal property." Consequently, § 263A(b)(2) applies to intangible, as well as tangible, property acquired by the taxpayer for resale. Reg. § 1.263A-3(a)(1).

The Code provides an exception from the capitalization rules of § 263A for personal property acquired for resale when the average of the taxpayer's gross receipts for the previous three taxable years does not exceed $10 million. IRC § 263A(b)(2)(B); Reg. § 1.263A-3(b). For purposes of this exception, gross receipts means the total amount, computed under the taxpayer's accounting method, received from all trades and businesses carried on by the taxpayer. Gross receipts do not include, however, amounts representing returns or allowances, receipts from sales not in the ordinary course of business, receipts from the sale or exchange of capital assets or interest, dividends, rent, annuities, or royalties not derived in the ordinary course of a trade or business.

As noted above, § 263A is applicable to real and tangible personal property "produced" by the taxpayer. Section 263A(g)(1) states that the term "produce" includes "construct, build, install, manufacture, develop, or improve." IRC § 263A(g)(1). *See also* Reg. § 1.263A-2(a)(1) (stating that the term "produce" includes "construct, build, install, manufacture, develop, improve, create, raise, or grow"). However, taxpayers must capitalize all direct and indirect costs allocable to the production of property even though production has not begun. Reg. § 1.263A-2(a)(3). Thus, for example, "a manufacturer must capitalize the costs of storing and handling raw materials before the raw materials are committed to production. In addition, a real estate developer must capitalize property taxes incurred with respect to property if, at the time the taxes are incurred, it is reasonably likely that the property will be subsequently developed." Reg. § 1.263A-2(a)(3)(ii). Similarly, indirect costs, such as storage and handling costs, incurred after production must also be capitalized. Reg. § 1.263A-2(a)(3)(iii).

In *Von-Lusk v. Commissioner*, 104 T.C. 207 (1995), a case involving taxable years prior to the effective date of the current Regulations, the Tax Court interpreted the term "produce" broadly in the context of costs incurred in the development of real property. The taxpayer in *Von-Lusk* challenged the Commissioner's denial of current deductions for the costs incurred for consultants, advertising, insurance, market research, and independent contractors in connection with a real estate development. The taxpayer contended that § 263A was inapplicable. According to the taxpayer, the costs were not incurred to produce property because no physical change had yet occurred on the property. Despite the "superficial appeal" of the taxpayer's argument, the Tax Court held that § 263A applied to the preliminary, nonphysical aspects of the development.

> While the pursuit of building permits and zoning variances, negotiating permit fees and similar activities may not readily spring to mind as examples of production activity, we think that upon reflection they are properly classifiable as such. Such activities are ancillary to actual physical work on the land and are as much a part of a development project as digging a foundation or completing a structure's frame. The project cannot move forward if these steps are not taken.
>
> Von-Lusk took purposeful steps to begin the development of the property. Petitioner attempts to place weight on the fact that Von-Lusk was formed with the stated purpose of managing, holding, and developing property for investment. Petitioner claims Von-Lusk's activities never went beyond managing and holding. The stipulated facts indicate otherwise. Meeting with government officials, obtaining building permits and zoning variances, negotiating permit fees, performing engineering and feasibility studies, drafting architectural plans, and appealing development conditions go beyond managing and holding. *These activities represent the first steps of development.*

Id. at 216 (emphasis in original). *See also Tsakopoulos v. Commissioner*, T.C. Memo. 2002-8 (holding that § 263A requires the capitalization of real estate taxes paid after the taxpayer filed a document with the local county outlining plans to subdivide the property and a request to change the applicable zoning); Rev. Rul. 2002-9, 2002-1 C.B. 614 (concluding that local impact fees incurred by a taxpayer in connection with the construction of a new residential rental building are capitalized costs allocable to the building under §§ 263(a) and 263A). *But see Hustead v. Commissioner*, T.C. Memo. 1994-374, *aff'd without pub. op.*, 61 F.3d 895 (3d Cir. 1995) (declining to broadly define the term "produce" to require the capitalization of costs incurred in settling a successful challenge to the constitutionality of a zoning ordinance that resulted in an increase in the value of the taxpayer's property).

However, a different rule applies in connection with the capitalization of interest under § 263A(f). Section 263(f) requires the capitalization of only interest incurred during the "production period" and then only in connection with real or personal property produced by the taxpayer that has a long useful life (i.e., real property or property with a class life of 20 years or more), in which the estimated production period exceeds two years, or in which the estimated production period exceeds one year and a cost in excess of $1 million. I.R.C. § 263A(f)(1); Reg. § 1.263A-8(a). Under the statutory language, the production period begins "on the date on which production of the property begins" and ends "on the date on which the property is ready to be placed in service or is ready to be held for sale." I.R.C. § 263A(f)(4)(B). The Regulations provide greater guidance concerning the commencement of the production period and state that, with respect to the production of real property, the production period begins when any physical production activities are undertaken, such as the clearing, grading, or excavating of raw land, the demolition or gutting of a building, or the construction of infrastructure including roads, sewers, sidewalks, cable, and wiring. Reg. §§ 1.263A-12(c)(2) and 1.263A-12(e). Physical production activities do not include soil testing, preparing architectural blueprints or models, obtaining building permits, or incidental repairs. The production period begins with respect to tangible personal property when the taxpayer's accumulated production expenditures are at least five percent of the taxpayer's estimated accumulated production expenditures. Reg. § 1.263A-12(c)(3).

If a taxpayer is required to capitalize interest under § 263A(f), the avoided cost method must be used under which "any interest that the taxpayer theoretically would have avoided if accumulated production expenditures . . . had been used to repay or reduce the taxpayer's outstanding debt must be capitalized . . . ." Reg. § 1.263A-9(a)(1). In other words, all of the taxpayer's debt is deemed to be financing the production expenditures and the interest on this debt to the extent of the production expenditures must be capitalized. The Regulations distinguish between traced and untraced debt. Interest incurred during the production period on traced debt must be capitalized into the basis of the property produced. Reg. § 1.236A-9(b). Interest incurred on untraced debt equal in amount to the excess expenditure amount (i.e., the amount of production expenditures in excess of the traced debt) must also be capitalized. Reg. §§ 1.263A-9(c)(1) and 1.263A-9(c)(5)(i). The Regulations provide extensive guidance in determining the average excess expenditures and the average weighted interest rate in order to properly determine the amount of interest incurred on untraced debt that must be capitalized. Reg. §§ 1.263A-9(c)(5)(ii) and 1.263A-9(c)(5)(iii).

PROBLEM FOR DISCUSSION

Problem 4-1. Problem Chicago Development Corp. (CDC) is in the business of developing commercial and residential projects in the greater Chicago area. It has located a parcel of property on which it plans to develop a retail shopping center and office building. CDC has entered into a purchase and sale agreement (P&S) with the current owner of the property that is expected to close in 90 days. CDC's in-house staff negotiated the terms of the P&S with the assistance of CDC's lawyers. CDC has already hired an engineering consultant and architect who are undertaking the design aspects of the project. Other consultants are conducting the due diligence work in investigating the property as permitted under the P&S. CDC's lawyers are working on due diligence matters and negotiating the financing terms with Citibank, CDC's lender. CDC's lawyers are also engaged with the city and state to obtain the zoning and other permits necessary to construct and operate the project. If all goes as currently scheduled, CDC expects to break ground 60 days after closing on the property. Are any of the costs that CDC has or will incur in the development of the project deductible or must they all be capitalized into the basis of the property?

§ 2.03. Tangible Assets

Prop. Treas. Reg. §§ 1.263(a)-1, 1.263(a)-2, and 1.263(a)-3

Following the language of § 263, the Regulations have long provided that no deduction is permitted for "[a]ny amount paid out for new buildings or for permanent improvements or betterments to increase the value of any property or estate" or for "[a]ny amount expended in restoring or in making good the exhaustion thereof for which an allowance is or has been made in the form of a deduction for depreciation [or] amortization. . . ." Reg. § 1.263(a)-1(a). The Regulations further explain that such expenditures include amounts paid or incurred "to add to the value, or substantially prolong the useful life, of property owned by the taxpayer" or "to adapt property to a new or different use." Reg. § 1.263(a)-1(b). Nevertheless, amounts paid or incurred for incidental repairs and maintenance of property need not be capitalized. *Id. See also* Reg. § 1.162-4 (allowing deductions under § 162 for the "cost of incidental repairs which neither materially add to the value of the property nor appreciably prolong it life, but keep it in an ordinarily efficient operating condition"). As described above, these regulatory provisions led to significant controversy between taxpayers and the Service in determining when expenditures were properly deductible as repairs or capitalized as improvements.

In order to provide greater guidance concerning the capitalization of amounts paid to acquire, produce, or improve tangible real and personal property, the Service released Proposed Regulations in 2006 that address each of these issues. With respect to amounts paid to acquire tangible real and personal property, the Proposed Regulations provide that, except in the case of dealers in property, commissions and other transaction costs paid to facilitate the sale of property generally must be capitalized and treated as a reduction in the amount realized. Prop. Reg. § 1.263(a)-1(c)(1). This provision applies only to transaction costs and does not include other amounts that might be paid for the purpose of selling property, such as amounts paid to repair or improve the property in preparation for a sale. The treatment of those amounts is governed by the general rules under the Proposed Regulations relating to improvements as described below.

With respect to amounts paid to acquire or produce tangible real and personal property, the Proposed Regulations require capitalization of amounts paid for property having a useful life substantially beyond the taxable year, including land and improvements to land, buildings, machinery and equipment, and furniture and fixtures. Prop. Reg. § 1.263(a)-2(d)(1). In determining whether property has a useful life substantially beyond the taxable year, the Proposed Regulations adopt a 12-month rule under which a taxpayer may deduct currently an amount paid for a benefit or paid for property having a useful life that does not extend beyond one year. Prop. Reg. § 1.263(a)-2(d)(4). Thus, this provision is consistent with some prior case law that had recognized such a rule. *See Mennuto v. Commissioner*, 56 T.C. 910 (1971), *acq.*; *Zelco, Inc. v. Commissioner*, 331 F.2d 418 (1st Cir. 1964); *International Shoe Co. v. Commissioner*, 38 B.T.A. 81 (1938). Interestingly, the Service declined to adopt a de minimis rule in connection with amounts incurred to acquire or produce tangible real and personal property, a rule that had been recognized by some courts. *See Union P. R. Co. v. United States*, 524 F.2d 1343 (Ct.

Cl. 1975) (permitting the use of the taxpayer's $500 de minimis rule, which was in accordance with the Interstate Commerce Commission (ICC) minimum rule and generally accepted accounting principles); *Cincinnati, N.O. & T. P. R. Co. v. United States*, 424 F.2d 563 (Ct. Cl. 1970) (same). *But see Alacare Home Health Serv. v. Commissioner*, T.C. Memo. 2001-149 (disallowing the taxpayer's use of a $500 de minimis rule because it distorted income).

With respect to amounts paid to produce tangible real and personal property, the Proposed Regulations are not intended to change the treatment of any amount that is specifically provided for under any provision of the Code or Regulations other than section 162(a) or section 212 and provide an exception for amounts paid for materials and supplies that are properly treated as deductions or deferred expenses under Reg. § 1.162-3. Prop. Reg. § 1.263(a)-2(c)(2). The Proposed Regulations also provide that a taxpayer must capitalize amounts paid to acquire or produce real or personal property for resale and cross-reference § 263A for guidance concerning the scope of the costs that must be capitalized in such situations. Prop. Reg. § 1.263(a)-2(d)(1). Finally, the Proposed Regulations require taxpayers to capitalize amounts paid to defend or perfect title to tangible property as well as amounts paid to facilitate the acquisition of real or personal property. Prop. Reg. §§ 1.263(a)-2(d)(2) and 1.263(a)-2(d)(3). Amounts capitalized under these provisions must be included in the basis of the property involved or included in inventory costs and recovered through depreciation, amortization, or the cost of goods sold. Prop. Reg. §§ 1.263(a)-2(e) and 1.263(a)-2(f).

The most extensive aspect of the Proposed Regulations concerns the treatment of amounts paid to improve tangible property. The Proposed Regulations generally provide that a taxpayer must capitalize the aggregate of related amounts paid that improve a unit of property, whether the improvements are made by the taxpayer or a third party. Prop. Reg. § 1.263(a)-3d)(1). A unit of property is improved if the expenditures "[m]aterially increase the value of the unit of property" or "restore the unit of property." Each of these terms is more fully discussed below. Again, amounts capitalized under these provisions must be included in the basis of the property involved or included in inventory costs and recovered through depreciation, amortization, or the cost of goods sold. Prop. Reg. §§ 1.263(a)-3(h) and 1.263(a)-3(i).

Importantly, the Proposed Regulations provide guidance in determining the proper unit of property for purposes of the analysis. The purpose of the unit of property rules under section 263(a) is to provide a starting point for determining whether an amount paid materially increases the value of, or restores, the unit of property. The Service concluded that the administrative burden associated with determining the appropriate unit of property could be reduced for both the Service and taxpayers by applying different rules, depending on the taxpayer's industry and the type of property at issue. Consequently, the Proposed Regulations provide different unit of property rules for four categories of property. Prop. Reg. § 1.263(a)-3(d)(2). However, an initial unit of property determination is based on a functional interdependence test under which the unit of property consists of components of property that are functionally interdependent. Prop. Reg. § 1.263(a)-3(d)(2)(ii). Under the Proposed Regulations, "[c]omponents of property are functionally interdependent if the placing in service of one component by the taxpayer is dependent on the placing in service of the other component by the taxpayer." Id. After the initial unit of property is determined, the additional unit of property rules are intended to result in a determination that either confirms the initial unit of property as the unit of property, or that separates one or more components of the initial unit of property into separate units of property.

The first and second categories of property are relatively straightforward. The first category of property applies to taxpayers in a regulated industry. If the taxpayer is in an industry for which a federal regulator has a uniform system of accounts (USOA) identifying a particular unit of property, the taxpayer must use the same unit of property for federal income tax purposes. Prop. Reg. § 1.263(a)-2(d)(2)(iii). The second category of property applies to buildings and their structural components and provides that a building and its structural components must be treated as one unit of property. Prop. Reg. § 1.263(a)-2(d)(2)(iv).

The third category of property applies to personal property that does not fall into the first category. The unit of property is determined based on a facts and circumstances test, under which four exclusive factors, none of which is dispositive or weighs more heavily than the others, are considered. Prop. Reg. § 1.263(a)-2(d)(2)(v). The first factor is whether the component is: (1) marketed separately to or acquired or leased separately by the taxpayer (from a party other than the seller/lessor of the property of which the component is a part) at the time it is initially acquired or leased; (2) subject to a separate warranty contract (from a party other than the seller/lessor of the property of which the component is a part); (3) subject to a separate maintenance manual or written maintenance policy; (4) appraised separately; or (5) sold or leased separately by the taxpayer to another party. The second factor is whether the component is treated as a separate unit of property in industry practice or by the taxpayer in its books and records. The third factor is whether the taxpayer treats the component as a rotable part. A rotable part is defined as a part that is removable from property, repaired or improved, and either immediately reinstalled on other property or stored for later installation. If the rotable part is a separate unit of property to the taxpayer and the taxpayer incorporates the rotable part into other property for resale, the rotable part will not necessarily be a separate unit of property to the purchaser. The fourth and final factor is whether the property of which the component is a part generally functions for its intended use without the component property.

The fourth category of property applies to real property not included in Category I or II. Prop. Reg. § 1.263(a)-2(d)(2)(vi). The unit of property determination under this category is based on a facts and circumstances test. The property subject to this category is primarily land and land improvements owned or leased by taxpayers not in a regulated industry. Unlike Category III, no specific factors are listed because land and land improvements are such unique assets that specific factors cannot uniformly provide appropriate results. Thus, the unit of property determination for property in this category may be based on some, all, or none of the factors listed in Category III for personal property, or may be based on other factors.

The Proposed Regulations provide an extensive number of examples illustrating the application of these rules. Prop. Reg. § 1.263(a)-2(d)(2)(vii) examples (1) through (15). Nevertheless, the Proposed Regulations provide that, if a taxpayer properly treats a component as a separate unit of property for any federal income tax purpose, the taxpayer must treat the component as a separate unit of property for purposes of § 263. Prop. Reg. § 1.263(a)-3(d)(2)(vii). The purpose of this rule is to prevent taxpayers from taking inconsistent positions by arguing that a component of property is a unit of property for one tax purpose and not a separate unit of property for capitalization purposes. For example, if a taxpayer does a cost segregation study on a building and properly identifies separate § 1245 property, the taxpayer must treat that separate property as the unit of property for capitalization purposes.

Once the appropriate unit of property is determined, the taxpayer must determine whether the expenditures paid or incurred improved the property either by materially increasing the value of the property or by restoring the property. With respect to the value of a unit of property, the Proposed Regulations provide an exclusive list of five tests for determining whether an amount paid materially increases value. Prop. Reg. § 1.263(a)-3(e)(1). Significantly, none of these tests actually considers any change in the actual fair market value of the property. The first test is whether the amount paid ameliorates a condition or defect that either existed prior to the taxpayer's acquisition of the unit of property or arose during the production of the unit of property. This rule is consistent with the concept that amounts paid to put property into ordinarily efficient operating condition must be capitalized. The second test is whether the work was performed prior to the date the property is placed in service by the taxpayer. This test is apparently based on the view that if the property cannot be placed in service prior to work being performed the work necessarily increases the value of the property. The third value test is whether the amounts paid adapt the property to a new or different use. The fourth value test is whether the amount paid results in a betterment or material addition to the unit of property. The fifth and final test is whether the amount paid results in a material increase in capacity, productivity, efficiency, or quality of output of the unit of property. In each case, the Proposed Regulations provide an exception to the value tests if the original economic useful life of the unit of property is 12 months or less and the taxpayer does not elect to capitalize amounts paid for the property. Prop. Reg. § 1.263(a)-3(e)(2).

In cases in which a particular event necessitates an expenditure, the valuation tests are applied by comparing the condition of the property immediately after the expenditure with the condition of the property immediately prior to the event necessitating the expenditure. Prop. Reg. § 1.263(a)-3(e)(3). When the event necessitating the expenditure is normal wear and tear, the condition of the property immediately prior to the event necessitating the expenditure is the condition of the property after the last time the taxpayer corrected the effects of normal wear and tear or, if the taxpayer has not previously corrected the effects of normal wear and tear, the condition of the property when placed in service by the taxpayer. Again, the Proposed Regulations provide an extensive number of examples illustrating the application of these rules. Prop. Reg. § 1.263(a)-2(e)(4) examples (1) through (17).

Finally, the Proposed Regulations provide that a taxpayer must capitalize amounts paid to restore property. Prop. Reg. § 1.263(a)-3(f)(1). Amounts are paid to restore property if the expenditures substantially prolong the economic useful life of the unit of property. Importantly, the economic useful life is not determined by reference to the recovery period under § 168 for the property. For taxpayers with an applicable financial statement (AFS), the economic useful life of the property is presumed to be the same as the useful life used by the taxpayer for purposes of determining depreciation in its AFS. Prop. Reg. § 1.263(a)-3(f)(2)(i). An AFS is a financial statement required to be filed with the Securities and Exchange Commission; a certified audited financial statement that is used for credit purposes, reporting to shareholders or partners, or any other substantial non-tax reason; or a financial statement other than a tax return required to be filed with federal or state governmental agencies. Prop. Reg. § 1.263(a)-3(f)(2)(iii). For taxpayers who do not have an AFS, the economic useful life is the period during which the property may reasonably be expected to be useful to the taxpayer. Prop. Reg. § 1.263(a)-3(f)(2)(ii). Several factors, including wear and tear and decay or decline from natural causes, the normal progress of the art, economic changes, inventions, and current developments in the taxpayer's trade or business, and climatic or other local conditions peculiar to the taxpayer's trade or business, are to be considered in determining the economic useful life of the property.

The Proposed Regulations then provide four rules for determining when an amount paid substantially prolongs the economic useful life of the property. Prop. Reg. § 1.263(a)-3(f)(3). The first rule requires capitalization when the amount paid extends the period during which the property may reasonably be expected to be useful to the taxpayer beyond the end of the taxable year immediately succeeding the taxable year in which the economic useful life of the property was originally expected to cease. Prop. Reg. § 1.263(a)-3(f)(3)(i). The second rule requires capitalization if a major component or a substantial structural part of the unit of property is replaced with either a new part or a part that has been restored to like-new condition. Prop. Reg. § 1.263(a)-3(f)(3)(ii). The third rule provides that amounts paid that restore a unit of property (or a major component or substantial structural part of the unit of property) to a like-new condition substantially prolong the useful life. Prop. Reg. § 1.263(a)-3(f)(3)(iii). The fourth rule relates to the restoration of a unit of property after the taxpayer has properly deducted a casualty loss under section 165 with respect to the property. Prop. Reg. § 1.263(a)-3(f)(3)(iv). Any amounts paid to repair property after a casualty loss must be capitalized. Again, the Proposed Regulations provide an extensive number of examples illustrating the application of these rules. Prop. Reg. § 1.263(a)-2(f)(4) examples (1) through (18).

Importantly, the Proposed Regulations do not incorporate the plan of rehabilitation doctrine under which deductible repair costs must be capitalized if they are incurred as part of a general plan of rehabilitation. The Service recognized that the doctrine had been the subject of considerable litigation and concluded that it was not "appropriate to capitalize as an improvement otherwise deductible repair costs solely because the taxpayer has a plan (written or otherwise) to perform periodic repairs or maintenance or solely because the taxpayer performs several repairs to the same property at one time." Notice of Proposed Rulemaking, 71 Fed. Reg. 48,590 (2006). Nevertheless, it stated that § 263A requires that all direct costs of an improvement and all indirect costs that directly benefit or are incurred by reason of the improvement must be capitalized and asserted that the requirements of § 263A are consistent with the application of the plan of rehabilitation doctrine as described in Rev. Rul. 2001-4, 2001-1 C.B. 295.

PROBLEM FOR DISCUSSION

Problem 4-2. Cross Country Movers, Inc. (CCM) has a fleet of various sized trucks that it uses to provide moving services for corporate executives who are being relocated by their companies. The trucks are scheduled for periodic inspection, maintenance, and repair, which depends on the size of the truck and the actual mileage since the last inspection. Every 50,000 miles, each truck is subject to a further inspection during which components of the truck might be rebuilt or replaced as necessary. Finally, trucks with more than 250,000 miles are subject to a complete overhaul during which major systems in the truck will be replaced. Can CCM deduct the costs of its maintenance program?

§ 2.04. Intangible Assets

Treas. Reg. §§ 1.162-14, 1.162-20(a)(2); 1.263(a)-4; 1.263(a)-5

In light of the continuing controversy concerning the capitalization requirement following the Supreme Court's decision in *INDOPCO, Inc. v. Commissioner*, 503 U.S. 79 (1992), particularly with respect to the treatment of intangible assets, the Service issued Regulations under § 263 to address specific categories of expenditures incurred to acquire or create intangible assets that taxpayers are required to capitalize. Importantly, the Regulations contain a number of safe harbors, simplifying assumptions, and de minimis rules to recognize the fact that expenditures that create or enhance intangible assets frequently do not create the type of future benefits for which capitalization under § 263 is appropriate, particularly when the administrative and recordkeeping costs associated with capitalization are weighed against the potential distortion of income.

The Regulations begin by requiring that amounts paid to acquire or create an intangible asset must be capitalized. The term "intangible asset" applies to a number of acquired and created intangible assets, which, as discussed below, are delineated in the Regulations. In addition, the Regulations adopt the language of the Supreme Court's decisions in *Commissioner v. Lincoln Sav. & Loan Ass'n*, 403 U.S. 345 (1971), and *INDOPCO* to require the capitalization of amounts paid to create or enhance a separate and distinct intangible asset as well as amounts paid to create or enhance a future benefit. Interestingly, the Regulations focus greater attention on the separate and distinct asset test than on the future benefits test. The Service reasoned that the separate and distinct asset test has not generated the same level of controversy as the future benefits test and, therefore, provides a more workable principle in practice. Finally, amounts paid to facilitate the acquisition or creation of certain intangible assets must also be capitalized.

The Regulations provide that a taxpayer must capitalize the following amounts in connection with intangible assets:

1. An amount paid to acquire an intangible asset;

2. An amount paid to create an intangible asset;
3. An amount paid to create or enhance a separate and distinct intangible asset;
4. An amount paid to create or enhance a future benefit; and
5. An amount paid to facilitate an acquisition or creation of an intangible asset.

Reg. § 1.263(a)-4(b)(1). Amounts that must be capitalized under the Regulations are not currently deductible but generally must be added to the basis of the intangible asset that is acquired or created. Reg. § 1.263(a)-4(g)(1).

With respect to amounts paid to acquire an intangible asset, the Regulations enumerate a multitude of types of intangible assets, the costs of which must be capitalized. The Regulations include the following assets:

1. An ownership interest in a corporation, partnership, trust, estate, limited liability company, or other entity;
2. A debt instrument or any other intangible asset treated as a debt instrument for tax purposes;
3. A financial instrument such as a notional principal contract, a foreign currency contract, a futures contract, a forward contract, an option, or any other financial derivative;
4. An endowment contract, annuity contract, or insurance contract;
5. Nonfunctional currency;
6. A lease;
7. A patent or copyright;
8. A franchise, trademark, or trade name;
9. Assembled workforce;
10. Goodwill or going concern value;
11. A customer list;
12. A servicing right, such as a mortgage servicing right;
13. A customer-based or supplier-based intangible asset;
14. Computer software; and
15. An agreement providing either party with the right to use, possess, or sell an intangible asset described in categories 1 through 5.

Reg. § 1.263(a)-4(c)(1).

With respect to amounts paid to create an intangible asset, the Regulations provide that taxpayers must capitalize amounts paid to another party to create, originate, enter into, renew, or renegotiate the types of financial interests described above in categories 1 through 5 and 15. Reg. § 1.263(a)-4(d)(2). In addition, a taxpayer must capitalize the following amounts:

1. Prepaid expenses, such as prepaid insurance or rent (Reg. § 1.263(a)-4(d)(3)).

2. Amounts paid to an organization to obtain, renew, renegotiate, or upgrade a membership or privilege from that organization such as rights to obtain lifetime staff privileges at a hospital or an initiation fee to obtain membership in a trade association (Reg. § 1.263(a)-4(d)(4)). This provision does not apply, however, to any amounts paid to obtain, renew, renegotiate, or upgrade certification of the taxpayer's products or processes.

3. Amounts paid to a governmental agency to obtain, renew, renegotiate, or upgrade its rights under a trademark, trade name, copyright, license, permit, franchise, or other similar right granted by that agency (Reg. § 1.263(a)-4(d)(5)). As illustrations of this provision, the Regulations describe amounts paid for a business license and a license to practice law within a particular state.

4. Amounts paid to another party to create, originate, enter into, renew, or renegotiate: (1) an agreement providing the taxpayer with the right to use, or the right to be compensated for the use of, tangible or intangible property; (2) the right to provide or to receive services; and (3) a covenant not to compete (Reg. § 1.263(a)-4(d)(6)). Importantly, an agreement will be deemed renegotiated if, in addition to modifying the terms of an existing agreement, the taxpayer terminates such an agreement and enters into a new agreement with the same party when the taxpayer could not have terminated the existing agreement without the consent of the other party and the other party would not have consented to the termination unless the taxpayer entered into the new agreement.

5. Amounts paid to another party to terminate certain types of agreements (Reg. § 1.263(a)-4(d)(7)). Such agreements include: (i) a lease of real or tangible personal property between the taxpayer (as lessor) and that party (as lessee); (ii) an agreement that grants that party the exclusive right to acquire or use the taxpayer's property or services or to conduct the taxpayer's business; or (iii) an agreement that prohibits the taxpayer from competing with that party or from acquiring property or services from a competitor of that party. The purpose of the rule is to require capitalization of termination payments that enable the taxpayer to reacquire some valuable right it did not possess immediately prior to the termination.

6. Amounts paid for real property if the taxpayer transfers ownership of the real property to another person and the real property can reasonably be expected to produce significant economic benefits to the taxpayer after the transfer (Reg. § 1.263(a)-4(d)(8)). As an example of this provision, the Regulations describe a taxpayer who pays a municipality $1 million to defray in part the cost of constructing a publicly owned bridge capable of accommodating the taxpayer's trucks. This provision does not apply, however, to impact fees or dedicated improvements to satisfy a state or local government's requirement against new development.

7. Amounts paid to another party to defend or perfect title to intangible property provided the other party challenges the taxpayer's title to the property (Reg. § 1.263(a)-4(d)(9)). The Regulations illustrate this provision through an example in which one party, U, challenges the validity of a patent held by another party, R. In settlement of the action, R pays U $100,000 in exchange for a release by U of all claims under the patent. Because the payment is an amount paid to defend or perfect R's title to the patent, it must be capitalized.

With respect to amounts paid to create or enhance a separate and distinct intangible asset, the Regulations require that such amount be capitalized if the property interest involved satisfies a three-part test. Reg. § 1.263(a)-4(b)(3). First, the property interest must be subject to protection under state, federal, or foreign law. Second, the property interest created must be transferable. Third, the property interest created must have an ascertainable and measurable value in money's worth. Despite the definition of a separate and distinct intangible asset, the Regulations specifically provide that amounts paid in performing services, developing computer software, or creating a package design are not treated as amounts that create a separate and distinct intangible asset.

With respect to amounts paid to create or enhance a future benefit, the Regulations state that provision is applicable only with respect to those assets or categories of assets that the Service identifies in published guidance as an intangible asset for which capitalization is required. Reg. § 1.263(a)-4(b)(1)(iv). The reference to "published" guidance refers only to guidance published in the *Federal Register* or the *Internal Revenue Bulletin*. In addition, this provision applies only to amounts paid on or after the date of publication of the guidance. Reg. § 1.263(a)-4(b)(2). To date, the Service has not provided any published guidance concerning the situations in which this provision is effective.

Finally, the Regulations provide that an amount is paid to facilitate a transaction involving the acquisition or creation of an intangible asset if the amount is paid "in the process of investigating or otherwise pursuing the transaction." Reg. § 1.263(a)-4(e)(1). Whether an amount is paid in the process of facilitating the acquisition or creation of an intangible asset is determined based on all of the facts and circumstances. Significantly, "[t]he fact that an amount would (or would not) have been paid but for the transaction is relevant, but not determinative," in determining whether the amount is paid to facilitate the transaction. *Id.* A transaction involving the acquisition or creation of an intangible asset includes:

> . . . [all] of the factual elements comprising an acquisition or creation of an intangible asset and includes a series of steps carried out as part of a single plan. Thus, a transaction can involve more than one invoice and more than one intangible asset. For example, a purchase of intangible assets under one purchase agreement may constitute a single transaction, notwithstanding the fact that the acquisition involves multiple intangible assets and the amounts paid to facilitate the acquisition are capable of being allocated among the various intangible assets acquired.

Reg. § 1.263(a)-4(e)(3). However, certain costs need not be capitalized under this provision. Compensation paid to employees (including salary, bonuses, and commissions), overhead, and de minimis costs are treated as amounts that do not facilitate the acquisition or creation of an intangible asset. Reg. §§ 1.263(a)-4(e)(4)(i) and 1.263(a)-4(e)(4)(ii). Facilitation costs other than employee compensation and overhead are treated as de minimis if, in the aggregate, they do not exceed $5,000. Reg. § 1.263(a)-4(e)(4)(iii).

The general capitalization requirements under the Regulations are subject to a simplifying convention referred to as the "12-month rule." Under this rule, taxpayers need not capitalize any amounts paid to create or to facilitate the creation of any right or benefit if that right or benefit does not extend beyond the earlier of: (1) 12 months after the date on which the taxpayer realizes the right or benefit or (2) the end of the taxable year following the taxable year in which the payment is made. Reg. § 1.263(a)-4(f)(1). As an example of the 12-month rule, the Regulations describe a corporation that makes payments to obtain a license to operate in a particular state for a five-year period. In addition to an up-front payment of $10,000, the taxpayer must pay annual fees of $500. The example concludes that, although the 12-month rule does not apply to the initial up-front fee, it does apply to the annual fees. Reg. § 1.263(a)-4(f)(8) example (5). However, in determining the duration of any right for purposes of this rule, the term includes any renewal period if there exists a reasonable expectancy of renewal during the taxable year in which the right is created. Importantly, the 12-month rule does not apply to amortizable § 197 intangible assets under § 197(c) or to any intangible asset of indefinite duration.

In addition to the Regulations applicable to the capitalization of costs incurred to acquire or create an intangible asset, another set of Regulations require that taxpayers capitalize expenditures paid to facilitate the acquisition of the assets of, or an ownership interest in, a trade or business, as well as the restructuring, recapitalization, or reorganization of the capital structure of a business entity. Reg. § 1.263(a)-5. An amount is paid to facilitate a transaction if "the amount is paid in the process of investigating or otherwise pursuing the transactions." Reg. § 1.263(a)-5(b)(1).

> Whether an amount is paid in the process of investigating or otherwise pursuing the transaction is determined based on all of the facts and circumstances. In determining whether an amount is paid to facilitate a transaction, the fact that the amount would (or would not) have been paid but for the transaction is relevant, but is not determinative. An amount paid to determine the value or price of a transaction is an amount paid in the process of investigating or otherwise pursuing the transaction. An amount paid to another party in exchange for tangible or intangible property is not an amount paid to facilitate the exchange.

Id. A simplifying convention treats employee compensation, overhead, and certain de minimis costs as amounts that do not facilitate a transaction. Reg. § 1.263(a)-5(d).

With the exception of payments that are "inherently facilitative," an amount that is paid by the taxpayer while in the process of investigating or pursuing certain "covered transactions" is treated as facilitating the transaction only if the payment relates to activities performed on or after the earlier of: (1) the date on which a letter of intent or similar written communication is executed by the acquirer and the target or (2) the date on which the material terms of the transaction are approved by the taxpayer's board of directors or appropriate governing officers of the taxpayer. Reg. § 1.263(a)-5(e)(1). Covered transactions include a taxable acquisition of assets that constitute a trade or business, a taxable acquisition of an ownership interest in a business entity if, immediately after the acquisition, the acquirer and the target are related within the meaning of § 267(b) or § 707(b), and reorganizations under §§ 368(a)(1)(A), 368(a)(1)(B), 368(a)(1)(C), or 368(a)(1)(D). Reg. § 1.263(a)-5(e)(3). Amounts that are considered inherently facilitative must be capitalized regardless of when incurred in the process of investigating or otherwise pursuing a transaction. Reg. § 1.263(a)-5(e)(2). Amounts are considered inherently facilitative if they are paid to: (1) secure an appraisal, formal written evaluation, or fairness opinion related to the transaction; (2) structure the transaction, including the negotiation of the transaction and the obtaining of tax advice; (3) prepare and review the documents that effectuate the transaction; (4) obtain regulatory approval of the transaction; (5) obtain shareholder approval of the transaction; or (6) convey property between the parties to the transaction. *Id. See also* Tech. Adv. Mem. 2005-12-021 (requiring the capitalization of a termination fee paid to cancel a merger agreement necessary to allow the taxpayer to merge with a second company; had the fee been paid after December 30, 2003, it would have been capitalized under Regulation § 1.263(a)-5(c)(8)); Tech. Adv. Mem. 2005-21-032 (same).

PROBLEMS FOR DISCUSSION

Problem 4-3. Faced with a declining market share as a result of significant competition from similar products, Pfizer, Inc. decided to change the marketing and promotional efforts for its mouthwash product, Listerine. Pfizer's marketing consultants conducted focus groups and demonstrated that a change in the shape of the bottle, bolder/brighter colors on the packaging, and a new advertising campaign would help Pfizer regain market share. The company even retained several well-known movie and television celebrities to appear in print and broadcast ads. Pfizer will unveil its "new" product with the major retail markets in the next month. Can Pfizer deduct the costs of its new promotional campaign?

Problem 4-4. Cross Country Movers, Inc. (CCM) has a fleet of various sized trucks that it uses to provide moving services for corporate executives who are being relocated by their companies. Its trucks must each be licensed in the states in which the truck operates. In most states, the license is for one year following an inspection, but, in a few states, the license is for two years. New licenses are obtained as they expire and most, if not all, licenses upon renewal continue beyond the end of CCM's taxable year. Can CCM deduct the license fees in the taxable year paid?

Problem 4-5. MegaCorp owns several companies that are involved in the beef industry. Although it is satisfied with its investments, MegaCorp decided several months ago to diversify into other food-related industries, such as chicken or pork, that would be counter-cyclical to the beef industry. After some initial marketing and industry research, MegaCorp decided to narrow its search of potential acquisitions to the chicken industry and identified several specific companies with a view to acquiring one or more of the companies. At that point, MegaCorp hired an investment banking firm to examine the books and evaluate the assets of each of the companies. MegaCorp also hired an accounting firm and a law firm at that time to begin drafting the acquisition documents and to plan the due diligence requirements for the acquisition. Based on the work of the investment banking firm, MegaCorp determined that it would acquire "Try Me Chicken" and instructed the law firm to prepare and submit a letter of intent to its board of directors. Thereafter, the officers of MegaCorp, along with its banking, accounting, and legal team, spent considerable time and money reviewing in detail the financial condition of "Try Me Chicken" and negotiating with its board over the terms of the sale, which eventually occurred. Can MegaCorp deduct the costs incurred in acquiring "Try Me Chicken"?

§ 2.05. Disputes and Litigation — Origin of the Claim

In the past, questions frequently arose concerning whether costs incurred in litigation of, or simply in negotiating a resolution to, a dispute were currently deductible or were properly capitalized under § 263. For a taxpayer engaged in a trade or business or in an activity for the production of income, attorney costs, for example, are frequently expenses deductible under § 162 or § 212. However, the Regulations generally provide that costs incurred in the acquisition or sale of property must be capitalized and specifically provide for the capitalization of the costs of defending or perfecting the title to property. Reg. §§ 1.212-1(k), 1.263(a)-2(a), and 1.263(a)-2(c). However, it was not always clear when a particular cost was incurred under these circumstances. In two decisions, *Woodward v. Commissioner*, 397 U.S. 572 (1970), which follows, and *United States v. Hilton Hotels Corp.*, 397 U.S. 580 (1970), the Supreme Court applied the "origin of the claim" test to make this determination. Under this test, litigation costs must be capitalized if the origin of the litigation "lies in the process of acquisition." The Court recognized, however, that the result of the origin of the claim test, like all tests, might be uncertain in borderline cases.

WOODWARD v. COMMISSIONER

Supreme Court of the United States
397 U.S. 572 (1970)

MR. JUSTICE MARSHALL delivered the opinion of the Court.

This case . . . involve[s] the tax treatment of expenses incurred in certain appraisal litigation.

Taxpayers owned or controlled a majority of the common stock of the Telegraph-Herald, an Iowa publishing corporation. The Telegraph-Herald was incorporated in 1901, and its charter was extended for 20-year periods in 1921 and 1941. On June 9, 1960, taxpayers voted their controlling share of the stock of the corporation in favor of a perpetual extension of the charter. A minority stockholder voted against the extension. Iowa law requires "those stockholders voting for such renewal . . . [to] purchase at its real value the stock voted against such renewal." Iowa Code § 491.25 (1966).

Taxpayers attempted to negotiate purchase of the dissenting stockholder's shares, but no agreement could be reached on the "real value" of those shares. Consequently, in 1962 taxpayers brought an action in state court to appraise the value of the minority stock interest. The trial court fixed a value, which was slightly reduced on appeal by the Iowa Supreme Court . . . . In July 1965, taxpayers purchased the minority stock interest at the price fixed by the court.

During 1963, taxpayers paid attorneys', accountants', and appraisers' fees of over $25,000, for services rendered in connection with the appraisal litigation. On their 1963 federal income tax returns, taxpayers claimed deductions for these expenses, asserting that they were "ordinary and necessary expenses paid . . . for the management, conservation, or maintenance of property held for the production of income" deductible under § 212 of the Internal Revenue Code of 1954 . . . . The Commissioner of Internal Revenue disallowed the deduction "because the fees represent capital expenditures incurred in connection with the acquisition of capital stock of a corporation." . . . .

Since the inception of the present federal income tax in 1913, capital expenditures have not been deductible. See Internal Revenue Code of 1954, § 263. Such expenditures are added to the basis of the capital asset with respect to which they are incurred, and are taken into account for tax purposes either through depreciation or by reducing the capital gain (or increasing the loss) when the asset is sold. If an expense is capital, it cannot be deducted as "ordinary and necessary," either as a business expense under § 162 of the Code or as an expense of "management, conservation, or maintenance" under § 212.

It has long been recognized, as a general matter, that costs incurred in the acquisition or disposition of a capital asset are to be treated as capital expenditures. The most familiar example of such treatment is the capitalization of brokerage fees for the sale or purchase of securities, as explicitly provided by a longstanding Treasury regulation . . ., Treas. (A)-2 (A)-2 (A)-2 Reg. on Income Tax § 1.263 (a)-2 (e), and as approved by this Court in *Helvering v. Winmill*, 305 U.S. 79 (1938), and *Spreckels v. Commissioner*, 315 U.S. 626 (1942). The Court recognized that brokers' commissions are "part of the acquisition cost of the securities," *Helvering v. Winmill*, [305 U.S. 79 (1938)], at 84, and relied on the Treasury regulation, which had been approved by statutory re-enactment, to deny deductions for such commissions even to a taxpayer for whom they were a regular and recurring expense in his business of buying and selling securities.

The regulations do not specify other sorts of acquisition costs, but rather provide generally that "the cost of acquisition . . . of . . . property having a useful life substantially beyond the taxable year" is a capital expenditure. [Reg. § 1.263(a)-2(a).] Under this general provision, the courts have held that legal, brokerage, accounting, and similar costs incurred in the acquisition or disposition of such property are capital expenditures. See, *e.g.*, *Spangler v. Commissioner*, 323 F.2d 913, 921 (C.A. 9th Cir. 1963); *United States v. St. Joe Paper Co.*, 284 F.2d 430, 432 (C.A. 5th Cir. 1960). . . . The law could hardly be otherwise, for such ancillary expenses incurred in acquiring or disposing of an asset are as much part of the cost of that asset as is the price paid for it.

More difficult questions arise with respect to another class of capital expenditures, those incurred in "defending or perfecting title to property." [Reg. § 1.263(a)-2(c).] In one sense, any lawsuit brought against a taxpayer may affect his title to property — money or other assets subject to lien. The courts, not believing that Congress meant all litigation expenses to be capitalized, have created the rule that such expenses are capital in nature only where the taxpayer's "primary purpose" in incurring them is to defend or perfect title. . . . This test hardly draws a bright line, and has produced a melange of decisions, which, as the Tax Court has noted, "it would be idle to suggest . . . can be reconciled." *Ruoff v. Commissioner*, 30 T.C. 204, 208 (1958).

Taxpayers urge that this "primary purpose" test, developed in the context of cases involving the costs of defending property, should be applied to costs incurred in acquiring or disposing of property as well. And if it is so applied, they argue, the costs here in question were properly deducted, since the legal proceedings in which they were incurred did not directly involve the question of title to the minority stock, which all agreed was to pass to taxpayers, but rather was concerned solely with the value of that stock.

We agree with the Tax Court and the Court of Appeals that the "primary purpose" test has no application here. That uncertain and difficult test may be the best that can be devised to determine the tax treatment of costs incurred in litigation that may affect a taxpayer's title to property more or less indirectly, and that thus calls for a judgment whether the taxpayer can fairly be said to be "defending or perfecting title." Such uncertainty is not called for in applying the regulation that makes the "cost of acquisition" of a capital asset a capital expense. In our view application of the latter regulation to litigation expenses involves the simpler inquiry whether the origin of the claim litigated is in the process of acquisition itself.

A test based upon the taxpayer's "purpose" in undertaking or defending a particular piece of litigation would encourage resort to formalisms and artificial distinctions. For instance, in this case there can be no doubt that legal, accounting, and appraisal costs incurred by taxpayers in *negotiating* a purchase of the minority stock would have been capital expenditures. See *Atzingen-Whitehouse Dairy Inc.* v. *Commissioner*, 36 T.C. 173 (1961). Under whatever test might be applied, such expenses would have clearly been "part of the acquisition cost" of the stock. *Helvering v. Winmill, supra*. Yet the appraisal proceeding was no more than the substitute that state law provided for the process of negotiation as a means of fixing the price at which the stock was to be purchased. Allowing deduction of expenses incurred in such a proceeding, merely on the ground that title was not directly put in question in the particular litigation, would be anomalous.

Further, a standard based on the origin of the claim litigated comports with this Court's recent ruling on the characterization of litigation expenses for tax purposes in *United States v. Gilmore*, 372 U.S. 39 (1963). This Court there held that the expense of defending a divorce suit was a nondeductible personal expense, even though the outcome of the divorce case would affect the taxpayer's property holdings, and might affect his business reputation. The Court rejected a test that looked to the consequences of the litigation, and did not even consider the taxpayer's motives or purposes in undertaking defense of the litigation, but rather examined the origin and character of the claim against the taxpayer, and found that the claim arose out of the personal relationship of marriage.

The standard here pronounced may, like any standard, present borderline cases, in which it is difficult to determine whether the origin of particular litigation lies in the process of acquisition. This is not such a borderline case. Here state law required taxpayers to "purchase" the stock owned by the dissenter. In the absence of agreement on the price at which the purchase was to be made, litigation was required to fix the price. Where property is acquired by purchase, nothing is more clearly part of the process of acquisition than the establishment of a purchase price. Thus the expenses incurred in that litigation were properly treated as part of the cost of the stock that the taxpayers acquired.

Affirmed.

PROBLEM FOR DISCUSSION

Problem 4-6. Do the recently promulgated Regulations under § 263, Reg. §§ 1.263(a)-4 and 1.263(a)-5, as well as Prop. Reg. § 1.263(a)-2 render the decision in *Woodward* superfluous?

§ 3. COST RECOVERY FOR TANGIBLE ASSETS

§ 3.01. In General

Once the determination is made that the expenditures incurred must be capitalized, the next question to be addressed is whether, and if so how, the capitalized costs can be recovered. For costs that must be capitalized under § 263A into the cost of goods sold of inventory held by the taxpayer, those costs will be recovered upon sale of the inventory. See I.R.C. § 471 and the Regulations thereunder (detailing the treatment of inventory accounting for tax purposes). For costs that must be capitalized under § 263 or § 263A into the basis of the property acquired or produced, those costs may be recovered over time through either depreciation or amortization if the property is used in the taxpayer's trade or business or for the production of income and the property is subject to exhaustion, wear or tear, or obsolescence under § 167. The mechanics of determining the annual amount of depreciation with respect to various types of tangible property are provided in § 168. More specifically, § 168 provides rules specifying the recovery period, depreciation method, and applicable conventions necessary to calculate the amount of depreciation. In addition, certain types of acquired, and some forms of self-created, intangible property are subject to amortization under § 197. Section 197 provides that such property is amortizable over a 15-year period beginning with the month in which the intangible property is placed in service by the taxpayer.

Importantly, however, Congress has provided that some types of expenditures or some portion of the basis of acquired property may be expensed in the taxable year in which the expenditures are paid or incurred or the property acquired. Congress typically does this for administrative reasons or to achieve certain social objectives. For example, § 179 permits the expensing of up to $125,000 of the cost of certain types of property acquired by the taxpayer and placed in service during the taxpayer year. This provision reduces administrative burdens on taxpayers by dispensing with the recordkeeping requirements that are applicable if the taxpayer had to depreciate such property. In addition, and as discussed above, expensing reduces the taxpayer's effective tax rate with respect to income generated by such property, thereby creating incentives to invest in such property. Congress has recently increased the amounts that may be expensed under § 179 to provide an added stimulus to a weak economy. Similarly, the expensing of environmental remediation expenditures under § 198 creates incentives for the clean-up of environmentally contaminated sites.

§ 3.02. Start-Up Expenditures

I.R.C. § 195

Treas. Reg. § 1.195-1

Generally, taxpayer expenses related to starting a new business, so-called start-up expenses, are not deductible under § 162 because the taxpayer is not yet engaged in carrying on the trade or business. Section 195, however, allows taxpayers to deduct up to $5,000 of any start-up expenditures in the taxable year in which the active trade or business begins and to ratably amortize any start-up expenditures in excess of this amount over a 180-month (15-year) period beginning with the month in which the active trade or business begins. I.R.C. § 195(b). The $5,000 amount is reduced, however, by the amount to which the start-up expenditures exceed $50,000.[1] The purpose of the $5,000 expense amount is to encourage the formation of new businesses that do not incur significant start-up expenditures while the 15-year amortization period is to coordinate the treatment of start-up expenditures under § 195 with the treatment of intangible assets under § 197. Section 195 applies not only to the start-up of a new trade or business by a taxpayer not previously engaged in a trade or business but also to the start-up costs of a new trade or business unrelated or only tangentially related to the trade or business in which the taxpayer is engaged.

Under § 195, start-up expenditures include any amount incurred in connection with: (1) investigating the creation or acquisition of an active trade or business, (2) creating an active trade or business, and (3) activities engaged in for profit and for the production of income before the date on which the active trade or business begins, in anticipation of becoming an active trade or business. I.R.C. § 195(c)(1)(A). According to the legislative history, the definition of "start-up expenditures" is intended to cover a broad range of costs.

> Under the provision, eligible expenses consist of investigatory costs incurred in reviewing a prospective business prior to reaching a final decision to acquire or to enter that business. These costs include expenses incurred for the analysis or survey of potential markets, products, labor supply, transportation facilities, etc. Eligible expenses also include startup

---

[1] As part of the Small Business Jobs Act of 2010, Pub. L. No. 111-240, § 2031(a), 124 Stat. 2504 (2010), Congress increased the $5,000 figure to $10,000 and the phase-out threshold from $50,000 to $60,000. I.R.C. § 195(b)(3). This change applies only for taxable years beginning in 2010, however.

> costs which are incurred subsequent to a decision to establish a particular business and prior to the time when the business begins. For example, startup costs include advertising, salaries and wages paid to employees who are being trained and their instructors, travel and other expenses incurred in lining up prospective distributors, suppliers or customers, and salaries or fees paid or incurred for executives, consultants, and for similar professional services.

H.R. Rep. No. 1278, 96th Cong., 2d Sess. 10–11 (1980); S. Rep. No. 1036, 96th Cong., 2d Sess. 11-12 (1980). Start-up expenditures are limited, however, to those expenditures that would be deductible if incurred in connection with the operation of an existing active trade or business. I.R.C. § 195(c)(1)(B). Thus, expenditures that would otherwise have to be capitalized under § 263 or § 263(a) are not start-up expenditures. In addition, expenditures for interest under § 163(a), taxes under § 164, and research and development under § 174 are specifically excluded from the definition of start-up expenditures and remain deductible to the extent permitted by these sections.

Section 195 does not define the term "active trade or business," but gives the Secretary the power to promulgate Regulations to determine when an active trade or business begins. In the absence of Regulations that have yet to be promulgated, the Service has relied on judicial definitions of the "carrying on" requirement under § 162 to determine when a business begins for purposes of § 195. Tech. Adv. Mem. 90-27-002. In particular, the Service has looked to the decision in *Richmond Television Corp. v. United States*, 345 F.2d 901 (4th Cir. 1965), as setting forth the test for when a taxpayer begins to carry on a trade or business. In *Richmond Television*, the taxpayer organized a business to operate a television station and, before receiving the necessary operating license, incurred expenses for employee training. The Fourth Circuit denied the taxpayer's claimed deductions under § 162 for these expenses. Because the court determined that a taxpayer engages in carrying on a trade or business only when it has "begun to function as a going concern and performed those activities for which it was organized," the court concluded that the taxpayer could not be carrying on a trade or business before it received a broadcast license.

The issue of when a trade or business begins also arises in distinguishing between the commencement of a new trade or business and the expansion of an existing trade or business. Importantly, § 195 does not apply to the costs of expanding an existing trade or business. According to the legislative history, the determination of whether expenditures are incurred in the expansion of an existing trade or business or the creation or acquisition of a new trade or business is to be based on all of the facts and circumstances of each case. H.R. Rep. 1278, 96th Cong., 2d Sess. 11 (1980); S. Rep. 1036, 96th Cong., 2d Sess. 12 (1980). In a Field Service Advice Memorandum considering the application of § 195, the Service recognized the difference in treatment between taxpayers who create or acquire a business and those who expand an existing business.

> Amortization under section 195 is available only to a taxpayer who creates or acquires a trade or business, not to a taxpayer who expands an existing business. Since expansion costs may be neither deductible nor amortizable

> while start-up expenses of a new business are amortizable under section 195, a taxpayer who starts a new business is in a much better tax position than a taxpayer who merely expands an existing one since expansion costs would be placed in the "black hole" of permanent capitalization.

Field Service Advice 1999-492 (undated). *See also* Tech. Adv. Mem. 2005-48-022 (concluding that the costs incurred by the taxpayer did not qualify as start-up expenditures under § 195 because they were incurred in connection with the expansion of an existing active trade or business); Field Attorney Advice 20040302F (dated September 23, 2003) (concluding that, "to a reasonable degree of certainty, § 195 applies only to the creation of a new business or acquisition of a business in a different field").

The definition of start-up expenditures under § 195 is the subject to the following Revenue Ruling. This Ruling was issued in 1999 at a time when § 195 permitted the amortization of start-up expenses over a period of 60 months. Section 195 was amended to extend the amortization period to 180 months in 2004.

REVENUE RULING 99-23

1999-1 C.B. 998

ISSUE

When a taxpayer acquires the assets of an active trade or business, which expenditures will qualify as investigatory costs that are eligible for amortization as start-up expenditures under § 195 of the Internal Revenue Code?

FACTS

Situation 1

In April 1998, corporation *U* hired an investment banker to evaluate the possibility of acquiring a trade or business unrelated to *U*'s existing business. The investment banker conducted research on several industries and evaluated publicly available financial information relating to several businesses. Eventually, *U* narrowed its focus to one industry. The investment banker evaluated several businesses within the industry, including corporation *V* and several of *V*'s competitors. The investment banker then commissioned appraisals of *V*'s assets and an in-depth review of *V*'s books and records in order to determine a fair acquisition price. On November 1,1998, *U* entered into an acquisition agreement with *V* to purchase all the assets of *V*. *U* did not prepare and submit a letter of intent, or any other preliminary agreement or written document evidencing an intent to acquire *V* prior to executing the acquisition agreement.

Situation 2

In May 1998, corporation *W* began searching for a trade or business to acquire. In anticipation of finding a suitable target to acquire, *W* hired an investment banker to evaluate three potential businesses and a law firm to begin drafting regulatory approval documents for a target. Eventually, *W* decided to purchase all the assets of corporation *X*. *W* and *X* entered into an acquisition agreement on December 1, 1998.

Situation 3

In June 1998, corporation *Y* hired a law firm and an accounting firm to assist in the potential acquisition of corporation *Z* by performing certain services that the parties labeled as "preliminary due diligence." These "due diligence" services included conducting research on *Z*'s industry (including information relating to competitors of *Z*), and analyzing financial projections for *Z* for 1998 and 1999. In September 1998, at *Y*'s request, the law firm prepared and submitted a letter of intent to *Z*. The offer contained in the letter of intent resulted from prior discussions between *Y* and *Z*, and specifically stated that a binding commitment with respect to the proposed transaction would result only upon execution of an acquisition agreement. Thereafter, the law firm and accounting firm continued to provide services labeled as "due diligence," including a review of *Z*'s internal documents relating to insurance policies, employee agreements, and lease agreements, an in-depth review of *Z*'s books and records, and preparation of an acquisition agreement. On October 10, 1998, *Y* entered into an acquisition agreement with *Z* to purchase all the assets of *Z*.

In each of the three situations, the trades or businesses of the targets are active trades or businesses unrelated to the trades or businesses of *U*, *W*, and *Y*. *U*, *W*, and *Y* each use an accrual method of accounting and a calendar taxable year. Each of the acquisition agreements entered into by *U*, *W*, and *Y* were subject to customary conditions of closing. Finally, *U*, *W*, and *Y* each completed the acquisitions in 1998 and timely elected on their 1998 federal income tax returns to amortize start-up expenditures over a period of not less than 60 months under § 195(b).

LAW AND ANALYSIS

Section 195(a) provides that, except as otherwise provided in § 195, no deduction is allowed for start-up expenditures.

Section 195(b) provides that start-up expenditures may, at the election of the taxpayer, be treated as deferred expenses that are allowed as a deduction prorated equally over a period of not less than 60 months (beginning with the month in which the active trade or business begins).

Section 195(c)(1) defines "start-up expenditure," in part, as any amount (A) paid or incurred in connection with investigating the creation or acquisition of an active trade or business, and (B) which, if paid or incurred in connection with the operation of an existing active trade or business (in the same field as the trade or business referred to in subparagraph (A)), would be allowable as a deduction for the taxable year in which paid or incurred. Thus, in order to qualify as start-up expenditures under § 195(c)(1), a taxpayer's "investigatory costs" must satisfy the requirements in both §§ 195(c)(1)(A) and (B). In addition, the term "start-up expenditure" does not include any amount with respect to which a deduction is allowable under § 163(a), 164, or 174.

Sections 162 and 1.162-1(a) of the Income Tax Regulations allow a deduction for all the ordinary and necessary expenses paid or incurred during the taxable year in carrying on any trade or business. Courts generally have construed § 162 as containing five conditions that an expenditure must meet to qualify for deduction. The expenditure must be (1) an expense, (2) ordinary, (3) necessary, (4) paid or incurred during the taxable year, and (5) made to carry on a trade or business. *See Commissioner v. Lincoln Savings and Loan Ass'n.*, 403 U.S. 345 (1971).

Sections 263 and 1.263(a)-1(a) provide that no deduction is allowed for any amounts paid out for new buildings or for permanent improvements or betterments made to increase the value of any property or estate. Section 1.263(a)-2(a) provides that capital expenditures include the cost of acquisition, construction, or erection of buildings, machinery and equipment, furniture and fixtures, and similar property having a useful life substantially beyond the taxable year.

Through provisions such as §§ 162(a) and 263(a), the Code generally endeavors to match expenses with the revenues of the taxable period to which the expenses are properly attributable, thereby resulting in a more accurate calculation of net income for tax purposes. *See, e.g., INDOPCO, Inc. v. Commissioner*, 503 U.S. 79 (1992).

In describing the law prior to § 195, Congress explained that "investigatory expenses," which were "costs incurred in seeking and reviewing prospective businesses prior to reaching a decision to acquire or enter any business," normally were not deductible because they were not incurred in carrying on a trade or business within the meaning of § 162. *See* H.R. Rep. No. 1278, 96th Cong., 2d Sess. 9 (1980) (House Report); S. Rep. No. 1036, 96th Cong., 2d Sess. 10 (1980) (Senate Report). The "carrying on a trade or business" requirement was not met where investigatory expenses were incurred by a taxpayer who was not yet carrying on any trade or business, or where a taxpayer was carrying on a trade or business but incurred costs to investigate the creation or acquisition of another, unrelated trade or business. *Id.* However, a taxpayer incurring costs to investigate the expansion of an existing business generally could deduct those costs under § 162, assuming the other requirements of that section were met. This disparity in the tax treatment of investigatory expenses resulting from the "carrying on a trade or business" requirement discouraged taxpayers from investigating the creation or acquisition of new trades or businesses. Section 195 was enacted, in part, to minimize this disparity and thereby encourage formation of new businesses by providing an amortization deduction for eligible investigatory expenses.

Accordingly, under § 195(c)(1)(B), expenditures described in § 195(c)(1)(A) that are incurred before the establishment of an active business are deemed to be paid or incurred in the operation of an existing active trade or business (in the same field as the business that the taxpayer is investigating whether to create or acquire), *i.e.*, they are deemed to satisfy the carrying on a trade or business requirement. However, because § 195(c)(1)(B) also requires that an expenditure described in § 195(c)(1)(A) be allowable as a deduction for the taxable year in which paid or incurred, the expenditure still must meet all the other requirements of § 162. Thus, the expenditure must be an ordinary expense under § 162, and not a capital expenditure, to be a start-up expenditure under § 195. "Section 195 did not create a new class of deductible expenditures for existing businesses . . . . [[I]n order to qualify under section 195(c)(1)(B), an expenditure must be one that would have been allowable as a deduction by an existing trade or business when it was paid or incurred." *FMR Corp. v. Commissioner*, 110 T.C. No. 30 (June 18, 1998). *See also* §§ 161 and 261 (deductions are allowed, subject to capitalization provisions). Whether an expenditure is an ordinary expense or is capital in nature is a question of fact that depends on the context in which the expenditure is incurred. *See Commissioner v. Idaho Power Co.*, 418 U.S. 1 (1974); *Deputy v. duPont*, 308 U.S. 488 (1940); *Welch v. Helvering*, 290 U.S. 111 (1933).

The legislative history of § 195 provides the following guidance regarding whether an expenditure is an ordinary investigatory cost that is an eligible start-up expenditure, or a capital acquisition cost:

> Eligible expenses consist of investigatory costs incurred prior to reaching a final decision to acquire or enter that business. These costs include expenses incurred for the analysis or survey of potential markets, products, labor supply, transportation facilities, etc.
>
> Start-up expenditures eligible for amortization do not include any amount with respect to which a deduction would not be allowed to an existing trade or business for the taxable year in which the expenditure was paid or incurred, . . . In addition, the amortization election for start-up expenditures does not apply to amounts paid or incurred as part of the acquisition cost of a trade or business. Also, start-up expenditures do not include amounts paid or incurred for the acquisition of property to be held for sale or property which may be depreciated or amortized based on its useful life . . . Whether an amount is consideration paid to acquire a business depends upon the facts and circumstances of the situation.

House Report at pages 10-11; Senate Report at pages 11-12.

Rev. Rul. 77-254, 1977-2 C.B. 63, which is specifically referenced by the legislative history of § 195 (House Report at 9, Senate Report at 10), considers which costs incurred in the potential acquisition of a new business are capital acquisition costs for purposes of §§ 165 and 263. That ruling provides that expenses incurred in the course of a general search for, or an investigation of, a business that relate to the decisions *whether* to purchase a business and *which* business to purchase are investigatory costs. However, once a taxpayer has focused on the acquisition of a specific business, expenses that are related to an attempt to acquire that business are capital in nature. Thus, the "final decision" referred to in the legislative history of § 195 is the point at which a taxpayer makes its decision *whether* to acquire a business, and *which* business to acquire, rather than the point at which a taxpayer and seller are legally obligated to complete the transaction.

Courts have long held that legal, brokerage, accounting, appraisal, and similar costs incurred to acquire a capital asset are capital expenditures under § 263. *Woodward v. Commissioner*, 397 U.S. 572 (1970) (when property is acquired by purchase, nothing is more clearly a part of the process of acquisition than the establishment of a purchase price); *United States v. Hilton Hotels Corp.*, 397 U.S.

580 (1970); *Beneficial Industrial Loan Corp. v. Handy*, 16 F. Supp. 110, 112 (D. Del. 1936), *aff'd*, 92 F.2d 74 (3d Cir. 1937); Rev. Rul. 73-580, 1973-2 C.B. 86.

For example, in *Ellis Banking Corp. v. Commissioner*, T.C. Memo. 1981-123, *aff'd in part & rem'd in part*, 688 F.2d 1376 (11th Cir. 1982), the taxpayer incurred expenses for office supplies, filing fees, travel, and accounting services in connection with its examination of target's books and records. The examination was performed pursuant to an acquisition agreement for the purchase of target's stock that was contingent on several terms and conditions, such as regulatory approval. The Tax Court concluded that the expenses were nondeductible capital expenditures incurred in the acquisition of a capital asset. The Court of Appeals for the Eleventh Circuit substantially affirmed, noting that the requirement that costs be capitalized extends beyond the price payable to include any costs incurred by the buyer in connection with the purchase, such as appraisals of the property or the costs of meeting any conditions of sale.

Accordingly, expenditures incurred in the course of a general search for, or an investigation of, an active trade or business, *i.e.*, expenditures paid or incurred in order to determine *whether* to enter a new business and *which* new business to enter (other than costs incurred to acquire capital assets that are used in the search or investigation), are investigatory costs that are start-up expenditures under § 195. Alternatively, costs incurred in the attempt to acquire a specific business are capital in nature and thus, are not start-up expenditures under § 195. The nature of the cost must be analyzed based on all the facts and circumstances of the transaction to determine whether it is an investigatory cost incurred to facilitate the *whether* and *which* decisions, or an acquisition cost incurred to facilitate consummation of the acquisition. The label that the parties use to describe the cost and the point in time at which the cost is incurred do not necessarily determine the nature of the cost.

In *Situation 1*, an examination of the nature of the costs incurred indicates that *U* made its decision to acquire *V* after the investment banker conducted research on several industries and evaluated publicly available financial information. The costs incurred to conduct industry research and review public financial information are typical of the costs related to a general investigation. Accordingly, the costs incurred to conduct industry research and to evaluate publicly available financial information are investigatory costs eligible for amortization as start-up expenditures under § 195. However, the costs relating to the appraisals of *V*'s assets and an in-depth review of *V*'s books and records to establish the purchase price facilitate consummation of the acquisition, and thus, are capital acquisition costs. The costs incurred to evaluate *V* and *V*'s competitors also may be investigatory costs, but only to the extent they were incurred to assist *U* in determining whether to acquire a business and which business to acquire. If the evaluation of *V* and *V*'s competitors occurred after *U* had made its decision to acquire *V* (for example, in an effort to establish the purchase price for *V*), such evaluation costs are capital acquisition costs.

In *Situation 2*, the costs incurred to evaluate potential businesses are investigatory costs eligible for amortization as start-up expenditures under § 195 to the extent they relate to the *whether* and *which* decisions. However, the costs incurred to draft regulatory approval documents prior to the time *W* decided to acquire *X* are not start-up expenditures under § 195. The costs related to such activities, even if the activities occurred during the period *W* is engaged in a general search for a business, were not incurred in order to investigate whether to acquire a business and which business to acquire, but rather to facilitate an acquisition.

In *Situation 3*, an examination of the nature of the costs incurred by *Y* indicates that *Y* made its decision to acquire *Z* in September 1998, around the time that *Y* instructed the law firm to prepare and submit the letter of intent. The costs related to the "preliminary due diligence" services provided prior to that time (including the costs of conducting research on *Z*'s industry and in reviewing financial projections of *Z*) are typical of the costs incurred during an investigation to determine whether to acquire a new business and which new business to acquire. Thus, these costs are investigatory costs that are eligible for amortization as start-up expenditures under § 195. The costs related to "due diligence" services provided after that time, however, relate to the attempt to acquire the business and must be capitalized under § 263 as acquisition costs. Thus, the "due diligence" costs incurred to review *T*'s internal documents, books and records, and to draft the acquisition agreements are not eligible for amortization under § 195.

HOLDING

Expenditures incurred in the course of a general search for, or investigation of, an active trade or business in order to determine *whether* to enter a new business and *which* new business to enter (other than costs incurred to acquire capital assets that are used in the search or investigation) qualify as investigatory costs that are eligible for amortization as start-up expenditures under § 195. However, expenditures incurred in the attempt to acquire a specific business do not qualify as start-up expenditures because they are acquisition costs under § 263. The nature of the cost must be analyzed based on all the facts and circumstances of the transaction to determine whether it is an investigatory cost incurred to facilitate the *whether* and *which* decisions, or an acquisition cost incurred to facilitate consummation of an acquisition.

PROBLEM FOR DISCUSSION

Problem 4-7. Have the new Regulations under § 263, Reg. §§ 1.263(a)-4, and 1.263(a)-5 modified the result in Rev. Rul. 99-23?

§ 3.03. Election to Expense Certain Business Assets

I.R.C. § 179

Treas. Reg. §§ 1.179-1; 1.179-2; 1.179-3; 1.179-4; 1.179-5

Section 179 allows taxpayers to treat the cost of any § 179 property as an expense and, therefore, as a deduction, for the taxable year in which the property is placed in service. I.R.C. § 179(a); Reg. § 1.179-1(a). Section 179 is principally directed at small businesses, and its purpose is twofold. First, it allows taxpayers to avoid the recordkeeping necessary in depreciating the property. Second, it reduces the taxpayers' cost of capital, creating an incentive for taxpayers to invest in more equipment and employ more workers. See Tax Relief Reconciliation Act of 2005, H.R. Rep. No. 109-304, 109th Cong., 1st Sess. 51-52 (2005).

Importantly, the expense deduction under § 179 is subject to certain limitations. However, Congress has modified these limitations frequently over the past several years in an effort to increase the incentives for taxpayers to invest in business equipment during periods of economic distress. For taxable years beginning in 2006, the amount of the deduction could not exceed $100,000 annually. In addition, the $100,000 limitation was reduced by the amount by which the cost of the § 179 property placed in service during the taxable year exceeded $400,000. Consequently, if the taxpayer placed into service during 2006 § 179 property with an aggregate cost of more than $500,000, the taxpayer would not be able to expense any portion of the cost of such property. Congress increased these limitations to $250,000 and $800,000 for taxable years beginning after 2006 and before 2010 and to $500,000 and $2,000,000 for taxable years beginning in 2010 and 2011. I.R.C. § 179(b)(1) and 179(b)(2). Under current law, the amount of the deduction is reduced to $25,000 annually for taxable years after 2011, and this figure is reduced by the amount by which the cost of the § 179 property placed in service during the taxable year exceeds $200,000. Importantly, the basis of any property that is not expensed under § 179 is eligible for depreciation under § 167 or § 168.

One additional limitation also applies. The amount of the expense for any particular taxable year cannot exceed the taxable income for that taxable year that is derived from the active conduct of the taxpayer's trade or business. I.R.C. § 179(b)(3)(A); Reg. § 1.179-2(c). However, any amount that is not allowed as a deduction because of the taxable income limitation may be carried forward to succeeding taxable years, subject to all other applicable limitations. I.R.C. § 179(b)(3)(B); Reg. § 1.179-3.

Section 179 property is generally defined as any tangible property that is depreciable under § 168 and to which § 1245 applies that is acquired by purchase for use in the active conduct of a trade or business. I.R.C. § 179(d)(1); Reg. § 1.179-4(a). Any purchase satisfies this latter requirement except a purchase of such property from either a related party or a member of a controlled group and the basis of the property in the hands of the transferee is determined in whole or in part by reference to the basis of the property in the hands of the transferor or under § 1014. Reg. § 1.179-4(c). The definition of § 179 property also includes so-called "off-the-shelf" computer software under § 197(e)(3)(A)(i) that is amortizable under § 167 and that is placed in service in a taxable year beginning after 2002 and before 2012. Off-the-shelf computer software must also satisfy the requirements involving § 1245 and have been acquired by purchase for use in the active conduct of a trade or business. Finally, for taxable years beginning in 2010 and 2011, § 179 property includes certain types of real property although not more than $250,000 of the aggregate cost of such property may be expensed in each of those years. I.R.C. § 179(f).

With respect to any § 179 held by a partnership or S corporation, § 179 applies at both the partnership or corporate level and the partner or shareholder level. I.R.C. § 179(d)(8). Thus, the limitations described above must be applied first at the partnership and corporate level. Any deductions attributable to § 179 property must then be separately allocated to each partner and shareholder. I.R.C. §§ 702 and 1366. The limitations are then applicable to each partner or shareholder based on the aggregate of all § 179 deductions claimed by each individual. Reg. §§ 1.179-2(b)(3) and 1.179-2(b)(4).

A recapture rule applies under § 179 if the business use of the property drops to 50 percent or less in any subsequent taxable year. § 179(d)(10); Reg. § 1.179-1(e). In such a situation, the taxpayer must treat as ordinary income the amount of the § 179 expense in excess of the amount that would have been allowable as a depreciation deduction under § 167 or § 168 for that and prior taxable years had no expense been taken under § 179. For all subsequent taxable years, depreciation under § 167 or § 168 will then be determined as if no expense been taken under § 179.

§ 3.04. Expensing of Certain Capital Expenditures

(a) Research and Experimental Expenses

I.R.C. § 174

Treas. Reg. §§ 1.174-1; 1.174-2; 1.174-3; 1.174-4

Under § 174, a taxpayer may elect to deduct currently all research and experimental expenditures made in connection with the taxpayer's trade or business or to amortize the expenditures over a period of not less than 60 months. I.R.C. §§ 174(a) and 174(b); Reg. §§ 1.174-3 and 1.174-4. If the taxpayer fails to treat the expenditures under one of these methods, then the research and experimental expenses are to be charged to a capital account.

For purposes of § 174, "research and experimental expenses" are limited to those expenditures incurred in connection with the taxpayer's trade or business that "represent research and development costs in the experimental or laboratory sense. The term generally includes all such costs incident to the development or improvement of a product." Reg. § 1.174-2(a)(1). The Regulations expand on this definition through the adoption of an "uncertainty test," conditioned on the quality of the information available to the taxpayer at the time that the expenditures are undertaken. The Regulations provide that:

> [e]xpenditures represent research and development costs in the experimental or laboratory sense if they are for activities intended to discover information that would eliminate uncertainty concerning the development or improvement of a product. Uncertainty exists if the information available to the taxpayer does not establish the capability or method for developing or improving the product or the appropriate design of the product. Whether expenditures qualify as research or experimental expenditures depends on the nature of the activity to which the expenditures relate, not the nature of the product or improvement being developed or the level of technological advancement the product or improvement represents.

Id. The Service has indicated that the uncertainty test applies in the design and development of a product only in connection with technological or scientific uncertainty and not in connection with business or marketing uncertainty.

> [T]he term "uncertainty" must be limited to technological or scientific uncertainty in that a taxpayer must be uncertain as to whether it will be able to develop or improve its product in the scientific or laboratory sense. Put differently, the taxpayer must be uncertain as to whether it will be able to achieve its product development objective through its research activities. Conversely, uncertainty attributable to business or market concerns is not determinative of the existence of research and experimentation for purposes of section 174.

Field Service Advice 200125019 (considering the treatment of expenditures incurred in the design, development, modification, and improvement of athletic footwear). In other words, the uncertainty confronting the taxpayer must arise from doubt concerning the technical feasibility of the product, or the manufacturing process to produce the product, and not from doubt concerning the marketability of the product. For purposes of the uncertainty test, the term "product" includes "any pilot model, process, formula, invention, technique, patent, or similar property, and includes products to be used by the taxpayer in its trade or business as well as products to be held for sale, lease, or license." Reg. § 1.174-2(a)(2).

While considerable uncertainty exists with respect to the precise contours of the definition of "research and experimental expenditures," the Regulations are clear that the costs of obtaining a patent, including such expenditures as attorneys' fees expended to make and perfect a patent application, are included within the definition. Reg. § 1.174-2(a)(1). The Regulations are also clear that certain costs incurred in the development of a product under § 174 do not qualify as research or experimental expenditures. For example, costs incurred for ordinary testing or inspection of materials for purposes of quality control, in addition to costs incurred for efficiency surveys, management studies, consumer surveys, advertising, or promotions do not qualify as research or experimental expenditures. Reg. § 1.174-2(a)(3). The costs of materials or labor used in the construction, installation, acquisition, or improvement of property are also excluded from the definition of "research or experimental expenditures." Reg. § 1.174-2(b)(4). In addition, § 174 does not apply to expenditures for the acquisition or improvement of land or depreciable property. I.R.C. § 174(c); Reg. § 1.174-2(b)(1). However, allowances for depreciation may be considered research or experimentation expenditures under § 174 to the extent that the property is used in connection with research or experimentation.

An election currently to deduct all research or experimental expenditures applies to all qualifying expenditures. I.R.C. § 174(a)(3); Reg. § 1.174-3(a). Nevertheless, with the permission of the Service, the taxpayer may change to the deferred method with respect to those expenditures attributable to a particular project or projects. In no event, however, may a taxpayer currently deduct some of the expenditures and defer and amortize other expenditures relating to the same project.

Importantly, § 174 is available to taxpayers who are not yet engaged in a trade or business. In *Snow v. Commissioner*, 416 U.S. 500 (1974), the Supreme Court held that § 174 does not require that the taxpayer actually be carrying on a trade or business in order to deduct otherwise qualified research and experimental expenditures. The Court based its decision in part on the fact that the statutory language refers to research and experimental expenditures paid or incurred "in connection with" the taxpayer's trade or business and distinguished this language as imposing a less stringent standard than the "carrying on" standard of § 162. In addition, the Supreme Court relied on statements contained in the legislative history that § 174 was intended to equalize the tax treatment of "small and growing business" with their "large and well-established competitors." As a result, a start-up business may deduct research and experimental expenditures under § 174 while its other costs may constitute nondeductible start-up expenditures under § 195. Nevertheless, the deductibility of such expenditures is not permitted under § 174 if the taxpayer does not have some realistic prospect of entering into a trade or business involving the technology under development or, in fact, never eventually enters into the active conduct of a trade or business. *See, e.g., Scoggins v. Commissioner*, 46 F.3d 950 (9th Cir. 1995) (taxpayer's objective intent and capability to enter into a business in connection with its research activities demonstrated a "realistic prospect" of subsequently entering into business such that research expenditures were deductible); *Mach-Tech, Ltd. v. Commissioner*, 95-2 U.S.T.C. ¶ 50,375 (5th Cir. 1995) (disallowing deductions under § 174 because the taxpayer was neither engaged in, nor had any realistic prospect of, entering into a trade or business).

NOTES AND COMMENTS

In Rev. Proc. 2000-50, 2000-2 C.B. 601, the Service concluded that the costs of developing computer software, whether or not the software is patented or subject to copyright protection, so closely resemble the types of research and experimental expenditures under § 174 that similar treatment should be provided for such costs.

> Accordingly, the Service will not disturb a taxpayer's treatment of costs paid or incurred in developing software for any particular project, either for the taxpayer's own use or to be held by the taxpayer for sale or lease to others, where:
>
> (1) All of the costs properly attributable to the development of software by the taxpayer are consistently treated as current expenses and deducted in full in accordance with rules similar to those applicable under § 174(a); or
>
> (2) All of the costs properly attributable to the development of software by the taxpayer are consistently treated as capital expenditures that are recoverable through deductions for ratable amortization, in accordance with rules similar to those provided by § 174(b) and the regulations thereunder, over a period of 60 months from the date of completion of the development or, in accordance with rules provided in § 167(f)(1) and the regulations thereunder, over 36 months from the date the software is placed in service.

Id. at § 5.01.

(b) Environmental Remediation Costs

I.R.C. § 198

Perhaps the most controversial of the Service's pronouncements following the Supreme Court's decision in *INDOPCO, Inc. v. Commissioner*, 503 U.S. 79 (1992), concerned the deductibility of environmental remediation costs that were largely considered in terms of the repair versus improvement distinction. In three Technical Advice Memoranda, the Service concluded that certain remediation costs incurred with respect to asbestos and PCB contamination must be capitalized. Tech. Adv. Mem. 94-11-002 (requiring the capitalization of expenditures incurred in the removal of asbestos-containing materials); Tech. Adv. Mem. 93-15-004 (requiring the capitalization of costs incurred in the remediation of PCB contamination); Tech. Adv. Mem. 92-40-004 (requiring the capitalization of costs incurred for the removal and replacement of asbestos insulation). The Service characterized remediation costs as improvements to the land rather than repairs. For example, with respect to the removal of asbestos-containing insulation, the Service noted that the expenditures increased the value of the taxpayer's equipment "by reducing or eliminating the human health risks posed by the presence of asbestos. . . ." Tech. Adv. Mem. 92-40-004. Similarly, in connection with the costs to clean up land and to treat groundwater contaminated with PCBs, the Service concluded that such costs could not be likened to incidental repairs. Rather, the Service found the costs to be in the nature of replacements because the "taxpayer's property will be more valuable in its business after it is cleaned of PCB residues than when it was in need of remediation." Tech. Adv. Mem. 93-15-004.

Despite these earlier Rulings, in Rev. Rul. 94-38, 1994-1 C.B. 35, which follows, the Service reversed its position and held that the costs to remedy environmental contamination were currently deductible. In Rev Rul 98-25, the Service extended the analysis of Rev. Rul. 94-38 1998-1 C.B. 998, to permit the deduction of the costs incurred to remove, clean, and dispose of underground storage tanks containing the waste by-products of the taxpayer's manufacturing process. In addition, the Service permitted the deduction of the costs of acquiring, installing, and filling the replacement underground storage tanks, as well as the costs of any ongoing monitoring of the replacement tanks. Importantly, however, under the facts of the Ruling, the taxpayer did not use the tanks to temporarily hold wastes, but the tanks, once filled, were sealed indefinitely. Nevertheless, in Rev. Rul. 2004-18, 2004-1 C.B. 509, the Service concluded that environmental remediation expenditures otherwise deductible under Rev. Rul. 94-38 and expenditures to replace underground storage tanks otherwise deductible under Rev. Rul. 98-25 must be included as inventory costs and capitalized under § 263A when incurred as part of a taxpayer's business activities in manufacturing inventory. *See also* Rev. Rul. 2005-42, 2005-2 C.B. 67 (treating environmental remediation costs incurred to clean up land that a taxpayer contaminated with hazardous waste as a result of the operation of the taxpayer's manufacturing activities as incurred by reason of the taxpayer's production activities and, thus, properly allocable to inventory under § 263A).

REVENUE RULING 94-38

1994-1 C.B. 35

ISSUE

Are the costs incurred to clean up land and to treat groundwater that a taxpayer contaminated with hazardous waste from its business deductible by the taxpayer as business expenses under § 162 of the Internal Revenue Code, or must they be capitalized under § 263?

FACTS

X, an accrual basis corporation, owns and operates a manufacturing plant. X built the plant on land that it had purchased in 1970. The land was not contaminated by hazardous waste when it was purchased by X. X's manufacturing operations discharge hazardous waste. In the past X buried this waste on portions of its land.

In 1993, in order to comply with presently applicable and reasonably anticipated federal, state, and local environmental requirements ("environmental requirements"), X decided to remediate the soil and groundwater that had been contaminated by the hazardous waste, and to establish an appropriate system for the continued monitoring of the groundwater to ensure that the remediation had removed all hazardous waste. Accordingly, X began excavating the contaminated soil, transporting it to appropriate waste disposal facilities, and backfilling the excavated areas with uncontaminated soil. These soil remediation activities started in 1993 and will be completed in 1995. X also began constructing groundwater treatment facilities which included wells, pipes, pumps, and other equipment to extract, treat, and monitor contaminated groundwater. Construction of these groundwater treatment facilities began in 1993, and the facilities will remain in operation on X's land until the year 2005. During this time, X will continue to monitor the groundwater to ensure that the soil remediation and groundwater treatment eliminate the hazardous waste to the extent necessary to bring X's land into compliance with environmental requirements.

The effect of the soil remediation and groundwater treatment will be to restore X's land to essentially the same physical condition that existed prior to the contamination. During and after the remediation and treatment, X will continue to use the land and operate the plant in the same manner as it did prior to the cleanup except that X will dispose of any hazardous waste in compliance with environmental requirements.

LAW AND ANALYSIS

Section 162 generally allows a deduction for the ordinary and necessary expenses paid or incurred during the taxable year in carrying on any trade or business. Even though a particular taxpayer may incur an expense only once in the lifetime of its business, the expense may qualify as ordinary and necessary if it is appropriate and helpful in carrying on that business, is commonly and frequently incurred in the type of business conducted by the taxpayer, and is not a capital expenditure.

Commissioner v. Tellier, 383 U.S. 687 (1966); Deputy v. du Pont, 308 U.S. 488 (1940); Welch v. Helvering, 290 U.S. 111 (1933). Section 162 has been applied to allow business expense deductions for the costs of removing and disposing of waste materials produced in a taxpayer's business. See H.G. Fenton Material Co. v. Commissioner, 74 T.C. 584 (1980).

Section 263 generally prohibits deductions for capital expenditures. Section 263(a)(1) provides that no deduction shall be allowed for any amounts paid out for new buildings or for permanent improvements or betterments made to increase the value of any property. Section 263(a)(2) provides that no deduction shall be allowed for any amount expended in restoring property or in making good the exhaustion thereof for which an allowance has been made in the form of a deduction for depreciation, amortization, or depletion. Section 1.263(a)-1(b) of the Income Tax Regulations provides that capital expenditures include amounts paid or incurred (1) to add to the value, or substantially prolong the useful life, of property owned by the taxpayer, such as plant or equipment, or (2) to adapt property to a new or different use. Section 1.263(a)-2(a) provides that capital expenditures include the cost of acquisition, construction, or erection of buildings, machinery and equipment, furniture and fixtures, and similar property having a useful life substantially beyond the taxable year.

Section 263A provides that the direct costs and indirect costs properly allocable to real or tangible personal property produced by the taxpayer shall be capitalized. Section 263A(g)(1) provides that, for purposes of section 263A, the term produce includes construct, build, install, manufacture, develop, or improve.

Pursuant to section 461(h), in determining whether an amount has been incurred for any item during the taxable year for an accrual method taxpayer, the all events test shall not be treated as met any earlier than when economic performance occurs.

Through provisions such as § 162(a), § 263(a), and related sections, the Internal Revenue Code generally endeavors to match expenses with the revenues of the taxable period to which the expenses are properly attributable, thereby resulting in a more accurate calculation of net income for tax purposes. See. e.g., INDOPCO, Inc. v. Commissioner, __U.S. __, 112 S. Ct. 1039, 1043 (1992); Commissioner v. Idaho Power Co., 418 U.S. 1, 16 (1974). Moreover, as the Supreme Court has specifically recognized, the "decisive distinctions [between capital and ordinary expenditures] are those of degree and not of kind," and a careful examination of the particular facts of each case is required. Welch v. Helvering, 290 U.S. at 114; Deputy v. du Pont, 308 U.S. at 496. In determining whether current deduction or capitalization is the appropriate tax treatment for any particular expenditure, it is important to consider the extent to which the expenditure will produce significant future benefits. See INDOPCO, Inc. v. Commissioner, 112 S. Ct. at 1044-45.

The groundwater treatment facilities constructed by X have a useful life substantially beyond the taxable year in which they are constructed and, thus, the costs of their construction are capital expenditures under §§ 263(a) and 1.263(a)-2(a). Moreover, because the construction of these facilities constitutes production within the meaning of § 263A(g)(1), X is required to capitalize under § 263A the direct costs and a proper share of allocable indirect costs of constructing these facilities. The costs of the groundwater treatment facilities are recoverable under applicable law (e.g., § 168).

Under these facts, X's soil remediation expenditures and ongoing groundwater treatment expenditures (i.e., the groundwater treatment expenditures other than the expenditures to construct the groundwater treatment facilities) do not produce permanent improvements to X's land within the scope of § 263(a)(1) or otherwise provide significant future benefits. Under the facts of this ruling, the appropriate test for determining whether the expenditures increase the value of property is to compare the status of the asset after the expenditure with the status of that asset before the condition arose that necessitated the expenditure (i.e., before the land was contaminated by X's hazardous waste). See Plainfield-Union Water Co. v. Commissioner, 39 T.C. 333, 338 (1962), nonacq. on other grounds, 1964-2 C.B. 8. X's soil remediation and ongoing groundwater treatment expenditures do not result in improvements that increase the value of X's property because X has merely restored its soil and groundwater to their approximate condition before they were contaminated by X's manufacturing operations.

No other aspect of § 263 requires capitalization of X's ongoing soil remediation or ongoing groundwater treatment expenditures. These expenditures do not prolong the useful life of the land, nor do they adapt the land to a new or different use. Moreover, since the land is not subject to an allowance for depreciation, amortization, or depletion, the amounts expended to restore the land to its original condition are not subject to capitalization under § 263(a)(2). Accordingly, the expenses incurred by X for the soil remediation and ongoing groundwater treatment do not constitute capital expenditures under § 263.

The soil remediation and ongoing groundwater treatment expenditures incurred by X represent ordinary and necessary business expenses within the scope of § 162. They are appropriate and helpful in carrying on X's business and are commonly and frequently required in X's type of business. Therefore, the costs incurred by X to evaluate and remediate its soil and groundwater contamination (other than the costs of constructing the groundwater treatment facilities) constitute ordinary and necessary business expenses that are deductible under § 162.

HOLDING

Under the circumstances described above, costs incurred (within the meaning of the economic performance rules of § 461(h)) to clean up land and to treat groundwater that a taxpayer contaminated with hazardous waste from its business (other than the costs attributable to the construction of groundwater treatment facilities) are deductible by the taxpayer as ordinary and necessary business expenses under § 162. Costs properly allocable to constructing the groundwater treatment facilities, as determined under § 263A and the regulations thereunder, are capital expenditures under § 263. These results are applicable whether the taxpayer plans to continue its manufacturing operations that discharge the hazardous waste or to discontinue those manufacturing operations and hold the land in an idle state.

NOTES AND COMMENTS

The treatment of certain environmental remediation costs was modified by Congress in 1997. Section § 198 provides taxpayers with an election to currently deduct any "qualified environmental remediation expenditure" paid or incurred during the taxable year. I.R.C. § 198(a). According to the legislative history, the purpose of this section is "[t]o encourage the cleanup of contaminated sites, as well as to eliminate uncertainty regarding the appropriate treatment of environmental remediation expenditures for Federal Tax law purposes. . . ." S. Rep. No. 33, 105th Cong., 1st Sess. 110 (1997).

A qualified environmental remediation expenditure is defined as any expenditure that is otherwise chargeable to a capital account and that is paid or incurred in connection with the abatement or control of hazardous substances at a qualified contaminated site. I.R.C. § 198(b)(1). A qualified contaminated site is defined as any area that is held by the taxpayer for use in the taxpayer's trade or business or for the production of income or which is stock in trade, inventory, or property held by the taxpayer primarily for sale to customers in the ordinary course of the taxpayer's trade or business and at or on which there has been a release (or threat of release) or disposal of any hazardous substance. I.R.C. § 198(c)(1). However, an area is treated as a qualified contaminated site only if the taxpayer has received a statement from an appropriate state agency that there has been a release (or threat of release) or disposal of any hazardous substance on the site. I.R.C. § 198(c)(3).

Qualified environmental remediation expenditures do not include depreciation expenses for property used in connection with the abatement or control of hazardous substances at a qualified contaminated site except for that portion of such expenses that may be allocated to the site under the principles of *Commissioner v. Idaho Power Co.*, 418 U.S. 1 (1974), and the uniform capitalization rules of § 263A. I.R.C. § 198(b)(2); S. Rep. No. 33, at 110; H.R. Conf. Rep. No. 220, 105th Cong., 1st Sess. 487 (1997). Importantly, however, all qualified environmental remediation expenditures are themselves to be treated as depreciation deductions subject to recapture as ordinary income under § 1245. I.R.C. § 198(e).

Although one of the purposes of § 198 was to provide "clear and consistent rules regarding the Federal tax treatment of certain environmental remediation expenses" (S. Rep. No. 33, at 110), the section does not apply to all of the situations that were the subject of earlier Rulings by the Service. As previously described, § 198 applies only to qualified contaminated sites. Consequently, the analysis contained in Rev. Rul. 94-38 and other Rulings remains relevant in those situations to which § 198 does not apply. The legislative history to § 198 specifically states that the election to deduct currently any qualified environmental remediation expenditures under § 198 creates no inference regarding the proper treatment of remediation expenditures not described therein. H.R. Conf. Rep. No. 220, at 487.

PROBLEM FOR DISCUSSION

Problem 4-8. Will the Proposed Regulations under § 263, Prop. Treas. Reg. §§ 1.263(a)-3, applicable to the treatment of costs incurred to improve tangible property, modify the result in Rev. Rul. 94-38 if they become final?

(c) Intangible Drilling Costs

I.R.C. § 263(c)

Treas. Reg. §§ 1.263(c)-1 and 1.612-4

Section 263(c) permits the deduction of intangible drilling and development costs (IDC) in the case of oil, gas, and geothermal wells in accordance with Regulations prescribed by the Secretary. Although the Regulations explicitly apply only to oil and gas wells, § 263(c) provides that the same rules apply to wells drilled for any geothermal deposit. A geothermal deposit is defined as "a geothermal reservoir consisting of natural heat which is stored in rocks or in an aqueous liquid or vapor." I.R.C. § 613(e)(2).

Under the Regulations, IDC include "all expenditures made by an operator for wages, fuel, repairs, hauling, supplies, etc., incident to and necessary for the drilling of wells and the preparation of wells for the production of oil and gas." Reg. § 1.612-4(a). Such expenditures are IDC if incurred in the "drilling, shooting, and cleaning of wells," in the "clearing of ground, draining, road making, surveying, and geological works," and in the construction of "derricks, tanks, pipelines, and other physical structures." Reg. § 1.612-4(a). The deduction of IDC is available only to an operator, who is defined as "one who holds a working or operating interest in any tract or parcel of land either as a fee owner or under a lease granting working or operating rights." In the absence of § 263(c), such expenditures would have to be capitalized and recovered through depreciation or depletion.

The Regulations are clear, however, that IDC do not include expenditures by which the taxpayer acquires tangible property that is ordinarily considered as having a salvage value. Reg. §§ 1.612-4(a) and 1.612-4(c)(1). "Examples of such items are the costs of the actual materials in those structures which are constructed in the wells and on the property, and the cost of drilling tools, pipe, casing, tubing, tanks, engines, boilers, machines, etc." Reg. § 1.612-4(c)(1). *See Harper Oil Co. v. United States*, 425 F.2d 1335 (10th Cir. 1970) (cost of casing in a well, even though cemented in the well to such an extent that it has no net salvage value, is a depreciable item, the cost of which may be recovered only through depreciation); Rev. Rul. 70-414, 1970-2 C.B. 132 (excluding from § 263(c) expenditures relating to the installation of equipment such as pumping equipment, flow lines, separators, storage tanks, treating equipment, and salt water disposal equipment). In addition, IDC do not include expenditures for wages, fuel, repairs, hauling, and supplies that are incident structures for storing or treating oil or gas. Such expenditures must be capitalized and recovered through depreciation.

The distinction between IDC and expenditures involving tangible property considered to have a salvage value has been the subject of considerable litigation. In Rev. Rul. 70-596, 1970-2 C.B. 68, superseded by Rev. Rul. 89-56, 1989-1 C.B. 83, the Service concluded that the acquisition costs of an off-shore drilling platform, constructed in accordance with operator's instructions, were not IDC although the costs incurred in transporting the platform to the well site, positioning and erecting the platform, and permanently anchoring it to the ocean bed were IDC. However, in *Exxon Corp. v. United States*, 547 F.2d 548 (Ct. Cl. 1970), the court allowed the taxpayer to treat the costs of fabricating standardized components of a drilling platform as IDC and held that the Regulations only excluded expenditures for "actual materials" such as the steel beams and pipes used to fabricate the platforms. *See also Texaco, Inc. v. United States*, 598 F. Supp. 1165 (S.D. Tex. 1984); *Gulf Oil Corp. v. Commissioner*, 87 T.C. 324 (1986). In *Standard Oil Co. v. Commissioner*, 77 T.C. 349 (1981), the Tax Court held for the taxpayer with respect to fabrication costs using a "risk analysis" based on the premise that Congress intended to include within the IDC option expenditures that are "at risk." According to the court, expenditures that ordinarily are economically unrecoverable should the well be dry are IDC, whether or not those expenditures are represented by physical property. *See also Stradlings Bldg. Materials, Inc. v. Commissioner*, 76 T.C. 84 (1981) (stating that IDC must be incurred "sufficiently early in the development stages so that the taxpayer is exposed to the unknown risks of development").

In light of its failure before the courts, the Service modified its position. In Rev. Rul. 89-56, 1989-1 C.B. 83, the Service adopted the following position with respect to fabrication costs.

> Design and fabrication expenditures may be treated as IDC if the evidence shows that the platform in question is incident to and necessary for the drilling of wells (even though subsequently used for production), that the platform is designed and constructed for use at a specific site, and that platforms of that type are not ordinarily reused or otherwise salvaged as a unit. To be considered site-specific, a platform must not ordinarily be usable at another site without extensive modifications. Design and fabrication expenditures are not disqualified by evidence that a type of platform could hypothetically be reused (with substantial modification and expense), or by evidence that platforms of that type have occasionally been salvaged in extraordinary circumstances.

Nevertheless, the expenditures for property acquired by purchase do not constitute IDC even if much of the cost would have been IDC if the taxpayer had incurred the fabrication costs directly.

IDC include only those expenditures incident to and necessary for drilling or development as opposed to production costs. See Rev. Rul. 70-414, 1970-2 C.B. 132 (stating that "[a] producing well is completed when the casing, including the so-called "Christmas tree," has been installed). Production costs include expenditures relating to production structures, facilities, and equipment, service facilities for production personnel, pumping equipment, flow lines, separators, storage tanks, treating equipment, and salt water disposal equipment. Such costs are either capitalized and recovered through depletion or depreciation or currently deducted as business expenses under § 162.

Finally, expenditures for geological and geophysical exploration incurred by the taxpayer for the purpose of obtaining and accumulating data that will serve as a basis for the acquisition or retention of properties are not IDC and must be capitalized as part of the basis of such properties. Rev. Rul. 77-188, 1977-1 C.B. 76. *See Louisiana Land & Exploration Co. v. Commissioner*, 7 T.C. 507 (1946), *aff'd*, 161 F.2d 842 (5th Cir. 1947); *Schermerhorn Oil Corporation v. Commissioner*, 46 B.T.A. 151 (1942). If no properties are acquired or retained on the basis of such exploration, the expenditures may be deducted as a loss under § 165. Rev. Rul.

83-105, 1983-2 C.B. 51. However, geological and geophysical expenditures incurred to prepare for the actual drilling of wells are IDC. Reg. § 1.612-4(a).

In lieu of a current deduction, taxpayers may elect to capitalize IDC and recover such costs through depreciation if such costs are related to physical property or through depletion if not. For example, costs incurred in the installation of casing and equipment and in the construction of derricks and other physical structures are recovered through depreciation. Reg. § 1.612-4(b)(2). Costs incurred in clearing ground, draining, road making, surveying, geological work, excavation, grading, and the drilling, shooting, and cleaning of wells are not considered as related to property and, thus, are recovered through depletion. Reg. § 1.612-4(b)(1). Alternatively, taxpayers may elect to recover capitalized IDC ratably over 60 months for regular tax purposes. I.R.C. § 59(e). Such an election also avoids treatment of IDC as a tax preference for purposes of the alternative minimum tax.

Several other provisions are applicable to IDC. A recapture rule applies under which gain on the disposition of an interest in oil, gas, or geothermal property is treated as ordinary income in an amount equal to the lesser of the gain realized or the sum of the IDC deducted under § 263(c) and all depletion taken with respect to the property excluding percentage depletion in excess of cost. I.R.C. § 1254(a). In addition, an integrated oil company can expense only 70 percent of its IDC. I.R.C. § 291(b)(1). The remaining 30 percent is deductible ratably over 60 months. I.R.C. § 291(b)(2). *See* Rev. Rul. 93-26, 1993-1 C.B. 50 (providing that a taxpayer that has begun amortizing IDC under § 291(b) must continue to amortize any undeducted IDC if the taxpayer ceases to be an integrated oil company in a later year and that the unamortized IDC amount is included in basis if the taxpayer disposes of the property during the amortization period). An integrated oil company is a producer of crude oil that also carries on refining or retailing operations. I.R.C. § 291(b)(4).

(d) Mining Exploration and Development

I.R.C. §§ 616 and 617

Treas. Reg. §§ 1.616-1, 1.616-2, 1.617-1, 1.617-2, 1.617-3, 1.617-4

Sections 616 and 617 allow taxpayers to expense explorations and development expenditures incurred in connection with any mine or other natural deposit other than an oil or gas well. Section 617 specifically applies to exploration expenditures that are defined as expenditures incurred for the purpose of "ascertaining the existence, location, extent, or quality of any deposit of ore or other mineral." I.R.C. § 617(a)(1). To fall within § 617, such expenditures must be incurred before the mine reaches the development stage. Section 616 specifically applies to development expenditures "paid or incurred after the existence of ores or minerals in commercially marketable quantities has been disclosed." I.R.C. § 616(a). Although both types of expenditures may be expensed, certain recapture rules apply with respect to exploration expenditures, as described below, that do not apply to development expenditures. Thus, distinguishing between the two types of expenditures remains important.

As previously noted, exploration expenditures must be incurred before the mine reaches the development stage. Under the Regulations, the development stage is reached when, based on all of the facts and circumstances, "deposits of ore or other minerals are disclosed in sufficient quantity and quality to reasonably justify commercial exploitation by the taxpayer." Reg. § 1.617-1(a). As examples of exploration expenditures, the Regulations refer to core drilling expenditures to ascertain the existence of commercially marketable ore as well as expenditures for exploratory drilling within a producing mine to ascertain the existence of a different ore deposit. *Id. See* Rev. Rul. 70-289, 1970-1 C.B. 147. In addition, exploration expenditures include expenditures incurred for "geological and geophysical investigations, reconnaissance, surveying, test-pitting, trenching, drilling, driving of exploration tunnels and adits, and similar types of work." Rev. Rul. 70-287, 1970-1 C.B. 146. However, core drilling expenditures to delineate the extent and location of an existing commercially marketable deposit to facilitate its development are development expenditures subject to § 616, not exploration expenditures under § 617. Reg. § 1.617-1(a); Rev. Rul. 70-288, 1970-1 C.B. 146. *See generally Estate of De Bie v. Commissioner*, 56 T.C. 876 (1971) (reviewing the distinction between exploration and development expenditures). Finally, exploration expenditures do not include expenditures that are reflected in improvements subject to depreciation or depletion or to amounts paid or incurred to acquire property. Reg. §§ 1.617-1(b)(2) and 1.617-1(b)(4).

Once the property reaches the producing stage, expenditures deducted under § 617(a) must be recaptured under one of two methods. The taxpayer may include in gross income the "adjusted exploration expenditures," an amount equal to the exploration expenditures less any amounts previously recaptured. I.R.C. § 617(b)(1)(A); Reg. § 1.617-3(a)(2). The amount included in income is then capitalized and can be recovered through depletion. Alternatively, depletion allowances otherwise allowable with respect to the property are disallowed until the amount of adjusted exploration expenditures is recaptured. I.R.C. § 617(b)(1)(B); Reg. § 1.617-3(a)(1).

Development expenditures are deductible under § 616(a) and arise once the development stage of the property, as described above, is reached. Reg. § 1.616-1(a). In lieu of deducting such expenditures, a taxpayer may elect to treat them as deferred expenses and deduct them ratably as the minerals are sold. I.R.C. § 616(b); Reg. § 1.616-2. Like exploration expenditures, development expenditures do not include expenditures that are reflected in improvements subject to depreciation or depletion. Reg. § 1.616-1(b)(2).

Importantly, development expenditures do not include operating expenditures. Reg. § 1.616-1(b)(1). The distinction between development and operating expenses is important because operating expenses cannot be deferred at the taxpayer's election and development expenditures, along with exploration expenditures but not operating expenses, are recaptured as ordinary income on disposition of the property. I.R.C. § 1254. In Rev. Rul. 77-308, 1977-2 C.B. 208, the Service distinguished between development expenditures and operating expenditures. According to the Service,

> [e]xpenditures that are deductible under section 616 of the Code for development are expenditures that benefit an entire mineral deposit or large areas of a mineral deposit. Such expenditures must provide benefits

> that extend over relatively long periods of extraction of the valuable ore or mineral. Determination of whether an expenditure is for development is essentially a determination of fact.

Operating expenditures, on the other hand, involve day-to-day operations or are "integrally related to extraction of a limited area of the coal to be mined." Based on this distinction, the Service concluded that the costs of stripping the overburden from a 100-acre tract in increments of 20 acres in order to strip-mine the underlying minerals were not development expenditures because "such removal is directly related to and tied in with the rate of the extraction of the mineral in the day-to-day mining cycle." Instead, such costs were operating expenditures to be taken into accounts as the cost of goods sold. *See also* Rev. Rul. 67-169, 1967-1 C.B. 159 (same); Rev. Rul. 86-83, 1986-1 C.B. 251 (treating the costs of stripping overburden as a development expenditure because the removal of the overburden was not related to the rate of extraction of the mineral in the daily mining cycle).

Several other provisions are applicable to exploration and development expenditures. A recapture rule applies under which gain on the disposition of an interest in mining property is treated as ordinary income in an amount equal to the lesser of the gain realized or the sum of the amounts deducted under §§ 616 and 617 and all depletion taken with respect to the property excluding percentage depletion in excess of cost. I.R.C. § 1254(a). In addition, a corporation can expense only 70 percent of its exploration and development expenditures. I.R.C. § 291(b)(1). The remaining 30 percent is deductible ratably over 60 months. I.R.C. § 291(b)(2). Finally, for purposes of the alternative minimum tax, exploration and development expenditures must be capitalized and amortized ratably over 120 months. I.R.C. § 59(e). An election to amortize exploration and development expenditures over 120 months is also available for regular tax purposes.

§ 3.05. Bonus Depreciation

I.R.C. § 168(k)

Treas. Reg. § 1.168(k)-1

Section 168(k) currently allows a temporary, 50-percent depreciation allowance for certain types of so-called "qualified property" acquired after December 31, 2007 and before January 1, 2011. § 168(k)(1). Congress originally enacted § 168(k) following the attacks on September 11, 2001, as part of the Job Creation and Worker Assistance Act of 2002, Pub. L. No. 107-147, § 101, 116 Stat. 22 (2002). The provision was intended to "accelerate purchases of equipment, promote capital investment, modernization, and growth, and . . . help to spur an economic recovery." H.R. Rep. No. 107-251, 107th Cong., 1st Sess. 20 (2002). As originally enacted, § 168(k) permitted a 30-percent depreciation allowance for qualified property acquired after September 10, 2001 and before September 11, 2004 provided the taxpayer's use of the property commenced after September 10, 2001. Congress subsequently extended and increased the provisions of § 168(k) as part of the Jobs and Growth Tax Relief Reconciliation Act of 2003, Pub. L. No. 108-27, § 201, 117 Stat. 756-757 (2003). First, Congress extended the date by which taxpayers had to acquire qualified property from September 11, 2004, to January 1, 2005, in order to obtain the 30-percent bonus depreciation. Second, Congress increased the amount of bonus depreciation available under § 168(k) from 30 percent to 50 percent for so-called "50-percent bonus depreciation property." Fifty-percent bonus depreciation property was defined as property that otherwise constituted qualified property under § 168(k) provided the original use of the property commenced with the taxpayer after May 5, 2003, the property was acquired by the taxpayer after May 5, 2003, and before January 1, 2005, and the property was placed in service before January 1, 2005.

Although § 168(k) lapsed for qualified property acquired after December 31, 2004, Congress re-enacted its provisions for property acquired after December 31, 2007 and before January 1, 2012, first as part of the Economic Stimulus Act of 2008, Pub. L. No. 110-185, § 103(a), 122 Stat. 618-619 (2008) (applicable to qualified property acquired after December 31, 2007 and before January 1, 2009), and then as part of the American Recovery and Reinvestment Tax Act of 2009, Pub. L. No. 111-5, § 1201(a)(1), 123 Stat. 115 (2009) (extending § 168(k) to qualified property acquired before January 1, 2010), and as part of the Small Business Jobs Act of 2010, Pub. L. No. 111-240, § 2022(a), 124 Stat. 2504 (2010) (extending § 168(k) to qualified property acquired before January 1, 2011). In September 2010, the Obama Administration proposed extending the benefits of § 168(k) to qualified property acquired before January 1, 2012, and increasing the bonus depreciation deduction from 50 to 100 percent of the basis of such property. There is no doubt that the extension and enhancement of § 168(k) since 2002 dramatically illustrates the widespread political belief that increased cost recovery deductions significantly affect economic investment.

Qualified property generally includes property that has a recovery period of 20 years or less for purposes of § 168. § 168(k)(2)(A). Section 168(k) also applies to qualified leasehold improvement property and to computer software as defined under § 167(f)(1)(B) for which a deduction is allowable under § 167(a). However, § 168(k) is currently available only in connection with property acquired during the period after December 31, 2007, and before January 1, 2011, and placed in service before January 1, 2011. This requirement is deemed satisfied with respect to self-created property if the taxpayer begins manufacturing, constructing, or producing the property after December 31, 2007, and before January 1, 2011. § 168(k)(2)(E)(i). In addition, the taxpayer must be the original user of the property, and the taxpayer's use must have commenced after December 31, 2007. The term "original use" means "the first use to which the property is put, whether or not that use corresponds to the use of the property by the taxpayer." Reg. § 1.168(k)-1(b)(3)(i). If these requirements are satisfied, a depreciation deduction equal to 50 percent of the adjusted basis of the qualified property may be taken in the taxable year that the property is placed in service. § 168(k)(1)(A). If the qualified property also satisfies the definition of § 179 property and the taxpayer elects to take advantage of § 179, the taxpayer must first expense all or a portion of the adjusted basis of the property under § 179 and then determine the additional depreciation deduction under § 168(k). *See* Reg. §§ 1.167(a)-14(b)(1) and 1.167(k)-1(d)(3) example (2). Any remaining basis may then be depreciated under § 167 or § 168. § 168(k)(1)(B).

§ 3.06. Modified Accelerated Cost Recovery System

I.R.C. § 167(a) and (b); 168(a), (b), (c), (d), (e), (f)

Treas. Reg. §§ 1.167(a)-2; 1.167(a)-5; 1.167(a)-9; 1.167(g)-1; 1.167(a)-1T; 1.168(b)-1T; 1.168(d)-1(a), (b)(2), and (b)(4); 1.168(d)-1T(b)(3)

Prop. Treas. Reg. §§ 1.168-1; 1.168-2(d)(3); 1.168-4(b); 1.168-5(b)(1)-(7), (f)(3), and (f)(4)

(a) General Principals

Section 167(a) provides the general rule that taxpayers are entitled to depreciate property used in a trade or business or held for the production of income that is subject to exhaustion, wear and tear, and obsolescence. Section 167(a) applies to both tangible and intangible property but does not apply to property held solely for personal use. Section 167(b) provides that the basis for the determination of any depreciation deduction is the adjusted basis of the property under § 1011 that applies in determining gain on the sale or other disposition of such property.

As might be imagined, taxpayers and the Services have engaged in innumerable controversies over the years regarding such questions as to whether a specific item of property is subject to exhaustion, wear and tear, or obsolescence such that depreciation is permissible and, if so, when the property is placed in service such that depreciation commences, what specific method of depreciation is applicable, the period over which the property is depreciable, and what, if any, salvage value the property might have at the end of its useful life that should be taken into account in determining the appropriate amount of depreciation deductions. Frequently, the dispute between taxpayers and the Service hinged on whether an asset had a determinable useful life and, if so, the length thereof. For example, in *Furst v. United States*, 678 F.2d 147 (Ct. Cl. 1982), the Court of Claims concluded that secret formulas are intangible assets subject to amortization under § 167 but were nevertheless nonamortizable under the facts of the case because they had no determinable useful life. However, in *Liquid Paper Corp. v. United States*, 83-1 U.S.T.C. ¶ 9305 (Ct. Cl. 1983), the court found that the taxpayer had sufficiently demonstrated that its secret formula had a determinable useful life because technical advances would render the formula obsolete by 1995.

In 1981, Congress enacted § 168 to address many of the factual issues that frequently generated controversies between taxpayers and the Service in connection with the depreciation of tangible property. The Congressional intent behind the enactment of § 168 was to simplify the determination of depreciation deductions by statutorily defining the available methods of depreciation, as well as the recovery period over which depreciation could be claimed, specifying when property will be placed in service for purposes of determining depreciation deductions, and providing that the salvage value of any property be treated as zero. At that time, § 168 was referred as implementing the accelerated cost recovery system (ACRS). In addition to simplifying the determination of depreciation, ACRS allowed taxpayers to use accelerated methods of depreciation over relatively short recovery periods, thus reducing the effective tax rate applicable to such property, as described previously. As stated in the legislative history, "[t]he committee believes that greater levels of investment are essential to a robust economic growth and that a new depreciation system is urgently needed to stimulate investment spending." H.R. Rep. No. 97-201, 97th Cong., 1st Sess. 73 (1981). *See* S. Rep. No. 97-144, 97th Cong., 1st Sess. 47 (1981) ("The committee agrees with numerous witnesses who testified that a substantial restructuring of depreciation deductions . . . will be an effective way of stimulating capital formation, increasing productivity and improving the nation's competitiveness in international trade.").

Congress reconsidered § 168 as part of the Tax Reform Act of 1986. At that time, Congress was concerned that ACRS in conjunction with the investment tax credit created inequities in the tax treatment of businesses depending on each business's mix of labor and capital. As stated in the legislative history,

> [u]nder present law, the tax benefits arising from the combination of the investment tax credit and accelerated depreciation are more generous for some equipment than if the full costs of the investment were deducted immediately — a result more generous than exempting all earnings on the investment from taxation. At the same time, assets not qualifying for the investment tax credit and accelerated depreciation bear much higher effective tax rates. The output attainable from our capital resources is reduced because too much investment occurs in tax-favored sectors and too little investment occurs in sectors that are more productive, but which are tax disadvantaged. The nation's output can be increased simply by a reallocation of investment, without requiring additional savings.

S. Rep. No. 313, 99th Cong., 2d Sess. 96 (1986). Congress retained the simplifications enacted in 1981 but modified the applicable depreciation methods and lengthened the recovery periods. As amended, § 168 is referred to as implementing the modified accelerated cost recovery system (MACRS).

Section 168 did not replace § 167 as the general provision allowing depreciation with respect to property used in a trade or business or held for the production of income. It simply provides specific rules applicable to the determination of depreciation deductions with respect to tangible property. The following decision resolves one of the interpretative questions that arose regarding the interplay of §§ 167 and 168 and the extent to which § 168 was intended to modify the requirements of § 167. Moreover, it addresses some fundamental issues regarding why depreciation is permissible and how property is to be conceptualized for purposes of applying the provisions of §§ 167 and 168.

SIMON v. COMMISSIONER

United States Tax Court

103 T.C. 247 (1994), aff'd, 68 F.3d 41 (2d Cir. 1995)

LARO, JUDGE:

Richard Simon and Fiona Simon petitioned the Court for a redetermination of respondent's determinations in a notice of deficiency issued to them on December 11, 1991. In the notice respondent determined a $21,198 deficiency in petitioners' 1989 Federal income tax and a $4,240 addition thereto under section 6662(a) of the

Internal Revenue Code in effect for 1989. . . .

Due to concessions by the parties, the sole issue for decision is whether petitioners are entitled to deduct depreciation claimed under the accelerated cost recovery system (ACRS) for the year in issue. Petitioners claimed depreciation on two 19th-century violin bows that they used in their trade or business as full-time professional violinists. As discussed below, we hold that petitioners may depreciate their violin bows during the year in issue.

FINDINGS OF FACT

* * *

In 1965, Richard Simon joined the New York Philharmonic Orchestra (Orchestra) and began playing in its first violin section. In 1981, he joined and began playing with the New York Philharmonic Ensembles (Ensembles) (hereinafter, the Orchestra and the Ensembles are collectively referred to as the Philharmonic). Since 1965, Richard Simon has maintained two careers, one as a player with the Orchestra (and later with the Philharmonic) and the second as a soloist, chamber music player, and teacher.

* * *

In 1985, Fiona Simon joined the Philharmonic and began playing in its first violin section. Since 1985, Fiona Simon has maintained two careers, one as a full-time player with the Philharmonic and a second as a soloist, chamber music player, teacher, and free-lance performer.

During the year in issue, petitioners were both full-time performers with the Philharmonic, playing locally, nationally, and internationally in the finest concert halls in the world. In 1989, petitioners performed four concerts per week with the Philharmonic, playing over 200 different works, and attended many rehearsals with the Philharmonic that were more demanding and more time-consuming than the concerts. Petitioners also carried out the busy schedules connected with their second careers.

Construction of a Violin Bow

A violin bow consists of a flexible wooden stick, horsehair, a frog, and a ferrule (screw). The stick, which varies in thickness, weight, and balance, is the working part of the bow and is an integral part in the production of sound through vibration. It is designed so that horsehair can be stretched between its ends.

* * *

Old violins played with old bows produce exceptional sounds that are superior to sounds produced by newer violins played with newer bows. The two violin bows in issue were made in the 19th century by François Xavier Tourte (1747-1835). François Tourte is considered the premier violin bow maker. In particular, he is renowned for improving the bow's design. (Hereinafter, the two bows in issue are separately referred to as Bow 1 and Bow 2, and are collectively referred to as the

Tourte bows.)

Purchase of the Tourte Bows

On November 13, 1985, petitioners purchased Bow 1 for $30,000; the bow was purchased from Moes & Moes, Ltd., a dealer and restorer of violins and violin bows. On December 3, 1985, petitioners purchased Bow 2 from this dealer for $21,500. The sticks, frogs, and screws were originals of François Tourte at the time of each purchase. No cracks or other defects were apparent in the sticks at the time of each purchase. The frogs and screws, however, were not in playable condition. Therefore, petitioners replaced them.

Petitioners acquired the Tourte bows for regular use in their full-time professional employment as violinists. Petitioners purchased the Tourte bows for their tonal quality, not for their monetary value. In the year of acquisition, petitioners began using the Tourte bows with the original sticks in their trade or business as full-time professional violinists. Petitioners continued to use the Tourte bows with the original sticks during the year in issue.

Depreciation Deductions Claimed for the Tourte Bows

On their 1989 Form 1040, petitioners claimed a depreciation deduction of $6,300 with respect to Bow 1 and $4,515 with respect to Bow 2; these amounts were in accordance with the appropriate ACRS provisions that applied to 5-year property. See sec. 168(b)(1). Respondent disallowed petitioners' depreciation deduction in full and reflected her disallowance in the notice of deficiency at issue here.

Conditions Affecting the Wear and Tear of Violin Bows

Playing with a bow adversely affects the bow's condition; when a musician plays with a bow, the bow vibrates up, down, sideways, and at different angles. In addition, perspiration from a player's hands enters the wood of a bow and ultimately destroys the bow's utility for playing. Cracks and heavy-handed bearing down while playing certain pieces of music also create wear and tear to a bow. A player who has a heavy hand may cause the stick to press against the horsehair; in turn, this may cause the bow to curve and warp. . . . Petitioners' use of the Tourte bows during the year in issue subjected the bows to substantial wear and tear.

Frequent use of a violin bow will cause it to be "played out", meaning that the wood loses its ability to vibrate and produce quality sound from the instrument. From the point of view of a professional musician, a "played out" bow is inferior and of limited use. The Tourte bows were purchased by petitioners, and were playable by them during the year in issue, only because the Tourte bows were relatively unused prior to petitioners' purchase of them; the Tourte bows had been preserved in pristine condition in collections. At the time of trial, the condition of the Tourte bows had deteriorated since the dates of their purchase. Among other things, the sticks on the Tourte bows were worn down.

Value of the Tourte Bows

On November 21, 1985, Bow 1 was appraised for insurance purposes as having a fair market value of $35,000. On December 3, 1985, Bow 2 was appraised for insurance purposes as having a fair market value of $25,000. Petitioners obtained both appraisals from Moes & Moes, Ltd.

In 1994, at the time of trial, the Tourte bows were insured with the Philharmonic for $45,000 and $35,000, respectively. These amounts are based on an appraisal dated May 14, 1990, from Yung Chin Bowmaker, a restorer and dealer of fine bows. The record does not indicate whether these appraised amounts were the fair market values of the Tourte bows or were their replacement values.

An independent market exists for the Tourte bows and other antique bows. Numerous antique bows (including bows made by François Tourte) are regularly bought and sold in this market. The Tourte bows are unadorned; they are not as lavish or decorative as some other bows (including other bows made by François Tourte) that are sold in the independent market. Adornments on other bows include engravings, gold, silver, ivory, and mother of pearl.

One factor that adds value to the Tourte bows is the fact that Pernambuco wood, the wood that was used to make the sticks, is now very scarce. The wood that is currently used to make the sticks of violin bows is inferior to Pernambuco wood.

OPINION

* * *

Taxpayers have long been allowed asset depreciation deductions in order to allow them to allocate their expense of using an income-producing asset to the periods that are benefited by that asset. The primary purpose of allocating depreciation to more than 1 year is to provide a more meaningful matching of the cost of an income-producing asset with the income resulting therefrom; this meaningful match, in turn, bolsters the accounting integrity for tax purposes of the taxpayer's periodic income statements.. . . Such a system of accounting for depreciation for Federal income tax purposes has been recognized with the approval of the Supreme Court for over 65 years; as the Court observed in 1927: "The theory underlying this allowance for depreciation is that by using up the plant, a gradual sale is made of it." *United States v. Ludey*, 274 U.S. 295, 301 (1927); . . . In this sense, an allocation of depreciation to a given year represents that year's reduction of the underlying asset through wear and tear. *United States v. Ludey, supra* at 300-301. Depreciation allocations also represent a return to the taxpayer of his or her investment in the income-producing property over the years in which depreciation is allowed. *Virginian Hotel Corp. v. Helvering*, 319 U.S. 523, 528 (1943); *Detroit Edison Co. v. Commissioner*, 319 U.S. 98, 101 (1943).

* * *

In the instant case, respondent determined that petitioners were not entitled to deduct depreciation for the Tourte bows. On brief, respondent supports her disallowance with two primary arguments. First, respondent argues that the useful lives of the Tourte bows are indeterminable because the bows are treasured works of art for which it is impossible to determine useful lives. According to respondent, the Tourte bows are works of art because the Tourte bows have existed for more than 100 years and have increased in value over that time; the presence of an independent market for the Tourte bows also gives them a value independent of their capacity to be used to play music, and serves to extend their useful lives indefinitely.

As an alternative to this first argument, respondent argues that the Tourte bows are depreciable under section 168 only if petitioners first prove that each bow has a determinable useful life within the meaning of section 167. In this regard, respondent contends that petitioners must prove a specific or reasonable estimate of the number of years that the Tourte bows will be useful in order to depreciate them under ACRS. Given that the Tourte bows have existed for more than 100 years, respondent concludes, petitioners may not depreciate the Tourte bows because petitioners cannot determine the number of remaining years during which the Tourte bows will continue to be useful.

Petitioners' argument is more straightforward. According to petitioners, they may claim depreciation on the Tourte bows because the Tourte bows: (1) Were necessary to their profession as full-time professional violinists, and (2) suffered wear and tear attributable to their use in that profession. In this regard, petitioners contend, the Tourte bows can be used to produce beautiful sounds superior to those produced by any newer bow, and the Tourte bows harmonize this beautiful music with the reputation of the Philharmonic as one of the most prestigious orchestras in the world.

* * *

Inasmuch as section 168(a) allows a taxpayer to deduct depreciation with respect to "recovery property", petitioners may deduct depreciation on the Tourte bows if the bows fall within the meaning of that term. The term "recovery property" is defined broadly under ERTA to mean tangible property of a character subject to the allowance for depreciation and placed in service after 1980. Accordingly, property is "recovery property" if it is: (1) Tangible, (2) placed in service after 1980, (3) of a character subject to the allowance for depreciation, and (4) used in the trade or business, or held for the production of income. Sec. 168(c)(1) . . . .

The Tourte bows fit snugly within the definition of recovery property. First, it is indisputable that the Tourte bows are tangible property, and that they were placed in service after 1980. Thus, the first two prerequisites for ACRS depreciation are met. Second, petitioners regularly used the Tourte bows in their trade or business as professional violinists during the year in issue. Accordingly, we conclude that petitioners have also met this prerequisite for depreciating the Tourte bows.

The last prerequisite for depreciating personal property under section 168 is that the property must be "of a character subject to the allowance for depreciation". The term "of a character subject to the allowance for depreciation" is undefined in the 1954 Code. Comparing the language that the Congress used in section 167(a) of the 1954 Code immediately before its amendment [in 1981], with the language that it used in section 168(a) and (c)(1) as added to the 1954 Code [in 1981], we believe that the Congress used the term "depreciation" in section 168(c)(1), to refer to the term "exhaustion, wear and tear (including a reasonable allowance for obsolescence)" that is contained in section 167(a). . . . Accordingly, we conclude that the term "of a character subject to the allowance for depreciation" means that property must suffer exhaustion, wear and tear, or obsolescence in order to be depreciated. Accordingly, petitioners will meet the final requirement under section 168 if the Tourte bows are subject to exhaustion, wear and tear, or obsolescence.

We are convinced that petitioners' frequent use of the Tourte bows subjected them to substantial wear and tear during the year in issue. Petitioners actively played their violins using the Tourte bows, and this active use resulted in substantial wear and tear to the bows.[7] Indeed, respondent's expert witness even acknowledged at trial that the Tourte bows suffered wear and tear stemming from petitioners' business; the witness testified that the Tourte bows had eroded since he had examined them 3 years before, and that wood had come off them. Thus, we conclude that petitioners have satisfied the final prerequisite for depreciating personal property under section 168, and, accordingly, hold that petitioners may depreciate the Tourte bows during the year in issue. Allowing petitioners to depreciate the Tourte bows comports with the text of section 168, and enables them to match their costs for the Tourte bows with the income generated therefrom. Refusing to allow petitioners to deduct depreciation on the Tourte bows, on the other hand, would contradict section 168 and vitiate the accounting principle that allows taxpayers to write off income-producing assets against the income produced by those assets.

With respect to respondent's arguments in support of a contrary holding, we believe that respondent places too much reliance on the fact that the Tourte bows are old and have appreciated in value since petitioners acquired them. Indeed, respondent believes that this appreciation, in and of itself, serves to prevent petitioners from claiming any depreciation on the Tourte bows. We disagree; section 168 does not support her proposition that a taxpayer may not depreciate a business asset due to its age, or due to the fact that the asset may have appreciated in value over time.[8] . . . Respondent incorrectly mixes two well-established, independent

---

[7] [11] In this regard, we do not believe that the Tourte bows are so-called works of art. We define a "work of art" as a passive object, such as a painting, sculpture, or carving, that is displayed for admiration of its aesthetic qualities. *See* Webster's New World Dictionary 1539 (3d coll. ed. 1988). The Tourte bows, by contrast, functioned actively, regularly, and routinely to produce income in petitioners' trade or business. Although a computer utilized by a child to play games is not a depreciable asset, the same computer becomes a depreciable asset if it is used actively, regularly, and routinely by a data processor in his or her trade or business. By the same token, the Tourte bows could have been a collector's item except for the fact that petitioners used them actively, regularly, and routinely in their full-time business.

[8] [12] Accounting for depreciation of assets is an annual offset to gross income by deductions that represent the exhaustion, wear and tear, or obsolescence of an income-producing asset. Depreciation occurs on a daily basis, and depreciation accounting reflects the daily diminution in value of the underlying asset through other than market conditions. Accounting for changes in the values of depreciable property because of market conditions, on the other hand, is reportable as gain or loss upon the sale of the depreciable asset. This concept accounts for the increase or decrease in the market value of an asset on account of fluctuations caused by inflation, scarcity, or the like; such fluctuations are independent of the decrease in value of an asset through depreciation. *Fribourg Navigation Co. v. Commissioner*, 383 U.S. 272, 277 (1966); *Macabe Co., Inc. v. Commissioner*, 42 T.C. 1105, 1109-1110 (1964).

concepts of tax accounting, namely, accounting for the physical depreciation of an asset and accounting for changes in the asset's value on account of price fluctuations in the market. . . . Moreover, we find merit in petitioners' claim that they should be able to depreciate an asset that receives substantial wear and tear through frequent use in their trade or business. Simply stated, the concept of depreciation is appropriately designed to allow taxpayers to recover the cost or other basis of a business asset through annual depreciation deductions.[9]

We also reject respondent's contention that the Tourte bows are nondepreciable because they have value as collectibles independent of their use in playing musical instruments, and that this value prolongs the Tourte bows' useful life forever. First, it is firmly established that the term "useful life" under pre-[1981] law refers to the period of time in which a particular asset is *useful to the taxpayer* in his or her trade or business. *Fribourg Navigation Co. v. Commissioner, supra* at 277; *Massey Motors, Inc. v. United States*, 364 U.S. 92 (1960) . . . . Thus, the fact that an asset such as the Tourte bows may outlive a taxpayer is not dispositive of the issue of whether that asset has a useful life for depreciation purposes under pre-ERTA law. Second, the same argument concerning a separate, nonbusiness value can be made of many other assets. Such types of assets could include, for example, automobiles, patented property, highly sophisticated machinery, and real property. For the Court to delve into the determination of whether a particular asset has a separate, nonbusiness value would make the concept of depreciation a subjective issue and would be contrary to the Congress' intent to simplify the concept and computation of depreciation.

With respect to respondent's contention that petitioners must prove a definite useful life of the Tourte bows, we acknowledge that the concept of useful life was critical under pre-[1981] law. Indeed, the concept of useful life was necessary and indispensable to the computation of depreciation because taxpayers were required to recover their investments in personal property over the estimated useful life of the property. . . . However, the Congress enacted [§ 168], in part, to avoid constant disagreements over the useful lives of assets, to shorten the writeoff periods for assets, and to encourage investment by providing for accelerated cost recovery through the tax law. S. Rept. 97-144, at 47 (1981), 1981-2 C.B. 412, 425. . . . To these ends, the Congress created two short periods of years over which taxpayers would depreciate tangible personal property used in trade or business; the 3-year and 5-year recovery periods, respectively, are the *deemed useful life* of personal property. After the taxpayer has written off his or her asset over this 3-year or 5-year period, the taxpayer's basis in that asset will be zero; thus, the taxpayer will need to purchase a new asset in order to receive a future tax deduction with respect thereto. Respondent's argument that a taxpayer must first prove the useful life of personal property before he or she may depreciate it over the 3-year or 5-year period would bring the Court back to pre-ERTA law and reintroduce the disagree-

---

[9] [13] We note that the Congress enacted sec. 1245 in 1962 to minimize any perceived inequities that may have occurred due to the fact that a taxpayer's depreciation deductions offset his or her ordinary income, but the taxpayer's gain on the sale of the depreciable asset was reportable as capital gain. Under sec. 1245, taxpayers must report as ordinary income any gain on a sale of depreciable personal property to the extent of the prior depreciation that they have taken on the property. *Fribourg Navigation Co. v. Commissioner, supra* at 285.

ments that the Congress intended to eliminate by its enactment of ERTA. This the Court will not do.

Respondent mainly relies on *Clinger v. Commissioner*, T.C. Memo. 1990-459, and *Browning v. Commissioner*, T.C. Memo. 1988-293, aff'd, 890 F.2d 1084 (9th Cir.1989), to support a holding contrary to the one that we reach today. We find both of these cases distinguishable. First, in *Clinger*, the taxpayer was a professional portrait artist who painted in the style of her former teacher and well-known portrait artist, Alvin Gittins. Based on the taxpayer's belief that she could further her studies of Gittins, establish her credentials as a painter, and facilitate the marketing of her paintings, the taxpayer purchased a painting by Gittins and displayed it among her own paintings that she had hanging in her studio. The taxpayer claimed deductions under ACRS with respect to the purchased painting.

We sustained respondent's determination that the taxpayer was not entitled to deductions on the painting under ACRS. In so doing, we rejected the taxpayer's argument that the concept of useful life was eliminated with the enactment of ACRS, and accepted respondent's argument that a taxpayer must prove a determinable useful life. Our holding there, however, is distinguishable from the case at hand; unlike the Tourte bows, the painting in *Clinger* was not an asset that suffered substantial wear and tear through its regular, active, and physical use in the taxpayer's trade or business. To the extent, however, that respondent relies on a broad reading of *Clinger* to support her proposition that petitioners must prove *the* useful life of the Tourte bows in order to depreciate them, respondent misconstrues our holding in *Clinger.* In *Clinger*, the Court merely held that ACRS required that the taxpayer had to prove *a* determinable useful life of her passive business asset that suffered no discernible wear and tear. Determinable means "that can be determined". Webster's New World Dictionary 375 (3d coll. ed. 1988). Accordingly, once a taxpayer establishes that an asset is subject to exhaustion, wear and tear, or obsolescence, we can determine whether its useful life is 3-year or 5-year class property under ACRS. As coherently and succinctly stated by this Court in a Court-reviewed opinion:

> Availability of deductions for depreciation on tangible property in this case is dependent solely upon compliance with section 168, which has only two requirements for deduction of depreciation. First, the asset (tangible) must be of a type which is subject to wear and tear, decay, decline, or exhaustion. * * * Second, the property must be used in the taxpayer's trade or business or held for the production of income. * * * The language of the section is unequivocal. [*Noyce v. Commissioner*, 97 T.C. at 689.]

Browning v. Commissioner, T.C. Memo. 1988-293, aff'd, 890 F.2d 1084 (9th Cir.1989), is also distinguishable. In *Browning*, the taxpayer was a musician who performed in nightclubs and bars and for private engagements. Prior to and during 1980 and 1981, the taxable years in issue there, the taxpayer purchased several expensive antique violins, including a Ruggeri, a Stradivarius, and a Gabrielli. The Ruggeri and the Stradivarius violins were purchased in 1978 and 1979, respectively, and were subject to the pre-[1981] rules for depreciation. The Gabrielli violin was purchased in 1981, and was subject to ACRS. During 1980 and 1981, the taxpayer claimed depreciation deductions with respect to the Ruggeri and Stradivarius violins; the taxpayer amended his petition in this Court to claim that section 168 of the 1954 Code, as added [in 1981], allowed him to deduct depreciation on the Gabrielli violin for his 1981 taxable year.

The Court in *Browning* sustained respondent's determination that the taxpayer was not entitled to any depreciation deductions on the violins. In so doing, the Court first stressed that the taxpayer had presented no credible evidence to support a contrary holding with respect to the Stradivarius violin. . . . With respect to the other two violins (including the one subject to ACRS), we held for respondent because the taxpayer failed to present any evidence with respect to those violins.

The record in the instant case, by contrast to the record in *Browning*, is replete with evidence showing clearly that the Tourte bows suffered substantial wear and tear while petitioners used them in their trade or business. Accordingly, unlike the taxpayer in *Browning*, petitioners have met their burden of proving wear and tear to their business asset. To state the obvious, violin bows are subject to wear and tear when in use by a professional violinist. Indeed, as stated by Publilius Syrus circa 42 B.C.: "The bow too tensely strung is easily broken." Bartlett, Familiar Quotations 1103 (12th ed. 1951).

* * *

HAMBLEN, CHIEF JUDGE, dissenting:

I must disagree with the majority opinion. I respectfully submit that the basis for the majority's allowance of a depreciation deduction in this instance is sophistical and wrong. The majority would create a tax shelter for musicians, which, in my judgment, is based on incorrect legal analysis and some findings of fact that are unsupported by the record. The statutory interpretation of sections 167 and 168 is wrong in this context. Pertinent legislative history regarding determinable useful life is ignored. The antique violin bows are treasured "works of art" that for 71 years the Internal Revenue Service has treated, with congressional acquiescence, as nondepreciable property because as instruments and collectibles they have an indeterminable useful life. The majority's holding is contrary to legal precedent. See *Browning v. Commissioner*, T.C. Memo. 1988-293, *affd.* 890 F.2d 1084 (9th Cir.1989); see also *Clinger v. Commissioner*, T.C. Memo. 1990-459.

* * *

GERBER, JUDGE, dissenting;

I must, to some extent, agree and disagree with both the majority's view and Chief Judge Hamblen's minority view. Both views are thoughtful, but each approach unnecessarily results in taxpayers' being entitled to all or none of the depreciation claimed. Both positions fail to consider that the bows may have two separate attributes-recoverable or depreciable and intrinsic attributes. If both are considered, the results that the majority and minority views advocate could, to some extent, be achieved. As I see this issue, under either section 167, permitting "a reasonable allowance for the exhaustion, wear and tear", or section 168, permitting depreciation for specific categories of "recovery property", a taxpayer should not be entitled to a depreciation deduction for intrinsic value, which is generally not subject to wear and tear and/or makes the life of the object indeterminable. The facts reveal, and neither viewpoint denies, that the bows are being subjected to wear and tear due to their use by professional musicians. It is also factually indisputable that, in spite of their use, the bows continue to increase in value from the original purchase price because of their unique qualities. The crucial point, which has not been addressed, concerns the effect of the wear and tear upon the intrinsic value inherent in the asset.

The majority reaches the conclusion that each entire bow constitutes recovery property as defined in section 168(c)(1). . . . I agree that the bows are tangible property placed in service after 1980, and that the bows were used in petitioners' trade or business. I do not agree, however, that petitioners have shown that all of the property is of a character subject to the allowance for depreciation. Admittedly, some portion of the bows is subject to wear and tear, but not the intrinsic value that may exist even if the bows can no longer be used as bows. The burden is on petitioners to show which portion of the bows is subject to wear and tear and, therefore, recovery property.

There are numerous situations in the tax law where property is composed of both depreciable and nondepreciable portions. One example of this concept may be found in situations where a business is purchased and some portion of the purchase price may be attributable to goodwill — the nondepreciable intrinsic value of a business. *Ithaca Indus., Inc. v. Commissioner*, 97 T.C. 253 (1991), *aff'd*, 17 F.3d 384 (4th Cir.1994). More specifically, our Court has considered the intrinsic value in works of art and musical instruments and not permitted depreciation attributable to that aspect. *Browning v. Commissioner*, T.C. Memo. 1988-293, *affd.* 890 F.2d 1084 (9th Cir.1989); *Clinger v. Commissioner*, T.C. Memo. 1990-459. On several occasions we have delineated the existence of depreciable business use and nondepreciable personal use in the same property. See, e.g., *International Artists, Ltd. v. Commissioner*, 55 T.C. 94 (1970); *Gudmundsson v. Commissioner*, T.C. Memo. 1978-299. Finally, and by way of analogy, bifurcation of property into depreciable and nondepreciable portions is entrenched in the tax treatment of improvements to realty, which may be depreciable even though the land upon which they rest is not subject to depreciation.

To better illustrate the concept of intrinsic value, let us assume that Elvis Presley had purchased a guitar for $1,000. Due to his fame, however, the value of the guitar immediately increases to $11,000. If Elvis Presley had used the guitar in his business, he would have been entitled to depreciate the $1,000 amount, either over its useful life or in accordance with its section 168 class life, as may have been appropriate. If, however, another musician purchases Elvis' guitar for $11,000, the portion of the guitar which would be subject to wear and tear or be recovery property would be about $1,000, more or less, depending upon how much Elvis had used it and/or the cost of a similar quality guitar at the time of purchase. The fact that it had been Elvis' guitar will sustain a premium value which is attributable to the guitar's intrinsic collector's value. Even if Elvis's guitar became unusable for commercial purposes, collectors would be willing to pay for the intrinsic value because it had belonged to Elvis. Usually, that value increases with time due to increased uniqueness attributable to scarcity or increased popularity. That intrinsic value could be affected by wear and tear, but the wear and tear will not necessarily eliminate the intrinsic value. Accordingly, under section 167 the remaining intrinsic value would be the equivalent of "salvage value". Because section 168 does not consider salvage value, the intrinsic value should not be considered recovery property.

These same principles apply to the bows under consideration. Some portion of the value and purchase price is attributable to the collector's value and is not recovery property within the meaning of section 168. Although Congress, by enacting section 168, intended to simplify the classification of depreciable property and permit shorter periods of writeoff, there was no intent to permit the writeoff of the portion of property attributable to the intrinsic collector's value of unique property. The burden rests with taxpayers to show that portion of the property which is depreciable or recovery property and which portion is intrinsic or investment. Petitioners in this case have not shown the cost portion or value of the bows which is subject to wear and tear and, accordingly, must fail here. Admittedly, it would be unfair to hold that petitioners did not have some depreciation attributable to their use of the bows. It would be equally unfair (to other taxpayers) to permit petitioners to write off the intrinsic value which is unaffected by wear and tear or use.

The majority's holding permits the opportunity for substantial unintended abuse. Taxpayers will be able to depreciate items with current business utility and intrinsic collector's value and, after 3 or 5 years, have the tax benefit of the entire cost, at a time when the value of the item has not decreased or may have increased. The process may be duplicated over and over, providing substantial writeoffs with the cost borne by the public fisc. Ultimately, the taxpayer accumulates numerous of these collector's items which are passed on to future generations because of their intrinsic collector's value, which is likely to have substantially appreciated.

For the reasons expressed, I respectfully dissent.

HALPERN, JUDGE, dissenting:

I agree with Chief Judge Hamblen, and I have joined his dissent. . . . Briefly stated, I believe that, to claim recovery property within the meaning of section 168(c)(1), petitioners would have to show not only that the bows here in question are subject to wear and tear but also that they have determinable useful lives (i.e., useful lives capable of being settled, fixed, or determined). I do not believe that they have done so. I write separately, however, only to address the suggestion of allocation raised by Judge Gerber.

Judge Gerber suggests that the bows are dual use property, having utility both as playables and as collectibles. Judge Gerber recognizes that the utility of the bows as collectibles will not be exhausted in any fixed or determinable period. He assumes that their utility as playables will be exhausted in a fixed period, which can be shown. Judge Gerber would allow a deduction under section 168 with respect to a taxpayer's basis in such dual use property properly allocated to the property's utility as a playable.

To be sure, section 1.167(a)-2, Income Tax Regs., provides:

> The depreciation allowance in the case of tangible property applies only to that part of the property which is subject to wear and tear, to decay or decline from natural causes, to exhaustion, and to obsolescence. * * *

We have allowed less than a full allowance for the exhaustion, wear and tear, and obsolescence of property where only a portion of the property was used in a trade or business or held for the production of income. See, e.g., *International Artists, Ltd. v. Commissioner*, 55 T.C. 94 (1970) (depreciation deduction allowed to the extent premises were used for business purposes and disallowed to the extent used for personal purposes); *Noyce v. Commissioner*, 97 T.C. 670 (1991) (similar allocation under ACRS, with respect to an airplane). It seems to me a different thing, however, to say that property can wear out for one purpose but not another, so that, in effect, we should treat the taxpayer as having purchased two pieces of property rather than one. We have characterized as "bizarre" the suggestion that the owner's life expectancy should determine the depreciable useful life of an asset whose inherent value does not terminate upon the owner's death. *Clinger v. Commissioner*, T.C. Memo. 1990-459 (quoting *Coussement v. Commissioner*, T.C. Memo. 1966-179, *affd.* 391 F.2d 227 (6th Cir.1968)). Judge Gerber would allow petitioners to carve out of the apparently indeterminable useful lives of the bows as a whole those particular lives that petitioners may (but did not) show to be limited, and get a depreciation deduction for the utility related to those lives. We do not, in general, allow the fee owner of land to fragment the varied utilities inherent in her ownership in order separately to depreciate those with a determinable useful life. I do not see why we should do so with respect to otherwise nondepreciable property, such as the bows.

NOTES AND COMMENTS

Although Congress amended § 168(c) as part of the Tax Reform Act of 1986, deleting the term and definition of "recovery property," the opinion's discussion of the relationship between §§ 167 and 168 remains relevant because § 168(a) refers explicitly to "the depreciation deduction provided by section 167 for any tangible property. . . ." As can be seen, the judges of the Tax Court were significantly split in the *Simon* decision. Of the 16 judges involved in the decision, 10 held for the taxpayer and seven held for the government. In addition to the majority opinion, there were two concurring opinions and four dissenting opinions. Although the Tax Court's decision was upheld on appeal before the Second Circuit, the Service did not acquiesce to the decision. 1996-2 C.B. 1. In a companion case, *Liddle v. Commissioner*, 103 T.C. 285 (1994), *aff'd*, 65 F.3d 329 (3d Cir. 1995), the Tax Court followed its decision in *Simon* and allowed a full-time professional musician to depreciate the cost of a seventeenth-century Ruggeri bass viol that the musician used in his trade or business.

(b) Mechanics of Depreciation

In order to determine the annual depreciation deductions under § 168 for any particular item of property, the following three issues must be determined:

- The applicable recovery period,

- The applicable depreciation method, and
- The applicable convention.

See § 168(a). Once these three issues have been determined, a schedule of the annual depreciation deductions attributable to the property can be calculated using the adjusted basis of the property.

The Applicable Recovery Period. The applicable recovery period for any particular asset is based on the class life of the property and not its estimated actual useful life in the taxpayer's trade or business. The class life for a variety of types of assets is provided in Rev. Proc. 87-56, 1987-2 C.B. 674, a portion of which is reproduced below. *See* § 168(i)(1). Based on the class life of the asset, § 168(e)(1) provides that the asset is treated as three-, five-, seven -, 10-, 15-, or 20-year property. For example, five-year property includes assets with a class life of more than four years but less than 10 years while seven-year property includes assets with a class life of 10 or more years but less than 16 years. The determination of some types of assets as three -, five -, seven-, 10-, 15-, or 20-year property is statutorily specified in § 168(e)(3). For example, five-year property includes any automobile or light general purpose truck as well as qualified technological equipment. § 168(e)(3)(B)(i) and (iv). Based on the type of property, § 168(c) then defines the applicable recovery period. Unsurprisingly, five-year property has a recovery period of five years, while 15-year property has a recovery period of 15 years.

Section 168(c) also explicitly provides the recovery period applicable to real property. The recovery period for residential rental property and nonresidential real property is 27.5 and 39 years, respectively. Residential rental property is defined as any building or structure if 80 percent or more of the gross rental income from the building or structure is rental income from dwelling units. § 168(e)(2)(A). Nonresidential real property is defined as § 1250 property that is not residential rental property or property with a class life of less than 27.5 years. § 168(e)(2)(B). However, a special rule applies in the case of "qualified restaurant property" under § 168(e)(3)(E)(v), which treats as 15-year property any such property placed in service before January 1, 2008. The justification for this rule was Congress's belief that, unlike other commercial buildings, restaurants are "specialized structures" that "experience considerably more traffic, and remain open longer than most retail properties." H.R. Rep. No. 108-548, 108 Cong., 2d Sess. 122 (2004). "This daily assault causes rapid deterioration of restaurant properties and forces restaurateurs to constantly repair and upgrade their facilities. As such, restaurants facilities have a much shorter life span than other commercial establishments." Qualified restaurant property is any § 1250 property that is an improvement to a building if the improvement is placed in service more than three years after the building is first placed in service and more than 50 percent of the building's square footage is devoted to the preparation of meals and to seating for the on-premises consumption of such meals. § 168(e)(7). Although such qualified restaurant property is 15-year property, it cannot be depreciated using the 150 percent declining balance method, as described below, but must be depreciated using the straight-line method. § 168(b)(3)(H).

The Applicable Depreciation Method. The method of depreciation that may be used in determining the depreciation deductions for a particular asset depends on the recovery period of the asset. Generally, the 200 percent declining balance method is available. § 168(b)(1). This is the most accelerated method of depreciation available under § 168. However, the 150 percent declining balance method must be used for certain types of 15- and 20-year property and for property used in a farming business. § 168(b)(2). In addition, a taxpayer can elect to use the 150 percent declining balance method for property that would otherwise be depreciable using the 200 percent declining balance method. §§ 168(b)(2)(C) and 168(b)(5). Finally, certain types of property, most importantly residential rental property and nonresidential real property, must be depreciated using the straight-line method. § 168(b)(3). Regardless of the actual depreciation method used, the salvage value of the property is treated as zero. § 168(b)(4). Thus, a taxpayer is permitted to depreciate the full basis of the property over the recovery period despite the fact that the property may retain some value at the end of its useful life in the taxpayer's trade or business.

The 200 and 150 percent declining balance methods are not that difficult to apply. Both are applied by first determining the rate at which the property at hand would be depreciated using the straight-line method. For example, if the property had a recovery period of five years, one-fifth or 20 percent of the property's basis would be recovered each year using the straight-line method. The 200 percent declining balance method simply increases this rate by 200 percent to 40 percent. Similarly, the 150 percent declining balance method simply increases this rate by 150 percent to 30 percent. This increased rate of depreciation is then multiplied by the adjusted basis of the asset each year, i.e., the original basis of the asset reduced by any depreciation deductions, to determine that year's depreciation deductions. In other words, the increased depreciation rate is applied to the "declining balance" of the asset's basis. For example, for property with a five-year recovery period and a basis of $100 using the 200 percent declining balance method, the first year of depreciation would be $40 (20 percent straight-line recovery rate x 200 percent x $100). The second year of depreciation would be $24 (20 percent straight-line recovery rate x 200 percent x $60). Alternatively, for property with a five-year recovery period and a basis of $100 using the 150 percent declining balance method, the first year of depreciation would be $30 (20 percent straight-line recovery rate x 150 percent x $100). The second year of depreciation would be $21 (20 percent straight-line recovery rate x 150 percent x $70). Because the 200 percent declining balance method results in greater depreciation deductions than the 150 percent declining balance method, the 200 percent declining balance method is a more accelerated method of depreciation than is the 150 percent declining balance method.

Of course, if the reduced basis of the asset is simply multiplied by the depreciation rate each year to determine that year's depreciation, the asset would never be fully depreciated; its basis and any resulting depreciation deductions would simply become smaller and smaller. Section 168(b)(1)(B) provides, however, that the straight-line method is to be used starting in the first taxable year in which the straight-line method, using the adjusted basis of the asset as of that taxable year and depreciating the asset over the remainder of its recovery period, provides a depreciation deduction that is greater than the depreciation deduction using the 200 or 150 percent declining balance method. The mechanics of this rule, as well as the implications of the applicable convention, are described in an example in § 6 of

Rev. Proc. 87-57, 1987-2 C.B. 687, provided below.

The Applicable Convention. As previously mentioned, one of the reasons for the enactment of § 168 was to simplify the determination of depreciation with respect to tangible property and to avoid controversies between taxpayers and the Service with regard to this issue. One of the common sources of controversy involved determining when the taxpayer placed the property in service during the taxable year, entitling the taxpayer to begin claiming depreciation deductions. As defined under § 168(d), the applicable convention avoids this difficulty. In the case of property other than residential rental property and nonresidential real property, the applicable convention is the half-year convention. Thus, the taxpayer is entitled to claim depreciation starting at the mid-point of the taxable year in which the property is actually placed in service. For a calendar-year taxpayer, depreciation may be claimed for the period from July 1 to December 31 for property placed in service in a particular year.

Because the recovery period begins at the mid-point of the year that the property is placed in service, the number of taxable years over which the taxpayer may claim depreciation deductions attributable to a particular asset will one year greater than the actual recovery period. For example, property with a five-year recovery period will actually be depreciable over six taxable years — six months of the taxable year in which the property is placed in service (Year 1), the full 12 months for taxable Years 2 through 5, and six months of taxable Year 6. Although depreciation is claimed in six taxable years, the total recovery period remains five years.

The availability of a half-year's depreciation regardless of when a taxpayer actually places property in service during a taxable year creates an incentive for taxpayers to defer acquisition of depreciable property to the later portion of the year. However, § 168 prevents taxpayers from benefiting in this way by providing that, if more than 40 percent of the aggregate basis of property depreciable under § 168 and placed in service during the taxable year is placed in service during the last three months of the taxable year, then the mid-quarter, rather than the half-year, convention is to apply. § 168(d)(3). If this rule is triggered, property placed in service during the first quarter of the taxable year will be treated as placed in service at the mid-point of the first quarter of the year, while property placed in service during the second quarter of the taxable year will be treated as placed in service at the mid-point of the second quarter of the year, and so forth. Thus, taxpayers will be prevented from claiming six months of depreciation with respect to the property placed in service during the fourth quarter of the taxable year.

The applicable convention is the mid-month convention in the case of residential rental property and nonresidential real property. § 168(d)(2). Thus, a taxpayer is entitled to claim depreciation starting at the mid-point of the month in which such property is actually placed in service. For example, if a calendar-year taxpayer places an apartment building in service in the month of April, the taxpayer will be entitled to depreciation for 10 and one-half months — half of April and all of May through December. Because the mid-month convention applies with respect to residential rental property and nonresidential real property, the concern underlying the imposition of the mid-quarter convention does not apply, and such property is not taken into account in determining whether the mid-quarter convention is applicable. § 168(d)(3)(B).

Importantly, the applicable convention applies for the taxable year in which the property is disposed of as well as the taxable year in which the property is placed in service. § 168(d)(4). Thus, if property that was depreciated using the half-year convention is sold on September 30 of a subsequent year, a calendar-year taxpayer would only be entitled to claim half of the depreciation that would otherwise be available in the year of disposition, despite the fact that the taxpayer held the property for nine of the 12 months during that year.

Illustration of Depreciation under § 168. In order to illustrate the mechanics of depreciation under § 168, consider the example from § 1.02. Assume that T pays $43,553 for the widget maker at the end of Year 0 and starts making widgets on January 1, Year 1. Assume further that the widget maker is five-year property so that for purposes of § 168 it has a recovery period of five years. Because it is five-year property, T may use the 200 percent declining balance method. Finally, assume that this is the only property that T places in service during the taxable year so that the half-year convention is applicable and that T does not expense the asset under § 179 or take advantage of bonus depreciation under § 168(k). Although T places the widget maker in service on January 1, Year 1, the half-year convention requires that T is entitled to claim only one-half of the depreciation in Year 1 that would otherwise be available using the 200 percent declining balance method. Because the five-year recovery period does not start until July 1 of Year 1, T will be allowed to claim depreciation for the first six months of Year 6 as well. Depreciation determined under § 168 is shown in Table 4.6.

Table 4.6

				Year				
	0	**1**	**2**	**3**	**4**	**5**	**6**	**Total**
Gross Income		10,000	10,000	10,000	10,000	10,000	10,000	60,000
Cost Recovery		8,711	13,937	8,362	5,017	5,017	2,509	43,553
Taxable Income		1,289	-3,937	1,638	4,983	4,983	7,491	16,447
Tax Liability @ 35%		451	-1,378	573	1,744	1,744	2,622	5,757
Present Value of Tax Liability		410	-1,139	431	1,191	1,083	1,480	3,456
Pre-Tax Income	-43,553	10,000	10,000	10,000	10,000	10,000	10,000	
IRR	10.00%							
After-Tax Income	-43,553	9,549	11,378	9,427	8,256	8,256	7,378	
IRR	7.08%							

As in Tables 4.1, 4.2, 4.4 and 4.5 in § 1.02, the total amount of gross income, cost recovery deductions, and net tax liability is the same as in Table 4.6. However, because the 200 percent declining balance method of § 168 is an accelerated method of depreciation as compared to economic depreciation, we would expect that the after-tax internal rate of return would be greater than the 6.5 percent result when using economic depreciation. Indeed, the internal rate of return is 7.08 percent, greater than that involving economic depreciation. This is equivalent to a drop in the effective tax rate from 35 percent to 29.2 percent.

Taxpayers can reduce the effective tax rate applicable to the income from depreciable property by combining cost recovery methods. For example, for property that qualifies for expensing under § 179 and bonus depreciation under § 168(k), these provisions can be applied first to recover the taxpayer's investment in such property. As previously described, these provisions may allow a taxpayer to recover all or a significant portion of the taxpayer's investment in such property in the year that the property is placed in service. Section 168 can then be applied to the extent that the taxpayer's investment is not recovered after application of these provisions.

REVENUE PROCEDURE 87-56

1987-2 C.B. 674

SECTION 1. PURPOSE

The purpose of this revenue procedure is to set forth the class lives of property that are necessary to compute the depreciation allowances available under section 168 . . . . Rev. Proc. 87-57 . . . describes the applicable depreciation methods, applicable recovery periods, and applicable conventions that must be used in computing depreciation allowances under section 168.

SEC. 2. GENERAL RULES OF APPLICATION

.01 IN GENERAL. This revenue procedure specifies class lives and recovery periods for property subject to depreciation under the general depreciation system provided in section 168(a) of the Code or the alternative depreciation system provided in section 168(g).

.02 DEFINITION OF CLASS LIFE. Except with respect to certain assigned property described in section 3 of this revenue procedure, for purposes of both the general depreciation system and the alternative depreciation system, the term 'class life' means the class life that would be applicable for any property as of January 1, 1986, under section 167(m) of the Code (determined without regard to paragraph 4 thereof and determined as if the taxpayer had made an election under section 167(m)). The class life that would be applicable for any property as of January 1, 1986, under section 167(m), is the asset guideline period (midpoint class life) for the asset guideline class in which such property is classified under Rev. Proc. 83-35, 1983-1 C.B. 745. However, for purposes of the alternative depreciation system, section 168(g)(3)(B) assigns a class life to certain property that is taken into account under section 168 rather than the class life that would be applicable as of January 1, 1986. The class life of property that is either determined as of January 1, 1986, under Rev. Proc. 83-35 or assigned under section 168(g)(3)(B) may be modified by the Secretary pursuant to authority granted under section 168(i)(1). See section 4 of this revenue procedure. . . .

.04 PROPERTY WITH NO CLASS LIFE. Property that is neither described in an asset guideline class listed in section 5 of this revenue procedure nor assigned a class life under section 168(g)(3)(B) of the Code is treated as property having no class life for purposes of section 168 unless and until a class life is prescribed by the Secretary pursuant to the authority granted under section 168(i)(1). See section 4 of this revenue procedure. The general and alternative depreciation systems contain separate rules for classifying property that does not have a class life.

SEC. 3. ASSIGNED PROPERTY WITH ASSIGNED CLASS LIVES, RECOVERY CLASSES, OR RECOVERY PERIODS

Under section 168(i)(1)(E) of the Code, the term 'assigned property' means property for which a class life, recovery class, or recovery period is assigned under section 168(e)(3) or section 168(g)(3)(B), (C), or (D), and the term 'assigned item' means the class life, recovery class, or recovery period assigned under section 168(e)(3) or section 168(g)(3)(B), (C), or (D). For purposes of the general depreciation system assigned property under section 168(c)(3) is assigned to a recovery class without regard to such property's class life. (See section 3.02 of Rev. Proc. 87-57, this Bulletin.) For purposes of the alternative depreciation system, certain assigned property is assigned a class life under section 168(g)(3)(B), notwithstanding such property's class life as set out in Rev. Proc. 83-35. See section 3.03 of Rev. Proc. 87-57, ... For purposes of the alternative depreciation system, certain assigned property is assigned a recovery period under section 168(g)(3)(C), (D), or (E), notwithstanding such property's class life (if any).

SEC. 4. PRESCRIPTION AND MODIFICATION OF CLASS LIVES

.01 Section 168(i)(1)(B) of the Code provides that the Secretary, through an office established in the Treasury, shall monitor and analyze actual experience with respect to all depreciable assets. Except in the case of section 1250 property that is residential rental property or nonresidential real property, the Secretary, through that office, (i) may prescribe a new class life for any property, (ii) in the case of assigned property, may modify any assigned item, or (iii) may prescribe a class life for any property that does not have a class life within the meaning of section 2.02 of this revenue procedure. Any class life or assigned item that is prescribed or modified pursuant to this authority shall be used for all purposes in determining depreciation allowances under the general depreciation system and the alternative depreciation system. In the case of assigned property as defined in section 168(i)(1)(E), no class life set forth in this revenue procedure nor any other assigned item may be modified, unless such modification reflects a shortening of such class life, for property placed in service prior to January 1, 1992.

.02 Prescription or modification of class lives under the authority granted in section 168(i)(1)(B) of the Code shall reflect the anticipated useful lives, and the anticipated decline in value over time (that is, economic depreciation) of an asset to the industry or other group. . . .

SEC. 5. TABLES OF CLASS LIVES AND RECOVERY PERIODS

.01 Except for property described in section 5.02, below, the class lives (if any) and recovery periods for property subject to depreciation under section 168 of the Code appear in the tables below. These tables are based on the definition of class life in section 2.02 of this revenue procedure and the assigned items described in section 3 of this revenue procedure.

.02 For purposes of depreciation under the general depreciation system, residential rental property has a recovery period of 27.5 years and nonresidential real property has a recovery period of [39] years. For purposes of the alternative depreciation system, residential rental and nonresidential real property each has a recovery period of 40 years. . . .

EXAMPLES. Qualified technological equipment as defined in section 168(i)(2) (class B) is assigned a recovery period of 5 years for both the general and alternative depreciation systems, notwithstanding such property's class life (if any). Property which is a computer or peripheral equipment, high technology telephone station equipment installed on the customer's premises or high technology medical equipment within the meaning of section 168(i)(2), may be described in asset guideline class 00.12 (class life 6 years), 48.13 (class life 10 years) or 57.0 (class life 9 years), respectively. Property used in connection with research and experimentation referred to in section 168(e)(3)(B) (class C) is assigned a recovery period of 5 years for the general depreciation system, notwithstanding its class life (if any). Such property's recovery period for the alternative depreciation system is based on its class life (if any). An item of property used in connection with research and experimentation has a class life if such property is contained in an asset guideline class.

.05 The following special rules are incorporated from Rev. Proc. 83-35, sections 2.02(iii) and (iv):

1. Asset guideline class 00.3, 'Land Improvements,' includes 'other tangible property' that qualifies under section 1.48-1(d) of the Income Tax Regulations. However, a structure that is essentially an item of machinery or equipment or a structure that houses property used as an integral part of an activity specified in section 48(a)(1)(B)(i) of the Code, if the use of the structure is so closely related to the use of the property that the structure clearly can be expected to be replaced when the property it initially houses is replaced, is included in the asset guideline class appropriate to the equipment to which it is related. . . .

Asset Class	Description of assets included	Recovery Periods (in years)		
		Class Life (in years)	General Depreciation	Alternative Depreciation
SPECIFIC DEPRECIABLE ASSETS USED IN ALL BUSINESS ACTIVITIES, EXCEPT AS NOTED:				
00.11	OFFICE FURNITURE, FIXTURES AND EQUIPMENT: Includes furniture and fixtures that are not a structural component of a building. Includes such assets as desks, files, safes, and communications equipment. Does not include communications equipment that is included in other classes	10	7	10
00.12	INFORMATION SYSTEMS: Includes computers and their peripheral equipment used in administering normal business transactions and the maintenance of business records, their retrieval and analysis. Information systems are defined as: 1) Computers: A computer is a programmable electronically activated device capable of accepting information, applying prescribed processes to the information, and supplying the results of these processes with or without human intervention. It usually consists of a central processing unit containing extensive storage, logic, arithmetic, and control capabilities. Excluded from this category are adding machines, electronic desk calculators, etc. and other equipment described in class 00.13 2) Peripheral equipment consists of the auxiliary machines which are designed to be placed under control of the central processing unit. Nonlimiting examples are: Card readers, card punches, magnetic tape fees, high speed printers, optical character readers, tape cassettes, mass storage units, paper tape equipment, keypunches, data entry devices, teleprinters, terminals, tape drives, disc drives, disc files, disc packs, visual image projector tubes, card sorters, plotters, and collators. Peripheral equipment may be used on-line or off-line.			

		Recovery Periods (in years)		
Asset Class	Description of assets included	Class Life (in years)	General Depreciation	Alternative Depreciation
SPECIFIC DEPRECIABLE ASSETS USED IN ALL BUSINESS ACTIVITIES, EXCEPT AS NOTED:				
	Does not include equipment that is an integral part of other capital equipment that is included in other classes of economic activity, i.e., computers used primarily for process or production control, switching, channeling, and automating distributive trades and services such as point of sale (POS) computer systems. Also, does not include equipment of a kind used primarily for amusement or entertainment of the user	10	7	10
00.12	DATA HANDLING EQUIPMENT, EXCEPT COMPUTERS: Includes only typewriters, calculators, adding and accounting machines, copiers, and duplicating equipment	6	5	6
00.21	AIRPLANES (AIRFRAMES AND ENGINES), EXCEPT THOSE USED IN COMMERCIAL OR CONTRACT CARRYING OF PASSENGERS OR FREIGHT, AND ALL HELICOPTERS (AIRFRAMES AND ENGINES)	6	5	6
00.22	AUTOMOBILES, TAXIS	3	5	5
00.23	BUSES	9	5	9
00.241	LIGHT GENERAL PURPOSE TRUCKS: Includes trucks for use over the road (actual unloaded weight less than 13,000 pounds)	4	5	5
00.242	HEAVY GENERAL PURPOSE TRUCKS: Includes heavy general purpose trucks, concrete ready mix-truckers, and ore trucks, for use over the road (actual unloaded weight 13,000 pounds or more)	6	5	6

. . .

Asset Class	Description of assets included	Recovery Periods (in years)		
		Class Life (in years)	General Depreciation	Alternative Depreciation
SPECIFIC DEPRECIABLE ASSETS USED IN ALL BUSINESS ACTIVITIES, EXCEPT AS NOTED:				
00.3	LAND IMPROVEMENTS: Includes improvements directly to or added to land, whether such improvements are section 1245 property or section 1250 property, provided such improvements are depreciable. Examples of such assets might include sidewalks, roads, canals, waterways, drainage facilities, sewers (not including municipal sewers in Class 51), wharves and docks, bridges, fences, landscaping, shrubbery, or radio and television transmitting towers. Does not include land improvements that are explicitly included in any other class, and buildings and structural components as defined in section 1.48-1(e) of the regulations. Excludes public utility initial clearing and grading land improvements as specified in Rev. Rul. 72-403, 1972-2 C.B. 102	20	15	20
. . .				
01.1	AGRICULTURE: Includes machinery and equipment, grain bins, and fences but no other land improvements, that are used in the production of crops or plants, vines, and trees; livestock; the operation of farm dairies, nurseries, greenhouses, sod farms, mushroom cellars, cranberry bogs, apiaries, and fur farms; the performance of agriculture, animal husbandry, and horticultural services	10	7	10
. . .				
01.21	CATTLE, BREEDING OR DAIRY	7	5	7
01.22	HORSES, BREEDING OR WORK	10	7	10
. . .				

Recovery Periods (in years)

Asset Class	Description of assets included	Class Life (in years)	General Depreciation	Alternative Depreciation
SPECIFIC DEPRECIABLE ASSETS USED IN ALL BUSINESS ACTIVITIES, EXCEPT AS NOTED:				
13.0	OFFSHORE DRILLING: Including assets used in offshore drilling for oil and gas such as floating, self-propelled and other drilling vessels, barges, platforms, and drilling equipment and support vessels such as tenders, barges, towboats and crewboats. Excludes oil and gas production assets	7.5	5	7.5
13.1	DRILLING OF OIL AND GAS WELLS: Includes assets used in the drilling of onshore oil and gas wells and the provision of geophysical and other exploration services; and the provision of such oil and gas field services as chemical treatment, plugging and abandoning of wells and cementing or perforating well casings. Does not include assets used in the performance of any of these activities and services by integrated petroleum and natural gas producers for their own account	6	5	6
. . .				
14.0	CONSTRUCTION: Includes assets used in construction by general building, special trade, heavy and marine construction contractors, operative and investment builders, real estate subdividers and developers, and others except railroads . . .	6	5	6

REVENUE PROCEDURE 87-57

1987-2 C.B. 687

SECTION 1. PURPOSE

.01 This revenue procedure provides guidance to taxpayers and Service personnel in computing depreciation allowances for tangible property under section 168 . . . . This revenue procedure describes the applicable depreciation methods, applicable recovery periods, and applicable conventions that must be used in computing depreciation allowances under section 168.

.02 Sections 2-7 of this revenue procedure prescribe the manner of computing depreciation allowances. Section 8 of this revenue procedure contains various tables that may be used by certain taxpayers in lieu of computing allowances in the manner described in sections 2-7.

SEC. 2. GENERAL RULES OF APPLICATION

.01 *Property to which section 168 applies.* This revenue procedure applies to all property to which section 168 of the Code applies. In general, section 168 applies to depreciable tangible property placed in service after December 31, 1986, except that the section does not apply to property described in section 268(f) . . . .

.02 *Property to which section 168 does not apply.* Transitional rule property and property described in section 168(f) of the Code are subject to depreciation not under section 168 but under the following applicable depreciation rules:

1. Transitional rule property is subject to depreciation under section 167 or section 168 of the 1954 Code, as in effect before the amendments made by . . . the [1986] Act, but as amended by . . . the Act.

2. Property that is described in section 168(f)(1) of the Code is subject to depreciation under section 167(a). . . .

3. Property that is described in section 168(f)(2) of the Code (that is, public utility property for which the taxpayer does not use a normalization method of accounting) is subject to depreciation under the rule prescribed in section 168(i)(9)(C).

4. Property that is described in section 168(f)(3) or (4) of the Code (that is, films and video tapes, and sound recordings, respectively) is subject to depreciation under section 167(a).

5. Property that is described in section 168(f)(5) of the Code (that is, certain churned property) is subject to depreciation under section 167 of the Code or section 168, as in effect before the [1986] amendments . . . .

.03 *Property subject to the general depreciation system of section 168(a).* In general, unless the alternative depreciation system in section 168(g) of the Code applies, depreciation allowances are computed under the general depreciation system prescribed in section 168(a) by use of the applicable depreciation method, applicable recovery period, and the applicable convention determined under section 168(b), (c) and (d) of the Code, respectively. See section 6 of this revenue procedure for rules determining the applicable depreciation method. See section 4 of this revenue procedure for rules determining the applicable recovery period. See section 5 of this revenue procedure for rules determining the applicable convention. However, for certain property section 168(g) provides the alternative depreciation system.

.04 *Property subject to the alternative depreciation system of section 168(g).* Under the alternative depreciation system prescribed in section 168(g) of the Code, depreciation allowances are computed by use of the applicable depreciation method, the applicable recovery period, and the applicable convention determined under section 168(g)(2).

1. *Required use of alternative depreciation system.* The alternative depreciation system must be used for:

(a) any tangible property that during the taxable year is used predominantly outside the United States, as determined under section 168(g)(4);

(b) any tax-exempt use property, as defined in section 168(h); . . .

(e) any property covered by an election made under section 168(g)(7); and

(f) any property used predominantly in a farming business and placed in service during any taxable year in which the taxpayer elects under section 263A(d)(3) not to have section 263A apply to certain costs. *See* section 263A(e)(2)(A).

2. *Elective use of alternative depreciation system.* A taxpayer may make an irrevocable election pursuant to section 168(g)(7) with respect to any recovery class of property for any taxable year to use the alternative depreciation system in lieu of the general depreciation system. The alternative depreciation system shall apply to all property in such class placed in service during such taxable year. See section 3.02 of this revenue procedure for determination of recovery classes. In the case of nonresidential real property or residential rental property, an election to use the alternative depreciation system in lieu of the general depreciation system may also be made separately with respect to each property. Elections to use the alternative depreciation system must be made as set out in section 2.10 of this revenue procedure.

.05 *Recovery period.* The recovery period for depreciation of an asset begins in the taxable year when the asset is placed in service and ends either when cumulative depreciation deductions (allowed or allowable) equal the cost or other basis of the asset or when the asset is disposed of or retired from service in a business activity. In general, the term 'placed in service' refers to the time that property is first placed by the taxpayer in a condition or state of readiness and availability for a specifically assigned function.

.06 *Salvage value.* For purposes of computing the depreciation allowance under section 168 of the Code, salvage value is treated as zero. Section 168(b)(4).

.07 *Earnings and profits and alternative minimum tax.* The adjustment to earnings and profits under section 312(k)(3) of the Code for depreciation of property with respect to which section 168 applies shall be made using the alternative depreciation system. Under section 56(a)(1)(A)(i), for purposes of determining alternative minimum taxable income, depreciation allowances are computed using the alternative depreciation system, as modified for such purpose by section 56(a)(1)(A)(ii). See section 7 of this revenue procedure.

.08 *Other cost recovery rules.* Depreciation allowances computed under section 168 of the Code and this revenue procedure may be limited under other provisions of the Code, such as section 280F, which limits depreciation deductions with respect to listed property. In addition, property that would otherwise be depreciable under section 168 may be eligible for other cost recovery provisions in lieu of section 168, such as expensing under section 179, amortization under section 169, and depletion under section 611. No depreciation deduction is allowed under section 168 of property that is not used in a trade or business or held for the production of income.

.09 *Additions or improvements.* Additions or improvements to any property are treated as separate property items for purposes of computing depreciation. The recovery period for any addition or improvement to property begins the later of (1) the taxable year in which the addition or improvement is placed in service, or (2) the taxable year in which the property with respect to which such addition or improvement was made is placed in service. The applicable recovery period, applicable convention, and applicable depreciation method for an addition or improvement to property shall be the same as those that would be applicable to the underlying property if the underlying property were placed in service at the same time as the addition or improvement and were subject to section 168 of the Code.

.10 *Time and manner for making elections.* Under section 5h.5(a)(2) of the temporary regulations, after April 14, 1987, an election described in this revenue procedure shall be made by the due date (taking extensions into account) of the tax return for the first taxable year for which the election is to be made. The tax return must be accompanied by a statement identifying the election by reference to Code or Act section and identifying the property items for which the election is being made.

SEC. 3. CLASSES OF PROPERTY

.01 *In general.* The general depreciation system and the alternative depreciation system classify property for purposes of determining the applicable depreciation method, applicable recovery period, and applicable convention. Under different rules for each system, property is classified based on the class life of the property or the assigned class life of the property. The class life of property is the class life (if any) that would be applicable with respect to the property as of January 1, 1986, under section 168(m) of the Code (determined without regard to paragraph (4) thereof and determined as if the taxpayer had made an election under section 167(m)). The class life or assigned class life of property may be modified by the Secretary pursuant to authority granted under section 168(i)(1). Rev. Proc. 87-56, page 674, this Bulletin, provides the rules and tables relating to class lives of property.

.02 *General depreciation system.* Property subject to the general depreciation system is classified based upon the property's class life (if any), unless a different recovery class is assigned under section 168(e)(2) or (3) of the Code:

1. Property that is not assigned a recovery class under section 168(e)(2) or (3) of the Code is assigned a recovery class under the following table:

Class Life (in years)	*Recovery Class*
4 or less	3-year property
more than 4, but less than 10	5-year property
10 or more, but less than 16	7-year property
16 or more, but less than 20	10-year property
20 or more, but less than 25	15-year property
25 or more	20-year property

2. Property is assigned under section 168(e)(2) of the Code to the recovery classes for residential rental property or nonresidential real property based on the following rules:

(a) *Residential rental property recovery class*: Only property that is described in section [168(e)(2)(A)]. Thus, a building or structure shall be considered to be residential rental property for any taxable year only if 80 percent or more of the gross rental income from the building or structure is rental income from dwelling units (within the meaning of section [168(e)(2)(A)(ii)(I)]). For purposes of the preceding sentence, if any portion of the building or structure is occupied by the taxpayer as a residence, the gross rental income from the building or structure shall include the rental value of the portion so occupied.

(b) *Nonresidential real property recovery class*: Only section 1250 property that is not residential rental property and that does not have a class life of less than 27.5 years.

3. The following property (not including property defined as residential rental property or nonresidential real property) is assigned under section 168(e)(3) of the Code to a recovery class notwithstanding its class life, if any:

(3) *3-year property recovery class*: Any race horse that is more than 2 years old at the time it is placed in service, and any horse that is not a race horse and that is more than 12 years old at the time it is placed in service. The 3-year property recovery class does not include any automobile or light general purpose truck.

(b) *5-year property recovery class*: Any automobile or light general purpose truck, any semi-conductor manufacturing equipment, any computer-based telephone central office switching equipment, any qualified technological equipment (as defined in section 168(i)(2)), any property used in connection with research and experimentation, and certain energy property described in section 168(e)(3)(B)(vi).

(c) *7-year property recovery class*: Any railroad track, any single-purpose agricultural or horticultural structure (within the meaning of section 48(p)), and any property that does not have a class life and is not otherwise classified in section 168(e)(2) or (3).

(d) *15-year property recovery class*: Any municipal wastewater treatment plant and any telephone distribution plant and comparable equipment used for 2-way exchange of voice and data communications.

(e) *20-year property recovery class*: Any municipal sewer.

.03 *Alternative depreciation system.* For purposes of the alternative depreciation system, section 168(g)(3)(B) of the Code assigns to certain property a class life that is to be taken into account instead of the class life (if any) determined under section 167(m) as of January 1, 1986. The following property is assigned class lives under section 168(g)(3)(B) for purposes of the alternative depreciation system:

(a) Any semi-conductor manufacturing equipment is assigned a class life of 5 years.

(b) Any computer-based telephone central office switching equipment is assigned a class life of 9.5 years.

(c) Any railroad track is assigned a class life of 10 years.

(d) Any single purpose agricultural or horticultural structure (within the meaning of section 48(p)) is assigned a class life of 15 years.

(e) Any municipal wastewater treatment plant is assigned a class life of 24 years.

(f) Any telephone distribution plant and comparable equipment used for 2-way exchange of voice and data communications is assigned a class life of 24 years.

(g) Any municipal sewer is assigned a class life of 50 years.

SEC. 4. APPLICABLE RECOVERY PERIODS

.01 *General depreciation system.* Under the general depreciation system, the applicable recovery period for property is determined under section 168(c) of the Code and is based on the classification of property among either recovery classes as set forth in the following table:

Class of Property	*Applicable Recovery Period*
3-year property	3 years
5-year property	5 years
7-year property	7 years
10-year property	10 years
15-year property	15 years
20-year property	25 years
Residential rental property	27.5 years
Non-residential rental property	[39] years

These recovery periods are 12-month periods and are not based on taxable years. The applicable recovery periods are not elective.

.02 *Alternative depreciation system.* Under the alternative depreciation system, the applicable recovery period for property is determined under section 168(g) of the Code and is based upon the table in section 168(g)(2)(C) or, if applicable, a recovery period assigned in section 168(g)(3). The applicable recovery period for property subject to the alternative depreciation system is set forth in the following table:

In the case of	*Applicable Recovery Period*
Property not described below	the class life (including class lives assigned in section 168(g)(3)(B)). See section 3.03 of this revenue procedure.
Personal property that has no class life and that is not described below	12 years
Qualified technological equipment (as defined in section 168(i)(2))	5 years
Any automobile or light general purpose truck	5 years
Nonresidential real and residential rental property (The same definitions apply as under the general depreciation system, see section 3.02 of this revenue procedure.)	40 years
Any section 1245 property (as defined in section 1245) that is real property with no class life	40 years

These recovery periods are 12-month periods and are not based on taxable years. The applicable recovery periods are not elective.

SEC. 5. APPLICABLE CONVENTIONS

.01 *Effect of conventions.* Section 168(d) of the Code prescribes the applicable conventions to be used in computing depreciation deductions under section 168 for the taxable year in which property is placed in service and the taxable year in which property is disposed of or retired from service. The applicable convention determines the portion of the taxable year for which depreciation is allowable. Thus, allowable depreciation in the taxable year in which a convention applies is a fraction of the amount of the depreciation that would be allowable under the applicable depreciation method for a full taxable year (that is, a taxable year in which property is in service for 12 full months). An applicable convention as determines how much of the applicable recovery period remains as of the beginning of the taxable year following the taxable year in which property is placed in service.

.02 *Determination of applicable conventions.* One of three applicable conventions (half-year, mid-month, and mid-quarter) applies to all property subject to depreciation under section 168. The applicable convention is not elective.

1. *Mid-month convention.* The applicable convention for all nonresidential real property and residential rental property under both the general and alternative depreciation systems is the mid-month convention. The mid-month convention does not apply to any other property.

2. *Half-year convention.* The applicable convention for all property other than

residential rental property and nonresidential real property, under both the general and alternative depreciation systems, is the half-year convention, unless the mid-quarter convention applies.

3. *Mid-quarter convention.* The mid-quarter convention is a special rule applicable to situations in which substantial property is placed in service during the last three months of the taxable year. The convention applies, for purposes of both the general and the alternative depreciation systems, to all property (other than residential rental property and non-residential real property) placed in service during a taxable year if the following is satisfied: The aggregate bases of property subject to depreciation under section 168 that is placed in service during the last 3 months of the taxpayer's taxable year exceed 40 percent of the aggregate bases of property subject to depreciation under section 168 that is placed in service during the entire taxable year. For purposes of determining whether the mid-quarter convention applies, the aggregate bases of property subject to the general and the alternative depreciation systems are aggregated, except that aggregate bases of nonresidential real property and residential rental property are not take into account. . . . If applicable to all property (other than residential rental property and nonresidential real property) placed in service during a taxable year, the mid-quarter convention applies to all such property in the year of its disposition or retirement.

.03 *Half year convention.* Under the half-year convention, property placed in service, disposed of, or retired at any time during the taxable year is treated as being placed in service, disposed of, or retired on the mid-point of such year. Thus, the amount of allowable depreciation in the taxable year in which the half-year convention applies is one-half of the amount that would be allowable under the applicable depreciation method for a full year. The remaining recovery period as of the beginning of the taxable year following the taxable year in which property is placed in service is equal to the applicable recovery period less one-half of a year.

Example. Assume that on March 1, 1987, a taxpayer filing returns on the basis of the calendar year placed in service office furniture and on August 1, 1987, the taxpayer placed in service additional office furniture. The office furniture is in the seven-year property class. Assume also that the taxpayer placed no other property in service during the taxable year ending December 31, 1987. On its tax return for the taxable year ending December 31, 1987, the taxpayer must use the half-year convention to compute the depreciation deductions for the seven-year property placed in service during the taxable year. Thus, the seven-year property is deemed to be placed in service on July 1, 1987. The taxpayer is entitled to one-half of the amount of depreciation that would be allowable under the applicable depreciation method for a full year. As of January 1, 1988, the remaining recovery period is 6 1/2 years.

.04 *Mid-month convention.* Under the mid-month convention, property placed in service, disposed of, or retired during any month is treated as being placed in service, disposed of, or retired on the mid-point of such month. Thus, regardless of when during the month a taxpayer places residential rental property or nonresidential real property in service, the property is deemed to be placed in service on the mid-point of such month. Under the mid-month convention, depreciation is allowable for a fraction of a year with respect to each item of property placed in service, disposed of, or retired during such year. The numerator of the fraction is equal to.5 plus the number of full months in the taxable year in which the property is in service. The denominator of the fraction is 12. Allowable depreciation in a taxable year in which the mid-month convention applies is that fraction of the amount that would be allowable under the applicable depreciation method of a full-year. The remaining recovery period as of the beginning of the taxable year following a taxable year in which property is placed in service is equal to the property's applicable recovery period less the fraction of the first year for which depreciation is allowable.

Example. Assume that on March 1, 1987, a taxpayer filing returns on the basis of the calendar year placed in service residential rental property. On its tax return for the taxable year ending December 31, 1987, the taxpayer is entitled to (9.5)/12 of the amount of depreciation that would be allowable under the applicable depreciation method for a full year. As of January 1, 1988, the remaining recovery period for the property is 26 years and 8 1/2 months (that is, 27 years and six months less the 9 1/2 months for which depreciation is allowable in 1987).

.05 *Mid-quarter convention.* Under the mid-quarter convention, property placed in service, disposed of, or retired during any quarter of a taxable year is deemed placed in service, disposed of, or retired on the mid-point of such quarter. Thus, under the mid-quarter convention, depreciation is allowable for a fraction of a year. The numerator of the fraction is equal to.5 plus the number of full quarters in the taxable year in which the property is in service. The denominator of the fraction is 4. Allowable depreciation in a taxable year in which the mid-quarter convention applies is that fraction of the amount of depreciation that would be allowable under the applicable depreciation method for a full year. The remaining recovery period as of the beginning of the taxable year following a taxable year in which property is placed in service is equal to the property's applicable recovery period less the fraction of the first year for which depreciation is allowable.

Example. Assume that on January 3, 1987, a taxpayer filing returns on the basis of the calendar year placed in service for use in its business an automobile that cost $10,000 and on November 1, 1987, the taxpayer placed in service for use in its business a dump truck that cost $100,000. Assume also that the taxpayer placed no other property in service for use in its business during the taxable year ending December 31, 1987. On its tax return for the taxable year ending December 31, 1987, the taxpayer must use the mid-quarter convention to compute the depreciation deductions for both the automobile and the truck. Thus, the automobile is deemed to be placed in service on February 15, 1987 (that is, the mid-point of the first quarter), and the truck is deemed to be placed in service on November 15, 1987 (that is, the mid-point of the fourth quarter). The taxpayer is entitled to 7/8 of the amount of depreciation that would be allowable with respect to the automobile under the applicable depreciation method for a full year and 1/8 of the amount of the depreciation that would be allowable with respect to the dump truck under the applicable depreciation method for a full year. As of January 1, 1988, the remaining recovery period for the automobile is 4 1/8 years, and the remaining recovery period for the truck is 4 7/8 years.

SEC. 6. APPLICABLE DEPRECIATION METHODS

.01 *General depreciation system.* Under the general depreciation system, applicable depreciation methods are prescribed for each property class of property. See sections 3 and 4 of this revenue procedure for rules relating to the classification of property among recovery classes and assignment of the applicable recovery period for each recovery class. For the 3-, 5-, 7- and 10-year property recovery classes, the applicable depreciation method is the 200 percent declining balance method, switching to the straight line method in the taxable year that maximizes the depreciation allowance. For the 15- and 20-year property recovery classes, the applicable depreciation method is the 150 percent declining balance method, switching to the straight line method in the taxable year that maximizes the depreciation allowance. For the residential rental and nonresidential real property recovery classes, the applicable depreciation method is the straight line method. No other depreciation method may be used for property subject to the general depreciation system. The applicable depreciation methods for each recovery class are not elective, except that a taxpayer may make an irrevocable election, pursuant to section 168(b)(5) of the Code, to use the straight line method in lieu of the otherwise applicable depreciation method for all property within a recovery class that is placed in service in a taxable year. Such an election would require use of the straight line method in combination with the applicable recovery period and convention determined under the general depreciation system. An election to use the straight line method in lieu of the otherwise applicable depreciation method must be made as set out in section 2.10 of this revenue procedure.

.02 *Alternative depreciation system.* Under the alternative depreciation system, except as modified for purposes of the alternative minimum tax (see section 7 of this revenue procedure), the applicable depreciation method for all property is the straight line method.

.03 *Determination of applicable depreciation rate.* Under each of the applicable depreciation methods, the depreciation allowance for a full taxable year (that is, a taxable year of 12 full months) is computed by applying the applicable depreciation rate to the unrecovered basis of the property for each taxable year. For this purpose, the unrecovered basis of the property is the cost or other basis of the property adjusted for depreciation previously allowed or allowable and for all other applicable adjustments under section 1016 or any other provision of law. Determination of the applicable depreciation rate under each applicable depreciation method is described in section 6.04,.05, and.06 of this revenue procedure. In no case may an applicable depreciation rate in any year exceed 100 percent. Computation of applicable depreciation rates must reflect a reasonable and consistent rounding convention that is exact to at least one-hundredth of a percent in the case of property with an applicable recovery period of less than 20 years and to at least one-thousandth of a percent in the case of property with an applicable recovery period of 20 years or greater. Under any rounding convention, a taxpayer may not recover more than 100 percent of the recoverable basis of the property.

.04 *Declining balance method.* Under the declining balance method, an applicable depreciation rate (in percentage terms) is determined by dividing the specified declining balance percentage (150 or 200 percent) by the applicable recovery period. This applicable depreciation rate is constant for each taxable year in which the declining balance method is used and is applied to the unrecovered basis of the property (that is, generally the cost or other basis adjusted for depreciation previously allowed or allowable and for all other applicable adjustments). For example, the 200 percent declining balance method applied to property with a 5-year recovery period results in an applicable depreciation rate of 40 percent (200/5) in each full taxable year. As a further example, the 150 percent declining balance method applied to property with a 7-year recovery period results in a depreciation rate of 21.43 percent (150/7) in each full taxable year. See section 6.03 of this revenue procedure for the rounding convention.

.05 *Straight line method.* Under the straight line method, a new applicable depreciation rate is determined for each taxable year in the applicable recovery period. For any taxable year, the applicable depreciation rate (in percentage terms) is determined by dividing 1 by the length of the applicable recovery period remaining as of the beginning of such taxable year. The rate is applied to the unrecovered basis of the property (that is, generally the cost or other basis adjusted for depreciation previously allowed or allowable and for all other applicable adjustments). If as of the beginning of any taxable year the remaining recovery period is less than 1 year, the applicable depreciation rate under the straight line method for that year is 100 percent. For example, the straight line method applied to property with a 5-year recovery period results in applicable depreciation rates of 20, 25, 33.33, 50, and 100 percent, computed for five full years.

.06 *Declining balance method switching to straight line method.* Under this applicable depreciation method, a taxpayer uses the specified percentage declining balance method but must switch to the straight line method in the taxable year in which use of the straight line method yields a depreciation allowance equal to or greater than the allowance yielded by use of the declining balance method. Thus, under this applicable depreciation method, for each taxable year, a taxpayer must compare the applicable depreciation rates for a full taxable year under the declining balance method and the straight line method, *after taking into account the applicable convention* for purposes of determining how much of the applicable recovery period remains as of the beginning of the next full taxable year.

Example. Assume that a taxpayer filing returns on the basis of the calendar year placed property with a basis of $100 in service in February 1987, the applicable recovery period is 5 years, the applicable convention is the half-year convention, and the applicable depreciation method is the 200 percent declining balance method, switching to the straight line method in the taxable year which maximizes the depreciation allowance. Also assume that the taxable year 1987 is a taxable year of 12 full months and that the property remains in service through the end of 1992. Under the half-year convention, depreciation is allowable for one-half of 1987, and allowable depreciation is one-half of the amount that would be allowable under the applicable depreciation method for a full taxable year. Under the applicable depreciation method, the taxpayer must compare the applicable depreciation rates for a full taxable year under both the 200 percent declining balance method and the straight line method. The 200 percent declining balance method yields an applicable depreciation rate of 40 percent (200 divided by 5) in each year, and the straight line method yields an applicable depreciation rate of 20 percent in the first year. Thus, in 1987 the taxpayer uses the 200 percent declining balance method and the half-year convention resulting in a 1987 depreciation allowance of $20 ($100 x.40 x.5). Also, the half-year convention results in 4.5 years of the recovery period remaining as of the beginning of 1988. In 1988, the applicable depreciation rate under the declining balance method remains 40 percent. The applicable depreciation rate under the straight line method, which takes into account application of the applicable half-year convention in determining the remaining recovery period, is 22.22 percent (1 divided by 4.5). Thus, the taxpayer's 1988 depreciation allowance is $32 ($80, the unrecovered basis in 1988, x.40). In 1989, the applicable depreciation rate under the declining balance method remains 40 percent. The applicable depreciation rate under the straight line method, taking into account 3.5 years remaining in the recovery period, is 28.57 percent (1 divided by 3.5). Thus, the taxpayer's 1989 depreciation allowance is $19.20 ($48, the unrecovered basis in 1989, x.40). In 1990, the applicable depreciation rate under the declining balance method remains 40 percent. The applicable depreciation rate under the straight line method, taking into account 2.5 years remaining in the recovery period, is also 40 percent (1 divided by 2.5). Since the applicable depreciation rate under the straight line method is equal to or greater than the applicable depreciation rate under the declining balance method, the taxpayer switches to the straight line method in 1990 and uses the straight line method for the remainder of the recovery period. In 1990, the taxpayer's depreciation allowance is $11.52 ($28.80, the unrecovered basis in 1990, x.40). In 1991, the applicable depreciation rate under the straight line method is 66.67 percent (1 divided by 1.5), and the depreciation allowance is also $11.52. In 1992, the applicable depreciation rate under the straight line method is 100 percent, since the remaining recovery period as of the beginning of that year is less than 1 year. Thus, the depreciation allowance in 1992 is $5.76, which is the unrecovered basis in 1992. Note that the rounding convention specified in section 6.03 of this revenue procedure applies to the applicable depreciation rates.

SEC. 7. ALTERNATIVE MINIMUM TAX

.01 Section 55(b)(2) of the Code provides that for purposes of the alternative minimum tax imposed by section 55, the term 'alternative minimum taxable income' means the taxable income of the taxpayer for the taxable year with certain adjustments. Section 56(g)(4)(A) provides that, for purposes of determining the amount of the alternative minimum taxable income for any taxable year an adjustment to taxable income must be made for depreciation. Section 56(a)(1)(A) provides that depreciation allowances are computed using the alternative depreciation system as modified in section 56(a)(1)(A)(ii). The applicable depreciation method for purposes of the alternative minimum tax is not elective.

.02 Under section 56(a)(1)(A)(ii) of the Code, the alternative depreciation system is modified by modifying the applicable depreciation method with respect to certain property. The modified applicable depreciation method applies, for purposes of the alternative minimum tax, to all property other than non-residential real property, residential rental property, and property for which the taxpayer is required to use or has elected to use the alternative depreciation system pursuant to section 168(g). For such property, the applicable depreciation method is the 150 percent declining balance method, switching to the straight line method at the time that maximizes the deductions. The modified applicable depreciation method is applied in conjunction with the applicable recovery period and applicable convention determined under section 168(g) and sections 4.02 and 5 of this revenue procedure.

.03 For purposes of the adjustment to alternative minimum taxable income for any taxable year beginning after 1989 with respect to adjusted current earnings for such year, special rules for computing depreciation allowances are provided in section 56(g)(4) of the Code.

SEC. 8. OPTIONAL TABLES

.01 This section contains optional depreciation tables that may be used by certain taxpayers in computing annual depreciation allowances under section 168 of the Code. The depreciation tables may be used with respect to any item of property placed in service in a taxable year. For all items of property placed in service in a taxable year for which the depreciation tables are not used, depreciation allowances must be computed in the manner prescribed in sections 2-7 of this revenue procedure.

.02 The optional depreciation tables specify schedules of annual depreciation rates to be applied to the *unadjusted basis* of property in each taxable year. If a taxpayer uses a table to compute the annual depreciation allowance for any item of property, the taxpayer must use the table to compute the annual depreciation allowances for the entire recovery period of such property. However, a taxpayer may not continue to use the table if there are any adjustments to the basis of the property for reasons other than (1) depreciation allowed or allowable or (2) an addition or an improvement to such property that is subject to depreciation as a separate item of property. Use of the tables in this revenue procedure to compute depreciation allowances does not require the filing of any notice with the Internal Revenue Service.

Taxpayers use the appropriate table for any property based on the depreciation system, the applicable depreciation method, the applicable recovery period, and the applicable convention. The tables lists the percentage depreciation rates to be applied to the unadjusted basis of property in each taxable year.

In Tables 1-5, for the general depreciation system, the listed depreciation rates reflect the 200 percent declining balance method switching to the straight line method for property with applicable recovery periods of 3, 5, 7 or 10 years and the 150 percent declining balance method switching to straight line method for property with applicable recovery periods of 15 and 20 years.

Table 1

General Depreciation System

Applicable Depreciation Method: 200 or 150 Percent Declining Balance Switching to Straight Line

Applicable Recovery Periods: 3, 5, 7, 10, 15, 20 years

Applicable Convention: Half-year

If the Recovery Year is:	and the Recovery Period is:					
	3-year	5-year	7-year	10-year	15-year	20-year
	the Depreciation Rate is:					
1	33.33	20.00	14.29	10.00	5.00	3.750
2	44.45	32.00	24.49	18.00	9.50	7.219
3	14.81	19.20	17.49	14.40	8.55	6.677
4	7.41	11.52	12.49	11.52	7.70	6.177
5		11.52	8.93	9.22	6.93	5.713
6		5.76	8.92	7.37	6.23	5.285
7			8.93	6.55	5.90	4.888
8			4.46	6.55	5.90	4.522
9				6.56	5.91	4.462
10				6.55	5.90	4.461
11				3.28	5.91	4.462
12					5.90	4.461
13					5.91	4.462
14					5.90	4.461
15					5.91	4.462
16					2.95	4.461
17						4.462
18						4.461
19						4.462
20						4.461
21						2.231

Table 2

General Depreciation System

Applicable Depreciation Method: 200 or 150 Percent Declining Balance Switching to Straight Line

Applicable Recovery Periods: 3, 5, 7, 10, 15, 20 years

Applicable Convention: Mid-quarter (property placed in service in first quarter)

If the Recovery Year is:	and the Recovery Period is:					
	3-year	5-year	7-year	10-year	15-year	20-year
	the Depreciation Rate is:					
1	58.33	35.00	25.00	17.50	8.75	6.563
2	27.78	26.00	21.43	16.50	9.13	7.000
3	12.35	15.60	15.31	13.20	8.21	6.482
4	1.54	11.01	10.93	10.56	7.39	5.996
5		11.01	8.75	8.45	6.65	5.546
6		1.38	8.74	6.76	5.99	5.130
7			8.75	6.55	5.90	4.746
8			1.09	6.55	5.91	4.459
9				6.56	5.90	4.459
10				6.55	5.91	4.459
11				0.82	5.90	4.459
12					5.91	4.460
13					5.90	4.459
14					5.91	4.460
15					5.90	4.459
16					0.74	4.460
17						4.459
18						4.460
19						4.459
20						4.460
21						0.557

Table 3

General Depreciation System

Applicable Depreciation Method: 200 or 150 Percent Declining Balance Switching to Straight Line

Applicable Recovery Periods: 3, 5, 7, 10, 15, 20 years

Applicable Convention: Mid-quarter (property placed in service in second quarter)

If the Recovery Year is:	and the Recovery Period is:					
	3-year	5-year	7-year	10-year	15-year	20-year
	the Depreciation Rate is:					
1	41.67	25.00	17.85	12.50	6.25	4.688
2	38.89	30.00	23.47	17.50	9.38	7.148
3	14.14	18.00	16.76	14.00	8.44	6.612
4	5.30	11.37	11.97	11.20	7.59	6.116
5		11.37	8.87	8.96	6.83	5.658
6		4.26	8.87	7.17	6.15	5.233
7			8.87	6.55	5.91	4.841
8			3.33	6.55	5.90	4.478
9				6.56	5.91	4.463
10				6.55	5.90	4.463
11				2.46	5.91	4.463
12					5.90	4.463
13					5.91	4.463
14					5.90	4.463
15					5.91	4.462
16					2.21	4.463
17						4.462
18						4.463
19						4.462
20						4.463
21						1.673

Table 4

General Depreciation System

Applicable Depreciation Method: 200 or 150 Percent Declining Balance Switching to Straight Line

Applicable Recovery Periods: 3, 5, 7, 10, 15, 20 years

Applicable Convention: Mid-quarter (property placed in service in third quarter)

If the Recovery Year is:	and the Recovery Period is:					
	3-year	5-year	7-year	10-year	15-year	20-year
	the Depreciation Rate is:					
1	25.00	15.00	10.71	7.50	3.75	2.813
2	50.00	34.00	25.51	18.50	9.63	7.289
3	16.67	20.40	18.22	14.80	8.66	6.742
4	8.33	12.24	13.02	11.84	7.80	6.237
5		11.30	9.30	9.47	7.02	5.769
6		7.06	8.85	7.58	6.31	5.336
7			8.86	6.55	5.90	4.936
8			5.53	6.55	5.90	4.566
9				6.56	5.91	4.460
10				6.55	5.90	4.460
11				4.10	5.91	4.460
12					5.90	4.460
13					5.91	4.461
14					5.90	4.460
15					5.91	4.461
16					3.69	4.460
17						4.461
18						4.460
19						4.461
20						4.460
21						2.788

Table 5

Applicable Depreciation Method: 200 or 150 Percent Declining Balance Switching to Straight Line

Applicable Recovery Periods: 3, 5, 7, 10, 15, 20 years

Applicable Convention: Mid-quarter (property placed in service in fourth quarter)

If the Recovery Year is:	and the Recovery Period is:					
	3-year	5-year	7-year	10-year	15-year	20-year
	the Depreciation Rate is:					
1	8.33	5.00	3.57	2.50	1.25	0.938
2	61.11	38.00	27.55	19.50	9.88	7.430
3	20.37	22.80	19.68	15.60	8.89	6.872
4	10.19	13.68	14.06	12.48	8.00	6.357
5		10.94	10.04	9.98	7.20	5.880
6		9.58	8.73	7.99	6.48	5.439
7			8.73	6.55	5.90	5.031
8			7.64	6.55	5.90	4.654
9				6.56	5.90	4.458
10				6.55	5.91	4.458
11				5.74	5.90	4.458
12					5.91	4.458
13					5.90	4.458
14					5.91	4.458
15					5.90	4.458
16					5.17	4.458
17						4.458
18						4.459
19						4.458
20						4.459
21						3.901

Table 6
General Depreciation System
Applicable Depreciation Method: Straight Line
Applicable Recovery Period: 27.5 years
Applicable Convention: Mid-month

If the Recovery Year is:	And the Month in the First Recovery Year the Property is Placed in Service is:											
	1	2	3	4	5	6	7	8	9	10	11	12
1	3.485	3.182	2.879	2.576	2.273	1.97	1.667	1.364	1.061	0.758	0.455	0.152
2	3.636	3.636	3.636	3.636	3.636	3.636	3.636	3.636	3.636	3.636	3.636	3.636
3	3.636	3.636	3.636	3.636	3.636	3.636	3.636	3.636	3.636	3.636	3.636	3.636
4	3.636	3.636	3.636	3.636	3.636	3.636	3.636	3.636	3.636	3.636	3.636	3.636
5	3.636	3.636	3.636	3.636	3.636	3.636	3.636	3.636	3.636	3.636	3.636	3.636
6	3.636	3.636	3.636	3.636	3.636	3.636	3.636	3.636	3.636	3.636	3.636	3.636
7	3.636	3.636	3.636	3.636	3.636	3.636	3.636	3.636	3.636	3.636	3.636	3.636
8	3.636	3.636	3.636	3.636	3.636	3.636	3.636	3.636	3.636	3.636	3.636	3.636
9	3.636	3.636	3.636	3.636	3.636	3.636	3.636	3.636	3.636	3.636	3.636	3.636
10	3.637	3.637	3.637	3.637	3.637	3.637	3.636	3.636	3.636	3.636	3.636	3.636
11	3.636	3.636	3.636	3.636	3.636	3.636	3.637	3.637	3.637	3.637	3.637	3.637
12	3.637	3.637	3.637	3.637	3.637	3.637	3.636	3.636	3.636	3.636	3.636	3.636
13	3.636	3.636	3.636	3.636	3.636	3.636	3.637	3.637	3.637	3.637	3.637	3.637
14	3.637	3.637	3.637	3.637	3.637	3.637	3.636	3.636	3.636	3.636	3.636	3.636
15	3.636	3.636	3.636	3.636	3.636	3.636	3.637	3.637	3.637	3.637	3.637	3.637
16	3.637	3.637	3.637	3.637	3.637	3.637	3.636	3.636	3.636	3.636	3.636	3.636
17	3.636	3.636	3.636	3.636	3.636	3.636	3.637	3.637	3.637	3.637	3.637	3.637
18	3.637	3.637	3.637	3.637	3.637	3.637	3.636	3.636	3.636	3.636	3.636	3.636
19	3.636	3.636	3.636	3.636	3.636	3.636	3.637	3.637	3.637	3.637	3.637	3.637

Table 6
General Depreciation System
Applicable Depreciation Method: Straight Line
Applicable Recovery Period: 27.5 years
Applicable Convention: Mid-month

If the Recovery Year is:	And the Month in the First Recovery Year the Property is Placed in Service is:											
	1	2	3	4	5	6	7	8	9	10	11	12
20	3.637	3.637	3.637	3.637	3.637	3.637	3.636	3.636	3.636	3.636	3.636	3.636
21	3.636	3.636	3.636	3.636	3.636	3.636	3.637	3.637	3.637	3.637	3.637	3.637
22	3.637	3.637	3.637	3.637	3.637	3.637	3.636	3.636	3.636	3.636	3.636	3.636
23	3.636	3.636	3.636	3.636	3.636	3.636	3.637	3.637	3.637	3.637	3.637	3.637
24	3.637	3.637	3.637	3.637	3.637	3.637	3.636	3.636	3.636	3.636	3.636	3.636
25	3.636	3.636	3.636	3.636	3.636	3.636	3.637	3.637	3.637	3.637	3.637	3.637
26	3.637	3.637	3.637	3.637	3.637	3.637	3.636	3.636	3.636	3.636	3.636	3.636
27	3.636	3.636	3.636	3.636	3.636	3.636	3.637	3.637	3.637	3.637	3.637	3.637
28	1.97	2.273	2.576	2.879	3.182	3.485	3.636	3.636	3.636	3.636	3.636	3.636
29	0.000	0.000	0.000	0.000	0.000	0.000	0.152	0.455	0.758	1.061	1.364	1.667

NOTES AND COMMENTS

When originally enacted, § 168 provided a recovery period for nonresidential real property of 31.5 years. Congress subsequently extended the recovery for such property to 39 years. In order to calculate depreciation in connection with nonresidential rental property, the following table may be used.

Table 4.7
General Depreciation System
Applicable Depreciation Method: Straight Line
Applicable Recovery Period: 39 years
Applicable Convention: Mid-month

If the Recovery Year is:	**And the Month in the First Year is: the Property is Placed in Service is:**											
	1	2	3	4	5	6	7	8	9	10	11	12
1	2.641	2.247	2.033	1.819	1.605	1.391	1.177	0.963	0.749	0.535	0.321	0.107
2-39	2.564	2.564	2.564	2.564	2.564	2.564	2.564	2.564	2.564	2.564	2.564	2.564

(c) Special Provisions

General Asset Accounts

I.R.C. § 168(i)(4)

Treas. Reg. § 1.168(i)-1

Taxpayers are permitted to elect to create general asset accounts under which properties in the same asset class under Rev. Proc. 87-56 and having the same applicable depreciation method and applicable convention that are place in service by the taxpayer in the same taxable year may be depreciated as a group. § 168(i)(4); Reg. § 1.168(i)-1(c)(2). Of course, if a taxpayer has expensed a portion of basis of an asset under, for example, § 179, only the unadjusted basis of the asset after reduction by the expensed amount is properly include in a general asset account. Reg. § 1.168(i)-1(c)(1). The purpose of the general asset account is to avoid the determination of depreciation on an asset by asset basis.

The regulations provide that, upon disposition of an asset in a general asset account, the basis of the asset is treated as zero. Reg. § 1.168(i)-1(e)(2). Thus, no loss is realized. Furthermore, any amount realized is treated as ordinary income to the extent that the sum of the unadjusted depreciable basis of the general asset account and any expensed cost for assets in the account exceeds amounts previously treated as ordinary income on the disposition of assets in the account. The characterization of any amount realized in excess of this amount is determined under provisions of the Code other than §§ 1245 and 1250. The determination of depreciation with respect to the general asset account is unaffected by the disposition of the asset. *See* Reg. § 1.168(i)-1(e)(2)(v) *Examples*. A disposition for this purpose includes a sale, exchange, retirement, physical abandonment, or destruction of an asset. Reg. § 1.168(i)-1(e)(1).

Upon disposition of all of the assets or the last asset in an account, the general asset account terminates, and gain or loss for the account is determined under § 1001(a) using the adjusted basis of the general asset account at the time of the disposition. Reg. § 1.168(i)-1(e)(3)(ii). The amount of gain treated as ordinary income is limited to the depreciation allowed or allowable for the general asset account plus any expensed cost in excess of the amount previously treated as ordinary income, as described above. The characterization of gain not treated as ordinary income is determined under provisions of the Code other than §§ 1245 and 1250.

Special rules apply in connection with the transfers of an asset from a general asset account if the transfer satisfies the definition of a qualifying disposition or occurs in certain nonrecognition transactions. Reg. § 1.168(i)-1(e)(3)(iii), (iv), and (v).

Improvements and Basis Redeterminations

I.R.C. § 168(i)(6)

Prop. Reg. § 1.168-2(d)

If the costs of improving property depreciable under § 168 must be capitalized under § 263 or § 263A, the basis of the improvement may itself be depreciated under § 168 in the same manner as the underlying property, computed as if the underlying property had been placed in service at the same time as the improvement. § 168(i)(6). Thus, a $200,000 improvement to the air-conditioning system of nonresidential real property made in Year 8 of the underlying property's 39-year recovery period is itself recovered over a new 39-year recovery period commencing in Year 8 as if the improvement were itself nonresidential real property.

The basis of depreciable property may be redetermined after the taxpayer begins to depreciate the property. The redetermined basis may be either greater than or less than the original basis of the property. In such situations, adjustments must be made with respect to future depreciation deductions. As examples of basis redeterminations, proposed regulations under § 168 refer to reductions in the basis of property attributable to purchase price adjustments under § 108(e)(5) and to increases in the basis of property attributable to contingent payments not originally included in basis. Prop. Reg. § 1.168-2(d)(3)(ii). When basis is redetermined, future depreciation deductions are equal to the "redetermined adjusted basis" multiplied by the "redetermined applicable percentage." Prop. Reg. § 1.168-2(d)(3)(i). The redetermined adjusted basis is equal to the original basis adjusted to reflect the redetermination less any depreciation previously allowed or allowable. The redetermined applicable percentage is equal to the depreciation rate otherwise applicable in that year multiplied by the unrecovered percentage as of the redetermination year (i.e., 100 percent minus the deprecation rate for years prior to the redetermination year). Thus, the increase or decrease in basis is accounted for over the remaining years of the recovery period.

For example, assume that in Year 1, A placed in service property with five-year recovery period and an unadjusted basis of $100,000. In addition to the $100,000, A agreed to pay the seller 25 percent of the gross profits from the operation of the property in the first year. On July 15, Year 2, A paid the seller an additional $10,000. The recovery allowance for the property in Year 1 is $20,000. In Year 2, the property's redetermined adjusted basis is $90,000 (i.e., ($100,000+$10,000)-$20,000)). The redetermined applicable percentage is 40 percent (.32/(1.00-.20)). Thus, the recovery allowance in Year 2 is $36,000 (i.e., $90,000 times.40). In Years 3, 4, 5, and 6, the redetermined applicable percentage is 24 percent (.192/(1.00-.20)), 14.4 percent (.1152/(1.00-.20)), 14.4 percent (.1152/(1.00-.20)), and 7.2 percent (.0576/(1.00-.20)), resulting in recovery allowances of $21,600, $12,960, $12,960, $6,480 in each of those years respectively.

Cost Segregation

As previously noted, the recovery period applicable to residential rental property and nonresidential real property is 27.5 and 39 years, respectively. § 168(c). In addition, residential rental property and nonresidential real property is depreciable only using the straight-line method. Consequently, taxpayers frequently look for means to reduce the recovery period and/or use an accelerated method of depreciation with respect to costs that might otherwise be allocable to the basis of residential rental property or nonresidential real property. If successful, such means can increase depreciation deductions, reducing the taxpayer's tax liability and improving its cash flow. One means of doing so is through the use of cost segregation studies.

Cost segregation studies provide a detailed listing of all of the assets that make up a building. The object of such studies is to establish that certain of the assets are properly classified as tangible personal property under § 1245 rather than real property under § 1250. This is important because residential rental property is defined as any building or structure if 80 percent or more of the gross rental income from the building or structure is rental income from dwelling units. § 168(e)(2)(A). Nonresidential real property is defined as § 1250 property that is not residential rental property or property with a class life of less than 27.5 years. § 168(e)(2)(B). To the extent that assets can be separately classified as tangible personal property, the accelerated depreciation methods and shorter recovery periods of § 168 may be available. Cost segregation studies are typically carried out immediately upon completion of construction or following a change in ownership or major capital improvement.

Prior to the enactment of ACRS in 1981, taxpayers were able to make use of so-called "component depreciation" under which the cost of a building was assigned to its basic component parts, each with a separate useful life. Each component was then depreciated as a separate item of property. In enacting ACRS, however, Congress specifically provided that component depreciation was no longer available. Former § 168(f)(1); Prop. Reg. § 1.168-2(e)(1). When enacting MACRS in 1986, Congress reiterated that component depreciation was not allowable. Nevertheless, in *Hospital Corp. of Am. v. Commissioner*, 109 T.C. 21 (1997), *acq.*, the Tax Court reinstated a form of component depreciation when it concluded that the statutory prohibition of component depreciation applied only to § 1250 property and that the enactment of ACRS and MACRS did not redefine § 1250 property to include property that had been § 1245 property for purposes of the investment tax credit ("ITC") under former § 48.

Based on the court's decision, the rules applicable to the ITC are critical in determining whether a taxpayer has properly classified property as § 1245 or § 1250 property. For purposes of the investment tax credit, the regulations provide that "tangible personal property" means "any tangible property except land and improvements thereto, such as buildings or other inherently permanent structures (including items which are structural components of such buildings or structures)." Reg. § 1.48-1(c). Tangible personal property is further defined to include:

> all property (other than structural components) which is contained in or attached to a building. Thus, such property as production machinery, printing presses, transportation and office equipment, refrigerators, grocery counters, testing equipment, display racks and shelves, and neon and other signs, which is contained in or attached to a building constitutes tangible personal property for purposes of the credit allowed by section 38. Furthermore, all property that is in the nature of machinery (other than structural components of the building or other inherently permanent structure) shall be considered tangible personal property even though located outside a building. Thus, for example, a gasoline pump, hydraulic

> car lift, or automatic vending machine, although annexed to the ground, shall be considered tangible personal property.

Id. See also S. Rep. No. 1263, 95th Cong., 2d Sess. 117 (1978) (including within the definition of personal property special lighting (including lighting to illuminate the exterior of a building or store, but not lighting to illuminate parking areas), false balconies, and other exterior ornamentation that have no more than an incidental relationship to the operation or maintenance of a building, floor coverings that are not an integral part of the floor itself such as floor tile generally installed in a manner to be readily removed, carpeting, wall panel inserts such as those designed to contain condiments or to serve as a framing for picture of the products of a retail establishment, beverage bars, ornamental fixtures, booths for seating, movable and removable partitions, and large and small pictures of scenery, persons, and the like). The regulations describe a "building" as:

> any structure or edifice enclosing a space within its walls and usually covered by a roof whereby the structure improves the land, and provides shelter or housing for work, office, display, or sales space. The term includes, for example, structures such as apartment houses, factory and office buildings, warehouses, barns, garages, railway or bus stations, and stores. Such term includes any such structure constructed by, or for, a lessee even if such structure must be removed, or ownership of such structure reverts to the lessor, at the termination of the lease.

Reg. § 1.48-1(e)(1). Furthermore, the term "structural components" includes:

> such parts of a building as walls, partitions, floors, and ceilings, as well as any permanent coverings therefor such as paneling or tiling; windows and doors; all components (whether in, on, or adjacent to the building) of a central air condition or heating system, including motors, compressors, pipes and ducts; plumbing and plumbing fixtures, such as sinks and bathtubs; electric wiring and lighting fixtures; chimneys; stairs, escalators, and elevators, including all components thereof; sprinkler systems; fire escapes; and other components relating to the operation or maintenance of a building.
>
> However, the term "structural components" does not include machinery the sole justification for the installation of which is the fact that such machinery is required to meet temperature or humidity requirements which are essential for the operation of other machinery or the processing of materials or foodstuffs. Machinery may meet the "sole justification" test provided by the preceding sentence even though it incidentally provides for the comfort of employees, or serves, to an insubstantial degree, areas where such temperature or humidity requirements are not essential. For example, an air conditioning and humidification system installed in a textile plant in order to maintain the temperature or humidity within a narrow optimum range which is critical in processing particular types of yarn or cloth is not included within the term "structural components".

Reg. § 1.48-1(e)(2). A structure that is essentially an item of machinery or equipment is specifically excluded from the definition of a building. Reg. § 1.48-

1(e)(1). *See also Boddie-Noell Enters. v. United States*, 36 Fed. Cl. 722 (1996), *aff'd without op.*, 132 F.3d 54 (Fed Cir. 1997) (concluding that acoustical tile ceilings, a portion of an electrical system and a plumbing system were structural components under the regulations); *La Petite Academy v. United States*, 95-1 U.S.T.C. ¶ 50,193 (W.D. Mo. 1995) *aff'd without op.*, 72 F.3d 133 (8th Cir. 1995) (concluding that wall panels, kitchen plumbing, bathroom accessories, and a portion of the electrical system were held to be structural components under the regulations).

Unfortunately, as the Service has noted, there are no bright-line tests for distinguishing § 1245 property from § 1250 property. IRS, *Cost Segregation*, Audit Techniques Guide (Jan. 14, 2005). The classification of assets is a factually intensive determination. The primary test for determining whether an asset is § 1245 property is whether or not it is a structural component of a building. If an asset is not a structural component of a building, then it can be considered to be § 1245 property. The structural component determination hinges on what constitutes an inherently permanent structure and how permanently the asset is attached to such a structure. In making this determination, a number of factors, referred to as the "*Whiteco* factors" after the decision in *Whiteco Industries, Inc. v. Commissioner*, 65 T.C. 664 (1975), are frequently considered:

1. Can the property be moved and has it been moved?
2. Is the property designed or constructed to remain permanently in place?
3. Are there circumstances that show that the property may or will have to be moved?
4. Is the property readily movable?
5. How much damage will the property sustain when it is removed?
6. How is the property affixed to land?

The factors appear to focus on the inherent permanency of the asset at issue. Nevertheless, in *L.L. Bean, Inc. v. Commissioner*, T.C. Memo. 1997-175, *aff'd*, 145 F.3d 53 (1st Cir. 1998), the court determined that, because a structure was designed to remain permanently in place, it was an inherently permanent structure despite the fact that the structure could be moved.

Once properly classified as § 1245 property, such property may then be depreciated under § 168 using the accelerated depreciation methods and shorter recovery periods applicable to tangible personal property.

Leasehold Improvements

I.R.C. §§ 168(b)(3)(G), 168(e)(3)(E)(iv), 168(e)(6), 168(i)(8), and 168(k)(3)

Leasehold improvements are generally depreciable in accordance with the MACRS rules without regard to the lease term. Thus, if the improvement is not property classified as tangible personal property under § 1245, the cost of any leasehold improvement is depreciable over a 39-year period despite the fact that the lease term may be shorter than 39 years. This general rule is modified by § 168(e)(3)(E)(iv), which treats as 15-year property any "qualified leasehold improvement property" placed in service before January 1, 2008. The justification for this rule was Congress's belief that the 39-year recovery period otherwise applicable extended well beyond the useful life of such assets. H.R. Rep. No. 108-548, 108 Cong., 2d Sess. 122 (2004). Although such property is 15-year property, it cannot be depreciated using the 150 percent declining balance method but must be depreciated using the straight-line method. § 168(b)(3)(G).

"Qualified leasehold improvement property" is defined as any improvement to the interior portion of a building that is not residential rental property made under or pursuant to a lease by the lessor, lessee, or sublessee. §§ 168(e)(6) and 168(k)(3)(A). However, if the improvement is made by the lessor, it will not qualify as qualified leasehold improvement property in the hands of any subsequent owner except under certain circumstances. § 168(e)(6)(A) and (B). In addition, the interior portion of the building must be occupied exclusively by the lessee or sublessee, and the improvement must be placed in service more than three years after the building is first placed in service. § 168(k)(3)(A). Finally, qualified leasehold improvement property does not include any expenditure attributable to the enlargement of a building, any elevator or escalator, any structural component benefitting a common area, or the internal structural framework of the building. § 168(k)(3)(B).

The Alternative Depreciation System

I.R.C. § 168(g)

In addition to the depreciation methods described above, property may be depreciated under § 168(g) using the alternative depreciation method system ("ADS") at the taxpayer's election. § 168(g)(7). In addition, ADS must be used in certain circumstances such as with respect to tangible property used predominately outside the United States or any tax-exempt use property. § 168(g)(1).

For purposes of ADS, the taxpayer is required to use the straight-line method with a recovery period equal to the class life of the property. § 168(g)(2). Class lives for certain types of property are statutorily defined. § 168((g)(3)(B). In the case of residential rental property and nonresidential property, the recovery period is 40 years. If no class life is available, the recovery period is 12 years.

Limitations on Depreciation

I.R.C. § 280F

Treas. Reg. § 1.280F-2T

Section 280F imposes certain limitations on the amount of depreciation deductions otherwise available under § 168 for luxury automobiles and listed property if the business use of the property does not exceed 50 percent. §§ 280F(a) and 280F(b). Through the enactment of § 208F, Congress determined that the investment incentives available through rapid cost recovery under § 168 should not apply under certain circumstances, apparently where the personal enjoyment of such property is substantial.

Section 280F(a) imposes absolute dollar limitations applicable to the depreciation of any passenger automobile. Although § 280F(a)(1) contains specific dollar amounts for the first, second, third, and each succeeding taxable year, they are actually adjusted each year for inflation under § 208F(d)(7). For taxable years beginning in 2008, these amounts are as follows:

1st Tax Year	$2,960
2nd Tax Year	$4,800
3rd Tax Year	$2,850
Each Succeeding Year	$1,775

Table 1 of Rev. Proc. 2008-22, 2008-12 I.R.B. 658. To the extent that § 208F limits the amount of depreciation that a taxpayer may otherwise claim, the disallowed depreciation may be carried over to succeeding taxable years subject to the limitations of § 208F in that succeeding taxable year. § 280F(a)(1)(B). Because a passenger automobile is five-year property for purposes of § 168 and is depreciable using the 200 percent declining balance method, these figures allow the maximum amount of depreciation under § 168 only if the original basis of the automobile does not exceed $14,800. Although § 280F(a) is intended to limit the amount of depreciation deductions available for "luxury" automobiles, it is hard to imagine that most people would consider a car costing only $14,800 as luxurious. Because the 50-percent depreciation allowance under § 168(k) is also available for automobiles placed in service in 2008, the § 280F(a)(1) limitation applicable to the first taxable year is increased to $10,960 to allow taxpayers to take advantage of § 168(k). Table 2 of Rev. Proc. 2008-22. *See also* § 168(k)(2)(F)(i) (increasing the first year depreciation allowed under § 280F(a)(1) by $8,000 for passenger automobiles to which the 50-percent additional first year depreciation deduction applies).

Importantly, the expensing of any portion of the cost of a passenger automobile under § 179 is subject to the limitations under § 280F(a). § 280F(d)(1). In addition, the figures above make the assumption that 100 percent of the use of the automobile occurs in the taxpayer's trade or business. If the automobile is used for both business and personal purposes, the limitations must be reduced by multiplying the limitation by the percentage attributable to the business use of the automobile in each year. § 280F(a)(2); Reg. § 1.280F-2T((i)(1). For example, if the business use of the automobile is 80 percent, the limitation must be reduced to 80 percent.

A "passenger automobile" is defined as any 4-wheeled vehicle manufactured primarily for use on public streets, roads, and highways that is rated at 6,000 pounds unloaded gross vehicle weight or less. § 280F(d)(5)(A). An exception is made for certain types of business vehicles. § 280F(d)(5)(B). As previously noted, the expensing of any portion of the cost of a passenger automobile under § 179 is also subject to the limitations under § 280F(a). Prior to 2004, automobile dealers would frequently entice buyers of vehicles to be used for business purposes to purchase certain types of automobiles that weighed in excess of 6,000 pounds, particularly sport utility vehicles, because such vehicles were not subject to the limitations under § 280F(a). In addition, because of the generous expense amounts available under § 179 at that time, the full cost of these vehicles could often be recovered in the year acquired. Congress reduced the attractiveness of such vehicles in 2004 by limiting the expense deduction available under § 179 in connection with any sport utility vehicle to $25,000. § 179(b)(6). As stated in the legislative history, the Senate

Finance Committee was concerned about "market distortions" under prior law and did not "believe that the United States taxpayers should subsidize a portion of such purchase[s]." S. Rep. No. 108-192, 108th Cong., 1st Sess. 195 (2003). Unlike the other figures under § 179, the $25,000 figure is not adjusted for inflation in subsequent years.

Section 280F(b) imposes a limitation on the depreciation of so-called "listed property" if the business use of the property is 50 percent or less. In such a situation, the taxpayer must use the alternative depreciation system ("ADS") under § 168(g) in that taxable year and any subsequent taxable year. § 280F(b)(1). If the business use of the property had previously been greater than 50 percent and the taxpayer used an accelerated method of depreciation under § 168, the taxpayer must switch to ADS for the taxable year in which the business use of the property drops to 50 percent or less and any subsequent taxable year. In addition, the taxpayer must recapture as ordinary income in the taxable year that the business use of the property drops to 50 percent or less the amount of depreciation taken in prior taxable years in excess of the amount that would have been allowed under ADS. § 280F(b)(2). The purpose of § 280F(b) is to take away the advantage of accelerated methods of depreciation for property that is not used predominately for business purposes.

PROBLEMS FOR DISCUSSION

Problem 4-9. On May 15, 2008, Sigma Corporation completed the installation of a new computer system for in-house accounting and record keeping. The hardware and software components of the computer system cost $2,000,000.

(a) Determine the maximum cost recovery deductions that Sigma Corp. will be allowed in connection with the computer system.

(b) Can Sigma elect to compute its depreciation deductions on a less accelerated basis?

(c) Would it make any difference if the installation were not completed until November?

Problem 4-10. Willy Loman, a traveling salesman, purchased a new $40,000 car in 2008 for use in his business in making calls on customers throughout his sales territory.

(a) Determine the maximum cost recovery deductions that Willy will be allowed in connection with the car.

(b) Determine the maximum cost recovery deductions that Willy will be allowed in connection with the car assuming that he uses the car 80 percent for business and 20 percent for personal purposes. (For purposes of this problem, assume that the limitations under § 280F are not applicable.) What will happen if he sells the car in Year 7 for $10,000?

(c) In part (b) above, what will happen in Year 3 if his business use of the car drops to 40 percent?

Problem 4-11. T transfers property to his wholly owned corporation in a transaction that qualifies under § 351. The property has a basis of $10,000 and a fair market value of $23,000. As part of the transaction, T receives $5,000 in cash. As a result, the basis of the property is $15,000 in the corporation's hands. Assume that the property was depreciable in T's hands and continues to be depreciable in the hands of the corporation. How will the corporation depreciate the basis of the property?

§ 3.07. Amortization of Intangible Assets

As previously discussed, § 167(a) permits, as a deduction, a "reasonable allowance for the exhaustion, wear and tear (including a reasonable allowance for obsolescence)" of any property used in a trade or business or held for the production of income. The amount that is subject to depreciation is the basis of the property. Because the costs incurred in the creation of many types of intangible assets are currently deductible as research or development expenditures under § 174 or as business expenses under § 162, a particular self-created intangible asset may have no basis that can be amortized. For example, the costs of creating a patentable invention or developing computer software may be currently deducted under § 174. Similarly, advertising expenses incurred in the creation of goodwill may be currently deducted under § 162. Thus, because the taxpayer has already recovered his investment in such assets for tax purposes, no amortization is permissible. However, and again as previously described, the costs incurred in the creation of some intangible assets may be capitalized as the basis of the asset under §§ 263 and 263A. In addition, the costs incurred in the acquisition of intangible assets must frequently be capitalized as the basis of such assets under § 263. A taxpayer may be entitled to recover his investment in such assets through amortization deductions.

Historically, § 167 allowed the amortization of any intangible asset that otherwise satisfied the general requirements of § 167 when the useful life of the asset could be reasonably estimated. According to the regulations:

> [i]f an intangible asset is known from experience or other factors to be of use in the business or in the production of income for only a limited period, the length of which can be estimated with reasonable accuracy, such an intangible asset may be the subject of a depreciation allowance. Examples are patents and copyrights. *An intangible asset, the useful life of which is not limited, is not subject to the allowance for depreciation.* No allowance will be permitted merely because, in the unsupported opinion of the taxpayer, the intangible asset has a limited useful life.

Reg. § 1.167(a)-3 (emphasis added). In addition, the regulations specifically provide that "[t]he cost or other basis of a patent or copyright shall be depreciated over its remaining useful life." Reg. § 1.167(a)-6(a). However, the regulations were explicit that goodwill was not amortizable, presumably because it had no determinable useful life. Reg. § 1.167(a)-3.

Taxpayers and the Service frequently engaged in debates about whether a particular intangible asset possessed a determinable useful life and, thus, was properly amortizable. In addition, the Service frequently claimed that a particular intangible was sufficiently similar to goodwill that it was nonamortizable as a matter of law. The Supreme Court addressed these two issues in *Newark Morning Ledger Co. v. United States*, 507 U.S. 546 (1993), a case involving the amortization of a subscriber list acquired by a newspaper as part of the acquisition of the assets of another newspaper. The government contended that the subscriber list was equivalent to goodwill and, thus, nonamortizable. The Court concluded, however, that the subscriber list was amortizable because the taxpayer was able to prove that the list possessed a limited useful life, thus distinguishing it from goodwill. The Court noted that difficult factual issues concerning the useful life of most assets would continue to arise.

> Although we now hold that a taxpayer able to prove that a particular asset can be valued and that it has a limited useful life may depreciate its value over its useful life regardless of how much the asset appears to reflect the expectancy of continued patronage, we do not mean to imply that the taxpayer's burden of proof is insignificant. On the contrary, that burden often will prove too great to bear.

Id. at 566. The Court went on to note that had the Government challenged the sufficiency of the taxpayer's proof regarding the limited useful life of the asset, "the District Court would have had a more difficult time deciding this case. . . . [T]he Government chose, rather, to rest its entire case on a legal argument that we now reject. This case was lost at trial." *Id.* at 568, n.14.

In response to the decision in *Newark Morning Ledger Co.* and the projected litigation that the decision would generate, Congress enacted § 197 in 1993. Section 197 permits taxpayers to amortize acquired goodwill, going concern value, and a number of other intangible assets that were not amortizable under prior law. Although generally applicable only to acquired intangible assets, § 197 also applies to certain self-created intangible assets, including governmental licenses and permits, covenants not to compete, and franchises, trademarks, and trade names. Under § 197, the basis of any "amortizable section 197 intangible" may be recovered on a straight-line basis over a 15-year period. Importantly, certain amortizable section 197 intangibles may have useful lives significantly shorter or longer than 15 years. Such assets must still be amortized over 15 years without regard to their useful lives.

Section 197 is not the only section of the Code applicable to the amortization of intangible assets. A variety of acquired intangible assets are excluded from § 197 and are, thus, amortized under § 167. In addition, certain types of computer software may be expensed under § 179. The following sections provide detailed discussion of the provisions applicable to the amortization of intangible assets.

(a) Section 197 Intangibles Assets

I.R.C. § 197(a)-(e), (f)(1)-(f)(3), (f)(7)

Treas. Reg. § 1.197-2(a)-(f), (g)(1)-(g)(2), and (k) examples (1) through (10)

Under § 197, certain intangible assets held in connection with a trade or business or an activity described in § 212, including acquired goodwill and going concern value, are amortizable over a period of 15 years. §§ 197(a) and 197(c)(1). The regulations under § 197 provide that the 15-year amortization period begins on the later of: (1) the first day of the month in which the § 197 intangible asset is acquired or (2) the first day of the month in which the active conduct of the trade or business or the activity begins. Reg. § 1.197-2(f)(1). The adjusted basis of the asset for amortization purposes is determined under § 1011, any salvage value is disregarded, and the property is not eligible for amortization in the month of disposition. Thus, amortization under § 197 is determined in a manner similar to the determination of depreciation under §§ 167 and 168 although § 197 does not adopt the concept of the applicable convention that applies under § 168.

The following acquired assets are generally amortizable under § 197:

1. Goodwill;
2. Going concern value;
3. Workforce in place, including the composition, terms, and conditions (contractual or otherwise) of employment;
4. Information base, including business books and records, operating systems, and information with respect to current or prospective customers;
5. Any patent, copyright, formula, process, design, pattern, know-how, format, or other similar item;
6. Any customer-based intangible asset;
7. Any supplier-based intangible asset;
8. Any license, permit, or other right granted by a governmental unit or instrumentality thereof;
9. Any covenant not to compete; and
10. Any franchise, trademark, or trade name.

§ 197(d)(1). A "customer-based intangible asset" includes composition of market, market share, and any other value resulting from the future provision of goods or services pursuant to relationships with customers in the ordinary course of business. § 197(d)(2)(A). Similarly, a "supplier-based intangible asset" includes any value resulting from the future acquisition of goods or services pursuant to relationships with suppliers of such goods or services to be used or sold by the taxpayer in the ordinary course of business. Section 197 does not apply to self-created intangible assets except governmental licenses and permits, covenants not to compete, and franchises, trademarks, and trade names. § 197(c)(2). Except as provided under § 197(a), no depreciation or amortization deduction is allowable with respect to any amortizable § 197 intangible.

The 15-year amortization period applies regardless of the taxpayer's ability or inability to establish the asset's estimated useful life. The use of such a uniform amortization period for all intangible assets covered by § 197 simplifies the treatment of these assets because it largely eliminates any incentives for taxpayers to manipulate the allocation of the purchase price of a trade or business to favor those § 197 intangible assets with shorter actual useful lives. As a result, the enactment of § 197 has helped to reduce many of the disputes, and their attendant costs, between the Service and taxpayers with respect to the treatment of intangible assets.

Importantly, § 197(e) provides that the definition of a § 197 intangible asset does not include certain financial interests and debt instruments, interests in land, off-the-shelf computer software, interests under leases of tangible property, and transaction costs. Off-the-shelf computer software is defined as software that: (1) is readily available for purchase by the general public, (2) is subject to a nonexclusive license, and (3) has not been substantially modified. In addition, a number of types of intangible assets that are otherwise included in the definition of a § 197 intangible asset are excluded from § 197 if they are acquired as part of the acquisition of assets constituting a trade or business. Such assets are frequently referred to as "separately acquired" assets. Such separately acquired assets include:

1. Computer software;
2. Any interest in a film, sound recording, videotape, book, or similar property;
3. Any right to receive tangible property or services under a contract or granted by a governmental unit, agency, or instrumentality;
4. Any interest in a patent or copyright;
5. To the extent provided by Regulation, any right under a contract or granted by a governmental unit, agency, or instrumentality if (1) the right has a fixed duration of less than 15 years or (2) the right is fixed in amount and would be recoverable under a method similar to the unit of production method;
6. Any right to service indebtedness secured by residential real property; and
7. Covenants not to compete.

The regulations provide that the acquisition of a group of assets constitutes a trade or business or a substantial portion thereof if their use would constitute a trade or business under § 1060. Reg. § 1.197-2(e)(1). In turn, the regulations under § 1060 provide that a group of assets constitutes a trade or business if goodwill or going concern value could under any circumstances attach to the assets. Reg. § 1.1060-1(b)(2). For this purpose, all the facts and circumstances, including any employee relationships that continue or covenants not to compete that are entered into as part of the transfer of the assets, are taken into account in determining whether goodwill or going concern value could attach to the assets. With certain limited exceptions, the acquisition of a franchise, trademark, or trade name will cause the transfer to be deemed the acquisition of a trade or business. Reg. § 1.197-2(e)(2).

Because of the relatively long amortization period under § 197, taxpayers frequently attempt to take advantage of the exclusions thereunder, particularly with respect to assets with relatively short useful lives. As described below, any assets excluded from § 197 may be amortizable under § 167. Section 197 contains several provisions designed to limit taxpayer efforts to avoid its provisions. For example, a taxpayer may not recognize a loss on the disposition of an amortizable § 197 intangible asset if the taxpayer retains any other amortizable § 197 intangible asset acquired in the same transaction. § 197(f)(1)(A); Reg. § 1.197-2(g)(1)(i). The unrecognized loss is allocated to the retained § 197 intangible assets and amortized over the remainder of the 15-year recovery period. In addition, no loss is recognized on the worthlessness of a covenant not to compete. § 197(f)(1)(B); Reg. § 1.197-2(g)(1)(iii). The taxpayer simply continues to amortize the covenant not to compete over its 15-year recovery period unless the taxpayer disposes of all interests acquired when the covenant was entered into. Finally, the license of a § 197 intangible asset when entered into as part of the acquisition of assets constituting a trade or business is itself an amortizable § 197 intangible asset. Reg. § 1.197-2(f)(3)(ii).

(b) Non-Section 197 Intangible Assets

I.R.C. § 167(f); 167(g)

Treas. Reg. §§ 1.167(a)-3; 1.167(a)-6(a); 1.167(a)-14

Prop. Reg. §§ 1.167(n)-1; 1.167(n)-2; 1.167(n)-3; 1.167(n)-4; 1.167(n)-5; 1.167(n)-6

Section 167 allows for the amortization of intangible assets not otherwise subject to amortization under § 197. Such assets include self-created intangible assets, the costs of which must be capitalized under § 263 or § 263A and are not otherwise expensed by the taxpayer. Such assets are amortizable if they possess a limited useful life. Reg. § 1.167(a)-3(a).

Section 167(f) specifically provides that computer software excluded from § 197 because it is either off-the-shelf computer software or separately acquired is amortizable using the straight-line method and a useful life of 36 months. § 167(f)(1); Reg. § 1.167(a)-14(b)(1). Importantly, the cost of an interest in computer software that is included, without being separately stated, in the cost of hardware or other tangible property may be treated as part of the hardware or other property. Reg. § 1.167(a)-14(b)(2); 1.197-2(g)(7). Other intangible assets excluded from § 197 because separately acquired are amortizable in accordance with regulations. § 167(f)(2); Reg. § 1.167(a)-14(c). For example, the cost of rights that are fixed in amount is recoverable in the same proportion that the amount received or delivered during the taxable year bears to the total amount to be received or delivered under the terms of the contract or grant. Reg. § 1.167(a)-14(c)(1)(i). With respect to rights of a fixed duration, amortization is permitted ratably over the period of the right. Reg. § 1.167(a)-14(c)(1)(ii).

The regulations provide a special rule with respect to separately acquired patents and copyrights. If the purchase price of a patent or copyright is payable on at least an annual basis as either a fixed amount per use or a fixed percentage of the revenue derived from the use of the patent or copyright, the depreciation deduction for a taxable year is equal to the amount of the purchase price paid or incurred during the year. Reg. § 1.167(a)-14(c)(4). Thus, the regulations adopt the method approved by the Tax Court in *Associated Patentees, Inc. v. Commissioner*, 4 T.C.

979 (1945), which is reproduced below. If the purchase price of the patent or copyright is not payable on at least an annual basis as either a fixed amount per use or a fixed percentage of the revenue derived from the use of the patent or copyright, the basis of the patent or copyright is depreciated either ratably over its remaining useful life or using the income forecast method under § 167(g). Finally, if a patent or copyright becomes valueless in any year before its legal expiration, its adjusted basis may be deducted in that year.

The regulations under § 167 also contain a safe harbor applicable to the amortization of certain intangible assets. Reg. § 1.167(a)-3(b). This safe harbor permits the amortization of such assets over a 15-year period unless amortization of the asset is otherwise specifically prescribed or prohibited by the Code, the asset has a useful life that can reasonably be estimated, the asset was acquired from another person, or the asset is one of a number of types of financial interests. The amortization period under this safe harbor is extended to 25 years for certain intangible assets related to real property.

ASSOCIATED PATENTEES, INC. v. COMMISSIONER

United States Tax Court
4 T.C. 979 (1945)

[Four individuals transferred to petitioner certain patents which they jointly owned in equal proportions under a contract obligating petitioner to pay them 80 percent of its income from licenses granted for their use. Under this contract petitioner paid them $42,209.76 in the taxable year and in its return deducted that amount as royalties paid.]

The value of the patents in question was far in excess of $42,209.76, the amount of the payments made by petitioner to the individuals for the calendar year 1940. These payments were capital expenditures in acquisition of legal and equitable title to the patents.

OPINION

LEECH, JUDGE:

* * *

Petitioner acquired the patents from four individuals. The patents had varying lives. The consideration to be paid for the patents was 80 percent of the yearly income received by petitioner from licenses granted by it to use the patents. The four individuals further contracted, in consideration of petitioner's agreement to make these annual payments, to perform services in keeping up the patents, all improvements thereon invented by them to become the property of the petitioner.

Thus the amount of $42,209.76, paid in 1940 by petitioner under the contract, in no sense constitutes the total cost of the patents. This cost includes the future payments which will be made and can not be determined until the expiration of the patents, at which time their value passes out. Of course, it is unquestioned that petitioner is entitled to recover this total cost through reasonable deductions for exhaustion over the period of their lives. The obstacle to computation of depreciation over the term of the lives of the patents in the ordinary way by a proration of total cost is the fact that we have here the first year of the term. It is impossible to determine in this year what the total cost will be, since it will include a percentage of earnings of petitioner in each year of that term. These earnings can not now be determined.

Under these conditions, it is respondent's contention that for the year 1940 there should be allowed as depreciation only a proportionate part of the $42,209.76 paid in that year, the balance of that cost to be prorated over the succeeding years of the lives of the patents, and that in each succeeding year there should be allowed depreciation upon payments made therein based upon the then remaining lives of the patents, petitioner to be allowed this amount plus the amount of depreciation allocated to such succeeding year from prior payments.

It will readily be seen that although this method of computation will give to the petitioner aggregate theoretical deductions for depreciation equaling the total ultimate cost, its practical result will be an entirely inadequate allowance for depreciation at the beginning of the term and excessive allowances for depreciation at the end. Actually, in the later years, the depreciation allowances would largely exceed income from the patents. Under such a method of computation the petitioner might not, in fact, recover its cost from income.

Petitioner's contention is that the cost payment made each year is subject to depreciation in its full amount because it is a cost pertaining to that year alone and measured by income over that period. It is argued that, with an allowance so made, at the close of the lives of the patents the petitioner will have recovered the amount of their cost prorated equitably over their lives.

Section 23(1) provides for 'a reasonable allowance' for depreciation. It provides no specific method for its computation. Respondent's regulations recognize the fact that there is no fixed rule, but that the cost should be apportioned over the useful life in such ratable amount as may reasonably be considered necessary to recover during the remaining useful life of the property the unrecovered cost or other basis. The situation here is unusual. But we think that the method for computing depreciation for which petitioner argues gives it a reasonable, and not more than a reasonable, allowance, whereas the method urged by respondent might deny petitioner the recovery of its cost and would unquestionably result in a distortion of income. . . .

Accordingly, we have found . . . that petitioner acquired legal and equitable title to the patents in question prior to the tax year. But we now hold that in computing its contested taxes for that year petitioner is entitled to a deduction for exhaustion of the patents equal to the total payments of $42,209.76 made in that year.

Decision will be entered for the petitioner.

Because the income generated by many types of intangible assets is seldom uniform over the life of the asset, amortization methods that allocate the cost of the asset over time, using either the straight-line method or an accelerated method, do not produce the matching of income and expenses necessary to accurately reflect income. In a number of Rulings and Pronouncements over the years, the courts generally favored the amortization of patents, copyrights, and other intangible assets using the income-forecast method over the period during which the taxpayer reasonably expected to derive income from the exploitation of the asset. *See, e.g., Abramson v. Commissioner*, 86 T.C. 360 (1986) (amortization of a film); G *reene v. Commissioner*, 81 T.C. 132 (1983) (same); *Wildman v. Commissioner*, 78 T.C. 943 (1982) (same); Schneider v. Commissioner, 65 T.C. 18 (1975) (amortization of a film and television program), *acq*. Indeed, in a number of Rulings, the Service required the use of the income-forecast method in connection with television films and motion pictures and encouraged its use in connection with the amortization of books, patents, sound recordings, and musical compositions when the taxpayer is able to demonstrate that the property generates an uneven flow of income. Rev. Rul. 79-285, 1979-2 C.B. 91, amplifying Rev. Rul. 64-273, 1964-2 C.B. 62, amplifying Rev. Rul. 60-358, 1960-2 C.B. 68; Rev. Rul. 78-28, 1978-1 C.B. 51.

As described in Rev. Rul. 60-358, 1960-2 C.B. 68, reprinted below, the income forecast method involves the use of a fraction, the numerator of which is the income from the asset for the taxable year and the denominator of which is the forecasted or estimated total income to be derived from the asset during its useful life. In determining this fraction, the term "income" refers to all income generated by the property, less any expenses other than depreciation. Because the purpose of using the income forecast method of depreciation is to appropriately match income with expenses for each period, the income to be used in the numerator of the fraction must reflect the same gross income used to compute taxable income for the same period.

Although the income forecast method of depreciation provides the taxpayer with the potential to depreciate the asset more quickly than the straight-line method would otherwise allow, the income forecast method is not without its difficulties. First, the income forecast method may be unavailable when it is difficult, if not impossible, to estimate reasonably the future income to be generated by the asset. Second, controversies may exist with respect to the determination of the amount of income that should appropriately be included as part of the numerator to the fraction and with respect to the basis of the property, particularly when certain capitalizable costs may be dependent on the net income generated by the property. Finally, under the income forecast method, a taxpayer has no depreciation deduction in a year in which no income is earned. Because the taxpayer must obtain the Service's consent before changing methods of depreciation, a taxpayer who has been depreciating an asset under the income forecast method but realizes no income in one year is precluded from switching to the straight-line method in order to obtain a deduction for that year.

REVENUE RULING 60-358

1960-2 C.B. 68

For Federal income tax purposes, the cost of leased or rented television films may be depreciated by use of the 'income forecast' method.

Advice has been requested as to the proper method for recovering the cost of leased or rented television films (including taped shows for reproduction) for Federal income tax purposes.

It has come to the attention of the Internal Revenue Service that the methods of computing depreciation described in section 167(b) of the Code are in most cases inadequate when applied to television films, resulting in a distortion of income on the returns filed by taxpayers deriving income from such films. This distortion is caused by a strikingly uneven flow of income, earned by groups of programs within the series, resulting from contract restrictions, methods of distribution and audience appeal of the programs. If the film series is a success, additional income will be forthcoming from reruns over a period of years, depending upon its popularity; whereas, unsuccessful film series may produce little or no income after the initial exhibition. Thus the usefulness of such assets in the taxpayer's trade or business is measurable over the income it produces and cannot be adequately measured by the passage of time alone. Therefore, in order to avoid distortion, depreciation must follow the 'flow of income.'

Some producers of television films have used the so-called 'cost recovery' method in reporting their income. By use of this method, no taxable income is reported until the income from the films exceeds the cost thereof. However, such 'cost recovery' method is not acceptable for Federal income tax purposes.

After an extensive study and consideration of the matter, the Service has concluded that the so-called 'income forecast' method is readily adaptable in computing depreciation of the cost of television films without producing any serious distortion of income. This method requires the application of a fraction, the numerator of which is the income from the films for the taxable year, and the denominator of which is the forecasted or estimated total income to be derived from the films during their useful life, including estimated income from foreign exhibition or other exploitation of such films. The term 'income' for purposes of computing this fraction means income from the films less the expense of distributing the films, not including depreciation. This fraction is multiplied by the cost of films which produced income during the taxable year, after appropriate adjustment for estimated salvage value. The 'income forecast' method may be illustrated as follows:

Example:

Certain television films which produced income within the first taxable year cost 800x dollars, after appropriate adjustment for estimated salvage value. The income therefrom for the first taxable year was 600x dollars; second year 150x dollars; and third year, 300x dollars. Total estimated income to be derived from the films 1200x dollars.

600x dollars/1200x dollars x 800x dollars=400x dollars (first year's depreciation)

150x dollars/1200x dollars x 800x dollars=100x dollars (second year's depreciation)

300x dollars/1200x dollars x 800x dollars=200x dollars (third year's depreciation)

If the estimated income from the television films should be less than the cost thereof, thus resulting in a loss, the use of the 'income forecast' method for computing depreciation will reflect such loss in the proper taxable years based on the amount of income from the films derived in each taxable year.

If in subsequent years it is found that the income forecast was substantially overestimated or underestimated by reason of circumstances occurring in such subsequent years, an adjustment of the income forecast for such subsequent years may be made. In such case, the formula for computing depreciation would be as follows: income for the taxable year divided by the revised estimated income (the current year's income and estimated future income), multiplied by the unrecovered depreciable film cost remaining as of the beginning of the taxable year.

The total forecast or estimated income to be derived from the films should be based on the conditions known to exist at the end of the period for which the return is made. This estimate can be revised upward or downward, as explained above, at the end of subsequent taxable periods based on additional information which became available after the last prior estimate.

Accordingly, it is the position of the Service that the 'income forecast' method described above constitutes an acceptable method for computing a reasonable allowance for depreciation of the cost of television films under section 167(a) of the Code.

In applying the above methods of depreciation, television films shall not be depreciated below a reasonable salvage value, such value being the amount which it is estimated will be realizable upon sale or other disposition of such films when they are no longer useful in the taxpayer's business or in the production of his income. The time when such films are no longer useful in the taxpayer's business, etc., may vary according to his policy with respect to the use thereof. If the taxpayer's policy is to dispose of the films after the initial showing, the salvage value may represent a relatively large proportion of the original cost of such films. However, if the taxpayer customarily uses the films after the initial showing for reruns, syndication, foreign exhibition, or other exploitation thereof, the salvage value may represent a relatively small proportion of the original cost. If there is a redetermination of the 'income forecast,' as explained above, salvage value may be redetermined based upon the known facts at the time of such redetermination of the 'income forecast.'

The principle of 'income forecast' as set forth in this Revenue Ruling is limited in its application to television films, taped shows for reproduction and other property of a similar character.

NOTES AND COMMENTS

The application of the income forecast method of depreciation has been significantly modified as a result of the enactment of § 167(g). Importantly, § 167(g)(6) specifically limits the application of the income forecast method of depreciation to motion picture films and videotapes, sound recordings, copyrights, books, patents, and other property as specified by Regulation. In addition, § 167(g)(6) specifically excludes any amortizable § 197 intangible asset from treatment under the income forecast method of depreciation.

Under § 167(g), depreciation deductions under the income forecast method are computed based on the ratio of current year income to forecasted total income from the property. Prop. Reg. §§ 1.167(n)-1(a) and 1.167(n)-4(a). Computation of depreciation under the income forecast method is elected on a property-by-property basis. Prop. Reg. § 1.167(n)-1(b). Current year income includes all income earned in connection with the property, determined in accordance with the taxpayer's method of accounting. Prop. Reg. § 1.167(n)-3(a)(1). Forecasted total income from the property is equal to the sum of current year income for the year in which the property is placed in service plus all estimated income to be earned in connection with the property up to and including the tenth taxable year following the year in which the property is placed in service. § 167(g)(1)(A); Prop. Reg. § 1.167(n)-3(b). The depreciation deduction following the tenth taxable year is the entire remaining adjusted basis of the property at the beginning of that taxable year. § 167(g)(1)(C); Prop. Reg. § 1.167(n)-4(d)(1).

The basis of the property subject to depreciation under the income forecast method is its cost basis under § 1011, determined in accordance with the taxpayer's method of accounting. Prop. Reg. §§ 1.167(n)-2(a)(1) and 1.167(n)-2(a)(2). In a change from the income forecast method of depreciation available under prior law, § 167(g) does not require that the cost basis of the property be reduced by any salvage value for purposes of calculating depreciation deductions. During the depreciation period, the taxpayer may be required to adjust the basis of the property because of intervening events. With respect to the basis of the property, if any cost is paid or incurred that must be capitalized and that cost is not treated as separate property, as described below, the basis of the property must be increased by the costs incurred (the "basis redetermination amount"). Reg. § 1.167(n)-2(b). In the year in which the basis of the property is redetermined and in all subsequent years, the redetermined basis must be used to determine the appropriate amount of depreciation. In addition, for the year in which the basis of the property is redetermined, an additional depreciation allowance is available in an amount equal to that portion of the basis redetermination amount that would have been recovered if the basis redetermination amount had been included in the basis of the property when the property was originally placed in service. Reg. § 1.167(n)-4(c)(1). See Prop. Reg. § 1.167(n)-4(c)(2) example. The purpose of this provision is to prevent the back-loading of deductions and diminish the amount of look-back interest that would otherwise occur.

During the depreciation period, the taxpayer may also be required to adjust the amount of forecasted total income because of intervening events. With respect to changes in forecasted total income, a taxpayer may decide to calculate depreciation deductions based on a revised estimate of forecasted total income. "[F]or example, a taxpayer using the income forecast method for a motion picture may revise upward the forecast of total income from the motion picture (to arrive at revised forecasted total income) in a taxable year wherein the taxpayer discovers that the motion picture is more popular than originally expected, and may thereafter use the revised computation to compute the allowance for income forecast depreciation for the motion picture." Reg. § 1.167(n)-4(b)(1). Revised forecasted total income is equal to "the sum of current year income for the taxable year and all prior taxable years, plus all income from the income forecast property that the taxpayer reasonably believes will be includible in current year income in taxable years after the current taxable year up to and including the 10th taxable year after the year in which the income forecast property is placed in service." Reg. § 1.167(n)-3(c). In such a situation, depreciation deductions are determined by multiplying the unrecovered basis of the property by a fraction, the numerator of which is the current year income and the denominator of which is the revised forecasted total income less the current year income from prior taxable years. Reg. §§ 1.167(n)-4(b)(1). The taxpayer must use the revised forecasted total income thereafter in the calculation of depreciation deductions for subsequent taxable years. A taxpayer must use the revised forecasted total income to determine depreciation deductions if, in any taxable year, the forecasted total income is less than 90 percent of the revised forecasted total income for the taxable year or greater than 110 percent of the revised forecasted total income for the taxable year. Prop. Reg. § 1.167(n)-4(b)(2).

Because the income forecast method of depreciation is based on an estimate of expected income at the time that the property is placed in service, § 167(g) incorporates a "look-back" rule under which interest is periodically computed in connection with any overpayment or underpayment of taxes should the forecasted total income on which the depreciation deductions were determined differ from actual income. §§ 167(g)(1)(D) and 167(g)(2); Prop. Reg. § 1.167(n)-6.

> Under the look-back method, taxpayers must pay interest on deductions accelerated by the underestimation of either forecasted total income or revised forecasted total income from income forecast property. Conversely, taxpayers are entitled to receive interest on deductions delayed by the overestimation of either forecasted total income or revised forecasted total income from income forecast property. If either forecasted total income or revised forecasted total income are overestimated or underestimated, interest may arise from basis redeterminations. The computation of adjusted tax liability as part of the look-back method is hypothetical; application of the look-back method does not require a taxpayer to adjust tax liability as reported on the taxpayer's tax returns, on an amended return, or as adjusted on examination for prior years.

Prop. Reg. § 1.167(n)-6(a). Importantly, the look-back rule applies only with respect to property with an adjusted basis of more than $100,000. § 167(g)(3); Prop. Reg. § 1.167(n)-6(f). Moreover, the provision does not apply if the forecasted total income for each preceding taxable year is greater than 90 percent of the revised forecasted total income for the taxable year that would otherwise be a recomputation year or less than 110 percent of the revised forecasted total income for the taxable year that would otherwise be a recomputation year. § 167(g)(4); Prop. Reg. § 1.167(n)-6(e)(2)(i).

Under the look-back rule, interest is computed in two "recomputation years," the third and the tenth taxable years beginning after the taxable year in which the property is placed in service. Reg. § 1.167(n)-6(e)(1). For each recomputation year, depreciation deductions for prior taxable years are recalculated using the current year income for the prior taxable years and the revised forecasted total income as of the end of the recomputation year. Reg. § 1.167(n)-6(c). Based on these recalculated depreciation deductions, a hypothetical overpayment or underpayment of tax liability for each prior taxable year is determined. Reg. § 1.167(n)-6(d).

Interest with respect to any such overpayment or underpayment is then calculated using the adjusted overpayment rate, compounded on a daily basis. Reg. §§ 1.167(n)-6(d)(2)(ii) and 1.167(n)-6(d)(3)(iii).

PROBLEMS FOR DISCUSSION

Problem 4-12. In Year 1, T acquired the assets of a trade or business including the land, building, manufacturing equipment, inventory, patents, trademarks, and goodwill of the business. In addition, T acquired a covenant not to compete from the prior owner. Of the total purchase price, T allocated the following amounts to the intangible assets acquired:

Patents	$600,000
Trademarks	$450,000
Goodwill	$1,500,000
Covenant Not to Compete	$300,000

The term of the covenant not to compete was three years. At the end of Year 7 when the basis of the patents was $320,000, T sold the patents for $200,000.

(a) How will T recover the cost of the intangible assets acquired?

(b) What if T had acquired only the patents for $600,000?

(c) What happens when the covenant not to compete expires at the end of Year 3?

(d) What happens when T sells the patents in Year 7 for $200,000?

Problem 4-13. In Year 1, Omega Corp. acquired a patent to manufacture and sell a newly developed industrial solvent from an unrelated party for $3,000,000. The patent will expire in Year 18, but Omega expects that the product will be obsolete within a decade. Nevertheless, Omega expects that the product will generate the following revenue over that time period:

Year	Revenues
1	$200,000
2	400,000
3	800,000
4	1,200,000
5	1,500,000
6	1,500,000
7	1,300,000
8	700,000
9	200,000
10	100,000
11	50,000
12	50,000
Total	$8,000,000

(a) How will Omega recover its investment in the patent?

(b) What happens if, in Year 4, the income earned over Years 1 through 4 is more than $2,600,000? What if the income earned is less than $2,600,000?

(c) What if instead of a lump-sum, up-front payment of $3,000,000, the seller of the patent agrees to receive 10 percent of the gross revenues each year?

§ 3.08. Depletion

I.R.C. §§ 611, 612, 613, 613A, and 614

Treas. Reg. §§ 1.611-1, 1.611-2(a)-(c), 1.612-1, 1.613-1, 1.613-2, 1.613-3, 1.613-4, 1.613-5

Depletion is the means through which holders of an economic interest in mines, oil and gas wells, other natural deposits, and timber recover their investment. Section 611(a) provides that taxpayers, in computing taxable income, may deduct "a reasonable allowance for depletion . . . according to the peculiar conditions of each case." The purpose of depletion, like depreciation, is to recognize that mineral deposits and timber, like most types of tangible property, are wasting assets. As stated by the Supreme Court in *Paragon Jewel Coal Co. v. Commissioner*, 380 U.S. 624, 631 (1965), "the purpose of the allowance for depletion is to compensate the owner of wasting mineral assets for the part exhausted in production, so that when the minerals are gone, the owner's capital and his capital assets remain unimpaired."

Taxpayers are generally entitled to determine the amount of depletion using one of two methods, whichever results in the greater deduction — cost depletion or percentage depletion. § 613; Reg. § 1.611-1(a). In either case, depletion is generally computed with respect to each separate interest owned by the taxpayer. § 614; Reg. § 1.614-1(a). Cost depletion is determined with respect to the taxpayer's basis in the mineral deposit. § 612 (referring to the taxpayer's adjusted basis under § 1011); Reg. § 1.612-1(a). If the taxpayer's basis in the mineral property includes land or depreciable equipment, the adjusted basis allocable only to the mineral deposit must be determined as only that basis is subject to depletion. Reg. § 1.612-1(b). The amount of the depletion deduction is determined on a unit basis, requiring that the taxpayer estimate the number of recoverable units in the mineral deposit. Reg. § 1.611-2(a). In the selection of the unit to be used, preference is given to the "principal or customary unit or units paid for in the products sold" and include such units as tons of ore, barrels of oil, or thousands of cubic feet of natural gas. The annual depletion allowance is equal to the adjusted basis of the mineral deposit multiplied by the ratio of the number of recovered units sold during the taxable year to the sum of the number of recovered units sold during the taxable year and the number of recoverable units remaining in the mineral deposit at the end of the taxable year. If, during any taxable year, information is obtained that results in a material change in the estimate of the remaining recoverable units, then the cost depletion allowance for that taxable year and subsequent taxable years will be based on the revised estimate. Reg. § 1.611-2(c)(2). Cost depletion in prior years is unaffected. The taxpayer's basis in the mineral deposit is reduced each year by the cost depletion allowance. § 1016(a)(2);

Reg. § 1.611-2(b). Once the taxpayer has fully recovered the basis of the mineral deposit, cost depletion is no longer available. However, the taxpayer may continue to claim the percentage depletion allowance.

Unlike cost depletion, percentage depletion is not determined with respect to the taxpayer's basis in the mineral deposit. Instead, percentage depletion is a statutorily defined percentage of the "gross income from the property," but in no event can the annual percentage depletion allowance exceed 50 percent (100 percent in the case of oil and gas wells) of the taxpayer's taxable income from the property computed without regard to the depletion allowance. § 613(a); Reg. § 1.613-1(a). Because it is unrelated to the taxpayer's investment in the mineral deposit, percentage depletion operates as an incentive to engage in oil, gas, and mineral exploitation. *See United States v. Swank*, 451 U.S. 571 (1981) (characterizing percentage depletion as a "special incentive"). The percentage depletion rates range from a high of 22 percent to a low of five percent depending on the particular type of mineral and, in some cases, the mineral's particular use. §§ 613(b) and 613A(b)(1); Reg. § 1.613-2. Percentage depletion is generally unavailable for oil and gas wells, except in the case of independent producers and royalty owners, regulated gas, and gas sold under fixed contracts. §§ 613(d) and 613A.

For purposes of computing percentage depletion, gross income from the property does not include any rents or royalties paid with respect to the property. § 613. The term "gross income from the property" is intended to refer only to gross income attributable to the mineral interests and not from any non-mining processing. Reg. § 1.613-4(c)(1). For oil and gas wells, gross income means "the amount for which the taxpayer sells the oil or gas in the immediate vicinity of the well." Reg. § 1.613-3. If the taxpayer does not sell the oil or gas without further refining or transportation, the gross income is equivalent to the representative market or field price prior to refining or transportation. In the case of minerals other than oil and gas, gross income is the "gross income from mining," which includes the extraction of the ores or minerals and treatment processes considered as mining. § 613(c); Reg. § 1.613-4.

As previously noted, the annual percentage depletion allowance cannot exceed 50 percent (100 percent in the case of oil and gas wells) of the taxpayer's taxable income from the property computed without regard to the depletion allowance. To compute taxable income from the property, the taxpayer begins with gross income from the property and subtracts all allowable deductions other than depletion that are attributable to mining processes. Reg. § 1.613-5(a). Deductible expenses include operating expenses, selling expenses, administrative overhead, depreciation, taxes, and losses. Expenses that are attributable to both mineral property and other activities must be properly apportioned between the mineral property and the other activities.

A depletion allowance is also available with respect to interests in timber, but timber qualifies only for cost depletion. § 611(a); Reg. § 1.611-3. The determination of the depletion allowance is somewhat more complicated in the case of timber than in the case or oil, gas, or mineral interests because trees grow and reproduce themselves. As a result, the amount of depletable timber must be redetermined annually. Like the determination of cost depletion for mineral interests, the amount of the depletion deduction for timber is determined on a unit basis, typically board feet, logs, or cords. Reg. § 1.611-3(e). As in the case of mineral interests, if the taxpayer's basis in the timber property includes land or depreciable equipment, the adjusted basis allocable only to the timber must be determined as only that basis is subject to depletion. § 612; Reg. §§ 1.611-3(d)(3) and 1.612-1(b). Moreover, the adjusted basis of timber for depletion purposes includes not only the original cost of the timber but also any capitalized expenditures incurred in preparing the site for planting or natural seeding and seedlings. Reg. § 1.611-3(a). Once the adjusted basis of the timber subject to depletion is known, the annual depletion allowance is equal to the adjusted basis of the timber multiplied by the ratio of the number of timber units cut during the taxable year to the sum of the number of timber units cut during the taxable year and the number of recoverable timber units remaining at the end of the taxable year. Reg. § 1.611-3(b).

Importantly, the depletion allowance is available only to the owner of an "economic interest" in a mineral deposit or standing timber. Reg. § 1.611-1(b)(1). According to the regulations:

> An economic interest is possessed in every case in which the taxpayer has acquired by investment any interest in mineral in place or standing timber and secures, by any form of legal relationship, income derived from the extraction of the mineral or severance of the timber, to which he must look for a return of his capital. . . . A person who has no capital investment in the mineral deposit or standing timber does not possess an economic interest merely because through a contractual relation he possesses a mere economic or pecuniary advantage derived from production. For example, an agreement between the owner of an economic interest and another entitling the latter to purchase or process the product upon production or entitling the latter to compensation for extraction or cutting does not convey a depletable economic interest.

Id. Thus, the holder of an economic interest need not actually "own" the mineral deposit or timber but must have made a capital investment in an interest that entitles him to profit from the exploitation of the mineral deposit or timber. In one opinion, the Supreme Court stated that an "[e]conomic interest does not mean title to the oil in place but the possibility of profit from that economic interest solely upon the extraction and sale of the oil." *Kirby Petroleum Co. v. Commissioner*, 326 U.S. 599, 604 (1946). The Tax Court has referred to an economic interest as requiring "a clear capital interest in the mineral that diminishes as the mineral is extracted, and the taxpayer must share directly in the economic productivity of the minerals and the market risk upon sale of the minerals." *Gulf Oil Corp. v. Commissioner*, 86 T.C. 115 (1986), *aff'd*, 914 F.2d 396 (3d Cir. 1990).

Numerous cases and rulings have considered the economic interest issue. Obviously, the owner of the mineral or timber rights will hold an economic interest. Similarly, a landowner who leased oil properties in return for a royalty and share of the lessee's net profits also holds an economic interest. *Kirby Petroleum Co. v. Commissioner*, *supra*. In addition, lessees of mineral property who exploit the mineral deposits hold an economic interest even though they are not regarded as owning the mineral deposits under local law. § 611(b)(1). *Palmer v. Bender*, 287 U.S. 551 (1933); *Lynch v. Alworth-Stephens Co.*, 267 U.S. 364 (1925); *Gulf Oil Corp. v. Commissioner, supra.* A lessee may hold an economic interest even if the lease is subject to termination on short notice. *United States v. Swank*, 451 U.S. 571 (1981) (lease subject to termination on 30 days' notice); Rev. Rul. 83-160, 1983-2 C.B. 99. However, a "mere economic advantage" from the production of mineral deposits may not be sufficient. For example, contract miners who sold coal for a fixed fee per ton did not hold an economic interest. *Paragon Jewel Coal Co. v. Commissioner*, 380 U.S. 624 (1965); *Parsons v. Smith*, 359 U.S. 215 (1959). Nevertheless, the Service concluded that a contract miner who received a 70 percent share of the net proceeds of the processed coal sold by the owner of the coal property held an economic interest in the coal. Rev. Rul. 84-88, 1984-1 C.B. 141. Finally, in *Helvering v. Bankline Oil Co.*, 303 U.S. 362 (1938), the Supreme Court concluded that an operator of a refining plant that separated gasoline from natural gas under contracts with producers of the natural gas did not hold an economic interest entitling him to depletion. Because the taxpayer held no interest in the gas in place, the taxpayer was only a processor and not a producer of the gas. Unfortunately, distinctions among the cases that find an economic interest and those that do not are not always so clear. Justice Frankfurter once referred to the distinctions drawn by the Court with respect to an economic interest as "gossamer lines . . . which hardly can be held in the mind longer than it takes to state them." *Burton-Sutton Oil Co. v. Commissioner*, 328 U.S. 25, 38 (1946).

§ 4. DEPRECIATION RECAPTURE

As described in Chapter 2, depreciable property used in a trade or business is not a capital asset for purposes of § 1221 but may be treated as a capital asset under § 1231 in certain instances. In the absence of §§ 1245 and 1250, gain attributable to depreciation deductions may be taxed at the preferential tax rates applicable to capital gain while the depreciation deductions previously taken would have reduced the taxpayer's ordinary income, otherwise taxable at the taxpayer's top marginal tax rate.

For example, assume that a taxpayer purchases depreciable equipment for use in his trade or business for $100,000 in Year 1. In Year 3, the taxpayer sells the equipment for $60,000. If the property has a five-year recovery period and is depreciable using the 200 percent declining balance method (and assuming that the taxpayer does not expense the asset under § 179 or take advantage of bonus depreciation under § 168(k)), the taxpayer will be entitled to depreciation deductions of $20,000 in Year 1, $32,000 in Year 2, and $9,600 in Year 3 (half of the otherwise available depreciation in Year 3 as a result of the half-year convention). At the time of disposition the property will have an adjusted basis of $38,400 ($100,000 - $61,600), resulting in gain of $21,600. Importantly, this gain is due solely to the fact that the taxpayer claimed depreciation deductions in excess of the actual decline in the fair market value of the equipment. More important, the depreciation deductions in excess of the actual decline in the fair market value of the property saved the taxpayer $7,560 in taxes if the taxpayer is in the top marginal tax bracket ($21,600 times 35 percent). If the gain realized on the sale of the equipment is treated as long-term capital gain under § 1231 taxable at only a 15 percent tax rate, our taxpayer will pay taxes of only $3,240 ($21,600 times 15 percent), saving him $4,320 due only to the difference in tax rates. In addition, the taxpayer enjoys the time value of money resulting from the deferral of tax liability due to the excess depreciation deductions.

In the early 1960s, Congress enacted §§ 1245 and 1250 to prevent taxpayers from realizing the benefit of deducting depreciation against income taxable at the marginal tax rates applicable to ordinary income and potentially treating the gain attributable to depreciation deductions as long-term capital gain taxable at preferential tax rates. Thus, capital gain treatment is generally available only to the extent that the sales price of the property exceeds its original cost basis. Gain attributable to depreciation deductions is "recaptured" as ordinary income and is not included in the § 1231 characterization process. Section 1245 is generally applicable to tangible and intangible personal property while § 1250 is generally applicable to real property. Although there are significant similarities between the two sections, there is at least one significant difference that makes § 1250 somewhat less burdensome from the taxpayer's perspective. Section 1250 recaptures as ordinary income only the gain attributable to depreciation deductions in excess of straight-line depreciation if the property is held for more than one year. Because straight-line depreciation under § 168 currently applies to most types of real property placed in service after 1986, § 1250 has only limited application. Thus, gain on the disposition of real property held for more than one year that is attributable to depreciation deductions may receive capital gain treatment. However, such gain is not taxed at the most preferential tax rates applicable to capital gain under § 1(h).

§ 4.01. Personal Property

I.R.C. § 453(i), 1245

Treas. Reg. §§ 1.1245-1(a)-(d), 1.1245-2(a)(1)-(4), 1.1245-3, 1.1245-4(a)-(d), 1.1245-5(a), 1.1245-6(a)

Section 1245(a) requires that, whenever any § 1245 property is disposed of, the amount by which the lesser of the recomputed basis of the property or the amount realized exceeds the adjusted basis of the property must be treated as ordinary income. Importantly, the provision also states that "[s]uch gain shall be recognized notwithstanding any other provision of this subtitle." Thus, § 1245 applies even if gain is not recognized on the transfer unless the transfer is specifically excepted from § 1245.

Section 1245 property is defined as any tangible or intangible personal property as well as certain types of real property that are depreciable under § 167. § 1245(a)(3). The recomputed basis of such property is equal to the adjusted basis of the property plus all reductions in basis attributable to deductions for depreciation or amortization. Deductions for depreciation or amortization include deductions under §§ 167 and 168, as well as deductions under § 179 and 197. §§ 197(f)(7) and 1245(a)(2)(C). Basis reductions under § 1017 attributable to discharge of indebtedness income under § 108 are also treated as deductions for depreciation or amortization. § 1017(d). Thus, gain realized on the disposition of § 1245 property to the extent of these types of deductions is treated as ordinary income because these deductions reduced the taxpayer's ordinary income. The amount of depreciation recapture is equal to the lesser of the recomputed basis or the amount realized in excess of the adjusted basis of the property. If there is no amount realized on the disposition of the property, the fair market value of the property is treated as the amount realized.

For example, assume that a taxpayer purchases depreciable equipment for use in his trade or business for $100,000 in Year 1. In Year 3, the taxpayer sells the equipment for $60,000. If taxpayer claimed depreciation deductions of $61,600 over this period, the equipment will have an adjusted basis of $38,400 ($100,000 - $61,600) at the time of disposition, resulting in gain of $21,600. Under § 1245, the equipment will have a recomputed basis of $100,000 ($38,400 + $61,600). The lesser of the recomputed basis or the amount realized is the amount realized, $60,000. Thus, of the $21,600 gain realized on the disposition of the equipment, $21,600 ($60,000 - $38,400) is treated as ordinary income. Alternatively, if the equipment were sold for $120,000 in Year 3, the taxpayer would realize a gain of $81,600 ($120,000 - $38,400). The recomputed basis would again be $100,000 ($38,400 + $61,600). The lesser of the recomputed basis or the amount realized this time is the recomputed basis, $100,000. Thus, of the $81,600 gain realized on the disposition of the equipment, $61,600 ($100,000 - $38,400) is treated as ordinary income, and the remaining $20,000 gain is eligible for capital gain treatment under § 1231.

Although § 1245 applies to all dispositions of property, certain statutory exceptions may prevent the recognition of ordinary income. Gifts and transfers at death do not trigger § 1245. § 1245(b)(1) and (2). In addition, depreciation recapture under § 1245 is recognized only to the extent that gain is recognized by the transferor in connection with any transaction under §§ 351, 721, and 731. § 1245(b)(3). However, § 1245 applies to the transferee on any subsequent disposition of the property to the extent of any depreciation deductions claimed by either the transferor or the transferee. The fact that the transferee is subject to § 1245 for depreciation claimed by the transferor is frequently referred to as the "§ 1245 taint." For example, assume that T acquired property with an original cost basis of $100,000 and claimed depreciation deductions of $20,000 in Year 1, reducing the basis of the property to $80,000. T then contributed the property to a corporation in a transaction under § 351. Assume further that the corporation claimed depreciation deductions of $41,600 in Years 2 and 3, reducing the basis of the property to $38,400. If, in Year 3, the corporation sold the property for $120,000, the recomputed basis of the property would be $100,000 ($38,400 + $20,000 + $41,600) even though the corporation claimed only $41,600 of depreciation. See § 1245(a)(2)(B) (stating that the recomputed basis is the property's adjusted basis deduction allowed or allowable "to the taxpayer *or to any other person* for depreciation or amortization" (emphasis added)). Thus, of the $81,600 gain realized on the disposition of the equipment, $61,600 ($100,000 - $38,400) is treated as ordinary income, and only the remaining $20,000 gain is eligible for capital gain treatment under § 1231.

With respect to any like-kind exchange under § 1031, depreciation recapture under § 1245 is generally recognized only to the extent that gain is recognized by the taxpayer. § 1245(b)(4). However, the § 1245 taint attributable to depreciation deductions claimed in connection with the relinquished property carries over to the replacement property. Thus, gain attributable to depreciation deductions claimed with respect to the relinquished property must be recaptured as ordinary income along with the gain attributable to depreciation deductions claimed with respect to the replacement property on the subsequent disposition of the replacement property in a taxable transaction.

Depreciation recapture under § 1245 is generally determined on an asset-by-asset basis. However, a special rule applies under § 1245 in connection with amortizable § 197 intangible assets. Under this rule, if more than one § 197 intangible asset is sold as part of a transaction or a series of related transactions, the amount of depreciation recapture is determined as if all of the § 197 intangible assets were a single asset. § 1245(b)(8)(A). This rule prevents taxpayers from manipulating the amount of consideration among the § 197 intangible assets so as to reduce the amount of gain characterized as ordinary income. The legislative history provides the following example:

> In year 1, a taxpayer acquires two section 197 intangible assets for a total of $45. Asset A is assigned a cost basis of $15 and asset B is assigned a cost basis of $30. The allocation is irrelevant for amortization purposes, as the taxpayer will be entitled to a total of $3 per year ($45 divided by 15 years).
>
> In year 6, the basis of A is $10 and the basis of B is $20. Taxpayer sells the assets for an aggregate sale price of $45, resulting in gain of $15. The character of this gain depends on the recapture amount, which depends in turn on the relative sales prices of the individual assets. Taxpayer has claimed $5 of amortization, and therefore has $5 of recapture potential, with respect to A. Taxpayer has claimed $10 of amortization, and therefore has $10 of recapture potential, with respect to B.
>
> Under present law, if the sale proceeds are allocated $15 to A and $30 to B, the gain on assets A and B will be $5 and $10, respectively. These amounts match the recapture potential for each asset so the full amount of the gain will be recaptured as ordinary income. However, if the sale proceeds instead are allocated $25 to A and $20 to B, the full $15 will be recognized with respect to A, and only $5 (full recapture potential with respect to A) will be recaptured as ordinary income. The remaining $10 of gain attributable to A will be treated as capital gain. No gain (and thus no recapture) will be recognized with respect to Asset B, and only $5 of the $15 recapture potential is recognized.
>
> Under the Act, the taxpayer calculates recapture as if assets A and B were a single asset. For purposes of the calculation, the proceeds are $45 and the gain is $15. Because a total of $15 of amortization has been claimed with respect to assets A and B, the full $15 gain is recaptured as ordinary income.

Staff of the Joint Committee on Taxation, Description and Technical Explanation of the Conference Agreement of H.R. 6, Title XIII, The "Energy Tax Incentives Act of 2005," 80-81 (JCX-60-05). Although the example suggests otherwise, this provision applies to the disposition of more than one § 197 intangible asset in the same or related transactions regardless of whether the assets were actually acquired in the same transaction. Thus, § 197 intangible assets acquired at different times and in different transactions, as well as self-created intangible assets amortizable under § 197, will be treated as a single asset for purposes of § 1245 if disposed of in the same or related transactions.

Importantly, this rule does not apply to the disposition of any amortizable § 197 intangible asset if its basis is greater than its fair market value. § 1245(b)(8)(B). Presumably, this exception ensures that the taxpayer recognizes the maximum amount of depreciation recapture and that any loss on the disposition of any § 197 intangible asset is potentially treated as a capital loss rather than as a reduction in the amount of depreciation recapture.

Finally, depreciation recapture under § 1245 is not eligible for installment sale reporting under § 453. § 453(i). All depreciation recapture is recognized in the year of the disposition, and only the gain in excess of any depreciation recapture may be taken into account under the installment method.

§ 4.02. Real Property

I.R.C. § 1(h), 453(i), 1250

Treas. Reg. § 1.453-12

Like § 1245, § 1250 requires the recapture of depreciation as ordinary income, but, unlike § 1245, it does not require that the entire amount of gain attributable to depreciation deductions to be treated as ordinary income; only the gain attributable to "additional depreciation" must be treated as ordinary income. Although the gain attributable to depreciation deductions in excess of any additional depreciation may be treated as long-term capital gain under § 1231, it is not eligible for the most preferential tax rates under § 1(h).

Section 1250 applies to § 1250 property. § 1250(a)(1)(A). Section 1250 property is any real property other than § 1245 property that is depreciable under § 167. § 1250(c). For purposes of § 1250, additional depreciation is defined as any depreciation deductions claimed with respect to § 1250 property, except that, if the property has been held for more than one year, additional depreciation is limited to the depreciation deductions claimed in excess of straight-line depreciation. § 1250(b)(1). This amount may be further limited because only the "applicable percentage" of the additional depreciation is treated as ordinary income. §§ 1250(a)(1)(A) and 1250(a)(1)(B). Because straight-line depreciation under § 168 currently applies to most types of real property placed in service after 1986, § 1250 has only limited application. Only if real property is disposed of within a year of its acquisition will § 1250 require that any portion of the gain be treated as ordinary income. However, straight-line depreciation for purposes of § 1250 is computed without regard for basis reductions under § 1017 attributable to discharge of indebtedness income under § 108. § 1017(d)(2). Thus, gain attributable to basis reductions under § 1017 will constitute additional depreciation under § 1250, characterized as ordinary income.

Like § 1245, § 1250 applies to all dispositions of property. § 1250(a)(1)(A). Nevertheless, § 1250 contains similar statutory exceptions to those contained in

§ 1245 that may prevent the recognition of ordinary income. Rules similar to those under § 1245 apply in the case of gifts, transfers at death, and nonrecognition transactions under §§ 351, 721, 731, and 1031. § 1250(d).

Although the gain attributable to depreciation deductions in excess of any additional depreciation may be treated as long-term capital gain under § 1231, it is not eligible for the most preferential tax rates under § 1(h). Section 1(h)(6) defines "unrecaptured § 1250 gain" as the amount of long-term capital gain not otherwise treated as ordinary income that would be treated as ordinary income if § 1250(b)(1) included all depreciation and the applicable percentage was 100 percent. In other words, the gain on the disposition of real property attributable to depreciation deductions in excess of additional depreciation, if any, is characterized as unrecaptured § 1250 gain and subject to a maximum tax rate of 25 percent under § 1(h). § 1(h)(1)(D). Of course, the actual amount of unrecaptured § 1250 gain that is taxed at a maximum rate of 25 percent is reduced by the excess of any collectibles loss, net short-term capital loss, and any long-term capital loss carryforward over any collectibles gain and § 1202 gain and is also limited to the amount of the taxpayer's net § 1231 gain and net capital gain for the taxable year. §§ 1(h)(1)(D)(i), 1(h)(6)(A)(ii), and 1(h)(6)(B).

Finally, depreciation recapture under § 1250 is not eligible for installment sale reporting under § 453. § 453(i). Any additional depreciation recapture is recognized in the year of the disposition, and only the gain in excess of any depreciation recapture may be taken into account under the installment method. If gain on the disposition of § 1250 property is reported using the installment method, the unrecaptured § 1250 gain is accounted before any gain in excess of the unrecaptured § 1250 gain. Reg. § 1.453-12.

§ 4.03. Mining Interests and Timber

I.R.C. § 1254

Treas. Reg. §§ 1.1254-1

Like §§ 1245 and 1250, a recapture rule applies under § 1254, which requires that gain on the disposition of an interest in oil, gas, or geothermal property be treated as ordinary income in an amount equal to the lesser of the gain realized or the sum of the IDC deducted under § 263(c) and all depletion taken with respect to the property, excluding percentage depletion in excess of cost. § 1254(a); Reg. § 1.1254-1. IDC deducted under the 10-year amortization rule of § 59(e) are included in the recapture amount as if they had been deducted under § 263(c). This recapture rule also applies to the deduction of mining exploration expenditures under §§ 616 and 617 incurred in connection with any mine or other natural deposit other than an oil or gas well. The recapture amount must be recognized even if the taxpayer disposes of the property in a nonrecognition transaction unless the disposition is specifically excepted from § 1254 under rules similar to those under § 1245(c). § 1254(b)(1); Reg. § 1.1254-2.

Chapter 5

NONRECOGNITION TRANSACTIONS

Generally, the gain or loss realized as a result of a transaction that constitutes a realization event is recognized by the taxpayer. § 1001(c). Nevertheless, the Code contains numerous provisions for the nonrecognition of gain or loss (or, sometimes, only loss), based on a Congressional policy judgment that, because the transaction involves a continuation of the taxpayer's investment, it is not an appropriate time to treat the taxpayer as recognizing gain or loss despite the existence of a realization event. Treas. Reg. § 1.1002-1(c). Some of the most important of these nonrecognition provisions apply in connection with transfers to controlled corporations under §§ 351 and 1032, transfers in corporate reorganizations under §§ 354, 355, 361, 368 and 1032, and transfers to and from partnerships under §§ 721 and 731. These provisions are covered in detail in corporate, partnership, or business entity tax courses. Sections 1 *Like Kind Exchanges* and 2 *Involuntary Conversion* of this Chapter describe the two principal nonrecognition provisions not covered by those courses, exchanges under § 1031 involving properties considered to be alike, and reinvestment under § 1033 of the proceeds from destruction or condemnation of property. Section 3 *Other Nonrecognition Provisions* describes similar provisions, including the limited exclusion of gain on sales of principal residences under § 121, which replaced an earlier provision for nonrecognition rollover of principal residences under former § 1034; and repossessions of real property on default of seller-provided financing, § 1038. In addition, Section 3 describes the nonstatutory exclusion, with statutory exceptions, of gain on appreciated property contributed to a charity. Although the Code contains other nonrecognition provisions applicable in specific situations, such as § 1041 allowing for the nonrecognition of gain or loss on transfers of property between spouses or between former spouses incident to divorce, this provision is more appropriately dealt with in connection with consideration of the tax consequences of divorce, and, thus, beyond the scope of this volume, except to the limited extent discussed in § 4.03(b) *Transfers in Satisfaction of a Claim* in Chapter 1 *Basis and Realization.*

Most nonrecognition provisions require an exchange of property in order to qualify for nonrecognition treatment. Thus, for example, a like-kind exchange under § 1031 will involve property given up by the taxpayer in the transaction, generally referred to as the *relinquished property*, and property received by the taxpayer in the transaction, generally referred to as the *replacement property*. Some nonrecognition provisions, such as § 1033, however, do not require that the taxpayer engage in an exchange of properties. Such provisions are referred to as rollover provisions, and require only that the taxpayer reinvest an amount equal to the proceeds received on the disposition of the relinquished property in the acquisition of replacement property within a certain period.

The term "nonrecognition" is misleading because nonrecognition almost inevitably requires that the replacement property receive a *substituted* basis, which means that the gain or loss is deferred until a subsequent taxable disposition of the replacement property. § 7701(a)(42). There are two types of substituted basis: *exchanged* basis, in which the basis of the relinquished property determines the basis of the replacement property, § 7701(a)(44), and *transferred* basis, in which the transferor's basis determines the basis for of the transferee, § 7701(a)(43). Although nonrecognition provisions in the corporate and partnership context usually involve both exchanged and transferred bases, the provisions considered in this chapter primarily involve only exchanged basis. Nonrecognition transactions also usually involve the "tacking" of holding periods for capital and section § 1231 assets, so that the holding period of the replacement property includes that of the relinquished property. § 1223.

Finally, the nonrecognition of gain or loss is permissible only when the transaction involves the receipt or acquisition of qualifying property. If the transaction also involves the receipt of cash or nonqualifying property, commonly called "boot," gain, at least in part, but not loss, is recognized.

§ 1. LIKE-KIND EXCHANGES

Under § 1031(a), no gain or loss is recognized "on the exchange of property held for productive uses in a trade or business or for investment, if such property is exchanged solely for property of like kind which is to be held either for productive use in a trade or business or for investment." Like many deceptively simple Code provisions, most of the words used have acquired meanings that are not necessarily intuitive. Section 1031(a) imposes three basic requirements that a transaction must satisfy for nonrecognition treatment. First, the transaction must involve an "exchange" of the relinquished property for the replacement property. The meaning of "exchange" is dealt with initially in § 1.01 *Exchange*, and further elaborated in § 1.03 *Multiparty Exchanges*, § 1.04 *Deferred (Starker) Exchanges*, and § 1.05 *Reverse (Starker) Exchanges*. Second, the relinquished property and the replacement property must be like kind. The meaning of "like kind," which is expansive for real property, but less so for personal property, is covered in § 1.06 *Like Kind.* Third, both the relinquished property and the replacement property must be held by the taxpayer "either for productive use in a trade or business or for investment." The issues of time and purpose of holding the relinquished and replacement properties are dealt with § 1.07 *Held*.

Section 1031(a) also refers to relinquished property exchanged "solely" for replacement property of like kind. Although this word suggests that the gain or loss attributable to the relinquished like-kind property in an exchange that also involves cash or nonlike-kind property, commonly referred to as "boot," would not be eligible for nonrecognition treatment, § 1031(b) provides that in such situations gain will be recognized but only to the extent of the fair market value of the boot received by the taxpayer while § 1031(c) prohibits the recognition of any loss attributable to the relinquished like-kind property. In many like-kind exchanges, liabilities secured by the relinquished or replacement properties are the most common form of boot. The treatment of such is covered in § 1.02 *Boot, Liabilities and Basis*, which also deals with the determination of the basis of the replacement property and the collateral effects of boot and gain.

Because related parties could engage in a like-kind exchange, exchanging Blackacre with a low basis for Greenacre with a high basis, prior to a sale of Blackacre to a third party and, thus, reducing the amount of gain on the disposition of Blackacre, § 1031(f) places limits on the use of § 1031 involving exchanges between related parties. These limitations are discussed in § 1.08 *Related Parties.*

There are essentially self-explanatory exceptions under § 1031(a)(2), which tend to exclude ordinary income property, § 1031(a)(2)(A), and stock, securities, and partnership interests, or other liquid assets, § 1032(a)(2)(B), (C), (D) and (E), and a less clear one for "choses in action," § 1031(a)(2)(F), which is not defined in the Code or regulations, and is generally defined as a right to receive consideration or property from another. Accounts receivable or similar assets, are, presumably, also excluded as choses in action, or under other principles, for example, as "assignment" of income. Accordingly, as a practical matter, § 1031 nonrecognition is primarily available for capital or section 1231 assets.

§ 1.01. Exchange

I.R.C. § 1031(a); Treas. Reg. § 1.1031(a)-1(a)

It is easy to recognize that there is an exchange when Blackacre is exchanged for Whiteacre, but § 1031(a) is not limited to such simple exchanges. The following two cases deal with sale-leasebacks, and reach seemingly inconsistent results. As discussed in § 1.06 *Like Kind*, the regulations provide that a leasehold of more than 30 years is like-kind to a fee, but that does not necessarily mean that a transaction involving the sale of Blackacre followed by a lease of Blackacre by the buyer to the seller, is an exchange for purposes of § 1031(a), even if the lease is for a term greater than 30 years. The first case concludes that a sale-leaseback is an exchange for purposes of § 1031, preventing the seller/lessee from deducting the loss resulting from the "sale" portion of the transaction. Without challenging this basic proposition, the second case concludes that, under the facts presented, there was no exchange. The opinions are not models of clarity as to why the results differ.

CENTURY ELECTRIC CO. v. COMMISSIONER

United States Court of Appeals, Eighth Circuit
192 F.2d 155 (8th Cir. 1951)

[The taxpayer corporation transferred land and a building that it used in its manufacturing business in a sale and lease-back transaction. The corporation was profitable. The sale and leaseback were with a "friendly" charity with a sale price of $150,000 and a 95-year term on the lease. The court denied the loss deduction on the ground that the transaction was a nonrecognition exchange under the predecessor of § 1031. In its opinion, the court stated:]

The questions presented are:

1. Whether the transaction stated was for tax purposes a sale of the foundry

property within the meaning of section 112 [1001] . . . on which petitioner realized in 1943 a deductible loss of $381,710.97 determined under section 111 [1001(a)] of the code (the adjusted basis of the foundry property of $531,710.97 less $150,000) as petitioner contends; or, as the Tax Court held, an exchange of property held for productive use in a trade or business for property of a like kind to be held for productive use in trade or business in which no gain or loss is recognized under sections 112(b)(1) and 112(e) [1031(a) and (c)] . . .

2. Whether if the claimed loss deduction is denied, its amount is deductible as depreciation over the 95-year term of the lease as the Tax Court held, or over the remaining life of the improvements on the foundry as the petitioner contends.

On the first question the Tax Court reached the right result. The answer to the question is not to be found by a resort to the dictionary for the meaning of the words "sales" and "exchanges" in other contexts, but in the purpose and policy of the revenue act as expressed in section 112 [1031]. . . . In this section Congress was not defining the words "sales" and "exchanges". It was concerned with the administrative problem involved in the computation of gain or loss in transactions of the character with which the section deals. Subsections 112(b)(2) and 112(e) [1031(a) and (c)] indicate the controlling policy and purpose of the section, that is, the nonrecognition of gain or loss in transactions where neither is readily measured in terms of money, where in theory the taxpayer may have realized gain or loss but where in fact his economic situation is the same after as it was before the transaction. *See Fairfield S.S. Corp. v. Commissioner*, 2 Cir. 157 F.2d 321, 323 [1946]; *Trenton Cotton Oil Co. v. Commissioner*, 6 Cir. 147 F.2d 33, 36 [1945]. For tax purposes the question is whether the transaction falls within the category just defined. If it does, it is for tax purposes an exchange and not a sale. So much is indicated by subsection 112(b)(1) [1031(a)] with regard to the exchange of securities of readily ascertainable market value measured in terms of money. Gain or loss on exchanges of the excepted securities is recognized. Under subsection 112(e) [1031(c)] no loss is recognized on an exchange of property held for productive use in trade or business for like property to be held for the same use, although other property or money is also received by the taxpayer. Compare this subsection with subsection 112 (c)(1) [1031(b)] where in the same circumstances gain is recognized but only to the extent of the other property or money received in the transaction. The comparison clearly indicates that in the computation of gain or loss on a transfer of property held for productive use in trade or business for property of a like kind to be held for the same use, the market value of the properties of like kind involved in the transfer does not enter into the equation.

The transaction here involved may not be separated into its component parts for tax purposes. Tax consequences must depend on what actually was intended and accomplished rather than on the separate steps taken to reach the desired end. The end of the transaction between the petitioner and the college was that intended by the petitioner at its beginning, namely, the transfer of the fee in the foundry property for the 95-year lease on the same property and $150,000.

It is undisputed that the foundry property before the transaction was held by petitioner for productive use in petitioner's business. After the transaction the same property was held by the petitioner for the same use in the same business. Both before and after the transaction the property was necessary to the continued operation of petitioner's business. The only change wrought by the transaction was in the estate or interest of petitioner in the foundry property. In Regulations 111, section 29.112(b)(1)-1 [1.1031(a)-1(c)], the Treasury has interpreted the words "like kind" as used in subsection 112(b)(1) [1031(a)]. Under the Treasury interpretation a lease with 30 years or more to run and real estate are properties of "like kind." With the controlling purpose of the applicable section of the revenue code in mind, we can not say that the words "like kind" are so definite and certain that interpretation is neither required nor permitted. The regulation, in force for many years, has survived successive reenactments of the internal revenue acts and has thus acquired the force of law. . . .

On the second question the Tax Court held that petitioner was not entitled to depreciation on the improvements on the foundry property over their useful life after December 1, 1943. The answer to this question depends upon whether as a result of the transaction under consideration the petitioner has an identifiable capital investment in the improvements on the land covered by the lease. Petitioner contends that the amount of its claimed loss, $381,710.97, should be apportioned between the land and improvements in proportion to their respective cost bases as of November 30, 1943. This would result in an allocation of $277,076.68 of petitioner's investment in the leasehold to the improvements and $104,634.29 to the land. The difficulty with petitioner's position is that it involves assumptions and inferences which find no support in the record. What the petitioner has done is to exchange the foundry property having an adjusted basis of $531,710.97 on December 1, 1943, for a leasehold and $150,000 in cash. Its capital investment is in the leasehold and not its constituent properties. Accordingly, we agree with the Tax Court that petitioner is entitled to depreciation on the leasehold. The basis for depreciation of the leasehold on December 1, 1943, is, therefore, $381,710.97 under section 113(a)(6) [1031(d)] of the revenue code, deductible over the term of the lease.

* * *

JORDAN MARSH CO. v. COMMISSIONER

United States Circuit Court of Appeals, Second Circuit
269 F.2d 453 (2d Cir. 1959)

* * *

The transactions giving rise to the dispute were conveyances by the petitioner in 1944 of the fee of two parcels of property in the city of Boston where the petitioner, then as now, operated a department store. In return for its conveyances the petitioner received $2,300,000 in cash which, concededly, represented the fair market value of the properties. The conveyances were unconditional, without provision of any option to repurchase. At the same time, the petitioner received back from the vendees leases of the same properties for terms of 30 years and 3 days, with options to renew for another 30 years if the petitioner-lessee should erect new buildings thereon. The vendees were in no way connected with the petitioner. The rentals to be paid under the leases concededly were full and normal rentals so that the leasehold interests which devolved upon the petitioner were of no capital value.

In its return for 1944, the petitioner, claiming the transaction was a sale under § 112(a) Internal Revenue Code of 1939 [§ 1001] sought to deduct from income the difference between the adjusted basis of the property and the cash received. The Commissioner disallowed the deduction, taking the position that the transaction represented an exchange of property for other property of like kind. . . .

Upon this appeal, we must decide whether the transaction in question here was a sale or an exchange of property for other property of like kind within the meaning of §§ [1031(a) and(c)] of the Internal Revenue Code cited above. If we should find that it is an exchange, we would then have to decide whether the Commissioner's regulation, declaring that a leasehold of property of 30 years or more is property "of like kind" to the fee in the same property, is a reasonable gloss to put upon the words of the statute. The judge in the Tax Court felt that *Century Electric Co. v. Commissioner* . . . , 8 Cir. 192 F.2d 155, certiorari denied . . . , was dispositive of both questions. In the view which we take of the first question, we do not have to pass upon the second question. For we hold that the transaction here was a sale and not an exchange.

The controversy centers around the purposes of Congress in enacting § 112(b) [§ 1031], dealing with non-taxable exchanges. The section represents an exception to the general rule, stated in § 112(e) [§ 1001], that upon the sale or exchange of property the entire amount of gain or loss is to be recognized by the taxpayer. The first Congressional attempt to make certain exchanges of this kind non-taxable occurred in Section 202(c), Revenue Act of 1921 . . . Under this section, no gain or loss was recognized from an exchange of property unless the property received in exchange had a "readily realizable market value." In 1924, this section was amended to the form in which it is applicable here. Discussing the old section the House Committee observed:

> "The provision is so indefinite that it cannot be applied with accuracy or with consistency. It appears best to provide generally that gain or loss is recognized from all exchanges, and then except specifically and in definite terms those cases of exchanges in which it is not desired to tax the gain or allow the loss. This results in definiteness and accuracy and enables a taxpayer to determine prior to the consummation of a given transaction the tax liability that will result." . . .

Thus the "readily realizable market value" test disappeared from the statute. A later report, reviewing the section, expressed its purpose as follows:

> "The law has provided for 12 years that gain or loss is recognized on exchanges of property having a fair market value, such as stocks, bonds, and negotiable instruments; on exchanges of property held primarily for sale; or on exchanges of one kind of property for another kind of property; but not on other exchanges of property solely for property of like kind. In other words, profit or loss is recognized in the case of exchanges of notes or securities, which are essentially like money; or in the case of stock in trade; or in case the taxpayer exchanges the property comprising his original investment for a different kind of property; but *if the taxpayer's money is still tied up in the same kind of property* as that in which it was originally invested, he is not allowed to compute and deduct his theoretical loss on the

exchange, nor is he charged with a tax upon his theoretical profit. The calculation of the profit or loss is deferred until it is realized in cash, marketable securities, or other property not of the same kind having a fair market value." . . .[4]

These passages lead us to accept as correct the petitioner's position with respect to the purposes of the section. Congress was primarily concerned with the inequity, in the case of an exchange, of forcing a taxpayer to recognize a paper gain which was still tied up in a continuing investment of the same sort. If such gains were not to be recognized, however, upon the ground that they were theoretical, neither should equally theoretical losses. And as to both gains and losses the taxpayer should not have it within his power to avoid the operation of the section by stipulating for the addition of cash, or boot, to the property received in exchange. These considerations, rather than concern for the difficulty of the administrative task of making the valuations necessary to compute gains and losses, were at the root of the Congressional purpose in enacting §§ 112(b)(1) and (3) [§§ 1031(a) and(c)]. Indeed, if these sections had been intended to obviate the necessity of making difficult valuations, one would have expected them to provide for nonrecognition of gains and losses in all exchanges, whether the property received in exchanges were "of a like kind" or not of a like kind. And if such had been the legislative objective, § 112(c) [§ 1031(b)] providing for the recognition of gain from exchanges not wholly in kind, would never have been enacted.

That such indeed was the legislative objective is supported by *Portland Oil Co. v. Commissioner* . . . , 1 Cir. 109 F.2d 479 [1940]. There Judge Magruder, in speaking of a cognate provision contained in § 112(b) [§ 351], said . . . :

> "It is the purpose of Section 112(b)(5) [351] to save the taxpayer from an immediate recognition of a gain, or to intermit the claim of a loss, in certain transactions where gain or loss may have accrued in a constitutional sense, but where in a popular and economic sense there has been a mere change in the form of ownership and the taxpayer has not really 'cashed in' on the theoretical gain, or closed out a losing venture."

In conformity with this reading of the statute, we think the petitioner here, by its unconditional conveyances to a stranger, had done more than make a change in the form of ownership: It was a change as to the quantum of ownership whereby, in the words just quoted, it had "closed out a losing venture." By the transaction its capital invested in the real estate involved had been completely liquidated for cash to an amount fully equal to the value of the fee. This, we hold, was a sale — not an exchange within the purview of § 112(b) [§ 1031].

The Tax Court apparently thought it of controlling importance that the transaction in question involved no change in the petitioner's possession of the premises: it felt that the decision in *Century Electric* . . . controlled the situation here. We think, however, that case was distinguishable on the facts. . . . [T]here was no finding that the cash received by the taxpayer was the full equivalent of the value of the fee which the taxpayer had conveyed to the vendee-lessor, and no finding that the lease back called for a rent which was fully equal to the rental value of the

[4] Emphasis supplied.

premises. Indeed, in its opinion the Court of Appeals pointed to evidence that the fee which the taxpayer had "exchanged" may have had a value substantially in excess of the cash received.[7] And in the *Century Electric* case, the findings showed . . . that the taxpayer-lessee, unlike the taxpayer here, was not required to pay "general state, city and school taxes" because its lessor was an educational institution which under its charter was exempt from such taxes. Thus the leasehold interest in *Century Electric* on this account may well have had a premium value.[8] In the absence of findings as to the values of the properties allegedly "exchanged," necessarily there could be no finding of a loss. And without proof of a loss, of course, the taxpayer could not prevail. Indeed, in the Tax Court six of the judges expressly based their concurrences on that limited ground. . . .

In the *Century Electric* opinion it was said . . . :

> "* * * Subsections [1031(a) and (c)] indicate the controlling policy and purpose of the section, that is, the nonrecognition of gain or loss in transactions where neither is readily measured in terms of money, where in theory the taxpayer may have realized gain or loss but where in fact his economic situation is the same after as it was before the transaction. *See Fairfield S.S. Corp. v. Commissioner*, 2 Cir. 157 F.2d 321, 323 [1946]; *Trenton Cotton Oil Co. v. Commissioner*, 6 Cir. 147 F.2d 33, 36 [1945]."

But the *Fairfield* case referred to was one in which the only change in taxpayer's ownership was through the interposition of a corporate title accomplished by transfer to a corporation wholly owned by the taxpayer. And in the *Trenton Cotton Oil* case, the court expressly relied on *Portland Oil Co.* . . . as stating correctly the purpose of § 112(b) [§ 1031(b)], but quoted only the first of the two requisites stated in *Portland*. As we have already observed, in that case Judge Magruder said that it was the purpose of § 112(b) [§ 1031] "to intermit the claim of a loss" not only where the economic situation of the taxpayer is unchanged but also "where * * * the taxpayer has not * * * closed out a losing venture." Here plainly the petitioner by the transfer finally closed out a losing venture. And it cannot justly be said that the economic situation of the petitioner was unchanged by a transaction which substituted $2,300,000 in cash for its investment in real estate and left it under a liability to make annual payments of rent for upwards of thirty years. Many bona fide business purposes may be served by such a transaction. . . .

In ordinary usage, an "exchange" means the giving of one piece of property in return for another — not, as the Commissioner urges here, the return of a lesser interest in a property received from another. It seems unlikely that Congress intended that an "exchange" should have the strained meaning for which the Commissioner contends. For the legislative history states expressly an intent to correct the indefiniteness of prior versions of the Act by excepting from the general rule "specifically and in definite terms those cases of exchanges in which it is not

---

[7] It said . . . : "The assessed value of petitioner's foundry building and land upon which it is located for 1943 was $205,000. There was evidence that in St. Louis real property is assessed at its actual value. There was also evidence introduced by petitioner before the Tax Court that the market value for unconditional sale of the foundry building, land and appurtenances was not in excess of $250,000."

[8] Under the leases received back by Jordan Marsh Company, the lessee was required to pay all local taxes.

desired to tax the gain or allow the loss."

But even if under certain circumstances the return of a part of the property conveyed may constitute an exchange for purposes of § 112 [1031], we think that in this case, in which cash was received for the full value of the property conveyed, the transaction must be classified as a sale. . . .

Reversed.

NOTES AND COMMENTS

These cases, particularly *Jordan Marsh*, give a fairly standard review of the history and the policy, such as it is, of § 1031. As indicated, they are more opaque on the relevance of a sale at fair market value in determining the applicability of § 1031. The distinction made in *Jordan Marsh* that an "exchange" means the giving of one piece of property in return for another — not, as the Commissioner urged, the return of a lesser interest in a property received from another seems to apply equally in *Century Electric*, because both cases involve a sale and leaseback. The basis for the distinction seems to be the finding that Jordan Marsh sold the property for fair market value and rented the property back at fair market value, while there was no indication that the price paid to Century Electric represented the property's value. When the leasehold has a value at the time of the transaction because the rent is below current rental value, it is easy to see that the seller-lessor has received property in exchange in addition to the purchase price, but when the rent for the lease is equal to the full rental value, it is difficult to see that anything in addition to the purchase price has been received by the seller-lessor in exchange for the property sold.

In *Crowley, Milner & Co. v. Commissioner*, 689 F.2d 635 (6th Cir. 1982), the principle that the lease must have a value in order for there to be an exchange was carried to what seems to be an extreme. The taxpayer was allowed a loss on the sale of building immediately on completion of construction that had been constructed for it, and for which it paid the construction cost under an arrangement entered into before the completion of construction that provided for a sale price equal to the lesser of the construction cost or a fixed price. The sale was followed by a leaseback by the purchaser at a fixed rent. Given the obvious financing nature of the transaction, it seems almost certain that if the sale contract had provided for a price equal to the actual construction cost, whatever it was, the purchaser-lessor would have insisted on an adjustment of the rent to reflect the higher price. Nevertheless, the Tax Court found that the rent was fair rental value and the payment of the excess construction cost was not a premium for the lease. The result was that Crowley, Milner was able to deduct the excess construction cost as an immediate loss instead of deducting it as rent over the life of the lease, or, as depreciation over the life of the building if it had not sold it. Although in a sense the result resembles that in *Jordan Marsh*, the loss deducted in *Jordan Marsh* probably reflected a decline in the value of real estate values over the period between the acquisition of the property and the sale, while in *Crowley, Milner* it represented an immediate deduction of what was, at best, an overpayment for the building. *Cf.*, § 167(e) (disallowing depreciation on a term interest in property when the remainder is held by a related person).

Section 1031 is an exchange provision, not a rollover provision, so that a sale for cash, even if followed immediately by a reinvestment of the proceeds in like-kind property, does not qualify for nonrecognition. Thus, in *Swaim v. United States*, 651 F.2d 1066 (5th Cir. 1981), the court found the transaction to be a sale, not an exchange, even though the contract between two parties provided for simultaneous closing of the sale by the Swains of the Hale parcel to the Zimmermans and Garys, and to purchase by him of the Maverick parcel from the Zimmermans and Garys by the Swains. When the Zimmermans and Garys could not comply with the conditions of sale at the closing date, the closing and payment for the Hale parcel was completed, and the deeds from the Zimmermans and Garys for the Maverick parcel were placed in escrow and replaced three months later when conditions met by new deed. The court viewed the Maverick transaction as still being conditional at the time of the closing of the Hale transaction, which it viewed as final. Similarly, in *Carlton v. United States*, 385 F.2d 238 (5th Cir. 1967), there was a sale — not an exchange — when a rancher gave an option on property to a developer, and received a cash payment, most of which was used as a deposit on two replacement parcels, even though he assigned the purchase contracts to the developer under terms of original contract for the ranch that indicated an intention to make a § 1031 exchange; which obligated the developer to pay the balance of the purchase price less the replacement properties. At the closing, however, to avoid multiple transfers of title, the developer paid the money to the rancher, who immediately paid it to the sellers of the replacement parcels. The intent to effect an exchange was not enough to overcome the rancher's role in the transactions. The case stands a lesson on how not to make an exchange. There are numerous other cases drawing indistinct lines between an exchange and a sale coupled with a purchase. *See Bell Lines, Inc. v. United States*, 480 F.2d 710 (4th Cir. 1973) (purchase of new trucks from manufacturer and sale of used trucks to dealer recommended by manufacturer was not an exchange, even though manufacturer guaranteed dealer against loss in a side agreement not known to trucker); *Estate of Bowers v. Commissioner*, 94 T.C. 582 (1990) (sale, not an exchange, when taxpayer agreed to sell oil and gas leases to a purchaser and, before closing of sale, contracted to buy a farm and arranged for purchaser to pay for the farm and assign it to the taxpayer, because taxpayer began operating the farm before the closing of the sale of the oil and gas lease and transfer of legal title to the farm, so that taxpayer had become tax owner of the farm before disposition of oil and gas leases). On the other hand, the step-transaction and other similar principles have been applied to find an exchange even where there is no direct exchange. *See Redwing Carriers, Inc. v. Tomlinson*, 399 F.2d 652 (5th Cir. 1968) (sale of used trucks by parent and purchase of new trucks from same source by a subsidiary treated as an exchange because the transactions were mutually dependent; results in eliminating § 1231 gain on sales and reducing depreciable basis of new trucks); Rev. Rul. 61-119, 1961-1 C.B. 395 (same result without the subsidiary, even though documentation treated transactions as separate). An exchange using a disregarded entity can also qualify as a § 1031 exchange. *See* Rev. Rul. 2004-86, 2004-2 C.B. 191 (§ 1031 exchange through a Delaware land trust treated as an investment trust qualifies); Priv. Ltr. Rul. 2001-18-023 (receipt of ownership interest in disregarded entity owning replacement property to avoid state transfer taxes qualifies under § 1031. As discussed in § 1.03 *Multiparty Exchanges*, and § 1.04 *Deferred Exchanges*, the requirement that a transaction must involve an actual exchange has become highly attenuated, creating great flexibility in tax planning.

PROBLEMS FOR DISCUSSION

Problem 5-1. In 20X1, Pubco arranged to construct an office building as its new headquarters to be known as the "Pubco Building." Because Pubco will only occupy 30 percent of the space, the remaining portion of the building will be rented by Pubco to third parties at prevailing market rents. To finance the construction of the Pubco Building, Pubco entered into a sale and leaseback transaction with Insurco, under which Pubco agreed to sell the Pubco Building, when completed, to Insurco for the estimated construction cost of $6,000,000, or the cost of construction, whichever was more, and lease it back for 40 years at a fixed rent for the 40 years, which would pay off $6,000,000 plus interest and the then-prevailing rate for such transaction, with an option for Pubco to extend for up to four additional 10-year terms at the then-prevailing per-square-foot rental levels for similar office buildings. The terms of the transaction are such that the lease will meet the standards for being treated as a lease for federal income tax purposes. During the construction, the famous architect who had been hired to design the building persuaded Pubco to add artistic touches that would make the office building an architectural gem that would add to Pubco's prestige. As a result, the actual cost of the Pubco Building was $7,000,000, all of which was paid by Insurco, but the annual rent was increased by $700,000. Nevertheless, Pubco and Insurco have received appraisals that the fair market value of the Pubco Building for rental purposes was only $6,000,000, because the artistic touches did not add to the rental value, so that Pubco will only be able to rent the remaining 70 percent for about $420,000, even though the allocable rent for that portion is, of course, $490,000, and which indicates that the real rental value of the portion occupied by Pubco (without taking into account "prestige" from the architectural "panache," is only $180,000, so that Pubco is "losing" $100,000 a year on the rent. What is tax treatment to Pubco and Insurco of the $1,000,000 excess construction cost and the $100,000 excess rent? *See Century Electric* (sale and leaseback treated as § 1031 exchange; no loss recognized for excess of adjusted basis over sale price); *Jordan Marsh* (loss allowed on sale and lease back when sale price equaled value); *Crowley, Milner* (loss allowed on sale and leaseback when construction cost exceed sale price fixed in advance).

Problem 5-2. In 20X1, Reel and Repp executed a contract providing for the sale of Blackacre by Reel to Repp for $100,000. Two weeks later, pursuant to negotiations that were in process at the time the Blackacre contract was executed, they executed a contract for the purchase by Reel from Repp of Whiteacre for $150,000, which, for convenience of both parties, was scheduled to (and did) close on July 1, 20X1, the date specified in the Blackacre sale contract. At the closing, Reel executed a deed of Blackacre to Repp, Repp executed a deed of Whiteacre to Reel, and Reel paid Repp the $50,000 excess of the price of Whiteacre over that of Blackacre. Both properties were used before and after the transaction by their respective owners as farms. Reel, who had a $50,000 unrealized gain in Blackacre, reported the transaction as a nonrecognition exchange under § 1031, while Repp, who had a $75,000 loss in Whiteacre, claimed a $75,000 section 1231 loss. (i) What is the proper tax treatment of the transaction to Reel and Repp? (ii) If you conclude that Reel was required to recognize gain, what changes should be made to provide nonrecognition? (iii) If you conclude that Repp was not allowed to recognize the loss, what changes should be made to allow her to do so? *See Swaim* (sale, not exchange, even though contract between two parties provided for simultaneous closing of mutual sales, when one sale delayed because of failure to meet contract conditions); *Carlton* (sale, not exchange when rancher received a cash payment for option used as a deposit on two replacement parcels under contract assigned to developer under that indicated an intention to make a § 1031 exchange; transactions not mutually dependent); *Bell Lines* (purchase of new trucks from manufacturer and sale of used trucks to dealer recommended by manufacturer was not an exchange, even though manufacturer guaranteed dealer against loss); *Bowers* (sale, not an exchange, when taxpayer agreed to sell oil and gas leases to a purchaser, and before closing of sale, contracted to buy a farm and arranged for purchaser to pay for the farm and assign it to the taxpayer; taxpayer began operating the farm before the closing of the sale of the oil and gas lease and transfer of legal title to the farm); *Redwing Carriers* (sale of used trucks by parent and purchase of new trucks from same source by subsidiary treated as an exchange); Rev. Rul. 61-119, 1961-1 C.B. 395 (same result without the subsidiary, even though documentation treated transactions as separate).

§ 1.02. Boot, Liabilities and Basis

I.R.C. § 1031(b), 1031(c), 1031(d); Treas. Reg. § § 1.1031(a)-1(a)(2), 1.1031(b)-1, 1.1031(c)-1, 1.1031(d)-1; Treas. **Reg. § 1.168(i)-6(c), (d), and (i).**

Section 1031(a) refers to relinquished property exchanged "solely" for replacement property of like kind. However, many, if not all, like-kind exchanges in real life involve the transfer or receipt of nonlike-kind property, most frequently cash and/or relief or assumption of liabilities. In addition, exchanges occur in which multiple properties are involved, not all of which are like-kind. Nonlike-kind property is frequently referred to as "boot," although that term does not appear in the Code. The term presumably was applied because the taxpayer received not only like-kind property, but something else "to boot" as part of the exchange.

Although the use of the word "solely" in § 1031(a) suggests that the gain or loss attributable to the relinquished like-kind property in an exchange that also involves cash or nonlike-kind property would not be eligible for nonrecognition treatment, § 1031(b) provides that in such situations gain attributable to relinquished like-kind property will be recognized, but only to the extent of the fair market value of the boot received by the taxpayer, while § 1031(c) prohibits the recognition of any loss attributable to the relinquished like-kind property even when boot is involved. Section 1.02(a), which follows, describes the implications of exchanges that involve boot in the form of cash and nonlike-kind property. Such exchanges may involve the transfer of boot by the taxpayer as well as the receipt of boot by the taxpayer. Of course, gain or loss attributable to nonlike-kind property transferred by the taxpayer will not be eligible for nonrecognition treatment under § 1031. In both situations, the inclusion of boot has implications for the determination of the basis of the like-kind and nonlike-kind property.

A significant complication arises when the relinquished property and/or the replacement property is subject to liabilities. The treatment of liabilities as boot is discussed in § 1.02(a) *Netting Liabilities*. When boot is paid over a period of time, the installment sales provisions may apply to defer recognition of the gain, as discussed in § 1.02(b) *Boot and Installment Sales*.

When there is boot, gain (but not loss) is recognized to the extent of the boot. The amount of gain recognized is the lesser of the unrealized gain in the relinquished property or the amount of the boot. Any gain resulting from boot is characterized as capital gain, section 1231 gain, or ordinary income — depending on the character of the relinquished property. Thus, if Reel exchanges Blackacre, held for investment with a basis of $10,000 and a value of $100,000, for Whiteacre with a value of $90,000 and $10,000 cash, Reel recognizes $10,000 of capital gain, if Blackacre is used in Reel's trade or business of farming. Reel has a basis of $95,000, only the unrealized gain of $5,000 is recognized, but it is § 1231 gain that goes into the main pot. If Blackacre, with a basis of $10,000 and a value of $100,000 is improved with barns and other farm buildings on which depreciation of $30,000 has been claimed for Whiteacre worth $90,000 and cash of $10,000, the $10,000 is unrecaptured section 1250 gain taxed at the 25 percent rate. If Reel trades in used machinery with a basis of $10,000 after $150,000 of depreciation and a value of $100,000 for new equipment with a value of $90,000 and cash of $10,000, the gain recognized is ordinary income as depreciation recapture.

Under § 1031(d), the basis of the replacement property is increased for the gain, and reduced for the boot received. It is increased for boot paid. When the boot exceeds the gain, so that there is no nonrecognition, the basis of the replacement property is its fair market value. When boot is less than the gain, the boot and gain wash, so that the basis of the replacement property is the same as the basis of the relinquished property, and the basis of the boot is its fair market value. If the relinquishing taxpayer pays boot, the basis of the replacement property is increased for the boot paid. Thus, when Reel exchanges Blackacre, held for investment with a basis of $10,000 and a value of $100,000 for Whiteacre with a value of $90,000 and $10,000, Reel's basis in Whiteacre is $10,000, the sum of the $10,000 basis in Blackacre and the $10,000 gain recognized, reduced by the $10,000 basis of the cash. This is appropriate because Reel has recognized $10,000 of the inherent gain in Blackacre and still has $80,000 unrecognized gain in Whiteacre ($90,000 value - $10,000 basis). If the exchange is also a nonrecognition exchange under § 1031 for Repp, who owned Whiteacre, and Repp's basis in Whiteacre is $20,000, the basis of Blackacre is $30,000, because the $10,000 cash is added to the $20,000 Whiteacre basis. This is, of course, appropriate because it preserves the $70,000 unrealized gain in Whiteacre ($90,000 value - $20,000 basis) in Blackacre's exchanged basis ($100,000 value - $30,000 basis).

When there is boot in a loss transaction, the boot reduces the basis of the replacement property. Thus, if in the preceding example the basis of Blackacre was $120,000 so that there was a $20,000 loss, the loss would not be recognized, and the basis of Whiteacre would be the $120,000 basis of Blackacre reduced by the $10,000 cash boot. This is appropriate because it leaves the unrealized loss of $20,000 in Whiteacre ($110,000 basis - $90,000 value). The boot always has a basis equal to its value. If in any of the examples the boot was a used car with a value of $10,000, the basis of the car for Reel is $10,000, the amount taken into account as its value.

When the properties exchanged in a nonrecognition exchange under § 1031 are depreciable properties that are subject to the Modified Accelerated Cost Recovery System (MACRS) discussed in § 3.06 *Modified Accelerated Cost Recovery System* of Chapter 4 *Capitalization and Cost Recovery*, the replacement MACRS property is depreciated over the remaining recovery period of, and using the same depreciation method and convention as, those that had been used for the relinquished MACRS property before the transaction, to the extent that the exchanged basis of the replacement property is the same as that of the relinquished property. Treas. Reg. § 1.168(i)-6(c)(i). The depreciation treatment by the prior owner is irrelevant. Treas. Reg. § 1.168(i)-6(c)(2). The regulations contain detailed rules for applying similar principles in determining the depreciation of the replacement property when the recovery periods or depreciation methods for the relinquished and replacement properties are not the same. Treas. Reg. § 1.168-(i)-6(c)(4). Any excess of the basis in the acquired MACRS property over the adjusted basis in the relinquished property is depreciated as new property. Treas. Reg. § 1.168(i)-6(d). The relinquishing party has an election not to apply these rules, in which case the relinquished property is treated as having been disposed of for its adjusted basis at the time of the exchange and the replacement property is treated as having been acquired at that time, but the nonrecognition exchange is not affected. Treas. Reg. § 1.168(i)-6(i)(1). The same principles apply to replacement property acquired to replace involuntarily converted property as discussed in § 2 *Involuntary Conversion*, of this Chapter.

§ 1.02(a). Liabilities

Treas. Reg. §§ 1.1031(d)-2

Under the principles of *Crane v. Commissioner*, 331 U.S. 1 (1947), and the Regulations under § 1001, liabilities transferred with mortgaged property are treated as part of the amount realized. Treas. Reg. § 1.1001-2(a). In addition, § 1031(d) specifically provides that the assumption by any other party to the exchange of any liability of the taxpayer is to be treated as money received by the taxpayer on the exchange. Consequently, the relief of any liability previously incurred by the taxpayer is treated as boot. A long-standing provision of what is now Treas. Reg. § 1.1031(d)-2, however, nets the amount of any relief of liabilities against the amount of any assumption of liabilities or cash paid, so that only the amount of any net relief of liabilities is treated as boot. Thus, if Reel exchanges Blackacre, held for investment with a basis of $10,000 and a value of $100,000, that is subject to a liability of $20,000 for Whiteacre with a value of $90,000 that is subject to a liability of $10,000, Reel has $10,000 of boot because $20,000 liability is transferred and only $10,000 of liability is assumed. As a result, Reel recognizes $10,000 of capital gain. If the exchange is also a nonrecognition exchange under § 1031 for Repp, who owned Whiteacre, there is no boot for Repp because the $20,000 liability assumed is more than the $10,000 liability transferred. If Repp's basis in Whiteacre was $20,000, the basis of Blackacre is $30,000, because the $10,000 excess liability is treated as boot paid.

The following case describes the degree to which the parties are free to arrange the liabilities to take advantage of this generous rule. The ruling that follows illustrates the seemingly inconsistent application of the netting principle when the party being relieved of an excess liability compensated the other party with a note, which is, of course, boot for the excess.

GARCIA v. COMMISSIONER

United States Tax Court

80 T.C. 491 (1983)

* * *

> [A major part of the opinion involves a fairly standard analysis of issues related to a three party exchange under § 1031, discussed in § 1.03 *Multiparty Exchanges,* in which the court found the transaction to qualify. In connection with the exchange, the other party increased the mortgage on the replacement property to an amount slightly in excess of the mortgage on the relinquished property.]

Having decided the central issue of the applicability of section 1031(a) for the petitioners, we now confront the corollary question of whether the provisions of sections 1031(b) and (d) apply to create any exception to the general nonrecognition afforded by section 1031(a). Section 1031(b) requires that, despite the nontaxable status of a like-kind exchange, gain must be recognized to the extent that money or other unqualified property (commonly referred to as "boot") is received in addition to qualified like-kind property. Under the basic refinements mandated by section 1031(d), relief from liability is considered as money received for purposes of determining boot. These "mortgage-boot" rules of sections 1031(b) and (d) combine to require under certain conditions that the assumption or acquisition of a transferor's mortgage liability by a transferee results in taxable boot to the transferor.

However, the mortgage-boot rule applies only where a transferor is relieved of liabilities without a corresponding assumption of liabilities from the transferee. Where liabilities are relieved and assumed on both sides of an exchange, they are netted against each other in determining the extent, if any, to which taxable boot has been received. This liability offset provision is logically required to uphold the purpose of section 1031 in deferring recognition of theoretical gains or losses and is embodied in section 1.1031(b)-1(c), Income Tax Regs., which provides in relevant part:

> Where, on an exchange described in section 1031(b), each party to the exchange either assumes a liability of the other party or acquires property subject to a liability, then, in determining the amount of "other property or money" for purposes of section 1031(b), consideration given in the form of an assumption of liabilities (or a receipt of property subject to a liability) shall be offset against consideration received in the form of an assumption of liabilities (or a transfer subject to a liability). * * *

Under the language of this regulation, petitioners are clearly entitled to offset the amount of their relieved liabilities by the amount of their assumed liabilities. It is undisputed that the St. Joseph property was encumbered throughout the relevant transactions with a mortgage of $106,463, and that the transfer of this property resulted in the relief of liabilities of $106,463 for the petitioners. However, the proper figure to be used to offset this $106,463 is in dispute. Petitioners claim they are entitled to use $107,250 as an offset figure, resulting in no taxable gain, while respondent claims that only $75,000 is eligible to offset, resulting in a taxable boot gain of $23,163, that being the difference between $106,463 and $75,000, further reduced by $8,300 cash which the petitioners had deposited into the escrow for the purchase of the Pine property. The varying amounts of $107,250 and $75,000 are drawn from the amounts of the mortgages with which the Pine property was encumbered at various times during the exchange procedures. Before entry into the exchange escrow, Colombi and Hayden held the Pine property subject to a mortgage of only $75,000. However, as a precondition to the exchange with the petitioners, Colombi and Hayden were required by the escrow agreement to obtain a "new deed of trust to record in amount of $107,200 at best terms available." They did, in fact, do so, securing a new first deed of trust in the amount of $100,000 and a second trust deed for the additional amount of $7,250. When the petitioners ultimately received the Pine property from Colombi and Hayden by way of the Grillos, they assumed all then-outstanding liabilities thereon totaling $107,250.

Respondent asserts that the $107,250 figure cannot be respected for tax purposes, arguing that it results from an artificial attempt to reallocate liabilities for the purpose of tax avoidance. In so arguing, respondent relied primarily upon this Court's recent decision in *Long v. Commissioner*, 77 T.C. 1045 (1981), and the cases cited therein. Respondent is correct that, in the *Long* case, we stated:

> In considering the validity of any adjustment agreed to by the parties so close in time to the date of the exchange, the documents and the transaction as a whole should be carefully scrutinized to make sure that the form accurately reflects the substance. The form will not be permitted to control over the substance where the form was chosen merely to alter the tax liabilities of the parties * * * . . . .

Respondent has failed, however, to understand properly the context in which that statement was made. The central issue in the relevant aspect of *Long* concerned not merely section 1031(b) standing alone, but rather its interplay with applicable Code provisions under subchapter K, relating to the taxation of partners and partnerships. . . . *Long* involved a reallocation of existing liabilities among partners rather than an assumption of new liabilities in connection with an exchange. The "adjustment" requiring "scrutiny" in the *Long* case was a reallocation of liabilities among partners which was found by the Court to be lacking in economic substance and undertaken solely for tax avoidance purposes. . . .

In the instant case, we have a situation where, as far as petitioners are concerned, there was an assumption of a debt which had independent economic substance. The fact that the debt was created at petitioners' instance is beside the point. . . . We hold that since the amount of liabilities assumed, $107,250, exceeds the amount of liabilities from which petitioners were relieved, $106,463, there was no "boot" and therefore no taxable gain under section 1031(b).

* * *

Rev. Rul. 79-44, 1979-1 C.B. 265

* * *

Two unrelated individuals, *A* and *B*, neither of whom are dealers in real estate, respectively owned undivided one-half interests in two separate parcels of land as tenants in common. Both parcels were used in the taxpayers' business of farming. One parcel was subject to a mortgage for which *A* and *B* were each personally liable in the face amount of 1,000x dollars.

A and *B* rearranged their interests so that each owned 100 percent of a separate parcel. At the time of the transaction, each parcel had a fair market value of $2,000 x dollars and an adjusted basis of 100x dollars. *A* received the parcel subject to the mortgage and *B* received the remaining parcel, which was free of debt. *B* also executed a promissory note to *A* in the amount of, and with a fair market value of, 500x dollars to compensate *A* for taking the property subject to the mortgage. *A* and *B* continued to use the parcels in their respective businesses of farming.

* * *

Rev. Rul. 73-476 . . . holds that any gain or loss realized by three taxpayers who each exchanged an undivided interest in three separate parcels of real estate that were not subject to mortgages for a 100 percent ownership of one parcel is not recognized pursuant to section 1031(a) of the Code.

In this case, the transfer of interests in real property held by tenants in common that resulted in the conversion of two jointly owned parcels into two individually owned parcels is an exchange. The provisions of section 1001(a) of the Code apply to the exchange for purposes of determining the amount of gain realized. However, because the property interest exchanged are like-kind property that were being used in the taxpayers' business of farming and have continued to be so used after the exchange, the provisions of section 1031 apply to determine to what extent, if any, the gain is to be recognized.

As a result of the exchange, *A* owns 100 percent of one parcel of real estate, with a fair market value of 2,000x dollars and subject to a mortgage of $1,000$x$ dollars. The value of the one-half interest received by *A* was 1,000x dollars, one-half of the fair market value of the real estate. The value of the mortgage liability assumed by *A* as a result of the change was 500x dollars. *A* also received a note from *B* for 500x dollars. The note received by *A* is other property for purposes of section 1031(b) of the Code. *A* realized a gain of 950x dollars computed as follows:

Value of property received		1,000 x dollars
Other property received (note)		500 x
Total consideration received		1,500 x
Less: Adjusted basis of property transferred (one-half of 100 x dollars)	50 x	
Liabilities to which new property is subject	500 x	550 x
Gain realized		950 x dollars

For purposes of section 1031(b) of the Code the amount of "other property or money" received by A is $500x$ dollars. Consideration received by A in the form of money or other property is not offset by consideration given in the form of an assumption of liabilities or receipt of property subject to a liability. Accordingly, under section 1031(b), $500x$ dollars of the $950x$ dollar gain will be recognized. *See* section 1.1031(d)-2 of the regulations.

B received 100 percent ownership of the parcel of real estate that was not subject to a mortgage. The value of the one-half interest received by B is $1,000x$ dollars, one-half of the fair market value of the real estate. B realized a gain of $950x$ dollars computed as follows:

Value of property received		$1,000x$ dollars
Liabilities subject to which old property was transferred		$500x$
Total consideration received		$1,500x$
Less: Adjusted basis of property transferred (one half of 100 x dollars)	$50x$	
Other property paid (note)	$500x$	$550x$
Gain realized		$950x$ dollars

For purposes of section 1031(b) of the Code, the amount of "other property or money" received by B is zero. Consideration received by B in the form of a transfer subject to a liability of $500x$ dollars is offset by consideration given in the form of other property. Accordingly, under section 1031(b), B will not recognize any of the gain to be realized from the exchange. *See* section 1.1031(d)-2 of the regulations.

* * *

The transfer of interests in real property held by tenants in common that resulted in the conversion of two jointly owned parcels into two individually owned parcels is an exchange under section 1001(a) of the Code.

Because the property interests that were exchanged are like-kind property that were being used in the taxpayers' business of farming and have continued to be so used after the exchange, the provisions of section 1031 of the Code apply. Under section 1031, A will recognize the gain realized from the exchange, but not in excess of the fair market value of the note received from B. B will not recognize any of the gain realized from the exchange.

NOTES AND COMMENTS

When there is boot as a result of an excess liability transferred or otherwise, gain (but not loss) is recognized to the extent of the boot. Under § 1031(d) the basis of the replacement property is increased for the gain, and reduced for the boot. As a practical matter, unless the boot exceeds the gain, so that there is no nonrecognition, and the basis of the replacement property is its fair market value, these two items wash. Accordingly, the basis of the replacement property is the same as the basis of the relinquished property. If the taxpayer pays boot, as in Rev.

Rul. 79-44, the basis of the replacement property is increased for the boot paid.

Whatever the purpose of the liability increase in *Garcia*, when the dust cleared, Colombi and Hayden had the cash, and Garcia had the liability. The *Long* case, distinguished in *Garcia*, involved an exchange of partnership interests before § 1031(a)(2) was amended to exclude such exchanges from § 1031. Like *Garcia*, the partnership interest was encumbered by a liability taken out immediately before the exchange, but that liability was incurred to acquire an equivalent amount of investment securities that were included in the partnership assets, obviously for the sole purposes of matching liabilities for netting. There was also a readjustment of shares of liabilities allocated to Long and another partner, Center, shortly before the exchange that was not taxable under the partnership rules. The claimed effect was to reduce the liabilities transferred for purpose of the netting rule, but the court decided the changes were properly disregarded, because they had no purpose other than tax avoidance. When the dust cleared following the exchange in *Long*, Long and Center were relieved of their entire share of liabilities in the relinquished partnership, and had additional assets to offset the increased liability in the replacement partnership interests. Their game was to treat the liabilities as reductions in basis instead of boot under the netting rule. The Tax Court refused to play.

On a technical level, Rev. Rul. 79-44 stands for the proposition that boot given can offset the boot aspect of an excess liability transferred, but that boot received cannot be offset by an excess liability transferred. This result appears to be a failure of proper tax planning for the exchange. If *B* had retained the liability on half of the mortgage on property transferred to A, the economics would have been the same, but the result would have been different. *See* Tech. Adv. Mem. 80-03-004 (relinquishing party entitled to offset liability on replacement property against liability transferred, even though the recipient of the relinquished property immediately repaid and refinanced the liability on the replacement property; it does not matter whether the taxpayer was deemed to have assumed the exchange party's mortgage on the replacement property or paid boot).

PROBLEM FOR DISCUSSION

Problem 5-3. Ant and Hopper, who are siblings, owned Blackacre and Whiteacre, which are adjacent, as tenants in common, having inherited their interests from their deceased parents. Ant lived and farmed on Blackacre, while Hopper lived and farmed on Whiteacre. Ant loved farming while Hopper longed for the lights of the big city, but could not practically dispose of Whiteacre as long as he owned only a tenancy in common. Ant also wanted to end the tenancy in common, because she wanted to be able to borrow on the value of Blackacre. As long as it was held in the tenancy-in-common, however, any borrowing required Hopper's consent, which he refused to give in order to pressure Ant to buy him out. When they inherited Blackacre and Whiteacre the two properties were subject to a mortgage to Countribanc, secured equally by both properties, with a principal balance of $1,000,000. Over the years, the mortgage had been reduced to $700,000, but Ant has made mortgage payments that resulted in $250,000 of the principal reduction, while Hopper has been responsible for only $50,000. Their agreement was that the differences will be taken into account on any disposition or partition.

Their agreement does not, however, affect Countribanc's lien on both properties. How should Ant and Hopper arrange their exchange of Ant's interest in Whiteacre for Hopper's interest in Blackacre so that Ant does not have tax on the $200,000 adjustment? *See Garcia* (even liability incurred to be netted offsets liability transferred); Rev. Rul. 79-44 (don't offset boot by liability increase); Tech. Adv. Mem. 80-03-004 (liability on replacement property immediately repaid and refinanced); *Long* (liability incurred to be netted does not offset liability transferred when matched by investment assets; tax avoidance).

§ 1.02(b). Boot and Installment Sales

I.R.C. § 453(f)(6); Prop. Treas. Reg. § 1.453-1(f)(1).

A like-kind exchange can be coupled with an installment sale, when the boot received as part of the exchange takes the form of a promissory note under which the taxpayer will receive payments in subsequent years. The issue that arises is how the rules regarding like-kind exchanges under § 1031 coordinate with the rules regarding installment sales under § 453. An installment sale for purposes of § 453 is defined as "any disposition of property where at least 1 payment is to be received after the close of the taxable year in which the disposition occurs." § 453(b)(1). Unless the taxpayer elects otherwise, the gain from an installment sale is taken into account under the installment method. § 453(a). The installment method allows the deferral of gain until the principal payments are received. Mechanically, the installment method involves establishing a "gross profit percentage" as the ratio of the seller's gross profit on the sale to the principal payments to be made under the contract of sale, whether as a down payment or as deferred payments. § 453(c); Treas. Reg. § 15A.453-1(b)(2). The portion of each payment corresponding to the gross profit percentage is recognized as gain on the sale when payment is received, with the remainder of the payment representing recovery of the seller's basis. When gain is recognized in a nonrecognition exchange under § 1031 (and other nonrecognition provisions) as a result of boot, and some of the consideration is to be paid in a tax year after the year the relinquished property is transferred, the gain may be reported under the installment method if, as is likely, the relinquished property qualifies for use of the installment method. When a like-kind exchange qualifies for nonrecognition in part and as an installment sale in part, modifications must be made in the determination of the gross profit percentage, because the receipt of the replacement property is not considered a payment for purposes of the installment method, as explained in the following excerpt from the legislative history to § 453(f)(6):

INSTALLMENT SALES REVISION ACT OF 1980

Sen. Rep. No. 1000; 96th Cong., 2d Sess.

* * *

II. EXPLANATION OF THE BILL

* * *

H. Receipt of Like Kind Property (. . . sec. 453(f)(7) of the Code)

Present law

Under present law, the transfer of property for cash payments and like kind property may qualify both for installment method reporting and, with respect to the gain attributable to the like kind exchange, nonrecognition treatment (Code sec. 1031 and Rev. Rul. 65-155 . . . In this case, the gain to be recognized under installment method reporting is the total gain realized on the transaction less the gain eligible for nonrecognition under the like kind exchange provision. However, the value of the like kind property received by the seller is taken into account in determining the amount of the selling price, the contract price, and payments received for purposes of the installment sale provision.[24] The value of the like kind property received in the taxable year in which the sale or exchange is made.

Reasons for change

The committee believes that, when like kind property and an installment obligation are received, the like kind property should not be treated as payment in order to achieve the basic purpose of installment sale reporting, *i.e.*, gain should be recognized as cash (and other property with respect to which gain is recognized) is received.

Explanation of provision

Under the bill, property permitted to be received without recognition of gain in an exchange described in Code section 1031 (b)[25] will not be treated as payment for purposes of reporting income under the installment method.

Thus, the reporting the gain on the exchange under the installment method where an installment obligation is received in addition to the like kind property, the gross profit will be the amount of gain which will be recognized on the exchange if the installment obligation were satisfied in full at its face amount. Also, the total contract price will not include the value of the like kind property but instead will consist solely of the sum of the money and fair market value of other property received plus the face amount of the installment obligation.

The basis of the like kind property received, (determined under section 1031(d))

---

[24] Rev. Rul. 65-155... A similar case under present law involves the treatment of an installment obligation received as "boot" in exchange by a shareholder under a plan of corporate reorganization (sec. 356(a)(1)). Present law is unclear whether the exchange qualifies for installment sale reporting.

[25] This provision includes like kind exchanges (sec. 1031), exchanges of certain insurance policies (sec. 1035), certain exchanges of stock of the same corporation (sec. 1036), and certain exchanges of United States obligations (sec. 1037).

will be determined as if the obligation had been satisfied at its face amount.[26] Thus, the taxpayer's basis in the property transferred will first be allocated to the like kind property received (but not in excess of its fair market value) and any remaining basis will be used to determine the gross profit ratio.

The bill also provides that similar treatment applies in the case of an exchange under a plan of corporate reorganization described in section 356(a) which is not treated as a dividend.

These provisions may be illustrated by the following example. Assume that the taxpayer exchanges property with a basis of $400,000 for like kind property worth $200,000, and an installment obligation for $800,000 with $100,000 payable in the taxable year of the sale and the balance payable in the succeeding taxable year. The example compares present law, which takes like kind property into account as payment, with the bill which reverses this rule.

	Rev. Rul. 65-155 — Like kind property taken into account	*Like kind property not taken into account*
Contract price	$1,000,000	$800,000
Gross profit	600,000	600,000
Gross profit ratio (percent)	(60)	(75)
Gain to be reported for		
1. Taxable year of sale:		
(a) 60% of $300,000 (payments "received" of $100,000 cash and $200,000 value of like property)	180,000	
(b) 75% of $100,000 (cash payments)		75,000
2. Succeeding taxable year:		
(a) 60% of $700,000 (cash received)	420,000	
(b) 75% of $700,000 (cash received)		525,000
Total gain recognized	600,000	600,000
3. Basis of like kind property received	200,000	200,000

* * *

NOTES AND COMMENTS

As the example in the Senate Report indicates, the basis of the relinquished property is applied first to the basis of the replacement property, which is consistent with § 1031(d), but not with the installment method, which allocates

26 This is the same rule as presently set forth in Rev. Rul. 65-155, *supra*.

basis ratably to payments in the year of sale and the deferred payments. Only when the basis of the relinquished property is greater than the fair market value of the replacement property is there basis to be allocated to the payments (boot). This is, of course, consistent with the general rule for like-kind exchanges under § 1031, which recognizes gain to the extent of any boot. Because the example does not involve liabilities, it does not illustrate the application of the liability netting rule, but there does not appear to be any reason that liability netting should not apply first in determining whether there is boot in determining the gain to be reported under the installment method.

There is a similar difference in approach in allocating basis to liabilities. Under the installment method, liabilities are applied first to basis, which has the effect of deferring more of the gain, except that any liabilities in excess of the basis of the property sold are treated as payments in the year of sale. On the other hand, except for the netting of liabilities discussed in § 1.02(a) *Netting Liabilities*, all relief of liabilities is treated as boot under § 1031(b). More than 25 years ago, the Service issued Prop. Treas. Reg. § 1.453-1(f)(1) to coordinate these approaches. Despite the passage of time, these proposed regulations have not been finalized or withdrawn. Although, under the installment sale provisions, the basis of property sold under the installment method is applied first to any liabilities transferred so that only liabilities in excess of the basis of the property sold are treated as payments in the year of sale, Treas. Reg. § 15A.453-1(b)(2)(iii) and (iv), under the proposed regulations, any net liabilities transferred are applied only to any excess of the basis of the relinquished property over the fair market value of the replacement property. This has the effect of reducing or eliminating deferred gain in the replacement property and increasing the likelihood that net liabilities transferred are treated as payments in the year of sale, because they exceed the remaining basis of the relinquished property. Any cash or other property transferred by the relinquishing party in addition to the qualifying property is netted against any liabilities transferred in making this determination. Prop. Treas. Reg. § 1.1031-1(f)(1)(iii) and (iv) Ex. 3. Thus, if Reel exchanges Blackacre, with a basis of $300,000 and value of $1,000,000, subject to a note and mortgage of $250,000, for Whiteacre that is unencumbered and worth $450,000 and deferred payments, with adequate stated interest of $300,000, the entire $300,000 of the basis of Blackacre is assigned to Whiteacre. As a result, Reel treats the $250,000 mortgage liability transferred as payment in the year of exchange, resulting in an equivalent amount of gain recognized at that time with an additional $300,000 gain realized as the deferred payments are received. Accordingly, Reel recognizes $550,000 of the inherent gain in Blackacre and defers only the remaining $150,000 gain in Whiteacre ($450,000 value - $300,000 basis). If the installment sale principle of applying basis first to the mortgage liability were applied, $250,000 of the Blackacre basis would be applied to the transfer of the mortgage liability, leaving only $50,000 for the basis of Whiteacre. Reel would recognize $300,000 of the $700,000 inherent gain in Blackacre as the deferred payments are received and defer the remaining $400,000 inherent gain in Whiteacre ($450,000 value - $50,000 basis).

PROBLEM FOR DISCUSSION

Problem 5-4. In 20X1, Reel exchanged Blackacre, worth $1,000,000, which has a basis of $350,000, and that is subject to a mortgage of $300,000 or a net value of $700,000, for Whiteacre, worth $250,000, with a basis of $100,000 and that is subject to a mortgage of $150,000, or a net value of $100,000, that was owned by Repp. Repp also issued an installment obligation for $500,000, payable in annual installments of $100,000, with adequate stated interest, beginning on the anniversary of the exchange in 20X2. (i) What are the tax consequences of the exchange to Reel and Repp? (ii) Is there anything they could or should have done to reduce or defer gain recognized? *See* § 453(f); Treas. Reg. §§ 1.1031(b)–1, (c)-1, and (d)-1 and –2; Prop. Treas. Reg. § 1.453-1(f); Sen. Rep. No. 1000, discussed in § 1.02(c) *Boot and Installment Sales*; *Garcia* (net even liability incurred to be netted); Rev. Rul. 79-44 (don't offset boot by liability increase); Tech. Adv. Mem. 80-03-004 (liability on replacement property immediately repaid and refinanced still netted).

§ 1.03. Multiparty Exchanges

If the exchange requirement of § 1031 could only be satisfied when the transaction involved a two-party exchange, the provision for nonrecognition of like-kind exchanges would have exceedingly limited application. It is rare to find two parties, each of whom happens to have a property the other wants. Fortunately for those looking to take advantage of the benefits of a like-kind exchange, the exchange requirement has not been interpreted in such a narrow manner. Taxpayers have successfully created three- and four-party exchanges that satisfy the requirements of § 1031. For example, when the owner of the relinquished property has an anxious purchaser, the purchaser can be persuaded to cooperate in acquiring the desired replacement property from a third party, turning a two-party exchange into a three-party transaction, as shown in the following two rulings. The rulings indicate the Service's willingness to cut through the substance to get at the form. The *Barker* case that follows shows an unsuccessful Service attempt to re-inject an element of substance, when the transaction is worked through an intermediary, so that the transaction has become a four-party one, so the case explains why form remains controlling.

Rev. Rul. 75-291, 1975-2 C.B. 332

* * *

Y, a corporation, desired to acquire a tract of land and a factory owned by *X*, an unrelated corporation engaged in the business of manufacturing certain products. *Y* entered into a written agreement with *X* for the acquisition of a tract of land and a factory owned by *X*. Pursuant to the agreement, *Y* acquired another tract of land and constructed a factory thereon solely for the purpose of exchanging the tract of land and new factory for *X*'s land and existing factory. Under the terms of the agreement, *Y* could terminate the agreement if the costs of purchasing the land and building the factory exceeded a specified amount. *Y* purchased the land, built the factory solely on its own behalf, and consummated the exchange. No personal property was involved in the exchange.

* * *

In the instant case *X* exchanged land and an existing factory for other land and a new factory that *Y* had respectively acquired and built solely for the purpose of making the exchange. With respect to *X*, a taxable exchange is not deemed to arise merely because *Y* acquired the property specifically to complete the exchange, if the transaction otherwise qualifies for nonrecognition of gain under section 1031(a) of the Code. *See Mercantile Trust Co* . . . . and *Alderson v. Commissioner*, 317 F.2d 790 (9th Cir. 1963), *rev'g* 38 T.C. 215 (1962), in which the transactions were treated as nontaxable exchanges even though property acquired in exchanges by the taxpayers had been acquired immediately prior thereto by the other parties to the exchanges. In each of those cases, as in the instant case, the party acquiring property to be exchanged with the taxpayer did so on his own behalf and not as an agent of the taxpayer.

Accordingly, as to *X*, the exchange of land and factories between *X* and *Y* qualifies for nonrecognition of gain or loss under section 1031(a) of the Code. However, any depreciation recaptured as a result of the exchange of *X*'s property is subject to tax as ordinary income under the provisions of section 1250(d)(4).

On the other hand, *Y* acquired the property transferred to *X* immediately prior to the exchange and did not hold such property for productive use in its trade or business or for investment. Thus, as to *Y*, the exchange does not qualify for nonrecognition of gain or loss under section 1031(a) of the Code.

Rev. Rul. 77-297, 1977-2 C.B. 304

* * *

A entered into a written agreement with *B* to sell *B* for 1,000x dollars a ranch (the "first ranch") . . . Pursuant to the agreement, *B* placed 100x dollars into escrow and agreed to pay at closing an additional 200x dollars in cash, to assume a 160 x dollar liability of *A*, and to execute a note for 540x dollars. The agreement also provided that *B* would cooperate with *A* to effectuate an exchange of properties should *A* locate suitable property. No personal property was involved in the transaction. *A* and *B* are not dealers in real estate.

A located another ranch (the "second ranch") . . . owned by *C*. *B* entered into an agreement with *C* to purchase the second ranch for 2,000x dollars. Pursuant to this agreement, *B* placed 40x dollars into escrow, agreed to pay at closing an additional 800x dollars, assume 400x dollars liability of *C*, and execute a note for 760x dollars. No personal property was involved in the transaction. *C* could not look to *A* for specific performance on the contract, thus, *B* was not acting as *A*'s agent in the purchase of the second parcel of property.

At closing, *B* purchased the second ranch as agreed. After the purchase, *B* exchanged the second ranch with *A* for the first ranch and assumed *A*'s liability of 160x dollars. With *C*'s concurrence, *A* assumed *C*'s 400x dollar liability and *B*'s note for 760x dollars. *C* released *B* from liability on the note. The escrow agent returned the 100x dollars to *B* that *B* had initially placed in escrow. This sum had never been available to *A*, since the conditions of the escrow were never satisfied.

* * *

Ordinarily, to constitute an exchange, the transaction must be a reciprocal transfer of property, as distinguished from a transfer of property for a money consideration only.

In the instant case *A* and *B* entered into a sales agreement with an exchange option if suitable property were found. Before the sale was consummated, the parties effectuated an exchange. Thus, for purposes of section 1031 of the Code, the parties entered into an exchange of property. *See Alderson* . . . , in which a similar transaction was treated as a like-kind exchange of property even though the original agreement called for a sale of the property. In addition, *A*'s 160x dollar liability assumed by *B* was offset by *B*'s liabilities assumed by *A* . . .

Accordingly, as to *A*, the exchange of ranches qualifies for nonrecognition of gain or loss under section 1031 of the Code. As to *B*, the exchange of ranches does not qualify for nonrecognition of gain or loss under section 1031 because *B* did not hold the second ranch for productive use in a trade or business or for investment. . . .

However, in the instant case, *B* did not realize gain or loss as a result of the exchange since the total consideration received by *B* of 2,160x dollars (fair market value of first ranch of 1,000x dollars plus *B*'s liabilities assumed by *A* of 1,160x dollars) is equal to *B*'s basis in the property given up of 2,000x dollars plus *A*'s liability assumed by *B* of 160x dollars. . . .

BARKER v. COMMISSIONER

United States Tax Court
74 T.C. 555 (1980)

* * *

> [A major part of the case opinion involves a fairly standard analysis of issues related to a multiple party § 1031 exchange that the court found to qualify. Barker transferred a property called the Demion property to Goodyear and acquired the Casa El Camino property, both through an intermediary.]

Respondent has an alternative argument which must be addressed since we have found that the transaction qualifies as a like-kind exchange under section 1031. As part of the transaction, and simultaneously with the exchange of the properties, petitioner's mortgage on the Demion property was satisfied and Goodyear took out a new mortgage on that property. Respondent characterizes the mortgage payment as cash boot to petitioner and contends that section 1031(b) requires petitioner to recognize realized gain up to the amount of the cash used to satisfy the mortgage. To analyze this issue we must explore the boot and boot-netting rules under section 1031(b).

Money or property other than "like-kind" property received in a section 1031 exchange is taxed as boot under section 1031(b). Furthermore, where property transferred by a taxpayer is subject to a mortgage, the amount of the mortgage is treated as boot received by the taxpayer. Treas. Regs. § 1.1031(b)-1(c) . . . The presence of boot in a like-kind exchange does not disqualify the transaction from section 1031 tax-free treatment. Under section 1031(b) gain is recognized on the transaction, but only in an amount not in excess of the boot received.[10]

Section 1031(b) speaks in terms of boot received but does not mention boot given.[11] However, the regulations under section 1031 allow the netting of boot in some situations. When there are mortgages on both sides of the exchange, the mortgages are netted and the difference becomes, for the purpose of determining how much gain is to be recognized, the "money or other property" received by the party transferring the property with the larger mortgage. Treas. Regs. §§ 1.1031(b)-1(c); 1.1031(d)-2, Examples (1) and (2).

The regulations have limits on netting of boot when the boot on one or both sides of the transaction consists of something other than reciprocal liabilities. While a taxpayer who receives boot by surrendering mortgaged property can offset the boot by any boot given, including cash, a taxpayer who receives consideration in the form of cash to compensate for a difference in net values in the properties (fair market value less mortgage) cannot offset the cash boot by boot given by virtue of receiving mortgaged property. Treas. Regs. § 1.1031(d)-2, Examples (1) and (2).

Thus, a taxpayer who receives cash consideration to compensate for a difference in net values must recognize gain realized to the extent of the sum of cash received and the net difference in favor of himself between the mortgage on the property transferred and the mortgage on the property received. . . . Furthermore, he cannot offset the cash boot received by the net of mortgages even if the property he receives has a larger mortgage. Conversely, a taxpayer who pays cash boot can use the cash paid to offset the net difference where the mortgage on the property transferred exceeds the mortgage on the property received.[13]

In the instant case, if petitioner had simply exchanged the Demion property for the Casa El Camino property (and paid money as she did to compensate for the larger net value (fair market value less mortgage) of the Casa El Camino property over the Demion property), it is clear that no gain would be recognized to petitioner under section 1031(b). Petitioner would be viewed as simply having moved her

---

[10] This Rule can be illustrated as follows. If *A* exchanges property worth $5,000 and subject to a mortgage of $3,000 for property worth $2,000, *A* has received $3,000 boot and he must recognize gain realized up to that $3,000.

[11] For purposes of this Opinion we adopt the following terminology: A taxpayer who assumes a liability or accepts property subject to a liability gives boot, and a taxpayer whose liability is assumed or who transfers property subject to a liability receives boot.

[13] Surrey, Warren, McDaniel and Ault, Federal Income Taxation, Cases and Materials, p. 873-874 (1972) contains the following illustrative example which we have paraphrased:

> If A exchanged property worth $55,000 but subject to a $20,000 mortgage for B's property worth $65,000 but subject to a $40,000 mortgage and $10,000 cash, A would recognize gain (to extent realized) only to the extent of the $10,000 cash received plus the net of mortgages if the net was favorable to A. Since A is taking subject to a $40,000 mortgage while being relieved of a $20,000 mortgage, the net of mortgages does not result in any boot to A. Thus, gain is recognized to the extent of the $10,000 cash. (Note, however, that if cash and mortgages were netted together, there would be no net boot to A. However, cash received cannot be netted against mortgages.)
>
> As for B, gain will be recognized only to the extent of $10,000 (the net of the $40,000 mortgage less the $20,000 mortgage and the $10,000 cash) since the cash transferred may be subtracted from the net of mortgages to reduce boot.

equity in the Demion property (which was subject to mortgages of $62,288.79) to the Casa El Camino property, which was subject to a larger liability, a classic case of no net boot to petitioner under the section 1031 regulations. Any gain realized by petitioner under this posture of the case need not be recognized since she received no cash or net cash equivalent. This result would obtain even if Goodyear then immediately paid off the liability on the Demion property.

This case does not exactly parallel the above scenario, however, because in reality the mortgage on the Demion property was not paid off by Goodyear after the exchange but was paid off contemporaneously with the exchange. On the facts of this case and for reasons developed *infra*, this distinction is not critical.

A taxpayer is not allowed to offset cash received by boot given in a case where the taxpayer has received two distinct assets — like-kind property (albeit mortgaged) and cash — and the taxpayer has an unfettered right to do with the cash as he pleases. *Coleman v. Commissioner*, 180 F.2d 758 (8th Cir. 1950). In that type of case the taxpayer can exit the transaction with non-like-kind property — the cash. It seems appropriate to trigger the recognition of gain in those circumstances.

But when liabilities are paid off contemporaneously with the exchange, the taxpayer does not obtain dominion and control over the cash, and the taxpayer's net investment in the new like-kind property is no less than his net investment in the old. Indeed, in the instant case the net effect mandated by the interdependent contractual arrangements among the parties was not simply to maintain petitioner's investment at the same level; her investment — now transferred to the Casa El Camino property — was actually increased since she paid additional money as part of the acquisition price of the Casa El Camino property. Moreover, the agreements among the parties were such that petitioner never received (nor did she ever have the option to receive) non-like-kind property, *i.e.*, unfettered cash. Conceptually, then, there is no reason that boot-netting should not be permitted in such situations and we think it proper to allow it. It follows under this approach that petitioner will be permitted to offset the Demion and Casa El Camino liabilities in mining net boot.

Respondent would answer that we have framed the issue incorrectly and that this contemporaneous transaction should be analyzed as if petitioner received the cash and paid off the liability on the Demion property prior to transferring that property. Even if we were convinced this characterization were appropriate, we think the same result would obtain. It is significant in this regard that the cash in the instant case was used to satisfy the liability on the property that the petitioner transferred (the Demion property) and that the petitioner was contractually bound to use the cash for that purpose. Under no circumstance would petitioner have been able to come away from the transaction with non-like-kind property in the form of cash. Moreover, the receipt of cash and satisfaction of the liability on the Demion property did not compensate petitioner for a larger net value (fair market value less mortgage) of the Demion property over the Casa El Camino property. The payment, standing alone, also would not enhance petitioner's wealth at all — prior to the exchange, to the extent one liability has been satisfied, petitioner has a corresponding obligation to the payor of the cash. In a sense petitioner was little more than a conduit for the monies used to pay off the mortgage on the Demion property and she had no option to put the monies to other use. Under this approach, since petitioner does not really benefit until the properties are exchanged, we would still find that petitioner could offset all boot received by boot given.

* * *

Accordingly, we hold that boot-netting is permissible in a case where, contemporaneously with the exchange of properties and where clearly required by the contractual arrangement between the parties, cash is advanced by the transferee (in this case Goodyear through Covington Brothers) to enable the transferor-taxpayer (petitioner) to pay off a mortgage on the property to be transferred by the taxpayer (here, the Demion property). Since these criteria have been met, we find that the exchange in this case was completely tax free to petitioner.

We hasten to add that there is nothing in this that is inconsistent with, or casts doubt upon, the regulations under section 1031 or the holding in *Coleman* . . . and in those examples the cash was paid to the taxpayer to compensate him for a difference in net values (fair market value less mortgage) in the properties exchanged and to enable him to pay off (or to compensate him for assuming) the mortgage on the property he was to receive. Where cash boot is paid to account for differences in net values in the properties, the taxpayer has received non-like-kind property — the cash — which he is free to dispose of as he wants. He may, but need not, use the money to pay off the mortgage on the property he has received. This is the key factor which distinguishes *Coleman* and the examples in the regulations from the case before us.

* * *

NOTES AND COMMENTS

Based on these authorities, the successful execution of a multiparty exchange is basically a matter of careful planning and drafting. As a practical matter, major real estate brokers, title insurers and financial institutions are happy to serve as intermediaries — for a fee — and provide drafts of the relevant documents. Although we have not conducted extensive research, we note that, except for the *Bowers* case, the cases discussed in the *Notes and Comments* in § 1.01 *Exchange*, in which the taxpayer wanted, but failed to achieve, a nonrecognition exchange, all antedate Rev. Rul. 75-291. Since that ruling, many multiparty exchanges have been determined to qualify despite facts that might raise questions about whether an exchange had occurred. Thus, in *Biggs v. Commissioner*, 632 F.2d 1171 (5th Cir. 1980), a complex exchange qualified for nonrecognition under § 1031, even though the relinquishing party advanced funds on the replacement property, used his attorney as intermediary, and the transferee of the relinquished property never acquired title to the replacement property, but transferred the contract to purchase the replacement property to the relinquishing party. *See* Rev. Rul. 90-34, 1990-1 C.B. 154 (exchange qualifies even if contract to purchase rather than title received in exchange); Priv. Ltr. Rul. 94-13-024 (exchange of ranch qualifies, even though the developer who was originally granted the option on the ranch under a contract providing for a § 1031 exchange transferred the option to a second developer, who, in turn, conveyed it to a third developer, who was to acquire a multi-unit apartment building to convey to the ranch owner as replacement property and was to make additional payments as housing units on ranch development were sold; the option payments were treated as boot in the year of the exchange; additional amounts to be paid as housing units were sold were also boot). As the decision in *Bowers* indicates, however, those who seek competent advice too late can foul up.

The multiparty exchange is a solution to the practical problem that an owner of property, often real property, who wishes to dispose of the property using a nonrecognition exchange, can rarely find an owner of property that the relinquishing party wants who also wants the relinquished property. Accordingly, the practical arrangement is that the relinquishing party, puts the relinquished property on the market, and eventually enters into an agreement with a purchaser that provides for a sale at the agreed price, but that contains a provision that the purchaser agrees to cooperate with the relinquishing party in carrying out a nonrecognition like-kind exchange under § 1031. The relinquishing party then enters into an exchange agreement with a qualified intermediary ("QI"), and assigns the rights and obligations under the agreement with the purchaser to the QI. QIs must not be agents of the relinquishing party, specifically disqualifying the relinquishing party's attorney, accountant, investment banker or broker, or real estate agent or broker, but not escrow agents, title insurers, or most banks. Treas. Reg. § 1.1031(k)-1(k)(1) and (2). Related parties as defined in §§ 267(b) and 707(b) (using 10% instead of 50% to measure the relationship) to the relinquishing party or to the specified disqualified agents are also disqualified. Treas. Reg. § 1.1031(k)-1(k)(3) and (4). The same bank can serve as a QI and as qualified trustee as described in the next paragraph. *See* Priv. Ltr. Rul. 2010-30-020.

Under the exchange agreement, the relinquishing party agrees to transfer the relinquished property to the QI in exchange for replacement property to be received from QI. The relinquishing party either has already located the replacement property or does so and enters into an agreement with the owner of the replacement property that also contains a provision for the seller of the replacement property to cooperate with relinquishing party in carrying out a nonrecognition like-kind exchange under § 1031. The relinquishing party assigns the rights and obligations under the agreement to acquire the replacement property to the QI. In a simultaneous exchange, the relinquishing party transfers the relinquished property to the QI (although it can directly deed the relinquished property to the purchaser under Rev. Rul. 90-34), who then sells the property to the purchaser. The proceeds are placed in a qualified trust or escrow account that secures the transferee of relinquished property's obligation to acquire the replacement property. Treas. Reg. § 1.1031(k)-1(g)(3). The QI uses the proceeds from its seller, and transfers the replacement property to the relinquishing party (although, once again, seller can directly deed the replacement property to the relinquishing party). Even though the deeds for the properties can be made directly between the relinquishing party and the purchaser or seller as the case may be — usually to save transfer taxes and other transfer costs — the purchase price must be paid to the QI and by the QI to the seller. The relinquishing party can never receive the purchase price and, after the agreement with the QI has been reached, can have no right to get the purchase price, unless the agreement with the seller of the replacement property fails.

For example, Reel owns Blackacre, which is highly appreciated and that she wants to sell, because she believes it does not have much potential for further appreciation, and locates Perch, who wants to use Blackacre for a project the he believes will make him a bundle. Reel and Perch agree on a price and enter into an agreement for Perch to pay $1,000,000 for Blackacre and to cooperate in a § 1031 exchange. Reel enters into agreement with QI under which Reel assigns the agreement with Perch to QI and agrees to transfer Blackacre to Perch at QI's direction, with QI to receive the $1,000,000 from Perch and use it to purchase replacement property. Under the agreement with QI, Reel has no right to receive the $1,000,000 from QI, which is to use it exclusively to acquire replacement property. Reel finds that Repp owns Whiteacre, which is perfect for her needs. She agrees to buy Whiteacre from Repp for $1,000,000, with Repp also agreeing to cooperate in a § 1031 exchange, and assigns that agreement to QI. On the closing date specified in both agreements, Perch pays $1,000,000 to QI. QI directs Reel to deed Blackacre to Perch. QI then pays the $1,000,000 to Repp and directs Repp to deed Whiteacre to Reel.

Unfortunately, in the financial crisis beginning in 2007-2008, a number of QIs defaulted on their obligation to acquire and transfer replacement property to the relinquishing taxpayer. In Rev. Proc. 2010-14, 2010-1 C.B. 456, the Service, in effect, deferred the tax consequences for transactions involving bankruptcy or similar proceedings for QIs until the confirmation of the QI's insolvency proceeding and receipt of payment by the relinquishing taxpayer, with the payments received becoming the proceeds from the sale of the relinquished property, which no longer can qualify for a nonrecognition exchange. Appropriate adjustments are made for any indebtedness satisfied by the QI from the proceeds of sale, with gain in the year of the satisfaction when the satisfied indebtedness exceeds the basis of the relinquished property. OID and imputed interest are measured from the date of the sale being the date of confirmation of the QIs plan.

PROBLEM FOR DISCUSSION

Problem 5-5. On Jan. 15, 20X1, Reel agreed to sell Blackacre, in which his basis was $50,000, and which was subject to a $80,000 mortgage loan owed to Countribanc, to Perch for $120,000. The Reel-Perch contract terms required that Perch to cooperate in a § 1031 like-kind exchange, with the $120,000 proceeds to be paid into an escrow account with Title, which was providing title insurance on Blackacre for Perch and on Whiteacre for Reel. Because of a due-on-sale clause that Countribanc was unwilling to waive, the Blackacre mortgage had to be paid at closing. On Feb. 1, 20X1, Reel orally agreed with Repp to purchase Whiteacre for $150,000 as the replacement property. The Reel-Repp oral contract required Repp to cooperate in a § 1031 like-kind exchange of Whiteacre for Blackacre. On Feb. 15, 20X1, Reel formally opened the escrow account with Title, assigned the agreements with Perch to Title, deeded Blackacre to Title, and issued written escrow instructions that provided that after using the proceeds of the sale of Blackacre to Perch to pay off the mortgage loan on Blackacre, Title was to transfer the remaining net proceeds after payment of its fees and expenses to Repp as the down payment on Whiteacre. Reel did not formally assign the oral agreement with Repp, and Repp never became a party to the escrow agreement, which remained solely among Reel, Perch, and Title. Reel did, however, orally advise Title of the Reel-Repp oral agreement. Both S&L and Title were advised that Reel would direct that the proceeds of the mortgaged be paid to Title as part of a § 1031 like-kind exchange. The sale of Blackacre to Perch and the purchase of Whiteacre from Repp both closed on Mar. 15, 20X1. Title deeded Blackacre to Perch and used $80,000 of the proceeds of the sale of Blackacre to Perch to pay off the Countribanc note and mortgage, leaving $35,000 net of fees and expenses that were paid to Repp on account of the $150,000 purchase price. The $115,000 balance of the purchase price Whiteacre was paid by Title from the proceeds of the S&L note and mortgage on Whiteacre executed by Title and Reel. On that date, as part of simultaneous closings held in the same office on Title's premises, the Reel-Perch transaction was closed in accordance with its terms; Reel executed a note and mortgage to S&L and S&L delivered a check for the $115,000 proceeds payable to Title. Title delivered to Reel a check payable to both Reel and Repp, for $150,000, representing the $35,000 balance of the net proceeds of the Reel-Perch transaction and the $115,000 proceeds of the S&L note and mortgage on Whiteacre, which, of course, Reel endorsed to Repp as the purchase price of Whiteacre. For convenience and to reduce transfer costs, the deed to Blackacre was delivered directly by Reel to Perch, and the one for Whiteacre was delivered directly by Repp to Reel. (i) Does Reel's disposition of Blackacre to Perch and acquisition of Whiteacre from Repp qualify for nonrecognition under § 1031? (ii) If it does, to what extent, if any, is the payment of the mortgage on Blackacre netted against the new mortgage on Whiteacre? Treas. Reg. §§ 1.1031(b)-1 and (2) and (k)-1(g) and (k); *see Barker* (multiparty exchange through intermediary); Rev. Rul. 75-291 (Service sanctions multiparty exchange involving property constructed to be replacement property); Rev. Rul. 77-297 (same with liability netting); *Swaim* (sale, not exchange, even though contract between two parties provided for simultaneous closing of mutual sales when once sale delayed because of failure to meet contract conditions); *Carlton* (sale, not exchange when rancher received a cash payment for option that was used as a deposit on two replacement parcels under contract assigned to developer that indicated an intention to make a § 1031 exchange; transactions not mutually dependent); *Biggs* (complex exchange qualifies even though taxpayer advanced funds on replacement property, used his attorney as intermediary and acquirer of the relinquished property, transferred the contract to the replacement property, not title); *Bell Lines* (purchase of new trucks from manufacturer and sale of used trucks to dealer recommended by manufacturer was not an exchange, even though manufacturer guaranteed dealer against loss); *Bowers* (sale, not an exchange, when taxpayer agreed to sell oil and gas leases to a purchaser, and before closing of sale, contracted to buy a farm and arranged for purchaser to pay for the farm and assign it to the taxpayer; taxpayer began operating the farm before the closing of the sale of the oil and gas lease and transfer of legal title to the farm); *Redwing Carriers* (sale of used trucks by parent and purchase of new trucks from same source by subsidiary treated as an exchange); Rev. Rul. 61-119 (same result without the subsidiary, even though documentation treated transactions as separate); Rev. Rul. 90-34 (exchange qualifies even if contract to purchase rather than title received in exchange); *Garcia* (net even liability incurred to be netted); Rev. Rul. 79-44 (don't offset boot by liability increase); Tech. Adv.

Mem. 80-03-004 (liability on replacement property immediately repaid and refinanced still netted).

§ 1.04. Deferred Exchanges

I.R.C. § 1031(a)(3); Treas. Reg. §§ 1.1031(k)-1; 1.468B-6.

The complexity of a multiparty exchange is significantly increased when the taxpayer transfers the relinquishing property prior to acquiring the replacement property. In many like-kind exchanges, the taxpayer may not even have located the replacement property before transferring the relinquished property. The following case, which deals with these issues, has given its name to deferred exchanges, so that they are now frequently referred to as *Starker* exchanges, even in newspaper real estate columns.

STARKER v. UNITED STATES

United States Court of Appeals, Ninth Circuit
602 F.2d 1341 (9th Cir. 1979)

* * *

On April 1, 1967, T. J. Starker and his son and daughter-in-law, Bruce and Elizabeth Starker, entered into a "land exchange agreement" with Crown Zellerbach Corporation (Crown). The agreement provided that the three Starkers would convey to Crown all their interests in 1,843 acres of timberland in Columbia County, Oregon. In consideration for this transfer, Crown agreed to acquire and deed over to the Starkers other real property in Washington and Oregon. Crown agreed to provide the Starkers suitable real property within five years or pay any outstanding balance in cash. As part of the contract, Crown agreed to add to the Starkers' credit each year a "growth factor", equal to six percent of the outstanding balance.

On May 31, 1967, the Starkers deeded their timberland to Crown. Crown entered "exchange value credits" in its books: for T. J. Starker's interest, a credit of $1,502,500; and for Bruce and Elizabeth's interest, a credit of $73,000.

Within four months, Bruce and Elizabeth found three suitable parcels, and Crown purchased and conveyed them pursuant to the contract. No "growth factor" was added because a year had not expired, and no cash was transferred to Bruce and Elizabeth because the agreed value of the property they received was $73,000, the same as their credit.

Closing the transaction with T. J. Starker, whose credit balance was larger, took longer. Beginning in July 1967 and continuing through May 1969, Crown purchased 12 parcels selected by T. J. Starker. Of these 12, Crown purchased 9 from third parties, and then conveyed them to T. J. Starker. Two more of the 12 (the Timian and Bi-Mart properties) were transferred to Crown by third parties, and then conveyed by Crown at T. J. Starker's direction to his daughter, Jean Roth. The twelfth parcel (the Booth property) involved a third party's contract to purchase. Crown purchased that contract right and reassigned it to T. J. Starker.

The first of the transfers from Crown to T. J. Starker or his daughter was on

September 5, 1967; the twelfth and last was on May 21, 1969. By 1969, T. J. Starker's credit balance had increased from $1,502,500 to $1,577,387.91, by means of the 6 per cent "growth factor". The land transferred by Crown to T. J. Starker and Roth was valued by the parties at exactly $1,577,387.91. Therefore, no cash was paid to T. J. Starker, and his balance was reduced to zero.

In their income tax returns for 1967, the three Starkers all . . . claimed that the transactions were entitled to nonrecognition treatment under section 1031 . . .

* * *

In the first of the two cases, *Bruce Starker v. United States* (*Starker I*). 75-1 U.S. Tax Cas. (CCH) § 8448 (D. Or. 1975), the trial court held that this court's decision in *Alderson v. Commissioner*, 317 F.2d 790 (9th Cir.1963), compelled a decision for the taxpayers. Bruce and Elizabeth Starker recovered the claimed refund. The government appealed, but voluntarily dismissed the appeal . . .

The government, however, did not capitulate in *T. J. Starker v. United States* (*Starker II*), the present case. The government continued to assert that T. J. Starker was not entitled to section 1031 nonrecognition. According to the government, T. J. Starker was liable not only for a tax on his capital gain, but also for a tax on the 6 per cent "growth factor" as ordinary income (interest or its equivalent).

The same trial judge who heard *Starker I* also heard *Starker II*. Recognizing that "many of the transfers here are identical to those in *Starker I*", the court rejected T. J. Starker's collateral-estoppel argument and found for the government. The judge said:

> "I have reconsidered my opinion in *Starker I*. I now conclude that I was mistaken in my holding as well in my earlier reading of *Alderson*. Even if *Alderson* can be interpreted as contended by plaintiff, I think that to do so would be improper. It would merely sanction a tax avoidance scheme and not carry out the purposes of § 1031." . . .

Judgment was entered for the government on both the nonrecognition and ordinary income (interest) issues, and this appeal followed.

* * *

The government, having lost its case against this taxpayer's son based on the same contract to transfer the same family lands, decided not to pursue an appeal in that case, but instead to pursue this taxpayer. Although T. J. Starker's transactions involving three of the parcels differed in a relevant way from those of his son, the legal issues and facts surrounding the other nine are so similar that collateral estoppel applies. Except as to the Bi-Mart, Timian, and Booth properties, the government should have been held collaterally estopped by *Starker I* from relitigation of the applicability of I.R.C. § 1031 in *Starker II*.

III. TIMIAN, BI-MART, AND BOOTH PROPERTIES

As to Timian, Bi-Mart, and Booth properties, the facts of *Starker I* are so different from those of this case that the entire issue of the applicability of section

1031 to them was properly before the district court in *Starker II*. The court therefore correctly went to the merits of the litigants' arguments as they pertained to these parcels. We now turn to those arguments.

. . . [N]one of these three properties was deeded to him at or near the time he deeded his timberland to Crown. . . . Thus, the question whether section 1031 requires simultaneity of deed transfers is presented as to all three. In addition, each of these parcels presents its own peculiar issues because of the differing circumstances surrounding their transfers.

A. Timian and Bi-Mart Properties.

The Timian property is a residence. Legal title to it was conveyed by Crown at T. J. Starker's request to his daughter, Jean Roth, in 1967. T. J. Starker lives in this residence, and pays rent on it to his daughter. The United States argues that since T. J. Starker never held legal title to this property, he cannot be said to have exchanged his timberland for it. Furthermore, the government contends, because the property became the taxpayer's personal residence, it is neither property "held for investment" nor of a like kind with such property under the meaning of the Code. On the other hand, the taxpayer argues that there was, in economic reality, a transfer of title to him, followed by a gift by him to his daughter.[7]

The Bi-Mart property, a commercial building, was conveyed by Crown to Roth in 1968. The government raises the same issue with regard to the Bi-Mart property: since T. J. Starker never had title, he did not effect an exchange. T. J. Starker points out, however, that he expended substantial time and money in improving and maintaining the structure in the three months prior to the conveyance of the property to his daughter, and he emphasizes that he controlled and commanded its transfer to her.

We begin our analysis of the proper treatment of the receipt of these two properties with a consideration of the Timian residence. T. J. Starker asserts that the question whether such property can be held "for investment" is unsettled. We disagree. It has long been the rule that use of property solely as a personal residence is antithetical to its being held for investment. Losses on the sale or exchange of such property cannot be deducted for this reason . . . A similar rule must obtain in construing the term "held for investment" in section 1031. . . . Thus, nonrecognition treatment cannot be given to the receipt of the Timian parcel.

Moreover, T. J. Starker cannot be said to have received the Timian or Bi-Mart properties in exchange for his interest in the Columbia County timberland because title to the Timian and Bi-Mart properties was transferred by Crown directly to someone else, his daughter. Under an analogous nonrecognition provision, section 1034 of the Code, the key to receiving nonrecognition treatment is maintaining continuity of title. Under section 1034, if title shifts from the taxpayer to someone other than the taxpayer's spouse, nonrecognition is denied. . . . Although in some cases a father and his daughter may be seen as having an identity of economic

---

[7] Apparently, T. J. Starker paid a gift tax in 1968 on the transfers of the Bi-Mart and Timian properties to his daughter, but the question whether he truly owed such a tax is not before us.

interests . . . , that unity is not sufficient to make transfer of title to one the same as transfer of title to the other. T. J. Starker has not shown that he has any legally cognizable interest in the Timian or Bi-Mart properties . . . In these circumstances, T. J. Starker cannot be said to have "exchanged" properties under section 1031, because he never received any property ownership himself.

B. Booth Property.

The Booth property is a commercial parcel, title to which has never been conveyed to T. J. Starker. The transfer of this property to him was achieved in 1968 by Crown's acquiring third parties' contract right to purchase the property, and then reassigning the right to T. J. Starker. In addition to emphasizing the lack of simultaneity in the transfers, the government points here to the total lack of deed transfer.

An examination of the record reveals that legal title had not passed by deed to T. J. Starker by the time of the trial. He continued to hold the third-party purchasers' rights under a 1965 sales agreement on the Booth land. That agreement notes that one of the original transferors holds a life interest in the property, and that legal title shall not pass until that life interest expires. In the meantime, the purchasers are entitled to possession, but they are subject to certain restrictions. . . .

. . . [W]e believe that what T. J. Starker received in 1968 was the equivalent of a fee interest for purposes of section 1031. Under Treas. Regs. § 1.1031(a)-1(c), a leasehold interest of 30 years or more is the equivalent of a fee interest for purposes of determining whether the properties exchanged are of a like kind. Under the assigned purchase rights, Starker had at least the rights of a long-term lessee, plus an equitable fee subject to conditions precedent. If the seller's life interest lasted longer than 30 years, the leasehold interest would be the equivalent of a fee; the fact that the leasehold might ripen into a fee at some earlier point should not alter this result. Thus, we hold that what T. J. Starker received in 1968 was the equivalent of a fee.

. . . Since the taxpayer did not receive the fee equivalent at the same time that he gave up his interest in the timberland, the same issue is presented as with the nine parcels on which the government was estopped, namely, whether simultaneity of transfer is required for nonrecognition treatment under section 1031.

The government's argument that simultaneity is required begins with Treas. Reg. § 1.1002-1(b). That regulation provides that all exceptions to the general rule that gains and losses are recognized must be construed narrowly . . . There are two problems, however, with applying this regulation to section 1031.

First, the "underlying purpose" of section 1031 is not entirely clear. The legislative history reveals that the provision was designed to avoid the imposition of a tax on those who do not "cash in" on their investments in trade or business property. Congress appeared to be concerned that taxpayers would not have the cash to pay a tax on the capital gain if the exchange triggered recognition. This does not explain the precise limits of section 1031, however; if those taxpayers sell their property for cash and reinvest that cash in like-kind property, they cannot enjoy the section's benefits, even if the reinvestment takes place just a few days after the sale. Thus, some taxpayers with liquidity problems resulting from a replacement of their business property are not covered by the section. The liquidity rationale must therefore be limited.

Another apparent consideration of the drafters of the section was the difficulty of valuing property exchanged for the purpose of measuring gain or loss. Section 1031(a) permits the taxpayer to transfer the basis of the property he or she gives up to the property he or she receives, thus deferring the valuation problem, as well as the tax, until the property received is sold or otherwise disposed of in a transaction in which gain or loss is recognized.

But this valuation rationale also has its limits. So long as a single dollar in cash or other non-like-kind property ("boot") is received by the taxpayer along with like-kind property, valuation of both properties in the exchange becomes necessary. In that case, the taxpayer is liable for the gain realized, with the maximum liability being on the amount of cash or other "boot" received, under I.R.C. § 1031(b). To compute the gain realized, one must place a value on the like-kind property received. Moreover, the nonrecognition provision applies only to like-kind exchanges, and not to other exchanges in which valuation is just as difficult. Therefore, valuation problems cannot be seen as the controlling consideration in the enactment of section 1031.

In addition to the elusive purpose of the section, there is a second sound reason to question the applicability of Treas. Regs. § 1.1002-1: the long line of cases liberally construing section 1031. If the regulation purports to read into section 1031 a complex web of formal and substantive requirements, precedent indicates decisively that the regulation has been rejected. *See Biggs v. Commissioner*, 69 T.C. 905, 913-14 (1978).[10] We therefore analyze the Booth transaction with the courts' permissive attitude toward section 1031 in mind.

---

[10] For example, courts have held that "three corner" exchanges qualify for section 1031 nonrecognition treatment. In *Biggs*, 69 T.C. 905 (1978), the court described these transactions and summarized the ease with which a taxpayer can use them to qualify for nonrecognition treatment:

> "* * * In such a transaction, the taxpayer desires to exchange, rather than to sell, his property. However, the potential buyer of the taxpayer's property owns no property the taxpayer wishes to receive in exchange. Therefore, the buyer purchases other suitable property from a third party and then exchanges it for the property held by the taxpayer.
>
> "In numerous cases, this type of transaction has been held to constitute an exchange within the meaning of section 1031. *E.g., Alderson v. Commissioner*, 317 F.2d 790 (9th Cir. 1963). . .. In so holding, the courts have permitted taxpayers great latitude in structuring transactions. Thus, it is immaterial that the exchange was motivated by a wish to reduce taxes. . .. The taxpayer can locate suitable property to be received in exchange and can enter into negotiations for the acquisition of such property. . .. Moreover, the taxpayer can oversee improvements on the land to be acquired . . . and can even advance money toward the purchase price of the property to be accepted by exchange . . . Provided the final result is an exchange of property for other property of a like kind, the transaction will qualify under section 1031.". . .

In *Biggs*, the Tax Court took this liberal treatment even further. It found that a "four corner" exchange qualified for section 1031 nonrecognition. The party to whom the taxpayer was deeding his property (the "second party") did not want to take title to the property the taxpayer ultimately desired. As a result, the taxpayer advanced money to a syndicate, which bought the desired property from a fourth party and transferred it directly to the taxpayer. The taxpayer then transferred his original property to the second party, and got back his cash advance to the syndicate, ultimately out of the pocket of the second party.

Two features of the Booth deal make it most likely to trigger recognition of gain: the likelihood that the taxpayer would receive cash instead of real estate, and the time gap in the transfers of the equivalents of fee title.

In assessing whether the possibility that T. J. Starker might receive cash makes section 1031 inapplicable, an important case is *Alderson v. Commissioner*, 317 F.2d 790 (9th Cir. 1963). There, this court held that a "three corner" exchange qualified for nonrecognition treatment. The taxpayer and Alloy entered into an agreement for the simple cash sale of the taxpayer's property, but later amended the agreement to provide that Alloy would purchase another parcel to effect a swap with the taxpayer. This amendment did not totally eradicate the possibility that the cash transaction would take place; it provided, in the words of the court, that "if the exchange was not effected by September 11, 1957, the original escrow re the purchase for cash would be carried out." . . . The exchange was effected when reciprocal deeds were recorded. Said the court:

> "True, the intermediate acts of the parties could have hewn closer to and have more precisely depicted the ultimate desired result, but what actually occurred on September 3 or 4, 1957, was an exchange of deeds between the petitioners and Alloy which effected an exchange of the Buena Park property for the Salinas property." *Alderson* . . . .

The court stressed that, although at the time the contract was amended there was a possibility that a cash sale would take place, there was from the outset no intention on the part of the taxpayer to sell his property for cash if it could be exchanged for other property of a like kind. Thus, *Alderson* followed *Mercantile Trust of Baltimore v. Commissioner*, 32 B.T.A. 82 (1935), a case in which the taxpayer could have required the other party to the exchange to pay cash if that other party was unable to purchase an identified parcel that the taxpayer desired. . . .

Coastal Terminals, Inc. v. United States, 320 F.2d 333 (4th Cir. 1963), held similarly. There, a "three corner" exchange was effected, with both the taxpayer and the other party to the exchange maintaining until the closing the option to cancel the exchange and bring about a cash sale instead. Citing *Alderson* with approval, the court noted that the taxpayer intended to sell the property for cash only if it was unable to locate a suitable piece of property to take in exchange. Because an exchange took place, nonrecognition treatment was granted.

The Fifth Circuit has indicated its agreement with this approach in *Carlton v. United States*, 385 F.2d 38 (5th Cir. 1967). There, the taxpayers gave General an option to purchase their property for cash, but maintained the right to require General to acquire land and transfer it to them in lieu of cash. From the outset, the taxpayers intended to get suitable property, and not cash, in return. As it turned out, at the closing, General transferred to the taxpayers a contract right to purchase two parcels, and enough cash to purchase them, in exchange for the taxpayers' land. Because of the form of payment, section 1031 was held not to apply. But the court noted that the government agreed that had the taxpayers followed the original plan,

---

Since the various transfers were all part of a single overall plan, the Tax Court found that section 1031 had been satisfied. . . .

with General acquiring title and then transferring it to the taxpayers, the section would have applied.

Thus, the mere possibility at the time of agreement that a cash sale might occur does not prevent the application of section 1031. Even in cases such as *Coastal Terminals*, where the taxpayers had the contract right to opt for cash rather than property, a preference by the taxpayer for like-kind property rather than cash has guaranteed nonrecognition despite the possibility of a cash transaction.[11]

In this case, the taxpayer claims he intended from the very outset of the transaction to get nothing but like-kind property, and no evidence to the contrary appears on the record. Moreover, the taxpayer never handled any cash in the course of the transactions. Hence, the *Alderson* line of cases would seem to control.

The government contends, however, that *Alderson* and other precedents of its type are distinguishable. It points out that in those cases, there may have been a possibility of a receipt of cash at the time of the exchange agreement, but there was no possibility of receiving cash at the time the taxpayer transferred the property pursuant to the agreement. This difference in timing, says the commissioner, renders the *Alderson* line of cases inapplicable.

At least one appellate decision indicates, however, that title may not have to be exchanged simultaneously in order for section 1031 to apply. In *Redwing Carriers, Inc. v. Tomlinson*, 399 F.2d 652 (5th Cir. 1968), the government argued successfully that mutual transfers of trucks that occurred "at or about" the same time were in fact an "exchange" under section 1031. In *Redwing Carriers*, the taxpayer was attempting to deduct a loss in the purchase of new trucks to replace old trucks; the government disallowed recognition of the loss on the ground that section 1031(c) applied. To keep its replacement transactions outside the scope of the section, a parent corporation transferred its old trucks to a subsidiary, bought new trucks for cash, and had the subsidiary sell the old trucks to the manufacturer for cash. The court viewed the transactions as a whole, and disallowed the loss under section 1031. Some lack of simultaneity was apparently "tolerated" by the commissioner and the court. As the court explained, the transfers to the subsidiary by the parent and to the parent by the manufacturer took place "at or about" the same time. . . . Nonetheless, the government urges this court to distinguish *Redwing Carriers*, and *Alderson* and its kin, on the ground that the transfers of title in T.J. Starker's case were separated by a "substantial" period of time. We decline to draw this line.

The government also argues that the contract right to receive property or cash was not "like" title to property, because it was like cash. It asks us to impose a "cash equivalency" test to determine whether section 1031 applies. One flaw to this argument is that title to land is no more or less equivalent to cash than a contract

[11] Of course, a mere intent to avoid taxation of the transaction is not sufficient. For example, in *Smith v. Commissioner*, 537 F.2d 972 (8th Cir. 1976), the taxpayer bought a parcel of Custer County land. Shortly thereafter, he decided to sever a cotenancy on other land with his brother. He conveyed the Custer County land to his brother for cash, and then his brother transferred the Custer County land back to him in exchange for the taxpayer's share of the cotenancy. The net result of the three transfers was that the taxpayer gave up his share of the cotenancy, and got the Custer County property.... The formal transfers of cash to and from the taxpayer's hands defeated the attempt to fit the exchanges within section 1031.

right to buy land. The central concept of section 1031 is that an exchange of business or investment assets does not trigger recognition of gain or loss, because the taxpayer in entering into such a transaction does not "cash in" or "close out" his or her investment. To impose a tax on the event of a deed transfer upon a signing of an exchange agreement could bring about the very result section 1031 was designed to prevent: "the inequity * * * of forcing a taxpayer to recognize a paper gain which was still tied up in a continuing investment of the same sort." *Jordan Marsh Co. v. Commissioner*, 269 F.2d 453, 456 (2nd Cir. 1959).

Against this background, the government offers the explanation that a contract right to land is a "chose in action", and thus personal property instead of real property. This is true, but the short answer to this statement is that title to real property, like a contract right to purchase real property, is nothing more than a bundle of potential causes of action: for trespass, to quiet title, for interference with quiet enjoyment, and so on. The bundle of rights associated with ownership are obviously not excluded from section 1031; a contractual right to assume the rights of ownership should not, we believe, be treated as any different than the ownership rights themselves. Even if the contract right includes the possibility of the taxpayer receiving something other than ownership of like-kind property, we hold that it is still of a like kind with ownership for tax purposes when . . . only like-kind property is ultimately received.

The metaphysical discussion in the briefs and authorities about whether the "steps" of the transactions should be "collapsed", and the truism that "substance" should prevail over "form", are not helpful to the resolution of this case. At best, these words describe results, not reasons. A proper decision can be reached only by considering the purposes of the statute and analyzing its application to particular facts under existing precedent. Here, the statute's purposes are somewhat cloudy, and the precedents are not easy to reconcile. But the weight of authority leans in T. J. Starker's favor, and we conclude that the district court was right in *Starker I*, and wrong in *Starker II*. Thus, on the merits, the transfer of the timberland to Crown triggered a like-kind exchange with respect to the Booth property.

IV. SIX PER CENT "GROWTH FACTOR"

The next issue presented is whether the 6 per cent "growth factor" received by T. J. Starker was properly treated as capital gain or as ordinary income. The government successfully argued below that this amount should be treated as ordinary income because it was disguised interest. The taxpayer, on the other hand, contends that the 6 per cent "growth" provision merely compensated him for timber growth on the Columbia County property he conveyed to Crown.

The taxpayer's argument is not without some biological merit, but he was entitled to the 6 per cent regardless of the actual fate of the timber on the property. He retained no ownership rights in the timber, and bore no risk of loss, after he conveyed title to Crown. We agree with the government that the taxpayer is essentially arguing "that he conveyed $1,502,500 to a stranger for an indefinite period of time [up to five years] without any interest." The 6 per cent "growth factor" was "compensation for the use or forbearance of money", that is, for the use of the unpaid amounts owed to Starker by Crown. Therefore, it was disguised interest. . . .

V. TIMING OF INCLUSION

Our final task, having characterized the proper nature of T. J. Starker's receipts, is to decide in which years they are includable in income. The Timian and Bi-Mart properties do not qualify for nonrecognition treatment, while the other 10 properties received do qualify. In this situation, we believe the proper result is to treat T. J. Starker's rights in his contract with Crown, insofar as they resulted in the receipt of the Timian and Bi-Mart properties, as "boot", received in 1967 when the contract was made. We hold that section 1031(b) requires T. J. Starker to recognize his gain on the transaction with Crown in 1967, to the extent of the fair market values of the Timian and Bi-Mart properties as of the dates on which title to those properties passed to his appointee.

We realize that this decision leaves the treatment of an alleged exchange open until the eventual receipt of consideration by the taxpayer. Some administrative difficulties may surface as a result. Our role, however, is not necessarily to facilitate administration. It is to divine the meaning of the statute in a manner as consistent as possible with the intent of Congress and the prior holdings of the courts. If our holding today adds a degree of uncertainty to this area, Congress can clarify its meaning.

As to the disguised interest, the district court erred in holding T. J. Starker liable for ordinary income in 1967. As a taxpayer reporting on the cash method, T. J. Starker was not liable for taxes on interest income until that interest was received. Although receipt may be actual or constructive, Crown's liability for the "growth factor" did not commence until after 1967 had expired. Had suitable properties been found for T. J. Starker in 1967 (as was the case with Bruce and Elizabeth), Crown would have owed T. J. Starker no "growth factor" at all. Therefore, the government should not have assessed an ordinary income tax on the "growth factor" in 1967. The proper years of inclusion would have been those in which the taxpayer received the interest. To the extent T. J. Starker paid the ordinary tax for 1967, he was entitled to his refund.

* * *

NOTES AND COMMENTS

The Timian and Bi-Mart properties raise issues not directly related to the court's discussion of the qualification of a deferred exchange as a like-kind exchange under § 1031. Those issues are considered in § 1.07 *Held*. Similarly, the court's discussion of estoppel is included because it is an essential part of the description of the transaction, it is not relevant to qualification of the transaction as a deferred exchange.

Congress reacted to what it perceived as the excessive flexibility for deferred (*Starker*) exchanges by amending § 1031 to add § 1031(a)(3), which implicitly codifies *Starker*, while placing significant limits on the time for identifying and acquiring the replacement property, essentially allowing a month and a half after the transfer of the relinquished property to identify the replacement property, and six months to acquire the replacement property. The latter requirement is particularly limiting when improvements are to be added to the replacement property, or when there are title, zoning, or other problems that need to be resolved before the closing on the replacement property. Because the period to satisfy the identification and receipt requirements begins on the date that the relinquished property is transferred, the actual time to locate the replacement property and resolve any problems is longer, depending on the amount of time between the date the purchase and sale agreement for the relinquished property is executed and the actual transfer of the relinquished property.

Recognition of deferred exchanges can lead to complex transactions qualifying as like-kind exchanges under § 1031. Thus, in Priv. Ltr. Rul. 94-13-006 a transaction qualified as a deferred exchange even though it involved a partnership that (i) contracted to sell rental real property to a purchaser; (ii) assigned the sale contract to a title company to become part of a § 1031 exchange agreement, under terms that provided for the partnership to convey the rental building directly to the purchaser with the purchase price to be paid to the title company, but did not allow the partnership to receive the proceeds before a specified date; but did allow the partnership to receive the proceeds if the exchange was not completed by the specified date; (iii) executed purchase agreement to acquire an industrial park property subject to the condition that the city owning the industrial park construct a building to the partnership's specification before the closing; (iv) assigned the purchase contract to the title company prior to the end of the identification period; so that when the building was finished, the title company paid the remaining sale proceeds to the city and the city conveyed the property to the partnership, which then leased it to another party on a long-term basis.

The Regulations provide a detailed roadmap for deferred exchanges. Treas. Reg. § 1.1031(k)-1. The exchange will not be respected if the relinquishing party has interim actual or constructive receipt of nonqualifying property, even if like-kind replacement property is ultimately received. Treas. Reg. § 1.1031(k)-1(f). Fortunately, the regulations provide a number of safe harbors through which actual or constructive receipt can be avoided through the use of qualified intermediaries, qualified escrows, or qualified trusts. Treas. Reg. § 1.1031(k)-1(g). These provisions must be followed assiduously because the Service applies them strictly. *See* Tech. Adv. Mem. 2001-30-001 (exchange did not qualify when the relinquishing party transferred the relinquished property to the purchasers directly without providing notice as required in the regulations, and when the agreement with the intermediary did not strictly comply with the requirements limiting the taxpayer's access to the funds until the end of the exchange period). A qualified escrow or trust must limit the relinquishing party's access to the funds until either the identification period has passed without proper identification or, after identification, the receipt period has expired through no fault of the relinquishing party. Treas. Reg. § 1.1031(k)-1(g)(3) and (6). A qualified intermediary must operate under an agreement that restricts the taxpayer's access to the funds as provided, and who is not the relinquishing party's accountant, attorney, investment banker or real estate broker, but who can be a title insurer or financial institution that provides routine services to the relinquishing party and is not related, under expanded versions of §§ 267(b) and 707(b). Treas. Reg. § 1.1031(k)-1(g)(4) and (k).

The regulations provide detailed guidance concerning the identification and receipt of the qualified replacement property within the required periods. Treas. Reg. § 1.1031(k)-1(b) to (e). The identification must be written, but can include alternate properties, provided there are not more than three alternate properties or any number of alternate properties with an aggregate value not in excess of twice the value of the relinquished property, with the actual selection to be made after the identification but, of course, prior to the required date for the receipt. Treas. Reg. § 1.1031(k)-1(c). There can be no material changes in the identified property prior to receipt. Treas. Reg. § 1.1031(k)-1(d). There are special rules when the replacement property is to be improved or modified prior to receipt, with any construction not completed or any property not produced by the time of receipt of the replacement property treated as boot, regardless of the reason for the noncompletion. Treas. Reg. § 1.1031(k)-1(e).

Because a deferred exchange almost inevitably means that that the qualified intermediary will receive the proceeds of the sale of the relinquished property before they are needed to pay the purchase price of the replacement property, there will be interim earnings on those funds. Consistent with *Starker*, the regulations treat interest or growth factors as ordinary income, in accordance with the taxpayer's method of accounting, and not as part of the § 1031 exchange. Treas. Reg. § 1.1031(k)-1(g)(5) and (h). The regulations under § 468B, not those under § 1031, provide for the treatment of the interim income of funds held by the qualified intermediary. Treas. Reg. § 1.103(k)-1(h)(2). Section 468B(g)(1) and Treas. Reg. § 1.468B-6 provide a general rule that the qualified intermediary or exchange facilitator is taxed currently on any interim income of the escrow funds, which are treated as loaned by the relinquishing party to the qualified intermediary. § 1.568B-6(c)(1) and (e) Ex. 8. The general rule is virtually swallowed up by an exception that taxes the relinquishing party when all of the earnings are paid to the relinquishing party under the agreement. Treas. Reg. § 1.468B-6(c)(2). Any funds used by the qualified intermediary to pay transactional expenses (including a fee of the qualified intermediary are treated as paid to the relinquishing party and, in effect, paid on the relinquishing party's behalf for the transactional costs or the fee. Treas. Reg. § 1.468B-6(c)(2) and (e) Exs. 2 and 3.

When a deferred exchange involves transferring the relinquished property in one year with a the replacement property to be received in the next year, any gain from boot is taxed in the later year when the replacement property and boot are received, or even if no qualified replacement property is received but there was a bona fide intent to have a nonrecognition exchange. Treas. Reg. § 1.1031(k)-1(j); *see Smalley v. Commissioner*, 116 T.C. 450 (2001) (installment sale provisions prevent taxation in year relinquished property transferred, even if no qualifying exchange in the later year). On the other hand, Rev. Rul. 2003-56, 2003-1 C.B. 985, in effect splits the difference when, in a deferred exchange, the liabilities relinquished and the liabilities received do not match, and the replacement property is not received until the tax year after the year in which the relinquished property is surrendered. Any net decrease in liability is taken into account at the end of the year the relinquished property was transferred, but any net increase is not taken into account until the replacement property and extra liability are received. The rationale is that the net decrease is attributable to the liability transferred on the relinquished property, but the liability increase is attributable to the transfer of the replacement property.

Deferred exchanges risk further complications because there may be changes in important circumstances between the time the relinquished property is transferred and the replacement property is received. For example, apparently, death of the relinquishing party before the completion of the exchange does not prevent completion by the successor. *See* Priv. Ltr. Rul. 98-29-025, holding that, when husband living in a community property state died after entering into a deferred exchange agreement through a bank as intermediary for two properties when only one replacement property had been identified and replacement property for the second property was then identified and the exchanges completed, the exchanges qualified under § 1031, the rights were not income in respect of a decedent under § 691 and the replacement property qualified for a basis step-up at death.

Multiparty deferred exchanges have moved from those involving single or a few properties to ongoing programs involving multiple properties over an extended period. Rev. Proc. 2003-39, 2003-1 C.B. 971 provides safe-harbors for multi-year like-kind exchange programs ("LKE"), that is, programs providing for ongoing exchanges involving 100 or more exchanges of tangible personal property using a single intermediary. To qualify, the taxpayer is required to have a master exchange agreement with the intermediary that limits the taxpayer's access to funds held by the intermediary, which may be in a joint account effectively controlled by the intermediary, and to follow the appropriate identification procedures in the appropriate periods and notify the other party of any sales or purchases of the assignment to the intermediary. Each identified match is treated is a separate exchange. The taxpayer can net funds owed by it against funds owed to it provided the intermediary has the total sales proceeds are transferred to the intermediary by the next business day. The taxpayer is also permitted to make arm's length loans to the buyer. *See* Priv. Ltr. Rul. 2002-36-026 (similar result; possibly basis for Rev. Proc. 2003-39).

PROBLEM FOR DISCUSSION

Problem 5-6. Reel owned Blackacre, purchased 15 years ago on the correct belief that eventually it would be worth a bundle for development, with a basis of $100,000 and a value of $1,000,000 subject to a nonrecourse mortgage of $600,000. Perch wanted to acquire the property for the purposes of subdividing it, but Reel was unwilling to recognize gain at the time. Accordingly, they agreed that Perch would locate suitable property for an exchange with a net value of $400,000 plus interest at the applicable federal rate (which was 10 percent annually) until the exchange was completed. Because Perch was anxious to begin subdividing, title to Blackacre was transferred on December 10, 20X1. The contract specified that Perch would cooperate in arranging a § 1031 exchange for Reel. The contract identified Greenacre, owned by Repp, as one of the properties to be received by Reel. Accordingly, on that date, Perch paid $400,000 to Broak, the real estate broker who brought Blackacre to his attention, under an escrow agreement also signed by Reel, which provided for $250,000 to be used to purchase Greenacre. Greenacre was worth $1,000,000, had a basis of $100,000, was subject to a mortgage of $250,000, and had been held by Repp for 10 years on the correct belief that someday it would be worth a lot of money. On March 10, 20X2, Perch arranged, through Broak, for Repp to transfer Greenacre to Reel in exchange for a transfer by Perch to Repp of Redacre, which Perch had owned for some time with an intention of subdividing it, and which he was planning to develop next when he made the deal for Blackacre, which he considered better. Redacre had a value of $450,000 and a basis of $100,000 was subject to a mortgage of $200,000. To reduce the net value of Greenacre to the $250,000 specified in the exchange agreement with Reel and the $250,000 net value of Redacre, the transfer of Greenacre was made subject to a newly-created, 20-year purchase money mortgage on which Perch was personally liable of $500,000 with interest at the AFR. Reel gave Perch an identical purchase money mortgage for $500,000 and Perch told Reel to save paperwork by making payments directly to Repp. Under the terms of the escrow agreement, Broak returned $250,000 of the amount paid by Perch to her.

The contract also identified Whiteacre as one of three other specified properties as suitable provided any of them could be acquired for no more than stipulated prices, which, in the case of Whiteacre, was $225,000. The aggregate gross fair market value of the identified properties (not including Greenacre) was $1,000,000, and their net fair market value after deducting mortgages was $400,000. On June 5, 20X2, Broak purchased Whiteacre at a price of $210,000 and transferred it to Reel. Because only $150,000 of the $400,000 originally deposited by Perch was left, Reel paid Broak $45,000 as his contribution and Perch paid the remaining $15,000 to bring the purchase price up to the $210,000 value of Whiteacre. Interest of $10,000 was earned on the escrow funds while Broak held them, which was retained by Broak as her fee for acting as intermediary.

These transactions may be summarized as follows:

			Gives			Receives	
	Basis	FMV	Mort.	Net	FMV	Mort.	Net (in thousands)
Reel							
12-10-20X1 Blackacre	100	1,000	600	400			
3-10-20X2 Greenacre				1,000	250		750
New Mortgage				500			
Cash				45			
6-5-20X2 Whiteacre					210	-0-	210
Totals				945			960
Perch							
12-10-20X1 Blackacre					1,000	600	400

			Gives			Receives	
	Basis	**FMV**	**Mort.**	**Net**	**FMV**	**Mort.**	**Net (in thousands)**
3-10-20X2 Redacre	100	450	200	250			
New Mortgage				500			500
Cash							45
6- 5-20X2 Whiteacre		210	-0-	210			
Totals				960			945
Repp							
3-10-X2 Greenacre	100	1,000	250	750			
New Mortgage							500
Redacre					450	200	250
Totals				750			750

What are the tax consequences of these transactions to each of Reel, Perch, Repp, and Broak, including any gain (or loss) recognized, the timing and character of any such recognition and the basis and holding period of any property owned when the dust clears? *See* Treas. Reg. §§ 1.1031(k)-1 and 1.1031(b) 1, (c)-1, and (d)-1 and 2; Prop. Treas. Reg. § 1.468B-6; *Starker* (deferred exchanges); *Smalley* (installment sale provisions prevent taxation in year relinquished property transferred, even if no qualifying exchange) *Garcia* (net even liability incurred to be netted); Rev. Rul. 79-44 (don't offset boot by liability increase); Tech. Adv. Mem. 80-03-004 (liability on replacement property immediately repaid and refinanced still netted).

§ 1.05. Reverse *Starker* Exchanges

The identification and receipt requirements applicable to deferred exchanges under § 1031(a)(3) assume that the taxpayer will transfer the relinquished property prior to receipt of the replacement property. However, a taxpayer could acquire the replacement property prior to transferring the relinquished property and, assuming that a multi-party transaction is properly arranged, an exchange between the taxpayer and a facilitator could be effectuated. Such exchanges are commonly referred to as "reverse *Starker* exchanges." Although some practitioners interpreted the requirements of § 1031(a)(3) as meaning that reverse *Starker* exchanges were implicitly prohibited, most disagreed. The Service confirmed the validity of reverse *Starker* exchanges in the following Rev. Proc., which places time limitations analogous to those of § 1031(a)(3) on them.

A significant difficulty encountered with reverse *Starker* exchanges is that the replacement property must be "parked" with a facilitator, because no exchange is possible, if the relinquishing taxpayer takes title before the relinquished property is transferred. For example, the taxpayer could decide which is to be exchanged for the replacement property even though no purchaser for that property has been located, exchange that property with the facilitator, and leave the relinquished property in the hands of the facilitator until a purchaser is found for the relinquished property. Alternatively, the taxpayer can have the facilitator acquire, and hold, the replacement property until a buyer is found for one of the properties held by the purchase. In either situation, the taxpayer must provide or obtain financing to allow the facilitator to acquire the replacement property. In addition, if the relinquished property is parked with the facilitator pending its sale, the taxpayer will want to retain possession of the relinquished property during this time, necessitating a leasing arrangement between the facilitator as lessor and the taxpayer as lessee. Alternatively, if the replacement property is parked with the facilitator pending the identification of the relinquished property and its transfer to a buyer, the taxpayer will want to enter into a lease of the replacement property in order to obtain immediate possession of the replacement property. The complicated nature of a reverse exchange made some practitioners wary of reverse *Starker* exchanges. In addition, some facilitators were unwilling to become title holders of either the relinquished or replacement properties despite indemnification agreements from the taxpayer. Rev. Proc. 2000-37 addresses many of these issues, including the types and extent of the relationship between the taxpayer and the facilitator that will be accepted by the Service while recognizing the facilitator as the owner of the property while it is parked with the facilitator.

Rev. Proc. 2000-37, 2000-2 C.B. 308, *as modified by* Rev. Proc. 2004-51, 2004-2 C.B. 294

This procedure provides a safe harbor under which the Service will not challenge (a) the qualification of property as either "replacement property" or "relinquished property" for purposes of section 1031 of the Code or (b) the treatment of the "exchange accommodation titleholder" as the beneficial owner of such property for federal income tax purposes, if the property is held in a "qualified exchange accommodation arrangement" (QEAA).

SECTION 1. PURPOSE

This revenue procedure provides a safe harbor under which the Internal Revenue Service will treat an exchange accommodation titleholder as the beneficial owner of property for federal income tax purposes if the property is held in a "qualified exchange accommodation arrangement" (QEAA), as defined in section 4.02 of this revenue procedure.

SECTION 2. BACKGROUND

.01 Section 1031(a)(1) provides that no gain or loss is recognized on the exchange of property held for productive use in a trade or business or for investment if the property is exchanged solely for property of like kind that is to be held either for productive use in a trade or business or for investment.

.02 Section 1031(a)(3) provides that property received by the taxpayer is not treated as like-kind property if it: (a) is not identified as property to be received in the exchange on or before the day that is 45 days after the date on which the taxpayer transfers the relinquished property; or (b) is received after the earlier of the date that is 180 days after the date on which the taxpayer transfers the relinquished property, or the due date (determined with regard to extension) for the transferor's federal income tax return for the year in which the transfer of the relinquished property occurs.

.03 Determining the owner of property for federal income tax purposes requires an analysis of all of the facts and circumstances. As a general rule, the party that bears the economic burdens and benefits of ownership will be considered the owner of property for federal income tax purposes. See Rev. Rul. 82-144, 1982-2 C.B. 34.

.04 On April 25, 1991, the Treasury Department and the Service promulgated final regulations under § 1.1031(k)-1 providing rules for deferred like-kind exchanges under § 1031(a)(3). The preamble to the final regulations states that the deferred exchange rules under § 1031(a)(3) do not apply to reverse-*Starker* exchanges (*i.e.*, exchanges where the replacement property is acquired before the relinquished property is transferred) and consequently that the final regulations do not apply to such exchanges. T.D. 8346, 1991-1 C.B. 150, 151; see *Starker* . . . . However, the preamble indicates that Treasury and the Service will continue to study the applicability of the general rule of § 1031(a)(1) to these transactions. T.D. 8346, 1991-1 C.B. 150, 151.

.05 Since the promulgation of the final regulations under § 1.1031(k)-1, taxpayers have engaged in a wide variety of transactions, including so-called "parking" transactions, to facilitate reverse like-kind exchanges. Parking transactions typically are designed to "park" the desired replacement property with an accommodation party until such time as the taxpayer arranges for the transfer of the relinquished property to the ultimate transferee in a simultaneous or deferred exchange. Once such a transfer is arranged, the taxpayer transfers the relinquished property to the accommodation party in exchange for the replacement property, and the accommodation party then transfers the relinquished property to the ultimate transferee. In other situations, an accommodation party may acquire the desired replacement property on behalf of the taxpayer and immediately exchange such property with the taxpayer for the relinquished property, thereafter holding the relinquished property until the taxpayer arranges for a transfer of such property to the ultimate transferee. In the parking arrangements, taxpayers attempt to arrange the transaction so that the accommodation party has enough of the benefits and burdens relating to the property so that the accommodation party will be treated as the owner for federal income tax purposes.

.06 Treasury and the Service have determined that it is in the best interest of sound tax administration to provide taxpayers with a workable means of qualifying their transactions under § 1031 in situations where the taxpayer has a genuine intent to accomplish a like-kind exchange at the time that it arranges for the acquisition of the replacement property and actually accomplishes the exchange within a short time thereafter. Accordingly, this revenue procedure provides a safe harbor that allows a taxpayer to treat the accommodation party as the owner of the property for federal income tax purposes, thereby enabling the taxpayer to accomplish a qualifying like-kind exchange.

SECTION 3. SCOPE

.01 *Exclusivity.* This revenue procedure provides a safe harbor for the qualification under § 1031 of certain arrangements between taxpayers and exchange accommodation titleholders and provides for the treatment of the exchange accommodation titleholder as the beneficial owner of the property for federal income tax purposes. These provisions apply only in the limited context described in this revenue procedure. The principles set forth in this revenue procedure have no application to any federal income tax determinations other than determinations that involve arrangements qualifying for the safe harbor.

.02 *No inference.* No inference is intended with respect to the federal income tax treatment of arrangements similar to those described in this revenue procedure that were entered into prior to the effective date of this revenue procedure. Further, the Service recognizes that "parking" transactions can be accomplished outside of the safe harbor provided in this revenue procedure. Accordingly, no inference is intended with respect to the federal income tax treatment of "parking" transactions that do not satisfy the terms of the safe harbor provided in this revenue procedure, whether entered into prior to or after the effective date of this revenue procedure.

.03 *Other issues.* Services for the taxpayer in connection with a person's role as the exchange accommodation titleholder in a QEAA shall not be taken into account in determining whether that person or a related person is a disqualified person (as defined in § 1.1031(k)-1(k)). Even though property will not fail to be treated as being held in a QEAA as a result of one or more arrangements described in section 4.03 of this revenue procedure, the Service still may recast an amount paid pursuant to such an arrangement as a fee paid to the exchange accommodation titleholder for acting as an exchange accommodation titleholder to the extent necessary to reflect the true economic substance of the arrangement. Other federal income tax issues implicated, but not addressed, in this revenue procedure include the treatment, for federal income tax purposes, of payments described in section 4.03(7) and whether an exchange accommodation titleholder may be precluded from claiming depreciation deductions (e.g., as a dealer) with respect to the relinquished property or the replacement property.

.04 *Effect of Noncompliance.* If the requirements of this revenue procedure are not satisfied (for example, the property subject to a QEAA is not transferred within the time period provided), then this revenue procedure does not apply. Accordingly, the determination of whether the taxpayer or the exchange accommodation titleholder is the owner of the property for federal income tax purposes, and the proper treatment of any transactions entered into by or between the parties, will be made without regard to the provisions of this revenue procedure.

SECTION 4. QUALIFIED EXCHANGE ACCOMMODATION ARRANGEMENTS

.01 *In general.* The Service will treat an exchange accommodation titleholder as the beneficial owner of property for federal income tax purposes if the property is held in a QEAA. Property held in a QEAA may, therefore, qualify as either "replacement property" or "relinquished property" (as defined in § 1.1031(k)-1(a)) in a tax-deferred like-kind exchange if the exchange otherwise meets the requirements for deferral of gain or loss under § 1031 and the regulations thereunder.

.02 *Qualified Exchange Accommodation Arrangements.* For purposes of this revenue procedure, property is held in a QEAA if all of the following requirements are met:

(1) Qualified indicia of ownership of the property is held by a person (the "exchange accommodation titleholder") who is not the taxpayer or a disqualified person and either such person is subject to federal income tax or, if such person is treated as a partnership or S corporation for federal income tax purposes, more than 90 percent of its interests or stock are owned by partners or shareholders who are subject to federal income tax. Such qualified indicia of ownership must be held by the exchange accommodation titleholder at all times from the date of acquisition by the exchange accommodation titleholder until the property is transferred as described in section 4.02(5) of this revenue procedure. For this purpose, "qualified indicia of ownership" means legal title to the property, other indicia of ownership of the property that are treated as beneficial ownership of the property under applicable principles of commercial law (e.g., a contract for deed), or interests in an entity that is disregarded as an entity separate from its owner for federal income tax purposes (e.g., a single member limited liability company) and that holds either legal title to the property or such other indicia of ownership;

(2) At the time the qualified indicia of ownership of the property is transferred to the exchange accommodation titleholder, it is the taxpayer's bona fide intent that the property held by the exchange accommodation titleholder represent either replacement property or relinquished property in an exchange that is intended to qualify for nonrecognition of gain (in whole or in part) or loss under § 1031;

(3) No later than five business days after the transfer of qualified indicia of ownership of the property to the exchange accommodation titleholder, the taxpayer and the exchange accommodation titleholder enter into a written agreement (the "qualified exchange accommodation agreement") that provides that the exchange accommodation titleholder is holding the property for the benefit of the taxpayer in order to facilitate an exchange under § 1031 and this revenue procedure and that the taxpayer and the exchange accommodation titleholder agree to report the acquisition, holding, and disposition of the property as provided in this revenue procedure. The agreement must specify that the exchange accommodation titleholder will be treated as the beneficial owner of the property for all federal income tax purposes. Both parties must report the federal income tax attributes of the property on their federal income tax returns in a manner consistent with this agreement;

(4) No later than 45 days after the transfer of qualified indicia of ownership of the replacement property to the exchange accommodation titleholder, the relinquished property is properly identified. Identification must be made in a manner consistent with the principles described in § 1.1031(k)-1(c). For purposes of this section, the taxpayer may properly identify alternative and multiple properties, as described in § 1.1031(k)-1(c)(4);

(5) No later than 180 days after the transfer of qualified indicia of ownership of

the property to the exchange accommodation titleholder, (a) the property is transferred (either directly or indirectly through a qualified intermediary (as defined in § 1.1031(k)-1(g)(4)) to the taxpayer as replacement property; or (b) the property is transferred to a person who is not the taxpayer or a disqualified person as relinquished property; and

(6) The combined time period that the relinquished property and the replacement property are held in a QEAA does not exceed 180 days.

.03 *Permissible Agreements.* Property will not fail to be treated as being held in a QEAA as a result of any one or more of the following legal or contractual arrangements, regardless of whether such arrangements contain terms that typically would result from arm's length bargaining between unrelated parties with respect to such arrangements:

(1) An exchange accommodation titleholder that satisfies the requirements of the qualified intermediary safe harbor set forth in § 1.1031(k)-1(g)(4) may enter into an exchange agreement with the taxpayer to serve as the qualified intermediary in a simultaneous or deferred exchange of the property under § 1031;

(2) The taxpayer or a disqualified person guarantees some or all of the obligations of the exchange accommodation titleholder, including secured or unsecured debt incurred to acquire the property, or indemnifies the exchange accommodation titleholder against costs and expenses;

(3) The taxpayer or a disqualified person loans or advances funds to the exchange accommodation titleholder or guarantees a loan or advance to the exchange accommodation titleholder;

(4) The property is leased by the exchange accommodation titleholder to the taxpayer or a disqualified person;

(5) The taxpayer or a disqualified person manages the property, supervises improvement of the property, acts as a contractor, or otherwise provides services to the exchange accommodation titleholder with respect to the property;

(6) The taxpayer and the exchange accommodation titleholder enter into agreements or arrangements relating to the purchase or sale of the property, including puts and calls at fixed or formula prices, effective for a period not in excess of 185 days from the date the property is acquired by the exchange accommodation titleholder; and

(7) The taxpayer and the exchange accommodation titleholder enter into agreements or arrangements providing that any variation in the value of a relinquished property from the estimated value on the date of the exchange accommodation titleholder's receipt of the property be taken into account upon the exchange accommodation titleholder's disposition of the relinquished property through the taxpayer's advance of funds to, or receipt of funds from, the exchange accommodation titleholder.

.04 *Permissible Treatment.* Property will not fail to be treated as being held in a QEAA merely because the accounting, regulatory, or state, local, or foreign tax treatment of the arrangement between the taxpayer and the exchange accommodation titleholder is different from the treatment required by section 4.02(3) of this revenue procedure.

.05 *Limitation.* This revenue procedure does not apply to replacement property held in a QEAA if the property is owned by the taxpayer within the 180-day period ending on the date of transfer of qualified indicia of ownership of the property to an exchange accommodation titleholder.

* * *

NOTES AND COMMENTS

Rev. Proc. 2000-37 provides a safe harbor for transactions that satisfy its requirements, but, as § 3.02 acknowledges, similar transactions that do not satisfy the safe harbor and other "parking" transactions may still qualify as § 1031 exchanges. On the other hand, taxpayers and their tax advisors who are forced to engage in an exchange that does not satisfy the safe harbor requirements should expect a challenge on audit, because many examining agents tend to view any transaction that is outside the safe harbor as being automatically subject to challenge. In Tech. Adv. Mem. 2000-39-005, issued and released shortly before Rev. Proc. 2000-37, but probably influenced by it, a transaction in which a taxpayer assigned a contract for sale of the relinquished property to an accommodator who would sell the relinquished property, and use the proceeds to acquire the replacement property, did not qualify as a § 1031 exchange when the sale of the relinquished property fell through, but the seller of the replacement property insisted on closing; although the replacement property was titled to the accommodator, because only the taxpayer was liable on the replacement property until a sale contract for the relinquished property was executed and assigned to the accommodator, the sale closed, and the replacement property was transferred to the taxpayer; because the Service determined that the accommodator was the taxpayer's agent — not a qualified intermediary. On the other hand, the Service has issued at least one private letter ruling finding a transaction that did not satisfy the safe harbor of Rev. Proc. 2000-37 nevertheless qualified as a § 1031 exchange. In Priv. Ltr. Rul. 2001-11-025, which was issued shortly after Rev. Proc. 2000-37, a transaction in which the relinquishing party granted a conservation organization an option to purchase the relinquished property under terms that required cooperation in a § 1031 exchange. Before the option was exercised — indeed the ruling was granted before the option was exercised — the relinquishing party arranged for an exchange accommodation titleholder (EAT) to acquire the replacement property. Although it is somewhat difficult to tell, the terms of the arrangement with the EAT seem to satisfy those for permissible agreements under § 4.03 of Rev. Proc. 2000-37. The terms seem to transfer to the relinquishing party most, but not all, risks and benefits of the property. If and when the conservation organization exercises the option, the option agreement is to be transferred to a qualified intermediary who will sell the property and receive the proceeds. Within the 45-day period, the relinquishing party will designate the replacement property held by the EAT and the § 1031 exchange will be completed. The ruling acknowledges that Rev. Proc. 2000-37 is not satisfied both because the deal was entered into before the effective date of the Rev. Proc. and because the acquisition of the replacement property does not satisfy the 180-day requirement. No other terms of the deal are stated to, or apparently do, fail to satisfy the other provision of Rev. Proc. 2000-37. In Priv. Ltr. Rul. 2007-18-028, the Service held that a transaction qualified under Rev. Proc. 2007-37 when a taxpayer who owned improved land (Parcel 1), assigned its rights to purchase similar land (Parcel 2) to an exchange accommodation titleholder (EAT) that acquired Parcel 2; taxpayer then agreed to sell Parcel 1, and entered into an exchange agreement with a qualified intermediary (QI) to which the rights to sell Parcel 1 were assigned; Parcel 1 was duly sold within 45 days of the transfer of Parcel 2 to the EAT, on the same date taxpayer identified to the EAT Parcel 1 as the relinquished property; the proceeds of the sale of Parcel 1 were transferred by the QI to the EAT and used to pay the purchase price of Parcel 2 within 180 days of the initial transfer of the right to purchase Parcel 2 to the EAT.

Other authority for reverse deferred exchanges that do not satisfy the Rev. Proc. 2000-37 safe-harbor is sparse; but there were some favorable determinations before the safe-harbor was issued. Thus, in *Rutherford v. Commissioner*, T.C. Mem. 1978-505, which was cited favorably in Priv. Ltr. Rul. 2001-11-025, a transaction in which farmer-cattle raiser received 12 half-blood heifers in exchange for agreeing to artificially inseminate them by a registered bull and deliver the first 12 three-quarter blood heifers to exchanging party qualified as a § 1031 exchange even though the half-blood heifers were received before the three quarter blood heifers were delivered. The court determined that the depreciable basis of the 12 heifers received was zero until the three-quarter blood heifers were delivered because it was determined by the basis of the three-quarter blood heifers when delivered. Similarly, in Priv. Ltr. Rul. 98-23-045, Priv. Ltr. Rul. 98-14 modifying -019, an arrangement to induce a public utility's relocation of transmission lines to facilitate a development project qualified as a § 1031 exchange, even though the utility was granted the new easements on which to relocate or underground its transmission lines before the old easement was surrendered, which was only after the new lines were constructed and tested, qualified. Such easements had been held to be real property under § 1031 in Rev. Rul. 72-549, 1972-2 C.B. 472. *But see Estate of Bowers v. Commissioner*, 94 T.C. 582 (1990) (proceeds of sale reinvested in a like-kind property do not qualify as § 1031 tax free exchange, when taxpayer agreed to sell oil and gas leases to a purchaser and, before closing of sale, contracted to buy a farm and arranged for purchaser to pay for the farm and assign it to the taxpayer, because taxpayer began operating the farm before the closing of the sale of the oil and gas lease and transfer of legal title to the farm, so that taxpayer had become tax owner of the farm before disposition of oil and gas leases). In *DeCleene v. Commissioner*, 115 T.C. 457 (2000), which was distinguished in Priv. Ltr. Rul. 2001-11-025, and which itself had distinguished Rev. Proc. 2000-37, taxpayer acquired the Lawrence property in 1992. Approximately one year later, in a transaction orchestrated by his accountant, taxpayer transferred the Lawrence property to Western Lime and Cement Co. (WLC) in exchange for a nonrecourse note and, three months later, received back the Lawrence property on which a building had been constructed by WLC, but paid for by the taxpayer, in exchange for the McDonald property and payment on the note. The court held that WLC did not acquire any of the benefits and burdens of ownership of the Lawrence property and, therefore, the Lawrence property was never transferred to WLC. It is difficult to see why the accountant could have advised that the transaction would work. If the Lawrence property was never transferred to WLC, then the only way in which the transaction could qualify for nonrecognition under § 1031 would be if the acquisition of the Lawrence property in 1992 was treated as part of an integrated plan to exchange it for the McDonald property. However, because at the time of the acquisition of the Lawrence property, taxpayer had not taken any steps to evidence an intent to enter into an exchange, such an integrated plan did not exist. As a result, the court did not reach the issue of the circumstances under which a parking transaction that is entered into as part of an integrated plan to accomplish a like-kind exchange qualifies for nonrecognition under § 1031.

PROBLEM FOR DISCUSSION

Problem 5-7. Reel, who was primarily engaged in owning and operating shopping centers, also owned Blackacre, which was improved with a warehouse complex, which he had acquired before he decided to concentrate on shopping centers. Reel believed Blackacre, with a basis of $2,500,000, was worth $4,000,000, but, because it was subject a $2,000,000 mortgage, the net value was $2,000,000. While he was trying to find a buyer, Reel was offered Whiteacre, which was improved with a shopping center that he considered a perfect addition to his holdings. Accordingly, based on legal advice, he decided to do a reverse *Starker* exchange under Rev. Proc. 2000-37. Accordingly, Reel arranged for the transfer of legal title of Whiteacre to an exchange accommodation titleholder ("EAT") satisfying the requirements of Rev. Proc. 2000-37, § 4.02(1), and entered into a qualified exchange accommodation agreement ("QEAA") satisfying the requirements of § 4.02(3). The purchase price of Whiteacre, which was subject to a $1,500,000 mortgage was $4,500,000, payable $500,000 in cash, $1,500,000 by taking it subject to the mortgage and $2,500,000 by a new 25-year mortgage. As permitted by § 4.03(1), Reel entered into an agreement with the EAT to serve as the qualified intermediary ("QI") for the exchange of Blackacre for Whiteacre, as it was qualified to do, and transferred legal title to Blackacre to the EAT/QI. In addition, as permitted by § 4.03(2) and (3), Reel loaned the EAT the $500,000 down payment on Whiteacre (with interest payable at the AFR), and guaranteed the EAT's note and mortgage for new 25-year purchase-money mortgage on Whiteacre. Similarly, as permitted by § 4.03(4) and (5), Reel leased Whiteacre on arm's-length terms, and entered into an agreement to manage Blackacre for a fee that was significantly less that the expected net earnings of Blackacre while held by the EAT. The EAT/QI was entitled to retain the excess of the net earnings of Blackacre over the management fee and the excess of the rental paid by Reel on Whiteacre over the interest on the loan from Reel for the down payment and the amounts paid on the old $1,500,000 mortgage on Whiteacre and on the new $2,500,000 purchase money mortgage. Similarly, as permitted by § 4.03(6), Reel granted the EAT a put for Whiteacre on the same terms as those on which the EAT purchased it. Reel and the EAT/QI also entered into an agreement that granted the EAT/QI a call on Blackacre at the price at which Reel proposed to sell it, subject to an agreement as permitted by § 4.03(7) to adjust for any difference between that value and the price on disposition of Blackacre. The expectation, of course was that the proceeds of Blackacre would be applied to the put price on Whiteacre. Unfortunately, no purchaser for Blackacre was found within 180 days. Accordingly, the EAT exercised its put option for Whiteacre. Reel paid by canceling his loan to the EAT/QI for the down payment, taking subject to the old $1,500,000 mortgage and assuming the $2,500,000, 25-year purchase money mortgage, which resulted in terminating the lease. Three months later Blackacre was finally sold for the $4,000,000 asking price, with $2,500,000 paid in cash. Because the seller of Whiteacre refused to allow any of the $2,500,000 purchase money mortgage to be paid off, $1,500,000 was used to prepay the assumed mortgage, and the $500,000 balance was retained by the EAT/QI to be used to make payments on the purchase-money mortgage under terms included in the original QEAA, which had provided that under no circumstances would Reel receive any cash from the sale of Blackacre, but that all proceeds would be applied to the purchase price of Whiteacre.

These transactions may be summarized as follows:

	Gives				*Receives*		
	Basis	*FMV*	*Mort.*	*Net*	*FMV*	*Mort.*	*Net*
		(in thousands)					
Whiteacre					4,500	1,500	3,000
New Mortgage				2,500			
Loan/Cash				500			
Blackacre	2,500	4,000	2,000	2,000	4,000	2,000	2,000
Totals				5,000			5,000

Blackacre Proceeds Applied	
Assumed Whiteacre Mortgage	1,500
New Whiteacre Mortgage (as due)	500

What are the tax consequences to Reel and the EAT/QI of the exchange of the Warehouse Complex for the Replacement Shopping Center, on the assumption that the failure to satisfy the 180-day period specified in § 4.02(5) and (6), does not prevent qualification under § 1031, including the effect of the EAT/QI's interim ownership of the Replacement Shopping Center and the Warehouse Complex and the receipts and payments under Reel's lease of the Replacement Shopping Center and the interest and mortgage payments on it, and Reel's management agreement for the Warehouse Complex. Does the transaction qualify under § 1031? How do the results change if it does not qualify? *See* Treas. Reg. §§ 1.1031(k)-1 and 1.1031(b) 1, (c)-1, and (d)-1 and 2; Treas. Reg. § 1.468B-6; Rev. Proc. 2000-37; Tech. Adv. Mem. 2000-39-005 (sale of relinquished property through an accommodator did not qualify as a § 1031 exchange when the sale of the relinquished property fell through, purchase of replacement property closed with title to the accommodator, since only the taxpayer was liable on the replacement property until sale of the relinquished property closed, and the replacement property was transferred to the taxpayer; the accommodator was the taxpayer's agent, and not a qualified intermediary); *Rutherford* (farmer-cattle raiser received 12 half-blood heifers in exchange for agreement to artificially inseminate them by a registered bull and deliver the first 12 three-quarter blood heifers to exchanging party was § 1031 exchange when 12 heifers received, but basis zero until full three-quarter blood heifers delivered); *Bowers* (sale, not an exchange, when taxpayer agreed to sell oil and gas leases to a purchaser, and before closing of sale, contracted to buy a farm and arranged for purchaser to pay for the farm and assign it to the taxpayer, because taxpayer began operating the farm before the closing of the sale of the oil and gas lease and because tax, but not legal owner); *Starker* (deferred exchange); *Garcia* (net even liability incurred to be netted); Rev. Rul. 79-44 (don't offset boot by liability increase); Tech. Adv. Mem. 80-03-004 (liability on replacement property immediately repaid and refinanced still netted).

§ 1.06. Like Kind

Treas. Reg. §§ 1.1031(a)-1(b), (c), and (d), 1.1031(a)-2; 1.1031(j)-1

The regulations state that the term "like kind" refers "to the nature or character of property and not to its grade or quality." Treas. Reg. § 1.1031(a)-1(b). The application of the like-kind requirement is extremely generous for real estate exchanges, treating improved and unimproved real estate as like kind, so that the Empire State Building and ex-President Bush's Crawford ranch would be considered like kind. As stated in the regulations, "[t]he fact that any real estate is improved or unimproved is not material, for that fact relates only to its grade or quality of the property and not to its kind or class." In addition, the regulations provide that a leasehold with 30 years or more remaining in the lease term is like kind to a fee. Treas. Reg. § 1.1031(a)-1(c). Real property located in the United States, however, is not like kind to real property located outside the United States. § 1031(h)(1).

The definition of "like kind" for personal property used in a trade or business or otherwise depreciable depends on the class of the property for depreciation purposes. Treas. Reg. § 1.1031(a)-2. The regulations provide a safe harbor under which depreciable tangible personal property is deemed like kind to other depreciable tangible personal property within the same general asset class or product class. Treas. Reg. § 1.1031(a)-2(b)(1). General asset classes are those contained in Rev. Proc. 87-56, 1987-2 C.B. 674. Treas. Reg. § 1.1031(a)-2(b)(2). Product classes are those described in the North American Industry Classification System. Treas. Reg. § 1.1031(a)-2(b)(3). Applying Treas. Reg. § 1.1031-2(b)(2)(a), which provides that property may be of like kind, even if not of like class. In Priv. Ltr. Rul. 2009-12-004, the Service held that cars, light duty trucks and vehicles that share characteristics of both cars and trucks are all like kind for purposes of exchanges by a leasing company. Like the treatment of real property, § 1031 is clear that personal property used predominantly in the United States is not like kind to personal property used predominantly outside the United States. § 1031(h)(2)(A).

The classification of intangible and nondepreciable personal property is much less clear and certain. The regulations state that no like classes are provided for such property. Treas. Reg. § 1.1031(a)-2(c)(1). With respect to intangible property, the regulations impose a two-pronged inquiry. First, the determination depends on "the nature or character of the rights involved (e.g., a patent or a copyright)." Treas. Reg. § 1.1031(a)-2(c)(2). Second, the determination depends on "the nature or character of the underlying property to which the intangible personal property relates." Thus, a copyright of one novel is like kind to a copyright of a different novel but a copyright of a novel is not like kind to a copyright of a song. Treas. Reg. § 1.1031(a)-2(c)(3). The application of the like-kind standard to nondepreciable personal property and to intangible property is illustrated by the following rulings.

Rev. Rul. 82-96, 1982-1 C.B. 113

* * *

An individual taxpayer, who is not a dealer in gold bullion or coins, purchased gold bullion in the cash market and held it as an investment. The taxpayer subsequently exchanged the gold bullion for Canadian Maple Leaf gold coins, which also were held for investment. . . .

The Canadian Maple Leaf gold coin is legal tender in Canada. However, the gold content of each coin greatly exceeds its face amount of $50. The Canadian Maple Leaf gold coin has no numismatic value.

* * *

In Rev. Rul. 74-218, 1974-1 C.B. 202, currency, in its usual and ordinary acceptation, is defined as gold, silver, other metals, or paper used as a circulating medium of exchange.

Rev. Rul. 76-214, 1976-1 C.B. 218, holds that the exchange of Mexican 50-peso bullion-type gold coins for Austrian 100-corona bullion-type gold coins qualifies for nonrecognition of gain under the provisions of section 1031(a) of the Code. The gold coins described in Rev. Rul. 76-214 were restrikes and were not circulating mediums of exchange in their respective countries and, therefore, were not currency, or money as that term is used in section 1031 of the Code.

In Rev. Rul. 76-249, 1976-2 C.B. 21, a taxpayer exchanged real property with a fair market value of $6,000 for United States silver coins with a face value of $2,000 and a fair market value of $6,000. The revenue ruling holds that silver coins received for the real property are to be treated as property and not as money. Therefore, the amount realized by the taxpayer from the exchange was the fair market value of the silver coins ($6,000) rather than the face amount of the coins ($2,000).

Rev. Rul. 79-143, 1979-1 C.B. 264, holds that the exchange of United States $20 gold coins (numismatic-type coins) for South African Krugerrand gold coins (bullion-type coins) does not qualify for nonrecognition of gain under section 1031(a) of the Code because the numismatic-type coins and the bullion-type coins are not property of like kind.

In the present case the taxpayer exchanged gold bullion for Canadian Maple Leaf gold coins, which are legal tender in Canada to the extent of their face value of $50 each. However, because the value of the gold content in each Canadian Maple Leaf gold coin greatly exceeds its face value, it is not a circulating medium of exchange. Therefore, the Canadian Maple Leaf gold coin is property rather than money for purposes of section 1031(a) of the Code. . . .

Because the Canadian Maple Leaf gold coins are bought and sold for their gold content, they are bullion-type coins. Therefore, the nature and character of the gold bullion and the Canadian Maple Leaf gold coins are the same, and they qualify as "like kind" property as that term is used in section 1.1031(a)-1(b) of the regulations.

Rev. Rul. 82-166, 1982-2 C.B. 190

* * *

An individual taxpayer, who is not a dealer in gold or silver bullion, purchased gold bullion in the cash market and held it as an investment. In 1980, after the gold bullion had appreciated in value, the taxpayer exchanged the gold bullion for silver bullion of equal total fair market value. A gain was realized by the taxpayer as a result of the exchange. The taxpayer holds the silver bullion as an investment.

* * *

Rev. Rul. 79-143, 1979-1 C.B. 264, holds that the exchange of United States $20 gold coins (numismatic-type coins) for South African Krugerrand gold coins (bullion-type coins) does not qualify for nonrecognition of gain under section 1031(a) of the Code because the numismatic-type coins and the bullion-type coins represent totally different types of underlying investment and thus are not property of like kind. The bullion-type gold coins, unlike the numismatic-type gold coins, represent an investment in gold on world markets rather than in the coins themselves.

In this case, the values of the silver bullion and the gold bullion are determined solely on the basis of their metal content. Although the metals have some similar qualities and uses, silver and gold are intrinsically different metals and primarily are used in different ways. Silver is essentially an industrial commodity. Gold is primarily utilized as an investment in itself. An investment in one of the metals is fundamentally different from an investment in the other metal. Therefore, the silver bullion and the gold bullion are not property of like kind.

* * *

The taxpayer's exchange of gold bullion for silver bullion does not qualify for nonrecognition of gain under section 1031(a) of the Code.

NOTES AND COMMENTS

Rev. Rul. 82-96, and the rulings cited in it, make distinctions between the "nature or character" of gold and silver, not on the basis of their chemical content, but on the basis of their function, as money, as collectibles, or as bullion. The Service adopted this position despite the fact that § 1031(a) only requires that the property be held for use in trade or business or investment, which means that investment property of like kind can be exchanged for business property, or vice versa. Rev. Rul. 82-166 adopted a narrower distinction between gold and silver bullion based on their general functions, even though, apparently, the taxpayer held both for investment.

There is, of course, a practical reason for a more restrictive definition of like kind for personal property than for real property underlying these rulings — a broad interpretation would allow taxpayers to change the nature of their assets radically without ever recognizing gain — thus avoiding realization. Thus, if personal property as different as improved and unimproved real estate could be exchanged without recognition, one could envision a business exchanging a used machine for a work of art, or the reverse, so that a broad barter economy could be used to avoid recognizing gain as long as the taxpayer could find property that could be labeled business or investment without ever recognizing gain. Of course, taxpayers would always seek to recognize losses.

The principle that any type of real estate improved or unimproved is like kind to any other real estate can result in what may seem to be excessively liberal results. Thus, for example, *Koch v. Commissioner*, 71 T.C. 54 (1978), *acq.*, held that an exchange of a fee interest in a golf course and in unimproved land for a remainder interest in land underlying condominium projects that was subject to 99-year leases that had more than 90 years to run, so that it was effectively primarily a right to receive the ground rent for 90 years also qualified as an exchange of like-kind property. Similarly, *Commissioner v. Crichton*, 122 F.2d 181 (5th Cir. 1941), held that an exchange of a partial interest in the mineral rights in unimproved rural land for a partial interest in the fee of an improved urban lot qualifies as an exchange of like-kind property because both are interests in real property, despite the significant differences in the uses of the property. Other examples involving mineral and timber interests with significantly different economic characteristics, but that are classified as real property, so that they qualify as nonrecognition exchanges, can also be cited. *See, e.g.*, Rev. Rul. 68-331, 1968-1 C.B. 352 (an exchange of a leasehold interest in a producing oil lease for a ranch and improvements qualified); Rev. Rul. 55-749, 1955-2 C.B. 295 (an exchange of perpetual water rights, classified as real estate under local law, for a fee also qualified); Priv. Ltr. Rul. 78-11-056 (exchanges by a paper manufacturer of timberland plus perpetual timber and grass rights to public lands for fee interests in public lands, some of which were covered by the exchanged timber and grass rights qualified); Priv. Ltr. Rul. 78-11-037 (perpetual timber cutting rights for a fee in land qualifies); and Priv. Ltr. Rul. 2005-41-037 (exchange of old growth timber held by an individual for investment for reproduction timber land held by a corporation whose business included harvesting timber and selling wood products and planned to harvest the old growth timber). As indicated despite the differences in the rights, because they were all classified as nonrecognition exchanges based on the broad language in § 1031(a) referring only to "like kind" as the qualification, in Treas. Reg. § 1.1031-1(b) defining "like kind" as based on "nature and character," not "grade or quality." Thus, as indicated, nonrecognition is available for exchanges that might be considered to involve such different economic rights that make it difficult to see why they are considered to represent a continuity of investment.

On the other hand, not every exchange of real property held for business or investment purposes for other real property qualifies under § 1031. To some degree the difference may involve differences in what is considered real property under state law. Thus in *Oregon Lumber Co. v. Commissioner*, 20 T.C. 192 (1953), *acq.*, an exchange of land for the right to cut timber on public land does not qualify, because the right to cut timber was personal property under local law. Priv. Ltr. Rul. 78-11-037, discussed in the previous paragraph, distinguished *Oregon Lumber* on the basis of the state law classification, but also noted that the timber cutting right was limited in the value of timber that could be cut, the time of harvesting, definition of timber that could be cut, etc. Similarly, in Tech. Adv. Mem. 95-25-002, an exchange of a right to remove all timber on a tract of land to be removed within two years for a fee interest in other timberland did not qualify for nonrecognition, even though the ruling apparently treats the right to remove as real property, but this is not explicit. *Wiechens v. United States*, 228 F. Supp. 2d 1080 (D. Ariz. 2002), held that an exchange of water rights that provided for a limited quantity, priority, and duration of water that could be used for fee interest in farm land did not qualify, even though term of the water rights was initially 50 years, with approximately 40 years remaining at the time of the exchange, and rights were interests in real property under local law, thus emphasizing the limitations, not the state law classification. *Cf. Smalley v. Commissioner*, 116 T.C. 450 (2001) (unnecessary to decide whether characterization of timber cutting real estate under state law made exchange of timber cutting rights for timberland qualified as a § 1031 exchange; installment sale provisions prevent taxation in year relinquished property transferred, even if no qualifying exchange). Thus, it is not clear from these decisions the degree to which the duration of the rights, or the characterization of the property as real or personal property under local law, is relevant and the degree and kinds of limitations that may prevent an exchange from qualifying for nonrecognition. To add further confusion, if that is possible, there is ambiguity about the importance of the duration of the limitations. As the *Century Electric* and *Jordan Marsh* cases discussed in § 1.01 *Exchange* emphasize, Treas. Reg. § 1.1031(a)-1(c) treats a leasehold of 30 or more years as equivalent to a fee. The Service has applied the same standards to life estates. Thus, in Rev. Rul. 78-4, 1978-1 C.B. 256, an exchange by a widow with a life expectancy of more than 30 years, who owned a life estate in one-half of each of two parcels of farm land and the fee to the other half of each, and who created a remainder out of her fee in all of one parcel, that she exchanged it for a life estate in all of the other, so that she ended up with a fee in all of one tract and life estate in the other qualified for nonrecognition. On the other hand, Rev. Rul. 72-601, 1972-2 C.B. 467, held that an exchange of a remainder interest (reserving a life estate) in one farm for a life estate in another by one whose life expectancy was less than 30 years did not qualify for nonrecognition. In addition, in *Wiechens*, a remaining term for water rights of about 40 years did not overcome other limitations. Thus, a term of 30 years or more may be a necessary condition for a real estate interest to qualify for nonrecognition, but it may not be a sufficient one.

Although partnership interests are not eligible for like-kind exchanges, § 1031(a)(2)(D), the Service has issued guidelines, in Rev. Proc. 2002-22, 2002-1 C.B. 733, for rulings on whether fractional interests in rental real property (other than mineral interests) packaged by a sponsor are co-ownership, and not interests in a partnership and, in doing so, specifically superseded Rev. Proc. 2000-46, 2000-2 C.B. 438, which had announced a no-ruling position on whether fractional interests qualified for § 1031 exchanges. Thus, although the guidelines are specifically directed toward determining whether a tenancy in common under local law is, nevertheless, a partnership for tax purposes, so that exchanges of interests cannot qualify for nonrecognition exchanges under § 1031(a)(2)(D), the clear point of the ruling is to describe arrangements that will create interests that can qualify for

§ 1031 exchanges, particularly as part of multiparty and deferred exchanges discussed in § 1.03 *Multiparty Exchanges*, § 1.04 *Deferred (*Starker*) Exchanges*, and § 1.05 *Reverse (*Starker*) Exchanges*.

The guidelines require interests that qualify as tenancies in common under state law, limit the number of co-owners to 35, and require (i) that the co-owners (directly or through disregarded entities) own direct interests in the real property (not through a single disregarded entity), (ii) that interests of the co-owners in assets and liabilities and profits and losses be proportionate, (iii) that the co-owners retain individual rights to dispose of their interests, subject only to fair market value rights of first refusal and options, and any bona fide creditor limits, (iv) that co-owners have the right to control (by unanimous vote) hiring any manager, sale, lease or mortgaging the property, but can submit to majority control for other matters, (v) that activities be limited to customary leasing activities and that leases be bona fide leases that may provide a percentage of receipts, but not profits, (vi) that management and brokerage arrangements be limited to one year, that dealings be at arm's-length prices, with any borrowing from unrelated persons, and (vii) that the operation never do anything as an entity, including filing partnership or corporate returns. Priv. Ltr. Rul. 2005-13-010 determined that the requirements of Rev. Proc. 2002-22 were satisfied even though the provision for unanimous approval of management agreement described in (iv) included an option for other co-owners to buy out objecting co-owners at fair market value, and a limited right of co-owner to opt out of management agreement if others did not purchase interest; specifically refers to qualification for § 1031 like-kind exchanges. Similarly, several rulings have held the requirement in (iii) for only fair market value rights of first refusal were satisfied by a fairly standard buy-sell agreement provision sometimes called the slice-the-pie or shotgun arrangement, under which one of equal co-owners could make an offer at a specified price and on specified terms with the other(s) having the right to accept the price and terms, or agree to sell on the same price and terms. As indicated, fractional interests satisfying the guidelines can provide convenient relatively marketable sources of replacement property for like-kind exchanges, making satisfying the timing and other requirements for deferred exchanges easier. This has the effect of further attenuating the substance of the exchange requirement, some would suggest to the point of disappearance.

In Priv. Ltr. Rul. 97-51-012 (and many subsequent rulings) the Service has treated ownership of relinquished or replacement properties through disregarded entities, usually single-member LLCs, as being the same as direct ownership by the owner of the disregarded entity for purposes of qualifying the exchange for nonrecognition under § 1031. Rev. Rul. 2004-86, 2004-2 C.B. 191, extended the liberalization of arrangements that can qualify for nonrecognition exchanges under § 1031 when it ruled that an exchange of interest in a Delaware Statutory Trust could qualify because the interest represented an interest in an investment trust that was a grantor trust for tax purposes in which the grantor-beneficiaries were deemed to be co-owners of the trust properties and not partners.

Intangible as well as tangible property may be transferred in a like-kind exchange under § 1031. The regulations adopt a relatively narrow test, requiring that the nature and character of the rights involved be considered as well as the nature and the character of the underlying property. Treas. Reg. § 1.1031(a)-2(c) applies a restrictive approach similar to that for intangible personal property, without, of course, use of the general asset class or product class scheme used for tangible personal property, and indicates that patents and copyrights can be exchanged for other patents and copyrights, but not for each other, and that the nature of the underlying property is relevant, but the regulation does not elaborate further. The examples indicate that, although a copyright of one novel is like kind to that of another novel, a copyright of a novel is not like kind to one for a musical composition. Tech. Adv. Mem. 2000-35-004 held the exchange of three radio licenses for a television license was an exchange of like-kind property, because both are rights to use a specific frequency of the electromagnetic spectrum although they are different portions of the spectrum; differences are in grade or quality, not in nature or character, but in follow-up Tech. Adv. Mem. 2002-24-004, the right to affiliate with a television network was held not to be part of the license, but was a separable property that was apparently boot. *See* Tech. Adv. Mem. 94-48-001 (in an exchange of businesses both of which apparently had franchise or affiliation contracts with a limited life, but of a type frequently renewed that had significant value; memo states that taxpayer failed to demonstrate the nature or character of the rights involved, and also that the nature or character of underlying property to which the intangible personal property relates were like kind, but because the nature of the intangibles is redacted, it is difficult to determine why). Nevertheless, the Service has ruled that baseball and football player contracts are § 1231 property that can qualify for like-kind exchanges under § 1031(a), apparently on the theory that while the individual players may be unique, the nature and character of the rights of the team under the contracts are sufficiently standard. *See* Rev. Rul. 67-380, 1967-2 C.B. 291; Rev. Rul. 71-137, 1971-1 C.B. 104. Tech. Adv. Mem. 2006-02-034 held that patents and unregistered intellectual property, such as designs and drawings, trade secrets and know-how, and software are like kind only if they relate to property in the same General Asset Class or the same Product Class. The regulations explicitly state that the goodwill and going concern value of each business is unique, and is not like kind to the goodwill and going concern value of another business. Treas. Reg. § 1.1031(a)-2(c)(2). *See also* Field Serv. Adv. 1999-51-006 (unsurprisingly, upholding the validity of Treas. Reg. § 1.1031(a)-2(c)(2) and distinguishing player contracts). Tech. Adv. Mem. 2006-02-034, also held that trademarks and trade names relate to goodwill so that they are never like kind, but that portion of the holding was repudiated by the Service in Chief Couns. Adv. 2009-11-006, 2009 TNT 48-18, which recognized that, except in rare and unusual situations, the trademark and similar intangibles could be separately described and valued apart from goodwill, relying on *Newark Morning Ledger Co. v. United States*, 507 U.S. 546 (1993), which held that an intangible asset was not goodwill for purposes of the depreciation rules if it could be separately described and valued apart from goodwill. The CCA emphasized that the property must satisfy all other requirements of § 1031, including the restrictive nature and character rules of section 1.1031(a)-2(c)(1) described above. Accordingly, the scope of the liberalization is not yet clear, particularly because neither technical advice memoranda nor chief counsel Advice are formal authority. As discussed in Chapter 4 *Capitalization and Cost Recovery*, § 3.07 *Amortization of Intangible Assets*, after the *Newark Morning Ledger* decision, Congress enacted § 197 to provide amortization of various intangibles including goodwill and other similar assets over a uniform 15-year period. Among other issues is the degree to which some of the other items listed in § 197 can be exchanged under § 1031.

Treas. Reg. § 1.1031(j)-1 provides rules for exchanges of multiple properties as part of the same transaction, for example when an entire branch, store, or other business operation is exchanged for another similar operation. Such exchanges are not uncommon following acquisition transactions, and may be required to satisfy regulatory or antitrust concerns. Because, following the approach of *Williams v. McGowan*, discussed in Chapter 1 *Basis and Realization*, § 4.01 *Overview*, any such transaction is not the exchange of a single asset, but of the individual assets and liabilities of the exchanged operations, the basic approach of the regulation is to group the assets by their kind or class, into exchange groups and a residual (boot) group. Treas. Reg. § 1.1031(j)-1(a)(2) and (b)(1) and (2)(i). The groups for personal property follow the same asset class or product class principles as for exchanges of individual assets, with real property being a single class. Any assets relinquished that cannot fit in a group with replacement assets falls into the residual (boot) group. Liabilities form their own group regardless of the exchange group to which they relate, so that all liabilities transferred and received are netted at once, with any excess of liabilities transferred added to the residual group, and any excess liabilities received allocated to the exchange groups in proportion to the value of the assets received in that group, in effect reducing that value. Treas. Reg. § 1.1031(j)-1(b)(2)(ii). Gain realized for an exchange group (excess of value over basis) is recognized to the extent of the exchange group deficiency — the excess of the value of the assets transferred in that group over the net value of the assets received, but, of course, losses are not recognized. Treas. Reg. § 1.1031(j)-1(b)(2)(iv) and (3). The usual basis rules apply. Treas. Reg. § 1.1031(j)-1(c). There are numerous helpful examples. Treas. Reg. § 1.1031(j)-1(d).

For example, Reel exchanges: (i) a computer with basis of $800 and value of $1,500; (ii) a car with basis of $900 and a value of $2,500 that is subject to a $500 liability for a net value of $2,000 and a truck with a basis of $700 and a value of $2,000; (iii) a truck with a basis of $700 and a value of $2,000, or assets with a net value of $5,000, all of which are used in Reel's business, with Repp for: (a) a better computer with a basis of $1,100 and a value of $1,600, (b) a better car, with a basis of $2,100 and a value of $3,100, but subject to a loan of $750, for a net value of $2,350; (c) a smaller truck with a basis of $600 and a value of $1,400, subject to a loan of $250, for a net value of $1,150 all of which are used in Repp's business, and (d) $400 cash to bring the net value to $5,500. Both Reel and Repp will use what they receive in the exchange in their businesses.

There are three exchange groups: (i) the computers (asset class 00.12); (ii) the cars (asset class 00.22); and (iii) the trucks (asset class 00.241). The liabilities are netted, with Reel becoming subject to, and Repp transferring, the $500 net excess. These liabilities are allocated among the exchange groups in proportion to the FMV (not netted for liabilities encumbering the assets) of the properties in the exchange group transferred by Repp, $131 to the computer group, $254 to the cars, and $115 to trucks, without regard to the assets encumbered or the relative net values of the groups.

In the computer exchange group, Reel has received a replacement computer with a value of $1,600 in exchange for the relinquished one with a value of $1,500 and $131 in excess liabilities, for an exchange group deficiency of $31 ($131 excess liabilities - $100 excess value received). In the car exchange group, Reel has received a replacement car with a value of $3,000 in exchange for a relinquished one with a value of $2,500 plus $254 in excess liabilities for an exchange group surplus of $346 ($500 excess value received - $254 excess liability). In the truck exchange group, Reel has received a replacement truck with a value of only $1,400 in exchange for the relinquished one worth 2,000 plus $115 excess liabilities for an exchange group deficiency of $715 ($600 excess value transferred + $115 excess liability). The net of the exchange group deficiencies and $131 + $715 (total $846) and the surplus $346) equals the $500 excess liabilities transferred. More important for Reel is that, as a result of this computation, the boot received is the sum of the $400 cash that is in the residual group, plus the $346 surplus in the car group, which, in effect, represents the portion of the value of the replacement car that is not part of the § 1031 exchange for the car relinquished. Accordingly, $31 of boot is allocated to the computer group and $715 to the truck for Reel. Because these amounts are less than the unrealized gain in each group — computer ($700 gain ($1,500 value - $800 basis)) and truck ($1,300 gain ($2,000 value- $700 basis)) — Reel recognizes $31 gain on the computer, offset by the $31 boot, but the $131 allocated excess liability increases the basis of the replacement computer from the $800 basis of the relinquished computer to $931; and $715 gain on the truck, offset by the boot, but the $115 excess liability increases the basis of the replacement truck from the $700 basis of the relinquished truck to $815). Because no boot is allocated to the car, there is no gain, but the basis of the replacement car is the $900 basis of the relinquished car, increased by the $254 allocated excess liabilities assumed and by the $346 surplus value of the car that is treated as boot so that it has a fair market value basis, for a total basis of the replacement of $1,500.

Repp's results mirror Reel's with adjustment for the $100 excess of the $500 liabilities transferred over the $100 cash paid, which is treated as the residual group. In the computer exchange group, the exchange group deficiency is the $100 excess value of the $1,600 computer relinquished over the $1,500 value of the replacement computer. In the car exchange group, the exchange group deficiency is the $600 excess of the $3,100 car relinquished over the $2,500 value of the replacement car. In the truck exchange group, the exchange group surplus is the $600 excess of the $2,000 value of the relinquished truck over the $1,500 value of the replacement truck. The net of exchange group deficiencies $100 + $600 and the surplus $600 equals the $100 residual group. More important for Repp is that the boot is the $700 sum of the sum of the exchange group surplus in the truck group that represents the excess of the value of the replacement truck that is not part of the § 1031 exchange, plus the $100 in the residual group that represents the net excess liability transferred. Accordingly, $100 of the boot is allocated to the computer group and $600 to the car group. Because these amounts are less than the unrealized gain in each group — computer ($500 gain ($1,600 - $1,100 basis)) and car ($1,000 gain ($3,100 value - $2,100 basis)) — Repp recognizes $100 gain on the computer offset by the $100 boot, so that basis of the replacement computer is the same $1,100 as the relinquished computer; and $600 gain on the car, offset by the $600 boot, so that the basis of the replacement car is the same $2,100 as the relinquished car. Because no boot is allocated to the truck, there is no gain, but the basis of the replacement truck is the $600 basis of the relinquished truck, increased by the $600 surplus value of the truck that is treated as boot so that it has a fair market value basis for a total basis of the replacement truck of $1,200.

PROBLEMS FOR DISCUSSION

Problem 5-8. In 20X1, Reel granted Repp the right for Repp to cut timber on Reel's 1,000-acre stand of young trees that will not be ready for cutting for at least five years, for Reel's right to cut timber on a 300-acre stand of mature trees on land owned by Repp that are ready for cutting immediately, although Reel is not required to cut at any particular time. As part of the exchange, Reel undertook all cultivation and care of the 1,000–acre stand of young trees on Repp's land until they are ready for cutting, which is to be completed by the end of 20X7, including the obligation under local conservation laws to plant seedlings after cutting. Is the exchange eligible for nonrecognition under § 1031 for Reel? For Repp? *See Crichton* (partial interest in the mineral rights in unimproved rural land for a partial interest in the fee of an improved urban lot qualifies); Rev. Rul. 55-749 (perpetual water rights, classified as real estate under local law exchanged for a fee qualifies); Priv. Ltr. Rul. 78-11-037 (timberland and perpetual timber and grass rights to public lands for fee interests in public lands, some of which were covered by the exchanged perpetual timber and grass rights); *Oregon Lumber Co.* (land exchanged for the right to cut timber on public land); *Wiechens* (water rights for limited quantity and priority with a 40-year remaining term that were interests in real property under local law exchanged for fee does not qualify); Tech. Adv. Mem. 95-25-002 (a right to remove all timber on a tract of land to be removed within two years exchanged for a fee interest in other timberland does not qualify); Priv. Ltr. Rul. 2005-41-037 (old growth timber (for cutting) for reproduction timber).

Problem 5-9. Rade owned many radio stations in small towns. She also owned a TV station in a bigger city. Because programming for city TV and small town radio is different, she arranged to exchange her TV station for four small-town radio stations in her service area with Mede, who operated city TV stations. The assets of the radio stations exchanged, included FCC licenses worth $100,000 each, network affiliation agreements worth $50,000 each, broadcast equipment worth $100,000 each, studio equipment worth $100,000 each, with any remaining value representing goodwill or other § 197 intangibles not recorded on the business's books. The assets of the TV station included an FCC license worth $500,000, a network affiliation agreement worth $150,000, broadcast equipment worth $300,000; studio equipment worth 300,000, and § 197 intangibles recorded on its books worth $150,000.

Thus, the exchanges are:

	Rade/TV	**Mede/Radio**
	Qualifying Exchanges	
Broadcast equipment.	$300,000	$600,000
Studio Equipment	300,000	---
FCC licenses	500,000	400,000

	Rade/TV	Mede/Radio
Affiliation agreements (if same rights)	150,000	200,000
Recorded § 197 Intangibles	150,000	
Unrecorded Goodwill & § 197 Intangibles		200,000
Totals	$1,400,000	$1,400,000

What is the tax effect of the exchange to Rade and Mede? *See* Tech. Adv. Mem. 2000-35-004 (exchange of a three radio licenses for a television license qualifies); Tech. Adv. Mem. 2002-24-004 (right to affiliate with a television network was not part of the license); Tech. Adv. Mem. 94-48-001 (exchange of businesses with unspecified affiliation contracts does not qualify); Tech. Adv. Mem. 2006-02-034 (trademarks and trade names); Chief Couns. Adv. 2009-11-006 (trademarks, trade names, and other intangibles separable from goodwill).

§ 1.07. Held

One of the requirements for a nonrecognition treatment under § 1031 is that both the relinquished and replacement property be held by the taxpayer for productive use in a trade or business or for investment. § 1031(a). Like the other requirements of § 1031, this requirement applies only to the relinquishing party. Whether the relinquished property will be held, or the replacement property was held, by the other party to the exchange for use in a trade or business or for investment is irrelevant. There is, however, no statutory or regulatory provision that specifies how long the relinquished property must have been held or how long the replacement property will be held for these purposes to satisfy this requirement. An issue that sometimes arises is whether a subsequent transfer or change in use of the replacement property will prevent the taxpayer from receiving nonrecognition treatment on the exchange. The following case considers whether the subsequent transfer of the replacement property in a second nonrecognition transaction to a partnership violates the requirement that the replacement property be held for use in a trade or business or for investment. In other words, can two rights make a wrong?

MAGNESON v. COMMISSIONER

United States Court of Appeals, Ninth Circuit
753 F.2d 1490 (9th Cir. 1985)

* * *

We are faced in this case with an issue of first impression in the Courts of Appeals: whether property acquired in a like-kind exchange with the intention of contributing it to a partnership under Internal Revenue Code § 721 is "held" for investment within the meaning of Internal Revenue Code § 1031(a).

* * *

The Magnesons were the sole owners of an apartment building in San Diego,

California (Iowa Street Property). They held the property for productive use in trade or business or for investment within the meaning of Section 1031(a). N.E.R. Plaza, Ltd. (NER) was the sole owner of commercial property in San Diego, California, known as the Plaza Property (Plaza Property).

Pursuant to a prearranged transaction . . ., the Magnesons transferred their fee interest in the Iowa Street Property to NER in exchange for a ten-percent undivided fee interest in the Plaza Property. Thereafter, on the same day, both the Magnesons and NER transferred their interests in the Plaza Property to U.S. Trust, Ltd. (U.S. Trust), a limited partnership under California law. In exchange for cash and their ten-percent interest in the Plaza Property, the Magnesons received a general partnership interest in U.S. Trust . . . U.S. Trust was formed for the purpose of acquiring, holding, and operating the Plaza Property. The Magnesons paid no tax on the gain realized from their exchange of the Iowa Street Property for the Plaza Property, claiming nonrecognition treatment under section 1031(a). They also paid no tax on the gain realized from their contribution of the Plaza Property to U.S. Trust, claiming nonrecognition treatment under section 721.

The parties agree that the contribution of the Plaza Property to U.S. Trust qualifies for nonrecognition of gain under section 721, which provides that "[n]o gain or loss shall be recognized to a partnership or to any of its partners in the case of a contribution of property to the partnership in exchange for an interest in the partnership." The parties also agree that the Iowa Street Property and the Plaza Property are like-kind properties within the meaning of section 1031(a) . . .

I. The Holding Requirement of Section 1031(a)

The Commissioner argues that the exchange of the Iowa Street Property for the Plaza Property cannot qualify for nonrecognition under section 1031(a) because the Magnesons did not "hold" the Plaza Property for investment. . . .

To qualify for nonrecognition treatment under section 1031(a), the taxpayer must, at the time the exchange is consummated, intend to hold the property acquired for investment. . . . Numerous cases have held that the taxpayers' intent at the time of the exchange to liquidate their interest in the property acquired disqualifies the exchange form nonrecognition under section 1031(a). . . . It is stipulated that the Magnesons intended at the time of the exchange to hold the property for contribution to U.S. Trust. Therefore, the Magnesons' exchange can only qualify under section 1031(a) if contributing property to a partnership in return for an interest in the partnership is "holding" the property for investment within the meaning of section 1031(a).

. . . Revenue Ruling 75-292, 1975-2 C.B. 333, relied on by the Commissioner, addresses a related question: whether a like-kind exchange followed by a transfer for stock under section 351 to a controlled corporation qualifies for nonrecognition under section 1031(a). The Service ruled that the property transferred to the corporation was no longer held by the taxpayer, and gain was recognized on the exchange. . . . Revenue rulings, however, are not binding on this court. *Richards v. Commissioner*, 683 F.2d 1219, 1224 & n. 12 (9th Cir. 1981) (rulings not dispositive although entitled to consideration as "body of experience and informed judgment").

More significantly, transfer to a corporation in exchange for shares is distinguishable from transfer to a partnership for a general partnership interest in several important ways.

First, a corporation is a distinct entity, apart from its shareholders, whereas a partnership is an association of its partner-investors. Shareholders have no ownership interest in the assets of a corporation; partners own the assets of a partnership. Shareholders have no participation in daily management of corporate assets and very little participation in long-term management; general partners are the managers of the partnership. Thus when the owner of property transfers it to a corporation in exchange for shares, he relinquishes ownership and control of the property. In contrast, he retains both in a transfer to a partnership for a general partnership interest.

Second, a like-kind exchange followed by a section 351 transfer, viewed as a whole, results in the exchange of property for stock. The parenthetical clause of section 1031(a) expressly excludes stock as property eligible for exchange, but there is no such prohibition on exchange of partnership interests. *Long v. Commissioner*, 77 T.C. 1045, 1966-68 (1981) (rejecting Commissioner's argument that partnership interests fit within exclusionary clause as choses in action or evidences of interests). [§ 1031(a)(2)(D) was enacted in 1984.] Revenue Ruling 75-292 is therefore inapplicable to this case.

The central purpose of both sections 721 and 1031(a), as stated by the Treasury Regulations, is to provide for nonrecognition of gain on a transfer of property in which the differences between the property parted with and the property acquired "are more formal than substantial," and "the new property is substantially a continuation of the old investment still unliquidated." Treas. Reg. 1.1002-1(c) . . . The regulations reflect the legislative history of the predecessor of section 1031(a). *See* . . . *Starker v. United States*, 602 F.2d 1341, 1352 (9th Cir. 1979) (section 1031 "designed to avoid the imposition of a tax on those who do not 'cash in' their investments in trade or business property"). Furthermore, as the Tax Court noted, the regulations unequivocally describe section 721 as representing a continuation, not a liquidation, of the old investment. The case law, the regulations, and the legislative history are thus all in agreement that the basis reason for nonrecognition of gain or loss on transfers of property under sections 1031 and 721 is that the taxpayer's economic situation after the transfer is fundamentally the same as it was before the transfer: his money is still tied up in investment in the same kind of property. . . . [T]his principle exactly described the Magnesons' situation. Before the two transactions, their investment was a fee interest in income-producing real estate. They exchanged this property for other income-producing real estate, which they held as tenants in common with NER. The Magnesons and NER then changed the form of their ownership of that real estate from tenancy in common to partnership. They still own the income-producing real estate, and they have taken no cash or non-like-kind property out of the transaction. The Magnesons' transactions therefore fit squarely within the central purpose of section 1031. They exchanged their investment property for like-kind investment property which they continue to hold for investment, albeit in a different form of ownership.

The Commissioner, and the dissenting Tax Court Judges, argue that the differences between ownership as tenants in common and ownership as a partnership are so substantial that the Magnesons cannot be regarded as having continued to hold the property for investment under section 1031(a) after the partnership contribution. Previous like-kind exchange cases have indeed looked to the nature of the taxpayer's ownership interest as well as to the nature of the property owned to determine if the section 1031(a) requirements are met. *See Estate of Meyer v. Commissioner*, 503 F.2d 556, 557-58 (9th Cir. 1974) (per curiam) (general partnership and limited partnership interests not like-kind property) . . . .

In application of federal tax statutes, state law controls in determining the nature of the legal interest the taxpayer holds in the property sought to be taxes. Federal law does not create or define property rights; it merely attaches tax consequences to the interests created by state law. . . . The dissent and the majority therefore correctly looked to California law to determine and compare the nature of tenancy in common and partnership ownership.

In California, a tenant in common owns an undivided interest in and is entitled to possession and enjoyment of the entire property. . . . Similarly, a partner is co-owner with his partners, as a tenant in partnership, of specific partnership property. . . . However, a partner's interest in specific partnership property is not assignable without concurrent assignment by all other partners, . . . nor subject to attachment except for partnership debt, . . . nor subject to marital property rights. . . .

The Tax Court minority concluded from these differences that the transformation of the Magnesons' tenancy in common into a partnership interest "so changed their legal relationship to that property as to disqualify the exchange from section 1031(a) treatment." We disagree. While there are significant distinctions, we do not believe that they are controlling in determining the holding for investment issue. First, we note that the crucial question in a section 1031(a) analysis is continuity of investment in like-kind property. Therefore, the critical attributes in the taxpayer's relationship to the property are those relevant to holding the property for investment. As both tenants in common and as general partners, the Magnesons owned an interest in the Plaza Property. As both tenants in common and as general partners, the Magnesons had the right to possess and control the property. While it is true that section 15025(2)(a) limits their possession and control to partnership purposes, the partnership purpose was to hold for investment. Under these circumstances their control as general partners is of the same nature as their control as tenants in common, in each case holding the property for investment.

The significant differences between the tenancy in common and the partnership interests lie in the voluntary and involuntary alienability of the property. Basically, the tenancy in common interest is freely alienable, but specific partnership property is not. Because the whole premise of section 1031(a) is that the taxpayer's intent is not to alienate the property, we believe that alienability distinctions are not dispositive. If at the time of the exchange, as here, the taxpayer intends to contribute the property to a partnership for a general partnership interest, and the partnership's purpose is to hold the property for investment, the holding requirement of section 1031(a) is satisfied despite the limited alienability of specific partnership property.

The Commissioner contends that the Tax Court majority, in focusing exclusively on the continuity of investment principle underlying section 1031(a), ignored the equally important technical requirements of the section itself. Treasury Regulation 1.1002-1(b) provides:

> The exceptions from the general rule requiring the recognition of all gains and losses . . . are strictly construed and do not extend either beyond the words or the underlying assumptions and purposes of the exception. Nonrecognition is accorded by the Code only if the exchange is one which satisfies both (1) the specific description in the Code of an excepted exchange, and (2) the underlying purpose for which such exchange is excepted from the general rule.

The Commissioner contends that this double test applies, and that even if this transaction satisfies the "underlying purpose" prong of the test, it still fails to qualify under the "specific description" prong because technically the partnership and not the taxpayers holds the acquired property. This circuit, however, rejected an analogous argument in *Starker* . . . refusing to give such a narrow construction. . . . Applying the *Starker* manner of construing the section, we decline to read into section 1031(a) the requirement that the taxpayer continue to hold the acquired property by the exact form of ownership in which it was acquired. So long as, as in this case, the taxpayers continue to own the property and to hold it for investment, a change in the mechanism of ownership which does not significantly affect the amount of control or the nature of the underlying investment does not preclude nonrecognition under section 1031(a).

II. The Step Transaction Doctrine

As an alternate position, the Commissioner contends that the step transaction doctrine should be applied in this case and would preclude section 1031(a) nonrecognition. Under this doctrine, the court must view the transaction as a whole even if the taxpayer uses a number of steps to consummate the transaction. *See Commissioner v. Court Holding C*o., 324 U.S. 331, 334 . . . (1945). A taxpayer may not secure, by a series of contrived steps, different tax treatment than if he had carried out the transaction directly. . . . Viewed as a whole, the Commissioner argues that the Magnesons have exchanged their fee interest in the Iowa Street Property for a partnership interest in U.S. Trust, which the Commissioner contends is not like-kind property under this court's decision in *Meyer*, 503 F.2d at 557-58 (general and limited partnership interests not like-kind). Initially, we note that it may not be appropriate to collapse the steps of this transaction, because it is not readily apparent that the transaction could have been achieved directly. The Magnesons started out with the Iowa Street Property, which was worth one tenth of the Plaza Property. NER owned 100% of the Plaza Property. NER and the Magnesons wanted to end up owning the Plaza Property together in a partnership, and the Magnesons wanted to pay for their share with the Iowa Street Property. The Magnesons could have sold the Iowa Street Property, used the proceeds to buy ten percent of the Plaza Property, and then formed the partnership with NER, but that would have added a step to the transaction, rather than being a more direct route than that taken. Alternatively, NER and the Magnesons could have formed the partnership with the Iowa Street Property and ninety percent of the Plaza Property, and then the partnership could have exchanged the Iowa Street Property for the remaining ten percent of the Plaza Property. Again, this is not more direct than the method by which the Magnesons chose to carry out the transaction. Between two equally direct ways of achieving the same result, the Magnesons were free to choose the method which entailed the most tax advantages to them. . . .

Even if we apply the step transaction doctrine, and view the transaction as an exchange of the Magnesons' fee interest in the Iowa Street Property for a partnership interest in the Plaza Property, we believe that the transaction qualifies under section 1031(a). The Commissioner argues that this case is controlled by *Meyer*, which held that a general partnership interest and a limited partnership interest were not like-kind although the underlying property in each partnership was like-kind. *Meyer* . . .

Meyer is not controlling in this case because, as discussed above, the rights of a fee owner and of a general partner to management and control are very similar. Rather than losing any participation in operating the investment property, as did the taxpayer in *Meyer*, the Magnesons as general partners are the managers of their investment, just as they were when they owned the Iowa Street Property in fee simple. Thus, we reject the Commissioner's argument that application of the step transaction doctrine disqualifies this exchange for section 1031(a) nonrecognition.

Finally, we note that a critical basis for our decision it [is] that the partnership in this case had as its underlying assets property of like kind to the Magnesons' original property, and its purpose was to hold that property for investment. . . .

Our holding in this case is limited to those situations in which the taxpayer exchanges property for like-kind property with the intent of contributing the acquired property to a partnership for a general partnership interest. Further, the taxpayer must show, as the Magnesons have here, that the purpose of the partnership is to hold the property for investment, and that the total assets of the partnership are predominantly of like-kind to the taxpayer's original investment.

AFFIRMED.

NOTES AND COMMENTS

To the extent that the court in *Magneson* relied on the special nature of the tenancy in partnership to conclude that the holding requirement had been satisfied, the Revised Uniform Limited Partnership Act may make the decision obsolete, because § 501 abolishes the concept of tenancy in partnership. On the other hand, under § 704(c), the Magnesons above and not the other partners are required to recognize any unrealized gain recognized by the partnership after the contribution. Nevertheless, if the holding in *Magneson* survives, the conclusion of Rev. Rul. 75-292, 1975-2 C.B. 333, that a nonrecognition transfer to a corporation violated the holding requirement, becomes questionable. The question is why the nonrecognition transfer to a corporation violates the holding requirement in view of the fact that nonrecognition for transfers to controlled corporations under § 351, like nonrecognition for transfers to a partnership under § 721, rests on continuity of investment. Although, as the court points out, differences exist in the relationship between shareholders and corporate property and that between partners and partnership property, these differences would appear irrelevant given the analogous treatment of transfers of property to a corporation and to a partnership under §§ 351 and 721. Thus, the earlier question remains: why do two rights — two successive nonrecognition transactions — make a wrong — a recognition transaction? Or to phrase the question more precisely, why do two rights in the partnership context not make a wrong when two rights in the corporate context make a wrong? In this connection, does, or should, the subsequent enactment of § 1031(a)(2)(D) in 1984, disallowing nonrecognition exchanges of partnership interests, change the result? Because the Service, in Rev. Rul. 84-52, 1984-1 C.B. 157, allows nonrecognition of what are, in effect, exchanges of interests in the same partnership, notwithstanding § 1031(a)(2)(D), and because *Magneson* involves a contribution to a partnership, not an exchange of partnership interests, the answer should be that § 1031(a)(2)(D) should not change the result in *Magneson*, even though the case cites the absence of such a provision as support for finding the holding requirement satisfied.

Bolker v. Commissioner, 760 F.2d 1039 (9th Cir. 1985), in an opinion written by the judge who wrote the opinion in *Magneson*, allowed nonrecognition in a situation quite similar to Rev. Rul. 77-337, 1977-2 C.B. 305, which determined that property was received in a liquidation under former § 333 — a limited nonrecognition provision that gave the shareholder an exchanged basis in the property received — did not satisfy the requirement that the relinquished property be held for business or investment before the exchange. The facts in *Bolker*, can be distinguished from those in Rev. Rul. 77-337, however. Although the exchange in *Bolker* was planned before the liquidation occurred, the taxpayer held the relinquished property for three months before the exchange was carried out. Although the *Bolker* court did not find *Magneson* controlling, it held that if a taxpayer owns property that he does not intend to liquidate or to use for personal pursuits, he is "holding" that property "for productive use in trade or business or for investment" within the meaning of section 1031(a). Moreover, the court stated that "the intent to exchange property for like-kind property satisfies the holding requirement, because it is *not* an intent to liquidate the investment or to use it for personal pursuits." Thus, the decision in *Bolker* could provide additional support for *Magneson*, even under the revised entity approach to partnership law. Rev. Rul. 84-121, 1984-2 C.B. 168, provides another liberal approach to the continuity of investment approach in holding that the relinquishing party qualified for nonrecognition under § 1031, even though the relinquished property was transferred pursuant to the terms of an option, issued for cash consideration that gave the option holder, not the property owner, the option to pay cash or replacement property with a value equal to the option exercise price. The option holder purchased and delivered replacement property. The option holder did not qualify for nonrecognition because replacement property was newly acquired, but no gain was recognized because its basis equaled its value.

The satisfaction of the holding requirement was also an issue in *Starker v. United States*, 602 F.2d 1341 (9th Cir. 1979), in connection with the Timian and Bi-Mart properties. The holding that the Timian property fails to satisfy the holding requirement because it was Starker's personal residence seems unassailable. Even though his daughter may have held the property for investment, because Starker paid rent, because he could not have paid rent to himself, *he* could not have held it for business or investment. On the other hand, with respect to the Bi-Mart property, the question is essentially the same as that in *Magneson*: whether a subsequent gift of the property should disqualify the exchange from nonrecognition treatment for failure to satisfy the holding requirement. Although title to the Bi-Mart property was transferred directly to the daughter, this could be considered equivalent to the delivery of a contract to purchase instead of title in Rev. Rul. 90-34. In other contexts, the Tax Court has resolved this issue by considering the amount of time that has elapsed between the exchange and the subsequent transfer through the application of the step transaction doctrine. *See Wagensen v. Commissioner*, 74 T.C. 653 (1980) (gift nine months after exchange did not disqualify exchange when no evidence that the taxpayer planned to make a gift of the property at the time of the exchange); *Click v. Commissioner*, 78 T.C. 225 (1982) (a gift seven months after the exchange to the taxpayer's children of properties the children had selected as their personal residences before the exchange indicated that the taxpayer never had an intent to hold the properties for investment); Priv. Ltr. Rul. 2005-21-002 (trust termination shortly after receipt of replacement property, with distribution of interests in disregarded entity owning replacement property to beneficiaries, does not violate the holding requirement of § 1031(a)).

PROBLEMS FOR DISCUSSION

Problem 5-10. Reel owned Blackacre, originally acquired three years earlier for $100,000 as a site for a commercial office building, but overbuilding in the area made her change her mind. She located Whiteacre in a nearby, rapidly growing community that she considered ideal for her purposes, but that would require zoning changes to be used for her purposes. To conserve cash, she wanted to make a nonrecognition exchange. Repp, who owned Whiteacre with a basis of $50,000, was also interested in a nonrecognition exchange, although he was not interested in Blackacre. Accordingly, they entered into an arrangement through a qualified intermediary (QI), under which Reel paid the qualified intermediary $20,000 as consideration for an option granted by Repp to the QI to purchase Whiteacre, for $200,000, which would be paid to Repp if he did not properly designate a replacement property for Whiteacre with a purchase price of $200,000 or less, within the 45-day period specified in § 1031(a)(3)(B). If Repp properly designated replacement property, the $20,000 would be applied to the purchase price of the designated replacement property. Under the terms of the option agreement, if Reel directed the QI to exercise the option, the QI, would direct Repp to transfer Whiteacre to Reel and Reel would transfer Blackacre to the QI. The QI would then sell Blackacre, and use the $20,000 option price and proceeds of the sale of Blackacre to acquire replacement property designated by Repp. If the proceeds of the sale of Blackacre were less than $180,000, Reel would be required to make up the difference, and if they were more, Reel would receive the excess. In due course Reel directed the QI to exercise the option, transferred Blackacre to the QI, who sold it for $210,000 and used $180,000 of the proceeds plus the $20,000 option payment to purchase Greenacre, which Repp had properly designated as the replacement property the day he conveyed Whiteacre to Reel. After purchasing Whiteacre and transferring it to Repp, the QI paid the $30,000 excess to Reel. What are the tax consequences of these transactions to Reel and Repp? *See* Treas. Reg. § 1.1031(k)-1; *Barker* (multiparty exchange through intermediary); *Garcia* (net even liability incurred to be netted); Rev. Rul. 84-121 (exchange of newly acquired replacement property pursuant to an option did not meet holding requirement, but qualified as replacement property for property relinquished under the option); Rev. Rul. 75-291 (Service sanctions multiparty exchange involving property constructed to be replacement property); Rev. Rul. 77-297 (same with liability netting); *Starker* (deferred exchange).

Problem 5-11. The facts are the same as in Problem 5-6, with the additional fact that four months after the exchange, following the birth of his first grandchild, Reel placed Greenacre in trust for the benefit of that grandchild and any future grandchildren, as he had contemplated when he insisted on the exchange. Does the gift disqualify the exchange? *See Magneson* (planned transfer to partnership does not disqualify replacement property); *Bolker* (planned transfer of relinquished property received in liquidation held three months before exchange qualified); *Starker* (Timian and Bi-Mart properties) *Wagensen* (gift of replacement property nine months after exchange does not disqualify exchange); *Click* (gift seven months after exchange to children of properties they had selected as their personal residences before the exchange indicated never an intent to hold properties for investment); Priv. Ltr. Rul. 2005-21-002 (trust termination shortly after receipt of replacement property, with distribution to beneficiaries, does not violate the "to be held" requirement); Rev. Rul. 75-292 (nonrecognition transfer to a corporation violated holding requirement).

§ 1.08. Related Parties

I.R.C. § 1031(f).

The exchanged basis aspect of § 1031(d) could allow related parties to reduce or eliminate gain on property intended for sale, by first exchanging the property for like-kind property with a higher basis held by the related party before the sale, and then having the related party sell the property to the third-party buyer. For example, Sail owns Blackacre with a basis of $10,000 and a fair market value of $100,000 that it plans to sell to Perch, an unrelated buyer. If Sail sells Blackacre to Perch, Sail realizes and recognizes $90,000 of gain. Fortunately, Sib, a party related to Sail, owns Whiteacre with a basis and fair market value of $100,000. In the absence of § 1031(f), Sail and Sib could take advantage of § 1031 and exchange Blackacre for Whiteacre. Following the exchange, Sail will then have a basis in Whiteacre of $10,000 — an amount equal to the basis of Blackacre — and Sib will have a basis in Blackacre of $100,000 — an amount equal to the basis of Whiteacre. Sib could then sell Blackacre to Perch for its fair market value and would not realize any gain on the sale, saving the related parties the tax liability that would otherwise have been incurred if Sail had sold Blackacre to Perch directly. Of course this works only if the related group is not troubled by having Sail own Whiteacre and having Sib have the proceeds of the sale of Blackacre, perhaps because they hope that there are legitimate means available for correcting the situation later, which is frequently the case for consolidated groups of corporations or for close family groups, particularly if one of the parties is a family trust.

Congress enacted § 1031(f) to prohibit such abusive transactions. As the following case indicates, however, the application of § 1031(f) becomes complicated in the context of multiparty exchanges effectuated through a qualified intermediary.

TERUYA BROS., LTD. v. COMMISSIONER

United States Tax Court
124 T.C. 45 (2005)

* * *

Teruya Brothers, Ltd. (Teruya), is a Hawaii corporation. Its business activities include purchasing and developing residential and commercial real property. During the taxable year in issue, Teruya owned 62.5 percent of the common shares of Times Super Market, Ltd. (Times).

I. *Exchanges of Properties*

In 1995, Teruya engaged in two separate real property exchange transactions, referred to herein as the Ocean Vista transaction and the Royal Towers transaction.

A. *Ocean Vista Transaction*

Teruya owned a fee simple interest in Ocean Vista, a parcel of land underlying the Ocean Vista Condominium complex in Honolulu, Hawaii. Teruya's ownership interest in Ocean Vista was subject to a long-term ground lease held by Golden Century Investments Co. (Golden), which in turn was subject to a sublease held by the Association of Apartment Owners of Ocean Vista (the Association).

In March 1993, the Association inquired about buying Teruya's fee simple interest in Ocean Vista. Teruya responded that its fee simple interest in Ocean Vista was not available. . . .

In June 1994, Teruya proposed buying Time's interest in "two pad sites" in Waipahu, Hawaii (these properties are hereinafter referred to collectively as Kupuohi II). Teruya's written proposal included these provisions:

> The purchase will be subject to a [section] 1031 four party exchange. . . . Teruya may cancel the proposed purchase of * * * [Times's] pad sites should the Ocean Vista transaction fail to proceed according to present plans.

Times accepted Teruya's proposal.

* * *

In August 1995, Teruya entered into an "exchange agreement" with T. G. Exchange, Inc. (TGE), whereby TGE agreed to act as an "exchange party to complete the exchange" of Ocean Vista for replacement property to be designated by Teruya, with the stated purpose of qualifying the exchange under section 1031.

TGE agreed to acquire the replacement property with proceeds from the sale of Ocean Vista and additional funds from Teruya as necessary to effect the acquisition. . . .

Pursuant to the exchange agreement, Teruya transferred Ocean Vista to TGE, and on September 1, 1995, TGE sold Ocean Vista to the Association for $1,468,500. At that time, Teruya had a $93,270 basis in Ocean Vista.

Also on September 1, 1995, TGE applied the proceeds from the sale of Ocean Vista, as well as $1,366,056 in additional cash from Teruya, to acquire Kupuohi II from Times for $2,828,000. Times had a $1,475,361 adjusted basis in Kupuohi II and recognized a $1,352,639 gain on the sale.

At some point, TGE transferred Kupuohi II to Teruya. As of the date the petition was filed, Teruya still owned Kupuohi II.

B. *Royal Towers Transaction*

In 1994, Teruya owned a fee simple interest in the Royal Towers Apartment building (Royal Towers) in Honolulu, Hawaii. On or about December 12, 1994, Teruya and Savio Development Co. (Savio) entered into a $13.5 million contract for the sale of Royal Towers. The contract stated that the sale was subject to the "Seller [Teruya] being able to consummate [a section 1031] exchange." Teruya and Savio later agreed to decrease the price for Royal Towers from $13.5 million to $11,932,000. In April 1995, Teruya's board of directors approved the sale of Royal Towers to Savio.

In anticipation of Teruya's sale of Royal Towers, Teruya and Times previously had agreed that Teruya would purchase Times's interests in two parcels of real property in Waipahu and Aiea, Hawaii (respectively, Kupuohi I and Kaahumanu). One of the purchase terms stated:

> The purchase will be subject to a [section] 1031 four party exchange. . . .

Early in 1995, the boards of directors of Times and Teruya approved the sale and purchase of Kupuohi I for $8.9 million and Kaahumanu for $3.73 million.

In August 1995, Teruya entered into an "exchange agreement" with TGE, whereby TGE agreed to act as an "exchange party to complete the exchange" of Royal Towers for replacement property to be designated by Teruya, with the stated purpose of qualifying the exchange under section 1031. TGE agreed to acquire the replacement property with proceeds from the sale of Royal Towers and additional funds from Teruya as necessary to effect the acquisition. . . .

Teruya transferred Royal Towers to TGE, and on August 24, 1995, TGE sold Royal Towers to Savio for $11,932,000. At that time, Teruya had a $670,506 basis in Royal Towers.

Also, on August 24, 1995, TGE applied the proceeds from the sale of Royal Towers, as well as $724,554 in additional funds from Teruya, to acquire Kupuohi I and Kaahumanu from Times for $8.9 million and $3.73 million, respectively. At the time of the sales, Times had a $15,602,152 adjusted basis in Kupuohi I and a $1,502,960 adjusted basis in Kaahumanu. Times realized a $6,453,372 capital loss on the sale of Kupuohi I but did not recognize this loss on its tax return because of the restriction on transactions between related taxpayers under section 267. Times realized and recognized a $2,227,040 gain on the sale of Kaahumanu.

At some point, TGE transferred Kupuohi I and Kaahumanu to Teruya. As of the date the petition was filed, Teruya still owned these properties.

* * *

This case presents an issue of first impression regarding the application of section 1031(f), which restricts nonrecognition of gain or loss with respect to like-kind exchanges between related persons.

I. *General Requirements for Like-Kind Exchanges*

Teruya used a qualified intermediary, TGE, to facilitate its transfers of Ocean Vista and Royal Towers and its acquisitions of Kupuohi II, Kupuohi I, and Kaahumanu. Respondent does not dispute that these transactions meet the general requirements for like-kind exchanges under section 1031(a)(1). Respondent contends, however, that section 1031(f) requires petitioner to recognize gains on the transactions.

II. *Rules Applicable to Related-Person Exchanges*

Section 1031(f)(1) provides generally that if a taxpayer and a related person exchange like-kind property and within 2 years either one disposes of the exchanged property, the nonrecognition provisions of section 1031(a) do not apply. Instead, any gain or loss must be taken into account as of the date of the disposition. As one of the few enumerated exceptions to this rule, section 1031(f)(2)(C) provides that a disposition of exchanged property will not be taken into account if "it is established to the satisfaction of the Secretary that neither the exchange nor such disposition had as one of its principal purposes the avoidance of Federal income tax."

It is undisputed that Times and Teruya were related persons within the meaning of the statute. Respondent makes no argument, however, that section 1031(f)(1) applies directly to the Ocean Vista and Royal Towers transactions.[10] Instead, respondent argues that petitioner has run afoul of section 1031(f)(4), which provides: "This section [1031] shall not apply to any exchange which is part of a transaction (or series of transactions) structured to avoid the purposes of this subsection [(f)]." Inasmuch as the statute does not directly identify or describe the purposes of subsection (f), we turn our attention to the legislative history.

---

[10] Respondent appears to acknowledge implicitly that sec. 1031(f)(1) applies only in the case of a direct exchange between related persons and that this case does not involve such a direct exchange. Consistent with such a view, the regulations provide that a "qualified intermediary is not considered the agent of the taxpayer for purposes of section 1031(a)." Sec. 1.1031(k)-1(g)(4)(i), Income Tax Regs.

III. *Legislative History: Purposes of Section 1031(f)*

Property acquired in a like-kind exchange generally takes the basis of the property relinquished. *See* sec. 1031(d). In other words, there is a "shifting" of tax basis between the relinquished property and the replacement property. . . .

Before 1989, Congress was concerned that because of this basis-shifting effect, "related parties * * * engaged in like-kind exchanges of high basis property for low basis property in anticipation of the sale of the low basis property in order to reduce or avoid the recognition of gain on the subsequent sale." H. Rept. 101-247, at 1340 (1989). In effect, because of basis shifting, related persons were able to "cash out" of their investments in property having an inherent gain at relatively little or no tax cost. . . . Also, in some cases, basis shifting allowed related persons to accelerate a loss on property that they ultimately retained. . . . Responding to these perceived abuses, Congress concluded that "if a related party exchange is followed shortly thereafter by a disposition of the property, the related parties have, in effect, 'cashed out' of the investment, and the original exchange should not be accorded nonrecognition treatment." . . . This policy is reflected in section 1031(f) . . . .

Congress was also concerned that related persons not be able to circumvent the purposes of this rule by using an unrelated third party:

> Nonrecognition will not be accorded to any exchange which is part of a transaction or series of transactions structured to avoid the purposes of the related party rules. For example, if a taxpayer, pursuant to a prearranged plan, transfers property to an unrelated party who then exchanges the property with a party related to the taxpayer within 2 years of the previous transfer in a transaction otherwise qualifying under section 1031, the related party will not be entitled to nonrecognition treatment under section 1031. . . .

Equating a qualified intermediary with the "unrelated party" referred to in the above-quoted example, respondent reads the example to mean that a deferred exchange between related parties, involving a qualified intermediary, should be recast as a direct exchange between the related parties. If section 1031(f)(1) would preclude nonrecognition treatment for the recast transaction, respondent concludes, then the deferred exchange should be deemed to have been structured to avoid the purposes of section 1031(f). Respondent suggests that such an analysis ends the inquiry under section 1031(f)(4).

Although respondent's argument has superficial appeal, it is only loosely grounded in the above-quoted, highly elliptical example in the legislative history. . . . Moreover, respondent's analysis fails to consider the non-tax-avoidance exception of section 1031(f)(2)(C).[11] Because this exception is subsumed within the purposes of section 1031(f), any inquiry into whether a transaction is structured to

[11] As previously discussed, in the context of a direct exchange between related parties, sec. 1031(f)(2)(C) allows the taxpayer to establish that neither the exchange nor the disposition had as one of its principal purposes the avoidance of Federal income tax.

avoid the purposes of section 1031(f) should also take this exception into consideration.

Petitioner seems to suggest that Congress intended section 1031(f) to apply only insofar as the taxpayer fails to "continue its investment" in property that it receives in a related-person deferred exchange. Petitioner seems to suggest that what happens to the relinquished property is of no consequence. We reject any such suggestion as flatly contrary to section 1031(f), which applies with equal force to post-exchange dispositions by either the taxpayer or the related person.

IV. *Analysis of the Ocean View and Royal Towers Transactions*

Teruya exchanged Ocean View and Royal Towers for like-kind replacement properties formerly owned by Times. A qualified intermediary immediately sold Ocean Vista and Royal Towers to unrelated third parties. Times received the proceeds, plus additional cash from Teruya.

These transactions are economically equivalent to direct exchanges of properties between Teruya and Times (with boot from Teruya to Times), followed by Times's sales of the properties to unrelated third parties. The interposition of a qualified intermediary in these transactions cannot obscure the end result. Petitioner offers no explanation for structuring the Ocean Vista and Royal Towers transactions as it did, and the record discloses no reason (other than seeking to avoid the section 1031(f) rules) for Teruya's using a qualified intermediary to accomplish the transactions. Under the circumstances, we are led to the conclusion that Teruya used the multiparty structures to avoid the consequences of economically equivalent direct exchanges with Times. As discussed below, petitioner has failed to establish that avoidance of Federal income taxes was not one of the principal purposes of the Ocean Vista and Royal Towers transactions.

V. *Non-Tax-Avoidance Exception*

Petitioner argues that Teruya's continued investment in like-kind properties meets the requirements of the non-tax-avoidance exception under section 1031(f)(2)(C), as subsumed within section 1031(f)(4). Section 1031(f)(2)(C) provides that there shall not be taken into account any disposition "with respect to which it is established to the satisfaction of the Secretary that neither the exchange nor such disposition had as one of its principal purposes the avoidance of Federal income tax."

With respect to both the Ocean Vista and Royal Towers transactions, petitioner contends that "there was no intent to disguise an actual sale of the relinquished property in order to reduce or avoid gain recognition on such sale, because a sale of the relinquished property was not intended in the first place." In other words, petitioner contends that from the outset of both transactions, Teruya intended to qualify for deferred like-kind exchange treatment and did not intend to make direct sales of the properties. Petitioner points to the fact that Teruya, Times, Golden, the Association, and Savio agreed in various documents that the Ocean Vista and Royal Towers transactions were conditional on effecting a section 1031 exchange.

Petitioner's contentions might be relevant in determining whether a transaction is in substance an exchange or a sale of like-kind property. *See Alderson v. Commissioner*, 317 F.2d 790 (9th Cir. 1963), *rev'g*. 38 T.C. 215 (1962). In the instant case, however, they have little relevance. In the first instance, respondent does not contend that the transactions in question were disguised sales or otherwise fail to meet the general requirements of section 1031(a)(1). More fundamentally, section 1031(f) presupposes that an exchange to which it applies otherwise meets the requirements of section 1031(a)(1). *See* sec. 1031(f)(1)(B). Even if Teruya never intended to make a direct sale of the relinquished properties, this does not mean that section 1031(f) is not implicated or that the deferred sale was not structured so as to avoid Federal income taxes. The economic substance of the transactions remains that the investments in Ocean Vista and Royal Towers were cashed out immediately and Times, a related person, ended up with the cash proceeds.

With respect to the Ocean Vista transaction, petitioner contends that there was no tax avoidance purpose because Times recognized a gain on its sale of Kupuohi II ($1,352,639) that was larger than the gain Teruya would have recognized ($1,345,169) had it sold Ocean Vista directly to the Association for cash. Although Times recognized a gain in the Ocean Vista transaction that slightly exceeded Teruya's gain deferral, it appears that Times paid a much smaller tax price for that gain recognition than Teruya would have paid if it had recognized gain in a direct sale of Ocean Vista. On its corporate income tax return for taxable year ending March 31, 1996, Teruya reported taxable income of $2,060,806. Consequently, if Teruya had made a direct sale of Ocean Vista, the gain recognized on that sale presumably would have been taxable at a 34-percent corporate income tax rate. *See* sec. 11(b)(1)(C). By comparison, on its Form 1120 for its taxable year ending April 25, 1996, Times reported a net operating loss (NOL) of $1,043,829. Thus, although Times recognized a considerable gain on the Ocean Vista transaction, because of offsetting expenses, it did not incur tax on that gain. Instead, the only tax consequences of Times's gain recognition were reductions of its NOL for its taxable year ending April 25, 1996, and of its NOL carryovers for subsequent taxable years.

In sum, petitioner has failed to persuade us that avoidance of Federal income tax was not one of the principal purposes of the Ocean Vista and Royal Towers transactions.

VI. *Conclusion*

Petitioner offers no explanation for Teruya's use of the qualified intermediary in the Ocean Vista and Royal Towers transactions. We infer that the qualified intermediary was interposed in an attempt to circumvent the section 1031(f)(1) limitations that would have applied to exchanges directly between related persons. Petitioner has failed to show that avoidance of Federal income tax was not one of the principal purposes of the Ocean Vista and Royal Towers transactions. We conclude that these transactions were structured to avoid the purposes of section 1031(f). Consequently, petitioner is not entitled, under section 1031(a)(1), to defer the gains that it realized on the exchanges of Ocean Vista and Royal Towers.

* * *

NOTES AND COMMENTS

The Service had previously issued a ruling reaching the same basic result as *Teruya.* Rev. Rul. 2002-83, 2002-2 C.B. 927. As the *Teruya* opinion indicates, § 1031(f) is a substance-over-form overlay to § 1031, which, with multiparty and deferred exchanges, has become a provision where the only substance is the form. The elaborate mechanism of Treas. Reg. § 1.1031(k)-1 is designed to allow relinquishing parties in substance to sell Blackacre and buy Whiteacre as long as they operate through a qualified intermediary, whose principal function is to receive and disburse the sale price and purchase price. Although the qualified intermediary must be contractually obligated to acquire the relinquished property from the taxpayer and transfer it to the buyer (the first leg of the exchange) and acquire the replacement property from the seller and transfer it to the taxpayer (the second leg of the exchange), so that intermediary is contractually liable to the buyer and seller if the relinquishing party defaults, the risks involved, create some substance, albeit small. Section 1031(f) places a two-year limit on resales of exchanged properties that, the court noted, Teruya Brothers did not violate. In *Teruya,* Times made a sale, but of property that it neither received nor transferred in a § 1031 exchange. On the other hand, as the court correctly points out, what the parties did was transfer the sale to the related party with the net operating loss carryover, as much tax avoidance as the basis shift that is the paradigm case under § 1031(f)(1). Nevertheless, if Times had used the proceeds of the sales to Teruya Bros. as part of its own § 1031 exchange, so that neither related party cashed out, the exchange through the qualified intermediary would not have invoked § 1031(f)(4). *Ocmulgee Fields, Inc. v. Commissioner,* 132 T.C. 105 (2009), *aff'd,* 613 F.3d 1360 (11th Cir. 2010) reached a similar result even though the basis of the property to the related party was considerably less than the $7.25 million sale price, but was still $1.75 million more than the basis of the property sold, when the related party's tax bracket was 15 percent versus the 34 percent bracket for the seller. The court did not consider the shift of the future gain to the higher bracket seller or lost depreciation deductions to offset the immediate $2+ million tax saving. On the other hand, Priv. Ltr. Rul. 2004-40-002 held that § 1031(f) does not apply when proceeds of sale of the relinquished property are used to purchase replacement property from related party that uses the proceeds for its own § 1031 exchange. In Priv. Ltr. Rul. 2007-12-013, the issue was whether nonrecognition treatment under § 1031 would apply to a transaction where (i) a relinquishing party purchased like-kind replacement property from an unrelated third party via an exchange accommodation titleholder; (ii) the relinquishing party sold the relinquished property to a related party for cash received by a qualified intermediary (QI); and (3) the related party disposed of the relinquished property within two years of the acquisition. The IRS held that the related party's disposal of the relinquished property within two years of the acquisition would not trigger taxable gains pursuant to § 1031(f)(1). The relinquishing party and the related party did not engage in a like-kind exchange. The relinquishing party transferred the relinquished property to the related party through a QI, who purchased replacement property from an unrelated third person. The relinquishing party's like-kind exchange was an exchange with the QI, who was not related to it. In addition, § 1031(f)(4) would not apply to prevent nonrecognition of the gain or loss in the exchange because the relinquishing party did not transfer the relinquished property to the related party to avoid the purposes of § 1031(f)(1). Although not stated, the apparent ground for the ruling is that there was no basis shift among related parties because the relinquishing party's basis in the replacement property is determined by its basis in the relinquished property and the related party's basis in its replacement property will be determined by its purchase price for the relinquished property, not the basis to the original relinquishing party. *See* Priv. Ltr. Rul. 2002-51-008 (in complex "parking" transaction under Rev. Proc. 2000-37, in which proceeds are to be used for improvements to be placed on a 32-year leasehold acquired from related party at fair rent, states no § 1031(f) problem as long as neither party cashes out within two years; rent to related party apparently not considered cashing out); Priv. Ltr. Rul. 2005-41-037 (cutting of old growth timber on timberland exchanged for land reproduction timber, by related party within two years does not trigger gain recognition because related party continued to hold the underlying land received in the exchange after harvesting the old growth timber).

PROBLEM FOR DISCUSSION

Problem 5-12. Widgetco owned Blackacre with a basis of $100,000 and a value of $1,000,000 that Perch agreed to buy. The sale agreement required that the transaction be structured as a like-kind exchange under § 1031, and provided that the proceeds of by sale of Blackacre be paid by Perch paid to QI, under terms that satisfied the requirements of Treas. Reg. § 1.1031-1(k). After the sale and within the periods of provided by § 1031(a)(3), Widgetco identified Whiteacre with a basis of $900,000 owned by Gadgetco as replacement property. Both Widgetco and Gadgetco are wholly owned subsidiaries of Conglom, but operate in completely different industries and have no intercompany dealings. Neither the employees of Widgetco nor of Gadgetco who worked on the transactions were aware that the other corporation was a Conglom subsidiary. Since Conglom had a net operating loss for the year of the Widgetco sale, the sale would not have resulted in tax on the Conglom consolidated return, even if it had not been arranged as a nonrecognition transaction. This was also unknown to all of those who arranged the transactions, because the arrangements were that each subsidiary provided its individual results to the Conglom tax department that prepared the consolidated return and, in due course, notified each profitable subsidiary what amount it was charged on the intercompany account for taxes. Is the Widgetco exchange disqualified under § 1031(f)? *See Teruya Bros.* (exchange with related party does not qualify even though use qualified intermediary); Rev. Rul. 2002-83 (same); *Ocmulgee Fields* (exchange with related party did not qualify even though substantial gain recognized by related party that had a lower tax rate); Priv. Ltr. Rul. 2007-12-013 (relinquished property sold through QI to related party that disposed of property within two years not subject to § 1031(f)); Priv. Ltr. Rul. 2004-40-002 (proceeds used to purchase replacement property from related party that uses the proceeds for its own § 1031 exchange); Priv. Ltr. Rul. 2002-51-008 (proceeds are to be used for improvements to placed on 32-year leasehold acquired from related party at fair rent); Priv. Ltr. Rul. 2005-41-037 (cutting of old growth timber on relinquished timberland by related party within two years).

§ 2. INVOLUNTARY CONVERSION

I.R.C. § 1033(a) and (b); Treas. Reg. §§ 1.1033(a)-1 to 3 and 1.1033(b)-1.

No exchange is required to qualify for nonrecognition of gain on an involuntary conversion. All that is required is that the taxpayer make a proper election and purchase qualifying replacement property or controlling stock of a corporation owning qualifying replacement property within two years after the close of the taxable year in which gain is realized as a result of the involuntary conversion. This period may, of course, be longer than two years after the taxable year in which the involuntary conversion occurs, since gain is not realized until some form of proceeds is received. § 1033(a)(2)(B)(i). In addition, the period can be extended for good cause. § 1033(a)(2)(B)(ii); Treas. Reg. § 1.1033(a)-2(c)(3). *See Dettmers v. Commissioner*, 430 F.2d 1019 (6th Cir. 1970) (entering into contract of purchase of replacement property, making a down payment, and putting a purchase money note in escrow within the required period was not enough to qualify as timely replacement because these items did not transfer benefits and burdens of ownership to the taxpayer, *Boyce v. United States*, 405 F.2d 526 (Ct. Cl. 1968) (replacement period began when taxpayer withdrew from court amount initially determined so that government could take over property, even though subject to reduction by further proceedings); *Aldridge v. Commissioner*, 51 T.C. 475 (1968) (same, even though taxpayer did not withdraw amount deposited in court, the taxpayer had constructive receipt of the funds); *R. A. Stewart & Co. v. Commissioner*, 57 T.C. 122 (1971) (period began when initial payment exceeded basis, even though final payment more than double). When there is a possibility of receiving additional proceeds, the owner of the involuntarily converted property must make a timely request for an extension of the replacement period. *See Shipes v. Commissioner*, T.C. Mem. 1997-304 (attempted election, when additional proceeds received five years after condemnation was too late when taxpayer received some proceeds immediately, but did not elect under § 1031 for those proceeds and no extension request made). In the absence of such an extension, the receipt of additional proceeds will result in the recognition of gain, because it is generally impossible to reinvest the proceeds within the period specified in 1033(a)(2)(B). If the taxpayer makes an election under § 1033 and reinvests more that the amount of the initial proceeds within the required period, an argument can be made that such reinvestment may be used to avoid gain on subsequent proceeds, but no authority has been located that deals with this rare situation.

Unlike § 1031, nonrecognition under § 1033 is not limited to situations involving property held only for use in a trade or business or investment, but includes personal use property as well. *See* Rev. Rul. 96-32, 1996-1 C.B. 177 (sale of land after house destroyed by disaster qualifies as involuntary conversion; house and land are a unitary property). The usual collateral consequences of nonrecognition, including the preservation of the unrecognized gain through an exchanged basis in the replacement property, apply. § 1033(b); Treas. Reg. § 1.1033(b)-1.

The term "involuntary conversion" is a shorthand phrase for destruction or theft and for condemnation or threat of condemnation. The meaning of destruction or theft is discussed in § 2.01 *Involuntary*. Owners of involuntarily converted property, who were also the users of that property, are required to replace it with property that meets a functional use test, frequently referred to as the "similar in service or use" test, as described in § 2.02 *Similar in Service or Use*. Investors who lease out property instead of using it themselves have a separate test to satisfy that is examined in § 2.03 *Investor-Lessors*. These two tests are generally more limiting than the like-kind standard of § 1031. Nevertheless, owners of real property held for business or investment that is condemned (but not if it is otherwise involuntarily converted) can qualify for nonrecognition under a like-kind test that is the same as that of § 1031, even though § 1031 is not expressly cross referenced in the Code. Treas. Reg. § 1.1033(g)-1(a). As discussed in § 2.04 *Like Kind Revisited*, this test, which should be the same as the test under § 1031, is sometimes broader and sometimes narrower than the similar in-service or use test or the investor-lessor tests.

The basis rules for involuntarily converted property under § 1033(b), parallel those for like-kind exchanges under § 1031(d) discussed in § 1.02(a) *Cash and Nonlike-Kind Property*. The basis of the replacement property is increased for any gain recognized because the entire amount of the proceeds of the involuntary conversion is not reinvested in qualifying replacement property, and reduced for any proceeds received that are not reinvested in the replacement property, essentially a wash. The basis of the replacement property is also increased for any amounts paid for the replacement property in excess of the proceeds. Thus, when Blackacre, held for investment by Invest, with a basis of $10,000 and a value of $100,000 is involuntarily converted, and Invest uses the $100,000 proceeds along with $10,000 to purchase Whiteacre, also held for investment, the basis of Whiteacre is $20,000 ($10,000 basis of Blackacre + $10,000 additional cash) because Invest still has $90,000 of the inherent gain in Whiteacre ($110,000 value and purchase price - $20,000 basis). If Invest only pays $90,000 for Whiteacre, Invest recognizes $10,000 gain for the $10,000 proceeds that were not reinvested and has a $10,000 exchanged basis in Whiteacre, which is appropriate because Invest still has a $80,000 unrecognized gain in Whiteacre ($90,000 value and purchase price - $10,000 basis. This is, of course, appropriate because it preserves the remaining inherent gain from Blackacre after the $10,000 gain was recognized for the unreinvested proceeds. Section 2.05 *Proceeds*, deals with determining the amounts related to involuntary conversions that that can be rolled over and the effect of liabilities on determining those amounts.

§ 2.01. Involuntary

I.R.C. § 1033(a) to (d) and (h),Treas. Reg. §§ 1.1033(a)-1 to 3 and 1.1033(b)-1.

One of the principal forms of involuntary conversion is destruction or damage to property as a result of a casualty. The following case interprets the casualty requirement liberally, even though the type of casualty involved was a common and expectable event in the taxpayer's business operations.

WILLAMETTE INDUSTRIES, INC. v. COMMISSIONER

United States Tax Court
118 T.C. 126 (2002)

GERBER, JUDGE: The parties filed cross-motions for partial summary judgment. The controversy concerns whether petitioner is entitled to defer gain resulting from the salvage (processing and sale) of damaged trees under section 1033. The parties have agreed on the salient facts. . . .

* * *

. . . Petitioner operates a vertically integrated forest products manufacturing business, which includes the ownership and processing of trees (raw materials) at various types of manufacturing plants, including lumber mills, plywood plants, and paper mills. The raw materials used in the manufacturing process are derived from petitioner's trees and from trees grown by others. Approximately 40 percent of petitioner's timber needs is acquired from petitioner's timberland, which comprises 1,253,000 acres of forested land.

Petitioner suffered damage to some of its standing trees during each of the years in issue, 1992-95. The damage was caused by wind, ice storms, wildfires, or insect infestations. The damage left part of petitioner's damaged trees standing and part of them fallen. The intended use of the trees was continued growth and cultivation until maturity, at which time the trees would have been systematically and efficiently harvested. The damage occurred prior to the intended time for harvest.

Petitioner salvaged its damaged trees to avoid further loss (from decay, insects, etc.) by means of the following steps: (1) Taking down damaged trees that remained standing; (2) cutting damaged trees into standard length logs; (3) stripping the branches from the logs; (4) dragging the logs to a pickup point; (5) grading and sorting the logs; (6) stacking the logs at a landing point; and (7) loading the logs onto trucks for further use or processing.

Petitioner chose to take the seven steps described in the preceding paragraph, rather than attempting to sell the damaged trees in place to a third party. Once it performed the seven steps, its options were to (1) attempt to sell the partially processed damaged trees to a third party; or (2) complete the processing of the damaged trees in its own plants in the ordinary course of its business. Petitioner chose the latter and completed the processing itself.

Petitioner relies on section 1033 for involuntary conversion treatment (deferral of gain). Petitioner did not realize income from harvesting and processing the damaged trees until it sold the products it manufactured from the damaged trees. Petitioner is seeking to defer only that portion of the gain attributable to the difference between its basis and the fair market value of the damaged trees as of the time its salvage of them began; that is, the value petitioner contends would have been recognized if it had sold the damaged trees on the open market instead of further processing and/or milling the damaged trees into finished products. Petitioner further contends that it is not attempting to defer any portion of the gain attributable to the processing, milling, or finishing of products.[5] Respondent determined that petitioner understated income by improperly deferring gain from the sale of the end product of the damaged trees, as follows: 1992–$647,953; 1993–$2,276,282; 1994–$3,592,035; and 1995–$4,831,462.

* * *

The specific question we consider is whether petitioner is disqualified from electing deferral of gain under section 1033 because it processed damaged trees into end or finished products rather than being compelled simply to sell the damaged trees.[6]

Respondent contends that under section 1033 the realization of gain must stem directly or solely from the damage and the involuntary conversion. More particularly, respondent asserts that petitioner's conversion was not "involuntary" because damaged trees were processed into end products in the ordinary course of its business. Respondent points out that section 1033 is a relief provision which does not or should not include petitioner's situation; i.e., where the damaged trees are processed in the same manner as undamaged trees. Finally, respondent contends that section 1033 was not intended for the long-term deferral of profits from petitioner's timber processing and manufacturing business.[7]

Petitioner argues that its factual situation complies literally with the requirements of section 1033 allowing deferral of gain realized from salvaging its damaged trees. Specifically, petitioner contends that it was compelled (in order to avoid further damage or loss) to salvage (process) the damaged trees resulting in an involuntary conversion within the meaning of section 1033. Petitioner also points out that the conversion was "involuntary" because the damaged trees were not scheduled for harvest at the time of the damage. In response to respondent's argument, petitioner contends that its choices for salvaging the damaged trees

---

[5] Based on a hypothetical example presented by petitioner, the majority of the gain deferred would appear to be attributable to the difference between the fair market value of the damaged trees and petitioner's basis. Petitioner posed a hypothetical example which included the premises that the damaged trees had a $100 basis and a $475 selling price if sold in place. If the damaged trees were processed into logs, the processing cost would be $25 resulting in a $500 selling price. Petitioner further posits that the cost of milling timber is $100 and that a finished product would have a $610 selling price, resulting in $10 of gain from milling. Petitioner argues that, under this hypothetical, respondent would have allowed a deferral of the $375 gain if petitioner had sold the damaged trees in place. Petitioner contends that respondent has denied any deferral whatsoever, even though the milling of timber into a final product adds only $10 of additional gain in the context of petitioner's hypothetical. We consider here only whether petitioner is entitled to use sec. 1033. The parties have left to another day the question of the amount of gain to be deferred if petitioner's motion for partial summary judgment is granted. . ..

[6] The parties have isolated this issue from other unresolved issues, including petitioner's substantiation of the quantity and value of the damaged trees; the amount of gain realized from sale of damaged trees; the amount of gain that may be deferred; and the determination of the correct year(s) for deferring the gain.

[7] Respondent's contention appears to address the possibility that petitioner reinvested the proceeds (and deferred gains) from the sale of the damaged trees in replacement property in the form of relatively young trees, thereby resulting in lengthy deferral of the subject gains. Respondent's contention, however, is more properly directed at the question of whether petitioner reinvested the proceeds in qualified replacement property, a question which is not at issue in the cross-motions for partial summary judgment.

should not preclude deferral of the portion of the gain that it was compelled to realize on account of the damage to its trees. Petitioner emphasizes that it is not attempting to defer gain from processing and/or milling the damaged trees. Petitioner seeks to defer only that portion of the gain attributable to the difference between its basis in the damaged trees and their fair market value at the time the process of salvaging the trees began.

Section 1033 provides, under certain prescribed circumstances, for relief from taxpayer's gains realized from involuntary conversion of property. The relief provided for under section 1033 is deferral of the gain from involuntary conversion, so long as the proceeds are used to acquire qualified replacement property.

The purpose of section 1033 was described, as follows:

> The purpose of the statute is to relieve the taxpayer of unanticipated tax liability arising from involuntary * * * [conversion] of his property, by freeing him from such liability to the extent that he re-establishes his prior commitment of capital within the period provided by the statute. The statute is to be liberally construed to accomplish this purpose. On the other hand, it was not intended to confer a gratuitous benefit upon the taxpayer by permitting him to utilize the involuntary interruption in the continuity of his investment to alter the nature of that investment tax free. * * *

Filippini v. United States, 318 F.2d 841, 844 (9th Cir. 1963).

* * *

From that limited legislative history, it can be gleaned that Congress intended relief from involuntary conversions only to the extent of the "proceeds of such conversion", and expected taxpayers to acquire replacement property within a reasonable time. Obviously, relief was intended only where the conversion was involuntary. Although Congress was concerned about the timeliness and "good faith" of efforts in seeking replacement property, there was no explanation or particular focus upon the use of damaged assets in the taxpayer's business.

Where the complete destruction or loss of property has occurred, there has been only a limited amount of litigation about whether a taxpayer should be allowed to defer the attendant gain. Where the destruction or loss to property is partial, however, additional questions have arisen.

In *C.G. Willis, Inc. v. Commissioner*, 41 T.C. 468 (1964), *aff'd.* 342 F.2d 996 (3d Cir. 1965), the taxpayer's ship was damaged in a 1957 collision, and the insurance company paid $100,000 to the taxpayer. The insurance payment was approximately $9,000 less than the taxpayer's basis in the ship, and, accordingly, no gain was realized for 1957. In 1958, however, the taxpayer sold the damaged, but unrepaired, ship for an amount which exceeded the remaining basis by approximately $86,000. Under those circumstances, it was held that the 1958 sale was not an "involuntary conversion" within the meaning of section 1033 so that the gain had to be recognized and could not be deferred. In so holding, it was explained that the damage to the taxpayer's ship was insufficient to compel the taxpayer to sell and, accordingly, the sale was not involuntary. . . . In that setting, "involuntary conversion" under section 1033 was defined to mean "that the taxpayer's property, through some outside force or agency beyond his control, is no longer useful or available to him for his purposes." . . . *[S]ee also Wheeler v. Commissioner*, 58 T.C. 459, 462-463 (1972) (where it was held that the taxpayer's choice to destroy his building was not an involuntary conversion).

In *S. H. Kress & Co. v. Commissioner*, 40 T.C. 142, 153 (1963), we held that condemnation of the taxpayer's property was imminent and unavoidable, and that the only realistic alternatives were to either await condemnation or to sell to an appropriate buyer. We found that those circumstances met the "compulsorily or involuntarily converted" requirement of section 1033, (citing *Masser v. Commissioner*, 30 T.C. 741 (1958)). Accordingly, even though a taxpayer has choices or alternatives a disposition may be deemed involuntary so that section 1033 relief remains available.

Masser v. Commissioner, supra, involved . . . (. . . [a] predecessor of section 1033). In *Masser*, the taxpayer operated an interstate trucking business from two proximately positioned pieces of business realty that were used as part of a single economic unit. One of the properties was subject to imminent condemnation, but the taxpayer sold both parcels. In that circumstance, we held that both pieces of realty were involuntarily converted and the gain from both could be deferred.

Those cases reveal two general elements as being necessary to qualify for deferral of gain under section 1033. First, a taxpayer's property must be involuntarily damaged, and second the property must no longer be available for the taxpayer's intended business purposes for the property.

The Commissioner issued a revenue ruling that specifically focused on whether gain from the sale of trees damaged by a hurricane qualified under section 1033. In that ruling it was held that the gain on sale of uprooted trees was "voluntary" and, in addition, that there was no direct conversion into money in the circumstances expressed in the ruling. *See* Rev. Rul. 72-372, 1972-2 C.B. 471. The principal rationale for the holding of Rev. Rul. 72- 372, *supra*, was that the hurricane did not cause the conversion of the trees into cash or other property directly resulting in gain from the damage.

In a second ruling, however, the 1972 ruling was revoked. See Rev. Rul. 80-175, 1980-2 C.B. 230. The 1980 ruling permitted deferral of gain from the sale of damaged trees. The factual predicate for both rulings was as follows:

> the taxpayer was the owner of timberland. As a result of a hurricane, a considerable number of trees were uprooted. The timber was not insured, and once downed, was subject to decay or being rendered totally worthless by insects within a relatively short period of time. The taxpayer was, however, able to sell the damaged timber and realized a gain from such sale. The proceeds of the sale were used to purchase other standing timber.

The rationale articulated in Rev. Rul. 80-175, *supra*, is that gain is "postponed on the theory that the taxpayer was compelled to dispose of property and had no economic choice in the matter" and that the taxpayer "was compelled by the destruction of the timber to sell it for whatever the taxpayer could or suffer a total loss." . . . . Accordingly, the taxpayer in the 1980 ruling was found to have met the two part test; i.e., that the damage was involuntary and the timber was no longer available for the taxpayer's intended business purpose. Most significantly, the 1980 ruling eliminated the requirement that the damage-causing event convert the property directly into cash or other property.

The 1980 ruling also contained a comparison with the holding in *C.G. Willis, Inc. v. Commissioner, supra*, as follows:

> In the present case, the downed timber was not repairable and was generally no longer useful to the taxpayer in the context of its original objective. The destruction caused by the hurricane forced the taxpayer to sell the downed timber for whatever price it could get. Unlike the situation in *Willis*, the sale of the downed timber was dictated by the damage caused by the hurricane. . . .

The taxpayer in the 1980 ruling apparently intended to grow trees and/or hold timberland for sale at a particular maturity. The hurricane caused the taxpayer to involuntarily sell/use the trees prior to the time intended for harvest or sale. The taxpayer's intended purpose or use was only affected as to timing, and the sale was prior to the time the taxpayer intended to sell or harvest.

Returning to the disagreement here, petitioner contends that, at the time of the damage, it did not intend to harvest the damaged trees, so that the conversion was involuntary and within the meaning of the statute. Petitioner argues that a taxpayer may not have a choice as to whether to dispose of damaged property, but a taxpayer may have a choice as to how to dispose of damaged property.

Respondent contends that petitioner should not be entitled to such deferral because of its choice to further process the trees into logs or finished products, its original intention. Respondent's position in this case is a reversion to the requirement of the 1972 ruling that the sale (conversion to cash) be the direct result of the damage-causing event. For more than 21 years, the Commissioner's ruling position has permitted section 1033 deferral even though the conversion is not directly into cash.

Petitioner in this case is effectively no different from the taxpayer in the 1980 ruling. Petitioner's conversion was involuntary, and petitioner was forced to act or suffer complete loss of the damaged trees. Section 1033 could be interpreted to permit either a direct or an indirect conversion. The case law permits indirect conversion, but the Commissioner's 1972 ruling denied relief because the trees damaged by the hurricane were sold by the taxpayer. The Commissioner, in revoking the 1972 ruling has permitted, since 1980, section 1033 relief where there is a sale (a voluntary act) of the damaged property. Respondent has denied relief here because petitioner processed rather than sold the damaged trees.

The critical factor is that petitioner was compelled to harvest the damaged trees prior to the time it had intended. The possibility that the partial damage to petitioner's trees might have been relatively small or resulted in a nominal amount of reduction in gain is not a reason to deny relief. In addition, if petitioner's salvage efforts were more successful than other taxpayers that is not a reason for denial of relief under section 1033.

Petitioner's circumstances fulfill the statutory purpose and intent. There was unanticipated tax liability due to various casualties that damaged the trees. Petitioner seeks to defer the gain that was occasioned by the damage and which it had reinvested in like property. Petitioner had not planned to harvest the damaged trees. Identical to the taxpayer's situation in the 1980 ruling, petitioner's trees were damaged by forces without its control, and petitioner was compelled to salvage its damaged trees prior to the intended date for harvest, sale, and/or processing into end products. Unlike the taxpayer in *C.G. Willis v. Commissioner, supra*, petitioner was forced to salvage (process or sell) the damaged trees or suffer a total loss.

Respondent's attempt to distinguish petitioner's situation from the ruling does not reconcile with the rationale of the 1980 ruling, the underlying statute, and case law. The taxpayer in the ruling and petitioner were both forced to salvage the damaged trees or suffer the imminent and total loss of the damaged trees. The taxpayer in the ruling and petitioner were prematurely forced to salvage (sell or use) the damaged trees. The damaged trees were used in their businesses, but not in the same manner as they would normally have done. In the 1980 ruling, the taxpayer was forced to sell the trees under unintended business conditions. Likewise, petitioner was forced to use the damaged trees, albeit in its manufacturing process, under unintended business conditions; i.e. before maturity and/or before the time at which the trees would normally be ready for efficient harvest.

Respondent also argues that petitioner is not entitled to defer gain because "there were no actual sales of damaged timber." Respondent argues that section 1033 requires a sale or conversion of the damaged property into money or property similar in use to the damaged property. Section 1033 simply requires that property be involuntarily converted into money or property. There is no requirement, as argued by respondent, that the deferred gain be derived in a particular manner; *i.e.*, only from a distress sale. Based on the holding of Rev. Rul. 80-175, 1980-2 C.B. 230, it is unlikely that respondent would have questioned the deferral of gain if petitioner had been forced to sell the damaged trees in place.

Finally, respondent contends that section 1033 was intended to provide relief for taxpayers who experience "destruction [of property] in whole or in part". Although respondent agrees that petitioner had a casualty, damage to the trees, and petitioner was compelled to salvage them, respondent infers that petitioner's situation is somehow not directly affected by the destruction. Respondent contends that petitioner's gain is voluntary or not caused by the damage because petitioner is able to process the logs into finished products.

Admittedly, petitioner's circumstances may appear more favorable than might have been expected after a "casualty", but the statute does not have a quantitative threshold. Petitioner is not seeking a windfall in the form of the deferral of gain from processing and/or making the finished products. Nor is petitioner attempting to "utilize the involuntary interruption in the continuity of his investment to alter the nature of that investment tax free." *Filippini v. United States*, 318 F.2d at 844. Petitioner is seeking to defer the unexpected gain that resided in trees that it had not, at the time of the damage, intended to harvest and to reinvest that gain in trees that will fulfill petitioner's intended purpose. Such deferral was the intended purpose for the enactment of section 1033.

* * *

Respondent would have this Court impose its own judgment as to which taxpayer deserves relief. So, for example, if a taxpayer, like the one in the 1980 ruling, was growing trees for eventual sale, relief is available even though the taxpayer sells the damaged trees to its usual customers. Under respondent's suggested approach, petitioner would not be entitled to relief because it had choices other than sale; i.e., to further process the damaged trees. Petitioner, under respondent's approach, would be deprived of relief from involuntarily generated gain merely because of happenstance. Under that type of reasoning, petitioner would be denied relief merely because it was a grower of trees and also a manufacturer of products using trees, whereas a similarly situated grower of trees without the ability to use the damaged trees to make products would be entitled to relief, even though its damaged trees might ultimately be manufactured into products by others. The line respondent asks us to draw would be illusive and a matter of conjecture.

Petitioner was growing its trees for harvest when they reached a certain maturity. The damage occurred outside of petitioner's control and forced petitioner to salvage its trees earlier than intended. That situation is indistinguishable from the circumstances set forth in Rev. Rul. 80-175, 1980-2 C.B. 230, where the taxpayer's trees were felled by a hurricane. The fact that the damage was sufficiently partial so as to result in a substantial amount of deferral is not a reason, under the statute, to deny relief.

* * *

NOTES AND COMMENTS

In view of the Service's position articulated in Rev. Rul. 80-175, it is difficult to see why the Service was contesting the taxpayer's position in *Willamette Industries*, or, at the very least, why it did so claiming that the conversion was not "involuntary." As a substantive matter, the Service obviously, and possibly justifiably, was concerned that Willamette essentially made the same profit on the lumber from the downed trees that it would have made from trees harvested in the ordinary course of business. On the other hand, the same is true of any involuntarily converted property. Although the authors know little about the economics of lumber production, the relative values in footnote 5, of the downed trees, the milling seems to ascribe too little value to the manufacturing operation and may indicate that Willamette is reaching in determining the portion of the value of the finished products attributable to the downed trees. On the other hand, the relative amounts may indicate that raising trees is a highly profitable business, because, as is the case for farmers' expenditures, many costs of tree cultivation are currently deductible, not capitalized. Although footnote 5 indicated that there would be a subsequent valuation proceeding, no report of the result of such a proceeding has been located. Nevertheless, as the Service implicitly conceded, there is little doubt that the trees were destroyed in part. It is also clear from the case, however, that such destruction of a substantial number of trees is a regular occurrence for a forest products company.

In the absence of actual or threatened condemnation, as discussed below, it is not enough that the disposition be involuntary; the disposition must also be a result of destruction, in whole or part, or theft. Thus, in *Wheeler v. Commissioner*, 58 T.C. 459 (1972), destruction of the building to make way for new improvements to be constructed by a third party who defaulted, did not qualify damages as an involuntary conversion, because the destruction was voluntary. Similarly, in Rev. Rul. 82-74, 1982-1 C.B. 110, a building destroyed by arsonist hired by the taxpayer was held not to be involuntarily converted into the cash insurance proceeds — apparently before the taxpayer's role in the fire was discovered. Other, less extreme elements of voluntariness can prevent qualification. Rev. Rul. 78-377, 1978-2 C.B. 208, held that § 1033 did not apply to the proceeds from the sale of portion of a shopping center that was still usable when the rest was partially destroyed by fire; only the insurance proceeds qualify under § 1033 to the extent reinvested in qualifying property. Similarly, Rev. Rul. 74-532, 1974-2 C.B. 270, § 1033 was held not to apply to the sale of rental property after repeated vandalism; because the sale was voluntary, not involuntary. The ruling follows Rev. Rul. 72-372 and *C.G. Willis, Inc.* both cited in *Willamette*. On the other hand, the ruling may be questionable in light of *Willamette* and Rev. Rul. 80-175. *See also* Priv. Ltr. Rul. 2004-08-027 (sale pursuant to FTC order as condition of FTC consent to merger of foreign parent with another foreign corporation is not an involuntary conversion).

Section 1033 contains a number of special rules for livestock sold as a result of disease, drought, and other weather conditions, including an expanded four-year replacement period. § 1033(d) and (e); Treas. Reg. §§ 1.1033(d)-1 and (e)-1. Section 1033(h) also provides special rules for property damaged in presidentially declared disaster areas, including automatic nonrecognition for insurance proceeds for unscheduled personal property, a four-year replacement period, more relaxed replacement standards, and special rules for principal residences. *See* Rev. Rul. 96-32, 1996-1 C.B. 177 (reinvestment of proceeds of insurance on house destroyed by disaster and of proceeds of subsequent sale of land qualifies for nonrecognition under § 1033; because, for a principal residence, house and land are a unitary property). In addition, another Code provision, § 139(g), provides exclusion from gross income for specified disaster mitigation payments, including payments for such disasters as 9/11 and the multiple hurricanes suffered by Florida in 2004. Payments for sale or disposition of property are not included. § 139(g)(3). Although excluded amounts do not need to be reinvested, they do not provide basis for property acquired as a result of reinvestment. § 139(g)(3).

For purposes of § 1033, an involuntary conversion also includes sales resulting from the condemnation of property as well as sales that occur under a threat of condemnation. In such situations, the standard of involuntariness is more relaxed. The threat does not require that condemnation be imminent, or even that any formal condemnation process be started. Thus in *S. & B. Realty Co. v. Commissioner*, 54 T.C. 863 (1970), a sale to a third party of property in an urban development district qualifies, even though the taxpayer had the option of retaining the property if he made repairs and improvements as determined by the development district. In addition, the condemnation does not have to be imminent, nor does the sale have to be made to the condemning authority. See Rev. Rul. 69-303, 1969-1 C.B. 201, *clarified by* Rev. Rul. 81-180, 1981-2 C.B. 161, a sale of property by a nonprofit organization cooperating with public agency, or even if to someone else, qualified for nonrecognition under § 1033, even when the owner notified property would be condemned only when funds became available). Emphasizing the permissible informality of the threat, Rev. Rul. 63-221, 1963-2 C.B. 332, held that there was a threat when the owner obtained information about the proposed condemnation from a newspaper article confirmed by a public official, with no official notice. The subsequent sale by a purchaser who buys knowing of the threat also qualifies, even though the purchaser knew that the property would be condemned, so that, in effect, the purpose of the purchase was to conduct the condemnation proceedings. Rev. Rul. 81-181, 1981-2 C.B. 162. The effect of this rule is that a taxpayer holding property under threat of condemnation who wants to avoid the risks and hassles of dealing with the condemnation process can sell the property and take advantage of § 1033 to a third party who seeks to profit from the risks of the condemnation process. On the other hand, not every government requirement is a condemnation. *Dorothy C. Thorpe Glass Mfg. Corp. v. Commissioner*, 51 T.C. 300 (1968), held that sale of a parcel of real estate required by the SBA as a condition of a loan to construct new facilities, was not involuntary conversion, even though SBA is government agency, loan requirements are not condemnation).

Not all acquisitions of property by the government constitute condemnations or the threat of condemnation. For example, the sale of property to a governmental unit to obtain favorable zoning or other benefits does not qualify as a condemnation. Thus, Rev. Rul. 69-654, 1969-2 C.B. 162, held that setting aside land to be sold as a school site as a condition of zoning approval for subdivision was not an involuntary conversion or condemnation, even though the agreement provided that the price would be fixed by condemnation if there was no agreement on the sale of the site.

PROBLEM FOR DISCUSSION

Problem 5-13. Owner's vacation house was severely damaged by a hurricane that was a presidentially declared disaster. Instead of rebuilding, Owner sold the vacation house, which had a basis of $50,000, and a pre-hurricane value of $500,000, but which was worth no more than $150,000 in its damaged state, plus the right to the insurance proceeds (the amount of which had not been determined) to Spec for $400,000. (i) Does the $400,000 qualify as an amount received by Spec as a result of an involuntary conversion under § 1033? (ii) If Spec collects $500,000 from the insurance company, does that qualify under § 1033? *See Willamette Industries* (timber knocked down by the wind); *Wheeler* (destruction of building to make way for new improvements to be constructed by a third party not involuntary conversion); *S & B Realty* (sale to third party of property in urban development district qualifies even though had option of retaining property); *Dorothy C. Thorpe Glass* (sale of a parcel of real estate required by the SBA as a condition of loan to construct new facilities not involuntary conversion); *C.G. Willis* (sale of damaged ship after insurance recovery less than basis not involuntary conversion); *S. H. Kress* (sale prior to imminent condemnation is involuntary conversion); *Masser* (sale of remaining parcel that was part of economic unit with condemned parcel is involuntary conversion); Rev. Rul. 82-74 (building destroyed by arsonist hired by owner not involuntarily converted into cash insurance proceeds); Rev. Rul. 81-181 (sale by a purchaser who buys knowing of condemnation threat is involuntary conversion); Rev. Rul. 80-175 (sale of damaged timber downed by hurricane qualifies); Rev. Rul. 78-377 (sale of a shopping center partially destroyed by fire when remainder usable, and destroyed part repairable is not involuntary conversion except for insurance proceeds); Rev. Rul. 74-532 (sale of rental property after repeated vandalism not involuntary conversion); Rev. Rul. 72-372 (sale of timber downed by hurricane not involuntary conversion; revoked by Rev. Rul. 80-175); Rev. Rul. 69-654 (setting aside land to be sold as a school site as a condition of zoning approval for subdivision was not involuntary conversion); Rev. Rul. 69-603, *clarified by* Rev. Rul. 81-180 (under threat where notified property would be condemned when funds available); Rev. Rul. 63-221 (threat if obtains information from public official or newspaper confirmed by public official).

§ 2.02. Similar in Service or Use

I.R.C. § 1033(a); Treas. Reg. §§ 1.1033(a)-1(a) and (2)(b)(9).

The basic test under § 1033(a) for replacement property is that it be "similar or related in service or use" to the involuntarily converted property. §§ 1033(a)(1) and § 1033(a)(2)(A). Fractional interests that satisfy the requirements of Rev. Proc. 2002-22 described in the *Notes and Comments* in § 1.06 *Like Kind* should qualify as replacement property for other property and vice versa. This is a functional use test that is quite different from the like-kind standard of § 1031, and is sometimes narrower and sometimes broader in its application. The Code and regulations do not define what the phrase "similar or related in service or use" means, although the regulations provide three cryptic examples of situations that do *not* qualify: (i) the proceeds of unimproved real estate acquired through condemnation invested in improved real estate, (ii) the proceeds of a conversion of real estate used to reduce the indebtedness incurred on a previously purchased leasehold; and (iii) the proceeds of requisitioned tugs used to purchase barges, each of which seems narrower than the like-kind standard. Treas. Reg. § 1.1033(a)-2(c)(9). On the other hand, as illustrated by the following ruling, improvements on land already owned, which are not like kind, may qualify.

Rev. Rul. 67-254, 1967-2 C.B. 269

* * *

A State condemned a portion of the land upon which the taxpayer's manufacturing plant was situated. The condemned portion had been used as a storage area for the taxpayer's product and also contained thereon a garage which housed the plant's delivery trucks. The taxpayer received an award for the condemned property, none of which was compensation for damages to the portion of the property which he retained.

Because of the prohibitive cost of acquiring land in the area suitable for storage, the taxpayer used part of the proceeds of the condemnation award in the year of its receipt to rearrange the layout of his plant facilities on the remainder of his land in order to create a new storage area. He used the remainder of the award to build a new garage (to house the plant's delivery trucks) on a small plot of land located nearby, which he had owned for several years.

Section 1033(a)[(2)](A) of the Code provides, in effect, that if property is compulsorily or involuntarily converted into money and the taxpayer, during the period specified, purchases other property similar or related in service or use to the property so converted, at the election of the taxpayer the gain shall be recognized only to the extent that the amount realized upon such conversion exceeds the cost of such other property.

Accordingly, based on these facts, to the extent that the taxpayer expended the condemnation proceeds in restoring the plant site so that it could be used in the same manner as it was used prior to the condemnation, he has acquired property similar or related in service or use to the property converted for purposes of section 1033(a)[(2)](A) of the Code. Whether all of the expenditures made by the taxpayer were necessary to restore the plant site to its original usefulness is a question of fact to be determined upon examination of his income tax return for the year in which the transaction occurred.

In addition, the garage erected on land already owned qualifies under section 1033(a)(3)(A) of the Code as property similar or related in service or use to the garage that was condemned.

NOTES AND COMMENTS

The similar-in-service-or-use test for the owner-user is a functional or end-use test — the character of the replacement property does not matter as long as it is devoted to the same business use. Accordingly, Rev. Rul. 83-70, 1983-1 C.B. 189, held that use of proceeds from condemnation of an office building and warehouses by the lessee under a net lease with a remaining term of 15 years to acquire a fee in land improved with a warehouse and an office building to be used by the taxpayer in the same business satisfied the functional use test, even though it did not satisfy the like-kind test, because the remaining term of the lease was less than 30 years. The functional use test has, however, been narrowly applied by the Service. For example, *McCaffrey v. Commissioner*, 275 F.2d 27 (3d Cir. 1960), held that a leased warehouse was not similar to a condemned leased parking lot; but this decision was before Rev. Rul. 64-237, discussed in § 2.03 *Investor-Lessor*). Similarly, Rev. Rul. 76-390, 1976-2 C.B. 243, held that a motel on land already owned that was constructed with the proceeds of a condemned mobile home park did not satisfy the similar use test, and in Rev. Rul. 76-319, 1976-2 C.B. 242, held that billiard center was not similar to bowling center destroyed by fire. *See also* Tech. Adv. Mem. 83-07-007 (shopping center on site of a former drive-in theater is not similar to condemned unimproved land intended for a drive-in theater because the condemned land had no established use).

The special rules for presidentially declared disasters treat any reinvestment of insurance proceeds of property held for business or investment in any tangible property so held as similar in service or use and treat any insurance proceeds on a personal residence or its contents as a single pool with any reinvestment in property similar in service or use to the residence or contents qualifying without regard to replacing specific items. *See* Rev. Rul. 95-22, 1995-1 C.B. 145 (aggregates the proceeds of insurance, including amounts received for the loss of the dwelling, unscheduled household goods, scheduled jewelry and scheduled silverware, so that the taxpayer has no taxable gain as long as an amount equal to the aggregate amounts received for the dwelling, jewelry and silverware is spent on qualified property, even if, for example, the jewelry and silver are not replaced). Similarly, when livestock is involuntarily converted as a result of drought or other weather conditions (but apparently not disease), the replacement farm property is treated as similar in service or use if replacement with livestock is not feasible; and if livestock is involuntarily converted as a result of soil or other environmental contamination, real property can be included. § 1033(f).

PROBLEM FOR DISCUSSION

Problem 5-14. Uze operated a drive-in theater on land that, luckily for him (because television had severely cut into the drive-in movie business) stood in the way of a road expansion project. He used the proceeds to acquire a closed drive-in theater on a 25-year leasehold, tear down the screen, and construct a movie theater. Does the replacement qualify as similar in service or use? *See* Rev. Rul. 67-254, (new storage and garage on land already owned); Rev. Rul. 83-70 (15-year leasehold v. fee); *McCaffrey* (leased warehouse v. leased parking lot); Rev. Rul. 76-390 (motel v. mobile home park); Rev. Rul. 76-319 (billiard center v. bowling center); Priv. Ltr. Rul. 96-19-028 (leveling and filing already owned unimproved land v. unimproved land held for investment); Tech. Adv. Mem. 83-07-007 (shopping center v. condemned unimproved land intended for a drive-in theater).

§ 2.03. Investor-Lessor

Although the Service originally made no distinction between owner-users and investor-lessors in applying the similar-in-service-or-use test under § 1033, it modified its position after a number of court defeats. The following ruling sets out the test for investor-lessors.

Rev. Rul. 64-237, 1964-2 C.B. 319

The Internal Revenue Service has reconsidered its position with respect to replacement property that is "similar or related in service or use" to involuntarily converted property within the meaning of section 112(f) of the Internal Revenue Code of 1939 and section 1033(a) of the Internal Revenue Code of 1954 in light of the decision of the United States Court of Appeals for the Second Circuit in the case of *Liant Record, Inc. v. Commissioner*, 303 Fed (2d) 326 (1962) and other appellate court decisions.

In previous litigation, the Service has taken the position that the statutory phrase, "similar or related in service or use," means that the property acquired must have a close "functional" similarity to the property converted. Under this test, property was not considered similar or related in service or use to the converted property unless the physical characteristics and end uses of the converted and replacement properties were closely similar. Although this "functional use test" has been upheld in the lower courts, it has not been sustained in the appellate courts with respect to investors in property, such as lessors.

In conformity with the appellate court decisions, in considering whether replacement property acquired by an investor is similar in service or use to the converted property, attention will be directed primarily to the similarity in the relationship of the services or uses which the original and replacement properties have to the taxpayer-owner. In applying this test, a determination will be made as to whether the properties are of a similar service to the taxpayer, the nature of the business risks connected with the properties, and what such properties demand of the taxpayer in the way of management, services and relations to his tenants.

For example, where the taxpayer is a lessor, who rented out the converted property for a light manufacturing plant and then rents out the replacement property for a wholesale grocery warehouse, the nature of the taxpayer-owner's service or use of the properties may be similar although that of the end users change. The two properties will be considered as similar or related in service or use where, for example, both are rented and where there is a similarity in the extent and type of the taxpayer's management activities, the amount and kind of services rendered by him to his tenants, and the nature of his business risks connected with the properties.

In modifying its position with respect to the involuntary conversion of property held for investment, the Service will continue to adhere to the functional test in the case of owner-users of property. Thus, if the taxpayer-owner operates a light manufacturing plant on the converted property and then operates a wholesale grocery warehouse on the replacement property, by changing his end use, he has so changed the nature of his relationship to the property as to be outside the nonrecognition of gain provisions.

NOTES AND COMMENTS

The similar-in-service-or-use test in the context of investors-lessors allows the gain on the disposition of the involuntarily converted property to qualify for nonrecognition treatment even though the replacement property may differ substantially in end use from the involuntarily converted property. In a fairly extreme case, *Davis v. United States*, 589 F.2d 446 (9th Cir. 1979), held that improvements in an industrial park leased to manufacturers, fabricators, equipment dealers, and warehouses is similar in use, under the investor-lessor test, to condemned land leased for agricultural use and a sea fishery, because risks and management were similar. Similarly, Rev. Rul. 80-184, 1980-2 C.B. 232, found a newly constructed rental warehouse on the remainder of land partly condemned and the purchase of additional land and construction of rental office building, all to replace land and building rented for retail stores, satisfied the similar-in-service-or-use test for the investor-lessor where unspecified risks and responsibilities remained the same; and Rev. Rul. 71-141, 1971-1 C.B. 211 held that a constructed rental gas station on land already owned is similar to condemned rental warehouse for a taxpayer who was investor-lessor in both.

It is not enough, however, that both properties be leased, if the investor-lessor's responsibilities under the leases are materially different. Thus, in Rev. Rul. 76-391, 1976-2 C.B. 243, an office building net leased to tenants, where the lessor was responsible for the parking lot and interior improvements to suit tenants, was not similar in service or use to unimproved farm land leased to tenant farmers, apparently based on different unspecified lessor responsibilities. Under the same approach, Priv. Ltr. Rul. 97-23-032 held that an owner-managed motel operation is not similar to owner-managed leased apartment building destroyed by fire, because the day-to-day responsibilities of operating a motel are significantly greater than those of finding tenants, maintaining grounds, overseeing repairs, and collecting rents.

Moreover, under Rev. Rul. 64-237, leasing becomes the functional use; it is not an additional or alternate way to qualify for nonrecognition. Accordingly, Rev. Rul. 79-261, 1979-2 C.B. 295, held than an office building is not similar to a leased office building destroyed by tornado to the extent that the replacement office building is used by the owner-lessor in its own banking business. Along the same lines, Rev. Rul. 70-466, 1970-2 C.B. 165, determined that a personal residence used by the owner is not similar to a residence rented to others; and Rev. Rul. 70-399, 1970-2 C.B. 164, held that a resort hotel operated by the taxpayer is not similar to net leased resort hotel operated by a tenant that had been destroyed by fire. According to the Service, unimproved land, although held for investment, has no established use, so that it cannot be replaced by improved land, even if held for investment, under the similar-in-service-or-use test. Applying this approach, Priv. Ltr. Rul. 96-19-028 held leveling and filling already owned unimproved land is not similar to condemned unimproved land held for investment, because leveling and filling changes the status of improved land, apparently even if improved land is held for investment, citing Treas. Reg. § 1.1033(a)-2(c)(9). *Cf.* Tech. Adv. Mem. 83-07-007 (shopping center on site of a former drive-in theater is not similar to condemned unimproved land intended for a drive-in theater because the condemned land had no established use).

PROBLEM FOR DISCUSSION

Problem 5-15. Invest owned an apartment building managed by a real estate management company, as her agent, who was responsible for providing heat, water, unattended parking, repairs, trash removal, and the cleaning of public areas, that was condemned for an urban renewal project. She used the proceeds to acquire a factory building that was net-leased to the manufacturer on terms that qualify as a bona fide lease for tax purposes. Does the replacement qualify for nonrecognition under the investor-lessor standard? *See Davis* (improvements in industrial park leased to users v. land leased for agricultural use and a sea fishery); *McCaffrey* (leased warehouse not similar to condemned leased parking lot; before Rev. Rul. 64-237); Rev. Rul. 80-184 (newly constructed rental warehouse and constructed rental office building on purchased land v. construction of rental warehouse v. rental office retail stores); Rev. Rul. 79-261 (leased office building v. partly leased, partly used office building); Rul. 76-391 (office building net leased to tenants v. unimproved farm land leased to tenant farmers); Rev. Rul. 71-41 (constructed rental gas station v. land and rental warehouse); Rev. Rul. 70-466 (residence rented to others v. owned/used residence); Rev. Rul. 70-399 (net leased resort hotel v. resort hotel operated by taxpayer); Rev. Rul. 64-237 (different kinds of rental real estate); Priv. Ltr. Rul. 97-23-032 (motel v. owner-managed leased apartment building).

§ 2.04. Like Kind Revisited

I.R.C. § 1033(g); Treas. Reg. § 1.1033-1(g)

As the preceding materials have demonstrated, the similar-in-service-or-use test is significantly different from the like-kind test of § 1031 — sometimes more restrictive and sometimes more lenient. Fractional interests that satisfy the requirements of Rev. Proc. 2002-22 described in the *Notes and Comments* in § 1.06 *Like Kind* should qualify as like kind for other real property and vice versa. Section 1031(g), however, allows use of the like-kind test, but only in connection with the condemnation of real property held for business or investment (including outdoor advertising displays if an election is made), and only if the property is not held primarily for sale. There is a true alternate test — a rollover under § 1033(a) is permitted if the reinvestment of such real property is either in similar-in service-or-use property or like-kind property as explained in the following ruling:

Rev. Rul. 67-255, 1967-2 C.B. 270

* * *

After 1957 land which the taxpayer held for investment was condemned. In the same year, the taxpayer expended the proceeds of the condemnation in the construction of an office building to be held for investment purposes on another site which he already owned.

The taxpayer also owned two separate tracts of unimproved rural land, one of which was condemned in a year after 1957. Immediately thereafter, the taxpayer invested the proceeds of the condemnation in the installation of storm drains, water systems, and roads on the remaining tract of rural land.

* * *

The effect of section 1033(g) of the Code is to extend the nonrecognition-of-gains benefits of section 1033(a) of the Code to a taxpayer who acquires property of a like kind to real property converted, but not necessarily similar or related in service or use to it.

In considering the "like kind" test, although the term "real estate" is often used to embrace land and improvements thereon, land and improvements are by nature not alike merely because one term is used to describe both. Land is not of the same nature or character as a building, or a storm drain, or a water system, or a road.

Applying the foregoing to the facts in the instant case, the building constructed on land already owned does not qualify as replacement property under section 1033(g) of the Code as being of a like kind to the land involuntarily converted. Nor do the storm drains, water systems and roads constructed on land already owned qualify as replacement property under section 1033(g) as being of a like kind to the land involuntarily converted. However, see Revenue Ruling 67-254 . . . for a situation where improvements constructed on land already owned qualify as replacement property under section 1033(a)(3)(A) of the Code.

Accordingly, the investment of the proceeds from an involuntary conversion of land held for investment purposes, in the construction of an office building to be held for investment purposes upon land already owned by the taxpayer, does not qualify as a "like kind" replacement of the converted property within the meaning of section 1033(g) of the Code.

Also, the investment of the proceeds from an involuntary conversion of unimproved rural land in the installation of storm drains, water systems and roads on other unimproved rural land already owned by the taxpayer, does not qualify as a "like kind" replacement of the converted property within the meaning of section 1033(g) of the Code.

* * *

NOTES AND COMMENTS

Rev. Rul. 67-255 holds that improvements constructed on land already owned is not like kind to land that was condemned, without referring to the broad definition of like kind in Treas. Reg. § 1.1031(a)-1(b), which states that the fact that land is improved or unimproved is not material to a like-kind determination. Thus, it seems to imply, without actually stating, that improvements alone are not like kind to unimproved land. It does not, however, address whether improvements can be like kind, in whole or part, to improved land, or even to improvements. Rev. Rul. 67-255 does, however, refer to Rev. Rul. 67-254, discussed in § 2.02 *Similar in Service or Use*, which indicates that improvements alone can be similar in service or use to improved land, thus reemphasizing that the similar-in-service-or-use test and the like-kind test are alternate, if overlapping, tests for nonrecognition under § 1033. Interestingly, Rev. Rul. 67-254, which was issued simultaneously, does not similarly refer to Rev. Rul. 67-255 and does not expressly state that replacement property constructed on the taxpayer's land is not like-kind to the condemned land, even though the replacement property would not be like kind under Rev. Rul. 67-255. One the other hand, the Service position, apparently, is that improvements constructed on land already owned is never like kind to condemned improved land, even though such improvements can be similar in service or use as illustrated by Rev. Rul. 67-254 and other authorities discussed in § 2.02 *Similar in Service or Use*. Rev. Rul. 71-41, discussed in *Notes and Comments* to § 2.03 *Investor-Lessor*, holding that constructed rental gas station on land already owned is similar in service or use to a condemned rental warehouse that qualifies for nonrecognition by a taxpayer who was an investor-lessor for both, even though that improvement was not like kind to land and improvements, but did not state the reason or why land improvements are not like kind to each other. Also interestingly, Rev. Rul. 71-41 does not refer to Rev. Rul. 67-255. G.C.M. 34284 which is apparently background to Rev. Rul. 71-41, which discussed, and rejected, a suggestion that Rev. Rul. 67-255 should be revoked. In doing so, G.C.M. 34284, addressed the relation between § 1031(a) and (g). It relied on G.C.M. 33256 (May 24, 1966), which is apparently the background to Rev. Rul. 67-255, and concluded that Rev. Rul. 67-255 should not be revoked, justifying this position on the ground that although land is unique, buildings are not. The G.C.M. determined that no allocation of the condemnation proceeds was necessary in Rev. Rul. 71-41, because the gas station was in its entirety (as opposed to only partially) a qualified replacement under section

1033(a), because it satisfied the test set forth in Rev. Rul. 64-237, discussed in § 2.03 *Investor-Lessor* and Rev. Rul. 67-254, § 2.02 *Similar in Service or Use*. It implied, but did not decide, that replacement of improvements with improvements might qualify as like kind, even if they did not satisfy the functional-use test. It noted that under the functional-use test there is no need to allocate proceeds of land and improvements when the reinvestment is in improvements that qualify, but there may be a need under the like kind test if part of the proceeds are invested in land and the balance is invested in improving already owned land. In *Asjes v. Commissioner*, 74 T.C. 1005 (1980), *acq. in result only*, the Tax Court rejected a Service position that the unallocated proceeds of condemnation of a nursery property that included improvements and growing plants (the growing costs of which had been deducted), did not have to be allocated, and that acquisition of replacement land with some improvements and some vegetation plus additional improvements qualified for nonrecognition under § 1033(g).

The Service position that improvements to land already owned do not satisfy the like-kind test was expressly stated in Rev. Rul. 76-390, 1976-2 C.B. 243 (a motel v. mobile home park); Priv. Ltr. Rul. 96-19-028 (leveling and filing already owned unimproved land v. unimproved land held for investment); and Tech. Adv. Mem. 83-07-007 (shopping center v. condemned unimproved land intended for a drive-in theater); all discussed in *Notes and Comments* in § 2.02 *Similar in Service or Use*, and Rev. Rul. 76-390, 1976-2 C.B. 243 (office building net leased to tenants v. unimproved farm land leased to tenant farmers), discussed in *Notes and Comments* in § 2.03 *Investor-Lessor*, all of which expressly held that the replacements were not like kind under § 1033(g). The other rulings discussed in those sections concluding that the replacement property did not qualify as similar in service or use did not discuss § 1033(g), presumably because they involved destruction rather than condemnation and § 1033(g) applies only to condemnations. On the other hand, acquisitions of additional interests in land may qualify improvements on that land for reinvestment under the like-kind test. Priv. Ltr. Rul. 96-20-010 held that purchase of the fee interest in property held under a lease for a term that was not specified, so that it is not clear whether the term was for more than 30 years, although Treas. Reg. § 1.1031(a)-1(c)(2) treating a lease of more than 30 years as equivalent to a fee was cited. Prior to the acquisition of the fee, the leased property was operated by the taxpayer as a shopping center. The cost of the fee and the much larger cost of the subsequent improvements to the shopping center after the acquisition qualified as replacement for proceeds from condemnation of a parcel on which an operation that was conceded not to be similar or related to a shopping center. The ruling does not address why improvements to newly acquired land qualify while those to already owned land do not. The ruling relies in part on Rev. Rul. 68-394, 1968-2 C.B. 338, which held that the purchase of 45-year leasehold on land already owned by the taxpayer that was used by the lessor as a mobile trailer park is like kind to condemned real estate held for investment. The ruling does not make it clear whether additional improvements were made after acquisition. Priv. Ltr. Rul. 81-19-029, held that the reinvestment of proceeds from the condemnation of land with a one-story retail building rented to separate retail stores to renovate a three-story building already owned by the taxpayer to be used for rental, in which the renovation is to provide better retail space on the first floors, and to provide rental office and professional facilities on the other two is not like kind to a condemned rented retail building, is another in this long line of authority. Although it repeats the litany that land and improvements are not alike, it does not explain why the improvements were not like kind to the improvements on the condemned land, and did not address the issue of apportioning part of the proceeds to the improvements on the condemned land that was discussed in G.C.M. 34284. In addition, although the caption refers to similar use, it did not explain why the reinvestment did not satisfy the similar-in-service-or-use test or the investor-lessor test. Accordingly, while it is clear that the Service position is that improvements to already owned land do not qualify as replacement of condemned land, it is not clear that improvements to purchased land do not qualify or that improvements to owned or purchased land do not qualify at least to the extent of the value of condemned improvements.

PROBLEMS FOR DISCUSSION

Problem 5-16. In 20X1, State condemned Blackacre, owned by Invest, which was improved by a mote net leased by Invest, that is, under terms requiring Invest's tenant to pay all taxes, insurance, and operating expenses in addition to the stipulated rent. The condemnation award was $1,500,000, allocating $1,200,000 to the plant and $300,000 to the land. Invest used the entire $1,500,000 to construct a motel on land she already owned that she proposes to operate. Can she defer the entire gain, or at least the gain on the manufacturing plant, under § 1031(g), on the ground that she invested the proceeds attributable improvements, which are real property, in other improvements? *See Asjes* (no allocation of proceeds of condemned nursery property on reinvestment in improved farm land); Rul. 80-184 (newly constructed rental warehouse and constructed rental office building on purchased land v. construction of rental warehouse v. rental office retail stores; Rev. Rul. 79-261 (leased office building v. partly leased, partly used office building); Rev. Rul. 76-391 (office building net leased to tenants v. unimproved farm land leased to tenant farmers); Rev. Rul. 76-390 (motel v. mobile home park); Rev. Rul.76-319 (billiard center v. bowling center); Rev Rul. 71-41 (constructed rental gas station on land already owned is similar in service or use to condemned rental warehouse, but replacement and condemned properties are not like kind); Rev. Rul. 70-399 (net leased resort hotel v. resort hotel operated by taxpayer); Priv. Ltr. Rul. 97-23-032 (motel v. owner-managed leased apartment building); Priv. Ltr. Rul. 96-19-028 (leveling and filing already owned unimproved land v. unimproved land held for investment); Tech. Adv. Mem. 83-07-007 (shopping center v. condemned unimproved land intended for a drive-in theater); Priv. Ltr. Rul. 81-19-029 (improvements to three-story building used for rental to provide better rental facilities is not like kind to condemned rented retail building); G.C.M. 34284 (land is unique, but buildings are not; does not decide whether improvements like kind to improvements).

§ 2.05. Proceeds

I.R.C. § 1033(i); Treas. Reg. § 1.1033-2(c)(10) and (11).

Section 1033(a)(2) provides nonrecognition of gain on the disposition of the involuntarily converted property only to the extent that the owner receives in exchange or, more commonly, purchases qualifying replacement property during the two-year period ending after the close of the taxable year in which any part of the gain on the disposition of the converted property is first realized. Accordingly, gain is recognized to the extent that the amount realized by the taxpayer on the disposition of the involuntarily converted property exceeds the cost of the qualifying replacement property. Because the amount required to be reinvested is measured by the amount realized, any liabilities transferred with the encumbered property are included in the amount required to be reinvested, even though they do not provide cash for reinvestment. Treas. Reg. § 1.1033-2(e)(11). A similar principle applies for the replacement property, including the full amount of the purchase price even if paid from borrowed funds. *See Cusak v. Commissioner*, 48 T.C. 156 (1967) (purchase of replacement property in full amount of price, even though the taxpayer was only paid an amount equal to part of the proceeds at the time, and sale subsequently rescinded); Rev. Rul. 68-642, 1968-2 C.B. 337 (lease of replacement property from a municipality that financed it with tax-exempt industrial development bonds qualifies a purchase of replacement property under § 1033 because terms of lease transferred benefits and burdens of ownership and equivalent of financing provided by municipality). There is no netting rule as there is for like-kind exchanges. *See* § 1.02(b) *Liabilities*. Thus, when Blackacre, held by Invest for use in business or for investment, with a basis of $10,000 and a value of $100,000, subject to a $30,000 mortgage is involuntarily converted, resulting in net cash proceeds of $70,000, and Invest purchases Whiteacre, also held for investment, for $100,000, paying $20,000 in cash and taking Whiteacre subject to an $80,000 mortgage, Invest does not recognize gain because the $100,000 purchase price of Whiteacre equals the $100,000 amount realized on the condemnation of Blackacre, even though she received $70,000 cash and only pays out $20,000 cash. The basis consequences when less than all proceeds are reinvested is discussed in the introductory section to this § 2 *Involuntary Conversion*.

Because condemnation payments may include payments that may not be directly related to the fair market value of the involuntarily converted property, including severance damages, and casualty insurance may include payments for loss of use and occupancy of the damaged property, it is not always easy to determine the amount of the proceeds that must be reinvested, or the amount of reinvestment that counts as being invested in qualifying property. The following case, involving payments for moving equipment from a condemned factory to a new location, illustrates a similar issue.

BUFFALO WIRE WORKS CO. INC. v. COMMISSIONER

United States Tax Court
74 T.C. 925 (1980)

* * *

Petitioner owned the real property at 308-320 Lower Terrace, Buffalo, New York, and used that property as a principal place of business until February 15, 1972. Such property (hereinafter the Lower Terrace property) consisted of land, buildings, and fixtures and was used by petitioner for the manufacture of wire and wire mesh products.

. . . In 1956 or thereabouts, petitioner informally learned that the City of Buffalo intended to acquire a large tract of real property, of which the Lower Terrace property was a part, in connection with the Project. During 1962, in anticipation of the condemnation of the Lower Terrace property, petitioner purchased a tract of land in West Seneca, New York, which was zoned for industrial use. Such property (hereinafter the West Seneca property) was intended as the site for a replacement facility . . .

By letter dated January 20, 1967, the City of Buffalo offered petitioner $399,330 for the Lower Terrace property. Petitioner did not accept the offer. Therefore, by petition dated February 28, 1967, the City of Buffalo commenced condemnation proceedings in the New York State Supreme Court. . . .

. . . [T]he court found that $195,000 would be just compensation for the land taken and that $440,000 would be just compensation for the buildings taken, but that there was insufficient evidence to determine the value of the fixtures which were to be removed or could be removed. For purposes of valuing such fixtures, the court directed the parties' attention to *Rose v. New York*, 24 N.Y.2d 80, 298 NYS.2d 968 (1969), wherein the proper method of valuation was described. In short, that opinion requires that the value of fixtures which are removed or could be removed is usually to be determined as the lesser of these two values: (1) the difference between salvage value of such items and their present value in place (i.e., reproduction cost less depreciation); or (2) the actual or contemplated costs of disassembly, trucking, and reassembling such items. . . . [T]he court determined that the value of fixtures in place for purposes of compensation in condemnation proceedings was at most $976,813. However, referring to the *Rose* case again, the court pointed out that the fixtures in place were found to be moveable and, therefore, the condemnation proceeds allocable to the fixtures in place were limited to the lower of $976,813 or the costs of disassembling, trucking, and moving them. . . .

By Order of Judgment dated December 24, 1969, judgment was entered in favor of Buffalo Wire Works Company, Inc., in accordance with the findings in the Memorandum dated December 10, 1969, with the proviso that the award for fixtures was subject to alteration. Specifically, Buffalo Wire Works Company, Inc., was awarded $635,000 for land and buildings and $976,813 for fixtures. The value of the fixtures was to be increased by any part of $178,605 that could be proved as expenses for carting, rigging, and installation of replacement fixtures. The value for fixtures so determined would constitute the award for fixtures unless the costs of moving, disassembling, trucking, reassembling, and relocating the existing fixtures were lower, in which case the award for fixtures would be the lower amount.

* * *

Due to changed circumstances between the date when petitioner acquired the West Seneca property and the end of 1970, petitioner decided to explore alternative relocation sites. Petitioner learned that a 24-year old facility located at 1165 Clinton Street in Buffalo was available and decided to acquire that property (hereinafter the Clinton property).

. . . The parties further agree that the Clinton property was acquired by petitioner to replace the Lower Terrace property and that the Clinton property is similar or related in service or use to the Lower Terrace property.

By Memorandum dated December 1, 1971, the New York State Supreme Court made its findings concerning the costs of moving petitioner's fixtures from the Lower Terrace property to the West Seneca property. The court determined that the costs of moving, disassembling, trucking, reassembling, and relocating the fixtures would be $480,744.87 . . .

Thus, based upon the rule set forth in the *Rose* case, the court had determined that the value of fixtures in place as measured by their fair market value less salvage value was $976,813, but that the value of fixtures in place as measured by the contemplated cost of disassembling, trucking, and reassembling the fixtures was $480,744.87. Thus, the total condemnation award was as follows:

Value of Land	$195,000.00
Value of Buildings	440,000.00
Value of Fixtures, not to exceed costs of moving	480,744.87
TOTAL	$1,115,744.87

* * *

Petitioner received checks totaling $1,141,072.45 as condemnation proceeds, which included a refund of taxes in the amount of $3,285.11, costs and disbursements in the amount of $22,042.47, and just compensation of $1,115,744.87. The parties agree that amounts received as a refund of taxes, which total $3,285.11, and amounts received as compensation for legal, engineering, and appraisal expenses, which total $139,438, do not constitute part of the amount realized by petitioner for purposes of section 1033 . . . . Thus, the maximum amount realized by petitioner upon the conversion of its property was $998,349 (rounded to the nearest dollar), calculated as follows:

Gross Award		$1,141,072
Less Refund of Property Tax:	$3,285	
Legal, Engineering, and appraisal expenses:	139,438	(142,723)
		$998,349

Petitioner made a timely election under section 1033 to recognize gain from the involuntary conversion of its property only to the extent that the amount realized upon the conversion of the property exceeds the cost of the replacement property. Petitioner expended $1,060,734 for replacement property and reported no gain from the involuntary conversion of its property.

Petitioner claimed deductions for moving expenses which it incurred during the taxable years 1965 through 1972 in the following amounts:

Taxable Year	*Amount*
1965	$23,377.81

Taxable Year	*Amount*
1966	11,863.57
1967	15,433.39
1968	14,387.62
1969	13,953.14
1970	-0-
1971	81,193.33
1972	257,842.52
TOTAL	$418,051.38

. . . None of the amounts which petitioner incurred as moving expense were included in the amount of $1,060,734 which petitioner expended for replacement property.

In his statutory notice of deficiency, the Commissioner determined that the amount of $418,052, which petitioner received as part of its condemnation award in 1972, constituted ordinary income to petitioner as a direct reimbursement of the moving expenses which had been incurred during and claimed as a deduction for the taxable years 1965 through 1972. The Commissioner determined further that petitioner received a net award of $430,162 as reimbursement for moving expenses, calculated as follows:

Award for Moving Expenses	$480,745
Portion Allocable to Legal, Engineering, and Appraisal Expenses	(50,583)
Net Award for Moving Expenses	$430,162

The Commissioner determined further that the difference of $12,110 between the amount of $418,052, which was received as a direct reimbursement of moving expenses, and the amount of $430,162, which was the net award, was not gain that qualifies for nonrecognition under section 1033 because it was not an award for condemned fixtures and it did not represent an amount paid for property which could be replaced. Accordingly, petitioner's taxable income for the taxable year 1972 was increased, additional investment credit was allowed to petitioner for that year, and no carryback of investment credit to the taxable years 1969, 1970, or 1971 was allowed. The basis of the Clinton property was also determined.

* * *

In summary, respondent has articulated three contentions:

(1) that $430,162 of the condemnation award constituted ordinary income to petitioner, part as reimbursement for moving expenses and part as excess reimbursement for moving expenses;

(2) that the moving expenses of petitioner for the taxable year 1972 are deductible only to the same extent that the condemnation award is includable as ordinary income to petitioner in that year; and

(3) that petitioner must restore to income in 1972 the amounts that were deducted as moving expenses in the taxable years 1965 through 1971 because such amounts were recovered by petitioner through its condemnation award. By placing respondent's contentions side-by-side, it can be seen that each of the three contentions is premised on the same crucial determination, namely that a portion of petitioner's condemnation award constituted reimbursement of moving expenses. Petitioner's sole contention is that no part of its condemnation award was received as reimbursement of moving expenses, but that the entire award (less refunded property tax and legal, engineering, and appraisal expenses) constitutes an amount realized upon the involuntary conversion of property into money. Thus, the basic issue to be decided in this case is whether the portion of the condemnation award which totaled $480,744.87 should be treated for purposes of Federal income taxation as reimbursement of moving expenses or as money into which property has been converted.

A similar issue was presented in *Graphic Press, Inc. v. Commissioner*, 60 T.C. 674 (1973), rev'd. 523 F.2d 585 (9th Cir. 1975). There, the California Department of Public Works notified the taxpayer that the State of California intended to condemn the taxpayer's property . . . . The State condemned the taxpayer's land, building, and fixtures. Upon condemnation of the fixtures, which included extensive machinery, the State was obliged to pay the taxpayer an amount equal to the fair market value of the fixtures unless the State could negotiate some relief from that obligation. Negotiations produced a settlement under which the taxpayer agreed to waive its right to receive an amount equal to the fair market value of the fixtures and also agreed to remove the fixtures. Correspondingly, the State agreed to compensate the taxpayer for the land, building, and fixtures in the amount of $725,000, and for moving expenses in the amount of $3,000. The Commissioner determined that $407,192 of the $725,000 condemnation award, less an allocable portion of legal fees, constituted ordinary income rather than money into which property has been converted.

In a Court-reviewed opinion, this Court decided that $407,192 of the condemnation award, less an allocable portion of legal fees, was received by the taxpayer in exchange for its waiver of the right to be compensated for the fair market value of the fixtures. Accordingly, it was held that such amount, less an allocable portion of legal fees, was includable in the taxpayer's income. On appeal to the United States Court of Appeals for the Ninth Circuit, our decision was reversed.

In its opinion, the United States Court of Appeals for the Ninth Circuit agreed that sufficient evidence existed to support a breakdown of the condemnation award into component parts, but disagreed that part of the condemnation award constituted payment for a waiver. In so holding, the court explained as follows:

> The state's right-of-way file reveals that the actual losses negotiated and compensated were moving expenses and business interruption costs. There was no evidence to indicate that any portion of the award was to pay for a waiver of the statutory right. . . .

The court then turned to the Commissioner's argument that the portion of the condemnation award which was allocable to moving expenses was not a payment for the property taken. After referring to *E. R. Hitchcock, Co. v. United States*, 514

F.2d 484 (2d Cir. 1975), *aff'g.* 382 F. Supp. 236 (C. Conn. 1974), and discussing generally section 1033, the court concluded as follows:

> We believe compensation in excess of land and building payments in this case qualifies for section 1033 treatment. From the taxpayer's viewpoint, he is being compensated for a loss due to the condemnation of his property. Whatever payment the taxpayer receives is attributable to the involuntary conversion. Where, as here, a payment is made for relocation costs in addition to land and building costs, as long as the condemnee reinvests the total award into other property similar or related in service or use within the statutory period, both the language and spirit of the statute have been met. . . .

Under the rule of *Golsen v. Commissioner*, 54 T.C. 742 (1970), *aff'd*, 445 F.2d 975 (10th Cir. 1971), we will follow the views of the United States Court of Appeals to which a case is appealable when that court has already expressed its views on an issue which is presented to us for decision. . . . In the instant case, the issue presented for decision is materially the same as that presented for decision in *Graphic Press* . . . However, appeal of our decision in this case would not be taken to the United States Court of Appeals for the Ninth Circuit, which reversed our decision in *Graphic Press*. Instead, appeal of our decision herein would be taken to the United States Court of Appeals for the Second Circuit, which has also decided a case involving the same issue.

In *Hitchcock, Co. v. United States*, 514 F.2d 484 (2d Cir. 1975), the court of appeals reviewed a decision by the United States District Court for Connecticut. On cross-motions for summary judgment, the district court had been faced with the question whether amounts received in a condemnation proceeding for disassembling, moving and reassembling machinery were part of the fair market value of the property taken and thus were amounts realized upon the conversion of property into money, or rather were a separate reimbursable item of damages for purposes of taxation. After reviewing Connecticut law on the determination of fair market value of condemned property, the district court held that the amounts attributable to the costs of moving were received by the taxpayer as part of the fair market value of the property taken. . . .

On appeal, the United States Court of Appeals for the Second Circuit affirmed the decision of the district court. In so doing, that court included the following statement:

> Without relying upon the state law concept of a condemnation award including moving expense as a factor in fair market value, it is an economic fact that this taxpayer received its moving expense money solely as a result of the condemnation and as a matter of state law. Its original property was actually converted by the condemnation into a sum (or sums) of money which the taxpayer utilized, concededly, for qualified replacement property purchase. Economically and substantively, . . . this money received for moving expense was part of the "amount realized" on the conversion. But for the conversion it would not have been realized. It was not just an integral part of the state award, it was to compensate the taxpayer for the

> property taken. To view the moving expense money as a separate, unrelated payment out of the blue, so to speak, is to exalt form over substance. * * * . . .

The court also noted that the deduction by the taxpayer of moving expenses was justified. . . .

Considering the rule of *Golsen* . . . , the opinion of the court of appeals in *E.R. Hitchcock Co.* . . . , and the facts of the instant case, we are compelled to hold that the portion of petitioner's condemnation award which was determined by reference to moving expenses constitutes an amount realized from the involuntary conversion of property into money rather than reimbursement for moving expenses. Accordingly, we hold that no part of petitioner's condemnation award constitutes ordinary income to petitioner as reimbursement for moving expenses or as excess reimbursement for moving expenses, that the moving expenses of petitioner for the taxable year 1972 are fully deductible in that year, and that petitioner need not restore to income amounts that were deducted as moving expenses in the taxable years 1965 through 1971.

* * *

There is not sufficient difference between the laws of Connecticut and New York to negate the applicability of *E.R. Hitchcock Co.* to the facts of this case. Under Connecticut law, the fixing of a condemnation award is done upon the basis of the fair market value of the property taken as of the day of the taking. . . . The costs of moving fixtures are not taken into account separately, but rather as an element which affects the fair market value of the property. . . . On the other hand, under New York law, the value of fixtures is determined as being the lower of two amounts: (1) the difference between their present value in place and their salvage value; and (2) the costs of disassembling, trucking, and reassembling the fixtures. *Rose* . . . Whichever amount is used, such amount becomes the value of fixtures which are removed or could be removed. Thus, as under Connecticut law, compensation is made from the value of the property taken. New York law is not different from Connecticut law in that respect; it is simply more definite than Connecticut law in the use of moving expense data. Nevertheless, in both states the use of moving expenses is as a measure of value, and it is upon that basis that the court of appeals made its decision in *E.R. Hitchcock Co.*

* * *

Respondent contends that if the decision . . . in *E.R. Hitchcock, Co.* is applied to the instant case, . . . the tax benefit rule should require that inclusion in petitioner's income of amounts which were recovered during the taxable year 1972 after being deducted in a previous taxable year. Respondent contends that amounts spent during the taxable year 1972 on moving expenses were spent with a right to reimbursement and, therefore, are not deductible. We disagree with both of the foregoing grounds.

With respect to . . . the tax benefit rule, we would point out the requirement that a taxpayer must make a recovery of an item which generated a deduction in an earlier taxable year. *See* sec. 111; sec. 1.111-1(a), Income Tax Regs. . . . Respondent correctly points out that petitioner claimed deductions for moving expenses in taxable years prior to 1972 and that such deductions resulted in a tax saving to petitioner. However, because of our holding that all of the condemnation award is properly categorized as an amount realized from the involuntary conversion of property into money, no part of that condemnation award constitutes a recovery of prior moving expenses. Without such a recovery, respondent's argument under the tax benefit rule must fail. *See* sec. 1.111-1(a)(2), Income Tax Regs.

We must reach a similar result with respect to respondent's argument that amounts expended for moving expenses during the taxable year 1972 were spent with a right to reimbursement. No part of the condemnation award represents reimbursement of moving expenses. The amounts expended by petitioner for moving expenses during the taxable year 1972 are deductible. . . .

Decisions will be entered for the petitioner.

NOTES AND COMMENTS

Although the Service obviously thought that something was wrong when Buffalo Wire both deducted the cost of moving the machinery and claimed nonrecognition on the amounts received that were measured by those same moving expenses, it properly did not challenge the moving expense deduction, because the costs of moving equipment previously placed in service are deductible as compared to the costs of shipping capital assets prior to the time they are placed in service, which must be capitalized. *See MacAdam & Foster, Inc. v. Commissioner*, 8 B.T.A. 967 (1927), *acq.* (cost of moving machinery purchased with a business and operated in place for two months to a new location is deductible); *Eastern Shoe Mfg. Co. v. Commissioner*, 8 B.T.A. 1169 (1927), *acq.* (same for moving plant). On the other hand, New York's sensible determination that Buffalo Wire should be paid only the $480,744 cost of moving its fixtures, instead of the $976,813 fair market value of the fixtures in place, should not obscure the fact that the amount was paid for the fixtures, not for the moving costs as such. Inclusion of the $480,744 in the proceeds of the condemnation of Buffalo Wire's factory required it to invest that amount in qualifying property at the new location in addition to what it received for its plant without counting the moving costs.

Other amounts that are not directly related to the involuntarily converted property may be included in the amount of the proceeds that, if invested in qualifying replacement property, will not result in the receipt of boot and the recognition of gain on the disposition of the involuntarily converted property. For example, when less than all of a parcel of property is condemned, the condemnation award may include severance damages — that is, amounts to compensate for the reduction in value of the retained property. The severance damages are considered as amounts paid for the condemned property in determining the proceeds eligible for reinvestment. *See* Rev. Rul. 80-184, 1980-2 C.B. 232 (reinvestment of severance damages in similar improvements constructed on remainder of land partly condemned, and similar improvements on land purchased and improved qualify for nonrecognition). Rev. Rul. 73-235, 1973-1 C.B. 519 (reinvestment of severance damages and proceeds of disposition of the remainder of the property that had become unprofitable to the taxpayer because of the condemnation in similar property all qualified for nonrecognition). In addition, governmental grants to assist businesses and others with disaster losses may qualify for nonrecognition under § 1033. *See* Rev. Rul. 2005-46, 2005-2 C.B. 120 (government disaster grant to business to reimburse losses incurred for destruction of real or personal property that is includible in gross income are treated as compensation for involuntary conversion); *but see* Rev. Rul. 74-206, 1974-1 C.B. 198 (condemnation award for damaged property measured by pre-disaster value includible in income to the extent of prior casualty loss deduction; balance is compensation for involuntary conversion).

Some fire and similar insurance policies include provisions compensating the business for the loss of the use of the premises as a result of the disaster, sometimes based on a flat per diem and sometimes based on lost profits. The Service generally treats per diem as proceeds of the involuntary conversion, but not those based on lost profits. *See* Rev. Rul. 86-12, 1986-1 C.B. 290, (although, in general, proceeds based on a flat per diem are subject to nonrecognition, if looking beyond the terms of the policy, the per diem amount is actuarially determined on the basis of lost profits, it is not compensation for the involuntary conversion).

Because condemnation and insurance proceeds are usually computed on the gross fair market value of the property without regard to encumbrances, the amount of money that must be invested in qualified replacement property must equal or exceed the full amount of the proceeds, even if the condemning authority or insurer pays a portion of the award to the holder of a mortgage. *See* Treas. Reg. § 1.1033-2(c)(11). *See Cusak v. Commissioner*, 48 T.C. 156 (1967) (purchase of replacement property in full amount of price, even though the taxpayer was only paid an amount equal to part of the proceeds at the time and sale subsequently rescinded); Rev. Rul. 68-642, 1968-2 C.B. 337 (acquisition of replacement property financed with industrial development bonds under a lease treated as a purchase is treated as a purchase of the property financed by the municipality).

Like § 1031, § 1033 contains a limitation similar to that of § 1031(f) on the acquisition of replacement property from a related party. § 1033(i). The scope limitation is broader under § 1033 than under § 1031, however. Under § 1033, nonrecognition is not permitted to the extent that the replacement property is acquired from a related party. This limitation only applies to C corporations, including partnerships with C corporation partners and to other owners of involuntarily converted property with more than $100,000 of unrealized gain. The limitation does not apply if the related party acquired the replacement property within the replacement period. *See* Priv. Ltr. Rul. 2004-11-001 (§ 1033(i) does not prevent qualification of replacement property acquired in a complex inter-company transaction when the replacement property was constructed for the related party by outsiders).

PROBLEMS FOR DISCUSSION

Problem 5-19. Bizz, whose operation was uninsured because insurance was very, very expensive as a result of its location in a coastal area prone to hurricanes and other natural disasters, suffered extensive damage as a result of a monster hurricane. She received various federal and state aid for property loss, decrease in value of real property, damage to physical infrastructure, damage to tangible assets and inventory, business interruption, overhead costs, and wages paid for work not performed, temporary relocation expenses, debris removal and other cleanup costs. In addition, Bizz agreed to condemnation of her property at its damaged value (in light of the other payments), and received reimbursement of costs of a permanent relocation of her operation to a site more than five miles from the coast to reduce the risk of subsequent damage. Which, if any, of these amounts is eligible for reinvestment under § 1033? Which, if any, can she deduct, notwithstanding eligibility for reinvestment? *See Buffalo Wire Works* (payment equal to cost of moving equipment to new site are proceeds). Rev. Rul. 80-184 (severance damages); Rev. Rul. 73-235 (severance damages and proceeds of disposition of the remainder of the property); Rev. Rul. 2005-46 (government disaster grant to business to reimburse losses); Rev. Rul. 74-206 (condemnation award for damaged property measured by pre-disaster value includible in income to the extent of prior casualty loss deduction); Rev. Rul. 86-12 (proceeds of use and occupancy insurance).

§ 3. OTHER NONRECOGNITION PROVISIONS

Although there are a number of other nonrecognition provisions in addition to those discussed above, most, including those relating to corporations and partnerships, are sufficiently limited in scope or applicability and similar in concept and result to those discussed in this chapter to make it appropriate to leave discussion of them to the courses dealing with those subjects. This section discusses some of the remaining nonrecognition provisions not likely to be dealt with elsewhere. Section 1038, which provides a nonrecognition provision for repossession of real property sold under the installment method, is the subject of § 3.01 *Installment Sale and Repossession*. Section § 3.02 *Principal Residences*, discusses § 121, which provides a limited exclusion of gain on sales of principal residences under § 121, which replaced an earlier provision for nonrecognition exchanges of principal residences under former § 1034. The exclusion can be combined with like-kind exchanges under § 1031 and involuntary conversions under § 1033. Finally, § 3.03 *Charitable Contributions*, briefly discusses the nonstatutory exclusion, with statutory exceptions, of gain on appreciated property contributed to charity.

§ 3.01. Installment Sales and Repossessions

§ 1038; Treas. Reg. § 1.1038-1

Although the general rule is that the foreclosure of a mortgage or other obligation secured by property is a taxable event for both the owner of the property and the creditor, *see* § 4.02 *Judicial Interpretation* in Chapter 2 *Capital Gains and Losses*, § 1038 provides a special rule that treats the reacquisition of real property by a seller who has financed a deferred payment sale as a nonrecognition transaction. The reacquisition results in no gain or loss for any difference between the basis of the debt and the value of the property and in no bad debt deduction for that difference. § 1038(b); Treas. Reg. § 1.1038-1(b). The basis of the repossessed property is generally the same as the basis at the time of sale, adjusted amounts paid by the seller in connection with the repossession.

§ 1038(c); Treas. Reg. § 1.1038-1(g). The transaction is treated as, in effect, a like-kind exchange by the seller of the property sold for the reacquired property, with any payments or other consideration received by the seller in the interim or on reacquisition treated as boot. This results in gain recognition for any payments or other consideration received that was treated as the recovery of basis between the time of the sale and the repossession. Thus, if Blackacre with a basis of $100,000 is sold by Sail to Perch for $1,000,000 with $200,000 paid at the time of sale and the balance to be paid over ten years in $80,000 installments with adequate stated interest, under the installment method, Sail reports the $900,000 gain ratably as payments are received. § 453(a), (b) and (c). Because the $900,000 gain is 90 percent of the sale price, 90 percent of each payment is reported as gain and 10 percent is a recovery of basis. Accordingly, Sail reports gain of $180,000 (90% of $200,000) in the year of sale and will report $72,000 of gain as she receives each $80,000 payment. If Perch makes no further payment and Sail repossesses Blackacre when its value is $600,000, instead of recognizing gain based on the $600,000 value, § 1038(b) treats $20,000, which is the excess of the $200,000 cash received on the sale over the $180,000 gain recognized at the time of the sale, as, in effect, boot, resulting in gain on the repossession. By no coincidence, this is the portion of the payment that was applied against the basis of Blackacre. The basis of Blackacre after repossession is the $100,000 basis at the time of sale. This is appropriate because Sail has recognized the entire $200,000 down payment as gain. As a result, the inherent gain in Blackacre is $500,000 ($600,000 value – $500,000 basis), the same as it would have been if Blackacre had never been sold.

The following case illustrates and explains the application of § 1038, with particular attention paid to determining whether certain of the payments received by the seller are properly considered boot.

GREENE v. COMMISSIONER

United States Tax Court
76 T.C. 1018 (1981)

* * *

On July 1, 1968, petitioner purchased approximately 145.23 acres of land in Walton County, Georgia . . . Upon conveyance petitioner signed a $20,000 promissory note in favor of the sellers. On December 17, 1968, petitioner purchased approximately 80.79 acres of land in Walton County, Georgia, from E. L. Hollis. In partial payment for the 80.79 acres of land, petitioner signed a promissory note for $32,025 in favor of the seller. These two parcels of land are adjacent and aggregate 226.02 acres in Walton County, Georgia. On July 26, 1974, petitioner's adjusted basis in the 226.02 acres was $70,329.55.

On April 20, 1974, petitioner contracted to sell the 226.02 acres to North Star Development Company, Robert A. Bick, president. Thereafter, North Star Development Company assigned the sales contract to Mr. Bick, John A. Nuzzulo, and George C. Robinson (Bick, Nuzzulo, and Robinson). On that date, the sale of the 226.02 acres between petitioner and Bick, Nuzzulo, and Robinson was consummated for $350,176. Petitioner received the sale proceeds as follows:

Item		*Amount*
Cash		$10,844.33
Note Payable from Bick, Nuzzulo, and Robinson (Payable August 9, 1974)		14,000.00
Real Estate Commissions		35,017.60
Neal Jackson Realty and Mortgage Co, (Cash)	$2,508.80	
Scenic Realty and Investment Co. (Note Payable from buyer January 24, 1975)	15,000.00	
Scenic Realty and Investment Co. (Note Payable from buyer July 25, 1975)	17,508.80	
Mortgage on Property to E. L. Hollis paid by Purchasers		9,208.29
Seller's Pro Rata Share of Real Property Taxes		592.28
Georgia Recording Tax		350.20
Recording Fee		22.50
Purchase Money Mortgage on Property from Bick, Nuzzulo, and Robinson		280,140.80
TOTAL		350,176.00

On their 1974 income tax return petitioners elected to report the gain from the sale of the land on the installment basis of accounting pursuant to section 453. They reported the gain as follows:

Item	*Amount*
1974 Real Estate: 226.02 Acres Walton County Georgia (7/26/74)	$350,176.00
Cost (Several Years Ago)	[2] 105,719.85
Potential Profit 69.80951%	244,456.15
Collected in 1974: $70,035.20 at 69.80951%	48,891.23

The $70,035.20 reported by petitioner as collected in 1974 consisted of the following items:

---

[2] The $105,719.85 used by petitioner as "Cost" of the property consisted of petitioner's stipulated adjusted basis in the property of $70,329.55, the $35,017.60 sales commissions paid for petitioner at the time of sale, the $350.20 Georgia recording tax, and the $22.50 recording fee. This method of handling the sales commissions and selling costs was technically incorrect since these amounts should have been deducted from the sales price received rather than added to the cost or basis of the property. Obviously, the result as to the gain in 1974 is the same under the method used by petitioner in this case as it would be had the commissions and selling expenses been properly used to reduce the sales price of the property. However, attention is directed to the incorrect method because of statutory provisions discussed later in this opinion.

Item	*Amount*
Cash	$10,844.33
Note Paid by Bick, Nuzzulo and Robinson on August 9, 1974	14,000.00
Real Estate Commissions Paid	35,017.60
Mortgage on the Property to E. L. Hollis Paid by Purchasers	9,208.29
Seller's Pro Rata Share of Taxes	592.28
Georgia Recording Tax	350.20
Recording Fees	22.50
TOTAL	70,035.20

Neither Bick, Nuzzulo, nor Robinson made any of the required payments on their notes and the purchase money mortgage during 1975 and 1976. On July 21, 1975, Robinson deeded his interest in the 226.02 acres to Bick. On May 18, 1976, Bick and Nuzzulo deeded the entire 226.02 acres back to petitioner in satisfaction of the $280,140.80 purchase money mortgage. At the time of repossession petitioner incurred a $25 fee for a title check on the 226.02 acres.

On their 1976 income tax return petitioners reported a loss of $14,271.33 upon the repossession of the land and an adjusted basis in the returned property of $84,600.88. Petitioners calculated the reported amounts as follows:

Item		*Amount*
1976 Repossession:		
1974 Sale Real Estate - Downpayment in 1974		$70,035.20
Income Reported		48,891.23
		21,143.97
Sales Commissions and Costs Paid at the Time of Sale - 1974	35,390.30	
Repossession Costs - 1976	25.00	
	35,415.30	
	(14,271.33)	
Loss on Repossession:		
Adjusted Property Basis:		
Cost of Land Taxpayer's Original Basis		70,329.55
Add - Repossession Costs		14,271.33
Adjusted Basis		84,600.88

In his statutory notice of deficiency, respondent determined that petitioners had a long-term capital gain of $10,559.49 on repossession of the property. Respondent computed this gain as follows:

Item	*Amount*
Amount of money received prior to the reacquisition	$70,035.20
Less: Gain on the sale of the property reported as income prior to reacquisition	48,891.23
Balance	21,143.97
Less: Cost of reacquisition of property	25.00
Net gain from reacquisition	21,118.97
Less: Section 1202 deduction	10,559.48
Increase in income	10,559.49

* * *

The parties agree that the general rule of section 1038(a) provides that no gain or loss results to a seller upon the reacquisition of previously sold property except as provided in subsections (b) and (d). Both parties recognize that the gain computed under the limitation provisions of section 1038(b)(2) would exceed the gain as computed by respondent under section 1038(b)(1) and recognize that the applicable section for computing gain in this case is section 1038(b)(1).

Respondent takes the position that the language of section 1038(b)(1) is mandatory, unambiguous, and mechanical in its application. He contends that the calculation formula of section 1038(b)(1) generates a reportable capital gain because it provides for the amount of money and fair market value of other property received prior to the reacquisition to be reduced only by the amount of gain previously reported and does not permit petitioners to reduce the money received by the sales commissions and costs paid at the time of the 1974 property sale. Respondent argues that petitioners will receive a tax benefit from the commissions and sales expenses paid in 1974 since the section 1038(c) basis calculation gives petitioners a stepped-up basis in their reacquired realty.

On the other hand, petitioners argue that they are entitled to report a loss as a result of the reacquisition of the realty. Petitioners emphasize that in 1974 they reported taxable profit of and paid taxes on $48,891.23 while they received only $35,017.60 in "money." On brief, they suggest that "gain on the repossession of the property is limited to this sum of 'money' " collected. Petitioners contend that respondent's interpretation of the statute and regulations unwarrantedly creates taxable income at the time of repossession.

Petitioners' interpretation of the facts as to the "money" they received in 1974 is in error. When the purchasers of the property paid the real estate agent the $35,017.60 sales commission owed by petitioner, petitioner received this $35,017.60 as if the cash had been handed to him and he had handed it to the real estate agent. In fact, petitioners recognized that they received the $35,017.60 when they showed on their 1974 return as the total collected from the property in that year the amount of $70,035.20.

Congress enacted section 1038 in 1964 with several purposes in mind. Congress intended to provide a uniform method of reporting gain upon the repossession of real property regardless of the method of accounting used by the taxpayer in reporting his gain or loss upon the initial sale. Recognizing the possibility that the realty might have appreciated in value between the time of the initial sale and the repossession, Congress aimed to reduce the likelihood that the initial seller-taxpayer, who might be illiquid upon repossession, would be responsible at that time for reporting large amounts of gain and paying taxes thereon. Congress directed that at repossession gain would not be measured by reference to the fair market value of the repossessed property. Moreover, Congress intended that the gain which a taxpayer would be responsible for reporting upon repossession should not exceed the payments he actually had received prior to that time.

Section 1038(b) directs the taxpayer to calculate by two methods the gain resulting from repossession, and the taxpayer is responsible for reporting on his income tax return in the taxable year of the reacquisition the lesser of the two gain calculations. Although section 1038(b)(2), the limitation subsection, specifically allows the taxpayer to reduce the gross sales price by the selling commissions, legal fees, and other expenses incident to the initial sale, subsection (b)(1) does not permit such a reduction.

If the mandatory language of section 1038(b) works a hardship on a taxpayer, who prior to repossession has not received cash in an amount equal to the reportable gain required by section 1038(b), such taxpayer is not excepted from the operations of section 1038(b)(1). These taxpayers are awarded relief by obtaining an increased adjusted basis in the repossessed property pursuant to section 1038(c). Under section 1038(c) petitioner's adjusted basis in the repossessed property will offset any gain he is required to report on the repossession.

* * *

NOTES AND COMMENTS

It is not clear why, having reported the payments of commissions and other items paid by the purchasers as amounts received in computing their gain in the year of sale, as they were required to do under the installment sales provisions, the taxpayers in *Greene* thought a different computation could be used under § 1038. When the dust clears, all of those amounts are, in effect, treated as boot and gain under § 1038. Not coincidentally, the $21,143.97 additional gain imposed on the repossession is exactly equal to the difference between the $70,035.20 reported as collected at the time of sale and the $48,891.23 reported as gain at that time. The $21,143.97 represents the amount collected that was applied against basis. The result is the same as if the $70,035.97 had been paid as a down payment, but the sale had never closed, except that under § 1038, the gain is determined by the character of the original sale, so that it is generally capital or § 1231 gain, § 453B(a); Treas. Reg. § 1.1038-1(d); Treas. Reg. § 1.453-9(a), while down payments or option payments that are forfeited are characterized as ordinary income, because there is no sale or exchange. Treas. Reg. § 1.1234-1(b); *see* §§ 4.03 *Extinguishment Doctrine*, and 4.04(b) *Loss on the Lapse of an Option* in Chapter 2 *Capital Gains and Losses*, for discussions of the requirement of a sale or exchange for capital or § 1231 gain. Although neither the *Greene* case nor the regulations state it expressly, § 1038 overrides the general installment sale principle that requires recognition of gain when an installment obligation is disposed of. § 453B.

In *Greene*, the purchasers did not make any significant improvements to the property before default and repossession. When purchasers make major improvements prior to repossession of the property by the seller, the treatment of the improvements is not spelled out in § 1038. In *Smith v. Commissioner*, 58 T.C. 874 (1972), the court held that when the purchaser improved property with fourplexes financed by a construction loan to which the purchase money mortgage had been subordinated, before default and repossession (subject to the construction loan), the entire tacked basis was allocated to repossessed land, so that the basis of the fourplexes was equal to an allocable share of the construction loan that the seller-repossessor would have to pay, and that there was no tacking of land holding period to the improvements. In *Conners v. Commissioner*, 88 T.C. 541 (1987), the court allowed nonrecognition of gain under § 1038 when seller accepted six condo units constructed on land sold in lieu of foreclosure on the entire parcel and distinguished *Smith* on the ground that the value of any improvements is implicitly entitled to nonrecognition under § 1038. In *Connors* the taxpayers were taxed on liabilities transferred as part of the original sale. The *Connors* case did expressly note that § 1038 creates an exception to recognition of gain under § 453 for the reacquisition of property. *See also Hovhannissian v. Commissioner*, T.C. Mem. 1997-444 (no loss on repossession of property even if incomplete construction decreased value of property; follows *Conners*). Thus, despite the absence of a "like kind" standard in § 1038, something very similar is being adopted and applied by the courts.

PROBLEMS FOR DISCUSSION

Problem 5-20. In 20X2, Land sold Blackacre to Perch, who intended to use it for a condo development. At the time of the sale, Blackacre was an unimproved parcel of urban land, with a basis of $50,000, subject to a mortgage loan of $150,000 incurred in early 20X1 to raise funds for another land acquisition. The sale price was $500,000, payable $50,000 down, $150,000 by taking the property subject to the mortgage and $300,000 payable at the rate of $50,000 a year beginning in 20X5, with mandatory prepayments equal to 50 percent of the excess of any cash payments received on sale of the condos over required prepayments on the financing Perch incurred for the construction of the condos. At the time of the sale, Land reported gain of $150,000, the sum of the $100,000 excess of the mortgage loan over the $50,000 basis plus the $50,000 down payment. Perch's construction financing, which was expected to refinance the $150,000 mortgage as well as provide construction funds, provided for mandatory prepayments of a portion of the sale price of the condos. In 20X4, when Perch was ready to begin selling the condos, the local condo market had collapsed as a result of overbuilding and changed economic circumstances. Accordingly, Perch defaulted on the payment due Land. To stave off foreclosure, Perch agreed to convey to Land condos with an appraised value of $1,000,000, subject to the related construction loans of $625,000, for a net value of $325,000. The extra $75,000 over the $250,000 balance of the original sale price of Blackacre was a hedge insisted on by Land, who was skeptical of the accuracy of the appraisal of the condos. What are the tax consequences to

Land of the transfer of the condos? § 453(f); Treas. Reg. §§ 1.1031(b) 1, (c)-1, and (d)-1 and 2; Prop. Treas. Reg. § 1.453-1(f); Sen. Rep. No. 1000, discussed in § 1.02(c) *Boot and Installment Sales. See Greene* (computation of gain on reacquisition); *Smith* (basis allocated only to land); *Connors* (condos constructed on reacquired land); *Hovhannissian* (no loss on reacquisition despite construction); *Garcia* (net even liability incurred to be netted); Rev. Rul. 79-44 (don't offset boot by liability increase).

§ 3.02. Principal Residences

I.R.C. § 121; Treas. Reg. § 1.121-1 to 4

Replacing a rollover provision for gain on sales of principal residences, former § 1034, § 121 now provides an exemption for up to $250,000 ($500,000 on a joint return, or for certain sales, after 2007, by surviving spouses within two years of death of the first spouse) of gain realized on the disposition of a principal residence. § 121(b); Treas. Reg. § 1.121-2. The amount of the exclusion is not indexed for inflation. A taxpayer only needs to have owned and actually used the property as his principal residence for two or more years out of the five years preceding the sale, thus allowing for a period of rental prior to sale, § 121(a); Treas. Reg. § 1.121-1(c), but the exclusion can only be used once every two years. § 121(b)(3). A reduced exclusion is available for taxpayers who fail to meet the basic requirements because of change of employment, health, or other unforeseen circumstances. § 121(c); Treas. Reg. § 1.121-4 and 5; *see* Priv. Ltr. Rul. 2005-04-012 (newly designated police K-9 officer who was required to maintain kennel at home for dog, who sold townhouse within two years of starting to use it as their principal residence because community rules did not permit a kennel, entitled to the reduced exclusion because appointment as K-9 was unforeseen circumstance even though he had applied for the position as a K-9 officer after execution of the contract but before purchase). Moreover, special provisions are also applicable in the case of the death of a spouse, divorce, military service, taxpayers who are incapable of caring for themselves, and other situations. § 121(d); Treas. Reg. § 1.121-3. The exclusion is only available for principal residences, not vacation or second homes, which can cause problems for "snowbirds" and others who divide their time between two or more residences. *See* Treas. Reg. § 1.121-1(b); *Guinan v. United States*, 2003-1 U.S.T.C. (CCH) § 50,475; 91 A.F.T.R.2d (RIA) 2174 (D. Ariz. 2003) (Wisconsin residence not principal residence when the taxpayer spent more time in first Georgia and then Arizona home during each of the five years prior to sale).

Requiring that the residence have been used as a principal residence for only two of the prior five years eliminates, as a practical matter, controversies that arose under prior law of the effect of renting a residence prior to sale. The Service position was that temporary rental was permissible when the taxpayer intended to return to the residence after a temporary absence, *see* Rev. Rul. 78-146, 1978-1 C.B. 260 (home leased for two years while taxpayer was on assignment in another city, continued to be principal residence, even though decided to sell on return without reoccupying; Rev. Rul. 59-72, 1959-1 C.B. 203 (whether former residence rented remains principal residence depends on all facts and circumstances), but that principal residence status terminated if the taxpayer claimed a loss on the rental of the residence for depreciation and expenses other than home mortgage interest and real estate taxes that are deductible without a profit motive. *See* Tech. Adv. Mem. 81-32-017 (§ 183 precluded claiming losses on the rental, even though § 183 is not customarily applied to rental of real property at a fair rental; intent to use former § 1034 precluded considering that the property had been converted to rental property). The courts were more generous. *See Bolaris v. Commissioner*, 776 F.2d 1428 (9th Cir. 1985) (temporarily renting the old residence after moving to a new one before selling it did not destroy its status as a principal residence for purposes of the nonrecognition rollover under former § 1034; allowing deductions for rental expenses in the meanwhile did not provide an impermissible windfall, taxpayers had the requisite profit motive to allow deduction of losses after depreciation during the interim rental).

When a principal residence has been rented or used for business purposes and depreciation deductions have been taken, any depreciation adjustments under § 1250(b)(3) are ineligible for the § 121 exclusion and will be included in gross income as unrecaptured § 1250 gain if treated as capital gain under § 1231. § 121(d)(6); Treas. Reg. § 1.121-1(d). Moreover, when a principal residence has also been used partly for business purposes, either as a home office or other business location simultaneously with its use as a residence, a distinction must be made between the gain attributable to the use of the property for business purposes and that attributable to the use of the property as a residence. In this situation, the portion of the gain attributable to the business use is ineligible for the § 121 exclusion. Treas. Reg. § 1.121-1(e). The requirement to allocate gain does not apply if both the residential and nonresidential portions of the property are within the same dwelling unit. Thus, no allocation of gain is necessary if the home office is located within the dwelling unit as opposed to a home office located in an appurtenant structure. Nevertheless, any gain, including depreciation adjustments under § 1250(b)(3), not eligible for exclusion under § 121 may be eligible for nonrecognition as an involuntary conversion (*see* § 121(d)(5); Treas. Reg. § 1.121-4(d)), or as part of a like-kind exchange, as illustrated by the following Revenue Procedure.

Beginning in 2009, however, § 121(b)(4)[5] prorates the exclusion for any portion of gain attributable to nonqualified use during the period of ownership after 2008, that is, any use other than as a qualified residence, including use as a vacation home or for rental, exclusions for: (i) any period after the taxpayers cease using it as a principal residence, (ii) any period of extended military or similar duty (under § 121(d)(9), and (iii) other period of temporary absence up to two years for employment, health conditions, or unforeseen circumstances. The proration applies even for periods before the five-year period used in determining whether the residence was a personal residence for two years, but, as indicated above, portions of the five-year period after the taxpayer's move out are not counted as nonqualified use. Although the provision seems designed to require proration when a vacation or rental property is converted to a principal residence to take advantage of the exclusion, its provisions, including the exclusion for the up to three years after moving out, make this purpose less than clear. Moreover, because what is disqualified is a portion of gain, not of the $250,000 exclusion, if the gain is large enough, there may be no bite. For example, if 60 percent of the period of ownership is nonqualified use, and the gain is $1,000,000, the entire $250,000 exclusion should apply because the effect of § 121(b)(4) is to disqualify 60 percent of the gain, or $600,000 gain, leaving $400,000 of gain eligible for exclusion. Thus a single taxpayer could take advantage of the entire $250,000 exclusion, although, of course, a married couple would lose $100,000 of the $500,000 exclusion otherwise available.

Rev. Proc. 2005-14, 2005-7 I.R.B. 528

* * *

SECTION 2. BACKGROUND

.01 Section 121(a) provides that a taxpayer may exclude gain realized on the sale or exchange of property if the property was owned and used as the taxpayer's principal residence for at least 2 years during the 5-year period ending on the date of the sale or exchange. Section 121(b) provides generally that the amount of the exclusion is limited to $250,000 ($500,000 for certain joint returns). Under § 121(d)(6), any gain attributable to depreciation adjustments (as defined in § 1250(b)(3)) for periods after May 6, 1997, is not eligible for the exclusion. This limitation applies only to depreciation allocable to the portion of the property to which the § 121 exclusion applies. *See* § 121-1(d)(1).

.02 Under § 1.121-1(e) of the Income Tax Regulations, a taxpayer who uses a portion of a property for residential purposes and a portion of the property for business purposes is treated as using the entire property as the taxpayer's principal residence for purposes of satisfying the 2-year use requirement if the residential and business portions of the property are within the same dwelling unit. The term "dwelling unit" has the same meaning as in § 280A(f)(1), but does not include appurtenant structures or other property. If, however, the business portion of the property is separate from the dwelling unit used for residential purposes, the gain allocable to the business portion of the property is not excludable unless the taxpayer has also met the 2-year use requirement for the business portion of the property.

.03 Section 1.121-1(e)(3) provides that, for purposes of determining the amount of gain allocable to the residential and business portions of the property, the taxpayer must allocate the basis and the amount realized using the same method of allocation the taxpayer used to determine depreciation adjustments (as defined in § 1250(b)(3)). Allocation based on the square footage of the residential and business portions of the property is an appropriate method of allocating the basis and the amount realized. *Poague v. United States*, 66 A.F.T.R.2d (RIA) 5825 (E.D. Va. 1990), *aff'd*, 947 F.2d 942 (4th Cir. 1991).

.04 Section 1031(a) provides that no gain or loss is recognized on the exchange of property held for productive use in a trade or business or for investment (relinquished property) if the property is exchanged solely for property of like kind (replacement property) that is to be held either for productive use in a trade or business or for investment. Under § 1031(b), if a taxpayer also receives cash or property that is not like-kind property (boot) in an exchange that otherwise qualifies under § 1031(a), the taxpayer must recognize gain to the extent of the boot. Section 1031 does not apply to property that is used solely as a personal residence.

.05 Section 1012 provides that the basis of property is its cost. The basis of property acquired in an exchange is its fair market value, unless otherwise provided in the Code or regulations (for example, § 1031(d)). *See Philadelphia Park Amusement Co. v. United States*, 126 F. Supp. 184 (Ct. Cl. 1954).

.06 Under § 1031(d), the basis of the replacement property is the same as the basis of the relinquished property, decreased by the amount of cash received and increased by the amount of gain recognized by the taxpayer in the exchange.

.07 Neither § 121 nor § 1031 addresses the application of both provisions to a single exchange of property. Section 121(d)(5)(B), however, provides rules for applying § 121 and another nonrecognition provision, § 1033, to a single replacement of property. Under § 1033, in general, gain is recognized only to the extent the amount realized from a compulsory or involuntary conversion of property exceeds the cost of qualifying replacement property, and the basis of the replacement property is its cost reduced by the amount of the gain not recognized.

.08 Section 121(d)(5)(B) provides that, in applying § 1033, the amount realized from the sale or exchange of property is treated as the amount determined without regard to § 121, reduced by the amount of gain excluded under § 121. Under § 121(d)(5)(B), the amount realized from an exchange of a taxpayer's principal residence for purposes of applying § 1033 is the fair market value of the relinquished property reduced by the amount of the gain excluded from gross income under § 121. Thus, Congress concluded that for exchanges meeting the requirements of both § 121 and § 1033, (1) the § 121 exclusion should be applied to gain from the exchange before the application of § 1033, (2) for purposes of determining gain that may be deferred under § 1033, the § 121 exclusion should be applied first against amounts received by the taxpayer that are not reinvested in the replacement property (amounts equivalent to boot that would result in gain recognition absent the application of § 121), and (3) the gain excluded under § 121 should be added in the calculation of the taxpayer's basis in the replacement property. . . .

* * *

SECTION 4. APPLICATION

.01 *In general.* Taxpayers within the scope of this revenue procedure may apply both the exclusion of gain from the exchange of a principal residence under § 121 and the nonrecognition of gain from the exchange of like-kind properties under § 1031 to an exchange of property by applying the procedures set forth in this section 4.

.02 *Computation of gain.*

(1) *Application of § 121 before § 1031.* Section 121 must be applied to gain realized before applying § 1031.

(2) *Application of § 1031 to gain attributable to depreciation.* Under § 121(d)(6), the § 121 exclusion does not apply to gain attributable to

depreciation deductions for periods after May 6, 1997, claimed with respect to the business or investment portion of a residence. However, § 1031 may apply to such gain.

(3) *Treatment of boot.* In applying § 1031, cash or other non-like kind property (boot) received in exchange for property used in the taxpayer's trade or business or held for investment (the relinquished business property), is taken into account only to the extent the boot exceeds the gain excluded under § 121 with respect to the relinquished business property.

.03 *Computation of basis.* In determining the basis of the property received in the exchange to be used in the taxpayer's trade or business or held for investment (the replacement business property), any gain excluded under § 121 is treated as gain recognized by the taxpayer. Thus, under § 1031(d), the basis of the replacement business property is increased by any gain attributable to the relinquished business property that is excluded under § 121.

SECTION 5. EXAMPLES

In each example below, the taxpayer is an unmarried individual and the property or a portion of the property has been used in the taxpayer's trade or business or held for investment within the meaning of § 1031(a) as well as used as a principal residence as required under § 121.

Example 1. (i) Taxpayer *A* buys a house for $210,000 that *A* uses as *A*'s principal residence from 2000 to 2004. From 2004 until 2006, *A* rents the house to tenants and claims depreciation deductions of $20,000. In 2006, *A* exchanges the house for $10,000 of cash and a townhouse with a fair market value of $460,000 that *A* intends to rent to tenants. *A* realizes gain of $280,000 on the exchange.

(ii) *A*'s exchange of a principal residence that *A* rents for less than 3 years for a townhouse intended for rental and cash satisfies the requirements of both §§ 121 and 1031. Section 121 does not require the property to be the taxpayer's principal residence on the sale or exchange date. Because *A* owns and uses the house as *A*'s principal residence for at least 2 years during the 5-year period prior to the exchange, *A* may exclude gain under § 121. Because the house is investment property at the time of the exchange, *A* may defer gain under § 1031.

(iii) Under section 4.02(1) of this revenue procedure, *A* applies § 121 to exclude $250,000 of the $280,000 gain before applying the nonrecognition rules of § 1031. *A* may defer the remaining gain of $30,000, including the $20,000 gain attributable to depreciation, under § 1031. *See* section 4.02(2) of this revenue procedure. Although *A* receives $10,000 of cash (boot) in the exchange, *A* is not required to recognize gain because the boot is taken into account for purposes of § 1031(b) only to the extent the boot exceeds the amount of excluded gain. *See* section 4.02(3) of this revenue procedure.

These results are illustrated as follows.

Amount realized	$470,000

Less:	Adjusted basis	$190,000
	Realized gain	$280,000
Less:	Gain excluded under § 121	$250,000
	Gain to be deferred	$30,000

(ii) *A*'s basis in the replacement property is $430,000, which is equal to the basis of the relinquished property at the time of the exchange ($190,000) increased by the gain excluded under § 121 ($250,000), and reduced by the cash *A* receives ($10,000)). *See* section 4.03 of this revenue procedure.

Example 2. (i) Taxpayer *B* buys a property for $210,000. The property consists of two separate dwelling units (within the meaning of § 1.121-1(e)(2)), a house and a guesthouse. From 2001 until 2006, *B* uses the house as *B*'s principal residence and uses the guesthouse as an office in *B*'s trade or business. Based on the square footage of the respective parts of the property, *B* allocates 2/3 of the basis of the property to the house and 1/3 to the guesthouse. In 2006, *B* exchanges the entire property for a residence and a separate property that *B* intends to use as an office. The total fair market value of *B*'s replacement properties is $360,000. The fair market value of the replacement residence is $240,000 and the fair market value of the replacement business property is $120,000, which is equal to the fair market value of the relinquished business property. From 2001 to 2006, *B* claims depreciation deductions of $30,000 for the business use. *B* realizes gain of $180,000 on the exchange.

(ii) Under § 121, *B* may exclude gain of $100,000 allocable to the residential portion of the house (2/3 of $360,000 amount realized, or $240,000, minus 2/3 of $210,000 basis, or $140,000) because *B* meets the ownership and use requirements for that portion of the property. Because the guesthouse is business property separate from the dwelling unit and *B* has not met the use requirements for the guesthouse, *B* may not exclude the gain allocable to the guesthouse under § 1.121-1(e). However, because the fair market value of the replacement business property is equal to the fair market value of the relinquished business property and *B* receives no boot, *B* may defer the remaining gain of $80,000 (1/3 of $360,000 amount realized, or $120,000, minus $40,000 adjusted basis, which is 1/3 of $210,000 basis, or $70,000, adjusted by $30,000 depreciation) under § 1031.

These results are illustrated as follows:

	Total property	**2/3 residential property**	**1/3 business property**
Amount realized	$360,000	$240,000	$120,000
Basis	$210,000	$140,000	$70,000
Depreciation adjustment	$30,000		$30,000
Adjusted basis	$180,000	$140,000	$40,000
Realized gain	$180,000	$100,000	$80,000
Gain excluded under ¶ 121	$100,000	$100,000	
Gain deferred under ¶ 1031	$80,000		$80,000

(iii) Because no portion of the gain attributable to the relinquished business property is excluded under § 121 and *B* receives no boot and recognizes no gain or loss in the exchange, *B*'s basis in the replacement business property is equal to *B*'s basis in the relinquished business property at the time of the exchange ($40,000). *B*'s basis in the replacement residential property is the fair market value of the replacement residential property at the time of the exchange ($240,000).

Example 3. (i) Taxpayer *C* buys a property for $210,000. The property consists of a house that constitutes a single dwelling unit under § 1.121-1(e)(2). From 2001 until 2006, *C* uses 2/3 of the house (by square footage) as *C*'s principal residence and uses 1/3 of the house as an office in *C*'s trade or business. In 2006, *C* exchanges the entire property for a residence and a separate property that *C* intends to use as an office in *C*'s trade or business. The total fair market value of *C*'s replacement properties is $360,000. The fair market value of the replacement residence is $240,000 and the fair market value of the replacement business property is $120,000, which is equal to the fair market value of the business portion of the relinquished property. From 2001 to 2006, *C* claims depreciation deductions of $30,000 for the business use. *C* realizes gain of $180,000 on the exchange.

(ii) Under § 121, *C* may exclude the gain of $100,000 allocable to the residential portion of the house (2/3 of $360,000 amount realized, or $240,000, minus 2/3 of $210,000 basis, or $140,000) because *C* meets the ownership and use requirements for that portion of the property.

(iii) The remaining gain of $80,000 (1/3 of $360,000 amount realized, or $120,000, minus $40,000 adjusted basis, which is 1/3 of $210,000 basis, or $70,000, adjusted by $30,000 depreciation) is allocable to the business portion of the house (the office). Under section 4.02(1) of this revenue procedure, *C* applies § 121 before applying the nonrecognition rules of § 1031. Under § 1.121-1(e), *C* may exclude $50,000 of the gain allocable to the office because the office and residence are part of a single dwelling unit. *C* may not exclude that portion of the gain ($30,000) attributable to depreciation deductions, but may defer the remaining gain of $30,000 under § 1031.

These results are illustrated as follows:

	Total property	**2/3 residential property**	**1/3 business property**
Amount realized	$360,000	$240,000	$120,000
Basis	$210,000	$140,000	$70,000
Depreciation adjustment	$30,000		$30,000
Adjusted basis	$180,000	$140,000	$40,000
Realized gain	$180,000	$100,000	$80,000
Gain excluded under ¶ 121	$150,000	$100,000	$50,000
Gain deferred under ¶ 1031	$30,000		$30,000

(iv) *C*'s basis in the replacement residential property is the fair market value of the replacement residential property at the time of the exchange ($240,000). *C*'s basis in the replacement business property is $90,000, which is equal to *C*'s basis in the relinquished business property at the time of the exchange ($40,000), increased by the gain excluded under § 121 attributable to the relinquished business property ($50,000). *See* section 4.03 of this revenue procedure.

* * *

NOTES AND COMMENTS

The basic principles adopted in Rev. Proc. 2005-14 for allocating the gain and basis on the residential and nonresidential portions of the property, so as to allow combining the exclusion for the residential portion under § 121 with the nonrecognition provision for like-kind exchanges under § 1031 for the nonresidential portion, are similar to those under § 121(d)(5) and Treas. Reg. § 1.121-4(d) relating to coordination with involuntary conversions. Rev. Proc. 2005-14 makes appropriate adjustment for the difference between involuntary conversions under § 1033, which cover the entire involuntarily converted property, and like-kind exchanges under § 1031, which cover only the portion of the residence used for business (or investment). Applying § 121 first, and, in particular, applying it to boot first is quite favorable to taxpayers, because it, in effect, reduces the amount of boot by the $250,000 or $500,000 exclusion under § 121(b), correspondingly reducing the gain recognized.

Where the taxpayer owns only a partial interest in the residence, the sale of that interest may qualify for the § 121 exclusion. Treas. Reg. § 1.121-4(e)(1); *see* Rev. Rul. 84-43, 1984-1 C.B. 27 (legal life estate that was taxpayer's sole interest qualified for the exclusion under the former version of § 121). If the taxpayer applies the exclusion to a sale of a remainder interest in the residence, the exclusion cannot also apply to the sale of the other interest, presumably a life estate. § 121(d)(8)(A); Treas. Reg. § 121-4(e)(2). A sale of a remainder to a related party, however, does not qualify for the exclusion. § 121(d)(8)(B); Treas. Reg. § 1.121-4(e)(2)(B). A sale of a residence held through a grantor trust, for example, qualifies, Treas. Reg. § 1.121-1(c)(3)(i), as does a sale by a bankruptcy trustee, with the benefit of the exclusion going to the bankruptcy estate, Treas. Reg. § 1.1398-3, but other sales by trusts or estates do not qualify.

PROBLEM FOR DISCUSSION

Problem 5-21. Ten years ago, Doc and her husband, Harry, a consultant (the Docs), purchased a single-family residence for $280,000 (paying $40,000 down and taking the property subject to a $240,000 mortgage). At the cost of $17,000, she refurbished two of the rooms in the house as her professional office. She has been properly treating 25 percent of the costs of operating the house (including insurance, taxes, mortgage interest, etc.) as business expenses and has depreciated the special improvements plus 25 percent of the cost of the purchase price allocable to the office (that is, $210,000 as the cost of the house, with the remaining $70,000 allocated to the land) plus the improvements under the straight-line method over a 40-year life as an additional business expense (total basis for depreciation purposes of $72,000). Because their children are now adults who own their own homes and the Docs are approaching retirement (he is now 63-years old and she is 61) they have been trying unsuccessfully to sell the house and move into smaller quarters.

Fortunately, their house stands in the way of progress in the form of a proposed interstate highway and was recently condemned. The proposed highway, and the fact that the Docs' property might be on the right-of-way, was first announced five years ago. Their condemnation award was $1,200,000 of which they received $980,000 in cash and the condemning authority paid off the $220,000 balance of the mortgage. They have purchased a new house within the required replacement period that had a larger portion (40%) allocated to the office for a total purchase price of $500,000, of which $100,000 was paid and cash and $400,000 by taking out a new mortgage, leaving them with net cash of $880,000.

After the highway plans were announced, but before the condemnation, and looking toward retirement, the Docs purchased a house in Florida four years ago for $250,000, $50,000 in cash $200,000 by taking the property subject to the existing mortgage. A smaller portion of the Florida house (20%) is devoted to an office Doc plans to use for a part-time practice in semi-retirement. Harry, who hates the cold, now spends the six or seven winter months in Florida, with Doc flying down for weekends. The Florida house will eventually be the only residence when Doc retires from her current practice in five years or so. Shortly after they purchased the Florida home, on the advice of their tax accountant, they changed their voting residence to Florida and started reporting Florida as their principal residence to save state income tax on their income other than that from the medical practice.

These facts may be summarized:

	Total	*Residence*	*Office*
Purchase Price:	$280,000	$210,000	$70,000
Mortgage	240,000	180,000	60,000
Net Cash Equity	$40,000	$30,000	$10,000
Adjusted Basis:			
Land	$60,000	$45,000	$15,000
Building	220,000	165,000	55,000
Improvements	17,000	-0-	-18,000
Adjusted Basis	$279,000	$210,000	$69,000
Proceeds	$1,600,000	$1,200,000	$400,000
Mortgage Payoff	220,000	165,000	55,000
Net Cash Proceeds	$1,380,000	$1.035,000	$345,000
Gain	$1,321,000	$990,000	$331,000
New House			
Purchase Price	$500,000	$300,000	$200,000
Mortgage	400,000	240,000	160,000
Cash Equity	$100,000	$60,000	$40,000

	Total	*Residence*	*Office*
Florida House:			
Purchase Price	$250,000	$200,000	$50,000
Mortgage	200,000	160,000	40,000

	Total	*Residence*	*Office*
Cash Equity	$50,000	$40,000	$10,000

Assuming the Docs make all appropriate elections for nonrecognition of gain and both new houses were acquired within appropriate periods, what are the tax consequences of these transactions? *See* § 121; Treas. Reg. § 1.121-1 and 4(d); Rev. Proc. 2005-14 (apply § 121 first, then like-kind exchange); *Guinan* (too much time in the sun); *Aagaard* (only the part of multi-family building used as residence qualifies under former § 1034); Rev. Rul. 82-26 (allocate the proceeds and defer gain on the pro rata portion of the gain allocable to the residence portion; no allocation required when business use terminated prior to sale);

§ 3.03. Charitable Contributions

§ 170(e); Treas. Reg. § 1.170-4A(a), (b)(1) and (2), and (d) Ex. 1.

Although no specific provision of the Code provides for the nonrecognition of gain or loss for any difference between the basis of property contributed in kind to a charity and the fair market value that is used to measure the charitable deduction, nonrecognition has long been the general rule. *See* Treas. Reg. § 1.170A-1(c)(2) (amount of contribution is equal to the value of the property contributed, implicitly assuming no gain recognized on the transfer); Rev. Rul. 55-410, 1955-1 C.B. 297 (contribution of property to satisfy a pledge of a specific dollar amount is not a realization event). The apparent basis for this result is that there is no amount realized on the charitable contribution, although the use of appreciated property to pay expenses typically results in gain recognition. The fact that gain is not recognized on the contribution of appreciated property to a charity means that, at high tax rates, a taxpayer could have more after-tax cash by making a charitable contribution of appreciated property than if the taxpayer had sold the property. For example, at a marginal tax rate of 60 percent, a charitable contribution of property with a fair market value of $1,000 will produce a tax savings of $600. Alternatively, if the property had a basis of $100 and a sale produced $900 of ordinary income, the taxpayer would have been subject to a tax liability of $540, leaving him with only $460 after taxes.

Not all taxpayers are able to avoid the realization and recognition of gain on the transfer of property to a charity, as shown in the following case:

HAVERLY v. UNITED STATES

United States Court of Appeals, Seventh Circuit
513 F.2d 224 (7th Cir. 1975)

Hastings, Senior Circuit Judge: This case presents for resolution a single question of law which is of first impression: whether the value of unsolicited sample textbooks sent by publishers to a principal of a public elementary school, which he subsequently donated to the school's library and for which he claimed a charitable deduction, constitutes gross income to the principal within the meaning of Section 61 of the Internal Revenue Code . . .

* * *

During the years 1967 and 1968 Charles N. Haverly was the principal of the Alice L. Barnard Elementary School in Chicago, Illinois. In each of these years publishers sent to the taxpayer unsolicited sample copies of textbooks which had a total fair market value at the time of receipt of $400. The samples were given to taxpayer for his personal retention or for whatever disposition he wished to make. The samples were provided, in the hope of receiving favorable consideration, to give taxpayer an opportunity to examine the books and determine whether they were suitable for the instructional unit for which he was responsible. The publishers did not intend that the books serve as compensation.

In 1968 taxpayer donated the books to the Alice L. Barnard Elementary School Library. The parties agreed that the donation entitled the taxpayer to a charitable deduction under . . . § 170, in the amount of $400, the value of the books at the time of the contribution.

The parties further stipulated that the textbooks received from the publishers did not constitute gifts within the meaning of . . . § 102 since their transfer to the taxpayer did not proceed from a detached and disinterested generosity nor out of affection, respect, admiration, charity or like impulses.

Taxpayer's report of his 1968 income did not include the value of the textbooks received, but it did include a charitable deduction for the value of the books donated to the school library. The Internal Revenue Service assessed a deficiency against the taxpayer representing income taxes on the value of the textbooks received. . . .

* * *

. . . The taxpayer concedes that receipt of the books does not fall within any of the specific exclusions from gross income set out in Sections 101 through 124 of Title 26. The only question remaining is whether the value of the textbooks received is included within "all income from whatever source derived."

The Supreme Court has frequently reiterated that it was the intention of Congress "to use the full measure of its taxing power" and "to tax all gains except those specifically exempted." . . . The Supreme Court has also held that the language of Section 61(a) encompasses all "accessions to wealth, clearly realized, and over which the taxpayers have complete dominion." . . .

There are no reported cases which have applied these definitions of income to the question of the receipt of unsolicited samples. The parties have cited to the court a number of cases applying income definitions to other fact situations. We have considered these cases, but we find them of no particular assistance in resolving the question before us. In view of the comprehensive conception of income embodied in the statutory language and the Supreme Court's interpretation of that language, we conclude that when the intent to exercise complete dominion over unsolicited samples is demonstrated by donating those samples to a charitable institution and taking a tax deduction therefor, the value of the samples received constitutes gross income.

The receipt of textbooks is unquestionably an "accession to wealth." Taxpayer recognized the value of the books when he donated them and took a $400 deduction therefor. Possession of the books increased the taxpayer's wealth. Taxpayer's receipt and possession of the books indicate that the income was "clearly realized." Taxpayer admitted that the books were given to him for his personal retention or whatever disposition he saw fit to make of them. Although the receipt of unsolicited samples may sometimes raise the question of whether the taxpayer manifested an intent to accept the property or exercised "complete dominion" over it, there is no question that this element is satisfied by the unequivocal act of taking a charitable deduction for donation of the property.

The district court recognized that the act of claiming a charitable deduction does manifest an intent to accept the property as one's own. It nevertheless declined to label receipt of the property as income because it considered such an act indistinguishable from other acts unrelated to the tax laws which also evidence an intent to accept property as one's own, such as a school principal donating his sample texts to the library without claiming a deduction. We need not resolve the question of the tax consequences of this and other hypothetical cases discussed by the district court and suggested by the taxpayer. To decide the case before us we need only hold, as we do, that when a tax deduction is taken for the donation of unsolicited samples the value of the samples received must be included in the taxpayer's gross income.

This conclusion is consistent with Revenue Ruling 70-498, 1970-2 Cum. Bull. 6, in which the Internal Revenue Service held that a newspaper's book reviewer must include in his gross income the value of unsolicited books received from publishers which are donated to a charitable organization and for which a charitable deduction is taken. This ruling was issued to supersede an earlier ruling, Rev. Rul. 70-330, 1970-1 Cum. Bull. 14, that mere retention of unsolicited books was sufficient to cause them to be gross income.

The Internal Revenue Service has apparently made an administrative decision to be concerned with the taxation of unsolicited samples only when failure to tax those samples would provide taxpayers with double tax benefits. It is not for the courts to quarrel with an agency's rational allocation of its administrative resources.

* * *

NOTES AND COMMENTS

Although the decision in *Haverly* explicitly applies only in connection with the charitable contribution of property received for services, § 170(e), which implicitly recognizes the general nonrecognition principle, now requires a reduction in the contribution for the amount of the unrecognized gain that would be treated as ordinary income for contributions of property not eligible for long-term capital gain on the sale at the time of the contribution, and of capital gain for a smaller list of contributions of property that would produce a capital gain on sale. The practical effect of this provision is to limit the amount of the charitable contribution deduction to the taxpayer's basis in the property. In Rev. Rul. 84-1, 1984-1 C.B. 39, a radio station was entitled to deduct contributions to charity of lodging and transportation that was provided by the hotels and airlines to the radio station in exchange for radio advertising. The station included the lodging in gross income at fair market value so that it had an equivalent basis in them. *See* § 3.01 *Capital Asset Defined*, in Chapter 2, for a discussion of what assets are eligible for capital gains.

PROBLEM FOR DISCUSSION

Problem 5-22. Rich contributes Property with a basis of $10,000 and a value of $150,000 to Favorite Charity to satisfy a $10,000 pledge. (i) What is the tax effect to Rich if Property is a capital asset? (ii) If it is an ordinary income asset? (iii) If Property is a right to receive compensation? (iv) In each case, how does the result to Rich and Favorite Charity compare with the result if Rich sold Property and contributed the after-tax proceeds to Favorite Charity? *See* § 170(e); *Haverly* (income on books contributed to charity); Rev. Rul. 84-1 (deduction of lodging and transportation received for advertising); Rev. Rul. 55-410 (no realization on property contributed to satisfy a pledge).

Chapter 6

EXECUTIVE COMPENSATION AND STOCK OPTIONS

In general, employers provide nonqualified deferred compensation for a variety of reasons, generally not tax-driven, such as encouraging and keeping the executives happy. From the employer's perspective, deferred compensation may be designed to provide incentives for the executives to use their maximum efforts and skills, and to encourage loyalty to the employer and its shareholders. Executives, however, have two principal goals; namely assuring they will not be taxed on the deferred compensation until receipt, and reducing the risk of nonpayment.

The lure of the capital gains preference provides an incentive for corporate executives and other highly compensated individuals to seek arrangements that improve on the advantage of deferring taxation on compensation until receipt of payment, and that permit them to receive corporate stock or other equity interests in a form that provides capital gain treatment: (i) with deferral of gain recognition and the tax rate advantages of equity investments, and (ii) with little or no amounts treated as compensation taxed as ordinary income. Stock options are a familiar form of such arrangements. The actual transfer of stock or other equity interests, usually subject to restrictions, is another common arrangement. Section 83, discussed in § 2 *Restricted Property*, provides for the valuation and timing of compensation paid in the form of property, and further provides the degree to which the appreciation is ordinary income or capital gain. Some of the incentive advantages of equity-based compensation can be achieved without actually making the employee a shareholder or other owner of equity (including rewarding of efforts by compensation based on increases in profits or in the value of equity), but with loss of the lure of capital gains, by the use of stock appreciation rights (SARs) or phantom stock discussed in § 2.01 *Stock Appreciation Rights (SARs)*. There are two basic types of compensatory stock options: (i) Incentive (or Statutory) Stock Options (ISOs); and (ii) options that do not meet the statutory requirements, called Nonstatutory Stock Options (NSOs), but sometimes called "nonqualified stock options" (NQOs) reflecting that the statutory predecessor of the ISO was the "qualified stock option" or that the term "qualified" encompasses employee stock purchase plans under § 423, as well as ISOs under § 422. Section 422 governs ISOs, and generally provides for no tax effect upon the exercise of the option and capital gain when the shares are sold, but imposes significant limitations on achieving this favorable treatment, which allows capital gain when the shares acquired on exercise of the ISO are sold. Nonstatutory Stock Options (NSOs) are, generally, subject to § 83 on exercise, which requires recognition of the difference between the value of the shares at exercise and the option price, but for subsequent appreciation to be treated as capital gain (or loss). NSOs are discussed in § 3 *Nonstatutory Stock Options (NSOs)*, which also discusses options granted to lenders or in other noncompensatory contexts, in § 3.03

Noncompensatory NSOs; and ISOs and employee stock purchase plans are discussed in § 4 *Incentive Stock Options (ISOs)*.

Except for noncompensatory NSOs, most forms of equity-based remuneration are a form of nonqualified deferred compensation, subject to statutory and other rules that are quite different from those governing qualified pension and profit-sharing plans and similar plans. Qualified pension plans allow the employer an immediate deduction for contributions to the plan, but, for most employees, these plans defer income earned in their high-earning years until later periods when their incomes may be taxed at lower rates and/or they are retired. An additional tax benefit is that the investment income is earned on funds held by qualified plans during the period of deferral, so that it is not taxed until distributed to the employee as part of the pension. Because of the importance of these tax incentives to qualified plans, the Code has become, as a practical matter, the principal source of regulating qualified plans in their role in pension policy. The Code provides strict coverage, participation, vesting, funding, nondiscrimination, and contribution limitations that do not allow major corporate executives to receive the amounts of deferred compensation that they desire solely under qualified plans. To prevent watering down the incentive effect of qualified plans, and for other policy reasons, §§ 83(h) (transfers of property) and 404(a)(5) (transfers of cash) defer the employer's deduction in the case of nonqualified deferred compensation until the (usually cash-method) employee includes the nonqualified deferred compensation in income. Section 1 *Deferred Compensation*, describes the principles that apply to deferred compensation generally paid in cash.

§ 1. DEFERRED COMPENSATION

The principles of nonqualified deferred compensation are, generally, applications of basic cash-method principles. The traditional approach to deferred compensation is discussed in § 1.01 *Traditional Deferred Compensation Principles*. Reflecting the corporate scandals of the beginning of the century, the American Jobs Creation Act of 2004 (2004 Act) placed significant new limits on nonqualified deferred compensation plans and now require immediate taxation of deferred compensation unless strict limitations are met. These requirements are summarized in § 1.02 *2004 Limitations — § 409A*.

§ 1.01. Traditional Deferred Compensation Principles

I.R.C. §§ 83(h); 404(a)(5) and (d)

For most of the last half century, the basic principles of nonqualified deferred compensation were based on the following ruling:

Rev. Rul. 60-31, 1960-1 C.B. 174, *modified by* Rev. Rul. 64-279, 1964-2 C.B. 121 and Rev. Rul. 70-435, 1970-2 C.B. 100

Advice has been requested regarding the taxable year of inclusion in gross income of a taxpayer, using the cash receipts and disbursements method of accounting, of compensation for services received under the circumstances described below.

(1) On January 1, 1958, the taxpayer and corporation *X* executed an employment contract under which the taxpayer is to be employed by the corporation in an executive capacity for a period of five years. Under the contract, the taxpayer is entitled to a stated annual salary and to additional compensation of $10x$ dollars for each year. The additional compensation will be credited to a bookkeeping reserve account and will be deferred, accumulated, and paid in annual installments equal to one-fifth of the amount in the reserve as of the close of the year immediately preceding the year of first payment. The payments are to begin only upon (a) termination of the taxpayer's employment by the corporation; (b) the taxpayer's becoming a part-time employee of the corporation; or (c) the taxpayer's becoming partially or totally incapacitated. Under the terms of the agreement, corporation *X* is under a merely contractual obligation to make the payments when due, and the parties did not intend that the amounts in the reserve be held by the corporation in trust for the taxpayer.

The contract further provides that if the taxpayer should fail or refuse to perform his duties, the corporation will be relieved of any obligation to make further credits to the reserve (but not of the obligation to distribute amounts previously contributed); but, if the taxpayer should become incapacitated from performing his duties, then credits to the reserve will continue for one year from the date of the incapacity, but not beyond the expiration of the five-year term of the contract. There is no specific provision in the contract for forfeiture by the taxpayer of his right to distribution from the reserve; and, in the event he should die prior to his receipt in full of the balance in the account, the remaining balance is distributable to his personal representative at the rate of one-fifth per year for five years, beginning three months after his death.

(2) The taxpayer is an officer and director of corporation *A*, which has a plan for making future payments of additional compensation for current services to certain officers and key employees designated by its board of directors. This plan provides that a percentage of the annual net earnings (before Federal income taxes) in excess of $4,000x$ dollars is to be designated for division among the participants in proportion to their respective salaries. This amount is not currently paid to the participants; but, the corporation has set up on its books a separate account for each participant and each year it credits thereto the dollar amount of his participation for the year, reduced by a proportionate part of the corporation's income taxes attributable to the additional compensation. Each account is also credited with the net amount, if any, realized from investing any portion of the amount in the account.

Distributions are to be made from these accounts annually beginning when the employee (1) reaches age 60, (2) is no longer employed by the company, including cessation of employment due to death, or (3) becomes totally disabled to perform his duties, whichever occurs first. The annual distribution will equal a stated percentage of the balance in the employee's account at the close of the year immediately preceding the year of first payment, and distributions will continue until the account is exhausted. However, the corporation's liability to make these distributions is contingent upon the employee's (1) refraining from engaging in any business competitive to that of the corporation, (2) making himself available to the corporation for consultation and advice after retirement or termination of his services, unless disabled, and (3) retaining unencumbered any interest or benefit under the plan. In the event of his death, either before or after the beginning of payments, amounts in an employee's account are distributable in installments computed in the same way to his designated beneficiaries or heirs-at-law. Under the terms of the compensation plan, corporation *A* is under a merely contractual obligation to make the payments when due, and the parties did not intend that the amounts in each account be held by the corporation in trust for the participants.

(3) On October 1, 1957, the taxpayer, an author, and corporation *Y*, a publisher, executed an agreement under which the taxpayer granted to the publisher the exclusive right to print, publish and sell a book he had written. This agreement provides that the publisher will (1) pay the author specified royalties based on the actual cash received from the sale of the published work, (2) render semiannual statements of the sales, and (3) at the time of rendering each statement make settlement for the amount due. On the same day, another agreement was signed by the same parties, mutually agreeing that, in consideration of, and notwithstanding any contrary provisions contained in the first contract, the publisher shall not pay the taxpayer more than $100x$ dollars in any one calendar year. Under this supplemental contract, sums in excess of $100x$ dollars accruing in any one calendar year are to be carried over by the publisher into succeeding accounting periods; and the publisher shall not be required either to pay interest to the taxpayer on any such excess sums or to segregate any such sums in any manner.

(4) In June 1957, the taxpayer, a football player, entered into a two-year standard player's contract with a football club in which he agreed to play football and engage in activities related to football during the two-year term only for the club. In addition to a specified salary for the two-year term, it was mutually agreed that as an inducement for signing the contract the taxpayer would be paid a bonus of $150x$ dollars. The taxpayer could have demanded and received payment of this bonus at the time of signing the contract, but at his suggestion there was added to the standard contract form a paragraph providing substantially as follows:

> The player shall receive the sum of $150x$ dollars upon the signing of this contract, contingent upon the payment of this 150 x dollars to an escrow agreement designated by him. The escrow agreement shall be subject to approval by the legal representatives of the player, the Club, and the escrow agent.

Pursuant to this added provision, an escrow agreement was executed on June 25,1957, in which the club agreed to pay $150x$ dollars on that date to the *Y* bank, as escrow agent, and the escrow agent agreed to pay this amount, plus interest to the taxpayer in installments over a period of five years. The escrow agreement also provides that the account established by the escrow agent is to bear the taxpayer's name; that payments from such account may be made only in accordance with the terms of the agreement; that the agreement is binding upon the parties thereto and their successors or assigns; and that in the event of the taxpayer's death during the escrow period the balance due will become part of his estate.

(5) The taxpayer, a theatrical performer, enters into an agreement with a producer whereby the taxpayer and the producer agree to share the profits and

losses from the production of a play. Under the agreement the producer is to furnish the cash necessary to produce the play and will assume the usual duties and obligations of a producer. The taxpayer will play the leading role in the production and will also direct the play. In addition, the taxpayer is responsible for supervising various aspects of the production itself, including the hiring of other performers and the designing of scenery. The agreement further provides that no more than 25 percent of the taxpayer's share of the net profits from the play are to be paid to him annually during the run of the play. The net profits accumulated for the taxpayer are to be paid him in equal amounts annually for a period of four years commencing with the closing of the play. Provision is also made for the actor to obtain periodic financial statements as to the income and expenditures relating to the production of the play.*

* * *

. . . [T]he following conclusions have been reached:

(1) The additional compensation to be received by the taxpayer under the employment contract concerned will be includible in his gross income only in the taxable years in which the taxpayer actually receives installment payments in cash or other property previously credited to his account. To hold otherwise would be contrary to the provisions of the regulations and the court decisions mentioned [below]. . . .

(2) For the reasons in (1) above, it is held that the taxpayer here involved also will be required to include the deferred compensation concerned in his gross income only in the taxable years in which the taxpayer actually receives installment payments in cash or other property previously credited to his account.

. . . Section 1.402(b)-1(a)(1) provides in part, with an exception not here relevant, that any contribution made by an employer on behalf of an employee to a trust during a taxable year of the employer which ends within or with a taxable year of the trust for which the trust is not exempt under section 501(a) of the Code, shall be included in income of the employee for his taxable year during which the contribution is made if his interest in the contribution is nonforfeitable at the time the contribution is made. Revenue Ruling 57-37 [1957-1 C.B. 18, *as modified by* Revenue Ruling 57-528 [1957-2 C.B. 263], held, *inter alia*, that certain contributions conveying fully vested and nonforfeitable interests made by an employer into separate independently controlled trusts for the purpose of furnishing unemployment and other benefits to its eligible employees constituted additional compensation to the employees includible . . . in their income for the taxable year in which such contributions were made. These Revenue Rulings are distinguishable from cases "(1)" and "(2)" in that . . . no trusts for the benefit of the taxpayers were created and no contributions are to be made thereto. Consequently, section 402(b) of the Code and section 1.402(b)-1(a)(1) of the regulations are inapplicable.

(3) Here the principal agreement provided that the royalties were payable substantially as earned, and this agreement was supplemented by a further concurrent agreement which made the royalties payable over a period of years. This

* As substituted by Rev. Rul. 70-435.

supplemental agreement, however, was made before the royalties were earned; in fact, it was made on the same day as the principal agreement and the two agreements were a part of the same transaction. Thus, for all practical purposes, the arrangement from the beginning is similar to that in (1) above. Therefore, it is also held that the author concerned will be required to include the royalties in his gross income only in the taxable years in which they are actually received in cash or other property.

(4) In arriving at a determination as to the includibility of the 150*x* dollars concerned in the gross income of the football player, under the circumstances described, in addition to the authorities cited above, consideration also has been given to Revenue Ruling 55-727, C.B. 1955-2, 25, and to the decision in *E.T. Sproull v. Commissioner*, 16 T.C. 244 [(1951)].

In Revenue Ruling 55-727, the taxpayer, a professional baseball player, entered into a contract in 1953 in which he agreed to render services for a baseball club and to refrain from playing baseball for any other club during the term of the contract. In addition to specified compensation, the contract provided for a bonus to the player or his estate, payable one-half in January 1954 and one-half in January 1955, whether or not he was able to render services. The primary question was whether the bonus was capital gain or ordinary income; and, in holding that the bonus payments constituted ordinary income, it was stated that they were taxable for the year in which received by the player. However, under the facts set forth in Revenue Ruling 55-727 there was no arrangement, as here, for placing the amount of the bonus in escrow. Consequently, the instant situation is distinguishable from that considered in Revenue Ruling 55-727.

In *E.T. Sproull* . . . , the petitioner's employer in 1945 transferred in trust for the petitioner the amount of $10,500. The trustee was directed to pay out of principal to the petitioner the sum of $5,250 in 1946 and the balance, including income, in 1947. In the event of the petitioner's prior death, the amounts were to be paid to his administrator, executor, or heirs. The petitioner contended that the Commissioner erred in including the sum of $10,500 in his taxable income for 1945. In this connection, the court stated:

> * * * it is undoubtedly true that the amount which the Commissioner has included in petitioner's income for 1945 was used in that year for his benefit * * * in setting up the trust of which petitioner, or, in the event of his death then his estate, was the sole beneficiary * * *.
>
> The question then becomes * * * was "any economic or financial benefit conferred on the employee as compensation" in the taxable year. If so, it was taxable to him in that year. This question we must answer in the affirmative. The employer's part of the transaction terminated in 1945. It was then that the amount of the compensation was fixed at $10,500 and irrevocably paid out for petitioner's sole benefit. * * *.

Applying the principles stated in the *Sproull* decision to the facts here, it is concluded that the 150*x*-dollar bonus is includible in the gross income of the football player concerned in 1957, the year in which the club unconditionally paid such amount to the escrow agent.

(5) In this case the individual performer and the producer are each acting in his own right; the proposed production of the play is a joint venture considered a partnership under section 761(a) of the Code and the taxpayer is neither an employee nor an independent contractor as to the producer. This joint venture is required to file a return for each taxable year under section 6031 of the Code, computing the taxable income of the partnership. . . . [E]ach partner is required, in determining his own income tax to take into account his distributive share (whether or not distributed) of each class or item of partnership income, gain, loss, deduction or credit, determined under the provisions of the partnership agreement . . . . The effect of this is that the performer taxpayer's distributive share of the net profits from the play is includible in his taxable income in his first taxable year ending with or after the first taxable year of the partnership, although the joint venture retains physical possession thereof by virtue of the arrangement with the taxpayer who, in substance, has thus authorized it to take possession and hold such net profits for him for distribution at a later time. Thereafter, the taxpayer's proportionate share of the net profits for each taxable year of the joint venture is includible in his gross income for each taxable year of his which ends with or after the taxable year of the joint venture.*

* * *

As previously stated, in each case involving a deferral of compensation, a determination of whether the doctrine of constructive receipt is applicable must be made upon the basis of the specific factual situation involved.

* * *

With respect to deductions for payments made by an employer under a deferred compensation plan, see section 404(a)(5) of the 1954 Code and section 1.404(a)-12 of the Income Tax Regulations.

In the application of those sections to unfunded plans, no deduction is allowable for any compensation paid or accrued by an employer on account of any employee under such a plan except in the year when paid and then only to the extent allowable under section 404(a). Thus, under an unfunded plan, if compensation is paid by an employer directly to a former employee, such amounts are deductible under section 404(a)(5) when *actually* paid *in cash or other property to the employee*, provided that such amounts meet the requirements of section 162 or section 212.

* * *

NOTES AND COMMENTS

Although § 409A, discussed in § 1.02 *2004 Limitations — § 409A*, places significant new restrictions on deferred compensation, the basic principles set forth in Rev. Rul. 60-31 remain the starting point for deferring compensation, because if the compensation deferral does not meet those requirements, the § 409A limitations generally are not relevant because the compensation is not deferred.

* As substituted by Rev. Rul. 70-435.

Rev. Rul. 60-31, particularly in the first two situations, confirmed that it was not necessary that the deferred compensation be forfeitable in order for cash-method employees to defer the income until receipt. When deferral does not satisfy the requirement that it be represented solely by an unfunded, unsecured contractual right against the recipient of the services, for example, the deferred compensation obligation is secured or is payable by a third party (other than a member of the employer's affiliated group, such as a parent corporation paying a subsidiary's employees), it is taxable under cash-method accounting principles, because the security or third-party obligation is considered payment of the compensation. Thus, although not a requirement for deferral under Rev. Rul. 60-31, a forfeiture restriction allows deferral even when security or a third-party obligation would otherwise make it taxable, because the compensation is not earned as long as it is forfeitable to the recipient of the services. Thus, in Rev. Rul. 77-420, 1977-2 C.B. 172, *amplifying* Rev. Rul. 69-50, 1969-1 C.B. 140, physicians who agreed with a health care insurer to defer receipt of a percentage of the fees otherwise payable to them by the insurer for services rendered to its subscribers were immediately taxable on the deferred amounts, even though the deferred payment was subject to a substantial risk of forfeiture, because forfeiture was to insurer, not to the patients, who were considered to be the recipients of the services, so that the insurer was a third-party obligor. On the other hand, in Rev. Rul. 69-474, 1969-2 C.B. 105, a pension provided under an arrangement for medical group partnership that agreed to provide medical services to a medical and hospital corporation's members was taxable to the physicians only on receipt. Although the medical group received capitation fees for its services, it had no contractual relation with the patients directly. The medical group established a pension plan for the physicians that provided rights to a pension contingent on the conditions of the plan being met when the payments were due to any particular physician.

Subsequent administrative guidance allows the employee to have limited additional assurances of payment as long as the creditors of the employer have priority over any funds set aside until payment. *See* Rev. Rul. 72-25, 1972-1 C.B. 127 (employer purchased and owned an annuity contract to fund its deferred compensation liability, but employee had no rights to annuity); Priv. Ltr. Rul. 81-13-107 (the "rabbi trust" ruling, a congregation funded a trust for the benefit of its rabbi, with the funds invested, but still subject to claims of creditors). In short, in these rulings, the employees, in effect, required the employers to have set aside funds for the future obligation, but remained at risk of the employer's business. The employee can obtain further security, provided the employee pays for it directly or indirectly, by including the costs of the security in income when incurred by the employer. Thus, in Priv. Ltr. Rul. 84-06-012, deferred compensation is not accelerated when the employee purchased a financial surety bond from an independent insurance company to pay the deferred compensation payments if the corporation could not pay for any reason, because the employer did not provide the security. A similar result was reached in Priv. Ltr. Rul. 93-44-038, which held that deferred compensation is not accelerated when the employer purchases a similar surety bond to back up the rabbi trust, and increased employee's salary by the amount of the premium, which employee included in income, in effect, paying the premium.

Rabbi trusts of the type described in Priv. Ltr. Rul. 81-13-107 have become sufficiently widespread that the Service issued Rev. Proc. 92-64, 1992-2 C.B. 422, containing a model grantor trust — that is, a trust, income of which is taxed directly to the creator under §§ 671 *ff.*, for use in executive compensation arrangements popularly referred to as "rabbi trust" arrangements, that must be adopted verbatim to obtain a favorable ruling, except where substitute language is expressly permitted: (i) the trustee of the trust must be an independent third party; (ii) the trust can be revocable or irrevocable, but must specify that it is a grantor trust, so that its income is taxed to the employer, and it must hold its assets separate from other corporate assets; (iii) the trust income can be distributed to the corporation or reinvested; (iv) but the trust must specify that the plan participants have no beneficial interest in the assets, and that the assets are subject to the claims of general creditors; (v) the trustee stops making payments when the corporation is insolvent. The trustee can be granted the power to invest in stock of the employer corporation, but only if the company expressly retains a right to substitute assets of equal value in a nonfiduciary capacity, making it clear that the trust is a grantor trust. Plan participants cannot direct investments. Rev. Proc. 92-65, 1992-2 C.B. 428, provides ruling guidelines that require the deferral election to be made before the beginning of the period of service for which compensation is payable; generally, the employee's taxable year for calendar year taxpayers, a position initially stated in Rev. Proc. 71-19, 1971-1 C.B. 698, with a 30-day grace period for newly eligible employees. Moreover, Rev. Proc. 92-65 limits early distributions and transferability of rights under the plan. Although not dealt with in the Rev. Procs., some companies reduce the earnings accumulated to reflect the tax imposed on the company's interim earnings. *See McAdams v. Mass. Mut. Life Ins. Co.*, 391 F.3d 287 (1st Cir. 2004) (such tax charge held legal).

In Priv. Ltr. Rul. 98-10-005, an arrangement for the benefit of a provider of services, apparently the Permanente group, provided for an irrevocable trust created, funded, and owned by a tax exempt organization to which the group provided services, apparently the Kaiser Foundation, to fund the group's nonqualified unfunded supplemental retirement benefit plan for the group's individual service providers. The contributions were made to the trust based on the actuarial value of retirement benefits to accrue at least two years after the contribution, and were paid to the group when the benefits became nonforfeitable — that is, when the individual service providers reached retirement age and completed required years of service. Amounts in the trust based on retirement benefits that were forfeited by individual service providers were forfeited to the trust. The amounts in trust were subject to the tax-exempt organization's creditors until they became nonforfeitable, so that the income was taxable to it or, presumably nontaxable because of its exempt status. The trust's assets were subject to the provider's creditors for the period between transfer from the trust to the provider and actual payment to the individual service providers, so that it was taxable to the group until paid. Thus the arrangement deferred taxation to the group of the benefits for the group's individual service providers to the extent the benefits were forfeitable by the group's individual service providers, achieving the benefits of a rabbi trust described below without having the income taxed to the group.[1] Although the ruling does not address the issue, the individual service providers were presumably not taxable on their benefits until paid. Although the ruling finds that the trust is a grantor trust, it does not cite Rev. Proc. 92-64, nor does it specify terms of the trust in sufficient detail to confirm that they satisfy the requirements of Rev. Proc. 92-64. In an extreme case, *Childs v. Commissioner*, 103 T.C. 634 (1994), *aff'd per curiam*, 89 F.3d 856 (11th Cir. 1996), the plaintiff's law firm was allowed to defer fees for a structured settlement that paralleled payments to the injured parties, because the court treated the liability insurers as the relevant obligors. In Tech. Adv. Mem. 93-36-001, the Service took a contrary position on what seems to be same facts as to annuity policies payment rights, applying the theory that obligation of the insurer was the obligation of a third party, and the obligations were not forfeitable.

Some authorities, nevertheless, determined that compensation could be deferred as long as the deferral election was made before the compensation became payable. Thus, in *Martin v. Commissioner*, 96 T.C. 814 (1991), the court held that an election to defer rights to payment for shadow stock benefits under new plan substituted for old one otherwise due on termination of employment, did not result in immediate compensation on termination, when the election was made by one executive two weeks before he was fired, and by another about four months before he quit, because amount was not ascertainable and due when election was made. Because most of the services had been performed before the revised deferral election, the decision seems questionable, even under prior law, and almost certainly does not survive enactment of § 409A, discussed in § 102 *2004 Limitations — § 409A*.

PROBLEM FOR DISCUSSION

Problem 6-1. Exec and other key employees of Ceeco are entitled to deferred compensation under a nonqualified deferred compensation plan, with assets placed in an irrevocable grantor (rabbi) trust that allows investment in Ceeco shares and satisfies all but one of the requirements of Rev. Proc. 92-64. Because Exec is a significant shareholder, instead of providing, as required by Rev. Proc. 92-64, that Ceeco shall have the right at any time, and from time to time in its sole discretion, to substitute assets of equal fair market value for any asset held by the Trust, the plan gives Ceeco the power to borrow from the rabbi trust with adequate security, but at a rate one-half a percentage point below the rate it pays on equivalent debt from third parties. This borrowing power is equivalent, under § 674 relating to grantor trusts, to the power specified in Rev. Proc. 92-64 to substitute assets in making the rabbi trust a grantor trust. In addition to the rabbi trust, Ceeco's obligations under the deferred compensation plan are secured by a letter of credit obtained by Ceeco from Countribanc, with the charges for the letter of credit allocated ratably in reduction of the amounts otherwise payable to Exec and the other key employees under the deferred compensation plan. The plan allows

[1] Although not directly relevant to the issues in the case, if the assumptions about the identity of the parties is correct, the arrangement solved a problem for the group created by the decision in *United States v. Basye*, 410 U.S. 441 (1973), which held that the partners in the group were taxable on benefits under an earlier similar arrangement even though the amounts payable to individual partners were forfeitable and unascertainable, because the benefits to the partnership were ascertainable.

employees to make or revoke elections to defer compensation at any time, provided the change applies only to compensation earned after the date the employee gives Ceeco notice of the change. At the beginning of 20X1, Exec elects to defer 10 percent of her salary and profit sharing bonus for 20X1. On June 30, when Exec determines that 20X1 will be a very good year, she increases her deferral to 20 percent of her salary for the last six months of the year and to 20 percent of as much of her bonus as relates to earnings for the last half of Ceeco's year. Her salary for 20X1 is $600,000 ($50,000 a month), and her bonus is $800,000, of which $300,000 is attributable to Ceeco earnings before June 30, and $500,000 to Ceeco earnings after July 1. How much, if any, of the $90,000 deferred from her salary ($30,000 up to June 30, and $60,000 after July 1) and of her bonus is deferred, and how much is currently taxable to her? *See* Rev. Rul. 60-31, *modified by* Rev. Rul. 64-279 and Rev. Rul. 70-435 (traditional deferred compensation); *Martin* (election to defer rights to payment for shadow stock benefits under new plan substituted for old one shortly before one executive was fired and another quit validly deferred amounts otherwise payable on termination); Rev. Rul. 72-25 (employer purchased an annuity contract to fund its deferred compensation liability); Priv. Ltr. Rul. 81-13-107 ("rabbi trust"); Priv. Ltr. Rul. 84-06-012 (employee purchase of financial surety bond from an independent insurance company did not accelerate deferred compensation); Priv. Ltr. Rul. 93-44-038 (employer purchased surety bond to back up rabbi trust increased employee's salary but did not accelerate deferred compensation); *Childs* (plaintiff's law firm was allowed to defer fees for a structured settlement); Tech. Adv. Mem. 93-36-001 (contrary Service position on similar facts).

§ 1.02. 2004 Limitations — § 409A

I.R.C. § 409A; Treas. Reg. §§ 1.409A-1 through 1.409A-3 and 1.409A-6; Prop Treas. Reg. § 1.409A-4.

In the 2004 Act, Congress responded to perceived abuses with deferred compensation, particularly as highlighted by the Enron, Tyco, WorldCom, and other corporate scandals. The new rules, found in I.R.C. § 409A, are a combination of statutory codifications of Service positions with respect to the requirements for deferring compensation under Rev. Rul. 60-31 and subsequent applications that had been challenged by aggressive, probably over-aggressive, taxpayers, including: (i) timing of deferral elections, (ii) limitations on early distribution, and (iii) limitations on funding arrangements. In addition, § 409A attempts to deal with corporate governance issues, and includes a provision that makes the acceleration of deferred compensation payments improper when there is a change in the employer's financial health. Treas. Reg. § § 1.409A-1 to –3, and –6 provide guidance on a number of issues under § 409A.

The new rules apply to very broadly defined "nonqualified deferred compensation plans," *see* § 409A(d)(1), Treas. Reg. § 1.409A-1(a), including arrangements with a single individual, § 409A(d)(3), Treas. Reg. § 1.409-1(c)(1), a position that the Service had taken earlier. In Rev. Rul. 88-68, 1988-2 C.B. 117, it held that amounts paid to an independent contractor pursuant to an individually negotiated arrangement that were spread over three years, were deferred compensation, with the result that the accrual method service recipient could not deduct the expense until the amounts were paid to the independent contractor. Deferral refers to having a legal right to compensation that is payable in a later year, rather than in the year when the legal right is created. Treas. Reg. § 1.409A-1(a). As discussed below with the relevant arrangements, some SARs, *see* § 2.01 *Stock Appreciation Rights (SARs)*, and NSOs, *see* § 3 *Nonstatutory Stock Options (NSOs)*, are subject to the new rules, Treas. Reg. § 1.409A-1(b)(5)(i), but ISOs, *see* § 4 *Incentive Stock Options (ISOs)*, are not, Treas. Reg. § 1.409A-1(b)(5)(ii), nor is restricted property subject to § 83, *see* § 2.02 *Restricted Property — § 83*, Treas. Reg. § 1.409A-1(b)(6), apparently on the assumption that those provisions provide their own satisfactory limitations. Amounts payable under nonqualified deferred compensation plans that do not satisfy the strict new limits for any participant are immediately includible in income to the extent the amount is not subject to "a substantial risk of forfeiture, that is, conditioned on future performance of substantial services." § 409A(a)(1) and (d)(4) (which tracks similar language in § 83(c)(1)), but as discussed below, the § 409A regulations are more restrictive in what constitutes a substantial risk of forfeiture. To the extent that amounts are deferred under nonqualified deferred compensation plans that do not satisfy the strict new limits, any deferred compensation received by any participant is subject to an increased underpayment interest rate and an additional 20 percent tax when included. § 409A(a)(1)(B).

The regulations under § 409A primarily address how to avoid having a "nonqualified deferred compensation arrangement" or, less obliquely, how to have a qualified deferred compensation arrangement. Although not a model of the drafter's art, if the participant recognizes that the plan does not satisfy the deferral requirements, and includes the amount in income when earned, or within 2½ months of the later of the end of the employer's or employee's year, even though not paid, the penalties should not apply because no amount was "deferred." This is not stated expressly in those terms in § 409A or the legislative history, but is implied in Treas. Reg. § 1.409A-1(b)(1) and (4); and because the provisions only refer to payments in the 2½-month period, they leave open the argument that an amount that is included in income, but that is not paid, may not be covered. Service recipients (employers) are required to report all amounts deferred under a nonqualified deferred compensation plans when earned, even though not paid. §§ 6041(g) and 6051(a)(13).

Generally, tracking the Service position on elective deferrals prior to the enactment of § 409A, § 409A(a)(4)(B) requires that an irrevocable election to defer compensation be made no later than the end of the year preceding the service year, that is, the year for performance of the services covered by the deferred compensation, Treas. Reg. § 1.409A-2(a)(1), or within 30 days of eligibility for the participant's first year of eligibility for a nonqualified deferred compensation plan, but only for compensation earned after the date of election. Treas. Reg. § 1.409A-2(a)(7). Even when the employer and employee are on different tax years, this apparently means by the end of the employee's earlier tax year when a bonus is based on performance during a calendar year — that is, by the end of 2010 for a bonus based on calendar year 2011 performance. Treas. Reg. § 1.409-2(a)(6). The regulation can, however, be read to mean that the election may have to be made a year earlier — that is, before the end of 2009. On the other hand, it is sufficient if, for example, a bonus received in 2011 is based on the corporation's fiscal year ending Sept. 30, 2011, which includes portions of calendar year 2010 and 2011, apparently making the election before the beginning of the fiscal year. Treas. Reg. § 1.409A-2(a)(9) Ex. 4.

A special rule allows an election no later than six months from the end of a period of at least 12 months in the case of performance-based compensation based on the employee's performance during the period. § 409A(a)(4)(B)(iii). Distributions of the deferred compensation can only be made on: (i) separation from service (or six months after separation for key employees, which appears to be a corporate governance provision); (ii) a scheduled time under the plan at the time of the deferral election; (iii) the participant's death, disability, or the occurrence of an unforeseen emergency; or (iv) a change in ownership, or effective control of the corporation, or ownership of a substantial portion of its assets. § 409(a)(2); Treas. Reg. § 1.409A-2(a)(8) and 1(e). Where a plan permits a subsequent delay or change in the form of payment, under § 409A(a)(4)(C): (i) the subsequent election cannot take effect for 12 months, Treas. Reg. § 1.409A-2(b)i); (ii) except for payments on death, disability, or unforeseeable emergency must require a further five-year deferral of distributions scheduled for a fixed date, Treas. Reg. § 1.409A-2(b)(2)(ii); (iii) for payments made for a specified time or on a specified schedule, must be made at least 12 months before the first specified payment, Treas. Reg. § 1.409A-2(b)(iii).

The definition of performance-based compensation is essentially the same as that under § 162(m) and Treas. Reg. § 1.162-27(e) relating to the limitation of the corporate deduction for compensation to specified employees to $1,000,000, but with a broad exception for performance-based compensation. Treas. Reg. §§ 1.162-27-(e)(2)(v) and 1.409A-1(e)(1) provide that compensation does not lose its status as performance-based compensation if it can be paid on death, disability, or change of control even when the performance goals have not been met, but that, if paid on those events, it loses its special status as performance-based compensation. Priv. Ltr. Rul. 1999-49-014 extended the exclusion to allow payment if the executive was terminated by the company without cause, or the executive terminated employment for good reason, before the achievement of the performance goals. Priv. Ltr. Rul. 2006-13-012 sanctioned a similar provision, although in that ruling only a pro rata portion of the award would be paid. The Service changed its position in Priv. Ltr. Rul. 2008-04-004, and ruled that such a provision would prevent any benefits under the plan qualifying as performance based, even when not paid under the exceptions for firing without cause or quitting for a good reason. After a storm of protest, the Service effectively withdrew the implicit retroactive effect of the change of position in Rev. Rul. 2008-13, 2008-1 C.B. 518, which reaffirmed the limitation of permissible payouts without achievement of the performance goals to the regulatory exceptions of death, disability, or change of control, but made it effective only for compensation periods beginning after Jan. 1, 2009.

The regulations do not specify the effect of the compensation's ceasing to be performance-based when it is paid on death, disability, or a change of control, but the consequence under Treas. Reg. § 1.162-27 is presumably that it is no longer exempt from the $1,000,000 limit on deduction provided by § 162(m)(4)(C). The effect under Treas. Reg. § 1.409A-1 is less clear, because the only effect of compensation's being performance based is that the election to defer can be made up to six months before the end of the period. § 409A(a)(4)(B)(iii); Treas. Reg. § 1.409A-2(a)(8). It seems to be unduly harsh to invalidate the election on death, making the compensation subject to the 20 percent penalty and the one percentage point interest penalty of § 409A(a)(B). Accordingly, those consequences should apply only if the compensation is not paid during the year of the triggering event.

Where a plan permits a subsequent delay or change in the form of payment, under § 409A(a)(4)(C) the subsequent election cannot take effect for 12 months and must require a further five-year deferral of distributions scheduled for a fixed date. Treas. Reg. § 1.409A-2(b)(1). Distributions of the deferred compensation can only be made on: (i) separation from service (or six months after separation for key employees, which appears to be a corporate governance provision); (ii) the participant's death, disability, or the occurrence of an unforeseen emergency; (iii) a scheduled time under the plan at the time of the deferral election; or (iv) a change in ownership, or effective control of the corporation, or ownership of a substantial portion of its assets. § 409(a)(2). Treas. Reg. § 1.409A-3(a).

Compensation is deferred if it is payable in a tax year later than the year in which the service provider has a legally binding right to the compensation, apparently without regard to whether it is subject to a substantial risk of forfeiture. Treas. Reg. § 1.409A-1(b)(1). On the other hand, the election only needs to be made at least 12 months before the substantial risk of forfeiture lapses. Treas. Reg. § 1.409A-2(a)(5). Because compensation is not earned as long as it is subject to a substantial risk of forfeiture — that is, a requirement of significant future services, it is not deferred compensation until the forfeiture restriction lapses. Thus, the definition of substantial risk of forfeiture not only prevents the devices used to allow easy acceleration, it also limits cases in which the recipient may claim that compensation is not deferred because it has not been earned. Although the statutory language in § 409A(d)(4) is substantially the same as that in § 83(c)(1), Treas. Reg. § 1.409A-1(b) is more limiting than the similar definition in Treas. Reg. § 1.83-3(c), requiring that the forfeiture condition be directly related to the service provider's performance for the service recipient or its business activities; and excluding noncompetition provisions and most forfeiture provisions imposed after the beginning of the service period. It also specifies that the risk be nondiscretionary and objective, Treas. Reg. § 1.409A-1(b)(1), but allow subjective criteria as long as the service provider does not control the determination. Treas. Reg. § 1.409A-1(b)(2). Like Treas. Reg. § 1.83-3(c)(3), they emphasize the lack of likelihood of enforcement of the forfeiture restriction when the executive owns substantial stock or is a key executive in a public corporation.

Reflecting a Service concern that some deferred compensation plans allowed participants to receive accelerated distributions upon request, "subject to a minimal amount of forfeiture" (i.e., a 'haircut' provision), which violated the spirit, if not the letter of the constructive receipt § 409A(a)(3), plans may not "permit the acceleration of the time or schedule of any payment," except as permitted by the Service. Consistent with the legislative history, nonelective distributions required by reasons beyond the participant's control, including (i) pursuant to a domestic relations order, (ii) to comply with federal conflict of interest statutes, or (iii) to pay payroll taxes, are permitted. Treas. Reg. § 1.409A-3(j). Treas. Reg. § 1.409A-3(h)(1) also states that waiver of a forfeiture restriction, such as an acceleration of vesting, is not an impermissible acceleration of distribution.

Responding to executives' desires to protect their deferred compensation, some rabbi trusts were apparently being funded by use of asset protection devices, particularly foreign trusts that would be difficult for the employer's creditors to reach. Section 409A(b)(1) responds to this concern by providing that if assets set aside for paying nonqualified deferred compensation are located outside the United States or are transferred outside the United States, or when transferred outside the United States, they are treated as compensation paid, subject to Service authority to provide regulatory exceptions. § 409(e)(3).

In a similar vein, responding to plans that restrict assets to payment of deferred compensation, if there is a change in the employer's financial health, § 409A(b)(2) also calls for immediate taxation of funds set aside for nonqualified deferred compensation at the earlier of the date when the plan first provides that assets will be restricted to the provision of such benefits "in connection with a change in the employer's financial health," to be defined by regulation, or when the assets are so restricted. The fact that the assets are subject to claims of general creditors is irrelevant under the statute. The Conference Report provides that the provision applies if a plan calls for transferring assets to a rabbi trust upon a change in financial health. H.R. Conf. Rep. No. 108-755, 108th Cong., 2nd Sess. 743 (2004). This seems to be more a corporate governance than tax provision, because the use of "plain vanilla" (especially domestic) rabbi trusts for nonqualified deferred compensation is not restricted by § 409A. The regulations allow acceleration of payments on termination of a plan, but not if the termination occurs "proximate to a downturn in the financial health of the service recipient." There is a similar limitation on acceleration to settle bona fide disputes as to rights of payment that are proximate to a downturn in the employer's financial health.

Proposed regulations issued in December 2008, Prop. Regs. 1.409A-4, address the computation of the relevant amounts. Prop. Treas. Reg. § 1.409A-4(a)(1) provides a seemingly simple calculation formula that the amount includible for any year is the total amount deferred in that year reduced by any amount subject to a substantial risk of forfeiture and by any amount previously included in income. For this purpose, amounts are subject to a substantial risk of forfeiture only if the forfeiture risk continues through the end of the year, Prop. Treas. Reg. § 1.409A-4(a)(2), and is included in income only if properly includible and actually included in an original or amended return. Prop. Treas. Reg. § 1.409A-4(a)(3). Amounts not so included may be considered deferred in subsequent years. Prop. Treas. Reg. § 1.409A-4(a)(1)(ii). There are complex calculation rules for the amounts deferred to be determined based on present values using reasonable actuarial assumptions and other relevant estimation methods that generally seek to maximize the amount deferred. Prop. Treas. Reg. § 1.409A-4(b). The amount so determined is subject to the 20 percent penalty for the taxable year in which it is required to be included. Prop. Treas. Reg. § 1.409A-4(c). It is also subject to an additional income tax at a premium rate of interest one percentage point higher that would have been incurred for the year includible that applies until the amount is actually included in income as a result of payment or otherwise, with complex rules for determining when that occurs. Prop. Treas. Reg. § 1.409A-4(d). The proposed regulations reserve the treatment of amounts includible under § 409(b) because of funding outside the United States. Prop. Treas. Reg. § 1.409A-4(e). Amounts included in income under § 409A are not included in income when they were to otherwise have been included in income on payment or otherwise. Prop. Treas. Reg. § 1.409A-4(f). The taxpayer is allowed a deduction when amounts included in income under § 409A are subsequently forfeited or the right to payment is otherwise permanently lost. Prop. Treas. Reg. § 1.409A-4(g). The proposed regulations are to be effective only when made final, Prop. Treas. Reg. § 1.409A-4(h), with the degree of interim reliance to be provided by administrative guidance. Preamble REG-148326-05, *Further Guidance on the Application of Section 409A to Nonqualified Deferred Compensation Plans*, 73 Fed. Reg. 74,380, 74,392 (12/9/2008).

Section 457A, added by the Emergency Economic Stabilization Act of 2008, provides additional acceleration of deferred compensation that is not subject to a substantial risk of forfeiture paid by tax-indifferent entities — that is, foreign entities not subject to U.S. tax or tax-exempt entities, so that they do not care about deduction for compensation, and that is attributable to services after December 31, 2008. For this purpose, a substantial risk of forfeiture is limited to one requiring future services; no other risks count. It is targeted primarily for offshore hedge funds, but the language is broad enough to apply to U.S. employees working abroad for foreign corporations and for some foreign citizens working abroad.

Section 409A does not change the results of the first two examples in Rev. Rul. 60-31, but the conditions in those examples become necessary but not sufficient conditions for deferral of compensation, because in addition, the requirements of § 409A(a) must be satisfied, including those prohibiting any subsequent relaxation of the provisions. The third example should be similarly affected, even though it relates to an independent contractor, not an employee, because, although most references in § 409A and the regulations are to employees, the definition of a nonqualified deferred compensation plan is not limited to employees. *See* Rev. Rul. 88-68, 1988-2 C.B. 117 (applies § 404(d), treating deferred payments to independent contractor pursuant to a special arrangement with him as deferred compensation). Because the fourth example finds current compensation, it is not affected. Because the fifth example, in effect, finds a partnership, although § 409A does not exempt partnerships, Notice 2005-1, 2005-1 C. B. 274, provides interim guidance regarding the application of § 409A to arrangements between partnerships and partners that, in effect, exempts grants of certain partnership interests, but that should not affect the application of the pass-through of partnership income when realized, as provided in the example. As indicated, above § 409A(b)(1) limits use of foreign trusts, but not "plain vanilla" domestic trusts.

PROBLEM FOR DISCUSSION

Problem 6-2. To what extent, if any, does § 409A change the results (or analysis) in Problem 6-1? *See* § 409A(4)(b), (d)(1) and (2), and Treas. Reg. §§ 1.409A-1 (a)(1), (2) and (3); (b)(1), (c), and (d)(1) and (2); 1.409A-2(a)(1).

§ 2. RESTRICTED PROPERTY

Most of the equity-based compensation arrangements contain restrictions on the executives' rights to the property for some period in order to provide incentive and act as some form of "golden handcuffs," tying the executive to the company. The restrictions may involve forfeiture, if the executive leaves prematurely, and usually involve restrictions on sale of the shares for a period of time, sometimes extending beyond the end of the forfeiture period. The equity compensation arrangements may be divided roughly into those that grant interests in stock and those that grant stock options.

§ 2.01. Stock Appreciation Rights (SARs)

Treas. Reg. §§ 1.61-2(d)(4); § 404(a)(5) and (b).

Not all equity-based compensation produces capital gains. The following ruling illustrates one form of deferred compensation, known as a stock appreciation right (SAR), that permits the executive or other employee to have some of the advantages (but not the capital gains preference) of increases in the value of a specified number of shares of the corporate stock over the value of that number of shares at the date of the grant, without investing in, or owning the shares. The employee usually has the right to determine when to collect on the appreciation after some period of time, but the SAR usually terminates, at the latest, on separation from service. Thus, there are three relevant dates: the date of grant, the date when the SAR becomes exercisable, and the date of exercise, as of which the employee receives the payment of the increase in value, usually in cash, but sometimes in a smaller number of shares with a value equal to the amount of the appreciation. The ability to give the employee a participation in increases in value of the stock without giving the rights of a shareholder can be particularly useful for closely held corporations. Although an SAR generally provides a free ride on the stock, it is not an option. *See* Priv. Ltr. Rul. 93-41-019 (SARs not taken into account as options in determining whether a redemption from an employee-shareholder is disproportionate under § 302(b)).

Rev. Rul. 80-300, 1980-2 C.B. 165

* * *

A corporation adopted a plan under which key employees of the corporation are granted stock appreciation rights (SAR's). An SAR entitles the employee to a cash payment equal to the excess of the fair market value of one share of the common stock of the corporation on the date of the exercise of the SAR over the fair market value of a share on the date the SAR was granted to the employee. An employee need not own any stock of the corporation to receive an SAR, and SAR's are granted without cost to the employee. To exercise an SAR, an employee must notify the corporation in writing. No SAR is exercisable before one year, and if not exercised by the employee within five years, the SAR's will be deemed to have been exercised on the fifth anniversary of the grant. At that time, the amount of the stock appreciation will automatically be paid to the employee. SAR's are not traded on an established market, and are nonassignable and nontransferable by the grantees.

In 1975, the corporation granted 10 SAR's to *A*, an employee of the corporation. On the date of the grant, the fair market value of the corporation's common stock was $30x$ dollars a share. In 1980, *A* exercised the SAR's when the fair market value of a share of the corporation's stock was $80x$ dollars. *A* received $500x$ dollars.

The courts and the Internal Revenue Service have recognized that a requirement of surrender or forfeiture of a valuable right is a sufficient restriction to make inapplicable the doctrine of constructive receipt. . . . See also Rev. Rul. 58-230, 1958-1 C.B. 204, which holds that a requirement of a six-month suspension from participation in an employees' profit sharing plan upon an employee's withdrawal of the employer's contributions and earnings thereon, and the employee's consequent loss of the benefit of the employer's contributions that would have been made for the six-month period, is a substantial limitation that precludes constructive receipt of the withdrawable amounts.

The forfeiture of a valuable right is a substantial limitation that precludes constructive receipt of income. The employee's right to benefit from further appreciation of stock, in this case, without risking any capital is a valuable right. However, once the employee exercises the stock appreciation rights, the employee loses all chance of further appreciation with respect to that stock and the amount payable becomes fixed and available without limitation. Accordingly, an employee will be in receipt of income on the date the SAR's are exercised.

* * *

An employee who possesses stock appreciation rights is not in constructive receipt of income by virtue of the appreciation of the employer's stock. The cash payment to which the employee is entitled is includible in gross income in the year a stock appreciation right is exercised. Thus, in the example above, the employee must include in gross income $500x$ dollars in 1980 because the SAR's were exercised in that year.

NOTES AND COMMENTS

Accordingly, an SAR is simply a deferred compensation arrangement, with the deferred compensation measured by change in stock value. As a result, the employer is entitled to its deduction at the end of the employee's tax year in which the compensation is paid. *See* Priv. Ltr. Rul. 2000-09-013 (deduction for S corporation that paid outstanding SARs the day before sale of stock and terminated S corporation status on June 30 allowed under § 404(a)(5) and Treas. Reg. § 1.404(b)-1T Q&A-2, during post-sale C corporation part of the year because that was when employee's calendar tax year ended). The grant of an SAR is not subject to payroll taxes, but the exercise is. Treas. Reg. § 31.3121(v)(2)-1(b)(4)(ii). SARs are deferred compensation subject to § 409A, except to the extent that they are structured to comply with its provisions. Treas. Reg. § 1.409A-1(b)(5)(i)(C), (D), and (E). Under the regulations, there is no deferral of compensation if the compensation payable on exercise of the SAR can never be more than the excess of the value of the underlying stock on the date of exercise over the value on the date of grant and there are no other deferral features. Treas. Reg. § 1.409A-1(b)(5)(i)(B). When the underlying stock is publicly traded, valuation is based on the trading price over a reasonable method using actual trading prices. Treas. Reg. § 1.409A-1(b)(5)(iv)(A). If not publicly traded, the value is determined by reasonable application of a reasonable valuation method, based on all the facts and circumstances — including asset values, anticipated cash flows, and stock of comparable corporations — and may include control premiums, marketability discounts, etc., provided they take into account all material information. Treas. Reg. § 1.409(A)-1(b)(5)(iv)(B)(1). Use of current independent appraisals, certain formulas used for nonlapse restrictions, and certain written appraisals of start-up corporations are presumed reasonable. Treas. Reg. § 1.409A-1(b)(5)(iv)(B)(2). Different methods can be used for grant and exercise, and once established cannot be modified, but if the stock becomes publicly traded between grant and exercise, only the trading price can used for exercise. Treas. Reg. § 1.409A-1(b)(5)(iv)(B)(3).

An SAR usually does not provide any right to receive, or be credited with, dividends paid between grant and exercise, but, if it does, and the right is contingent on exercise, it generally converts the SAR into deferred compensation, because it either increases the compensation to more than the spread or reduces the price. Treas. Reg. § 1.409A-1(b)(5)(i)(E). A dividend right that is not contingent on exercise does not disqualify the SAR, but any dividend payable may be deferred compensation when a dividend is declared, presumably unless the dividend is payable (and taxable) immediately. Some plans, labeled phantom stock plans, involve payment by the employee of the value of the shares at grant, and receipt of the value of the shares, not just the appreciation, at exercise, but the employee does not own any stock under state law. *See* Priv. Ltr. Rul. 94-13-023 (compensation realized under such a plan when becomes exercisable, because right to full value of shares means that exercise does not result in surrender of valuable rights); *cf.* Priv. Ltr. Rul. 98-03-023 (rights under phantom stock plan do not create a second class of stock for purposes of qualification as an S corporation under Treas. Reg. § 1.1361-1(b)(4)). Grant of phantom stock under which the employee is to receive the initial value of the stock on exercise is subject to payroll tax at that time. Treas. Reg. § 31.3121(v)(2)-1(b)(5) Ex. 8.

PROBLEM FOR DISCUSSION

Problem 6-3. Essco, an S corporation, which is, of course, not publicly traded, in accordance with an election made by Exec in 20X1, granted Exec in 20X2 a nontransferable, nonassignable certificate that allows Exec to receive an amount equal to any excess of the appraised value of 1,000 Essco shares (less than 5% of the outstanding Essco shares), as determined by qualified independent appraisers, on the date of exercise, increased by an amount equal to a ratable share of any distributions to Essco shareholders after the award, at any time she elects after the anniversary of the award in 20X4, or her earlier death, disability, unforeseeable emergency, or separation from service, until the anniversary of the award in 20X7. The qualified appraisers valued the Essco shares at $100 per share in 20X1. In 20X3, Essco made a $5 per share distribution to its shareholders, so that $5 was added to the amount distributable to Exec. The qualified appraisers determined the value of the Essco shares was $120 per share for 20X3. In 20X4, when Exec's right first became exercisable, the qualified appraisers valued the Essco shares at $115. Essco made a $3 per share distribution to shareholders in 20X4 (properly treated as distributions and not as compensation to the Essco shareholders), so that the amount distributed to Exec became $123 per share, or $123,000 total. Exec did not exercise her right until 20X6 after further distributions of $4 per share in 20X5 and $9 per share in 20X6. The appraised value of the shares in 20X6, when Exec exercised her right, was $140, so that she was entitled to $161,000, including the addition for distributions. In accordance with a provision of the plan, giving Essco the right to distribute the amount in cash or Essco shares with a value equal to the amount of the distribution, Essco distributed to Exec, 1,150 Essco shares with an appraised value of $161,000. (i) Not taking into account § 409A, when does Exec realize income and in what amounts? (ii) If Exec has income before exercise, what is the effect of the distribution of the shares in 20X6? (iii) When is Essco entitled to a deduction (or other allowance)? *See* Rev. Rul. 80-300 (grant of SAR not income, because having to give up a substantial right — the ride — precludes constructive receipt); Priv. Ltr. Rul. 94-13-023 (compensation realized under phantom stock plan when becomes exercisable); Priv. Ltr. Rul. 98-03-008 (S Corp. phantom stock plan); Priv. Ltr. Rul. 2000-09-013 (deduction of S corporation that paid outstanding SARs the day before sale of stock and terminated S corporation status on June 30, allowed under § 404(a)(5) at end of calendar year). (iv) How, if at all, does § 409A affect the analysis? *See* § 409A(a)(1)(A), (2)(A), (4)(A) and (B), and (d)(1); Treas. Reg. § 1.409A-1(b)(5)(i)(B), (C) and (E), and (iv)(B): Treas. Reg. § 31.3121(v)(2)-1(b)(4)(ii).

§ 2.02. Restricted Property — § 83

I.R.C. § 83; Treas. Reg. §§ 1.83-1 to 6 and 8; § 7872(c)(1)(B)

Under the basic realization principle, a taxpayer does not generally recognize income when a restriction on ownership or disposition lapses or terminates. For example, an investor who purchases shares in a private placement, subject to "investment letter" restrictions, does not have a realization event when those restrictions lapse with the passage of time. Taxpayer attempts to use similar principles for compensatory stock before the current Code provisions had mixed success. Thus, taxpayers would take the position that shares that would be forfeited if the employee left the company before the end of a specified period were not compensation because of the forfeiture risk. *See Kuchman v. Commissioner*, 18 T.C. 154 (1952). They would then claim that the lapse of the restriction was not a realization event. *See Lehman v. Commissioner*, 17 T.C. 652 (1951). Finally, when the shares were sold, they would claim capital gains because they held the shares as investors, not employees. For example, if Ceeco transferred 1,000 shares worth $10,000 a share to Exec on Jan. 1, 20X1, subject to forfeiture if Exec was not employed by Ceeco on Jan. 1, 20X4, Exec would not report any income on receipt because of the risk of forfeiture if employment terminated within three years. If Exec was still employed on Jan. 1, 20X4, when the shares were worth $15,000, she would not report income on the ground that the lapse of the restriction was not a realization event. On the disposition of the shares in 20X6 for $20,000, Exec would claim the entire $20,000 as capital gain, because they had been held for the qualifying period.

The Service issued regulations that required recognizing income when the restriction lapsed, but in an amount equal to the lesser of the value at transfer or of the value at lapse. This provided a considerable advantage for the employee who deferred income until the shares were free of restrictions, and who might well have a considerable built-in capital gain if the shares had appreciated in the meanwhile. Thus, in the preceding example, Exec would be required to report $10,000 of compensation for 20X4 when the restriction lapsed, and $10,000 capital gain when the shares were sold because the basis became $10,000 when income was reported in 20X4. Thus, there seems to have been an underlying assumption that there could be one, and only one, compensatory event in the transfer of property — that is, that it would be improper to treat the value of the property determined, taking into account the restrictions as compensation at the time of transfer and to treat the difference in value when the restrictions lapse as additional compensation, or as negative compensation if the forfeiture occurred. Carrying on the preceding example, that, if the value of the shares; at the time of grant taking into account the restrictions was $6,000, Exec would include that amount in income at the time of grant, and an additional $9,000 ($15,000 - $6,000 included in income at grant) when the restriction lapsed. Of course, under this approach, if the shares were forfeited Exec should be entitled to a deduction of $6,000 on forfeiture.

Section 83 changes all of that by, generally, requiring that any compensatory transfer of restricted stock or other property be included in gross income at the time of transfer, with the value determined without regard to any restrictions that may lapse, including even forfeiture restrictions that may deprive the employee of any benefit from the shares when an election under § 83(b), as discussed below, applies. § 83(a); Treas. Reg. § 1.83-1(a). Thus, in the example above, Exec would have $10.000 compensation on the grant, if instead of the forfeiture restriction there was a nontransfer restriction that reduced the value of the shares to $7,000. The constitutionality of this arguably extreme valuation was upheld in *Sakol v. Commissioner*, 574 F.2d 694 (2nd Cir. 1978). Apparently, the unrestricted value of the property as measuring the amount taxable at transfer was adopted, in part, because Congress thought it had to get the tax then, because, under the realization principle, it might be unable to tax any increase in value when the restrictions lapsed. The valuation principle can also be justified as limiting deferral. Even restrictions imposed by law or not otherwise part of the compensation arrangement are disregarded in valuing the compensation received on transfer of property. *See Pledger v. Commissioner*, 641 F.2d 287 (5th Cir. 1981) (same result when restrictions were imposed by federal securities laws, not terms imposed by the employer); *Grant v. United States*, 15 Cl. Ct. 38 (Cl. Ct. 1988) (shares valued at $23 public trading price without regard to restrictions, even though sold in a private sale on the date of purchase subject to those restrictions for $14). The valuation date is when the employee becomes the beneficial owner of the property, not a possibly later date when legal title to the property is transferred. *See Theophilos v. Commissioner*, 85 F.3d 440 (9th Cir. 1996) (value shares on the date employee undertook a binding contract to purchase, not the higher value when paid the purchase price).

Shares that are subject to a substantial risk of forfeiture and are nontransferable by the service provider are not considered transferred until they become either nonforfeitable or transferable. *Robinson v. Commissioner*, 805 F.2d 38 (1st Cir. 1986), *rev'g* 82 T.C. 467 (1984), held that the requirement to resell shares to the company at the purchase price if the shares transferred within one year of purchase was substantial risk of forfeiture; legend on stock certificates stating restriction made shares nontransferable, reversing a Tax Court decision that held the resale requirement to not be a substantial risk of forfeiture, and that the legend did not make shares nontransferable. Section 83(c)(3) treats restrictions under § 16(b) of the Securities Exchange Act as forfeiture restrictions, delaying compensation until the restrictions lapse. Accordingly, Tech. Adv. Mem. 87-06-009 determined that shares purchased by a former executive on exercise of nonstatutory stock options that were subject to § 16(b) requirements were subject to forfeiture restrictions, even though § 16(b) restrictions were held to be lapse restrictions under prior law. Rev. Rul. 2005-48, 2005-2 C.B. 259, however, held that shares acquired on exercise of an nonstatutory stock option were not subject to a substantial risk of forfeiture under § 16(b), even though Treas. Reg. § 1.83-3(j) states that § 16(b) applies for "six months after the purchase," reflecting that in 1991 the Securities and Exchange Commission had changed its rules so that in the case of most options the six-month period begins at the grant of the option, and, in the ruling, the exercise was more than six months after the grant. The ruling announced an intention to amend the regulations to explicitly set forth its holding, but, of course, to date no such amendment has been proposed.

In addition, when the restriction is one that may result in forfeiture of the stock or other property, or that prevents transfer, the stock (or other property) is not owned by the service provider until the forfeiture or transfer restrictions lapse — in effect it is like phantom stock — so that the compensation is postponed until the forfeiture or transfer restriction lapses, with the value measured at that time. § 83(a) (flush language); Treas. Reg. § 1.83-1(a)(1), and 3(a)(1). *See* Rev. Proc. 80-11; 1980-1 C.B. 616 (interim dividends on nonvested stock treated as compensation, not dividends). In the continuing example, because the restriction at grant for Exec was a forfeiture restriction, there is no compensation recognized at grant, but $15,000 compensation when the restriction lapses (compared with $10,000 under the former regulations).

Even though the transferee of property subject to a substantial risk of forfeiture is not the tax owner until the risk lapses, this may not prevent a sale or other transfer under state law. If the transfer is an arm's-length sale, any excess of the proceeds over any basis in the property is compensation at that time, and the transferee is not taxed further when the purchaser disposes of the property. Treas. Reg. § 1.83-1(b). If the transfer is not at arm's length, any excess consideration is still compensation at the time of the transfer but the potential compensation remains with the original recipient of the forfeitable property to be realized when the forfeiture restriction lapses or when there is an arm's-length transfer. Treas. Reg. § 1.83-1(c).

A restriction that will never lapse — for example, a requirement that an employee sell shares to the employer on separation from service, whenever it occurs, at a formula price — is taken into account in determining the amount included in gross income, § 83(a)(1) and (d); Treas. Reg. § 1.83-5(a). Such valuation formulas are frequently used when stock of a corporation that is not publicly traded is transferred to employees. In Tech. Adv. Mem. 97-44-001 and *Riverton Inv. Corp. v.* United States, 170 F. Supp. 2d 608 (W.D. Va. 2001), a corporation issued stock to management employees subject to terms that required them to sell the shares back to the corporation at the higher of the purchase price or 60 percent of book value on termination of employment. Neither the corporation nor the employees treated the issuance as a taxable event. When the shares were subsequently redeemed, the corporation treated the redemption price as a compensation deduction and the employees reported it as compensation income. There was a provision that stated that the provisions relating to termination of employment did not apply to liquidations and reorganizations. The TAM rejected the company's argument that the provision only meant that such an event was not a termination of employment, but that the other limitations continued, and concluded that the restrictions were lapse restrictions, so that any compensation had occurred when the shares were issued. It did not mention that the employees had reported the income when the corporation deducted it, so that they should have been entitled to refunds. The court, however, determined that the provision allowed the management employees to receive the same consideration as other shareholders in a liquidation or merger, but that what they received would remain subject to the buy-back provisions, so that they were nonlapse restrictions. Accordingly, the management shareholders never became owners of the shares for tax purposes and the redemption payments were compensation that was properly deducted by the corporation, and properly included by the employees on redemption, although, of course, the employees were not before the court. Even under the court's interpretation, there may, however, be additional compensation if the restriction is subsequently terminated in connection with a liquidation or merger (or otherwise), unless the termination is not compensatory. Treas. Reg. § 1.83-5(b)

The regulations may also convert what appears to be a transfer of restricted property under § 83 into an NSO, when a purchase is financed by a nonrecourse loan, particularly, a loan by the service recipient, so that the service provider has no risk of loss. Treas. Reg. § 1.83-3(a)(2). *See* § 3.02 *Grant, Exercise and Lapse of NSOs*, for a discussion of the consequences of treating a sale of restricted property financed by a nonrecourse loan as an option.

If the recipient makes an election under § 83(b) and Treas. Reg. § 1.83-2 within 30 days of the transfer, the value of the restricted stock (or other property) is included in gross income on transfer and the service provider becomes the immediate owner of the restricted stock or other property. Because the possibility of forfeiture is a restriction that will lapse, Treas. Reg. § 1.83-2(a) and –3(h) and (i), the amount included as compensation is determined without regard to the risk of forfeiture. Moreover, there is no deduction for the amount included in income if the forfeiture occurs. § 83(b)(1) (flush language); Treas. Reg. § 1.83-2(a). *See Kadillak v. Commissioner*, 127 T.C. 184 (2006), *aff'd*, 534 F.3d 1197 (9th Cir. 2008) (when taxpayer forfeited stock acquired on exercise of ISO for which he made § 83(b) election resulting in recognition of income for purposes of the AMT (although not for regular tax), election was valid, even though nonvested shares held in escrow; capital loss for AMT purposes, but no deduction for amount previously included in income under § 83(b) election when shares forfeited). Under the continuing example, if Exec made an election under § 83(b), she would recognize $10,000 compensation income in 20X1, compared with $15,000 compensation income in 20X4 when the restriction lapsed if she did not. If, however, her employment terminated in 20X2, she would not be entitled to deduct the $10,000 included in income, making a § 83(b) election a substantial risk if the property has a significant value at receipt. Restricted property is subject to Social Security and Medicare taxes when earned, or, if subject to a substantial risk of forfeiture, when the risk lapses. § 3121(v)(2); Treas. Reg. § 31.3121(v)(2)-1. Because there is no special provision on withholding, the employer is required to withhold when the compensation arises. Under the regulations, the deduction or other allowance is contingent on reporting the payment to the Service, including on Form W-2. Treas. Reg. § 1.83-6(a)(2). *See* Rev. Rul. 83-22, 1983-1 C.B. 17 (interim dividends paid on restricted stock for which an election under § 83(b) made are taxed as dividends).

Although nonlapse restrictions are not taken into account in valuation, other valuation factors, such as blockage, may be. *See Robinson v. Commissioner*, T.C. Memo. 1985-275 (before reversal, determined that an 18 percent blockage discount based on expert testimony reduced the value of the shares to Robinson); *Theophilos v. Commissioner* (considers lack of voting rights and lack of control in valuation).

The employer's deduction or other allowance generally occurs at the time the recipient includes the income, whether at transfer because the restrictions are not forfeiture restrictions or because of a § 83(b) election, or when a forfeiture restriction lapses (when there is no § 83(b) election) without regard to the employer's method of accounting, or economic performance, etc. § 83(h); Treas. Reg. § 1.83-6. If the employee makes a § 83(b) election and subsequently forfeits the stock or other property, the employer is required to include the amount of any deduction in income, or to reverse any capitalization, even though the employee has no offsetting allowance. Treas. Reg. § 1.83-6(d)(2). In short, Ceeco is entitled to a deduction (or entitled to capitalize) the amount Exec includes in income, whenever that is. Under Treas. Reg. § 1.83-6(a)(2), the requirement that the employee include the amount in income is satisfied if the employer reports the compensation to the Service. *See Robinson v. United States*, 335 F.3d 1365 (Fed. Cir. 2003) (employer's deduction was allowable based on the amount includible in the employee's income when employer sold restricted stock to its chief operating officer, who made a § 83(b) election reporting no income because the value of the stock was equal to the price paid and notified employer by giving notice to himself; when he was terminated and the owners of the employer discovered the situation, the corporation filed an amended W-2, reporting a stock value of more than $25,000,000; court rejected the argument that the refund depended on the final outcome of the employee's case, holding that "included" meant "includible"); *Venture Funding v. Commissioner*, 110 T.C. 236 (1998), *aff'd by order*, 198 F.3d 248 (6th Cir. 1999), *cert. denied*, 530 U.S. 1205 (2000) (no deduction when employer did not report transfers and employees did not include amounts in income).

Thus, there are two key dates: (i) the date of transfer for property subject to lapse or nonlapse restrictions that are no forfeiture or transfer restrictions or if there is a § 83(b) election event if there are such restrictions; and (ii) the date of lapse or transfer, if there is no § 83(b) election. The employee realizes compensation on the date of transfer measured by the value of the property at that time without regard to lapse restrictions, but taking into account nonlapse restrictions and valuation factors that are not restrictions. A § 83 election makes the date of transfer the compensation and valuation date for property subject to forfeiture or transfer restrictions, with the restrictions disregarded in valuation even though there is a risk of forfeiture, because the risk of forfeiture will lapse. When the compensation is realized on the date lapse and transfer restrictions end, the value is likely to be considerably more than even the unrestricted value at the date of the initial transfer, or, at least, that is what all the parties hope will be the case.

The scope of § 83 is quite broad as illustrated by the following case.

ALVES v. COMMISSIONER

United States Court of Appeals, Ninth Circuit
734 F.2d 478 (9th Cir. 1984)

. . . The appeal raises an unusual question under section 83 of the Internal Revenue Code . . . Section 83 requires that an employee who has purchased restricted stock in connection with his "performance of services" must include as ordinary income the stock's appreciation in value between the time of purchase and the time the restrictions lapse, unless at the time he purchased the stock he elected to include as income the difference between the purchase price and the fair market value at that time. The issue here is whether section 83 applies to an employee's purchase of restricted stock when, according to the stipulation of the parties, the amount paid for the stock equaled its full fair market value, without regard to any restrictions. . . .

General Digital Corporation (the company) was formed in April, 1970, to manufacture and market micro-electronic circuits. At its first meeting, the company's board of directors resolved to issue 90,000 shares of its common stock to its company president, and 66,000 shares to the company underwriter. The board also voted to sell an additional 264,000 shares of common stock to seven named individuals, including Alves. All seven became company employees.

Alves joined the company as vice-president for finance and administration. As part of an employment and stock purchase agreement dated May 22, 1970, the company agreed to sell Alves 40,000 shares of common stock at ten cents per share "in order to raise capital for the Company's initial operations while at the same time providing the Employee with an additional interest in the Company. . . . " . . . The six other named individuals signed similar agreements on the same day. The agreement divided Alves's shares into three categories: one-third were subject to repurchase by the company at ten cents per share if Alves left within four years; one-third were subject to repurchase if he left the company within five years; and one-third were unrestricted. In addition, the company retained an option to repurchase up to one-half of the shares for their fair market value at any time between July 1, 1973 and July 1, 1975.

In transactions not at issue here, Alves sold some of his shares to friends and relatives. In 1973 he sold 4,667 four-year shares to Technology Ventures, Inc. (TVI), the assignee of General Digital's repurchase option, for $18 per share, and in 1974 he sold TVI 2,240 five-year shares for $4 per share.

On July 1, 1974, when the restrictions on the four-year shares lapsed, Alves still owned 4,667 four-year shares that had a fair market value at that time of $6 per share. On March 24, 1975, the restrictions on the 7,093 remaining five-year shares lapsed with the fair market value at $3.43 per share.

Although Alves reported the $8,736 of gain on the sale of the 2,240 five-year shares to TVI as ordinary income on his 1974 tax return, he did not report the difference between the fair market value of the four and five-year shares when the restrictions ended, and the purchase price paid for the shares. . . .

In proceedings before the Tax Court, the parties stipulated that: (1) General Digital's common stock had a fair market value of 10 cents per share on the date Alves entered into the employment and stock purchase agreement; (2) the stock restrictions were imposed to "provide some assurance that key personnel would remain with the company for a number of years;" (3) Alves did not make an election under section 83(b) when the restricted stock was received; (4) the free shares were not includable in gross income under section 83; and (5) the four and five-year restricted shares were subject to a substantial risk of forfeiture until July 1, 1974, and March 24, 1974, respectively.

* * *

Resolution of the legal issue presented here requires an understanding of section 83's background and operation. Congress enacted section 83 in 1969 in response to the existing disparity between the tax treatment of restricted stock plans and other types of deferred compensation arrangements. . . . Prior to 1969, an individual purchasing restricted stock was taxed either when the restrictions lapsed or when the stock was sold in an arm's length transaction. Tax was imposed upon the difference between the purchase price and the fair market value at the time of transfer or when the restrictions lapsed, whichever was less. *See Cohn v. Commissioner*, 73 T.C. 443, 446 (1979). This had both tax deferral and tax avoidance advantages over, for example, employer contributions to an employee's pension or profit sharing trust, which were immediately taxable in the year of receipt. . . .

Section 83 resolved this disparity by requiring the taxpayer either to elect to include the "excess" of the fair market value over the purchase price in the year the stock was transferred, or to be taxed upon the full amount of appreciation when the risk of forfeiture was removed. . . . By its terms, the statute applies when property is: (1) transferred in connection with the performance of services; (2) subject to a substantial risk of forfeiture; and (3) not disposed of in an arm's length transaction before the property becomes transferable or the risk of forfeiture is removed. In the present case, it is undisputed that the stock in question was subject to a substantial risk of forfeiture, that it was not disposed of before the restrictions lapsed, and that Alves made no section 83(b) election. Alves's contention is that because he paid full fair market value for the shares, they were issued as an investment, rather than in connection with the performance of services.

The Tax Court concluded that Alves obtained the stock "in connection with the performance of services" as company vice-president. To the extent that this conclusion is a finding of fact, it is not clearly erroneous. . . . Although payment of full fair market value may be one indication that stock was not transferred in connection with the performance of services, the record shows that until the company sold stock to TVI, it issued stock only to its officers, directors, and employees, with the exception of the shares sold to the underwriter. Alves purchased the stock when he signed his employment agreement and the stock restrictions were linked explicitly to his tenure with the company. In addition, the parties stipulated that the restricted stock's purpose was to ensure that key personnel would remain with the company. Nothing in the record suggests that Alves could have purchased the stock had he not agreed to join the company.

Alves maintains that, as a matter of law, section 83(a) should not extend to purchases for full fair market value. He argues that "in connection with" means that the employee is receiving compensation for his performance of services. In the unusual situation where the employee pays the same amount for restricted and unrestricted stock, the restriction has no effect on value, and hence, Alves contends, there is no compensation.

The plain language of section 83(a) belies Alves's argument. The statute applies to all property transferred in connection with the performance of services. No reference is made to the term "compensation." Nor is there any statutory requirement that property have a fair market value in excess of the amount paid at the time of transfer. Indeed, if Congress intended section 83(a) to apply solely to restricted stock used to compensate employees, it could have used much narrower language. Instead, Congress made section 83(a) applicable to all restricted "property," not just stock; to property transferred to "any person," not just to employees; and to property transferred "in connection with . . . services" not just compensation for employment. . . . As the Second Circuit has noted, Congress drafted section 83(a) as a "blanket rule" in an effort to create "a workable, practical system of taxing employees' restricted stock options." . . .

Section 83's legislative history also reveals that while Congress was concerned primarily with the favorable tax treatment afforded restricted stock plans, it also was concerned that such plans were a means of allowing key employees to become shareholders in businesses without adhering to requirements in other sections of the Code. The Senate Report stated:

> To the extent that a restricted stock plan can be considered a means of giving employees a stake in the business, the committee believes the present tax treatment of these plans is inconsistent with the specific rules provided by Congress in the case of qualified stock options, which were considered by Congress as the appropriate means by which an employee could be given a shareholder's interest in the business.

. . . The legislative history reveals that Congress perceived restricted stock as more than a problem of deferred compensation. It also demonstrates that Congress intended section 83 to apply to taxpayers like Alves who allege that they purchased restricted stock as an investment.

Alves suggests that the language of section 83(b) indicates that Congress meant for that section to apply only to bargain purchases and that section 83(a) should be interpreted in the same way. Section 83(b) allows taxpayers to elect to include as income in the year of transfer "the excess" of the full fair market value over the purchase price. Alves contends that a taxpayer who pays full fair market value would have "zero excess," and would fall outside the terms of section 83(b).

Section 83(b), however, is not a limitation upon section 83(a). Congress designed section 83(b) merely to add "flexibility," not to condition section 83(a) on the presence or absence of an "excess." . . .

Moreover, nothing in section 83(b) precludes a taxpayer who has paid full market value for restricted stock from making an 83(b) election. Treasury Regulations promulgated in 1978 and made retroactive to 1969[4] specifically provide that section 83(b) is available in situations of zero excess:

> If property is transferred . . . in connection with the performance of services, the person performing such services may elect to include in gross income under section 83(b) the excess (if any) of the fair market value of the property at the time of transfer . . . over the amount (if any) paid for such property . . . The fact that the transferee has paid full value for the property transferred, realizing no bargain element in the transaction, does not preclude the use of the election as provided for in this section.

§ 1.83.2(a)(1983) (emphasis supplied). These regulations are consistent with the broad language of section 83 and, as the Tax Court stated, simply make "more explicit a fact which is inherent in the statute itself." . . .

Alves last contends that since every taxpayer who pays full fair market value for restricted stock would, if well informed, choose the section 83(b) election to hedge against any appreciation, applying section 83(a) to the unfortunate taxpayer who made no election is simply a trap for the unwary. The tax laws often make an affirmative election necessary. Section 83(b) is but one example of a provision requiring taxpayers to act or suffer less attractive tax consequences. A taxpayer wishing to avoid treatment of appreciation as ordinary income must make an affirmative election under 83(b) in the year the stock was acquired.

Other courts have considered and rejected even stronger attacks on the broad application of section 83. . . . In the present case, the statutory language, legislative history, applicable regulations and the consistent refusal of courts to create exceptions to the statute's coverage, all compel the conclusion that section 83(a) applies to the income Alves received when the restrictions on his stock lapsed in 1974 and 1975. The decision of the Tax Court is affirmed.

NOTES AND COMMENTS

Thus, *Alves* finds that a requirement to resell property at the purchase if employment terminates within a specified period is a forfeiture restriction even when the property is purchased at fair market value as indicated by the price paid by nonemployee purchasers at the same time. In view of Alves' purchase at fair

---

[4] Treas. Reg. § 1.83.8(b)(1)(1983). The Commissioner has statutory authority under 26 U.S.C. § 7805(b) to prescribe the retroactivity of regulations. . . .

market value, albeit a low ten cents a share, he could have avoided both the income, which was measured by the appreciated value when the restriction lapsed, and the litigation by making the election under § 83(b), since there would have been no excess to include in income. Similarly, the resale at the price he paid would not leave him with any loss on forfeiture. Recognizing the uncertainty concerning the scope of § 83(b) represented by the *Alves* case, Congress subsequently provided a retroactive election for those who received property in similar circumstances before the date of the Tax Court decision. The Tax Reform Act of 1986, P.L. 99-514 § 1855(b). A warning of the need for tax practitioners to keep up-to-date on the latest cases and other authorities!

The case also indicates the substantial valuation uncertainties in technological companies. Alves sold shares at various times during the five-year restriction period at prices per share ranging from $3.43, ironically when the final five-year restriction lapsed, to $18 per share during the third year of the restriction period, on exercise of the company's fair market value repurchase right. In any event, not a bad return on a $4,000 investment.

Although the § 83(b) election is made by the employee-transferee of restricted property, the employer, in *Alves* case, General Digital, has a substantial interest, since it hopes to be entitled to a big deduction when Alves had income, which it loses if Alves makes a § 83(b) election. Depending on relative tax brackets, it may be to General Digital's advantage to have Alves not make the election even it must compensate him for the tax cost by paying him for the difference between ordinary income and capital gain, particularly, if he expects to sell the shares when the forfeiture restriction lapses, since his cost is only the difference between ordinary income and capital gain, the corporation's loss is the entire deduction. At the extreme, Alves sold 4,667 shares with a basis of $467, for $84,000 during 1973, resulting in a little less than $84,000 compensation income with a corresponding deduction for General Digital under the decision. If he had made the § 83(b) election he would avoid that income, but pay capital gain tax on the gain of $16,800 at a 20% capital gains rate. Without the § 83(b) election, the tax at 35% would be about $29,400, a difference of $12,600 for Alves, but with a deduction worth the full $29,400 for General Digital at 35%. If General Digital agrees to pay Alves a bonus of $19,400, which leaves him with $12,600 to pay the tax difference, he is not worse off. On the other hand, General Digital is $16,800 better off ($29,400 tax savings on the $84,000 deduction - $12,600 after tax cost of the bonus to Alves). The computation is more complex if Alves is still to hold the shares when the restriction lapses, since he incurs tax of $29,600 at that time, but does not save on the capital gains tax on sale of the shares until he would otherwise dispose of the shares. A bonus of $45,500 to allow him to pay his full tax overpays him with no after tax cost, but does not account for his future saving of $16,800 in capital gains tax. A bonus only for the difference leaves Alves temporarily $16,800 out of pocket until he sells the shares.

As indicated in *Alves*, a substantial risk of forfeiture is a restriction conditioned on the performance of future services or the occurrence of a condition related to the purpose of the transfer. § 83(c); Treas. Reg. § 1.83-3(c)(1). The importance of the restrictions being imposed in connection with a transfer of property to the service provider is emphasized in Rev. Rul. 2007-49, 2007-2 C.B. 237. In the familiar three situation ruling pattern, a shareholder-employee who had included shares received in income, agreed to new forfeiture restrictions after the shares had appreciated significantly that required sale of the shares to the employer-corporation if the employee-shareholder terminated employment before a specified date at the lesser of the value of the shares when the restriction was placed on them or when the forfeiture occurred. In *Situation* 1, restrictions similar to those in *Alves*, were placed on shares in connection with receipt of needed financing by the outside investor, but the ruling holds that, because there was no transfer of new shares to the shareholder-employee, § 83 does not apply to subsequent appreciation. *See* Priv. Ltr. Rul. 2002-04-005 (restrictions placed on member interests in an LLC taxed as a partnership in connection with a public offering of shares of stock of a corporation wholly-owned by the LLC prior to the offering that required substantial forfeiture if the member ceased to be employed by the LLC within four years were not subject to § 83, because the members owned their interests prior to the imposition of the restrictions, there was no transfer of property for purposes of § 83). In *Situation 2*, the restrictions were placed on shares received in a nonrecognition reorganization, and the employee-shareholder made a § 83(b) election. Because the price paid for the newly restricted shares was the value on the date of the reorganization, the amount of income reported under the § 83(b) election was zero. In *Situation 3*, the exchange is for half-stock, half-cash in what is stated to be a fully taxable transaction, apparently because it is in the form of a reverse-subsidiary merger with too much boot. Naturally, there is no discussion why the transaction was not structured as a nonrecognition forward subsidiary merger. In any event, the inherent gain in the shares is recognized on the transaction, no income is realized if a § 83(b) election is made, but if not, all of the shares whether received for cash or stock are subject to § 83(b) with compensation income measured by value when the restrictions lapse. *See* Priv. Ltr. Rul. 2008-28-016 (similarly § 83 does not apply when restrictions imposed following a reincorporation treated as a F reorganization, in connection with a new investment; apparently on ground that reincorporation did not involve new issuance).

Although not an issue in *Alves*, the requirement that the forfeiture risk be substantial prevents use of unrealistic conditions to defer compensation, particularly, compensation paid in a form that is unlikely to appreciate substantially. *See Ludden v. Commissioner*, 68 T.C. 826 (1977), *aff'd on another issue*, 620 F.2d 700 (9th Cir. 1980) (forfeiture only upon discharge for cause under a plan for shareholder officers of closely-held corporation that did not qualify as an exempt plan was not substantial risk on the facts); *Richardson v. Commissioner*, 64 T.C. 621 (1975) (deferred compensation, placed in trust with provision added at employee's request for forfeiture if he failed, without cause, to provide post-retirement consulting, held nonforfeitable, where no showing of real likelihood of employee's being ever called on to consult).

Treas. Reg. § 1.409A-1(b)(6) excludes restricted property under § 83 from § 409A, in effect, recognizing that, under § 409A(a)(1)(i)(II), delaying realization of compensation until the lapse of a forfeiture or transfer restriction is not a deferral of compensation.

PROBLEMS FOR DISCUSSION

Problem 6-4. Why does § 83 not apply to SARs of the type discussed in Rev. Rul. 80-300? *See* Treas. Reg. § 1.83-3(e).

Problem 6-5. Because General Digital expects the price of its stock to take off, it offers to agree that when the forfeiture restriction lapses, it will pay Alves a bonus of amount equal to the amount of compensation he recognizes when the restriction lapses, multiplied by twice the difference between the capital gain rate and the top ordinary income rate if he agrees not to file a § 83(b) election. (i) Is this a good deal for Ives if he expects to sell the shares when the forfeiture restriction lapses? (ii) If he expects to continue to hold the shares for a substantial period after the restrictions lapse? (iii) Is this is a good deal for General Digital? *See* § 83(a), (b), and (h); Treas. Reg. § 1.83-1(a), (b) and (e); 2(a); and 6(a)(1) and (4), and (c); § 3121(v)(2); Treas. Reg. § 31.3121(v)(2)-1.

Problem 6-6. Exec, the newly hired CEO of Ceeco, was granted 100,000 Ceeco shares, then selling at $20 per share, that were free of contractual restrictions, as an incentive, and to align her interests with those of the Ceeco public shareholders. Exec was, however, required to execute an "investment letter" that recognized that the shares could only be sold in accordance with the federal securities law. In addition, under § 16(b) of the Securities and Exchange Act of 1934, because of Exec's status as an officer, Ceeco is entitled to any profits (specially computed) if Exec sells the Ceeco shares within six months of acquisition. Exec obtained valid appraisals from highly qualified appraisers that show that the investment letter reduced the value of the shares by 20 percent from $2,000,000 to $1,600,000, and that as a result of "blockage," that is, the shares cannot be absorbed in a single trade, but must be dribbled out over several weeks, the value of the shares was reduced by an additional 10 percent, or $200,000, to $1,400,000. She did not make a § 83(b) election. Exec became the owner of the Ceeco shares under state law, whether she was the owner of the shares for federal income tax purposes or not. Ceeco pays a quarterly dividend of 25 cents a share. Accordingly, Exec received dividends of $50,000 (100,000 shares x $.50) before the restrictions under § 16(b) lapsed, and $20,000 (80,000 shares x $.50) or $80,000 a year after that. (i) What, if any, amount is included in Exec's income under § 83 when the 100,000 Ceeco shares are granted? On the date that the restriction under § 16(b) lapsed, when the Ceeco shares were selling for $25, but the investment letter restrictions still applied, Exec sold 20,000 Ceeco shares to Perch for $20 a share (total $400,000), under terms that required Perch to sign an investment letter. The price reflected the disadvantage to Perch as a result of those restrictions. (ii) What, if any, amount of compensation does Exec recognize when the § 16(b) restriction lapses and Exec sells 20,000 shares to Perch. (iii) How, if at all, would an election under § 83(b) affect the results in (i) and (ii)? *See* § 83(c)(3); Treas. Reg. § 1.83-1(a); *Pledger* (securities law restrictions are lapse restrictions); *Theophilos* (shares valued at the time of binding obligation to purchase, taking into account lack of voting rights and lack of control), *Robinson* (determined that an 18 percent blockage discount based on expert testimony reduced the value of the shares to Robinson); *Grant* (value shares at unrestricted value, even though immediately sold at lower restricted value); Rev. Proc. 80-11 (dividends on forfeitable shares are compensation); Rev. Rul. 83-22 (dividends on forfeitable shares with § 83(b) election are dividends); Tech. Adv.

Mem. 87-06-009 (stock valued at the date of acquisition under prior law).

§ 2.03. Shareholder Grants

Particularly in closely held corporations, and even in public corporations that have a controlling, or major, shareholder, a shareholder may transfer shares to a favored employee. This may be a result of disagreement with other shareholders and directors as to whether the transfer is wise, so that the transferring shareholder can receive the consideration for the shares, or for some other reason. Because the employer, not the transferring shareholder, receives the value of the services, it is entitled to the corresponding deduction, but the reduction in the holdings of the transferring shareholder must also be accounted for. The following ruling spells out these consequences, where it is assumed that there is no element of gift involved in the transfer.

Rev. Rul. 80-76, 1980-1 C.B. 15

* * *

On January 2, 1979, *A*, an individual who owned a majority of the outstanding shares of *P*, a domestic corporation, transferred 10 shares of *P* stock to *B*. *B* was a key employee of *S*, also a domestic corporation and controlled by *P* within the meaning of section 368(c) of the Internal Revenue Code. The fair market value of the 10 shares on the date of transfer was 75x dollars. *B*'s rights in the *P* stock were not subject to a substantial risk of forfeiture. The total compensation received by *B* in 1979, including the fair market value of the *P* stock, was reasonable compensation for services performed by *B* for *S*. Both *S* and *B* file federal income tax returns on a calendar year basis.

* * *

Section 1.83-6(a)(1) of the regulations provides that, in the case of a transfer of property in connection with the performance of services, a deduction is allowable under section 162 or 212 of the Code, to the person for whom the services were performed. The amount of the deduction is equal to the amount includible as compensation in the gross income of the service provider, but only to the extent the amount meets the requirements of section 162 or 212 and the regulations thereunder.

Section 1.83-6(a)(2) of the regulations provides that, if the service provider is an employee of the person for whom services are performed, the deduction is allowed only if the employer deducts and withholds upon the amount in accordance with section 3402 of the Code.

HOLDINGS

(1) No gain or loss is recognized by *A* as a result of the transfer of the 10 shares of *P* stock; however *A* must allocate *A*'s basis in the transferred stock to *A*'s remaining shares of *P* stock.

(2) The fair market value of the stock on January 2, 1979, 75x dollars, is includible

in *B*'s gross income under section 83(a) of the Code for 1979 and is subject to the withholding of income tax at source on wages.

(3) Pursuant to section 83(h), *S* is allowed a deduction under section 162 of 75*x* dollars for 1979.

(4) Because section 83 applies to the transfer of the *P* stock to *B*, *S* does not recognize gain or loss on the transfer of the *P* stock.

The above principles would also apply had *B*'s rights in the *P* stock been subject to a substantial risk of forfeiture.

* * *

NOTES AND COMMENTS

Under Treas. Reg. § 1.83-6(d), when a shareholder transferor receives consideration, the transfer is routed through the corporation, so that the consideration is treated as, in effect, a redemption of the transferred shares from the shareholder. *See Estate of Schneider v. Commissioner*, 88 T.C. 906 (1987) (a principal shareholder sold stock to employees applying their cash bonuses to the purchase price paid to him at the formula based on book value treated as having redemptions that were equivalent to dividends); Priv. Ltr. Rul. 2002-19-016 (transfer of NSO by shareholder-director to a corporate employee treated as a surrender of the NSO to the corporation and issue of a new NSO to the transferee, so that any compensation realized on exercise would be taxable only to the transferee and deductible by the corporation); Rev. Rul. 84-68, 1984-1 C.B. 31 (similar result of deduction by a subsidiary for cash bonuses paid to subsidiary employees by the corporate parent; § 83 held not applicable because cash paid). Even though a transferring shareholder, who is not the sole shareholder, does not receive the full benefit of the value of the compensated services, the fact that the employer does prevents the transfer from being a gift. See Rev. Rul. 80-196, 1980-2 C.B. 32. Correspondingly, any loss in relative value as a result of the non-pro rata transfer is not a currently realized loss. *See Commissioner v. Fink*, 483 U.S. 89 (1987).

PROBLEMS FOR DISCUSSION

Problem 6-7. Ceeco is a closely-held corporation owned 60 percent by the Stock family and 40 percent by the Share family. Eighty percent of the Stock family's shares are owned by Sam Stock. The shares of Ceeco are subject to a buy-sell agreement, under which any shareholder who wishes to sell Ceeco shares must first offer them to other members of the shareholder's family at a formula price based on book value and, to the extent that the family is unwilling to purchase, the shares are then offered to Ceeco at the formula price, and, if Ceeco does not purchase, to the members of the other family at the formula price with the right to sell to a third party if none of the shareholders or Ceeco purchase. At Sam Stock's suggestion, Ceeco amended its profit-sharing plan to allow key employees to elect to use all or any part of the bonus to purchase restricted Ceeco shares, at the formula price, from any Ceeco shareholder, or, if none were willing to sell, from

Ceeco. Under the bonus plan, the employees were required to offer to sell the Ceeco shares on termination of employment under the buy-sell agreement to the shareholder from whom purchased, then to the family of that shareholder, and, if no member of that family agreed to purchase, to Ceeco. The formula price for the employees was modified to provide that if the termination was within five years of the purchase, the price would be the purchase price plus 20 percent of the increase in book value. Most eligible employees elected to purchase the Ceeco stock, because book value was increasing rapidly. Sam was the only shareholder who offered shares for sale. When employees terminated employment, Sam usually waived his right to purchase in favor of family members, to whom he sometimes made gifts to allow the purchase. (i) What is the effect on the employees, Ceeco, Sam, and other members of the Stock family of purchases under the plan? (ii) Of repurchases from employees? *See* § 83(h); Treas. Reg. § 1.83-6(d); *Schneider* (employee purchases from shareholder with cash bonuses treated as redemption equivalent to a dividend); *Fink* (transfer of shares by major, not sole shareholder to employee treated as contribution to capital); Rev. Rul. 80-76 (shares transferred gratuitously by shareholder to corporate employee taxed to employee, deductible by corporation; no gain to transferor); Rev. Rul. 80-196 (transfer not a gift).

§ 3. NONSTATUTORY STOCK OPTIONS (NSOs)

Nonstatutory stock options (NSOs) are compensatory options that do not meet the requirements of § 422 for Incentive Stock Options (or § 423 for Employee Stock Purchase plans), which is why they are called nonstatutory. Section 83(e)(3) excludes the grant of most NSOs from the provisions of § 83, which leaves the transfer of stock or other property on exercise of such NSOs subject to § 83. Thus, the grant of most NSOs is treated as not being a transfer of "property." Before discussing the tax treatment of NSOs in detail in § 3.02 *Grant, Exercise and Lapse of NSOs*, § 3.03 *Transfers of NSOs*, and § 3.05 *Valuing NSOs*. § 3.01 *Purchased Options*, summarizes the contrasting tax treatment of purchased options. Noncompensatory options that are issued in financing and other transactions are discussed in § 3.04 *Noncompensatory NSOs*.

§ 3.01. Purchased Options

I.R.C. §§ 1234 and 1233; Treas. Reg. § 1.1234-1(a)(1) and (b)

Options, warrants, and other arrangements based on the value of corporate or partnership equity, including SARs and phantom stock, are types of derivative contracts — that is, rights whose value depends on the value of the underlying security. They are derivative because the value of the derivative contract is interdependent on the value of the underlying stock, although the value of the derivative does not change in direct relation to the value of the underlying stock. An option or warrant usually gives the right to the holder to acquire an interest in the underlying stock at a specified exercise price, sometimes called the strike price, particularly for publicly traded options. If the value of the underlying stock increases, the value of the option increases, although for complex financial reasons, not necessarily dollar for dollar. When the value of the stock is more than the option price, the option is said to be "in-the-money," although the holder of the option cannot make a profit from exercise unless the value of the underlying stock is equal to the exercise price plus any amount paid for the option, called a premium, that cannot be applied against the purchase price. As a practical matter, the option will only be exercised when the value of the underlying stock is, at least, equal to the strike price. When the option is assignable, some profit (or loss reduction) can be realized by selling, instead of exercising, the option. An option to purchase stock is also called a "call." There are also "puts," in which the owner of stock will pay a premium for the right to sell the stock at a specified price, thus protecting some profit against a decline in value. There are also "naked" puts and calls, in which an investor sells a call or put without owning the underlying stock, expecting to acquire the stock at or before exercise at a price that is more favorable than the strike price. This is a form of short sale. Premiums received for issuing puts and calls are, generally, treated as open transactions, that is they are not included in income when received, but are taxed as part of the purchase or sale transaction when the put or call is exercised, or as income when the option lapses without exercise. The sale of the put or call is, of course, a recognition event.

Thus, there are four key events for an option: (i) the writing, issue, or grant of the option, (ii) the exercise of the option, (iii) the sale of the option, and (iv) the lapse of the option without exercise. There are also two key players: the writer of the option and the holder. Sections 1233 and 1234 provide some of the rules governing the tax consequences of options. There is an active market in puts and calls, with the Chicago Board Options Exchange, the primary U.S. market. The following ruling spells out in detail the tax consequences of dealings in purchased options.

Rev. Rul. 78-182, 1978-1 C.B. 265

* * *

Advice has been requested concerning the Federal income tax consequences to the holders and writers of "puts", "calls", and "straddles" purchased, sold or "closed out" in transactions on the Chicago Board Options Exchange, Incorporated (CBOE).

The purchaser of a "call" option pays a sum of money to the writer of said option for the right to purchase from the writer, at any time before a specified future date, a stated number of shares of stock at a specified price. The holder of the option is not obligated to purchase the stock that is the subject of the option. Thus, if the market value of such stock were to fall below the price specified in the option contract, the holder normally would not exercise the option and would allow it to lapse. On the other hand, if the market value of the underlying stock were to rise above the price specified in the option contract, the holder probably would exercise the option before it lapses.

The purchaser of a "put" option pays a sum of money to the writer of said option for the right to sell to the writer, at any time before a specified future date, a stated number of shares of stock at a specified price. As is the case with a call of option, the holder of a put is not obligated to exercise the option. Thus, if the market value of the stock that is the subject of the option were to rise above the price specified in the option contract, the holder of the put normally would not exercise the option and would allow it to lapse. On the other hand, if the market value of the underlying stock were to fall below the price specified in the option contract, the holder most likely would exercise the put before it lapses.

* * *

The CBOE is a national securities exchange that has established a national market in option contracts for the purchase and sale of puts, calls, and straddles. The Chicago Board Options Exchange Clearing Corporation (OCC) is a subsidiary of the CBOE and functions as a clearing house for all transactions on the CBOE.

Before formation of the CBOE, option contracts for the purchase and sale of stock could not be purchased through organized exchanges. The writer and holder of an option transacted over-the-counter are tied together in a direct contractual relationship where the writer is personally obligated to respond to the decision of a particular holder, and that holder may demand performance only from that particular writer.

By marketing through the CBOE, the writer of a put or call deals directly with the OCC. Thus, the writer is paid by the OCC for writing the option, and is obligated only to the OCC to perform in the event the option is exercised.

Through the medium of the CBOE, the OCC sells an option for each option it acquires. The purchaser of an option looks only to the OCC for performance in the event that the purchaser should elect to exercise the option. There is no direct contractual relationship between the writer and holder of an option. However, if a holder of an option were to obligate the OCC by exercising the option, then the OCC would cause a writer of an equivalent option to perform.

The CBOE has also established a procedure whereby the writer of an option may terminate the contract. The writer of an option accomplishes this by declaring a closing transaction, whereupon the OCC will purchase an equivalent option either from a new writer or from a holder wishing to terminate the contract. The OCC will pay to the writer or terminating holder of the equivalent option an amount representing the fair market value of such option at that time, and such amount will likewise be paid to the OCC by the closing writer. The closing writer will thereupon be released from the obligation under the option written.

The following rulings are based on the assumption that, with respect to the tax consequences to the holder, the securities that are the subject of the options are capital assets in the hands of the holder or would be if acquired by the holder, and with respect to the tax consequences to the writer, the option is not granted in the course of the writer's trade or business of granting options.

A. Holder of a call

1. Ruling: **The cost of the call is a nondeductible capital expenditure.**

Analysis: Rev. Rul. 58-234, 1958-1 C.B. 279, states . . . that it is evident from the nature and consequences of put and call option premiums and obligations, that there is no Federal income tax incident on account of either the receipt or the payment of such option premiums, that is, from the standpoint of either the optionor or the optionee, unless and until the options have been terminated, by failure to exercise, or otherwise, with resultant gain or loss.

2. Ruling: **If the call is sold prior to exercise, any gain or loss recognized to the holder is capital gain or loss, and is short-term or long-term, depending upon the holding period of the call.**

Analysis: Section 1234(a)(1) . . . provides that gain or loss attributable to the sale or exchange of, or loss attributable to failure to exercise, an option to buy or sell property shall be considered gain or loss from the sale or exchange of property that has the same character as the property to which the option relates has, or would have, in the hands of the taxpayer. Thus, if the stock to which the option relates would be a capital asset in the hands of the option holder, capital gain or loss results from the sale of a call prior to its exercise. Under section 1222, such capital gain or loss would be long-term or short-term depending on how long the taxpayer held the call prior to its sale.

3. Ruling: **If the call is allowed to expire without exercise, the expiration is treated as a sale or exchange of the call on the expiration date. The resultant loss is a capital loss, and is short-term or long-term, depending on the holding period of the call.**

Analysis: Section 1234(a)(2) of the Code provides that if a loss is attributable to the failure to exercise an option, the option shall be deemed to have been sold or exchanged on the day it expired. Thus, under the rules of sections 1234(a)(1) and 1222, the loss will be treated as long-term or short-term capital loss depending on the holding period of the call.

4. Ruling: **If the call is exercised, its cost is added to the basis of the stock purchased.**

Analysis: Rev. Rul. 58-234 states . . . that when an option to buy property (a call) is exercised, the option cost (premium) should be included by the optionee, with the option price thereupon paid or accrued, in determining the (total) cost basis of the property that the optionee purchased pursuant thereto, for subsequent gain or loss purposes.

B. Writer of a call

1. Ruling: **The premium received for writing the call is not included in income at the time of receipt, but is carried in a deferred account until (1) the writer's obligation expires through the passage of time, (2) the writer sells the underlying stock pursuant to the exercise of a call, or (3) the writer engages in a clos** ing transaction.

Analysis: Rev. Rul. 58-234 states . . . that there is no Federal income tax incident on account of either the receipt or the payment of such option premium, that is, from the standpoint of either the optionor or the optionee, unless and until the options have been terminated, by failure to exercise, or otherwise, with resultant gain or loss.

2. Ruling: **If the writer's obligation expires through the passage of time, the premium is short-term capital gain to the writer upon such expiration.**

Analysis: . . . [S]ection 1234(b)(1) of the Code provides that any gain to the grantor of an option arising from the failure of the holder to exercise it shall be treated as gain from the sale or exchange of a capital asset held not more than . . . 1 year . . .

3. Ruling: **If the writer sells the underlying stock pursuant to exercise of a call, the premium received by the writer increases the amount realized upon the sale of such stock in determining gain or loss. Such gain or loss is short-term or long-term depending upon the holding period of the stock.**

Analysis: Rev. Rul. 58-234 provides . . . that when a call option is exercised, the amount (premium) received by the writer (issuer or optionor) for granting it is includible by the writer, with the option price, which the writer received for the securities involved upon its exercise, in the total amount realized for the securities that the writer sold pursuant thereto for the purpose of determining gain or loss on their sale. Because the stock is a capital asset in the hands of the taxpayer, the capital gain or loss resulting from the sale is short-term or long-term depending on how long the taxpayer held the stock prior to the sale under section 1222 of the Code.

4. Ruling: **Section 1233(b) of the Code does not apply when a call is written, but only when stock is sold short or a put is purchased. Consequently, if a call is written at a time when the underlying stock (or a call thereon) has been held by the taxpayer for . . . 1 year or less . . . or if the underlying stock (or a call thereon) is acquired after a call is written and before exercise or expiration of the call so written, the writing of the call does not affect the holding period of the underlying stock (or of the call thereon).**

Analysis: Section 1233(b), relating to gains and losses from short sales, applies only where substantially identical property is sold short, or where a put is acquired giving the owner the right to sell substantially identical property. It does not apply where, instead of selling short or purchasing a put, the taxpayer writes a call.

5. Ruling: **If the writer of a call enters into a closing transaction by payment of an amount equivalent to the value of the call at the time of such payment, the difference between the amount so paid and the premium received is short-term capital gain or loss.**

Analysis: . . . [S]ection 1234(b)(1) of the Code provides that in the case of the grantor of an option, gain or loss from any closing transaction shall be treated as a gain or loss from the sale or exchange of a capital asset held not more than . . . 1 year . . . Section 1234(b)(2)(A) defines "closing transaction" as any termination of the taxpayer's obligation under any option in property other than through the exercise or lapse of the option.

C. Holder of a put

1. Ruling: **The cost of a put is a nondeductible capital expenditure.**

Analysis: Rev. Rul. 71-521, 1971-2 C.B. 313, holds that the purchase of a put is a transaction entered into without respect to any particular acquisition of shares of the stock named, for which reason the cost of a put upon its acquisition should not be entered as a part of the purchase price of any particular block of stock, but should be carried in a deferred account as a capital expenditure made in an uncompleted transaction entered into for profit.

2. Ruling: **If the put is sold prior to exercise, any gain or loss recognized to the holder is a capital gain or loss, and is short-term or long-term, depending on the holding period of the put.**

Analysis: Section 1234(a)(1) of the Code provides that gain or loss attributable to the sale or exchange of, or loss attributable to failure to exercise, an option to buy or sell property shall be considered gain or loss from the sale or exchange of property that has the same character as the property to which the option relates has, or would have, in the hands of the taxpayer. Thus, if the stock to which the option relates would be a capital asset in the hands of the option holder, capital gain or loss results from the sale of a put prior to its exercise. Under section 1222, such capital gain or loss would be long-term or short-term depending upon how long the taxpayer held the put prior to its sale.

3. Ruling: **If the put is allowed to expire without exercise, the expiration is treated as a sale or exchange of the put on the expiration date. The resultant loss is a capital loss and is short-term or long-term, depending on the holding period of the put.**

Analysis: Section 1234(a)(2) of the Code provides that if a loss is attributable to the failure to exercise an option, the option shall be deemed to have been sold or exchanged on the day it expired. Thus, under the rules of sections 1234(a)(1) and 1222, the loss will be treated as short-term or long-term capital loss, depending on the holding period of the put.

4. Ruling: **If the put is exercised, its cost reduces the amount realized upon the sale of the underlying stock in determining gain or loss. Such gain or loss is capital gain or loss and is short-term or long-term, depending on the holding period of the stock involved.**

Analysis: Rev. Rul. 71-521 holds that if the taxpayer exercises the put, thereby causing the sale of stock involved in the put, the cost of the put is offset against the price received for the stock in order to compute the amount realized by the taxpayer for purposes of determining gain or loss on the sale of the stock. Because the stock is a capital asset in the hands of the taxpayer, the capital gain or loss resulting from the sale of the stock is short-term or long-term, depending on how long the taxpayer held the stock prior to the sale, under section 1222 of the Code.

5. Ruling: **For purposes of section 1233(b) of the Code, the acquisition of a put is a short sale and the exercise, sale or expiration of the put is a closing of the short sale. If the put is acquired at a time when the underlying stock has been held by the taxpayer for . . . 1 year or less . . . or if shares of the**

underlying stock are acquired after acquisition of the put and before its exercise, sale or expiration, any gain on exercise, sale or expiration of the put is short-term capital gain, and the holding period of the underlying stock begins to run on the earliest of (1) the date such stock is disposed of, (2) the date the put is exercised, (3) the date the put is sold, or (4) the date the put expires.

Analysis: Section 1233(b) of the Code provides that the acquisition of a put is a short sale and the exercise or failure to exercise such option shall be considered as a closing of such short sale. Section 1233(b) also provides that if the put is acquired at a time when the underlying stock has been held by the taxpayer for . . . 1 year or less . . . or if the underlying stock is acquired after acquisition of the put and before the taxpayer exercises, or fails to exercise the put, any gain on such closing is short-term capital gain, and the holding period of the related stock begins to run on the date (1) the taxpayer disposes of such stock, (2) the taxpayer exercises the put, or (3) the taxpayer "fails to exercise" the put, whichever date occurs first. For purposes of section 1233(b), the failure to exercise a put includes the lapse of the put or the sale of the put.

6. Ruling: **If a put and the stock identified to be used in its exercise are acquired on the same day, the acquisition of the put is not a short sale for purposes of section 1233(b) of the Code. If the put is exercised and if the identified stock is delivered pursuant to the exercise, the premium paid for the put reduces the amount realized on the sale. If the put is not exercised, the premium paid for the put is added to the basis of the identified stock.**

Analysis: Section 1233(c) of the Code provides that if a put and the stock identified to be used in its exercise are acquired on the same day, section 1233(b) does not apply and the acquisition of the put is not a short sale. Under Rev. Rul. 71-521, if the put is exercised and if the identified stock is delivered, the premium paid reduces the amount realized on the sale of the stock. If the put is not exercised, the premium paid is added to the basis of the identified stock.

D. Writer of a put

1. Ruling: **The premium received for writing the put is not included in income at the time of receipt, but is carried in a deferred account until the writer's obligation expires through the passage of time, until the writer purchases the underlying stock pursuant to the exercise of a put, or until the writer engages in a closing transaction.**

Analysis: Rev. Rul. 58-234 states, at page 283, that there is no Federal income tax incident on account of either the receipt or the payment of such option premium, that is, from the standpoint of either the optionor or the optionee, unless and until the options have been terminated, by failure to exercise, or otherwise, with resultant gain or loss.

2. Ruling: **If the writer's obligation expires through the passage of time, the premium is short-term capital gain to the writer upon such expiration.**

Analysis: . . . [S]ection 1234(b)(1) of the Code provides that any gain to the grantor of an option arising from the failure of the holder to exercise it shall be treated as gain from the sale or exchange of a capital asset held not more than . . . 1 year . . .

3. Ruling: **If the writer purchases the underlying stock pursuant to the exercise of a put, the premium received decreases the writer's basis in such stock. The holding period of the underlying stock begins on the date of its purchase, rather than on the date the put was written.**

Analysis: Rev. Rul. 58-234 states . . . that if a writer purchases stock by reason of the exercise of a put, the premium received reduces the cost of the stock so purchased. The period of time during which the writer of a put option was obligated under the option may not be added to the period of ownership of the stock in determining the holding period of the stock acquired pursuant to the holder's exercise of the put.

4. Ruling: **Section 1233(b) of the Code** does not apply when a put is written, but only when stock is sold short or a put is purchased.

Analysis: Section 1233(b) applies only when substantially identical property is sold short, or when a put is acquired giving the owner the right to sell substantially identical property. It does not apply when instead of selling short or purchasing a put, the taxpayer writes a put.

5. Ruling: **If the writer of a put enters into a closing transaction by payment of an amount equivalent to the value of the put at the time of such payment, the difference between the amount so paid and the premium received is short-term capital gain or loss.**

Analysis: . . . [S]ection 1234(b)(1) of the Code provides that in the case of the grantor of an option, gain or loss from any closing transaction shall be treated as a gain or loss from the sale or exchange of a capital asset held not more than . . . 1 year . . . Section 1234(b)(2)(A) defines "closing transaction" as any termination of the taxpayer's obligation under any option in property other than through the exercise or lapse of the option.

* * *

NOTES AND COMMENTS

Thus, the rulings set out in Rev. Rul. 78-182 are simply application of the basic statutory and common law realization and capital gain principles. The grant of an option is not a sale of all or part of the underlying property, but is an open transaction. Nevertheless, the option itself becomes property that can be disposed of by the holder in a realization event, with gain or loss independent of gain or loss on the underlying property, although the character may be determined by the underlying property. Even though Rev. Rul. 78-182 deals with puts and calls on traded stock or securities, the same principles apply to options on closely-held stock or securities, real estate, or other property. *See, e.g., Commissioner v. Dill Co.*, 294 F.2d 291 (3d Cir. 1961) (amount received to extend option for licensee to purchase a zero basis trademark, with the extension payment applied against the option price if the option was exercised, was not income until option exercised); *Virginia Iron Coal & Coke Co. v. Commissioner*, 99 F.2d 919 (4th Cir. 1938) (payment for option to purchase stock of subsidiary not income until option lapsed); *Ahadpour v. Commissioner*, T.C. Memo. 1999-9 (the amount received was deposit on contract of sale of real property that did not close because of title defect not income until rights resolved).

PROBLEM FOR DISCUSSION

Problem 6-8. In late 20X1, Invest paid Share $25,000 for an option to purchase Share's 20 percent interest in Hi-Tech for an additional $500,000. Hi-Tech owned technology that Invest believed could be useful in his business, but that Hi-Tech had refused to sell to Invest on reasonable terms. The management of Hi-Tech was controlled by the Stock family, which owned 35 percent of the shares of Hi-Tech. Until recently, Share, who was a founder of Hi-Tech, and who acquired the Hi-Tech shares for $10,000, had been allied with the Stock family, but became disgruntled when they raised their own compensation significantly, without providing a pro rata increase for Share. Other Hi-Tech shareholders are investors who provided venture capital. Invest intends to seek control of Hi-Tech, but purchased the option to see if he could obtain control before buying Share's and others' Hi-Tech stock. In 20X2, after he was successful in obtaining options from other Hi-Tech shareholders or commitments from them to join him in ousting the Stocks from management, he exercised the option, paying $500,000 for Share's Hi-Tech stock. What are the tax consequences to Invest and Share of the grant and exercise of the option in 20X1 and 20X2? How, if at all, would the result change for each of them, if the option payment applied against the $500,000 purchase price? How, if at all, would the result change for each of them, if Invest was unsuccessful in his efforts and option lapsed in 20X2? How, if at all, would the result change for each of them, if Invest sold the option in 20X2 for $50,000 to Munn, one of the venture capitalists, who was making a similar effort, and who exercised the option? How, if at all, would the result change for each of them, if Share found out about Munn's efforts and paid Invest $50,000 in 20X2 to cancel the option, so that Share could join with Munn? *See* § 1234; Treas. Reg. § 1.1234-1(a)(1) and (b); Rev. Rul. 78-182 (CBOE ruling); *Dill* (amount received for option not income on receipt); *Virginia Iron Coal & Coke* (same); *Anhadpour* (deposit on contract of sale not income until rights resolved).

§ 3.02. Grant, Exercise and Lapse of NSOs

Treas. Reg. § 1.83-7

Consistency with the principles for purchased options — that the purchase of an option is a capital expenditure that gives the purchasers property with its own tax characteristics (albeit with its character statutorily related to the character of the underlying property) — would suggest that the grant of compensatory option would result in immediate income. The tax principle relating to compensatory options, however, has taken a different approach — that the exercise, not the grant, is the compensatory event — which, generally, means much more compensation later than if the grant was the taxable event. At one time, there was an argument that the grant of an option to a key employee could be, in effect, an investment by the employee in the company, if its purpose was to encourage the employee to act like an owner of the corporation, much as seems to have been the situation in the *Alves* case, discussed in § 2.02 *Restricted Property — § 83*. The following case, in addition to explaining why that argument is invalid, also deals with the timing issue.

COMMISSIONER v. LO BUE

Supreme Court of the United States
351 U.S. 243 (1956)

Mr. Justice Black delivered the opinion of the Court.

This case involves the federal income tax liability of respondent LoBue for the years 1946 and 1947. From 1941 to 1947 LoBue was manager of the New York Sales Division of the Michigan Chemical Corporation, a producer and distributor of chemical supplies. In 1944 the company adopted a stock option plan making 10,000 shares of its common stock available for distribution to key employees at $5 per share over a 3-year period. LoBue and a number of other employees were notified that they had been tentatively chosen to be recipients of nontransferable stock options contingent upon their continued employment. LoBue's notice told him: "You may be assigned a greater or less amount of stock based entirely upon your individual results and that of the entire organization." About 6 months later he was notified that he had been definitely awarded an option to buy 150 shares of stock in recognition of his "contribution and efforts in making the operation of the Company successful." As to future allotments he was told "It is up to you to justify your participation in the plan during the next two years."

LoBue's work was so satisfactory that the company in the course of 3 years delivered to him 3 stock options covering 340 shares. He exercised all these $5 per share options in 1946 and in 1947, paying the company only $1,700 for stock having a market value when delivered of $9,930. Thus, at the end of these transactions, LoBue's employer was worth $8,230 less to its stockholders and LoBue was worth $8,230 more than before. The company deducted this sum as an expense in its 1946 and 1947 tax returns but LoBue did not report any part of it as income. Viewing the gain to LoBue as compensation for personal services the Commissioner levied a deficiency assessment against him, relying on § 22(a) [§ 61(a)] of the Internal Revenue Code of 1939 . . . , which defines gross income as including "gains, profits, and income derived from . . . compensation for personal service . . . of whatever kind and in whatever form paid. . . ."

LoBue petitioned the Tax Court to redetermine the deficiency, urging that "The said options were not intended by the Corporation or the petitioner to constitute additional compensation but were granted to permit the petitioner to acquire a proprietary interest in the Corporation and to provide him with the interest in the successful operation of the Corporation deriving from an ownership interest." The Tax Court held that LoBue had a taxable gain if the options were intended as compensation but not if the options were designed to provide him with "a proprietary interest in the business." Finding after hearings that the options were granted to give LoBue "a proprietary interest in the corporation, and not as compensation for services" the Tax Court held for LoBue. 22 T. C. 440, 443. Relying on this finding the Court of Appeals affirmed, saying: "This was a factual issue which it was the peculiar responsibility of the Tax Court to resolve. From our examination of the evidence we cannot say that its finding was clearly erroneous." 223 F.2d 367, 371. Disputes over the taxability of stock option transactions such as this are longstanding. We granted certiorari to consider whether the Tax Court and the Court of Appeals had given § 22(a) too narrow an interpretation.

We have repeatedly held that in defining "gross income" as broadly as it did in § 22(a) Congress intended to "tax all gains except those specifically exempted." *See, e. g., Commissioner v. Glenshaw Glass Co.*, 348 U.S. 426, 429-430. The only exemption Congress provided from this very comprehensive definition of taxable income that could possibly have application here is the gift exemption of § 22(b)(3) [102]. But there was not the slightest indication of the kind of detached and disinterested generosity which might evidence a "gift" in the statutory sense. These transfers of stock bore none of the earmarks of a gift. They were made by a company engaged in operating a business for profit, and the Tax Court found that the stock option plan was designed to achieve more profitable operations by providing the employees "with an incentive to promote the growth of the company by permitting them to participate in its success." 22 T. C. at 445. Under these circumstances the Tax Court and the Court of Appeals properly refrained from treating this transfer as a gift. The company was not giving something away for nothing.

Since the employer's transfer of stock to its employee LoBue for much less than the stock's value was not a gift, it seems impossible to say that it was not compensation. The Tax Court held there was no taxable income, however, on the ground that one purpose of the employer was to confer a "proprietary interest." But there is not a word in § 22(a) which indicates that its broad coverage should be narrowed because of an employer's intention to enlist more efficient service from his employees by making them part proprietors of his business. In our view there is no statutory basis for the test established by the courts below. When assets are transferred by an employer to an employee to secure better services they are plainly compensation. It makes no difference that the compensation is paid in stock rather than in money. Section 22(a) taxes income derived from compensation "in whatever form paid." And in another stock option case we said that § 22(a) "is broad enough to include in taxable income any economic or financial benefit conferred on the employee as compensation, whatever the form or mode by which it is effected." *Commissioner v. Smith*, 324 U.S. 177, 181. LoBue received a very substantial economic and financial benefit from his employer prompted by the employer's desire to get better work from him. This is "compensation for personal service" within the meaning of § 22(a).

LoBue nonetheless argues that we should treat this transaction as a mere purchase of a proprietary interest on which no taxable gain was "realized" in the year of purchase. It is true that our taxing system has ordinarily treated an arm's length purchase of property even at a bargain price as giving rise to no taxable gain in the year of purchase. *See Palmer v. Commissioner*, 302 U.S. 63, 69. But that is not to say that when a transfer which is in reality compensation is given the form of a purchase the Government cannot tax the gain under § 22(a). The transaction here was unlike a mere purchase. It was not an arm's length transaction between strangers. Instead it was an arrangement by which an employer transferred valuable property to his employees in recognition of their services. We hold that LoBue realized taxable gain when he purchased the stock.[6]

A question remains as to the time when the gain on the shares should be measured. LoBue gave his employer promissory notes for the option price of the first 300 shares but the shares were not delivered until the notes were paid in cash. The market value of the shares was lower when the notes were given than when the cash was paid. The Commissioner measured the taxable gain by the market value of the shares when the cash was paid. LoBue contends that this was wrong, and that the gain should be measured either when the options were granted or when the notes were given.

It is of course possible for the recipient of a stock option to realize an immediate taxable gain. *See Commissioner v. Smith*, 324 U.S. 177, 181-182. The option might have a readily ascertainable market value and the recipient might be free to sell his option. But this is not such a case. These three options were not transferable and LoBue's right to buy stock under them was contingent upon his remaining an employee of the company until they were exercised. Moreover, the uniform Treasury practice since 1923 has been to measure the compensation to employees given stock options subject to contingencies of this sort by the difference between the option price and the market value of the shares at the time the option is exercised. We relied in part upon this practice in *Commissioner v. Smith*, 324 U.S. 177, 324 U.S. 695, and in its 1950 Act affording limited tax benefits for "restricted stock option plans" Congress adopted the same kind of standard for measurement of gains. . . . 421, Internal Revenue Code of 1954. . . . Under these circumstances there is no reason for departing from the Treasury practice. The taxable gain to LoBue should be measured as of the time the options were exercised and not the time they were granted.

It is possible that a bona fide delivery of a binding promissory note could mark the completion of the stock purchase and that gain should be measured as of that date. Since neither the Tax Court nor the Court of Appeals passed on this question the judgment is reversed and the case is remanded to the Court of Appeals with instructions to remand the case to the Tax Court for further proceedings.

Reversed and remanded.

* * *

MR. JUSTICE HARLAN, whom MR. JUSTICE BURTON joins, concurring in part and dissenting in part.

In my view, the taxable event was the grant of each option, not its exercise. When the respondent received an unconditional option to buy stock at less than the

---

[6] Since . . . the transactions in question here occurred prior to 1950 the 1950 statute establishing special tax treatment for "restricted stock option plans" has no relevance. See § 130A, Internal Revenue Code of 1939, as amended. And see § 421, Internal Revenue Code of 1954, [the predecessor of current § 421 ff., which are substantially different. Ed.]

market price, he received an asset of substantial and immediately realizable value, at least equal to the then-existing spread between the option price and the market price. It was at that time that the corporation conferred a benefit upon him. At the exercise of the option, the corporation "gave" the respondent nothing; it simply satisfied a previously-created legal obligation. That transaction, by which the respondent merely converted his asset from an option into stock, should be of no consequence for tax purposes. The option should be taxable as income when given, and any subsequent gain through appreciation of the stock, whether realized by sale of the option, if transferable, or by sale of the stock acquired by its exercise, is attributable to the sale of a capital asset and, if the other requirements are satisfied, should be taxed as a capital gain.[1] Any other result makes the division of the total gains between ordinary income (compensation) and capital gain (sale of an asset) dependent solely upon the fortuitous circumstance of when the employee exercises his option.[2]

* * *

NOTES AND COMMENTS

An important underlying premise of *LoBue* is that there can be only one compensatory event — that either the grant or the exercise, but not both, can give rise to compensation. The Court decides that the event is exercise, while Justice Harlan would opt for grant, but neither suggested that, for example, the value of the option could be compensation, with additional compensation realized on exercise, and to carry it to an extreme, still more compensation on eventual sale or other disposition of the stock. The same can, of course, be said about the taxation of purchased options to the writer. The open transaction treatment assumes that it would be improper to characterize the premium on receipt, either as consideration for the stock, or as income, with adjustment when it is known whether the option is

---

[1] *Commissioner* v. *Smith*, 324 U.S. 177, 324 U.S. 695, does not require an opposite result. In that case Smith's employer, Western, had undertaken the management of a reorganized corporation, Hawley, under a contract by which Western was to receive as compensation for its managerial services a specified amount of stock in Hawley if it was successful in reducing Hawley's indebtedness by a stated amount. Western, in turn, gave Smith, who was active in the Hawley reorganization, an option to buy, at the then-existing market price, a fixed share of any Hawley stock received under the management contract. The management contract was successfully performed, and a part of the Hawley stock received by Western — the value of which was of course substantially enhanced by the performance of the contract — was sold to Smith at the option price. Under the peculiar facts of that case — more analogous to an assignment to an employee of a share in the anticipated proceeds of a contract than to the usual employee stock option plan — the Tax Court's finding that the gain that would accrue to Smith upon the successful performance of the management contract was intended as "compensation" to him for his services was no doubt amply justified. But as the Court expressly stated in upholding that finding: "It of course does not follow that in other circumstances not here present the option itself, rather than the proceeds of its exercise, could not be found to be the only intended compensation.". . .

[2] Suppose two employees are given unconditional options to buy stock at $5, the current market value. The first exercises the option immediately and sells the stock a year later at $15. The second holds the option for a year, exercises it, and sells the stock immediately at $15. Admittedly the $10 gain would be taxed to the first as capital gain; under the Court's view, it would be taxed to the second as ordinary income because it is "compensation" for services. I fail to see how the gain can be any more "compensation" to one than it is to the other.

exercised. More to the point, § 83 reflects the same approach, assuming that restricted property is either income when received or when forfeiture or transfer restrictions lapse, rather than treating the value subject to the restrictions as income, with additional income when they lapse, except in the narrow case of nonlapse restrictions that are subsequently cancelled.

Whether the current approach is a necessary result of the realization principle is debatable, but it is clearly established. In the context of NSOs, § 83(e)(3) provides that the grant (transfer) of an NSO without a readily ascertainable fair market value is not subject to § 83, and (e)(4) provides the same for the transfer of property on exercise of an option with such a value, so that § 83(e)(3) and (e)(4) read together provide that if an option has a readily ascertainable fair market value when granted, the recipient must recognize ordinary income at the time of grant, but not at the time of exercise or disposal; if an option does not have a readily ascertainable fair market value when granted, the recipient must recognize ordinary income at the time of exercise or disposal, but not at the time of grant. Correspondingly, the grant of NSO is not subject to payroll taxes, but the exercise is. Treas. Reg. § 31.3121(v)(2)-1(b)(4)(ii) and (b)(5) Ex. 7. The "readily ascertainable [fair] market value" distinction, of course, codifies *Smith* and *LoBue*. The result is that the compensation is realized (or, more accurately, that § 83 applies) on grant for the rare option with a readily ascertainable fair market value and on exercise for an option without. Because Treas. Reg. § 1.83-7(b) makes it virtually impossible for an NSO to have a readily ascertainable fair market value, the practical result is that § 83 applies to the exercise of almost all compensatory NSOs. Thus, in *Pagel, Inc. v. Commissioner*, 905 F.2d 1190 (8th Cir. 1990), an underwriter who received NSO from a company whose stock it underwrote was taxable, not when the option was issued, but on exercise, because the NSO did not have a readily ascertainable value, even though a number of recognized option valuation formulas were capable of measuring the fair market value of a restricted option at the time of the option's grant, because the valuation formulas did not satisfy the Treas. Reg. § 1.83-7(b)(2) definition of "readily ascertainable fair market value." The definition in Treas. Reg. § 1.83-7(b)(2) adopts a policy of requiring reasonable accuracy in the valuation of nonpublicly traded options, that is in sharp contrast, the disregard of accuracy of valuation under § 83 that applies when an NSO is exercised, but remains subject to restrictions. Thus, Rev. Rul. 2005-48, 2005-2 C.B. 259, held that shares received on exercise of an NSO when the sale of shares subject to insider trading restrictions, the violation of which could result in termination of employment, were valued at unrestricted value, because the restrictions were not a risk of forfeiture under § 83(c), so that they were lapse restrictions. It did not discuss whether they could be considered valuation adjustments, like the blockage discount allowed in *Robinson*, discussed in § 2.02 *Restricted Property — § 83*.

Because § 83(e) excludes the grant of such an option without a readily ascertainable fair market value from § 83, no § 83(b) election is available, although a 1976 Senate report suggested that the Service consider providing an equivalent election by regulation, which it has never done. Thus, *Cramer v. Commissioner*, 64 F.3d 1406 (9th Cir. 1995), held that taxpayers who sold NSOs several years after grant of the NSOs for stock that was not publicly traded had ordinary income, not capital gain. They had filed § 83(b) elections claiming a zero value for the NSOs, despite legal advice that this was contrary to Treas. Reg. § 1.83-7. Their claim of capital gains on the sale was made without referring to the § 83(b) election and, in some cases, using what can only be described as "creative" [misleading] reporting. The court also upheld imposition of penalties for disregard of the rules and regulations, and for substantial understatement, refusing to treat the 1976 legislative history as providing substantial authority for the reporting position.

Although Treas. Reg. § 1.83-2(a)(2) indicates that a transfer of property may be considered an option when it is financed by a nonrecourse loan, so that the service provider has no risk of loss, taxpayer attempts to treat arrangements for "cashless" exercises as options, particularly when the value of stock declined in value have been rejected. For example, in *United States v. Tuff*, 469 F.3d 1249 (9th Cir. 2006), the taxpayer exercised stock options, presumably NSOs, by borrowing through a brokerage account on a margin loan the option price and the withholding tax required to be paid to the employer under the terms of the option. The funds were remitted to the employer, and the taxpayer duly reported the spread as income on his joint return for the year of exercise. Two years later after the high tech bubble burst, he filed a claim for refund on the basis that the exercise was taxable because it was an option under Treas. Reg. § 1.83-2(a)(2). The court rejected the argument, noting that unlike the example, the employer received cash for the purchase price and the withholding tax. It also rejected a claim that the taxpayer was not the owner because he had no risk of loss, because the terms of the margin loan provided for a sale of the shares when the price dropped to 1.33 times the amount borrowed. It also found that blackout periods of restriction on sale of the shares, usually designed to prevent violation of insider trading and other securities law violations are not forfeiture or lapse restrictions, because they do not relate to the incentive purpose for issuing the restricted shares. A similar result was reached in *Miller v. United States*, 345 F. Supp. 2d 1046 (N.D. Ca. 2004), *aff'd*, 209 Fed. Appx. 690 (9th Cir 2006) (cites *Tuff*), in which the taxpayer exercised Microsoft NSOs through a Microsoft-arranged broker cashless exercise program with similar terms and effect. Priv. Ltr. Rul. 98-22-012 illustrates another form of cashless exercise under which a employee electing cashless exercise of an NSO in the form of the number of shares of the corporation on the date of exercise that the appreciation in the NSO shares, less applicable taxes would buy at the fair market value of the shares on the date of exercise. The ruling treats the exercise as having the tax consequences of receipt of the number of shares covered by the exercise of the NSO, not the net number of shares held after the cashless exercise. Treas. Reg. § 1.409A-1(b)(5)(i)(A) excludes NSOs from § 409A as long as: (i) the exercise price at least equals the value of the underlying stock on date of a grant (that is, it is not "in the money" at grant), (ii) the transfer or exercise is subject to § 83, and (iii) there is no other deferral feature. The receipt, transfer, or exercise of the option is, however, subject to taxation under § 83, so that the only deferral is the delay of realization of compensation until exercise (or disposition) of the NSO. That delay is justified, because what is received on exercise is property subject to a forfeiture or transfer restriction. Treas. Reg. § 1.409A-1(b)(5)(iv) sanctions the use of the same valuation methods as for SARs as discussed in *Notes and Comments* in § 2.01 Stock Appreciation Rights (SARs). The Service has a general no ruling position as to when compensation is realized by a person who, in connection with the performance of services, is granted a nonstatutory option without a readily ascertainable fair market value to purchase stock at a price that is less than the fair market value of the stock on the date the option is granted — that is, an option that is "in the money." *See, e.g.*, Rev. Proc. 2010-3 § 4.01(4), 2010-1 I.R.B. 110 (continues a position that has been in effect for many years). There have been similar issues involving ISOs, which, even though not taxable on exercise, give rise to alternative minimum tax liability. *See* § 4.02 *Alternative Minimum Tax on Exercise of ISOs*, for a discussion of this issue.

PROBLEMS FOR DISCUSSION

Problem 6-9. In 20X1, Exec exercised an NSO to purchase 20,000 shares of Hi-Tech stock at $10 a share for a total purchase price of $200,000. At the time, Hi-Tech shares were selling at $60 a share, so that the value of the shares was $1,200,000. Accordingly, Exec was able to exercise the options without actually paying any cash, using an arrangement made available by Broak, Hi-Tech's investment bankers, under which she obtained a margin loan for the $200,000 exercise price plus an additional $250,000 in withholding and other payroll taxes, and paid the proceeds to Hi-Tech. Although Exec signed a recourse note for the margin loan, there was no real risk of a default, because, under the terms of the margin loan, if the value of the Hi-Tech shares declined below $800,000, Broak would sell the Hi-Tech shares and pay off the loan if Exec failed to provide additional collateral within three business days. Unfortunately for Exec, a precipitous decline occurred early in 20X2, when Hi-Tech's auditors discovered that the three highest ranking officers had been "cooking the books" and "raiding the cookie jar." Broak sold the shares for $550,000, leaving Exec with $150,000 less $30,000 interim interest on the margin loan, or a net of $120,000. Hi-Tech did not pay any dividends in the period between exercise and sale. (i) What are the tax effects to Exec of these events? *See* § 83(a), (e)(3), and (4); Treas. Reg. § 1.83-3(a)(2); Treas. Reg. § 31.3121(v)(2)-1(b)(4)(ii) and (b)(5) Ex. 7 (payroll taxes); *Theophilos* (discussed in § 2.02 *Restricted Property — § 83*) (shares valued when binding obligation to purchase, taking into account lack of voting rights and lack of control); *Miller* (cashless exercise of NSO); *Grant* (discussed in § 2.02 *Restricted Property — § 83*) (value shares at unrestricted value even though immediately sold at lower restricted value); Rev. Rul. 2005-48 (exercise of NSO more than six months after grant is taxable even if sale of shares subject to insider trading restrictions); *United States v. Tuff*, 469 F.3d 1249 (9th Cir. 2006); *Miller v. United States*, 345 F. Supp. 2d 1046 (N.D. Ca. 2004), *aff'd*, 209 Fed. Appx. 690 (9th Cir 2006) (cites *Tuff*); *Merlo v. Commissioner*, T.C. Memo. 2005-178, *aff'd*, 492 F.3d 618 (5th Cir. 2007) (where violation of insider trading rules did not allow company to return shares to issuer, but resulted in disciplinary action, including firing, shares acquired on exercise of an ISO were not subject to a substantial risk of forfeiture, so that the spread at exercise was subject to AMT). (ii) How, if at all, does § 409A affect the analysis? *See* Treas. Reg. § 1.409A-1(b)(5)(ii)(A) and (iv).

Problem 6-10. Exec was granted an NSO to purchase 10,000 Ceeco shares at $8 a share in 20X1 when Ceeco shares are selling for $10 on NASDAQ. She exercises the option in 20X3 when Ceeco shares are selling at $16 a share. When and how much compensation does Exec recognize in connection with the Ceeco option? *See* Treas. Reg. § 1.83-7(b); Rev. Proc. 2007-3 § 4.01(4) (no ruling position for "in the money" NSOs). How, if at all, does § 409A affect the analysis? *See* Treas. Reg. § 1.409A-1(b)(5)(ii)(A) and (iv).

§ 3.03. Transfers of NSOs

Treas. Reg. §§ 1.83-1(b) and (c); 1.83-7(a); 1.1032-3

When compensatory NSOs are sold in an arm's length transaction, the consideration received on the sale is taxed as compensation. § 1.83-1(b). When the transfer is an intrafamily or a related-party transfer, not at arm's length, any consideration received is compensation, but the transferor remains taxable on the additional compensation, under assignment of income and § 83 principles, when the NSO is exercised or transferred in an arm's length transaction by the family or related-party transferee. Treas. Reg. § 1.83-1(c). The following case illustrates some of surprising consequences these principles.

WEIGL v. COMMISSIONER

United States Tax Court
84 T.C. 1192 (1985)

[The taxpayers were shareholders and, with one exception, also employees of Federman Inc., a securities firm involved in underwriting hi-tech issues. In connection with several underwritings, it received warrants to purchase securities of the issuers. Some of the prospectuses described the warrants as compensation while others did not. In some cases, Federman Inc. paid a few hundred or a few thousand dollars for the warrants. There were limits on the transfers of the warrants and the underlying stock or securities. Warrants were assigned to shareholders and employees. Several of the warrants were exercised or sold. One of the shareholders, Federman, arranged the establishment of a foreign trust for the benefit of his wife and transferred some of the warrants to the trust for a private annuity. Shortly afterwards, the warrant was exercised and the stock sold pursuant to negotiations that had begun prior to establishment of the trust. Although the nominal beneficiary of the foreign trust was Federman's wife Sylvia, she did not even know of its existence. The taxpayers first, unsuccessfully argued that the warrants were never owned by Federman, Inc., but by its shareholders. This argument was summarily rejected.]

* * *

Issue No. 2: Were the Warrants Received by Federman Inc. as Compensation for Services Rendered?

The Court having found that the warrants were received by Federman Inc. as the owner thereof, petitioners argue that the receipt of the warrants represented a stock investment by Federman Inc. in exchange for the price paid therefor. . . .

Again, the documentation associated with each underwriting transaction, involved herein establishes the compensatory nature of the receipt by Federman Inc. of the warrants. Self-serving testimony by the individual petitioners herein that the warrants were not received as compensation for underwriting services does not begin to overcome the extensive documentation to the contrary.

Petitioners argue that the fact that Federman Inc. paid some cash for the "purchase" of most of the warrants demonstrates the non-compensatory nature thereof. In fact, the purchase price of the warrants was nominal under any measurement, even taking into account the restrictions placed on the warrants.

* * *

Under section 1.61-15(b)(2), Income Tax Regs., if a nonqualified option or warrant to acquire stock has a readily ascertainable value within the meaning of section 1.421-6, Income Tax Regs., [equivalent to Reg. § 1.83-7] the recipient of the non-qualified option or stock warrant may be able to establish that the option or warrant was not received as compensation for services by showing that the amount of money paid for the option or warrant equaled the fair market value thereof thereby avoiding any compensatory element on receipt of the warrants. This argument, however, is not available to petitioners herein since they concede on brief that the stock warrants in question would not be treated as having a readily ascertainable fair market value at the time of receipt of the warrants . . .

* * *

Issue 3: When Must Federman Inc. Recognize and Determine the Amount of the Compensation Income it Received as a Result of the Receipt of the Stock Warrants?

Petitioners contend that regardless of the valuation criteria of section 1.83-7(b)(2), Income Tax Regs., as in effect during the years involved herein, the stock warrants in question had a readily ascertainable fair market value upon receipt by Federman Inc. Petitioners therefore contend that the value of the warrants must be determined and includible in petitioners' income at that time. Petitioners' contentions are based on the argument that the regulations are invalid insofar as they make the valuation rules set forth therein applicable to independent contractors and that the specific rules provided in the regulations for stock options and warrants are invalid.

* * *

Petitioners refer to a number of the early changes made to sections 1.61-15, and to section 1.421-6 [1.83-7], Income Tax Regs., and petitioners infer therefrom that the Treasury initially doubted the propriety of applying the valuation rules of section 1.421-6 [1.83-7], Income Tax Regs., to independent contractors. . . .

Contrary to petitioners' contention, the significance, if any, to be drawn from the background of section 1.61-15, Income Tax Regs., is that the instant question received considerable attention prior to the finalization of the regulations in 1963. For example, the identical argument asserted by petitioner herein (namely, that the tax treatment of stock options received by independent contractors for services rendered should be different from the tax treatment of stock options received by employees) was made in 1960, in Fleischer & Meyer, "Tax Treatment of Securities

Compensation: Problems of Underwriters," . . . That argument was rejected in 1963 by the adoption of section 1.61-15, Income Tax Regs. . . .

* * *

In *Frank* . . . a statement also was made concerning the policy underlying and the validity of the valuation rules of section [1.83-7(b)(3)], Income Tax Regs., as follows:

> Surely, it cannot be considered unreasonable to require reasonable accuracy in the valuation of stock options. To hold otherwise would be to encourage estimates of fair market value of such rights on the basis of pure speculation and surmise. . . .

That policy is as applicable to options received by independent contractors at it is to options received by employees. . . .

* * *

Under the valuation rules of section [1.83-7(b)(2)], Income Tax Regs., the stock warrants in question herein must be held not to have had an ascertainable fair market value upon receipt by Federman Inc. since (1) they were not traded on an established securities market, (2) they were not transferable by Federman Inc. except under very limited conditions, (3) they were not immediately exercisable and (4) the value of the option privilege could not have been readily ascertained.

Since the stock warrants involved herein did not have a readily ascertainable fair market value at the time of receipt by Federman Inc., under section [1.83-7(b(2)], Income Tax Regs., the receipt thereof by Federman Inc. was not taxable at that time. Rather, the warrants generally would be taxable to Federman Inc. at the time of exercise of the warrants, or if an arm's-length transfer of the warrants occurred before exercise of the warrants, at the time of the arm's-length transfer.

If a non-arm's-length transfer of the warrants occurred before exercise of the warrants, receipt of the warrants would be taxable to Federman Inc. at the time of exercise of the warrants by the transferee, and the amount of compensation income to Federman Inc. (in the year of exercise by the transferee) would be measured by the difference between the fair market value of the stock received by the transferee on exercise of the warrants and the exercise price of the warrants. Sec. [1.83-7(b)(3)], Income Tax Regs. The rationale for deferral of the taxation with respect to options and warrants until exercise thereof, where a non-arm's length transfer of options or warrants occurs, is the same rationale (previously discussed herein) for the deferral of taxation of options and warrants upon original receipt thereof where the fair market value of options and warrants at the time of original receipt is not readily ascertainable.

The periodic transfers on the books of Federman Inc. of the warrants from Federman Inc. to the shareholder and/or employee investment accounts were not made at arm's length. The amounts charged to the shareholders on the books were simply pro rata portions of the nominal amounts Federman Inc. had paid for the warrants. No attempt was made by Federman Inc. or by the shareholder transferees of the warrants to value the warrants or to negotiate the amount to be charged to the shareholder accounts at the time the warrants were credited thereto.

* * *

A portion of the Vernitron and NPDC warrants involved herein were sold by Federman Inc. and/or by the shareholders prior to exercise of the warrants. To the extent those sales were made in arm's-length transactions, Federman Inc. is taxable in the year of those sales based on the amount realized from the sales over its adjusted basis in the warrants. The net amount realized on the sales is taxable to Federman Inc. as compensation income.

Some of the NPDC warrants were contributed by the shareholder/employees to charitable organizations. Since a charitable contribution is not an arm's-length transaction, . . . Federman Inc. is not to be taxed on the warrants at the time of the contributions of the warrants, but Federman Inc. is taxed on the warrants at the time the recipients of the contributions either exercise the warrants or transfer them in an arm's-length transaction.

As described more fully in our findings of fact, on July 3, 1968, H. L. Federman's interest in the SCC convertible debenture warrant was transferred to a foreign situs trust in return for annual annuity payments for his life of $40,612.17. Additionally, on July 10, 1968, the other shareholders with interests in the SCC convertible debenture warrant sold their interests therein to the same foreign trust. Although the facts are not entirely clear, it appears that the price paid by the foreign trust for the purchase of the shareholders' interests in the SCC convertible debenture warrant and for the annuity obligation given to H. L. Federman was reached at arm's length and reflected the underlying market value of the stock.

Our conclusion as to the arm's-length nature of the value placed on the SCC warrant by the foreign trust pertains solely to the instant issue. See our opinion herein, *infra*, concerning the tax effect of the annuity transaction.

Accordingly, with respect to the SCC convertible debenture warrant, Federman Inc. will be taxed in 1968 on the amount realized by H. L. Federman from the sale of his interest in the warrant (namely, $475,000 reduced by costs) and on the net amount realized by the other shareholders on their sale of their interest in the warrant (namely, $325,000 reduced by costs) to the foreign trust. To the extent respondent disagrees as to the arm's-length nature of the amount paid by the foreign trust or of the value placed on the annuity, respondent should notify the Court and a further hearing will be held with respect thereto . . .

The remaining Vernitron, NPDC and DPA warrants (that were exercised directly by Federman Inc. or by the shareholders) will be taxable to Federman Inc. in the year the respective warrants were exercised, and the compensation income to be taxed to Federman Inc. will be calculated based on the difference between the costs associated with the acquisition of the stock (namely, warrant price plus exercise price) and the fair market value of the stock received.

Issue 4: Did the Shareholders Realize Dividend Income Upon the Transfer by Federman Inc. of the Warrants to Them? If so, How Is That Income to Be Measured?

This issue of whether the shareholders of Federman Inc. (individual petitioners herein) are to be taxed on the transfer by Federman Inc. of the warrants to acquire the stock turns, in part, on whether the options were transferred to the individual petitioners as compensation for services rendered. If so, the receipt of the stock warrants by the shareholders is governed by section 1.61-15(b) and section 1.421-6 [1.83-7], Income Tax Regs. (the validity and application of which previously have been discussed herein), and the shareholders would not realize ordinary income at the time their investment accounts were credited with the shares but at the time of a subsequent exercise of arm's-length transfer of the warrants.

Based on our examination of the evidence, it is concluded that the warrants were not transferred to the shareholders as compensation for services rendered but as a distribution of corporate property. This conclusion is supported by the essentially pro rata nature of the distributions of the warrants to the shareholders of Federman Inc., and by the extensive documentation in evidence which consistently refers to the transfer to the warrants to the shareholders as dividend distributions.

The Federal income tax consequences of distributions of corporate property are governed generally by the rules of sections 301 and 317. . . .

It follows from the above statutory provisions that a distribution by a corporation to its shareholders of options to acquire stock in another corporation is a dividend if the distributing corporation has sufficient earnings and profits. As explained by the Supreme Court in *Commissioner v. Gordon*, 391 U.S. 83, 89 (1968)–

> Whether the actual dividend occurs at the moment when valuable rights [such as stock options and warrants] are distributed or at the moment when their value is realized through sale or exercise, it is clear that when a corporation sells corporate property to stockholders or their assignees at less than its fair market value, thus diminishing the net worth of the corporation, it is engaging in a "distribution of property" as that term is used in § 316. . . .

The time when a dividend distribution must be included in income of the shareholder and the amount of the distribution are determined according to section 1.301-1(b), Income Tax Regs., as follows:

> (b) Time of inclusion in gross income and of determination of fair market value. — A distribution made by a corporation to its shareholders shall be included in the gross income of the distributees when the cash or other property is unqualifiedly made subject to their demands. However, if such distribution is a distribution other than in cash, the fair market value of the property shall be determined as of the date of distribution without regard to whether such date is the same as that on which the distribution is includible in gross income.

Generally, pursuant to the above regulation, the value to a shareholder of a dividend distribution will be determined at the time of the distribution. Under the open transaction doctrine of *Burnet v. Logan*, . . . however, the amount to a shareholder of a dividend of property other than cash will be determined at a later time if, as of the date of the dividend or of the declaration thereof, the fair market value of the property distributed cannot be ascertained. *Baumer v. United States*, 580 F.2d 863 (5th Cir.), *rehearing denied* 585 F.2d 520 (1978).

Only "in rare and extraordinary cases does property have no fair market value." Sec. 1.453-6 [1.83-7], Income Tax Regs. In "those rare circumstances where no fair market value of the property [distributed] can be ascertained * * * the courts have found it necessary to treat the transaction as 'open' until the value can be ascertained." . . .

Respondent argues that the valuation rules of section 1.421-6 [1.83-7], Income Tax Regs. (the specific provisions of which have been explained in connection with our discussion of the taxability to Federman Inc. of its receipt of the warrants), as a matter of law, should govern our determination under section 1.301-1(b), Income Tax Regs., of the value of the warrants that were distributed to the shareholders. Respondent points out that if the valuation rules of section 1.421-6 [1.83-7], Income Tax Regs., are not applied to our determination of the amount of the dividend distribution of the warrants, the anomalous result may be produced that the warrants are not taxed to Federman Inc. as compensation income until the time of exercise of the warrants (under the valuation rules of section 1.421-6 [1.83-7], Income Tax Regs.), but the warrants are taxed to the shareholders as dividend income at the time of the shareholder distributions (under section 1.301-1(b), Income Tax Regs.).

There is some authority that the valuation rules of section 1.421-6 [1.83-7], Income Tax Regs., may be relevant to determine the valuation of property under section 1.301-1(b), Income Tax Regs. . . . We are not convinced at this point, however, that the valuation rules of section 1.421-6 [1.83-7], Income Tax Regs., as a matter of law, should govern the valuation necessary under section 1.301-1(b), Income Tax Regs., and we defer ruling on that specific point.

In this case the parties have not yet submitted evidence as to the fair market value, at any point in time, of the warrants in question, and they have stipulated that all questions of fair market value will be deferred until resolution of the other issues addressed herein. Accordingly, the parties are to notify the Court as to whether it will be necessary to schedule for further hearings this issue concerning the value of the dividend distributions along with other valuation issues.

Issue No. 5: Annuity Transaction

The final issue requires us to determine the Federal income tax consequences to petitioners H. L. Federman and Sylvia Federman of the sale of a 64-percent equitable interest in the SCC convertible debenture warrant to the foreign trust and of the subsequent sale of the stock acquired by the foreign trust as a result of the exercise of the warrant. Petitioners H. L. Federman and Sylvia Federman contend that H. L. Federman sold his interest in the warrant to the trust in exchange for an annual annuity and that the gain on the sale should be recognized only when the annual annuity payments are received. . . . Respondent counters that the transaction did not constitute a bona fide exchange for an annuity. Instead, respondent argues that the transfer of the 64-percent interest in the warrant and the subsequent sale of the stock by the trust constituted, in substance, nothing more than the sale of that stock by H. L. Federman in his individual capacity and should be taxed accordingly. For the reasons set forth below, we agree with respondent that H. L. Federman's transfer of his interest in the warrant was not a bona fide exchange for an annuity. However, . . . we find instead that H. L. Federman transferred the warrants in trust and that based on his relationship to the foreign trust he is taxable on the trust's income pursuant to the grantor trust rules of sections 671 through 678.

The pivotal question is whether H. L. Federman retained control and beneficial enjoyment of the warrants transferred to the trust. . . .

In determining whether a series of related transactions that took the form of a sale of property to a trust in exchange for an annuity was, in substance, a transfer in trust by a grantor-owner, this Court has looked at several factors, including: (1) The relationship between the creation of the trust and the transfer of property to the trust; (2) the relationship between the income generated by the transferred property and the amount of the annuity payments; (3) the degree of control over the transferred properties exercisable by the annuitant; (4) the nature and extent of the annuitant's continuing interest in the transferred properties; (5) the source of the annuity payment; and (6) the arm's-length nature of the annuity/sale arrangement. . . .

In the context of the instant case, we find that this issue can be decided primarily on the basis of the degree of control Federman maintained over the transferred property. . . .

* * *

In this case it is clear that H. L. Federman retained effective control of his interest in the SCC debenture warrant. For example, one of the trust provisions allows Mrs. Federman, as the beneficiary of the trust, to exercise her power of appointment over the trust assets in favor of H. L. Federman. Since H. L. Federman made all of Mrs. Federman's business and financial decisions, this provision of the trust effectively preserved control over the transferred property in H. L. Federman.

H. L. Federman's continuing control of the transferred property is also evidenced by other trust provisions that permit the trustee to lend Sylvia Federman money on an unsecured, interest-free basis and to distribute all of the corpus or income to her. While those decisions would have to be made by the trustee, the evidence in this case demonstrates that the trustee maintained little, if any, independence from H. L. Federman. . . .

* * *

In summary, based primarily on H. L. Federman's control over the trust and, therefore, over the SCC debenture warrant after it was transferred to the trust and on the tie-in between the annuity payments and the trust's income, we conclude that the transaction was in substance a transfer in trust subject to retained control and beneficial enjoyment of the property.

In view of the above holding, we also find that H. L. Federman was the settlor of the trust and that the named settlor, Yaacov Meridor, H. L. Federman's friend and business associate, was the settlor in name only. . . .

Finally, since H. L. Federman was in substance the grantor of the trust, the grantor trust rules of sections 671 through 678 come into play. Under those rules, H. L. Federman is taxable on the income attributable to any portion of a trust over which he is deemed to be the "owner." . . .

To reflect the foregoing,

An appropriate order will be entered.

Reviewed by the Court.

Fay, J., dissenting: I respectfully dissent as to the majority's holding that "the readily ascertainable fair market value" rules of sections 1.61-15 and 1.421-6 [1.83-7], Income Tax Regs., are valid insofar as they apply to stock warrants received as compensation by independent contractors. I disagree with what I consider to be the majority's conclusory analysis and its expansive use of prior case law the resolve this issue.

* * *

For the following reasons, I would conclude that sections 1.61-15 and 1.421-6 [1.83-7], Income Tax Regs., are invalid to the extent they make the rules of section 1.421-6 [1.83-7], Income Tax Regs., applicable to options received as compensation by independent contractors. Accordingly, I would hold that the amount of the corporation's income arising from the receipt of such warrants must be determined at the time the warrants were received, not when the warrants were subsequently exercised or transferred in an arm's-length transaction.

* * *

Sections 1.61-15 and 1.421-6 [1.83-7], Income Tax Regs., were promulgated to deal with the administrative difficulties respondent faced in attempting to value nonstatutory options not traded on an established market. It is a basic rule under our tax laws that property received as compensation for services must be included in income to the extent of its fair market value at the time of receipt. See sec. 1.61-2(d)(1), Income Tax Regs. Only in rare and extraordinary cases will property not have an ascertainable value. . . . In promulgating sections 1.61-15 and 1.421-6 [1.83-7], Income Tax Regs., respondent took the position that the receipt of options as compensation can be one of these "rare and extraordinary" cases.

The rules contained in sections 1.61-15 and 1.421-6 [1.83-7], Income Tax Regs., were certainly not derived from any specific statutory language. Section 421 provides special tax treatment for certain qualifying options granted to employees; however, no provision is made for options, such as the warrants herein, which do not so qualify. . . .

The origin of these regulations can be traced instead to a series of cases which culminated in the Supreme Court's decision in *Commissioner v. LoBue* . . . In *LoBue*, the Court was faced with the question of the taxability of options granted to employees. The options at issue were nontransferable and their exercise was conditioned upon the continued employment of the recipient. In holding that the options constituted compensation income to the extent of the difference between the option price and the fair market value of the stock acquired upon the exercise of the options, the Supreme Court stated:

> It is of course possible for the recipient of a stock option to realize an immediate taxable gain. . . . The option might have a readily ascertainable market value and the recipient might be free to sell his option. But this is not such a case. These three options were not transferable and LoBue's right to buy stock under them was contingent upon his remaining an employee of the company until they were exercised. Moreover, the uniform Treasury practice since 1923 has been to measure the compensation to employees given stock options subject to contingencies of this sort by the difference between the option price and the market value of the shares at the time the option is exercised. (Emphasis added.) . . .

Clearly, the distinction made in section 1.421-6 [1.83-7], Income Tax Regs., between options with and without a "readily ascertainable fair market value" was derived from this language in *LoBue*. However, neither *LoBue* nor any of the preceding cases in this area ever indicated that these rules should be applied, as they are under section 1.61-15, Income Tax Regs., to options received by independent contractors. . . . For the following reasons, the rationale in *LoBue* strongly suggests that at least in the typical independent contractor situation the Court would have reached the opposite conclusion.

In *LoBue*, the Court emphasized that the stock options at issue were nontransferable and the employee' right to exercise them was contingent upon his remaining in the employment of the company. When both of these restrictions are imposed, I think it is clear that the intent of the employer and employee is that the value of the "bargain purchase" made at the time of the exercise of the option, rather than the option itself, will constitute compensation. Through his continued employment, an employee contributes to the appreciation in the value of the stock subject to the option from the date the option is received until the date it is exercised. Thus, in the employee stock option situation there is justification for viewing the "bargain purchase" as compensation. Moreover, where the employee is required to remain in the employment of the company as a condition to exercising the option, there is a real possibility that this condition will not be satisfied and that the option will never even be exercisable. Thus, when such a condition is imposed, it is not inappropriate to defer taxation until the time when the condition is satisfied and the option is in fact exercised.

In contrast, the two factors emphasized in *LoBue* are not present in the typical independent contractor situation. For example, the corporation herein was not under any obligation to perform services after it received the warrants and, thus, exercise of the warrants could not be made contingent upon continued rendering of services. Although there were various restrictions on the transferability of the warrants and the corporation was generally not allowed to exercise them for a certain period of time, these restrictions were not imposed by the issuers to ensure continued rendering of services but instead were primarily intended to satisfy SEC requirements. Therefore, such restrictions do not change the intent of the parties that the value of the warrants themselves constitute the compensation for the services rendered. Moreover, the sole restriction on exercise of the warrants in this case was the lapse of time, a condition which was certain to eventually be satisfied. Thus, the uncertainty as to whether the warrants would become exercisable which was present in *LoBue*, wherein exercisability was contingent upon future employment, is simply not present here. Finally, since the corporation was not under any obligation to render services after it received the warrants, it certainly could not have been assumed that the corporation would thereafter contribute to any appreciation in the value of the stock subject to the warrants or to the resulting appreciation in the value of the warrants themselves. Thus, to treat any part of that appreciation as compensation income strikes me being unreasonable and inconsistent with the plain meaning of the phrase "compensation for services" in section 61.

It is also noteworthy that measuring compensation income on the basis of the "bargain purchase" made at the time of the exercise of the option, rather than by the value of the option when it is received, can have substantial harsh consequences. The corporation herein will be forced to include as ordinary income, rather than capital gain, the appreciation in the stock subject to the warrants, even though such appreciation resulted from the steep rise in stock market prices and was wholly unrelated to the services rendered by the corporation. The following example is helpful in understanding the unfairness of this result.

Assume that an attorney performs services worth approximately $1,000 for a client and, instead of cash, is given warrants similar to the ones given to the corporation herein. The attorney performs no further services for the client. If the attorney exercises the warrants when the underlying stock has a fair market value of $50,000, he will, under the majority's holding, have $50,000 of ordinary income at the time of exercise even though his services were only worth approximately $1,000 and he never again dealt with the client. Since the $49,000 increase in value had no relationship to the value of the services rendered, I believe the correct and fair result is for taxability to be governed by section 1.61-2(d), Income Tax Regs., under which receipt of the warrants would be the taxable event, with the measure of income being the fair market value of the warrants on the date received. Thus, in my example, the attorney would include $1,000 in ordinary income at the time the warrants were received, and the $49,000 increase in value would ultimately be taxed as a capital gain. Following this rationale, identical tax consequences would result whether the attorney received warrants for his services or, instead, was paid cash which he then used to purchase such warrants.

The majority states . . . that the policy underlying the valuation rules of section 1.421-6 [1.83-7], Income Tax Regs., is to require reasonable accuracy in the valuation of stock options and asserts that such policy is as applicable to independent contractors as it is to employees. Thus, the majority apparently believes that the application of section 1.421-6 [1.83-7], Income Tax Regs., to the warrants received by the corporation herein is valid because its purpose is to defer taxability to the time when the value of such warrants can be accurately determined. However, its position is contradicted by its discussion . . . concerning the question of when the shareholders must recognize dividend income. Therein, the majority refuses to accept respondent's argument that, as a matter of law, the rules of section 1.421-6 [1.83-7], Income Tax Regs., must be followed in determining the taxability of the shareholders with respect to the distribution of the warrants to them. In so doing, it acknowledges that the warrants may in fact be valued at some time prior to their exercise. If, as the majority implies, the warrants may be valued prior to exercise for purposes of determining taxability to the shareholders, I see no reason why they cannot similarly be valued prior to exercise for the purpose of determining the taxability of the corporation.

Furthermore, the majority states that under *Burnet v. Logan*, . . . "the amount to a shareholder of a dividend of property other than cash will be determined at a later time if, as of the date of the dividend or of the declaration thereof, the fair market value of the property distributed cannot be ascertained." The majority also acknowledges, and subsequent case law has made it clear, that a transaction will be treated as "open" only in rare and extraordinary cases where the fair market value of the property cannot be ascertained. However, the majority fails to articulate why this might be one of those "rare and extraordinary" cases. I do not believe that the open transaction doctrine of *Burnet v. Logan* . . . is applicable to the facts before us. I would conclude, consistent with my previous analysis with respect to the corporation, that the warrants can and should be valued when they were assigned to the shareholders.

* * *

NOTES AND COMMENTS

Weigl highlights a number of differences between the consequences of a transfer by the holder of a compensatory option and a purchased or other noncompensatory option. One of the more striking is the application of the special valuation rule that requires that a noncompensatory option have a readily ascertainable fair market value to be included in income, while most other provisions of the Code require realization of income at the time an amount is realized, even a contingent amount that is capable of valuation. *Weigl* upholds Treas. Reg. § 1.83-7(b)'s rejection of this principle for compensatory NSOs. It then, seemingly inconsistently, requires the Weigl shareholders to treat the distribution of the NSO-warrants as dividends at their fair market value. Although at the time of the *Weigl* case, the distribution was not taxable to Federman, Inc., under § 311(b)(1), as amended in 1986, such a distribution is now a recognition event, presumably resulting in ordinary income under § 83(a) and Treas. Reg. § 1.83-1(a) and (c). Nevertheless, the transferred NSOs are "sticky" so that Federman (and its S corporation shareholders) remains subject to additional compensation, when those same shareholders make an arm's-length disposition, or, if the shareholders make a further non-arm's length disposition, when the transferees make an arm's length disposition. *See* Priv. Ltr. Rul. 96-16-035 (transfer of NSO by employee under a plan that permits transfers to members of the employee's immediate family is not a disposition under Treas. Reg. § 1.83-7(a) so that compensation will be realized by the employee when the option is exercised by the transferee; family member's basis in shares is fair market value at exercise); Priv. Ltr. Rul. 97-22-022 (similar conclusions).

On the other hand, when the transfer is in a divorce, § 1041 trumps § 83. Thus, in Rev. Rul. 2002-22, 2002-1 C.B. 849, the Service ruled that, under § 1041 there is no compensation to an employee on transfer of NSO in a divorce; so that the transferee spouse is taxable on the compensation realized when the NSO is exercised, Rev. Rul. 2004-60, 2004-1 C.B. 1051, carries the analysis one step further, dealing with the payroll tax consequences of the exercise by the transferee spouse, holding that when the compensation taxed to transferee spouse is subject to payroll tax; the transferee spouse entitled to credit for any tax withheld, but transferor-employee spouse receives credit for Social Security wages. Obviously, these are matters to be dealt with in the separation or divorce agreement.

Because the court determined that the transfers by Federman to its shareholder-employees were dividends, not compensation, it did not have to deal with the consequences of a transfer of NSOs to employees as compensation. Under Treas. Reg. § 1.83-7(a), to the extent the employees were not 20 percent-plus shareholders, the transfer would be an arm's-length transfer resulting in the recognition of compensation income by the employer/transferor (Federman). On the other hand, because gain is recognized only when the transferee recognizes income, the employer is entitled to the deduction (or other allowance) only at that time. *See* Treas. Reg. § 1.83-6(b). It is unclear, however, whether the transfer of a compensatory NSO on stock other than that of the employer to a service provider has the same effect as a grant of an NSO on stock of the employer (or an affiliate). Treas. Reg. § 1.83-7(a) refers to a grant of an option not covered by § 421, which, in turn, refers to § 422. Section 422(b) defines an ISO as one on the stock of the granting corporation that is granted to an employee of the granting corporation, or an affiliate. On the other hand, the principles of *Commissioner v. Smith*, 324 U.S. 177 (1945); and *Commissioner v. Lo Bue*, 351 U.S. 243 (1956), suggest that the compensation should not be recognized until the option is exercised, especially when, as is likely, the NSO is transferred to an employee who participated in the deal that led to the granting of the NSO, so that the consequences of the exercise of the option for both, the original grantee and the issuer, are delayed until, and valued when, the transaction is successful. A corporation does not realize gain when its shares are issued on exercise of an NSO granted to its employees, but it may recognize gain under the Service's "zero basis" approach when the shares are transferred to an affiliate's employees, if the affiliate had beneficial ownership of the shares between the grant of the NSO and the exercise or lapse of the option. *See* Treas. Reg. § 1.1032-3(c), (d), and (e) Exs. 6 to 9; Rev. Rul. 99-57, 1999-2 C.B. 678 (when gain recognized by partnership on compensatory stock to partnership employee, gain allocated to partner corporation is nontaxable under § 1032, but gain allocated to other partners is taxable). Although the Service revoked Rev. Rul. 74-503, 1974-2 C.B. 117 in Rev. Rul. 2006-2, 2006-1 C.B. 261, it did not state what the proper result is, but only that the issue is still under study. Moreover, it did not revoke Rev. Rul. 99-57.

When the grantor of an NSO is involved in a merger or other reorganization: (i) the acquiring corporation may grant a substitute option, usually, on terms similar to those provided under § 424 and Treas. Reg. § 1.424-1(a) with respect to ISOs; or (ii) the NSO may terminate (a) requiring the employee to exercise it if it is exercisable (or becomes exercisable as a result of the transaction) and is in the money; or (b) the acquiring or target corporation may pay the employee an amount to offset the lost compensation. The assumption of the NSO is a nonevent for tax purposes, because both the old NSO and the new NSO are open transactions. Exercise of the NSO, of course, has the usual compensation and deduction consequences. *See* Rev. Rul. 2002-1, 2002-1 C.B. 268 (neither parent nor subsidiary recognized gain on lapse of the restrictions or exercise of the options on NSOs of the parent held by employees of both parent and subsidiary converted to NSOs of both parent and subsidiary in a subsidiary spin-off, with the eventual deductions belonging to the employer, not the issuer of the shares). Similarly, payment to terminate the option is compensation to the employee (and is sometimes grossed up to help the employee pay tax on the exercise), and deductible (or capitalizable) by the grantor/target, under the principle of *Commercial Sec. Bank v. Commissioner*, 77 T.C. 145 (1981), discussed in Chapter 3, *Liabilities*, § 4.03 *Deductible Items*, whether the amount is paid by the target or the acquiring corporation. *See* Rev. Rul. 2003-98, 2003-2 C.B. 378 (NSOs, issued by a target corporation before the cash acquisition of its stock (with no § 338 election), but exercised or paid out after, are deductible by the target corporation after the acquisition at the time when the employee is taxed on the income); Tech. Adv. Mem. 92-06-004 (amounts paid by "new" target, following a § 338 election, to cancel "old" target employee nonstatutory stock options deductible by old target under Treas. Reg. § 1.83-6(a)(3) and the *Commercial Security* principle, because § 83(a) applies to compensation on the disposition of an NSO); Tech. Adv. Mem. 94-38-001 (same for NSOs and SARs). On the other hand, when the payment is determined to be related to post-acquisition operations, it may be deductible by the acquiring corporation. *See* Tech. Adv. Mem. 97-21-002 (severance payment obligations to employees of old target for downsizing immediately after acquisition treated as deductible expense of purchaser, not a liability of old target); Tech. Adv. Mem. 97-31-001 (increased severance payment obligations negotiated as part of stock acquisition to provide protection to continuing employees are deductible and not required to be capitalized as purchase price); Priv. Ltr. Rul. 2007-28-034 (distribution of restricted stock of entities spun off under § 355 to holders of restricted stock granted by parent company is disregarded so that stock that does not vest on spinoff date remains subject to substantial risk of forfeiture under § 83).

PROBLEMS FOR DISCUSSION

Problem 6-11. InvBanque received warrants for 100,000 Ceeco shares in connection with acting as underwriter of a second round of financing for Ceeco in 20X1. The warrant price is $10, which is 20 percent more than the public offering price of Ceeco shares, but the warrants are not exercisable until 18 months after grant and have a term of five years thereafter (six and one-have years after grant). InvBanque transferred warrants for 10,000 shares to Exec, a key employee who is not a shareholder of InvBanque, and transferred the remaining shares: 30,000 each to Stock, Share, and Munn, its equal shareholders, who are also key executives, in 20X2, when they first became exercisable. At the time of the transfers, Ceeco shares were selling for $13, and the appraised value of the warrants was $5 for each underlying Ceeco share or $500,000 in total. In 20X4, when Ceeco was selling for $15 and the warrants were appraised at $7, Munn made a bargain sale of his

30,000 Ceeco warrants to PetChar, a tax-exempt charity, for $3 for each underlying Ceeco share. Accordingly, Munn claimed a charitable deduction of $120,000 (30,000 warrants x $4 each for the bargain). At the same time, Share sold her 30,000 Ceeco warrants to FamTrust for $3 a share, and paid a gift tax of $60,000 on the $120,000 gift. The gift tax is included in FamTrust's basis under § 1015(d). Stock held on to hers. Exec, Stock, PetChar, and FamTrust all exercised the warrants in 20X6 when Ceeco was selling at $20, so that each realized a profit of $10 per Ceeco share. They each sold the Ceeco shares a little more than one year later in 20X7 for $22. (i) What is the tax effect of each of these transactions on InvBanque, Exec, Stock, Share, Munn, PetChar, and FamTrust? *See* § 83(a)(2), (e)(3) and (4); Treas. Reg. §§ 1.83-1(b) and (c), and 1.83-7(a); *Weigl* (underwriters' warrants distributed); *Pagel* (underwriter's options taxable on exercise, not grant); Priv. Ltr. Rul. 96-16-035 (transfer of NSO by employee to members of the employee's immediate family is not a disposition, so that compensation will be realized by the employee when the option is exercised by the transferee); Priv. Ltr. Rul. 97-22-022 (similar conclusions). (ii) How, if at all, does § 409A affect the analysis? *See* Treas. Reg. § 1.409A-1(b)(5)(ii)(A) and (iv).

Problem 6-12. Exec was granted an NSO by Ceeco for 10,000 shares at $10 a share in 20X1. In connection with a divorce from Spouse in 20X3, he transferred the NSO to the extent of the right to purchase 5,000 Ceeco shares to Spouse, and to the extent of an additional 2,000 shares to KidzTrust. At the time the Ceeco shares were worth $15. In 20X5 when the Ceeco shares were selling for $18, Spouse exercised her option and caused KidzTrust to exercise its shares. In connection with the exercise, Ceeco was required to collect $10,000 withholding tax for Spouse's shares, $4,000 withholding tax for KidzTrust shares, and to pay 2,400 Social Security (FICA) tax and $600 Medicare tax for the employee's portion of those taxes on Spouse's shares and $1,000 and $240 on KidzTrust shares. (i) What is the effect of exercise on Exec, Spouse, and KidzTrust of the spread at exercise, the withholding taxes, and the FICA and Medicare taxes? *See* § 3121(v)(2); Treas. Reg. § 31.3121(v)(2)-1(a)(1) and (2)(ii) and (b)(1) and (3)(ii) (payroll taxes); Rev. Rul. 2002-22 (no compensation to employee on transfer of NSO in divorce; transferee spouse taxable when NSO exercised); Rev. Rul. 2004-60 (compensation taxed to transferee spouse is subject to payroll tax;). (ii) How, if at all, does § 409A affect the analysis? *See* Treas. Reg. § 1.409A-1(b)(5)(ii)(A) and (iv).

§ 3.04. Noncompensatory NSOs

Treas. Reg. § 1.61-15. [Note that Treas. Reg. § 1.421-6 referred in Treas. Reg. § 1.61-15 is the very similar predecessor of Treas. Reg. § 1.83-7 so that it should be read to refer to Treas. Reg. § 1.83-7, although the Service has never gotten around to making the correction]

Not all options without a readily ascertainable fair market value are granted to employees or other service providers. Options granted to others may be called noncompensatory NSOs. Many are granted to lenders in connection with loans to those with less than prime rate credit as "equity kickers," as "bond and warrant packages," or as investment units. Noncompensatory NSOs granted in such transactions are not governed by the provisions of § 83, but by the tax principles that govern the transactions in which they are granted. Others may be granted to customers, suppliers, or others as parts of major business relationships or transactions. Section 3.04(a) *Determining Whether NSO is Compensatory or Noncompensatory*, discusses how the distinction is made, and the consequences of the transaction, which frequently involve valuing the option when granted. Although the grant of the noncompensatory NSO is the taxable event, when the value of the noncompensatory NSO cannot be determined at grant and some cases, primarily involving technology companies, treat the exercise as the taxable event. These situations are discussed § 3.04(b) *Noncompensatory Options Taxed on Exercise*.

§ 3.04(a). Determining Whether NSO Is Compensatory or Noncompensatory

When noncompensatory NSOs are granted to lenders or otherwise in conjunction with the issuance of debt obligations, the consideration for the package is usually equal to the principal amount of the debt obligation, but, in any event, a portion of the consideration must be allocated to the option or warrant. This usually means that the portion of the value of the package allocated to the warrant results in original issue discount for the debt obligation. Treas. Reg. § 1.1273-2(h). In *Custom Chrome, Inc. v. Commissioner*, 217 F.3d 1117 (9th Cir. 2000), the appellate court determined that warrants issued to a bank that provided funds for a leveraged buy-out were required to be valued when issued, even though neither issuer nor bank valued them when issued. In doing so, the court reversed a Tax Court decision, T.C. Memo. 1998-317, which had accepted a Service argument that warrants could not be valued at grant, and remanded the case for the Tax Court to determine the value. The appellate court suggested that the value be determined, under *Monarch Cement Co. v. United States*, 634 F.2d 484 (10th Cir. 1980), based on the difference in interest rates between a loan with and without warrants. In Tech. Adv. Mem. 2000-43-013, dealing with warrants issued to a lender in connection with financing provided to a company emerging from bankruptcy reorganization, the Service determined that the warrants were not for payment of services under § 83, because they were compensation for making the loan, with any involvement by the lender in the business of the debtor being to protect the lender's interest, not to provide services to the debtor, so that the value of warrant at issue gave rise to OID, for the issuer. It further determined that the value of the warrants was a option premium under Rev. Rul. 78-182, discussed in § 3.01 *Purchased Options*; so that under § 1032, the issuer would not recognize gain or loss on lapse or termination of the option); *see* Field Serv. Adv. 2000-11-006 (if lender warrants cannot be valued at issue, the value at exercise would measure the amount deductible or capitalized).

Determining whether an NSO is compensatory or noncompensatory is not always as easy as for those issued in lending transactions. Treas. Reg. § 1.61-15(b)(1)(ii) places on the holder the burden of demonstrating that an option without a readily ascertainable fair market value is noncompensatory, with Treas. Reg. § 1.16-15(c) supplying detailed reporting requirements. Even so, it is not always easy to determine whether an option has been issued for services or use of capital, as demonstrated by the following case.

CENTEL COMMUNICATIONS CO., INC. v. COMMISSIONER

United States Tax Court

92 T.C. 612 (1989), *aff'd,* 920 F.2d 1335 (7th Cir. 1990)

* * *

Founded in 1913 by relatives of Lloyd K. Davis, Electric is engaged in the electrical contracting business, serving commercial, industrial, and residential markets. Davis and his family own a majority of the outstanding stock in Electric, and Davis has been Electric's president since 1954.

In the late 1960's, the Federal Communications Commission issued the Carter Phone decision, [which] allowed non-telephone companies to enter the "telephone interconnect business," which consists of the sale, leasing, installation, and maintenance of private and commercial telephone systems. After the *Carter Phone* decision . . . Electric organized Fisk Telephone Systems, Inc. . . . to engage in the telephone interconnect business. . . .

* * *

Beginning in 1973, Telephone entered into a series of loan agreements to obtain additional funds that were essential for its operations. . . . Beginning with the initial loan agreement in September 1973 and continuing until March 24, 1980, petitioners Davis and Grey each executed continuing guarantees of the repayment by Telephone of the various bank loans and notes executed by Telephone under its loan agreements (the "personal guarantees"). . . . The banks required the personal guarantees as a condition for making the loans to Telephone.

In addition to requiring the personal guarantees of Davis and Grey, the banks also required certain guarantees of Electric, referred to generally as "performance guarantees," before making the loans to Telephone. . . .

In addition to the performance guarantees, the banks also required Electric to execute a subordination agreement in connection with the loans to Telephone (the "subordinations"). . . .

The personal guarantees, performance guarantees, and subordinations were entered into by petitioners Davis, Grey, and Electric voluntarily and without the expectation of any compensation from Telephone. . . .

* * *

In early 1975, Grey approached Davis and suggested that he and Davis should have some additional stock in Telephone for the increased risk they each had assumed under the personal guarantees. . . .

Davis had been a member of Telephone's board of directors since its inception and served as Telephone's president from 1972 through 1976. . . . Grey served as Telephone's chairman of the board from 1975 through 1979. Davis and Grey's involvement in Telephone's day-to-day operations was limited, and both generally served Telephone only in a consulting capacity. . . . However, Davis and Grey were not employees of Telephone, and neither person could or did participate in Telephone's employee stock option plan.

* * *

. . . In its regular meeting held on April 26, 1978, the [Telephone] board adopted a resolution authorizing the issuance to Davis, Grey, and Electric of warrants to purchase 50,000 shares of Telephone common stock each. On May 1, 1978, Telephone granted to each (Davis, Grey, and Electric) warrants to purchase 50,000 shares of Telephone common stock for $1 per share. The warrants could be exercised, in whole or in part, from time to time, at any time prior to May 1, 1982. The warrants were issued in consideration of, or in recognition of, the increased risks assumed by Davis, Grey, and Electric under the personal guarantees, performance guarantees, and subordinations. . . .

On March 24, 1980, Centel acquired Telephone in a tax-free reorganization under section 368(a)(2)(D). . . . On February 29, 1980, Davis, Grey, and Electric had exercised their Telephone stock warrants, each receiving 50,000 shares of Telephone common stock in exchange for $50,000. . . . [I]n connection with the merger each Telephone shareholder received.605613 shares of Centel common stock for each Telephone share held. As of February 29, 1980 and March 24, 1980, the closing price on the New York Stock Exchange of Centel common stock was $22.875 and $22.1659 per share, respectively.

Immediately subsequent to the merger, Centel agreed to have Davis, Grey, and Electric released from their obligations under the personal guarantees and performance guarantees. In the event that the releases could not be obtained, Centel agreed to indemnify Davis, Grey, and Electric with respect to these obligations.

. . . On the return for the period ended March 24, 1980, Centel as the successor to Telephone decided to claim a deduction under section 83(h) attributable to the exercise of the warrants by Davis, Grey, and Electric. . . .

On August 18, 1980, prior to the filing of Telephone's return for the period ended March 24, 1980, Centel's officers met to discuss this proposed $1,863,665 deduction under section 83(h). At this meeting Centel's officers decided to claim the deduction with respect to the warrants issued to Grey and Electric, but not to claim the portion of the deduction attributable to the warrants issued to Davis. The decision to forgo the deduction with respect to the Davis warrants was reached because Centel wanted "to retain Mr. Davis' goodwill and his potential for helping Fisk Telephone in its business, which [Centel] had just acquired." Centel's director of taxes at that time assured the other officers that Centel's position would not be jeopardized by postponing the deduction since it could be claimed on an amended return filed in a later year. . . .

In any event, Telephone claimed a deduction for two-thirds of the amount of $1,863,665, totaling $1,242,443, on its March 24, 1980 return. However, on March 4, 1982, Telephone filed an amended return for its taxable period ended March 24, 1980. In this amended return Telephone claimed an additional deduction of $621,222 for the remaining one-third of the warrants (Davis' warrants). As its explanation for claiming the $621,222 deduction, the amended return stated:

> Upon the filing of the original return, the taxpayer inadvertently failed to take into account the exercise of a group of stock warrants. The additional

deduction shown on this amended return reflects the Section 83 deduction attributable to the exercised stock warrants not taken into account on the original return.

The statement that the taxpayer "inadvertently failed" to claim that group of warrants was untrue.

* * *

In November 1980, Davis, Grey, and Electric each filed an amended income tax return for 1978. These amended returns stated that the respective taxpayers either "inadvertently omitted" (Davis and Electric) or "failed to include" (Grey) the value of the warrants on their respective 1978 returns. The record does not establish what prompted the filing of these amended returns. The amount reported on these amended returns was $35,000, computed on the basis of an appraisal of the warrants made by the firm of Underwood, Neuhaus & Co., Inc. of Houston, Texas. The appraisal report, dated September 16, 1980, opined that the fair market value of each warrant at April 30, 1978 was $.70. Davis, Grey, and Electric did not report any income with respect to their exercise of the warrants on their respective 1980 Federal income tax returns.

* * *

. . . In order to avoid being "whipsawed," respondent has taken inconsistent positions with respect to petitioner Centel, on the one hand, and petitioners Davis, Grey, and Electric, on the other, as to the applicability of section 83. If we find that section 83 applies to the warrants, we must then decide whether the warrants had a readily ascertainable fair market value when they were issued in 1978. . . .

* * *

ULTIMATE FINDINGS OF FACT

1. The stock warrants in this case were not compensatory in nature.

2. The stock warrants were not transferred in connection with, or in recognition of, the performance of services.

OPINION

The principal issue we must decide is whether section 83 applies to the Telephone stock warrants issued to petitioners Davis, Grey, and Electric. If we conclude that section 83 applies to the warrants, then we must further decide whether the warrants had a readily ascertainable fair market value at the time they were issued in 1978. If so, income from the warrants would be reportable by Davis, Grey, and Electric in 1978 and a deduction in a like amount would be available to Telephone that year; if not, income from the warrants would be reportable by them in 1980 when the warrants were exercised and the deduction in a like amount would be available that year to Centel as Telephone's successor in interest. This being a "whipsaw" situation, respondent has taken inconsistent positions, but is basically in the position of a stakeholder, seeking to collect additional tax either from Centel (successor in interest to Telephone), on the one hand, or from Davis, Grey, and Electric, on the other hand.

* * *

In order for section 83 to apply to the transfer of the warrants in this case, it must be shown that the warrants were transferred "in connection with the performance of services" by Davis, Grey, and Electric. . . .

As detailed in our findings of fact, the warrants were granted to Davis, Grey, and Electric in recognition of the increased risks they had assumed under the various personal guarantees, performance guarantees, and subordinations. Based on this finding, we think that the warrants were transferred "in connection with" the personal guarantees, performance guarantees, and subordinations given by Davis, Grey, and Electric. However, we further think the crux of this issue is whether assumption of the increased financial risks by Davis, Grey, and Electric under the guarantees and subordinations constituted "the performance of services" under section 83.

Unfortunately, the term "the performance of services," and specifically "services," is not defined in section 83. Moreover, the regulations under section 83 provide little assistance. . . . Thus, we look to the legislative history of section 83 for any guidance it may provide.

. . . The primary impetus behind the enactment of section 83 was to equate the tax treatment of restricted stock plans involving employers and employees to the tax treatment accorded other types of deferred compensation arrangements. . . . Both the House Report . . . and the Senate Report . . . describe restricted stock plans as follows:

> A restricted stock plan, generally, is an arrangement under which an employer transfers stock to one or more of his employees (often without the payment of any consideration), where the stock is subject to certain restrictions which affect its value. A restricted stock plan may cover only one employee or it may cover a number of employees. The stock transferred under a plan may be stock in the employer corporation, stock of another company — often an unrelated growth company — or even shares of a mutual fund.

* * *

Reading the clear statutory language, section 83 was intended by Congress to apply to property transferred by an employer to an employee in connection with the performance of services by the employee. It is also clear that section 83 applies in the case of services performed by independent contractors as well as employees. . . . Petitioners Davis, Grey, and Electric argue that since they were neither employees nor independent contractors of Telephone, section 83 does not apply to the warrants they received. This argument rather assumes the answer. . . . However, what constitutes the performance of services under section 83 is not addressed by Congress in the legislative history or in the language of the statute itself. It is also not addressed by the pertinent regulations. Thus, we turn to relevant case law.

. . . In *Alves v. Commissioner*, 734 F.2d 478 (9th Cir. 1984), *affg.* 79 T.C. 864 (1982). Alves argued that since he paid the fair market value for the shares, he did not obtain the stock "in connection with the performance of services." This Court and the Ninth Circuit rejected his argument, concluding that the plain language of the statute did not require that the property be transferred as "compensation" for the performance of services but only "in connection with" the performance of services. In affirming this Court's holding that the stock was obtained in connection with performance of services, the Ninth Circuit looked to the facts that Alves purchased the stock when he signed his employment agreement and that the stock restrictions were linked explicitly to his tenure with the company. . . .

In *Bagley v. Commissioner*, 806 F.2d 169 (8th Cir. 1986), *affg.* 85 T.C. 663 (1985), the taxpayer (Bagley) entered into an employment contract with Spencer Foods, Inc. (Spencer) in which Bagley agreed to work for Spencer for five years as vice president of its fabricating division. . . . A separate stock option agreement was executed which granted Bagley the option to purchase 10,000 shares of Spencer common stock at five dollars per share. Three years later Bagley and Spencer terminated their employment relationship when all of Spencer's outstanding common stock was acquired by another corporation. As part of the termination Spencer received $70,000 for the 10,000 shares subject to the option. . . .

In determining whether the $70,000 received by Bagley was transferred to him in connection with the performance of services within the meaning of section 83, the Tax Court looked to several factors. Those factors included: the fact that the grant of the option was provided for in the employment agreement, pursuant to which Bagley agreed to render services as an employee of Spencer; that the option was granted under the option agreement, which referred to Bagley as a "key employee;" that the sole consideration furnished by Bagley in exchange for the option was his promise to render services as an employee; and that Spencer's intent in granting the option was to compensate and better secure Bagley's services as its employee while simultaneously providing Bagley additional incentive to put forth maximum effort for the success of the business. . . .

The facts in the present case, however, are wholly distinguishable from those in *Alves* and *Bagley*. In both *Alves* and *Bagley* the taxpayers were employees and received their restricted stock options in connection with executed employment agreements wherein they agreed to perform services as employees for their respective employers. In the present case there were no employment agreements executed between Telephone and either Davis, Grey, or Electric. It is undisputed that Davis, Grey, and Electric were not employees of Telephone. . . . In the present case Telephone granted the stock warrants to Davis, Grey, and Electric in their capacity as shareholders and in recognition of the increased financial risks these shareholders had assumed under the personal guarantees, performance guarantees, and subordinations.

* * *

The personal guarantees, performance guarantees, and subordinations were essentially an assumption of additional financial risk on the part of Davis, Grey, and Electric in their role as shareholders or investors. We think these are shareholder/investor actions to protect their investment in Telephone and as such do not constitute the performance of services and do not arise "in connection with the performance of services" within the meaning of section 83. The parties have not cited, and we have not found, any case exactly on point under section 83 or under other Code sections. The parties rely on various cases by analogy.

* * *

Petitioners Davis, Grey, and Electric argue that, by giving the guarantees and agreeing to the subordinations, they were in effect substituting their own credit for that of Telephone. *Cf., Bank of America v. United States*, 230 Ct. Cl. 679, 689 F.2d 142, 149 (1982). While Bank of America did not involve section 83, we think the case has some relevance to our issue of whether the guarantees and subordinations constituted the performance of services.

The issue in *Bank of America* was whether, for purposes of computing the section 901 foreign tax credit, certain commissions received by the taxpayer-bank were United States source income or foreign source income. A portion of the commissions received by the bank was related to transactions in which the bank "confirmed" letters of credit issued by foreign banks. The essence of these confirmation transactions was the substitution of the taxpayer-bank's credit for that of the foreign banks. . . . In order to determine whether these "confirmation commissions" were United States or foreign source income, it was necessary for the court to analogize the commissions to one of the classes of income listed in sections 861 and 862, specifically whether it was income from interest or income from personal services. The Government . . . argued that the bank received the commissions for services, which would have made the commissions United States source income (which would have reduced the bank's foreign tax credit). The bank, on the other hand, argued that it was not being paid for personal services but instead for the use of its credit. Analogizing the transaction to a loan, the bank claimed the commissions it received were similar to interest received on a loan. If the commissions were considered interest, they would have been foreign source income (which would have increased the bank's foreign tax credit). In holding that the confirmation transactions resembled loans, and that therefore the commissions should be considered received as interest and not in return for services, the Court stated:

> Thus, from the moment of confirmation the plaintiff has made an enforceable promise to pay regardless of any change in the foreign bank's financial condition. As in acceptance and loan transactions, the plaintiff here has acted as an intermediate, has assumed the risk of default of the foreign bank, and has assured the draft's holder of payment.
>
> * * * Thus, it is apparent what plaintiff was really charging for was not the services performed but the substitution of its own credit for that of the foreign bank. The predominant feature of the confirmation transactions was the substitution of plaintiff's credit for that of the foreign banks. The services performed were subsidiary to this. Therefore due to the similarities between a confirmation and a loan transaction, we hold that the confirmation commissions should be sourced by analogy to interest. . . .

Davis, Grey, and Electric simply signed guarantees and subordinations; they performed no services "subsidiary" to them. We think *Bank of America* . . . lends some support to the view that the guarantees and subordinations given by Davis, Grey, and Electric did not constitute the performance of services under section 83.

In arguing that the guarantees and subordinations do constitute the performance of services under section 83, petitioner Centel cites several reasonable compensation cases. . . .

In deciding the issue of whether reasonable compensation was paid, the court in each of these cases made a passing reference to the fact that the employee had guaranteed corporate obligations. . . .

We do not find the reasonable compensation cases cited by Centel particularly helpful in deciding the issue in the present case. In those cases there was no dispute that services had been rendered by an employee. While the regulations under section 162 provide that to be deductible as compensation for personal services, the payment must be both reasonable in amount and a payment "purely for services" (sec. 1.162-7(a), Income Tax Regs.), once it is determined that services have been rendered by an employee, the courts then appropriately focus on whether the amount paid was reasonable. . . .

However, other cases involving a shareholder who has guaranteed a corporate loan, while not arising under section 83, may provide a closer analogy. We have in mind cases where the shareholder-guarantor has been compelled to pay under his guarantee. A shareholder-guarantor's payment of a corporate debt typically gives rise to a nonbusiness bad debt deduction. *Putnam v. Commissioner*, 352 U.S. 82 (1956). . . . [T]o have a business deduction, a shareholder must show that his payment of corporate debt or expense was made to protect his own separate trade or business rather than to protect his own separate trade or business rather than to protect his investment in the stock of the corporation. *United States v. Generes*, 405 U.S. 93, 100-103 (1973). Neither Davis, Grey, or Electric was in the business of guaranteeing debts or guaranteeing performance. Davis and Grey were not in the business of being employees, i.e., they were not corporate executives with a salary to protect. . . . Thus had Telephone not prospered as it did and had Davis and Grey been called upon to pay Telephone's debts or its other expenses, any deduction no doubt would have been limited to a nonbusiness (investment) bad debt or capital loss.

* * *

. . . We think that in this case their personal guarantees, performance guarantees, and subordinations do not constitute the performance of services by an employee or independent contractor, but instead have more of a shareholder/investment aura. When the stock warrants were ultimately exercised, there was a realignment of the equity interest in the corporation, giving Davis, Grey, and Electric a greater equity interest and diluting the interest of the other shareholders. The transfer of stock warrants in this case is more akin to, or in recognition of, the shareholders' making additional contributions to capital. *Cf. Commissioner v. Fink*, 483 U.S. 89 (1987), involving a non-pro-rata surrender of stock in a closely held corporation as a contribution to capital.

* * *

. . . Centel argues that through the operation of section 1.61-15, Income Tax Regs., the rules of section 1.83-7, Income Tax Regs., are still applicable to the warrants in the present case. Centel argues that section 1.61-15, Income Tax Regs., in effect serves as a "safety net" to assure that the rules of section 1.83-7, Income Tax Regs., and thus section 83 itself, apply to all compensatory stock options. However, we have concluded that the warrants in this case were not compensatory in nature and that the warrants were not transferred either as compensation for, or in connection with, the performance of services. . . .

. . . In general, section 1.61-15, Income Tax Regs., . . . extends the rules of section 1.421-6, Income Tax Regs., which pertain to options granted by employers to employees in connection with their employment, to options received by any person in payment of an amount constituting compensation of such person . . . "for purposes of determining when income is realized in connection with such option and the amount of such income." We think implicit in section 1.61-15(a), Income Tax Regs., is that the options or warrants be transferred (or received) in connection with the performance of services. This is borne out by section 1.61-2(d)(6)(i), which restricts the application of section 1.61-15, Income Tax Regs., for transfers of property occurring after June 30, 1969. Section 1.61-2(d)(6)(i) provides:

> (6) Certain property transferred, premiums paid, and contributions made in connection with the performance of services after June 30, 1969. (i) *Exception.* Paragraph (d)(1), (2), (4), and (5) of this section and § 1.61-15 do not apply to the transfer of property (as defined in § 1.83-3(e)) after June 30, 1969, unless § 1.83-8 (relating to applicability of section 83 and transitional rules) applies. If section 83 applies to a transfer of property, and the property is not subject to a restriction that has a significant effect on the fair market value of such property, then the rules contained in paragraph (d)(1), and (2), and (4) of this section and § 1.61-15 shall also apply to such transfer to the extent such rules are not inconsistent with section 83. [Added emphasis indicated by underscoring.]

Since the warrants in the present case were not transferred either as compensation for, or in connection with, the performance of services, we reject petitioner Centel's argument that the rules of section 83 apply to the warrants in this case through the operations of section 1.61-15, Income Tax Regs.[14]

---

[14] . . . [W]e think Centel's "safety net" argument has some merit in the right circumstance. Such a circumstance is our recent opinion in *Pagel, Inc.* . . . In *Pagel,* we had to decide whether a warrant received in connection with the performance of services had a readily ascertainable fair market value for purposes of section 83. In footnote 15 we recognized that a technical reading of the statute and regulations would have resulted in the warrant in issue in that case not being subject to any regulation provision. . . . This was so because section 83(e)(3) states that section 83 does not apply to the transfer of an option (warrant) without a readily ascertainable fair market value, and section 83(a), by its terms, applies only to a transfer of property in connection with the performance of services. Thus, we recognized that a warrant without a readily ascertainable value at the time it was transferred by the recipient of services was not subject to taxation under section 83 and that the section 83 regulations did not appear to provide the authority to tax the performer of the services. Realizing that in this instance section 61, by default, should control taxation of the property, but also noting that under the transition

* * *

NOTES AND COMMENTS

In *Centel*, the Service claimed deficiencies against both the shareholder/guarantors and the issuer to prevent whipsaw, because Telephone's new owners decided to claim a deduction on exercise of the NSOs. In *Robinson v. Commissioner*, 82 T.C. 467 (1984) *rev'd*, *Robinson v. Commissioner*, 805 F.2d 38 (1st Cir. 1986), discussed in § 2.02 *Restricted Property — § 83*, the Service similarly made inconsistent determinations to prevent whipsaw. There is no similar record of a claim against the issuer in *Weigl v. Commissioner*, 84 T.C. 1192 (1985) or *Pagel, Inc. v. Commissioner*, 905 F.2d 1190 (8th Cir. 1990), presumably, because the "services" of the underwriters were in connection with selling the issuers' shares, so that they were nondeductible costs of issuing shares. In *Kimberlin v. Commissioner*, 128 T.C. 163 (2007), warrants issued to settle a claim for breach of a contract to employ an underwriter as an exclusive private placement agent that arose when the issuer placed the shares itself were determined not to be received as compensation for services since no services were performed. The warrants were issued pursuant to a settlement agreement relating to breach of the placement agreement, but not pursuant to its liquidated damages clause. The court determined that the private placement agreement was not applicable since the settlement agreement superseded it. Nevertheless, because what the taxpayer was required to do under the private placement agreement was essentially similar to what the taxpayers did in *Weigl* and *Pagel*, the decision seems inconsistent with those cases, but the opinion indicates the court's determination that the Service essentially botched its case. The warrants were determined, on the basis of expert testimony, to have an ascertainable value at date of issue, so that income was realized in that amount, and at that time, not at the substantially higher value on exercise. Treas. Reg. § 1.61-15 was not cited.

In footnote 14 of the *Centel* case, the Tax Court judge distinguishes the Tax Court's decision in *Pagel* (which was subsequently affirmed on the ground that it was in connection with the performance of services, not the use of capital). Many, if not most underwritings, however, are firm commitment underwritings, which means that the underwriters agree to purchase the shares, even if they cannot resell them to the public. Although underwriters usually protect themselves against that risk, the risk can become real, if, for example, the underwriter miscalculates, or, when unforeseen situations not covered by the underwriting contract's protective limitations come into play. Apparently, the argument that

---

rules of sections 1.61-15(a) and 1.61-2(d)(6)(i), Income Tax Regs., these section 61 regulations did not technically apply either, we went on to state:

> We nevertheless believe that the regulatory scheme is intended to apply to options taxable under both section 83 and section 61. We thus shall apply the scheme of the section 83 regulations as if it technically applied to options which fell out of the provisions of section 83 into those of section 61. . . .

However, the present case is distinguishable from the situation in *Pagel*. Section 83 does not apply to the warrants in the present case because they were not transferred in connection with the performance of services. Here the warrants were not compensatory, but were issued in recognition of something akin to contributions to capital. Thus, neither section 83 nor section 61 applies.

underwriter warrants were issued for use of capital, not services, was not raised in either case, or subsequently.

When the issuer of a noncompensatory NSO is involved in a merger or other reorganization, as discussed in § 3.03 *Transfers of NSOs*, the acquirer may assume the noncompensatory NSO, or may make payments to terminate the noncompensatory NSOs. Payments made by the acquirer are generally part of the purchase price, with any deduction belonging to the target, and, of course, the tax consequences to the holder are the same as if terminated by the target. *See* Tech. Adv. Mem. 92-06-004 (amounts paid by "new" target, following a § 338 election, to cancel "old" target lender options deductible by old target under § 1234(b)(1) and under the *Commercial Security* principle, discussed in § 4.03 *Deductible Items* of Chapter 3 *Liabilities: Discharge of Indebtedness; Mortgaged Property*; but may be deductible by the acquirer if the option is not terminated). *See* Rev. Rul. 2003-98, 2003-2 C.B. 378 (NSOs, issued by a target corporation before the cash acquisition of its stock (with no § 338 election), but exercised or paid out after, are deductible by the target corporation (now owned by acquirer) after the acquisition when the employee is taxed on the income; deductible by acquirer if target is liquidated).

PROBLEM FOR DISCUSSION

Problem 6-14. In 20X1, InvBanque received a warrant in connection with the underwriting of an IPO of Ceeco in 20X1. The underwriting was a firm commitment underwriting, which meant that InvBanque would be forced to purchase any IPO shares it could not sell to customers. This is, in substance, a guarantee. The warrant gave InvBanque the right to buy 50,000 Ceeco shares at scheduled prices that ranged from 10 percent to 30 percent above the IPO price, but restricted InvBanque from exercising or disposing of the warrant for 13 months after its grant. At the time of receipt, Ceeco options were not publicly traded, although Ceeco shares became publicly traded as a result of the offering. The value of the warrant when granted was $10,000. The value was determined by a qualified financial expert using the Black-Scholes formula, which has been used by the Service for valuation of options in other contexts. The financial expert took into account the value of the Ceeco share at offering, the probability of that value increasing or decreasing, and the length of the option period, all of which are factors in the formula, InvBanque exercised the Ceeco warrant in 20X4 when the Ceeco shares were selling at $6 a share above the exercise price. Although denying the warrants were received in connection with the performance of services, InvBanque made a "protective" § 83(b) election and reported the $10,000 as income realized on the receipt of the warrants. InvBanque did not report any additional income when it exercised the warrant. (i) Was InvBanque's income $10,000 in 20X1 or $300,000 in 20X4? (ii) Why? *See* 83(a) and (e)(3) and (4); Treas. Reg. §§ 1.83-7(b) and 1.61–15; *Weigl* (underwriters' warrants received and distributed); *Pagel* (underwriter's options taxable on exercise, not grant); *Kimberlin* (warrants issued to settle breach of private placement agreement taxed on receipt) *Cramer* (no § 83(b) election for NSOs), (iii) How, if at all, does § 409A affect the analysis? *See* Treas. Reg. § .1409A.

Problem 6-15. In 20X1, Ceeco issued warrants to purchase 100,000 Ceeco shares at $11 per share at any time up to 2X10 when Ceeco shares were selling at

$10, to Countribanc in connection with Countribanc's 10–year $1,000,000 loan to Ceeco due in 2X10, with interest at two percent above the prime rate, because Ceeco was far from a prime credit risk. Under the loan documents, the warrants were valued at $24,900, which, not by coincidence, is the largest amount that satisfies the de minimis provision of § 1.1273-1(d)(2) so that neither party was required to report OID. In internal documents, Countribanc valued the warrants at $150,000. In 20X9, when Ceeco shares were selling at $16, Countribanc exercised the Ceeco warrants, reporting no taxable income. It sold the Ceeco shares in 2X10, when Ceeco refinanced the loan at the prime rate reflecting its improved financial status, for $18, reporting a profit of $675,100 ($7 x 100,000 = $700,000 - $24,900 assigned warrant value). Ceeco claimed $500,000 deduction for additional contingent interest when Countribanc exercised the warrants on the ground that the assigned value indicated that the warrants really had no value when exercised. (i) What is the proper tax treatment of the grant and exercise of the Ceeco warrants for both parties? *See* Treas. Reg. §§ 1.61-15 and 1.1273-2(h); *Custom Chrome* (lender warrants must be valued at issue); *Monarch Cement* (lender warrants may be valued based on differential interest rates); Tech. Adv. Mem. 2000-43-013 (lender warrants are OID at issue, not at termination).

§ 3.04(b). Noncompensatory Options Taxed on Exercise

Although Treas. Reg. § 1.61-15 distinguishes between compensatory and noncompensatory NSOs, and seems to assume that the value of the noncompensatory NSO at grant is the relevant amount, it does not say so expressly. Moreover, it does not deal directly with the valuation of a noncompensatory NSO, which, by definition, does not have a readily ascertainable fair market value. Despite the general approach of the Service to require valuation of consideration received as income "except in rare and extraordinary circumstances," as its argument in *Custom Chrome v. Commissioner*, T. C. Memo 1998-317, *rev'd*, 217 F.3d 1117 (9th Cir. 2000), demonstrates, it seems more willing to argue that an option cannot be valued at grant, so that the tax consequences are determined at exercise. In the following case, in which the grantor of the option claimed a deduction for the spread at exercise, the Service argued unsuccessfully that the spread at exercise was required to be capitalized, but did not argue that the value of the warrants at grant was the proper measure of the tax consequences. Neither party seems even to have mentioned Treas. Reg. § 1.61-15.

SUN MICROSYSTEMS, INC. v. COMMISSIONER

United States Tax Court

T.C. Memo. 1993-467

[Sun Microsystems, Inc. (SMS) developed, manufactured, and sold computer workstations and related computer peripheral equipment primarily to universities, research laboratories, government agencies, and other individual companies and customers. SMS wanted to grow primarily by focusing its sales efforts on original equipment manufacturers (OEMs) of computers and computer products, including OEMs that engaged in the computer-assisted design (CAD), computer-assisted manufacturing (CAM), and computer-assisted engineering (CAE) business. Computervision Corporation (CV) was an OEM engaged in the business of developing, producing, and selling computer hardware and software products in the CAD, CAM, and CAE field. It was one of the largest producers and sellers of CAE/CAD/CAM products in the world. CV wanted to establish a long-term contractual relationship with a supplier for certain computer workstations. SMS considered the opportunity to sell computer workstations to CV was vital because CV was the first potential OEM customer of significant size for SMS. CV sought to minimize the price at which it would purchase workstations by maximizing the discount from SMS's list price for such products. SMS offered a 45% discount from list, but CV pressed for a higher discount, although it was aware that, in the computer industry, a 45-percent discount was on the high end of normal purchase discounts. SMS did not think that it could make a cash profit if it allowed CV a discount greater than the one offered. The parties discussed stock warrants during the negotiations as a means of affording CV greater discounts. The eventual agreements provided that the relationship between SMS and CV would encompass an exchange of current product technologies; cooperation on future product developments; and investment participation in SMS by CV. The investment agreement provided that SMS would grant to CV two stock warrants and a convertible debenture (the debenture). The warrants were exercisable only if CV purchased specified dollar amounts of work stations under the purchase agreement. CV and SMS regarded the warrants as an incentive for CV to purchase computer workstations from SMS. SMS claimed a deduction in the total amount of $4,912,500 with respect to the warrants issued to CV. However, this deduction was not reflected as an expense in petitioners' 1987 financial statements. At the time that the parties entered into the agreements, both parties viewed their new relationship as potentially long-term. In holding that the warrants were purchase discounts, the court stated:]

* * *

TANNENWALD, JUDGE.

* * *

We must determine the correct tax treatment of the warrants issued by SMS to CV. Petitioners contend that the value of the warrants, *i.e.*, the excess of the value of SMS stock over the exercise price (an amount which is not in dispute), constitutes a sales discount or allowance, excludable from gross sales or, alternatively, an ordinary and necessary business expense deductible under section 162. Respondent contends that such value was not a sales discount or allowance, but rather represented an "investment opportunity" for CV, with the result that it is neither excludable from gross sales as a sales discount or allowance nor deductible under section 162.

Initially, we note that respondent has renounced any claim that section 1032 applies so as to deny SMS the tax benefit flowing from either of its positions. . . . Nor does respondent contend that the warrants (or the stock issued pursuant to their exercise) are not property which can be the subject of a sales discount or allowance or a deductible expense. . . . Finally, the parties are in agreement that, because of the contingent nature of the warrants, 1987 is the earliest year, under the all-events test, for determining their tax consequences. . . .

Essentially, petitioners' position is based on the proposition that, since the purpose of the warrants was to reduce the cost of a customer's purchases, the value of the warrants must necessarily be a sales discount or allowance or a deductible expense. Respondent's position is equally categoric, namely, that the issuance of the warrants represents an "investment opportunity" which is capital in nature and therefore precludes characterization of their value at the time of exercise as a sales discount or allowance or a deductible expense. Our view differs from the simplistic positions adopted by the parties and derives from an analysis of the totality of the facts and circumstances of the relationship between SMS and CV in order to determine the intent and purpose of the parties and thus proper tax treatment of the item in question.

The parties have focused on our pronouncement in *Pittsburgh Milk Co. v. Commissioner*, 26 T.C. 707, 716-717 (1956):

> It does not follow, of course, that all allowances, discounts, and rebates made by a seller of property constitute adjustments to the selling prices. Terminology, alone, is not controlling; and each type of transaction must be analyzed with respect to its own facts and surrounding circumstances. Such examination may reveal that a particular allowance has been given for a separate consideration — as in the case of rebates made in consideration of additional purchases of specified quantity over a specified subsequent period; or as in the case of allowances made in consideration of prepayment of an account receivable, so as to be in effect a payment of interest. The test to be applied, as in the interpretation of most business transactions, is: What did the parties really intend, and for what purpose or consideration was the allowance actually made? Where, as here, the intention and purpose of the allowance was to provide a formula for adjusting a specified gross price to an agreed net price, and where the making of such adjustment was not contingent upon any subsequent performance or consideration from the purchaser, then, regardless of the time or manner of the adjustment, the net selling price agreed upon must be given recognition for income tax purposes.

See also Max Sobel Wholesale Liquors v. Commissioner, 630 F.2d 670 (9th Cir. 1980), *affg.* 69 T.C. 477 (1977).

While we agree that the *Pittsburgh Milk* test is relevant to our inquiry herein, we think it is important to note that is not the determinative standard for decision.

* * *

We first note that the subject matter of the adjustment herein is warrants for the purchase of stock. Respondent's concession as to the nonapplicability of section 1032 . . . does not preclude taking into account the fact that stock, rather than some other type of property, *i.e.*, cash or merchandise, was used and that stock conveys an aura of investment. Clearly, however, this fact standing alone is not determinative. . . .

Respondent attaches great importance to the fact that the warrants were dealt with as an "investment participation" by CV in SMS and were grouped with the note and debentures representing capital transactions, *i.e.*, loans from CV to SMS, not only in the memo of understanding but also in the investment agreement, rather than in the purchase agreement covering the purchase of the workstations. While we recognize that this factor cannot be ignored, we do not give it the same weight as respondent. Whatever significance might otherwise attach to respondent's form-over-substance argument, it is counteracted by the totality of the facts and circumstances, which we consider the proper standard to be applied herein, and particularly by the stipulations of the parties that the various elements of the arrangements between CV and SMS were integrated and that the inclusion of the note, debenture, and warrants in the same agreement represented simply a more convenient way to deal with the requirements in Federal and State law relating to the issuance of securities.

Respondent further asserts that the arrangement cannot qualify under the *Pittsburgh Milk* test because it (1) did not provide a formula for "an agreed net price" and (2) was "contingent upon * * * subsequent performance or consideration from" CV. . . . In support of her position, respondent points to the fact that the claimed sales discount or allowance was dependent upon the value of the warrants at a future date, namely, when CV had purchased the requisite dollar amounts of workstations and that, since that value was speculative, there could not be "an agreed net price". In respect of the contingent performance, respondent points to the fact that the exercise of the warrants was not only dependent upon the purchase by CV of the designated amounts of workstations, which was optional with CV, but also upon CV's payment for the stock represented by the warrants.

* * *

We . . . do not view *Pittsburgh Milk* as creating an exclusive test for determining the existence of a sales discount or allowance. . . . *Pittsburgh Milk* did not say the presence of these elements is enough irrespective of other facts, nor did it say that the literal language of the test must be satisfied.

In our opinion, a specified dollar amount at the inception of a purchase arrangement is not a necessary ingredient of an "agreed net price. . . . It is enough if a mechanism for establishing such a price is established in the arrangement. . . . To be sure, the mechanism left the determination of the dollar amount to future events, and such amount could vary from zero to a very large figure depending on the value of SMS stock over the exercise price. But we are not persuaded that a potentially large amount necessarily precludes characterization as a sales discount or allowance.[9] Although an adjustment to income under such circumstances conceivably could reduce a taxpayer's taxable income to zero or even to a negative figure, the fact of the matter is that, from a financial point of view, the earnings of

[9] In the instant case, the amount claimed as a discount by SMS is $4,912,500 against discounted sales of $30 million to CV, gross sales of $459,556,429, gross profit of $226,694,139, and taxable income of $42,211,832 for the taxable year at issue.

the taxpayer would not be affected since the issuance of the stock would represent a nonexpenditure item which would be reflected as capital on the balance sheet. When this factor is taken into account along with the fact that the appropriate time to evaluate the arrangement is at its inception, it is difficult to conclude that the reasonableness of the amount involved was so open to question as to cause it to lose characterization as a sales discount. . . .

As far as the elements of performance are concerned, the need for CV to purchase the designated dollar amount of workstations is an element of performance present in every volume discount arrangement. Similarly, the facts that the warrants had to be exercised and the warrant price paid are no different from the conditions attaching to warrants and stock options generally. . . .

* * *

In a similar vein, we reject respondent's attempt to relate the warrants to what she claims were the favorable financial terms of the note and convertible debenture. The stipulations of the parties, *see infra* note 13, and the testimony of the officials of SMS and CV stand as clear rebuttal to the assertion that the warrants were related in any way to the note or the debenture.

* * *

Finally, we must consider the extent to which the warrants should be attributed to the development of a long-term customer relationship with CV and should be capitalized in accordance with the "new look", which respondent asserts has been accorded the issue of business expense versus capital expenditure by the Supreme Court in *INDOPCO, Inc. v. Commissioner*, 503 U.S. [79] (1992). We find it unnecessary to refine this claimed "new look" for the purpose of our decision herein. In the first place, *INDOPCO* stands primarily for the proposition that a separate asset is not necessary in order to characterize a payment as a capital expenditure. In the second place, *INDOPCO* articulated this proposition in the context of a situation which clearly involved a capital transaction. Finally, the Supreme Court recognized that, while realization of future benefits is important in determining existence of a capital expenditure, "the mere presence of an incidental future benefit — '*some* future aspect' — may not warrant capitalization". . . . Our evaluation of the record herein, including particularly the stipulations of the parties and the testimony of the officials of SMS and CV involved in the negotiations, clearly shows that the warrants were included as an incentive to purchase $20 million and $30 million worth of workstations. . . .

We conclude that the instant situation falls within the "incidental future benefit" category reflected in *INDOPCO*. *Cf.* . . . Rev. Rul. 92-80, 1992-2 C.B. 57 (*INDOPCO* does not preclude deduction of advertising expenses having a future benefit). . . . Indeed, the long-term benefits herein appear to be no different than those present in stock options given to employees which were held not to impair their compensatory character even before the enactment of the statutory framework that now exists. *See Commissioner v. LoBue* . . .

In sum, the hard fact is that the stipulations of the parties[13] and the testimony of officials of SMS and CV involved in the negotiations clearly show that the warrants were included as an incentive to the purchase of the workstations and not a capital item. This conclusion is reinforced by the fact that the parties have stipulated that CV "did not intend to purchase or hold the stock of SMS if the Stock Warrants became exercisable and had value" . . . and that CV sold the warrants within a very short time after they became exercisable.

Based on an evaluation of all the facts and circumstances, we conclude that the value of the warrants represented a sales discount or allowance by SMS to CV. . . .

* * *

NOTES AND COMMENTS

Whether as a result of the Computervision and similar deals, or otherwise, Sun Microsystems' strategy seems to have paid off since it is now a major computer company. Whatever force this has for the analysis of whether the grant was a deductible sales discount or capitalizable, other than the parenthetical references to possible increases in value of Sun Microsystems stock in Stipulations 43, 45, and 47 quoted in note 13, the only statement in the *Sun Microsystems* opinion that addresses why the discount was measured by the spread at exercise instead of the initial value of the warrants as in, for example, *Centel Communications* (warrants issued for guaranty not for services), and *Custom Chrome* (lender warrants valued

---

[13] Among the stipulations are the following:

22. In May 1983, SMS offered a package of incentives to CV as part of its new offer to supply the workstations to CV.

* * *

28. During the negotiations between CV and SMS, CV sought to minimize the price at which it would purchase workstations from SMS by maximizing the discount from SMS's list price for such products. SMS sought to maximize the price at which it sold workstations, and to minimize the amount of the discount from its list price. * * * * * *

40. CV and SMS regarded the Stock Warrants as an incentive for CV to purchase computer workstations from SMS.

41. CV and SMS regarded the Stock Warrants as a mechanism which could potentially reduce the effective cost to CV of the computer workstations that CV purchased from SMS.

42. The Stock Warrants were "part and parcel" of CV's purchase of workstations from SMS.

43. From CV's perspective, the Stock Warrants were a mechanism by which the effective cost of the computer workstations purchased by CV could be reduced if the Stock Warrants increased in value (i.e., if SMS's stock increased in value).

* * *

45. CV and SMS intended that if SMS's stock increased in value, the Stock Warrants would provide an opportunity for CV to reduce the effective cost of the computer workstations that CV purchased from SMS.

* * *

47. CV viewed the Stock Warrants as an opportunity to reduce the cost of the workstations purchased from SMS if the value of the Stock Warrants increased (i.e., if the value of the SMS stock increased), and did not intend to purchase or hold the stock of SMS if the Stock Warrants became exercisable and had value.

at issue) is that the parties agreed that because of the contingent nature of the warrants, the year they became exercisable and were exercised was the earliest year under the all events test for determining the consequences. For that matter, Treas. Reg. § 1.61-15 concentrates more on determining whether NSOs are compensatory or noncompensatory, with the focus, in the valuation portions of paragraph (c), on public trading, even though the primary focus of the regulation being options without a readily ascertainable fair market value. Two possible explanations are the "intent" test of *Commissioner v. Lo Bue*, 351 U.S. 243 (1956), and *Commissioner v. Smith*, 324 U.S. 177 (1945), and the "impossible to value" at grant test adopted by the Service and the Tax Court in *Custom Chrome* that was rejected by the Court of Appeals. Neither is entirely satisfactory, since hope for appreciation is the basis of any option transaction (except the questionable rare one, in which the option is in the money at grant), and since valuation difficulty delays tax consequences only in "rare and extraordinary circumstances," but the opinion does not discuss what those circumstances might be. A possible basis for the distinction in that in *Centel* and *Custom Chrome*, the guarantee and loan were completed when the warrants were issued, while in *Sun Microsystems*, the purchases were not completed until a later year.

The *Sun Microsystems* approach was applied to the other party to the transactions in *Computervision Int'l Corp. v. Commissioner*, T.C. Memo. 1996-131, where the issue was whether the lower value on the date the warrants became exercisable was the proper measure, with the difference between that value, and the higher value when the warrants were sold treated as capital gain. The Tax Court rejected Computervision's attempt to treat the entire spread as capital gain on the ground that the warrant was a trade discount, and followed *Convergent Technologies v. Commissioner*, T.C. Memo. 1995-320, in which manufacturer/seller's discount was also measured by the value at the date of exercise, not the higher value on the date they become exercisable, on the ground that the all events test had not been satisfied until then. Nevertheless, since none considered valuing the options at grant, none provide any useful guidance on the tax consequences of when a noncompensatory NSO should be valued at grant, and when at exercise. If the reason for delaying the income and deduction is completion of all events, exercisability, not exercise should be the time for valuation. The *Sun Microsystems* approach was rejected in Custom Chrome, Inc. v. Commissioner, 217 F.3d 1117 (9th Cir. 2000), dealing with warrants issued in a loan transaction on the ground that the warrants were required to be valued in determining OID as a part of the loan transaction, and in Field Serv. Adv. 1999-41-018, dealing with warrants issued as part of the consideration for a technology license agreement, denying a deduction on exercise of the warrants after the license had been abandoned by the issuer of the warrants, on the ground that the warrants could be and were valued by the parties, so that the deduction should have been the unamortized value of the warrants at grant when the license was abandoned. In addition, in an undated Field Serv. Adv., 1999 TNT 110-39, the Service held that warrants issued to customers allowing exercise after the holder had made specified purchases were required to be capitalized under *INDOPCO*. Although the fact pattern seems to be similar to *Sun Microsystems*, *Convergent Technologies* and *Conputervision*, none were cited by the Service, possibly suggesting that the Field Serv. Adv. was issued before those cases were decided or might even had been addressed to one of them.

On the other hand, Tech. Adv. Mem. 2006-22-046 treated a receipt of a noncompensatory warrant as ordinary income in the year of receipt, when the warrant was received in connection with a transfer of telecommunications customer traffic to the issuer. The Service held the receipt currently taxable despite a condition subsequent, considering the transaction as not satisfying the rare and unusual circumstances for open transaction treatment, requiring current inclusion whether the receipt was in exchange for an intangible asset, or an incentive to enter the deal, and was not a purchase discount with deferral under the foregoing cases that were labeled the "workstation cases."

An issuer may pay consideration for canceling noncompensatory NSOs to facilitate another transaction, for example, a public offering of its securities or a financial reorganization. Although the tax consequences to the holder are, presumably, determined by the tax status of the original transaction, some cases have determined that the consequences to the issuer should be determined under the origin-of-the claim test, by the nature of the facilitated transaction. *See Jim Walter Corp. v. United States*, 498 F.2d 631 (5th Cir. 1974) (cost of repurchasing warrants, originally issued to partners of a predecessor partnership as part of incorporation to facilitate public offering, was capitalized into the cost of offering or as capital restructuring cost of ending the obligation to issue shares; purpose of issuing the warrants was irrelevant; does not state whether the warrants were taxed on issue); Field Serv. Adv. 2000-11-006 (warrants to purchase stock issued by a corporation in financial difficulty to lenders, who agreed to convert deferred interest into preferred stock, were costs to be amortizable over the life of the restructured loans; when the restructured loans were discharged early, the unamortized cost attributable to the portion paid in cash was deductible, but the unamortized costs allocated to a portion exchanged for preferred stock was a cost of issuing the stock; if the lender warrants could not be valued at issue, value at exercise would measure the amount deductible or capitalized; when lender warrants were exchanged for common stock, the termination of the lender warrants did not give rise to a deduction and was not a closing transaction under § 1234). The issue is similar to the one discussed in *Notes and Comments* in § 3.03 *Transfers of NSOs*, as to when payments to retire NSOs issued by the target or similar compensatory payments by the acquiring corporation are part of the purchase price and when they are deductible expenses of the acquirer.

PROBLEMS FOR DISCUSSION

Problem 6-16. In 20X1, Ceeco acquired a nonexclusive license for technology from Hi-Tech for $100,000 in cash and granting Hi-Tech a 10-year option to purchase 10,000 Ceeco shares then appraised at $10 (although there was no active market for Ceeco shares). Ceeco hoped to go public at $11 (or more), when conditions were right at any time up to 20X6. Hi-Tech reported the license consideration as $110,000, including $10,000 for the option. Ceeco recorded its amortizable basis as the $100,000 cash consideration. Hi-Tech exercised the option in 20X6 after Ceeco had gone public and its shares were selling at $20. Ceeco claimed a $90,000 deduction for the spread on the option when Hi-Tech exercised it in 20X6. Which, if either, of Ceeco and Hi-Tech reported the option transaction correctly? *See* Treas. Reg. § 1.61-15, *Custom Chrome* (lender warrants must be valued at issue); Tech. Adv. Mem. 2000-43-013 (lender warrants are OID at issue, not at termination); *Centel Communications* (options for providing guarantee are for the use of capital, not services; valued at grant); *Weigl* (underwriters' warrants distributed); *Pagel* (underwriter's options taxable on exercise, not grant); Field Serv. Adv. 1999-41-018 (warrants for technology license capitalized as part of license cost); *Sun Microsystems* (warrants as purchase discount valued at exercise); *Computervision Int'l* (warrants as purchase discount valued by recipient at exercise price, not lower value when became exercisable); *Convergent Technologies* (warrants as purchase discount valued by issuer at exercise price, not higher value when became exercisable); Field Serv. Adv., 1999 TNT 110-39 (value of warrants is capitalized; apparently issued on *Sun Microsystems* facts before the decision); Tech. Adv. Mem. 2006-22-046 (value of warrant received for transfer of telecommunications traffic taxed when received; distinguishes "workstation" cases).

Problem 6-17. In 20X1, Ceeco issued: (i) warrants for 10,000 Ceeco shares at $10 to Countribanc in connection with a loan that provided Ceeco needed funds, (ii) warrants for an additional 10,000 Ceeco shares at $10 to Munn as consideration for guaranteeing the Countribanc loan, and (iii) warrants for an additional 10,000 Ceeco shares at $10 to VenCap to induce it to convert a convertible debenture into Ceeco shares, in order to improve Ceeco balance sheet in connection with the Countribanc loan. In 20X3, to facilitate a public offering, it paid each of them $50,000 to cancel the warrants. (i) What, if any, are the tax consequences to Ceeco, Munn, Countribanc and VenCap of the grant of the warrants in 20X1? (ii) What, if any are the tax consequences to each of the $50,000 payment in 20X3? *See Jim Walter* (cost of repurchasing warrants originally issued to partners of a predecessor partnership as part of the incorporation to facilitate public offering was capitalized into cost of offering or as capital restructuring cost of ending the obligation to issue shares; purpose of issuing the warrants was irrelevant; does not state whether the warrants were taxed on issue); Field Serv. Adv. 2000-11-006; Tech. Adv. Mem. 2000-43-013 (lender warrants are OID at issue, not at termination). Tech. Adv. Mem. 92-06-004 (severance payment obligations to employees of old target for downsizing immediately after acquisition treated as deductible expense of purchaser, not a liability of old target); Tech. Adv. Mem. 2006-22-046 (value of warrant received for transfer of telecommunications traffic taxed when received; distinguishes "workstation" cases); Tech. Adv. Mem. 97-21-002 (severance payment obligations to employees of old target for downsizing immediately after acquisition treated as deductible expense of purchaser, not a liability of old target); Tech. Adv. Mem. 97-31-001 (increased severance payment obligations negotiated as part of stock acquisition to provide protection to continuing employees not required to be capitalized as purchase price) (last two discussed in § 3.03 *Transfers of NSOs*).

§ 3.05. Valuing NSOs

As indicated by the preceding materials, compensatory and noncompensatory NSOs may be transferred in a number of circumstances requiring that NSOs be valued, either to determine the consequences of the transfer of NSOs, or to determine collateral consequences, including the amount of a gift, charitable contribution, dividend, or other tax effects. Because such NSOs are rarely, if ever, publicly traded, and because the value of an NSO is almost always more than the spread between the exercise price and the value of the underlying stock, even for publicly traded stocks, valuing the NSO is a difficult and controversial exercise. Rev. Proc. 98-34, 1998-1 C.B. 983, sets out valuation principles for gifts of nonstatutory stock options similar to those of the Statement of Financial Accounting Standards No. 123 (FAS 123). Under FAS 123, the fair value of a stock option granted by a public entity is estimated using an option pricing model (for example, the Black-Scholes model or a binomial model) that takes into account as of the option grant date: (1) the exercise price of the option; (2) the expected life of the option; (3) the current price of the underlying stock; (4) the expected volatility of the underlying stock; (5) the expected dividends on the underlying stock; and (6) the risk-free interest rate for the expected term of the option. The Rev. Proc. applies only to nonpublicly-traded compensatory stock options on stock that is publicly traded on an established securities market. The Rev. Proc. sets forth a number of additional conditions and requirements. Rev. Proc. 2002-13, 2002-1 C.B. 549, provides a safe-harbor valuation structure for determining the value of NSOs under the golden parachute provision of § 280G. It applies generally to publicly traded corporations and expressly excludes NSOs covered by Rev. Proc. 98-34. Rev. Proc. 2002-13 does not explain how its formula differs from that in Rev. Proc. 98-34 or why different formulas are appropriate for NSOs in the different contexts.

Priv. Ltr. Rul. 96-16-035 held that transfer by employee of an NSO under a plan that permits transfers to members of the employee's immediate family and other related entities is a completed gift, even though the time of exercise might be accelerated if the employee terminates his employment because of retirement, physical disability, or death, because these acts are of independent significance, and any affect such termination may have on the exercise of the options is only collateral or incidental to termination of employment. In valuing the option, factors, such as the possibility that the terms of the options may permit the options to be exercised without payment and the possibility that the committee may allow exercise of the options without payment, should be considered in valuing the options for gift tax purposes. Priv. Ltr. Rul. 97-22-022 reached a similar conclusion by ducking the valuation. On the other hand, Rev. Rul. 98-21, 1998-1 C.B. 975, held that a gift of an NSO to members of the employee's immediate family was not a completed gift at the time the transfer was made if it was exercisable only after the employee performed additional services, even though the transfer was valid under state law and the donee had control of when the option would be exercised; transfer is a completed gift when the donee's right to exercise the option is no longer conditioned on the performance of services by the transferor.

PROBLEMS FOR DISCUSSION

Problem 6-18. Ceeco, which is not publicly traded, grants Exec an NSO for 10,000 Ceeco shares at $10 per share, which is based on a formula that will also be applied to purchase of the Ceeco shares if Exec exercises the NSO and subsequently terminates employment with Ceeco, including termination at death or on disability. As permitted by the terms of the grant, Exec makes a gift of the NSO for 2,000 of the Ceeco shares to a family trust. (i) How should the shares be valued? *See* Priv. Ltr. Rul. 96-16-035 (transfer by employee of an NSO to members family is a completed gift); Priv. Ltr. Rul. 97-22-022 (similar conclusion). (ii) How, if at all, is the result changed, if, at the time of the transfer, the NSO was subject to forfeiture if he voluntarily terminated employment during a period that did not end for one year after the gift? *See* Rev. Rul. 98-21 (no completed gift on transfer of option when exercise conditioned on further services by transferring employee).

§ 4. INCENTIVE STOCK OPTIONS (ISOs)

§§ 421 to 424; Treas. Reg. §§ 1.421-1 and 2, 1.422-1 to 5, 1.424-1

As previously discussed, NSOs are called nonstatutory to distinguish them from those compensatory options that, nevertheless, provide the employee with what LoBue sought — no compensation on exercise and the desired capital gains on disposition of the shares, but at the price of satisfying significant statutory requirements. § 421(a)(1). Interestingly, neither § 421 nor any other Code or regulations provision excludes income on grant — implicitly endorsing the *Lo Bue/Smith* position that exercise, not grant, is the potential compensatory event, implying that the position is so ingrained that it presumably does not require statement. Similarly, no provision expressly provides capital gain on sale. One major statutory price is that the employer is denied any deduction for the grant, exercise, or disposition of the shares. § 421(a)(2) and (3). The current version of a statutory stock option for key employees is, under § 422, is called an Incentive Stock Option ("ISO"). There are similar provisions under § 423 for broad-based employee stock purchase plans. The employer is required to file a return on exercise of an ISO or option under an employee stock purchase plan and to furnish the employee with information relating to stock transferred each year on exercise of options, including dates of grant and exercise of the options, the exercise price per share, and the number of shares and value of the shares exercised, which are intended to be sufficient to enable the employee to calculate the tax obligations on exercise and disposition of the shares. § 6039, Treas. Reg. § 1.6039-1(a) and (b) and 2(a) and (b); Prop. Treas. Reg. § 1.6039-1(a) and (b) and 2(a) and (b).

The requirements qualification of an employee stock option as an ISO, and the income tax effect of grant and exercise of an ISO, and of disposition of shares acquired on exercise of an ISO are covered in § 4.01 *ISO Requirements and Effects*. Even though, or perhaps because, extraordinary tax benefits are granted for ISOs, the exercise of an ISO is treated as an item of tax preference for purposes of the alternative minimum tax (AMT) which is imposed to limit the benefits of specified special tax provisions without eliminating those benefits for regular income tax purposes. The AMT effect of exercise of an ISO is discussed in § 4.02 *Alternative Minimum Tax on Exercise of ISOs* in Chapter 9 Alternative Minimum Tax.

§ 4.01. ISO Requirements and Effects

The major requirements for an option to qualify as an ISO are that it: (i) be granted pursuant to a shareholder-approved plan that specifies the number of shares and class of employees covered; (ii) be granted within 10 years of the adoption of the plan; (iii) have a maximum term of 10 years from grant; (iv) have a price equal to the value of the underlying stock when granted; (v) be nontransferable except on death; (vi) must not become exercisable in any calendar year for more than $100,000 of stock (determined at the date of grant); and (vii) if granted to a 10 percent shareholder, have a price 110 percent of value and be limited to five years. § 422(b); Treas. Reg. § 1.422-2. The exercise must occur while the grantee is still employed or within three months of termination (or one year if terminated for disability). § 422(a)(2); Treas. Reg. § 1.422-1(a)(1)(i)(B). It is far from clear how these requirements relate to the extraordinary capital gain benefit.

The requirement that the option price equals the value (110% of the value for 10% shareholders) of the underlying stock at grant is relaxed to provide that it is satisfied if there is a good faith effort to value the stock. § 422(c)(1); Treas. Reg. § 1.422-(f) and (e)(2). The regulations validate any reasonable method, including those appropriate for estate tax purposes, with a facts and circumstances qualification. Treas. Reg. § 1.422-2(e)(2)(i). For publicly traded stock, the estate tax method seems to be the only relevant fact. Treas. Reg. § 1.422-2(e)(2)(ii). This does not necessarily prevent key executives from conveniently receiving ISO (and NSO) grants shortly before the announcement of good news (or their selling out before bad). On the other hand, back-dating options should disqualify them and make them subject to § 409A. For nonpublicly traded stock, expert appraisal is blessed, but minority discounts (or control premia) are permitted. Treas. Reg. § 1.422-2(e)(2)(iii). In neither case, however, are lapse restrictions taken into account. Treas. Reg. § 1.422-2(e)(2)(iv).

The $100,000 limit on ISOs is a limit on initial exercisability during a calendar year, not a limit on grant or exercise. *See Montgomery v. Commissioner*, 127 T.C. 43 (2006) ($100,000 limit applies, even though taxpayer made disqualifying disposition of stock acquired in the same year as exercise). Thus, an executive can receive, in one year, a grant of ISOs with a total exercise price of $1,000,000, if the options become exercisable at the rate of 10% ($100,000) a year over 10 years, and the executive can exercise all of the options in the tenth year. Treas. Reg. § 1.422-4(a) and (d) Ex. 1. The value of the stock at exercise is irrelevant, so that it does not matter whether the profit on exercise is $1,000,000 or $200,000,000 or any other amount. NSOs and any other equity based compensation do not count in applying the $100,000 limit. Treas. Reg. § 1.422-4(b)(2). As a practical matter, most plans simply limit grants to those within the $100,000 limit. When they do not, qualification is generally determined by the order of grant, with a special rule when an option is accelerated as a result of a change in control or otherwise. Treas. Reg. § 1.422-4(b)(3) and (d) Exs. 2 to 5. When a single grant exceeds the limit, the option is bifurcated into an ISO and an NSO. A corporation may designate each part by a separate certificate or otherwise, and, if it does not, the first exercises are ISOs up to the limit. Treas. Reg. § 1.422-4(c)(2) and (d) Ex. 6. When an ISO is modified or otherwise disqualified as a result of cancellation or transfer in violation of § 1.421-1b(2), it, nevertheless, remains outstanding for the purpose of the $100,000 limit until the end of the year of its original exercisability, effectively preventing later granted options from qualifying for that period. Treas. Reg. § 1.422-4(b)(5).

A single deferred compensation or stock option plan can provide for issuance of more than one type of stock-based compensation — ISOs, NSOs, SARs, phantom stock, and restricted stock. If all are granted under the same plan, either the maximum number of ISOs, or the maximum number of shares covered by the plan, including ISOs, must be specified. Treas. Reg. § 1.422-2(b)(1) and (3). A tandem arrangement is one providing an employee with rights to two (or more) kinds of stock based compensation, with a provision that the exercise of one right cancels the right to the other, for example, the grant of an SAR on 100 shares of stock and an NSO on 100 shares, when the exercise of the SAR cancels the NSO, or vice versa. The tandem nature of the arrangement, in effect, allows the employee to choose which one to exercise, with the tax consequences determined at the time of the exercise and governed by the type of stock-based compensation exercised. Rev. Rul. 82-121, 1982-1 C.B. 79. On the other hand, when an ISO is part of the package, concern about the pricing and other requirements of an ISO limits the permissible tandem arrangements. Specifically, a tandem arrangement, under which the exercise of the alternate arrangement could result in benefits that are greater than those permitted for an ISO, disqualifies the ISO. Treas. Reg. § 1.422-5(d). Thus, although a tandem ISO and SAR is permissible if they are both at the same price, Treas. Reg. § 1.422-5(d)(3), a tandem ISO and NSO does not qualify when the NSO has a longer term than is permissible for an ISO, or is transferable, or contains other terms not allowed for an ISO. Treas. Reg. § 1.422-5(d)(2).

Section 423 contains a provision for broad-based employee stock purchase plans. The requirements for employee stock purchase plans are that: (i) the options by limited to employees of the issuer or its affiliates; (ii) they be granted under a stockholder approved plan; that they not be granted more than five percent shareholders of the issuer or its affiliates; (iii) all employees be covered with exceptions for those who have been employed less than two years and for part-time employees and highly compensated employees; (iv) the terms for all employees have the same rights, except that the number of shares covered may be proportional to compensation and there may be a maximum on the number of shares that can be purchased under the plan; (v) the option price be at least 85 percent of the value of the stock at grant or exercise; (vi) the term of the option not exceed five years from the date of grant when the option price is at least 85 percent of the value at date of exercise, or 27 months if not, presumably when the price is fixed based on value at date of grant; (vii) an employee's rights to purchase stock under the plan not exceed $25,000 for each calendar year of the option is outstanding; (viii) the option be exercisable only by the employee or by a transferee under the employees will or by intestacy. § 423(b); Treas. Reg. § 1.423-1. When the price is less is than full value at grant, the spread between the option price and the value of the stock at grant, limited to the spread at exercise, is taxed as compensation at exercise. § 423(c); Treas. Reg. § 1.423-1(k). ISOs and employee stock purchase plans are excluded from the provisions of § 83. § 83(e)(1). Similarly, Treas. Reg. § 1.409A-1(b)(5)(ii) excludes ISOs and employee stock purchase plans from § 409A.

If there is a gain in excess of the amount treated as compensation, presumably when the sale price exceeds the fair market value of the shares at exercise, the excess is generally treated as capital gain, short-term or long-term depending on the period between the exercise and the sale. Because the benefits of an ISO are lost, the employer has a deduction for the year the employee makes the disqualifying disposition. Although the apparent purpose of the holding period requirement is to condition the employee's ability to realize the extraordinary benefits of ISOs on the employee's satisfying the "proprietary" purpose, at least, for a minimum period, as the following case shows, even an involuntary transfer can be a disqualifying disposition.

SCHUMANN v. COMMISSIONER

United States Court of Appeals for the District of Columbia Circuit
857 F.2d 808 (D.C. Cir. 1988)

* * *

. . . On September 7, 1973, Warren Schumann was granted a qualified stock option to purchase shares of his employer, Kaiser Industries Corporation ("Kaiser"). On May 27, 1976, Schumann exercised his option and acquired such stock. The option price was $7.00 per share, while the price on the American Stock Exchange on the date of exercise was $13.25 per share.

On April 20, 1977, . . . the shareholders adopted a plan of complete liquidation. Schumann voted against the plan. Following adoption of the plan, Schumann received a partial distribution of $14.30 per share on June 3, 1977 (when the market price was $17.50 per share), and $1.00 per share on October 3, 1977 (when the market price was $4.50 per share). In 1978, 1979, and 1980, Schumann received distributions of $3.00, $0.75, and $1.90 per share, respectively. Throughout the period that these distributions were being made, Schumann retained his stock certificates. Kaiser stock continued to be listed and traded on the American Stock Exchange until March 21, 1980 at which time the price was $2.13 per share. . . .

The Internal Revenue Commissioner determined that the relevant partial distributions to Schumann constituted a disposition of his shares within the meaning of section 425(c) of the Code. Since taxpayers seeking capital gains treatment under section 421 must hold their shares for three years, the Commissioner determined that Schumann was ineligible for such treatment and instead was subject to taxation at ordinary rates. . . .

* * *

A. The Partial Liquidation Dividend

Schumann argues that because he retained physical possession of his Kaiser stock certificates after the partial liquidation distribution in 1977, the distribution could not be considered a disposition of the stock. Schumann's argument is inconsistent with the statute. Section 425(c) of the Code defines "disposition" as "includ[ing] a sale, exchange, gift, or a transfer of legal title." (Emphasis added). In addition, section 331(a)(2) provides:

> [a]mounts distributed in partial liquidation of a corporation . . . shall be treated as in part or full payment in *exchange* for the stock.

. . . (Emphasis added). Since Schumann accepted a distribution in partial liquidation of Kaiser in 1977, such acceptance in accordance with the above statute constituted an "exchange" of a proportionate interest in his stock holdings in the corporation. He thus exchanged his stock within the meaning of section 331(a)(2) and disposed of it within the meaning of section 425(c).

Schumann's physical possession of the stock certificates until the liquidation process was completed in 1980 is legally irrelevant. The value of the shares decreased proportionately with each liquidating dividend that constituted an "exchange" as defined by the statute. . . . The ordinary meaning of "exchange" supports the conclusion that the distributions to Schumann flowed to him in reimbursement for his shares. . . .

B. Disqualifying Disposition of Stock

Schumann argues that even if his receipt of the liquidation distribution is found to be a disposition, it should not be considered disqualifying, because Schumann voted against the liquidation plan and the disposition was not voluntary on his part. Schumann relies on *Brown v. United States*, 427 F.2d 57 (9th Cir.1970), which held that a disqualifying disposition . . . required a "voluntary, affirmative act" of a shareholder, and would not result from a shareholder's "involuntary disposition of his shares pursuant to a company's liquidation plan. In *Brown*, . . . Brown . . . was granted a stock option which he exercised. The company was liquidated and its shareholders were paid pursuant to a liquidation plan. . . .

The *Brown* court held that there was no disqualifying disposition, and that Brown remained entitled to capital gains tax treatment. The court held that "the term[s] 'disposition . . . *made by him* [the taxpayer]' manifest[] Congress' intent that some affirmative, voluntary act of the option holder-taxpayer is required to constitute a disqualifying disposition." . . . (Emphasis added). The court reasoned that Congress' use of the words "made by him evidenced an intention to include within the meaning of "disposition" only affirmative acts of the taxpayer to sell, exchange or transfer his interest.

The Ninth Circuit's interpretation of the statute as articulated in *Brown* is flawed and we therefore decline to adopt it. *Brown*'s definition of disqualifying disposition is . . . unduly restrictive. Schumann's disposition of his stock constitutes an "exchange" within the meaning of section 425(c) . . . In that statute Congress provided that a disqualifying "disposition includes a sale, exchange, gift, or transfer of legal title." (Emphasis added). . . . Congress' use of the word "includes" supports the conclusion that a broad rather than a restrictive interpretation of this provision of the statute should apply rather than the narrow definition applied by the Ninth Circuit. . . .

In addition, Congress expressly exempted certain involuntary dispositions (such as stock transfers made from decedents by bequest or inheritance) from the category of "disqualifying dispositions," but did not exempt dispositions made pursuant to corporate liquidation plans. . . . The *Brown* court erroneously inferred that Congress intended to exempt all arguably involuntary disposition because the statute exempts certain specified involuntary dispositions from the disqualifying disposition category. However, under the maxim *expressio unius exclusio alterius*, Congress' specific enumeration of certain exceptions indicates that no other exceptions were intended. . . .

Brown incorrectly interpreted the phrase "disposition . . . made by him" in former section 422(a)(1) to exclude "exchanges" implicitly effectuated by virtue of the corporation's action and the "relinquishment" by the taxpayer of a portion of his rights in the shares. Neither the statute nor its legislative history supports an artificial distinction between voluntary and involuntary dispositions by shareholders. . . . When a shareholder receives a distribution in liquidation of his stock holdings, he has effectively "made" a disposition — an exchange as defined by the statute and a relinquishment within the ordinary meaning of "disposition."

* * *

NOTES AND COMMENTS

The seemingly harsh result of *Schumann* is an almost inevitable result of a statutory process that uses stated conditions to achieve policy results. In the legislative process, Congress, or the legislative drafter(s), inevitably has a picture of the specific kind of transaction intended to be covered, but cannot foresee everything. On the other hand, too broad an attempt by the Service or the courts to seek to achieve "justice" can easily defeat the purpose of the statutory limits. Although Schumann lost out, as discussed in the *Notes and Comments* in § 3.03 *Transfers of NSOs*, the parties to reorganizations and mergers often provide additional compensatory payments to employees, who lose the expected tax benefits of the SARs, and NSOs, and even ISOs as a result of the transactions. For example, in Tech. Adv. Mem. 95-27-005, when a management buy-out of a target corporation, provided that stock options, including ISOs, would be terminated — essentially forcing exercise of the options — the target paid a special bonus to certain management employees, some of whom were to participate in the acquiring corporation. The special bonus essentially put each of the recipient employees in an after-tax position equivalent to the result that would have occurred if the shares to be acquired on exercise of the ISOs had been disposed of by the recipient employees in a transaction qualifying for long-term capital gains treatment. The bonuses were deductible by the target, because of their relation to the pre-existing options that arose out of the employment relationship. As a matter of statutory construction and tax administration it is probably best to leave such adjustments to the parties as was done in the situation described in the technical advice and many others, where the adjustment can be adapted by the specific circumstances. For whatever reason, Kaiser decided not to make such an adjustment for Schumann.

Other circumstances after the grant of an ISO can result in the ISO's ceasing to meet the statutory requirements, so that, if the option remains outstanding, it becomes an NSO. Thus, an option granted to an employee of a subsidiary that is no longer a subsidiary as a result of sale of the stock, ceases to be an ISO if not exercised within three months of the sale. *See* Treas. Reg. § 1.421-1(b)(3) and (h)(2) and (4) Ex. 1. Similarly, transfer of an ISO in a divorce violates the requirement that the ISO be exercisable only by the employee, §§ 422(b)(5) and 423(b)(9), so that the ISO becomes an NSO, with the tax consequences discussed in *Notes and Comments* in § 3.03 *Transfers of NSOs*. If the transfer to the ex-spouse is delayed until the ISO is exercised, but the shares acquired on exercise are transferred instead of the ISO, the transfer of the shares is not a disqualifying disposition, but the transferee-spouse succeeds to the tax status of the transferor. § 424(c)(4); *see* Priv. Ltr. Rul. 2005-19-011 (the divorcing spouse having a beneficial interest in ISO shares, realizes any alternative minimum tax on exercise, and any other income on disposition, even if the shares are held in the name of the employee spouse).

One of the practical problems of exercising ISOs is financing the purchase price. Although there is a similar problem with NSOs, it is more acute for ISOs because the advantages of an ISO are lost if there is a disqualifying disposition, while a sale of NSO shares does not affect the tax effect of exercise. The regulations sanction a type of "cashless exercise," in which previously owned shares of the issuer are used in an nonrecognition exchange under § 1036 to acquire a larger number of shares under an ISO. Treas. Reg. § 1.422-5(b)(1) to (3) and (e) Ex. 1; *see* Rev. Rul. 80-244, 1980-2 C.B. 234 (when employee, who had both qualified and nonstatutory stock options, exercised the qualified stock option (the predecessor of the ISO) and subsequently used some of the shares acquired on exercise to pay the option price under the NSO for twice the number of shares surrendered, receipt of the shares under the NSO was a nonrecognition exchange under § 1036 to the extent of one-half of the shares acquired under the NSO; exchange was not a disposition of the qualified stock option shares which had a basis equal the exercise price under the qualified stock option; the other half of the shares received on exercise of the NSO were compensation under § 83 for the full value (without any allocation of the option price) with a basis equal to the amount included in income). The ISO shares in a qualifying tandem arrangement are subject to the same holding period and disqualifying disposition rules that would apply to an exercise for cash. Treas. Reg. § 1.422-5(b)(2) and (e) Exs. 2 and 3. The nonrecognition exchange, however, means that the basis of the number of ISO shares equal to the number of shares used to pay the price is measured by the basis of the shares surrendered, and the basis of the remaining shares is zero. Treas. Reg. § 1.422-5(b)(3) and (e) Ex. 1. The use of the ISO shares to pay the price, however, would be a disqualifying disposition. *See* Treas. Reg. § 1.422-5(b)(2) and (e) Ex. 2; Treas. Reg. § .1.424-1(c)(3). The tax advantage of an ISO can be lost if the shares received on exercise are disposed of within a year of exercise, or within two years of the grant of the option, except as a result of death, divorce, or insolvency. In a broad sense, this provision indirectly confirms capital gain treatment on any other disposition. As long as the holding period for long-term capital gain is one year, *see* Chapter 2, § 5.01 *Overview*, the effect of a disqualifying disposition is likely to be significant only for options exercised within one year of grant. If the holding period requirements for shares received on exercise of an ISO are not satisfied, the employee realizes income for the year of the disposition of the lesser of the spread between the value of the shares and the exercise price at the time of exercise, or the excess of the sale price over the exercise price. Thus, there is no risk of ordinary income and capital loss, as happened in *Grant v. United States*, 15 Cl. Ct. 38 (Cl. Ct. 1988) (similar result for restricted property sold for less than the unrestricted fair market value), discussed in discussed in § 2.02 *Restricted Property — § 83*.

Although not expressly sanctioned by the ISO regulations, other forms of cashless exercise discussed in *Notes and Comments* in § 3.02 *Grant, Exercise and Lapse of NSOs*, may be arranged. *Merlo v. Commissioner*, T.C. Memo. 2005-178, *aff'd*, 492 F.3d 618 (5th Cir. 2007), discussed in § 4.02 *Alternative Minimum Tax on Exercise of ISOs*, involves such a transaction.

Modifications of ISOs, or of options under employee stock purchase plans, are generally treated as grants of new options, so that the statutory requirements, including the requirements as to minimum price, must be satisfied at the time of the modification. If the modified option does not satisfy the ISO requirements, the modified, "new" option is presumably an NSO that is subject to the provisions of § 409A. Treas. Reg. § 1.409A-1(b)(5)(ii). This places some restraints on repricing options when the price falls, but only if the number of shares or other time limits of the plan may prevent new options, because the modification does not restore the original shares to the option pool. § 424(h)(1); Treas. Reg. § 1.424-1(e)(2).

Adjustments to reflect corporate reorganizations and similar transactions that do not increase the aggregate spread in the options and do not give any other additional benefits are usually not considered modifications. § 424(a) and (h)(3)(A); Treas. Reg. § 1.424-1(a). *See* Rev. Rul. 71-166, 1971-1 C.B. 135 (removal of provision in a qualified stock option (the predecessor of the ISO) that limited adjustments for stock dividends to those over four percent was a modification under § 424(h)(3), because it conferred an additional benefit, even though the regulations provide that adjustments for stock dividends and stock splits are not modifications when included in the original terms), *but see* Priv. Ltr. Rul. 2000-07-033 (failing to adjust ISOs as provided in their terms for a reverse stock split was not modification, because the reverse stock split was intended to offset the effect of a large special dividend of the proceeds of certain businesses; the two events are the equivalent of a pro rata redemption of shares, so that the adjustment reflected a "corporate transaction," even though then Treas. Reg. § 1.425-1(a)(1)(ii) seemed to require corporate transactions to involve employee transfers or discharges; even though the sale of the businesses may have had that effect, the ruling does not rely on this, but stated that the change conformed the ISOs to original intent; it distinguished Rev. Rul 71-166 as involving a change in terms that were intended to harm employees). Treas. Reg. § 1.424-1(a)(3)(ii) seems to allow adjustments for any distribution other than an ordinary dividend.

The existence of the array of stock-based compensation including restricted stock, SARs, NSOs, and ISOs creates a complex menu of planning options that requires careful weighing of the differences among them and adapting them to the particular situation; there is no one-size-fits-all. *See, e.g.*, Knoll, *The Tax Efficiency of Stock-Based Compensation*, 103 Tax Notes 203 (Apr. 12, 2004).

PROBLEMS FOR DISCUSSION

Problem 6-19. Ceeco adopted a shareholder-approved employer equity-based compensation plan in 20X1 that provides for granting stock appreciation rights (SARs), nonstatutory stock options (NSOs), and Incentive Stock Options (ISOs) specifying a maximum number of shares that can be granted under the plan and that no more than one-half of that number can be ISOs. In 20X1, Ceeco granted Exec, its CEO, an ISO for 50,000 Ceeco shares at $10 a share, the quoted market price, initially exercisable at 40 percent (20,000 share) on the second anniversary of the grant, and in 20 percent (10,000 share) increments beginning each subsequent anniversary, with a final exercise date of the tenth anniversary of the date of the grant in 2X11. At the same time, it also granted Exec an NSO for 50,000 shares, exercisable in full beginning the first anniversary of the grant and an SAR for 100,000 shares, initially exercisable 50 percent on the first anniversary of the grant and the balance on the second anniversary of the grant, both expiring 15 years from the date of grant in 2X16. Immediately following the anniversary date in 20X4, when Ceeco shares are selling at $16, Exec exercised the NSO for 10,000 shares and immediately sold the shares making a $600,000 profit. On the same date, she collected an additional $600,000 by exercising 10,000 shares of the SAR. Finally, just before the end of 20X4, she exercised the ISO for 10,000 shares when Ceeco shares were down to $14. (i) What is the effect of the exercises in 20X4 on Exec and Ceeco? Do not consider any possible application of the AMT. *See* Treas. Reg. § 1.422-5(d); Rev. Rul. 82-121 (consequences of exercise of tandem option determined by portion exercised). (ii) How, if at all, does § 409A affect the analysis? *See* § 409A(a)(1)(A), (2)(A) and (4)(A) and(B), and (d)(1); Treas. Reg. § 1.409A-5(b)(i) and (ii); *Montgomery* ($100,000 limitation applies notwithstanding disqualifying disposition).

Problem 6-20. The Ceeco plan in Problem 6-19 also allows tandem arrangements — that is, a combination of an NSO and SAR under terms that provide that the exercise of the NSO cancels the SAR and vice versa. It also allowed tandem ISOs and SARs and tandem ISOs and NSOs, with the same mutual cancellation consequences. In 20X1, Ceeco grants Exec, its CEO, an ISO for 50,000 Ceeco shares at $10 a share, the quoted market price initially exercisable in 20 percent increments beginning on the first anniversary of the grant. At the same time, it also grants Exec an NSO for 80,000 shares, exercisable in full beginning on the first anniversary of the grant and an SAR for 100,000 shares, initially exercisable 50 percent on the first anniversary of grant, and the balance on the second anniversary of the grant. The options are mutually dependent, so that any exercise of the ISO requires surrender of a corresponding number of shares of the NSO, and vice versa. To the extent there are no remaining shares of the ISO, any exercise of the NSO requires surrender of an equivalent number of shares of the SAR. Similarly, any exercise of the SAR requires surrender of an equivalent number of shares of the NSO, and if none remain, of the ISO. Any surrender of shares is allocated to those that vest latest, so that the first ISO shares surrendered are those that become exercisable in 20X6, with corresponding provisions for the others. Immediately following the anniversary date in 20X3, when Ceeco shares are selling for $16, Exec exercises the NSO for 10,000 shares and immediately sells the shares, making a $600,000 profit. This requires surrender of the ISO for 10,000 shares that first become exercisable in 20X6. On the same date, she collects an additional $600,000 by exercising 10,000 of the SAR, which requires surrender of 10,000 shares of the NSO that are already exercisable. Finally, just before the end of 20X4, she exercises the ISO for 10,000 shares when Ceeco shares are down to $14, which requires surrender of an additional 10,000 shares of the NSO. *See* Treas. Reg. § 1.422-5(d); Rul. 82-121 (consequences of exercise of tandem option determined by portion exercised). What is the effect of the exercises in 20X2 on Exec and Ceeco? Do not consider any possible application of the AMT. How, if at all, does § 409A affect the analysis? *See* § 409A(a)(1)(A), (2)(A) and (4)(A) and(B), and (d)(1); Treas. Reg. § 1.409A-1(b)(5)(i) and (ii).

§ 4.02. Alternative Minimum Tax ("AMT") and ISOs

I.R.C. §§ 55, 56, 57, 59. [§§ 53; 55 (other than 55(b)(1)(B), 55(d)(2),and 55(e)); 56(a)(1)(A), (a)(2), (a)(4), (b), (d), (e)(1) and (2); 57(a)(1), (a)(2), (a)(5), (a)(7), (b)

The Alternative Minimum Tax ("AMT") amounts to a semi-autonomous tax system that runs parallel to the regular income tax system, taking much of its structure from the regular tax system, but having its own significant concepts and principles. It significantly complicates an already overcomplex tax system, and requires that taxpayers have a second set of tax accounting records.

The individual AMT is imposed only to the extent that the amount computed at the AMT rate on the alternative minimum taxable income, called the tentative minimum tax, exceeds the regular income tax, § 55(a), so that, in a sense, the tax is still an add-on tax, and not an alternative tax. Individual taxpayers have no choice between the two systems — they end up paying whichever of the two taxes is higher. There is, however, a limited credit carryforward from years in which the regular tax is higher than the AMT. § 53. In recent years, the AMT has applied to increasing numbers of middle-income taxpayers who do not make extensive use of tax gimmicks and who were apparently not intended to be subject to the AMT under the original justifications for its enactment.

In its current form, the AMT is different from the "regular" tax system, because: (i) it is imposed on a different, and broader, tax base — alternative minimum taxable income (AMTI) — that subjects to tax numerous items that are not taxed by regular tax either as a result of deductions or exclusions; (ii) it has a different tax rate structure with only two brackets — 26 percent and 28 percent — after an exemption amount that varies depending on whether taxpayers file a joint return, married filing separately, single individuals, and estates and trusts that phase out; and (iii) without many, but not all, of the regular tax credits. There is a separate maximum tax rate on capital gains. § 402(a) *Computing the AMT* deals with the computation of the AMT in general, as background for the application of the AMT to ISOs, which is the subject of § 4.02(b) *The AMT and ISOs*. Section 402(c) *Net Operating Loss ("NOL") Carryovers Under the AMT ("ATNOL") and ISOs* deals with net operating loss carryover issues, when the ISO shares are sold for less than the basis of the shares for AMT purposes.

§ 4.02(a). Computing the AMT

The computation of the AMT or, more accurately, determining the tentative minimum tax, § 55(b)(1), requires applying the statutory rates — 26 percent to the first $175,000 ($87,5000 for married individuals filing separately) and 28 percent to the balance, § 55(a)(1), but with maximum capital gain rates, § 55(b)(3), to the taxable excess, § 55(A)(1)(ii), which is the excess of the alternative minimum taxable income ("AMTI"), § 55(b)(2), over the exemption amount, § 55(d). Even though it is labeled an alternative tax, the computation of AMTI starts with the computation of taxable income for regular tax purposes. The next step is making a series of adjustments that, in effect, broaden the AMT tax base. Under § 55(b)(2), taxable income is subject to adjustments specified in §§ 56 and 58, and increased by tax preferences specified in § 57.

The adjustments listed in § 56 are a miscellaneous grab bag: Under § 56(a) all taxpayers make the following adjustments, the first four of which generally delay deductions allowed for regular tax purposes of what would otherwise be capitalized costs; the fourth limits deferral of income allowed for regular tax purposes. For present purposes the important adjustment item is § 56(b)(3), which makes the exclusion from income of the spread on exercise of an ISO provided by § 421 not applicable for AMT purposes, so that AMTI includes the spread on incentive stock options taxed for AMT purposes even though excluded for regular tax purposes, as discussed in the opening paragraph of § 4 *Incentive Stock Options (ISOs)*. The effect is to convert the potential capital gain into current ordinary AMTI. The inclusion results in an AMT basis for the stock acquired on exercise that is increased for the amount included in AMTI.

Once the AMTI is computed by adjusting taxable income for regular tax purposes by the specified preferences and adjustments, the next computation is the taxable excess, which is the excess of the AMTI over the exemption amount. The statutory exemption amounts are $45,000 for married taxpayers ($22,500 for those filing separately and $33,750 for unmarried individuals, which are not adjusted for inflation). On the other hand, in recent years they have been adjusted almost annually be Congress, to prevent the AMT from effectively nullifying the so-called Bush tax cuts. For 2009 the exemption amounts were $70,950 for married taxpayers ($35,475 if filing separately) and $46,700 for singles. These are less than the exemption amounts that would apply if the AMT exemption had been adjusted for inflation taxpayers ($41,000 if filing separately) and $61,500 for singles. If adjusted for 2010, there would be a small, if any, inflation adjustment. The exemption amounts phase out when AMTI (not the taxable excess) exceeds $150,000 for married taxpayers ($75,000 if filing separately) and $112,500 for singles. Because these amounts have not been increased, the phase-out starts relatively quickly. As previously indicated, the rates are 26 percent for the first 175,000 of taxable excess and 28 percent thereafter. The preferential rates for long-term capital gains and qualified dividends are, however, preserved by § 55(b)(3).

A specially computed foreign tax credit is allowed against the AMT under § 59(a), which is basically the regular foreign tax credit adjusted to reflect AMTI principles. In addition, § 55(c)(3) obliquely indicates other credits that are allowed in part — that is, that are not limited under § 26(a) to the excess of the regular tax over the tentative minimum tax. These include the adoption credit in § 23, the child credit in § 24, and the saver's credit in § 25B.

The AMT is the excess of the tentative minimum tax over the regular tax for the taxable year, so that the individual taxpayer pays the greater of the regular tax or the AMT.

Because many of the adjustments in computing AMTI are timing adjustments, § 53 allows a credit against regular tax for AMT paid in prior years, which reduces whipsawing the taxpayer. For example, in early years of depreciable assets life, the AMT may be imposed because of the lower depreciation, while in later years regular tax may be higher because the accelerated depreciation has expired, giving rise to the § 53 AMT credit, in effect only reducing the timing advantage of the accelerated deductions. Accordingly, the credit is, in effect, reduced under § 53 for what are called exclusion preferencs, including such items as the disallowance of itemized deductions, the standard deduction, personal exemptions, the reduction in medical deductions, the inclusion of interest on private activity bonds, and the excess of percentage depletion over cost depletion.

NOTES AND COMMENTS

The status of the AMT as a tax system that is largely separate from, but parallel to, the regular tax system was emphasized in Priv. Ltr. Rul. 93-21-063, in which a taxpayer made large charitable contributions that were subject to the percentage limitations, some of which were available as carryovers and some of which expired unused, and a large amount of AMTI. The Service emphasized that the AMT is a separate and distinct tax system. Accordingly, the Service held that the charitable contribution base limitations under section 170(b)(1) of the Code must be computed separately for purposes of computing AMTI to reflect applicable AMT adjustments and preferences. The AMTI charitable contribution base allows a different charitable contribution deduction for AMT purposes than for regular tax purposes. This difference will be maintained in different charitable contribution carryovers for regular tax and AMT. In short, it achieve the same result as for the NOL under § 56(a)(4) without an express statutory provision. Presumably, the same principle will apply for other carryovers and, perhaps, in other contexts as well. On the other hand, *Allen v. Commissioner*, 118 T.C. 1 (2002), limited the application of the separate and parallel system concept of the AMT when it thought that it conflicted with the plain meaning of the words of the Code. The taxpayers were shareholders of an S corporation that paid wages eligible for the targeted jobs credit ("TJC") provided by § 280C, and the credit was passed through to the shareholders. Wages for which a credit is allowed are not deductible in determining taxable income, so that the S corporation income passed through was higher by that amount. There is also a limitation to the credit based on AMTI. The court rejected the taxpayers' argument that because the TJC is not allowed for purposes of the AMT, the corresponding wages should be deductible in determining AMTI.

PROBLEM FOR DISCUSSION

Problem 6-21. Taxpayer is a single, calendar year taxpayer in 2009. Assume that the following occurred in 2009 and, for simplicity's sake, assume that the personal exemption amount is $2,000. Other than the income and deductions below, she has $200,000 of gross income and $50,000 of § 162 business deductions, which are deductible under § 62. In January 1998 she purchased an apartment house with inherited funds at a cost of $650,000, $100,000 of which is for the land. She gives some investment land, worth $30,000, that was purchased several years ago for $10,000, to her alma mater. She receives $8,000 of interest on a "qualified bond" under § 141(e)(1)(B) which is a private activity bond (issued in 2004) but is exempt from regular income tax under § 103(a). She also owns an unencumbered building acquired prior to 1987 on which she properly takes $30,000 of depreciation during the year when straight-line depreciation would have been only 327,500. She has $10,000 of miscellaneous expenses above the two percent floor and she pays state and local property taxes of $10,000 on her personal use property. She has no business or investment indebtedness. Compute taxpayer's tax liability for the year, assuming she pays regular tax at a flat 20 percent rate.

§ 4.02(b). The AMT and ISOs

I.R.C. §§ 53, 55, 56(b)(3)

Even though the exercise of an ISO does not result in compensation for regular income tax purposes, it does result in income for alternative minimum tax purposes. As discussed in § 4.02(a) *Computing the AMT*, the AMT is, in effect, a separate and distinct tax system and determinations under the regular tax system do not necessarily control those under the AMT. The following case addresses how to value the spread at exercise of an ISO in view of the fact that § 83 does not apply to the exercise. § 83(e)(1).

GRESHAM v. COMMISSIONER

United States Court of Appeals, Tenth Circuit
752 F.2d 518 (10th Cir. 1985)

* * *

Louis Gresham (taxpayer) was president, a director, and a member of the executive committee of General Energy Corporation (GEC). During 1974, 1975, and 1976, taxpayer acquired unregistered stock of GEC by exercising a qualified stock option granted to him by GEC in 1973.

In order for the transaction granting taxpayer this option to be exempt from federal securities registration requirements, each time taxpayer exercised his option he was required to execute an investment letter. . . . Additionally, taxpayer agreed that a stop transfer order would be placed against the shares with GEC's transfer agent. Finally, the stock certificates bore a legend. . . .

By executing the investment letter, taxpayer was prohibited, under SEC rulings, from selling or transferring the stock for a period of two years, unless a registration statement was in effect with respect to the shares. . . . In any private placement of the option stock, the SEC would also have required the purchaser to execute a similar investment letter.

During the years in question, taxpayer calculated his minimum tax liability by first determining the bid prices for GEC stock traded on the over-the-counter market on the dates he exercised the option and then discounting the total value of each block of shares purchased by 33-1/3 percent, reporting this discounted value as the "fair market value" of the shares so acquired. (This discounted value represented the value taxpayer would receive if he sold the shares in a private placement.) Taxpayer then subtracted from this discounted value his cost for the option shares; this amount taxpayer reported as his tax preference income.

In determining deficiencies for the years 1975 and 1976, the Commissioner of Internal Revenue (Commissioner) valued the option shares using the over-the-counter, rather than the private placement, value of the shares. The Commissioner thus ignored the effect of the investment letter restrictions on the basis of Treas.

Reg. § 1.57-1(f)(3). The parties stipulated that if section 1.57-1(f)(3) is valid and applicable, taxpayer will concede the deficiencies as assessed in the statutory notice. Conversely, they have stipulated that if, as the Tax Court concluded, section 1.57-1(f)(3) is invalid or inapplicable, the fair market value of the option shares is the discounted value as contended by taxpayer.

Section 56 of the Code imposes a minimum tax, in addition to all other taxes imposed by the Code, on "items of tax preference." Section 57 of the Code lists those items of tax preference subject to the minimum tax, tax, and section 57(a)(6), which is at issue in this appeal, provides as follows:

§ 57. Items of tax preference.

(a) In general. — For purposes of this part, the items of tax preference are —

* * *

(6) Stock options. — With respect to the transfer of a share of stock pursuant to the exercise of a qualified stock option (as defined in section 422(b)) or a restricted stock option (as defined in section 424(b)), the amount by which the *fair market value* of the share at the time of exercise exceeds the option price. (Emphasis added.)

"Fair market value" is not defined in section 57. It is defined, however, in Treas. Reg. section 1.57-1(f)(3), which utilizes the valuation principles of section 83 of the Code. Section 1.57-1(f)(3) provides, in relevant part, that "[i]n accordance with the principles of section 83(a)(1), the fair market value of a share of stock received pursuant to the exercise of a qualified or restricted stock option is to be determined without regard to restrictions (other than non-lapse restrictions within the meaning of § 1.83-3(h))." (Emphasis added.) It is undisputed that the investment letter restrictions of taxpayer's option stock are restrictions which, by their terms, might lapse. It follows, then, that unless section 1.57-1(f)(3) is invalid or inapplicable, the deficiencies assessed against taxpayer under the authority of section 1.57-1(f)(3) is invalid or inapplicable, the deficiencies assessed against taxpayer under the authority of section 1.57-1(f)(3) must be upheld. In making this determination, we must not simply defer to the Commissioner's construction of section 57(a)(6), although that construction is entitled to great deference. . . . Treasury regulations are not absolute rules of law; consequently, they should not be followed when they are inconsistent with the purpose of the Code section in question or exceed the administrative authority granted. . . .

Though it cannot be disputed that section 57(a)(6) does not contain the language in section 83(a)(1) directing that fair market value be determined without regard to restrictions which by their terms might lapse, we should infer such, argues the Commissioner, because the sections were designed to achieve similar results. Both sections were added to the Code by the Tax Reform Act of 1969. . . . The minimum tax bill was designed to distribute more fairly the tax burden by taxing items of "economic income." . . . Here, according to the Commissioner, taxpayer realized economic income when he exercised his stock option in the amount of the bargain element — the difference between fair market value and option price — of the option shares. Were it not for the preferential treatment accorded by sections 421 and 422, this bargain element would be subject to immediate income tax under section 83(a)(1). In an effort to limit the tax avoidance prospects of these sections for high bracket taxpayers, argues the Commissioner, Congress enacted the minimum tax, which subjects this bargain element to a tax in addition to other taxes imposed by the Code. Consequently, reasons the Commissioner, it is incongruous to think Congress would have defined "fair market value" differently in section 57(a)(6) from the way it is defined in section 83(a)(1) if, by doing so, high bracket taxpayers could avoid the minimum tax simply by subjecting the option shares to restrictions such as those that are at issue here.

* * *

Having rejected the view that section 1.57-1(f)(3) was adopted by acquiescence, we are left to speculate on the meaning of "fair market value" in section 57(a)(6). The Commissioner concedes that "fair market value" in other provisions of the Code is generally determined using the "willing buyer/willing seller" test . . . (The Commissioner apparently does not dispute the fact that use of this test would result in the private placement value being used as the "fair market value.") He contends, however, that even though fair market value has a well-defined meaning elsewhere in the Code, that meaning should not be applied here because it is inconsistent with the purpose behind section 57(a)(6) of taxing "economic income."

While we agree that section 57(a)(6) was designed to reach economic income, we do not agree that taxpayer received economic income when he exercised his stock option. Unlike the restrictions in *Harrison* [*Harrison v. United States*, 475 F. Supp. 408 (E.D.Pa.1979)], and *Kolom* [*Kolom v. Commissioner*, 71 T.C. 235 (1978)], the letter investment restrictions here precluded taxpayer from selling his shares except in a private placement. That private placement value was substantially below the public trading price for those same shares. Consequently, by requiring taxpayer to compute fair market value by using the full public trading value for his option shares, the Commissioner's method of valuation has the effect not of taxing "economic income," but of taxing "value" which taxpayer has not received and might never receive.

Given that Congress could have achieved this result in 1969 simply by including the section 83 fair market value language in section 57(a)(6), we agree with Justice Powell that "the failure to include any similar qualification in § 57 strongly suggests that [Congress] intended to use "fair market value" in its traditional and well-established sense." . . . We also agree with Justice Powell's statement, adopted by the Tax Court majority, explaining from a policy standpoint the different use of language in these sections: "It is this policy of encouraging employee stock ownership that explains why the language of section 57 and section 83 differs." . . . Since the Commissioner concedes that "Congress did, of course, encourage the use of qualified stock options with the passage of Section 421 [and 422]," . . . we reject the Commissioner's construction of section 57(a)(6) as inconsistent with the congressional intent of encouraging employee stock ownership.

The Commissioner draws our attention to section 555 of the Tax Reform Act of 1984, which amended section 57(a)(10) to provide that in the case of incentive stock options, "the fair market value of a share of stock shall be determined [for minimum tax purposes] without regard to any restriction other than a restriction which, by its terms, will never lapse." Subsequent legislation is entitled to some weight in determining what a previous Congress meant. . . . Here, however, to read into the plain language of section 57(a)(6) the section 83 meaning of "fair market value" is to reject the "willing buyer-willing seller test of fair market value [which] is nearly as old as the federal income, estate, and gift taxes themselves . . . " . . . We decline to do so without a clear expression of legislative intent.

Affirmed

NOTES AND COMMENTS

Although there is no direct equivalent of the § 57(d)(10) provision referred to in *Gresham* in the current AMT, § 56(b)(3), by providing that § 421 does not apply to the exercise of an ISO, it means that the exclusion of ISOs under § 83(e)(3) does not apply, so that § 83 does. It also applies for corresponding basis adjustment for AMT purpose to the stock acquired on exercise. In Tech. Adv. Mem. 2003-38-010, the Service applied these principles literally, holding that the exercise of an ISO resulted in AMT income for the spread at exercise, even though the shares were subject to restrictions under the securities laws (but not § 16(b), because the options had been granted more than six months before exercise) that blocked all sales by the taxpayer during a lock-up period under an underwriting agreement, and under a company insider trading program allowed sales only during a two-week trading window. The trading restrictions were disregarded on the grounds that they were not forfeiture restrictions and were lapse restrictions. This position, of course, anticipates the similar position for NSOs in the *Tuff* and *Miller* cases discussed in *Notes and Comments* in § 3.02 *Grant, Exercise and Lapse of NSOs* in Chapter 6 *Executive Compensation and Stock Options*.

The AMT on the spread on exercise of an ISO is avoided (but at the price of inclusion for regular tax purposes), if there is a disqualifying disposition in the year of exercise but, as many who exercised ISOs before the collapse of the Internet bubble discovered to their horror, not when there is no disqualifying disposition, or even a disqualifying disposition in the next year.

MERLO v. COMMISSIONER

United States Tax Court

T.C. Memo. 2005-178 (2005), *aff'd*, 492 F.3d 618 (5th Cir. 2007)

* * *

. . . The issues for decision are: (1) Whether petitioner's rights to shares of stock of Exodus Communications, Inc. (Exodus) he acquired during 2000 as a result of exercising an incentive stock option (ISO) were subject to a substantial risk of forfeiture; and (2) whether petitioner is entitled to an alternative tax net operating loss (ATNOL) deduction under section 56(d).

* * *

On July 2, 1999, petitioner commenced work for Service Metrics, Inc. (SMI), as Vice President of Marketing. On July 14, 1999, SMI granted petitioner a stock option to purchase 275,000 shares of SMI common stock.

On November 19, 1999, petitioner entered into an employment agreement with Exodus. On November 23, 1999, Exodus acquired SMI. Pursuant to the reorganization agreement, petitioner's SMI stock option was assumed by Exodus and was converted into an option to purchase shares of Exodus common stock.

According to the Exodus prospectus entitled "Stock Options Granted Under the Service Metrics, Inc. 1998 Stock Option Plan Assumed by Exodus Communications, Inc.":

> The Service Metrics Plan generally does not impose any restrictions on the resale of shares of Common Stock purchased under the Service Metrics Plan. * * *
>
> In accordance with federal law and Exodus' policy prohibiting insider trading, you [petitioner] are always prohibited from trading in Exodus securities when you [petitioner] have inside information.

The Exodus Procedures and Guidelines Governing Securities Trades by Company Personnel (Exodus Procedures) states in pertinent part:

> It is illegal for any Director, officer or employee of Exodus communications, Inc. (the "Company"), to trade in the securities of the Company while in the possession of material nonpublic information about the Company. * * *
>
> * * *
>
> Violation of this policy or federal or state insider trading or tipping laws by any Director, officer or employee may subject a Director to dismissal proceedings and an officer or employee to disciplinary action by [Exodus] up to and including termination for cause.

The Exodus Procedures contain no requirement that petitioner return the stock to Exodus if he attempted to sell his stock in violation of its insider trading policy.

On August 28, 2000, petitioner and Exodus entered into a Settlement Agreement and General Release, effective as of August 4, 2000, under which petitioner ceased to hold the position of Vice President, Marketing of Exodus. On December 21, 2000, petitioner exercised his ISO to purchase 46,125 shares of Exodus common stock. Petitioner's employment with Exodus terminated on December 31, 2000.

Exodus filed bankruptcy on September 26, 2001. In a press release dated November 12, 2001, Exodus announced that the company's common stock had no value.

On his 2000 Form, 1040, U.S. Individual Income Tax Return, petitioner included in his alternative taxable income for alternative minimum tax (AMT) purposes $452,025, the excess of the price for Exodus common stock reported on NASDAQ on April 15, 2001, over the price he paid for the stock. Petitioner did not use the stock's fair market value on the December 21, 2000, ISO exercise date. Instead, petitioner filed Form 8275-R, Regulation Disclosure Statement, disclosing that he relied on proposed legislation H.R. 2794, 107th Cong., 1st Sess. (2001), then pending in Congress, to use the stock's fair market value on April 15, 2001. The proposed legislation would have allowed taxpayers to use the difference between the amount paid for shares purchased pursuant to the exercise of an ISO during 2000 and the fair market value of such shares on April 15, 2001, for purposes of computing their AMT. H.R. 2794, 107th Cong., 1st Sess. (2001), was never enacted.

On November 13, 2003, respondent mailed petitioner a notice of deficiency, in which respondent determined a deficiency of $4,833 in petitioner's 1999 Federal income tax and a deficiency of $169,510 in petitioner's 2000 Federal income tax. In the notice of deficiency respondent stated:

> The fair market value of Exodus Communications, Inc. common stock, at the date that certain stock options were exercised (December 21, 2000) was $23.25 per share instead of the amount used to compute the adjustments/preferences on [F]orm 6251 of the income tax return. Therefore, the amount of the adjustment/preference is $1,057,415.00 instead of the $452,025.00 reported on the return. * * *

On December 4, 2003, prior to filing a petition for redetermination of the notice of deficiency, petitioner filed a Form 1040X, Amended U.S. Individual Income Tax Return for 2000, reducing his alternative taxable income for AMT purposes by $452,025, the excess of the price for Exodus common stock reported on NASDAQ on April 15, 2001, over the price he paid for the stock, thereby eliminating the $116,973 of AMT reported on his 2000 Federal income tax return and claiming a tax refund of $149,757. Under Part II, Explanation of Changes to Income, Deductions, and Credits, of the 2000 amended Federal income tax return, petitioner stated: "Return adjusted to reflect shares subject to substantial risk of forfeiture and non-transferable."

* * *

Petitioner admits that petitioner's stock option meets the requirements of section 422 and qualifies as an ISO. Under section 421(a), a taxpayer is allowed to defer regular tax on income resulting from a stock option meeting the requirements of section 422 or 423 until the taxpayer sells the shares of stock. Were our inquiry to end here petitioner would not have been required to recognize any gain until he disposed of the shares of stock he acquired by exercising his ISO. Our inquiry cannot end here because of the application of the AMT.

Under section 56(b)(3), "Section 421 shall not apply to the transfer of stock acquired pursuant to the exercise of an incentive stock option (as defined in section 422)." Therefore, for AMT purposes, shares of stock acquired by exercising a stock option that qualifies as an ISO under section 422 are treated as shares of stock acquired by means of exercising a nonqualified stock option under section 83. See sec. 56(b)(3); sec. 1.83-7(a), Income Tax Regs.; see also *Speltz v. Comm'r*, 124 T.C. 165. . . .

Under section 83, a taxpayer generally must recognize income when he exercises a compensatory stock option to the extent that the fair market value of the shares of stock transferred to him exceeds the price he pays at the time he exercises the option if the taxpayer's rights in the shares are transferable or not subject to a substantial risk of forfeiture. . . .

* * *

Case law establishes that a restriction on the transferability of property does not affect the timing of income inclusion or the amount of income required to be included under section 83 if the property is not subject to a substantial risk of forfeiture. *See Pledger* . . . ; *Sakol.* . . .

* * *

A taxpayer's right to his shares of stock may be subject to a substantial risk of forfeiture if his rights to full enjoyment of the shares of stock is conditioned upon the future performance of substantial services. Sec. 83(c)(1). The record is devoid of any facts that show petitioner's right to full enjoyment of his shares of Exodus stock was conditioned upon the future performance of substantial services.

Petitioner alleges his shares of Exodus stock were subject to a substantial risk of forfeiture and not freely transferable because they were blacked out from trading by reason of Exodus's insider trading policy. In his brief, petitioner relies on *Robinson*. . . .

The Court of Appeals for the First Circuit in *Robinson* . . . held that a taxpayer's shares of stock were subject to a substantial risk of forfeiture until a 1-year sellback provision lapsed. The employer in Robinson could have compelled its employee to sell the shares of stock back to it at the price the employee paid at the time he exercised his stock option if the employee attempted to sell the shares of stock within a year of exercising his stock option.

Robinson is distinguishable from the instant case on its facts. Petitioner has not shown that Exodus could have ever compelled him to return his shares of stock. The remedy chosen expressly by Exodus to enforce its insider trading policy was not a forfeiture of the shares, but disciplinary proceedings against the offending employee, up to and including involuntary termination of employment.

The Court of Appeals for the Ninth Circuit, citing section 1.83-3(c)(1), Income Tax Regs., has noted that "The risk of forfeiture analysis requires a court to determine the chances the employee will lose his rights in property transferred by his employer." *Theophilos*. . . .

The evidence in the instant case shows that petitioner had no substantial risk of losing the rights to his shares of Exodus stock. There is no evidence that Exodus could have ever compelled petitioner to return his shares after he exercised his ISO; no sellback provision is present; nor is there any evidence that Exodus could have compelled petitioner to forfeit his shares of stock.

In consequence of the foregoing, we hold that petitioner's rights to his shares of Exodus stock were not subject to a substantial risk of forfeiture. . . .

Petitioner also alleges that he is entitled to an ATNOL deduction under section 56(d). An ATNOL deduction is the net operating loss deduction allowable for the taxable year under section 172 and is computed by taking into consideration all the adjustments to taxable income under sections 56 and 58 and all the preference items under section 57 (but only to the extent that the items increased the net operating loss for the year for regular tax purposes). Sec. 56(d)(1). Section 172 defines the net operating loss as "the excess of the deductions allowed by this chapter over the gross income." Sec. 172(c). In the case of a noncorporate taxpayer, the amount deductible on account of losses from sales or exchanges of capital assets shall not exceed the amount includable on account of gains from sales or exchanges of capital assets. Sec. 172(d)(2)(A). In addition, where deductions are not attributable to the taxpayer's trade or business the deductions generally will be allowed only to the extent of the amount of the gross income not derived from the taxpayer's trade or business. Sec. 172(d)(4).

Determination of whether petitioner is entitled to such deduction is based upon facts and circumstances which are not before the Court. Granting of the motion for summary judgment with respect to this issue would be premature, because material issues of fact exist, not the least of which is whether petitioner was engaged in his activity as an investor or trader. . . .

NOTES AND COMMENTS

A subsequent proceeding in *Merlo v. Commissioner*, 126 T.C. 205, *aff'd*, 492 F.3d 618 (5th Cir. 2007) dealing with AMT issues arising from the subsequent loss on the shares acquired under the ISO is discussed in § 4.02(c) *Net Operating Loss ("NOL") Carryovers Under the AMT ("ATNOL")*.

Because the spread on an ISO frequently produces a significant amount of income for AMT purposes that is not matched by any equivalent regular tax item, it may produce an AMT, which allows a credit against regular tax when the regular tax for a year exceeds the tax under the AMT for that year, so that the ultimate tax liability is the regular tax. In the case of ISOs, the offsetting regular tax usually comes when the stock acquired under an ISO is disposed of. In the case of taxpayers like Merlo (and Tuff and Miller), for whom the bursting of the tech bubble meant that such delayed income was unlikely, the potential credit did not provide significant relief. Congress has provided some relief. Although § 53(e) is not specifically addressed to ISOs, the legislative history makes it clear that ISOs were a major impetus. It provides a limited refund of long-term unused minimum tax credits, for tax years beginning after Jan. 1, 2007 and before Jan. 1, 2013. To be long-term, the credit has to have been generated more than three years before it is used. The refundable credit is the lesser 50 percent of the credit (originally 20%, but increased to 50% in the 2008 Act), or $5,000 (or any remaining unused credit), and was initially phased out using the same percentage as for phasing out personal exemptions under § 151, but the phase-out was eliminated in the 2008 Act. As a result, such taxpayers are likely to be able to recover part of their AMT on ISOs on stock that proved to be of little value over that period, of course, without interest.

Section 53(f) provides limited relief specifically addressed to ISOs. It abates any remaining outstanding tax, penalties, and interest attributable to ISOs exercised for taxable years beginning before Jan. 1, 2008, still outstanding on the date of enactment, Oct. 3, 2008 (as part of the legislative response to the financial crisis). It also provided a refundable credit for 50 percent of any interest and penalties already paid that would have been abated if not paid for the 2008 and 2009 tax years.

PROBLEM FOR DISCUSSION

Problem 6-22. In 20X1 Affiliated Enterprises granted to Edward Exec an Incentive Stock Option ("ISO") for 12,000 shares at $11.00 a share and a stock appreciation right ("SAR") for 12,000 shares under which Exec was entitled upon exercise to be paid, in cash or stock at the corporation's option, an amount equal to the difference between the value of Affiliated's stock on the date of exercise and the value of such stock on the date of grant — that is, $11.00 a share, with a provision that the two would only be exercised for a total of 12,000 shares. At the time of the grant of the option, Affiliated stock was selling for $11.00 a share. The ISO and the SAR become exercisable for one-half of the shares in 20X2 and one-half in 20X3.

At the same time, Associated Enterprises granted to Edna Exec (who was married to Edward Exec) a nonstatutory option ("NSO") for 10,000 shares at $12.00. At the time of the grant, Associated stock was selling for $13.00 and freely transferable options to purchase Associated stock at $12.00 a share were selling at $3.00 per option. Edna's options, however, were nontransferable and Edna, therefore, could not sell them.

The ISO, NSO, and SAR, if paid in stock, will be paid by delivery of stock that is restricted stock within the meaning of the federal securities laws. This means that the Execs' ability to dispose of it will be limited by the provisions of Rule 144. In addition, both Execs are sufficiently senior officers to be subject to the application of § 16(b) of the Securities Exchange Act. It can be demonstrated that restricted stock has a fair market value of approximately 20 percent less than the quoted market price.

On December 31, 20X1, the quoted market price of both Affiliated and Associated stock was $15.00 a share. On September 15, 20X2, when the price of Associated stock was $18.00 a share, Edna exercised her NSO. March 15, 20X3, when the § 16(b) restrictions expired for Edna, the value was $19.00 a share.

On December 31, 20X2, the quoted market price of Affiliated stock was $14.00 a share. On January 31, 20X3, when the price of Affiliated stock was $16.00, Edward exercised his incentive stock option with respect to 6,000 shares and his stock appreciation right for the remaining 6,000. The corporation paid him for the SAR by delivering 1,875 shares of affiliated stock. On July 31, 20X3, when the § 16(b) restrictions expired for Edward, the value was $15.00 a share.

For each of the years 20X1 through 20X4, Edward and Edna each received salaries of $150,000, and the Execs together received investment income of $40,000 (including municipal bond interest of $15,000, $4,000 of which was from specified private activity bonds), capital gains of $50,000, and incurred itemized deductions of $180,000 ($30,000 of which were miscellaneous itemized deductions), including home equity interest of $10,000, investment interest of $50,000, and charitable contributions of $35,000.

What is the tax effect of the foregoing transactions of the Execs and Affiliated and Associated Enterprises? Take into account the alternative minimum tax. What is the basis in the shares acquired by the Execs?

§ 4.02(c). Net Operating Loss ("NOL") Carryovers Under the AMT ("ATNOL") and ISOs

I.R.C. §§ 172(a), (c), and (d); 1211(b); 1212(b)

The AMT has its own separate and parallel net operating (and presumably, other) system of carryovers from one tax year to the other. Although § 57(a) states that the ATNOL is computed using AMTI and not regular tax principles, Rev. Rul. 87-44, 1987-1 C.B. 3, tied the two together in holding that a taxpayer's election under § 172(b)(3) to relinquish the carryback period is effective for purposes of both the regular tax net operating loss deduction and the alternative tax net operating loss deduction. Thus, the only way for a taxpayer to relinquish the carryback period in computing the AMT net operating loss deduction is by making the election under § 172(b)(3)(C) for regular tax purposes. On the other hand, Priv. Ltr. Rul. 93-17-002 held that in computing an NOL carryback from 1989 for AMT purposes, the ATNOL was computed under current law without deducting deferral preferences even though the carryback was to 1986 under prior law when such items did not reduce the NOL. It relied in part on the Supreme Court's decision in *Reo Motors, Inc. v. Commissioner*, 338 U.S. 442 (1950), which held that a taxpayer who sustained a loss in 1941 that did not produce an NOL could not carry a loss forward to 1942 even though the loss would have been permitted under 1942 law, in part on the ground that any other rule would not permit a fixed determination of a loss for any year.

The AMT treatment of the spread on exercise of ISOs discussed in the preceding section resulted in major pressure on the carryover system as discussed in the following case dealing with the loss produced when ISO stock acquired prior to the bursting of the tech bubble produced losses.

SPITZ v. COMMISSIONER

United States Tax Court
T.C. Memo. 2006-168

* * *

Petitioner began employment with Seagate Software, Inc. (Seagate), on March 6, 1995. After Veritas Software Corp. (Veritas) acquired Seagate on May 28, 1999, petitioner stayed on as a full-time employee of Veritas until April 23, 2001.

As part of his compensation from both companies, petitioner was granted options to acquire common stock, all of which qualified as incentive stock options (ISO). Petitioner's Seagate ISOs were converted to Veritas ISOs when Veritas took over Seagate, but the converted ISOs continued to be governed by the original Seagate stock option grants and retained the Seagate grant number. Petitioner was granted additional ISOs by Veritas which were governed by the Veritas 1993 Equity Incentive Stock Option Plan.

Petitioner was not a dealer or trader in securities. He exercised Veritas ISOs and acquired 34,948 shares in a series of transactions beginning November 30, 1999, and ending May 1, 2001. Petitioner paid $115,954 to exercise the ISOs and acquired the shares, which had a fair market value (FMV) of $4,476,973 at the various dates of exercise. Between February 28, 2000, and December 27, 2002, petitioner sold all of the Veritas shares acquired by exercising ISOs. In 2000, the market value for Veritas stock began to fall and continued to decline thereafter. The proceeds petitioner received from the sale of the Veritas shares totaled $1,267,468.

* * *

Petitioner timely filed his 2000 Federal income tax return, which was prepared by a certified public accountant. The return reported wages from Veritas of $137,261, capital gains of $425,161, miscellaneous income of $8,104, and, after itemized deductions of $88,844, taxable income of $481,682. The return reported regular tax of $165,719 and AMT of $898,914 for a total tax liability of $1,064,611, after deducting a foreign tax credit of $22.

On June 12, 2002, relying on the advice of Brian G. Isaacson, a tax attorney, petitioner filed a Form 1040X, Amended U.S. Individual Income Tax Return, amending his 2000 Federal income tax return (2000 amended return) with a Form 8275, Disclosure Statement. The Internal Revenue Service (IRS) accepted the 2000 amended return that Mr. Isaacson prepared.

The 2000 amended return reported wages from Veritas of $563,974 rather than the $137,261 initially reported. The increase of $426,713 in wages was attributable to sales of Veritas stock by petitioner which did not qualify for capital gain treatment and had to be included in ordinary income, a subject discussed in more detail later in this opinion. As a result, for regular tax purposes, petitioner reported $44,914 in capital gains rather than the $425,161 initially reported, miscellaneous income remained the same at $8,104, and itemized deductions were increased by $204,703 to total $293,547. The changes resulted in taxable income of $616,992. The 2000 amended return reported regular income tax of $103,058 and AMT of $869,828, for a total tax liability of $972,864, after deducting a foreign tax credit of $22. Petitioner's total tax liability was reduced from $1,064,611 to $972,864 resulting in a $91,747 refund claim.

Respondent issued the notice of deficiency in dispute on November 29, 2004. With respect to the income tax liability for 2000, the notice of deficiency increased capital gains by $87,735, reduced wages by $134,023, and denied $204,709 of itemized deductions, resulting in a determined deficiency of $183,743. . . .

* * *

Mr. Isaacson prepared petitioner's 2001 Federal income tax return with an attached Form 8275 setting out his legal position. The return reported wages from Veritas of $70,939, capital gain of $698,312, miscellaneous income of $6,555, and itemized deductions of $41,625, resulting in taxable income of $734,181. The return reported regular income tax of $148,209, no alternative minimum tax, and a credit for the prior year's minimum tax of $138,957, resulting in a $9,252 tax liability.

The notice of deficiency issued on November 29, 2004, with respect to 2001 reduced the credit for the prior year's minimum tax from $138,957 to $62,730, resulting in a determined deficiency of $76,227 el.

* * *

Section 421(a) provides that, if the requirements of section 422(a) are met, a taxpayer does not recognize income either upon the granting of an ISO to the taxpayer or when the stock is transferred 6 to the taxpayer upon exercise of an ISO. Recognition of income is deferred until the disposition of the stock. Sec. 421(a); sec. 14a.422A-1, Q&A-1, Temporary Income Tax Regs. . . . Gain on the sale of the stock is characterized as capital gain if the holding requirements under section 422(a)(1) are satisfied. Secs. 1221 and 1222; sec. 14a.422A-1, Q&A-1, Temporary Income Tax Regs., supra.

In order to qualify for capital gain treatment, the taxpayer must hold the stock he acquires by exercising an ISO for a period ending no earlier than 2 years after the grant date or 1 year after the transfer of the stock to him. Sec. 422(a)(1). Selling a share of stock before the holding period expires results in a disqualifying disposition. Sec. 421(b). If a disposition is disqualified, recognized gain on the sale of the stock is characterized as ordinary income up to the fair market value (FMV) of the stock at the date the option is exercised, and the balance, if any, is treated as capital gain. Sec. 421(b); sec. 14a.422A-1, Q&A-2(a), Temporary Income Tax Regs. . . . If the amount realized on a disqualified disposition is less than the FMV at the date of exercise, the taxpayer recognizes gain only to the extent of the sale price over the option price, not the FMV over the option price at the date of exercise. Sec. 422(c)(2).

Petitioner's 2000 amended returns reported Veritas stock sales resulting in qualifying and disqualifying dispositions. The disqualifying dispositions were the result of selling shares within 1 year of transfer. Petitioner's 2001 return and amended return reported that all Veritas shares sold during the tax year were qualifying dispositions.

2. The AMT and Its Impact on the Exercise of ISOs

For regular tax purposes, section 421 defers the recognition of income on the exercise of an ISO until the disposition of the stock. However, for AMT purposes, section 421 does not apply. Sec. 56(b)(3). Instead, the exercise of an ISO results in the recognition of income under section 83. See sec. 56(b)(3). . . . Consequently, if the stock's FMV exceeds the option price on the date of exercise, a taxpayer recognizes ordinary income for AMT purposes in the year an ISO is exercised. Secs. 55(b)(2), 56(b)(3), 83(a). . . .

If a taxpayer makes a disqualifying disposition in the same year the ISO is exercised and the amount realized is less than the FMV at the exercise date, the regular tax rules of section 422(c)(2) apply for AMT purposes. Thus, the amount the taxpayer includes as AMTI will not exceed the amount realized over the adjusted basis. Secs. 56(b)(3), 422(c)(2).

* * *

For regular tax purposes, the taxpayer's basis in stock acquired by exercising an ISO is the exercise price. Secs. 421(a), 1012. However, for AMT purposes, a taxpayer's basis in stock acquired by exercising an ISO is the FMV of the stock at the date of exercise. Secs. 56(b)(3), 83(a), 1012. Thus, when stock is sold in a tax year subsequent to the year in which the ISO was exercised, the amount of gain (or loss) recognized for AMT purposes will vary from the amount of gain (or loss) recognized for regular tax purposes.

This anomaly may create inequitable results when a taxpayer (such as petitioner) finds himself holding stock that has decreased in value in the year after a year in which he recognized large amounts of AMT. In this situation, the AMT imposed on the gain from exercise of the ISO results in payment of tax on income the taxpayer may never actually receive.

In an attempt to avoid these harsh results petitioner asserts: (1) The capital loss limitations under sections 1211(b) and 1212(b) do not apply to the computation of AMTI; (2) he is entitled to carry back capital losses as an ATNOL to reduce his AMTI in the years at issue; and (3) he is not liable for accuracy-related penalties under section 6662 for the tax years at issue.

* * *

Starting on November 30, 1999, and ending May 1, 2001, petitioner exercised Veritas stock options and recognized large amounts of ordinary income for AMT purposes. However, market values fell, and petitioner sold, over a period extending from February 28, 2000, through December 27, 2002, all of the Veritas stock he had acquired by exercising the ISOs. Petitioner sold most of the shares at prices below FMV at the date of exercise. As a result, petitioner recognized large AMT capital losses with minimal AMT capital gains. Petitioner contends that the capital loss limitations of sections 1211(b) and 1212(b) do not apply to AMT capital losses for purposes of calculating AMTI.

In general, all the Code provisions that apply in computing regular taxable income also apply when determining a taxpayer's AMTI, except as otherwise provided by statute, regulation, or other publication issued by the Commissioner. . . . . Section 55 is unambiguous. The computation of AMTI requires a taxpayer to first compute his regular taxable income and then adjust that amount to reflect the items described in sections 56, 57, and 58. . . .

There are no provisions within sections 55 through 58 and the accompanying regulations excluding capital loss limitations under sections 1211(b) and 1212(b) from the calculation of an individual's AMTI. To the contrary, as explained by the Joint Committee on Taxation:

> For most purposes, the tax base for the new alternative minimum tax is determined as though the alternative minimum tax were a separate and independent income tax system.
>
> In certain instances, the operation of the alternative minimum tax as a separate and independent tax system is set forth expressly in the Code.
>
> * * *
>
> In other instances, however, where no such express statement is made, Congress did not intend to imply that similar adjustments were not necessary. Thus, for example, for [alternative] minimum tax purposes it was intended that section 1211 (limiting capital losses) be computed using [alternative] minimum tax basis * * *. [Staff of Joint Comm. on Taxation,

General Explanation of the Tax Reform Act of 1986, at 438 . . .]

Therefore, the capital loss limitations of sections 1211(b) and 1212(b) apply in calculating a taxpayer's AMTI, and petitioner may not carry back the excess AMT capital losses recognized in 2001 and 2002 to reduce his AMTI in 1999, 2000, and 2001. *See Merlo v. Commissioner*, 126 T.C. 205, 212 (2006).

C. ATNOL

Petitioner asserts he is entitled to an ATNOL deduction for AMT capital losses recognized in 2001 and 2002 and he is entitled to carry back the losses to reduce his AMTI.

Generally, a taxpayer may carry back a net operating loss (NOL) back to the 2 taxable years preceding the loss, then forward to each of the 20 taxable years following the loss. . . . Section 172(c) defines an NOL as "the excess of the deductions allowed by this chapter over the gross income", as modified by section 172(d). . . . As a result, excess capital losses are not subject to section 172 and are excluded when computing an NOL under section 172(c).

For AMT purposes, the ATNOL deduction is applied in lieu of section 172 in determining AMTI. Sec. 56(a)(4). An ATNOL deduction is defined as "the net operating loss deduction allowable for the taxable year under section 172," subject to exceptions under section 56(d). Sec. 56(d). Thus, an ATNOL is computed under section 172 and then adjusted pursuant to section 56(d)(2). Sec. 56(d)(1)(B)(i). There is no exception under section 56(d) that modifies section 172(c) or (d) to allow excess capital losses to be used as deductions under section 172(c), or to allow excess capital losses to be carried forward or back under section 172(b). See Merlo v. Commissioner, supra at 212 213. Instead, remaining capital losses are governed by a separate carryover scheme prescribed in section 1212(b), as described above.

Therefore, the Court finds petitioner's excess AMT capital losses are excluded for purposes of calculating his ATNOL deduction. As a result, petitioner cannot carry back his AMT capital losses realized in 2001 and 2002 under sections 56 and 172(b).

* * *

To reflect the foregoing and the concessions of the parties,

Decision will be entered under *Rule 155*.

NOTES AND COMMENTS

The *Merlo* case referred to in the *Spitz* opinion is not the one included above, but the one referred to in the *Notes and Comments* after it, which reached the same result as in *Spitz*, although earlier and with a less informative discussion. In *Pierce v. United States*, 76 Fed. Cl. 638 (2007), rejected the taxpayer's attempt to treat the loss on sale of the ISO stock for less than its basis, reflecting the inclusion of the spread on exercise in AMTI, as a "negative AMT adjustment" for purposes of the ATNOL under § 56(b)(4). See *Guzak v. United States*, 75 Fed. Cl. 304 (2007)

($3,000 limitation on capital losses also applied for AMT purpose, relying on the legislative history of the 2006 adoption of § 56(e) referred to in the *Notes and Comments* in § 4.02(b) *The AMT and ISOs*. In *Palahnuk v. Commissioner*, 127 T.C. 118 (2006), the court rejected another creative argument seeking to avoid the problem of AMT income on exercise of ISOs that was eventually offset by an AMT capital loss on sale of dubious tax benefit. In this case, the taxpayers tried to exclude the regular tax capital gain they realized on sale of the ISO stock, which, of course, resulted in a large AMTI capital loss, in determining their AMTI and, apparently avoiding the $3,000 limit on capital losses and increasing their § 53 minimum tax credit, but the court did not agree. The regular tax treatment of capital losses is discussed in § 2.01(d) *Capital Loss Limitations*.

Although the acceleration represented by current inclusion of the spread on ISOs in AMTI on exercise was clearly intentional, the problem of the limited capital loss on the sale after the burst of the bubble that cannot be carried back was probably not intended in the adoption of the AMT. As the greater amount of litigation indicates, the problem involves much greater impact — AMT in the hundreds of thousands or even millions of dollars. Although as discussed in the *Notes and Comments* in § 4.02(b) *The AMT and ISOs*, the problem did attract Congress's attention, but the result was a limited and temporary patch, not an attempt to reform the AMT.

At one time some commentators saw the adoption of the AMT as a possible way station toward a general broadening of the tax base. Although there is no sign as yet of that happening, the effects discussed in these two sections indicate that it has had that result, although on a spotty and inconsistent basis. A cynic might suggest that Congress may like it that way, because the AMT remains less visible and, therefore, less political than the regular income tax, so that the government can reap the benefit of increased taxes without as much political heat. Some have described taxation as the art of "pluck[ing] feathers from the [colonial] goose with a minimum of squawking," a statement attributed to British Prime Minister Charles Townshend in connection with the adoption of the Townshend Acts, which did not have the desired effects, because they helped foment the American Revolution.

Chapter 7

ADVANCED CHARACTERIZATION PROBLEMS

Chapter 2, *Capital Gains and Losses*, deals with the most basic tax characterization issue: the classification of property as ordinary income property, or as a capital asset, or its cousin, section 1231 property. There are of course, other important classifications — between property that is permanently capitalized, and that which is depreciable, depletable, or amortizable; or among property that is held for use in a trade or business, for investment, or for personal use. In contrast to those determinations, this chapter focuses on transactions involving partial interests in property, including long-term leasing transactions and special issues relating to intangible property, particularly property created by personal effort or with other characteristics closely tied to personal services. A cliché in first-year property courses is that ownership of property involves a bundle of rights that can be separated. When some of those rights are held by one person, and some by one or more others, it may not be easy to determine which is the tax owner of property, entitled to tax benefits that depend on ownership, particularly because the Code assumes that, for example, only the owner is entitled to claim depreciation. The tax determination is a federal one not governed by state law legal title or other labels. State law does determine the legal rights of the parties, but it is federal tax law that characterizes those rights for federal tax purposes.

Perhaps the most basic partial interest, the right to current possession by one not the "owner" of the property, is covered in § 1 *Reality of Sale (Sale v. Lease)*, which considers who is the tax (as distinguished from the legal) owner of the property. Tax ownership is frequently described as having the benefits and burdens of the property, but, as always, the question is which benefits and which burdens are determinative. The tax consequences of transfers of partial interests, leaseholds, rights to income from property, and other arrangements that separate the principal from the income are covered in § 2 *Transfers of Partial Interests.* There are even more vexing problems of transfers of rights to intangible assets, including patents and copyrights as well as additional assets, such as goodwill and going concern value, and distinguishing them from contract rights to income. These issues as well as a number of special provisions for artists, inventors, and franchises, are covered in § 3 *Intangibles — Contract Rights, Self-Created Property, Goodwill, and Going Concern Value.* Finally, § 4 *Related Taxpayers — § 482*, looks at the transactions among related parties that may have a similar effect of directly or indirectly transferring income from property.

§ 1. REALITY OF SALE (SALE v. LEASE)

As was discussed in § 3.02 *Contingencies* in Chapter 3, *Liabilities: Discharge of Indebtedness; Mortgaged Property*, nonrecourse and other arrangements — in which nonrecourse purchase price obligations are significantly in excess of the value of the property — raise issues of whether the liabilities should be recognized as such for tax purposes. Implicit in *Estate of Franklin v. Commissioner*, 544 F.2d 1045 (9th Cir. 1976) (nonrecourse liability for 100% of purchase price in tax-shelter sale and leaseback not recognized to support interest and depreciation deductions), and materials discussed there, is that the nominal legal owner is not the tax owner of the underlying property. On the other hand, *Crane v. Commissioner*, 331 U.S. 1 (1947); *Mayerson v. Commissioner*, 47 T.C. 340 (1966) (nonrecourse liability for 100% of purchase price not contingent), and similar authorities discussed in the same section, found that a nonrecourse obligation did not automatically prevent tax ownership. Both *Franklin* and *Mayerson* involve a transaction that can be described as a "bootstrap sale," in which the seller provides 100 percent "nonrecourse financing" allowing the purchaser to "lift himself by his own bootstraps." An earlier form of bootstrap sale involving a sale to a charity to take advantage of the charity's tax-exempt status is examined in § 1.01 *Bootstrap Sales.* Special principles for natural resource properties are considered in § 1.02 *Natural Resource Interests.* When a purchaser does not need, or want, immediate possession of the purchased property, or when the seller is not prepared to part with the use of the property for a period of time but the purchaser desires to secure its right to eventual possession of the property without risking the seller's change of heart, or a change in market conditions, it can be difficult to determine whether the transaction is more appropriately characterized as a sale of only a remainder interest in the property or as a sale and leaseback of the property. Distinguishing between these two types of transactions is the topic of § 1.03 *Retained Interest v. Amount Realized.*

The most obvious means of separating the right to possession from the other rights of ownership is through a lease when the property is tangible, or a license when the property is intangible. Although leases or licenses are usually of limited duration, long-term leases, particularly of personal property, but even of real property, can be of such long duration that they effectively consume substantially all of the economic benefits of the property. In tax law, as in commercial law, the issue then becomes distinguishing a long-term lease from a financing arrangement. If the lease is respected as a lease, the lessor, as owner of the property, is entitled to the tax benefits of ownership. On the other hand, the economic relationship may be such that the lessee is more appropriately viewed as the owner of the property and, thus, entitled to the tax benefits of ownership. In this situation, the lessor is viewed as simply providing financing to the lessee. The parties to the lease may be using the lease as a means to move the tax benefits of ownership, such as depreciation and interest deductions, from the lessee, who may be not be able to use such tax benefits because it is either tax exempt or otherwise subject to a low effective tax rate, to the lessee who is subject to a high effective tax rate. The standards for making the determination when the transaction is between a manufacturer or retailer of the property and the user of (usually) personal property, are considered in § 1.04 *Lease v. Sale.* When dealing with "big ticket" items, the financing is often supplied by a third party lender-lessor, but with the lender-lessor relying more on the creditworthiness of the lessee-user, than on the value of the property. The reliance is usually based on what is called a "hell-or-high-water" lease in which the lessee-user is obligated to continue making the lease payments to the lessor-lender, without regard to normal tenant defenses, and even if the property is completely destroyed. The standards for tax characterization of these three-party transactions, whether of personal property or real property, are the subject of § 1.05 *Leveraged Leasing.*

§ 1.01. Bootstrap Sales

The issue in the following case, which, like *Mayerson* and *Franklin*, discussed in § 3.02 *Contingencies*, of *Chapter 3, Liabilities: Discharge of Indebtedness; Mortgaged Property*, involved a sale with 100 percent nonrecourse financing, with an additional aspect of a price based on the earnings of the property, deals with the seller's side of the transaction but does involve the right to claim depreciation and interest deductions. Instead, the issue is whether the profit on the transaction was taxable as ordinary income or as capital gain. As described in the case, the economics of the transaction depended on the charitable purchaser's ability to receive most of the income from the property tax-free, increasing its ability to pay a high purchase price. Notwithstanding the acknowledged tax motivation for the transaction, the Court found the transaction to be a sale, rejecting the Service's argument that a "sale" requires risk shifting. As you read the Supreme Court's decision, see if you can identify what a sale requires when the purchaser has no risk.

COMMISSIONER v. BROWN

Supreme Court of the United States
380 U.S. 563 (1965)

MR. JUSTICE WHITE delivered the opinion of the Court.

In 1950, when Congress addressed itself to the problem of the direct or indirect acquisition and operation of going businesses by charities or other tax-exempt entities, it was recognized that in many of the typical sale and lease-back transactions, the exempt organization was trading on and perhaps selling part of its exemption. . . . For this and other reasons the Internal Revenue Code was accordingly amended in several respects, of principal importance for our purposes by taxing as "unrelated business income" the profits earned by a charity in the operation of a business, as well as the income from long-term leases of the business. The short-term lease, however, of five years or less, was not affected and this fact has moulded many of the transactions in this field since that time, including the one involved in this case.

* * *

This case is one of the many in the course of which the Commissioner has questioned the sale of a business concern to an exempt organization. The basic facts are undisputed. Clay Brown, members of his family and three other persons owned substantially all of the stock in Clay Brown & Company, with sawmills and lumber interests near Fortuna, California. Clay Brown, the president of the company and spokesman for the group, was approached by a representative of California

Institute for Cancer Research in 1952, and after considerable negotiation the stockholders agreed to sell their stock to the Institute for $1,300,000, payable $5,000 down from the assets of the company and the balance within 10 years from the earnings of the company's assets. It was provided that simultaneously with the transfer of the stock, the Institute would liquidate the company and lease its assets for five years to a new corporation, Fortuna Sawmills, Inc., formed and wholly owned by the attorneys for the sellers.[4] Fortuna would pay to the Institute 80% of its operating profit without allowance for depreciation or taxes, and 90% of such payments would be paid over by the Institute to the selling stockholders to apply on the $1,300,000 note. This note was noninterest bearing, the Institute had no obligation to pay it except from the rental income and it was secured by mortgages and assignments of the assets transferred or leased to Fortuna. If the payments on the note failed to total $250,000 over any two consecutive years, the sellers could declare the entire balance of the note due and payable. The sellers were neither stockholders nor directors of Fortuna but it was provided that Clay Brown was to have a management contract with Fortuna at an annual salary and the right to name any successor manager if he himself resigned.

The transaction was closed on February 4, 1953. Fortuna immediately took over operations of the business under its lease, on the same premises and with practically the same personnel which had been employed by Clay Brown & Company. Effective October 31, 1954, Clay Brown resigned as general manager of Fortuna and waived his right to name his successor. In 1957, because of a rapidly declining lumber market, Fortuna suffered severe reverses and its operations were terminated. Respondent sellers did not repossess the properties under their mortgages but agreed they should be sold by the Institute with the latter retaining 10% of the proceeds. Accordingly, the property was sold by the Institute for $300,000. The payments on the note from rentals and from the sale of the properties totaled $936,131.85. Respondents returned the payments received from rentals as the gain from the sale of capital assets. The Commissioner, however, asserted the payments were taxable as ordinary income and were not capital gain . . .

In the Tax Court, the Commissioner asserted that the transaction was a sham and that in any event respondents retained such an economic interest in and control over the property sold that the transaction could not be treated as a sale resulting in a long-term capital gain. . . .

[T]he Commissioner now admits that there was real substance in what occurred between the Institute and the Brown family. The transaction was a sale under local law. The Institute acquired title to the stock of Clay Brown & Company and, by liquidation, to all of the assets of that company, in return for its promise to pay over money from the operating profits of the company. If the stipulated price was paid, the Brown family would forever lose all rights to the income and properties of the company. Prior to the transfer, these respondents had access to all of the income of the company; after the transfer, 28% of the income remained with Fortuna and the Institute. . . . Any rights to control the management were limited to the manage-

---

[4] The net current assets subject to liabilities were sold by the Institute to Fortuna for a promissory note which was assigned to sellers. The lease covered the remaining assets of Clay Brown & Company. Fortuna was capitalized at $25,000, its capital being paid in by its stockholders from their own funds.

ment contract between Clay Brown and Fortuna, which was relinquished in 1954.

Whatever substance the transaction might have had, however, the Commissioner claims that it did not have the substance of a sale within the meaning of § 1222(3). His argument is that since the Institute invested nothing, assumed no independent liability for the purchase price and promised only to pay over a percentage of the earnings of the company, the entire risk of the transaction remained on the sellers. Apparently, to qualify as a sale, a transfer of property for money or the promise of money must be to a financially responsible buyer who undertakes to pay the purchase price other than from the earnings or the assets themselves or there must be a substantial down payment which shifts at least part of the risk to the buyer and furnishes some cushion against loss to the seller.

To say that there is no sale because there is no risk-shifting and that there is no risk-shifting because the price to be paid is payable only from the income produced by the business sold, is very little different from saying that because business earnings are usually taxable as ordinary income, they are subject to the same tax when paid over as the purchase price of property. This argument has rationality but it places an unwarranted construction on the term "sale," is contrary to the policy of the capital gains provisions of the Internal Revenue Code, and has no support in the cases. We reject it.

"Capital gain" and "capital asset" are creatures of the tax law and the Court has been inclined to give these terms a narrow, rather than a broad, construction. . . . A "sale," however, is a common event in the non-tax world; and since it is used in the Code without limiting definition and without legislative history indicating a contrary result, its common and ordinary meaning should at least be persuasive of its meaning as used in the Internal Revenue Code. "Generally speaking, the language in the Revenue Act, just as in any statute, is to be given its ordinary meaning, and the words 'sale' and 'exchange' are not to be read any differently." . . .

"A sale, in the ordinary sense of the word, is a transfer of property for a fixed price in money or its equivalent," . . . ; it is a contract "to pass rights of property for money, — which the buyer pays or promises to pay to the seller . . ." The transaction which occurred in this case was obviously a transfer of property for a fixed price payable in money.

* * *

As of January 31, 1953, the adjusted net worth of Clay Brown & Company as revealed by its books was $619,457.63. . . . The appraised value as of that date, however, relied upon by the Institute and the sellers, was $1,064,877, without figuring interest on deferred balances. Under a deferred payment plan with a 6% interest figure, the sale value was placed at $1,301,989. The Tax Court found the sale price agreed upon was arrived at in an arm's-length transaction, was the result of real negotiating and was "within a reasonable range in light of the earnings history of the corporation and the adjusted net worth of the corporate assets." . . .

Obviously, on these facts, there had been an appreciation in value accruing over a period of years, . . . and an "increase in the value of the income-producing property." . . . This increase taxpayers were entitled to realize at capital gains rates on a cash sale of their stock; and likewise if they sold on a deferred payment plan taking an installment note and a mortgage as security. Further . . . the gain itself could be reported on the installment basis.

In the actual transaction, the stock was transferred for a price payable on the installment basis but payable from the earnings of the company. Eventually $936,131.85 was realized by respondents. This transaction, we think, is a sale, and so treating it is wholly consistent with the purposes of the Code to allow capital gains treatment for realization upon the enhanced value of a capital asset.

The Commissioner, however, embellishes his risk-shifting argument. Purporting to probe the economic realities of the transaction, he reasons that if the seller continues to bear all the risk and the buyer none, the seller must be collecting a price for his risk-bearing in the form of an interest in future earnings over and above what would be a fair market value of the property. Since the seller bears the risk, the so-called purchase price must be excessive and must be simply a device to collect future earnings at capital gains rates.

We would hesitate to discount unduly the power of pure reason and the argument is not without force. But it does present difficulties. In the first place, it denies what the tax court expressly found — that the price paid was within reasonable limits based on the earnings and net worth of the company. . . . We do not have, therefore, a case where the price has been found excessive.

Secondly, if an excessive price is such an inevitable result of the lack of risk-shifting, it would seem that it would not be an impossible task for the Commissioner to demonstrate the fact. However, in this case he offered no evidence whatsoever to this effect. . . .

Thirdly, the Commissioner ignores as well the fact that if the rents payable by Fortuna were deductible by it and not taxable to the Institute, the Institute could pay off the purchase price at a considerably faster rate than the ordinary corporate buyer subject to income taxes, a matter of considerable importance to a seller who wants the balance of his purchase price paid as rapidly as he can get it. . . .

Furthermore, risk-shifting of the kind insisted on by the Commissioner has not heretofore been considered an essential ingredient of a sale for tax purposes. In *LeTulle v. Scofield*, 308 U.S. 415 [(1940)], one corporation transferred properties to another for cash and bonds secured by the properties transferred. The Court held that there was "a sale or exchange upon which gain or loss must be reckoned in accordance with the provisions of the revenue act dealing with the recognition of gain or loss upon a sale or exchange,," . . . since the seller retained only a creditor's interest rather than a proprietary one. "[That] the bonds were secured solely by the assets transferred and that, upon default, the bondholder would retake only the property sold, [did not change] his status from that of a creditor to one having a proprietary stake." . . . To require a sale for tax purposes to be to a financially responsible buyer who undertakes to pay the purchase price from sources other than the earnings of the assets sold or to make a substantial down payment seems to us at odds with commercial practice and common understanding of what constitutes a sale. . . .

The Commissioner relies heavily upon the cases involving a transfer of mineral interests, the transferor receiving a bonus and retaining a royalty or other interest in the mineral production. . . . *Thomas v. Perkins* [301 U.S. 655 (1937)] is deemed particularly pertinent. There a leasehold interest was transferred for a sum certain payable in oil as produced, and it was held that the amounts paid to the transferor were not includable in the income of the transferee but were income of the transferor. We do not, however, deem either *Thomas v. Perkins* or the other cases controlling.

First, "Congress . . . character of the business of extracting natural resources, ". . . which is viewed as an income-producing operation and not as a conversion of capital investment, . . . but one which has its own built-in method of allowing through depletion a tax-free return of the capital consumed in the production of gross income through severance, *Anderson v. Helvering*, 310 U.S. 404 at 407 [(1940)], but one which has its own built-in method of allowing through depletion "a tax-free return of the capital consumed in the production of gross income through severance," . . . which is independent of cost and depends solely on production, . . . The Commissioner, however, would assess to respondents as ordinary income the entire amount of all rental payments made by the Institute, regardless of the accumulated values in the corporation which the payments reflected and without regard for the present policy of the tax law to allow the taxpayer to realize on appreciated values at the capital gains rates.

Second, . . . [t]he Court in *Anderson v. Helvering* . . . pointed out that it was still possible for the owner of a working interest to divest himself finally and completely of his mineral interest by effecting a sale. In that case the owner of royalty interest, fee interest and deferred oil payments contracted to convey them for $160,000 payable $50,000 down and the balance from one-half the proceeds which might be derived from the oil and gas produced and from the sale of the fee title to any of the lands conveyed. . . . Since the transferor in *Anderson* had provided for payment of the purchase price from the sale of fee interest as well as from the production of oil and gas, ". . . there was held to be an outright sale of the properties, all of the oil income therefrom being taxable to the transferee notwithstanding the fact of payment of part of it to the seller. . . .[8]

There is another reason for us not to disturb the ruling of the Tax Court and the Court of Appeals. In 1963, the Treasury Department . . . proposed a change in the law which would have taxed as ordinary income the payments on the sale of a capital

---

[8] Respondents place considerable reliance on the rule applicable where patents are sold or assigned, the seller or assignor reserving an income interest. In Rev. Rul. 58-353, 1958-2 Cum. Bull. 408, the Service announced its acquiescence in various Tax Court cases holding that the consideration received by the owner of a patent for the assignment of a patent or the granting of an exclusive license to such patent may be treated as the proceeds of a sale of property for income tax purposes, even though the consideration received by the transferor is measured by production, use, or sale of the patented article. The Government now says that the Revenue Ruling amounts only to a decision to cease litigating the question, at least temporarily, and that the cases on which the rule is based are wrong in principle and inconsistent with the cases dealing with the taxation of mineral interests. We note, however, that in Rev. Rul. 60-226, 1960-1 C.B. 26, the Service extended the same treatment to the copyright field. . . .

These developments in the patent field obviously do not help the position of the Commissioner. Nor does I.R.C. 1954, § 1235, which expressly permits specified patent sales to be treated as sales of capital assets entitled to capital gains treatment. We need not, however, decide here whether the extraction and patent cases are irreconcilable or whether, instead, each situation has its own peculiar characteristics justifying discrete treatment under the sale and exchange language of § 1222. . . .

asset which were deferred over more than five years and were contingent on future income. Payments, though contingent on income, required to be made within five years would not have lost capital gains status nor would payments not contingent on income even though accompanied by payments which were. . . .

Congress did not adopt the suggested change[9] but it is significant for our purposes that the proposed amendment did not deny the fact or occurrence of a sale but would have taxed as ordinary income those income-contingent payments deferred for more than five years. . . .

* * *

MR. JUSTICE HARLAN, concurring.

Were it not for the tax laws, the respondents' transaction with the Institute would make no sense, except as one arising from a charitable impulse. However the tax laws exist as an economic reality in the businessman's world, much like the existence of a competitor. Businessmen plan their affairs around both, and a tax dollar is just as real as one derived from any other source. The Code gives the Institute a tax exemption which makes it capable of taking a greater after-tax return from a business than could a nontax-exempt individual or corporation. Respondents traded a residual interest in their business for a faster payout apparently made possible by the Institute's exemption. The respondents gave something up; they received something substantially different in return. If words are to have meaning, there was a "sale or exchange."

* * *

One may observe preliminarily that the Government's remedy for the so-called "bootstrap" sale — defining sale or exchange so as to require the shifting of some business risks — would accomplish little by way of closing off such sales in the future. It would be neither difficult nor burdensome for future users of the bootstrap technique to arrange for some shift of risks. . . .

The force underlying the Government's position is that the respondents did clearly retain some risk-bearing interest in the business. Instead of leaping from this premise to the conclusion that there was no sale or exchange, the Government might more profitably have broken the transaction into components and attempted to distinguish between the interest which respondents retained and the interest which they exchanged. The worth of a business depends upon its ability to produce income over time. What respondents gave up was not the entire business, but only their interest in the business' ability to produce income in excess of that which was necessary to pay them off under the terms of the transaction. The value of such a residual interest is a function of the risk element of the business and the amount of

[9] It did, however,, accept and enact another suggestion made by the Treasury Department. Section 483, which was added to the Code, provided for treating a part of the purchase price as interest in installment sales transactions where no interest was specified. The provision was to apply as well when the payments provided for were indefinite as to their size, as for example "where the payments are in part at least dependent upon future income derived from the property." . . . This section would apparently now apply to a transaction such as occurred in this case.

income it is capable of producing per year, and will necessarily be substantially less than the value of the total business. Had the Government argued that it was that interest which respondents exchanged, and only to that extent should they have received capital gains treatment, we would perhaps have had a different case.

I mean neither to accept nor reject this approach, or any other which falls short of the all-or-nothing theory specifically argued by the petitioner, specifically opposed by the respondents, and accepted by the Court as the premise for its decision. . . .

Mr. Justice Goldberg, with whom The Chief Justice and Mr. Justice Black join, dissenting.

* * *

At first glance it might appear odd that the sellers would enter into this transaction, for prior to the sale they had a right to 100% of the corporation's income, but after the sale they had a right to only 72% of that income and would lose the business after 10 years to boot. This transaction, however, afforded the sellers several advantages. The principal advantage sought by the sellers was capital gain, rather than ordinary income, treatment for that share of the business profits which they received. Further, because of the Tax Code's charitable exemption and the lease arrangement with Fortuna, the Institute believed that neither it nor Fortuna would have to pay income tax on the earnings of the business. Thus the sellers would receive free of corporate taxation, and subject only to personal taxation at capital gains rates, 72% of the business earnings until they were paid $1,300,000. Without the sale they would receive only 48% of the business earnings, the rest going to the Government in corporate taxes, and this 48% would be subject to personal taxation at ordinary rates. In effect the Institute sold the respondents the use of its tax exemption, enabling the respondents to collect $1,300,000 from the business more quickly than they otherwise could and to pay taxes on this amount at capital gains rates. In return, the Institute received a nominal amount of the profits while the $1,300,000 was being paid, and it was to receive the whole business after this debt had been paid off. In any realistic sense the Government's grant of a tax exemption was used by the Institute as part of an arrangement that allowed it to buy a business that in fact cost it nothing. I cannot believe that Congress intended such a result.

* * *

In dealing with what constitutes a sale for capital gains purposes, this Court has been careful to look through formal legal arrangements to the underlying economic realities. Income produced in the mineral extraction business, which "resemble[s] a manufacturing business carried on by the use of the soil," . . . is taxed to the person who retains an economic interest in the oil. Thus, while an outright sale of mineral interests qualifies for capital gains treatment, a purported sale of mineral interests in exchange for a royalty from the minerals produced is treated only as a transfer with a retained economic interest, and the royalty payments are fully taxable as ordinary income. . . .

* * *

I believe that the sellers here retained an economic interest in the business fully as great as that retained by the seller of oil interests in *Thomas v. Perkins*. The sellers were to be paid only out of the proceeds of the business. If the business made money they would be paid; if it did not, they would not be paid. In the latter event, of course, they could recover the business, but a secured interest in a business which was losing money would be of dubious value. There was no other security. The Institute was not bound to pay any sum whatsoever. The Institute, in fact, promised only to channel to the sellers a portion of the income it received from Fortuna.

Moreover, in numerous cases this Court has refused to transfer the incidents of taxation along with a transfer of legal title when the transferor retains considerable control over the income-producing asset transferred. . . . Control of the business did not, in fact, shift in the transaction here considered. Clay Brown, by the terms of the purchase agreement and the lease, was to manage Fortuna. Clay Brown was given power to hire and arrange for the terms of employment of all other employees of the corporation. . . .

I would conclude that on these facts there was not a sufficient shift of economic risk or control of the business to warrant treating this transaction as a "sale" for tax purposes. Brown retained full control over the operations of the business; the risk of loss and the opportunity to profit from gain during the normal operation of the business shifted but slightly. If the operation lost money, Brown stood to lose; if it gained money Brown stood to gain, for he would be paid off faster. . . . I do not believe that Congress intended this recurrent receipt of ordinary business income to be taxed at capital gains rates merely because the business was to be transferred to a tax-exempt entity at some future date. . . .

* * *

Although the Court implies that it will hold to be "sales" only those transactions in which the price is reasonable, I do not believe that the logic of the Court's opinion will justify so restricting its holding. If this transaction is a sale under the Internal Revenue Code, entitling its proceeds to capital gains treatment because it was arrived at after hard negotiating, title in a conveyancing sense passed, and the beneficial ownership was expected to pass at a later date, then the question recurs, which the Court does not answer, why a similar transaction would cease to be a sale if hard negotiating produced a purchase price much greater than actual value. . . . Such transactions would have the same degree of risk-shifting, there would be no less a transfer of ownership, and consideration supplied by the buyer need be no less than here.

* * *

NOTES AND COMMENTS

Although the Court rejected the Service's risk-shifting requirement, it is less clear what requirement the Court believed must be satisfied for a transaction to be a sale. Perhaps the transaction constituted a sale because the charity had the possibility in the future benefit of becoming the sole owner of the property, although, as things turned out, it only received eight percent of the income from the business and 10 percent of the proceeds of the sale. Had things turned out differently and the full $1.3 million of payments been made, Brown would have had no further interest in the business. Accordingly, a key factor seems to be the one that was also key in *Mayerson* (nonrecourse liability for 100% of purchase price not contingent), a finding that the price was the fair market value of the property, so that, unlike *Franklin* (nonrecourse liability for 100% of purchase price in tax-shelter sale and leaseback not recognized for tax purposes), there was a significant likelihood that the payments of the purchase would be made, despite the absence of personal liability or risk.

The Court accepted a Tax Court finding that the "price paid was within reasonable limits based on the earnings and net worth of the company." *Brown*, 380 U.S. at 573. It did not, however, directly address the Service's contention that the price had to include an element to compensate the sellers for the risk that was not shifted with the potential benefit of ownership, although, at one point, it seemed to treat the risk as minor, because the charity's exemption simply allowed a faster payoff out of earnings. In *Berenson v. Commissioner*, 507 F.2d 262 (2d Cir. 1974), which involved a transaction similar to that in *Brown*, the Tax Court found the agreed price to be more than twice the amount that would be paid by a nonexempt purchaser. On that basis, the Court of Appeals determined that only the amount that would be paid by a nonexempt purchaser was entitled to capital gain treatment, and that the balance was taxable as ordinary income, but it did not indicate what the ordinary income represented, that is, why it was paid, for example, as interest, as compensation, and if so for something else.

Another aspect of the sale in *Brown* that has been subsequently changed is having the price paid by a non-interest-bearing note to avoid interest income and maximize capital gain. Current law provides that, in absence of a stated interest at least, at a minimum rate known as the applicable federal rate ("AFR") in a deferred payment sale of property, the interest will be imputed. § 1274. In addition, Congress eliminated the gimmick in *Brown*, by making the earnings of a charity on the "lease" of business assets taxable. *See* §§ 512(b)(4) and 514.

PROBLEM FOR DISCUSSION

Problem 7-1. Share proposes to sell the stock of Ceeco, a highly profitable corporation, to Lossco — a public corporation with enormous net operating loss carryovers from a failed biotech project that has left it with very little cash — for a price, with adequate stated interest, that is 150 percent more than any profitable public corporation would pay. Lossco can avoid paying tax on Ceeco's future earnings by filing a consolidated return. Lossco has little hope of making use of its net operating loss carryover except by acquiring a profitable business, and has no cash to buy such a business, so that, as a practical matter, it must make a bootstrap purchase, paying the price in specified installments of principal and interest over the five years after the purchase in amounts equal to 80 percent of Ceeco's profits (which it intends to distribute to Lossco as dividends that are tax-free under the consolidated return regulations). The agreement limited required payments to Ceeco's earnings, with a carryover to future years of any specified payments that are not earned. Any purchase price payments not earned are carried to the sixth and seventh years, with any amount not paid at the end of the seventh year cancelled. Is Share entitled to capital gains for the entire purchase price? For the amount equal to the portion of the price that would be paid by a profitable corporation? If the latter, what is the nature of the remaining payments? Could Share hope to make the same deal on a sale of shares of Wal-Mart, that is, a sale to Lossco for 150 percent of the NYSE quoted price? Why or why not? What is the effect of the purchase price to Lossco? How, if at all, does Lossco treat the "extra" purchase price differently from the basic price? *See Brown* (bootstrap sale valid); *Berenson* (excess of price on sale to charity over fair market value is ordinary income); *Mayerson* (nonrecourse liability for 100% of purchase price not contingent); *Franklin* (nonrecourse liability for 100% of purchase price in tax-shelter sale and leaseback not recognized for tax purposes). To the extent that you conclude that Share does not have capital gain on the sale of the Ceeco shares, how should the transaction be changed to provide the desired capital gain?

§ 1.02. Natural Resource Interests

Treas. Reg. § 1.611-1(b)(1)

In *Brown*, the Service relied on cases involving the definition of sales in the natural resources industry, but the Court treated them as inapplicable outside the natural resources context. The rules involving natural resources developed when percentage depletion — which bases the allowance for recovery of capital on a percentage of gross income from the property, significantly, without limitation to cost — made the realization of ordinary income more advantageous than the realization of capital gain. Although significant limitations have been placed on the determination of percentage depletion over the years, it is still important. The following case and ruling explain the rules.

WOOD v. UNITED STATES

United States Court of Appeals, Fifth Circuit
377 F.2d 300 (5th Cir. 1967)

* * *

Mr. and Mrs. Wood own 14,088 acres of land in Crosby County, Texas. Since the date of purchase in 1950, Mr. Wood has used the land for ranching. . . .

Negotiations between Wood and Prentice resulted in a contractual agreement, entitled Sand, Gravel and Rock Lease, whereby Wood did "grant, lease, and let" to Prentice the exclusive right to mine sand, gravel and rock on his ranch for an indefinite period.[3] . . . In 1958, 1959, and 1960 Wood received as consideration

[3] The contract between taxpayer and Prentice provided:

* * *

(4) First Party agrees to protect the Second Party in the peaceful possession of the premises here let, for the purpose of mining, processing and removing sand, gravel and rock only for so long as sand, gravel and rock is produced from said land and the First Party receives a minimum of $15,000.00 per year from royalty from sales of sand, gravel and rock and/or supplemental payment by Second Party to produce said annual minimum if royalty payments above are insufficient to meet said annual minimum royalty guarantee. . . .

under the agreement the respective sums of $85,078.32, $140,426.72, and $114,006.72 which, less annual allowances for depletion of five per cent, were reported in his income tax returns as gravel royalties and taxed as such by the Commissioner.[4]

In March, 1962, Wood filed amended returns . . . based on the theory that the royalty receipts under the lease agreement were actually income from the sale of a capital asset. . . .

The central question upon which appellant's tax liability must turn is whether he has, by his contractual relation, retained an interest in the minerals which must be classified as an "economic interest." *Palmer v. Bender*, 1933, 287 U.S. 551 . . . The Supreme Court has stated that an economic interest exists where a taxpayer has: "(1) 'acquired, by investment, any interest in * * * [the minerals] in place,' and (2) secured by legal relationship 'income derived from the extraction of * * * [the mineral], to which he must look for a return of his capital.' " *Commissioner . . . v. Southwest Explor. Co.*, 1956, 350 U.S. 308. . . .[6]

It should be noted that the controlling concept of "economic interest" was enunciated and refined by the Supreme Court in cases involving oil and gas leases. A study of hard mineral cases indicates that its application by other courts has been far from consistent outside of the field of oil and gas, although there would appear to be no apparent justification for a difference in approach depending upon the nature of the mineral involved. . . .

Some hard mineral cases reject the applicability of the test as developed in the oil and gas area. . . . More prevalent, however, are cases in which a decision has been reached by acknowledging the relevancy of the economic interest test . . .

I. The "economic interest" test as developed by the Supreme Court clearly supports the classification of the funds involved here as ordinary income. In *Burnet v. Harmel*, 1932, 287 U.S. 103 . . . the Supreme Court dealt with the precise issue now before this Court, although the contractual agreement there involved dealt with the extraction of oil and gas. The assertion of the taxpayer was the same — that the lease agreement was actually a sale of the minerals in place and that he was therefore entitled to capital gains treatment. . . . The Court recognized that the purpose behind capital gains treatment is to avoid the hardship of taxing as income in one year the entire gain due to appreciation of value of a capital asset over a considerable period of time. It was noted, however, that "taxation of the receipts of the lessor as income does not ordinarily produce the kind of hardship aimed at by

* * *

[4] Likewise, these amounts were treated and reported by the lessee as royalty expenses in its corporate income tax returns . . .

[6] This definition of "economic interest" has been faithfully adopted by the Treasury Department. Treas. Reg. § 1.611-1(b)(1) (1960). The "economic interest" test, of course, has wide application throughout the tax law. Use of that term in this opinion, however, specifically refers to its development and application as the standard by which the issue before this court is to be resolved — *i.e.*, when will proceeds arising out of agreements calling for the exploitation of mineral deposits be considered ordinary income and when will they be taxed as proceeds from the sale of a capital asset.

the capital gains provision of the taxing act." The Court continued by pointing out that the capital gains provision "speaks of a 'sale,' and these leases would not generally be described as a 'sale' of the mineral content of the soil, using the term either in its technical sense or as it is commonly understood."

It can thus be stated that *Harmel* stands for the proposition that an agreement in the nature of a mineral "lease" is not entitled to tax treatment as a sale of capital assets. Yet, *Harmel* did not set forth any criteria to facilitate a determination of whether a given agreement contains those characteristics which render that decision controlling. The needed standard was supplied by the economic interest test of *Palmer v. Bender* . . . The issue in *Palmer*, dissimilar to that in *Harmel*, was whether a lessee under an oil and gas lease who subsequently conveyed certain of his lease interests to a third party was entitled to depletion on that consideration paid him by the third party. The Court held that he was entitled to depletion since he had retained by his stipulation for royalties with the third party "an economic interest in the oil, [and gas] in place." The provisions of the agreement, the Court held, retained in the original lessee "an economic interest in the oil, in place, identical with that of a lessor." This interest was "depleted by production" and this reliance upon production for gain under the agreement was clearly the critical factor in the Court's reasoning.

Subsequent Supreme Court cases have shown that the test for determination of whether proceeds are taxable as capital gains or ordinary income is the same as that for determining whether proceeds are subject to depletion. . . .

* * *

The agreement here involved is on its face a typical mineral lease.[14] Yet, the taxpayer bases his claim upon the presence of an allegedly uncommon provision which stipulates royalty payments of a fixed amount per cubic yard of mineral removed, rather than of a certain percentage of market value, sales price, or some similar quantity. Contrary to taxpayer's position, royalty payment measurement, as in the lease under consideration, is anything but uncommon in hard mineral cases. In fact, such a provision appears to be typical. . . . Under the economic interest test, the critical consideration is whether payment is dependent upon extraction, not the method by which that payment is calculated. Thus, the difference in the typical measurement of payment under oil and gas and hard mineral leases should not affect the application of the economic interest test.

Taxpayer next argues that, even if the royalty payments are based upon production, the presence of minimum guaranteed royalty provisions in the agreement, requires a finding that his income was not based solely upon production as required by the economic interest test. This contention is without merit as the

---

[14] Of course, by the use of the term "typical" we do not mean that all, or most, mineral leases are substantially identical. They are not. However, certain characteristics of such agreements are typical in the sense of being quite common. That the present lease is typical may be shown by a comparison of its terms with lease characteristics discussed in 42 Texas Jurisprudence 2d, Oil and Gas . . . See also *Douglas v. Commissioner* . . . wherein the Supreme Court dealt with a hard mineral lease substantially identical to the one here under consideration. Clearly, the lease in *Douglas* retained an economic interest in the lessor.

courts have stated many times that a minimum royalty, such as that present in this case, is merely an advancement for future payments in the form of a guarantee and does not render payment dependent upon a factor other than extraction or production.

* * *

II. We now pass to a consideration of the hard mineral cases decided by the courts of appeals. The two most recent decisions that deal with the issue at hand lend strong support to the government's position. *Rabiner v. Bacon*, 8th Cir., 1967, 373 F.2d 537, the Eighth Circuit dealt with a "Lease Contract" for the removal of sand and gravel. Aside from the fact that it stipulated no minimum royalty and was for a definite period of time, the lease was substantially identical to the one at bar. The payments to the lessor were to be measured by a fixed price per unit of mineral removed. The Court, placing primary reliance upon *Burnet v. Harmel* and *Palmer v. Bender*, held that the contract was a lease and not a sale of the minerals in place and that landowner's compensation under the lease was ordinary income. As in the present case, the taxpayer emphasized the presence of a fixed rate of compensation. The court rejected the contention that when so measured, royalty payments cannot be considered as a retained economic interest . . .

* * *

Taxpayer cites *Linehan v. Commissioner* . . ., 1st Cir., 1961, 297 F.2d 276, in support of the contention that his contract effected a sale of the minerals in place. In *Linehan* the taxpayer had a small tract of land which was zoned for industrial use only. Pursuant to his desire to develop the land, he entered into a contract with a gravel company whereby the company agreed to excavate all sand and gravel down to a specific grade. The minerals thus removed were to be paid for at a fixed rate per cubic yard and the approximate amount to be removed was determined by a quantity survey. . . . [T]he court found that a sale of the minerals had been effected. Aside from questioning the reasoning used by the court to reach this conclusion, we also deem *Linehan* clearly distinguishable from the present case on its facts. In *Linehan* the gravel company was obligated to remove all of the sand and gravel down to a specific grade. Furthermore, the primary purpose of the contract, in the taxpayer's mind, was to make the land suitable for industrial use by lowering the grade. . . . Consequently, we do not consider *Linehan* as persuasive authority for taxpayer's position.

* * *

Gowans v. Commissioner . . . , 9th Cir., 1957, 246 F.2d 448, involved an agreement worded in terms of a sale and obligating the "buyer" to remove all sand on taxpayer's land. By subsequent agreement, the payments for the sand removed were secured by a bank note. Viewing these facts, the court found that a sale had been effectuated. Strong emphasis was given to the fact that taxpayer's purpose in entering the contract was to prepare his land for subdivision development, not to exploit the sand deposits. The court further noted that under the agreement the buyer was obligated to remove all of the sand and that the quantity of the sand had been determined "with great accuracy" prior to execution of the agreement. The court also felt that the execution of a bank note as security for the buyer's performance gave the seller a source other than production from which to obtain his compensation under the contract. . . . None of the factors which the Ninth Circuit viewed as removing the case from the general rule are present in the instant controversy. . . .

United States v. White, 10th Cir., 1967, 311 F.2d 399 . . . [involved] the tax treatment to be given a large down payment received by the landowner under an instrument entitled "Mineral Deed." This instrument granted to the vendee thereunder all mineral interests except oil and gas. An initial payment of $175,000 was stipulated, along with future payments of 10% of gross value of all minerals removed. The court had before it only the question of the taxability of the initial $175,000 down payment (which was in no way tied to, or dependent upon, extraction of any mineral). Viewing the language of the instrument and the size of the initial payment, the court concluded that taxpayer could treat the $175,000 as capital gain. . . . [T]he court expressly stated that no implication concerning the taxability of possible future royalty payments under the mineral deed should be drawn from the opinion.

* * *

It should be noted that each court of appeals decision relied upon by taxpayer involved factors not present in the instant case. In each case, these factors, here missing, were critical to the court's decision to allow capital gains treatment. In *Linehan* . . . and *Gowans* . . . the courts were influenced by the fact that preparation of the land for another use, not extraction of the minerals, was the primary motive of the landowners' action in entering into the contracts covering the minerals. The courts in the same two cases were influenced by a requirement in the respective agreements that all of the minerals covered by the contracts be removed. In *United States v. White*, the court felt that a large down payment in no way tied to extraction was indicative of a sale. In . . . *Gowans*, . . . [and] *White* . . . , the deciding courts were strongly influenced by the fact that the respective agreements were couched in terms of absolute conveyances or contracts of sale.[28]

* * *

Rev. Rul. 69-352, 1969-1 C.B. 34

* * *

This Revenue Ruling relates to whether a lump-sum payment received by a taxpayer purportedly for fee simple title to all minerals in and under certain land owned by him, but in conjunction with which he reserved a royalty interest in any minerals produced from the land, is ordinary income under section 61 of the Internal Revenue Code of 1954, or is the proceeds from the sale of a capital asset.

* * *

The Supreme Court of the United States has repeatedly taken the position that

[28] Whether or not any or all of these factors should be material under the economic interest test we do not here decide. An awareness of their influence in prior cases and their absence upon the facts of the present case, however, serve to illustrate the strength of the government's position.

where, in consideration of a lump-sum payment and stipulated royalties payable out of production, a grantor extends to a grantee a right to enter upon land for purposes of exploitation of the minerals therein, the lump-sum payment constitutes an advance royalty, taxable as ordinary income, and not proceeds from a sale of a capital asset. . . .

The cases cited show that the ordinary income character of such a cash payment is not dependent upon the retention by the grantor of ownership or any other form of legal interest in the mineral content of the land, and that it is not affected by the fact that the transaction may be cast in the form of a sale or that under local law title to the mineral in place passes immediately to the grantee upon execution of the instrument. In addition, the ordinary income character of such a cash payment is not dependent on the presence or absence of any dominating purpose of the parties to secure development and operation of the property. In this respect, there need not be any existing production of mineral, nor any practical assurance thereof in the future; nor is it necessary that the grantor have the right to compel the drilling of wells. In such transactions, the grantor merely extends to the grantee exclusive exploitation privileges, retaining as his (grantor's) share of the whole reservoir of mineral, a right, upon production, to a portion of such mineral with all burdens of development and the operating costs to be borne by the grantee. So considered, the view that a grantor parts with no capital interest in the mineral, though the grantee acquires one, presents no logical difficulties since, though it may be a potentially highly valuable mineral interest, the grantee's interest ordinarily achieves such value as the result of the investment incident to exploitation, or by reason of discovery.

Accordingly, it is held that irrespective of the presence, or absence, of a dominating purpose of the parties to secure development and operation of the property, the lump-sum payment received by the taxpayer-grantor of the mineral rights in the instant case, in conjunction with the retention by him of a royalty interest, is ordinary income and not proceeds from the sale of a capital asset.

* * *

NOTES AND COMMENTS

Although cast in terms of whether the transaction is a sale or lease, the special treatment under these authorities seems to be based more on the notion that what the taxpayer receives is not consideration for the transfer, but payment on a retained interest. This, of course, begs the question of what is the consideration for the fee interest transferred to the other party. To some degree, this is answered by a concept not discussed directly in *Wood* or Rev. Rul. 69-352: that the arrangement is a pool of capital, more or less analogous to a partnership or joint venture. This pool of capital notion is implicit in the statement in Rev. Rul. 69-352: "the view that a grantor parts with no capital interest in the mineral, though the grantee acquires one, presents no logical difficulties since, though it may be a potentially highly valuable mineral interest, the grantee's interest ordinarily achieves such value as the result of the investment incident to exploitation, or by reason of discovery." Although a detailed discussion of the joint venture approach is beyond the scope of this volume, it is worth noting that similar concepts are encountered in determining whether amounts supplied by others represent liabilities discussed in the *Notes and Comments* in § 3.3, *Speculative Security* of Chapter 3 *Liabilities: Discharge of Indebtedness; Mortgaged Property;* not coincidentally, immediately after *Brountas v. Commissioner*, 692 F.2d 152 (1st Cir. 1982) (nonrecourse notes secured by production from wildcat wells are too speculative to be given tax effect), which also deals with some of the special rules applicable to natural resource interests. Similar issues are involved in *Commissioner v. P. G. Lake, Inc.*, 356 U.S. 260 (1958), discussed in § 2.02, *Sales of Partial Interests — Ordinary Income Substitute.*

Cast in terms of whether there was a transfer or a retention, it is not as clear, as the Court suggested in *Brown* that the concepts are that different. After all, Brown was to be paid solely from the charity's receipts from the lease back of the business to Brown, which can be viewed as a retention almost as well as consideration for a transfer. Justice Harlan's concurrence makes this point, but notes that the Service did not cast the issue in those terms. Nevertheless, the notion that natural resource interests are different is deeply ingrained in the tax law. Perhaps one important factor is that when mineral operations cease, the transferor still has the land for whatever it is worth, for purposes other than mineral production, while Brown and Berenson have no continuing interest in the business assets once the stipulated payments are made.

PROBLEM FOR DISCUSSION

Problem 7-2. The Clampett family has been farming on a large tract of land for generations. In 20X1, oil was found on the neighboring farm and Oilco has made the Clampetts an offer of $1,000,000 for the land, pointing out the glories of the 15 percent capital gain rate. Being naturally suspicious, Clampett Sr. has consulted a lawyer and proposes to transfer the fee to land, for $500,000 in cash, plus retaining a royalty of up to an additional $1,500,000, plus an amount equal to interest on any unpaid balance at the applicable federal rate; all payable only out of 20 percent of the gross proceeds of any oil, gas, or other hydrocarbons produced from the property. Under the arrangement, the Clampetts are not to be charged with any development or other costs or expenses, but are to receive their payments out of the gross proceeds. The agreement further provided that, if the Clampetts had not received the full $1,500,000 plus applicable interest within 10 years of the transaction, the land would be sold and the balance would be paid out of 100 percent of the portion of the purchase price allocable to the oil and gas rights to the property. (i) What are the tax consequences to the Clampetts and Oilco as a result of the proposed arrangement? (ii) If the Clampetts are entitled to depletion of 22 percent, is the deal better than the original offer? (iii) If they are not entitled to depletion? If they are not entitled to depletion, what are the minimum changes needed to make them entitled? *See Wood* (economic interest in sand and gravel); Rev. Rul. 69-352 (lump sum payment plus royalty interest is ordinary income); *Southwest Explor. Co.*, (economic interest must look solely to mineral extraction for return of investment); *Anderson* (not economic interest if any other source of payment); *Thomas v. Perkins* (ascertainable amount payable only out of extraction is economic interest); *Palmer v. Bender* (royalty interest is economic interest);

Rabiner v. Bacon (lease even though fixed rate of payment); *Linehan* (obligation to remove sand and gravel to fit land for another use is not an economic interest); *Gowans* (required removal of sand and gravel is a sale). (iv) To the extent that you conclude that the Clampetts are not entitled to depletion, how should the transaction be changed to allow the desired result?

§ 1.03. Retained Interest v. Amount Realized

I.R.C. § 167(e)

Property, particularly real property, may be placed on the market before the owner is ready to vacate the premises, in part, at least, to avoid having to carry the property for an extended period after moving out while waiting to find a purchaser. Similarly, a purchaser may be willing to commit to purchase property before actually needing it, to assure its availability when needed. The interim period may be viewed as a current sale of a future interest in the property, or as a current sale of the property, with a leaseback, usually rent free. Drawing the line between the two is not easy, particularly when the parties do not expressly focus on the tax consequences, and do not expressly provide which of these two approaches they intend to employ. The following case draws the thin line for parties who were not careful enough to specify what they meant, and who took inconsistent positions.

ALSTORES REALTY CORP. v. COMMISSIONER

United States Tax Court
46 T.C. 363 (1966)

* * *

Petitioner, Alstores Realty Corp., is a corporation organized . . . to engage in various aspects of the real estate business. . . . Since its organization, petitioner has been a wholly owned subsidiary of Allied Stores Corp., a Delaware corporation, engaged in the ownership and operation directly and through subsidiaries of a large number of retail department stores. . . .

Stern Brothers, Inc. (hereinafter sometimes referred to as Stern Bros.) . . . was . . . 98-percent owned by Allied Stores Corp. Stern Bros. operated a retail department store on 42nd Street in New York City. Under the charter of Allied Stores Corp., the subsidiary corporations which operate retail department stores are subject to a restriction which prevents them from financing purchase of real estate. Stern Bros. was subject to this restriction. Alstores Realty Corp. was a nonrestricted subsidiary and, in fact, was organized for the purpose of acquiring and financing purchases of real property to be used by restricted subsidiaries.

Steinway & Sons, a New York corporation (hereinafter sometimes referred to as Steinway), was, prior to February 1, 1957, owner of certain real property . . . (hereinafter sometimes referred to as the subject property), part of which it leased to tenants and part of which it used in its own manufacturing operations. . . . Prior to the transaction here in question, portions of this building were leased by Steinway to Stern Bros.; as of October 4, 1956, Stern Bros. had a total of 59,178 square feet under lease . . . Steinway also leased approximately 500 square feet to

Nathan Manufacturing Co., which was not related to any of the corporations here involved. . . .

During the period 1956 through the middle of 1959, Steinway & Sons was in process of consolidating its manufacturing and other facilities at another location, and it decided to sell the subject . . . property. However, . . . until such time as the new facilities were ready for occupancy, Steinway & Sons required the continued use of considerable space in the subject property.

In 1956 and 1957, Stern Bros. was in process of building a new store in Bergen Mall Shopping Center in Paramus, N.J. In anticipation of the opening of this store on November 1, 1957, Stern Bros., Alstores Realty Corp., and Allied Stores Corp. began consideration of methods of acquiring additional warehouse space in order to handle the merchandise that would be needed for sale in the Paramus store.

Preliminary negotiations were entered into in the spring of 1956 looking toward a possible sale of the subject property by Steinway & Sons to petitioner for use by Stern Bros. . . .

Steinway's original asking price for the subject premises was $1,250,000; this was later lowered to $1 million. However, because Steinway at the time of these negotiations was not yet prepared to remove its manufacturing operations from the subject building, it would not at that time have agreed to a sale unless an arrangement could be made permitting it to retain possession of a portion of the building until its new plant would be ready for occupancy. Eventually, in 1956, the parties agreed to a transaction under which petitioner (Alstores) would pay $750,000 cash for title to the building and Steinway would retain occupancy of a portion of the building for 2-1/2 years from the date of conveyance, without further payment of rent.

* * *

On October 4, 1956, two agreements were executed by petitioner and Steinway & Sons with respect to the subject property. The first agreement can, for convenience, be called the sale contract and the second agreement can, for convenience, be called the space occupancy agreement. The two agreements were executed and delivered by the parties simultaneously and were expressly made interdependent one upon the other. . . .

The space occupancy agreement contains, *inter alia*, the following provisions:

* * *

1. Alstores as Landlord, agrees to provide Steinway as Tenant, *without further payment* by Steinway therefor, with space, services and facilities in the premises to be conveyed under the aforesaid contract of sale, all as more fully set forth in the following schedule and paragraphs. . . .

2. . . . In addition, Alstores, as Landlord, shall provide Steinway, as Tenant, during the term set forth above, without additional charge therefor, with heat, electricity and water. . . .

3. It is understood and agreed that if any portion of the space to be used and occupied by Steinway as hereinabove provided for shall, during the term set forth above, be so damaged or destroyed by fire or other cause as to render same unusable by Steinway . . . , Alstores shall, during any such period, pay to Steinway, on the 1st day of each and every month, during the balance of the term above set forth, a sum equivalent to six and one-quarter (6-1/4) cents per square foot for that portion of the space so affected.

4. Steinway, as Tenant, shall have the right, from time to time, to terminate the tenancy, . . . in which event, Alstores shall pay to Steinway on the 1st day of each and every month during the balance of the term, a sum equivalent to six and one-quarter (6-1/4) cents per square foot for that portion or portions of the space as to which Steinway's tenancy has been so terminated. . . .

* * *

[Emphasis supplied.]

. . . At the closing, petitioner . . . completed the cash consideration of $750,000 specified in the sale contract. . . . Steinway's attorney affixed to the deed revenue stamps in the amount of $1,103.85, reflecting a consideration for the transaction of $1,003,090.75. The difference between $1,003,090.75 and the $750,000 total cash consideration, or $253,090.75, was the fair rental value of the space in the subject premises which Steinway was to occupy "without further payment," pursuant to the above-described occupancy agreement, measured at a rate of 6-1/4 cents per square foot per month. This was the same rate then being paid to Steinway by Stern Bros. under existing lease for portions of the subject property.

* * *

Beginning in early 1958 and from time to time thereafter Steinway, by agreement with Stern Bros., vacated portions of the space in the subject property which it had been occupying and received payment from Stern Bros. at a rate of 6-1/4 cents per square foot per month for the space so vacated. . . .

After consummation of the transaction here in question, Steinway, which kept its books and records and filed its tax returns on an accrual basis, made an entry in its general ledger showing prepaid rent as of February 1, 1957, in the amount of $253,090.75. . . . Over a period of 30 months subsequent to February 1, 1957, Steinway deducted a total of $163,644.39 as rent in its Federal income tax returns, this sum representing the difference between the prepaid rent item of $253,090.75 and the $89,446.36 which Steinway received as aforesaid from Stern Bros. in connection with Steinway's vacating portions of the space . . .

* * *

Steinway & Sons reported the transaction as a sale on which the "amount realized" within the meaning of section 1001(b) was not only the $750,000 cash received, but also included the fair market value of the rent-free space-occupancy agreement; said fair market value was determined to be $253,090.75. This amount was "capitalized" on the books of Steinway and amortized (with adjustments for payments from Stern Bros. as detailed above) over the 2-1/2-year term of the space-occupancy agreement.

* * *

There are two approaches to analyzing the transaction here involved. One approach is to say that there was a purchase by petitioner of the entire fee interest in the subject premises and at the same time a lease of a portion of the premises back to the seller for a 2-1/2-year term. This is the approach taken by the respondent herein.

Petitioner contends that even if the space-occupancy agreement should be regarded as a lease, there was, nonetheless, no income produced to the "lessor" since the "lease" was rent free. While it may be true that no rent was due or to be paid after Steinway's occupancy was to begin as petitioner's tenant, the agreement of the parties recognizes that it was because prepayment had been made by Steinway. . . . The answer to petitioner's contention here is that although there were no cash payments to petitioner designated as rent after the property was deeded to it, Steinway's right of occupancy thereafter was a valuable one for which petitioner must have received consideration in some form, and that consideration was in the form of Steinway's conveyance to petitioner of fee title to the entire building — to the extent that the purchase price of the building exceeded the $750,000 cash paid therefor, or $253,090.75 . . .

The alternative analysis of the situation looks to the substance of the transaction. Petitioner here argues that, although in form there may have been a sale and leaseback, in substance there was a conveyance of a future interest with Steinway reserving to itself, or carving out, a term of 2-1/2 years in a portion of the property. Hence, Steinway in substance retained its right to occupancy not as a lessee of petitioner, but as a legal owner of a reserved term for years. . . .

Although at first blush petitioner's argument is an appealing one, we conclude that it must be rejected and we must hold for respondent. Steinway did not in form or substance reserve an estate for years.

An analogous situation was presented in *McCulley Ashlock*, 18 T.C. 405 (1952). There the building in question was subject to a lease to a third party at the time it was purchased by the taxpayer. The contract of sale provided that the buyer would pay $40,000 cash but the seller was to retain "possession" of the premises and all the rights to the rental income from the lessee until the expiration of the primary term of the existing lease (about 28 months from date of the sale contract). The Commissioner determined that the rent received by the seller subsequent to conveyance of title to the taxpayer purchaser was really taxable income to the taxpayer purchaser. We rejected the Commissioner's approach in that case, holding that the seller had reserved an ownership interest in the property (an estate for years) and that the rents received were income to the seller for occupancy of what was still his property — not income to the purchaser, who did not then have a present legal ownership interest but only a future interest. The essence of our reasoning in the *Ashlock* case was as follows . . .

> Here, the trustees [the sellers of the property] not only retained the rents legally but they also retained control and benefits of ownership. Under the

> contract of sale on April 18, 1945, the trustees specifically agreed to pay property taxes, insurance premiums, and "all normal maintenance items and expenses," so that the property would be delivered to * * * [the buyer] in the present condition except for normal wear and tear. Furthermore, the June 11, 1945, agreement stated that in the event that the property was damaged or destroyed, and loss of income during the period of repair or reconstruction would be the trustees' loss. It further provided that insurance proceeds would be devoted to restore and repair the property, except in the event of total destruction petitioner would have the option of rebuilding the premises or compensating the trustees for unpaid rent. Thus the trustee bore the risks of ownership of the rents and managed the property. Larger expenses or a cessation of rents were risks incurred by the trustees. * * *

A directly analogous problem, solved by the same type of reasoning may be found in the "oil payment" line of cases in which the question is whether or not the vendor of an oil lease retains an economic interest in the oil in place. *See Thomas v. Perkins*, 301 U.S. 655 (1937).

The same factors which we looked to in *Ashlock* in deciding in favor of the purchaser, analyzed in the factual posture of the instant case, dictate the opposite result here. Petitioner, the buyer, assumed control of the premises and the benefits of ownership. Petitioner, the buyer, specifically agreed to pay for and supply to Steinway, the seller, heat, electricity, and water. The space-occupancy agreement stated that in the event the property was damaged or destroyed and Steinway's occupancy was thereby destroyed or impaired the burden of loss would be upon petitioner (with petitioner agreeing to pay Steinway 6-1/4 cents per square foot per month for space so affected). It is clear in the instant case that the buyer bore the risks and burdens of ownership during the term of the space-occupancy agreement. . . .

Furthermore, the rights of Steinway, the seller, as occupant were not those of a holder of a legal estate for years but were specifically limited to those of a lessee. . . .

Of key significance in this case is the fact that petitioner was required to pay to Steinway 6-1/4 cents per square foot per month for space which Steinway was entitled to occupy but which it may have been unable to occupy by reason of an act of God or the fault of petitioner, or which it may have elected to vacate during the last one-half year of the space occupancy agreement. This arrangement is entirely inconsistent with the theory that Steinway had a reserved estate for years . . . What we really have here is a provision for reimbursement of prepaid rent . . .

Petitioner emphasizes the fact that it received no cash rental payments at any time; it merely purchased real estate for cash. This is partly true, but one need not receive cash to have received income. . . . [P]etitioner received, in exchange for the lease interest granted to Steinway, rent income in the amount of the excess of the value of the property that petitioner received over the cash which it paid.

* * *

Possibly the result in the instant case would be different if the parties had in fact intended to carve out a reserved term for years in Steinway and had structured their transaction in that form. . . . We do not agree with petitioner, however, that to hold that there was a sale of the fee and a simultaneous leaseback here is to exalt form over substance. The so-called space-occupancy agreement placed the two parties' rights, obligations, and risks as they would be allocated in a typical lease arrangement. Hence, the arrangement was a lease in substance as well as in form.

* * *

Petitioner has raised the alternative argument that if it is deemed to have received rent income upon purchase of the subject premises its cost basis of said premises should be increased by the amount of such income and, consequently, its annual depreciation deduction increased. Petitioner originally treated the entire premises as having a basis of $750,000, the amount of cash paid, and it had taken depreciation on the portion of that amount allocable to the depreciable building. Respondent objects to any increase in petitioner's basis as a result of a determination that petitioner realized rent income, however, he presents no argument on this point.

* * *

We hold that petitioner's cost basis in the subject premises includes the $253,090.75 fair market value of the space-occupancy agreement. This sum must be allocated between the land and the building in the same proportions as the $750,000 cash consideration was allocated. . . .

* * *

NOTES AND COMMENTS

It is not easy to identify the factor or factors that the court believes distinguish *Ashlock* from *Alstores*, but the key seems to be that Alstores immediately assumed the risks of operation of the premises, even though it did not have the benefit of possession or any other economic benefit, other than a reduction in price. This, however, was equally consistent with the value of deferred possession. The similar assumption of the risks of operation helps distinguish *Mayerson* (nonrecourse liability for 100% of purchase price not contingent) from *Franklin* (nonrecourse liability for 100% of purchase price in tax-shelter sale and leaseback not recognized for tax purposes). In *Steinway & Sons v. Commissioner*, 46 T.C. 375 (1966), the seller's side of the *Alstores*, Steinway was allowed to deduct the $253,090.75 allocated to the leaseholder over the 2½-year term.

In *Wagner v. Commissioner*, 518 F.2d 655 (10th Cir. 1975), a seemingly inconsistent opinion that did not cite *Ashlock* or *Alstores/Steinway*, a purchaser of real estate who allowed the seller to retain all rent under the existing lease and required it to pay all expenses during the remaining lease term, with a deferred portion of the purchase price that would bear interest only after the end of the lease term, was allowed to depreciate the building during the lease term, even though the seller apparently reported the interest and expenses, but it is not stated whether the seller claimed depreciation during that period. The court cited the fact that the purchaser accepted the condition of the premises on the date of the contract, which the court treated as assuming the benefits and burdens of ownership. Although not stated by the court, depreciation is generally recognized to be based on investment in the property, rather than ownership, particularly investments by lessees, even in the construction of buildings owned by the lessor, *see* Treas. Reg. §§ 1.162-11(b) and 1.167(a)-4(a), which could be used to justify *Wagner*, but the justification is weak one, because Wagner did not pay any amount allocable to the period of beneficial ownership retained by the seller.

At one time, taxpayers arranged to depreciate otherwise nondepreciable land, by transferring the fee to a related corporation subject to a retained term of years, or by transferring a term of years to the related corporation while retaining the fee, or by joint purchases of the term and remainder by related persons. In *Lomas Santa Fe, Inc. v. Commissioner*, 693 F.2d 71 (9th Cir 1982), the court disallowed the taxpayer's claim of an amortization of a 40-year term retained on conveyance of land to a related golf-course corporation that developed the golf course as an adjunct to a residential development, because the taxpayer's fragmentation of interest did not provide depreciable basis in term. The court determined that the taxpayer could establish a cost basis in the term by allocating its pre-transaction basis in the land between fee and term permitted. Section 167(e) confirms the disallowance by denying a depreciation deduction for term interests when the fee is held by a related person, with the disallowed deduction increasing the basis of the fee interest, unless the term interest is held by a person not subject to tax.

PROBLEMS FOR DISCUSSION

Problem 7-3. Ceeco owns and operates a farm on land with a basis of $1,000,000 that is worth $10,000,000 as agricultural land. Ceeco's farm is subject to condemnation for use as part of an environmental cleanup project to protect the local water supply. In the nature of government projects, the planning and appropriation of funds for the cleanup project are expected to take five or more years. The condemning authority has land available that it does not need and that it is prepared to transfer immediately to pay the condemnation price. Although not directly relevant, the exchange will qualify under § 1033, as discussed in § 2, *Involuntary Conversion*, of Chapter 5, *Nonrecognition Exchanges*. Accordingly, the condemning authority and Ceeco have agreed that Ceeco will immediately receive eight acres of government-owned land for each of the 10 acres that is being condemned. Under the agreement, Ceeco is entitled to continue its farming operation for five years without payment on the condemned land. In addition, Ceeco has the option to continue its farming operation after the five years, until the land is actually needed for the cleanup project, but if Ceeco continues to use the land after the five years, it is required to make rental payments based on a formula that is not determined by the rental value of the land. During the period it continues its farming operations, Ceeco is obligated to pay all expenses and taxes on the land, comply with all environmental and other laws and regulations relating to its operations on the land and, of course, is entitled to all of the income from the land and is also entitled to make any changes or improvements to the land provided they will not interfere with the eventual use of the land for the cleanup project. During the period Ceeco farms the land, the condemning authority has rights of inspection to make sure Ceeco is complying with its duties. Ceeco intends to allocate 20 percent ($400,000) of its $2,000,000 basis in the land to the five-year period and amortize it, and to allocate the remaining $1,600,000 as its basis for the replacement land, even though it believes the present value of the profits it will make during the five-year period is $3,500,000. What are the tax effects of the Ceeco's rights to farm the land: (i) during the initial five-year period in which it is not obligated to make any payments? and (ii) if it continues to farm the land thereafter, during the period it makes the formula payments? *See* § 167(e); *Ashlock* (retained right to rent converts sale to a remainder); *Alstores* (retained right of possession does not convert sale to a remainder); *Steinway & Sons* (same); *Wagner* (purchaser can depreciate building notwithstanding seller's retained right to rents); *Lomas Santa Fe* (retained term on conveyance of fee is not amortizable).

Problem 7-4. Invest transferred a commercial building to Perch for $500,000 in cash, and a right to up to an additional $1,500,000, plus an amount equal to interest on any unpaid balance at the applicable federal rate. All but the $500,000 down payment was payable only out of 20 percent of the gross rentals received by Perch from the commercial building. Invest was not to be charged with any costs or expenses, and was to receive her payments out of the gross rentals. The agreement further provided that, if Invest had not received the full $1,500,000 plus applicable interest within 10 years of the transaction, the land would be sold and the balance would be paid out of 100 percent of the portion of the purchase price allocable to the then-existing leases and any renewals. What are the tax consequences to Invest and Perch of the transaction? *See Brountas* (discussed in Chapter 3, § 3.3, *Speculative Security*) (nonrecourse notes secured by speculative oil and gas properties); *Brown* (bootstrap sale valid); *Berenson* (excess of price on sale to charity over fair market value is ordinary income); *Wood* (economic interest in sand and gravel); *Wagner* (purchaser can depreciate building notwithstanding seller's retained right to rents); Rev. Rul. 69-352 (lump sum payment plus royalty interest is ordinary income); *Southwest Explor. Co.* (economic interest must look to mineral extraction for return of investment); *Anderson* (not economic interest if any other source of payment); *Thomas v. Perkins* (sum certain payable only out of extraction is economic interest); *Palmer v. Bender* (royalty interest is economic interest); *Harmel* (oil and gas lease not a sale, but no standard for distinguishing); *Rabiner v. Bacon* (lease even though fixed rate of payment); *Linehan* (obligation to remove sand and gravel to fit land for another use is not a lease); *Gowans* (required removal of sand and gravel is a sale); *Mayerson* (nonrecourse liability for 100% of purchase price not contingent).

Problem 7-5. Stock is the sole shareholder of Ceeco, a small but highly successful airline. His basis in Ceeco is $100,000. Ceeco has produced after-tax income of approximately $100,000 a year (pre-tax income of a little more than $200,000 a year) over each of the past three years. In the next few years, however, its pre-tax results are expected to increase dramatically because its fleet, although fully operational, has been almost fully depreciated for tax purposes (as a result of accelerated depreciation). For similar reasons, the book value of the airline is under $500,000. Stock has been seeking to sell the airline for a price of $1,500,000, but the best offer he has received so far has been $1,000,000. He has been approached by Lossco, which has offered to meet his asking price of $1,500,000 provided it can pay the purchase price over a period of time based on the earnings of Ceeco. Lossco has available to it accumulated net operating losses of $1,500,000 and anticipates incurring at least another $1,000,000 to $1,500,000 of losses before it reaches turnaround in approximately 15 years. It anticipates that a substantial portion of its current and anticipated losses, at least $2,000,000, is likely to expire unutilized unless it acquires a profit-making venture. Specifically, Lossco proposes to issue its note for the purchase price of $1,500,000, payable in five annual installments of $300,000 each together with interest at the AFR, and with the proviso that the annual installment of principal and interest would not exceed 75 percent of the pre-tax earnings of Ceeco (which would be kept as a separate subsidiary). Any amount deferred in any one year would then be payable in the first available year in which 75 percent of the pre-tax earnings of Ceeco exceed the installment (including interest) otherwise due in that year. Because on the basis of the projected earnings of Ceeco, the purchase price should be fully paid in five years, Lossco also proposes that if the full purchase price has not been paid at the end of seven years, it would have no further obligation to make payment. Lossco is, of course, willing to make payment based on pre-tax earnings because it does not anticipate paying any tax, in view of its net operating loss carryover and expectancy of future losses. Stock is interested in the Lossco proposal because he is confident that the earnings will justify the purchase price, but he does not like the risk that the total price may not be paid. Lossco is insistent on the cutoff, but has offered to increase the maximum price to $1,750,000. Stock has countered that, if he is going to take some risk on the downside, he wants to have some opportunity to participate in any substantial appreciation. Accordingly, he has proposed that the price remain $1,500,000, but that he is to have the right to purchase a 25 percent interest in the company for $400,000 at the end of five years. Lossco, of course, wants Stock to continue to run the airline for, at least the payout period, and Stock, obviously, wishes to continue to operate it to protect his interest. He will receive a salary commensurate with the salary he has received in the past and equivalent to the salaries of other comparable executives of Lossco. What are the tax consequences to Stock if he enters into a contract along the final terms proposed by him? *See Brown* (bootstrap sale to charity); *Ashlock* (retained right to rent converts sale to a remainder); *Alstores* (retained right of possession does not convert sale to a remainder); *Steinway* (same); *Wagner* (purchaser can depreciate building notwithstanding seller's retained right to rents); *Lomas Santa Fe* (retained term on conveyance of fee is not amortizable).

§ 1.04. Lease versus Sale

Under a long-term lease, the lessee has the use of the property without an immediate capital expenditure, and pays rent over the term of the lease that is deductible when paid or accrued. The lessor, on the other hand, receives the rental income and enjoys the tax benefits of owning the property, principally depreciation and interest deductions, when the property is acquired with borrowed funds. Of course, the depreciation and interest deductions are significantly larger in the early years of the lease, providing a time value of money advantage. Thus, the lessor will be servicing the debt with the cash flow generated from the rents received from the lessee. If the lease is of personal property, the lessor owner usually has substantial tax losses in the early years, particularly when the depreciation deductions may be determined using an accelerated method under § 168. In addition, interest deductions on loans are typically larger in the early years of the loan and subsequently decrease as the principal of the loan is amortized. Thus, if the rents are level over the term of the lease, the lessor usually has tax losses in the early years of the lease that will be offset by substantial income in the later years. The advantage of the early losses exceeds the cost of the later income when the time value of money is taken into account.

Alternatively, a long-term lease can be conceptualized as a financing arrangement under which the "lessee" is the owner of the property entitled to the tax benefits of ownership, such as depreciation and interest deductions, while the "lessor" provides financing to the lessee. The "rent" in such a situation is a payment of interest and principal to the "lessor." If the "lessor" acquired the property with borrowed funds, the "lessor" will again be servicing the debt with the cash flow generated from the "rents" received from the "lessee." In this case, the "lessee" is deemed the true borrower, and the "lessor" is treated as a conduit for payments to the third-party lender.

A lessee is likely to favor a lease over a purchase for nontax reasons, when, for example, it cannot finance the purchase price, because of limits on its ability to incur financing, due to a poor credit status or if, for some other reason, incurring the debt or owning the property is undesirable. A lease arrangement may be tax motivated, however, when the "lessee" is tax exempt or has other deductions that prevent obtaining immediate tax benefit from the depreciation and interest deductions. In such instances, the lease arrangement may simply be a mechanism to transfer the tax benefits of ownership to the lessor, who is subject to a high effective tax rate. The parties typically share the value of the tax benefits through the determination of the "rent" to be paid.

Generally, commercial, bankruptcy, and banking law, as well as accounting principles and the tax law, respect the form of the transaction as structured. Nevertheless, they respect the form within limits, and treat at least some long-term leases as rental arrangements, although they all draw a line somewhere, on the other side of which a purported lease is treated as financing. The following ruling attempts to deal with this troublesome issue, not by drawing a bright line, but by trying to highlight the facts and circumstances relevant to the determination in a number of different arrangements involving personal property supplied by the "lessor" to the "lessee."

Rev. Rul. 55-540, 1955-2 C.B. 39

* * *

Sec. 2. Background.

.01 Many new and unique types of agreements concerning the use and disposition of equipment have been developed to meet the needs and purposes of the users of industrial and business equipment. The lessor, in devising these agreements, is primarily interested in disposing of his wares to customers. (Here and elsewhere in this ruling the terms "lessor" and "lessee" are used for convenience, without intending to suggest the proper characterization of any agreement.) The lessee, on the other hand, may have one or more reasons for leasing instead of purchasing the equipment. He may have use for the equipment for only a comparatively short period of time. He may wish to experiment with a new process or product which requires equipment he does not own. He may have insufficient capital or credit with which to make an outright purchase, or have other needs for his working capital. A significant motive may, in some cases, be the tax advantages which might result because of the different timing of the deductions for rent as compared to depreciation.

.02 The agreements are generally cast in the form of chattel leases and are as varied as the reasons for entering into such arrangements. An approximate pattern is discernible, however, and many of the agreements may be loosely defined and grouped as follows:

(a) Short-term agreements which usually concern mobile equipment or relatively small articles of equipment. The "compensation for use" provisions in these agreements are usually expressed in terms of an hourly, daily, or weekly rental, and the rental rates are relatively high in relation to the value of the article. There may be an option to purchase the equipment at a price fixed in advance which will approximate the fair market value of the equipment at the time of the election to exercise the option. In this type of agreement, all costs of repairs, maintenance, taxes, insurance, etc., are obligations of the lessor.

(b) Agreements entered into by taxpayers engaged in the business of leasing personal property to others either as their principal business activity or incidental thereto. Under the terms of these agreements the amounts payable, called rental rates, are ordinarily based on normal operations or use, plus a surcharge for operations in excess of the normal stated usage. In some instances the rental is based on units produced or mileage operated. Termination of the agreement at stated periods is provided upon due notice by either party. If the agreement includes an option to purchase, the option price has no relation to the amounts paid as rentals.

(c) Agreements providing for a "rental" over a comparatively short period of time in relation to the life of the equipment. The agreed "rental" payments fully cover the normal purchase price plus interest. Title usually passes to the lessee upon the payment of a stated amount of "rental" or on termination of the agreement upon the payment of an amount which when added to the "rental" paid approximates the normal purchase price of the equipment plus interest.

(d) Agreements which provide for the payment of "rental" for a short original term in relation to the expected life of the equipment, with provision for continued use over substantially all of the remaining useful life of the equipment. During the initial term of the agreement, the "rental" approximates the normal purchase price of the equipment, plus interest, while the "rentals" during the remaining term or renewal period or periods are insignificant when compared to the initial rental. These agreements may or may not provide for an option to acquire legal title to the equipment upon the termination of the initial period or at any stated time thereafter.

(e) Agreements similar to the arrangement in (d) above, but with the added factor that the manufacturer of the equipment purports to sell it to a credit or finance company, which either takes an assignment of such an existing agreement with the user or itself later enters into such an agreement with the user. In some instances, the lessor may be a trustee acting for or on behalf of the original vendor.

SEC. 3. Nature of the Problem.

.01 Section 162(a)(3) of the Internal Revenue Code of 1954 provides that there shall be allowed as a deduction all ordinary and necessary expenses paid or incurred during the taxable year in carrying on any trade or business, including rentals or other payments required to be made as a condition to the continued use or possession, for the purposes of the trade or business of the taxpayer, of property to which the taxpayer has not taken or is not taking title or in which he has no equity. . . .

.02 In deciding whether a taxpayer is entitled to a deduction for any payments claimed to represent rentals under the provisions of the Code . . . , it is necessary to determine whether by virtue of the agreement the lessee has acquired, or will acquire, title to or an equity in the property. The determination of that question with respect to agreements of the type here involved will ordinarily depend upon whether the particular agreement should be treated as in reality a lease or a conditional sale contract.

SEC. 4. Determination Whether an Agreement Is a Lease or a Conditional Sales Contract.

.01 Whatever interest is obtained by a lessee is acquired under the terms of the agreement itself. Whether an agreement, which in form is a lease, is in substance a conditional sales contract depends upon the intent of the parties as evidenced by the provisions of the agreement, read in the light of the facts and circumstances existing at the time the agreement was executed. In ascertaining such intent no single test, or any special combination of tests, is absolutely determinative. No general rule, applicable to all cases, can be laid down. Each case must be decided in the light of its particular facts. However, from the decisions cited below, it would appear that in the absence of compelling persuasive factors of contrary implication an intent warranting treatment of a transaction for tax purposes as a purchase and sale rather than as a lease or rental agreement may in general be said to exist if, for example, one or more of the following conditions are present:

(a) Portions of the periodic payments are made specifically applicable to an equity to be acquired by the lessee. . . .

(b) The lessee will acquire title upon the payment of a stated amount of "rentals" which under the contract he is required to make. . . .

(c) The total amount which the lessee is required to pay for a relatively short period of use constitutes an inordinately large proportion of the total sum required to be paid to secure the transfer of the title. . . .

(d) The agreed "rental" payments materially exceed the current fair rental value. This may be indicative that the payments include an element other than compensation for the use of property. . . .

(e) The property may be acquired under a purchase option at a price which is nominal in relation to the value of the property at the time when the option may be exercised, as determined at the time of entering into the original agreement, or which is a relatively small amount when compared with the total payments which are required to be made. . . .

(f) Some portion of the periodic payments is specifically designated as interest or is otherwise readily recognizable as the equivalent of interest. . . .

.02 The fact that the agreement makes no provision for the transfer of title or specifically precludes the transfer of title does not, of itself, prevent the contract from being held to be a sale of an equitable interest in the property.

.03 Conditional sales of personal property are, in general, recordable under the various State recording acts if the vendor wishes to protect its lien against claims of creditors. However, the recording or failure to record such a sales contract is usually discretionary with the vendor and is not controlling insofar as the essential nature of the contract is concerned for Federal tax purposes. . . .

.04 Agreements are usually indicative of an intent to rent the equipment if the rental payments are at an hourly, daily, or weekly rate, or are based on production, use, mileage, or a similar measure and are not directly related to the normal purchase price, provided, if there is an option to purchase, that the price at which the equipment may be acquired reasonably approximates the anticipated fair market value on the option date. Thus, agreements of the type described in section 2.02(a) and (b), above, will usually be considered leases, in the absence of other facts or circumstances which denote a passing of title or an equity interest to the lessee.

.05 In the absence of compelling factors indicating a different intent, it will be presumed that a conditional sales contract was intended if the total of the rental payments and any option price payable in addition thereto approximates the price at which the equipment could have been acquired by purchase at the time of entering into the agreement, plus interest and/or carrying charges. Agreements of the type described in section 2.02(c), above, will generally be held to be sales of the equipment.

.06 If the sum of the specified "rentals" over a relatively short part of the expected useful life of the equipment approximates the price at which the equipment could have been acquired by purchase at the time of entering into the agreement, plus interest and/or carrying charges on such amount, and the lessee may continue to use the equipment for an additional period or periods approximating its remaining estimated useful life for relatively nominal or token payments, it may be assumed that the parties have entered into a sale contract, even though a passage of title is not expressly provided in the agreement. Agreements of the type described in section 2.02(d), and (e), above, in general, will be held to be sales contracts.

SEC. 5. Reporting of Income and Deductions by a Lessor or a Vendor.

.01 The amounts paid for the use of equipment under an agreement which is determined, under the foregoing principles, to be a lease will be held to be rental income to the lessor. . . . [T]he lessor will be allowed a deduction for depreciation determined pursuant to the provisions of section 167 of the Code of 1954. If the lessee under the contract pays to the lessor a stipulated rental, and in addition pays certain other expenses which are properly payable by the lessor, the lessor is deemed to have received as rental income not only the stipulated rental but also the amount of such other expenses paid by the lessee to, or for the account of, the lessor . . .

.02 If the agreement is determined to be a sale, the amounts received under the contract by the vendor will be considered to be payments on the sales price of the equipment to the extent such amounts do not represent interest or other charges.

SEC. 6. Deductions Allowable to Lessee or Purchaser.

.01 If it is held, under the foregoing principles, that an agreement is a lease, the lessee may deduct the amount of rent paid or accrued, including all expenses which under the terms of the agreement the lessee is required to pay to, for, or on account of the lessor. . . . If the payments are so arranged as to constitute advance rental, such payments will be duly apportioned over the lease term. In computing the term of the lease, all options to renew shall be taken into consideration if there is a reasonable expectation that such options will be exercised.

.02 If under the provisions of this Revenue Ruling the agreement is to be treated as a sale, the amounts paid to the vendor will be considered as payments for the purchase of the equipment to the extent such amounts do not represent interest or other charges. Expenditures treated as payments for the purchase of the equipment may be recovered over the life of the asset through appropriate depreciation deductions.

NOTES AND COMMENTS

Although not explicitly cast in terms of who has the benefits and burdens of ownership, in light of *Brown* and *Alstores/Steinway*, § 4 of Rev. Rul. 55-540 is clearly designed to make the classifications, at least in the easy cases, on such a determination. Needless to say, Rev. Rul. 55-540 was not effective in eliminating controversy, and probably did little to reduce it. The following case deals with the same issue — interestingly, without reference to Rev. Rul. 55-540.

EST. OF STARR v. COMMISSIONER

United States Court of Appeals, Ninth Circuit
274 F.2d 294 (9th Cir. 1959)

* * *

Yesterday's equities in personal property seem to have become today's leases. This has been generated not a little by the circumstance that one who leases as a lessee usually has less trouble with the federal tax collector. At least taxpayers think so.

But the lease still can go too far and get one into tax trouble. While according to state law the instrument will probably be taken (with the consequent legal incidents) by the name the parties give it, the internal revenue service is not always bound and can often recast it according to what the service may consider the practical realities.[1] We have so held in *Oesterreich v. Commissioner*, 9 Cir., 226 F.2d 798, and *Commissioner . . . v. Wilshire Holding Corporation*, 9 Cir., 244 F.2d 904, *certiorari denied* 355 U.S. 815 . . . The principal case concerns a fire sprinkler system installed at the taxpayer's plant at Monrovia, California, where Delano T. Starr, now deceased, did business as the Gross Manufacturing Company. The 'lessor' was 'Automatic' Sprinklers of the Pacific, Inc., a California corporation. The instrument entitled 'Lease Form of Contract' (hereafter 'contract') is just about perfectly couched in terms of a lease for five years with annual rentals of $1,240. But it is the last paragraph thereof, providing for nominal rental for five years, that has caused the trouble. It reads as follows:

> At the termination of the period of this lease, if Lessee has faithfully performed all of the terms and conditions required of it under this lease, it shall have the privilege of renewing this lease for an additional period of five years at a rental of $32.00 per year. If Lessee does not elect to renew this lease, then the Lessor is hereby granted the period of six months in which to remove the system from the premises of the Lessee.'

Obviously, one renewal for a period of five years is provided at $32.00 per year, if Starr so desired. Note, though, that the paragraph is silent as to status of the system beginning with the eleventh year. Likewise the whole contract is similarly silent.

The tax court sustained the commissioner of internal revenue, holding that the five payments of $1,240, or the total of $6,200, were capital expenditures and not pure deductible rental. Depreciation of $269.60 was allowed for each year. Generally, we agree.

Taxpayers took the deduction as a rental expense under trade or business pursuant to Section 23(a) [§ 162(a)] of the Internal Revenue Code. . . .

The law in this field for this circuit is established in *Oesterreich v. Commissioner*, *supra*, and *Robinson v. Elliot*, 9 Cir., 262 F.2d 383. There we held that for tax purposes form can be disregarded for substance and, where the foreordained practical effect of the rent is to produce title eventually, the rental agreement can be treated as a sale.

In this, Starr's case, we do have the troublesome circumstance that the contract does not by its terms ever pass title to the system to the 'lessee.' Most sprinkler systems have to be tailor-made for a specific piece of property and, if removal is required, the salvageable value is negligible. Also, it stretches credulity to believe that the 'lessor' ever intended to or would 'come after' the system. And the 'lessee'

[1] Thus it shifts rental payments of a business (fully deductible) to a capital purchase for the business. If the nature of the property is wasting, then depreciation may be taken, but usually not all in one year.

would be an exceedingly careless businessman who would enter into such contract with the practical possibility that the 'lessor' would reclaim the installation. He could have believed only that he was getting the system for the rental money. And we think the commissioner was entitled to take into consideration the practical effect rather than the legal, especially when there was a record that on other such installations the 'lessor', after the term of the lease was over, had not reclaimed from those who had met their agreed payments. It is obvious that the nominal rental payments after five years of $32.00 per year were just a service charge for inspection.

Recently the Court of Appeals for the Eighth Circuit has decided *Western Contracting Corporation v. Commissioner*, 1959, 271 F.2d 694, reversing the tax court in its determination that the commissioner could convert leases of contractor's equipment into installment purchases of heavy equipment. The taxpayer believes that case strongly supports him here. We think not.

There are a number of facts there which make a difference. For example, in the contracts of Western there is no evidence that the payments on the substituted basis of rent would produce for the 'lessor' the equivalent of his normal sales price plus interest. There was no right to acquire for a nominal amount at the end of the term as in *Oesterreich* and the value to the 'lessor' in the personalty had not been exhausted as in Starr's case. And there was no basis for inferring that Western would just keep the equipment for what it had paid. It appears that Western paid substantial amounts to acquire the equipment at the end of the term. There was just one compelling circumstance against Western in its case: What it had paid as 'rent' was apparently always taken into full account in computing the end purchase price. But on the other hand, there was almost a certainty that the 'lessor' would come after his property if the purchase was not eventually made for a substantial amount. This was not even much of a possibility in *Oesterreich* and not a probability in Starr's case.

In *Wilshire Holding Corporation v. Commissioner*, 9 Cir., 262 F.2d 51, we referred the case back to the tax court to consider interest as a deductible item for the lessee. We think it is clearly called for here. Two yardsticks are present. The first is found in that the normal selling price of the system was $4,960 while the total rental payments for five years were $6,200. The difference could be regarded as interest for the five years on an amortized basis. The second measure is in clause 16 (loss by fire), where the figure of six per cent per annum discount is used. An allowance might be made on either basis, division of the difference (for the five years) between 'rental payments' and 'normal purchase price' of $1,240, or six per cent per annum on the normal purchase price of $4,960, converting the annual payments into amortization. We do not believe that the 'lessee' should suffer the pains of a loss for what really was paid for the use of another's money, even though for tax purposes his lease collapses.

We do not criticize the commissioner. It is his duty to collect the revenue and it is a tough one. If he resolves all questions in favor of the taxpayers, we soon would have little revenue. However, we do suggest that after he has made allowance for depreciation, which he concedes, and an allowance for interest, the attack on many of the 'leases' may not be worth while in terms of revenue.

Decision reversed for proceedings consistent herewith.

NOTES AND COMMENTS

As indicated by *Starr*, litigation on the lease versus sale issue continues unabated. Thus, in *Lester v. Commissioner*, 32 T.C. 711 (1959), a company that sold equipment and also leased similar equipment, with the purchaser having an option to purchase at the same price as the sale price with rental payments applied to the purchase price if the option was exercised, was required, as the Service determined, to treat payments received prior to exercise as rentals, based on a finding that the rentals were fair rental prices and that the agreement was intended as rents, noting that the company depreciated the equipment until the option was exercised. On the other hand, in *M & W Gear Co. v. Commissioner*, 446 F.2d 841 (7th Cir. 1971), the court upheld a Service determination that a purported lease of farm land was a sale on the basis that the annual rent for five years was about twice the rental value, while the option price was less than the fair market value of the farm at the time the lease with option was granted. There was also evidence of computations indicating that an interest factor was included in determining the option price. Yet in *Highland Farms v. Commissioner*, 106 T.C. 237 (1996), the Tax Court upheld the Service's determination that sales of cluster houses in a retirement community on land leased to the purchasers were sales, not leases, so that the operator of the retirement community could not claim depreciation, even though the seller-operator was required to repurchase the cluster houses at a price equal to at least 76 percent of the initial sale price, and the purchasers were required to sell at that price, giving the seller-operator the benefit of any appreciation, but protecting the purchasers from the detriment of decline in value. In addition, the purchasers were required to pay the real estate taxes and, apparently, claimed interest and tax deductions. On this basis. and in reliance on local law, the transactions were held to be sales. None of the cases mentioned Rev. Rul. 55-540. There does not seem to be any common thread among these decisions except that the Service won them all. The taxpayers were stuck with their contractual characterizations in *Lester* and *Highland Farms*, but the Service was allowed to reject the taxpayers' contractual characterization in *M & W Gear.*

PROBLEM FOR DISCUSSION

Problem 7-6. How would *Starr* (sprinkler lease); *Lester* (equipment lease with option to purchase treated as lease until option exercised), *M & W. Gear* (lease of farm land with option is a sale), and *Highland Farms* (cluster houses on leased land were sales) come out if the standards of Rev. Rul. 55-540 were applied?

§ 1.05. Leveraged Leasing

The finance aspect of long-term leases is on stark display in leveraged leases. These differ from the leases considered in the preceding section in two significant, interrelated aspects: (i) they almost inevitably involve "big ticket" items — very expensive equipment or real estate; and (ii) the property involved is financed by a (usually nonrecourse) loan to the lessor that, effectively, relies more on the credit of the lessee-user than on that of the lessor-lender. In other words, the primary security for the financing loan to the lessor is the lease, which is usually in the form of a "hell-or-high-water lease," under which the user promises to pay the specified rent to the lessor (and indirectly to the lender) regardless of any default by the lessor in its obligations under the lease or any other circumstances that interfere with the lessee's use of the property, including destruction or condemnation. The leases are also usually "triple net" leases, in which the lessee agrees to pay all expenses of operating the leased property, all taxes, and all insurance, so that the rent is pure profit, subject, of course to the principal and interest payments owed by the lessor on the financing. The transactions sometimes involve financing the initial acquisition of the property and sometimes are sale-leasebacks in which the user deliberately recognizes the unrealized gain on the property for accounting purposes without losing the use of the property.

The parties to leveraged lease transactions agree on two major things: (i) the lessee should have as much as possible of the benefits and burdens of the property and (ii) the lessor should have the tax benefits of ownership. A major purpose of leveraged leasing is to pass on those tax benefits from the lessee who cannot use them to the lessor who can, with the understanding that the lessor will pass some of those benefits back to the lessee in the form of reduced rents. On the other hand, the lessee wants to be absolutely sure that it has complete control over the use of the property, including, as a practical matter, any residual economic benefit of the property at the conclusion of the lease term. The lessor, on the other hand, usually has no interest in using the property or obtaining those residual economic benefits as long as the lease rentals during any primary term are sufficient to provide it with an adequate return on its money. Accordingly, the lessee is happy to take the risk and residual, and the lessor is happy to get rid of them. Unfortunately for the parties, the tax law conditions the lessor's entitlement to the tax benefits of ownership on its bearing the benefits and burdens of tax ownership that it does not want, but the lessee is quite willing to accept. Thus, there is no real conflict between the parties to the transaction, but a conflict between each party's own tax goals and its economic desires, which must be resolved by giving the lessor the minimum benefits and burdens necessary to satisfy the tax requirements (and any similar requirements to achieve the desired accounting, commercial law, bankruptcy, or other governing legal treatment). *See* Charles I. Kingson, *The Confusion Over Tax Ownership*, 93 Tax Notes 409 (2001) ((i) the assignment of tax attributes should follow tax ownership; (ii) the criteria for determining such ownership should not vary for different kinds of property; (iii) those criteria should be risk and reward in the property; and (iv) whether transactions between unrelated parties should be treated as steps in a single transaction should be determined as an issue of tax ownership). The following is the leading Supreme Court case on leveraged leasing.

FRANK LYON CO. v. UNITED STATES

Supreme Court of the United States
435 U.S. 561 (1978)

MR. JUSTICE BLACKMUN delivered the opinion of the Court.

This case concerns the federal income tax consequences of a sale-and-leaseback in which petitioner Frank Lyon Company (Lyon) took title to a building under construction by Worthen Bank & Trust Company (Worthen) of Little Rock, Ark., and simultaneously leased the building back to Worthen for long-term use as its headquarters and principal banking facility.

* * *

Lyon is a closely held Arkansas corporation engaged in the distribution of home furnishings . . . Worthen in 1965 was an Arkansas-chartered bank and a member of the Federal Reserve System. Frank Lyon was Lyon's majority shareholder and board chairman; he also served on Worthen's board. Worthen at that time began to plan the construction of a multistory bank and office building to replace its existing facility in Little Rock. About the same time Worthen's competitor, Union National Bank of Little Rock, also began to plan a new bank and office building. . . . It became a matter of competition, for both banking business and tenants, and prestige as to which bank would start and complete its building first.

Worthen initially hoped to finance, to build, and to own the proposed facility at a total cost of $9 million . . . This was to be accomplished by selling $4 million in debentures and using the proceeds in the acquisition of the capital stock of a wholly owned real estate subsidiary. This subsidiary would have formal title and would raise the remaining $5 million by a conventional mortgage loan on the new premises. Worthen's plan, however, had to be abandoned for two significant reasons:

1. As a bank chartered under Arkansas law, Worthen legally could not pay more interest on any debentures it might issue than that then specified by Arkansas law. But the proposed obligations would not be marketable at that rate.

2. Applicable statutes or regulations of the Arkansas State Bank Department and the Federal Reserve System required Worthen, as a state bank subject to their supervision, to obtain prior permission for the investment in banking premises of any amount (including that placed in a real estate subsidiary) in excess of the bank's capital stock or of 40% of its capital stock and surplus. . . . Worthen, accordingly, was advised by staff employees of the Federal Reserve System that they would not recommend approval of the plan by the System's Board of Governors.

Worthen therefore was forced to seek an alternative solution that would provide it with the use of the building, satisfy the state and federal regulators, and attract the necessary capital. In September 1967 it proposed a sale-and-leaseback arrangement. The State Bank Department and the Federal Reserve System approved this approach, but the Department required that Worthen possess an option to purchase the leased property at the end of the 15th year of the lease at a set price, and the federal regulator required that the building be owned by an independent third party.

Detailed negotiations ensued with investors that had indicated interest, namely, Goldman, Sachs & Company; White, Weld & Co.; Eastman Dillon, Union Securities & Company; and Stephens, Inc. Certain of these firms made specific proposals.

Worthen then obtained a commitment from New York Life Insurance Company to provide $7,140,000 in permanent mortgage financing on the building, conditioned upon its approval of the titleholder. At this point Lyon entered the negotiations and it, too, made a proposal.

Worthen submitted a counterproposal that incorporated the best features, from its point of view, of the several offers. . . . Worthen selected Lyon as the investor. After further negotiations, . . . Lyon in November 1967 was approved as an acceptable borrower by First National City Bank for the construction financing, and by New York Life, as the permanent lender. In April 1968 the approvals of the state and federal regulators were received.

In the meantime, on September 15, before Lyon was selected, Worthen itself began construction.

B

In May 1968 Worthen, Lyon, City Bank, and New York Life executed complementary and interlocking agreements under which the building was sold by Worthen to Lyon as it was constructed, and Worthen leased the completed building back from Lyon.

1. Agreements between Worthen and Lyon. Worthen and Lyon executed a ground lease, a sales agreement, and a building lease.

Under the ground lease dated May 1, 1968, . . . Worthen leased the site to Lyon for 76 years and 7 months through November 30, 2044. The first 19 months were the estimated construction period. The ground rents payable by Lyon to Worthen were $50 for the first 26 years and 7 months and thereafter in quarterly payments:

12/1/94 through 11/30/99 (5 years)	$100,000 annually
12/1/99 through 11/30/04 (5 years)	$150,000 annually
12/1/04 through 11/30/09 (5 years)	$200,000 annually
12/1/09 through 11/30/34 (25 years)	$250,000 annually
12/1/34 through 11/30/44 (10 years)	$10,000 annually.

Under the sales agreement dated May 19, 1968, . . . Worthen agreed to sell the building to Lyon, and Lyon agreed to buy it, piece by piece as it was constructed, for a total price not to exceed $7,640,000, in reimbursements to Worthen for its expenditures for the construction of the building.[2]

---

[2] This arrangement appeared advisable and was made because purchases of materials by Worthen (which then had become a national bank) were not subject to Arkansas sales tax. . . . Sales of the

Under the building lease dated May 1, 1968, . . . Lyon leased the building back to Worthen for a primary term of 25 years from December 1, 1969, with options in Worthen to extend the lease for eight additional 5-year terms, a total of 65 years. During the period between the expiration of the building lease (at the latest, November 30, 2034, if fully extended) and the end of the ground lease on November 30, 2044, full ownership, use, and control of the building were Lyon's, unless, of course, the building had been repurchased by Worthen. . . . Worthen was not obligated to pay rent under the building lease until completion of the building. For the first 11 years of the lease, that is, until November 30, 1980, the stated quarterly rent was $145,581.03 ($582,324.12 for the year). For the next 14 years, the quarterly rent was $153,289.32 ($613,157.28 for the year), and for the option periods the rent was $300,000 a year, payable quarterly. . . . The total rent for the building over the 25-year primary term of the lease thus was $14,989,767.24. That rent equaled the principal and interest payments that would amortize the $7,140,000 New York Life mortgage loan over the same period. When the mortgage was paid off at the end of the primary term, the annual building rent, if Worthen extended the lease, came down to the stated $300,000. Lyon's net rentals from the building would be further reduced by the increase in ground rent Worthen would receive from Lyon during the extension.[3]

The building lease was a "net lease," under which Worthen was responsible for all expenses usually associated with the maintenance of an office building, including repairs, taxes, utility charges, and insurance, and was to keep the premises in good condition, excluding, however, reasonable wear and tear.

Finally, under the lease, Worthen had the option to repurchase the building at the following times and prices:

11/30/80 (after 11 years)	$6,325,169.85
11/30/84 (after 15 years)	$5,432,607.32
11/30/89 (after 20 years)	$4,187,328.04
11/30/94 (after 25 years)	$2,145,935.00

These repurchase option prices were the sum of the unpaid balance of the New York Life mortgage, Lyon's $500,000 investment, and 6% interest compounded on that investment.

2. Construction financing agreement. By agreement dated May 14, 1968, . . . City Bank agreed to lend Lyon $7,000,000 for the construction of the building. This loan was secured by a mortgage on the building and the parking deck, executed by

---

building elements to Lyon also were not subject to state sales tax, since they were sales of real estate. . . .

[3] This, of course, is on the assumption that Worthen exercises its option to extend the building lease. If it does not, Lyon remains liable for the substantial rents prescribed by the ground lease. This possibility brings into sharp focus the fact that Lyon, in a very practical sense, is at least the ultimate owner of the building. If Worthen does not extend, the building lease expires and Lyon may do with the building as it chooses.

The Government would point out, however, that the net amounts payable by Worthen to Lyon during the building lease's extended terms, if all are claimed, would approximate the amount required to repay Lyon's $500,000 investment at 6% compound interest.

Worthen as well as by Lyon, and an assignment by Lyon of its interests in the building lease and in the ground lease.

3. Permanent financing agreement. By Note Purchase Agreement dated May 1, 1968, . . . New York Life agreed to purchase Lyon's $7,140,000 6 3/4% 25-year secured note to be issued upon completion of the building. Under this agreement Lyon warranted that it would lease the building to Worthen for a noncancelable term of at least 25 years under a net lease at a rent at least equal to the mortgage payments on the note. Lyon agreed to make quarterly payments of principal and interest equal to the rentals payable by Worthen during the corresponding primary term of the lease. . . . The security for the note was a first deed of trust and Lyon's assignment of its interests in the building lease and in the ground lease. . . . Worthen joined in the deed of trust as the owner of the fee and the parking deck.

In December 1969 the building was completed and Worthen took possession. . . . The actual cost of constructing the office building and parking complex (excluding the cost of the land) exceeded $10,000,000.

* * *

On audit of Lyon's 1969 return, the Commissioner of Internal Revenue determined that Lyon was "not the owner for tax purposes of any portion of the Worthen Building," and ruled that "the income and expenses related to this building are not allowable . . . for Federal income tax purposes." . . . In other words, the Commissioner determined that the sale-and-leaseback arrangement was a financing transaction in which Lyon loaned Worthen $500,000 and acted as a conduit for the transmission of principal and interest from Worthen to New York Life.

* * *

After trial without a jury, the District Court, in a memorandum letter-opinion setting forth findings and conclusions, ruled in Lyon's favor and held that its claimed deductions were allowable. . . . It concluded that the legal intent of the parties had been to create a bona fide sale-and-leaseback in accordance with the form and language of the documents evidencing the transactions. It rejected the argument that Worthen was acquiring an equity in the building through its rental payments. It found that the rents were unchallenged and were reasonable throughout the period of the lease, and that the option prices, negotiated at arm's length between the parties, represented fair estimates of market value on the applicable dates. It rejected any negative inference from the fact that the rentals, combined with the options, were sufficient to amortize the New York Life loan and to pay Lyon a 6% return on its equity investment. It found that Worthen would acquire an equity in the building only if it exercised one of its options to purchase, and that it was highly unlikely, as a practical matter, that any purchase option would ever be exercised. It rejected any inference to be drawn from the fact that the lease was a "net lease." It found that Lyon had mixed motivations for entering into the transaction, including the need to diversify as well as the desire to have the benefits of a "tax shelter." . . .

The United States Court of Appeals for the Eighth Circuit . . . held that the Commissioner correctly determined that Lyon was not the true owner of the building and therefore was not entitled to the claimed deductions. . . . It stressed the following: (a) The lease agreements circumscribed Lyon's right to profit from its investment in the building by giving Worthen the option to purchase for an amount equal to Lyon's $500,000 equity plus 6% compound interest and the assumption of the unpaid balance of the New York Life mortgage. (b) The option prices did not take into account possible appreciation of the value of the building or inflation. (c) Any award realized as a result of destruction or condemnation of the building in excess of the mortgage balance and the $500,000 would be paid to Worthen and not Lyon. (d) The building rental payments during the primary term were exactly equal to the mortgage payments. (e) Worthen retained control over the ultimate disposition of the building through its various options to repurchase and to renew the lease plus its ownership of the site. (f) Worthen enjoyed all benefits and bore all burdens incident to the operation and ownership of the building so that, in the Court of Appeals' view, the only economic advantages accruing to Lyon, in the event it were considered to be the true owner of the property, were income tax savings of approximately $1.5 million during the first 11 years of the arrangement. . . . The court concluded . . . that the transaction was "closely akin" to that in *Helvering v. Lazarus & Co.*, . . . "In sum, the benefits, risks, and burdens which [Lyon] has incurred with respect to the Worthen building are simply too insubstantial to establish a claim to the status of owner for tax purposes. . . . The vice of the present lease is that all of [its] features have been employed in the same transaction with the cumulative effect of depriving [Lyon] of any significant ownership interest." . . .

* * *

This Court, almost 50 years ago, observed that "taxation is not so much concerned with the refinements of title as it is with actual command over the property taxed — the actual benefit for which the tax is paid." . . . In a number of cases, the Court has refused to permit the transfer of formal legal title to shift the incidence of taxation attributable to ownership of property where the transferor continues to retain significant control over the property transferred. . . . Nor is the parties' desire to achieve a particular tax result necessarily relevant. . . .

In the light of these general and established principles, the Government takes the position that the Worthen-Lyon transaction in its entirety should be regarded as a sham. The agreement as a whole, it is said, was only an elaborate financing scheme designed to provide economic benefits to Worthen and a guaranteed return to Lyon. The latter was but a conduit used to forward the mortgage payments, made under the guise of rent paid by Worthen to Lyon, on to New York Life as mortgagee. This, the Government claims, is the true substance of the transaction as viewed under the microscope of the tax laws. Although the arrangement was cast in sale-and-leaseback form, in substance it was only a financing transaction, and the terms of the repurchase options and lease renewals so indicate. It is said that Worthen could reacquire the building simply by satisfying the mortgage debt and paying Lyon its $500,000 advance plus interest, regardless of the fair market value of the building at the time; similarly, when the mortgage was paid off, Worthen could extend the lease at drastically reduced bargain rentals that likewise bore no relation to fair rental value but were simply calculated to pay Lyon its $500,000 plus interest over the extended term. Lyon's return on the arrangement in no event could exceed 6% compound interest (although the Government conceded it might well be less . . .).

Furthermore, the favorable option and lease renewal terms made it highly unlikely that Worthen would abandon the building after it in effect had "paid off" the mortgage. The Government implies that the arrangement was one of convenience which, if accepted on its face, would enable Worthen to deduct its payments to Lyon as rent and would allow Lyon to claim a deduction for depreciation, based on the cost of construction ultimately borne by Worthen, which Lyon could offset against other income, and to deduct mortgage interest that roughly would offset the inclusion of Worthen's rental payments in Lyon's income. If, however, the Government argues, the arrangement was only a financing transaction under which Worthen was the owner of the building, Worthen's payments would be deductible only to the extent that they represented mortgage interest, and Worthen would be entitled to claim depreciation; Lyon would not be entitled to deductions for either mortgage interest or depreciation and it would not have to include Worthen's "rent" payments in its income because its function with respect to those payments was that of a conduit between Worthen and New York Life.

The Government places great reliance on *Helvering v. Lazarus & Co.* . . . and claims it to be precedent that controls this case. The taxpayer there was a department store. The legal title of its three buildings was in a bank as trustee for land-trust certificate holders. When the transfer to the trustee was made, the trustee at the same time leased the buildings back to the taxpayer for 99 years, with option to renew and purchase. The Commissioner, in stark contrast to his posture in the present case, took the position that the statutory right to depreciation followed legal title. The Board of Tax Appeals, however, concluded that the transaction between the taxpayer and the bank in reality was a mortgage loan and allowed the taxpayer depreciation on the buildings. This Court, as had the Court of Appeals, agreed with that conclusion and affirmed. It regarded the "rent" stipulated in the leaseback as a promise to pay interest on the loan, and a "depreciation fund" required by the lease as an amortization fund designed to pay off the loan in the stated period. Thus, said the Court, the Board justifiably concluded that the transaction, although in written form a transfer of ownership with a leaseback, was actually a loan secured by the property involved.

The *Lazarus* case, we feel, is to be distinguished from the present one and is not controlling here. Its transaction was one involving only two (and not multiple) parties, the taxpayer-department store and the trustee-bank. The Court looked closely at the substance of the agreement between those two parties and rightly concluded that depreciation was deductible by the taxpayer despite the nomenclature of the instrument of conveyance and the leaseback. . . .

The present case, in contrast, involves three parties, Worthen, Lyon, and the finance agency. The usual simple two-party arrangement was legally unavailable to Worthen. Independent investors were interested in participating in the alternative available to Worthen, and Lyon itself (also independent from Worthen) won the privilege. Despite Frank Lyon's presence on Worthen's board of directors, the transaction, as it ultimately developed, was not a familial one arranged by Worthen, but one compelled by the realities of the restrictions imposed upon the bank. Had Lyon not appeared, another interested investor would have been selected. The ultimate solution would have been essentially the same. Thus, the presence of the third party, in our view, significantly distinguishes this case from *Lazarus* and removes the latter as controlling authority.

III

It is true, of course, that the transaction took shape according to Worthen's needs. As the Government points out, Worthen throughout the negotiations regarded the respective proposals of the independent investors in terms of its own cost of funds. . . . It is also true that both Worthen and the prospective investors compared the various proposals in terms of the return anticipated on the investor's equity. But all this is natural for parties contemplating entering into a transaction of this kind. Worthen needed a building for its banking operations and other purposes and necessarily had to know what its cost would be. The investors were in business to employ their funds in the most remunerative way possible. And, as the Court has said in the past, a transaction must be given its effect in accord with what actually occurred and not in accord with what might have occurred. *Commissioner v. National Alfalfa*. . . .

There is no simple device available to peel away the form of this transaction and to reveal its substance. The effects of the transaction on all the parties were obviously different from those that would have resulted had Worthen been able simply to make a mortgage agreement with New York Life and to receive a $500,000 loan from Lyon. Then *Lazarus* would apply. Here, however, and most significantly, it was Lyon alone, and not Worthen, who was liable on the notes, first to City Bank, and then to New York Life. Despite the facts that Worthen had agreed to pay rent and that this rent equaled the amounts due from Lyon to New York Life, should anything go awry in the later years of the lease, Lyon was primarily liable. No matter how the transaction could have been devised otherwise, it remains a fact that as the agreements were placed in final form, the obligation on the notes fell squarely on Lyon. Lyon, an ongoing enterprise, exposed its very business well-being to this real and substantial risk.

The effect of this liability on Lyon is not just the abstract possibility that something will go wrong and that Worthen will not be able to make its payments. Lyon has disclosed this liability on its balance sheet for all the world to see. Its financial position was affected substantially by the presence of this long-term debt, despite the offsetting presence of the building as an asset. To the extent that Lyon has used its capital in this transaction, it is less able to obtain financing for other business needs.

In concluding that there is this distinct element of economic reality in Lyon's assumption of liability, we are mindful that the characterization of a transaction for financial accounting purposes, on the one hand, and for tax purposes, on the other, need not necessarily be the same. . . . Accounting methods or descriptions, without more, do not lend substance to that which has no substance. But in this case accepted accounting methods, as understood by the several parties to the respective agreements and as applied to the transaction by others, gave the transaction a meaningful character consonant with the form it was given.[14] Worthen was not

[14] We are aware that accounting standards have changed significantly since 1968 and that the

allowed to enter into the type of transaction which the Government now urges to be the true substance of the arrangement. Lyon and Worthen cannot be said to have entered into the transaction intending that the interests involved were allocated in a way other than that associated with a sale-and-leaseback.

Other factors also reveal that the transaction cannot be viewed as anything more than a mortgage agreement between Worthen and New York Life and a loan from Lyon to Worthen. There is no legal obligation between Lyon and Worthen representing the $500,000 "loan" extended under the Government's theory. And the assumed 6% return on this putative loan — required by the audit to be recognized in the taxable year in question — will be realized only when and if Worthen exercises its options.

The Court of Appeals acknowledged that the rents alone, due after the primary term of the lease and after the mortgage has been paid, do not provide the simple 6% return which, the Government urges, Lyon is guaranteed . . . Thus, if Worthen chooses not to exercise its options, Lyon is gambling that the rental value of the building during the last 10 years of the ground lease, during which the ground rent is minimal, will be sufficient to recoup its investment before it must negotiate again with Worthen regarding the ground lease. There are simply too many contingencies, including variations in the value of real estate, in the cost of money, and in the capital structure of Worthen, to permit the conclusion that the parties intended to enter into the transaction as structured in the audit and according to which the Government now urges they be taxed.

It is not inappropriate to note that the Government is likely to lose little revenue, if any, as a result of the shape given the transaction by the parties. No deduction was created that is not either matched by an item of income or that would not have been available to one of the parties if the transaction had been arranged differently. While it is true that Worthen paid Lyon less to induce it to enter into the transaction because Lyon anticipated the benefit of the depreciation deductions it would have as the owner of the building, those deductions would have been equally available to Worthen had it retained title to the building. The Government so concedes. . . . The fact that favorable tax consequences were taken into account by Lyon on entering into the transaction is no reason for disallowing those consequences.[15] We

---

propriety of Worthen's and Lyon's methods of disclosing the transaction in question may be a matter for debate under these new standards. . . .

Then-existing pronouncements of the Internal Revenue Service gave Lyon very little against which to measure the transaction. The most complete statement on the general question of characterization of leases as sales, Rev. Rul. 55-540, . . . by its terms dealt only with equipment leases. . . .

The Service announced more specific guidelines, indicating under what circumstances it would answer requests for rulings on leverage leasing transactions, in Rev. Proc. 75-21. . . . These guidelines are not intended to be definitive, and it is not clear that they provide much guidance in assessing real estate transactions. . . .

[15] Indeed, it is not inevitable that the transaction, as treated by Lyon and Worthen, will not result in more revenues to the Government rather than less. Lyon is gambling that in the first 11 years of the lease it will have income that will be sheltered by the depreciation deductions, and that it will be able to make sufficiently good use of the tax dollars preserved thereby to make up for the income it will recognize and pay taxes on during the last 14 years of the initial term of the lease and against which it will enjoy no sheltering deduction.

cannot ignore the reality that the tax laws affect the shape of nearly every business transaction. See *Commissioner v. Brown* . . . (Harlan, J., concurring). Lyon is not a corporation with no purpose other than to hold title to the bank building. It was not created by Worthen or even financed to any degree by Worthen. We cannot ignore the reality that the tax laws affect the shape of nearly every business transaction.

The conclusion that the transaction is not a simple sham to be ignored does not, of course, automatically compel the further conclusion that Lyon is entitled to the items claimed as deductions. Nevertheless, on the facts, this readily follows. As has been noted, the obligations on which Lyon paid interest were its obligations alone, and it is entitled to claim deductions therefor under § 163(a). . . .

As is clear from the facts, none of the parties to this sale-and-leaseback was the owner of the building in any simple sense. But it is equally clear that the facts focus upon Lyon as the one whose capital was committed to the building and as the party, therefore, that was entitled to claim depreciation for the consumption of that capital. The Government has based its contention that Worthen should be treated as the owner on the assumption that throughout the term of the lease Worthen was acquiring an equity in the property. In order to establish the presence of that growing equity, however, the Government is forced to speculate that one of the options will be exercised and that, if it is not, this is only because the rentals for the extended term are a bargain. We cannot indulge in such speculation in view of the District Court's clear finding to the contrary. We therefore conclude that it is Lyon's capital that is invested in the building according to the agreement of the parties, and it is Lyon that is entitled to depreciation deductions, under § 167. . . .

IV

We recognize that the Government's position, and that taken by the Court of Appeals, is not without superficial appeal. One, indeed, may theorize that Frank Lyon's presence on the Worthen board of directors; Lyon's departure from its principal corporate activity into this unusual venture; the parallel between the payments under the building lease and the amounts due from Lyon on the New York Life mortgage; the provisions relating to condemnation or destruction of the property; the nature and presence of the several options available to Worthen; and the tax benefits, such as the use of double declining balance depreciation, that accrue to Lyon during the initial years of the arrangement, form the basis of an argument that Worthen should be regarded as the owner of the building and as the recipient of nothing more from Lyon than a $500,000 loan.

We, however, as did the District Court, find this theorizing incompatible with the substance and economic realities of the transaction: the competitive situation as it existed between Worthen and Union National Bank in 1965 and the years immediately following; Worthen's undercapitalization; Worthen's consequent inability, as a matter of legal restraint, to carry its building plans into effect by a conventional mortgage and other borrowing; the additional barriers imposed by the state and federal regulators; the suggestion, forthcoming from the state regulator, that Worthen possess an option to purchase; the requirement, from the federal regulator, that the building be owned by an independent third party; the presence of several finance organizations seriously interested in participating in the transaction and in the resolution of Worthen's problem; the submission of formal proposals by several of those organizations; the bargaining process and period that ensued; the competitiveness of the bidding; the bona fide character of the negotiations; the three-party aspect of the transaction; Lyon's substantiality and its independence from Worthen; the fact that diversification was Lyon's principal motivation; Lyon's being liable alone on the successive notes to City Bank and New York Life; the reasonableness, as the District Court found, of the rentals and of the option prices; the substantiality of the purchase prices; Lyon's not being engaged generally in the business of financing; the presence of all building depreciation risks on Lyon; the risk, borne by Lyon, that Worthen might default or fail, as other banks have failed; the facts that Worthen could "walk away" from the relationship at the end of the 25-year primary term, and probably would do so if the option price were more than the then-current worth of the building to Worthen; the inescapable fact that if the building lease were not extended, Lyon would be the full owner of the building, free to do with it as it chose; Lyon's liability for the substantial ground rent if Worthen decides not to exercise any of its options to extend; the absence of any understanding between Lyon and Worthen that Worthen would exercise any of the purchase options; the nonfamily and nonprivate nature of the entire transaction; and the absence of any differential in tax rates and of special tax circumstances for one of the parties — all convince us that Lyon has far the better of the case.[18]

In so concluding, we emphasize that we are not condoning manipulation by a taxpayer through arbitrary labels and dealings that have no economic significance. Such, however, has not happened in this case.

In short, we hold that where, as here, there is a genuine multiple-party transaction with economic substance which is compelled or encouraged by business or regulatory realities, is imbued with tax-independent considerations, and is not shaped solely by tax-avoidance features that have meaningless labels attached, the Government should honor the allocation of rights and duties effectuated by the parties. Expressed another way, so long as the lessor retains significant and genuine attributes of the traditional lessor status, the form of the transaction adopted by the parties governs for tax purposes. What those attributes are in any particular case will necessarily depend upon its facts. It suffices to say that, as here, a sale-and-leaseback, in and of itself, does not necessarily operate to deny a taxpayer's claim for deductions.

* * *

MR. JUSTICE STEVENS, dissenting.

In my judgment the controlling issue in this case is the economic relationship between Worthen and petitioner, and matters such as the number of parties, their reasons for structuring the transaction in a particular way, and the tax benefits

---

[18] Thus, the facts of this case stand in contrast to many others in which the form of the transaction actually created tax advantages that, for one reason or another, could not have been enjoyed had the transaction taken another form. . . . Indeed, the arrangements in this case can hardly be labeled as tax-avoidance techniques in light of the other arrangements being promoted at the time. . . .

which may result, are largely irrelevant. The question whether a leasehold has been created should be answered by examining the character and value of the purported lessor's reversionary estate.

For a 25-year period Worthen has the power to acquire full ownership of the bank building by simply repaying the amounts, plus interest, advanced by the New York Life Insurance Company and petitioner. During that period, the economic relationship among the parties parallels exactly the normal relationship between an owner and two lenders, one secured by a first mortgage and the other by a second mortgage. If Worthen repays both loans, it will have unencumbered ownership of the property. What the character of this relationship suggests is confirmed by the economic value that the parties themselves have placed on the reversionary interest.

All rental payments made during the original 25-year term are credited against the option repurchase price, which is exactly equal to the unamortized cost of the financing. The value of the repurchase option is thus limited to the cost of the financing, and Worthen's power to exercise the option is cost-free. Conversely, petitioner, the nominal owner of the reversionary estate, is not entitled to receive any value for the surrender of its supposed rights of ownership.[2] Nor does it have any power to control Worthen's exercise of the option.

"It is fundamental that 'depreciation is not predicated upon ownership of property *but rather upon an investment in property.*' No such investment exists when payments of the purchase price in accordance with the design of the parties yield no equity to the purchaser." *Estate of Franklin* . . . Here, the petitioner has, in effect, been guaranteed that it will receive its original $500,000 plus accrued interest. But that is all. It incurs neither the risk of depreciation, nor the benefit of possible appreciation. Under the terms of the sale-leaseback, it will stand in no better or worse position after the 11th year of the lease — when Worthen can first exercise its option to repurchase — whether the property has appreciated or depreciated. And this remains true throughout the rest of the 25-year period.

Petitioner has assumed only two significant risks. First, like any other lender, it assumed the risk of Worthen's insolvency. Second, it assumed the risk that Worthen might *not* exercise its option to purchase at or before the end of the original 25-year term. If Worthen should exercise that right *not* to repay, perhaps it would *then* be appropriate to characterize petitioner as the owner and Worthen as the lessee. But speculation as to what might happen in 25 years cannot justify the *present* characterization of petitioner as the owner of the building. Until Worthen has made a commitment either to exercise or not to exercise its option, I think the Government is correct in its view that petitioner is not the owner of the building for tax purposes. At present, since Worthen has the unrestricted right to control the

---

[2] It is worth noting that the proposals submitted by two other potential investors in the building . . . did contemplate that Worthen would pay a price above the financing costs for acquisition of the leasehold interest. For instance, Goldman, Sachs & Company proposed that, at the end of the lease's primary term, Worthen would have the option to repurchase the property for either its fair market value or 20% of its original cost, whichever was the greater. . . . A repurchase option based on fair market value, since it acknowledges the lessor's equity interest in the property, is consistent with a lessor-lessee relationship. . . .

residual value of the property for a price which does not exceed the cost of its unamortized financing, I would hold, as a matter of law, that it is the owner.

In effect, Worthen has an option to "put" the building to petitioner if it drops in value below $500,000 plus interest. Even if the "put" appears likely because of bargain lease rates after the primary terms, that would not justify the present characterization of petitioner as the owner of the building.

I therefore respectfully dissent.

NOTES AND COMMENTS

Lyon seems to be a strange case for the Service to have sought and been granted certiorari by the Supreme Court because it involved recourse financing, while virtually all tax shelter cases, including *Franklin* (nonrecourse liability for 100 percent of purchase price in tax-shelter sale and leaseback not recognized for tax purposes), discussed in § 3.02, *Contingencies* of Chapter 3, *Liabilities: Discharge of Indebtedness; Mortgaged Property;* and in *Brountas* (nonrecourse notes secured by production from wildcat wells are too speculative to be given tax effect), discussed in § 3.03 *Speculative Security* of Chapter 3, involve nonrecourse financing. Apparently, as a result, the Court found that the transaction was a true lease, in part on the basis that Lyon had the burden in the form of the risk of the liability for the financing of the Worthen building, even though it did not have the benefit of a meaningful residual in the building. On the other hand, this can be viewed as a case that was won in the trial court. Note, particularly, the paragraph beginning "[a]fter trial without a jury . . . " Although these findings may strain credulity, they are the findings of the trier of fact that are hard to overcome on appeal. The court of appeals, nevertheless, did so, but the Supreme Court accepted them. The decision leaves considerable uncertainty, however, in view of the 25 factors listed in the third from last paragraph of Justice Blackmun's opinion. Even the final summary in the last paragraph provides little guidance from which to draw any standard from the decision. Putting *Brown* and *Lyon* together — *Brown* concluded that a benefit in the form of an expected residual value, without risk, gives ownership, while *Lyon* concluded that risk, in the form of a liability if Worthen defaulted on the lease, without any real benefit in the form of expected residual value if Worthen exercised its option (subject to the trial court's dubious finding that it was unlikely as a practical matter that Worthen would do so) gives ownership. Moreover, the Court distinguished the decision in *Lazarus* on the ground that Lyon was a three-party deal, while *Lazarus* was a two-party deal. This is also true of *Brown* and the transactions in Rev. Rul. 55-540, but that cannot be the deciding factor. But then, what is?

The practical gap between the unusual recourse loan in *Lyon* and the usual nonrecourse leveraged lease was addressed in *Hilton* v. *Commissioner*, 74 T.C. 305 (1980), *aff'd per curiam* 671 F.2d 316 (9th Cir. 1982), *cert. denied*, 459 U.S. 907 (1982), although not in those terms. In *Hilton*, a large department store chain that had used sale-and-leaseback financing stores for many years, apparently, because of accounting, financial covenant considerations, as well as insurance regulatory considerations of the lender, arranged an insurance company sale and leaseback transaction (with a triple net lease) through a single-purpose financing corporation as lessor. All of the basic terms of the deal were arranged between the department store chain and the insurance companies and the tax shelter promoter as lessor before the tax shelter investors came on the scene. Indeed, the stores were built and occupied before then. The capital contributions made by Hilton and the other tax-shelter participants, mostly medical doctors, for interests in the lessor partnerships were primarily used to pay fees and compensation to the promoters; none of their contributions were used for the construction of the stores. The Tax Court translated the *Lyon* opinion as imposing four requirements for a leasehold arrangement to be respected. According to the court, a transaction must be tested to see that it be: (i) "genuinely multiple-party," (ii) "with economic substance," (iii) "compelled or encouraged by business realities" (no "regulatory" realities claimed), and (iv) "imbued with tax independent considerations, which are not shaped solely by tax avoidance features." *Hilton*, 74 T.C. at 347. In dealing with the economic substance of the transaction, without expressly acknowledging that it was doing so, the Tax Court substituted an analysis of whether the investors had a genuine hope for economic gain — that is, a *residual* analysis, because the use of the special purpose financing corporation and other financing terms eliminated any *risk* of the type borne by Lyon. It noted several significant differences from *Lyon*, without necessarily spelling out why they were significant: (i) the *Lyon* rent during the initial lease term completely amortized the underlying mortgage principal, while the *Hilton* rent amortized only 90 percent, leaving a sizable balloon at the end; (ii) the *Lyon* rent was fair rental value, while the *Hilton* rent was not; (iii) the buyer-lessor in *Lyon* paid $500,000 of its own funds to the seller-lessee, while all of the tax shelter investors' money in *Hilton* went to the promoters, with none to the project; (iv) the buyer-lessor in *Lyon* stood to realize a substantial gain in the event the seller-lessee exercised its repurchase option,* while the *Hilton* investors could not dispose of the property at a profit; (v) the buyer-lessor in *Lyon* was a substantial corporate entity that participated actively in negotiating the terms and conditions of the sale and leaseback, while in *Hilton* the entire "deal" was packaged as a financing transaction by the orchestrator and marketed as a tax shelter; (vi) the buyer-lessor in *Lyon* was personally liable on the mortgage while the absence of personal liability was considered a neutral factor in *Hilton*. Accordingly, the Tax Court concluded that the taxpayers had failed to satisfy its four-factor test and that its investment vehicle was a mere conduit for funds flowing from the department store chain to the insurance companies.

Because of the importance of the lessor's ability to realize the tax benefits of ownership for the economics of leveraged lease transactions, lessors frequently condition the deal on obtaining a tax ruling. Even if a ruling is not actually obtained, the position of the Service is often crucial to structuring leveraged leasing transactions. The following revenue procedure sets forth the Service's current ruling guidelines. Even though, as stated in § 3, the guidelines are not rules of law, or even significant legal authority, they achieve significant legal effect because many lessors are unwilling to risk deviating from them.

---

* This factor is questionable since the repurchase option during the initial term was a price equal to the mortgage balance + Lyon's $500,000 investment + 6% interest on that investment.

Rev. Proc. 2001-28, 2001-1 C.B. 1156

SECTION 1. PURPOSE

This revenue procedure provides guidelines that the Internal Revenue Service will use for advance ruling purposes in determining whether certain transactions purporting to be leases of property are, in fact, leases for federal income tax purposes. . . .

SECTION 2. BACKGROUND

Section 4.01 of Rev. Rul. 55-540, 1955-2 C.B. 39, sets forth certain conditions that, in the absence of compelling factors of contrary implication, would warrant treatment of a transaction for federal income tax purposes as a conditional sales contract rather than a lease of equipment. . . .

SECTION 3. SCOPE

This revenue procedure applies in the case of transactions commonly called "leveraged leases." Such leases generally involve three parties: a lessor, a lessee and a lender to the lessor. In general, these leases are net leases, the lease term covers a substantial part of the useful life of the leased property, and the lessee's payments to the lessor are sufficient to discharge the lessor's payments to the lender.

The guidelines set forth in this revenue procedure clarify the circumstances in which an advance ruling recognizing the existence of a lease ordinarily will be issued solely to assist taxpayers in preparing ruling requests and the Service in issuing advance ruling letters as promptly as practicable. These guidelines do not define, as a matter of law, whether a transaction is or is not a lease for federal income tax purposes and are not intended to be used for audit purposes.

SECTION 4. GUIDELINES

Unless other facts and circumstances indicate a contrary intent, for advance ruling purposes only, the Service will consider the lessor in a leveraged lease transaction to be the owner of the property and the transaction a valid lease if all the guidelines described below are met. If all of these guidelines are not met, the Service nevertheless will consider ruling in appropriate cases on the basis of all the facts and circumstances.

.01 *Minimum unconditional "at risk" investment*

The lessor must have made a minimum unconditional "at risk" investment in the property (the "Minimum Investment") when the lease begins, must maintain such Minimum Investment throughout the entire lease term, and such Minimum Investment must remain at the end of the lease term. The Minimum Investment must be an equity investment (the "Equity Investment") that, for purposes of this revenue procedure, includes only consideration paid, and personal liability incurred, by the lessor to purchase the property. The net worth of the lessor must be sufficient to satisfy any such personal liability. In determining the lessor's Minimum Investment, the following rules will be applied:

(1) *Initial Minimum Investment.* When the property is first placed in service or use by the lessee, the Minimum Investment must be equal to at least 20 percent of the cost of the property. The Minimum Investment must be unconditional. . . . [T]he lessor must not be entitled to a return of any portion of the Minimum Investment through any arrangement, directly or indirectly, with the lessee, a shareholder of the lessee, or any party related to the lessee . . . (the "Lessee Group"). . . .

(2) *Maintenance of Minimum Investment.* The Minimum Investment must remain equal to at least 20 percent of the cost of the property at all times throughout the entire lease term. That is, the excess of the cumulative payments required to have been paid by the lessee to or for the lessor over the cumulative disbursements required to have been paid by or for the lessor in connection with the ownership of the property must never exceed the sum of (i) any excess of the lessor's initial Equity Investment over 20 percent of the cost of the property plus (ii) the cumulative *pro rata* portion of the projected profit from the transaction (exclusive of tax benefits).

(3) *Residual Investment.* The lessor must represent and demonstrate that an amount equal to at least 20 percent of the original cost of the property is a reasonable estimate of what the fair market value of the property will be at the end of the lease term. For this purpose, fair market value must be determined (i) without including in such value any increase or decrease for inflation or deflation during the lease term, and (ii) after subtracting from such value any cost to the lessor for removal and delivery of possession of the property to the lessor at the end of the lease term. In addition, the lessor must represent and demonstrate that a remaining useful life of the longer of one year or 20 percent of the originally estimated useful life of the property is a reasonable estimate of what the remaining useful life of the property will be at the end of the lease term.

.02 *Lease Term and Renewal Options*

For purposes of this revenue procedure, the lease term includes all renewal or extension periods except renewals or extensions at the option of the lessee at fair rental value at the time of such renewal or extension.

.03 *Purchase and Sale Rights*

No member of the Lessee Group may have a contractual right to purchase the property from the lessor at a price less than its fair market value at the time the right is exercised. When the property is first placed in service or use by the lessee, the lessor may not have a contractual right (except as provided in section 4.01(1) above) to cause any party to purchase the property. The lessor must also represent that it does not have any present intention to acquire such a contractual right. The effect of any such right acquired at a subsequent time will be determined at that time based on all the facts and circumstances. A provision that permits the lessor to abandon the property to any party will be treated as a contractual right of the lessor to cause such party to purchase the property.

.04 *Investment by Lessee*

(1) *Permitted Investments.* Except as otherwise specifically provided in paragraphs (2) and (3) below, no part of the cost of the property or the cost of improvements, modifications, or additions to the property ("Improvements"), may be furnished by any member of the Lessee Group. Property that could itself be separately leased in a transaction eligible for an advance ruling under this revenue procedure does not constitute an Improvement. For example, assume *X* leases a chemical plant from *Y*. Assume further, that after the plant is placed in service, *X* wishes to erect and own additional tanks that will be used to store the output of the plant. Although the tanks will be used in conjunction with *X*'s plant, they constitute separate items of property that could be used in conjunction with other facilities and therefore do not constitute limited use property under section 5.02 of this revenue procedure. If a third party owned the tanks, it could lease them to *X* in a transaction eligible for an advance ruling. Thus, the tanks do not constitute an Improvement.

(2) *Severable Improvements.* A member of the Lessee Group may furnish amounts to pay for the cost of an Improvement that is owned by a member of the Lessee Group, and is readily removable without causing material damage to the leased property ("Severable Improvement"), provided that such Improvement is not subject to a contract or option for purchase or sale between the lessor and any member of the Lessee Group at a price other than fair market value at the time of such purchase or sale. At the commencement of the term of the lease, a Severable Improvement to the leased property must not be required in order to render the leased property complete for its intended use by the lessee. However, property will be considered to be complete even though the lessee may add as Severable Improvements ancillary items of equipment of a kind that customarily are selected and furnished by purchasers or lessees of property of the kind subject to the lease. Thus, for example, to the extent an item of equipment such as the boiler for a leased, steam powered vessel otherwise constituted a Severable Improvement, the vessel would not, for purposes of this section, be considered complete without the boiler. On the other hand, a leased airplane would be considered complete without items of equipment such as aviation electronics and a leased vessel would be considered complete without such ancillary items such as radar, lines, or readily removable fittings, and will be eligible for an advance ruling even though such items of equipment are to be added by the lessee.

(3) *Nonseverable Improvements.* A member of the Lessee Group may furnish amounts to pay for the cost of Improvements that are not readily removable without causing material damage to the property ("Nonseverable Improvements") if they are described in subparagraph (a) below and

the conditions of subparagraph (b) are met.

(a) A Nonseverable Improvement is described in this subparagraph if either:

(i) it is furnished in order to comply with health, safety, or environmental standards of any government or governmental authority having relevant jurisdiction (or any industry-wide standard recognized by such government or governmental authority);

(ii) it does not increase the productivity (or capacity) of the leased property to more than 12.5 percent of its productivity (or capacity) when first placed in service, or modify the leased property for a materially different use. For this purpose, separate units that are subject to one lease (*e.g.*, ten boxcars subject to one lease) are each considered "the leased property;" or

(iii) the cost of the Nonseverable Improvement, when added to the cost of Nonseverable Improvements that previously have been made to the property (other than those described in subparagraph (i) above) does not exceed 10 percent of the cost of the property. For purposes of this subparagraph, the cost of a Nonseverable Improvement will be considered to be the actual cost multiplied by a fraction, the numerator of which is the Implicit Price Deflator for Fixed Nonresidential Investment (published by the Department of Commerce in the Survey of Current Business) for the year in which the property was placed in service, and the denominator of which is the Implicit Price Deflator for Fixed Nonresidential Investment for the year in which the Improvement is made. As indicated in section 4.04(5) of this revenue procedure, ordinary maintenance and repair does not constitute an Improvement.

(b) The following conditions must be satisfied:

(i) At the commencement of the term of the lease, a Nonseverable Improvement must not be required in order to complete the property for its intended use by the lessee;

(ii) The Nonseverable Improvement must not cause the leased property to become limited use property within the meaning of section 5.02 of this revenue procedure; and

(iii) The furnishing of the cost of the Nonseverable Improvement must not constitute an equity investment by a member of the Lessee Group in the property. For this purpose, the lessee's right to use the Improvement during the lease term in which such improvement is made does not constitute an equity investment in the property. The furnishing of such cost will be considered an equity investment in the property if a member of the Lessee Group may receive compensation, directly or indirectly, for its interest in such Nonseverable Improvement. A member of the Lessee Group will be regarded as having made an equity investment in the property if, for example:

— the lessor is obligated to purchase the Nonseverable Improvement or reimburse a member of the Lessee Group for the cost or the fair market value of the Nonseverable Improvement;

— any option price or renewal rental rate to a member of the Lessee Group is adjusted downward to reflect any portion of the cost or fair market value of the Nonseverable Improvement; or

— the lessor is obligated to share with a member of the Lessee Group a portion of the proceeds of any sale or lease of the property to a third party.

(4) *Cost Overruns and Modifications.* If the cost of property exceeds the estimate on which the lease was based, the lease may provide for adjustments of rent to compensate the lessor for such additional cost.

(5) *Maintenance and Repair.* If the lease requires the lessee to maintain and keep the property in good repair during the term of the lease, ordinary maintenance and repairs performed by a member of the Lessee Group will not constitute an Improvement.

.05 *No Lessee Loans or Guarantees*

No member of the Lessee Group may lend to the lessor any of the funds necessary to acquire the property, or guarantee any indebtedness created in connection with the acquisition of the property by the lessor. A guarantee by any member of the Lessee Group of the lessee's obligation to pay rent, properly maintain the property, or pay insurance premiums or other similar conventional obligations of a net lease does not constitute a guarantee of the indebtedness of the lessor.

.06 *Profit Requirement*

The lessor must represent and demonstrate that it expects to receive a profit from the transaction, apart from the value of or benefits obtained from the tax deductions, allowances, credits, and other tax attributes arising from such transaction. This requirement is met if:

(1) *Overall Profit.* The aggregate amount required to be paid by the lessee to or for the lessor over the lease term plus the value of the residual investment referred to in section 4.01(3) of this revenue procedure exceed an amount equal to the sum of the aggregate disbursements required to be paid by or for the lessor in connection with the ownership of the property and the lessor's Equity Investment in the property, including any direct

costs to finance the Equity Investment; and

(2) *Positive Cash Flow.* The aggregate amount required to be paid to or for the lessor over the lease term exceeds by a reasonable amount the aggregate disbursements required to be paid by or for the lessor in connection with the ownership of the property.

SECTION 5. OTHER CONSIDERATIONS

.01 *Uneven Rent Test.* Leveraged lease transactions that satisfy the guidelines set forth in section 4 of this revenue procedure and that contain uneven rent payments may be subject to § 467 and the regulations thereunder relating to the accounting treatment for certain leases with prepaid or deferred rent. In addition, § 1.467-3(c)(4) of the Income Tax Regulations provides an uneven rent test. A lease meeting this uneven rent test will not be treated as a disqualified leaseback or long-term agreement for purposes of § 467. How the lease is treated under § 467, including whether or not the uneven rent test of § 1.467-3(c)(4) is met, will not affect the ability of a taxpayer to obtain an advance ruling under this revenue procedure.

.02 *Limited Use Property.*

(1) *In General.* Section 4.01(3) of this revenue procedure requires the lessor to represent and demonstrate certain facts relating to the estimated fair market value and estimated remaining useful life of the property at the end of the lease term. This requirement is intended, in part, to assure that the purported lessor has not transferred the use of the property to the purported lessee for substantially its entire useful life. In the case of such "limited use" property, at the end of the lease term there will probably be no potential lessees or buyers other than members of the Lessee Group. As a result, the lessor of limited use property will probably sell or rent the property to a member of the Lessee Group, thus enabling the Lessee Group to enjoy the benefits of the use or ownership of the property for substantially its entire useful life. See Rev. Rul. 55-541, 1955-2 C.B. 19, for an example of a transaction in which property was determined to be leased for substantially its entire useful life and the conclusion that such a transaction transfers equitable ownership. Accordingly, the Service will not issue advance rulings concerning whether certain transactions purporting to be leases of property are, in fact, leases for federal income tax purposes when the property is limited use property.

(2) *Examples.* The following examples illustrate the types of property the Service considers to be limited use property, and the types of property the Service does not consider to be limited use property.

(a) *X* builds a masonry smokestack attached to a masonry warehouse building owned by Y, and leases the smokestack to Y for use as an addition to the heating system of the warehouse. The lease term is 15 years; the smokestack has a useful life of 25 years, and the warehouse has a remaining useful life of 25 years. It would not be commercially feasible to disassemble the smokestack at the end of the lease term and reconstruct it at a new location. The smokestack is considered to be limited use property.

(b) *X* builds a complete chemical production facility on land owned by *Y* and leases the facility to *Y*, a manufacturer of chemicals. The lease term is 24 years, and the facility has a useful life of 30 years. The land is leased to *X* pursuant to a ground lease for a term of 30 years. The technical "know-how" and trade secrets *Y* possesses are necessary elements in the commercial operation of the facility. At the time the lease is entered into, no person who is not a member of the lessee group possesses the technical "know-how" and trade secrets necessary for the commercial operation of the facility. The taxpayers submit to the Service the written opinion of a qualified expert stating it is probable that by the expiration of the lease term of the facility third parties who are potential purchasers or lessees of the facility will have independently developed such "know-how" and trade secrets. The facility is considered to be limited use property. In reaching this conclusion, the Service will not take into account such expert opinion because such opinions are too speculative for advance ruling purposes.

(c) The facts are the same as in example (b) except *X* has an option, exercisable at the end of the lease term of the facility, to purchase from *Y* the "know-how" and trade secrets necessary for the commercial operation of the facility, and it would be commercially feasible at the end of such lease term for *X* to exercise the option and operate the facility itself. The facility is not considered to be limited use property.

(d) The facts are the same as in example (b) except it would be commercially feasible for the lessor at the end of the lease term to make certain structural modifications of the facility that would make the facility capable of being used by persons not possessing any special technical "know-how" or trade secrets. Furthermore, if such modifications were made, it would be commercially feasible, at the end of the lease term, for a person who is not a member of the lessee group to purchase or lease the facility from *X*. The facility is not considered to be limited use property.

(e) *X* builds an electrical generating plant on land owned by *Y* and leases the plant to *Y*. The lease term is 40 years, and the plant has an estimated useful life of 50 years. The land is leased to *X* pursuant to a ground lease for a term of 50 years. The plant is adjacent to a fuel source that it is estimated will last for at least 50 years. Access to this fuel source is necessary for the commercial operation of the plant, and *Y* has recently obtained the contractual right to acquire all fuel produced from the source for 50 years. *Y* will use the plant to produce and generate electrical power for sale to a city located 500 miles away. The plant is synchronized into a power grid that makes the sale of electrical power to a number of potential markets commercially feasible. It would not be commercially feasible to disassemble the plant and reconstruct it at a new location. The electrical generating plant is considered to be limited use property because access to the fuel source held exclusively by *Y* is necessary for the commercial operation of the plant.

(f) The facts are the same as in example (e) except *X* has an option, exercisable at the end of the lease term of the plant, to acquire from *Y* the contractual right to acquire all fuel produced from the fuel source for the 10-year period commencing at the end of such lease term. It would be commercially feasible at the end of such lease term for *X* to exercise this option. Furthermore, it would be commercially feasible, at the end of such lease term, for a person who is not a member of the lessee group to purchase the contractual right to the fuel from *X* for an amount equal to the option price and purchase or lease the plant from *X*. The plant is not considered to be limited use property.

* * *

NOTES AND COMMENTS

As indicated, although it is only a ruling guideline, the standards of Rev. Proc. 2001-28 become practical rules of law when an advance ruling is considered essential to a transaction. It is worth noting how the guidelines solve the risk versus residual dichotomy by requiring both. It is worth rereading the conditions to determine which require residual, which risk, and which have some other function.

PROBLEMS FOR DISCUSSION

Problem 7-7. Would the taxpayer in *Frank Lyon Co.* (leveraged lease not a sale) be able to obtain a ruling under Rev. Proc. 2001-28 (ruling guidelines for leveraged leases)? If not, what is the justification for the Guidelines in § 4 of Rev. Proc. 2001-28?

Problem 7-8. Treating the transaction in *Brown* (bootstrap sale) as a leveraged lease, would Brown and the Institute be able to obtain a ruling under Rev. Proc. 2001-28 (ruling guidelines for leveraged leases) that the Institute was the owner and Brown the lessee?

Problem 7-9. Developer owns a parcel of urban land, on which he was planning to build an office building for production of rental income. Data Processing Company, Inc. has now approached Developer with a proposal that Developer instead erect a building according to its specifications and lease the entire building to it. The terms of the agreement proposed by Data are that if the cost of construction will exceed the expenditures that Developer would have incurred in constructing the building originally proposed, Data will pay the excess. The original cost estimate by Developer was $40,000,000. As it eventually turned out, Data paid excess construction costs of $25,000,000. Under the proposed lease, Data is to pay rent at the rate of $12,000,000 a year for 25 years and has an option to renew for four successive 10-year periods, with rent at the rate of $7,000,000 a year thereafter. In addition, Data is to pay all the taxes, insurance, and other expenses of the property so that the lease is absolutely net to Developer. Data will, of course, pay all repair costs and also has the right to make any alterations that do not appreciably reduce the amount of rentable space in the building. Data has the right to assign the lease and to sublease the premises. Data has the obligation to restore the premises if they are damaged or destroyed during the term of the lease, whether or not the damage is covered by insurance, which Data, of course, would have maintained. In the event of condemnation, Data is to receive an amount equal to the depreciated portion of its investment in the premises. Developer is to receive an amount equal to the depreciated portion of its investment in the premises, plus an amount of $20,000,000 as the estimated value of the land, and the balance of any condemnation award is to be divided equally between Data and the Developer. Data also has an option to purchase the premises any time after the twenty-fifth year. The option price is $60,000,000, which is the sum of the estimated present value of the land, plus the investment made by Developer in the building. In addition, in the event of condemnation, Data has the right to exercise the option at the same purchase price. Data expects to put a large amount of special purpose computer equipment into the building. At the expiration of the lease, Data is required to surrender the premises in good order and to remove all of its special purpose equipment. It is currently estimated that such removal could cost it in excess of $40,000,000.

Would Data and Developer be able to obtain a ruling under Rev. Proc. 2001-28 (ruling guidelines for leveraged leases)? Would the lease qualify as a lease under *Frank Lyon Co.* (leveraged lease not a sale)? Under *Hilton* (leveraged sale and leaseback not recognized)?

§ 2. TRANSFERS OF PARTIAL INTERESTS

Capital assets are not limited to the entire interest in property. A partial interest — for example, the interest of a lessor under a long-term lease — can be a capital or § 1231 asset. *See, e.g.*, Rev. Rul. 77-414; 1977-2 C.B. 299 (gain on sale of development right for property used in farming that restricts use of land to designated agricultural purposes qualifies under § 1231); Rev. Rul. 73-341, 1973-2 C.B. 306 (sale of interest in water rights underlying land used in farming qualifies under § 1231); Rev. Rul. 72-95, 1972-1 C.B. 429 (sale of leasehold interest in land and improvements qualifies as sale of § 1231 property, even though leasehold in land not depreciable or amortizable because of indefinite life); Rev. Rul. 68-226, 1968-1 C.B. 362 (interest of a lessee in oil and gas property qualifies under § 1231); Rev. Rul. 59-121, 1959-1 C.B. 212 (gain on granting easement qualifies under § 1231); Priv. Ltr. Rul. 2008-50-010 (gains on sales of term interest and remainder to separate buyers qualify under § 1231).

§ 2.01. Gratuitous Transfers of Partial Interests

Although gratuitous transfers of partial interests in property belong primarily to the subject of taxation of the family, particularly intrafamily assignments of income, because the principles relating to sales and other compensated transfers of such interests derive from the cases dealing with family transfers, it is useful to review them. Section 2.01(a) *Income from Services*, deals with the basic principle that earned income is taxed to the earner, with minor variations for services performed as an agent for another or for gratuitous services performed usually for a family member or a charity. Section 2.01(b) *Income from Property*, discusses when taxation of future income from property can be transferred to the donee without transferring the entire property and when the transfer is inadequate to keep the donor from having to recognize the income collected by the donee. Although unrealized gain is transferred to the recipient of a gratuitous transfer of property, § 2.01(c) *Appreciated Property v. Realized Income (How Ripe is the Fruit?)*, deals with the principle that the donor remains taxable on gain that has been realized in an economic sense, even if unrealized for tax purposes. When money or property is held by a court fund or in escrow pending determination of who is entitled to it, the income is taxed to depositor or the fund, as described in § 2.01(d) *Escrows*.

§ 2.01(a). Income from Services

The classic case of *Lucas v. Earl*, which is the fountainhead of the assignment of income law and lore, is notable, among other things, for the succinctness of Justice Holmes' opinion and for the persistent "fruit and tree" imagery he used.

LUCAS v. EARL

Supreme Court of the United States
281 U.S. 111 (1930)

* * *

MR. JUSTICE HOLMES delivered the opinion of the Court.

This case presents the question whether the respondent, Earl, could be taxed for the whole of the salary and attorney's fees earned by him in the years 1920 and 1921, or should be taxed for only a half of them in view of a contract with his wife which we shall mention. . . .

By the contract, made in 1901, Earl and his wife agreed "that any property either of us now has or may hereafter acquire . . . in any way, either by earnings (including salaries, fees, etc.), or any rights by contract or otherwise, during the existence of our marriage, or which we or either of us may receive by gift, bequest, devise, or inheritance, and all the proceeds, issues, and profits of any and all such property shall be treated and considered and hereby is declared to be received, held, taken, and owned by us as joint tenants, and not otherwise, with the right of survivorship." The validity of the contract is not questioned, and we assume it to be unquestionable under the law of the State of California, in which the parties lived. . . .

The Revenue Act of 1918 . . . imposes a tax upon the net income of every individual including "income derived from salaries, wages, or compensation for personal service . . . of whatever kind and in whatever form paid," . . . The provisions of the Revenue Act of 1921 . . . are similar to those of the above. A very forcible argument is presented to the effect that the statute seeks to tax only income beneficially received, and that taking the question more technically the salary and fees became the joint property of Earl and his wife on the very first instant on which they were received. We well might hesitate upon the latter proposition, because however the matter might stand between husband and wife he was the only party to the contracts by which the salary and fees were earned, and it is somewhat hard to say that the last step in the performance of those contracts could be taken by anyone but himself alone. But this case is not to be decided by attenuated subtleties. It turns on the import and reasonable construction of the taxing act. There is no doubt that the statute could tax salaries to those who earned them and provide that the tax could not be escaped by anticipatory arrangements and contracts however skillfully devised to prevent the salary when paid from vesting even for a second in the man who earned it. That seems to us the import of the statute before us and we think that no distinction can be taken according to the motives leading to the arrangement by which the fruits are attributed to a different tree from that on which they grew.

Judgment reversed.

NOTES AND COMMENTS

The contract between the Earls presumably had no tax avoidance, or at least, no federal income tax avoidance motive, because it was executed after the Civil War income tax had been declared unconstitutional, and well before the adoption of the Sixteenth Amendment in 1913. Despite the ringing nature of the Holmes opinion, the Court, later in the same year in *Poe v. Seaborn*, 282 U.S. 101 (1930), allowed taxpayers in community property states to split their incomes on the ground that state law made the earnings the property of the community, whereas in *Earl* the earnings were, under state law, Mr. Earl's. The resulting lack of uniformity between community property and other states was not considered unconstitutional and persisted until joint returns were authorized in 1948.

In a business context, the right to service income can be assigned without being taxed to the service provider if the services are considered rendered on behalf of the person to whom the earnings are transferred. Thus, in Rev. Rul. 64-90, 1964-1 C.B. 226, fees for services rendered by law firm partners in their individual capacities for services similar to those of the partnership, and turned over to the partnership pursuant to the partnership agreement, were determined to be properly income of the firm. The same result was reached in Rev. Rul. 74-581, 1974-2 C.B. 25, for clinical legal fees received by faculty members and turned over to a law school. *See* Rev. Rul. 76-479, 1976-2 C.B. 20 (same for physicians); Rev. Rul. 80-338, 1980-2 C.B. 30 (same for executor's fees turned over by accountant to firm, because firm cannot serve as executor, and services provided by executor are within the range of services undertaken by accountants). This approach was carried further in Rev. Rul. 83-127, 1983-2 C.B. 25, which held that compensation received by a member of religious order under vows of poverty for teaching services for an affiliated organization was not taxable to the teacher who treated as an agent of the order. In *Schneer v. Commissioner*, 97 T.C. 643 (1991), fees turned over by a partner in law firm, Firm #2, whose partnership agreement required him to turn over to Firm #2 referral fees he collected from his former employer, Firm #1, under an agreement to give him a percentage of the fees it collected from clients he brought to Firm #1 that were not collected and paid over until he became a partner in Firm #2, are taxed to Firm # 2, not the partner, as representing an implicit pooling of income for partners. A concurring opinion reached the same result by concluding that if he was required to include the amount in income, he was entitled to an offsetting deduction. A dissenting opinion would have characterized the payment as a nondeductible contribution to capital, leaving the entire fee taxable to the partner. The service provider is taxed, however, if the services are considered to be rendered in an individual capacity and not on behalf of the business entity. Other service providers have not been as successful. Thus, in *Leavell v. Commissioner*, 104 T.C. 140 (1995), a basketball player was taxed personally on salary paid to personal service corporation. Similarly in *Blassie v. Commissioner*, 394 F.2d 628 (8th Cir. 1968), a union official who qualified as an insurance broker was taxed individually on a brokerage commission he earned and turned over to the union, but there was no discussion of any possible deduction for turning over commissions; *See* Priv. Ltr. Rul. 95-14-008 (income on exercise of NSO received by employee shareholder of an incorporated law firm as a director of a client corporation turned over to firm as required by agreement was income of attorney because he served in his individual capacity); *Fogarty v. United States*, 780 F.2d 1005 (Fed. Cir. 1986) (Jesuit under vow of poverty taxed individually on salary as faculty member of a secular university turned over to the order; not agent of order when teaching).

In addition, a taxpayer is not taxed for rendering gratuitous services to family members or charities. *See* Treas. Reg. § 1.61-2(c) (gratuitous service to charitable organization); Rev. Rul. 66-167, 1966-1 C.B. 20 (service as executor when fees waived shortly after starting to serve estate of family member); Rev. Rul. 71-33, 1971-1 C.B. 30 (consultation relating to manuscript of memoirs assigned to foundation that had arranged publication with all royalties to foundation); Rev. Rul. 68-503, 1968-2 C.B. 44 (professional entertainer performing at a political fundraiser not taxed); Rev. Rul. 77-121, 1977-1 C.B. 17 (race track not taxed on net proceeds of "charity day" event turned over to charity that acted as promoter, handled advertising, and agreed to cover any losses); *Alexander* v. *Commissioner*, 194 F.2d 921 (5th Cir. 1952) (cattle and grazing land taxable to 14-year-old daughter where father continued to manage cattle and land with his own cattle and land). The line is a narrow one, however, so that the service provider is taxed when the services are rendered to a third party, with the proceeds paid to the charity. Treas. Reg. § 1.61-2(c) (does not discuss possible charitable deduction for amounts turned over); Rev. Rul. 72-542, 1972-2 C.B. 37 (race track taxed on "charity day" proceeds turned over to charity, but entitled to deduction within applicable limits).

PROBLEMS FOR DISCUSSION

Problem 7-10. Lex, a well known estate planning guru, who is a partner in MegaFirm, has been appointed the executor of her father-in-law's very large and complex estate. The MegaFirm agreement requires her to turn executor's fees over to the firm. Her initial instinct was to serve without claiming the statutory fee, to reduce sibling rivalry. At the urging of her law professor husband, however, she has agreed to claim the fee to reduce estate taxes, and to make gifts to her siblings of her after-tax share, equivalent to the fee charged, because that would leave them all with more money, because the income tax rate is less than the estate tax rate. At the suggestion of the executive committee of MegaFirm, she has agreed to reduce her share of income by 10 percent during the period of administration of the estate to reflect that she will not be able to devote her full time to MegaFirm during that period because of the demands of her role as executor. Megafirm has agreed that she will not be required to turn over even her retained share of the fee. What are the tax consequences to Lex, MegaFirm, and the estate under these arrangements? *See Lucas v. Earl* (assignment of earned income; fruit and tree); *Poe v. Seaborn* (income split under community property); Rev. Rul. 64-90 (individual legal fees turned over to firm); Rev. Rul. 74-581 (clinical legal fees turned over to law school); Rev. Rul. 76-479 (same for physicians); Rev. Rul. 80-338 (executor's fees turned over by accountant to firm); Rev. Rul. 83-127 (member of religious order performing services for an affiliated organization treated as agent); *Schneer* (share of fees from prior firm turned over to current firm); *Leavell* (basketball player taxed personally on salary paid to personal service corporation); *Blassie* (union official turned over insurance commissions to union); Priv. Ltr. Rul. 95-14-008 (NSO income earned as director turned over to law firm); *Fogarty* (faculty salary of Jesuit under vow of poverty).

Problem 7-11. Famous Actress agrees to star without compensation in a movie being produced and directed by Chip, her son, once a rising star whose career is on the skids as a result not only of substance abuse, but also of being caught quite publicly, but who is trying to start fresh after rehab. What are the tax consequences to Famous and Chip of this arrangement? *See Lucas v. Earl* (assignment of earned income; fruit and tree); *Poe v. Seaborn* (income split under community property); Treas. Reg. § 1.61-2(c) (gratuitous service to charitable organization); Rev. Rul. 66-167 (waiver of executor fees); Rev. Rul. 71-33 (consultation for memoirs turned over to foundation); Rev. Rul. 68-503 (professional entertainer performing at political fundraiser); Rev. Rul. 77-121 (charity day proceeds at race track); Rev. Rul. 72-542 (another charity day at race track); *Alexander* (cattle and grazing land for daughter).

§ 2.01(b). Income from Property

I.R.C. § 1286

The contract between the Earls covered not only Mr. Earl's salary but the Earls' earnings from their property. At the time of execution, Mrs. Earl's property was worth $30,000, and Mr. Earl's is described in the Board of Tax Appeals opinion as "substantial." The Service did not attack the splitting of the property income. Despite the Service's apparent acquiescence to the splitting of the Earls' income from property, the Service subsequently challenged other assignments of income from property, particularly shares of trust income interests. In the following three cases, the taxpayers won in one and lost in two. What serves as the basis for the different result in each of these three cases?

BLAIR v. COMMISSIONER

Supreme Court of the United States
300 U.S. 5 (1937)

[The taxpayer, who was the life beneficiary of a trust, assigned to his daughter the right to receive a specific dollar amount of income in each future year. The Court held that the assignment was effective to transfer to the daughter the taxability of the assigned income, stating:]

* * *

Our decisions in *Lucas v. Earl*, 281 U.S. 111, and *Burnet v. Leininger*, 285 U.S. 136, are cited. . . . These cases are not in point. The tax here is not upon earnings which are taxed to the one who earns them. Nor is it a case of income attributable to a taxpayer by reason of the application of the income to the discharge of his obligation. *Old Colony Trust Co. v. Commissioner*, 279 U.S. 716, ... There is here no question of evasion or of giving effect to statutory provisions designed to forestall evasion; or of the taxpayer's retention of control. . . .

In the instant case, the tax is upon income as to which, in the general application of the revenue acts, the tax liability attaches to ownership. See *Poe v. Seaborn*, 282 U.S. 101. . . .

* * *

The will creating the trust entitled the petitioner during his life to the net income of the property held in trust. He thus became the owner of an equitable interest in the corpus of the property. . . . By virtue of that interest he was entitled to enforce the trust, to have a breach of trust enjoined and to obtain redress in case of breach. The interest was present property alienable like any other, in the absence of a valid restraint upon alienation. . . . The beneficiary may thus transfer a part of his interest as well as the whole. See Restatement of the Law of Trusts . . . The assignment of the beneficial interest is not the assignment of a chose in action but of the "right, title and estate in and to property." . . .

We conclude that the assignments were valid, that the assignees thereby became the owners of the specified beneficial interests in the income, and that as to these interests they and not the petitioner were taxable for the tax years in question. . . .

Reversed.

HELVERING v. HORST

Supreme Court of the United States
311 U.S. 112 (1940)

* * *

MR. JUSTICE STONE delivered the opinion of the Court.

* * *

In 1934 and 1935 respondent, the owner of negotiable bonds, detached from them negotiable interest coupons shortly before their due date and delivered them as a gift to his son who in the same year collected them at maturity. . . .

* * *

The holder of a coupon bond is the owner of two independent and separable kinds of right. One is the right to demand and receive at maturity the principal amount of the bond representing capital investment. The other is the right to demand and receive interim payments of interest on the investment in the amounts and on the dates specified by the coupons. Together they are an obligation to pay principal and interest given in exchange for money or property which was presumably the consideration for the obligation of the bond. Here respondent, as owner of the bonds, had acquired the legal right to demand payment at maturity of the interest specified by the coupons and the power to command its payment to others, which constituted an economic gain to him.

Admittedly not all economic gain of the taxpayer is taxable income. From the beginning the revenue laws have been interpreted as defining "realization" of income as the taxable event, rather than the acquisition of the right to receive it. And "realization" is not deemed to occur until the income is paid. But the decisions and regulations have consistently recognized that receipt in cash or property is not the only characteristic of realization of income to a taxpayer on the cash receipts basis. Where the taxpayer does not receive payment of income in money or property realization may occur when the last step is taken by which he obtains the fruition of the economic gain which has already accrued to him. *Old Colony*. . . .

. . . [T]he rule that income is not taxable until realized has never been taken to mean that the taxpayer even on the cash receipts basis, who has fully enjoyed the benefit of the economic gain represented by his right to receive income, can escape taxation because he has not himself received payment of it from his obligor. The rule, founded on administrative convenience, is only one of postponement of the tax to the final event of enjoyment of the income, usually the receipt of it by the taxpayer, and not one of exemption from taxation where the enjoyment is consummated by some event other than the taxpayer's personal receipt of money or property. . . . This may occur when he has made such use or disposition of his power to receive or control the income as to procure in its place other satisfactions which are of economic worth. . . . If the taxpayer procures payment directly to his creditors of the items of interest or earnings due him . . . or if he sets up a revocable trust with income payable to the objects of his bounty, he does not escape taxation because he did not actually receive the money. . . .

Underlying the reasoning in these cases is the thought that income is "realized" by the assignor because he, who owns or controls the source of the income, also controls the disposition of that which he could have received himself and diverts the payment from himself to others as the means of procuring the satisfaction of his wants. The taxpayer has equally enjoyed the fruits of his labor or investment and obtained the satisfaction of his desires whether he collects and uses the income to procure those satisfactions, or whether he disposes of his right to collect it as the means of procuring them. . . .

Although the donor here, by the transfer of the coupons, has precluded any possibility of his collecting them himself, he has nevertheless, by his act, procured payment of the interest as a valuable gift to a member of his family. . . . Even though he never receives the money, he derives money's worth from the disposition of the coupons which he has used as money or money's worth in the procuring of a satisfaction which is procurable only by the expenditure of money or money's worth. The enjoyment of the economic benefit accruing to him by virtue of his acquisition of the coupons is realized as completely as it would have been if he had collected the interest in dollars and expended them for any of the purposes named. . . .

* * *

The power to dispose of income is the equivalent of ownership of it. The exercise of that power to procure the payment of income to another is the enjoyment, and hence the realization, of the income by him who exercises it. We have had no difficulty in applying that proposition where the assignment preceded the rendition of the services, *Lucas v. Earl*. . . . But it is the assignment by which the disposition of income is controlled when the service precedes the assignment, and in both cases it is the exercise of the power of disposition of the interest or compensation, with the resulting payment to the donee, which is the enjoyment by the donor of income derived from them.

This was emphasized in *Blair v. Commissioner*, 300 U.S. 5, on which respondent relies, where the distinction was taken between a gift of income derived from an obligation to pay compensation and a gift of income-producing property. In the circumstances of that case, the right to income from the trust property was thought to be so identified with the equitable ownership of the property, from which alone the beneficiary derived his right to receive the income and his power to command disposition of it, that a gift of the income by the beneficiary became effective only as a gift of his ownership of the property producing it. Since the gift was deemed to be a gift of the property, the income from it was held to be the income of the owner of the property, who was the donee, not the donor — a refinement which was unnecessary if respondent's contention here is right, but one clearly inapplicable to gifts of interest or wages. Unlike income thus derived from an obligation to pay interest or compensation, the income of the trust was regarded as no more the income of the donor than would be the rent from a lease or a crop raised on a farm after the leasehold or the farm had been given away. *Blair v. Commissioner*. . . .

The dominant purpose of the revenue laws is the taxation of income to those who earn or otherwise create the right to receive it and enjoy the benefit of it when paid. . . . The tax laid by the 1934 Revenue Act upon income "derived from . . . wages, or compensation for personal service, of whatever kind and in whatever form paid, . . . ; also from interest . . . " therefore cannot fairly be interpreted as not applying to income derived from interest or compensation when he who is entitled to receive it makes use of his power to dispose of it in procuring satisfactions which he would otherwise procure only by the use of the money when received.

* * *

Nor is it perceived that there is any adequate basis for distinguishing between the gift of interest coupons here and a gift of salary or commissions. The owner of a negotiable bond and of the investment which it represents, if not the lender, stands in the place of the lender. When, by the gift of the coupons, he has separated his right to interest payments from his investment and procured the payment of the interest to his donee, he has enjoyed the economic benefits of the income in the same manner and to the same extent as though the transfer were of earnings, and in both cases the import of the statute is that the fruit is not to be attributed to a different tree from that on which it grew. *See Lucas v. Earl.* . . .

HARRISON v. SCHAFFNER

Supreme Court of the United States
312 U.S. 579 (1941)

[The taxpayer, who was the life beneficiary of a trust, assigned to his children the right to receive a specific dollar amount of income for the following year. The Court held that the assignment was not effective to transfer to the children the taxability of the assigned income, stating:]

* * *

. . . Taxation is a practical matter and those practical considerations which support the treatment of the disposition of one's income by way of gift as a realization of the income to the donor are the same whether the income be from a trust or from shares of stock or bonds which he owns. It is true, as respondent argues, that where the beneficiary of a trust had assigned a share of the income to another for life without retaining any form of control over the interest assigned, this Court construed the assignment as a transfer *in praesenti* to the donee, of a life interest in the corpus of the trust property, and held in consequence that the income thereafter paid to the donee was taxable to him and not the donor. *Blair v. Commissioner*. . . . But we think it quite another matter to say that the beneficiary of a trust who makes a single gift of a sum of money payable out of the income of the trust does not realize income when the gift is effectuated by payment, or that he escapes the tax by attempting to clothe the transaction in the guise of a transfer of trust property rather than the transfer of income, where that is its obvious purpose and effect. We think that the gift by a beneficiary of a trust of some part of the income derived from the trust property for the period of a day, a month or a year involves no such substantial disposition of the trust property as to camouflage the reality that he is enjoying the benefit of the income from the trust of which he continues to be the beneficiary, quite as much as he enjoys the benefits of interest or wages which he gives away as in the *Horst* and *Eubank* cases. Even though the gift of income be in form accomplished by the temporary disposition of the donor's property which produces the income, the donor retaining every other substantial interest in it, we have not allowed the form to obscure the reality. Income which the donor gives away through the medium of a short term trust created for the benefit of the donee is nevertheless income taxable to the donor. *Helvering v. Clifford* [309 U.S. 331]. . . .

Nor are we troubled by the logical difficulties of drawing the line between a gift of an equitable interest in property for life effected by a gift for life of a share of the income of the trust and the gift of the income or a part of it for the period of a year as in this case. "Drawing the line" is a recurrent difficulty in those fields of the law where differences in degree produce ultimate differences in kind. See *Irwin v.*

Gavit, 268 U.S. 161, 168. It is enough that we find in the present case that the taxpayer, in point of substance, has parted with no substantial interest in property other than the specified payments of income which, like other gifts of income, are taxable to the donor. Unless in the meantime the difficulty be resolved by statute or treasury regulation, we leave it to future judicial decisions to determine precisely where the line shall be drawn between gifts of income-producing property and gifts of income from property of which the donor remains the owner, for all substantial and practical purposes. . . .

Reversed.

NOTES AND COMMENTS

Although the decisions do not address the issue directly, one interesting aspect of *Blair* and *Schaffner* is that the taxpayers only had an income interest, only a right to the fruit, and no interest in the tree (the trust corpus or the bonds) itself. Nevertheless, *Blair* effectively transfers taxation of the fruit, while *Schaffner* does not. *Horst*, of course had both the fruit (the coupons) and the tree (the bond), but did not successfully transfer taxation of the fruit.

What Horst did by transferring the coupons separately from the bonds became a popular financial transaction at one time. Because of the separate accounting, the sale of the principal right while retaining the coupons could produce a loss if the entire basis was allocated to the rights sold. For example, the discounted value of the principal of a $1,000 20-year bond providing interest at 10 percent is only $149 with the $851 ($1,000 - $149) balance representing the right to collect $100 a year for 20 years until maturity. If the entire $1,000 purchase price is allocated as basis to the principal portion of the bond, the principal portion of the bond could be sold for its $149 value, resulting in a $851 loss on the sale. That loss would be offset, of course, by a $851 gain if the right to all the interest payments is sold for its $851 value, with no basis allocated to it. Taxpayers would sell only the loss-generating portion of the bond, however, and would wait until future years to realize income on the gain-generating portion of the bond or, occasionally, would reverse the sequence to realize the income portion, initially, to offset expiring losses. Thus, under the traditional basis allocation, separating the right to principal and right to interest allowed sophisticated taxpayers to recognize an artificial current loss (or income). Section 1286(b) prevents this result by requiring allocation of basis between the rights sold and the rights retained when the coupons are stripped. Section 1286(a) then treats the retained rights and the stripped rights as obligations that have original issue discount ("OID"). The result is that both holder of the principal and the holder of the interest coupons are taxed on their obligations for the difference between the stated amounts of the obligations they own and their basis during the period between the time of the transaction and the time they collect the principal or interest payments, respectively. Because § 1286 applies only to purchases of stripped bonds, or stripped coupons, it does not affect gifts like the one in *Horst.*

PROBLEMS FOR DISCUSSION

Problem 7-12. What would be the result if Mr. Horst had stripped and given all of the coupons on the bonds to his son, not merely those for the year? If this would not work, what would he have to do to transfer taxability of the income? *See Blair* (transfer of trust interest); *Horst* (gift of interest coupons detached from the bonds to a family member); *Schaffner* (transfer of trust income).

Problem 7-13. (i) How would *Horst* (gift of bond coupons to son) come out under § 1286(b) if it applied to gifts? (ii) What would be an outcome of *Blair* (transfer of trust interest); and *Schaffner* (transfer of trust income) if § 1286 were expanded to cover transfers of trust interests? Would these be more sound tax results? (iii) Could § 1286 be feasibly expanded to cover *Lucas v. Earl* (assignment of income; fruit and tree); and *Poe v. Seaborn* (income split under community property)?

§ 2.01(c). Appreciated Property versus Realized Income (How Ripe is the Fruit?)

Gifts and other gratuitous transfers of appreciated property (transfer of the tree) effectively transfer the taxation of the unrealized gain and future income, while transfers of rights to income (the fruit) do not. When property is sold shortly after gratuitous transfer pursuant to arrangements that were in process at the time of the transfer, the issue is whether the tree had become nothing more than a basket of fruit. The following case deals with determining how ripe the sale had become.

FERGUSON v. COMMISSIONER
United States Court of Appeals, Ninth Circuit
174 F.3d 997 (9th Cir. 1999)

[The Fergusons were officers and directors of American Health Companies, Inc. ("AHC") which had acquired their closely held business in exchange for about 18% of AHC stock. On July 28, 1988, AHC entered into a merger agreement with CDI Holding, Inc. ("CDI"). The tender offer and merger were conditioned on the acquisition by DC Acquisition of at least 85% of the outstanding shares of AHC by the expiration date of the tender offer. Slightly over half the shares were tendered by Aug. 31, with most of the rest coming in on Sept. 9, the extended tender date as a result of a fire that completely destroyed AHC's product manufacturing plant on Aug. 25. On the final day of the tender offer, the Fergusons exchanged a significant amount of their AHC stock for CDI common and preferred stock, pursuant to an oral agreement, and they tendered the remainder of their AHC stock pursuant to the tender offer. On Sept. 12, DC Acquisition announced its acceptance of all tendered AHC shares.

In the meanwhile the Fergusons transferred some of their AHC stock to three charitable organizations ("Charities"): the Church of Jesus Christ of the Latter Day Saints ("Church"), and two private foundations they formed on Aug. 26, 1988. Working with Brett Floyd of Merrill Lynch, on Aug. 15 and 16, the Fergusons executed nonbinding donation-in-kind records for

60,000+ shares to the Church. Some more binding documents were signed by Aug. 21, but were destroyed and replaced by others in connection with the exchanges of some of the Fegusons' shares with CDI. They also transferred their AHC shares into street name new accounts at Merrill Lynch. Their shares were subject to restrictive legends. The in-house journal entry to transfer the shares to the Church and the private foundations was made on Sept. 8, and the final letters of authorization were signed on Sept. 9.]

* * *

The key issue here is whether the Fergusons had completed their contributions of the appreciated AHC stock before it had ripened from an interest in a viable corporation into a fixed right to receive cash. If the Fergusons had done so, then they cannot be taxed on the gain realized when the stock ripened; if they had not, then they can. Because the evidence in the record and the applicable law support the conclusion that the Fergusons' contributions were not completed until after the appreciated AHC stock had ripened, we affirm the Tax Court's decision.

1. *Completion of the Contributions Under Treas. Reg. § 1.170A-1(b)*

The parties and the Tax Court relied upon Treas. Reg. § 1.170A-1(b) to determine the exact date that the Fergusons' contributions were completed. I.R.C. § 170 deals with tax deductions for the payment of charitable contributions, and Treas. Reg. § 1.170A-1(b) deals with the timing of such contributions as follows:

> Ordinarily, a contribution is made at the time delivery is effected. . . . If a taxpayer unconditionally delivers or mails a properly endorsed stock certificate to a charitable donee or the donee's agent, the gift is completed on the date of delivery or, if such certificate is received in the ordinary course of the mails, on the date of mailing. If the donor delivers the stock certificate to his bank or broker as the donor's agent, or to the issuing corporation or its agent, for transfer into the name of the donee, the gift is completed on the date the stock is transferred on the books of the corporation.

The most relevant provision here, focused upon by the Tax Court and both parties, is the second sentence of the regulation, which deals with the delivery of stock to either a charitable donee or the donee's agent.

The Fergusons make two contentions with respect to this provision. First, they contend that the date of delivery directly to the Charities, was the date that Brett Floyd made the in-house journal entries on Merrill Lynch's computers: September 8, 1988. Second, they contend alternatively (and preferably for them) that Brett Floyd was acting as the Charities' agent, or as trustee of a voluntary trust created for the benefit of the Charities, and that the dates of delivery to the Charities' agent therefore were the dates that the Fergusons purportedly executed the alleged original letters of authorization: August 15, 1988 (transfer from Michael Ferguson to the Church); August 21, 1988 (transfer from Roger and Sybil Ferguson to the Church); and August 26, 1988 (transfer from the Fergusons to their foundations on the earliest date possible - the date of the Charities' formation).

However, the evidence in the record does not support any of the Fergusons' contentions but instead supports a finding that the Fergusons' contributions were not completed until September 9, 1988, the date that they executed their final letters of authorization.

The evidence shows that Brett Floyd was not acting on behalf of the Charities (as their agent, as the trustee of a voluntary trust created for their benefit, or in any other capacity) until the time that the Merrill Lynch clearance process had been completed, the AHC stock had been transferred on the books of Merrill Lynch from the Fergusons' account to the Charities' account, and the Fergusons had authorized the transfer, finally and effectively. Even if Brett Floyd had ceased to be acting under the control of the Fergusons at any time, not until Merrill Lynch's legal department had completed its two-week clearance process, would he even have been capable of acting at the Charities' behest with respect to any disposition of the AHC stock, which still remained in the Fergusons' personal accounts. . . .

Furthermore, contrary to the Fergusons' assertion, Brett Floyd's testimony as to the existence of the original letters of execution and as to the intended purpose of those letters, if they indeed existed, was not uncontroverted. The total absence of any trace of the original letters and the "substantial documentary evidence" that the Tax Court relied upon in its decision, easily could have supported a finding that Brett Floyd was not a credible supporting witness. . . .

Therefore, in the absence of Brett Floyd's role as anything other than an agent of the Fergusons or Merrill Lynch, there could have been no contribution until the delivery of the AHC stock to the Charities' account had been completed. And in the absence of any earlier letters of authorization that were intended to be final and effective, there was no completed delivery to the Charities, no transfer that was legally binding and irrevocable, until the date that the Fergusons' letters of authorization were finally and effectively executed - September 9, 1988.

2. *The Ripening of the AHC Stock*

Under the anticipatory assignment of income doctrine, once a right to receive income has "ripened" for tax purposes, the taxpayer who earned or otherwise created that right, will be taxed on any gain realized from it, notwithstanding the fact that the taxpayer has transferred the right before actually receiving the income. *See Jones v. United States*, 531 F.2d 1343, 1346 (6th Cir. 1976); *Kinsey v. Commissioner*, 477 F.2d 1058, 1063 (2nd Cir. 1973); *Hudspeth v. Commissioner*, 471 F.2d 275, 280 (8th Cir. 1972) . . .

While the Ninth Circuit has not addressed the issue of "ripening" yet, several other courts (both tax and appellate) have considered the issue, as shown by the citations above. In light of the soundness of their reasoning and that of the Tax Court in the present case, we now adopt the doctrine as followed by those courts.

To determine whether a right has "ripened" for tax purposes, a court must consider the realities and substance of events to determine whether the receipt of income was practically certain to occur (i.e., whether the right basically had become a fixed right). . . . While the finding of a mere anticipation or expectation of the receipt of income has been deemed insufficient to conclude that a fixed right to income existed, . . . courts also have made it quite clear that the overall determination must not be based on a consideration of mere formalities and remote hypothetical possibilities. . . .

In the present case, the Tax Court determined that the realities and substance of the ongoing tender offer and the pending merger agreement indicated that the AHC stock already had ripened from an interest in a viable corporation into a fixed right to receive cash, by August 31, 1988 - the first date by which over 50% of the AHC share had been tendered. To wit, the Tax Court determined that by August 31, 1988, it was practically certain that the tender offer and the merger would be completed successfully and that all AHC stock, even untendered stock, either already had been converted into cash (via the tender offer) or imminently would be converted into cash (via the merger).

The Fergusons contend that until September 12, 1988, the date when DC Acquisition formally announced its acceptance of over 95% of the outstanding AHC shares, the tender offer and the merger still could have been derailed and their AHC stock thus had not ripened. However, in support of their many contentions, the Fergusons raise only possibilities that the Tax Court correctly considered to be remote and hypothetical and therefore irrelevant.

Before turning to a contention-by-contention analysis, it is worth noting that in defending its selection of August 31, 1988, as the relevant date for the ripening of the AHC stock, the Tax Court considered whether, as of that date, the surrounding circumstances were sufficient to indicate that the tender offer and the merger would proceed, as if both had to be completed as of or on that date. For example, the Tax Court initially noted that, as of August 31, 1988, over 50% of the outstanding AHC shares had been tendered, and then the Tax Court noted that the receipt of this amount alone was sufficient to ensure that DC Acquisition would accept the tendered stock and thus unilaterally could and would proceed with the merger. . . .

Turning to the Fergusons' individual contentions, we find them to be unpersuasive. First, the Fergusons correctly point out that in the majority of the anticipatory assignment of income cases, some kind of formal shareholder vote (approving a merger, liquidation, or distribution) already had occurred by the time that the stock was deemed to have ripened. . . . However, the language of these cases does not suggest that such formalities are a prerequisite of finding that a ripening has occurred. . . . Indeed, the language of these cases only indicates that such formalities are sufficient, not that they are necessary. . . .

Second, the Fergusons contend that prior to DC Acquisition's acceptance of the tendered stock on September 12, 1988, either of two occurrences might have blocked the successful completion of the tender offer and the merger: (1) the Fergusons, the Charities, or the other shareholders might have withdrawn their tendered shares or simply not tendered their shares; or (2) DC Acquisition might have decided not to accept the tendered stock because the minimum tender condition had not been met yet and because the material change condition had not been waived yet. However, by August 31, 1988, the surrounding circumstances indicate that it was quite unlikely that any of the relevant parties would back out of the tender offer or the merger, and it also was quite unlikely that the requisite number of shares would not be tendered by the close of the tender offer window. . . . [B]y August 31, 1988, the tender offer already had gained a great deal of momentum. Moreover, all of the relevant parties seemed to be getting what they wanted. The Fergusons were receiving a fair amount of cash, generous stock incentives, and assurances that they would continue to play major active roles in the management of their business. CDI, through DC Acquisition, was receiving a very successful business and assurances from the Fergusons that they would continue to be involved extensively in the management and ownership of their business. And the minority shareholders were receiving a fair price for their AHC stock, at a substantial premium over its pre-merger price. Therefore, since the clearly stated intentions and expectations of all of the relevant parties, and the surrounding circumstances as of August 31, 1988, suggest that the receipt of cash (as either tender offer or merger proceeds) was practically certain to occur, the Fergusons' AHC stock had ripened by that date. . . .

Third, the Fergusons and at least one commentator . . . contend that the Tax Court's analysis of the likelihood that as of August 31, 1988, the merger would proceed, was fundamentally flawed because it failed to take into account the bilateral nature of a merger. More specifically, they claim that as of August 31, 1988, even though more than 50% of the AHC shareholders had expressed their tacit approval of the pending merger by tendering their shares, there was still a significant possibility that DC Acquisition's own shareholders might not approve of the merger - a threat until 90% ownership had been obtained by DC Acquisition, thereby eliminating the need for any formal shareholder vote. However, further analysis shows that it is the Fergusons' and the one commentator's analyses that are fundamentally flawed. Both make it sound as if there was much uncertainty as to how the many shareholders of DC Acquisition would vote. Both seem to have completely forgotten that DC Acquisition's sole shareholder was CDI, and that CDI's board of directors (along with DC Acquisition's single director - another corporate insider) therefore effectively could approve the merger without turning to any outside shareholders. And for the reasons discussed above, it was most unlikely as of August 31, 1988, that CDI's board of directors was not fully committed to approving the merger once the tender offer had been completed. Thus, the Tax Court's analysis was sound.

Fourth, the Fergusons attempt to draw analogies to the tax treatment associated with a taxpayer's selection of different accounting methods or with the death of a taxpayer. However, as the government rightly points out, these contexts do not present the same policy considerations as the present one does. Here, but not there, a real danger exists that taxpayers might seek to shift their income to other taxpayers - the very danger that was addressed by the creation of the anticipatory assignment of income doctrine. *See Lucas v. Earl*, 281 U.S. 111 . . . (1930).

On a final note, the Fergusons raise two policy considerations, but these considerations do not support their contentions. First, the Fergusons rightly point out that there is a distinction between tax evasion (i.e., choosing an impermissible path) and tax avoidance (i.e., choosing the least costly permissible path) and that so long as they are acting in accordance with the existing tax laws, the motives for their actions should not dictate the consequences of their actions. However, simply because the Fergusons have the right to choose the least costly path (from a tax perspective) upon which to walk, they do not have the right to be free from taxation if they decide to walk the line between what is and what is not permissible, and happen to stray across it, as they have here. Second, the Fergusons note that the logic of the Tax Court's decision implies that their AHC stock already might have ripened by some date even earlier than August 31, 1988. In essence, they note that there is no clear line demarcating the first date upon which a taxpayer's appreciated stock has ripened into a fixed right to receive cash pursuant to a pending merger. However, from the perspective of taxpayers, walking the line between tax evasion and tax avoidance seems to be a patently dangerous business. Any tax lawyer worth his fees would not have recommended that a donor make a gift of appreciated stock this close to an ongoing tender offer and a pending merger, especially when they were negotiated and planned by the donor. . . . Therefore, we will not go out of our way to make this dangerous business any easier for taxpayers who knowingly assume its risks. Moreover, from the perspective of judging such cases, there is no special reason that we should curtail the application of this doctrine simply because it requires "engaging in an exercise in line drawing, a difficult task which nevertheless is part of the daily grist of judicial life." . . .

Conclusion

Thus, because the Fergusons' contributions of their AHC stock were not completed until September 9, 1988 - at least nine days after the stock had ripened, we affirm the Tax Court's decision holding the Fergusons taxable on the gain in the appreciated stock.

AFFIRMED.

NOTES AND COMMENTS

Yielding to adverse court opinions, the Service now has a more lenient approach to charitable contributions of corporate stock followed by a prearranged redemption of the donated stock, taxing the donor only if the charity was legally obligated to surrender the shares. Rev. Rul. 78-197, 1978-1 C.B. 83. This liberal approach was carried further in *Rauenhorst v. Commissioner*, 119 T.C. 157 (2002), which held that the donor of stock warrants to charities was not taxed on the profit realized by the charitable donees on the sale of donated warrants when the warrants were sold shortly after the transfer in connection with a sale of all the stock of the issuing corporation to third parties even though the sale was pursuant to an offer that had been received by the issuer-donor before the transfer, but that had not been agreed to at the time of the transfer because neither the charities nor third parties were bound to complete the transaction; the gift of warrants to charity was valid. The court refused to allow the Service to take a position it considered contrary to Rev. Rul. 78-197 even though it acknowledged that revenue rulings are not binding on the courts. *See S. C. Johnson & Son, Inc. v. Commissioner*, 63 T.C. 778 (1975) (donor of forward currency contract that appreciated when British pound revalued not taxed when charity sold contract with built-in gain shortly after donation; gift of appreciated property not previously disposed of). The courts and Service have been less generous to donees when there was a binding or agreed right to the proceeds under a contract or similar right. For example, in *Doyle v. Commissioner*, 147 F.2d 769 (4th Cir. 1945), the donor, and not the family-member donees, was taxed on proceeds of litigation when the gift of claim to proceeds after denial of certiorari, but before payment, because at the time of the transfer, the claim was practically assured. *See Malkan v. Commissioner*, 54 T.C. 1305 (1970), *acq.* (donor taxed on proceeds of public offering, including shares given to family trust after terms of public offering agreed to, but before actual contract signed and offering made). The courts have also adopted a similar result when there was a practical reality that the disposition would occur, but no binding agreement, treating a right to proceeds as having ripened for contributions, following adoption of a plan of corporate liquidation, particularly one under former § 337, which made following through a virtual certainty because any gain on the sale of corporate assets was avoided if the liquidation occurred within 12 months, effectively treating the shareholder vote as the turning point. Accordingly, in *Hudspeth v. United States*, 471 F.2d 275 (8th Cir. 1972), the court found that transfers to charities of corporate stock after adoption of a plan of liquidation by the directors and shareholders was an anticipatory assignment of the liquidation proceeds; because the shareholder adoption of the plan was the critical event, stating that "the realities and substance of the events must govern our determination, rather than formalities and remote hypothetical possibilities." *See Kinsey v. Commissioner*, 477 F.2d 1058 (2d Cir. 1973) (donee could not stop liquidation); *Jones v. United States*, 531 F.2d 1343 (6th Cir. 1976) (assignment of anticipatory liquidation proceeds; follows *Hudspeth* and *Kinsey*); *Allen* v. *Commissioner*, 66 T.C. 340 (1976) (same even though donee had power to stop liquidation when liquidation had proceeded to point of declaration of liquidating dividend before donation; situs of control is only one of the factors). On the other hand, in *Keck v. Commissioner*, 415 F.2d 531 (6th Cir. 1969), the proceeds of liquidation from corporate stock owned by a decedent was not income in respect of decedent, even though sale of the corporate assets was agreed before his death and liquidation were contemplated, because the sale was subject to government approval that did not occur until after death so that the decedent lacked control over the corporation's liquidation, and absence of entitlement to receive any proceeds from the contemplated liquidation. In contrast, in *Estate of Bickmeyer v. Commissioner*, 84 T.C. 170 (1985), proceeds of liquidation of corporate shares of sole shareholder of two corporations that had adopted plans of liquidation under former § 337, but died after government paid amounts of its appraisal, some of which were distributed, but before the litigation on proper value was resolved, and additional amounts received and distributed in liquidation were income in respect of a decedent who did not receive a step-up at death; *Keck* was distinguished on the basis that the sale in that case involved contingencies.

PROBLEM FOR DISCUSSION

Problem 7-14. Exec is a shareholder of Tarr, which has recently announced an agreement in principle for a cash merger with Ack on terms that will provide $20 per share for each Tarr share. Exec and his wife own approximately 60,000 shares or 10 percent of Tarr, a public corporation, which Exec helped found, so that the basis in their shares is only $1 per share. Other directors (also founders) and their families collectively own another 25 percent. Exec proposes to make a substantial charitable contribution of Tarr shares and naturally desires to do so on a basis that avoids his being taxed on the inherent gain. It is anticipated that the market price for Tarr shares, which is now $14 per share, will be $16 immediately after execution of the definitive merger agreement, $18 when the proxy statement is mailed, $19 on the record date for the shareholder vote, and $19.50 immediately after the shareholder vote. Before taking into account any expected tax effect of the gift, the Execs have adjusted gross income of $250,000 and taxable income of $200,000. When would you advise Exec to make the gift? Do not consider the AMT. *See Ferguson* (gift of target stock to charity before merger); Rev. Rul. 78-197 (prearranged redemption of stock donated to charity); *Rauenhorst* (warrants donated to charity); *S. C. Johnson & Son* (built-in gain on forward currency contract donated to charity); *Doyle* (gift of litigation claim); *Malkan* (gift of shares after public offering agreed to); *Hudspeth* (gift of shares after adoption of plan of liquidation); *Kinsey* (anticipatory assignments of the liquidation proceeds; gift when donor could not stop liquidation); *Jones* (same); *Allen* (same, but donor could stop liquidation); *Keck* (basis step-up for stock under contract of sale before death, but subject to contingencies); *Bickmeyer* (no basis step-up on death after plan of liquidation adopted).

§ 2.01(d). Escrows

I.R.C. § 468B(g); Treas. Reg. § 1.468B-1 to 4; –7, –9 Prop. Treas. Reg. § 1.468B-8

Despite the comprehensiveness of § 61's definition of gross income, when the ownership of money or property is unknown or in dispute, it is difficult to determine to whom the interim earnings generated by the property should be taxable. Some old rulings held that no one was taxable on the income until the owner became known. *See* Rev. Ruls. 70-567, 1970-2 C.B. 133 (interim income of the escrow of wrongful death proceeds pending a court determination of the proper disposition of and to distribute fund to approved claimants not taxed); Rev. Rul. 71-119, 1971-1 C.B. 163 (income on the settlement fund deposited with the Court upon agreement in securities litigation was not subject to tax; neither the court, nor the special master was required to file a return); both, *declared obsolete by* Rev. Rul. 92-51, 1992-2 C.B. 102. Not surprisingly, Congress found this unsatisfactory and provided in § 468B(g) that someone, to be determined by the Service, had to pay tax on the income currently. The application of this provision to funds held by a qualified intermediary was discussed in § 1.04, *Deferred Exchanges* of Chapter 5, *Nonrecognition Exchanges*.

Treas. Reg. § 1.468B-1 through 5 provide detailed rules for taxing qualified settlement funds, which are those established in court to settle specified litigation, including gain recognition and deductibility by the transferor and taxability of distributions to claimants; essentially, under general tax principles, and generally, taxing the income to the fund. In addition, the regulations provide that the purchaser in a pre-closing escrow is taxed on the income, but a pre-closing escrow is defined as one, in which the income is distributed for the purchaser's benefit. Treas. Reg. § 1.468B-7. When the escrow is contingent-at-closing, the purchaser is taxed on income until the contingencies are removed, and thereafter the purchaser and seller, on the basis of their interests in the escrow. Prop. Treas. Reg. § 1.468B-8. When the escrow is for disputed ownership funds, the escrow is taxed as a C corporation on the earnings, unless it is a qualified settlement fund, in which all of its assets are passive investment assets, so that in the latter case it is taxed at the highest individual rate, or it is taxed to the transferor who claims ownership of the property transferred. Treas. Reg. § 1.468B-9.

PROBLEMS FOR DISCUSSION

Problem 7-15. Pubco deposited $10,000,000 into a United States District Court to settle claims that were asserted against the corporation in several lawsuits brought by shareholders who alleged misstatements and omissions in registration statements filed pursuant to the Securities Act of 1933 by the corporation. The funds are to be distributed to Pubco shareholders who owned their shares during the periods of 20X1 and 20X2 after the alleged misstatements were made and before Pubco made adequate correcting statements. A special master will invest the funds in U.S. Treasury securities, determine the validity and amount of claims (subject to court confirmation) and distribute the funds pro rata to the claimants. In the unlikely event that the funds exceed valid claims, the balance will be returned to Pubco. How is the income taxed? *See* § 468B(g); Treas. Reg. § 1.468B-1, -2, and -9; Rev. Rul. 71-119 *declared obsolete* (settlement proceeds deposited in court).

Problem 7-16. Impare's insurance company paid $1,000,000 (the policy limit) to CountriBanc to hold in escrow as the damages of a wrongful death action by survivors of Vic, resulting from an auto accident, in which Impare was held liable. The funds are to be held while Vic's survivors arbitrate who is entitled to how much. CountriBanc is to invest the funds in U.S. Treasury securities while the arbitration goes on. How is the income of the fund taxed? *See* § 468B(g); Treas. Reg. § 1.468B-1, -2, and -9; Rev. Rul. 70-567 *declared obsolete* (escrow of wrongful death proceeds pending determination of claims).

§ 2.02. Sales of Partial Interests — Ordinary Income Substitute

I.R.C. §§ 631, 636, 1001(e), and 1231(b); Treas. Reg. § 1.1014-4

Some sales or other taxable dispositions of partial interests in property are taxed as ordinary income, while others are entitled to capital gain or section 1231 treatment. The phrase "assignment of income" is frequently used to describe the transactions taxed as ordinary income, but it has quite a different meaning in this context. In the context of gratuitous transfers, the question is: to whom is the income taxed? When partial interests are transferred for consideration, however, it is clear that the transferor is indicated as the one taxed and the question is the character of the income. Nevertheless, as explained at the beginning of this section, generally the character of gain (or loss) on sale of a partial interest as ordinary income or capital gain is essentially the same as for the underlying property.

Amounts realized from the disposition of partial interests in property are treated as ordinary income when they are considered to be substitutes for ordinary income from the property. This is indisputable for the sale of partial interests representing income that has accrued economically, as, for example, rents or interest for past periods, but has not been realized for tax purposes, usually because the taxpayer uses the cash method of accounting. When the income has not yet accrued economically, treating amounts realized from disposition as ordinary income on the gain realized from the disposition of property as ordinary income because it represents an anticipation of ordinary income proves too much, because the value of any asset is represented by the income or gain that might be realized from holding it. As Lord Coke is widely quoted as stating: "For what is the land, but the profits thereof?" Obviously, as long as there is a capital gains preference, some intermediate line must be drawn. The following cases grapple with where and how to do the line drawing.

HORT v. COMMISSIONER

Supreme Court of the United States
313 U.S. 28 (1941)

* * *

Mr. Justice Murphy delivered the opinion of the Court.

We must determine whether the amount petitioner received as consideration for cancellation of a lease of realty in New York City was ordinary gross income as defined in § [61] . . . and whether, in any event, petitioner sustained a loss through cancellation of the lease which is recognized in § [165].

Petitioner acquired the property, a lot and ten-story office building, by devise from his father in 1928. At the time he became owner, the premises were leased to a firm which had sublet the main floor to the Irving Trust Co. In 1927, five years before the head lease expired, the Irving Trust Co. and petitioner's father executed a contract in which the latter agreed to lease the main floor and basement to the former for a term of fifteen years at an annual rental of $25,000, the term to commence at the expiration of the head lease.

In 1933, the Irving Trust Co. found it unprofitable to maintain a branch in petitioner's building. After some negotiations, petitioner and the Trust Co. agreed to cancel the lease in consideration of a payment to petitioner of $140,000. Petitioner did not include this amount in gross income in his income tax return for 1933. On the contrary, he reported a loss of $21,494.75 on the theory that the amount he received as consideration for the cancellation was $21,494.75 less than the difference between the present value of the unmatured rental payments and the fair rental value of the main floor and basement for the unexpired term of the lease. He did not deduct this figure, however, because he reported other losses in excess of gross income.

The Commissioner included the entire $140,000 in gross income, disallowed the asserted loss, made certain other adjustments not material here, and assessed a deficiency. . . .

Petitioner apparently contends that the amount received for cancellation of the lease was capital rather than ordinary income and that it was therefore subject to [Subchapter P] . . . which govern[s] capital gains and losses. Further, he argues that even if that amount must be reported as ordinary gross income he sustained a loss which § [165] authorizes him to deduct. We cannot agree.

The amount received by petitioner for cancellation of the lease must be included in his gross income in its entirety. Section [61] . . . expressly defines gross income to include "gains, profits, and income derived from . . . rent, . . . or gains or profits and income derived from any source whatever." Plainly this definition reached the rent paid prior to cancellation just as it would have embraced subsequent payments if the lease had never been canceled. It would have included a prepayment of the discounted value of unmatured rental payments whether received at the inception of the lease or at any time thereafter. Similarly, it would have extended to the proceeds of a suit to recover damages had the Irving Trust Co. breached the lease instead of concluding a settlement. . . . That the amount petitioner received resulted from negotiations ending in cancellation of the lease rather than from a suit to enforce it cannot alter the fact that basically the payment was merely a substitute for the rent reserved in the lease. So far as the application of § [165] is concerned, it is immaterial that petitioner chose to accept an amount less than the strict present value of the unmatured rental payments rather than to engage in litigation, possibly uncertain and expensive.

The consideration received for cancellation of the lease was not a return of capital. We assume that the lease was "property," whatever that signifies abstractly. Presumably the bond in *Helvering v. Horst*, 311 U.S. 112, and the lease in *Helvering v. Bruun*, 309 U.S. 461, were also "property," but the interest coupon in *Horst* and the building in *Bruun* nevertheless were held to constitute items of gross income. Simply because the lease was "property" the amount received for its cancellation was not a return of capital, quite apart from the fact that "property" and "capital" are not necessarily synonymous in the Revenue Act of 1932 or in common usage. Where, as in this case, the disputed amount was essentially a substitute for rental payments which § [61] expressly characterizes as gross income, it must be regarded as ordinary income, and it is immaterial that for some purposes the contract creating the right to such payments may be treated as "property" or "capital."

For the same reasons, that amount was not a return of capital because petitioner acquired the lease as an incident of the realty devised to him by his father. Theoretically, it might have been possible in such a case to value realty and lease separately and to label each a capital asset. . . . But that would not have converted into capital the amount petitioner received from the Trust Co., since § 1[02] . . . would have required him to include in gross income the rent derived from the property, and that section, like § [61], does not distinguish rental payments and a payment which is clearly a substitute for rental payments.

We conclude that petitioner must report as gross income the entire amount received for cancellation of the lease, without regard to the claimed disparity between that amount and the difference between the present value of the unmatured rental payments and the fair rental value of the property for the unexpired period of the lease. The cancellation of the lease involved nothing more than relinquishment of the right to future rental payments in return for a present substitute payment and possession of the leased premises. Undoubtedly it diminished the amount of gross income petitioner expected to realize, but to that extent he was relieved of the duty to pay income tax. Nothing in § [165] indicates that Congress intended to allow petitioner to reduce ordinary income actually received and reported by the amount of income he failed to realize. . . . We may assume that petitioner was injured insofar as the cancellation of the lease affected the value of the realty. But that would become a deductible loss only when its extent had been fixed by a closed transaction. . . .

The judgment of the Circuit Court of Appeals is Affirmed.

MCALLISTER v. COMMISSIONER

United States Court of Appeals, Second Circuit

157 F.2d 235 (2d Cir. 1946)

[The taxpayer was life beneficiary of a trust. She released her interest to the remainderman for a specified sum and reported a loss on the sale. In upholding the taxpayer, the court stated:]

* * *

Petitioner's right to income for life from the trust estate was a right in the estate itself. Had she held a fee interest, the assignment would unquestionably have been regarded as the transfer of a capital asset; we see no reason why a different result should follow the transfer of the lesser, but still substantial, life interest. . . .

* * *

The Tax Court and the government have attempted to distinguish both the *Bell* and the *Blair* cases on grounds which seem to us to lack either substance or reality. The principal ground seems to be the form the transaction assumed between the parties. Thus the Court says that petitioner received the payment for "surrendering" her rights to income payments, and "she did not assign her interest in the trust, as did petitioners in the *Bell* case." But what is this more than a distinction in words? Both were cases where at the conclusion of the transaction the remaindermen had the entire estate and the life tenants had a substantial sum of money. There surely cannot be that efficacy in lawyers' jargon that termination or cancellation or surrender carries some peculiar significance vastly penalizing laymen whose counsel have chanced to use them. . . .

* * *

. . . Here the line of demarcation between the *Blair* and the *Hort* principles is obviously one of some difficulty to define explicitly or to establish in borderline cases. Doubtless all would agree that there is some distinction between selling a life estate in property and anticipating income for a few years in advance. It is the kind of distinction stressed in *Harrison v. Schaffner* . . . where the Court said: "Nor are we troubled by the logical difficulties of drawing the line between a gift of an equitable interest in property for life effected by a gift for life of a share of the income of the trust and the gift of the income or a part of it for the period of a year as in this case." The distinction seems logically and practically to turn upon anticipation of income payments over a reasonably short period of time and an out-and-out transfer of a substantial and durable property interest, such as a life estate at least is. . . . Where the line should be finally placed we need not try to anticipate here. But we are clear that distinctions attempted on the basis of the various legal names given a transaction, rather than on its actual results between the parties, do not afford a sound basis for its delimitation. More rationally, to accept the respondent's contention we ought frankly to consider the *Blair* case as overruled, . . . a position which, as we have seen, the Supreme Court itself has declined to take.

* * *

FRANK, CIRCUIT JUDGE (dissenting).

* * *

We must, then, ascertain the intention of Congress expressed in those provisions — especially § [1221] — in the light of the language it employed and the policy there embodied, i.e., we must determine whether Congress intended that a taxpayer who receives income in those circumstances should come within that exception.

My colleagues avoid a direct discussion of that problem. Instead, they rely on *Blair* . . . , which they hold to be controlling. But the court in the *Blair* case had no occasion to, and did not, consider § [1201]; it considered solely the interpretation of § [61(a)]. There, the . . . only question was whether thereafter the donor, notwithstanding the gift, should be regarded, under § [61(a)], as the recipient annually of that part of the income which was the subject of the gift and, consequently, should be taxed each year thereon. In other words, no capital gain or loss was involved, and the one issue was whether the donor or donee was annually taxable. The only conceivable ground for holding the donor liable was- . . . that which moved the Court in *Helvering v. Clifford* . . . i.e., that, in terms of "non-material satisfactions" the donor had not, by the gift, changed his position and, because of his continued "enjoyment of the economic benefit," . . . must still be regarded, within § [61(a)], as receiving the income actually paid to the donee. In the *Horst* and *Schaffner* cases, the Court said the donor was thus within § [61(a)]; in the *Blair* case, because the gift transferred the income for the duration of the donor's life, the Court held he was not. . . .

Since the Court in the *Blair* case was not called on to say (as we are here) whether the taxpayer was liable under either § [61(a)] or under § [1201], but only whether taxpayer was liable, if at all, under § [61(a)], the *Blair* case sheds no light on the construction of § [1201]. Surely it does not follow merely (1) because one who makes a gift of a life estate does not retain such "non-material satisfactions" as to be liable under § [61(a)], that (2) one who disposes of a life estate for a valuable consideration is to be treated as having disposed of a "capital asset" under § [1201(a)(1)] and is therefore entitled to the peculiar, exceptional, treatment accorded by the capital gains provisions. So, when it was argued that an interest which, pursuant to the *Horst* case, was "property" for purposes of § [61(a)] must be "capital" for purposes of the capital gains provisions, the Supreme Court answered that " 'property' and 'capital' are not necessarily synonymous in the Revenue Act of 1932 or in common usage"; *Hort* . . .

* * *

The policy of the capital gains provisions is not in doubt: Congress believed that the exaction of income tax on the usual basis on gains resulting from dispositions of capital investments would undesirably deter such dispositions. To put it differently, Congress made an exception to § [61(a)], in order to give an incentive to the making of such transfers. Having regard to that purpose, the courts have been cautious in interpreting the clauses creating that exception. They have refused to regard as "capital" transactions for that purpose divers sorts of transfers of "property," especially those by which transferors have procured advance payments of future income.

Those cases and *Hort* . . . seem to me to render it somewhat doubtful whether any transfer of a life estate for a valuable consideration is within § [1201]. The consideration paid for such a transfer is a substitute for future payments which would be taxable as ordinary income, and resembles the advance payment of dividends, interest or salaries. . . .

* * *

It suggests far more strongly that we cannot reasonably extrapolate the language of § [1201] to include the transaction before us in the instant case. In the *Hort* case, the Supreme Court held that the "prepayment of the discounted value of unmatured rental payments" to a landlord on the cancellation of a lease constituted "ordinary income," coming within § [61(a)], and not within the capital gains clauses. The Court said, " . . . The cancellation of the lease involved nothing more than the relinquishment of the right to future rental payments in return for a present substitute payment and possession of the leased premises * * *" . . .

* * *

METROPOLITAN BUILDING CO. v. COMMISSIONER

United States Court of Appeals, Ninth Circuit
282 F.2d 592 (9th Cir. 1960)

[The taxpayer, lessee of a large tract, had subleased a portion to Olympic. When the main lease and sublease had about two years to run, Olympic, in order to obtain a new long-term lease offered to start paying higher rent to the fee owner. The taxpayer agreed to release the remainder of its interest in the lease to the owner of the property for a lump sum consideration of based on its expected profit. Apparently the subtenant actually provided the consideration. In holding that the payment was capital gain and distinguishing *Hort*, the court stated:]

In that case the Trust Company did not acquire any interest of its lessor. It simply compromised and liquidated its rental obligation under the lease. The sum received by the lessor . . . was not compensation for acquisition of any interest of the lessor.

In the case before us, the sums paid to Metropolitan were not simply a discharge of Olympic's obligation to pay rental. They were paid for the purchase of Metropolitan's entire leasehold interest. The case is not one of a liquidation of a right to future income as is *Hort*, but rather it is one of a disposition of income-producing property itself. . . .

In *Golonsky* the court stated the problem of the case as follows:

> "A tenant in possession of premises under a lease, upon receipt of payment by the landlord, and pursuant to an agreement made with the landlord, 'vacated and surrendered the premises' before the date at which the lease expired." . . .

It was held that the proceeds of the transaction constituted capital gain.

The Commissioner would (and the Tax Court did) distinguish *Golonsky* upon the ground that in the instant case the consideration passed not from the lessor but from the sublessee, the very party obliged to pay rental to the recipient, and that such consideration represented the amount which the recipient felt it would otherwise have received under the sublease. . . .

We are not impressed by this proposed distinction. The lease clearly had value over the amount of rentals due by virtue of the fact that its acquisition was of importance to Olympic. . . . The Commissioner seems to concede[1] that if the consideration had been paid by the University or if the lease had been assigned to a third party the transaction would have constituted a sale by the lessee.

It is not the person of the payor which controls the nature of the transaction in our view. Rather, it is the fact that the transaction constituted a bona fide transfer, for a legitimate business purpose, of the leasehold in its entirety. It did not constitute a release or transfer only of the right to future income under the sublease. . . .

* * *

COMMISSIONER v. P. G. LAKE, INC.

Supreme Court of the United States
356 U.S. 260 (1958)

MR. JUSTICE DOUGLAS delivered the opinion of the Court.

* * *

. . . Lake is a corporation engaged in the business of producing oil and gas. It has a seven-eighths working interest[1] in two commercial oil and gas leases. In 1950 it was indebted to its president in the sum of $600,000 and in consideration of his cancellation of the debt assigned him an oil payment right in the amount of

---

[1] "In 1954 the taxpayer sold the remainder of the Metropolitan Tract lease to a third party, and the Tax Court held that the proceeds of the sale were taxable under Section [1201] as gain realized from the sale of property. From this adverse decision, the Commissioner has not appealed."

[1] An oil and gas lease ordinarily conveys the entire mineral interest less any royalty interest retained by the lessor. The owner of the lease is said to own the "working interest" because he has the right to develop and produce the minerals.

In *Anderson v. Helvering*, . . . we described an oil payment as "the right to a specified sum of money, payable out of a specified percentage of the oil, or the proceeds received from the sale of such oil, if, as and when produced." . . . A royalty interest is "a right to receive a specified percentage of all oil and gas produced" but, unlike the oil payment, is not limited to a specified sum of money. The royalty interest lasts during the entire term of the lease. . . .

$600,000, plus an amount equal to interest at 3 percent a year on the unpaid balance remaining from month to month, payable out of 25 percent of the oil attributable to the taxpayer's working interest in the two leases. At the time of the assignment it could have been estimated with reasonable accuracy that the assigned oil payment right would pay out in three or more years. It did in fact pay out in a little over three years.

In its 1950 tax return Lake reported the oil payment assignment as a sale of property producing a profit of $600,000 and taxable as a long-term capital gain . . . In the *O'Connor* case the assignors of the oil payments owned royalty interests rather than working interests. But these differences are not material to the question we have for decision.

The *Weed* case is different only because it involves sulphur rights, rather than oil rights. . . .

* * *

The *Fleming* case is a bit more complicated and presents an additional question not in the other cases. Here oil payment assignments were made, not for cash but for real estate. Two transactions are involved. Fleming and others with whom he was associated made oil payment assignments, the rights and interests involved being held by them for productive use in their respective businesses of producing oil. Each oil payment was assigned for an interest in a ranch. Each was in an amount which represented the uncontested fair value of the undivided interest in the ranch received by the assignor, plus an amount equal to the interest per annum on the balance remaining unpaid from time to time. The other transaction consisted of an oil payment assignment by an owner of oil and gas leases, held for productive use in the assignor's business, for the fee simple title to business real estate. This oil payment assignment, like the ones mentioned above, was in the amount of the uncontested fair market value of the real estate received, plus interest on the unpaid balance remaining from time to time.

First, as to whether the proceeds were taxable as long-term capital gains under § [1221] or as ordinary income subject to depletion. The Court of Appeals started from the premise, laid down in Texas decisions . . . that oil payments are interests in land. We too proceed on that basis; and yet we conclude that the consideration received for these oil payment rights (and the sulphur payment right) was taxable as ordinary income, subject to depletion.

The purpose of § [1221] was "to relieve the taxpayer from . . . excessive tax burdens on gains resulting from a conversion of capital investments, and to remove the deterrent effect of those burdens on such conversions." See *Burnet v. Harmel*. . . . And this exception has always been narrowly construed so as to protect the revenue against artful devices. See *Corn Products*. . . .

We do not see here any conversion of a capital investment. The lump sum consideration seems essentially a substitute for what would otherwise be received at a future time as ordinary income. The pay-out of these particular assigned oil payment rights could be ascertained with considerable accuracy. Such are the stipulations, findings, or clear inferences. In the *O'Connor* case, the pay-out of the assigned oil payment right was so assured that the purchaser obtained a $9,990,350 purchase money loan at 3 1/2 percent interest without any security other than a deed of trust of the $10,000,000 oil payment right, he receiving 4 percent from the taxpayer. Only a fraction of the oil or sulphur rights were transferred, the balance being retained.[5] Except in the *Fleming* case, which we will discuss later, cash was received which was equal to the amount of the income to accrue during the term of the assignment, the assignee being compensated by interest on his advance. The substance of what was assigned was the right to receive future income. The substance of what was received was the present value of income which the recipient would otherwise obtain in the future. In short, consideration was paid for the right to receive future income, not for an increase in the value of the income-producing property.

These arrangements seem to us transparent devices. Their forms do not control. Their essence is determined not by subtleties of draftsmanship but by their total effect. See *Helvering v. Clifford* . . . ; *Harrison v. Schaffner*. . . . We have held that if one, entitled to receive at a future date interest on a bond or compensation for services, makes a grant of it by anticipatory assignment, he realizes taxable income as if he had collected the interest or received the salary and then paid it over. That is the teaching of *Helvering v. Horst* . . . and *Harrison v. Schaffner* . . . ; and it is applicable here. As we stated in *Helvering v. Horst*, . . . "The taxpayer has equally enjoyed the fruits of his labor or investment and obtained the satisfaction of his desires whether he collects and uses the income to procure those satisfactions, or whether he disposes of his right to collect it as the means of procuring them." There the taxpayer detached interest coupons from negotiable bonds and presented them as a gift to his son. The interest when paid was held taxable to the father. Here, even more clearly than there, the taxpayer is converting future income into present income.

---

[5] Until 1946 the Commissioner agreed with the contention of the taxpayers in these cases that the assignment of an oil payment right was productive of a long-term capital gain. In 1946 he changed his mind and ruled that "consideration (not pledged for development) received for the assignment of a short-lived in-oil payment right carved out of any type of depletable interest in oil and gas in place (including a larger in-oil payment right) is ordinary income subject to the depletion allowance in the assignor's hands." G.C.M. 24849. . . . In 1950 a further ruling was made that represents the present view of the Commissioner. I.T. 4003 . . . reads in relevant part as follows:

> "After careful study and considerable experience with the application of G.C.M. 24849 . . . it is now concluded that there is no legal or practical basis for distinguishing between short-lived and long-lived in-oil payment rights. It is, therefore, the present position of the Bureau that the assignment of any in-oil payment right (not pledged for development), which extends over a period less than the life of the depletable property interest from which it is carved, is essentially the assignment of expected income from such property interest. Therefore, the assignment for a consideration of any such in-oil payment right results in the receipt of ordinary income by the assignor which is taxable to him when received or accrued, depending upon the method of accounting employed by him. Where the assignment of the in-oil payment right is donative, the transaction is considered as an assignment of future income which is taxable to the donor at such time as the income from the assigned payment right arises.
>
> "Notwithstanding the foregoing, G.C.M. 24849 . . . and I.T. 3935 . . . do not apply where the assigned in-oil payment right constitutes the entire depletable interest of the assignor in the property or a fraction extending over the entire life of the property."

The pre-1946 administrative practice was not reflected in any published ruling or regulation. It therefore will not be presumed to have been known to Congress and incorporated into the law by re-enactment. . . . Moreover, prior administrative practice is always subject to change "through exercise by the administrative agency of its continuing rule-making power." See *Helvering v. Reynolds* . . .

Second, as to the *Fleming* case. The Court of Appeals in the *Fleming* case held that the transactions were tax-free under § [1031(a)] which provides:

> "No gain or loss shall be recognized if property held for productive use in trade or business or for investment (not including stock in trade or other property held primarily for sale, nor stocks, bonds, notes, choses in action, certificates of trust or beneficial interest, or other securities or evidences of indebtedness or interest) is exchanged solely for property of a like kind to be held either for productive use in trade or business or for investment."
>
> In the alternative and as a second ground, it held that this case, too, was governed by § [1201].

We agree with the Tax Court . . . that this is not a tax-free exchange under § [1031(a)]. Treasury Regulations . . . [§ 1.1031(a)-1(b)] as respects the words "like kind," as used in § [1031(a)], that "One kind or class of property may not . . . be exchanged for property of a different kind or class." The exchange cannot satisfy that test where the effect under the tax laws is a transfer of future income from oil leases for real estate. As we have seen, these oil payment assignments were merely arrangements for delayed cash payment of the purchase price of real estate, plus interest. Moreover, § [1.1002-1(c)] states that the "underlying assumption of these exceptions is that the new property is substantially a continuation of the old investment still unliquidated." Yet the oil payment assignments were not conversions of capital investments, as we have seen.

Reversed.

NOTES AND COMMENTS

As indicated, these cases echo the gratuitous "assignment of income" cases. *Hort* (payment to lessor for cancellation of future rent is ordinary income) is analogous to *Horst* (gratuitous assignment of bond coupons by holder of right to bond principal representing future interest does not transfer taxability of interest coupons), which it cites, while *McAllister* (sale of entire trust income interest is taxable as capital gain) is analogous to *Blair* (gratuitous assignment of an undivided share of trust income interest transfers taxability of assigned income), which it cites copiously, and *Schaffner* (assignment of limited portion of income interest for a short time does not transfer taxability of income), which it distinguishes. *Metropolitan Building* (receipt of payment by tenant for cancellation of remaining term of lease — all tenant owned — terminating right to collect rent from subtenant is capital gain) is also analogous to *Blair* (gratuitous assignment of an undivided share of trust income interest transfers taxability of assigned income), which it does not cite, and properly distinguishes *Hort*). *See* Priv. Ltr. Rul. 2000-45-019 (payments, including legal fees and taxes by a landlord to a tenant to completely terminate a lease under a local rent control law that applied only to residential properties (although there was some business use) were entitled to capital gain treatment under § 1221 or 1231; ruling also referred to § 1241). *P.G. Lake* also appears to be similar to *McAllister* and *Metropolitan Building* in that the taxpayer sold all he had, but neither case is cited — possibly poor tax lawyering? — and the result is different. Interestingly, *P.G. Lake* does cite *Horst* (but not *Hort*), and *Schaffner* to support its result. Although Justice Douglas indicates that the interest sold was a right to receive future income, the same is true in *McAllister* and *Metropolitan Building*, which, nevertheless, allowed capital gain. Perhaps a clue is found in Justice Douglas' emphasis on the fact that the amounts receivable were calculable with reasonable accuracy, but what is the significance of that fact? One possible explanation, not justified by anything stated in Justice Douglas' opinion, is the word "receive," which accurately reflects that the taxpayers did not have to do anything more to *earn* the right to collect the income, so that the amounts were economically earned, even though not yet realized or otherwise recognizable for tax purposes. In contrast, even though Ms. McAllister, as a trust beneficiary, did not have to do anything to earn her share of the future income, the trust did, using the capital in which she had an interest.

Congress modified the result in *McAllister* by enacting § 1001(e), which does not address the capital gain issue, but does require that the entire amount realized be treated as gain by denying the holder of the term interest a share of the basis of the underlying property. Under the "uniform basis" rules, Treas. Reg. §§ 1.1014-4 and -5, the basis of inherited property held in trust is allocated between the holders of life or term interests and the holder of the remainder interest in proportion to actuarial values, with the basis shifting to the remainder with the passage of time. The holder of the life or term interest is not entitled to amortize the allocated basis against the income. Accordingly, the allocated basis to the holder of the life or term interest is only significant on the sale of the interest. Section 1001(e) allows the holder of the life or term interest to offset the basis against an allocable amount of the proceeds when the sale is part of a sale of the entire property, but does not allow it for a sale of the life or term interest alone, whether to the holder of the remainder or otherwise. For example, if parents establish a trust with securities with a basis and value of $1,000,000 to pay income to their daughter for life with a remainder to her children, at a time when the actuarial value of Dora's life interest is 70 percent of the value of the trust, the initial basis of her interest is $700,000 and the initial basis of the children's remainder is $300,000. A few years later when the basis of the trust's assets is still $1,000,000, but the actuarial value of the daughter's interest has declined to 60 percent, she and her children sell their interests in the trust to a unrelated purchaser for its value of $1,200,000 with $720,000 (60% of $1,200,000) paid to the daughter and $480,000 (40% of $1,200,000) to the children. The daughter realizes gain of $120,000 ($720,000 proceeds - $600,000 (60% of $1,000,000) basis) and her children realize gain of $80,000 ($480,000 proceeds - $400,000 (40% of $1,000,000) basis), because under the uniform basis rules, the initial basis gradually shifts from the daughter to her children as the actuarial value of her interest declines with age. If, on the other hand, the daughter sold her interest to her children for $720,000, her gain would be $720,000, because, under §1001(e) she is not allowed to offset any portion of her share of the uniform basis.

The result in *P. G. Lake* has also been modified by the enactment of § 636, discussed in *Brountas* (nonrecourse notes secured by production from wildcat wells are too speculative to be given tax effect), discussed in § 3.03, *Speculative Security* of Chapter 3 *Liabilities: Discharge of Indebtedness; Mortgaged Property.* Because, unlike *Brountas*, as Justice Douglas indicates, the carved-out oil payment in *P.G. Lake* was hardly speculative, under § 636, it would represent the equivalent of a secured note issued by P.G. Lake, Inc., to its president, so that it would be paying its debt with a new secured debt, realizing no income, ordinary or capital gain, although the president would if the debt was an obligation for compensation that he had not included in income.

PROBLEMS FOR DISCUSSION

Problem 7-17. What is the effect to the payer of the payment? (i) In *Hort* (payment to escape burdensome lease); (ii) In *McAllister* (purchase of life interest by remainder); (iii) In *Metropolitan Building Co.* (lump sum payment from surrender of lease by tenant; funds supplied by subtenant); and (iv) *P.G. Lake, Inc.* (oil payment rights in cancellation of debt)?

Problem 7-18. Lucky won the big prize in the state lottery in a state that does not provide the alternative of taking a lump sum. Believing that he could use the money better in his "private account," he sold the right to all the future proceeds to Invest for an amount equal to the discounted value at the high grade bond rate. (i) What is the tax effect of the sale to Lucky? (ii) To Invest? *See Lattera* (sale of right to lottery proceeds) discussed in § 3.02 *Definition of Property* of Chapter 2, *Capital Gains and Losses*; *Hort* (payment to escape burdensome lease); *McAllister* (payment for life estate); *Metropolitan Building Co.* (payment for termination of leaseholder interest); and *P.G. Lake, Inc.* (debt repaid with oil payment rights).

§ 3. INTANGIBLES — CONTRACT RIGHTS, SELF-CREATED PROPERTY, AND GOODWILL (AND GOING CONCERN VALUE)

As vexing as distinguishing rights to ordinary income from the inherent profit-making potential of all income-producing property may be, the issues are perhaps even more vexing when the transfer is of rights to intangible assets. Intangible assets include not only statutorily protected forms of intellectual property — patents, copyrights, and trademarks — but also a vast array of contract rights, ranging from management contracts to contracts to acquire property, and noncontractual value known as goodwill or going concern value. The tax issue that frequently arises is the proper characterization of the gain realized on the transfer of such assets as either capital gain or ordinary income. An underlying issue in many cases is the element of personal effort that went into creating the intangible property, with an unstated assumption that the gain attributable to personal efforts is inherently ordinary income.

A first cut at classifying contract rights between those entitled to capital gain and those that give rise to ordinary income is made in § 3.01, *Contract Rights.* The classification, particularly relating to management and service contracts, is refined in § 3.02, *Future Services versus Goodwill,* which recognizes that goodwill and going concern value are rights to earn income. The statutory allocation of the purchase price of a business, resulting from *Williams v. McGowan*, 152 F.2d 570 (2d Cir. 1945), discussed in § 4.01 *Overview* of Chapter 1 *Basis and Realization.* Recognizing that case law was not adequate, Congress has enacted several specific

Code provisions to deal with the tax treatment of intellectual property that are covered in § 3.03 *Artists, Inventors, Franchises.*

§ 3.01. Contract Rights

I.R.C. §§ 1241; 1234A

The following famous, and controversial, opinion involves the characterization of gain associated with the transfer of certain contract rights in connection with a complex contractual arrangement also involving a significant element of personal services. The opinion was authored by an excellent judge who freely acknowledged that he was no tax lawyer. His approach is that of a common-law lawyer to this technical tax issue. Whatever the effects of his lack of tax expertise, it provides a good review of the case law and of the underlying tax problem.

COMMISSIONER v. FERRER

United States Court of Appeals, Second Circuit
304 F.2d 125 (2d Cir. 1962)

FRIENDLY, CIRCUIT JUDGE.

This controversy concerns the tax status of certain payments received by Jose Ferrer with respect to the motion picture "Moulin Rouge" portraying the career of Henri de Toulouse-Lautrec. The difficulties Mr. Ferrer must have had in fitting himself into the shape of the artist can hardly have been greater than ours in determining whether the transaction here at issue fits the rubric "gain from the sale or exchange of a capital asset . . . " . . . or constitutes ordinary income . . . We have concluded that neither party is entirely right, that some aspects of the transaction fall on one side of the line and some on the other, and that the Tax Court must separate the two.

In 1950 Pierre LaMure published a novel, "Moulin Rouge," based on the life of Toulouse-Lautrec. He then wrote a play, "Monsieur Toulouse," based on the novel. On November 1, 1951, LaMure as "Author" and Ferrer, a famous actor but not a professional producer, as "Manager" entered into a contract, called a Dramatic Production Contract, for the stage production of the play by Ferrer.

The contract was largely on a printed form recommended by the Dramatists Guild of the Authors League of America, Inc. However great the business merits of the document, . . . for a court, faced with the task of defining the nature of the rights created, it exemplifies what a contract ought not to be. Its first six pages include eleven articles, some introduced by explanatory material whose contractual status is, to say the least, uncertain. Here the last of these pages was preceded by three single-spaced typewritten pages of "Additional Clauses," one with a still further insert. Finally come 15 pages of closely printed "Supplemental Provisions," introduced by explanatory material of the sort noted. We shall thread our way through this maze as best we can.

By the contract the Author "leased" to the Manager "the sole and exclusive right" to produce and present "Monsieur Toulouse" on the speaking stage in the

United States and Canada, and gave certain rights for its production elsewhere. . . . Five hundred dollars were paid as an initial advance against Author's royalties; the Manager was required to make further advances . . . Royalties were to be paid the Author on all box-office receipts, on a sliding scale percentage basis.

Article Seventh said that "In the event that under the terms hereof the Manager shall be entitled to share in the proceeds of the Motion Picture and Additional Rights hereafter referred to, it is agreed that the Manager shall receive" 40% for the first ten years and diminishing percentages thereafter. . . .

For the beginning of an answer whether the Manager would be so entitled, we turn to Article IV, § 2, of the Supplemental Provisions. This tells us that "In the event the Manager has produced and presented the play for the 'Requisite Performances and Terms,' the Negotiator shall pay the Manager" the above percentages "of the proceeds, from the disposal of the motion picture rights." . . .

Further provisions put flesh on these bones. . . . Article VIII says, . . . "The Author shall retain for his sole benefit, complete title, both legal and equitable, in and to all rights whatsoever (including, but not by way of limitation, the Motion Picture Rights * * * Radio and Television Rights * * *)," other than the right to produce the play. The Motion Picture Negotiator, a person appointed by the Council of the Dramatists Guild, Article V, §§ 1 and 6, has power to dispose of the motion picture rights. However, he may not do this without the written consent of both Author and Manager "prior to the time the play has been playing for any of the respective periods of time referred to in Article XIII, Section 9(b) hereof," Article IV, § 1(b). This prohibition serves a double purpose — it protects the Manager from dilution of the value of the right to produce the play through too early exhibition of a picture, and it promotes realization of the enhancement of the value of the motion picture rights normally resulting from successful dramatic production. . . . Article V, § 1(b), decrees that the Manager shall "have no right, title or interest, legal or equitable, in the motion picture rights, other than the right to receive the Manager's share of the proceeds * * *" Article V, § 1(c), lays down that if the Manager deems "himself aggrieved by any disposition of motion picture rights, . . . "the Manager's sole recourse * * * shall be against the Author and only by arbitration as provided hereunder." . . .

Having been somewhat upstaged by these provisions, the Manager then returns toward the center under other clauses. The Negotiator must confer with him, as well as with the Author, on every step in the disposition of the motion picture rights. . . . If the Manager does not like an offer the Negotiator is planning to accept, he has an opportunity to turn up a better one . . . An insert to one of the "Additional Clauses" provides that if the Manager desires, the Author, not later than three weeks after the New York opening of the play, will "discuss a proposed deal for the Manager to acquire" the motion picture rights. Finally, another "Additional Clause" prescribes that "All dramatic, motion picture, radio and television rights in the novel MOULIN ROUGE shall merge in and with the play during the existence of this contract," and if the Manager produces and presents the play for a sufficient period, "throughout the copyright period of the play."

Shortly after signature of the Dramatic Production Contract, John Huston called Ferrer to ask whether he would be interested in playing Toulouse-Lautrec in a picture based upon "Moulin Rouge." On getting an affirmative indication, Huston said he would go ahead and acquire the motion picture rights. Ferrer replied, in somewhat of an exaggeration, "When you get ready to acquire them talk to me because I own them."

Both Huston and Ferrer then had discussions with LaMure. Ferrer expressed a willingness "to abandon the theatrical production in favor of the film production, provided that, if the film production were successful, I would be recompensed for my abandoning the stage production." On the strength of this, LaMure signed a preliminary agreement with Huston's corporation. In further negotiations, Huston's attorney insisted on "either an annulment or conveyance" of the Dramatic Production Contract. LaMure's lawyer prepared a letter of agreement . . . whereby Ferrer would cancel and terminate the Contract. Ferrer signed the letter but instructed his attorney not to deliver it until the closing of a contract between himself and the company that was to produce the picture. . . .

Meanwhile . . . Ferrer entered into a contract with Huston's company, Moulin Productions, Inc. ("Moulin"), hereafter the Motion Picture Contract. This was followed by an agreement and assignment . . . whereby LaMure sold Huston all motion picture rights to his novel . . .

The Motion Picture Contract said that Romulus Films Limited, of London, proposed to produce the picture "Moulin Rouge," . . . and that Moulin on behalf of Romulus was interested in engaging Ferrer's service to play the role of Toulouse-Lautrec. Under clause 4(a), Ferrer was to receive $50,000 to cover 12 weeks of acting, payments to be made weekly as Ferrer rendered his services. . . . By clause 4(b), Ferrer was to receive $10,416.66 per week for each additional week, but this, together with an additional $50,000 of salary provided by clause 4(c), was "deferred and postponed" and was payable only out of net receipts. Finally, clauses 4(d) and (e) provided "percentage compensation" equal to stipulated percentages of the net profits from distribution of the picture. . . . If Ferrer's services were interrupted by disability or if production of the picture had to be suspended for causes beyond Moulin's control, but the picture was thereafter completed and Ferrer's "acts, poses and appearances therein" were recognizable to the public, he was to receive a proportion of the compensation provided in clauses 4(c), (d) and (e). . . . The absence of any similar provision with respect to termination for Ferrer's wilful refusal or neglect to perform services indicates that all his rights, except that for compensation already due under clause 4(a), would be forfeited in that event. . . . Ferrer offered testimony by Huston's attorney, who was also president of Moulin, that in the negotiation "it was said that the ultimate percentage payment to be made to Ferrer would be his compensation for giving up his interest in the dramatization guild," and a letter from the same attorney . . . confirming that in the negotiations with Ferrer's attorney "for the sale of the dramatic rights held by you to the property entitled 'MONSIEUR TOULOUSE' and the novel 'MOULIN ROUGE,' is was understood that the consideration for such sale price was the payments due, or to become due, to you under Clause 4(d) and Clause 4 (e)," and also that LaMure "refused to sell the motion picture rights for the production of the motion picture known as 'MOULIN ROUGE' unless you sold the aforesaid dramatic rights." Ferrer's agent testified . . . that the largest salary Ferrer had previously received for a moving picture appearance was $75,000.

Moulin's books showed $109,027.74 as a salary payment to Ferrer in August, 1953, and $178,751.46 at various later dates in 1953 as the payment of "Participating Interests" under clause 4(d). Ferrer's 1953 return reported the former as ordinary income, and the latter, less expenses of $26,812.72, as a long-term capital gain. . . .

Section . . . § 1221 . . . tells us, not very illuminatingly, that " 'capital asset' means property held by the taxpayer (whether or not connected with his trade or business), but does not include" four (now five) types of property therein defined. However, it has long been settled that a taxpayer does not bring himself within the capital gains provision merely by fulfilling the simple syllogism that a contract normally constitutes "property," that he held a contract, and that his contract does not fall within a specified exclusion, *C.I.R. v. Gillette Motor Transport, Inc.*, 364 U.S. 130, 134-135 . . . (1960). This is easy enough; what is difficult, perhaps impossible, is to frame a positive definition of universal validity. . . .

Perhaps we can get more help from analyzing the fact situations in cases in adjacent areas, including those decided since Judge Smith's careful review in *C.I.R. v. Pittston Co.*, 252 F.2d 344, *cert. denied*, 357 U.S. 919 . . . (1958), than from the language of the opinions. Putting aside . . . *C.I.R. v. Starr Bros., Inc.*, 204 F.2d 673, 674 (2 Cir. 1953) . . . the principal relevant authorities on the two sides of the line in the Supreme Court and in the courts of appeals are as follows: There is no sale or exchange of a capital asset when a lessor receives payment for releasing a lessee from an obligation to pay future rent, *Hort v. C,I.R.*, 313 U.S. 28. . . . (1941). The same was true of the cancellation of an exclusive distributorship, *C.I.R. v. Starr Bros., Inc.*, 204 F.2d 673, 674 (2 Cir. 1953); *Leh v. C.I.R.*, 260 F.2d 489 (9 Cir. 1958), although § 1241 . . . now rules otherwise if the distributor has a substantial capital investment therein. The transfer of exclusive agency rights to a third person likewise did not qualify, *General Artists Corp. v. Commissioner*, 205 F.2d 360(2 Cir.), *cert. denied*, 346 U.S. 866 . . . (1958); whether it now does if the capital investment requirement of § 1241 is met is another question. The sale of oil payment rights, *C.I.R. v. P.G. Lake, Inc.* 356 U.S. 260 . . . (1958), the temporary taking of a taxpayer's right to use his own transportation assets, *C.I.R. v. Gillette Motor Transport, Inc., supra*, and the surrender of an exclusive contract to purchase coal, *C.I.R. v. Pittston Co., supra*,. do not meet the statutory test. Neither does the receipt of a lump sum in liquidation of a percentage of the gross receipts of motion pictures otherwise payable to a producer solely in return for personal services not yet performed, *Holt v. C.I.R.*, 303 F.2d 687 (9 Cir. 1962). On the other hand, a lessee's surrender of his lease to the lessor, *C.I.R. v. Golonsky*, 200 F.2d 73 (3 Cir. 1952), *cert. denied*, 245 U.S. 939 . . . (1953); *C.I.R. v. McCue Bros. & Drummond, Inc.* 210 F.2d 752 (2 Cir.) *cert. denied*, 348 U.S. 829 . . . (1954), now in effect ratified by § 1241 of the 1954 Code, his relinquishment of a right to restrict the lessor's renting to another tenant in the same business, *C.I.R. v. Ray*, 210 F.2d 390 (5 Cir.), *cert. denied*, 348 U.S. 829 . . . (1954), and his release of his entire interest to a sublessee, *Metropolitan Bldg. Co.*, 282 F.2d 592 (9 Cir. 1960), but see *Voloudakis v. C.I.R.*, 274 F.2d 209 (9 Cir. 1960), constitute the sale or exchange of a capital asset. So does the abandonment of an option to acquire a partnership interest, *Dorman v. United States*, 296 F.2d 27 (9 Cir. 1961).

One common characteristic of the group held to come within the capital gain provision is that the taxpayer had either what might be called an "estate" in

(*Golonsky, McCue, Metropolitan*) or an "encumbrance" on (*Ray*), or an option to acquire an interest in (*Dorman*), property which, if itself held, would be a capital asset. In all these cases the taxpayer had something more than an opportunity, afforded by contract, to obtain periodic receipts of income, by dealing with another (*Starr, Leh, General Artists, Pittston*), or by rendering services (*Holt*), or by virtue of ownership of a larger "estate (*Hort, P.G. Lake*). We are painfully aware of the deficiencies of any such attempt to define the wavering line even in this limited area, but it is the best we can do. We add, with greater confidence, that more recent cases, such as *McCue & Drummond, Ray, Metropolitan*, and *Dorman*, have moved away from the distinction relied upon to some extent in *Starr Brothers* and *General Artists*, between a sale to a third person that keeps the "estate" or "encumbrance" alive, and a release that results in its extinguishment. Indeed, although reasoning from another section of a statute so full of anomalies is rather treacherous business, we take § 1241 of the 1954 Code as indicating Congressional disenchantment with this formalistic distinction. In the instant case we can see no sensible business basis for drawing a line between a release of Ferrer's rights to LaMure for a consideration paid by Moulin, and a sale of them, with LaMure's consent, to Moulin or to a stranger who would then release them. Moulin's attorney, as we have seen, did not care a fig whether there was "an annulment or conveyance" of the Dramatic Production Contract. Tax law is concerned with the substance, here the voluntary passing of "property" rights allegedly constituting "capital assets," not with whether they are passed to a stranger or to a person already having a larger "estate." So we turn to an analysis of what rights Ferrer conveyed.

* * *

When Huston displayed an interest in the motion picture rights . . . , Ferrer was possessed of a bundle of rights, three of which are relevant here. First was his "lease" of the play. Second was his power, incident to that lease, to prevent any disposition of the motion picture rights until . . . December 1, 1952, and for a period thereafter if he produced the play, and to prevent disposition of the radio and television rights even longer. Third was his 40% share of the proceeds of the motion picture and other rights if he produced the play. All these, in our view, Ferrer "sold or exchanged," although the parties set no separate price upon them. To be sure, Moulin had no interest in producing the play. But Ferrer did, unless a satisfactory substitute was provided. Hence Moulin had to buy him out of that right, as well as to eliminate his power temporarily to prevent a sale of the motion picture, radio and television rights and to liquidate his option to obtain a share of their proceeds.

(1) Surrender of the "lease" of the play sounds like the transactions held to qualify for capital gain treatment in *Golonsky* and *McCue Bros. & Drummond*, see § 1241 of the 1954 Code. [C]ourts would have enjoined LaMure, or anyone else, from interfering with this . . . Ferrer thus had an "equitable interest" in the copyright of the play.

The Commissioner did not suggest . . . that this interest or, indeed, any with which we are concerned in this case, fell within . . . § 1221(3), excluding from the term "capital asset" "a copyright; a literary, musical, or artistic composition; or similar property; held by —

"(i) a taxpayer, whose personal efforts created such property * * *."

He was right in not doing this. . . . [T]he legislative history . . . shows that § [1221(3)] . . . was intended to deal with personal efforts and creation in a rather narrow sense. . . . Ferrer's role as producer, paying large sums to the theatre, the actors, other personnel, and the author, is not analogous to that of the writer or even the "creator" of a radio program mentioned by the Committee. . . .

We see no basis for holding that amounts paid Ferrer for surrender of his lease of the play are excluded from capital gain treatment because receipts from the play would have been ordinary income. The latter is equally true if a lessee of real property sells or surrenders a lease from which he is receiving business income or subrentals; yet *Golonsky* and *McCue Bros. & Drummond* held such to be the sale or exchange of a capital asset, as § 1241 now provides. Likewise we find nothing in the statute that forbids capital gain treatment because the payment to Ferrer might be spread over a number of years rather than coming in a lump sum; although prevention of the unfairness arising from applying ordinary income rates to a "bunching" of income may be one of the motivations of the "capital gain" provisions, the statute says nothing about this. Compare *Burnet v. Logan*, 282 U.S. 404 . . . (1931). . . .

(2) Ferrer's negative power, as an incident to the lease, to prevent any disposition of the motion picture, radio and television rights until after production of the play, was also one which . . . would be protected in equity unless he had contracted to the contrary, and would thus constitute an "equitable interest" in this portion of the copyright. Although we should not regard Articles IV, § 1(a) and VIII as outlawing equitable relief to protect the rights granted as to the play, a literal reading of Article V, § 1(c), quoted above, would negate Ferrer's power to enjoin disposition of the motion picture rights prior to production of the play and would remit him to arbitration — a consequence serious from the standpoint of definition of a capital asset, especially in view of the emphasis we placed in *Pittston*, 352 F.2d at 348, on the unavailability of injunctive relief there . . . As a practical matter, this feature of the Dramatic Production Contract "clouded" LaMure's title, despite the Contract's contrary assertion. . . . Ferrer's dissipation of the cloud arising from the negative covenant seems analogous to the tenant's relinquishment of a right to prevent his landlord from leasing to another tenant in the same business, held to be the sale or exchange of a capital asset . . . What we have said in (1) with respect to possible grounds for disqualification as a capital asset is *a fortiori* applicable here.

(3) We take a different view with respect to the capital assets status of Ferrer's right to receive 40% of the proceeds of the motion picture and other rights if he produced "Monsieur Toulouse."

We assume, without deciding, that there is no reason in principle why if the holder of a copyright grants an interest in the portion of a copyright relating to motion picture and other rights contingent on the production of a play, or, to put the matter in another way, gives the producer an option to acquire such an interest by producing the play, the option would not constitute a "capital asset" unless the producer is disqualified by . . . § 1221(1). Although the copyright might not be such an asset in the owner's hands because of that section or . . . § 1221(3)(A), the latter disqualification would not apply to the producer for reasons already discussed, and the former would not unless the producer was a professional. However, it is equally possible for the copyright owner to reserve the entire "property" both legal and equitable in himself and agree with the producer that a percentage of certain avails shall be paid as further income from the lease of the play—just as the lessor of real estate might agree to pay a lessee a percentage of what the lessor obtained from other tenants attracted to the building by the lessee's operations. In both instances such payments would be ordinary income. . . .

Here the parties were at some pains to do exactly that. LaMure was to "retain for his sole benefit, complete title, both legal and equitable, in and to all rights whatsoever" other than the right to produce the play. Ferrer was to "have no right, title or interest, legal or equitable, in the motion picture rights, other than the right to receive the Manager's share of the proceeds"; even as to that, he was to have "no recourse, in law or in equity" against a purchaser, a lessee, or the Negotiator, but only a right to arbitration against the Author. We cannot regard all this as mere formalism. The Contract is full of provisions designed to emphasize the Negotiator's freedom to act — provisions apparently stemming from a fear that, without them, the value of the motion picture rights might disintegrate in controversy. . . .

It follows that if Ferrer had produced the play and LaMure had sold the motion picture, radio and television rights for a percentage of the profits, Ferrer's 40% of that percentage would have been ordinary income and not the sale or exchange of a capital asset. The decisions in *Hort* and *Holt* point to what would seem the inevitable corollary that if, on the same facts, Ferrer had then sold his rights to a percentage of the profits for a lump sum, that, too, would have been ordinary income . . . The situation cannot be better from Ferrer's standpoint because he had merely a contingent right to, or an option to obtain, the 40% interest. . . .

The situation is thus one in which two of the rights that Ferrer sold or exchanged were "capital assets" and one was not. Although it would be easy to say that the contingent contract right to a percentage of the avails of the motion picture, radio and television rights was dominant and all else incidental, that would be viewing the situation with the inestimable advantage of hindsight. In 1952 no one could tell whether the play might be a huge success and the picture a dismal failure, whether the exact opposite would be true, whether both would succeed or both would fail. We cannot simply dismiss out of hand the notion that a dramatic production, presenting an actor famous on the speaking stage and appealing to a sophisticated audience, might have had substantial profit possibilities, perhaps quite as good as a film with respect to a figure, not altogether attractive and not nearly so broadly known then as the success of the picture has made him now, which presumably would require wide public acceptance before returning production costs. At the very least, when Ferrer gave up his lease of the play, he was abandoning his bet on two horses in favor of a bet on only one.

In such instances, where part of a transaction calls for one tax treatment and another for a different kind, allocation is demanded . . . If it be said that to remand for this purpose is asking the Tax Court to separate the inseparable, we answer that no one expects scientific exactness; that however roughly hewn the decision may be, the result is certain to be fairer than either extreme. . . .

Still we have not reached the end of the road. The Commissioner contends that, apart from all else, no part of the payments here can qualify for capital gain treatment, since Ferrer could receive "percentage compensation" only if he fulfilled his acting commitments, and all the payments were thus for personal services. . . .

* * *

On the basis of this evidence the Tax Court found that the percentage compensation was not "to any extent the consequence of, or consideration for, petitioner's personal services." In one sense, this is hardly so. Under the Motion Picture Contract, Ferrer would receive no percentage compensation if he wrongfully refused to furnish acting services, and none or only a portion if, for reasons beyond his control, he furnished less than all. Since that must have been as plain to the Tax Court as to us, we read the finding to mean rather that Ferrer and Moulin adopted the percentage of profits formula embodied in clauses 4(d) and (e) as an equivalent and in lieu of a fixed sum payable in all events for the release of the Dramatic Production Contract. If they had first agreed on such a sum and had then substituted the arrangement here made, it would be hard to say that although payments under their initial arrangement would not be disqualified for capital gain treatment, payments under the substituted one would be. . . .

* * *

NOTES AND COMMENTS

In determining which of Ferrer's rights qualify for capital gain treatment, Judge Friendly dismissed the "disappearing asset" issue inherent in the requirement that there be a "sale or exchange," not merely a "disposition," of property, as exemplified by *Pounds* (no capital gain on payment by obligor for purchased right to share of proceeds from sale of property) discussed in § 4.03 *Extinguishment Doctrine* of Chapter 2 *Capital Gains and Losses.* In doing so, he relied principally on § 1241, one of the many Code provisions treating a transaction as a "sale or exchange" when it might not otherwise be one. As he indicated, § 1241 provides exchange treatment for amounts received on cancellation of a lease or of a distributorship agreement, in which the distributor has a substantial investment. A subsequently enacted broader provision, § 1234A, covering the termination of a right or obligation with respect to property that is or would be a capital asset in the hands of the holder eliminates most, if not all, of what is left of the sale or exchange requirement, although Ferrer does not appear to have any substantial investment, which may be why Judge Friendly characterizes it as a "lease." A more normal distributorship agreement was involved in Rev. Rul. 2007-37, 2007-1 C.B. 1390, dealing with an automobile manufacturer who discontinued a model of a car and paid amounts to cancel distributorship agreements, for which the distributor had originally made payments on acquisition, and had substantial capital investments in inventory. In the case of distributorships acquired after the effective date of § 197 discussed in § 3.07 *Amortization of Intangible Assets* of Chapter 4, *Capitalization and Cost Recovery*, the payment was determined to be a sale or exchange of the distributorship agreement qualifying under § 1241, but because the distributorship agreement was an amortizable § 197 intangible, the gain was on a §1231 asset, not a capital asset, and subject to depreciation recapture under § 1245. A subsequently enacted broader provision, § 1234A, covering termination of right or obligation with respect to property that is or would be a capital asset in the hands of the holder, eliminates most, if not all, of what is left of the sale or exchange requirement, is discussed in § 4.03(c) *Amounts Received on the Cancellation of a Lease* of Chapter 2 *Capital Gains and Losses.*

Commissioner v. Pittston Co., 252 F.2d 344 (2d Cir. 1958), referred to and substantially relied on by Judge Friendly, held that an amount received by a holder of a contract to purchase all of the coal from a particular mine for resale under terms that, in effect, provided the holder with an eight percent commission, was properly treated as ordinary income. In reaching its conclusion the majority admitted that courts had not been consistent in determining whether lump sum payments for the termination of jural relations were entitled to capital gains treatment. The court reviewed *McAllister* (sale of life estate to remainder owner), *Commissioner v. Starr Bros., Inc.*, 204 F.2d 673 (2d Cir. 1953) (no capital gain on payment for cancellation of exclusive agency); *General Artists Corp. v. Commissioner*, 205 F.2d 360 (2d Cir. 1953) (payment for transfer of contract as exclusive booking agent for a singer was ordinary income); *Commissioner v. McCue Bros. & Drummond, Inc.*, 210 F.2d 752 (2d Cir. 1954) (payment to lessee to terminate lease subject rent control was capital gain); and *Commissioner v. Golonsky*, 200 F.2d 72 (3d Cir. 1952) (payment to lessee from landlord to cancel lease was capital gain). It based its conclusion on a determination that the contract right did not give the taxpayer any interest in the mine while the taxpayers in *McAllister*, *McCue*, and *Golonsky* owned property that had more "substance" than mere contract rights in *Starr* and, by implication, *General Artists.*

Ferrer is hardly the last word on the vexing problem of contract rights tied up with personal services. In *Martin v. Commissioner*, 50 T.C. 341 (1968), *acq*, the Tax Court concluded that amounts received on the transfer of the producer's subsidiary rights to a share of the proceeds of the motion picture rights for *Guys and Dolls* following the successful production of the play, were ordinary income, but that amounts received for the motion picture rights for *The Boy Friend*, purchased from the author, gave rise to capital gain. On the other hand, in *Bellamy v. Commissioner*, 43 T.C. 487 (1965), the Tax Court concluded that payment for an actor's surrender of rights to prevent reruns was ordinary income because the rights arose out of his acting in the TV series — that is, personal services. In cases with a lesser personal service element, capital gain is easier to achieve. *See, e.g., Anderson v. United States*, 468 F. Supp. 1085 (D. Minn. 1979), *aff'd without op.*, 624 F.2d 1109 (8th Cir. 1980) (amounts paid for release of right of first refusal on franchise for operation of a Holiday Inn in a specified territory are capital gain; follows *Ferrer*); *Foy v. Commissioner*, 84 T.C. 50 (1985) (capital gain on the transfer of rights to a franchise network in which the taxpayers held a veto over new franchises and rights to a share of sale proceeds in addition to the rights to a share of the sale proceeds; follows *Ferrer*).

PROBLEM FOR DISCUSSION

Problem 7-19. What, if anything, would be the effect of §§ 1241 and 1234A on *Ferrer* (some rights capital assets; some ordinary income); *Hort* (payment to escape burdensome lease); *Starr* (sprinkler lease); *P.G. Lake* (payment for oil production payment); *Gillette* (proceeds received for the temporary taking of the taxpayer's business facilities during World War II was not capital gain); *Pittston Co.* (amount received by a holder of a contract to purchase coal for resale under terms that, in effect, provided it with an eight percent commission was ordinary income); *Martin* (amounts paid for the producer's subsidiary rights to share of motion picture rights for *Guys and Dolls,* after producing the play were ordinary income, but amounts received for motion picture rights for *The Boy Friend* purchased from the author were capital gain); and *Bellamy* (payment for an actor's surrender of rights to prevent reruns not capital gain); *Pounds* (no capital gain on payment by obligor for purchased right to share of proceeds from sale of property); *Anderson* (amounts paid for release of right of first refusal on franchise for operation of a Holiday Inn in a specified territory are capital gain); *Foy* (capital gain on rights to franchise network where taxpayers owned, in addition to a share of the income, a veto over new franchises and a share of sale proceeds).

§ 3.02. Future Services versus Goodwill

Goodwill is the value of a business that represents an expectation of continued customer patronage, and going concern value is the related value of having an ongoing business structure. By their nature, goodwill and going concern value are initially a result of the normal conduct of a business, but no portion of a business's ordinary operating expenses is required to be capitalized, as these intangible assets develop. For example, advertising expenses are generally deductible under § 162 despite the fact that at least a portion of such expenses generate name recognition and, presumably, goodwill that will continue to exist beyond the current taxable year. Accordingly, unless purchased as part of an acquisition of an ongoing business, these intangible assets usually have a zero basis. The existence of goodwill as a separate asset is usually easy to establish for a manufacturing or retail business, although there may be valuation difficulties as discussed in § 4.02, *§ 1060 and Residual Allocation for Goodwill,* of Chapter 1, *Basis and Realization.* When a service business is sold, however, there is a greater difficulty in determining whether the consideration paid was for goodwill or going concern value or was simply a substitute for ordinary income to be received in the future. The following case struggles with this issue and, interestingly, represents the third substantive attempt to resolve the issue by the same court of appeals (although different panels) within a two-year period. Is there any further need for evidence of the difficulty of the issue?

BISBEE-BALDWIN CORP. v. TOMLINSON

United States Court of Appeals, Fifth Circuit

320 F.2d 929 (5th Cir. 1963)

WISDOM, CIRCUIT JUDGE.

The question for decision is whether payments the taxpayer received for the termination of mortgage servicing contracts are taxable as ordinary income or as capital gains.[1]

---

[1] The tax treatment of assignment of income is examined intensively in Lyon & Eustice, *Assignment*

This Court has recently decided three other cases concerning the tax effects of the termination of similar contracts: *Nelson Weaver Realty Co. v. Commissioner*, 5 Cir. 1962, 307 F.2d 897; *United States v. Eidson*, 5 Cir. 1962, 310 F.2d 311; *Commissioner v. Maurice L. Killian*, 5 Cir. 1963, 314 F.2d 852. In *Weaver*, Judge Cameron, for the majority of the Court, held: "It cannot be doubted that the sum total of the ingredients of (the mortgage company's) longstanding relationship with * * * (its) clientele constitutes a property right which is the equivalent of goodwill * * * a capital asset * * * entitled to capital gain treatment" on its sale. Judge Rives dissented: The "part alloca(ble) to the right to receive service fees should be taxable as an ordinary income." . . . In *Eidson* Judge Tuttle, for the Court, held that it "makes no difference whether the assignment (of rights under the contract) * * * be denominated a sale" the taxpayers assigned the right to receive "net profit of operations during the remainder of the life of the contract" which must be treated as ordinary income. . . .

* * *

Bisbee-Baldwin, the taxpayer, is in the mortgage banking business. Most of its loans are secured by mortgages on residential property in Jacksonville, Florida. After making a loan, the company invariably assigns the mortgage to an institutional investor. The essential profit-making element is the investor's agreement to employ the mortgage company as its agent to service the mortgages. The company receives no profit on the assignment of a mortgage but earns an annual commission of one-half of one per cent of the principal outstanding balance of the mortgages serviced. The servicing activities generate other business. For example, the company often writes fire insurance on the property mortgaged, acts as real estate broker when the property is sold, and serves as property manager when a mortgage is foreclosed. Escrow deposits by the mortgagors enhance its credit standing, a substantial benefit since the company must borrow large sums from the banks in the operation of its affairs. Thus the success of the mortgage servicing business depends upon the amount of mortgage indebtedness it services.

The taxpayer had no right to assign the servicing agreement and could not demand any payment from a successor servicing agent if the investor transferred its business to another company. The taxpayer was not the exclusive agent for any investor, even in the Jacksonville area serviced by it. Each investor had the right to enter into similar agreements with other servicing agents, and the taxpayer had the right to assign and service mortgages for other investors.

During the fiscal year ending April 30, 1957, various investors cancelled servicing agreements with the taxpayer, and gave the business to other agents. When an investor cancels such an agreement without cause, it is customary for the investor to pay a termination fee equal to one per cent of the principal balance of the mortgages then being serviced by the mortgage company. In this case, several of the taxpayer's agreements with investors expressly provided for such a termination fee. The taxpayer received net termination fees of $206,454.63. The investors paid this sum to Bisbee-Baldwin, but were reimbursed by the new servicing agents for

---

of Income: Fruit and Tree as Irrigated by the P. G. Lake Case, 17 TAX L. REV. 295 (1962). See especially pages 346-353, 393-397. . . .

the amount of the termination fees paid to the taxpayer. In substance, therefore, the mortgage servicing was transferred from Bisbee-Baldwin to other agents for, as the district court found, the cancellations would not have taken place had the successor mortgage servicing agents not agreed to reimburse the investors in the amount of the termination fees.

The district court found that:

> "Plaintiff kept extensive files containing information concerning the mortgages which it serviced. When an investor canceled an agreement the files containing information concerning the mortgages assigned to that investor were turned over either to the investor or to the new servicing agent designated by the investor. Those files were of value to the Plaintiff in obtaining the (indirect) advantages (of servicing mortgages)."

* * *

The fact that contractual rights in a mortgage servicing agency constitute a species of "property" under state law affords no assistance in determining whether such rights are capital assets. . . . :

In *Hort* v. *Commissioner*, 1941, 311 U.S. 328, . . . the Court held that amounts received in cancellation of a lease were taxable as ordinary income to a lessor. . . .

* * *

The question is, what do the mortgage servicing rights under the contracts represent. If they represent the right to earn future income in the form of commissions for services rendered, then the sum received for the cancellation of the contracts and the transfer of rights is ordinary income.

In *Roscoe* v *Commissioner*, 5 Cir. 1954, 215 F.2d 478, a sum received by taxpayers for their real-estate corporation stock in excess of the amount received by other shareholders was held to be ordinary income representing the commission which the taxpayers would have been entitled to had the land represented by the stock been sold directly. . . .

The line between contractual rights representing capital assets and those representing the right to receive future income is far from clear. Judge Friendly, for the Second Circuit, after an extremely able, thorough survey of all the relevant cases, reached the following conclusion:

> "One common characteristic of the group held to come within the capital gain provision is that the taxpayer had either what might be called an 'estate' in (*Golonsky, McCue, Metropolitan*), or an 'encumbrance' on (Ray), or an option to acquire an interest in (*Dorman*), property which, if itself held, would be a capital asset. In all these cases the taxpayer had something more than an opportunity, afforded by contract, to obtain periodic receipts of income, by dealing with another (*Starr, Leh, General Artists, Pittston*), or by rendering services (*Holt*), or by virtue of ownership of a larger 'estate' (*Hort, P. G. Lake*)." *Commissioner v. Ferrer*. . . .

In Judge Friendly's analysis, as in Judge Rives' analysis in *Weaver*, some components of the "bundle" of contractual rights held by a taxpayer are capital assets while others represent a substitute for future income. . . . We agree with this analysis. As Judge Rives said in *Weaver*:

> "It seems to me, however, that a substantial part of the $121,841.11 paid to the Mortgage Company was for the right to receive service fees for the remaining years of the outstanding loans. To that extent the Mortgage Company was simply converting future income into present income. *Commissioner v. P. G. Lake*. . . .
>
> "The sale of 'all of the rights, title, obligations and benefits pertaining to the servicing contract,' like the sale of any going business, should, I think, be comminuted into its fragments and the 'purchase price' should be allocated among the various assets sold. *Williams v. McGowan*. . . . I would agree that a part of the $121,841.11 represented the purchase price of capital assets."

Applying these principles to the factual situation before us, we find that the basic rights Bisbee-Baldwin sold were the annual servicing commissions on the principal balance outstanding on the mortgages. Indeed, the termination fee of one per cent of the mortgages serviced by the taxpayer was equivalent to two years gross income in commissions and was, to our minds, a substitute for the income which would have been earned by Bisbee-Baldwin had the contracts not been transferred.

This holding is, of course, in direct conflict with *Nelson Weaver*. . . . In an almost identical situation *Weaver* held that compensation for the assignment of a mortgage-servicing agency should be treated as capital gain. In reaching its decision, the Court relied heavily upon the fact that the amount paid the taxpayer "bore no convincing resemblance to the amount the purchaser would actually collect out of the service contract sold since the purchaser had to pay the cost of collection." It is equally true in the present case that the net income from commissions over a two year period would be much smaller than the sum received by Bisbee-Baldwin. But, as this Court recently stated in *Eidson*, "while, of course, the sum of $170,000 which (the taxpayers) received in the taxable year at issue was doubtless much larger than the income they received in any year for a current year's operation, this clearly resulted from the fact that they were assigning, * * * not a capital asset whose value had enhanced or accrued over several years, but the right to receive this net profit of operations during the remainder of the life of the contract." Since, according to undisputed testimony, the primary value of these mortgage correspondent relationships lay in the right to receive annual percentage commissions, there can be little doubt that the bulk of the sum paid to Bisbee-Baldwin was compensation for the loss of such commissions. In such a situation, the statement by the Supreme Court in *Commissioner v. P. G. Lake*. . . . is applicable.

> "The substance of what was assigned was the right to receive future income. The substance of what was received was the present value of income which the recipient would otherwise obtain in the future. In short, consideration was paid for the right to receive future income, not for an increase in the value of the income-producing property."

The taxpayer seeks to distinguish between the right to receive future income and the right to earn future income. This distinction finds no support in the decisions. Indeed, in *Roscoe* v *Commissioner*, 5 Cir. 1954, 215 F.2d 478, the very fact that the taxpayer's ten per cent commissions on the sale of real estate had to be earned by the taxpayer's efforts caused the compensation for this right to be classified as ordinary income.

* * *

Still, some parts of the "bundle" of contractual rights transferred by Bisbee-Baldwin were capital assets. The mortgage correspondent relationships have value in addition to the rights to servicing commissions. It acts as a "feeder" for related businesses, such as insurance and real estate, frequently engaged in by mortgage bankers. The monthly escrow deposits made by the mortgagors considerably enhance the servicing agent's credit standing. Moreover, as the dissenting opinion in *Nelson Weaver* recognized, there is a sale of "good will". The mortgage portfolio of the mortgage banker tends to increase each year as both the mortgagors and the investors look to the mortgaging servicing agent for further funds and further outlets for investment. The taxpayer's extensive files and equipment are in the nature of capital assets. (Most of these were retained by the taxpayer.) These items are closely related to the everyday business operations of the taxpayer. They are not so integrally related, however, as to be insusceptible of separate valuation.

We summarize. Essentially, the contract was a management contract for the employment of personal services. The consideration received for the right to earn future servicing commissions must be regarded as a substitute for such future ordinary income. This important part of the bundle of rights sold or exchanged can be separated from the other parts and should be taxed for what it is — not for what it is not. . . .

The case should be remanded to allow the district "Court to allocate the amount (of the purchase price) according to the realities of the transaction." *Nelson Weaver* . . . (dissent).

* * *

Looking only at the form of the transaction, it might be said that the payments fail to qualify for capital gains treatment because there was no "sale or exchange" as required in Section 1221. Thus, the Commissioner argues that on termination of the contracts, Bisbee-Baldwin's rights vanished; nothing survived to be transferred. *Commissioner v. Starr Bros.*, 2 Cir. 1953, 204 F.2d 673, 674, held that cancellation of an exclusive agency did not result in capital gain. Such release not only ended the promisor's previously existing duty but also destroyed the promisee's rights. They were not transferred to the promisor; they merely came to an end and vanished.

* * *

In the fact pattern this case presents, where the "realities of the transaction" undeniably show a market value for the bundle of rights said to have vanished, we feel compelled to look through form to substance. In substance the transaction was a two-party transfer. The investors were conduits. Bisbee-Baldwin received the payments; the transferees paid through the investors. Something was transferred. What Bisbee-Baldwin transferred was a bundle of rights under its contracts to service certain mortgages. For a price, the transferees stepped into Bisbee-Baldwin's shoes. It is irrelevant that the investors' approval was required, that the consideration was fixed in the contract or by trade custom, and that instead of assignment the transfer was effected by termination of the old contracts and execution of new contracts. These circumstances do not extinguish the fact that Bisbee-Baldwin gave up mortgage servicing commissions and other profits for a consideration. . . .

We hold therefore that property rights passed by sale or exchange from the taxpayer to the successor agents. This holding is circumscribed by our decision that not all of the sticks making up the bundle of rights constituted capital assets. As in *Ferrer*, although the whole bundle was sold or exchanged, the parties set no separate price upon each stick.

We therefore affirm the judgment below in part, reverse it in part, and remand the case for the district court to determine (1) what part of Bisbee-Baldwin's compensation was a substitute for future earnings, and therefore taxable as ordinary income and (2) what part or parts, if any, were capital assets, sold or exchanged, entitled to capital gains treatment.

GRIFFIN B. BELL, CIRCUIT JUDGE (dissenting).

I dissent. I would affirm the judgment of the District Court without reaching the capital asset question, either as presented here or in *Nelson Weaver*. . . . The sale or exchange there was undoubted. Weaver sold his mortgage banking business. The sole question was whether what was sold constituted capital assets.

Here there is a preliminary or threshold question of whether there was a sale or exchange. In fact, Bisbee-Baldwin refused to sell. Four out of several lending institutions represented by Bisbee-Baldwin shortly thereafter terminated their relationship with Bisbee-Baldwin. Two paid a termination fee required by contract. Two paid a negotiated fee in an amount customary in the trade. Three of the lending institutions chose the mortgage banker to represent them who had attempted to purchase their accounts from Bisbee-Baldwin, while the other chose a third mortgage banker.

* * *

In my view, the judgment of the District Court should be affirmed for the reason that there was no sale or exchange. Any question as to the correctness of the *Nelson Weaver* capital asset rule should be postponed until a case presenting the question reaches us.

NOTES AND COMMENTS

As Judge Wisdom indicates, *Nelson Weaver Realty Co. v. Commissioner*, 307 F.2d 897 (5th Cir. 1962) held that amounts received for sale of rights under a mortgage servicing agreement were capital gain. In reaching the conclusion, the court noted that the purchaser acquired not only the right to service the mortgages, but also all of the records relating to them that provided a ready-made market and that represented a property right, which is the equivalent of goodwill — the probability that the old customers will resort to the old place. It distinguished *P.G. Lake* as involving the sale of the right to receive money in the future, the sales price being almost the exact equivalent of the income that was to be produced in the future. *Killian* essentially follows *Nelson Weaver* on facts that did not involve any bundle of rights because the court determined that the payments in question were for goodwill. In *United States v. Eidson*, 310 F.2d 111 (5th Cir. 1962), a different panel of the same circuit determined that a transfer of a contract to manage an insurance company, as part of a transaction in which another insurance company took over the business of the one being managed by the taxpayer, resulted in ordinary income. It emphasized that whatever the seller would have earned under the contract would be ordinary income and determined that, even though no income would be received without performing substantial services, this did not affect the nature of the payment. It relied on *P.G. Lake* and the statement in *Gillette Motor* that capital gain arises in situations typically involving the realization of appreciation in value accrued over a substantial period, and concluded that the interest sold was not a capital asset, the value of which had enhanced or accrued over several years, but the right to receive profit of operations during the remainder of the life of the contract. It distinguished *Nelson Weaver* on the ground that it involved a sale of a business including goodwill, a circumstance it did not find present in *Eidson*. Because *Bisbee-Baldwin* is not an *en banc* decision, all three apparently remain valid authority.

Judge Wisdom rejects the distinction between the right to collect income in the future and the opportunity to earn income in the future in distinguishing between ordinary income and capital gain. In doing so, he relied on the decision in *Roscoe* v *Commissioner*, 215 F.2d 478 (5th Cir. 1954), but that case involved a payment of an amount that was the equivalent to a commission on a completed transaction, so that it was, at best, a payment for foregoing a right to collect income, not a payment for an opportunity to earn income in the future that would require use of capital or future effort. Stated another way, if goodwill is the value of expected continued patronage, how can that value be realized except by providing the future customers with the desired goods or services? Indeed, the items listed in the opinion as generating capital gain — the value of the mortgage correspondent relationships as a "feeder" for related businesses, the enhancement of the servicing agent's credit standing from the escrow deposits, and the increase of the mortgage portfolio — all have value only as the opportunity to earn income.

For that matter, the sublease in *Metropolitan Building* (payment for termination of leaseholder interest), represented only the opportunity to earn income. *See Stewart Trust v. Commissioner*, 63 T.C. 682 (1975), *acq.* , (a mortgage-servicing contract was property entitled to nonrecognition under former § 337 and presumably other provisions, and was not assignment of income)Rev. Rul. 77-190, 1977-1 C.B. 88, *declared obsolete by* Rev. Rul. 95-71, 1995-2 C.B. 323 (follows *Stewart*, although recognizing that mortgage-servicing rights might not be a capital asset and distinguishing *Eidson* as requiring gain that admittedly was recognized on a sale to be characterized as ordinary income). Similarly, in Tech. Adv. Mem. 2000-49-009, a power plant operator had a long-term supply contract that preceded deregulation with a utility that provided rates that were highly advantageous rates to the power plant operator. A payment by a third party for the contract was capital gain or § 1231 property, even though the purchaser entered into a new contract with the utility to supply a greater amount of power at lower rates. The memorandum emphasizes contract transferred, not extinguished. In addition, the Service has recognized that even a professional practice can have goodwill entitled to capital gains. *See* Rev. Rul. 64-235, 1964-2 C.B. 18 (finding goodwill to be taxable as capital gain on sale of a professional practice); Rev. Rul. 70-45, 1970-1 C.B. 17 (partial transfer of goodwill even on admission of a new partner).

On the other hand, consideration received for the transfer of rights to income that has already been earned, even if the amount of such income is in dispute at the time of sale, is properly ordinary income. Thus, in *Nahey v. Commissioner*, 196 F.3d 866 (7th Cir. 1999), *aff'g* 111 T.C. 256 (1998), the amount received in settlement of claim acquired as part of a purchase of assets in a leveraged buy-out (but with a zero basis because the claim was considered speculative) is ordinary income because based on lost profits of the predecessor. The Tax Court also relied on a disappearing asset or extinguishment analysis. *See* Tech. Adv. Mem. 2000-49-009 (payment to power plant operator that had a long-term supply contract with a utility that preceded deregulation and provided highly advantageous rates by third party for the contract was for capital asset or § 1231 property, even though purchaser entered into a new contract with the utility to supply a greater amount of power at lower rates). The holding in *Lattera v. Commissioner*, discussed in § 3.02 *Definition of Property* of Chapter 2 *Capital Gains and Losses*, holding that the lottery winner was selling the right to income that was earned when the winning ticket was drawn may be considered consistent with treating the proceeds of sale of a right to service mortgages as ordinary income. The argument for this approach is that, because the originator normally continues to service the mortgage after disposition, usually into a mortgage pool, the act of originating the mortgage, in effect, is the key event in earning future mortgage servicing income. This may be illustrated, although in a different context, by Rev. Rul. 91-46, 1991-2 C.B. 358, in which the originator of mortgages sold them into a pool at their original principal amount even though subsequent drops in interest rates made them worth a premium, but, as part of the same deal, entered into a contract to service the mortgages for fees that the Service determined were in excess of arm's-length servicing fees. It recharacterized the excess fees into a retained right to a portion of the interest on the mortgages, which, under § 1286, required allocation of a portion of the basis in the mortgages to the retained right, resulting in immediate gain on the mortgages sold, instead of the deferred income from the service fees.

Although *Bisbee-Baldwin*, *Nelson Weaver*, and *Eidson* did not have to deal with the purchaser's side of the transactions, the purchaser confronts a similar issue in determining the nature of the assets acquired. For example *First Pennsylvania Banking & Trust Co. v. Commissioner*, 56 T.C. 677 (1971), involved the purchaser of a mortgage servicing business. At the time of the transaction, the seller was servicing nearly 18,000 mortgages with an outstanding principal of more than $175 million, primarily for Metropolitan Life, but also for others. The purchaser made a careful study of the financial aspects of the servicing arrangement, including factors affecting servicing fee income, late charges, that were, customarily, retained by the servicing agent, and escrow deposits, before agreement to pay $2 million for the business, even though it had no assurance that Metropolitan or the other lenders would continue to use its services. The purchaser claimed that the basis of the acquired rights was amortizable over the estimated remaining service lives of the mortgages. The court recognized that the situation was the flip side of cases like *Bisbee-Baldwin*, in which the courts held that the sale was the transfer of goodwill and the right to future income. Based on expert testimony, the court made a similar allocation of the purchase price, reflecting the fact that the purchaser acquired not only the right to continue servicing existing loans but also the possibility that it could secure the right to service future mortgages from Metropolitan Life and the other lenders. Although the consideration paid for the right to continue servicing existing loans had to be capitalized, the court allowed the taxpayer to amortize the basis of this asset over the estimated average life spans of the classes of mortgages and their related escrows. The court treated the right to service future mortgages as goodwill. On the other hand, the right to provide future services on existing contracts was not treated as goodwill, but was amortizable over the remaining lives of the existing mortgages.

At the time of *First Pennsylvania* and the other decisions discussed in the preceding paragraphs, purchased goodwill was a nonamortizable capital asset, as were other assets with no ascertainable life. That was changed in 1993 with the enactment of § 197, which allows goodwill, going concern value, and other intangible assets to be amortized over 15 years. Section 197 is discussed in § 3.06, *Amortization of Intangible Assets*, of Chapter 4, *Capitalization and Cost Recovery*. Among the assets that must be amortized under § 197 are rights under covenants not to compete. On the other hand, the distinction for sellers is between sales of goodwill that are eligible for capital asset treatment and of rights under a covenant not to compete that produce ordinary income. The Tax Court has held that payments received by a father and son on the sale of a division of a company were attributable to their covenants not to compete instead of the sale of a customer list. In *Solomon v. Commissioner*, T.C. Memo. 2008-102, the court rejected a creative attempt to claim capital gain on amounts paid to corporate shareholders in connection with the sale of a corporate business. The shareholders claimed that the amounts were for sales of customer lists that belonged to them as the ones who maintained customer relations. The court determined that the customers were the property of the corporation and that any rights to the customer base they had were distributed by the corporation as dividends.

Payments to terminate contracts and leases raise similar issues as to whether they must be capitalized, or are currently deductible. The authorities seem to allow current deduction for termination payments made to reduce expenses that are currently deductible. Thus in Rev. Rul. 69-511, 1969-2 C.B. 24, a lessee's payment to cancel a burdensome lease was held to be currently deductible; as was a payment by a utility company to terminate a supply contract that required purchase of a specified amount of a product by paying a specified amount per unit in order to buy the product at lower prices in the spot market in Priv. Ltr. Rul. 91-23-004 (payment by a utility company to terminate a supply contract that required purchase of a specified amount of a product by paying a specified amount per unit in order to buy the price at lower prices in the spot market was currently deductible). The result seems consistent with *Hort*, treating the lessor's receipt of the lessee's payment to terminate a burdensome lease as ordinary income.

On the other hand, payments to increase income are not deductible when made. Thus, in *Darlington-Hartsville Coca-Cola Bottling Co. v. United States*, 273 F. Supp. 229 (D.S.C. 1967), *aff'd*, 393 F.2d 494 (4th Cir. 1968), amounts paid by two bottling companies to the Coca-Cola company to eliminate a nonproductive middleman, which allowed the bottling companies to receive indefinite contracts to purchase the syrup from Coca-Cola at a price up to that paid by the eliminated middleman were for an intangible business advantage to improve the taxpayers' profits in future years, could not be currently deducted; but the case did not discuss amortization. Priv. Ltr. Rul. 91-23-004 distinguished *Darlington* on the ground that the utility terminated the contract to reduce operating costs rather than increase income. Payments that are not may be amortizable. Thus, in *Rodeway Inns of America v. Commissioner*, 63 T.C. 414 (1974), a payment to cancel a territorial franchise agreement that had been granted to an unrelated corporation so that franchisor could develop territory was capital expenditure amortizable over the life of the cancelled agreement, while in Rev. Rul. 71-283, 1971-2 C.B. 168, a payment by a lessor to terminate a lease in order to use leased premises itself was a capital expenditure amortizable over the remaining term of the cancelled lease. Section 167(c)(2) now provides, however, that when property is acquired subject to a lease, the entire price is allocated to the property, with no portion of the price able to be allocated to the lease, so that it can be amortized over the remaining life of the lease. As a result, in *Union Carbide Foreign Sales Corp. v. Commissioner*, 115 T.C. 423 (2000), when a lessee in a complex leasing transaction for a cargo ship that had been manufactured to its specifications, found that when the lessee exercised a right to purchase the ship because the price was less than that of an alternate right to terminate the lease by paying a stipulated amount the lessee could not deduct the $94,000,000 excess of the $108,000,000 purchase price over the $14,000,000 value of the ship even though reduced expenses, § 167(c)(2) applied even though by its nature the lease terminated with the purchase. Accordingly, the entire $108,000,000 price would be the depreciable cost of the ship.

PROBLEMS FOR DISCUSSION

Problem 7-20. (i) How, if at all, would § 1234A affect *Bisbee-Baldwin Corp.* (payment for termination of mortgage servicing contracts was combination of goodwill (capital gain) and right to future income (ordinary income)? *Nelson Weaver* (payment for termination of mortgage servicing contracts all capital gain)? *Eidson* (payment to terminate management contract all ordinary income)? *Stewart* (amounts realized for mortgage servicing contract excluded under former § 337)? Rev. Rul. 77-190 (Service follows *Stewart* but also *Eidson*)? *Nahey* (amounts received in settlement of claim acquired as part of a purchase of assets are ordinary income because based on lost profits of the predecessor only)? and Tech. Adv. Mem. 2000-49-009 (capital or § 1231 gain on payment to power plant operator to terminate long-term supply contract with a utility capital gain property, even though new contract with the utility to a supply of a greater amount of power at lower rates) or the basis on which they were decided? (ii) What is the proper treatment of the purchasers in those cases on the basis on which they were decided? (iii) Would any change under § 1234A affect the purchasers? (iv) What, if any is the effect of § 197 on the purchaser in any of these cases. (v) How, if at all, would § 197 affect *First Pennsylvania* (purchase price of mortgage service business allocated between right to continue servicing existing loans (amortizable over remaining terms of mortgages) and possibility to secure right to service future mortgages of the lenders was goodwill (not amortizable at the time). (vi) How, if at all, would § 1234A affect the seller in *First Pennsylvania*? (vii) How, if at all, would § 197 affect the seller in *First Pennsylvania*?

Problem 7-21. Under the terms of a leveraged lease of a ship, Les has the option to terminate the lease for a termination payment of $8,000,000 to Own, or, in the alternative, to purchase the ship from Own for $10,000,000. Assuming the ship is not worth more than $8,000,000, from a purely tax standpoint, what should Les do and why? Should Own care what Les does? If so, by how much should Own be willing to adjust the terms to split the difference with Les? *See* Rev. Rul. 69-511 (lessee's payment to cancel burdensome lease is currently deductible); Priv. Ltr. Rul. 91-23-004 (payment by a utility company to terminate a supply contract that required purchase of a specified amount of product by paying a specified amount per unit to buy at lower prices in the spot market was currently deductible); *Darlington-Hartsville Coca-Cola Bottling Co.* (amounts paid to Coca-Cola company to eliminate a nonproductive middleman were for an intangible business advantage to improve the taxpayers' profits in future years that could not be deducted currently); *Metropolitan Building* (payment for termination of leaseholder interest); *Rodeway Inns of America* (payment to cancel territorial franchise agreement so that franchisor could develop territory was capital expenditure amortizable over the life of the cancelled agreement); Rev. Rul. 71-283 (payment by lessor to terminate lease in order to use leased premises itself is capital expenditure amortizable over remaining term of cancelled lease); *Union Carbide Foreign Sales Corp.* (payment by lessee in a complex leasing transaction for a cargo ship to purchase ship at lesser amount than stipulated payment required to terminate the lease was part of the depreciable cost of the ship; § 167(c)(2)).

§ 3.03. Artists, Inventors, Franchises

The characterization issue with respect to ordinary income from transactions involving personal services versus capital gain from transactions involving property is, probably, at its extreme in connection with the creation of intellectual property, particularly including copyrights and patents. For years, Congress expressed a clear preference for science over the arts because § 1221(a)(3) provides that a copyright or artistic composition is never a capital asset in the hands of the creator while § 1235 provides a safe harbor for capital gain for inventors. In 2006, however, Congress made a limited modification to this broad preferences when amended § 1221(b)(3) to provide that capital gain treatment may, at the taxpayer's election, apply to the sale or exchange of a musical composition or copyrights in musical works. Other copyrights or artistic compensations continue to be denied capital asset status. Of course, in the hands of purchaser, a copyright or patent can be a capital asset or § 1231 property — think of the late Michael Jackson's ownership of Beatles' copyrights.

Because patents and copyrights are frequently disposed of for contingent consideration depending on the future proceeds from the exploitation of the patent or copyright, distinguishing between a license and a sale can be difficult. If a license is found, the payments will be ordinary income to the recipient and frequently deductible by the payor. However, if a sale is found and the patent or copyright is a capital asset or § 1231 property, the recipient may be entitled to capital gain treatment while the payor may be required to capitalize and amortize such payments over a prescribed period. Similar, problems arise when the grant of rights to a patent or copyright is limited to a portion of the geographic area, for example, a transfer of the rights under a patent for use in only the six New England states, or to a specific area of use, for example, a transfer of the rights to a novel to be used to make a movie while retaining the paperback rights or a transfer of the rights to a new automobile carburetor for use in boat engines, while retaining all other rights, including its use in automobiles. The following materials address this sale versus license distinction in situations involving copyrights, patents, trade names and franchises.

§ 3.03(a). Copyrights

I.R.C. § 1221(a)(3) and 1221(b)(3); Treas. Reg. § 1.1221-1(c); § 197(a), (c)(1) and (2), (d)(1)(C)(iii), and (e)(4)(C); Treas. Reg. § 1.197-2(b)(5) and (c)(7)

The following rulings show the evolution of the Service's treatment of copyrights, first allowing sale treatment for division by the field of use, but not if the consideration was contingent, and, then, later in the same year, recognizing the validity of the splitting the income by gifts.

Rev. Rul. 54-409, 1954-2 C.B. 174

A grant of less than all of a copyright proprietor's right may confer a license or constitute a transfer of property. A grant of the exclusive right to exploit a copyrighted work in a medium of publication throughout the life of the copyright transfers a property right; a grant of less confers a license. If the consideration received for a grant transferring a property interest is not measured by a percentage of the receipts from the sale, performance, or publication of the copyrighted work, is not measured by the number of copies sold, performances given, or exhibitions made of the copyrighted work, and is not payable periodically over a period generally coterminous with grantee's use of the copyrighted work, it is to be treated as proceeds from a sale of property and not as rentals or royalties.

I.T. 2735, C.B. XII-2, 131 (1933), is modified insofar as it holds that copyrights are incapable of division into separate properties.

* * *

I.T. 2735, *supra*, holds that a copyright is not divisible into separate properties and that a grant of less than all the rights conferred by a copyright must be a license (the consideration received therefor is rental or royalty income) and cannot be a sale. However, it was held in the *Herwig* case [*Herwig v. United States*, 105 F. Supp. 384 (Ct. Cls. 1952)] that a copyright proprietor who granted only the exclusive motion picture rights in a copyrighted work had made a sale of property.

In the market in which copyrights are traded, the exclusive rights to copyrighted works in one medium of publication are purchased and sold as separable properties according to practices so well established that they have been the subject of judicial notice. *Pelham G. Wodehouse* v. *Commissioner*, 166 Fed. (2d) 986, *reversed on other grounds*, 337 U.S. 369. . . .

Although it is well established that the grantee of less than all the rights conferred by a copyright is a "licensee" and not an "assignee" and cannot, therefore, sue for infringement, the rule is purely procedural. . . .

For the purposes of the Internal Revenue Code, a trademark may be divided, according to the usage of the market in which trademarks move, into separately salable fractions. . . . The Copyright Act, 61 Stat. 652 (Title 17 U.S.C.), itself suggests that the same is true of copyrights.

* * *

That a copyright proprietor's grant effects a transfer of property does not necessarily mean that the consideration received for the grant is in the nature of proceeds from a sale. *Burnet* v. *Henry Harmel*, 287 U.S. 103, Ct. D. 611, C.B. XI-2, 210 (1932). Therefore, it is held that, when the proprietor of a copyright grants the exclusive right to exploit the copyrighted work throughout the life of the copyright in a medium of publication or expression for a consideration which is not measured by a percentage of receipts from the sale, performance, exhibition, or publication of the copyrighted work, is not measured by the number of copies sold, performances given or exhibitions made of the copyrighted work, and is not payable periodically over a period generally coterminous with the grantee's use of the copyrighted work, the consideration is to be treated as the proceeds of a sale of property and not as rentals or royalties.

Whether a copyright is a capital asset within the meaning of section 117 [1221] of the Internal Revenue Code of 1939 and when the provisions of section 107(b) [a special income averaging provision with no current equivalent] of the Code with respect to copyrights would apply are separate and distinct questions. The taxability of the income of a nonresident alien derived from a copyrighted work is also distinct from the question dealt with here. *Commissioner* v. *Pelham G. Wodehouse*, *supra*. To the extent that I.T. 2735 . . . holds copyrights to be indivisible, it is modified. . . .

Rev. Rul. 54-599, 1954-2 C.B. 52

Revenue Ruling 54-409 . . . holds that copyrights are divisible into separate properties and that a grant of the exclusive right to exploit a copyrighted work in a specific medium such as radio, television, movies or the stage, throughout the life of the copyright transfers a property right. Accordingly, where a taxpayer by deed of gift transfers and divests himself of all rights, title, and interest in the dramatization rights to his novel necessary for its production in a specific medium, such as radio, television, motion pictures or on stage, he is not liable for Federal income tax with respect to any income deriving from his former interest in these rights. Any income from such dramatization rights would be taxable to the donee to the extent provided by the Internal Revenue Code of 1939. *Cf. Edward T. Blair* v. *Commissioner*, 300 U.S. 5 . . .

NOTES AND COMMENTS

Rev. Rul. 60-226, 1960-1 C.B. 26, *modified* Rev. Rul. 54-409 to remove the limitation that the consideration not be measured by a percentage of the receipts from the sale, performance, exhibition, or publication of the copyrighted work, or by the number of copies sold, performances given, or exhibitions made of the copyrighted work, or be payable over a period generally coterminous with the grantee's use of the copyrighted work. It relied on Rev. Rul 58-353, 1958-2 C.B. 408, which held that the consideration received by the owner of a patent for the assignment of the patent, or the granting of an exclusive license to a patent, may be treated as the proceeds of a sale of property, even though the consideration received by the transferor is measured by production, use, or sale of the patented article. It noted, however, that when the copyright proprietor retains interests that resemble royalties, along with other rights in the transferred interest, the transaction may, under some conditions, fail to have the required characteristics of a sale.

The *Wodehouse* case cited in Rev. Rul. 54-409, is only one of several cases involving P.G. Wodehouse, the creator of Bertie Wooster and Jeeves. In two other cases, *Wodehouse v. Commissioner*, 177 F.2d 881 (2d Cir. 1949), and *Wodehouse v. Commissioner*, 178 F.2d 987 (4th Cir. 1949), the British author assigned to his wife half-interests in two manuscripts and their copyrights. The Second Circuit held that, as a result of the assignment, the author's wife was taxable on the royalty income she received, but the Fourth Circuit reached the opposite conclusion. The different courts were, apparently, involved because of a shift of the place of jurisdiction over nonresident aliens. In both cases there was also an issue of whether royalties allocable to Canadian serial rights were subject to U.S. taxation of a nonresident alien. Again the courts split. On this issue, the Second Circuit held (two to one) that they were because, even though six percent of the magazine sales were in Canada, this was not sufficient evidence of the value of the Canadian rights absent allocation in the contract. The Fourth Circuit, on the other hand, held that a separate valuation of the Canadian rights was required, but did not hold that six percent was necessarily the right allocation. Despite the conflicting results, apparently, neither Wodehouse nor the government applied for certiorari.

In view of § 1221(a)(3), the question of the divisibility of a copyright is of interest to the creator, only for purposes of the assignment of income, as in the *Wodehouse* cases, and for purposes of capital gain, so that Rev. Rul. 54-409 and Rev. Rul. 60-226 are of interest primarily to publishers and others to whom the copyrights are assigned by the creators.

PROBLEM FOR DISCUSSION

Problem 7-22. In 20X1, Pubb acquired the worldwide copyright for Ides' *Great American Novel,* as a result of agreeing to publish the *Great American Novel,* subject to Pubb's standard royalties on all gross proceeds from exploiting the novel in any medium anywhere in the world with a payment equal to 10 percent of Pubb's gross receipts from exploiting the *Great American Novel.* (a) Which, if any of the following forms of transfer of rights to the *Great American Novel* by Pubb to Ack, subject to the amounts due Ides in 20X3 would give rise to capital gains? (i) An undivided one-half interest in the rights to the *Great American Novel*; (ii) The right to exploit the *Great American Novel* from 20X3 to 20X8, including the rights to grant licenses, etc; (iii) The right to exploit the *Great American Novel* in the motion picture industry, which is a major portion of the use of any bestseller; (iv) The right to exploit the *Great American Novel* in the area of the United States east of the Mississippi; (v) The right to exploit the *Great American Novel* in Switzerland? (b) How would the transferee treat the payments in each case? (c) How, if at all, would the result differ if the consideration for the transfer included an additional payment based on five percent of the transferee's gross receipts from exploiting the *Great American Novel*? (d) How, if at all, would the results differ if the transferor in each case was Ides? *See* Rev. Rul. 54-409 (capital gain on sale of copyright interest only for particular medium); Rev. Rul. 54-599 (assignment of copyright for a particular medium transfers income); Rev. Rul. 60-226 (removes no contingent payments limit); *Wodehouse* 2d Cir. (assignment of half-interest in copyright transferred taxability of income to wife; income allocable to Canadian rights taxable to nonresident alien); and *Wodehouse* 4th Cir. (assignment of half-interest in copyright did not transfer taxability of income to wife; income allocable to Canadian rights not taxable to nonresident alien); *Hort* (payment to escape burdensome lease); *McAllister* (sale of life estate to remainder owner); *Metropolitan Building Co.* (payment for termination of leaseholder interest); *P.G. Lake* (payment for oil production payment); and *Metropolitan Building Co.* (payment for termination of leaseholder interest).

§ 3.03(b). Patents

I.R.C. § 1235; Treas. Reg. § 1.1235-1 and 2(a), (b), (c) and (f)(1), (3) and (4); § 197(a), (c)(1) and (2), (d)(1)(C)(iii), and (e)(4)(C); Treas. Reg. § 1.197-2(b)(5), (c)(7) and (k) Examples 7 and 10

Unlike the mere artist, the inventor of a patent has a safe harbor providing for capital gain treatment under § 1235(a), even for deferred payment sales, with payments contingent on the proceeds of use of the patent. This provision is available even for professional inventors whose sales might otherwise fall within § 1221(a), but only when the transfer is of "all substantial rights" to the patent. It is not essential that the invention be patented, only that it be patentable. Treas. Reg. § 1.1235-2(a). The safe harbor does not, however, apply to a sale to a related party. § 1235(d). The following case deals with the meaning of "all substantial rights."

KUENEMAN v. COMMISSIONER

United States Court of Appeals, Ninth Circuit
628 F.2d 1196 (9th Cir. 1980)

This case was submitted to the Tax Court on stipulated facts which may be summarized as follows:

Taxpayers Don Kueneman and John Kueneman were the principal investors of a type of rock-crushing machine for which they obtained patents in the 1940's. In 1946, they entered into an agreement which altered the ownership of the patents so that John Kueneman, Don Kueneman, Alma Harrell, and Cyril Kenville, held specified undivided ownership interests. In November, 1948, John Kueneman, who was authorized to act on behalf of the others, entered into a licensing agreement with Pennsylvania Crusher Co., (Crusher), a New York corporation. In return for specified royalty payments, the license granted Crusher the exclusive right to make, vend, and use the patented machinery throughout Puerto Rico, eastern Canada, and all of the United States east of North Dakota, South Dakota, Nebraska, Kansas, Oklahoma, and Texas, during the lives of the patents.

* * *

The sole issue is whether appellants' exclusive transfer of their patent rights within a specified geographical area was a transfer of "all substantial rights" to the patent within the meaning of § 1235. If so they are entitled to treat royalty payments as long-term capital gains. We conclude that it was not such a transfer.

* * *

Appellants argue . . . that they thereby relinquished the monopoly right conferred by the patents to make, use, and sell the patented invention within the specified geographic area. . . . Their position is that Congress intended for an exclusive geographic transfer of patent rights to qualify for capital gains treatment under § 1235. Conceding that a patent transfer subject to a field-of-use restriction does not constitute the sale of a capital asset, *see Mros v. Commissioner* [493 F.2d 813 (9th Cir. 1974)]; . . . they argue that the rationales of these cases are inapplicable to an exclusive geographic transfer.

The Seventh Circuit appears to be the only appellate court which has considered the tax consequences of a geographically limited transfer of patent rights and the validity of Treasury Regulation § 1.1235-2(b)(i). *Estate of Klein v. Commissioner*, 507 F.2d 617, 621 (7th Cir. 1974) . . . held that an exclusive transfer of a patented process for the production of organic compost in certain eastern states did not relinquish "all substantial rights" to the patent within the meaning of § 1235. The Court said that the statutory requirement that "all substantial rights" be transferred indicated Congress' intent that a transfer of a part only of the patent rights should not be considered a sale or exchange of a capital asset. It found support for this conclusion in the Senate Committee Report excluding geographically limited transfers from consideration under § 1235 as an "undivided interest." . . . Treasury Regulations § 1.1235-2(b)(i) was seen as consistent with the statutory language and underlying Congressional intent.

The Seventh Circuit also found support in our decision *Mros*. . . . In *Mros*, we reversed the Tax Court and held that the transfer of patent rights to a gear reduction device for a limited industrial field-of-use did not transfer "all substantial rights" in the patent under § 1235. . . . [W]e adopted a two-prong test to determine whether a taxpayer is entitled to § 1235 benefits: (1) What did the taxpayer actually give up by the transfer; that is, was there an actual transfer of the monopoly rights in a patent; and (2) what did the taxpayer retain after the transfer; that is, are any substantial rights retained. . . . Since the patent in *Mros* had potential value in fields-of-use other than the field that was the subject of the transfer, we concluded that such a transaction could not qualify for capital gains treatment. The legislative history supported this conclusion, and we also upheld Treasury Regulation 1.1235-2(b)(i) as a valid implementation of § 1235.

Appellants argue that geographic divisions are fundamentally distinguishable from field-of-use divisions. We agree and recognize that *Mros* is not controlling in this case. . . . But this is not to say that the approach used in *Mros* is inapposite to a transfer subject to a geographical restriction. The *Mros* analysis embodies the language of § 1235 and its underlying legislative history. Field-of-use and geographical divisions must both comply with § 1235 as construed in accordance with the legislative history in order to qualify for capital gains. Accordingly, we conclude that the standard embraced in *Mros* in the context of a field-of-use transfer for determining whether a taxpayer is entitled to § 1235 benefits applies also to an exclusive geographical transfer. . . .

Thus, applying our two-prong analysis, it is clear that appellants' geographically limited transfer does not entitle them to capital gains treatment under § 1235. A patent gives the patent holder the monopoly right to make, use, and sell the patented invention throughout the United States during the life of the patent . . . and to exclude others from doing so. To qualify for the capital gains advantage it is this right that must be transferred, and in the context of a geographical transfer it must include all areas of the United States in which the patented invention has potential value. Appellants relinquished their monopoly rights in the patented rock-crushing machine only in the eastern portion of the United States. They transferred less than all the monopoly rights represented by the patent, retaining the exclusive rights to make, use, and vend the patented machine in the western portion of the United States. The record does not indicate that these retained monopoly rights were not substantial. Consequently, we find that appellants have failed to establish that their exclusive geographical transfer disposed of "all substantial rights" to their patents within the meaning of § 1235. . . . Congress enacted § 1235 as an incentive to inventors and to assure them that their license royalties would be afforded capital gains treatment whether payments were payable periodically or contingent on the use of the property transferred. . . . This was, however, conditioned on the transfer by the patent holder of property consisting of all substantial rights to a patent. A transfer of patent right limited to a geographical area is not a transfer of "all substantial rights." In *Mros* . . . we found this instructive language from the Senate Report:

> "It is the intention of your committee to continue this realistic test, whereby the entire transaction, regardless of formalities, should be examined in its factual context *to determine whether or not substantially all rights of the owner in the patent property have been released to the*

> *transferee*, rather than recognizing less relevant verbal touchstones. . . . *Furthermore, retention by the transferor of rights in the property which are not of the nature of rights evidenced by the patent and which are not inconsistent with the passage of ownership*, such as a security interest (e.g., a vendor's lien) or a reservation in the nature of a condition subsequent (e.g., a forfeiture on account of non-performance) are not to be considered as such a retention as will defeat the applicability of this section." . . .

(Emphasis added)

We believe Congress used the phrase "all substantial rights to the patent property" to refer to the monopoly rights represented by the patent throughout the United States. . . . This conclusion is fortified by the legislative history which explains the language of § 1235 providing that capital gain treatment is proper where a patent owner transfers "an undivided interest." The Senate Committee Report states:

> "By *'undivided interest' a part of each property right represented by the patent* (constituting a fractional share of the whole patent) *is meant (and not, for example, a lesser interest such as* a right to income, *or a license limited geographically*, or a license which conveys some, but not all, of the claims or uses covered by the patent)." . . .

(Emphasis added) A transfer limited geographically was to be excluded from consideration as an "undivided interest" because it does not convey a "fractional share of each property right represented by the patent." Therefore, transfer of such a "lesser interest" does not transfer "all substantial rights" to the patent — the entirety of each property right evidenced by the patent.

* * *

We conclude, as did the Seventh Circuit, that this regulation represents the proper interpretation of § 1235. . . .

* * *

NOTES AND COMMENTS

Because Reg. § 1235 provides a safe harbor, sales of patents by anyone other than the inventor, or by inventors who do not qualify under § 1235 because the sale is to a related party or otherwise, can still qualify for capital gains. Treas. Reg. § 1.1235-1(b); *see* Rev. Rul. 69-482, 1969-2 C.B. 164 (inventor who transferred all substantial rights to a patent to a corporation, in which he was a one-third shareholder for a contingent consideration, was entitled to capital gain treatment, even though he did not qualify under § 1235). It is interesting that *Kueneman*, apparently, did not cite Treas. Reg. § 1.1235-1(b), but instead chose to rely on the invalidity of Treas. Reg. § 1.1235-2(b), which defines all substantial rights restrictively. It contains a list of rights that are substantial, those that are not substantial, and those that may be substantial. Nevertheless, the ultimate question is whether the rights transferred are only the rights to royalties, or whether they include a sufficient interest in the patent to qualify as a sale or transfer of enough of the rights in the patent to qualify for capital gain or to effectively assign the income. *See Heim v. Fitzpatrick*, 262 F.2d 887 (2d Cir. 1959) (assignment to the taxpayer's wife and two children of a 25 percent undivided interest in the retained rights each was effective to transfer taxation of the income because the retained rights included not only the right to receipt of royalties, but also the right to negotiate for royalties on future related patents and the right to terminate the transfer if royalties were less than a specified amount); *Commissioner v. Reece*, 233 F.2d 30 (1st Cir. 1956) (assignment of rights to contingent proceeds from sale of invention transferred income to wife; right to proceeds was property).

The seller-inventor's obtaining capital gain, frequently, means that the purchaser has paid the purchase price of an asset, albeit an amortizable one. Fortunately for the purchaser, *Associated Patentees, Inc. v. Commissioner*, 4 T.C. 979 (1945), discussed in § 7.03(b) *Non-Section 197 Intangible Assets*, of Chapter 4 *Capitalization and Cost Recovery*, in effect, allows the purchaser to deduct contingent payments as the equivalent of current depreciation. The court reasoned that because the payment in the year of transfer was not the total cost of the patent, it would provide inadequate depreciation in the early years to amortize each payment over the remaining life of the patent for the period following the payment. It concluded that although that method allowed a full recovery of cost, it distorted income. The Service reached the same result, applying *Associated Patentees*, in Rev. Rul. 67-136, 1967-1 C.B. 58. For further discussion of the treatment of the purchaser, *see* § 3.06, *Amortization of Intangible Assets*, of Chapter 4, *Capitalization and Cost Recovery*.

PROBLEM FOR DISCUSSION

Problem 7-26. In 20X1, Ides transferred the following rights to his "Black Box," which does truly wondrous things, to Ack on a basis that provided her with a payment equal to 10 percent of Ack's gross receipts from exploiting the patent rights. (a) Which, if any of the following forms of transfer would give rise to capital gains? (i) An undivided one-half interest in the rights to the patent; (ii) The right to receive all royalties during the next five years including the rights to grant licenses, etc.; (iii) The right to exploit the patent in the automotive industry, which is a major portion of the use of the Black Box; (iv) The right to exploit the Black Box in the area of the United States east of the Mississippi; (v) The right to exploit the Black Box in Switzerland? (b) How would the transferee treat the payments in each case? (c) How, if at all, would the results differ if the transferor was Manu, which acquired worldwide rights to the Black Box as a result of manufacturing Black Boxes, giving Ides standard royalties on all gross proceeds from exploiting the Black Boxes in any medium anywhere in the world? *See Kueneman* (§ 1235 does not apply to geographically limited interest in patent); *Mros* (§ 1235 does not apply to interest in patent limited by field of use); *Heim* (assignment of a 25% undivided interest in the retained rights to each of three family members was effective to transfer taxation of the income); *Reece* (assignment of rights to contingent proceeds from sale of invention transferred income to wife; right to proceeds was property); *Associated Patentees* (purchaser deducts contingent payments as depreciation in year of payment), *Hort* (discussed in § 2.02, *Sales of*

Partial Interests — Ordinary Income Substitute (payment to escape burdensome lease)); *McAllister* (discussed in § 2.02, *Sales of Partial Interests — Ordinary Income Substitute* (payment for life estate); *P.G. Lake, Inc.* (discussed in § 2.02, *Sales of Partial Interests — Ordinary Income Substitute* (payment for oil production payment); and *Metropolitan Building Co.* (discussed in § 2.02, *Sales of Partial Interests — Ordinary Income Substitute* (payment for termination of leaseholder interest).

§ 3.03(c). Franchises and Trade Names

I.R.C. § 1253; § 197(a), (c)(1) and (2), (d)(1)(F), and (f)(4); Treas. Reg. § 1.197-2(b)(10), (d)(2)(iii), (e)(2), (f)(3)(iv)(A), and (4)(i), (g)(6), and (k) Examples 5 and 8

Unlike § 1221(a)(3), which denies artists capital gain treatment in the case of most copyrights regardless of the form of the transaction, and § 1235, which grants inventors capital gain treatment if they transfer all substantial rights to a patent, even for consideration contingent on future exploitation, but without substantially prejudicing the purchaser's depreciation or amortization deduction, § 1253 denies transferors of franchises, trademarks and trade names capital gain treatment if they retain "any significant power, right, or continuing interest" in the franchise, trademark, or trade name. This may reflect a brokered arrangement because, unlike §§ 1221(a)(3) and 1235, which deal only with the characterization of gain on the seller's side, § 1253, ties the treatment for the transferee to the treatment for the transferor, by denying capital gain treatment by the transferor for contingent payments but generally allowing a deduction to the transferee for certain contingent payments. § 1253(c) and (d)(1). The following case deals with the meaning of any significant right.

STOKELY USA, INC. v. COMMISSIONER
United States Tax Court
100 T.C. 439 (1993)

. . . Petitioner is in the business of processing, canning, and marketing canned and frozen vegetables, fruits, tomato products, and juices. Its principal products are canned corn, beans, peas, and beets. . . .[2]

During the years in issue, roughly half of petitioner's net sales (and 26 percent of total sales) were made under the trademarks and trade names Stokely's or Stokely's Finest. Products sold by petitioner under the Stokely trademarks and trade names carry a higher price than those sold under its other labels and generate a higher unit profit margin for petitioner.

Petitioner initially obtained the right to use the Stokely's Finest trademarks and trade names in a 1983 license agreement with Stokely-Van Camp, Inc. (SVC), an unrelated Indiana corporation that also owned the rights to other trademarks and

[2] There were two trademarks using the name Stokely's Finest with registration numbers 999,795 and 277,037, respectively. Petitioner did not obtain the rights to use the trademark Stokely's, registration number 994,422, in this license agreement.

trade names, including Stokely's, Stokely-Van Camp's Finest, and Van Camp's. In 1983, petitioner also purchased production facilities related to the Stokely's Finest trademarks that it licensed from SVC. All SVC's trademarks, trade names, and registrations included rights of use for a variety of canned and frozen food products, including pork and beans. Petitioner was also interested in obtaining SVC's pork and beans product lines and related trademarks; however, SVC specifically retained its Stokely-Van Camp's and Van Camp's trademarks and trade names and prohibited petitioner from using the Stokely's Finest trademarks on pork and beans products. At no time prior to its negotiations with SVC did petitioner produce pork and beans products. As of June 1983, SVC's share of the market for canned pork and beans in the United States was about 33 percent, totaling about $150,000,000 annually in sales.

In September 1983, the Quaker Oats Co. (Quaker Oats) acquired all the assets of SVC. . . .

* * *

Petitioner and Quaker Oats eventually agreed to the transfer of certain trademarks owned by Quaker Oats. On November 5, 1984, Quaker Oats transferred to the Quaker Oats Foundation (the Foundation), a private foundation controlled by Quaker Oats, the trademarks that it intended to transfer to petitioner. On November 15, 1984, the Foundation and petitioner entered into a trademark transfer agreement pursuant to which, for a lump-sum payment of $1,584,500, the Foundation:

> [transferred], [sold] and [assigned] to * * * [petitioner] * * * THE FOUNDATION'S right, title and interest, both statutory and at common law, in The Trademarks and the registrations thereof, subject to * * * [certain restrictions] * * * including the right to sue for and collect damages for any past infringement * * *.

The trademarks referred to in the agreement were Stokely's, Shellie, Bavarian Style, and the two Stokely's Finest trademarks (the Stokely trademarks). Also under the agreement, petitioner's royalty obligations to SVC for the latter two trademarks were canceled.[6] The restrictions mentioned in the agreement were as follows: (1) Because of prior agreements with SVC, petitioner's rights were subject to the rights of two other companies in various Stokely trademarks; . . . and (4) The agreement also contained the following restrictions:

> 2.1 * * * [Petitioner] shall not use The Trademarks on * * * [pork and beans, and products containing beans and wieners (such wieners being composed of either beef, pork, chicken or poultry or a combination thereof) for] * * * [20 years]. * * * . . .

* * *

---

[6] The Stokely-Van Camp's and Van Camp's trademarks and trade names were not transferred and remained in use by Quaker Oats

> 2.4 The FOUNDATION shall have the right to disapprove any assignment of [Petitioner's] right, title and interest in the Trademarks for a period of five years.

* * *

In January 1985, petitioner changed its name to Stokely USA, Inc. On December 24, 1986, petitioner acquired from the American National Co. a number of processing plants, including one used for pork and beans, as well as an inventory of pork and beans. Petitioner . . . continued production of pork and beans products at the acquired plants for several months under other trade names and trademarks. . . . However, petitioner was soon forced to discontinue production of pork and beans due to the lack of a major brand name and consequent low profitability for those products. Had petitioner been able to use the Stokely trademarks on pork and beans products, or obtain rights to the Van Camp's trademarks, petitioner would have continued pork and beans production and converted the other plant for such production.

Quaker Oats continued selling pork and beans under the Van Camp's label. During the years after the agreement between petitioner and the Foundation, Van Camp's pork and beans products accounted for approximately 28 percent of the United States market for such products. . . .

* * *

The only issue is whether petitioner is entitled to amortize the $1,584,500 payment it made for the purchase of the Stokely trademarks. Section 1253(d)(2)(A) provides for amortization of the cost of a trademark over a 10-year period if, pursuant to section 1253(a), the transfer of the trademark is not treated as a sale or exchange of a capital asset.[10] . . .

* * *

Petitioner contends that the Foundation's 5-year right to disapprove any assignment of petitioner's right, title, and interest in the trademarks and the 20-year prohibition on petitioner's use of the trademarks with respect to pork and beans (the pork and beans restriction), represent powers, rights, or continuing interests retained by the Foundation. We agree with petitioner that the Foundation's right to disapprove transfer of the trademarks by petitioner during the first 5 years after the transfer constitutes a retained power, right, or continuing interest with respect to the subject matter of the trademarks. Respondent does not dispute this. Respondent's only argument with respect to this retained power, right, or interest is that it is not "significant" within the meaning of section 1253(a).

Respondent argues, however, that the pork and beans restriction does not constitute a retained power, right, or continuing interest, but rather, merely defines the assets that petitioner purchased. In essence, respondent contends that petitioner simply did not purchase the right to use the Stokely trademarks for pork and beans. According to respondent, petitioner purchased the right to use the Stokely trademarks on everything except pork and beans. . . .

---

[10] In some cases, the amortization period may be shorter. Sec. 1253(d)(2)(A). . . .

Respondent's analysis begs the question. It is clear that petitioner did not "purchase" the right to use the Stokely trademarks on pork and beans (for 20 years). It is equally clear that the Foundation retained no right to continue to use the specific trademarks that were transferred to petitioner. However, the relevant statutory language of section 1253 refers to neither of these factors. Rather, section 1253(a) refers to a "transfer of a * * * trademark". This reference to the transfer of a trademark contemplates all transfers, including those with substantial restrictions and limited durations.[13]

Section 1253(a) states that such "transfer" "shall not be treated as a sale or exchange of a capital asset if the transferor retains any significant power, right, or continuing interest *with respect to the subject matter of the * * * trademark*". (Emphasis added.) The subject matter of the Stokely trademarks included the ability to use them in the marketing of food products. Trademarks and trade names represent goodwill. . . . Petitioner purchased the Stokely trademarks with the expectation that potential customers would be more likely to purchase petitioner's products if they were identified by the Stokely trademarks. Stokely trademarks could have been used to market pork and beans. . . . While petitioner acquired less than the full use of the Stokely trademarks, this was the direct result of the pork and beans restriction, through which the Foundation was able to prevent petitioner from using the trademarks on pork and beans products.

The statute contains examples that show the error of respondent's reliance on the fact that petitioner did not purchase the right to use the trademarks on pork and beans. Section 1253(b)(2) lists several significant retained powers, rights, or continuing interests. One of these is the right of the transferor to disapprove any transfer. . . . The purchaser of a trademark encumbered by this type of restriction clearly does not "purchase" the unencumbered right to transfer the trademark. Nevertheless, it is clear that this type of restriction was to qualify as a retained power within the meaning of section 1253. . . .

* * *

Based on the foregoing factors, we find that the pork and beans restriction was a retained power, right, or continuing interest with respect to the subject matter of the Stokely trademarks.

* * *

Petitioner's primary argument is that the Foundation's right to disapprove assignment of the Stokely trademarks for 5 years is, as a matter of law, "significant". . . . The powers, rights, or continuing interests specified in section 1253(b)(2) are deemed significant by the terms of the statute. If a retained power, right, or continuing interest falls within the rights listed in section 1253(b)(2), no further inquiry is necessary. This list, however, is nonexclusive and does not preclude the possibility that other retained powers, rights, or continuing interests may be "significant".

---

[13] That temporal limitations were contemplated in such transfers is clear from the language of sec. 1253(d)(2)(A) and (B), which refers to "the period of the transfer agreement", and sec. 1253(b)(3), which describes a "renewal of a franchise, trademark, or trade name" as a "transfer".

Petitioner contends that the Foundation's right to disapprove assignment of the Stokely trademarks for 5 years is "A right to disapprove any assignment of such interest, or any part thereof" within the meaning of subparagraph (A) of section 1253(b)(2). Respondent counters by pointing out that the Foundation's right to disapprove assignments was limited to the 5-year period following the transfer, whereas petitioner's rights in the transferred trademarks were for an unlimited duration. . . . In essence, the parties ask us to decide whether the words "any assignment" in the statute mean all assignments (suggested by respondent), or some assignments (suggested by petitioner).

* * *

The parties' arguments present us with a conundrum. Subparagraph (A) refers to "*any* assignment of such interest, or *any* part thereof." (Emphasis added.) The second "any" in subparagraph (A) can only mean "some". It would be arguably inconsistent to interpret the first "any" in a single sentence to mean "all" and the second "any" to mean "some". Yet, if the first "any" means "some", the interpretative problems noted by respondent arise.

The better course, and the one we adopt, is to interpret subparagraph (A) in light of the statute as a whole. Section 1253(b)(2) contains a list of retained rights upon which Congress conferred significance as a matter of law. . . . However, unless the retained rights listed in subsection (b)(2) are coextensive in duration with the interest transferred, it can readily be seen that any one of them could be objectively insignificant if the time period during which the transferor could exercise such right was restricted. Courts would then be faced with the dilemma of either interpreting the statute in a way that would produce absurd results or making a case-by-case determination of the actual significance of whatever temporal limits had been placed on the retained right. Neither approach is satisfactory or in keeping with the legislative objective of subsection (b)(2). We believe, therefore, that the retained rights enumerated in subsection (b)(2) must be exercisable for a period of time that is coextensive with the duration of the interest that was transferred. This interpretation is consistent with the language in section 1253, the legislative history, and the objective of the statute.

The language of section 1253 makes a literal distinction between the object of a significant retained right referred to in subsection (a) and the object of the specifically described rights in subsection (b)(2). Section 1253(a) refers to retained rights "with respect to the *subject matter* of the franchise, trademark, or trade name." (Emphasis added.) While a transferred interest in a franchise, trademark, or trade name may itself have a specifically limited duration, the "subject matter" of these intangibles, including the goodwill associated with them, would not likely have an ascertainable limit. In contrast, section 1253(b)(2), which lists specifically defined rights, refers to rights retained "with respect to the *interest* transferred". (Emphasis added.) The "interest transferred" can encompass less than the subject matter of a franchise, trademark, or trade name. The "interest transferred" can be, and often is, for a limited period.[18] . . . Thus, the duration of a retained right takes

---

[18] For example, a typical restaurant franchise, which encompasses trademarks and trade names, is generally granted for a specified period of years. . . . As previously noted, sec. 1253(b)(3) defines

on added importance "with respect to the interest transferred" under subsection (b)(2). Our interpretation of the statute recognizes that importance.

The legislative history of section 1253 also emphasizes the importance of duration in regard to the retained rights enumerated in subsection (b)(2). . . .

One of the objectives of Congress in enacting section 1253 was to provide a simple, uniform method for determining whether the transfer of a trademark, franchise, or trade name should receive capital gains treatment. . . . Courts had previously conducted detailed factual analyses of such transfers to determine the significance of rights retained by the transferor. These factual analyses led to divisions of authority among courts about the significance of many retained rights. . . . If, as suggested by petitioner, the duration of the retained rights listed in subsection (b)(2) need not be coextensive with the duration of the interest transferred, two potential interpretative scenarios follow.

Under the first scenario, a retained right listed in subsection (b)(2) would be deemed significant regardless of its duration. If we were to adopt this approach, a 1-month or 1-week right to disapprove the assignment of a 20-year franchise would, as a matter of law, be considered significant for purposes of section 1253(b)(2). . . . This is clearly not what Congress intended . . . and could easily lead to absurd results. . . .

Under the second scenario, a retained right listed in subsection (b)(2) might or might not have significance, depending upon an analysis of the facts and circumstances in order to determine whether its duration was adequate. This type of analysis leads directly back to the problems and resulting uncertainty that existed prior to the enactment of section 1253, and therefore, subverts the intent of Congress. . . .

Based on the foregoing analysis, we hold that those powers, rights, or continuing interests retained by a transferor that are enumerated in subsection (b)(2) must be coextensive with the duration of the interest transferred. It follows that the Foundation's 5-year transfer disapproval right is not a significant right within the meaning of section 1253(b)(2).

This does not mean that the Foundation's disapproval right is not significant for purposes of section 1253(a). The list in subsection (b)(2) is nonexclusive, and therefore, retained rights not included in subsection (b)(2) may still qualify under subsection (a) so as to entitle petitioner to amortize its payment. Whether a retained right not specifically enumerated in section 1253(b)(2) is "significant" for purposes of section 1253(a) must be determined in light of all the facts and circumstances at the time of the transfer.

There is very little evidence regarding the impact on petitioner as a result of the 5-year disapproval right. . . . Absent such evidence, we are unprepared to find that this disapproval right, on its own, should be characterized as a significant power, right, or continuing interest for purposes of section 1253(a).

Petitioner next argues that the 20-year restriction on using the Stokely

---

"transfer" to include "the *renewal* of a franchise, trademark, or trade name" (emphasis added). . . .

trademarks on pork and beans products is itself a "significant" retained power, right, or continuing interest. Respondent contends that this restriction is not significant for two reasons. First, respondent asserts that the name "Stokely" is barely visible on Quaker Oats' well-known line of Van Camp's pork and beans products. This, according to respondent, belies the claim that the Stokely trademarks could have been used by petitioner to successfully market pork and beans products. Second, respondent notes that petitioner was not in the business of producing pork and beans products at the time it entered the transaction to acquire the trademarks. From this, respondent argues that the restriction had no significance for petitioner's business or its use of the Stokely trademarks. We disagree.

The restriction clearly had significance for Quaker Oats. The specific reason for its inclusion in the contract was to protect the company's Van Camp's line. Because of the close connection in the public mind between the Van Camp's and Stokely names, Quaker Oats' management believed that the Van Camp's mark would be "seriously diluted", and Quaker Oats' sales of pork and beans products materially and adversely affected, if petitioner were allowed to use the Stokely trademarks for these products. On brief, respondent agrees that the Stokely and Van Camp's names have been associated with one another in the minds of the public. Thus, it is probable that the use of the Stokely trademarks on pork and beans products would have had considerable importance in any effort by petitioner to market such products.

Moreover, petitioner wanted to enter into the market for pork and beans. Petitioner initially approached Quaker Oats regarding the purchase of the Stokely-Van Camp's trademark, but was rejected. Petitioner wanted to use the Stokely trademarks on pork and beans products and would have done so but for the restriction. Despite the restriction, petitioner attempted to sell pork and beans for a short period under another label. Petitioner was forced to abandon its plans for that market due to the lack of a strong brand name. Stokely could have been that name.

* * *

In light of these facts, the pork and beans restriction carried undoubted significance for the Foundation, Quaker Oats, and petitioner. The trademark transfer agreement states this clearly: [Petitioner] recognizes and acknowledges that such use of The Trademarks before expiration of the applicable time period would result in immediate and irreparable injury to the FOUNDATION, which could not be adequately compensated by payment of money damages, and hence injunctive relief would be appropriate in favor of the FOUNDATION or its designees to prevent use of The Trademarks in such manner.

* * *

Section 1.1253-2(d), Proposed Income Tax Regs., . . . lists nine rights that are considered to be "significant". Six of the rights listed in the proposed regulations are identical to those listed in section 1253(b)(2). The right listed in section 1.1253-2(d)(9), Proposed Income Tax Regs. . . . is: "Any other right which permits the transferor to exercise continuing, active, and operational control over the transferee's trade or business activities." Respondent argues that active, operational control is the sine qua non of significance. We observe, however, that the proposed regulation itself belies respondent's conclusion. It introduces its list with the caveat that "The term 'significant power, right, or continuing interest' *includes, but is not limited to*, the following rights". . . . (Emphasis added.)

. . . We believe the pork and beans restriction allows the Foundation control of the transferee's activities and operations in that it prevents petitioner from using its trademarks for a significant market that petitioner could have and would have otherwise entered. This constitutes a "significant [condition] or [restriction]". . . .

We recognize that the pork and beans restriction is not coextensive with the duration of petitioner's rights in the trademarks. The restriction lasts for 20 years, whereas petitioner acquired its right, title, and interest in the trademarks in perpetuity. Section 1253(a) provides that a transfer "not be treated as a sale or exchange of a capital asset if the transferor retains any significant power, right, or continuing interest with respect to the *subject matter of the franchise, trademark, or trade name.*" (Emphasis added.) As previously noted, the subject matter of a trademark may be broader than the "interest transferred" referred to in section 1253(b)(2). Section 1253(a) is therefore distinguishable from section 1253(b)(2). Unlike section 1253(b)(2), section 1253(a) contains no specifically enumerated criteria for determining the significance of a retained right. While the duration of a restriction may be an important factor, the ultimate determination of whether a retained right is "significant" for purposes of section 1253(a) must be based on all the facts and circumstances. In the context of petitioner's business, 20 years is a significant period.

* * *

NOTES AND COMMENTS

The proposed regulations referred to in the *Stokely* opinion were withdrawn in 1993, more than 20 years after they were first proposed, apparently as no longer needed or not to be pursued in the foreseeable future. Although it is possible that the withdrawal was based the enactment of § 197, which applies to the transferee's side of most transfers, requiring capitalization under § 1253(d)(2) and 15-year amortization under § 197, this would attribute an unprecedented degree of speed to the Service in its response to new legislation, particularly because the withdrawal proposal preceded the enactment of § 197. Section 1253 continues, however, to apply in certain situations to the transferee's side of the transaction, allowing the deduction of contingent serial payments are payable at least annually and that are substantially equal in amount or determined under a fixed formula. Because § 197 does not apply to the seller's side, 1253(d)(1). Sections 1253(a) and (c) continue to apply to the transferor's side of the transaction. This means that the transferor has ordinary income in any case in which significant power, right, or interest is retained and also for any contingent payments. Thus, *Stokely*, which is a transferee case, now has primary relevance to the transferor.

PROBLEM FOR DISCUSSION

Problem 7-27. In 20X1, Ides transferred the following rights to the trade name "Black Box" on a basis that provided him with an annual payment of $100,000 plus an amount equal to 10 percent of the transferee's gross receipts from exploiting the name "Black Box." (a) Which, if any, of the following forms of transfer would give rise to capital gains for the transferor? (i) An undivided one-half interest in the rights to the name "Black Box"; (ii) The right to receive all royalties during the next five years including the rights to grant licenses, etc.; (iii) The right to exploit the name "Black Box" in the electronics industry, which is a major portion of the use of the name "Black Box"; (iv) The right to exploit the name "Black Box" in the area of the United States east of the Mississippi; (v) The right to exploit the name "Black Box" in Switzerland; (b) How would the transferee treat the annual payments in each case? (c) How, if at all, would the result differ if the payments were substantially equal in the amount? (d) How, if at all, would the result differ if the consideration included only the $100,000 annual payment? *See* § 1253; *Stokely USA* (trademark is a capital asset in the hands of the transferee; exclusion of a significant market is a substantial right); *Kueneman* (§ 1235 does not apply to geographically limited interest in patent); *Mros* (§ 1235 does not apply to interest in patent limited by field of use); *Heim* (assignment of a 25% undivided interest in the retained rights to three family members was effective to transfer taxation of the income); *Reece* (assignment of rights to contingent proceeds from sale of invention transferred income to wife; right to proceeds was property); *Associated Patentees* (purchaser deducts contingent payments as depreciation in year of payment); *Hort* (discussed in § 2.02, *Sales of Partial Interests — Ordinary Income Substitute* (payment to escape burdensome lease)); *McAllister* (discussed in § 2.02, *Sales of Partial Interests — Ordinary Income Substitute* (payment for life estate)); *P.G. Lake, Inc.* (discussed in § 2.02, *Sales of Partial Interests — Ordinary Income Substitute* (payment for oil production payment); and *Metropolitan Building Co.* (discussed in § 2.02, *Sales of Partial Interests — Ordinary Income Substitute* (payment for termination of leaseholder interest)).

§ 4. RELATED TAXPAYERS

Transactions between related taxpayers do not reflect the results of arm's-length bargaining by parties with adverse interests, which partially validates allocations in sales between unrelated parties. Consequently, transactions between related parties may involve the potential for shifting income and changing the character of the income. This potential for abuse has led Congress to enact a number of statutory provisions designed to allow the Service to recharacterize the transactions and impose the consequences that would have resulted from arm's-length dealings on transactions between related parties, regardless of the formal terms adopted by them. The scope of these provisions is discussed in § 4.01, *§ 482 — Applicability,* while § 4.02, *§ 482 — Applied,* illustrates the effect of imposing the arm's-length requirement.

§ 4.01. § 482 — Applicability

I.R.C. §§ 482; 269A; 707(e) and 1366(e)

Section 482 provides the Service with broad authority to allocate income, deductions, and credits among two or more trades or businesses owned directly or indirectly by the same interests to prevent evasion of taxes or to clearly reflect income. The provision is notable for its brevity and lack of definition of any of the key terms, which reflects that it is an old provision, antedating the Internal Revenue Code of 1939. The result is broad Service authority, but also significant scope for taxpayer defense. The following case, in its multiple iterations, deals with the application of § 482 to the reverse of the "reasonable compensation" issue, that is, whether a senior family member as a shareholder-employee, claiming too little compensation, indirectly shifted service income, effecting the kind of transfer that Mr. Earl, in *Lucas v. Earl*, discussed in § 2.01(a) *Income from Services*, was not allowed to make.

FOGLESONG v. COMMISSIONER

United States Court of Appeals, Seventh Circuit
621 F.2d 865 (7th Cir. 1980)

* * *

The facts here are not in substantial dispute. Frederick H. Foglesong, the taxpayer, was a sales representative for the Plymouth Tube division of the Van Pelt Corporation ("Plymouth Tube") and for the Pittsburgh Tube Company ("Pittsburgh Tube"), two manufacturers of cold drawn steel tubing. Taxpayer entered into an agreement to become the Eastern sales representative of Plymouth Tube in 1962. He sold Plymouth Tube's products within a defined territory for a commission. In 1963, taxpayer entered into a similar agreement with Pittsburgh Tube.

. . . There was evidence that taxpayer had an impressive reputation as a salesman, and this was one of the principal reasons he was retained as a sales representative by Plymouth Tube and Pittsburgh Tube.

On August 30, 1966, taxpayer incorporated his business as Frederick H. Foglesong Company, Inc. . . . Of the one hundred shares of common stock issued by the Corporation (for a total subscription price of $1,000), taxpayer held 98 shares and his wife and accountant held 1 share each. The Corporation paid no dividends on its common stock during the taxable years in question, 1966 through 1969.

The Corporation also issued preferred stock to the taxpayer's four minor children (for which the total subscription price was $400). The four children received dividends totaling $32,000 over the period beginning September 1, 1966 and ending December 31, 1969.

At or about the time the Corporation was organized, the taxpayer notified Plymouth Tube and Pittsburgh Tube that the Corporation was being formed and asked that any commissions due under his agreements with them be paid to the Corporation. Both suppliers agreed to this request. As a result, certain commissions earned for services rendered before the date of incorporation were paid to the Corporation. In addition, the Corporation adopted a fiscal year ending August 31, and the taxpayer received no salary from the Corporation during the months of September through December 1966 although he continued to work as a salesman servicing Plymouth Tube and Pittsburgh Tube during that period.

On his personal income tax return for the calendar year 1966, taxpayer reported a net profit from his business as a sales representative in the amount of $86,665.88, all of which was derived from commissions paid to him personally during the months of January through August, 1966, by his principals. The Corporation made its first salary payment to taxpayer on January 9, 1967, and he received a regular monthly salary after that date during the years which are relevant here. Taxpayer's salary income from the Corporation during calendar year 1967 was $56,500. In that year and in the succeeding relevant calendar years, he reported no personal income from any business as a sole proprietor. The respective net receipts of the Corporation from sales commissions and its deductions for compensation paid to taxpayer for the four taxable years in question are as follows:

Taxable Year Ending	Net Receipts from Commissions Before Payment of Compensation to Taxpayer[4]	Compensation to Taxpayer Deducted
August 31, 1967	$148,486.70	$41,500.00
August 31, 1968	100,482.023	55,000.00
August 31, 1969	99,429.35	65,000.00
August 31, 1970	121,018.24	73,700.00

After the formation of the Corporation, all commissions from Plymouth Tube and Pittsburgh Tube were paid to the Corporation. But a written agreement with Pittsburgh Tube was not executed until May 19, 1969, or with Plymouth Tube until January 1, 1971.

Taxpayer testified that he wished to incorporate his business in order to obtain the limited liability protection afforded by a corporate structure and also to provide a better vehicle for his planned expansion into several new business ventures. Subsequent to the formation of the Corporation, taxpayer interviewed a prospective salesman to help him in the New England area, but these negotiations were unsuccessful. The Corporation did, however, employ a secretary during its taxable years ending August 31, 1969 and 1970, paid her a salary and took corresponding deductions. . . .

The Corporation paid taxpayer a regular salary as a salesman, paid all of taxpayer's expenses incurred in connection with his sales activities, maintained a bank account, carried its own insurance coverage, maintained a company automobile and complied with all the formalities required of corporations in the state of New Jersey. . . .

During the years in question here taxpayer did not enter into any written

[4] These figures show the total net commission income (before payment of compensation to taxpayer) as reported by the Corporation on its tax returns for the taxable years in issue. They thus include the income generated on certain sales made within the Corporation's exclusive sales territories, but without any selling effort on taxpayer's part. Approximately two percent of the total commissions received by the Corporation during the taxable years in question resulted from these exclusive territorial arrangements. . . .

employment contracts with the Corporation nor did he enter into a covenant not to compete with the Corporation.

During these years taxpayer's only gainful activity was as an employee of the Corporation. He had no legal rights under the representation contracts with Plymouth Tube and Pittsburgh Tube subsequent to the formation of the Corporation. . . .

The Tax Court, *inter alia*, concluded on balance that, although there was no attempt by taxpayer to form a corporation to take advantage of losses incurred by a separate trade or business, tax avoidance considerations "far outweighed any genuine business concerns taxpayer may have had in setting up [the Corporation]." Nonetheless, the Commissioner conceded, and the Tax Court found, that the Corporation was a viable, taxable entity and not a mere sham during the years in issue.

But, in spite of its finding of viability (and strongly influenced by the apparent flagrancy of the tax avoidance), the Tax Court, in effect, substantially disregarded the Corporation for tax purposes. It found that during the years in question control over 98% of the commission income remained with taxpayer so as to cause such income to be taxable to him (as the person who earned it through his personal sales efforts) and not to the Corporation. The Tax Court based this result on Section 61 of the Internal Revenue Code and the assignment of income doctrine of *Lucas v. Earl*, [281 U.S. 111 (1930). With respect to those commissions which were received by taxpayer solely because of the exclusive territorial rights assigned to the Corporation under its agreements with Plymouth Tube and Pittsburgh Tube (amounting to approximately 2% of the total), the Tax Court held that the Corporation, not the taxpayer, was the party earning this income, and, hence, such commissions should be taxed to it.

The Tax Court found it unnecessary to reach the question whether the Commissioner was authorized to allocate the commission income to taxpayer under Section 482 of the Internal Revenue Code, which permits the Commissioner to reallocate income and expenses among commonly controlled "organizations, trades or businesses."

Personal service corporation tax cases reveal a tension between "the principle of a graduated income tax * * * and the policy of recognizing the corporation as a taxable entity distinct from its shareholders in all but extreme cases." *Rubin v. Commissioner*, 429 F.2d 650, 652 (2d Cir. 1970). The impact of the graduated income tax is eroded when income is split artificially among several entities or over several tax years. The assignment of income doctrine under Section 61 of the Internal Revenue Code (as formulated in *Lucas v. Earl*) seeks to recognize "economic reality" by cumulating income diffused among several recipients through "artificial" legal arrangements. The attribution of income to its "true earner" is simply a species of recognizing "substance" over "form." . . .

But, if the issue is one of attributing the income of a corporation to its sole stockholder-employee who "really" earned it, we encounter the important policy of the law favoring recognition of the corporation as a legal person and economic actor.

As Mr. Justice Holmes said *in Klein. v. Board of Supervisors*, 282 U.S. 19, 24 . . . (1930):

> But it leads nowhere to call a corporation a fiction. If it is a fiction it is a fiction created by law with intent that it should be acted on as if true. The corporation is a person and its ownership is a nonconductor that makes it impossible to attribute an interest in its property to its members.

In the instant case, the following circumstances, among others, are present: (1) the Corporation and not the taxpayer is the party to the contracts under which services are performed, (2) the Corporation is recognized to be a viable, taxable entity and not a mere sham, (3) non-tax business purposes are present even though tax avoidance is apparently a major concern, (4) the Corporation has not been formed for the purpose of taking advantage of losses incurred by a separate trade or business, (5) the corporate form (and the status of the Corporation as an actual operating enterprise) has been consistently honored by the taxpayer and other parties to the transactions giving rise to the income, (6) the taxpayer does not render services as an employee to any entity other than the Corporation, (7) the Corporation is not disqualified from performing the services required of it by contact because the law requires these services to be performed by an individual, (8) the entities paying or providing the income are not controlled or dominated by the taxpayer, and (9) as will appear, other and more appropriate legal bases exist for attacking apparent tax avoidance than broad-scale disregard of the corporate form through application of assignment of income theory. We note especially that the Tax Court did not find the Corporation to be a pure tax avoidance vehicle.

Under the circumstances of the instant case, we think it inappropriate to attempt to weight "business purposes" against "tax avoidance motives" in a determination whether the assignment of income doctrine of *Lucas v. Earl* should apply, in effect, to substantially disregard the corporate form. Ostensibly this inquiry has been made in order to question the validity of a transaction purportedly entered into by a corporation, rather than the validity of the corporation itself. . . . But to apply *Lucas v. Earl* in this fashion under the circumstances present here is effectively (and more realistically) to nullify the determination that the Corporation is a viable, taxable entity and not a sham. *See Moline Properties v. Commissioner*, 319 U.S. 436 . . . (1943); *National Carbide v. Commissioner*, 336 U.S. 422 (1949).

In *Moline Properties* . . ., the Supreme Court confronted the question whether the gain on sale of certain real estate held by a corporation as security was to be taxed to the corporation or to its sole shareholder. The Court perceived the problem as determining whether the corporate form might be disregarded for tax purposes as a sham or unreal. The Court said that the corporation was a viable taxable entity so long as the purpose of its creation is the equivalent of business activity or its creation is followed by the carrying on of business by the corporation. In *Moline Properties*, the question of purpose to evade or avoid income taxes (through the use of a corporation) was addressed as part of the theretofore live issue whether the corporation was a viable taxable entity or a sham. Although, as a practical matter the "viability" objection has apparently now fallen into general disuse, the *Moline Properties* analysis is still fundamental. . . . We think it inappropriate, in light of *Moline Properties* . . . , except on more extreme facts than appear here, to achieve, through recourse to the assignment of income doctrine, essentially the same result as would follow from treating the Corporation as a "sham" for tax purposes. . . .

The instant case is not unlike the early case of *Fontaine Fox v. Commissioner*, 37 B.T.A. 271 (1938), where a cartoonist transferred to his corporation his cartoon copyrights and various contracts pursuant to which he earned royalties and entered into an agreement with the corporation to render his services exclusively to it for a fixed salary. The corporation, in turn, made a contract with a distributor, who made payments to the corporation based on the percentage of sales of newspapers carrying taxpayer's cartoons. In *Fontaine Fox*, the Board of Tax Appeals distinguished *Lucas v. Earl* on the grounds that, rather than an assignment of income, *Fox* involved an assignment of property (the contracts with distributors); subsequent income arising from such property was income not of the assignor but of the assignee. *Accord*, *Laughton v. Commissioner*, 40 B.T.A. 101 (1939), *rem'd* 113 F.2d 103 (9th Cir. 1940).[12]

Although we do not regard the point as decisive, the Tax Court here found that, with respect to the contracts to perform sales services for Plymouth Tube and Pittsburgh Tube, there had been not only an assignment but a novation, with the corporation's becoming the sole party obligated to perform sales services and entitled to be compensated for such performance. Hence, this case is in essential concept quite distinguishable from *Lucas v. Earl*, where only income was assigned, and cannot be plausibly distinguished from *Fontaine Fox*, where the service contracts were assigned. Here not only the fruit but the tree itself was transferred to the Corporation.

In *Rubin* . . . the Tax Court held that income was taxable to an individual who owned a 70% interest in a personal service corporation, which performed management services for another company. The same individual also controlled the company for which services were to be performed. The Tax Court attempted to analyze the problem both as one in which from differed from substance (the individual being held to work "directly" for the company) and in which the earning of the income was controlled by the individual rather than his corporation and was, therefore, taxable to the individual under the doctrine of *Lucas v. Earl*. In *Rubin*, the Tax Court suggested that the difference between the form over substance analysis and the assignment of income approach was only semantic. Thus it attempted to determine whether the form of the transaction, involving the personal service corporation, served any economic purpose and also whether the individual, in fact, controlled the earning of the income. The Tax Court found, first, that the income was properly taxable to the individual and distinguished both *Fox* and *Laughton* on the grounds that in *Rubin* the taxpayer was not contractually bound to (and in fact did not) render services exclusively to the personal service corporation (as he was bound to and did in *Fox* and *Laughton*). Second, in *Rubin*,

---

[12] *Laughton* was remanded for consideration "whether Laughton's hiring of himself to (a personal service corporation) for a salary substantially less than the compensation for which the corporation supplied his services as its employee to various motion picture producers, constituted, in effect, a single transaction by Laughton in which he received indirectly the larger sum paid by the producers." 133 F.2d 104. The Ninth Circuit relied on *Higgins v. Smith*, 308 U.S. 473 . . . (1940), decided after the Tax Court decision.

the taxpayer controlled not only the personal service corporation, but also the corporation to which services were rendered; in *Fox* and *Laughton* only the personal service corporations themselves were controlled.

On the second point — taxpayer's control of the company receiving services — the instant case is like *Fox* and *Laughton* in that taxpayer here had no control over Plymouth Tube and Pittsburgh Tube. On the first point, although taxpayer here was not contractually bound to render services exclusively for the Corporation, he did in fact do so.

Rubin was later reversed on appeal by the Second Circuit, through Judge Friendly, who was of the view that "references to 'substance over form' and the 'true earner' of income merely restate the issue in cases like this: Who is the 'true earner'? What is substance and what is form?" . . . Judge Friendly felt that Section 482 of the Internal Revenue Code (providing for reallocation of the gross income of controlled taxpayers) was a more appropriate tool for use in this kind of case than "common law" tax doctrines such as assignment of income under *Lucas v. Earl*. In any event, Judge Friendly believed that the two bases on which the Tax Court distinguished *Fox* (and *Laughton*) were not relevant with respect to § 61 of the Internal Revenue Code. . . .

We think that the Tax Court determination in *Rubin* might be easily distinguished here on the grounds that the taxpayer in the instant case worked exclusively for his personal service corporation (although he was not under contract to do so). Further, he did not own or control Pittsburgh Tube or Plymouth Tube, the entities to which services were rendered. Fundamentally, however, we believe that both *Rubin* and the instant case are more like *Fox* and *Laughton* than they are unlike those leading cases. In the resolution of the instant case we accord considerable deference to Judge Friendly's holding in *Rubin*.

* * *

We believe that, where the issue is application of the assignment of income doctrine to effectively set aside the corporation, under the particular circumstances of this case (which we have carefully delineated), an attempt to strike a balance between tax avoidance motive and "legitimate" business purposes is an unproductive and inappropriate exercise. Such an approach places too low a value on the policy of the law to recognize corporations as economic actors except in exceptional circumstances. This is true whether the analysis used to dismantle the corporation pursues the rubric of assignment of income or substance over form. Here there are other more precise devices for coping with the unacceptable tax avoidance which is unquestionably present in this case. But there is no need to crack walnuts with a sledgehammer. . . .

In the instant case, Section 482 of the Internal Revenue Code appears available to allocate among controlled taxpayers "gross income, deductions, credits or allowances" to prevent evasion of taxes or to clearly reflect the income of the controlled taxpayers. Other statutory provisions and "common law" doctrines, structured for more limited application, may also be available to remedy potential tax abuse. Thus, the dividends paid to taxpayer's children, any undue accumulation of earnings by the Corporation, the assignment of commissions already earned before formation of the Corporation on September 1, 1966, and non-payment of taxpayer's salary for the balance of 1966 after September 1 may each be subject to attack via one or a combination of the following routes: the assignment of income doctrine, the Code provisions governing the improper accumulation of surplus (I.R.C. §§ 531-537) and the doctrine of constructive receipt. We think that the very aggressive tax avoidance measures which taxpayer employed here are vulnerable, but we express no opinion as to what statutory provisions or "common law" principles may properly address them.

We believe that, where all of the criteria set forth here are met, it is inappropriate to weigh "legitimate" business purposes against tax avoidance motivations in determining the application of the *Lucas v. Earl* assignment of income doctrine essentially to set aside a corporation for tax purposes. In the instant case, the Tax Court did not find that the Corporation was organized as a pure tax avoidance vehicle. Nor has the Tax Court perceived any flouting of the corporate form in the way business has been conducted. Pittsburgh Tube and Plymouth Tube entered into contracts requiring the Corporation to provide them services, for which they paid the Corporation. Taxpayer then worked exclusively for the Corporation in enabling it to carry out its responsibilities as a sales representative. The corporate tree seems sturdy enough to become fruit-bearing, subject, of course, to whatever pruning (radical or otherwise) by the tax collector appears appropriate.

We think that our approach in this case of recognizing some vitality in personal service corporations accords with congressional intent. "A history of legislation targeted at personal service corporations, the absence of any special exclusion of such corporations from corporate taxation and the personal holding company tax provisions indicate that to some extent Congress has sanctioned the incorporation of service businesses for tax purposes." . . .

We, therefore, remand to the Tax Court for consideration of the issues surrounding the Commissioner's claim under Section 482 and other claims if available. For those purposes we do not disagree with the Tax Court's basic findings of fact in this case. But we do not intimate any conclusive view on what specific results with respect to these claims should be.

REVERSED AND REMANDED.

FOGLESONG v. COMMISSIONER

United States Court of Appeals, Seventh Circuit
691 F.2d 848 (7th Cir. 1982)

PELL, CIRCUIT JUDGE: Appellant Frederick H. Foglesong (taxpayer) appeals from a decision of the United States Tax Court assessing deficiencies in income taxes for four taxable years. The Tax Court held that the Commissioner of Internal Revenue could properly allocate the income received by the taxpayer's personal service corporation to the taxpayer pursuant to 26 U.S.C. § 482.

* * *

On November 16, 1981, the Tax Court issued an opinion holding that section 482 applied and that 98% of the corporation's taxable income was allocable to the taxpayer. . . .

The issue in this case is whether section 482 can properly be applied to allocate the income received and reported by the company to the taxpayer and, if so, whether the amount of the allocation was proper.

* * *

This court extensively set out the facts of this case in its prior decision . . . and, because they are not disputed, we need not reiterate them. . . .

* * *

Section 482 provides that the Commissioner may allocate income, to prevent evasion of taxes, in the case of "two or more organizations, trades, or businesses . . . owned or controlled directly or indirectly by the same interests." The crux of the case is whether the taxpayer and his personal service corporation constitute two "organizations, trades, or businesses."

There is no doubt that section 482 was intended to be broadly interpreted. The section was intended to apply and has been applied to cases where the profits of one business have been offset against the losses of another to reduce or escape tax liability. . . .

Furthermore, the regulations define "organization" to include "a sole proprietorship, a partnership, a trust, an estate, an association, or a corporation." Treas. Reg. 1. 482-1(a)(1). Accordingly, courts have held that the two businesses requirement is satisfied when an individual engages in a business that is distinct from or in addition to the business in which the personal service corporation is engaged. *See, e.g.*, *Borge v. Commissioner*, 405 F.2d 673 (2d Cir. 1968), cert. denied. . . .

In recent decisions, however, the Tax Court has gone beyond this to hold that section 482 is designed "to cover any type of entity or enterprise which has independent tax significance," *Keller v. Commissioner*, 77 T.C. 1014, 1022 (1991), when evasion of taxes is perceived. Thus a corporation and its sole employee, even though the employee works exclusively for it in the same business – carrying on no outside business activity – may be deemed to be in a separate trade or business so as to meet the dual business requirement of section 482. Once the two business threshold is passed, the test of whether section 482 allocation is permissible is whether the compensation package the individual received from the corporation was less than what he would have received absent incorporation. *See Pacella v. Commissioner*, 78 T.C. 604 (1982) (holding invalid the Commissioner's allocation under section 482 when the compensation package was substantially equivalent).[3]

[3] *Keller* similarly held the Commissioner's allocation improper because the compensation was substantially equivalent. We note that Congress has sought to overturn this result in *Keller* by a new statute that allows allocation where "substantially all of the services of a personal service corporation are performed for (or on behalf of) 1 other corporation, partnership, or other entity." . . . § 269A. The House Conference Committee report said that the provision was aimed at situations "where the corporation served no meaningful business purpose other than to secure tax benefits which would not otherwise be available." . . . This section does not affect this case because it is effective for taxable years beginning after December 31, 1982.

We disagree with the Tax Court's expansive interpretation of section 482. The Tax Court in large part seems to have a Congressional committee report that the provision was designed to encompass "all kinds of business activity." . . . The Tax Court did not consider the statement in context, however. The committee made the remark in explaining why it was adding "organizations" to "trades or businesses". "While it is believed that the language of the present law is broad enough to include "organizations", this word is added to remove any doubt as to the application of this section to all kinds of business activity." Reliance on the committee's phrase "all kinds of business activity" must therefore be tempered by the recognition that Congress decided to amend the statute by adding "organizations" rather than a much broader phrase like "all entities with independent tax significance."

As section 482 is written, we do not believe that the statute can be stretched as far as the Tax Court contends. Rather, we believe that it is appropriate to hold that an individual who does not work exclusively for his personal service corporation may have the income earned by it allocated to him under section 482. The section should not apply, however, to one who does work exclusively for his corporation. This interpretation of section 482 satisfies both the terms of the statute — one who does not work exclusively for his corporation may rightly be said to be engaging in a separate business — and the policy that legitimate personal service corporations should be recognized. . . .

Virtually all of the cases upholding the application of section 482, many of which the appellee and the Tax Court rely upon to support their position, have done so either in situations involving an attempt to offset the profits of one business with the losses of another or in situations in which the individual performed work other than that he did on behalf of the corporation. A case involving both situations is *Borge*. . . . In that case, the taxpayer was a successful entertainer who also ran a poultry farm that suffered losses. He organized a corporation and transferred to it all of the assets of the poultry business. He then entered into an agreement to work for the corporation as an entertainer and thereby offset the poultry farm's losses by entertainment profits.

The court held that the section 482 dual business requirement was satisfied because despite the entertainment contract between *Borge* and his corporation, Borge in fact remained in a separate business. Instead of putting all of his entertainment revenues into the corporation, he put in only a percentage. "[Taxpayer] was not devoting his time and energies to the corporation; he was carrying on his career as an entertainer, and merely channeling a part of his entertainment income through the corporation." . . . An indicium that Borge, not the corporation, was running the entertainment business was that the parties seeking his services as an entertainer required that he, not the corporation, guarantee the contracts. . . . The court concluded that the only purpose of the arrangement between the taxpayer and his corporation was to offset poultry business losses with profits from the entertainment business. . . .

The instant case is markedly different. The taxpayer and his corporation were engaged in the identical business and Foglesong worked exclusively for the corporation. He did no consulting on the side nor did he engage in any other business. Furthermore, he instructed everyone to pay the corporation, not him.

Finally, there was no attempt to evade taxes by offsetting the profits of one business against the losses of another.

* * *

Another case stressing the significance of exclusivity is *Rubin*. . . . There, the taxpayer formed a corporation to do business with another corporation, and he performed the required work. The Tax Court held section 482 applicable. In holding that mere employment status is not a trade or business, however, the court indicated the importance of determining whether the taxpayer performed work in addition to that he did for the corporation. It stated

> that where the particular facts of a case are such as to justify a finding that a shareholder operated an independent business *and merely assigned to the corporation a portion of the income therefrom*, the business activity of the taxpayer may constitute a trade or business to which allocation of all or part of the income attributable to his efforts is authorized under section 482.

. . . (emphasis added). The court in an earlier ruling in that case noted that taxpayer performed more than $25,000 worth of other work unrelated to the work for his controlled corporation. . . .[5]

* * *

We hold that the Tax Court erred in its decision that . . . § 482 should be applied to allocate income received by Foglesong' personal service corporation to Foglesong. Because the taxpayer did work exclusively for the corporation and because there was no shifting of profits we reverse the judgment of the Tax Court. We remand the case for a consideration of whether assignment of income principles may be employed to allocate the dividends and preferred stock received by Foglesong's children to Foglesong as well as commission income earned by Foglesong before incorporation but paid to the company after incorporation.

REVERSED AND REMANDED.

Final Note on *Foglesong*

From discussion with attorneys for Fred Foglesong: The case was subsequently settled out of court, with the IRS conceding that Section 482 was inapplicable, so that all monies earned after incorporation would be considered those of the service corporation. The taxpayer did agree to have pre-incorporation monies earned by him assigned back and included in his income. It was also agreed that preferred stock dividends would be treated as additional compensation paid by the corporation to Foglesong. After receiving a deduction for this additional compensation (something that was unavailable when these amounts were treated as "dividends"), the total amount owed by Fred and his service corporation amounted to a little more

[5] The Second Circuit's brief per curiam opinion affirming the Tax Court suggested that it would not disapprove of a holding that mere employee status is a separate trade or business under section 482, but it did not so hold. . . .

than $3,500 plus interest (finally about $10,000). This compares to more than $300,000 in deficiencies outstanding when the out-of-court settlement was initially instigated.

NOTES AND COMMENTS

Thus, we have another situation in which two panels of the same Circuit hold differing opinions, but this time on the same set of facts: the first holding that § 482 was the applicable legal standard to apply, not the assignment of income doctrine, and the second rejecting § 482 on the ground that being an employee is not a separate trade or business, but remanding for application of a less virulent form of assignment of income. In all of this, the fact that $32,000 of dividends, plus an uncertain build-up in the value of their interest, was transferred to the children without any discussion of any possible gift tax implications seems to have passed unnoticed. In Rev. Rul. 88-38, 1988-1 C.B. 246, the Service announced that it would not follow the final Seventh Circuit holding that an employee is not engaged in a trade or business separate from that of the corporation and that, therefore, the "two or more organizations, trades, or businesses" requirement of § 482 is not met. It stated that the dual trade or business requirement of § 482 is satisfied because the corporation is in the business of providing goods or services to customers and the employee is in the business of providing services to the corporation.

As the second panel of the Seventh Circuit indicates, § 269A now provides for allocation of income between an employee-owner and a personal service corporation. Ironically, § 269A was narrowly drafted to catch personal service corporations like that in *Keller* that served as members of a professional partnership. It would not have applied to *Foglesong*, because it applies only if the personal service corporation provides services to "1" other entity, and Foglesong served as a representative for two manufacturers, Plymouth and Pittsburgh. As a further irony, the same statute that enacted § 269A also eliminated the differences between qualified pension benefits available to self-employed individuals, including partners, and those available for corporate employees that was one of the major reasons to incorporate a personal service corporation. Nevertheless, § 269A remains as a device to attack other benefits of personal service corporation, many of which are conveniently catalogued in Prop. Treas. Reg. § 1.269A-1(b)(6), another proposed regulation that remains unadopted after 20 years. Its basic approach of requiring allocation of income between an entity and an owner-employee echoes earlier provisions for family partnerships, § 704(e), and S corporations, § 1366(e). Thus, there remains a statutory gap, leaving § 482 and the assignment of income doctrine as the only applicable principles for owner-employees of C corporations that are not personal service corporations. It is less than clear how well, if at all, these principles can be used against the benefits listed in Prop. Treas. Reg. § 1.269A-1(b)(6).

Whatever the deficiencies of the two *Foglesong* opinions in clarifying these principles, the decisions provide a useful review of some of the principal cases and issues relating to personal service corporations. As the cases cited in the two *Foglesong* opinions indicate, there have been, and continue to be, numerous cases in which professionals, athletes, entertainers, artists, and other high income earners find it useful to incorporate their activities to take advantage of certain differences in the taxation of corporations and individuals. *See, e.g.*, *Johnson v. Commissioner*, 78 T.C. 882 (1982) (Charles (not Magic) Johnson taxed on earnings as NBA player paid to his corporation; no contract between team and corporation); *Leavell v. Commissioner*, 104 T.C. 140 (1995) (same; even though contract with corporation where player guaranteed to perform on behalf of corporation); *Sargent v. Commissioner*, 929 F.2d 1252 (8th Cir. 1991) (corporations, not hockey players, taxed on earnings paid to corporations, with most of the balance, after pensions contributions, paid to players as salaries).

PROBLEM FOR DISCUSSION

Problem 7-28. Lex, a highly successful sole practitioner tax lawyer and estate planner, forms Lex, P.A., a C corporation, to conduct her practice. Her daughter, Doris, a public interest lawyer, is a 40 percent shareholder, but does not provide any services. Lex, P.A. shares office space and administrative staff with two other sole practitioners, one a real estate lawyer, and the other a probate litigator. They do not share clients or fees, although each refers clients to another office mate when appropriate. Lex takes advantage of all of the items listed in Prop. Treas. Reg. § 1.269A-1(b)(6) that she can, plus a few others, like the inapplicability of the investment interest limits of § 163(d). Lex, of course, draws a salary sufficient for her living expenses, puts the maximum amount in pension and other tax advantaged savings plans and uses Lex, P.A. as an investment vehicle, building up value for herself (and Doris). Is any of Lex, P.A.'s undistributed income taxed to Lex? *See* §§ 61(1), 162(a)(1), 269A, 482, 707(e) or 1366(e); *Foglesong* (§ 482 does not apply to allocate income from a personal service corporation to a shareholder-employee); *Johnson* (Charles (not Magic) Johnson taxed on earnings as NBA player paid to his corporation; no contract between team and corporation); *Leavell* (same even though contract with corporation where player guaranteed to perform on behalf of corporation); *Sargent* (corporations, not hockey players, taxed on earnings paid to corporations, with most of the balance, after pensions contributions, paid to players as salaries); *Rubin* (§ 482 applied to allocate income to shareholder-employee of management company); *Fontaine Fox* (cartoonist not taxed on income of corporation that held copyrights to cartoons under contracts with distributor for payments based on percentage of sales of newspapers carrying cartoons); *Borge* (§ 482 applied to tax entertainer taxed on portion of entertainment earning transferred to losing poultry corporation); *Pacella* (no allocation of personal service corporation income when compensation to shareholder-employee is equivalent to earnings, although different character); *Keller* (same); Rev. Rul. 88-38 (Service will not follow *Fogelsong* and will apply § 482).

§ 4.02. § 482 — Applied

Treas. Reg. § 1.482-1(a); I.R.C. §§ 1551, 1552, 1561, 1563; 1239, 707(b)

The basic approach of § 482's arm's-length standard is to treat each of the related parties as if they participated in a transaction had occurred between unrelated parties. Section 482 is frequently applied in the international context to transactions between U.S. corporations and foreign affiliates, principally foreign affiliates of U.S. parents, but also U.S. affiliates of foreign parents. Reg. §§ 1.482-2 to –8 contain detailed rules for the application of § 482 to related party transactions involving the transfer of tangible property, intangible property, and services, principally, in this context. Fortunately for the authors, a detailed discussion of these regulations is beyond the scope of this volume. This section is concerned solely with dealings among closely held U.S. corporations or other entities. The following case involves a typical situation, a downtown department store that opens a separately incorporated suburban store.

HAMBURGERS YORK ROAD, INC. v. COMMISSIONER

United States Tax Court
41 T.C. 821 (1964)

* * *

The petitioner in docket No. 92388 is the Isaac Hamburger & Sons Co. (hereinafter called Hamburger & Sons), a Maryland corporation, organized in July 1922, and having its principal place of business at Baltimore and Hanover Streets in the downtown section of the city of Baltimore. It kept its books of account and filed its Federal income tax returns in accordance with an accrual method of accounting and for fiscal years ended January 31.

The petitioner in docket No. 92387 is Hamburger York Road, Inc. (hereinafter called York Road), a Maryland corporation, organized in January 1955, and having its principal place of business at York Road and Walker Street in the suburbs of the city of Baltimore. It likewise kept its books of account and filed its Federal income tax returns in accordance with an accrual method of accounting and for fiscal years ended January 31.

* * *

Hamburger & Sons conducts the oldest and largest retail men's wear business in Baltimore. Its business was founded in 1850; and its present corporate form dates from 1922. . . .

The . . . stockholders were members of three family groups. Sidney Berney and Robert Berney were father and son, respectively; Isaac Hamburger and Betty Hamburger were husband and wife, and Isaac was Sidney Berney's first cousin; Albert, Henry, and Richard Berney were brothers, nephews of Sidney, and first cousins of Robert Berney. Sidney Berney had retired from active participation in the business operations of the Hamburger & Sons store some time prior to January 31, 1955; and Richard Berney at no time took any part in the business operations of said store.

For several years prior to 1955, the stockholders of Hamburger & Sons had been considering opening a store in the Baltimore suburbs. A merchandising trend had set in following World War II for an ever-increasing amount of goods and services to be purchased in the suburban section, due to the movement of population to suburbs. As a result of this trend, the sales of Hamburger & Sons had been steadily decreasing before 1955. Other business concerns in Baltimore (and throughout the country generally) had opened suburban stores in order to maintain their sales position in the face of the population shift and the concomitant merchandising trend. By the fall of 1954, a decision had been reached by the Hamburger & Sons stockholders to open a suburban store.

Consideration was given by the Hamburger & Sons stockholders to the question of whether said store should be operated as a division of Hamburger & Sons, or as a corporate subsidiary, or as a separate sister corporation. The principal advocates of opening the new store and the persons most interested in getting it underway were the above-mentioned Berney brothers, Albert and Henry; and it was their desire that they be permitted to have a larger proportionate interest in the suburban store than they had in the downtown store. The other Hamburger & Sons stockholders were amenable to the Berney brothers' wishes. Each of the stockholders of Hamburger & Sons had received his stock by gift, purchase, or inheritance from relatives who were previously active in the business; and it had been largely the practice to let the ownership of the business follow the persons who were active in its operation. It was finally decided that, of the three alternatives above mentioned, the separate sister corporation approach would be utilized. The Hamburger & Sons stockholders were advised by their accountants and attorneys that one of the benefits that would flow from this approach would be that the new corporation would get an additional surtax exemption, and thus enjoy a lower rate of tax on the first $25,000 of the taxable income of the enterprise.

* * *

The following table shows a comparison of the percentage of ownership in each of the petitioner corporations, which was held by each of the above-mentioned family groups:

	Percentage of ownership	
Family group	Hamburger & Sons	York Road
Sidney and Robert Berney	42.03	30
Isaac and Betty Hamburger	25.6	30
Albert, Henry, and Richard Berney	32.01	40
Total	100.0	100

The officers of York Road were the same as those of Hamburger & Sons; and the directors of the former were the same as those of the latter, except that Sidney Berney (who . . . had retired from active participation in business operations) did not serve as a director of York Road.

The York Road stockholders acquired their stock for $10 per share, or an aggregate of $20,000. York Road also obtained additional working capital in the beginning, by means of two loans: One for $40,000 from a Baltimore bank (which was guaranteed by the York Road directors in their individual capacities); and the other for $25,000 from Sidney Berney and his wife, which was evidenced by York Road's unsecured promissory note. Hamburger & Sons did not, at or immediately following the organization of York Road, make any formal transfer of assets, tangible or intangible, to the latter corporation. Hamburger & Sons did permit York Road to employ the name "Hamburgers" for its own use, without any charge therefor.

* * *

A lease agreement was entered into by York Road and the owner of the new store premises. . . . By a separate agreement, Hamburger & Sons guaranteed performance of the lease by York Road.

* * *

Betty Hamburger also caused advertising brochures to be prepared announcing that the same specified brands of quality merchandise sold at Hamburger & Sons, and the famous Hamburger label backed by 105 years of experience, would be found at the new store; and that "your Hamburger charge account is good at both stores." Advertisements to the same effect were placed in the newspapers, one of which stated that "Hamburgers-York Road is a new addition of Hamburgers main store." The advertisements also emphasized that customers would receive the same painstaking, courteous service at "our" new store that has built "our" reputation for 105 years.

. . . The trade name "Hamburgers" was displayed on the front of the York Road store in a sign of similar design to that displayed on the downtown store. Both stores had the same telephone number; and telephone service to both stores was handled through a PBX switchboard located in the downtown store.

. . . [T]he officers of the corporations operating the two stores were the same individuals. These officers made their headquarters at the downtown store, and spent most of their working time at that location. . . . The York Road store had its own store manager, who was not an officer, stockholder, or director of either of the Hamburger corporations.

Each of the stores had its own staff of sales clerks; but the store buyers, who had supervision over the sales personnel and the purchase and display of the merchandise, were the same individuals for both stores. . . . These buyers were compensated on the basis of a percentage commission of the sales in their departments; and in computing the commissions payable to a particular buyer (except in the men's clothing departments), the sales of his department in each store were added together, and the appropriate percentage figure was applied to the sum total.

The pension trust established by Hamburger & Sons was also used for the employees who worked at the York Road store.

* * *

. . . York Road did not carry its own customer accounts receivable. Instead they were "sold" daily at full face value to Hamburger & Sons, so that the related debit entry to the sales income credit entry was to the above-mentioned intercompany account with Hamburger & Sons; and the latter company would take the accounts of the York Road's customers into its own accounts receivable and credit the intercompany account with the amounts thereof.

. . . Hamburger & Sons handled the billing and collection of the customer accounts receivable which had originated in both stores. At the end of each month it would make a charge to the York Road store of approximately 1 1/2 percent of the accounts taken over from York Road during the month to defray the estimated costs of billing and collecting the accounts receivable which had originated in the York Road store, and also to defray any losses on said York Road receivables. Accounting wise, this monthly charge would be handled through the intercompany accounts. The normal cost in the Baltimore area for the commercial factoring of accounts receivable during the taxable years was approximately 9 percent of the face amount of any receivables sold to a factor.

. . . Following the opening of the York Road store, the format of the advertising copy remained practically identical. . . . The only differences were: . . . [T]he specially designed script legend for the word "Hamburgers" was supplemented only by the address of the downtown store; following the opening of the York Road store, said script legend was supplemented by the addresses for both the downtown and the suburban stores. . . .

A single customer list was used by both stores for advertising and charge accounts. . . . Billings to the customers were made by Hamburger & Sons in its trade name; and all purchases made at both stores by a customer were included on one invoice.

* * *

Most of the alterations required on clothing sold at the York Road store were performed at the downtown store by the latter store' employees. The downtown store charged the York Road store for such services with a proportionate part of the alterations department costs and expenses; and in doing this it again utilized the intercompany account procedure outlined above.

* * *

As regards the various and sundry overhead expenses which applied to both stores (such as advertising, expenses of the store buyers' trips, telephone service, bookkeeping services, and supplies), there was no accurate system for the division of these expenses between the two stores. . . .

The sales income of each corporation was reflected on its books of account in the conventional manner.

* * *

The operations of Hamburger & Sons in its downtown store and those of York Road in its suburban store were all part of a single integrated business enterprise; and the suburban store was operated substantially as a branch of the downtown store. There would not have been any substantial difference in Hamburger & Sons operations, and no substantially different records would have been required by it if it had operated York Road store as a division without York Road having been incorporated.

The taxable income of said single integrated business enterprise, which was reported partly by Hamburger & Sons and partly by York Road on their separate income tax returns for each of the taxable years here involved, was produced by and due to the long-established business reputation and goodwill of Hamburger & Sons, its business organization and procedures, the brands of merchandise which it handled, and its advertising program.

There was no substantial business purpose for the separate incorporation of York Road, which in its operation served merely as a division of Hamburger & Sons.

The principal purpose for the incorporation of York Road was to avoid Federal income taxes by securing the benefit of an additional surtax exemption.

The business transactions between Hamburger & Sons and York Road were not those of an uncontrolled taxpayer dealing at arm's length with another uncontrolled taxpayer.

The Commissioner, in attributing to Hamburger & Sons all of the taxable income of the single integrated business enterprise, did not act arbitrarily, capriciously, or unreasonably.

The action of the Commissioner, in allocating to Hamburger & Sons all of the taxable income of said single integrated business enterprise, was necessary in order to prevent evasion of taxes and clearly to reflect the taxable income (if any) of each corporation here involved, within the meaning of section 482 of the 1954 Code.

* * *

. . . It is at once apparent that there is here present the requisite common ownership and control over the two corporate business organizations involved. The same individuals served in the same officer capacities in both corporations. The directors were the same persons in both corporations, with the exception of Sidney Berney who was a director of Hamburger & Sons but not of York Road. And both corporations had the same stockholders.

Common control, however, is not the end of the matter; for, . . . "taxpayers owned or controlled by the same interests may enter into transactions inter se and if fair, or resulting from arm's length bargaining, such transactions will be undisturbed." . . .

The evidence establishes that the operation of the two stores here involved was substantially the function of Hamburger & Sons. Betty Hamburger, who had many years' experience as public relations director and advertising manager for the downtown store, placed all advertisements for both stores, and continued to employ the same tried and tested format that Hamburger & Sons had used prior to the organization of York Road. The selection of merchandise for both stores, the supervision over the display thereof at both stores, and also the supervision over the sales forces of both stores, were all handled by the department manager located at the downtown store, except in the case of one department at the suburban store which had its own manager. And even as to this exception, we believe it reasonable to infer that the overall merchandising supervision given by Isaac Hamburger and Albert Berney to all departments at both stores assured that Hamburger & Sons' long-established experience would be applied also to that one exceptional department.

In addition, the compensation paid to the department managers of both stores was computed on a sliding scale, based on the combined sales of both stores. Employees of Hamburger & Sons made the alterations on clothing sold at York Road. The downtown store furnished the telephone switchboard service for both stores. Moreover, Hamburger & Sons acted as the paymaster and disbursing agent for both stores; its employees kept the books for both stores; and all daily cash receipts of York Road were turned over to Hamburger & Sons for deposit in the latter's bank account for all 3 years here involved, except the first 9 months of the new store's operation. Hamburger & Sons also took over all the customers' accounts receivable which arose at the York Road store; and it billed and collected the same along with its own accounts receivable. Thus, the conclusion is a compelling one, that the two stores (which in form were operated by two separate corporations) were in substance and in fact, actually parts of a single, integrated retail men's clothing business — with the downtown store of Hamburger & Sons serving as the headquarters, and with the suburban York Road store serving merely as a branch or division.

Our inquiry will now focus on what Hamburger & Sons contributed to this integrated business enterprise, and what (if anything) York Road contributed. For more than 100 years, the founders of Hamburger & Sons, and their successors, had, through their labors, established one of the most outstanding men's wear businesses in the Baltimore area. The success of the business which they thus developed was due principally, not merely to the racks and display cases filled with merchandise, but rather to the reputation established for dependable and courteous service to the public and to the skills employed by its organization in selecting merchandise with an eye to high quality, right quantity, and salable style. And all these could only be assured through use of a knowledgeable purchasing and merchandising organization and through application of long years of experience. The name "Hamburgers" had, over the many years prior to 1955, become a hallmark for business integrity, and it was the focal point for a goodwill of great value which was primarily responsible for producing both sales volume and business success. Likewise, the customer lists and the sales organization of Hamburger & Sons were additional assets and attributes of very substantial value in the retail clothing business.

All of the foregoing assets and attributes were contributed to the integrated and unitary enterprise which was operated after the establishment of the new suburban store in 1955; and the record herein clearly establishes that the York Road segment of the enterprise made full use of the same. The two stores were at all times represented to the public as "Hamburgers." The promotional advertising for both stores was continuously presented in one format, using the "Hamburgers" name; and after the York Road store was opened, the trade name "Hamburgers" was displayed on the front in a sign of similar design to that displayed on the downtown store, and a shield-shaped emblem was placed on the front door on which appeared the legend "since 1850." Also, existing customers of the downtown store were informed that their charge accounts at the downtown store could thereafter be used for purchases made either at the downtown store or at the York Road suburban store.

Notwithstanding the foregoing facts and circumstances, petitioners here contend that the net profits of York Road should be fixed by charging against the sales of that store only the net current operating cost of such store, without any consideration being given to the above-mentioned factors of goodwill, trade name, experienced buying and selling organizations, customer lists, and advertising format which Hamburger & Sons furnished for the use of York Road. We are confident that Hamburger & Sons would not have permitted such an arrangement, if it had dealt with York Road at arm's length. For such use of its business organization and assets, Hamburger & Sons would, we believe, have claimed for itself the profits in their entirety of the York Road segment of the integrated business.

To be sure, York Road contributed to the integrated enterprise an attractive business location, and a modest amount of capital. But, when we examine these more closely, in their context in this case, their power to command any portion of the profits of the York Road segment of the integrated enterprise is quickly perceived to be more apparent than real. As regards the location, the findings of fact establish that the lease on the premises was acquirable by York Road only on the strength of its affiliation with Hamburger & Sons and on the strength of that corporation's guaranteeing York Road's performance of its lease obligations. In short, Hamburger & Sons could have acquired the lease itself, and we believe that, in arm's-length dealing with a stranger (rather than with its sister corporation), it would have refused to yield any profits of the York Road segment as a consequence of York Road having the lease on the attractive business location.

As regards the capital of the York Road corporation, we find that it totaled only $85,000, consisting of $20,000 paid in for stock and $65,000 borrowed from two sources: (1) $25,000 from Sidney Berney and his wife on York Road's unsecured promissory note and (2) $40,000 from a bank on York 's note which was guaranteed by its directors. Here again, we are led to conclude that Hamburger & Sons could have used its own capital funds to open the new suburban store; it was not compelled to seek outside financing for that purpose. In fact $45,000 came from Hamburger & Sons stockholders; and they would surely just as readily put such funds (assuming the need for the same) directly into Hamburger & Sons, rather than into a separate corporation. No doubt the bank's loan of $40,000 to York Road took into consideration that Hamburger & Sons' business organization, assets, and attributes were being made available to the new store. Hence the loans (that of the bank and that of the Berneys), realistically considered, were worth only the interest charges required to obtain them; and York Road's deductions for such interest have not been disturbed by the respondent. Those loans, and the paid-in capital, would not in our judgment have merited a share of the profits of the York Road segment of the integrated enterprise.

It must also be observed that there was no pressing business need requiring a separate corporation to operate the York Road suburban store. We have hereinabove found as an ultimate fact, after considering and weighing all the relevant evidence, that there would not have been any substantial difference in Hamburger & Sons operations, and no substantially different records would have been required, if it had operated the suburban store as a division of the Hamburger & Sons corporation. Thus, we are convinced, and we have likewise found as an ultimate fact, that the principal purpose for the separate corporation was to avoid Federal income tax by securing the benefit of an additional surtax exemption — which would be applied against that portion of the profits of the integrated, unitary enterprise that would be shifted over to York Road. True enough, under York Road's lease, the rental payable was in part pegged to the gross sales at the York Road store; and York Road was required to maintain such accounting records as would enable the lessor to verify the sales at that store. But separate incorporation was not required in order to permit compliance with these lease terms. Ascertainment of the sales of a divisional branch (or even a branch's net operating profit) is a familiar technique of convention accounting for such branches. . . .

Petitioner has argued in defense of the separate incorporation of York Road, that this was necessary in order to accommodate the desire of Albert and Henry Berney for a larger interest in the York Road store than they had in the downtown store. But this argument is not realistic. The evidence establishes, in the light of the close family relationship prevailing in the ownership and operation of Hamburger & Sons, the retired status of Sidney Berney, and the historical pattern of keeping the ownership in the family and permitting such ownership to follow those who were actively participating in the Hamburger & Sons enterprise, that the Berney brothers' desire could have been met by appropriate adjustments in Sidney's stockholdings in Hamburger & Sons, without having to form a new corporation.

The petitioners have argued also that what was done here by the respondent amounted to effecting a consolidated return for Hamburger & Sons and York Road. . . .

. . . The Second Circuit [in another case] rejected the taxpayer's consolidated return argument, as follows:

> At first blush, this regulation would seem to support the petitioner's position but analysis shows the contrary. The effect of such an interpretation would be to exclude from the applicability of Sec. [482] fact situations like the present one if the separate entities involved were all corporations and the Commissioner had sought to allocate all of the income from each to one of them, since this "would produce a result equivalent to a computation of consolidated net income . . . Whatever valid interpretation may be given this regulation, the unsoundness of that of the petitioner is illustrated by the fact that it would exclude from the "policing" provisions of Sec. [482] the most flagrant evasion by arbitrary shifting of income. It would let the Commissioner reallocate the income of these separate entities, to reflect the income of each correctly, if the amount involved, however great, did not equal their total combined income but he could not apply Sec. 45 at all if the taxpayers succeeded in constructing a situation where, in order to prevent tax evasion or properly to reflect income, it were necessary to attribute all of the income of the separate entities to one of them, as was done here.

Thus tax evasion could be so complete as to make itself invulnerable, a proposition whose statement discloses its fallacy.

* * *

NOTES AND COMMENTS

The court in *Hamburgers* upholds allocating all of the income of York Road to the original Hamburgers. It would seem to have been more appropriate to have charged York Road with arm's length fees for the services rendered by Hamburgers to it. Such "creation of income" is proper under § 482 even though its express terms only refer to allocations of income or deductions. *See Latham Park Manor, Inc. v. Commissioner*, 69 T.C. 199 (1977) (when operating subsidiaries borrowed money and loaned the funds interest free to the holding company that used the funds in a shareholder buy-out that did not generate any income, § 482 applied to "create" interest income for the subsidiaries); Treas. Reg. § 1.482-1(d)(4) and 1.482-2(a)(1), reaching this result, are valid); *Powers v. Commissioner*, 724 F.2d 64 (7th Cir. 1983) (poor financial condition of tenant does not justify controlling shareholder's leasing property from one controlled corporation at an inflated rent and releasing it to another corporation at a rent that was less than fair market value; § 482 applies to readjust shareholder's rents, increasing rent from tenant corporation and reducing rent to owning corporation).

In *Hamburgers*, the new corporation was capitalized without a direct transfer of assets from the old and was not a subsidiary of the old, but what is sometimes called a brother-sister arrangement, with the same controlling shareholders, even if in slightly different percentages. One of the stated advantage of such an arrangement was to lower the group's effective tax rate because each corporation was taxed at lower brackets on part of its income. Under current law, this advantage is limited by §§ 1551, 1552, 1561, and 1563. There are elaborate elective consolidated return provisions for parent-subsidiary affiliated groups under §§ 1501-04, and the regulations under them.

When there are dealings between parent and subsidiary corporations, particularly those that do not file consolidate returns, there can be a conflict between the principles of § 482, which require arm's length dealings, and § 351, which permits assignment of income and deductions, within limits, to a controlled corporation. One aspect of this implicit assignment of income and deductions principle under § 351 transactions is discussed in § 1.02 *Tax Amount* of Chapter 3, *Liabilities: Discharge of Indebtedness; Mortgaged Property; At Risk*, and is implicit in Rev. Rul. 80-198, 1980-2 C.B. 113, and Rev. Rul. 80-199, 1980-2 C.B. 122, which are discussed therein. In a deleted part of Rev. Rul. 80-198, the Service limited its conclusions by stating that the assignment of income doctrine or § 482 is applicable to transfers under § 351 in certain circumstances, citing *Brown v. Commissioner*, 40 B.T.A. 565 (1939), *aff'd*, 115 F.2d 337 (2d Cir. 1940), in which an attorney transferred to a controlled corporation that was not a law firm, part of a claim to income from for legal services performed in his individual capacity in order to provide the controlled corporation with capital. The Service cited *Brown*, as exemplifying cases in which the assignment of income principles would tax the fees, when collected, to the contributor. The Service also cited *Rooney v. United States*, 305 F.2d 681 (9th Cir. 1962), in which a farming operation was incorporated after the expenses of the crop had been incurred but before the crop had been sold and income realized. Section 482 was applied in that case to allocate the expenses of the farming operation to the corporation. Rev. Rul. 80-198, of course, recognized that in *Hempt Bros., Inc. v. United States*, 490 F.2d 1172 (3d Cir. 1974), *cert. denied*, 419 U.S. 826 (1974), the nonrecognition transfer of receivables was proper. The standard seems to be that nonrecognition is proper if the income is related to the business being conducted by the corporation but not if the transfer is not related to that business. *Compare Huber Homes, Inc. v. Commissioner*, 55 T.C. 598 (1971) (§ 482 does not apply to sale by a parent corporation of single family homes that it constructed but had difficulty selling at cost to its subsidiary that rented them; excess of value of homes over price was properly contribution to capital) with *National Sec. Corp. v. Commissioner*, 137 F.2d 600 (3d Cir. 1943) (predecessor of § 482 disallows loss realized by a subsidiary on the sale of stock shortly after contribution that had it received from its parent corporation when the value of the stock was less than its transferred basis; loss was reallocated to the parent that could not use it, which was the reason for the contribution).

There are also a number of provisions disallowing losses on transactions between related parties that are discussed in § 3.02(b) *Related Parties* of Chapter 5 *Nonrecognition Transactions.* Still other provisions put two parties, even some not ordinarily considered related, on the same method to prevent what is considered a timing distortion. *See* Chapter 6, *Executive Compensation and Stock Options*, for discussions of the provisions that coordinate the employer's deduction or other allowance with the employee's income for deferred compensation, restricted property, and disqualifying dispositions of stock acquired exercise of incentive stock options; *Notes and Questions* in § 3.01 *Cash, Notes, Checks and Credit Cards*, of Chapter 2, *The Cash Receipts and Disbursements Method of Accounting*, in the Federal Tax Accounting volume of this Graduate Tax Series, for a discussion of the application of § 267 to related parties; § 2.01, *Original Issue Discount ("OID")*, of Chapter 5, *Interest, Original Issue Discount, and the Time Value of Money*, for a discussion of the application of § 1272, which puts both parties on the accrual method of original issue discount, both in the Federal Tax Accounting volume of this Graduate Tax Series.

PROBLEMS FOR DISCUSSION

Problem 7-26. What should the taxpayers have done in *Hamburgers York Road* to avoid the application of § 482?

Problem 7-27. In 20X1, Doc, a physician, bought Blackacre, a parcel of undeveloped land beyond the suburbs of the city where he practiced, because he believed it would become suitable for development. In the meanwhile, he leased Blackacre for farming, to obtain a lower tax appraisal and rate, which required a ten-year commitment to agricultural use. On audit, the interest on his Blackacre mortgage was determined to be investment interest, because he was not currently holding the land for development. In 20X9, he determined that the time was right for development. He formed a joint venture corporation, Jointcorp, with Develcorp, the largest local developer of residential communities. Because he was more bullish on the project than Develcorp, in order to obtain 60 percent of the stock of Jointcorp, a C corporation, while realizing substantial cash, he agreed to sell Blackacre for 50 percent of its appraised value to Jointcorp. What are the tax consequences of the sale? *See* §§ 351 and 482; *Huber* (§ 482 does not apply to sale by a parent corporation of single family homes that it constructed but had difficulty selling at cost to its subsidiary that rented them; excess of value of homes over price was property contribution to capital); *National Securities Corp.* (predecessor of § 482 disallows loss realized by a subsidiary on the sale of stock shortly after contribution that had it received from its parent corporation when their value less than the transferred basis; loss reallocated to parent that could not use it, which was the reason for the contribution); *Brown* (attorney on claim for legal services performed in his individual capacity to provide capital for the controlled corporation, which was not a law firm); and *Rooney* (§ 482 applied to allocate to corporation expenses of the crop had been incurred before farming operation was incorporated where crop sold shortly after incorporation); Rev. Rul. 80-198 (unrealized receivables and payables transferred without recognition on incorporation of a business); *Powers* (poor financial condition of tenant does not justify controlling shareholder's leasing property from one controlled corporation at an inflated rent and releasing it to another corporation at a rent that was less than fair market value). *Latham Park* (§ 482 applied to "create" interest income for the subsidiaries that loaned borrowed funds interest-free to parent that used the funds in a shareholder buyout). How, if at all, would the result differ if the joint venture vehicle was Jointco, an LLC taxed as a partnership?

Chapter 8

LIMITATIONS ON DEDUCTIONS AND LOSSES

§ 1. INTRODUCTION

Taxpayers are generally allowed to deduct losses and other expenses to reduce gross income in the determination of adjusted gross income or taxable income. Under § 165, losses not compensated by insurance or otherwise are generally allowable. I.R.C. § 165(a). In the case of individuals, however, such losses must have been incurred in either a trade or business or a transaction entered into for profit. I.R.C. § 165(c)(1) and (2). Individuals are allowed deductions for personal losses only if such losses arise in a casualty (e.g., fire, storm, shipwreck, or theft), but such deductions are subject to particular limitations. I.R.C. § 165(c)(3) and (h).

Despite the general rules applicable to the deduction of losses under § 165, the Code includes a number of provisions that further limit or defer such losses in particular circumstances. An example of such a limitation is found in § 1211 under which, as described in § 2.01(d), the deduction of capital losses is limited for both corporate and individual taxpayers. *See* I.R.C. § 165(f). Section 2 below describes the operation of § 1091, which limits the deduction of losses incurred in the sale of stock or securities when the taxpayer acquires substantially similar stock or securities within 30 days before or after the sale. Under such circumstances, the taxpayer is not deemed to have incurred the economic loss associated with the stock or securities because the taxpayer's acquisition of substantially similar property represents a continuation of the original investment. Similarly, as described in § 3, the deduction of losses on the sale of property between related parties is deferred under § 267 because the realized loss does not necessarily represent an actual economic loss when the taxpayer and the related party are viewed as an economic unit.

The Code also defers the deduction of losses generated by taxpayers engaged in certain activities to reduce the income generated by other activities. In these situations, the losses involved are not measured by the excess of basis over the amount realized on the sale or exchange of property, but by the excess of otherwise deductible expenses from the activities over the income generated by these same activities. This latter type of loss may arise solely because of the way in which the deductible expenses are determined for tax purposes and may not represent actual economic losses incurred by the taxpayer. Congress enacted these limitations in order to reduce the incentives that the tax law otherwise creates encouraging taxpayers to investing in activities that generate such tax losses in order to shelter other income from taxation. For example, § 465 prohibits certain taxpayers from deducting losses generated by an activity except to the extent that the taxpayer is "at risk" for any actually economic loss from the activity. In a similar manner, § 469 prohibits certain taxpayers from deducting losses generated by so-called "passive activities" except to the extent of any income generated by the taxpayer's other passive activities. The details and complexity of the at-risk and passive loss rules are described in §§ 4 and 5.

Finally, § 6 describes a recently enacted set of loss limitation rules applicable to leasing transactions involving tax-exempt parties that were structured to generate tax losses and, thus, tax benefits to investors. These rules replicate the approach adopted by the passive loss rules and provide that any "tax-exempt use loss" from such a transaction is not allowed but may be carried forward to be deducted to the extent of any income generated by the same leasing transaction in the future. As a result, taxpayers are unable to use the tax losses generated by these leasing transactions to reduce the income generated by other leasing or non-leasing transactions.

§ 2. WASH SALES OF SECURITIES

I.R.C. § 1091

Treas. Reg. §§ 1.1091-1, 1.1091-2

To prevent a perceived abuse inherent in the realization system, § 1091 disallows or, more accurately, rolls over losses realized on sales of stock or securities when substantially identical stock or securities are purchased within 30 days before or after the sale. Section 1091 does not apply, however, in the case of a noncorporate taxpayer if the sale or other disposition of stock or securities is made in connection with the taxpayer's trade or business or, in the case of a corporation that is a dealer in stock or securities, if the sale or other disposition of stock or securities is made in the ordinary course of its business as a dealer. Treas. Reg. § 1.1091-1(a). A sale or other disposition that falls within § 1091 is frequently referred to as a "wash sale" because the realized loss is disallowed but preserved through basis adjustments in the substantially identical securities. Thus, § 1091 may be considered as a nonrecognition provision although it applies only in the case of realized losses and not realized gains.

The purpose and operation of § 1091 can be illustrated through a simple example. Assume that T owns 100 shares of common stock in Acme, Inc. with a basis of $10,000. If T sells the 100 shares on March 15 for $6,500, T will realize a $3,500 loss on the sale. If, however, T buys 100 common shares of Acme, Inc. stock on April 8, the loss on the prior sale will be disallowed under § 1091. In such a situation, T's economic situation has not sufficiently changed to allow deduction of the loss. If the loss is disallowed, § 1091(d) provides that the basis of the new shares is equal to the basis of the old shares, increased or decreased by the difference between the acquisition price of the new shares and the sale price of the old shares. In this case, if T purchased the 100 shares of common stock for $6,800, T's basis in the new shares will be $10,300 ($10,000 basis of the shares sold plus $300, the difference between the acquisition price of the new shares, $6,800, and the sale price of the old shares, $6,500), thereby preserving the $3,500 disallowed loss. *See* Treas. Reg. § 1.1091-2(a) example (1). When a loss is disallowed as a result of § 1091, the holding period of the stock giving rise to the disallowed loss is added to the holding period of the substantially identical stock. § 1223(3).

Of course, one of the most significant issues with respect to the application of § 1091is whether the stock or securities acquired within the 61-day period are "substantially identical" to the stock or securities that gave rise to the loss. This phrase is not further defined in either the statute or the Regulations. Nevertheless, the Service has provided the following description of when bonds will be deemed substantially similar:

> Generally, respective bonds are "substantially identical" . . . if they are not substantially different in any material feature (unaffected by any related material feature, or as affected by such other feature or features), or because of differences in several material features considered together. On the other hand, they are not "substantially identical," within such meaning, if they are substantially different in any material feature (unaffected by any related material feature, or as affected by such other feature or features), or because of differences in several material features considered together (*i.e.*, even though each of such differences considered alone might not be regarded as substantial). In determining whether or not bonds purchased were substantially identical to bonds sold, the bonds purchased must, of course, be compared as they existed when purchased with the bonds sold as they existed when sold.
>
> The fact that bonds of one series have the same, or approximately the same, market value on a particular day, or days, as bonds of another series of the same obligor, equally secured, and bearing interest at the same rate, does not necessarily establish that the respective bonds are "substantially identical," for that market situation can occur even if such respective series of bonds have substantially different maturity dates (unaffected, or as affected, by earlier call provisions) but, where they so differ, their market prices often are substantially higher on the substantially longer term series (than on the substantially shorter term series) when the market for the bonds is strong (usually during periods of generally low interest rates) and the reverse frequently occurs when the market for the bonds is weak (usually during periods of generally high interest rates).

Rev. Rul. 58-211, 1958-1 C.B. 529. In its Ruling, the Service concluded that United States Treasury 2¼ percent coupon (bearer) bonds maturing December 15, 1962, but callable on and after December 15, 1959, at par (face amount) and accrued interest, were substantially identical to United States Treasury 2¼ percent registered bonds, of equal face (principal) amount, maturing June 15, 1962, but callable on and after June 15, 1959, at par and accrued interest. *See Hanlin v. Commissioner*, 108 F.2d 429 (3d Cir. 1939) (bonds from different land banks were substantially identical, even though the collateral security underlying the bond issues were physically distinct). *But see* Rev. Rul. 76-346, 1976-2 C.B. 247 (6? percent Treasury bonds maturing in 1982 and not redeemable at par with accrued interest for payment of estate taxes not substantially similar to 4¼ percent Treasury bonds maturing in 1992 and redeemable at par with accrued interest for payment of estate taxes); Rev. Rul. 60-195, 1960-1 C.B. 300 (3.45 percent bonds not substantially similar to 4.5 percent bonds); Rev. Rul. 58-210, 1958-1 C.B. 523

(Treasury bonds not redeemable for application in payment of Federal estate taxes and eligible for unrestricted investment by commercial banks not substantially identical to Treasury bonds redeemable for application in payment of federal estate taxes and not eligible for unrestricted investment by commercial banks).

Presumably, when comparing different classes of stock, the voting, dividend, and liquidation rights of the classes of stock must be considered. *See Kidder v. Commissioner*, 30 B.T.A. 59 (1934) (voting trust certificates for common stock were substantially identical to common stock). However, different types of stock will not necessarily fail to satisfy the substantially identical requirement. For example, in Revenue Ruling 77-201, 1977-1 C.B. 250, the Service concluded that the sale of shares of common stock followed by a purchase of convertible preferred shares of the same corporation that were convertible into an equivalent number of common shares was a wash sale when the preferred stock and the common stock were traded at prices that did not vary significantly from the conversion ratio. In reaching this conclusion, the Service relied primarily on Regulation § 1.1233-1(d), which provides that bonds or preferred stock of a corporation are not ordinarily considered substantially identical to the common stock of the same corporation, but that where the preferred stock or bonds are convertible into common stock of the same corporation, the relative values, price changes, and other circumstances may be such as to make such bonds or preferred stock and the common stock substantially identical property.

Importantly, a transaction is a wash sale if, within the 61-day statutory period, the taxpayer acquires substantially identical stock or securities or "enters into a contract or option . . . to acquire" such property. Although an argument could be made that a contract or option to reacquire substantially identical stock or securities is economically different from the reacquisition of, or an obligation to reacquire, such property, § 1091 treats the transactions in the same manner. Section 1091 will apply even if the option is unlikely to be exercised. For example, the Service has held that § 1091 applies even in the context of an employee of a corporation who was granted an option to purchase stock of the corporation under the terms of a restricted stock option plan that would be forfeited if the employment relationship terminated. Rev. Rul. 56-452, 1956-2 C.B. 525. *See also* Rev. Rul. 77-201, 1977-1 C.B. 250 (concluded that the sale of shares of common stock followed by a purchase of convertible preferred shares of the same corporation was a wash sale because the acquisition of the convertible preferred shares is considered to be an option to acquire stock of the issuing corporation within the meaning of § 1091 when such stock is convertible at the shareholder's election and there are no restrictions with respect to such election); Rev. Rul. 56-406, 1956-2 C.B. 523 (concluding that a stock warrant is an option to acquire stock of the issuing corporation within the meaning of § 1091). If an option to acquire the stock or securities is exercised, no gain or loss will be recognized with respect to the option, and the disallowed loss will become part of the basis of the stock or securities acquired. If the option lapses, the basis of the option, equal to the disallowed loss plus the option premium, will then be deductible.

The Service has also considered whether a "put option" (i.e., an obligation to acquire property) with respect to substantially identical stock or securities will constitute a contract to acquire such property for purposes of § 1091. Rev. Rul.

85-87, 1985-1 C.B. 268. The facts of the Ruling were as follows:

> On December 3, 1984, *A*, an individual, sold 100 shares of *X* corporation stock and realized a loss with respect to the shares. On December 4, 1984, *A* sold a put option obligating A to buy 100 shares of *X* corporation stock prior to February 1, 1985, at a particular price (the "exercise price") if the holder of the put option exercised the option. When the put was sold by *A*, the market price of the stock was substantially less than the exercise price of the put. In light of the spread at the time the put was sold between the value of the underlying stock and the exercise price of the put, the term of the put, the premium paid, the historic volatility in the value of the stock, and other objective factors, there was, at that time, no substantial likelihood that the put would not be exercised. Because the fair market value of the stock at the time the put was sold was less than the exercise price of the put, the put option sold by *A* is referred to as an "in-the-money" put.

The Service concluded that because there was no substantial likelihood that the put would not be exercised at the time that it was sold, the put was in substance a contract to acquire stock for purposes of § 1091.

The following decision considers the application of § 1091 in the context of the sale of stock for a loss when the taxpayer subsequently enters into a contract to acquire the same stock in a transaction designed to generate a capital loss to offset capital gain realized as part of an unrelated transaction.

ESTATE OF ESTROFF v. COMMISSIONER

United States Tax Court
47 T.C.M. (CCH) 234, T.C. Memo. 1983-666

DRENNEN, *JUDGE:*

After concessions, the sole issue is whether Maxwell J. Estroff and petitioner Naomi Estroff are entitled to deduct a capital loss resulting from their sale of First Railroad and Banking Co. of Georgia common stock to a personal friend who resold it to them 34 days later.

Petitioner Naomi Estroff (petitioner) and Dale Toporek (Toporek) are executrixes of the estate of Maxwell J. Estroff (Estroff), deceased. Petitioner and Toporek both legally resided in Augusta, Ga., on the date the petition was filed herein.

Estroff and petitioner were married and filed joint Federal income tax returns for the taxable years 1974 and 1975 with the Internal Revenue Service Center, Chamblee, Ga.

In 1974, Estroff and his close personal friend and business associate, Jack E. Fink (Fink), jointly owned various corporations which manufactured and sold clothing for the Army-Air Force exchange system and for the general public. Prior to September 1974, Estroff and Fink disposed of their interests in three of their jointly owned corporations. Estroff reported $216,161 of long-term capital gain from the sale on his 1974 joint Federal income tax return.

Prior to September, 1974, Estroff, petitioner, and Fink had acquired common stock of the First Railroad and Banking Company of Georgia, (First Railroad). At that time, Estroff, petitioner, and Fink owned 13,601, 14,073, and 23,504 shares of First Railroad common stock, respectively.

In late Sept., 1974, a meeting was held between, Estroff and A.J. Kilpatrick (Kilpatrick) of the firm, A.J. Kilpatrick & Co., Investment Securities, (Investment Securities). At the meeting, Kilpatrick suggested that Estroff sell his First Railroad stock to Fink with the understanding that he would later repurchase it. Kilpatrick believed the transaction would create tax losses which could be used by Estroff and Fink to offset the substantial capital gains they had realized earlier in the year.

Sometime after the meeting, Estroff and Fink orally agreed that Estroff would sell 21,559 shares of First Railroad to Fink using Investment Securities as the broker. Estroff agreed to loan Fink the money to purchase the stock, and Fink agreed to sell the stock back to Estroff after a minimum of 30 days and to use the proceeds from that sale to repay the loan. The sale price for both sales was to be market price.

On Oct. 1, 1974, Estroff sold 7,486 shares of his First Railroad stock over the counter to Fink. On the same date, petitioner sold her 14,073 shares of First Railroad stock over the counter to Fink. The stock was sold through Investment Securities at its market price on that date of $6.25 per share for a total of $134,743.75, less a $750 broker's commission paid to Investment Securities. Petitioner and Estroff had a combined cost basis in the 21,559 shares of $323,943.69 on the date of sale.

Estroff loaned Fink $135,000 by check dated Oct. 8, 1974, which Fink used to purchase the 21,559 shares of First Railroad stock. No interest was charged by Estroff and Fink did not put up any collateral for the loan. The shares purchased by Fink were registered in his name and a credit entry in the amount of $133,993.75 was made in the Investment Securities ledger card in the name of Estroff to reflect the sale of 21,559 shares of First Railroad stock.

Fink held the 21,559 shares of stock for approximately 34 days. During that time, Fink received a dividend of $2,100 on the stock, which he retained. On November 4, 1974, Fink sold the 21,559 shares through Investment Securities back to Estroff for $6.25 per share. The stock was sold to Estroff at this price, even though the low bid was 6-3/4 and the high ask was 7-1/2 on the date of the sale. Estroff paid a total of $134,743.75 for the shares, of which $133,933.75 was paid over to Fink, and $750 of which was paid to Investment Securities as a broker's commission. Fink, immediately after receiving the sale proceeds from the 21,559 shares of First Railroad stock, repaid the $135,000 he had borrowed from Estroff.

Estroff and petitioner claimed a loss on the sale of the First Railroad stock in the amount of $189,949.94 on their 1974 Federal income tax return. Respondent disallowed the loss in its entirety.

The sole issue is whether Estroff and petitioner are entitled to a loss deduction on the sale of their First Railroad stock. Respondent contends that the sale of the

21,559 shares of First Railroad stock to Fink was a sham and lacked economic substance; also that the sale was a "wash sale" within the purview of section 1091(a). . . .

We agree with respondent. . . . Briefly, with regard to the first ground, the stipulated facts clearly indicate that the Estroffs' only purpose in entering into this transaction with Fink was to obtain a capital loss that could be offset against Estroff's capital gain from the sale of his business. The terms of the agreement were such that it was very unlikely that the Estroffs would realize a profit or a loss on the transaction. After reacquiring the stock from Fink they were in the same economic position they were in prior to the sale, with regard to both the stock and the cash loan. The retention by Fink of the dividend paid on the stock while it was in his name was probably just icing on the cake to make the transaction look real. While there is no evidence to prove it, we believe the circumstances warrant the assumption that Estroff was acting as agent for his wife when he dealt with her stock. The courts will not allow a taxpayer to deduct a loss from a transaction that "did not appreciably affect his beneficial interest except to reduce his tax * * *." *Knetsch v. United States*, 364 U.S. 361, 366 (1960). See also *Gregory v. Helvering*, 293 U.S. 465 (1935); *Higgins v. Smith*, 308 U.S. 473 (1940); *Goldstein v. Commissioner*, 364 F.2d 734 (2nd Cir. 1966), *affg.* 44 T.C. 284 (1965).

Turning now to respondent's second ground, we agree with respondent that Estroff was acting for both himself and his wife when he entered into the agreement with Fink to sell Fink 21,559 shares of First Railroad stock and to repurchase those shares from Fink not less than 30 days later. The record does not disclose what arrangements Estroff had with petitioner, but Estroff did not own 21,559 shares in his own name so petitioner had to be a party to the transaction. Neither does the record disclose whether the 14,073 shares owned by petitioner were reregistered in her name after Estroff repurchased them. Absent any evidence to the contrary we assume petitioner's stock was reregistered in her name after it had served their purposes. Since petitioner and Estroff filed a joint return for 1974, the return sheds no light on the subject. . . .

Section 165(c)(2) in conjunction with section 165(a) allows a deduction for losses incurred in any transaction entered into for profit, though not connected with a trade or business. However, section 1091(a) prohibits the deduction of a loss on the sale of stock if substantially identical stock is acquired or if the taxpayer enters into a contract or option to acquire substantially identical stock within 30 days prior to or 30 days subsequent to the sale.

On the assumption that Estroff was acting as agent for his wife, . . . Estroff sold 21,559 shares of First Railroad stock to Fink on October 1, 1974. Sometime between late September and the date of the sale, Estroff and Fink agreed that Fink would sell the stock back to Estroff after a minimum of 30 days. Thus, within 30 days of the time of the sale to Fink, Estroff entered into a contract to acquire substantially identical stock to that which he had sold. Accordingly, section 1091(a) by its express terms prohibits the deduction of the loss realized by Estroff on the sale of his stock to Fink.

However, petitioner maintains that under State law oral understandings or agreements to purchase stock or securities are unenforceable and, accordingly, the wash-sale rules were not triggered. We disagree. Section 1091(a) requires only that the taxpayer have a contract to purchase substantially identical securities. Although under Ga. Ann. Code, section 11-8-319(a) (1982), the contract may not have been enforceable at the time it was first entered into, the parties still had a *contract.* This is not a case where the contract was void *ab initio*, and furthermore, under Ga. Ann. Code, section 11-8-319(b) (1982), to the extent delivery of the stock was accepted, or payment had been made, the contract was enforceable. Section 1091(a) requires only that the taxpayer have a contract to purchase substantially identical securities. Therefore, we hold that section 1091(a) prohibits the loss deduction on the sale of the 21,559 shares of First Railroad stock by Estroff to Fink. . . .

NOTES AND COMMENTS

1. In addition to stock and securities, § 1091 applies to "contracts or options to acquire or sell stock or securities." This expansion of § 1091 was enacted in 1989 in response to the decision of the Tax Court in *Gantner v. Commissioner*, 91 T.C. 713 (1988), *aff'd*, 905 F.2d 241 (8th Cir. 1990), concluding that the phrase "stock or securities" did not include options to acquire stock. The Tax Court's decision was based on the explicit statutory language at the time.

> The statute speaks in terms of the sale or disposition only of "shares of stock or securities"; however, the reacquisition event is described as occurring if "the taxpayer has acquired * * *, *or has entered into a contract or option so to acquire*, substantially identical stock or securities." (Emphasis supplied.) Implicit in that statutory language is that *a contract or option to acquire* stock or securities is not the same as an *acquisition of* stock or securities. To say that entry into a contract or option to acquire stock or securities is tantamount to the acquisition of stock and securities would be to render superfluous the above-emphasized clause in section 1091(a).

Gantner v. Commissioner, 91 T.C. at 720–721. As amended, § 1091(a) now treats options, puts, and convertible securities in the same manner as stock. Importantly, such interests need not be "in the money" (i.e., that the option price be such that it is currently profitable to exercise the option, put, or conversion right) in order to trigger the application of § 1091. The expansion of § 1091 to include contracts or options to acquire or sell stock or securities raises considerable issues in the application of the "substantially identical" requirement. Presumably, however, a contract or option to buy stock or securities will be substantially identical to the stock or securities themselves. Thus, § 1091 will apply to disallow the loss on the sale of an option to buy stock if the stock itself is acquired within 30 days before or after the sale. Despite the statutory expansion of its scope, § 1091 does not apply to transactions involving foreign currency or commodity futures. Rev. Rul. 74-218, 1974-1 C.B. 202 (foreign currency); Rev. Rul. 71-568, 1971-2 C.B. 312 (commodity futures).

2. The literal language of § 1091 would apply to the situation in which a taxpayer purchases a block of shares that subsequently declines in value, and the taxpayer sells a portion of the block within 30 days of the purchase date. The

Service has declined to apply § 1091 in such a situation as inconsistent with Congressional intent.

> Congressional discussions and reports refer consistently to the "new acquisition" and to "repurchasing" and "buying back" stock or securities. These terms indicate an intent on the part of Congress to prevent a taxpayer's taking losses for tax purposes while giving up his position in a security for only a few days or not at all. However, they do not indicate an intent to disallow a loss sustained in a bona fide sale of securities made to reduce the taxpayer's holdings, even though the sale is made within 30 days after the securities were purchased.

Rev. Rul. 56-602, 1956-2 C.B. 527. However, the loss will be disallowed if the taxpayer, in another transaction occurring within the period beginning 30 days before the date of the sale and ending 30 days after such date, acquires or enters into a contract or option to acquire, additional substantially identical stock or securities.

3. The Regulations provide that when a taxpayer has several purchases and sales of substantially identical stock or securities, § 1091 applies "to the losses in the order in which the stock or securities the disposition of which resulted in the respective losses were disposed of (beginning with the earliest disposition." Treas. Reg. § 1.1091-1(b). For example, assume that T owns 250 shares of XYZ stock, each share having a basis of $20. T executes the following transactions involving XYZ shares:

August 23	Sale of 50 shares for $15 per share
September 4	Purchase of 100 shares for $10 per share
September 29	Sale of 100 of the original 250 shares for $5 per share

The purchase of substantially identical shares on September 4 requires that the $5 loss per share realized as a result of the August 23 sale be disallowed under § 1091. Although T purchased 100 shares of substantially identical stock within 30 days of the sale on September 20 at a loss of $15 per share, only the loss on 50 of the shares will be disallowed under § 1091.

4. There is no rule similar to that of § 1091 applicable to the sale of stock or securities that result in a gain, so that a taxpayer who will not be currently taxable on the gain from the sale of stock, for example because of an otherwise expiring net operating loss carryover, can sell stock and then buy substantially identical stock, thus stepping up its basis without the payment of tax. Assuming that any gain is subject to limited taxation in their country of residence, nonresident aliens moving to the U.S. are often advised to sell and repurchase substantially identical stock in order to obtain a step-up in the basis of their stock, because assets do not acquire a fair market value basis on change of status from nonresident alien to resident alien or U.S. citizen.

PROBLEMS FOR DISCUSSION

Problem 8-1. Invest sold 1,000 shares of Pubco stock with a basis of $10 per share for $5 per share and purchased 500 shares of Subco stock that can be exchanged for Pubco stock on a share-for-share basis at $5, but the exchange is a taxable transaction. Can Invest deduct her loss?

Problem 8-2. T owns 100 shares of common stock in Acme, Inc. with a basis of $10,000 and sells the 100 shares on March 15 for $6,500, realizing a $3,500 loss. T then buys 100 common shares of Acme, Inc. stock on April 8, for $6,250. What is T's basis in the newly acquired stock?

Problem 8-3. Using the facts of the example in note 3 above, determine the basis of the various groups of shares of XYZ stock.

§ 3. LOSSES BETWEEN RELATED PARTIES

I.R.C. § 267(a)(1), (b), (c), (d) and (g); 1041

Treas. Reg. §§ 1.267(b)-1, 1.267(c)-1, and 1.267(d)-1

As described in the previous section, § 1091 disallows losses on the sale of stock or securities when the taxpayer reacquires substantially identical stock within a 61-day period because the taxpayer's economic situation has not sufficiently changed so that such a loss should be deductible for tax purposes. Losses could also be deductible without a sufficient change in the taxpayer's economic situation if the taxpayer transferred property to a related party. Viewing the taxpayer and the related party as an economic unit, the realization of a loss on the transfer of property from the taxpayer to the related party would not affect the economic situation of the two parties. Recognizing the potential for taxpayer abuse through related party sales, § 267(a)(1) disallows the deduction of any loss on the sale or exchange of property between related parties. As the Supreme Court has stated:

> [Section 267] states an absolute prohibition — not a presumption — against the allowance of losses on any sales between the members of certain designated groups. The one common characteristic of these groups is that their members, although distinct legal entities, generally have a near-identity of economic interests. It is a fair inference that even legally genuine intra-group transfers were not thought to result, usually, in economically genuine realizations of loss, and accordingly that Congress did not deem them to be appropriate occasions for the allowance of deductions.

McWilliams v. Commissioner, 331 U.S. 694, 699 (1947). Thus, § 267(a)(1) applies even if the property is sold for its fair market value, and there is no evidence of taxpayer manipulation to understate the sale price. *Johnson v. Commissioner*, 42 T.C. 441 (1964) (loss disallowed on sales to related corporation in ordinary course of business even though similar losses incurred on sales to third parties). The loss realized by the transferor taxpayer is not completely disallowed for tax purposes, however, as the related party's gain on a subsequent transfer is reduced to the extent of the disallowed loss. § 267(d).

Two requirements must be satisfied in order for § 267(a) to apply: (1) there must be a sale or exchange of property that results in a recognized loss and (2) the transferor and transferee must be related parties. With respect to the first requirement, a sale or exchange for purposes of § 267(a)(1) presumably has the same meaning as a sale or exchange for purposes of §§ 1001(c) and 1222. However, if a sale or exchange of economically depreciated property between related parties does not result in a recognized loss, § 267(a) does not apply. For example, no gain or loss is recognized on the sale or exchange of property between spouses under § 1041. As a result, § 267(a) would not apply. *See* § 267(g) (specifically stating that § 267(a)(1) does not apply to transfers under § 1041). With respect to the second requirement, § 267(c) provides a list of the situations under which the transferor and transferee of property will be deemed related parties. For example, the transferor and certain members of his family, such as his ancestors, descendants, and siblings, are related parties. §§ 267(b)(1) and (c)(4). In addition, the transferor and a corporation in which he owns more than 50 percent of the value of the stock are related parties. § 267(b)(2). *But see* § 267(a)(1) (exempting any loss incurred by the corporation or its shareholder on a distribution in complete liquidation). Related parties also include two corporations that are members of the same consolidated group; the grantor and fiduciary of any trust; the fiduciary and any beneficiary of the same trust; and the fiduciary and beneficiary of a different trust if the same person is the grantor of both trusts. §§ 2687(b)(3) through (b)(7). *But see Widener, Trust No. 5 v. Commissioner*, 80 T.C. 304 (1983), *acq.* (concluding that § 267 was inapplicable to transfers between two trusts with a common beneficiary but with different grantors and contingent beneficiaries). Finally, two S corporations and an S corporation and a C corporation are related parties if the same person owns more than 50 percent of the value of the stock of each corporation. §§ 267(b)(11) and (b)(12). In determining the ownership of stock for purposes of § 267(b), a number of constructive ownership rules apply under § 267(c).

Although the asserted justification for denying the deduction of any loss on the sale or exchange of property under § 267(a)(1) is the assumed economic unity of the related parties, the disallowance is mandatory even if the related parties can demonstrate hostility of interest. In *Miller v. Commissioner*, 75 T.C. 182 (1980), two brothers argued that because they had a hostile relationship they should not be considered brothers for purposes of § 267. Relying on the ordinary rules of statutory construction and the lack of any such indication in the legislative history, the court rejected the argument that a hostility exception applied under the statute: "Congress obviously did not want the courts to face the difficult task of looking behind the sales. Instead, Congress made its prohibition absolute in reach, believing that this would be fair to the great majority of taxpayers." *Id.* at 189.

The related party rules are also applied without regard to whether the sale is voluntary or forced. *See Hassen v. Commissioner*, 599 F.2d 305 (9th Cir. 1979) (loss disallowed following foreclosure sale when bank, pursuant to nonbinding arrangement, sold the property to a corporation owned by the taxpayers for a price that covered its costs of the defaulted loan and the foreclosure); *Merritt v. Commissioner*, 400 F.2d 417 (5th Cir. 1968) (loss disallowed on sale of property seized to pay a federal income tax deficiency when purchaser at sale was the taxpayer's wife). Because determining whether an involuntary sale with an independent intermediary is covered involves a step-transaction analysis, some taxpayers have been allowed losses. *See McNeill v. Commissioner*, 251 F.2d 863 (4th Cir. 1958) (loss not disallowed when property seized for nonpayment of taxes and sold to a corporation controlled by the taxpayer six years later after governing authority unsuccessfully tried to sell it in the meanwhile); *McCarty v. Cripe*, 201 F.2d 679 (7th Cir. 1953) (loss not disallowed when property seized for nonpayment of taxes was purchased at public auction by corporation controlled, but not wholly owned by taxpayer, which made the highest of 25 bids, even though taxpayer provided funds).

Section 267 also applies to indirect sales of property between related parties, even when the different property is received and the sale is effectuated through a public market. In *McWilliams v. Commissioner*, 331 U.S. 694 (1947), the Supreme Court concluded that § 267 disallowed the loss on the sale of stock held in the husband's account when the same stock, but different shares, were purchased and held in the wife's account, despite the fact that the transfers took place through an exchange in which the identities of the persons buying from the husband and those selling to the wife were not known. According to the Court:

> We conclude that the purpose of the purpose of [§ 267] was to put an end to the right of taxpayers to choose, by intra-family transfers and other designated devices, their own time for realizing tax losses on investments which, for most practical purposes, are continued uninterrupted.
>
> We are clear as to this purpose, too, that its effectuation obviously had to be made independent of the manner in which an intra-group transfer was accomplished. Congress, with such purpose in mind, could not have intended to include within the scope of [§ 267] only simple transfers made directly or through a dummy, or to exclude transfers of securities effected through the medium of the Stock Exchange, unless it wanted to leave a loop-hole almost as large as the one it had set out to close.

Id. at 700–701. Nevertheless, in *United States v. Norton*, 250 F.2d 902 (5th Cir. 1958), the court distinguished between contemporaneous sales and purchases of the same stock as occurred in *McWilliams*, and sales followed by subsequent purchases of the same stock. Although § 267 does not contain an explicit time limit between the sale and subsequent purchase as found under the wash sale rules of § 1091, the Fifth Circuit noted the Supreme Court's recognition in *McWilliams* of the difficulty the lack of an explicit time period presented in properly applying § 267.

> Normally there can be a sale from A to B only at a single point of time, whether that sale be direct or indirect. The Supreme Court has held that such a sale and purchase exist when an order is given simultaneously for sale by A and purchase by B, to be executed on the stock exchange contemporaneously. . . . It has not been held, and we do not think it can be, that such sale and purchase exists when A sells on the market and no action is taken or contemplated for 28 days, at which time B determines to buy the same amount of stock and does so at a different price. The fact that there is a complete break in the control by the members of the related group prevents this purchase from being a sale between A and B, either direct or indirect. Of course, Congress could extend the wash sales prohibitions to purchases by related persons if it saw fit to do so, but it has

> not accomplished this result in [267]. Dealing only with the facts here, we must hold that a sale of fungible stocks . . . , followed by the purchase [by a related party] 28 days later at a lower price was not a sale or exchange of property directly or indirectly between [related parties], within the contemplation of [267].

Id. at 909. *See also Shethar v. Commissioner*, 28 T.C. 1222 (1957) (§ 267 disallowed losses on sale of different stock by husband and wife that was preceded by one day by the purchase by the husband and wife of the same stock to be sold by the other); *Lincoln v. Commissioner*, 24 T.C. 669 (1955), *nonacq.*, *aff'd per curiam*, 242 F.2d 748 (6th Cir. 1957) (the decision in *McWilliams* did not apply to disallow losses to a shareholder on the redemption of stock despite the fact that the corporation contemporaneously issued stock to a member of the shareholder's family because "[t]he plan was not conceived and carried out for the primary purpose of establishing tax losses for the stockholders").

If a loss is disallowed on the sale or exchange of property under § 267(a)(1), any gain realized by the transferee on a subsequent sale of the property is not recognized to the extent of the previously disallowed loss. § 267(d). For example, assume that A sells property with an adjusted basis of $100,000 to B, a related party, for $80,000, and the $20,000 loss is disallowed under § 267. If B sells the property three years later for $115,000, only $15,000 of the $35,000 gain realized ($115,000 amount realized minus $80,000 adjusted basis) will be recognized ($35,000 gain realized minus $20,000 previously disallowed loss). Alternatively, if B sells the property for only $95,000, none of the $15,000 gain realized ($95,000 amount realized minus $80,000 adjusted basis) will be recognized ($15,000 gain realized minus $15,000 of the $20,000 previously disallowed loss). The previously disallowed loss in excess of the gain not recognized on the subsequent sale is permanently disallowed. Similarly, B sells the property three years later for $55,000, B will realize and recognize a loss of $25,000 ($55,000 amount realized minus $80,000 adjusted basis). The previously disallowed loss of $20,000 is permanently disallowed. The results under § 267(d) are similar to those involving a gift of economically depreciated property under § 1015.

The application of § 267(a)(1) is considerably more complicated when multiple properties, some with inherent gain and others with inherent loss, are transferred between related parties as part of the same transaction. The following Revenue Ruling provides guidance in such situations.

Rev. Rul. 76-377, 1976-2 C.B. 89

* * *

In 1975, the taxpayer was president of *X* corporation and owned more than 50 percent of its stock, the remainder of stock being owned by members of the taxpayer's family. As of December 31, 1974, the taxpayer owed $71x$ dollars to *X*. During 1975, the taxpayer transferred to *X*, in partial satisfaction of the debt, shares of stock in *Y* corporation, a publicly held corporation, with a fair market value of $65x$ dollars. The transaction resulted in gain with respect to some of the shares of the stock and loss with respect to other shares. Computing the gain or loss on the sale of each block of stock separately, it was found that losses aggregated $10x$ dollars and gains aggregated $9x$ dollars; and that, considering the transfers as a whole, a net loss of $1x$ dollars was sustained.

Section 267(a) . . . provides, in part, that no deduction shall be allowed in respect of losses from sales or exchanges of property (other than losses in case of distributions in corporate liquidations), directly or indirectly, between persons specified within any one of the paragraphs of subsection (b).

Subsection (b) of section 267 of the Code provides at paragraph (2) that among the persons referred to in subsection (a) is an individual and a corporation more than 50 percent in value of the outstanding stock of which is owned, directly or indirectly, by or for such individual.

In *Morris Investment Corporation v. Commissioner*, 156 F.2d 748 (3rd Cir. 1946), aff'g 5 T.C. 583 (1945), *cert. denied*, 329 U.S. 788 (1946), a corporation sold certain securities to its controlling stockholder at a lump sum and claimed a net loss on the transaction by using the losses on some of the securities to offset the gain on others. The United States Circuit Court of Appeals held that the transaction must be construed as a number of distinct sales of the various securities, and since the purchaser owned more than 50 percent of the corporation's stock, losses were not deductible. However, the corporation was held taxable on any gains from the sales.

The question has been raised whether all of the *Y* stock transferred to *X* should be considered as a unit resulting in a net loss of $1x$ dollars or whether each block of stock should be considered as a separate transaction and the gains and losses treated separately.

In view of the decision in *Morris Investment Corporation* and the specific provisions of section 267 of the Code to the effect that no deduction shall be allowed in respect of losses from the sales or exchanges of property between an individual and a corporation more than 50 percent in value of the outstanding stock of which is owned by such individual, the losses sustained by the taxpayer by virtue of the transfer of stock to the corporation may not be offset against the gains derived from such transfer. To allow an offset would permit the deduction of losses specifically prohibited by statute and frustrate the legislative purpose of section 267. Thus, each block of stock transferred should be considered as a separate transaction and the gains and losses treated separately.

Accordingly, in the instant case, the aggregate gain of $9x$ dollars must be reported in gross income by the taxpayer. No deduction from gross income is allowed with respect to the losses of $10x$ dollars pursuant to section 267 of the Code.

* * *

NOTES AND COMMENTS

1. As Revenue Ruling 76-377 indicates, § 267(a)(1) is a loss disallowance rule; there is no netting of gain and loss realized in the same transaction. Thus, the seller may be taxed on more gain than the net gain on the overall sale. In addition to the decision in *Morris Investment Corp. v. Commissioner* cited in the Ruling, see

Kaplan v. Commissioner, 21 T.C. 134 (1953), *acq.* (concluding that the sale of 172 blocks of stock must be treated separately with gains being taxable and losses disallowed under § 267). Although the related purchaser's basis in the transferred property is the cost of the property, § 267(d), in effect, will allow the purchaser to reduce gain on a subsequent sale of the property by the amount of the disallowed loss, but not allow the seller to take advantage of the loss at the time of the original sale.

2. By its terms, § 267 does not apply to sales or exchanges of property between a taxpayer and a partnership in which the taxpayer is a member. Nevertheless, § 707(b)(1) contains a similar provision that disallows the deduction of any loss on the sale or exchange of property between a partnership and any person who owns more than 50 percent of the capital or profits interest in the partnership and between any two partnerships in which the same persons own more than 50 percent of the capital or profits interest in the partnerships. See *Davis v. Commissioner*, 866 F.2d 852 (6th Cir. 1989) (partnership's loss on foreclosure of property disallowed under § 707(b)(1)(B) when purchaser at the foreclosure sale sold the property 41 days later to a second partnership controlled by the same persons as part of a prearranged plan). Section § 707(b)(1) specifically cross-references § 267(d) to allow the nonrecognition of gain on a subsequent disposition of the property by the transferee as if the loss had been disallowed under § 267(a)(1).

3. Losses may be disallowed, even if not expressly covered by § 267(a)(1), under the principle of *Higgins v. Smith*, 308 U.S. 473 (1940), which disallowed a loss on a sale to a controlled corporation before the enactment of the predecessor of § 267. The legislative history to § 267 expressly recognized that fictitious losses may be disallowed without resort to § 267. S. Rep. No. 558, 73rd Cong., 2d Sess. (1934) (§ 267 "is not intended . . . to imply any legislative sanction of claiming deductions for losses on sales or exchanges in cases not covered thereby, where the transaction lacks the elements of good faith or finality, generally characterizing sales and exchanges of property").

PROBLEM FOR DISCUSSION

Problem 8-4. In Year 1, Fred sold a plant that was obsolete for use in his business, which had an adjusted basis of $575,000, but a fair market value of $400,000, to his daughter Sharon, for its $400,000 value for use in her start-up operation. The plant's useful life was 39 years for Sharon even though Fred had used it for more than 20 years. As of the beginning of Year 9, after approximately 12½ percent of the basis of the plant had been depreciated, Sharon sold the plant. What is the tax effect to Sharon of a sale for: (i) $250,000; (ii) $450,000; (iii) $650,000? How, if at all, would the result differ if Fred had given the plant to Sharon?

§ 4. AT-RISK RULES

I.R.C. §§ 465, 49(a)(1)(D)(iv)Treas. Reg. §§ 1.465-8, 1.465-20, 1.465-27Prop. Treas. Reg. §§ 1.465-1, 1.465-2, 1.465-3, 1.465-4, 1.465-5, 1.465-6, 1.465-7, 1.465-9, 1.465-11, 1.465-12, 1.465-13, 1.465-22, 1.465-23, 1.465-24, 1.465-25, 1.465-38, 1.465-41, 1.465-66

§ 4.01. In General

The at-risk rules under § 165 and the passive loss limitations under § 469 apply generally to prevent taxpayers from deducting losses incurred in one activity against the income incurred in another activity. Prior to the enactment of these provisions, individuals were able to deduct expenses, generally in the form of depreciation and interest, in excess of the actual income earned in certain investment activities to reduce their taxable income from compensation or other business activities. In other words, the losses from these investment activities would "shelter" otherwise taxable income, thus reducing the individual's overall tax liability. Such tax shelter investments proliferated in the 1970s and early 1980s, despite the enactment of the at-risk rules in 1976 and their expansion in 1978. Only with the enactment of the passive loss limitations in 1986 were these tax shelter investments finally brought under control.

The basic structure of these tax shelter investments can be illustrated through a relatively simple example. Assume that T acquires a widget-making machine on January 1 of Year 1. The machine costs $1 million, which T finances by obtaining a $900,000 nonrecourse loan, along with $100,000 of his own money. The loan requires only the annual payment of interest at 10 percent, payable on December 31 of each year. Upon acquisition of the machine, T immediately leases it to a widget-making company. Rent under the lease is $90,000 payable on December 31 of each year. The lessee will be responsible for all costs of maintaining and insuring the machine. Because the annual interest on the loan and the rent are equal, T will receive no net cash flow except that generated by any tax benefits that may be available. T does not expect that the widget-making machine will either increase or decrease in value over the foreseeable future and that he can sell the machine in the year immediately following the year in which tax benefits have been exhausted. The widget-making machine is five-year property under § 168, you can use the mid-year convention, and T does not take advantage of any deduction available under either § 168(k) or § 179. Finally, T's marginal tax rate is 35 percent.

From a non-tax perspective, the widget-making machine is an unwise investment. T will not receive any positive cash flow while holding the machine nor is the machine expected to increase in value. However, as shown in Table 8-1, the investment is attractive when considered from an after-tax perspective. The widget-making machine generates a loss each year equal to the depreciation deduction that is available to T in that year. Assuming that T has other income against which this loss can be deducted, T saves $70,000 in taxes in Year 1 alone. Of course, the depreciation deductions in Years 1 through 6 will reduce the basis of the widget-making machine to zero at the end of Year 6. If T sells the widget-making machine at the beginning of Year 7 when the machine has been fully depreciated for its original purchase price of $1 million, he will have gain of $1 million under § 1001, all of which will be ordinary income under § 1245. At that time, T will have to repay the $900,000 loan with $900,000 of the $1 million sale proceeds and incur an additional $250,000 expense in paying the $350,000 tax liability. Nevertheless, the widget-maker will have generated a 65.77 percent internal rate of return over its life for T, all attributable to tax benefits.

Table 8.1

								Year
		1	**2**	**3**	**4**	**5**	**6**	**7**
Down Payment	100,000							
Debt	900,000							
Total	1,000,000							
Interest Rate	10%							
Depreciation Rate		20.00%	32.00%	19.20%	11.52%	11.52%	5.76%	
Rent		90,000	90,000	90,000	90,000	90,000	90,000	
Interest		90,000	90,000	90,000	90,000	90,000	90,000	
Depreciation		200,000	320,000	192,000	115,200	115,200	57,600	
Taxable Income		-200,000	-320,000	-192,000	-115,200	-115,200	-57,600	
Tax Rate		35%	35%	35%	35%	35%	35%	
Tax Liability		-70,000	-112,000	-67,200	-40,320	-40,320	-20,160	
Amount Realized								1,000,000
Adjusted Basis								0
Gain								1,000,000
Deprec. Recapture								1,000,000
Tax Rate								35%
Tax Liability								350,000
Cash Flow	-100,000	70,000	112,000	67,200	40,320	40,320	20,160	-250,000
IRR	65.77%							

The reason that T is able to generate a positive internal rate of return on an investment that does not appreciate in value or produce a positive cash flow over its life is that the depreciation expense for tax purposes is in excess of the economic depreciation of the widget-making machine. As shown in Table 8.2, the internal rate of return would be even greater had T taken advantage of expensing and bonus depreciation under §§ 179 and 168(k). In this situation, T would have received tax benefits in Year 1 alone almost 2½ times his initial $100,000 investment. The ability to deduct depreciation in excess of actual economic depreciation and postpone the realization of gain attributable to such deductions is referred to as "deferral."

Table 8.2

								Year
Down Payment	100,000							
Debt	900,000							
Total	1,000,000							
Interest Rate	10%							
Depreciation Rate		20.00%	32.00%	19.20%	11.52%	11.52%	5.76%	
		1	2	3	4	5	6	7
Rent		90,000	90,000	90,000	90,000	90,000	90,000	
Interest		90,000	90,000	90,000	90,000	90,000	90,000	
§ 179 Expense		250,000						
Bonus Depreciation		375,000						
Depreciation		75,000	120,000	72,000	43,200	43,200	21,600	
Taxable Income		-700,000	-120,000	-72,000	-43,200	-43,200	-21,600	
Tax Rate		35%	35%	35%	35%	35%	35%	
Tax Liability		-245,000	-42,000	-25,200	-15,120	-15,120	-7,560	
Amount Realized								1,000,000
Adjusted Basis								0
Gain								1,000,000
Deprec. Recapture								1,000,000
Tax Rate								35%
Tax Liability								350,000
Cash Flow	-100,000	245,000	42,000	25,200	15,120	15,120	7,560	-250,000
IRR	164.90%							

T's return on his investment in the widget maker would have been further enhanced if he could have converted gain on the sale of the widget maker into capital gain taxed at a preferential tax rate. In this instance, T's depreciation deductions would have generated tax savings at his top marginal tax rate of 35 percent, which would have been repaid through gain on the sale of the widget maker at a preferential rate as low as 15 percent. Although § 1245 requires that the gain on the sale be taxed as T's top marginal rate of 35 percent, conversion may still be achieved under current law if T had invested in real property rather than equipment. In that case, the depreciation deductions would have generated tax savings at T's top marginal tax rate of 35 percent, but, assuming that the property was depreciated using the straight-line method, the gain attributable to those deductions would not have been recaptured as ordinary income under § 1250. Instead, the gain would have been taxed at 25 percent as unrecaptured § 1250 gain under § 1(h). The ability to treat gain generated by deductions against ordinary income taxed at the taxpayer's top marginal tax rate as capital gain taxed at a preferential rate is referred to as "conversion."

Finally, T's after-tax return on the widget maker was also increased through his ability to finance the acquisition of the widget maker through the use of debt. Although T made no principal payments on the debt, he was able to include the full amount of the debt in the basis of the widget maker. The inclusion of debt in basis provided T with the benefit of depreciation deductions in excess of his actual investment. Moreover, T was able to acquire the widget maker with nonrecourse debt. Thus, T did not face the personal liability for the debt should the widget maker actually decline in value. As described in the following excerpt from a report produced by the Joint Committee on Taxation, these three factors — deferral, conversion, and leverage — were the defining characteristics of the typical tax shelter. Despite the fact that the top marginal tax rates have been substantially reduced since 1975 when this report was written, the concepts of deferral, leverage, and conversion remain applicable today.

Staff of the Joint Committee on Taxation

Overview of Tax Shelters

1975

General

Since 1969, . . . there has been a substantial growth in the promotion of investments which are advertised as "tax shelters." Although they take a great variety of forms, in general, they allow taxpayers to offset certain "artificial losses" (that is, noneconomic losses but losses which are available as deductions under the present tax laws) not only against the income from those investments but also against the taxpayer's other income, usually from his regular business or professional activity. A major purpose of these investments for most taxpayers is to reduce the tax liability on their regular income.

There are several elements that make up a tax shelter investment (though not all of these elements are found in all shelters). The first is the "deferral" concept where deductions are accelerated in order to reduce the tax liability of an individual in early years of the transaction instead of matching the deductions against the income which is eventually generated from the investment. This deferral of tax liability from earlier years to later years, in effect, results in an interest-free loan by the Federal Government, repayable when, and as, the investment either produces taxable income, is sold, or is disposed of.

The second element of a tax shelter is "leverage" whereby a taxpayer maximizes his tax benefits, as well as his economic situation, by using borrowed funds in his investments to pay the expenses for which accelerated deductions are received. The individual's position is enhanced when borrowing on a nonrecourse basis, which means that he is not personally liable to repay the loan, but his personal investment risk is limited to his equity investment. Limited partnerships generally are used in tax shelter investments so that the taxpayer can invest as a limited partner with no liability other than the amount of equity that he has advanced with his own funds.

In addition, a third shelter element for many investments is "conversion' of ordinary income to capital gains at the time of subsequent sale or other disposition of the asset. Conversion occurs when the portion of the gain which reflects the accelerated deductions taken against ordinary income is taxed as capital gains. (Also, if the taxpayer is in a lower income tax bracket in the later years, he effectively "converts" the tax rate too.)

The following discussion deals generally with tax shelter investments as an overview to the whole area. . . . This discussion will cover the elements of a tax shelter investment and the entities used for such investments. . . .

Elements of a Tax-Shelter Investment

Deferral

Deferral commonly arises in situations where taxpayers make investments in activities or businesses which use cash basis methods of accounting and are permitted to take certain deductions . . . for tax writeoffs in the first year and the other early years of the tax shelter investment before the investment produces any income. Deferral also occurs where taxpayers are permitted to accelerate certain deductions (such as depreciation) to the early years of an investment transaction.

The 'bunching" of deductions in the first years, rather than ratably over the life of the property, is used to offset (shelter) an individual's other income. The excess accelerated deductions result in losses used against his other investment and earned income and may significantly reduce the individual's tax liability. However, the taxes that are reduced in the earlier years may be shifted to later years when the investment begins to generate income, and many of the offsetting deductions have been used up. Taxpayers in this situation have found it advantageous to invest in another tax shelter to provide a "rollover" or further deferral of the taxes.

The net effect of deferral is that the taxpayer grants himself an interest-free loan from the Federal Government during the period of the tax deferral. Over a period of years, this loan can be worth a substantial amount of money. For example, if a taxpayer has $100,000 of accelerated deductions and invests the tax savings in 7%

tax-exempt bonds (with interest compounded annually) his money will double in less than 11 years. In other words, deferral can be worth as much as total tax forgiveness after a period of time.

In addition, in many cases, especially where leverage is used, as discussed below, a tax shelter investment also results in a taxpayer completely recovering his investment (and in some cases more) by the acceleration of deductions. This is often the case for taxpayers in the 50-percent or higher tax brackets. Thus, not only does the Federal Government provide an interest-free loan, but in a sense the Government provides risk capital to high bracket taxpayers to enter into these investments.

It is important to note that this deferral treatment benefits those in higher tax brackets proportionately more than it benefits those in lower tax brackets. For example, for each $100 deduction, a taxpayer in the 70-percent bracket will save $70 by taking that deduction against his income. On the other hand, a taxpayer in the 20-percent bracket will save only $20 when that $100 deduction is used to offset his income. This is particularly important in a tax shelter investment because of the various risks that are involved. In other words, the interest free loan for the upper income taxpayer is $70; the interest free loan for the lower bracket taxpayer is considerably less.

It should be noted that the tax benefits from deferral are greater in some tax shelters than in others simply because the deferral is for a longer period than for other investments; that is, taxes are deferred over a longer period of time. In the case of shorter deferrals it is possible for an individual to rollover his investment; that is, to make another tax shelter investment to provide new accelerated deductions and thus defer tax liability further into the future.

* * *

Leverage

The second element of a tax shelter investment is "leverage," which is the use of borrowed money by an individual in the investment. Generally, an individual will borrow money (or money will be borrowed on his behalf) which will equal or exceed his equity investment. There are two benefits to the use of borrowed funds, the first being an economic benefit and the second being a tax benefit. From an economic standpoint, the more that an individual can use borrowed money for an investment the more he can use his own money for other purposes (including other investments) and the more he can make on an investment that is profitable. From a tax standpoint, borrowed funds are treated in the same manner as a taxpayer's own funds that he has put up as equity in an investment. Since a taxpayer is allowed deductions not only with respect to his own equity but also on the borrowed funds, he can maximize deferral by incurring deductible expenditures which exceed his equity investment.

A simple illustration of the use of leveraging in a tax shelter investment is as follows. Assume the investment requires $100,000 of capital. If an individual invests $10,000 of his own money and is able to borrow $90,000 to meet the $100,000 requirement, for tax purposes he is treated as having $100,000 in the investment.

This means that if there are accelerated deductions of $20,000 in the first year, the individual, if he is in the 70-percent bracket, would be reducing his tax liability by $14,000. In this case, the tax deductions in the initial year ($20,000) would be $10,000 more than the equity capital invested and his tax savings would be $4,000 more than the amount originally invested ($10,000). This individual would be financing his investment completely with what can be referred to in effect as an interest-free loan from the Federal Government. In this example above, a taxpayer in the 50-percent bracket would recover his entire investment in the initial year; that is, if he invests $10,000 of his own money and is allowed to deduct $20,000, he receives back by way of reduction of his tax liability the $10,000 he invested. This is the reason why most tax shelter investments are advertised for taxpayers in the 50-percent bracket and above.

A taxpayer in the 20-percent tax bracket who invests the same $10,000, as in the above example, would only receive back $4,000 from the same $20,000 tax write-off in the first year and, therefore, he is still out of pocket $6,000 in the first year. Not only is the low bracket taxpayer less likely to have the funds to invest in these investments but the Federal Government does not provide him the same subsidy as it does for the high bracket individual.

As can be seen from this example, in the initial years, the risks to a high bracket taxpayer are minimal because in the normal tax shelter investment, he or she would recover the amount of his own investment in the year it is made through tax deductions. It should be noted, however, that even if the investment fails, there is usually some recovery (and sometimes substantial recovery) of previous writeoffs where the investor would be liable on the constructive income he is required to recognize when the shelter terminates. This is often referred to as the "phantom gain"; where there is gain for tax purposes, even though the investment does not generate economic income or positive cash flow. In other words, the taxpayer is required to repay his interest free loan from the Government, at least to the extent of any nonrecourse borrowings which he was previously able to deduct. (Sometimes this repayment must be made in full, and sometimes only in part, if there is a "conversion" feature to the shelter, as discussed below.)

The use of leverage has increased significance when an investor is not even liable on the borrowed money, which is often the case in tax shelter investments. This is what is referred to as "nonrecourse financing." Where a partnership (usually a limited partnership) is being used as the investment vehicle, a loan may be made to the partnership so that the partnership assets are subject to liability but the investors are not personally liable for the loan. However, under partnership tax regulations, the limited partner investor is entitled to increase his basis in his investment by the amount which is treated as his proportionate share of the liability (even though in fact he has no such liability). (A partner may deduct partnership losses to the extent of his basis.) Thus, the investor is able to take tax write-offs on account of the accelerated deductions not only for the money he invested (on which he is at risk) but, more significantly, also on his share of the nonrecourse loans (on which he is not at risk). (Nonrecourse loans are discussed below in connection with limited partnerships.)

Conversion of ordinary income into capital gains

A third aspect which is present in some tax shelter investments is referred to as "conversion," which is the process of converting ordinary income deductions into capital gains.

When a taxpayer depreciates an asset, he takes a deduction against his ordinary income (and thus reduces taxable ordinary income) for depreciation. If the asset is a capital asset when it is sold and the proceeds exceed basis, there is a taxable gain. However, even though the previous reduction in basis (depreciation) reduced ordinary income, this gain may be taxed as capital gain. When the gain is capital gain, the effect of the sale is to convert ordinary income, that is the income which was reduced by previous accelerated deductions at the marginal bracket of the taxpayer, to capital gains taxed at the preferential capital gains tax rates.

In several case, Congress has dealt with this situation by requiring a portion of the gain on the sale or other disposition to be treated as ordinary income rather than capital gains, to the extent of accelerated depreciation deductions (and in the case of personal property, to the extent of all depreciation). This is what is referred to a "recapture." The taxes on the ordinary income that have been deferred through the taking of accelerated deductions in earlier years are recaptured at the time the property is disposed of. Although there are several recapture rules in present law today, the recapture rules do not apply to all tax shelter investments. (In addition, the "recapture" applies only to prevent the conversion of ordinary income into capital gains; it does not apply to the deferral factor.)

Use of Limited Partnerships

The form of entity most commonly used to maximize tax benefits in a tax shelter investment is a limited partnership. . . . In general, a partnership is not considered a separate entity for tax purposes; rather the individual partners are taxed currently on their share of the partnership gains and can deduct partnership losses to the extent of the basis of their partnership interest.

When an investor enters a partnership, his basis in the partnership generally includes the amount he invested and his share, if any, of the partnership liabilities. In this regard, the income tax regulations . . . provide that a limited partner may include in the basis of his partnership interest his share of the nonrecourse loans to the partnership even though he is not personally liable on the debt. (Such loans usually are secured only by the partnership property.) Nonrecourse financing facilitates the use of limited partnerships for tax shelter investments because the investor is able to limit the his liability to the amount he has actually invested but use nonrecourse loans obtained by the partnership to substantially increase his basis and thus increase his tax deductions.

More specifically, these general principles apply to limited partnerships in tax shelter investments:

1. The limited partnership is not a taxpaying entity, but instead is a tax conduit, the partners reporting their distributive shares of partnership income or loss.

2. Subject to the restriction that [its allocations have substantial economic effect], a limited partnership agreement may provide for the manner in which the partnership's items of income, gain, loss, deduction or credit will be allocated among the partners.

3. The amount of losses which a partner may deduct for a particular year is limited to the amount of the adjusted basis of his partnership interest at the end of the year. At the inception of the partnership, the adjusted basis of the partner's partnership interest equals the sum of his capital contribution to the partnership plus his share, if any, of partnership liabilities. In the case of a limited partnership, a limited partner's share of partnership liabilities is his . . . share . . . of all liabilities with respect to which there is no personal liability ("nonrecourse liabilities"). This rule, where a limited partner's adjusted basis in his partnership interest is increased by a [share] of nonrecourse liability, is one of the cornerstones of tax shelter investments, allowing the investor, in many cases, to currently deduct amounts in excess of his actual investment.

The limited partnership is generally preferred over the general partnership because the limited partners, who are passive investors in most cases, have limited liability for the debts or claims against the partnership. [Editors note: The preferred vehicle for investments since the later 1980s has become the limited liability company which provides all of its members with limited liability for the debts and claims against the partnership and is treated as a partnership for federal tax purposes unless the LLC elects otherwise.]

Corporations

The corporate form of doing business generally does not lend itself to tax shelter investments by individuals since the corporation is the taxpaying entity and, therefore, the tax incidents of its operation remain at the corporate level and do not pass through to its shareholders. The one exception to this treatment is for Subchapter S corporations. To a great extent, the tax incidents of a Subchapter S corporation's operations pass through to its shareholders. However, there are certain tax limitations applicable to the Subchapter S corporation which are not imposed on a limited partnership under the partnership provisions.

As previously noted, one of the principal tax shelter benefits obtained under the partnership tax provisions is that the adjusted basis of an individual partner in his partnership interest not only includes his cash investment but also a . . . share of any nonrecourse liability of the partnership. By contrast, the adjusted basis of the shareholders of a Subchapter S corporation in their stock includes their investment in the stock and any loans they may have made to the corporation, but, most significantly, does not include any portion of the corporation's liabilities. In both cases, that of the Subchapter S corporation shareholder and the limited partner, it is the adjusted basis in partnership interest or stock, as the case may be, which serves as an upper limit on the amount of loss that may be deducted by the shareholder (partner) in a given year. Thus, in comparison to the limited partner, the Subchapter S corporation shareholder is severely limited in terms of the amount of losses, and therefore tax shelter, available.

* * *

Economic Effects and Background of Tax Shelters and Their Public Syndication

Tax shelters are not a new form of investment, nor were they created by the public syndicators of interests in real estate or other limited partnerships. The advantage of owning an apartment building, for example, both for current income and for accelerated depreciation, has long been familiar to doctors, lawyers, and other high-income professionals and businessmen. Real estate syndicates of individuals have been formed for many years, usually involving a builder and a small group of individuals who personally know each other. However, the widespread public sales of shares in investments in real estate, farming, oil drilling, motion pictures and the like (many of which involve registering the offering with the Securities and Exchange Commission and selling it like a stock interest) has been a phenomenon of recent years, reflecting efforts by promoters to pass through tax shelter benefits to passive outside investors.

This form of mass merchandising, which has received much publicity in recent years, is basically a reflection rather than a cause of tax shelter benefits in present law. Some critics of tax shelters believe, however, that the public syndication of specialize investments to absentee owners has created a preoccupation with tax benefits (rather than with the economic merits and risks of the project) to the neglect of future tax liabilities.

Some of those who share this view argue that the tax provisions which Congress intended as incentives work well so long as they are not carried to extremes, but when an investment is made chiefly to intensify "tax write-offs," the tax rules become distorted and cease to work as they were intended.

NOTES AND COMMENTS

One of the first attempts to limit the impact of tax shelters was the enactment of the at-risk rules in 1976. The at-risk rules generally limit a taxpayer's deduction of losses only to the extent that a taxpayer is "at risk" in an activity. For this purpose, losses are defined as the amount of any deductions in excess of the income from the activity. § 465(d). As described in greater detail below, a taxpayer is deemed to be at-risk only to the extent that the taxpayer may be personally liable for any economic losses that may be incurred as a result of the activity. Thus, as a general matter, the at-risk rules attempt to prevent taxpayers from generating tax benefits attributable to nonrecourse debt.

Under the at-risk rules, a taxpayer is denied the deduction of any losses in excess of his at-risk amount. § 465(a)(1); Prop. Treas. Reg. § 1.465-1(a). Importantly, § 465 only limits the deduction of losses generated by the activity. Section 465 does not prohibit a taxpayer from deducting expenses incurred in the activity to the extent of any income generated by that activity. Prop. Treas. Reg. §§ 1.465-2(a) and 1.465-11(a). Any losses incurred in excess of the taxpayer's at-risk amount must be carried forward to succeeding taxable years and are deductible in future years only to the extent of the income generated by the activity in that taxable year and any additional amount by which the taxpayer is at-risk in the activity at that time. § 465(a)(2); Prop. Treas. Reg. § 1.465-2(b).

The effect of the at-risk rules is illustrated in Table 8.3. Table 8.3 assumes the same investment as depicted in Table 8.2, in which T acquires a widget-making machine on January 1 of Year 1. The machine costs $1 million, which T finances by obtaining a $900,000 nonrecourse loan, along with $100,000 of his own money. The loan requires only the annual payment of interest at 10 percent, payable on December 31 of each year. Upon acquisition of the machine, T immediately leases it to a widget-making company for annual rent of $90,000 payable on December 31 of each year. T will receive no net cash flow except that generated by any tax benefits that may be available and does not expect that the widget-making machine will either increase or decrease in value over the foreseeable future. T takes advantage of expensing under § 179 and bonus depreciation under § 168(k) in Year 1 and depreciates the remaining basis of the widget maker as five-year property under § 168.

Under § 465, T will be deemed at-risk only to the extent of the $100,000 investment in the activity. Because T is not personally liability for repayment of the $900,000 nonrecourse loan, this liability has no effect on the amount that T is considered to be at risk. Because T earns $90,000 of income in the form of rent, T will be permitted to deduct $90,000 of the interest, § 179 expense, and depreciation expenses incurred in Year 1. In addition, because T's at-risk amount is $100,000, he will be permitted to deduct an additional $100,000 of the interest, § 179 expense, and depreciation expenses incurred in Year 1. This $100,000 loss will generate tax savings for T of only $35,000, as compared to the $245,000 in tax savings in the absence of the at-risk rules as shown in Table 8.2. However, the deduction of the $100,000 loss will reduce T's at-risk amount to zero, and T will be prohibited from deducting any portion of the remaining $600,000 loss against other income. This loss will be carried forward to Year 2, but, because T's at-risk amount remains at zero, he will not be permitted to deduct the $600,000 suspended loss from Year 1 or the $120,000 loss incurred in Year 2. Likewise, the losses incurred in Years 3 through 6 will not be deductible because T's at-risk amount remains at zero. When T disposes of the widget maker in Year 7, generating a gain of $1,000,000, the $900,000 of suspended losses will be deductible. The $100,000 of taxable income in Year 7 will result in a tax liability of $35,000. Of the $1,000,000 in proceeds on the sale of the widget maker, T will pocket $65,000 after paying the outstanding balance of the $900,000 loan and the $35,000 tax liability. As a result of the at-risk rules, T's only after-tax return on his $100,000 investment is $35,000 in Year 1 and $65,000 in Year 7. Thus, the internal rate of return on T's investment is 0 percent. By removing the tax benefits of this investment by prohibiting the deduction of tax losses generated by the widget maker against other income, the at-risk rules have made an investment with no positive pre-tax return but a positive after-tax return into an investment with no positive pre-tax or after-tax return.

Table 8.3

Down Payment	100,000							
Debt	900,000							
Total	1,000,000							
Interest Rate	10%							
Depreciation Rate		20.00%	32.00%	19.20%	11.52%	11.52%	5.76%	
							Year	
		1	**2**	**3**	**4**	**5**	**6**	**7**
Rent		90,000	90,000	90,000	90,000	90,000	90,000	
Interest		90,000	90,000	90,000	90,000	90,000	90,000	
§ 179 Expense		250,000						
Bonus Depreciation		375,000						
Depreciation		75,000	120,000	72,000	43,200	43,200	21,600	
Taxable Income		-700,000	-120,000	-72,000	-43,200	-43,200	-21,600	
At-Risk Amount		100,000	0	0	0	0	0	
Suspended Loss		-600,000	-720,000	-792,000	-835,200	-878,400	-900,000	
Allowable Loss		-100,000	0	0	0	0	0	
Tax Rate		35%	35%	35%	35%	35%	35%	
Tax Liability		-35,000	0	0	0	0	0	
Amount Realized								1,000,000
Adjusted Basis								0
Gain								1,000,000
Deprec. Recapture								1,000,000
Suspended Loss								-900,000
Tax Rate								35%

Tax Liability								35,000
Cash Flow	-100,000	35,000	0	0	0	0	0	65,000
IRR	0.00%							

Before considering the details of the determination of a tax-payer's at-risk amount, it is important to note that § 465 is not applicable to all taxpayers. By its terms, § 465 applies only to individuals and certain closely held C corporations. §§ 465(a)(1)(A) and 465(a)(1)(B). A closely-held C corporation is one that is taxed under Subchapter C of the Code and that satisfies the ownership requirements of a personal holding company under § 542(a)(2), albeit with certain modifications. *See* § 465(a)(3). Because the taxable income of trusts and estates is determined as if they were individuals under § 641(b), § 465 applies to them as well. In addition, the at-risk rules apply to these taxpayers if their activities are carried on indirectly as partners in a partnership or as shareholders in an S corporation.

When originally enacted, § 465 applied only to certain covered activities that were typically used as tax-shelter investments. These were activities that the taxpayer engaged in as a trade or business or for the production of income of: (1) holding, producing, or distributing motion picture films or videotapes; (2) farming; (3) leasing of § 1245 property; and (4) exploring for, or exploiting, oil and gas resources or geothermal deposits. § 465(c)(1). Currently, covered activities for purposes of § 465 have been expanded to any activity engaged in by a taxpayer as a trade or business or for the production of income. § 465(c)(3). However, the at-risk rules do not apply to closely held corporations engaged in equipment leasing under certain circumstances. §§ 465(c)(4) and 465(c)(5).

Importantly, the at-risk rules apply on an activity-by-activity basis. Losses for which the taxpayer is not at risk cannot be deducted against the income generated by a different activity. Consequently, taxpayers must separately identify each activity. With respect to the originally covered activities, each film or videotape, leased § 1245 property, farm, and oil or gas and geothermal property is a separate activity. § 465(c)(2)(A). Under certain circumstances, separate activities may be aggregated and treated as a single activity. § 465(c)(2)(B); Temp. Treas. Reg. § 1.465-1T. Activities other than the original covered activities that constitute a trade or business are treated as one activity if the taxpayer materially participates in the management of the trade or business or if the trade or business is carried on by a partnership or S corporation and 65 percent of the or more of the losses are allocable to persons who materially participate in the management of the trade or business. § 465(c)(3)(B). The identification of each activity and ability to aggregate separate trades or business into a single activity is important because losses incurred in one trade or business may be deducted against the income earned in another trade or business without regard to the amount that the taxpayer is at risk only if the two trades or businesses comprise a single activity.

§ 4.02. At-Risk Amount

As previously noted, losses incurred in an activity are deductible by a taxpayer against the income generated by a different activity only to the extent that the taxpayer is at risk in the activity. § 465(a). A taxpayer is at risk in an activity to the extent of any money contributed to the activity plus the adjusted basis of any property contributed to the activity. § 465(b)(1)(A); Prop. Treas. Reg. §§ 1.465-22(a) and 1.465-23(a). In addition, a taxpayer is at risk for any amounts borrowed with respect to an activity to the extent that the taxpayer is personally liable for the repayment of the borrowed amounts or has pledged property, other than property used in the activity, as security for the borrowed amounts. § 465(b)(1)(B) and 465(b)(2); Prop. Treas. Reg. §§ 1.465-24(a)(1) and 1.465-25(a)(1). Finally, income from the activity in excess of the deductible expenses from the activity for the taxable year will increase the taxpayer's at-risk amount. Prop. Treas. Reg. § 1.465-22(c)(1). A taxpayer's at-risk amount is reduced, however, to the extent that the taxpayer withdraws money or property from the activity and to the extent of any losses that are otherwise deductible under § 465(a). § 465(b)(5); Prop. Treas. Reg. §§ 1.465-22(b), 1.465-22(c)(2), and 1.465-23(c).

Generally, the issue involved in applying the at-risk rules is whether the taxpayer is "personally liable" for the repayment of borrowed amounts incurred in the activity. The Proposed Regulations provide that a taxpayer is not considered at risk with respect to borrowed amounts to the extent that "the taxpayer is protected against loss. . . ." Prop. Treas. Reg. § 1.465-6(a). For example, a partner is not at risk with respect to any partnership liability to the extent that the partner is entitled to contribution from the other partners. Prop. Treas. Reg. §§ 1.465-6(b) and 1.465-24(a)(2). The Proposed Regulations also provide that a taxpayer is not at risk with respect to contingent liabilities "if the likelihood of the contingency occurring is such that the taxpayer is effectively protected against loss." Prop. Treas. Reg. § 1.465-6(c).

In *Pritchett v. Commissioner*, 827 F.2d 644 (9th Cir. 1987), the Ninth Circuit held that the "critical inquiry" in this regard is whether the taxpayer is "the obligor of last resort" and that "in determining who has the ultimate economic responsibility for the loan, the substance of the transaction controls." *Id.* at 647 (quoting *Melvin v. Commissioner*, 88 T.C. 63, 75 (1987)). In *Pritchett*, the taxpayers were limited partners in a partnership formed to conduct oil and gas operations. The partnership paid cash and executed a 15-year recourse note to a third party that agreed to drill, develop, and exploit any productive wells. The note was to be paid from the income earned by the partnership if the drilling operations were successful. Although only the general partners were personally liable under the note, the partnership agreement provided that if the note was not paid at maturity, the limited partners would be personally obligated to make additional capital contributions to cover the deficiency when called upon to do so by the general partners. The Tax Court had concluded that the limited partners were not at risk in the first year of the partnership because it was not known whether the partnership's income would be sufficient to pay off the note or even whether the general partners would in fact exercise their discretion to make a capital call on an unpaid balance of the note 15 years in the future. The Tax Court characterized the limited partners' obligation as "indirect and secondary" and "merely a contingency." The Court of Appeals reversed, concluding that the limited partners, "by virtue of their contractual obligations," had ultimate responsibility for the debt. The Court reasoned that, if the notes were not paid at maturity, the partnership agreement made the call for additional capital mandatory and that "economic reality" dictated that the general partners would make such a call.

In determining whether a taxpayer is "the obligor of last resort," a complete examination of the circumstances under which the taxpayer would be liable for repayment of any debt is necessary. In the following opinion, the Tax Court considered whether a deficit restoration obligation required under the Regulations to § 704 to ensure that any special allocation of partnership income or loss has substantial economic effect is sufficient to determine that a member of a limited liability company is at risk with respect to an obligation of the LLC.

HUBERT ENTERPRISES, INC. v. COMMISSIONER

United States Tax Court
95 T.C.M. (CCH) 1194, T.C. Memo. 2008-46

LARO, *JUDGE*:

This case is before the Court on remand from the Court of Appeals for the Sixth Circuit. . . . See *Hubert Enters., Inc. v. Commissioner*, 230 Fed. Appx. 526 (6th Cir. 2007), *affg. in part, vacating in part and remanding,* 125 T.C. 72 (2005). The Court of Appeals for the Sixth Circuit vacated the . . . decision and remanded the case to this Court to decide, after allowing the parties to develop the record more fully, whether the deficit capital account restoration obligation (DRO) included in the amended and restated operating agreement of Leasing Co., L.L.C. (LCL), a limited liability company, rendered LCL's members payors of last resort under the law applicable in the Sixth Circuit. . . .

We hold that the DRO did not render HBW a payor of last resort under the applicable law. . . .

FINDINGS OF FACT

LCL was formed as a Wyoming limited liability company on April 30, 1998, and was treated as a partnership for Federal income tax purposes. LCL operated on the basis of a fiscal year ended July 31, and it filed Forms 1065, U.S. Return of Partnership Income, to report its operations for Federal income tax purposes. During the relevant years, LCL engaged in equipment leasing activities and purchased equipment subject to a lease. LCL partially financed its purchases of that equipment using promissory notes. Some portions of the notes were recourse; the remaining portions were nonrecourse.

LCL's members were HBW and HCC. HBW owned 99 of LCL's 100 membership units, and HCC owned the remaining unit. During the subject years, HBW was a wholly owned subsidiary of HHC and a member of its affiliated group. HCC also was connected with that group.

Relevant Equipment Leasing Activities

In 1998, LCL purchased some equipment from Capital Resources Group, Inc. (CRG). In connection with this purchase, LCL signed four promissory notes. Two of the notes were nonrecourse; the other two notes were partially recourse. Neither LCL member signed any of these notes or otherwise guaranteed repayment of the notes.

In 2000, LCL purchased other equipment from CRG. In connection with this purchase, LCL signed two promissory notes. Both notes were partially recourse. Neither LCL member signed either of these notes or otherwise guaranteed repayment of the notes.

The DRO

Section 4.2 of LCL's initial operating agreement (initial operating agreement) states that "No Member shall be liable as such for the liabilities of the Company". On March 28, 2001, LCL's two members amended and restated the initial operating agreement in its entirety (revised operating agreement) and stated in the revised operating agreement that it was effective as of January 1, 2000. The revised operating agreement is construed under Wyoming law, and only the parties that signed the revised operating agreement (and their successors in interest) have any rights or remedies under that agreement. The revised operating agreement states that the life of LCL is 30 years from the date of the filing of its articles of organization with the Wyoming secretary of state. The revised operating agreement states that neither LCL member is required to make any additional capital contribution to LCL.

Section 7.7 of the revised operating agreement contains the DRO.[1] That provision states as follows:

> *Deficit Capital Account Restoration.* If any Partner has a deficit Capital Account following the liquidation of his, her or its interest in the partnership, then he, she or it shall restore the amount of such deficit balance to the Partnership by the end of such taxable year or, if later, within 90 days after the date of such liquidation, for payment to creditors or distribution to Partners with positive capital account balances.

Provision Concerning Potential Third-Party Beneficiaries

The revised operating agreement contains a provision concerning potential third-party beneficiaries. As stated in section 20.9 of that agreement:

> Nothing express or implied in this Agreement is intended or shall be construed to confer upon or to give any person or entity, other than the parties or their successors-in-interest in accordance with the provision of this Agreement, any rights or remedies hereunder or by reason hereof.

At-Risk Bases of HBW

For its taxable years ended in July 2000 and 2001, HBW took into account its proportionate share of LCL's recourse debt in computing its at-risk amounts under section 465(b). Respondent determined that HBW was not entitled to increase its at-risk amounts on account of that debt. Accordingly, respondent determined, HBW

---

[1] [4] A partnership (or another type of entity treated as a partnership) typically includes a DRO in its operating agreement so that the allocations of income, gain, loss, deduction, or credit (or item thereof) stated in the agreement have "substantial economic effect" within the meaning of sec. 704(b)(2). See generally sec. 1.704-1(b), Income Tax Regs., and especially par. (2)(ii)(*b*)(*3*) thereof.

was not entitled to deduct losses that it claimed with respect to LCL's leasing activities because those losses exceeded the amounts for which HBW was at risk with respect to those activities.

OPINION

Petitioner argues that the DRO rendered HBW a payor of last resort as to LCL's recourse debt for purposes of applying the at-risk rules of section 465(b). Respondent argues that HBW was not a payor of last resort as to LCL's recourse debt because the DRO did not render HBW personally liable as to that debt. We agree with respondent. . . .

The parties agree that the recourse notes signed by LCL did not in and of themselves create personal liability for HBW. See also Wyo. Stat. Ann. sec. 17-15-113 (2007) (providing that "the members of a limited liability company * * * are [not] liable under a judgment, decree or order of a court, or in any other manner, for a debt, obligation or liability of the limited liability company"). The parties dispute whether the DRO made HBW personally liable on those notes for purposes of applying the at-risk rules of section 465. Petitioner argues that LCL's recourse creditor could in a worst case situation obtain a judgment against LCL and cause the DRO to be enforced against HBW so that the recourse creditor could then receive from HBW payments on the recourse notes. Petitioner asserts that Wyo. Stat. Ann. sec. 17-15-121(a) and (c) allows a member of a limited liability company to promise to contribute additional capital to the company and permits a creditor of the company to enforce that promise in order to receive payment on a debt owed to the creditor by the company.

As discussed in detail below, we disagree with petitioner's argument and assertion as applied to the facts at hand. First, from a factual point of view, HBW did not through the DRO make an unconditional promise to contribute additional capital to LCL. To the contrary, the DRO requires that HBW contribute additional capital to LCL only if: (1) HBW liquidates its interest in LCL and (2) then has a deficit in its capital account. For this purpose, as discussed further below, LCL's recourse creditor has no right to force HBW to liquidate its interest in LCL to cause an additional contribution under the DRO. Hence, HBW's personal liability for repayment of LCL's recourse debt is neither fixed nor definite but is generally contingent on HBW voluntarily causing a liquidation of its interest in LCL. Even then, HBW's contribution of additional capital is required under the DRO only if HBW then has a deficit capital account. Second, even if both conditions are met, the DRO does not impose on HBW an obligation to contribute funds in the amount necessary to satisfy its proportionate share of any unpaid debt owed by LCL; the DRO simply requires that HBW contribute funds equal to the amount of the deficit in HBW's capital account, which may or may not be the same as the amount of HBW's proportionate share of LCL's recourse debt. Third, even if HBW actually makes an additional contribution to LCL's capital under the DRO, the DRO does not require that any of the additional contribution be paid to one or more of LCL's creditors. The DRO states specifically that LCL may transfer the additional contribution to its members with positive capital accounts.

Congress enacted section 465 to limit the use of artificial losses created by deductions from certain leveraged investment activities. Section 465(a)(1) provides that a taxpayer who is engaged in certain activities may deduct losses occurring from these activities only to the extent that the taxpayer is "at risk" for such activities at the close of a taxable year. Equipment leasing, which is the type of activity involved in this case, comes within the terms of these at-risk activities. See sec. 465(c)(1)(C).

Under section 465(b)(1)(A), a taxpayer is at risk for amounts of money and the adjusted basis of other property contributed by the taxpayer to the designated activity. The basis of property, under section 1012, is generally defined as cost and that cost is increased or decreased, i.e., adjusted, as permitted pursuant to section 1016. Under section 465(b)(2), a taxpayer also is at risk for amounts borrowed for use in the activity to the extent that the taxpayer is "personally liable for the repayment of such amounts" or to the extent that the taxpayer has pledged property, other than the property used in the activity, as security for such borrowed amounts. A taxpayer is not at risk with respect to amounts protected against loss through nonrecourse financing, guaranties, stop loss agreements, or other similar arrangements. See sec. 465(b)(4). The mere fact that a debt of a partnership (or similar entity) is payable in a later year by the partner does not necessarily mean that the partner must exclude the amount of that debt from the computation of the partner's at-risk amount with respect to the partnership. See *Melvin v. Commissioner*, 88 T.C. at 73-74.

This case is appealable to the Court of Appeals for the Sixth Circuit. That court has analyzed the at-risk provisions of section 465 in the setting of leases in three primary opinions; namely, *Pledger v. United States*, 236 F.3d 315 (6th Cir. 2000), *Martuccio v. Commissioner*, 30 F.3d 743, 750-751 (6th Cir. 1994), revg. T.C. Memo. 1992-311, and *Emershaw v. Commissioner*, 949 F.2d 841 (6th Cir. 1991), *affg.* T.C. Memo. 1990-246. In each of these cases, the court applied the "payor of last resort" test that it first adopted in *Emershaw*. That test essentially asks in the setting of section 465(b) whether the taxpayer has a fixed and definite obligation to use personal funds to pay a debt in a worst case scenario. See also *Pritchett v. Commissioner*, 827 F.2d 644, 647 (9th Cir. 1987) (a taxpayer is not at risk if the taxpayer's obligation to repay borrowed funds is contingent), revg. on other grounds 85 T.C. 580 (1985). Under this test, if a taxpayer is a payor of last resort, then the taxpayer is at risk for the purpose of section 465(b).

In determining whether the taxpayers in *Emershaw v. Commissioner, supra*, were payors of last resort, the Court of Appeals for the Sixth Circuit initially referenced a Tax Court opinion stating that whether a taxpayer is at risk for purposes of section 465(b) " 'must be resolved on the basis of who realistically will be the payor of last resort if the transaction goes sour and the secured property associated with the transaction is not adequate to pay off the debt.' " *Id.* at 845 (quoting *Levy v. Commissioner*, 91 T.C. 838, 869 (1988)). The Court of Appeals gave detailed consideration to the Commissioner's argument that the taxpayers' investment could not be at risk because there was not a realistic possibility that the taxpayers would ever be called upon to make payments on the debt. *Id.* The court dismissed that argument as unpersuasive and found that the taxpayers were at risk because they could ultimately be required to make payment. *Id.* at 850. The court concluded that the taxpayers were payors of last resort because they might have to pay the debt.

Here, in a worst case scenario, HBW is not a payor of last resort as to LCL's recourse debt. In such a scenario, LCL defaults on the debt without any assets to repay any of the debt. LCL's default, however, does not mean that the recourse creditor can simply turn to HBW to collect any part of the debt. HBW's obligation under the DRO requires in part that HBW liquidate its interest in LCL, and LCL's default on its payment of its recourse debt does not trigger a liquidation of HBW's interest in LCL (or of LCL itself). Nor in a worst case scenario could LCL's recourse creditor recover directly from HBW or compel a dissolution of LCL so as to force a liquidation of HBW's interest in LCL. The revised operating agreement states that LCL shall be liquidated upon its "dissolution" and that dissolution occurs "only as provided by the Wyoming LLC Act." Under that act, the dissolution of a limited liability company occurs only upon the happening of one of three events, none of which is the company's default on the payment of a debt. See Wyo. Stat. Ann. sec. 17-15-123(a). Thus, LCL's default on its obligation to repay the recourse notes would not entitle LCL's recourse creditor to compel the dissolution of LCL. The DRO also would not apply to HBW if LCL defaulted on its debt and HBW had a positive capital account following a liquidation of HBW's interest in LCL. Given that the DRO requires additional capital contributions only when a member "has a deficit Capital Account following the liquidation of * * * its interest" in LCL and that no creditor of LCL could compel a liquidation of HBW's interest in LCL, we conclude that HBW is not a payor of last resort because HBW is not "personally liable for the repayment" of any of LCL's recourse debt within the meaning of section 465(b)(2)(A). In other words, we conclude that HBW is not personally liable for the repayment of any of LCL's recourse debt because HBW's obligation to contribute additional funds to LCL is not unavoidable in that HBW can avoid contributing additional capital under the DRO simply by not liquidating. See *Callahan v. Commissioner*, 98 T.C. at 283.

Petitioner relies erroneously on Wyo. Stat. Ann. sec. 17-15-121(a) and (c), to support a contrary conclusion. As petitioner sees it, that section allows a member of a limited liability company to promise to contribute additional capital to the company and permits a creditor of the company to enforce that promise in order to receive payment on a debt owed by the company to the creditor. We disagree with petitioner's application of this section to the facts at hand. As stated above, the operation of the DRO hinges on a liquidation of a member's interest in LCL, and a creditor of LCL has no right to compel such a liquidation. Further, the revised operating agreement does not require LCL to pay the restored deficit to creditors; it allows this amount to be distributed to members with positive capital account balances. Further, the revised operating agreement does not confer any rights on a creditor of LCL. The agreement states specifically that nothing express or implied therein "shall be construed to give to any person or entity, other than the parties or their successors-in-interest * * *, any rights or remedies hereunder or by reason hereof." We also note the illogic of petitioner's argument that the DRO in and of itself makes HBW at risk for the repayment of LCL's recourse debt. As we have stated, a DRO is routinely inserted into a partnership agreement to meet the substantial economic effect requirements of section 704(b). If a member of a limited liability company is automatically "at risk" for repayment of the company's recourse debt simply by inserting a DRO in the operating agreement in order to meet the requirements of section 704(b), then the at-risk rules of section 465 have little purpose in that seemingly every member of a limited liability company is at risk for the repayment of the company's recourse debt.

The limited amount of any capital contribution under the DRO further supports our conclusion that HBW was not a payor of last resort as to LCL's recourse debt. Under the DRO, HBW's obligation is limited to restoring the amount of any deficit in its capital account. However, the amount of that deficit, if in fact one occurs, is not necessarily the same amount as HBW's proportionate share of LCL's recourse debt. Moreover, as just noted, the revised operating agreement does not require LCL to pay any or all of the restored deficit to creditors; it allows LCL to distribute any restored funds to members with positive capital account balances.

We hold that the DRO did not render HBW a payor of last resort under the applicable law. Instead, the person who bears the risk of loss on a default on LCL's recourse obligations is LCL's recourse creditor itself. Such a fact is not surprising, however, in that it is that creditor that chose to deal with LCL in its status as a limited liability company and through the terms of the promissory notes agreed to seek repayment solely from the assets of LCL rather than also from the assets of one or more of LCL's members. . . .

NOTES AND COMMENTS

1. Despite the fact that a taxpayer may be personally liable for amounts borrowed with respect to an activity, a liability will not be included in a taxpayer's at-risk amount if the lender has an interest in the activity other than that of a creditor or if the lender is related to a person with an interest in the activity other than that of a creditor. § 465(b)(3); Treas. Reg. § 1.465-8(a). A person is generally deemed related to the lender by applying the related party rules of § 267(b) or § 707(b)(1) but with the ownership requirements reduced from 50 percent to 10 percent. § 465(b)(3)(C).

The statutory language "interest (other than an interest as a creditor)" is not defined in § 465 or in the legislative history of the Tax Reform Act of 1976, which enacted § 465. However, the General Explanation of the Tax Reform Act of 1976 states that the language was intended to include any person who stands to receive financial gain from the activity. Staff of Joint Comm. on Taxation, General Explanation of the Tax Reform Act of 1976, at 39, 1976-3 C.B. (Vol. 2) 51. The Regulations do not adopt as expansive a definition of a prohibited interest as might be expected. Under the Regulations, a prohibited interest is limited to either a capital interest in the activity or an interest in the net profits of the activity. Treas. Reg. § 1.465-8(b)(1). A capital interest is an interest in the assets of the activity which is distributable to the owner of the capital interest on the liquidation of the activity. Treas. Reg. § 1.465-8(b)(2). A person may have a prohibited profits interest in the activity even though he has no incidents of ownership in the activity as, for example, an employee or independent contractor whose compensation may be determined in whole or in part by the net profits of the activity. Treas. Reg. § 1.465-8(b)(3). *See Pritchett v. Commissioner*, 56 T.C.M. (CCH) 1070, T.C. Memo.

1989-21, *aff'd in an unpublished op.*, 944 F.2d 908 (9th Cir. 1991) (applying the capital and a net profits interest test under the Regulations as proposed to determine if a prohibited interest existed). *See also Levy v. Commissioner*, 91 T.C. 838 (1988); *Larsen v. Commissioner*, 89 T.C. 1229 (1987), *aff'd in part, rev'd in part and remanded sub nom., Casebeer v. Commissioner*, 909 F.2d 1360 (9th Cir. 1990); *Bennion v. Commissioner*, 88 T.C. 684 (1987); *Waddell v. Commissioner*, 86 T.C. 848 (1986), *aff'd*, 841 F.2d 264 (9th Cir. 1988); and *Jackson v. Commissioner*, 86 T.C. 492 (1986), *aff'd*, 864 F.2d 1521 (10th Cir. 1989).

2. Although losses from an activity cannot be deducted in excess of a taxpayer's at-risk amount, the at-risk amount can become negative if the taxpayer withdraws money or property from the activity or is relieved of personal liability, in whole or in part, for a liability that was previously included in the taxpayer's at-risk amount. Prop. Treas. Reg. § 1.465-3. Section 465(e) requires that the taxpayer include an amount in gross income in the current taxable year equal to the amount that, at the close of a taxable year, the taxpayer's at-risk amount is negative. § 465(e)(1)(A). Thus, § 465(e) requires that a taxpayer recapture as gross income the deduction of any previously allowed losses to the extent that the taxpayer is no longer at-risk for those losses as measured by his at-risk amount. In no event, however, is the income inclusion to exceed the amount of losses previously allowed under § 465, minus any income inclusion under § 465(e) in a prior year. § 465(e)(2). In the following taxable year, the taxpayer will be allowed to claim as an additional deduction from the activity an amount equal to the inclusion in gross income in the prior year. § 465(e)(1)(B). The effect of this rule is to allow the taxpayer to deduct the recaptured loss in the future if the taxpayer subsequently has a positive at-risk amount. Importantly, the taxpayer is not permitted to offset the amount included in gross income under § 465(e) with losses from the current taxable year or with suspended losses from any prior taxable year. Thus, the income inclusion under § 465(e) will increase the taxpayer's taxable income and generate an increased tax liability. Although § 465(e)(1)(A) specifies only that the recaptured amount is includable in the taxpayer's gross income, this result is attributable to the statutory language under § 465(d) providing that the income inclusion is not to be taken into account for purposes of computing the loss generated by the activity for the taxable year. *See* S. Rep. No. 96-498, 96th Cong., 1st Sess. 43-44 (1980) (describing the enactment of the parenthetical phrase "determined without regard to subsection (e)(1)(A)" in § 465(d)).

Section 465 as originally enacted did not include § 465(e), which was not enacted until 1978. Prior to that time, recourse liabilities of the activity would be included in the taxpayer's at-risk amount, allowing the taxpayer to deduct losses generated by the activity. The liabilities were frequently structured to become nonrecourse, relieving the taxpayer of personal liability, in the future, typically coinciding with the time that the activity was no longer generating losses. At the time that the liability converted from being recourse to nonrecourse, the taxpayer's at-risk amount would frequently become negative as a result of the deduction of losses in prior years. In the absence of § 465(e), however, taxpayers suffered no adverse tax impact although they had previously deducted losses for tax purposes for which they no longer confronted an economic risk of loss. The Proposed Regulations attempted to distinguish between recourse liabilities with such a conversion feature which could properly be included the taxpayer's at-risk amount and those that could not by considering whether the reasons for entering into such an arrangement were primarily business motivated as opposed to tax motivated and whether the arrangement was consistent with normal commercial financing practices. Prop. Treas. Reg. § 1.465-5. The Service also issued a number of Revenue Rulings with respect to this issue. *See, e.g.*, Rev. Rul. 82-225, 1982-2 C.B. 100 (concluding that an investor will not be considered "at risk" for a recourse note that may be converted into a nonrecourse note where the criteria for conversion do not require that the underlying property be of sufficient value to cover the amount of the note); Rev. Rul. 81-283, 1981-2 C.B. 115 (concluding an investor will not be considered at risk where the reason for requiring the investor to be personally liable during the initial seven-year period was to increase the investor's amount at risk in the activity and that the option permitting the investor to convert the liability into a nonrecourse obligation was available only at a point where the property has reached the end of the life used for depreciation purposes). The recapture provision of § 465(e) largely eliminates the issues encountered in this regard.

§ 4.03. Stop Loss Agreements

A taxpayer's at-risk amount does not include any amount contributed to the activity or debt for which the taxpayer is personally liable if the taxpayer is protected from the economic risk of loss through any "nonrecourse financing, guarantees, stop loss agreements, or other similar arrangements." § 465(b)(4). In describing this aspect of the bill, the legislative history stated that "a taxpayer's capital is not 'at risk' in the business, even as to the equity which he has contributed to the extent he is protected against economic loss of all or part of such capital by reason of an agreement or arrangement for compensation or reimbursement to him of any loss which he may suffer." S. Rep. No. 94-938, 94th Cong., 2d Sess. 49 (1976).

As an example of a "stop loss" agreement, the legislative history referred to livestock feeding operations in which commercial feedlots offered to reimburse investors against any loss sustained on sales of the fed livestock above a stated dollar amount per head. Under § 465, the investor would only be considered to be at risk to the extent that he was not entitled to reimbursement. *Id.* As an example of other similar arrangements, the legislative history referred to limited partnership investments involving the breeding or livestock, in which the limited partnership agreed to repurchase, at the limited partner's election, the partner's partnership interest for a stated minimum dollar amount that was usually less than the partner's original capital contribution. In such a situation, the limited partner would be considered at risk only to the extent that the capital contribution exceeded the guaranteed repurchase price. *Id.* Finally, the legislative history also described the situation in which a limited partner who assumes personal liability on a loan to the partnership is indemnified by the general partner against some or all of any loss that might arise. In such a situation, the limited partner is at risk only to the extent of the indebtedness in excess of the minimum amount covered by the indemnity agreement. *Id.* n.5.

Importantly, the assumption is to be made that, in each of these situations, the agreement or arrangement will be fully honored and that the amount due the taxpayer will be paid. The possibility that the other guaranteeing or indemnifying party will fail to carry out the agreement because of insolvency or other financial difficulty is not material "unless and until the time when the taxpayer becomes unconditionally entitled to payment and, at that time, demonstrates that he cannot recover under the agreement." *Id.* at 50, n.6.

The following decision considers the application of § 465(b)(4) in the context of a sale-leaseback transaction. The statements in the legislative history were crucial to the court's analysis. Although the Ninth Circuit concluded that the sale-leaseback transaction constituted an "other similar arrangement" for purposes of § 465(b)(4), the Sixth Circuit reached the opposite conclusion on substantially identical facts in a subsequent decision.

AMERICAN PRINCIPALS LEASING CORP. v. UNITED STATES

United States Court of Appeals, Ninth Circuit
904 F.2d 477 (9th Cir. 1990)

WIGGINS, CIRCUIT JUDGE.

American Principals Leasing Corporation (APLC) and twenty-four limited partnerships, debtors in a bankruptcy case, appeal the district court's dismissal for lack of bankruptcy jurisdiction of that portion of their complaint seeking to adjudicate the tax consequences of partnership activities or the tax liabilities of non-debtor partners. The United States appeals the district court's judgment for Richard and Mearice Baldwin, partners in one of the limited partnerships, in their tax refund suit for the 1982 taxable year. We have jurisdiction of both cases under 28 U.S.C. § 1291 (1982). We consolidate the cases, affirm the judgment in *American Principals*, and reverse the judgment in *Baldwin*.

BACKGROUND

The facts relevant to these appeals are largely undisputed. APLC is the sole and managing general partner of the limited partnerships and three investment trusts involved in the bankruptcy case. APLC set up the partnerships between 1981 and 1983 to purchase and lease computer equipment. The partnerships have a total of approximately 600 individual partners. . . .

On their federal income tax returns for the 1981, 1982, and 1983 taxable years, the partners in the various limited partnerships each claimed a distributive share of the partnership losses and deductions from the leasing activities. The IRS disallowed these losses and deductions. The Commissioner determined, in part, that the leasing activities were not profit motivated, that the partnerships did not have the benefits and burdens of ownership, that the transactions lacked economic reality, and that the partners were not at risk under I.R.C. § 465. Most of the partners filed petitions in the tax court contesting the Commissioner's determination.

The Baldwins, however, paid their deficiency and sued for refund in the district court. Apparently the leasing transaction underlying the *Baldwin* case is not atypical, and the parties expected that suit to serve as a test case of the tax liability issues. The case arose as follows: The Baldwins were limited partners in June Partners, Ltd., a partnership that APLC formed in 1982 to acquire IBM computer equipment from Softpro, Inc., and lease it to Finalco, Inc. Prior to March 17, 1982, IBM had been leasing certain computer equipment to Southwestern Bell Telephone Company. Between March 17, 1982 and April 1, 1982, the following transactions occurred: IBM sold the equipment to Southwestern for $2,583,288. Southwestern then sold the equipment to Finalco for the same price. Finalco leased the equipment back to Southwestern for 24 months at $106,811 per month. Finalco borrowed $2,089,033 from NSCC Leasing Corporation to finance its purchase and NSCC took a security interest in the equipment and lease to Southwestern. Southwestern's payments to Finalco on the lease equalled Finalco's payments to NSCC on its note and were sufficient to pay that note in 24 months.

On May 28, 1982, the following transactions occurred: Finalco sold the equipment (subject to the lease and to NSCC's security interest) to Softpro; Softpro sold the equipment (subject to the same interests) to June Partners; and June Partners leased the equipment back to Finalco. Softpro paid $4,843,012 to Finalco, consisting of $20,000 in cash, a short-term recourse note for $516,000, and a long-term recourse note for $4,307,012. June Partners paid $4,863,012 to Softpro, consisting of $20,000 in cash, a short-term recourse note for $536,000, and a limited recourse long-term note for $4,307,012. The Baldwins later assumed personal liability for up to $120,000 of June Partners' obligations to Softpro.

Finalco leased the equipment from June Partners for 91 months, at the rate of $43,070.12 per month for the first 31 months and $95,807.10 per month for the remaining 60 months. In addition, Finalco would pay June Partners 75% of net rentals received from Finalco's subleasing the equipment to any third-party user (including Southwestern Bell) for months 22 through 91 of the lease.

Both the long-term note that Softpro gave to Finalco and the long-term note that June Partners gave to Softpro provided for 31 interest only monthly payments of $43,070.12, followed by 60 principal and interest monthly payments of $95,807.10. Thus, the payments on June Partners' long-term note to Softpro, the payments on Softpro's long-term note to Finalco, and the minimum payments on Finalco's lease from June Partners were all identical. No party had sufficient resources to make its payments without receiving the payments due it. The parties, therefore, satisfied the three equal obligations each month by offsetting bookkeeping entries. No cash ever changed hands.

On the parties' cross-motions for partial summary judgment, the district court determined that the Baldwins were at risk for their assumption of up to $120,000 of June Partners' obligations to Softpro. In the bench trial that followed, the district court decided that the transaction had economic substance, that it was entered into with a reasonable expectation of profit, and that the purchase price of the equipment was at fair market value.

Following judgment for the Baldwins, the United States informed the partnerships that it planned to appeal the decision in *Baldwin*. Since the facts of the leasing transactions might vary, the United States also made clear that it planned to litigate individually the tax consequences of each partnership's activities. Desiring a quick and integrated resolution of the tax issues, APLC and the partnerships then filed in the district court, sitting in bankruptcy, a complaint for declaratory relief concerning the tax consequences for APLC and the other partners of the various partnerships' activities. The district court granted the government's motion to dismiss for lack of bankruptcy jurisdiction as to all plaintiffs but APLC.

DISCUSSION

* * *

The Internal Revenue Code provides that a taxpayer generally may take a deduction from leasing depreciable property only to the extent that he is at risk in the leasing activity. I.R.C. § 465(a)(1), (c)(1)(C). A taxpayer is at risk for the amount of cash he has contributed to an activity and for the amount he has borrowed with personal liability for use in the activity. I.R.C. § 465(b)(1), (2). The government agrees that the Baldwins borrowed with personal liability $120,000 for use in June Partners when the Baldwins assumed up to $120,000 liability on June Partners' recourse long-term note to Softpro. The government argues, however, that June Partners' debt to Softpro, and thus the Baldwins' assumption of part of that debt, falls within two of section 465's express exclusions from at risk treatment.

The government first argues that the circular nature of the obligations of June Partners, Softpro, and Finalco protected the Baldwins from ever being required to satisfy their liability on June Partners' note, and thus constituted a loss-limiting arrangement excepted from at risk treatment by I.R.C. § 465(b)(4), which provides:

> (4) Exception. Notwithstanding any other provision of this section, a taxpayer shall not be considered at risk with respect to amounts protected against loss through nonrecourse financing, guarantees, stop loss agreements, or other similar arrangements.

The statute nowhere explains the phrase "other similar arrangements" and on the parties' cross-motions for partial summary judgment, the district court rejected the government's argument, stating "if Finalco became insolvent the partners could still be called upon to make payments on the debt for which they had assumed responsibility." Memorandum Decision and Order Granting Partial Summary Judgment at 10-11. We review de novo a district court's findings on summary judgment. *In re Walker*, 861 F.2d 597, 599 (9th Cir. 1988).

We believe that although the district court's analysis of whether a taxpayer would legally be responsible for his debt in a worst-case scenario is proper to determine whether under subsection 465(b)(2) a taxpayer is personally liable for amounts he has borrowed for use in an activity, *Pritchett v. Commissioner*, 827 F.2d 644, 647 (9th Cir. 1987) (quoting *Melvin v. Commissioner*, 88 T.C. 63, 75 (1987), *affirmed*, 894 F.2d 1072 (9th Cir. 1990)), such analysis is improper to determine whether the taxpayer has engaged in a loss-limiting arrangement prohibited by subsection 465(b)(4). For example, contrary to the district court's rationale, the legislative history of subsection 465(b)(4) shows that Congress intended to exclude the possibility that financial difficulty would prevent a guarantor from reimbursing a taxpayer for a loss from the subsection 465(b)(4) calculus:

> For purposes of [subsection 465(b)(4)], it will be assumed that a loss-protection guarantee, repurchase agreement or insurance policy will be fully honored and that the amounts due thereunder will be fully paid to the taxpayer. The possibility that the party making the guarantee to the taxpayer, or that a partnership which agrees to repurchase a partner's interest at an agreed price, will fail to carry out the agreement (because of factors such as insolvency or other financial difficulty) is not to be material unless and until the time when the taxpayer becomes unconditionally entitled to payment and, at that time, demonstrates that he cannot recover under the agreement.

S. Rep. No. 938, 94th Cong., 2d Sess. 50 n. 6 (1976) . . . . And subsection 465(b)(4)'s use of the term "arrangement" rather than "agreement" indicates that a binding contract is not necessary for this subsection to be applicable. . . .

Rather, the purpose of subsection 465(b)(4) is to suspend at risk treatment where a transaction is structured — by whatever method — to remove any realistic possibility that the taxpayer will suffer an economic loss if the transaction turns out to be unprofitable. *See Melvin*, 894 F.2d 1072, slip op. at 666. A theoretical possibility that the taxpayer will suffer economic loss is insufficient to avoid the applicability of this subsection. We must be guided by economic reality. *See id.* 894 F.2d 1072, slip op. at 668; *Pritchett*, 827 F.2d at 647. If at some future date the unexpected occurs and the taxpayer does suffer a loss, or a realistic possibility develops that the taxpayer will suffer a loss, the taxpayer will at that time become at risk and be able to take the deductions for previous years that were suspended under this subsection. I.R.C. § 465(a)(2).

The Baldwins base their argument that subsection 465(b)(4) does not countenance their situation on the theoretical possibility that Finalco could refuse to pay its rent and, since its refusal would not compromise its right to enforce Softpro's obligations to it or Softpro's right to enforce June Partners' obligations to Softpro, June Partners could still be called upon to satisfy its obligations to Softpro. It is true that the government has directed this court to no evidence that June Partners' note to Softpro is contingent upon Finalco discharging its obligations to June Partners. We believe, however, that the Baldwins nevertheless fall within subsection 465(b)(4).

No realistic possibility exists that June Partners (and, thus, the Baldwins) would suffer any economic loss if its leasing transaction turned out unprofitable. All three parties to the transaction lacked the independent means to pay their obligations, and so they satisfied their circular obligations each month by offsetting bookkeeping entries. The Baldwins point to no circumstance under which one of the parties would break the chain of "payments," or even demand that its obligee satisfy its obligations in cash (or sell its note to an outside party who would demand a cash payment). Indeed, no party could expect any benefit from doing so. Given that no party had the means to meet its obligations without its obligee's payments, if one party failed to "pay", he could only expect a chain reaction resulting in his obligor's ceasing "payment" as well. And if one party demanded cash payments from its obligee, he could only expect a similar chain reaction resulting in his obligor's demand for a cash payment, which he would be unable to make.

We find, therefore, that the Baldwins were not at risk for their assumption of personal liability for up to $120,000 of June Partners' obligations to Softpro and the district court erred in concluding to the contrary. Our resolution of the applicability of subsection 465(b)(4) to the Baldwins' case makes consideration of the government's second argument unnecessary.

HUG, CIRCUIT JUDGE, dissenting:

* * *

I. *Summary*

This is not the case of a sham tax shelter arrangement. The district court found, after hearing reliable expert testimony, that the $4,863,012 purchase price for the computer equipment represented fair market value. The district court further found that the transaction had economic substance and that it was entered into with a reasonable expectation of profit. The Government does not contest these findings on appeal.

The June Partners' partnership is clearly at risk. The note is a recourse note, and if the lease payments are not made, the partnership is still liable on the note. The majority erroneously interprets section 26 U.S.C. § 465(b)(4) to apply because the lease payments, if they are made, will pay off the note. Section 465(b)(4) was designed to apply to a situation where the taxpayer's risk is eliminated by non-recourse financing, insurance, a guarantee, or some other type of collateral agreement that would preclude the taxpayer from suffering a loss. For example, if there were an agreement that liability on the June Partners' note would be extinguished if the lease payments were not made, then this would be the type of stop-loss agreement contemplated by section 465(b)(4). The section was not designed to apply to the normal business arrangement where a taxpayer procures a loan to buy equipment, leases it and pays off the loan with the lease payments.

II. *Detailed Analysis*

We are here concerned with interpretation of 26 U.S.C. § 465 as applied to this case. Section 465(a) provides that when a taxpayer engages in an activity to which section 465 applies, any loss from such activity for a taxable year shall be allowed only to the extent of the aggregate amount that the taxpayer is "at risk" for such activity at the close of the taxable year. Section 465(b)(1) provides that a taxpayer is "at risk" for the amount of money and the adjusted basis of property contributed. Section 465(b)(2) provides that the taxpayer is also "at risk" for the amounts of money borrowed for use in the activity to the extent he is personally liable for the repayment of such amounts. There are then certain exclusions and exceptions. Section 465(b)(3)(A) excludes from the borrowed amounts considered "at risk" amounts that are borrowed from a person who has an interest in such activity, other than an interest as a creditor. Section 465(b)(4) creates an exception to the above "at risk" provisions. It provides that "notwithstanding any other provisions of this section, a taxpayer shall not be considered at risk with respect to the amounts protected against loss through nonrecourse financing, guarantees, stop loss agreements, or other similar arrangements."

In personally assuming a $120,000 portion of June Partners' $4,307,012 recourse long-term loan, the Baldwins are clearly at risk within the terms of section 465(b)(2) because they are personally liable for repayment. The question is whether either subsection (b)(3)(A) or (b)(4) precludes the transaction from being treated as one in which the taxpayers are "at risk."

Because the majority relies on section 465(b)(4) in reversing the district court, I will first discuss the application of that section. Section 465(b)(4) provides for disallowance of "at risk" treatment for borrowed funds when the taxpayer is "protected against loss through nonrecourse financing, guarantees, stop loss agreements, or other similar arrangements." It is clear that the transaction here in issue does not involve nonrecourse financing, guarantees, or stop-loss agreements. Thus, in order for this section to apply, this transaction must be determined to be an "other similar arrangement."

The majority considers the arrangement whereby the lease payments from Finalco to June Partners are utilized to pay the Softpro note as being "similar" to protection against loss by a guarantee or stop-loss agreement, despite the fact that there is no provision that excuses performance under the note or protects against the loss if the lease payment is not made.

The lease itself is not a similar arrangement. A guarantee and a stop-loss agreement are both binding legal agreements that are directed to protect the borrower against loss on the note itself, and insure against his having to pay it. The note in issue in this case is a negotiable instrument with recourse against the borrower and there is no such binding agreement to protect against loss on the note. All we have here is a lease, the payments on which are sufficient to pay off the loan. There is nothing to prevent Softpro from negotiating June Partners' note to a third party who could collect despite the nonpayment of rent. The obligations are separate. June Partners and, in turn, the Baldwins remain at risk whether the lease payment is made or not.

Suppose, for example, Softpro finds that it needs cash for some business purpose. It can legally factor the note to a third party, perhaps at a discount. Softpro would intend to continue making its payments to Finalco out of its business proceeds. The new noteholder would look to the repayment of the note from June Partners and to the personal liability of the Baldwins for the portion of the indebtedness they assumed. If for some reason Finalco cannot or does not pay the lease payments, perhaps because Softpro does not make payment on its note to Finalco, the noteholder would ultimately look to June Partners' and the Baldwins' personal liability.

The fact that Finalco is legally obligated to pay the rent under the lease is no guarantee that taxpayers will suffer no loss on the note. It is true that, so long as the rent payments are made, June Partners has the funds to pay Softpro. But many things can go wrong and the key is that June Partners and, in turn, the Baldwins are neither absolved on the note nor protected against loss.

We must examine what it is about this arrangement that the Government contends makes it similar to a guarantee or an agreement that the June Partners will not suffer a loss. The fact that they contracted for lease payments to cover the loan cannot be the reason. If June Partners had obtained its loan from a bank and also entered into a lease that was in an amount necessary to make those payments, no one would contend that this constituted another arrangement similar to a guarantee or stop-loss agreement. This is true even if the lessee was a solid Fortune 500 company. This would be just a simple prudent business arrangement.

Does then the fact that the credit and lease arrangement is circular disqualify this under section 465(b)(4)? There is certainly nothing in the statute or legislative history that so provides. Even assuming that Finalco lent directly to June Partners, there is no more of a guarantee, stop-loss or similar agreement than in the situation where the loan was from the bank. Now, of course, if there were an agreement that the liability on the note would be extinguished if the rent was not paid, then there would be a stop-loss type of agreement. A circular arrangement could well involve such an agreement, but the point is that in this case there was none. Indeed, there was such a binding setoff provision in the case of *Klagsbrun v. Commissioner*, 1988 T.C. Memo. 364, 55 T.C.M. (CCH) 1519, relied upon by the majority but that is the crucial feature which distinguishes that case from this one.

Furthermore, in this case we do not have a true circular arrangement because Softpro is the lender to June Partners and June Partners receives the rent from Finalco. The district court found that Softpro is an independent business corporation. There are no organizational ties between Softpro and Finalco — Softpro is not a subsidiary; it does not have interlocking directors; it is an independent computer dealer that buys and sells equipment. It had purchased and sold $140,000,000 in computer equipment.

To have an effective stop-loss agreement in this case there would have to have been a stop-loss or setoff provision in both the June Partners' note to Softpro and the Softpro note to Finalco. There was no such provision.

The third contention of the Government seems to be based on the method of payment. Surely it cannot be seriously contended that the fact that payment was made by offsetting bookkeeping entries rather than sending monthly checks through the mail can have any effect on the underlying legal relationships. No authority is cited for such a proposition and it would indeed be the paragon of form over substance to so hold.

The simple fact of the matter is that section 465(b)(4) was not designed to cover this type of arrangement at all. It was not designed to cover a situation in which the payments on a loan were going to be made from a lease of the equipment, which the loan financed. This is the normal business relationship in most circumstances. Rather, section 465(b)(4) was designed to cover the situation in which the borrower was protected by some collateral arrangement whereby he was protected by an insurance policy, a guarantee, or an agreement that insured that he would not have to pay his note or would be reimbursed if he did.

The Tax Court recognized this in *Gefen v. Commissioner*, 87 T.C. 1471 (1986). In that case, the taxpayer was also a limited partner who had assumed personal liability for a pro rata share of a partnership's recourse indebtedness. The equipment financed was leased to Exxon, and the lease payments covered the loan payments. The Tax Court stated:

> [The Commissioner] argues, however, that because Exxon was a strong credit risk and not likely to default on its lease obligations during the years in question, petitioner was protected against loss and was therefore not at risk within the meaning of section 465 for her pro rata share of the partnership's recourse indebtedness. We reject this argument because we perceive nothing in section 465 or its legislative history that requires an owner of property to enter into a transaction with a party that is a poor credit risk in order to be "at risk" within the meaning of section 465.

The majority misconstrues our recent opinion in *Melvin v. CIR*, 894 F.2d 1072 (9th Cir. 1990). In that case, a limited partner had claimed a loss for the full amount of his recourse note, but we held, in affirming the Tax Court, that he was limited to his pro rata share of the loss because California statutory provisions gave him a legally binding right of contribution against his copartners. We recognized this as a statutory collateral protection against loss and, thus, within the meaning of section 465(b)(4). We noted the legislative history of the section:

As the Senate Finance Committee explained:

> A taxpayer's capital is not . . . "at risk" . . . to the extent he is protected against economic loss of all or part of such capital by reason of an agreement or arrangement for compensation or reimbursement to him of any loss which he may suffer. Under this concept, an investor is not "at risk" if he arranges to receive insurance or other compensation for an economic loss after the loss is sustained, or if he is entitled to reimbursement for part or all of any loss by reason of the binding agreement between himself and another person.

S.Rep. No. 938, 94th Cong., 2d. Sess. 49 (1976) ("Senate Report").

It is important to note that this explanation refers to an arrangement for protection from loss by means of insurance or other compensation "after the loss is sustained." In our case, no loss would be sustained until after the lease payment was not made. The type of protection contemplated by Congress in section 465(b)(4) is protection that comes into play after the loss has been sustained. The statutory right of contribution among partners was such later collateral protection.

The majority acknowledges that the district court was correct in determining that the Baldwins were at risk for purposes of section 465(b)(2) because they bore the ultimate responsibility of Finalco's financial difficulty and nonpayment of the rent. However, the majority states that for purposes of section 465(b)(4) the lease must be evaluated under a different standard and that the possibility of Finalco's inability to pay the lease cannot be considered. The legislative history cited by the majority clearly applies, not to the basic lease transaction but to the collateral insurance against loss arrangements. If a taxpayer obtains this type of loss protection insurance, Congress did not want a collateral issue to be raised concerning the solvency of the insurer or guarantor.

It would make no sense to evaluate the basic lease transaction under section 465(b)(2) and then again under section 465(b)(4). In *Melvin*, we specifically stated that for protection against loss under section 465(b)(4) "we apply the same principles of logic as used to determine a taxpayer's risk in a transaction," (the section 465(b)(2) standard). 894 F.2d at 1075.

The other case relied upon by the majority, *Capek v. Commissioner*, 86 T.C. 14 (1986), involved a third party in effect insuring against a loss on the notes involved. The Tax Court noted the legislative history pertaining to section 465(b)(4).

> [A] taxpayer's capital is not "at risk" in the business, even as to the equity capital which he has contributed to the extent he is protected against economic loss of all or part of such capital by reason of an agreement or arrangement for compensation or reimbursement to him of any loss which he may suffer. Under this concept, an investor is not "at risk" if he arranges to receive insurance or other compensation for an economic loss after the loss is sustained, or if he is entitled to reimbursement for part or all of any loss by reason of a binding agreement between himself and another person.
>
> . . . .
>
> if a taxpayer is personally liable on a mortgage but he separately obtains insurance to compensate him for any payments which he must actually make under such personal liability, the taxpayer is at risk only to the extent of the uninsured portion of the personal liability to which he is exposed. . . . [S. Rept. 94-938, *supra*, 1976-3 C.B. (Vol. 3) at 87-88; fn. refs. omitted.]

Id. at 52.

It is apparent Congress is speaking of a collateral protection against loss — insurance or compensation for loss "after the loss is sustained" or reimbursement for the loss by a binding agreement. The Tax Court noted that it is in this type of collateral agreement that reimburses for the loss after it is sustained that we do not look to the potential insolvency of the party providing the loss protection. *Id.*

In summary, in this case we have no collateral agreement providing reimbursement for or insurance against loss after it is sustained. We have only the lease from Finalco, which is not an arrangement similar to a guarantee or stop-loss agreement. Section 465(b)(4) does not apply.

The majority does not reach the Government's argument that section 465(b)(3)(A) precludes "at risk" treatment and, thus, my discussion will be brief. The Government contends that Softpro was merely a strawman and, thus, ignores it in the transaction. It contends that Finalco is the real lender to June Partners and that it has a prohibited interest under that section. The district court found that Softpro was an independent computer dealer that bought the equipment and then sold it to June Partners. It had the legal responsibilities of a buyer and a seller. The Government's argument that it operated simply as a broker is not supported by the actual legal relationships that were created. There were liabilities and responsibilities undertaken by the purchase and sale of the equipment and Softpro also stood to lose if June Partners did not pay its note. Section 465(b)(3)(A) does not apply.

I would affirm the district court.

NOTES AND COMMENTS

In *Emershaw v. Commissioner*, 949 F.2d 841 (6th Cir. 1991), the Sixth Circuit considered the application of § 465(b)(4) to a sale-leaseback arrangement substantially similar to that in *American Principals Leasing Corp.* In this transaction, CIS Leasing Corporation (CIS) acquired computers and computer peripherals that it leased to several end-users. CIS sold the computers to Program Leasing Corporation (Program) subject to the leases to the end-users, and Program, in turn, sold the computers to Leasing Equipment Associates-83 (LEA). LEA then leased the computers back to CIS. The taxpayers involved, the Emershaws, were partners in LEA. The transaction set up a round-robin of payments among CIS, LEA, and Program. CIS owed LEA rent, LEA owed Program $2,850,300 on a partial recourse promissory note, and Program owed CIS the same amount on a full recourse promissory note. The monthly rental was exactly equal to the amount LEA owed Program and Program owed CIS. No cash actually changed hands as all "payments" were bookkeeping transactions. As in *American Principals Leasing Corp.*, the question was whether the sale-leaseback transaction was a loss-limiting arrangement under § 465(b)(4) such that the Emershaws, as partners in LEA, were not at-risk for their share of the partnership liability between LEA and Program.

The Sixth Circuit rejected the Ninth Circuit's conclusion that an "economic reality" standard applied under § 465(b)(4) rather than the "payor of last resort" standard under § 465(b)(2). According to the Court, "the issue of whether a taxpayer is 'at risk' for purposes of 26 U.S.C. § 465(b)(4) 'must be resolved on the basis of who realistically will be the payor of last resort if the transaction goes sour and the secured property associated with the transaction is not adequate to pay off the debt.' " *Id.* at 845 (quoting *Levy v. Commissioner*, 91 T.C. 838, 869 (1988)). With respect to whether the sale-leaseback transaction itself was a loss-limiting arrangement, the Sixth Circuit found Judge Hug's dissenting opinion in *American Principals Leasing Corp.* "the better reasoned view."

> We do not consider the circular, off-setting group of obligations established by the sale-leaseback transaction at issue here to be, by itself, a loss-limiting arrangement within the meaning of § 465(b)(4). The structure of the obligations of the parties to this transaction does not seem to be a loss-limiting device of any sort. The parties have arranged their transaction to minimize the need for the LEA partners to provide a great deal of cash "up front" in order to participate in the purchase and leasing of computer equipment. Nonetheless, if CIS becomes insolvent because the end-users stop paying rent or for some other reason, the Emershaws and other LEA partners will be called on to satisfy the terms of the partial recourse note. Therefore, their investment is at risk. Consistent with the . . . dissent [in *American Principals Leasing Corp.*], we reject the interpretation of the legislative history of § 465(b)(4) that leads to the opposite conclusion. We see no reason for dismissing the possible bankruptcy of CIS as a mere

theoretical possibility. In fact, it has already occurred, as we learned during oral argument.

* * *

We agree with the conclusion of the . . . dissent [in *American Principals Leasing Corp.*] . . . that a loss-limiting arrangement within the meaning of § 465(b)(4) is a collateral agreement protecting a taxpayer from loss after the losses have occurred, either by excusing him from his obligation to make good on losses or by compensating him for losses he has sustained. . . . Once the taxpayer has entered into such an arrangement, it is improper to inquire into the solvency of the insurer or guarantor in determining whether the taxpayer's investment is "at risk." . . . This is the significance of the passage . . . from the legislative history of § 465(b)(4). That passage states that the solvency of a guarantor or insurer is irrelevant in determining whether a taxpayer's capital is at risk. The [*American Principals Leasing Corp.*] majority and the Commissioner have interpreted the passage by reading it as if it referred to the insolvency of any party to an investment transaction. We think this incorrect. In the main, the passage speaks of collateral agreements. Even when the passage presents a hypothetical case in which one limited partner buys out another in order to protect the latter from loss, such an arrangement must be considered in the nature of a collateral guarantee.

* * *

We see no reason to extend the logic of the passage from the Senate Report . . . beyond its explicit discussion of the effect of a collateral arrangement on the "at risk" status of an investment. For a taxpayer, the potential insolvency of a company on which an investment depends is the critical risk affecting an investment decision. The Emershaws have invested, albeit indirectly, in CIS. The risk they have assumed is that CIS will fail. As the . . . dissent [in *American Principals Leasing Corp.*] astutely suggests, they are in the position of an investor who buys rental property with a bank loan and then rents the property out for a sum equal to his monthly installment on the loan. . . . If such a transaction were within the terms of § 465, no one would argue that the investor was not at risk for the amount he had borrowed, even though he is "protected" as long as the lessee pays, and even though the lessee is creditworthy. If the lessee defaults on the rent, the investor must still make payments on the note.

In this case, the Commissioner has presented no collateral agreement that would relieve the Emershaws of their obligations under LEA's partial recourse note should CIS stop paying rent or that would satisfy the Emershaws' obligations for them. For this reason, we hold that they were "at risk" within the meaning of 26 U.S.C. § 465 for their pro rata share of LEA's partial recourse note.

* * *

The Commissioner's brief makes it clear that what he finds most unsettling about the sale-leaseback transaction in this case is the circle of off-setting obligations and payments and the fact that the payments are made by bookkeeping entries. The . . . majority [in *American Principals Leasing Corp.*] argues that in such a case there is no realistic possibility that a part in the position of LEA would suffer any economic loss if the transaction turned out unprofitable, because all three parties lacked the independent means to pay their obligations. See [*American Principals Leasing Corp.*], 904 F.2d at 483. Therefore, the . . . majority [in *American Principals Leasing Corp.*] said, they satisfied them by means of off-setting bookkeeping entries. Since none of them has independent means, none has any interest in disrupting the circle of payments by demanding cash from the others or withholding its own fictitious payments.

In this case, the Commissioner asserts that LEA had no independent means to satisfy any of its obligations other than the rental payments from CIS, which it received in the form of bookkeeping entries. He concedes that he does not know if Program and CIS were in the same position. Nonetheless, he concludes, as the . . . majority [in *American Principals Leasing Corp.*] did, that because of the circle of off-setting obligations, the Emershaw are not "at risk," because there is no "realistic possibility that the taxpayer will suffer any out-of-pocket loss if the transaction is unsuccessful." Brief for the Appellant, at 20 (citing [*American Principals Leasing Corp.*], 904 F.2d at 483).

We are at a loss to understand this argument. [An] example will illustrate our perplexity. Let us imagine that instead of using a system of off-setting bookkeeping entries, the three entities in this transaction paid each other by check. CIS would write a check to LEA for the rent. LEA would endorse the check over to Program as payment on its installment note. Finally, Program would endorse the same check over to CIS as payment on its note. We do not see how such an arrangement is essentially different from a sequence of off-setting bookkeeping transactions. We further do not see how either arrangement exempts the transaction from risk. Ultimately, the end-users of the computers and the equipment in this case must come up with cash to pay CIS so that it can pay IBM. If this does not occur, CIS becomes insolvent; the investment goes sour; and the LEA partners are called upon to pay on the partnership's note.

The structure of the transaction in this case minimizes the need for a large initial cash outlay by any of the LEA partners. It does not minimize the risk that "the taxpayer will suffer any out-of-pocket loss if the transaction is unsuccessful." That risk depends on whether or not CIS loses its end-user leases and becomes bankrupt. If it does, the LEA partners will be called on to pay their share of LEA's obligations to Program. The circle of off-setting obligations does nothing to affect this risk, let alone eliminate it, realistically, probably, or otherwise. It is true, as the Commissioner contends, that none of the entities that are party to this transaction have an incentive to demand cash from any other entity. Neither do they have an incentive to introduce cash payments into the circle of off-setting obliga-

> tions by selling any of the promissory notes in the transaction. We do not see the relevance of these facts. Plainly, this sale-leaseback was structured so as to avoid the need for investors to commit large sums of cash to it. As a result, they have little cash "at risk" in this transaction, but the tax code makes it quite clear that an investor is "at risk" not only for the cash contributed to an activity but for "amounts borrowed with respect to such activity . . . for which he is personally liable." 26 U.S.C. § 465(b)(1)(B) & (b)(2)(A). In other words, the tax code recognizes that a taxpayer may invest not only cash but also credit. When the Commissioner asserts that LEA has no "independent means" to satisfy its obligations, he can only mean that it has no present cash income. He is ignoring the fact that the LEA partners, including the Emershaws, have invested their credit in this transaction and that LEA can call on them to pay its note to Program. At that time, they will have to come up with cash. For this reason, the LEA partners are the "payors of last resort," and they are "at risk" in this transaction for sums represented by the partial recourse note LEA issued to Program.

Id. at 848–851.

Interestingly, one judge on the three-judge panel dissented, citing the majority opinion in *American Principals Leasing Corp.* as support for his conclusion. In Judge Cohn's view, "section 465's 'at risk' requirement looks to a realistic possibility that the taxpayer may be required to make good on the partial recourse note involved here. . . . In short, the circular sale-leaseback transaction at issue in this case removed any realistic possibility that the investors would suffer an economic loss." *Id.* at 851.

§ 4.04. Qualified Nonrecourse Financing

Prior to 1987, the at-risk rules did not apply to the activity of holding real estate. When enacted in 1976, § 465 applied only to certain covered activities described in § 465(c)(1). In 1978, when Congress expanded the scope of the at-risk rules to apply to all activities engaged in by a taxpayer in carrying on a trade or business or for the production of income under § 465(c)(3) in addition to the originally covered activities under § 465(c)(1), a specific exception was enacted that excluded the holding of real property. As a result, the at-risk rules reduced the attractiveness of certain tax shelter investments, but tax shelters involving real estate investments continued to proliferate throughout the early 1980s.

As described in § 5 below, Congress subsequently addressed the specific problem of real estate tax shelters as well as some of the inadequacies of the at-risk rules in limiting tax shelter investments more generally in 1986 through the enactment of the passive loss limitations under § 469. At that time, Congress also extended the scope of the activities covered by the at-risk rules to include the holding of real property. However, Congress provided a significant exception from the requirements of § 465 for so-called "qualified nonrecourse financing" under § 465(b)(6). Under this provision, a taxpayer is considered at-risk with respect to any qualified nonrecourse financing, despite the fact that the taxpayer is not personally liable for the repayment of such financing, provided the financing is incurred in an activity of holding real property and is secured by real property used in the activity. § 465(b)(6)(A); Treas. Reg. § 1.465-27(a). As a general matter, this provision was intended principally to exclude from the at-risk determination nonrecourse financing by the seller of real property because of concerns regarding the incentives of both the buyer and seller in such instances to overvalue the property in order to generate tax benefits. H.R. Rep. No. 426, 99th Cong., 1st Sess. 293 91986). As stated in the House Report:

> The committee believes it is appropriate to apply the at-risk rules to real estate activities so as to limit the opportunity for overvaluation of property (resulting in inflated deductions.) . . .
>
> Nonrecourse financing by the seller of real property (or a person related to the seller) is not treated as an amount at risk under the bill, because there may be little or no incentive to limit the amount of such financing to the value of the property. In the case of an arm's length third party commercial financing secured solely by the real property, however, the lender is much less likely to make loans which exceed the property's value or which cannot be serviced by the property; it is more likely that such financing will be repaid and that the purchaser consequently has or will have real equity in the activity.

Id. Thus, § 465(b)(6) resolves much of the concern regarding the overvaluation of property in transactions involving seller-provided nonrecourse financing that were addressed in such cases as *Estate of Franklin v. Commissioner*, 544 F.2d 1045 (9th Cir. 1976), and *Pleasant Summit Land Corp. v. Commissioner*, 863 F.2d 263 (3d Cir. 1988), in which the courts considered the extent to which nonrecourse debt should be included in basis for purposes of determining depreciation and interest deductions.

Qualified nonrecourse financing includes any financing that is borrowed by the taxpayer with respect to the activity of holding real property from a qualified person for which no person is personally liable and which is not convertible debt. § 465(b)(6)(B); Treas. Reg. § 1.465-27(b)(1). In addition to a loan from a qualified person, the lender of qualified nonrecourse financing may be any federal, state, or local government or a loan guaranteed by any federal, state, or local government. A qualified person is any person who is actively and regularly engaged in the business of lending money to a person related to the taxpayer, the person from whom the property is acquired, or a person who receives a fee with respect to the taxpayer's investment in the property. §§ 49(a)(1)(D)(iv) and 465(b)(6)(D)(i). Financing will still be deemed qualified nonrecourse financing if the lender is related to the taxpayer provided the financing is commercially reasonable and on substantially the same terms as loans from unrelated persons. § 465(b)(6)(D)(ii). A partner's share of any qualified nonrecourse financing obtained by the partnership is determined under the rules of § 752. § 465(b)(6)(C).

PROBLEM FOR DISCUSSION

Problem 8-5. On January 1 of Year 1, T acquires a widget-making machine for $1,000,000, paying $100,000 of his own funds and the proceeds of a $900,000 nonrecourse loan from a third-party lender. Interest on the loan is at 10 percent compounded annually. The loan is payable over a 10-year period with annual principal and interest payments of $146,471 per year payable on December 31 of each year. Upon acquisition, T immediately leases the machine to a widget-making company for a term of 10 years with annual rent of $160,000 payable on December 31 of each year. The lessee will be responsible for all costs of maintaining and insuring the machine. The widget-making machine is five-year property under § 168, but T will take no deduction under either § 168(k) or § 179. T's marginal tax rate is 35 percent.

(a) What will happen under § 465 if T retains the property through Year 10?

(b) What will happen under § 465 if the loan is recourse? What does it mean to be a recourse loan? How might T structure the loan to be recourse yet expose himself to as little risk as possible?

(c) What if, instead of the investment being made by T, an individual, it is made by a corporation? By an S corporation? By a partnership?

(d) What will happen in (a) if, at the beginning of Year 7, the lessee goes bankrupt, T defaults on the loan, and the mortgagee forecloses?

(e) How is the answer in (a) affected if, instead of a widget-making machine, T acquires real property for $1,000,000? What if the loan is a purchase money mortgage from the seller of the property?

§ 5. PASSIVE LOSSES

I.R.C. § 469

Regs. §§ 1.469-1T(a) through (e)(3), (e)(6), (f), (g)(1) through (4); 1.469-2T(a) through (c)(4), (c)(7), (d)(1) through (d)(6), (d)(8), (e)(1), (f)(1) through (f)(3), (f)(7); 1.469-4; 1.469-5T; 1.469-9 (through example (3))

The Temporary Regulations under § 469 cross reference certain portions of the Regulations that have been finalized. Where this occurs in the assigned portions of the Temporary Regulations, please read those portions of the final Regulations that are cross-referenced.

§ 5.01. In General

The at-risk rules under § 465 were inadequate to prevent taxpayers from engaging in investments that were viewed as abusive tax shelters. In the early 1980s, with an increasing federal deficit, Congress considered whether tax shelters owned by individuals were improperly eroding federal tax revenues. One popular form of tax shelter at the time involved rental real estate, the acquisition of which was frequently financed through nonrecourse loans from third-party lenders. Promoters and syndicators would create limited partnerships to hold such properties, and the limited partnership interests were sold as investments to the public. Frequently, the tax benefits to be realized through such investments were the principal attraction for such investments. Tax losses attributable to depreciation and interest deductions in excess of rental income generated by the real estate held by these partnerships were allocable under the rules of Subchapter

K of the Code to the limited partners. Because the at-risk rules did not apply to real estate investments prior to 1987, the losses were deductible by the limited partners against income from other sources, such as salary and investment income. Although the limited partners would subsequently realize taxable income from their investments as the interest and depreciation deductions declined in future years or upon disposition of the real estate by the partnership, the deductible losses in the early years of the investment generated significant benefits through deferral. However, if the real estate held by the partnership actually increased in value, the sale proceeds in excess of loan balance might be sufficient to pay the resulting tax liability without the limited partners having to contribute additional funds of their own. Importantly, as limited partners, the liability of the investors in such partnerships was limited to the investors' initial capital contributions to the partnership.

The proliferation of tax shelters of this type persuaded Congress in 1986 to enact the passive loss rules under § 469, which prohibit the deduction of losses generated by passive activities against non-passive or investment income of the taxpayer. A passive activity is generally defined as an activity in which the taxpayer does not materially participate. Material participation is determined by examining whether the taxpayer is involved in the operations of the activity on a regular, continuous, and substantial basis. § 469(h)(1). In addition, an activity is generally treated as passive if the taxpayer is involved in the activity only as a limited partner. § 469(h)(2). Finally, rental activities for most taxpayers are passive activities regardless of the level of the taxpayer's participation in the activity. § 469(c)(2) and (4).

The purpose of § 469 and its reliance on the taxpayer's level of participation in the operations of the activity in determining the tax implications of the taxpayer's investment in that activity is described in the following excerpt from the Senate Report of the 1986 Tax Reform Act.

S. Rep. No. 99-313, 99th Cong., 2d Sess. 713-718 (1986)

A. Limitations on Losses and Credits from Passive Activities . . .

Present Law

In general, no limitations are placed on the ability of a taxpayer to use deductions from a particular activity to offset income from other activities. Similarly, most tax credits may be used to offset tax attributable to income from any of the taxpayer's activities.

* * *

In the absence of more broadly applicable limitations on the use of deductions and credits from one activity to reduce tax liability attributable to other activities, taxpayers with substantial sources of positive income are able to eliminate or sharply reduce tax liability by using deductions and credits from other activities, frequently by investing in tax shelters. Tax shelters commonly offer the opportunity to reduce or avoid tax liability with respect to salary or other positive income, by making available deductions and credits, possibly exceeding real economic costs or losses currently borne by the taxpayer, in excess or in advance of income from the shelters.

Reasons for Change

In recent years, it has become increasingly clear that taxpayers are losing faith in the Federal income tax system. This loss of confidence has resulted in large part from the interaction of two of the system's principal features: its high marginal rates (in 1986, 50 percent for a single individual with taxable income in excess of $88,270), and the opportunities it provides for taxpayers to offset income from one source with tax shelter deductions and credits from another.

* * *

Such patterns give rise to a number of undesirable consequences, even aside from their effect in reducing Federal tax revenues. Extensive shelter activity contributes to public concerns that the tax system is unfair, and to the belief that tax is paid only by the naive and the unsophisticated. This, in turn, not only undermines compliance, but encourages further expansion of the tax shelter market, in many cases diverting investment capital from productive activities to those principally or exclusively serving tax avoidance goals.

The committee believes that the most important sources of support for the Federal income tax system are the average citizens who simply report their income (typically consisting predominantly of items such as salaries, wages, pensions, interest, and dividends) and pay tax under the general rules. To the extent that these citizens feel that they are bearing a disproportionate burden with regard to the costs of government because of their unwillingness or inability to engage in tax-oriented investment activity, the tax system itself is threatened.

Under these circumstances, the committee believes that decisive action is needed to curb the expansion of tax sheltering and to restore to the tax system the degree of equity that is a necessary precondition to a beneficial and widely desired reduction in rates. So long as tax shelters are permitted to erode the Federal tax base, a low-rate system can provide neither sufficient revenues, nor sufficient progressivity, to satisfy the general public that tax liability bears a fair relationship to the ability to pay. In particular, a provision significantly limiting the use of tax shelter losses is unavoidable if substantial rate reductions are to be provided to high-income taxpayers without disproportionately reducing the share of total liability under the individual income tax that is borne by high-income taxpayers as a group.

The question of how to prevent harmful and excessive tax sheltering is not a simple one. One way to address the problem would be to eliminate substantially all tax preferences in the Internal Revenue Code. For two reasons, however, the committee believes that this course is inappropriate.

First, while the bill reduces or eliminates some tax preference items that the committee believes do not provide social or economic benefits commensurate with their cost, there are many preferences that the committee believes are socially or economically beneficial. This is especially true when such preferences are used primarily to advance the purposes upon which Congress relied in enacting them, rather than to avoid taxation of income from sources unrelated to the preferred activity.

Second, it would be extremely difficult, perhaps impossible, to design a tax system that measures income perfectly. For example, the statutory allowance for depreciation, even under the normative system used under the bill for alternative minimum tax purposes, reflects broad industry averages, as opposed to providing precise item-by-item measurements. Accordingly, taxpayers with assets that depreciate less rapidly than the average, or that appreciate over time (as may be the case with certain real estate), may engage in tax sheltering even under the minimum tax, unless Congress directly addresses the tax shelter problem.

Even to the extent that rules for the accurate measurement of income can theoretically be devised, such rules may involve undue complexity from the perspective of many taxpayers. For example, a system that required all taxpayers to use a theoretically pure accrual method of accounting (e.g., including unrealized appreciation, and allowing only the amount of depreciation actually incurred for each specific asset in each taxable year) would create serious difficulties in both compliance and administration.

However, when the tax system, in order to avoid such complexity, permits simpler rules to be applied (e.g., generally not taxing unrealized gain, and allowing depreciation based on broad industry averages), opportunities for manipulation are created. Taxpayers may structure transactions specifically to take advantage of the situations in which the simpler rules lead to undermeasurement or deferral of income.

The question of what constitutes a tax shelter that should be subject to limitations is closely related to the question of who Congress intends to benefit when it enacts tax preferences. For example, in providing preferential depreciation for real estate or favorable accounting rules for farming, it was not Congress's primary intent to permit outside investors to avoid tax liability with respect to their salaries by investing in limited partnership syndications. Rather, Congress intends to benefit and provide incentives to taxpayers active in the businesses to which the preferences were directed.

In some cases, the availability of tax preferences to nonparticipating investors has even harmed the industries that the preferences were intended to benefit. For example, in the case of farming, credits and favorable deductions have often encouraged investments by wealthy individuals whose principal or only interest in farming is to receive an investment return, largely in the form of tax benefits to offset tax on positive sources of income. Since such investors may not need a positive cash return from farming in order to profit from their investments, they have a substantial competitive advantage in relation to active farmers, who commonly are not in a position to use excess tax benefits to shelter unrelated income. This has significantly contributed to the serious economic difficulties presently being experienced by many active farmers.

The availability of tax benefits to shelter positive sources of income also has harmed the economy generally, by providing a non-economic return on capital for certain investments. This has encouraged a flow of capital away from activities that may provide a higher pre-tax economic return, thus retarding the growth of the sectors of the economy with the greatest potential for expansion.

The committee believes that, in order for tax preferences to function as intended, their benefit must be directed primarily to taxpayers with a substantial and *bona fide* involvement in the activities to which the preferences relate. The committee also believes that it is appropriate to encourage nonparticipating investors to invest in particular activities, by permitting the use of preferences to reduce the rate of tax on income from those activities; however, such investors should not be permitted to use tax benefits to shelter unrelated income.

There are several reasons why it is appropriate to examine the materiality of a taxpayer's participation in an activity in determining the extent to which such taxpayer should be permitted to use tax benefits from the activity. A taxpayer who materially participates in an activity is more likely than a passive investor to approach the activity with a significant nontax economic profit motive, and to form a sound judgment as to whether the activity has genuine economic significance and value.

A material participation standard identifies an important distinction between different types of taxpayer activities. In general, the more passive investor is seeking a return on capital invested, including returns in the form of reductions in the taxes owed on unrelated income, rather than an ongoing source of livelihood. A material participation standard reduces the importance, for such investors, of the tax-reduction features of an investment, and thus increases the importance of the economic features in an investor's decision about where to invest his funds.

Moreover, the committee believes that restricting the use of losses from business activities in which the taxpayer does not materially participate against other sources of positive income (such as salary and portfolio income) addresses a fundamental aspect of the tax shelter problem. As discussed above, instances in which the tax system applies simple rules at the expense of economic accuracy encourage the structuring of transactions to take advantage of the situations in which such rules give rise to undermeasurement or deferral of income. Such transactions commonly are marketed to investors who do not intend to participate in the transactions, as devices for sheltering unrelated sources of positive income (e.g., salary and portfolio income). Accordingly, by creating a bar against the use of losses from business activities in which the taxpayer does not materially participate to offset positive income sources such as salary and portfolio income, the committee believes that it is possible significantly to reduce the tax shelter problem.

Further, in the case of a nonparticipating investor in a business activity, the committee believes that it is appropriate to treat losses of the activity as not realized by the investor prior to disposition of his interest in the activity. The effort to measure, on an annual basis, real economic losses from passive activities gives rise to distortions, particularly due to the nontaxation of unrealized appreciation and the mismatching of tax deductions and related economic income that may occur, especially where debt financing is used heavily. Only when a taxpayer disposes of his interest in an activity is it possible to determine whether a loss was sustained over the entire time that he held the interest.

The relationship to an activity of an investor who does not materially participate may be little different from the relationship of a shareholder to a corporation. So long as the investor retains an interest in the activity, any reduction in the value of such interest not only may be difficult to measure accurately, but has not been realized by the investor to a greater extent than in the context of a C corporation. In the case of a C corporation, losses and expenses borne by the corporation, and any decline in the value of the corporation's stock, do not give rise to the recognition of any loss on the part of shareholders prior to disposition of their stock.

The distinction that the committee believes should be drawn between activities on the basis of material participation bears no relationship to the question of whether, and to what extent, the taxpayer is at risk with respect to the activities. In general, the fact that a taxpayer has placed a particular amount at risk in an activity does not establish, prior to a disposition of the taxpayer's interest, that the amount invested, or any amount, has as yet been lost. The fact that a taxpayer is potentially liable with respect to future expenses or losses of the activity likewise has no bearing on the question whether any amount has as yet been lost, or otherwise is an appropriate current deduction or credit.

At-risk standards, although important in determining the maximum amount that is subject to being lost, are not a sufficient basis for determining whether or when net losses from an activity should be deductible against other sources of income, or for determining whether an ultimate economic loss has been realized. Congress' goal of making tax preferences available principally to active participants in substantial businesses, rather than to investors seeking to shelter unrelated income, can best be accomplished by examining material participation, as opposed to the financial stake provided by an investor to purchase tax shelter benefits.

In certain situations, however, the committee believes that financial risk or other factors, rather than material participation, should be the relevant standard. . . .

A further area in which the material participation standard is not wholly adequate is that of rental activities. Such activities predominantly involve the production of income from capital. For this reason, rental income generally is not now subject to the self-employment tax, whether or not the activity constitutes a trade or business. . . . Rental activities generally require less ongoing management activity, in proportion to capital invested, than business activities involving the production or sale of goods and services. Thus, for example, an individual who is employed full-time as a professional could more easily provide all necessary management in his spare time with respect to a rental activity than he could with respect to another type of business activity involving the same capital investment. The extensive use of rental activities for tax shelter purposes under present law, combined with the reduced level of personal involvement necessary to conduct such activities, make clear that the effectiveness of the basic passive loss provision could be seriously compromised if material participation were sufficient to avoid the limitations in the case of rental activities.

A limited measure of relief, however, is believed appropriate in the case of certain moderate-income investors in rental real estate, who otherwise might experience cash flow difficulties with respect to investments that in many cases are designed to provide financial security, rather than to shelter a substantial amount of other income.

Further, additional considerations apply in the case of limited partnerships. In order to maintain limited liability status, a limited partner generally is precluded from materially participating in the business activity of the partnership; in virtually all respects, a limited partner more closely resembles a shareholder in a C corporation than an active business entrepreneur. Moreover, limited partnerships commonly are used as vehicles for marketing tax benefits to investors seeking to shelter unrelated income. In light of the widespread use of limited partnership interests in syndicating tax shelters, the committee believes that losses from limited partnership interests should not be permitted, prior to a taxable disposition, to offset positive income sources such as salary.

§ 5.02. Passive, Non-Passive, and Investment Activities

Section 469 applies to an individual, estate or trust, any closely held C corporation and any personal holding corporation. § 469(a)(2); *see* § 469(j)(1) and (2) (defining a closely held C corporation and a personal service corporation, respectively). Although § 469 does not apply to S corporations or partnerships, it does apply to shareholders of S corporations and partners of both general and limited partnerships. As described in § 5.04, § 469 also applies to members of a limited liability company who are treated as limited partners of a partnership.

A taxpayer subject to § 469 must separate the business and investment activities in which he is involved into separate activities. An activity includes the conduct of a trade or business under § 162 or an activity the expenses of which are deductible under § 212. § 469(c)(1)(A) and 469(c)(6). Activities are generally deemed passive if the taxpayer does not materially participate in the activity. If the taxpayer materially participates in the activity, then the activity is deemed non-passive.

As previously mentioned, a passive activity loss is not deductible by the taxpayer to reduce the taxpayer's income from other sources. A passive activity loss is defined as the aggregate losses from all passive activities in excess of the aggregate income from all passive activities for the taxable year. § 469(d)(1). As a result, losses from a passive activity in excess of the income from that passive activity are deductible only to the extent of the net income from other passive activities. If a taxpayer's losses from all passive activities exceed the taxpayer's income from all passive activities, the losses in excess of income are suspended and carried forward to the subsequent taxable year. § 469(b). Thus, the effect of § 469 is not to permanently disallow, but only to defer to future taxable years, losses generated by the taxpayer's passive activities.

Importantly, § 469 applies without affecting the character of the income or the expenses generated by a passive activity. Temp. Treas. Reg. § 1.469-1T(d)(1). Thus, a deduction from a passive activity that is not disallowed under § 469 may nevertheless be disallowed under another provision of the Code. The Regulations contain an example in which a individual taxpayer has $10,000 of ordinary income from passive activity X and $12,000 capital loss from passive activity Y. Treas. Reg. § 1.469-1T(d)(2) example. Under § 469, the taxpayer has a $2,000 passive loss that is suspended and carried forward to the succeeding taxable year. The $10,000 ordinary income from passive activity X is included in the taxpayer's gross income and $10,000 of the $12,000 capital loss from passive activity Y is deductible subject to the limitations of § 1211. If the taxpayer has no capital gain, only $3,000 of the $10,000 capital loss allowable under § 469 will be deductible under § 1211. The $7,000 remaining capital loss will be carried forward under § 1212.

The Regulations also contain an example in which the taxpayer's only income and loss from a passive activity for the taxable year is a $10,000 capital gain from passive activity X and a $12,000 ordinary loss from passive activity Y. Temp. Treas. Reg. § 1.469-1T(d)(1) example. In addition, the taxpayer has a $10,000 capital loss that is not from a passive activity. Under § 469, the taxpayer has a $2,000 passive loss that is suspended and carried forward to the succeeding taxable year. The $10,000 capital gain from passive activity X is included in the taxpayer's gross income and $10,000 of the $12,000 ordinary loss from passive activity Y is deductible. Because the $10,000 capital gain from passive activity X is included in the taxpayer's gross income, the taxpayer will be entitled to deduct the $10,000 capital loss under § 1211(b). The capital gain from passive activity X retains its character as capital gain after moving through § 469 for purposes of the limitations on the deduction of capital losses under § 1211.

Because § 469 simply defers the deduction of expenses and losses generated by a passive activity but does not affect the character of the expenses and losses, a taxpayer must identify which of the expenses and losses are actually disallowed under § 469 in order to ensure that the character of the disallowed expenses or losses is maintained when the disallowed expenses and losses are carried forward to succeeding taxable years. The Regulations contain detailed rules regarding the proper identification of the disallowed expenses and losses generated by different passive activities, some of which are generating net income and some of which are generating net loss. Temp. Treas. Reg. § 1.469-1T(f)(2)(i). In addition, the Regulations contain detailed rules for identifying which of the expenses or losses are disallowed within an activity. Temp. Treas. Reg. § 1.469-1T(f)(2)(ii). Importantly, a taxpayer needs to account separately for an expense or loss within an activity only if that expense or loss would result in a different income tax liability in a succeeding taxable year if not taken into account separately. Temp. Treas. Reg. § 1.469-1T(f)(2)(iii). Among other items of expense or loss, this rule applies to losses from capital assets and losses from § 1231 property.

Section 469 contains a special rule to prevent taxpayers from deducting passive losses against investment, or so-called portfolio, income. Gross income in the form of interest, dividends, annuities, or royalties not derived in the ordinary course of a trade or business is not considered in determining the income or loss from any activity. § 469(e)(1); Temp. Treas. Reg. § 1.469-2T(c)(3). The same rule applies to expenses, including interest, that is allocable to such income and to gains or losses not derived in the ordinary course of a trade or business on the disposition of property producing such income or property held for investment. Thus, a taxpayer's income and loss can be separated into three types: passive income or loss, non-passive income or loss, and portfolio income or loss. Section 469 prevents any passive loss from reducing non-passive or portfolio income.

Although the statute is generally silent with respect to the determination of each activity, the Regulations contain some guidance to taxpayers in determining what trades or businesses or groupings of trades or businesses constitute a separate activity. Generally, taxpayers face a conflict in the determination of each activity. On one hand, a taxpayer is more likely to materially participate in an activity that is broadly defined. On the other hand, because suspended losses from a passive activity are deductible when the taxpayer disposes of its entire interest in an activity, a taxpayer will want to narrowly define the scope of each of its activities. The Regulations provide that one or more trades or businesses may be treated as a single activity if they constitute "an appropriate economic unit for the measurement of gain or loss" for the purposes of § 469. Treas. Reg. § 1.469-4(c)(1). A facts and circumstances test is applied, and a taxpayer may use any reasonable method of applying the relevant facts and circumstances in grouping activities. Treas. Reg. § 1.469-4(c)(2). The factors to be considered in making this determination include: (1) the similarities and differences in the types of trades or business, (2) the extent of common control, (3) the extent of common ownership, (4) geographical location, and (5) interdependencies between or among the activities. The Regulations provide an example of a taxpayer owning a bakery and movie theater in Baltimore and a bakery and movie theater in Philadelphia. The regulations recognize that there is more than one reasonable grouping of the activities: a single activity; a movie theater activity and a bakery activity; a Baltimore activity and a Philadelphia activity; or four separate activities. Treas. Reg. § 1.469-4(c)(3) example (1). Once a taxpayer has grouped its activities, it may not regroup the activities in a subsequent year. Treas. Reg. § 1.469-4(e)(1). A taxpayer may only regroup its activities if the "original grouping was clearly inappropriate or a material change in the facts and circumstances has occurred that makes the original grouping clearly inappropriate." Treas. Reg. § 1.469-4(e)(2). In addition, Revenue Procedure 2010-13, 2010-4 I.R.B. 329, requires taxpayers to report to the Service their groupings and regroupings of activities and the addition of specific activities within their existing groupings of activities for purposes of § 469.

Importantly, however, the Regulations provide that a rental activity may not be grouped with a trade or business activity unless the rental activity is insubstantial as compared with the trade or business activity, the trade or business activity is insubstantial as compared to the rental activity, or each owner has the same proportionate interest in the trade or business and the rental activity, in which case the rental activity that involved the rental of property used in the trade or business may be grouped with the trade or business. Treas. Reg. § 1.469-4(d)(1). In addition, the rental or real property and the rental of personal property may not be treated as a single activity. Treas. Reg. § 1.469-4(d)(2). Finally, an interest in an activity held as a limited partner may only be grouped with other activities in the same type of business. Treas. Reg. § 1.469-4(d)(3).

Once a taxpayer has grouped trades or businesses as a single activity, the taxpayer cannot regroup those activities in subsequent taxable years. Treas. Reg. § 1.469-4(e)(1). Only if it is determined that the taxpayer's original groupings were inappropriate or a material change in the facts or circumstances makes the original groupings inappropriate will the taxpayer be permitted to regroup the activities. Treas. Reg. § 1.469-4(e)(2). Nevertheless, the Commissioner may regroup a taxpayer's activities if the grouping is inappropriate and a principal purpose of the taxpayer's grouping was to circumvent the underlying purposes of § 469. Treas. Reg. § 1.469-4(f)(1).

§ 5.03. Material and Significant Participation

The distinction between a passive and non-passive activity is generally determined by whether or not the taxpayer materially participates in the activity. § 469(h)(1). Material participation is defined as "regular, continuous, and substantial" involvement by the taxpayer in the operations of the activity. This vague standard is given greater content under the Regulations, which provide a number of safe-harbors that, if satisfied, will be deemed to constitute material participation. Temp. Treas. Reg. § 1.469-5T(a). These safe-harbors are based on the amount of time that the taxpayer devotes to the operations of the activity. A taxpayer will be deemed to materially participate in an activity if any of the following tests are met:

(1) The taxpayer participates in the activity for more than 500 hours during such year;

(2) The taxpayer's participation in the activity for the taxable year constitutes substantially all of the participation in the activity of all individuals;

(3) The taxpayer participates in the activity for more than 100 hours during the taxable year, and the taxpayer's participation in the activity for the taxable year is not less than the participation in the activity of any other individual for such year;

(4) The taxpayer participates in the activity for more than 100 hours but not more than 500 hours (defined as a significant participation activity) during the taxable year, and the taxpayer's aggregate participation in all significant participation activities during such year exceeds 500 hours;

(5) The taxpayer materially participated in the activity for any five (whether or not consecutive) of the 10 taxable years that immediately precede the taxable year;

(6) The activity is a personal service activity and the taxpayer materially participated in the activity for any three taxable years (whether or not consecutive) preceding the taxable year; or

(7) Based on all of the facts and circumstances, the taxpayer participates in the activity on a regular, continuous, and substantial basis during such year.

Temp. Treas. Reg. § 1.469-5T(a)(1) through (7). If the taxpayer participates in the activity for less than 100 hours during the taxable year, the taxpayer will not be deemed to materially participate in the activity under the general "regular, continuous, and substantial" standard. Temp. Treas. Reg. § 1.469-5T(b)(2)(iii).

Certain types of involvement in the operations of the activity are not deemed participation for purposes of these rules. For example, work that is not customarily performed by an owner of an activity and one of the principal purposes for the performance of such work is to avoid the disallowance of losses under § 469 is not to be considered. Temp. Treas. Reg. § 1.469-5T(f)(2)(i). Similarly, work performed in the capacity of an investor in an activity is not be considered as participation in the activity for purposes of § 469 unless the individual is directly involved in the day-to-day management or operations of the activity. Temp. Treas. Reg. § 1.469-5T(f)(2)(ii). Work done in the capacity as an investor includes studying and reviewing financial statements or reports on operations of the activity, preparing or compiling summaries or analyses of the finances or operations of the activity for the individual's own use, and monitoring the finances or operations of the activity in a non-managerial capacity.

Participation by the taxpayer's spouse in an activity during the taxable year is deemed to be participation by the taxpayer without regard to whether the spouse owns an interest in the activity or whether the spouses file a joint return for the taxable year. § 469(h)(5); Temp. Treas. Reg. § 1.469-5T(f)(3). Participation by the taxpayer or the taxpayer's spouse may be established by any reasonable means. Although contemporaneous daily time reports, logs, or similar documents are not required, the Regulations provide that "reasonable means" for this purpose include, but are not limited to, "the identification of services performed over a period of time and the approximate number of hours spent performing such services during such period, based on appointment books, calendars, or narrative summaries." Temp. Treas. Reg. § 1.469-5T(f)(4).

Section 469 generally provides that, if a limited partnership interest is held in an activity, the activity is deemed one in which the taxpayer does not materially participate. § 469(h)(2); Temp. Treas. Reg. § 1.1469-5T(e)(1). However, the statutory provision is subject to regulatory modification, and the Regulations provide that a limited partner will be deemed to materially participate in an activity if he satisfies tests (1), (5), or (6), described above. Temp. Treas. Reg. § 1.1469-5T(e)(2). As described in the Senate Report accompanying the Tax Reform Act of 1986, this approach was intended to reflect the fact that, "[i]n order to maintain limited liability status, a limited partner generally is precluded from materially participating in the business activity of the partnership. . . ." S. Rep. No. 99-313, 99th Cong, 2d Sess. 718 (1986). Apparently, Congress intended to place limited partners in the difficult position of risking their limited liability status in order to materially participate in the activity. Although this may have been the effect under state partnership law in 1986, the most recent version of the Uniform Limited Partnership Act allows limited partners to be active in partnership management and operations without loss of their limited liability status.

In addition to the evolution of state partnership law since 1986 when § 469 was enacted, the intervening years have also witnessed the rise of the limited liability company. LLCs provide their members with limited liability for entity-level liabilities and allow all members to be actively involved in management and operations without loss of their limited liability status. In addition, LLCs are generally treated as partnerships under Subchapter K. Although § 469 does not explicitly refer to members of an LLC as LLCs were relatively unknown in 1986, the Service has taken the position that the definition of a limited partner under the Regulations is sufficiently expansive to cover members of an LLC. The Regulations provide that a partnership interest is treated as a limited partnership interest if the interest is designated a limited partnership interest in the limited partnership agreement or the certificate of limited partnership or "[t]he liability of the holder of such interest for obligations of the partnership is limited, under the law of the State in which the partnership is organized, to a determinable fixed amount (for example, the sum of the holder's capital contributions to the partnership and contractual obligations to make additional capital contributions to the partnership)." Temp. Treas. Reg. § 1.469-5T(e)(3)(i). Based on this language, the Service has argued that interests as a member of an LLC are treated in the same manner as interests of a limited partner in a limited partnership. Thus, the Service has adopted the position that, in order to be deemed to materially participate in the operations of an LLC, a member of an LLC must satisfy tests (1), (5), or (6), described above. As described in the following opinion, the Service's argument has not been accepted by the courts.

THOMPSON v. UNITED STATES

United States Court of Federal Claims
87 Fed. Cl. 728 (2009)

BLOCK, *JUDGE.*

I. Introduction

The nub of this case is whether the government is collecting more taxes than written law and regulation allow. More precisely, plaintiff James R. Thompson structured his business activity in the form of a limited liability company ("LLC") under the laws of the State of Texas. LLCs are hybrid entities that under state law are neither partnerships nor corporations. Nevertheless, under the Treasury Regulations, an LLC must choose to be taxed as either one or the other.[2] *See* 26 C.F.R. ("Treas. Reg.") §§ 301.7701-2(a), -3(b)(1)(i). To avoid the two-tier system of corporate taxation, most LLCs elect partnership taxation.[3] See Gregg v. United States, 186 F. Supp. 2d 1123, 1126 (D. Or. 2000).

The parties ask this court to decide whether a member interest in an LLC electing partnership taxation is a limited partnership interest for purposes of applying the passive activity rules of 26 U.S.C. ("I.R.C." or the "Code") § 469 and the regulations thereunder. This is a question of first impression for the court. The issue arises when a member of an LLC claims a share of the LLC's losses. If the member's ownership interest is a limited partnership interest, as defendant

---

[2] [1] Technically, the LLC must choose whether or not it will be taxed as a corporation. Otherwise, it is taxed as a partnership by default. See Treas. Reg. § 301.7701-3(b)(1)(i). This is what happened in the case at bar. See infra section II.

[3] [2] Under partnership taxation law, the LLC and its members are not separately taxable. . . . Instead, the LLC serves as a conduit; its income and losses pass through to its members, who take the losses and income into account in calculating their own taxable income.

contends, then the member has fewer means by which he can demonstrate his material participation in the business. See Treas. Reg. § 1.469-5T(e)(2). This is important because unless the member can demonstrate his material participation, the Code will deem his share of the LLC's losses to be a "passive activity" loss rather than an ordinary loss. See I.R.C. § 469(c)(1)(B). Passive activity losses are less advantageous than ordinary losses because they may only offset passive activity income. See I.R.C. § 469 (a)(1), (d)(1). In the instant case, plaintiff's share of his LLC's losses exceeds his passive activity income.

[T]he parties stipulated that if plaintiff's member interest is a limited partnership interest, then plaintiff cannot demonstrate his material participation in the LLC and I.R.C. § 469 limits his losses. . . . Likewise, the parties also stipulated that if plaintiff's member interest is not a limited partnership interest, then plaintiff can demonstrate his material participation in the LLC and § 469 does not limit his losses. Because the parties do not disagree as to the amount of the tax and because the parties stipulated that deciding their cross-motions for partial summary judgment will, in fact, resolve the case entirely, the court deems the parties' cross-motions for partial summary judgment to be cross-motions for summary judgment.

Perhaps demonstrating once again that "[l]ogic and taxation are not always the best of friends," Sonneborn Bros. v. Cureton, 262 U.S. 506, 522 (1923) (McReynolds, J., concurring), the court rejects defendant's position because, among other reasons, the tax code and the applicable regulations literally cannot be read to transfigure plaintiff's member interest in his LLC into one of a limited partnership. Accordingly, this court grants plaintiff's motion for summary judgment and denies the government's motion.

II. Factual and Procedural Background

On March 19, 2002, plaintiff formed Mountain Air Charter, LLC ("Mountain Air")[4] under the laws of the State of Texas. . . . Plaintiff directly holds a 99% member interest in Mountain Air and indirectly holds the remaining 1% through JRT Holdings, Inc., a Subchapter S corporation.[5] Significantly, Mountain Air's articles of organization[6] designate plaintiff as its only manager.

Because Mountain Air did not elect to be treated as a corporation for federal tax purposes, by default the Code treats it as a partnership, see Treas. Reg. §§ 301.7701-2(a), -3(b)(1)(i). On his 2002 and 2003 individual income tax returns, plaintiff claimed Mountain Air's losses of $1,225,869 and $939,878, respectively. After reviewing plaintiff's returns, an IRS auditor disallowed all of plaintiff's

[4] [3] Mountain Air owns and operates a single aircraft for on-demand air charter services.

[5] [4] An S corporation is a business entity with shareholders, rather than members or partners, and is taxed in a pass-through manner as if it were a partnership or sole proprietorship. . . . Unlike limited partnerships, however, all S corporation shareholders enjoy limited liability regardless of their level of participation in the business.

[6] [5] Organizers must file an LLC's "articles of organization" with the appropriate state authority before the state will formally recognize the LLC. . . . The articles include, *inter alia*, whether management power is vested in specific managers or its members generally.

claimed losses in 2002 and $783,878 of plaintiff's claimed losses in 2003. The IRS assessed plaintiff additional tax liability and interest amounting to $437,186 for 2002 and $308,055 for 2003. On September 9, 2005, plaintiff paid the IRS $863,124 in tax and interest stemming from his 2002 and 2003 income tax returns. On the same day plaintiff submitted his payment, he also submitted a tax refund claim for the same amount. The IRS denied plaintiff's claim on March 2, 2006. Compl. Ex. B at 1.

According to the IRS auditor, he disallowed the claimed losses because plaintiff did not materially participate in the business operations of Mountain Air. The IRS auditor rested his conclusion on Treasury Regulation § 1.469-5T, which sets forth the test for what constitutes taxpayer material participation for purposes of applying I.R.C. § 469's passive activity rules. See Treas. Reg. § 1.469-5T (titled "Material participation"). To the auditor, § 1.469-5T "explicitly treats interests in any entity which limits liability as limited partnership interests." Because plaintiff enjoyed limited liability as an LLC member, the auditor concluded that plaintiff's interest was identical to a limited partnership interest. The IRS then deemed plaintiff's share of Mountain Air's losses to be a passive activity loss. . . .

III. Discussion

[T]he parties' cross-motions ask this court to determine whether plaintiff held a limited partnership interest in Mountain Air for purposes of applying the passive activity rules of I.R.C. § 469 to plaintiff's share of Mountain Air's losses. A "passive activity loss" occurs where "the aggregate losses from all *passive activities* for the taxable year, exceed the aggregate income from all passive activities for such year." I.R.C. § 469(d)(1) (emphasis added). A passive activity is "any activity which involves the conduct of a trade or business, and in which the taxpayer does not *materially participate.*" I.R.C. § 469(c)(1)(B) (emphasis added).

A taxpayer materially participates in an activity only if he is involved in the activity's operations on a regular, continuous, and substantial basis. I.R.C. § 469(h)(1). Generally, an individual may establish his material participation for a given taxable year by demonstrating any of the following:

(1) The individual participate[d] in the activity for more than 500 hours during such year;

(2) The individual's participation in the activity for the taxable year constitute[d] substantially all of the participation in such activity of all individuals . . . for such year;

(3) The individual participate[d] in the activity for more than 100 hours during the taxable year, and such individual's participation in the activity for the taxable year [was] not less than the participation in the activity of any other individual . . . for such year;

(4) The activity [was] a significant participation activity . . . for the taxable year, and the individual's aggregate participation in all significant participation activities during such year exceed[ed] 500 hours;

(5) The individual materially participated in the activity . . . for any five taxable years . . . during the ten taxable years that immediately pre-

cede[d] the taxable year;

(6) The activity is a personal service activity . . . , and the individual materially participated in the activity for any three taxable years . . . preceding the taxable year; or

(7) Based on all of the facts and circumstances . . . , the individual participate[d] in the activity on a regular, continuous, and substantial basis during such year.

Treas. Reg. § 1.469-5T(a).

The Code treats limited partners differently because it presumes that they do *not* materially participate in their limited partnerships. See I.R.C. § 469(h)(2) ("Except as provided in regulations, no interest in a limited partnership as a limited partner shall be treated as an interest with respect to which a taxpayer materially participates."). In fact, under the Treasury Regulations implementing § 469, if a taxpayer holds a limited partnership interest, only three of the seven tests described above — (1), (5), and (6) — are available to measure the taxpayer's material participation in the partnership. Treas. Reg. § 1.469-5T(e)(2). Treasury Regulation § 1.469-5T(e)(3) determines whether a taxpayer is holding a limited partnership interest. See Treas. Reg. § 1.469-5T(e)(3) (titled "Limited partnership interest"). The regulation provides:

(i) In general. Except as provided in paragraph (e)(3)(ii) of this section, for purposes of [I.R.C. §] 469(h)(2) and this paragraph (e), a partnership interest shall be treated as a limited partnership interest if —

(A) Such interest is designated a limited partnership interest in the limited partnership agreement or the certificate of limited partnership, without regard to whether the liability of the holder of such interest for obligations of the partnership is limited under the applicable State law; or

(B) The liability of the holder of such interest for obligations of the partnership is limited, under the law of the State in which the partnership is organized, to a determinable fixed amount (for example, the sum of the holder's capital contributions to the partnership and contractual obligations to make additional capital contributions to the partnership).

(ii) Limited partner holding general partner interest. A partnership interest of an individual shall not be treated as a limited partnership interest for the individual's taxable year if the individual is a general partner in the partnership at all times during the partnership's taxable year ending with or within the individual's taxable year (or the portion of the partnership's taxable year during which the individual (directly or indirectly) owns such limited partnership interest).

Id.

As noted above, both parties agree that I.R.C. § 469's passive activity rules limit plaintiff's share of Mountain Air's losses if he holds a limited partnership interest under § 1.469-5T(e)(3) and only § 1.469-5T(a)(1), (5), and (6) are available to measure his material participation. The parties also agree that I.R.C. § 469 does not limit plaintiff's share of Mountain Air's losses if plaintiff does not hold a limited partnership interest under § 1.469-5T(e)(3) and all seven tests under § 1.469-5T(a) are available to measure his material participation. Therefore, the instant case turns on the proper application of Treasury Regulation § 1.469-5T(e)(3) to plaintiff's interest in Mountain Air.

As a threshold matter, it is important to note that an LLC is not a partnership. While LLC members may participate directly in the management of the company, all members enjoy limited liability regardless of their respective levels of involvement. Limited partnerships, on the other hand, must distinguish between: (1) their limited partners, who have limited liability but are unable to participate in the management of the partnership; and (2) their general partners, who may participate in the management of the partnership but are personally liable for its debts.

Defendant argues that it was nevertheless proper for the IRS to treat plaintiff's interest in Mountain Air as a limited partnership interest under Treasury Regulation § 1.469-5T(e)(3)(i)(B) because plaintiff elected to have Mountain Air taxed as a partnership for income tax purposes and because plaintiff's liability is limited under the laws of the state in which Mountain Air was organized (Texas). Plaintiff's response is a simple one: because Mountain Air is not a limited partnership, his ownership interest cannot be that of a limited partner. Moreover, plaintiff contends that even if Mountain Air could be properly analogized to a limited partnership, his interest is more akin to a general partner's interest under § 1.469-5T(e)(3)(ii) than a limited partner's interest under 1.469-5T(e)(3)(i), given the high degree of control he exerts over Mountain Air's business operations as its sole manager.

The court notes that the canons of statutory construction apply equally to regulations. . . . Thus, this court begins with the language of § 1.469-5T(e)(3), and derives its plain meaning from its text, structure, and purpose.[7]

The language from § 1.469-5T(e)(3) upon which defendant relies states that "a partnership interest shall be treated as a limited partnership interest if . . . [t]he liability of the holder of such interest for obligations of the partnership is limited, *under the law of the State in which the partnership is organized.*" Treas. Reg. § 1.469-5T(e)(3)(i)(B) (emphasis added). The emphasized portion of the regulation thus literally requires that the ownership interest be in a business entity that is, in fact, a partnership under state law — not merely taxed as such under the Code. This provision is unambiguous. As such, this court must enforce its plain meaning. . . .

---

[7] [7] Defendant argues that this court owes substantial deference to an agency regulation promulgated in accordance with an express congressional mandate and to an agency's reasonable interpretation of such a regulation. However, plaintiff agrees that the regulation is valid, . . . and defendant has not set forth, nor is this court aware of, any official IRS interpretation extending § 1.469-5T(e)(3) to include membership interests in LLCs. Therefore, this court owes no deference to defendant's proffered interpretation, and the court may proceed unhindered in applying the appropriate canons of construction. See Bowen v. Georgetown Univ. Hosp., 488 U.S. 204, 212-13 (1988) (holding that where the agency itself has articulated no position on the question, "[d]eference to what appears to be nothing more than an agency's convenient litigating position would be entirely inappropriate"); see also Am. Express Co. v. United States, 262 F.3d 1376, 1383 (Fed. Cir. 2001) (holding that a "mere audit determination . . . may not draw deference").

Moreover, the relevant section of the Code, upon which Treasury Regulation § 1.469-5T(e)(3) is predicated, states: "Except as provided in regulations, no interest in a limited partnership *as a limited partner* shall be treated as an interest with respect to which a taxpayer materially participates." I.R.C. § 469(h)(2) (emphasis added). Thus for this provision even to apply, the taxpayer must actually be a limited partner. See Garnett [v. Commissioner, 132 T.C. 368, 376-77 (2009)] ("The operative condition for applying § 469(h)(2) is not simply that there be an 'interest in a limited partnership' but an 'interest in a limited partnership *as a limited partner.*' "). Of course, Mountain Air is organized under Texas state law as an LLC, not a limited partnership, and plaintiff is a member of an LLC, not a limited partner.

Defendant also ignores the possibility that plaintiff meets the general partner exception under § 1.469-5T(e)(3)(ii). This is remarkable considering that the provision upon which defendant bases its argument, § 1.469-5T(e)(3)(i), begins: "Except as provided in paragraph (e)(3)(ii) . . . ." Section 1.469-5T(e)(3)(ii) provides, in part, that "[a] partnership interest of an individual shall not be treated as a limited partnership interest . . . if the individual is a general partner in the partnership at all times during the partnership's taxable year." In other words, plaintiff's ownership interest would not be a limited partnership interest under the regulations if plaintiff could show that he were a general partner at all times during the 2002 and 2003 tax years.

Again, plaintiff was both a member and a manager of an LLC, not a partner in a limited partnership. However, defendant twice conceded at oral argument that plaintiff would be a general partner if Mountain Air were a limited partnership. Defendant asks this court to equate plaintiff's interest in Mountain Air to that of a limited partner's interest in a limited partnership under § 1.469-5T(e)(3)(i)(B), but also deny plaintiff the possible benefit of § 1.469-5T(e)(3)(ii)'s general partner exception. According to defendant, the legal fiction created by the Code — that an LLC electing partnership taxation is a limited partnership — does not extend to § 1.469-5T(e)(3)(ii). This position strikes the court as entirely self-serving and inconsistent. If an LLC member could hold a limited partner's interest under § 1.469-5T(e)(3)(i), then, alternatively, that same member could hold a general partner's interest under § 1.469-5T(e)(3)(ii).

Defendant further argues that between the two types of partnership interests plaintiff could possess — limited or general — plaintiff must hold a limited partnership interest because at the time I.R.C. § 469 and Treasury Regulation § 1.469-5T were promulgated, "there was universal agreement among the states that the *sine qua non* of a limited partnership interest was limited liability." Plaintiff takes the opposite position, contending that the key feature or attribute differentiating the two interests is the ability to participate in the control of the business. After reviewing the state of limited partnership law at the time Congress enacted § 469, this court agrees with plaintiff.

When Congress passed I.R.C. § 469 in 1986, the limited partnership was not a novel business entity. In 1916, the National Conference of Commissioners on Uniform State Laws drafted the first Uniform Limited Partnership Act ("ULPA"). By the 1970s, a majority of the states had adopted the ULPA. In 1976, the National

Conference created the Revised Uniform Limited Partnership Act ("RULPA"). Further amendments followed in 1985. By 1986, almost every state, including Texas, had adopted either the ULPA or the RULPA.

The ULPA provides that "[a] limited partner shall not become liable as a general partner unless, in addition to the exercise of his rights and powers as a limited partner, *he takes part in the control of the business.*" ULPA § 7 (1916) (emphasis added). Likewise, the 1976 version of the RULPA provides that "a limited partner is not liable for the obligations of a limited partnership unless he is also a general partner or, in addition to the exercise of his rights and powers as a limited partner, *he takes part in the control of the business.*" RULPA § 303(a) (1976) (emphasis added). The 1985 version of the RULPA offers no material change, providing that "a limited partner is not liable for the obligations of a limited partnership unless he is also a general partner or, in addition to the exercise of his rights and powers as a limited partner, *he participates in the control of the business.*" RULPA § 303(a) (1985) (emphasis added).

In sum, when Congress enacted I.R.C. § 469, there was general agreement among state laws that a limited partner would lose his limited liability status if he participated in the control of the business.[8] Stated another way, a limited partner's level of participation in the business dictated whether or not he enjoyed limited liability. But the converse is not true. Under the ULPA, a limited partner who "takes part in the control of the business" becomes "liable as a general partner." ULPA § 7 (1916). The same is true under the RULPA, which makes a limited partner "liable for the obligations of a limited partnership" if "he participates in the control of the business." See RULPA § 303(a) (1985). To be sure, the loss of limited liability under state law likely deterred many limited partners from participating in the control of their businesses, but limited liability is not the *sine qua non* of a limited partnership interest.

Moreover, the surrounding statutory and regulatory framework does not support a "dividing line between the two types of [partnership] interests [based on] limited liability," as defendant suggests, but rather a dividing line based on participation. Defendant loses sight of what the Treasury Secretary drafted § 1.469-5T to define — namely, what constitutes "material participation" in an activity. See I.R.C. § 469(l)(1) ("The [Treasury] Secretary shall prescribe regulations . . . to carry out the provisions of this section, including regulations which specify what constitutes an activity, material participation, or active participation . . . ."); Treas. Reg. § 1.469-5T (titled "Material participation"). Deciding whether a taxpayer materially participated in an activity is but one step in the ultimate determination of whether the taxpayer was involved in a "passive activity." See I.R.C. § 469(c)(1). These terms — "material participation" and "passive activity" — indicate that Congress was primarily concerned with the taxpayer's level of involvement in the activity in question. If Congress desired a test that turned on a taxpayer's level of liability, it surely would have included the word "liability" somewhere in the statute. However,

---

[8] [12] Defendant argues that the Uniform Limited Partnership Act of 2001 ("ULPA 2001") eliminated the control rule, in part, to bring limited partnerships into parity with LLCs. The glaring deficiency in this argument is that the National Conference drafted ULPA 2001 fifteen years after Congress enacted I.R.C. § 469. Even today, only fourteen states have adopted ULPA 2001. Texas is not one of them.

as defendant's counsel admitted at oral argument, the word "liability" does not appear in I.R.C. § 469.

Defendant's appeal to § 469's legislative history is no more persuasive. Defendant cites two committee prints and argues that Congress passed § 469 to stem the use of limited liability pass-though entities as tax shelters. But "[t]he starting point in discerning congressional intent is the existing statutory text," Lamie v. United States Trustee, [540 U.S. 526, 534 (2004)], not the legislative history, see Hoechst Aktiengesellschaft v. Quigg, 917 F.2d 522, 526 (Fed. Cir. 1990) ("It is well settled law that the plain and unambiguous meaning of the words used by Congress prevails in the absence of a clearly expressed legislative intent to the contrary."). As described above, the text of § 469 does not demonstrate that Congress cared about a taxpayer's level of liability. And, as defendant's counsel conceded, shareholders in an S corporation enjoy limited liability and pass-through taxation, just as members in an LLC, yet the regulations do not hold them to the same standard for demonstrating their material participation. If Congress were, in fact, trying to stem the use of limited liability pass-though entities as tax shelters, the disparate treatment of S corporations and LLCs would be inexplicable.

Ironically, even if this court required § 469's legislative history to shed light on the issue at bar, the legislative history supports plaintiff's position, not defendant's. While Congress may have been concerned about the "proliferation of a variety of tax-driven transactions," Def.'s Br. at 10 (citing Staff of J. Comm. on Taxation, 100th Cong., General Explanation of the Tax Reform Act of 1986 at 209 (Comm. Print 1987)), it does not follow that "limited liability [was] central to the reasons that [§] 469 was enacted." Defendant's own sources undermine its arguments. One of the two committee prints that defendant cites states:

> In general, a tax shelter is an investment in which a significant portion of the investor's return is derived from the realization of tax savings with respect to other income, as well as the receipt of tax-favored (or, potentially, tax-exempt) income from the investment itself. Generally tax shelters are passive investments *in the sense that the investor is not involved in actively managing a business.*

Staff of J. Comm. On Taxation, 99th Cong., Tax Reform Proposals: Tax Shelters and Minimum Tax 2 (Comm. Print 1985) (emphasis added). The print identifies three "elements of a tax shelter," none of which involve limited liability. See id. (stating that tax shelters typically permit taxpayers to: (1) defer tax liability to future years; (2) convert ordinary income to tax-favored income; and (3) leverage their investments to maximize the benefit of deductions). The second committee print states:

> The distinction that Congress determined should be drawn between activities on the basis of material participation was viewed as unrelated to the question of whether, and to what extent, the taxpayer was at risk with respect to the activities.
>
> * * *
>
> At-risk standards, although important in determining the maximum amount that is subject to being lost, were viewed as not a sufficient basis for determining whether or when net losses from an activity should be

> deductible against other sources of income, or for determining whether an ultimate economic loss has been realized. Congress concluded that its goal of making tax preferences available principally to active participants in substantial businesses, rather than to investors seeking to shelter unrelated income, was best accomplished by examining material participation, as opposed to the financial stake provided by an investor to purchase tax shelter benefits.

General Explanation of the Tax Reform Act of 1986 at 213.

The only piece of legislative history that aids defendant is a Senate Finance Committee report, which arguably suggests that Congress may have intended to vest the Treasury Secretary with the regulatory authority to treat "substantially equivalent entities" as limited partnerships for purposes of § 469(h)(2). See S. Rep. No. 99-313, at 731-32 (1986). However, the Senate report is far from clear on this point. The relevant section states:

> Under the bill, the Secretary of the Treasury is empowered to provide through regulations that limited partnership interests in certain circumstances will *not* be treated (other than through the application of the general facts and circumstances test regarding material participation) as interests in passive activities.
>
> * * *
>
> The exercise of *such authority* might also be appropriate where taxpayers sought to avoid limited partnership status with respect to substantially equivalent entities.

S. Rep. No. 99-313 at 731-32 (emphases added). "[S]uch authority" appears to refer to the authority to treat a taxpayer's limited partnership interest as *not* an interest in a passive activity. However, if that were true, the second sentence in the above-quoted passage would make little sense. How "such authority" could be used in an effort to press limited partnership status upon a taxpayer's ownership interest in a substantially equivalent activity is unclear.

Notwithstanding whatever the Senate report was attempting to convey, defendant's interpretation conflicts with the plain language of the statute. Section 469 states: "Except as provided in regulations, no interest in a limited partnership as a limited partner shall be treated as an interest with respect to which a taxpayer materially participates." I.R.C. § 469(h)(2). Thus, the purpose of Congress's grant of regulatory authority was to provide *exceptions* to — not *expand* upon — the Code's presumption that limited partners do not materially participate in their limited partnerships.

Finally and most importantly, an LLC is not "substantially equivalent" to a limited partnership. As discussed above, unlike a limited partnership, an LLC allows all members to participate in the business while retaining limited liability. In other words, "LLCs are designed to permit active involvement by LLC members in the management of the business." Gregg, 186 F. Supp. 2d at 1128. It makes little sense, therefore, to extend the Code's presumption concerning limited partners' lack of participation in their limited partnerships to plaintiff and his LLC.[9] Once Treasury Regulation § 1.469-5T(e)(3) is read in context and with due regard to its text, structure, and purpose, it becomes abundantly clear that it is simply inapplicable to a membership interest in an LLC.[10] See Gregg, 186 F. Supp. 2d at 1128 ("Plaintiffs argue that the limited partnership test, as set forth in . . . Treasury Regulation § 1.469-5T(e)(3)(i)(B) . . . , is obsolete when applied to LLCs and their members . . . . I agree.").

And even if Treasury Regulation § 1.469-5T(e)(3) could apply to plaintiff and this court had to categorize his membership interest as either a limited or a general partner's interest, it would best be categorized as a general partner's interest under § 1.469-5T(e)(3)(ii). Accord Garnett [v. Commissioner, 132 T.C. at 380-81] (recognizing the legal "fiction of treating an . . . [LLC] as a 'limited partnership' " and holding that "the legislative purposes of the special rule of [§] 469(h)(2) are more nearly served by treating . . . [LLC] members as general partners"). At best, defendant has identified an ambiguity in § 1.469-5T(e)(3) as it applies to LLCs. However, the court should decide such ambiguities in favor of the taxpayer. Accordingly, plaintiff may demonstrate his material participation in Mountain Air using all seven § 1.469-5T(a) tests.

This holding also accords with *Gregg*, wherein the plaintiff was a member of an LLC "formed to create a network of credentialed alternative medicine practitioners." He claimed an ordinary flow-through loss of $230,723 on his income tax return, which the IRS disallowed on the basis that it should have been characterized as a passive activity loss. The plaintiff paid the resulting deficiency amount, filed a claim for refund, and ultimately brought suit in district court. As in the instant case, defendant argued that the plaintiff's losses were passive activity losses because the plaintiff was a limited partner under Treasury Regulation § 1.469-5T(e)(3)(i)(B). The *Gregg* court disagreed, holding:

> In the absence of any regulation asserting that an LLC member should be treated as a limited partner of a limited partnership, defendant's conclusion is inappropriate. Therefore, the higher standard of material participation test for limited partners should not be applied to plaintiff. Plaintiff materially participated in the activity of [his LLC] "if and only if" he satisfies one of the seven tests set forth in . . . Treasur[y] Regulation § 1.469-5T(a)(1)-(7).

[Gregg, 186 F. Supp. 2d at] 1129.

Defendant raised the same argument in *Garnett*, a recent United States Tax Court case in which the petitioners owned interests in both LLCs and limited liability partnerships ("LLPs"). [Garnett v. Commissioner, 132 T.C. at 376] ("Because of [their] limited liability, respondent contends, each [LLP] and [LLC] interest in question is a 'limited partnership interest' under the temporary

---

[9] [15] When Congress debated the Tax Reform Act of 1986, only one state, Wyoming, had adopted an LLC statute. Therefore, it is unlikely that Congress could have envisioned applying § 469(h)(2"s presumption to LLCs.

[10] [16] As Judge Wolski stated at oral argument: "We don't have a living breathing tax code, or, at least, we shouldn't."

regulations."). Like the district court in *Gregg*, the *Garnett* court rejected defendant's argument, holding:

> We do not believe that this rationale properly extends to interests in [LLPs] and [LLCs]. . . . [M]embers of [LLPs] and [LLCs], unlike limited partners in [s]tate law limited partnerships, are not barred by State law from materially participating in the entities' business. Accordingly, it cannot be presumed that they do not materially participate. Rather, it is necessary to examine the facts and circumstances to ascertain the nature and extent of their participation. That factual inquiry is appropriately made, we believe, pursuant to the general tests for material participation under [I.R.C. §] 469 and the regulations thereunder. We anticipate that this examination will occur in subsequent phases of this proceeding.

[Id. at 380.]

Unlike *Garnett*, no subsequent determination is necessary in this case to establish whether plaintiff meets one of the seven general tests for material participation set forth under Treasury Regulation § 1.469-5T(a). As noted above, the parties have stipulated that if plaintiff does not hold a limited partnership interest under § 1.469-5T(e)(3), then I.R.C. § 469 does not limit his share of Mountain Air's losses. Plaintiff does not hold a limited partnership interest. Therefore, § 469 does not limit plaintiff's share of Mountain Air's losses and the IRS's conclusion to the contrary is in error.

NOTES AND COMMENTS

1. An LLP is a general partnership that, by making an appropriate filing or registration under state law, is able to obtain a form of limited liability for its general partners. In other respects, however, an LLP is generally subject to the provisions of the applicable general partnership statute. Thus, under state law, the holder of an interest in an LLP, like a member in an LLC, may be actively involved in the business activities of the entity.

The *Thompson* decision cited and discussed two other decisions that have addressed the question regarding the application of § 469 and the material participation standard to holders of an interest in an LLC and an LLP, all of which reached the same conclusion albeit by adopting slightly different rationales. In *Gregg v. United States*, 186 F. Supp. 2d 1123 (D. Or. 2000), a federal district court judge applied minimal analysis and simply concluded that "[t]he limited partnership test is not applicable to all LLC members, because LLCs are designed to permit active involvement by LLC members in the management of the business." *Id.* at 1128. Similarly, in *Garnett v. Commissioner*, 132 T.C. 368 (2009), the Tax Court concluded that all seven of the material participation tests were available to a taxpayer who held interests in several LLPs and LLCs. The court did not adopt the narrow construction of Treasury Regulation § 1.469-5T(e)(3)(i) subsequently adopted by the Court of Federal Claims in *Thompson*, acknowledging the congressional grant of authority under § 469(h)(2) to the Secretary to treat "substantially equivalent entities" as limited partnerships could apply to both LLPs and LLCs. Assuming that an interest in an LLP or LLC could be characterized as an interest in a limited partnership, the court nevertheless concluded that the exception under § 1.469-5T(e)(3)(ii) for general partnership interests would be applicable because partners in an LLP and members in an LLC may participate in the business activities of the entity. In addition, the court refused to make "threshold factual inquiries" into the specific nature and extent of the taxpayer's authority to act on behalf of the LLPs and LLCs in order to determine if the interests involved were properly considered as general partnership interests. "These threshold factual inquiries . . . seem closely akin to factual inquiries appropriately made under the general tests for material participation. To import them into the per se rule of section 469(h)(2) would tend, we believe, to blur that special rule and the general rules for material participation in a manner that is at odds with the statutory framework and legislative intent." *Id.* at 379. *See also Newell v. Commissioner*, T.C. Memo. 2010-23, 99 T.C.M. (CCH) 1107 (following *Garnett* in a case involving an LLC under California law in which the taxpayer was the managing member of the LLC).

The Service subsequently acquiesced with respect to the result in *Thompson*, citing the decisions in *Gregg* and *Garnett*. AOD 2010-14, 2010 AOD LEXIS 2. The Service has also acknowledged the need to provide taxpayers with greater guidance in this area.

2. In addition to material participation, the Regulations recognize the concept of significant participation. Significant participation activities are those in which the taxpayer participates in the activity for more than 100 hours but not more than 500 hours during the taxable year. Temp. Treas. Reg. § 1.469-5T(c). The identification of significant participation activities is important for two reasons. First, as described above, a taxpayer will be deemed to materially participate in significant participation activities if the taxpayer's aggregate participation in all significant participation activities during such year exceeds 500 hours. Temp. Treas. Reg. § 1.469-5T(a)(4). Second, income in excess of losses from significant participation activities in which the taxpayer does not materially participate will be treated as income from a non-passive activity. Temp. Treas. Reg. § 1.469-2T(f)(2). Thus, if significant participation activities in which the taxpayer does not materially participate generate a net loss, the loss will be considered as a passive loss subject to the limitations on passive losses under § 469. However, if significant participation activities in which the taxpayer does not materially participate generate net income, the net income will be considered as arising from a non-passive activity and the taxpayer will not be allowed to offset such income with other passive losses. The purpose of this provision is to prevent taxpayers from manipulating the amount of time they devote to significant participation activities to make such activities passive if they generate net income.

§ 5.04. Rental Activities

Several special rules apply under § 469 in connection with rental activities. First, rental activities are typically deemed passive per se. § 469(c)(2); Temp. Treas. Reg. § 1.469-1T(e)(3)(i). The Regulations provide significant detail in defining a rental activity and contain a number of exceptions depending on the average period of customer use and the extent of personal services that may be combined with the rental of property. Treas. Reg. § 1.469-2(e)(3)(iii); Temp. Treas. Reg. § 1.469-1T(e)(3)(ii) through (viii).

Second, a rental real estate activity will not be deemed passive if the taxpayer is engaged in real property trades or business and satisfies certain tests in connection therewith. § 469(c)(7). To satisfy the requirements: (1) the taxpayer must perform more than 750 hours of services in real property trades of business in which the taxpayer materially participates, and (2) more than half of the personal services performed by the taxpayer during the taxable year must be performed in real property trades or businesses in which the taxpayer materially participates. § 469(c)(7)(B). In making this determination, the taxpayer may treat each rental real estate activity as a separate activity or treat all rental real estate activities as one activity. § 469(c)(7)(A). Real property trades or business include "any real property development, redevelopment, construction, acquisition, conversion, rental, operation, management, leasing, or brokerage trade or business." § 469(c)(7)(C). Participation by the taxpayer's spouse is not considered in determining whether the requirements of § 469(c)(7) are satisfied.

Section 469(c)(7) was not originally part of § 469 but was subsequently enacted in 1993. The purpose of this provision was to relax the characterization of rental real estate activities as passive per se with respect to individuals who were significantly engaged in real estate activities. *See* H.R. Rep. No. 103-111, 103d Cong., 1st Sess. 613 (1993) (stating that "[t]he committee considers it *unfair* that a person who performs personal services in a real estate trade or business in which he materially participates may not offset losses from rental real estate activities against income from nonrental real estate activities or against other types of income such as portfolio investment income (emphasis added). As described in the decision in *Bailey v. Commissioner*, T.C. Memo. 2001-296, 82 T.C.M. (CCH) 868, the taxpayer must jump through a number of hurdles to take advantage of the benefits of § 469(c)(7).

Third, the passive loss rules do not apply to rental real estate activities held by individuals who actively participate in such activities. § 469(i)(1). However, the aggregate losses allowable under this provision are limited to $25,000 in any taxable year, and this amount is reduced by 50 percent of the amount by which the taxpayer's adjusted gross income exceeds $100,000. § 469(i)(2) and (3). Thus, a taxpayer with an adjusted gross income in excess of $150,000 will not be eligible to deduct losses from these activities. An individual will not be deemed to actively participate in a rental real estate activity if the individual owns less than 10 percent of the interests by value in the activity. § 469(i)(6)(A). In addition, an activity in which the taxpayer holds a limited partnership interest will not be treated as an activity in which the taxpayer actively participates. § 469(i)(6)(C). Like material participation, active participation includes the participation of the taxpayer's spouse. § 469(i)(6)(D).

BAILEY v. COMMISSIONER

United States Tax Court

82 T.C.M. (CCH) 868, T.C. Memo. 2001-296

COHEN, JUDGE:

Respondent determined deficiencies of $12,094 and $11,651 in petitioners' Federal income tax for 1996 and 1997, respectively. After concessions, the remaining issues for decision are: (1) Whether petitioner Judy Bailey (petitioner) was a real estate professional under section 469(c)(7) during 1997 and (2) whether petitioners materially participated in the operation of their Lake Arrowhead property during 1996 and 1997. . . .

FINDINGS OF FACT

Petitioners resided in La Jolla, California, at the time they filed their petition. Petitioners filed joint individual income tax returns for 1996 and 1997.

Petitioners are both attorneys admitted to practice in California. Petitioner is an employee of Judy R. Bailey, a professional corporation, and practices in San Diego, California.

During 1996 and 1997, petitioners owned the following real estate properties, all of which were located in California: (1) A condominium located at Arapaho Way, Indian Wells (Indian Wells condominium); (2) a unit in a planned unit development located at Arapaho Drive, Indian Wells (Indian Wells unit); (3) two four-plex buildings located at Elderwood Court, Riverside (Elderwood properties); and (4) a single-family house located at Caribou Drive, Lake Arrowhead (Lake Arrowhead property). Petitioners filed an election, with their income tax return in 1994, to treat all interests in rental real estate as a single rental real estate activity pursuant to section 469(c)(7)(A).

Petitioner kept daily calendars for 1996 and 1997 that contained various appointments related to her law practice and real estate activities. In preparation for trial, petitioner prepared a separate summary report of her calendars for 1996 and 1997. Each summary report provided an estimate of the total number of hours spent on activities related to each rental property and gave a general description of the activities performed by petitioner. The summary report also provided a general list of the legal activities performed by petitioner and estimated that she spent 876 hours in the practice of law in 1997.

INDIAN WELLS PROPERTIES

Petitioner estimated that in 1997 she spent approximately 311 hours on activities related to the Indian Wells properties. Petitioner summarized her activities for 1997 as "re-rented, cleaned, did gardening, showed property to prospective renters, inspected repairmen's work". She also "started [the] process to sell by drawing up option[s] to purchase for prospective buyers [and] holding open houses." Petitioner's 1997 calendar indicates that she made 13 visits to the Indian Wells properties,

7 of which were in conjunction with matters relating to her law practice.

Petitioner had a commission agreement with Shirley Baughan and Associates to handle the rental of the Indian Wells condominium. The Indian Wells condominium was rented to a tenant from January 1 through 31, 1997, and to another tenant from February through December 1997. The residential lease agreement directed the tenants to remit their rent to Shirley Baughan's address. Shirley Baughan and Associates collected the rent payments, paid itself the agreed commission, reimbursed itself for expenses and repairs related to the rental property, and issued a check for the remaining amount to petitioners. Some of the expenses paid by Shirley Baughan and Associates were for shower parts, a water hose, a dryer vent hose, labor, the water bill, and keys. Petitioners deducted the commission expense that they paid to Shirley Baughan and Associates in the amount of $1,367 on Schedule E, Supplemental Income and Loss, of their 1997 joint income tax return.

Petitioners reported the rents received and expenses from the Indian Wells properties on Schedule E of their 1997 joint income tax return as follows:

	Indian Wells Condominium	Indian Wells Unit	Total
Rents received	$13,805	$10,900	$24,705
Less: Expenses	29,255	10,487	39,742
Income/(Loss)	(15,450)	413	(15,037)

ELDERWOOD PROPERTIES

Petitioner estimated that in 1997 she spent approximately 412 hours on activities related to the Elderwood properties. During 1997, the Elderwood properties were vacant, and petitioner conducted open houses to sell the Elderwood properties. Petitioner summarized her activities for 1997 as "arranged for repairs, did gardening and cleaning and inspected properties on a regular basis." Petitioner encountered several problems with the Elderwood properties in 1997 such as roof leaks that damaged the painting and carpeting, vandalism, trespassing by neighborhood children, and the eviction of a homeless person. Petitioner made nine visits to the Elderwood properties, five of which were in conjunction with matters relating to her law practice.

Petitioners reported the rents received and expenses from the Elderwood properties on Schedule E of their 1997 joint income tax return as follows:

	Elderwood 4-plex #1	Elderwood 4-plex #1	Total
Rents received	$-0-	$-0-	$-0-
Less: Expenses	11,227	7,837	19,064
Income/(Loss)	(11,227)	(7,837)	(19,064)

LAKE ARROWHEAD PROPERTY

Petitioner estimated that she spent 197.5 hours and 214 hours in 1996 and 1997, respectively, on activities related to the Lake Arrowhead property. The average period of customer use for the Lake Arrowhead property was 5 days per customer and 3.86 days per customer during 1996 and 1997, respectively. In 1996, petitioner supervised the repairmen and contractors, made selections and supervised interior design work, purchased household furnishings and supplies, and cleaned the property. Petitioner summarized her activities for 1997 as "re-rented, cleaned, gardening, showed property to prospective renters, inspected repairmen's work" and "started process to sell by holding open houses". In 1996, petitioner made 10 visits to the Lake Arrowhead property, 9 of which were in conjunction with matters relating to her law practice. In 1997, petitioner made three visits to the Lake Arrowhead property, two of which were in conjunction with matters relating to her law practice.

Petitioner had a commission agreement with Mountain Country Realty, Inc. (Mountain Country), to handle the rental of the Lake Arrowhead property during 1996 and 1997. Mountain Country located renters and showed the property to prospective renters. Mountain Country collected the rent payments, paid itself the agreed commission, reimbursed itself for expenses and repairs related to the rental property, and issued a check for the remaining amount to petitioners. Mountain Country handled the repairs related to the Lake Arrowhead property. Petitioners deducted the commission expenses paid to Mountain Country in the amounts of $2,471 and $1,881 in 1996 and 1997, respectively, on Schedule E of their joint income tax return.

Petitioners reported the rents received and expenses from the Lake Arrowhead property on Schedule E of their 1996 and 1997 joint income tax return as follows:

	1996	1997
Rents received	$9,855	$9,935
Less: Expenses	18,861	16,361
Income/(Loss)	(9,006)	(6,426)

* * *

OPINION

The parties have stipulated that petitioner was a real estate professional pursuant to section 469(c)(7) in 1996 and that petitioners are entitled to deduct $29,716 in rental losses in 1996 with respect to the Indian Wells properties and Elderwood properties.

Whether the remaining rental losses claimed by petitioners in 1996 and 1997 constitute passive activity losses under section 469 depends on: (1) Whether petitioner was a real estate professional under section 469(c)(7) during 1997 and (2) whether petitioners materially participated in the operation of their Lake Arrowhead property during 1996 and 1997.

Section 469 generally disallows for the taxable year any passive activity loss. Sec. 469(a). A passive activity loss is defined as the excess of the aggregate losses from all passive activities for the taxable year over the aggregate income from all passive activities for that year. Sec. 469(d)(1). A passive activity is any trade or business in which the taxpayer does not materially participate. Sec. 469(c)(1). Rental activity is treated as a per se passive activity regardless of whether the taxpayer materially participates. Sec. 469(c)(2), (4). Under section 469(c)(7)(B), the rental activities of a taxpayer in the real property business (real estate professional) are not per se passive activities under section 469(c)(2), but are treated as a trade or business and subject to the material participation requirement of section 469(c)(1). See also sec. 1.469-9(e)(1).

REAL ESTATE PROFESSIONAL

Petitioners assert that they are entitled to deduct their rental losses in 1997 and that such losses are not subject to the passive activity loss limitations under section 469. Petitioners contend that petitioner qualifies as a real estate professional under section 469(c)(7) for 1997, and, thus, their rental activities are exempt from being passive activities under section 469(c)(2).

Respondent's position is that petitioners are not entitled to deduct their rental losses in 1997 because their rental activities are passive activities under section 469(c)(2). Respondent maintains that petitioners have not presented adequate evidence to support their assertion that petitioner was a real estate professional pursuant to section 469(c)(7) in 1997.

Under section 469(c)(7)(B), a taxpayer qualifies as a real estate professional and a rental real estate activity of the taxpayer is not a passive activity under section 469(c)(2) if:

(i) more than one-half of the personal services performed in trades or businesses by the taxpayer during such taxable year are performed in real property trades or businesses in which the taxpayer materially participates, and

(ii) such taxpayer performs more than 750 hours of services during the taxable year in real property trades or businesses in which the taxpayer materially participates.

In the case of a joint return, the above requirements are satisfied if and only if either spouse separately satisfied these requirements. Sec. 469(c)(7)(B). Thus, if either spouse qualifies as a real estate professional, the rental activities of the real estate professional are exempt from being a passive activity under section 469(c)(2). Instead, the real estate professional's rental activities would be treated as a passive activity under section 469(c)(1) unless the taxpayer materially participated in the activity. Sec. 1.469- 9(e)(1).

For purposes of determining whether a taxpayer is a real estate professional, a taxpayer's material participation is determined separately with respect to each rental property, unless the taxpayer makes an election to treat all interests in rental real estate as a single rental real estate activity. Sec. 469(c)(7)(A); sec. 1.469-9(e)(1).

Here, petitioners made an election in 1994 to treat their rental properties as a single activity. According to section 1.469-9(g)(1), this election is binding for the taxable year in which it is made and, unless duly revoked by the taxpayer, for all future years in which the taxpayer is a real estate professional, even if there are intervening years in which the taxpayer is not a real estate professional.

Whether petitioner qualifies as a real estate professional under section 469(c)(7) is based on petitioner's activities related to the Indian Wells condominium, Indian Wells unit, and Elderwood properties. Petitioners argue that the Lake Arrowhead property is rental real estate that should be included in determining whether petitioner is a real estate professional. We disagree.

Petitioner's activities that are related to the Lake Arrowhead property are disregarded for purposes of determining whether she was a real estate professional, because the Lake Arrowhead property is not "rental real estate" as defined in section 1.469-9(b)(3). Section 1.469-9(b)(3) defines "rental real estate" as "any real property used by customers or held for use by customers in a rental activity within the meaning of section 1.469-1T(e)(3)." Section 1.469-1T(e)(3) states that, except as otherwise provided, an activity is a "rental activity" for a taxable year, if "during such taxable year, tangible property held in connection with the activity is used by customers or held for use by customers". See also sec. 469(j)(8). As provided in section 1.469-1T(e)(3)(ii)(A), an "activity involving the use of tangible property is not a rental activity for a taxable year if for such taxable year * * * [the] average period of customer use for such property is seven days or less".

The average period of customer use for the Lake Arrowhead property was less than 7 days during 1996 and 1997. Thus, the rental of the Lake Arrowhead property is not a "rental activity" as defined in section 1.469-1T(e)(3)(ii)(A), not "rental real estate" under section 1.469-9(b)(3), and not included in the election under section 469(c)(7) to treat all interests in rental real estate as a single rental real estate activity. See *Scheiner v. Commissioner*, T.C. Memo. 1996-554 (where average period of customer use less than 7 days, condominium hotel activity was not rental activity under section 469(j)(8) and not considered a passive activity under section 469(c)(2)); *Mordkin v. Commissioner*, T.C. Memo. 1996-187.

Respondent maintains that petitioner is not a real estate professional for 1997 because: (1) Petitioners have not substantiated through a reasonable means that petitioner performed more than 750 hours of service in relation to her rental activities and (2) petitioner's personal services performed in her rental activities during 1997 do not exceed the 876 hours that she spent in her practice of law.

With respect to the evidence that may be used to establish hours of participation, section 1.469-5T(f)(4) provides:

> The extent of an individual's participation in an activity may be established by any reasonable means. Contemporaneous daily time reports, logs, or similar documents are not required if the extent of such participation may be established by other reasonable means. Reasonable means for purposes of this paragraph may include but are not limited to the identification of services performed over a period of time and the approximate number of

hours spent performing such services during such period, based on appointment books, calendars, or narrative summaries.

Petitioner kept a daily calendar for 1997 that indicated the number of visits made to the rental properties, but the calendar did not quantify the number of hours that she spent on her rental activities. Petitioner attempted to summarize the activities that were noted in her 1997 calendar into a summary report, in which she generally explained the activities performed at the rental properties and provided an annual estimate of the hours spent on each rental property. Excluding petitioner's estimate of the hours that she spent on activities directly related to the Lake Arrowhead property, petitioner's summary report estimated that she spent 827 hours performing services related to the rental properties during 1997 and consisted of the following: (1) Indian Wells properties, 311 hours; (2) Elderwood properties, 412 hours; and (3) general activities for all real estate properties (including the Lake Arrowhead property), 104 hours. We believe that the methods that petitioner used to approximate the time that she spent performing these services during 1997 are not reasonable within the meaning of section 1.469-5T(f)(4), Temporary Income Tax Regs., supra. Petitioner's estimates are uncorroborated and do not reliably reflect the hours that she devoted to her rental real estate activities. Petitioner assigned hours to activities years later, and in preparation for trial, based solely on her judgment and experience as to how much time the activities must have taken her. This Court has previously noted that, while the regulations are somewhat ambivalent concerning the records to be maintained by taxpayers, they do not allow a post event "ballpark guesstimate". *Carlstedt v. Commissioner*, T.C. Memo. 1997-331; *Speer v. Commissioner*, T.C. Memo. 1996-323; *Goshorn v. Commissioner*, T.C. Memo. 1993-578. Petitioner has not distinguished the facts of this case from those cited, and we conclude that they are not distinguishable.

The following factors further diminish the credibility and accuracy of the summary report prepared by petitioner: (1) The number of hours claimed appears excessive in relation to the tasks described; (2) petitioner testified that she usually combined a trip to the rental properties with a trip related to her law practice; (3) the Elderwood properties were vacant during 1997; (4) the Elderwood properties and Indian Wells properties were for sale during 1997; and (5) petitioner had a commission agreement with Shirley Baughan and Associates to manage the rental of the Indian Wells condominium during 1997.

Additionally, petitioner's personal services performed in her rental activities of 827 hours do not exceed the 876 hours that she spent in 1997 in her practice of law. Petitioner therefore does not qualify as a real estate professional under section 469(c)(7), and the rental activities of the Indian Wells properties and Elderwood properties are passive activities under section 469(c)(2) during 1997 regardless of material participation by petitioner in these activities. See sec. 469(c)(4).

LAKE ARROWHEAD PROPERTY

Respondent maintains that petitioners are not entitled to deduct losses generated from their Lake Arrowhead property in 1996 and 1997, because the Lake Arrowhead property is real estate held in a trade or business subject to section 469(c)(1), rather than a rental activity under section 469(c)(2), and petitioners have not established that they materially participated in the trade or business of renting their Lake Arrowhead property as required by section 469(c)(1)(B).

Petitioners argue that they properly filed an election pursuant to section 469(c)(7)(A)(ii) to treat all of their interests in rental real estate as a single rental real estate activity and that their activities related to the rental of their Lake Arrowhead property should be considered in aggregate with their other rental properties. As previously explained, petitioners' argument fails because the election to treat all rental properties as one activity is limited to the purpose of determining whether a taxpayer is a real estate professional under section 469(c)(7). Here, the average period of use of the Lake Arrowhead property was less than 7 days in 1996 and 1997; thus, the rental of the Lake Arrowhead property is not a rental activity as defined in section 469(j)(8) and is not a passive activity under section 469(c)(2). See *Scheiner v. Commissioner*, supra; *Mordkin v. Commissioner*, supra. Nevertheless, petitioners' operations at the Lake Arrowhead property during each year in issue constitute an activity that is treated as a trade or business under section 469(c)(6). Consequently, petitioners' operations at the Lake Arrowhead property will constitute a passive activity under section 469(c)(1) unless petitioners establish that they materially participated in that activity during the taxable years in issue. Petitioners argue in the alternative that the activities related to the Lake Arrowhead property were not a passive activity under section 469(c)(1) because petitioners met the material participation requirements.

Material participation is defined as involvement in the operations of the activity that is regular, continuous, and substantial. Sec. 469(h)(1). As explained in section 1.469-5T(a), a taxpayer can satisfy the material participation requirement if the individual meets any one of the seven regulatory tests:

(1) The individual participates in the activity for more than 500 hours during such year;

(2) The individual's participation in the activity for the taxable year constitutes substantially all of the participation in such activity of all individuals (including individuals who are not owners of interests in the activity) for such year;

(3) The individual participates in the activity for more than 100 hours during the taxable year, and such individual's participation in the activity for the taxable year is not less than the participation in the activity of any other individual (including individuals who are not owners of interests in the activity) for such year;

(4) The activity is a significant participation activity * * * for the taxable year, and the individual's aggregate participation in all significant participation activities during the year exceeds 500 hours;

(5) The individual materially participated in the activity * * * for any five taxable years (whether or not consecutive) during the ten taxable years that immediately precede the taxable year;

(6) The activity is a personal service activity * * *, and the individual materially participated in the activity for any three tax years (whether or not

consecutive) preceding the taxable year; or

(7) Based on all facts and circumstances * * *, the individual participates in the activity on a regular, continuous, and substantial basis during such year.

"Participation" generally means "all work done in an activity by an individual who owns an interest in the activity". Sec. 1.469-5T(f). Work done by an individual in the individual's capacity as an investor in an activity is not generally treated as participation in the activity. Sec. 1.469-5T(f)(2)(ii)(A). Additionally, work done by the individual is not treated as participation in the activity if such work is not of a type that is customarily done by an owner of such activity and one of the principal purposes for performing such work is to avoid the passive activity limitations of section 469. Sec. 1.469-5T(f)(2)(i).

In determining whether a taxpayer materially participates, the participation of the spouse of the taxpayer shall be taken into account. Sec. 469(h)(5). Petitioners' reply brief argues that they both spent time in the activity in issue; however, Bruce Bailey did not testify or even appear at trial. Petitioners' assertion that Bruce Bailey spent time in the activity appears to be an afterthought; such participation is not mentioned in the testimony of petitioner, who described only her own actions. Thus, we are unable to take into account the hours, if any, spent by Bruce Bailey in the operation of the Lake Arrowhead property.

Petitioners contend that they meet several of the material participation tests under section 1.469-5T(a). Petitioner's summary report estimated that she spent 197.5 hours and 214 hours in 1996 and 1997, respectively, on activities related to the Lake Arrowhead property. Petitioner's calendars indicated the number of visits made to the Lake Arrowhead property in 1996 and 1997, but those calendars do not quantify the number of hours that petitioner spent on activities related to the Lake Arrowhead property. For the reasons stated previously, we do not accept petitioner's summary reports that estimated the hours spent on activities related to the Lake Arrowhead property. See *Carlstedt v. Commissioner*, T.C. Memo. 1997-331; *Speer v. Commissioner*, T.C. Memo. 1996-323; *Goshorn v. Commissioner*, T.C. Memo. 1993-578.

Even if such hours were accurate, petitioners would not meet any of the material participation tests. Petitioners have not spent more than 500 hours in the activity. Petitioner's commission agreement with Mountain Country to manage the rental of the Lake Arrowhead property would preclude petitioners' activities from being substantially all of the participation in the activity. Petitioners have not presented evidence to establish that the participation by Mountain Country did not exceed petitioners' participation. Petitioners have not presented evidence of their material participation in the Lake Arrowhead property for 5 of the prior 10 years.

Petitioners also fail the facts and circumstances test based on petitioner's commission agreement with Mountain Country to operate the rental of their Lake Arrowhead property. The realty company found tenants, showed the property, collected rents, and paid for repairs. See *Barniskis v. Commissioner*, T.C. Memo. 1999-258 (taxpayers did not materially participate where taxpayers utilized a management company to handle the rental of their resort condominium); *Chapin v. Commissioner*, T.C. Memo. 1996-56 (taxpayers' participation did not constitute participation on a regular, continuous, and substantial basis where taxpayers used a rental agent to handle all leasing arrangements, cleaning between tenants, and routine repairs and maintenance).

We conclude that petitioners did not materially participate in the operation of the Lake Arrowhead property during 1996 and 1997, and, accordingly, petitioners' trade or business relating to the Lake Arrowhead property is a passive activity under section 469(c)(1). The losses incurred with respect to the Lake Arrowhead property are subject to the passive loss limitations imposed by section 469 and are disallowed in 1996 and 1997.

* * *

We have considered all of the remaining arguments that have been made by petitioners for a result contrary to that expressed herein, and, to the extent not discussed above, they are without merit.

§ 5.05. Self-Charged Items

When enacting § 469, Congress recognized that, under certain circumstances, a taxpayer may be engaged in activities with a pass-through entity in which he owns an interest that result in non-passive income to the taxpayer and that generate passive losses for the entity. One example is a loan from a limited partner to the partnership under which the interest paid by the partnership generates portfolio income to the limited partner and an interest expense that would increase a loss at the partnership level. The limited partner's allocable share of the partnership loss would be a passive loss that the limited partner could not use to offset the non-passive interest income despite the fact that the limited partner was, in effect, paying himself a portion of the interest income. The legislative history referred to such situations as involving "self-charged" interest and provided that the Treasury Department should issue Regulations providing appropriate relief to taxpayers. § 469(l)(2); H.R. Rep. No. 99-841, 99th Cong., 2d Sess. II-146-47 (1986). Although referring explicitly to situations involving loans between a taxpayer and a related pass-through entity, the legislative history recognized that other situations should be accorded similar relief.

The Service issued Proposed Regulations addressing the treatment of interest income and interest expense in lending transactions between a taxpayer and a pass-through entity in 1991. The Proposed Regulations did not provide taxpayer relief in other similar situations. In the following case, the taxpayer argued that similar relief should be allowed in the context of real estate management services that he provided to a number of related pass-through entities for which he received non-passive compensation for services income that generated losses at the entity level. The Tax Court agreed with the taxpayer that relief should be granted despite the fact that no Regulations addressing situations other than lending transactions had been issued. *Hillman v. Commissioner*, 114 T.C. 103 (2000). The court relied on prior case law under which the court found language similar to that of § 469(l)(2) to be self-executing. According to the court, "the Treasury's failure to provide the needed guidance should not deprive taxpayers of the benefit or relief Congress intended." *Id.* at 111. In the following opinion, however, the Fourth Circuit reversed the Tax Court's decision, finding it inconsistent with the plain meaning of § 469. The Appeals Court's opinion is an important example of statutory interpretation under the Code.

Subsequent to the Fourth Circuit's opinion in *Hillman*, the Service and the Treasury Department considered comments to the Proposed Regulations to expand their scope to address management fees and salaries. In promulgating the final Regulations, the Service and the Treasury Department declined to do so. As stated in the Supplementary Information to the final Regulations, the Service and the Treasury Department found such relief unnecessary in light of the enactment of § 469(c)(7).

> Noting that Congress authorized the Secretary to identify other situations in which self-charged treatment is appropriate, several commentators suggested that self-charged treatment be extended to other transactions involving rental real estate activities, such as the payment of management fees and salaries. After publication of the proposed regulations, Congress considered the impact of section 469 on rental real estate transactions and enacted specific relief in section 469(c)(7) for certain real estate professionals for taxable years beginning after 1993. There was no indication in the legislative history of section 469(c)(7) that Congress considered additional relief for real estate transactions necessary or desirable. Moreover, there is less justification for the complexity of a self-charged rule in this area after the enactment of section 469(c)(7) because that change substantially reduced the number of real estate transactions that would benefit from a self-charged rule. Accordingly, the regulations do not extend the self-charged treatment to other transactions involving rental real estate.

T.D. 9013, 67 Fed. Reg. 54,088 (2002).

HILLMAN v. INTERNAL REVENUE SERVICE

United States Court of Appeals, Fourth Circuit
263 F.3d 338 (4th Cir. 2001)

HAMILTON, SENIOR CIRCUIT JUDGE:

I.

In mid-July 1997, David and Suzanne Hillman (the Hillmans) received written notice from the Commissioner of the United States Internal Revenue Service (the Commissioner) that a deficiency existed in the amount of federal income taxes they had paid for taxable years 1993 and 1994. According to the notice, the Hillmans still owed the government $294,556.00 in federal income taxes for taxable year 1993 and $309,696.00 in federal income taxes for taxable year 1994. The Hillmans contested the full amounts of these deficiencies by filing a timely petition for redetermination in the United States Tax Court (the Tax Court). At the time the Hillmans filed their petition, they were residents of Bethesda, Maryland.

The parties submitted this case to the Tax Court on the following stipulated facts.

During taxable year 1993, David Hillman was the sole shareholder of Southern Management Corporation (SMC), a corporation taxed under Subchapter S of the Internal Revenue Code (IRC).[11] During taxable year 1994, David Hillman owned 94.43 percent of SMC's stock.

SMC provided real estate management services to approximately ninety entities, including joint ventures, limited partnerships, and Subchapter S corporations, which were involved in real estate rental activities.[12] At all times relevant to the issues in this appeal, David Hillman owned, either directly or indirectly, interests in each of these entities (the Passthrough Entities). The general partner of each limited partnership was either David Hillman or an upper tier partnership or Subchapter S corporation in which he owned an interest.

During taxable years 1993 and 1994, the Hillmans did not participate in the activities of the Passthrough Entities. The Hillmans did, however, participate in the activities of SMC by performing real estate management services SMC had contracted to perform for the Passthrough Entities. Indeed, David Hillman materially participated in SMC's real estate management activity in excess of 500 hours.

The Hillmans reported as income the compensation paid to them for their real estate management services offered through SMC for taxable years 1993 and 1994. In computing their taxable income for 1993 and 1994, the Hillmans deducted the total amounts of the management fee expenses of the Passthrough Entities for taxable years 1993 and 1994 from the gross income they received during those years through SMC for providing the management services that gave rise to the management fee expenses. The notice of deficiency disallowed this deduction, thus resulting in the claimed tax deficiencies at issue in this appeal.

On April 18, 2000, the Tax Court entered a final decision fully in favor of the Hillmans. The Tax Court accompanied its final decision with a published opinion holding the Hillmans properly deducted the management fee expenses of the Passthrough Entities from their related management fee income for purposes of lowering the amounts of their taxable income for taxable years 1993 and 1994. The Commissioner filed a timely appeal. We have appellate jurisdiction pursuant to 26 U.S.C. § 7482(a)(1).

Judge Wilkins and Judge Williams join in this part of the opinion.

II.

In this appeal, we are presented with the following question of law: May the Hillmans legally deduct their passive management fee expenses from their related

[11] [1] Shareholders of a corporation taxed under Subchapter S of the IRC may elect a passthrough taxation system, under which the corporation's profits pass through directly to its shareholders on a *pro rata* basis and are reported on each shareholder's individual federal income tax returns. 26 U.S.C. § 1366(a)(1)(A).

[12] [2] For purposes of federal income tax liability, joint venturers and partners are taxed under a passthrough taxation system. 26 U.S.C. § 701-04, 761(a). Thus, each joint venturer or partner is individually taxed on his distributive share of joint venture or partnership income. *Id.*

nonpassive management fee income for purposes of lowering their taxable income for taxable years 1993 and 1994? We review this question of law *de novo*. *Balkissoon v. Commissioner*, 995 F.2d 525, 527 (4th Cir. 1993).

The Commissioner insists this question is easily answered by applying the plain language of IRC § 469(a), which prohibits individuals, estates, trusts, closely held C corporations, and personal service corporations from deducting passive activity losses or passive activity credits from nonpassive gains in an effort to lower taxable income. 26 U.S.C. § 469(a). Specifically, IRC § 469(a) provides:

> (a) Disallowance. —
> (1) In General. — If for any taxable year the taxpayer is described in paragraph (2), neither —
> (A) the passive activity loss, nor
> (B) the passive activity credit, for the taxable year shall be allowed.
> (2) Persons described. — The following are described in this paragraph:
> (A) any individual, estate, or trust,
> (B) any closely held C corporation, and
> (C) any personal service corporation.

Id. For purposes of IRC § 469, the term "passive activity" is defined as an activity involving the conduct of a trade or business in which the taxpayer does not materially participate. *Id.* § 469(c)(1). With certain exceptions not relevant here, rental activity is a passive activity. *Id.* § 469(c)(2). Also for purposes of IRC § 469, the term "passive activity loss" is defined as "the amount (if any) by which — (A) the aggregate losses from all passive activities for the taxable year, exceed (B) the aggregate income from all passive activities for such year." *Id.* § 469(d)(1). The Commissioner points out that the somewhat harsh result of applying IRC § 469(a) in a self-charged or wash transaction is tempered by IRC § 469(b), which provides that "any loss or credit from an activity which is disallowed under subsection (a) shall be treated as a deduction or credit allocable to such activity in the next taxable year." *Id.* § 469(b).

The Hillmans do not dispute, nor could they, that straightforward application of the plain language of IRC § 469(a) prohibits them from deducting the management fee expenses of the Passthrough Entities for taxable years 1993 and 1994 from their related management fee income for those same respective years. However, the Hillmans take the position that the plain language of IRC § 469(a) should not so apply. The Hillmans' position is based upon their argument that, when IRC § 469(l)(2) is read together with certain portions of IRC § 469's legislative history, it is clear that Congress directed the Secretary of the Treasury (the Secretary) to issue a regulation excepting self-charged management fees resulting in no accretion of the taxpayer's actual wealth from operation of IRC § 469(a), and the Secretary's failure to comply with this direction does not prevent them from avoiding operation of IRC § 469(a). The Tax Court's reasoning in support of its ruling in favor of the Hillmans essentially tracks this argument made by the Hillmans.

IRC § 469(l)(2), relied upon by the Hillmans, provides that the Secretary "shall prescribe such regulations as may be necessary or appropriate to carry out provisions of [IRC § 469], including regulations — . . . which provide that certain items of gross income will not be taken into account in determining income or loss from any activity (and the treatment of expenses allocable to such income) . . . ." 26 U.S.C. § 469(l)(2). The following excerpt from the House Conference Report for the Tax Reform Act of 1986 is the legislative history of IRC § 469 upon which the Hillmans rely:

> Self-charged interest. — A further issue with respect to portfolio income arises where an individual receives interest income on debt of a passthrough entity in which he owns an interest. Under certain circumstances, the interest may essentially be "self-charged," and thus lack economic significance. For example, assume that a taxpayer charges $100 of interest on a loan to an S corporation in which he is the sole shareholder. In form, the transaction could be viewed as giving rise to offsetting payments of interest income and passthrough interest expense, although in economic substance the taxpayer has paid the interest to himself.
>
> Under these circumstances, it is not appropriate to treat the transaction as giving rise both to portfolio interest income and to passive interest expense. Rather, to the extent that a taxpayer receives interest income with respect to a loan to a passthrough entity in which he has an ownership interest, such income should be allowed to offset the interest expense passed through to the taxpayer from the activity for the same taxable year.
>
> * * *
>
> The conferees anticipate that Treasury regulations will be issued to provide for the above result. Such regulations may also, to the extent appropriate, identify other situations in which netting of the kind described above is appropriate with respect to a payment to a taxpayer by an entity in which he has an ownership interest. Such netting should not, however, permit any passive deductions to offset non passive income except to the extent of the taxpayer's allocable share of the specific payment at issue.

H.R. Conf. Rep. No. 99-841, at II-146-47 (1986). The Secretary has promulgated no permanent regulations exempting self-charged items of income and expenses from operation of IRC § 469(a), and has only issued one proposed regulation in this regard. That proposed regulation deals *only* with the self-charged interest situation specifically discussed in the just quoted legislative history of IRC § 469 and the reverse of that situation (*i.e.*, when a passthrough entity loans money to its owner). Prop. Treas. Reg. § 1.469-7, 56 Fed. Reg. 14,034 (April 5, 1991).

We hold IRC § 469(a) prohibits the Hillmans from legally deducting their passive management fee expenses from their related nonpassive management fee income for purposes of lowering their taxable income for taxable years 1993 and 1994. The threshold problem with the Hillmans' position is that nothing in the plain language of IRC § 469 suggests that an exception to IRC § 469(a)'s general prohibition against a taxpayer's deducting passive activity losses from nonpassive activity gains exists where, as in the present case, the taxpayer essentially paid a management fee to himself. The general rule is that unless there is some ambiguity in the language of a statute, a court's analysis must end with the statute's plain language (the Plain

Meaning Rule). *Caminetti v. United States*, 242 U.S. 470, 485, 37 S. Ct. 192, 61 L. Ed. 442 (1917) ("The rules which are to aid doubtful meanings need no discussion" when the statutory language is clear and unambiguous.); *United States v. Morison*, 844 F.2d 1057, 1064 (4th Cir. 1988) ("When the terms of a statute are clear, its language is conclusive and courts are not free to replace that clear language with an unenacted legislative intent." (internal quotation marks and alteration marks omitted)).

The Hillmans' argument calling for us to ignore the plain language of IRC § 469(a) implicates two extremely narrow exceptions to the Plain Meaning Rule. The first exception applies when literal application of the statutory language at issue produces an outcome that is demonstrably at odds with clearly expressed congressional intent to the contrary. *Sigmon Coal Co. v. Apfel*, 226 F.3d 291, 304 (4th Cir. 2000). The second exception implicated by the Hillmans' argument applies when literal application of the statutory language at issue "results in an outcome that can truly be characterized as absurd, *i.e.*, that is so gross as to shock the general moral or common sense . . . ." *Id.* (internal quotation marks omitted). If either of these exceptions apply, "then we can look beyond an unambiguous statute and consult legislative history to divine its meaning." *Id.* Again, the instances in which either of these exceptions to the Plain Meaning Rule apply "are, and should be, exceptionally rare." *Id.*

When considering the applicability in the case before us of the first described exception to the Plain Meaning Rule, we must consider whether clearly expressed congressional intent exists to the effect that taxpayers such as the Hillmans are exempt from operation of IRC § 469(a) in a self-charged or wash transaction involving passive management fee expense and related nonpassive management fee income. Unfortunately for the Hillmans, no such clearly expressed congressional intent exists. First, no statutory language, including the statutory language of IRC § 469(l)(2), is of help to the Hillmans in this regard. Second, the legislative history of IRC § 469 does not clearly express the congressional intent the Hillmans need in order to prevail on their argument. Indeed, the only situation the legislative history of IRC § 469 specifies that deserves exception from operation of IRC § 469(a) is one involving self-charged interest. H.R. Conf. Rep. No. 99-841, at II-146 (1986). Moreover, the legislative history further states, without qualification, that the Secretary has discretion to identify other situations in which offsetting otherwise prohibited under IRC § 469(a) will be allowed. H.R. Conf. Rep. No. 99-841, at II-146-47 (1986). Without clearly expressed congressional intent, contrary to the result produced by literally applying the plain language of IRC § 469(a) to the factual situation presented in this case, the Hillmans cannot avail themselves of the first described exception to the Plain Meaning Rule.

The Hillmans also cannot avail themselves of the second described exception to the Plain Meaning Rule — that literal application of the statutory language at issue produces an absurd result. Literal application of the plain language of IRC § 469(a) to the factual situation before us does not produce a result that is so gross as to shock our general moral or common sense. In this regard, we point out that the somewhat harsh result created by literally applying IRC § 469(a) to the wash transaction at issue here is considerably tempered by the fact that IRC § 469(b) allows the Hillmans to carry forward the passive management fee expenses for taxable years 1993 and 1994 to subsequent taxable years as deductions allocable to the activity of the Passthrough Entities for those next years. We do note, however, that we see no reason why the factual situation before is not deserving of exemption from operation of IRC § 469(a) as proposed by the Secretary with regard to an interest payment in a self-charged transaction, *see* Prop. Treas. Reg. § 1.469-7. But, this is an inequity in the United States Tax Code that only Congress or the Secretary (as the holder of delegated authority from Congress) has the authority to ameliorate.

In summary, we hold that IRC § 469(a) prohibits the Hillmans from legally deducting their passive management fee expenses from their related nonpassive management fee income for purposes of lowering their taxable income for taxable years 1993 and 1994.

Judge Wilkins and Judge Williams join in this part of the opinion.

§ 5.06. Disposition of a Passive Activity

Upon disposition of a taxpayer's entire interest in a passive activity in which gain or loss is recognized, all previously suspended losses are allowed. This result is accomplished by treating gain on the disposition of the activity as passive income and allowing the taxpayer to deduct previously suspended losses from the activity disposed of to the extent of that gain. If the gain realized on disposition is greater than the previously suspended losses from the activity, the net passive income may allow suspended losses from other passive activities to be deducted. If the disposition of the activity results in a loss or results in gain that is less than the previously suspended losses from the activity, the loss resulting from the disposition of the activity or the net loss after allowance of the previously suspended losses will then be allowable to the extent of any passive income in excess of passive expenses and losses from other passive activities in the taxable year. Finally, any loss from the activity disposed of in excess of this amount is treated as a loss that is not from a passive activity. § 469(g)(1).

Special rules apply on disposition of a passive activity on the death of the taxpayer or by gift from the taxpayer. A transfer of a passive activity on the death of the taxpayer allows the taxpayer to deduct any previously suspended losses to the extent that such losses exceed the basis of the property in the hands of the transferee over the basis of such property in the hands of the taxpayer immediately before the taxpayer's death. § 469(g)(2)(A). Thus, the decedent taxpayer is typically allowed to deduct suspended losses that exceed the step-up in basis of the devised property under § 1014. Any previously suspended losses to the extent of any such step-up in basis are permanently disallowed. § 469(g)(2)(B). If there is a step down in basis under § 1014, the entire amount of previously suspended losses are deductible. In the case of a transfer by gift, any suspended losses are not allowed as a deduction by the donor in the year of disposition, but the donee is permitted to increase the donee's basis in the property by the amount of the suspended losses. § 469(j)(6). For purposes of determining loss on any subsequent disposition of the activity by the donee, the donee's basis may not exceed the fair market value of the activity at the time of the gift. S. Rep. No. 99-313, 99th Cong., 2d Sess. 726 n.12 (1986).

Finally, if a passive activity is disposed of through an installment sale under which gain is recognized under § 453, any suspended losses are allowable only in proportion to the gain that is recognized each year. § 469(g)(3).

PROBLEMS FOR DISCUSSION

Problem 8-6. On January 1, Year 1, T bought a residential apartment building for $3.5 million, paying $700,000 in cash and obtaining a nonrecourse mortgage from the seller for $2.8 million. The loan requires interest payments of eight percent each year, with principal payable at the end of 15 years. At the time of acquisition, the fair market value of the building was $3 million and the land was $500,000. T hired a management company to lease and manage the property. In Year 1, T received rent of $520,000 and incurred the following expenses:

Rent	$520,000
Expenses:	
Interest	$224,000
Management Costs	80,450
Taxes	175,000
Insurance	26,000
Depreciation	104,550
Total	$610,000

(a) How do the at-risk rules under § 465 limit T's deductions in Year 1? To what extent is T at-risk with respect to the property?

(b) How do the passive loss rules under § 469 limit T's deductions in Year 1?

(c) Assume that T owns another residential apartment building that generates rental income in excess of expenses (including depreciation) of $50,000 in Year 1 and that T receives $30,000 in dividends on his investment portfolio in Year 1. Does this affect his deductions under § 469?

(d) What if T owns several apartment buildings generating the following rental income and deductions?

	A	B	C	Total
Rental Income	520,000	360,000	525,000	1,405,000
Deductions	610,000	420,000	475,000	1,505,000
Net Income (Loss)	(90,000)	(60,000)	50,000	(100,000)

What limitations apply with respect to the deductions from each of these activities?

Problem 8-7. On January 1, Year 11, T decides to sell the residential apartment building he purchased in Year 1. T's basis in the property is $2,413,700. T sells the property to an unrelated party for $4,000,000. T has suspended losses attributable to this rental activity of $300,000.

(a) How does the sale of the building affect the deductibility of the previously suspended losses?

(b) What difference would it make in (a) if T had losses of $50,000 from a different passive activity in Year 11?

(c) What difference would it make in (a) if T sold the building in an installment sale in which the buyer paid $800,000 in the year of the sale and $800,000 in each of the following four years?

(d) What difference would it make in (a) if T sold the building for $2,000,000? Would it matter if T had $100,000 of passive income from other activities?

(e) What if, instead of selling the building, T gave the building to his son? What if T died and his son inherited the building?

Problem 8-8. T is an accountant with gross income in excess of $100,000 in Year 1 from her practice. Can T deduct the losses from the following activities against that income?

(a) T spends more than 600 hours operating business A with income of $250,000 and deductions of $275,000. T has several full-time employees.

(b) Same as (a) except that T spends 450 hours and T's spouse spends 150 hours.

(c) Same as (a) except that T spends only 350 hours running the business.

(d) Same as (c) except that T has only part-time employees, none of whom spends more than 300 hours in the business.

(e) Same as (c) except that T also runs business B and business C (both with full-time employees) and T spends 250 hours running business A, 150 hours running business B, and 120 hours running business C.

(f) Same as (e) except that T spends 200 hours running business A, 150 hours running the business B, and 120 hours running business C. What if business C has gross income excess of deductions of $20,000 for the year?

(g) T is a limited partner in a partnership that operated business A, and T is not involved in the daily activities of the business. What if T is a member of an LLC that operates business A, and T is not involved in the daily activities of the business? What if T is a member of an LLC that operates business A, and T spends more than 600 hours in business activities?

(h) T owns several rental apartment buildings with deductions in excess of income. T spends 1,200 hours in her accounting practice and 1,300 hours managing the apartment buildings.

§ 6. LIMITATIONS ON LOSSES FROM LEASING TRANSACTIONS

I.R.C. §§ 168(g)(1)-(3), 168(h)(1)-(4); 470; 7701(e)

Treas. Reg. § 1.168(i)-2

Following the expansion of § 465 and the enactment of § 469, tax shelter transactions evolved from those designed especially for individual investors to those designed for corporate taxpayers who were not subject to the constraints of those provisions. One type of transaction that generated significant opportunities for the sheltering of income by corporations was the leasing of both personal and real property. Under these transactions, corporate taxpayers with high effective tax rates acquired and leased property to taxpayers with low effective rates rather than the lessees acquiring the property directly, thus maximizing the value of the depreciation and interest deductions associated with the ownership of such property. The tax benefits of such arrangements were described in Chapter 7.

Congress had long been concerned with leasing transactions involving so-called "tax indifferent parties" — tax-exempt and governmental entities and foreign persons and entities. Because these persons or entities are exempt from U.S. taxation, U.S. taxpayers can engage in leasing transactions that will generate tax benefits for U.S. tax purposes. In 1984, Congress limited the tax benefits from such transactions through the denial of accelerated depreciation deductions for tangible property that was predominantly used outside the United States and for any tax-exempt use property. § 168(g)(1)(A) and (B). Such property is depreciable only by using the straight-line method under the alternative depreciation system. Tax-exempt use property includes personal and most types of real property leased to a tax-exempt entity. § 168(h)(1) and (2). In addition, Congress imposed significant limitations on the ability of lessees and lessors to structure rental terms so as to maximize tax benefits. § 467.

Notwithstanding these provisions of the Code, taxpayers devised methods to structure leasing arrangements that continued to generate substantial tax benefits. One such structure, referred to as a SILO transaction, refocused congressional attention on leasing transactions and whether restrictions should be enacted to curtail the use of such transactions. The Service identified SILO transactions as abusive in 2005-1 C.B. 630, Notice 2005-13. The structure of a SILO transaction is described in the following excerpt from the Treasury Department's revenue proposals for the 2005 fiscal year.

U.S. TREASURY DEPARTMENT

General Explanations of the Administration's Fiscal Year 2005 Revenue Proposals 124-126 (February 2004)

Reform the Tax Treatment for Leasing Transactions with Tax Indifferent Parties

Leasing plays an important role as an affordable source of capital. Recently, arrangements have been entered into with tax-indifferent parties, such as foreign and domestic municipalities and tax-exempt organizations, that purport to be leasing transactions but, in substance, provide no financing to the tax-indifferent party aside from a fee. These arrangements have no meaningful financial or economic utility other than the transfer of tax benefits to a U.S. taxpayer (by means of a purported "sale" of property) in exchange for the payment of an accommodation fee to the tax-indifferent party. These arrangements are known as SILOs, or sale-in/lease out arrangements.

For example, a U.S. taxpayer ("Lessor") may purport to "purchase" an existing asset, such as a subway line, stadium, or waste water facility, from a tax-indifferent party for $100 million and simultaneously lease the property back to the tax-indifferent party.[13] No interruption or change occurs in the actual use, operation, or control of the property. Under the terms of the arrangement, the tax-indifferent party has an option to "repurchase" the property from the Lessor for a predetermined price at the end of the lease.

Approximately 85 percent of the Lessor's $100 million "purchase" price is financed with non-recourse debt. Virtually all (in this example $96 million) of the "purchase" price is set aside in defeasance arrangements and other investments for the benefit of the Lessor and the nonrecourse lender (often in an account at a bank related to the lender). These arrangements are structured to provide the necessary funds to pay the rent due under the lease and to fund the exercise by the tax-indifferent party of its "purchase option" at the end of the lease term. Thus, without any further cost or expenditure, the tax-indifferent party may continue to use the property for the entire lease term and retain all rights to the property at the end of that term. In return for its participation, the tax-indifferent party receives the $4 million difference between the "purchase" price and the amount set aside for the benefit of the Lessor. In essence, the $4 million amount is an accommodation fee received by the tax-indifferent party for selling tax benefits (depreciation on the $100 million "purchase" price) to the Lessor.

In addition to the defeasance arrangements described above, Lessors have used other arrangements, including "loop debt" or "loan backs" by the tax-indifferent party to the Lessor (or an affiliate), collateralized letters of credit, payment undertakings, lease prepayments, deposit agreements, and sinking funds, that are designed to eliminate the Lessor's risk and monetize the tax-indifferent party's tax benefits. Although nominally different, in each case the tax-indifferent party sets aside the capital normally provided or made available to the lessee by a lease transaction. The only capital retained by the tax-indifferent party is the $4 million accommodation fee.

These arrangements also include features designed to ensure that the Lessor will not lose money if the property declines in value. As discussed above, the tax-indifferent party has an option to "reacquire" the property for a predetermined price that is funded as a result of the defeasance arrangements. If the "purchase option" is exercised, the Lessor will recover its equity investment and a fixed return on that investment. It is reasonable to expect a municipality to exercise a funded "purchase option" to prevent the transfer of a public asset, such as a subway line, stadium, or waste water facility, to a private party. Moreover, from a practical and political standpoint, the tax-indifferent party is unlikely to surrender control of an asset such as a subway. Nevertheless, the parties take the position that the "purchase option" is not likely to be exercised.

If the "purchase option" is not exercised by the tax-indifferent party, the Lessor has two other alternatives under the terms of the arrangement. First, the Lessor

---

[13] [44] Because of the nature of the asset, the tax-indifferent party may not be able to transfer title to the asset to the Lessor. In that case, the "sale" takes the form of a lease by the tax-indifferent party to the Lessor for a period in excess of the expected useful life of the asset, which is treated as a sale for federal tax purposes.

may take possession of the property. Second, the Lessor may require the tax-indifferent party to locate a third party to enter into a service contract, the terms of which were agreed to at the inception of the arrangement. The third party must agree to receive services to be provided by the Lessor using the leased property.[14] In return, the third party must agree to make payments to the Lessor. The payments required by the service contract provide the Lessor with funds to repay the remaining balances of the nonrecourse loans and to enable the Lessor to recoup its equity investment and a return on that investment. If the tax-indifferent party does not locate a third party, the tax-indifferent party (or, in certain cases, an affiliate) must agree to receive services and make the required payments. The service contract is used to shorten the lease term, which results in a shorter tax depreciation recovery period. Whether the "purchase option" or the service contract is selected, the practical effect is that the Lessor recovers its investment plus a return and the Lessor's risk of loss is eliminated.[15]

Considering the totality of the circumstances, the substance of the arrangement is the payment of a small fee to the tax-indifferent party in exchange for tax benefits. No real financing occurs and there is no change in the control, use, operation of, or beneficial interest in, the asset.

Many of these arrangements involve foreign property and provide no benefits to state or local governments or charities in the United States. Even when the arrangement involves U.S. property, the tax benefits purchased by the Lessor, and the corresponding cost to U.S. taxpayers in lost tax revenues, exceed the fee paid to the tax-indifferent party.

Existing rules have proved ineffective in preventing U.S. taxpayers from entering into these and similar arrangements that result in the monetization of tax benefits rather than financing for the tax-indifferent party. Additional rules are necessary to expand the types of assets covered by the existing rules and to limit the ability of a U.S. taxpayer to acquire tax benefits through such arrangements. At the same time, leasing arrangements that provide real financing to tax-indifferent parties should be permitted to continue.

* * *

Congress responded to the Treasury Department's proposals through amendments to the depreciation rules applicable to tax-exempt use property and through

---

14 [45] As part of any service contract arrangement, it is contemplated that the Lessor will enter into an operating agreement engaging a third party to operate the leased property. The service recipient will be required to reimburse the Lessor for monthly operating expenses in addition to making the minimum payments required under the service contract.

15 [46] Similar arrangements take advantage of the shorter depreciation periods available for computer software and qualified technological equipment, which comprise a growing proportion of the assets involved in these leasing arrangements. In these arrangements, the Lessor purports to "purchase" equipment having a useful life substantially longer than the recovery period for qualified technological equipment and related software. The terms of these arrangements are similar to the example discussed above. In lieu of a service contact, however, the tax-indifferent party may be required to purchase residual value insurance if it fails to exercise an early buyout option. The residual value insurance requirement, like the service contract, ensures that the Lessor will recoup its equity investment and a return on that investment.

the enactment of § 470 as part of the American Jobs Creation Act of 2004. Section 470 is modeled on § 469 and prohibits the deduction of any tax-exempt use loss. § 470(a). Such losses are carried forward and treated as a deduction in the following taxable year. § 470(b). A tax–exempt use loss is the excess of the deductions from any tax-exempt use property over the income from such property. § 470(c)(1). Unlike § 469, which applies on an aggregate basis to all passive activities so that losses from one passive activity can offset income from a different passive activity, the limitation of the deduction of losses under § 470 applies on property-by-property basis. For purposes of § 470, the definition of tax-exempt use property is the same as that under § 168(h), with certain modifications. Thus, a taxpayer may deduct expenses allocable to property leased to a tax-exempt person or entity only to the extent of the income from that property. The excess deductions may not be used to reduce the amount of taxable income from other sources.

Nevertheless, § 470 does not apply to leases of property that satisfy certain requirements. First, defeasance arrangements may not exceed 20 percent of the property's adjusted basis at the time the lease is entered into. § 470(d)(1). Second, the lessor must have an equity investment in the leased property of at least 20 percent of the property's adjusted basis at the time the lease is entered into. § 470(d)(2). Third, the lessee may not bear more than minimal risk of loss with respect to the property. § 470(d)(3). These requirements were intended to ensure that the limitations of § 470 apply to the typical structure of the abusive SILO transactions that motivated the enactment of § 470 but that its limitations do not apply to more legitimate leasing transactions.

The following excerpt from the Conference Committee Report for the American Jobs Creation Act of 2004 describes amendments to the depreciation rules applicable to tax-exempt use property and the details of the requirements under § 470.

H.R. Rep. No. 108-755, 108th Cong., 2d Sess. 654–663 (2004)

29. Reform of tax treatment of certain leasing arrangements and limitation on deductions allocable to property used by governments or other tax-exempt entities

. . .

PRESENT LAW

Overview of depreciation

A taxpayer is allowed to recover, through annual depreciation deductions, the cost of certain property used in a trade or business or for the production of income. The amount of the depreciation deduction allowed with respect to tangible property for a taxable year is determined under the modified accelerated cost recovery system ("MACRS"). Under MACRS, different types of property generally are assigned applicable recovery periods and depreciation methods based on such property's class life. The recovery periods applicable to most tangible personal property (generally tangible property other than residential rental property and nonresidential real property) range from 3 to 25 years and are significantly shorter than the property's class life, which is intended to approximate the economic useful life of the property. In addition, the depreciation methods generally applicable to tangible personal property are the 200-percent and 150-percent declining balance methods, switching to the straight-line method for the taxable year in which the depreciation deduction would be maximized.

Characterization of leases for tax purposes

In general, a taxpayer is treated as the tax owner and is entitled to depreciate property leased to another party if the taxpayer acquires and retains significant and genuine attributes of a traditional owner of the property, including the benefits and burdens of ownership. No single factor is determinative of whether a lessor will be treated as the owner of the property. Rather, the determination is based on all the facts and circumstances surrounding the leasing transaction.

A sale-leaseback transaction is respected for Federal tax purposes if "there is a genuine multiple-party transaction with economic substance which is compelled or encouraged by business or regulatory realities, is imbued with tax-independent considerations, and is not shaped solely by tax-avoidance features that have meaningless labels attached."[16]

Recovery period for tax-exempt use property

Under present law, "tax-exempt use property" must be depreciated on a straight-line basis over a recovery period equal to the longer of the property's class life or 125 percent of the lease term.[17] For purposes of this rule, "tax-exempt use property" is tangible property that is leased (other than under a short-term lease) to a tax-exempt entity.[18] For this purpose, the term "tax-exempt entity" includes Federal, State and local governmental units, charities, and, foreign entities or persons.[19]

In determining the length of the lease term for purposes of the 125-percent calculation, several special rules apply. In addition to the stated term of the lease, the lease term includes options to renew the lease or other periods of time during which the lessee could be obligated to make rent payments or assume a risk of loss related to the leased property.

Tax-exempt use property does not include property that is used by a taxpayer to provide a service to a tax-exempt entity. So long as the relationship between the parties is a bona fide service contract, the taxpayer will be allowed to depreciate the property used in satisfying the contract under normal MACRS rules, rather than the rules applicable to tax-exempt use property.[20] In addition, property is not

---

16 [596] *Frank Lyon Co.* v. *United States*, 435 U.S. 561, 583–84 (1978).

17 [597] Sec. 168(g)(3)(A). Under present law, section 168(g)(3)(C) states that the recovery period of "qualified technological equipment" is five years.

18 [598] Sec. 168(h)(1).

19 [599] Sec. 168(h)(2).

20 [600] Sec. 7701(e) provides that a service contract will not be respected, and instead will be treated

treated as tax-exempt use property merely by reason of a short-term lease. In general, a short-term lease means any

lease the term of which is less than three years and less than the greater of one year or 30 percent of the property's class life.[21]

Also, tax-exempt use property generally does not include qualified technological equipment that meets the exception for leases of high technology equipment to tax-exempt entities with lease terms of five years or less.[22] The recovery period for qualified technological equipment that is treated as tax-exempt use property, but is not subject to the high technology equipment exception, is five years.[23]

The term "qualified technological equipment" is defined as computers and related peripheral equipment, high technology telephone station equipment installed on a customer's premises, and high technology medical equipment.[24] In addition, tax-exempt use property does not include computer software because it is intangible property.

HOUSE BILL

Overview

The House bill modifies the recovery period of certain property leased to a tax-exempt entity, alters the definition of lease term for all property leased to a tax-exempt entity, expands the short-term lease exception for qualified technological equipment, and establishes rules to limit deductions associated with leases to tax-exempt entities if the leases do not satisfy specified criteria.

Modify the recovery period of certain property leased to a tax-exempt entity

The House bill modifies the recovery period for qualified technological equipment and computer software leased to a tax-exempt entity[25] to be the longer of the property's assigned class life (or assigned useful life in the case of computer software) or 125 percent of the lease term. The House bill does not apply to

---

as a lease of property, if such contract is properly treated as a lease taking into account all relevant factors. The relevant factors include, among others, the service recipient controls the property, the service recipient is in physical possession of the property, the service provider does not bear significant risk of diminished receipts or increased costs if there is nonperformance, the property is not used to concurrently provide services to other entities, and the contract price does not substantially exceed the rental value of the property.

21 [601] Sec. 168(h)(1)(C).

22 [602] Sec. 168(h)(3). However, the exception does not apply if part or all of the qualified technological equipment is financed by a tax-exempt obligation, is sold by the tax-exempt entity (or related party) and leased back to the tax-exempt entity (or related party), or the tax-exempt entity is the United States or any agency or instrumentality of the United States.

23 [603] Sec. 168(g)(3)(C).

24 [604] Sec. 168(i)(2).

25 [605] The House bill defines a tax-exempt entity as under present law. Thus, it includes Federal, State, local, and foreign governmental units, charities, foreign entities or persons.

short-term leases, as defined under present law with a modification described below for short-term leases of qualified technological equipment.

Modify definition of lease term

In determining the length of the lease term for purposes of the 125-percent calculation, the House bill provides that the lease term includes all service contracts (whether or not treated as a lease under section 7701(e)) and other similar arrangements that follow a lease of property to a tax-exempt entity and that are part of the same transaction (or series of transactions) as the lease.[26]

Under the House bill, service contracts and other similar arrangements include arrangements by which services are provided using the property in exchange for fees that provide a source of repayment of the capital investment in the property.[27] This requirement applies to all leases of property to a tax-exempt entity.

Expand short-term lease exception for qualified technological equipment

For purposes of determining whether a lease of qualified technological equipment to a tax-exempt entity satisfies the present law 5-year short-term lease exception for leases of qualified technological equipment, the House bill provides that the term of the lease does not include an option or options of the lessee to renew or extend the lease, provided the rents under the renewal or extension are based upon fair market value determined at the time of the renewal or extension. The aggregate period of such renewals or extensions not included in the lease term under this provision may not exceed 24 months. In addition, this provision does not apply to any period following the failure of a tax-exempt lessee to exercise a purchase option if the result of such failure is that the lease renews automatically at fair market value rents.

Limit deductions for certain leases of property to tax-exempt parties

The House bill also provides that if a taxpayer leases property to a tax-exempt entity, the taxpayer may not claim deductions for a taxable year from the lease transaction in excess of the tax-payer's gross income from the lease for that taxable year. This provision does not apply to certain transactions involving property with respect to which the low-income housing credit or the rehabilitation credit is allowable.

---

[26] [606] A service contract involving property that previously was leased to the tax-exempt entity is not part of the same transaction as the preceding leasing arrangement (and, thus, is not included in the lease term of such arrangement) if the service contract was not included in the terms and conditions, or contemplated at the inception, of the preceding leasing arrangement.

[27] [607] For purposes of the House bill, a service contract does not include an arrangement for the provision of services if the leased property or substantially similar property is not utilized to provide such services. For example, if at the conclusion of a lease term, a tax-exempt lessee purchases property from the taxpayer and enters into an agreement pursuant to which the taxpayer maintains the property, the maintenance agreement will not be included in the lease term for purposes of the 125-percent computation.

This provision applies to deductions or losses related to a lease to a tax-exempt entity and the leased property.[28] Any disallowed deductions are carried forward and treated as deductions related to the lease in the following taxable year subject to the same limitations. Under rules similar to those applicable to passive activity losses (including the treatment of dispositions of property in which less than all of the gain or loss from the disposition is recognized),[29] a taxpayer generally is permitted to deduct previously disallowed deductions and losses when the taxpayer completely disposes of its interest in the property.

A lease of property to a tax-exempt party is not subject to the deduction limitations of this provision if the lease satisfies all of the following requirements:[30]

(1) Tax-exempt lessee does not monetize its lease obligations

In general, the tax-exempt lessee may not monetize its lease obligations (including any purchase option) in an amount that exceeds 20 percent of the taxpayer's adjusted basis[31] in the leased property at the time the lease is entered into.[32] Specifically, a lease does not satisfy this requirement if the tax-exempt lessee monetizes such excess amount pursuant to an arrangement, set-aside, or expected set-aside, that is to or for the benefit of the taxpayer or any lender, or is to or for the benefit of the tax-exempt lessee, in order to satisfy the lessee's obligations or options under the lease. This determination shall be made at all times during the lease term and shall include the amount of any interest or other income or gain earned on any amount set aside or subject to an arrangement described in this provision. For purposes of determining whether amounts have been set aside or are expected to be set aside, amounts are treated as set aside or expected to be set aside only if a reasonable person would conclude that the facts and circumstances indicate that such amounts are set aside or expected to be set aside.[33]

---

[28] [608] Deductions related to a lease of tax-exempt use property include any depreciation or amortization expense, maintenance expense, taxes or the cost of acquiring an interest in, or lease of, property. In addition, this provision applies to interest that is properly allocable to tax-exempt use property, including interest on any borrowing by a related person, the proceeds of which were used to acquire an interest in the property, whether or not the borrowing is secured by the leased property or any other property.

[29] [609] See Sec. 469(g).

[30] [610] Even if a transaction satisfies each of the following requirements, the taxpayer will be treated as the owner of the leased property only if the taxpayer acquires and retains significant and genuine attributes of an owner of the property under the present-law tax rules, including the benefits and burdens of ownership.

[31] [611] For purposes of this requirement, the adjusted basis of property acquired by the taxpayer in a like-kind exchange or involuntary conversion to which section 1031 or section 1033 applies is equal to the lesser of (1) the fair market value of the property as of the beginning of the lease term, or (2) the amount that would be the taxpayer's adjusted basis if section 1031 or section 1033 did not apply to such acquisition.

[32] [612] Arrangements to monetize lease obligations include defeasance arrangements, loans by the tax-exempt entity (or an affiliate) to the taxpayer (or an affiliate) or any lender, deposit agreements, letters of credit collateralized with cash or cash equivalents, payment undertaking agreements, prepaid rent (within the meaning of the regulations under section 467), sinking fund arrangements, guaranteed investment contracts, financial guaranty insurance, or any similar arrangements.

[33] [613] It is anticipated under the House bill that the customary and budgeted funding by tax-exempt entities of current obligations under a lease through unrestricted accounts or funds for general working

The Secretary may provide by regulations that this requirement is satisfied, even if a tax-exempt lessee monetizes its lease obligations or options in an amount that exceeds 20 percent of the taxpayer's adjusted basis[34] in the leased property, in cases in which the creditworthiness of the tax-exempt lessee would not otherwise satisfy the taxpayer's customary underwriting standards. Such credit support would not be permitted to exceed 50 percent of the taxpayer's adjusted basis in the property. In addition, if the lease provides the tax-exempt lessee an option to purchase the property for a fixed purchase price (or for other than the fair market value of the property determined at the time of exercise of the option), such credit support at the time that such option may be exercised would not be permitted to exceed 50 percent of the purchase option price.

Certain lease arrangements that involve circular cash flows or insulation of the taxpayer's equity investment from the risk of loss fail this requirement without regard to the amount in which the tax-exempt lessee monetizes its lease obligations or options. Thus, a lease does not satisfy this requirement if the tax-exempt lessee enters into an arrangement to monetize in any amount its lease obligations or options if such arrangement involves (1) a loan (other than an amount treated as a loan under section 467 with respect to a section 467 rental agreement) from the tax-exempt lessee to the taxpayer or a lender, (2) a deposit that is received, a letter of credit that is issued, or a payment undertaking agreement that is entered into by a lender otherwise involved in the transaction, or (3) in the case of a transaction that involves a lender, any credit support made available to the taxpayer in which any such lender does not have a claim that is senior to the taxpayer.

(2) Taxpayer makes and maintains a substantial equity investment in the leased property

The taxpayer must make and maintain a substantial equity investment in the leased property. For this purpose, a taxpayer generally does not make or maintain a substantial equity investment unless (1) at the time the lease is entered into, the taxpayer initially makes an unconditional at-risk equity investment in the property of at least 20 percent of the taxpayer's adjusted basis in the leased property at that time,[35] (2) the taxpayer maintains such equity investment throughout the lease term, and (3) at all times during the lease term, the fair market value of the property at the end of the lease term is reasonably expected to be equal to at least 20 percent of such basis.[36] For this purpose, the fair market value of the property at the end of the lease term is reduced to the extent that a person other than the

---

capital needs will not be considered arrangements, set-asides, or expected set-asides under this requirement.

[34] [614] For purposes of this requirement, the adjusted basis of property acquired by the taxpayer in a like-kind exchange or involuntary conversion to which section 1031 or section 1033 applies is equal to the lesser of (1) the fair market value of the property as of the beginning of the lease term, or (2) the amount that would be the taxpayer's adjusted basis if section 1031 or section 1033 did not apply to such acquisition.

[35] [615] The taxpayer's at-risk equity investment shall include only consideration paid, and personal liability incurred, by the taxpayer to acquire the property. Cf. Rev. Proc. 2001–28, 2001–2 C.B. 1156.

[36] [616] Cf. Rev. Proc. 2001–28, sec. 4.01(2), 2001–1 C.B. 1156. The fair market value of the property must be determined without regard to inflation or deflation during the lease term and after subtracting the cost of removing the property.

taxpayer bears a risk of loss in the value of the property.

This requirement does not apply to leases with lease terms of 5 years or less.

(3) Tax-exempt lessee does not bear more than a minimal risk of loss

The tax-exempt lessee generally may not assume or retain more than a minimal risk of loss, other than the obligation to pay rent and insurance premiums, to maintain the property, or other similar conventional obligations of a net lease.[37] For this purpose, a tax-exempt lessee assumes or retains more than a minimal risk of loss if, as a result of obligations assumed or retained by, on behalf of, or pursuant to an agreement with the tax-exempt lessee, the taxpayer is protected from either (1) any portion of the loss that would occur if the fair market value of the leased property were 25 percent less than the leased property's reasonably expected fair market value at the time the lease is terminated, or (2) an aggregate loss that is greater than 50 percent of the loss that would occur if the fair market value of the leased property were zero at lease termination.[38] In addition, the Secretary may provide by regulations that this requirement is not satisfied where the tax-exempt lessee otherwise retains or assumes more than a minimal risk of loss. Such regulations shall be prospective only.

This requirement does not apply to leases with lease terms of 5 years or less.

* * *

CONFERENCE AGREEMENT

The conference agreement follows the House bill, with the following modifications.

Definition of tax-exempt entity

The conference agreement expands the present-law definition of tax-exempt entity for this purpose to include certain Indian tribal governments in addition to Federal, State, local, and foreign governmental units, charities, foreign entities or persons.

---

[37] [617] Examples of arrangements by which a tax-exempt lessee might assume or retain a risk of loss include put options, residual value guarantees, residual value insurance, and service contracts. However, leases do not fail to satisfy this requirement solely by reason of lease provisions that require the tax-exempt lessee to pay a contractually stipulated loss value to the taxpayer in the event of an early termination due to a casualty loss, a material default by the tax-exempt lessee (excluding the failure by the tax-exempt lessee to enter into an arrangement described above), or other similar extraordinary events that are not reasonably expected to occur at lease inception.

[38] [618] For purposes of this requirement, residual value protection provided to the taxpayer by a manufacturer or dealer of the leased property is not treated as borne by the tax-exempt lessee if the manufacturer or dealer provides such residual value protection to customers in the ordinary course of its business.

Modify the recovery period of certain property leased to a tax-exempt entity

The conference agreement also modifies the recovery period for certain intangibles leased to a tax-exempt entity to be the no less than 125 percent of the lease term.[39] The conference agreement modification does not apply to short-term leases, as defined under present law with a modification described below for short-term leases of qualified technological equipment.

Limit deductions for leases of property to tax-exempt parties

The conference agreement provides an additional requirement that must be satisfied to avoid the deduction limitations for certain leases of property to tax-exempt parties. This requirement provides that the tax-exempt lessee may not have an option to purchase the leased property for any stated purchase price other than the fair market value of the property (as determined at the time of exercise of the option). This requirement does not apply to (1) property with a class life (as defined in section 168(i)(1)) of seven years or less, or (2) any fixed-wing aircraft or vessels (i.e., ships).

[39] [621] In the case of computer software and intangible assets, this rule is applied by substituting useful life and amortization period, respectively, for class life.

TABLE OF CASES

[*References are to pages.*]

A

A.E. Staley Mfg. Co. v. Commissioner . . 62; 64, 65
Aagaard v. Commissioner 152
Abramson v. Commissioner 435
Ahadpour v. Commissioner 624
Aizawa v. Commissioner. 278
Alabama Mineral Land Co. v. Commissioner. . .117
Alacare Home Health Serv. v. Commissioner. . .338
Albany Car Wheel Co. v. Commissioner. . .57; 246, 247
Albany Car Wheel Co. v. Commissioner. . . 57; 247
Albertson's v. Commissioner 191
Alderson v. Commissioner . 475; 484; 487, 488; 530
Aldridge v. Commissioner. 533
Alexander v. Commissioner 755
Allen v. Comm'r. 678
Allen v. Commissioner. 768
Allen v. Courts 260
Alstores Realty Corp. v. Commissioner. 713
Alvary v. United States 174
Alves v. Commissioner. 607; 651
Am. Express Co. v. United States. 911
Amerada Hess Corp. v. Commissioner. 19
American Auto. Ass'n v. United States 325
American Principals Leasing Corp. v. United States 882
Anderson v. Helvering. 701
Anderson v. United States. 790
Arkansas Best Corp. v. Commissioner . . 88; 90, 91; 93; 97; 120; 122; 129; 176
Arrowsmith v. Commissioner. 58
Asjes v. Commissioner. 551
Associated Patentees, Inc. v. Commissioner . . . 432, 433; 809
Atzingen-Whitehouse Dairy Inc v. Commissioner. 350

B

Bagley v. Commissioner. 651
Bailey v. Comm'r. 919, 920
Balding v. Commissioner. 40
Balkissoon v. Commissioner. 931
Baltimore, Mercantile Trust of v. Commissioner. 488
Bank of America v. United States. 652
Barker v. Commissioner. 476
Barniskis v. Commissioner. 927
Barrios, Estate of v. Commissioner 118
Basye; United States v. 592
Baumer v. United States. 637
Bear Manufacturing Co. v. United States. 217
Beaver Dam Coal Co. v. United States 8
Becker v. Commissioner. 153
Bell Lines, Inc. v. United States. 460
Bellamy v. Commissioner 790
Beneficial Industrial Loan Corp. v. Handy 358
Bennion v. Commissioner 880
Berenson v. Commissioner. 705
Beth W. Corp. v. U. S. 40
Beth W. Corp. v. United States 40
Bickmeyer, Estate of v. Commissioner 768
Biedenharn Realty Co. v. United States. . .101, 102; 106; 115; 118
Biggs v. Commissioner. 479; 487
Billy Rose's Diamond Horseshoe, Inc. v. United States. 142; 148
Bisbee-Baldwin Corp. v. Tomlinson. 791
Black & Decker Corp. v. United States. 197
Blair v. Commissioner 757; 759; 804
Blassie v. Commissioner. 755
Boddie-Noell Enters. v. United States. 424
Boehme v. Comm'r. 88, 89; 94
Bolaris v. Commissioner. 570
Bolger v. Commissioner. 247
Bolker v. Commissioner. 522
Borge v. Commissioner 826
Boston E. R. Co. v. Commissioner. 36
Bowen v. Georgetown Univ. Hosp. 911
Bowers v. Kerbaugh-Empire Co. 200
Bowers, Estate of v. Commissioner 460; 503
Boyce v. United States. 533
Bradford v. Commissioner. 202
Bramblett v. Commissioner 119
Briarcliff Candy Corp. v. Commissioner 317
Brooks v. Commissioner. 325
Brountas v. Commissioner 252; 712
Brown v. Commissioner. 839
Brown; Commissioner v. 251; 697; 705
Brown v. United States 671
Browne v. United States. 119
Browning v. Commissioner. 383–385
Buffalo Wire Works Co. v. Comm'r. 553
Burbank Liquidating Corp. v. Commissioner. . . 128
Burnet v. Harmel. 69; 707; 803
Burnet v. Leininger. 757
Burnet v. Logan 787

[*References are to pages.*]

Burnet v. Sanford & Brooks Co. 200
Burton-Sutton Oil Co. v. Commissioner 444

C

C.G. Willis, Inc. v. Commissioner . . . 537; 539, 540
C.I.R. v. (see name of defendant). . . . .
California Casket Co. v. Commissioner. 314
Callahan v. Commissioner. 878
Caminetti v. United States. 932
Cannon v. University of Chicago 28
Capek v. Commissioner 890
Carlson v. Comm'r. 288
Carlstedt v. Commissioner. 925; 927
Carlton v. United States 460; 488
Carnegie Productions, Inc. v. Commissioner . . . 259
Casebeer v. Commissioner. 880
Caspe v. United States. 151
Cenex, Inc. v. United States 100; 123
Centel Communications Co. v. Commissioner . . 647
Centennial Sav. Bank FSB; United States v.. . .204; 295
Central Texas Sav. & Loan Asso. v. United States. 317; 319
Century Electric Co. v. Commissioner. . . .453; 456
Chapin v. Commissioner. 927
Chicago, B.&Q.R. Co; United States v.. 323
Childs v. Commissioner 592
Childs Co., In re. 43
Chronicle Publishing Co. v. Internal Revenue . . 126
Cincinnati, N.O. & T. P. R. Co. v. United States. 338
Cinergy Corp. v. United States 315
Citizen's Nat'l Bank v. United States. 158
Citron v. Commissioner. 136; 140; 234
Clark Oil & Refining Corp. v. United States. . . .65
Click v. Commissioner. 523
Clinger v. Commissioner 383–385; 387
Clopton v. Comm'r. 89; 91; 94; 96
Coastal Terminals, Inc. v. United States. 488
Cohan v. Comm'r. 52
Cohn v. Commissioner. 608
Cole v. Commissioner 289
Coleman v. Commissioner. 478
Collins v. Commissioner. 218
Coltec Indus. v. United States. 197
Columbus & G. R. Co. 246
Comm'r v. Lo Bue 625; 643; 663
Commercial Sec. Bank v. Commissioner . . 281; 644
Commissioner v. (see name of defendant) . . . . . .
Commissioner of Internal Revenue v. (see name of defendant). . . . .
Computervision Int'l Corp. v. Commissioner. . .663
Concord Control, Inc. v. Commissioner 51; 54
Conners v. Commissioner 568
Continental Can Co. v. United States. 102
Convergent Technologies v. Commissioner. . . .663
Cook v. United States 208
Corn Prods. Refining Co. v. Commissioner. .69; 99, 100; 120, 121; 129; 176
Correll; United States v.. 28
Cottage Sav. Ass'n v. Commissioner. 25; 26
Court Holding Co.; Commissioner v.. 520
Coussement v. Commissioner 387
Covey v. Commercial Nat'l Bank. 295
Cramer v. Commissioner. 629
Crane v. Commissioner. .43, 44; 222; 235; 464; 696
Crane; Commissioner v.. 44
Crawford v. Commissioner 174
Crichton; Commissioner v.. 509
Crowley, Milner & Co. v. Commissioner. 459
Cummings; Commissioner v. 154
Curtis Co. v. Commissioner. 118
Cusak v. Commissioner 553; 561
Custom Chrome v. Commissioner. 646; 657
Custom Chrome, Inc. v. Commissioner. . .646; 657; 663

D

Dallas Transfer & Terminal Warehouse Co. v. Commissioner. 289
Darlington-Hartsville Coca-Cola Bottling Co. v. United States 800
Daugherty v. Commissioner. 101
David R. Webb Co., Inc. v. Commissioner. .61; 285
Davidson v. Tomlinson. 102
Davis v. Comm'r. 88, 89; 91; 94
Davis v. Commissioner 857
Davis v. United States. 547
Davis; United States v. 20; 39
De Bie, Estate of v. Commissioner 372
DeCleene v. Commissioner 503
Denman Tire & Rubber Co. v. Commissioner . . 208
Denver & R. G. W. R. Co. v. United States 57
Deputy v. Du Pont. 196; 318; 330; 357; 366
Detroit Edison Co v. Commissioner. 323; 379
Dettmers v. Commissioner. 533
Dial v. Commissioner 123
Diedrich v. Commissioner. 39
Dill Co; Commissioner v. 187; 623
Dobson v. Commissioner 326
Doggett v. Burnet 330

[*References are to pages.*]

Dominion Resources, Inc. v. United States. . . . 313
Dorman v. United States. 785
Dorothy C. Thorpe Glass Mfg. Corp. v. Commissioner. 543
Doyle v. Commissioner 767
Draper v. Commissioner. 152
Dresser Industries, Inc.; United States v. . 87; 91; 94, 95; 142
Duberstein; Commissioner v.. 10

E

E. I. du Pont de Nemours & Co. v. United States. .9
E. R. Hitchcock, Co. v. United States. . . . 557, 558
E.T. Sproull v. Commissioner. 588
Eagle Asbestos & Packing Co. v. United States . 208
Eastern Shoe Mfg. Co. v. Commissioner. 560
Eidson; United States v.. . . . . 87; 792; 797
Eisner v. Macomber. 23; 28
Elliott v. United States 96
Ellis Banking Corp. v. Commissioner. 358
Emershaw v. Commissioner 877; 891
Encyclopaedia Britannica, Inc. v. Commissioner.315; 328
Estate of (see name of party) . . . .
Estroff, Estate of v. Commissioner 847
Exch. Nat'l Bank of Chi. v. Touche Ross & Co.. .93
Exxon Corp. v. United States 369

F

Fackler v. Commissioner. 174
Fairbanks v. United States. 134
Fairfield S.S. Corp. v. Commissioner 454; 458
Farid-Es-Sultaneh v. Commissioner. 40
Farley v. Commissioner 102; 117
Fashion Park, Inc. v. Commissioner. 201; 237
Fasken v. Commissioner 8
Faura v. Commissioner. 329
Federal Nat'l Mortgage Ass'n v. Commissioner . 123
FedEx Corp. v. United States 314
Ferber, Estate of v. Commissioner. 102
Ferguson v. Commissioner. 762
Ferrer; Commissioner v.. . . . 86; 96; 127; 141; 782
Fields v. Commissioner 125
Filippini v. United States. 537; 540
Fink; Commissioner v.. . . . . 615; 653
First Pennsylvania Banking & Trust Co. v. Commissioner. 798
FMR Corp. v. Commissioner 357
Focht v. Commissioner. 191
Fogarty v. United States. 755
Fogel v. Commissioner. 151
Foglesong v. Commissioner 819; 825
Fontaine Fox v. Commissioner 823
Foy v. Commissioner 87; 790
Frank Lyon Co. v. United States. 731; 941
Franklin, Estate of v. Commissioner. . 248; 696; 895
Frazier v. Commissioner. 281
Freeland v. Commissioner 136; 234
Fribourg Navigation Co. v. Commissioner . 381, 382
Friedland v. Comm'r. 202
Frierdich v. Commissioner. 187
Fulton Gold Corp. v. Commissioner. 238; 261
Furst v. United States 375

G

Gannon v. Commissioner 136
Gantner v. Commissioner 850
Garcia v. Commissioner. 465
Gefen v. Commissioner 888
Geftman v. Commissioner. 187
General Artists Corp. v. Commissioner. . . 141; 785; 790
General Bancshares Corp. v. Commissioner.320, 321
General Ins. Agency, Inc. v. Commissioner 55
Generes; United States v.. 653
Gershkowitz v. Commissioner. 262
Gillette Motor Transport, Inc.; Commissioner v. . 86, 87; 90; 135; 163; 785
Gilmore; United States v.. 350
Gladden v. Comm'r. 3; 86
Glen v. Commissioner. 126
Glenshaw Glass Co.; Commissioner v..24; 183; 216; 626
Goldberg v. Commissioner. 118
Goldstein v. Commissioner 849
Golonsky; Commissioner v. . 86; 142; 147; 785; 790
Golsen v. Commissioner. 558
Gordon; Commissioner v.. 636
Gordy v. Commissioner 119
Goshorn v. Commissioner 925; 927
Gould Securities Co. v. United States 18
Gowans v. Commissioner 709
Grace Bros., Inc. v. Commissioner 101
Gracey; Commissioner v.. 155
Grant v. United States 603; 673
Graphic Press, Inc. v. Commissioner 557
Greene v. Commissioner. 563
Gregg v. United States 907; 915–917

[*References are to pages.*]

Gregory v. Helvering. 849
Gresham, Estate of v. Commissioner 679
Grier v. United States 174
Gudmundsson v. Commissioner. 385
Gulf Oil Corp. v. Commissioner. . . . 370; 443; 444
Guzak v. United States. 692

H

H.G. Fenton Material Co. v. Commissioner. . . .366
Hahn v. Comm'r. 288
Hall; United States v.. . . . . .214–216; 218
Hamburgers York Road, Inc. v. Commissioner. . 831
Hamlin's Trust v. Commissioner 55
Hanlin v. Commissioner. 845
Harper Oil Co. v. United States. 369
Harrison v. Schaffner. 760
Harrison v. United States 681
Hassen v. Commissioner. 853
Haverly v. United States. 578
Hawaiian Gas Products, Ltd. v. Commissioner. . 135
Heim v. Fitzpatrick. 809
Heininger; Commissioner v.. 62
Heller Trust v. Commissioner 117
Helvering v. American Dental Co. 208
Helvering v. Bankline Oil Co.. 444
Helvering v. Bruun. 24; 772
Helvering v. Clifford. 760
Helvering v. Hammel. 135; 140
Helvering v. Horst. 24; 26; 29; 757; 772
Helvering v. Nebraska Bridge Supply & Lumber Co.. 135
Helvering v. San Joaquin Fruit & Inv. Co. 153
Helvering v. Tex-Penn Oil Co. 18
Helvering v. William Flaccus Oak Leather Co.. . 134
Helvering v. Winmill. 28; 349, 350
Hempt Bros., Inc. v. United States. 189; 840
Hertz Corp v. United States 323
Herwig v. United States 803
Higgins v. Smith 823; 849; 857
Highland Farms v. Commissioner. 729
Hillard v. Commissioner. 102
Hillman v. Commissioner 928
Hillman v. IRS. 929
Hilton v. Commissioner 742, 743
Hilton Hotels Corp.; United States v. 348; 357
Hirsch v. Commissioner. 260
Hoechst Aktiengesellschaft v. Quigg 914
Hollywood Baseball Asso. v. Commissioner . . . 175
Holt v. Commissioner. 86; 96; 785
Homes by Ayres v. Commissioner. 175
Hort v. Commissioner. . . 86; 90; 94; 771; 785; 793
Hospital Corp. of Am. v. Commissioner 422
Hoven v. Commissioner. 154
Huber Homes, Inc. v. Commissioner 840
Hubert Enters., Inc. v. Commissioner. 874
Hudson v. Commissioner 274
Hudspeth v. Commissioner. 249; 764; 768
Hustead v. Commissioner 335
Hutcheson v. Commissioner. 136

I

Idaho Power Co. v. Commissioner 323
Idaho Power Co.; Commissioner v.. . 315; 318; 321; 329, 330; 357; 366; 368
Illinois Tool Works, Inc. v. Commissioner . . 58; 62; 285
In re (see name of party) . . . .
Inaja Land Co. v. Commissioner. 5; 7, 8; 23
INDOPCO v. Commissioner. . 61; 64, 65; 307; 313; 316; 342; 356; 364; 366; 661
Ingram Indus. Inc. v. Commissioner. 313, 314
International Artists, Ltd. v. Commissioner. 385; 387
International Freighting Corp. v. Commissioner. . 37
International Shoe Co. v. Commissioner 337
International Shoe Machine Corp. v. United States. 101, 102; 176
Interstate Transit Lines v. Commissioner 318
Irwin v. Gavit. 760
Ithaca Indus. v. Commissioner. 385

J

Jackson v. Commissioner 275
Jackson v. Commissioner 880
Jacobson; Commissioner v.. 206–208
Jelle v. Comm'r. 219; 297
Jim Walter Corp. v. United States. 664
Johns v. Comm'r 88
Johnson v. Commissioner. 281
Johnson v. Commissioner 830
Johnson v. Commissioner 852
Jones v. Commissioner. 313
Jones v. United States 764; 768
Jordan Marsh Co. v. Commissioner. 455; 490

K

Kadillak v. Comm'r 605
Kadillak v. Comm'r 605

[*References are to pages.*]

Kaplan v. Commissioner 857
Keck v. Commissioner 768
Keller v. Commissioner 826
Kentucky & I. T. R. Co. v. United States 208
Kidder v. Commissioner 846
Kimberlin v. Comm'r 655
Kinsey v. Commissioner 764; 768
Kirby Lumber Co.; United States v. . . 199; 206; 216; 238; 288
Kirby Lumber Corp. v. Phinney 102
Kirby Petroleum Co. v. Commissioner 443
Klagsbrun v. Commissioner 888
Klein. v. Board of Supervisors 822
Klein, Estate of v. Commissioner 806
Knetsch v. United States 849
Knoxville v. Knoxville Water Co 323
Koch v. Commissioner 509
Kochansky v. Commissioner 40
Kolom v. Commissioner 681
Kortright v. Cady 44
Kuchman v. Commissioner 602
Kueneman v. Commissioner 806

L

L.L. Bean Inc. v. Commissioner 424
La Petite Academy v. United States 424
La Rue v. Commissioner 135
La Salle Trucking Co. v. Commissioner 314
Lakeland Grocery Co. v. Commissioner . . . 238; 290
Lamie v. United States Trustee 914
Larsen v. Commissioner 880
Latham Park Manor, Inc. v. Commissioner 839
Lattera v. Comm'r 88
Laughton v. Commissioner 823
Laughton; Commissioner v. 823
Leavell v. Commissioner 755; 830
Leh v. Commissioner 785
Lehman v. Commissioner 602
Lehr v. Commissioner 128
Lessinger v. Commissioner 268
Lester v. Commissioner 729
LeTulle v. Scofield 700
Levine, Estate of v. Commissioner 229
Levy v. Commissioner 877; 880; 891
Liant Record, Inc. v. Commissioner 546
Liddle v. Commissioner 387
Lincoln v. Commissioner 855
Lincoln Sav. & Loan Ass'n; Commissioner v. . . 312; 317–319; 325; 342; 356
Linehan v. Commissioner 709
Liquid Paper Corp. v. United States 375
Lo Bue v. Commissioner 626
Lo Bue; Commissioner v. 626
Lockwood v. Commissioner 36; 136
Lomas Santa Fe, Inc. v. Commissioner 719
Long v. Commissioner 466; 518
Lorillard v. Pons 28
Louisiana Land & Exploration Co. v. Commissioner 370
Lucas v. Earl 753; 757; 766; 821
Ludden v. Commissioner 612
Ludey; United States v. 379
Luna v. Commissioner 98
Lynch v. Alworth-Stephens Co 444
Lynch v. Hornby 24

M

M & W Gear Co. v. Commissioner 729
Macabe Co., Inc. v. Commissioner 381
MacAdam & Foster, Inc. v. Commissioner 560
Mach-Tech, Ltd. v. Commissioner 363
Madorin v. Commissioner 234
Maginnis; United States v. 88–92; 94; 97
Magneson v. Commissioner 516
Maher v. Commissioner 275; 277
Malat v. Riddell 101; 103
Malkan v. Commissioner 768
Mansfield Journal Co. v. Commissioner 121
Marr v. United States 28, 29
Martin v. Commissioner 154
Martin v. Commissioner 592
Martin v. Commissioner 790
Martuccio v. Commissioner 877
Masser v. Commissioner 538
Massey-Ferguson, Inc. v. Commissioner 36
Massey Motors, Inc. v. United States 382
Mathews v. Commissioner 103
Maurice L. Killian; Commissioner v. 792
Max Sobel Wholesale Liquors v. Commissioner . 659
Mayerson v. Commissioner 242; 248; 696
McAdams v. Mass. Mut. Life Ins. Co 591
McAllister v. Commissioner 96; 98; 142; 773
McCaffrey v. Commissioner 545
McCarty v. Cripe 854
McCue Bros. & Drummond, Inc.; Commissioner v. 86; 142; 147; 785; 790
McNeill v. Commissioner 854
McWilliams v. Commissioner 852; 854

[*References are to pages.*]

Melvin v. Commissioner . . 873; 877; 884; 885; 889
Mennuto v. Commissioner. 337
Meredith Corp. v. Commissioner. 57
Merkel v. Commissioner. 293
Merlo v. Comm'r. 631; 673; 682; 686
Merrill v. Commissioner. 154
Merritt v. Commissioner. 853
Mesta; Commissioner v.. 39
Metropolitan Bldg. Co. v. Commissioner . . 775; 785
Meyer, Estate of v. Commissioner. 519, 520
Middleton v. Commissioner 140
Midland Empire Packing Co. v. Commissioner. .313
Midland-Ross Corp.; United States v. 86; 93
Milenbach v. Comm'r 181; 185
Miller v. Commissioner 853
Miller v. United States. 630, 631
Mississippi Chemical Corp.; United States v.. . .319
Moline Properties v. Commissioner. 822
Monarch Cement Co. v. United States 646
Montana Power Co. v. United States. 39
Montgomery v. Comm'r. 668
Mordkin v. Commissioner 924; 926
Morison; United States v.. 933
Morris Inv. Corp. v. Commissioner 856
Morris Investment Corporation v. Commissioner.856
Morrison v. Commissioner. 126
Moss v. Commissioner. 314
Mros v. Commissioner. 806
Mt. Morris Drive-In Theatre Co. v. Commissioner. 313
Mt. Morris Drive-in Theatre Co. v. Commissioner. 313

N

N. Sobel, Inc. v. Commissioner 213; 216
Nahey v. Commissioner. 63; 66; 142; 798
National Alfalfa Dehydrating & Milling Co; Commissioner v.. 201
National Carbide v. Commissioner 822
National Muffler Dealers Ass'n v. United States. .27
National Sec. Corp. v. Commissioner. 840
National Starch & Chemical Corp. v. Commissioner. 317
NCNB Corp. v. United States 317
Nelson Weaver Realty Co. v. Commissioner. . .792; 796
New Colonial Ice Co. v. Helvering 318
Newark Morning Ledger Co. v. United States. . .50; 429; 512
Newell v. Comm'r. 918
Niagara Mohawk Power Corp. v. United States. . .6
Norton; United States v.. 854
Norwest Corp. v. Commissioner. 315
Noyce v. Commissioner 383; 387

O

Ocmulgee Fields, Inc. v. Comm'r. 531
Oesterreich v. Commissioner 727
Old Colony R. Co. v. Commissioner 196; 325
Old Colony Trust Co. v. Commissioner. 757
Oregon Lumber Co. v. Commissioner. 509
Osteopathic Med. Oncology & Hematology, P.C. v. Commissioner. 133
Owen v. Commissioner 275

P

P.G. Lake, Inc.; Commissioner v.. . . 87; 90, 91; 94; 712; 776; 785
Pacella v. Commissioner. 826
Pacific Transport Co. v. Commissioner . . 57; 63; 66
Pagel, Inc. v. Commissioner. 629; 655
Palahnuk v. Comm'r. 693
Palmer v. Bender. 444; 707
Palmer v. Commissioner. 626
Paragon Jewel Coal Co. v. Commissioner. .441; 444
Parker v. Delaney 228
Parsons v. Smith 444
Paul v. Commissioner 152
Payne v. Commissioner 201
Pelham G. Wodehouse v. Commissioner 803
Peracchi v. Commissioner 274
Phellis; United States v.. . . . . .28, 29
Philadelphia Park Amusement Co. v. United States 15; 572
Philber Equipment Corp. v. Commissioner. . . . 102
Philip Morris Inc. v. Commissioner. 208
Pierce v. Underwood 28
Pierce v. United States. 692
Pike v. United States. 123
Piper v. Commissioner. 6
Pittsburgh Milk Co. v. Commissioner. 659
Pittston Co.; Commissioner v. . . 141; 785; 787; 790
Plainfield-Union Water Co. v. Commissioner . . 313; 367
Plastic Eng'g & Tech. Servs., Inc. v. Commissioner. 333
Pleasant Summit Land Corp. v. Commissioner . 251; 895
Pledger v. Commissioner. 603

[*References are to pages.*]

Pledger v. United States 877
Plotinsky v. Comm'r. 209
Plow Realty Co. v. Commissioner. 5
Poague v. U.S.. 571
Poe v. Seaborn 754; 757
Portland Oil Co. v. Commissioner. 457
Pounds v. United States 143
Powers v. Commissioner. 839
Preslar v. Commissioner 218; 264
Pritchett v. Commissioner. .873; 877; 879; 884, 885
Proesel v. Commissioner 36
Professional Equities v. Commissioner 268
Prussin v. Commissioner. 251
Putnam v. Commissioner. 653

R

R. A. Stewart & Co. v. Commissioner 533
Rabiner v. Bacon. 709
Rail Joint Co; Commissioner v.. . . . . 201; 237
Rauenhorst v. Comm'r. 767
Ray; Commissioner v. 86; 142; 147; 785
Recordak Corp. v. United States. 102
Redwing Carriers, Inc. v. Tomlinson. 460; 489
Reece; Commissioner v.. 809
Reo Motors, Inc. v. Commissioner 688
Reves v. Ernst & Young. 93
Rhodes' Estate v. Comm'r 95
Ricards v. United States 517
Richardson v. Commissioner. 612
Richmond Television Corp. v. United States . . . 353
Rider v. Commissioner. 125
Riverton Inv. Corp. v. United States. 605
Robinson v. Commissioner. 604; 606; 655
Robinson v. Elliot 727
Robinson v. United States 606
Robinson Knife Mfg. Co. v. Commissioner. . . .333
Rodeway Inns of America v. Commissioner . . . 800
Rooney v. United States 840
Roscoe v. Commissioner 793; 795; 797
Rose v. New York 554
Rubin v. Commissioner 821
Ruoff v. Commissioner. 350
Russo v. Commissioner 152

S

S. & B. Realty Co. v. Commissioner 542
S. C. Johnson & Son, Inc. v. Commissioner . . . 767
S. H. Kress & Co. v. Commissioner 538
S.S. White Dental Mfg. Co.; United States v. . . . 36
Sakol v. Commissioner. 603
Salina Partnership L.P. v. Commissioner 186
Sargent v. Commissioner. 830
Saviano v. Commissioner 259
Scheiner v. Commissioner 924; 926
Schermerhorn Oil Corp. v. Commissioner 370
Scheuber v. Commissioner. 102
Schlude v. Comm'r. 325
Schneer v. Commissioner 754
Schneider v. Commissioner 435
Schneider, Estate of v. Commissioner. 615
Schroeder v. Commissioner 314
Schumann v. Commissioner. 670
Scoggins v. Commissioner. 363
Seas Shipping Co. v. Commissioner 19
Sharp v. United States. 21
Sherman; Commissioner v. 216
Shethar v. Commissioner. 855
Sigmon Coal Co. v. Apfel. 933
Simon v. Commissioner. 376
Simon v. Commissioner. 376
Simpson v. Comm'r. 88; 93
Sirbo Holdings, Inc. v. Commissioner. 148
Smalley v. Comm'r. 493; 510
Smith v. Comm'r. 314
Smith v. Commissioner 103
Smith v. Commissioner 489
Smith v. Commissioner 568
Smith; Commissioner v.. . . . . . .626–628; 643; 663
Smith; United States v.. 65
Snow v. Commissioner. 362
Solomon v. Comm'r. 799
Sonneborn Bros. v. Cureton 908
Southwest Explor. Co.. 707
Sovereign v. Commissioner 103
Spangler v. Commissioner. 349
Spartan Petroleum Co. v. United States. 207
Speer v. Commissioner. 925; 927
Speltz v. Comm'r. 684
Spitz v. Comm'r. 688
Spreckels v. Commissioner 349
Springfield Productions, Inc. v. Commissioner. . .36
St. Joe Paper Co; United States v.. 349
Standard Oil Co. v. Commissioner 370
Starker v. United States. 483; 518; 522
Starr Bros., Inc.; Commissioner v.. . .141; 785; 790; 795
Starr, Estate of v. Commissioner 726
Steinway & Sons v. Commissioner. 718

[*References are to pages.*]

Stewart Trust v. Commissioner 797
Stoeltzing v. Commissioner 314
Stokely USA, Inc. v. Commissioner. 810
Stoller v. Commissioner 142
Stradlings Bldg. Materials, Inc. v. Commissioner.370
Suburban Realty Co. v. United States . 101; 103; 116
Sun Microsystems v. Commissioner. 657
Sutphin v. United States. 260
Swaim v. United States 460
Swank; United States v. 442; 444

T

Taft v. Bowers. 11
Tellier; Commissioner v.. . . . . . .62; 318; 330; 366
Teruya Bros. v. Comm'r. 525
Texaco, Inc. v. United States 370
Theophilos v. Commissioner. 603
Thomas v. Perkins 701; 717
Thompson v. Commissioner. 103
Thompson v. United States 907
Tibbals v. United States 119
Towne v. Eisner. 24
Trenton Cotton Oil Co. v. Commissioner . . 454; 458
Trs. of Graceland Cemetery Improv. Fund v. United States 330
Trust of (see name of party). . . . .
Tsakopoulos v. Commissioner. 335
Tuff; United States v.. . . . . .630, 631
Tufts; Commissioner v.. . . . .44; 136; 185; 206; 235
Tunnell v. United States. 95
Turner v. Commissioner. 158
Turner; Commissioner v.. 158
Turzillo v. Commissioner 142
2925 Briarpark, Ltd. v. Commissioner 264

U

Union Carbide Foreign Sales Corp. v. Commissioner 8; 800
Union P. R. Co. v. United States 337
United States v. (see name of defendant). . . . . . .
United States Freight Co. v. United States 148
United States Freightways Corp. v. Comm'r. 61; 315
United States Steel Corp. v. United States 201

V

Vaaler v. United States 98
Venture Funding v. Commissioner. 606
Venture Funding, Ltd. v. Commissioner. 606
Virginia Iron Coal & Coke Co. v. Commissioner. 186; 624
Virginian Hotel Corp. v. Helvering 379
Voloudakis v. C.I.R. 785
Von-Lusk v. Commissioner 334
Vukasovich, Inc. v. Commissioner. 216; 219

W

W. C. & A. N. Miller Dev. Co. v. Commissioner.175
Waddell v. Commissioner 880
Wagensen v. Commissioner 523
Wagner v. Commissioner 718
Walker, In re 884
Walling, Estate of v. Commissioner. 313
Weeden, Estate of v. Commissioner. 274
Wehrli; United States v. 314; 331
Weigl v. Commissioner 655
Weir v. Commissioner. 154
Weiss v. Stearn 28, 29
Welch v. Helvering 318; 357; 366
Wells Fargo & Co. v. Commissioner. 61
Western Contracting Corporation v. Commissioner, 1959. 728
Wheeler v. Commissioner 538; 542
White; United States v. 710
Whiteco Industries, Inc. v. Commissioner. 424
Widener, Trust No. 5 v. Commissioner 853
Wiechens v. United States. 510
Wildman v. Commissioner. 435
Willamette Indus. v. Comm'r 535
Williams v. McGowan. 47; 781
Williams v. United States 103
Wilshire Holding Corporation v. Commissioner . 728
Winthrop; United States v.. . . . . 101; 103; 106
Wiseman v. Halliburton Oil Well Cementing Co. . 86
Wodehouse v. Commissioner 804
Wolff v. Commissioner. 142
Wood v. Commissioner 103
Wood v. United States. 706
Woodsam Associates, Inc. v. Commissioner 42
Woodward v. Commissioner 324; 348; 357

Y

Yale Ave. Corp. v. Commissioner. 208
Yarbro v. Commissioner. 140; 234
Young v. Comm'r. 40

[*References are to pages.*]

Z

Zappo v. Commissioner. 219; 275; 297
Zarin v. Commissioner 210; 211
Zelco, Inc. v. Commissioner. 337

TABLE OF STATUTES

[References are to chapter numbers followed by section/subsection numbers in brackets.]

AMERICAN JOBS CREATION ACT OF 2004

Generally . . . . 6[1]; 8[6]

AMERICAN RECOVERY AND REINVESTMENT TAX ACT OF 2009

Generally . . . . 2[2.01(a)]
§ 1201(a)(1) . . . . 4[3.05]

BANKRUPTCY REFORM ACT OF 1978 (BANKRUPTCY CODE)

Generally . . . . 3[5.01]
§ 101(26) . . . . 3[5.01]
§ 108(d)(3) . . . . 3[5.01]

BANKRUPTCY TAX ACT OF 1980

Generally . . . . 3[5.01]

COPYRIGHT ACT

Generally . . . . 7[3.03(a)]

ECONOMIC STIMULUS ACT OF 2008

Pub. L. No. 110-185, § 103(a) . . . . 4[3.05]

ENERGY TAX INCENTIVES ACT OF 2005

H.R. 6, Title XIII . . . . 2[6.01]

INSTALLMENT SALES REVISION OF ACT OF 1980

Sen. Rep. No. 1000; 96th Cong., 2d Sess. 5[1.02(b)]

INTERNAL REVENUE CODE

I.R.C.

§ 1 . . . . 2[1]; 2[2.01(a)]; 2[2.01(b)]; 2[2.02]
§ 1.197-2(c)(7) . . . . 7[3.03(a)]
§ 1.752-1(e) . . . . 3[4.01]
§ 1(h) . . . . 1[4.01]; 2[2.01(a)]; 2[2.01(b)]; 2[2.02]; 2[3.03(f)]; 2[6.01]; 2[6.02(c)]; 2[6.03(c)]; 4[1.01]; 4[4]; 4[4.02]; 8[4.01]
§ 1(h)(1) . . . . 2[1]
§ 1(h)(1)(A) . . . . 2[2.01(a)]; 2[2.01(b)]
§ 1(h)(1)(B) . . . . 2[1]; 2[2.01(a)]
§ 1(h)(1)(C) . . . . 2[1]; 2[2.01(a)]
§ 1(h)(1)(D) . . . 1[4.02]; 2[1]; 2[2.01(a)]; 2[6.01]; 4[4.02]
§ 1(h)(1)(D)(i) . . . . 4[4.02]
§ 1(h)(1)(E) . . . . 2[1]; 2[2.01(a)]
§ 1(h)(2) . . . . 2[2.01(b)]
§ 1(h)(3) . . . . 2[2.01(a)]; 2[2.01(b)]
§ 1(h)(4) . . . . 2[2.01(a)]; 2[2.01(b)]
§ 1(h)(5)(A) . . . . 2[2.01(a)]
§ 1(h)(5)(B) . . . . 2[2.01(c)]
§ 1(h)(6) . . . . 2[2.01(a)]; 2[6.01]; 4[4.02]
§ 1(h)(6)(A)(i) . . . . 2[2.01(b)]
§ 1(h)(6)(A)(ii) . . . . 2[2.01(b)]; 4[4.02]
§ 1(h)(6)(B) . . . . 4[4.02]
§ 1(h)(7) . . . . 2[2.01(a)]
§ 1(h)(8) . . . . 2[6.02(d)]
§ 1(h)(9) . . . . 2[1]; 2[2.01(c)]
§ 1(h)(10) . . . . 2[1]; 2[2.01(c)]
§ 1(h)(11) . . . . 2[2.01(b)]
§ 1(h)(11)(A) . . . . 2[2.01(a)]
§ 11 . . . . 2[1]; 2[2.02]
§ 11(b)(1) . . . . 2[2.02]
§ 11(b)(1)(A) . . . . 2[2.02]
§ 11(b)(1)(B) . . . . 2[2.02]
§ 11(b)(1)(C) . . . . 2[2.02]; 5[1.08]
§ 22(a) . . . . 6[3.02]
§ 22(b)(3) . . . . 6[3.02]
§ 23 . . . . 6[4.02(a)]
§ 23(1) . . . . 4[3.07(b)]
§ 23(a) . . . . 7[1.04]
§ 23(f) . . . . 1[2.06]
§ 24 . . . . 6[4.02(a)]
§ 25B . . . . 6[4.02(a)]
§ 26(a) . . . . 6[4.02(a)]
§ 38 . . . . 4[3.06(c)]
§ 45 . . . . 7[4.02]
§ 48 . . . . 4[3.06(c)]
§ 48(a)(1)(B)(i) . . . . 4[3.06(b)]
§ 48(p) . . . . 4[3.06(b)]
§ 49(a)(1)(D)(iv) . . . . 8[4]; 8[4.04]
§ 53 . . . 6[4.02]; 6[4.02(a)]; 6[4.02(b)]; 6[4.02(c)]
§ 53(e) . . . . 6[4.02(b)]
§ 53(f) . . . . 6[4.02(b)]
§ 55 . . . . 6[4.02]; 6[4.02(b)]; 6[4.02(c)]
§§ 55–58 . . . . 6[4.02(c)]
§ 55(a) . . . . 6[4.02]
§ 55(a)(1) . . . . 6[4.02(a)]
§ 55(A)(1)(ii) . . . . 6[4.02(a)]
§ 55(b)(1) . . . . 6[4.02(a)]
§ 55(b)(1)(B) . . . . 6[4.02]
§ 55(b)(2) . . . . 4[3.06(b)]; 6[4.02(a)]
§ 55(b)(3) . . . . 6[4.02(a)]

[*References are to chapter numbers followed by section/subsection numbers in brackets.*]

§ 55(b)(3)(B) . . . . 2[2.01(a)]
§ 55(b)(3)(C) . . . . 2[2.01(a)]
§ 55(b)(3)(D) . . . . 2[2.01(a)]
§ 55(c)(3) . . . . 6[4.02(a)]
§ 55(d) . . . . 6[4.02(a)]
§ 55(d)(2) . . . . 6[4.02]
§ 55(e) . . . . 6[4.02]
§ 56 . . . 6[4.02]; 6[4.02(a)]; 6[4.02(b)]; 6[4.02(c)]
§ 56(a) . . . . 6[4.02(a)]
§ 56(a)(1)(A) . . . . 4[3.06(b)]; 6[4.02]
§ 56(a)(1)(A)(i) . . . . 4[3.06(b)]
§ 56(a)(1)(A)(ii) . . . . 4[3.06(b)]
§ 56(a)(2) . . . . 6[4.02]
§ 56(a)(4) . . . . 6[4.02]; 6[4.02(a)]; 6[4.02(c)]
§ 56(b) . . . . 6[4.02]
§ 56(b)(2) . . . . 6[4.02(c)]
§ 56(b)(3) . . . . . 6[4.02(a)]; 6[4.02(b)]; 6[4.02(c)]
§ 56(b)(4) . . . . 6[4.02(c)]
§ 56(d) . . . . 6[4.02]; 6[4.02(b)]; 6[4.02(c)]
§ 56(d)(1) . . . . 6[4.02(b)]
§ 56(d)(1)(B)(i) . . . . 6[4.02(c)]
§ 56(d)(2) . . . . 6[4.02(c)]
§ 56(e) . . . . 6[4.02(c)]
§ 56(e)(1) . . . . 6[4.02]
§ 56(e)(2) . . . . 6[4.02]
§ 56(g)(4) . . . . 4[3.06(b)]
§ 56(g)(4)(A) . . . . 4[3.06(b)]
§ 57 . . . 6[4.02]; 6[4.02(a)]; 6[4.02(b)]; 6[4.02(c)]
§ 57(a) . . . . 6[4.02(c)]
§ 57(a)(1) . . . . 6[4.02]
§ 57(a)(2) . . . . 6[4.02]
§ 57(a)(5) . . . . 6[4.02]
§ 57(a)(6) . . . . 6[4.02(b)]
§ 57(a)(7) . . . . 2[2.01(a)]; 6[4.02]
§ 57(a)(10) . . . . 6[4.02(b)]
§ 57(b) . . . . 6[4.02]
§ 57(d)(10) . . . . 6[4.02(b)]
§ 58 . . . . 6[4.02(a)]; 6[4.02(b)]; 6[4.02(c)]
§ 59 . . . . 6[4.02]
§ 59(a) . . . . 6[4.02(a)]
§ 59(e) . . . . 4[3.04(c)]; 4[3.04(d)]; 4[4.03]
§ 59(g) . . . . 6[4.02(c)]
§ 61 . . 3[2.03]; 3[5]; 6[3.04(a)]; 7[1.02]; 7[2.01(d)]; 7[2.02]; 7[4.01]
§ 61(1) . . . . 7[4.01]
§ 61(a) . 2[3.02]; 2[4.03]; 3[1.01]; 5[3.03]; 6[3.02]; 7[2.02]
§ 61(a)(3) . . . . . 1[2.01]; 1[2.02]; 1[3.01]; 1[3.06]; 2[2.01(b)]; 3[3.01(b)]
§ 61(a)(12) . . . . 3[2.01]; 3[2.03]; 3[5.01]
§ 62 . . . . 2[2.01(b)]; 2[2.01(d)]; 6[4.02(a)]
§ 62(a)(3) . . . . 2[2.01(b)]
§ 62(m)(4)(C) . . . . 6[1.02]
§ 83 . . . 6; 6[1.02]; 6[2.02]; 6[2.03]; 6[3]; 6[3.02]; 6[3.03]; 6[3.04]; 6[3.04(a)]; 6[4.01]; 6[4.02(b)]; 6[4.02(c)]
§ 83(a) . . . . . . 6[2.02]; 6[2.03]; 6[3.02]; 6[3.03]; 6[3.04(a)]; 6[4.02(c)]
§ 83(a)(1) . . . . 6[2.02]; 6[4.02(b)]
§ 83(a)(2) . . . . 6[3.03]
§ 83(b) . . . . 6[2.02]; 6[3.02]; 6[3.04(a)]
§ 83(b)(1) . . . . 6[2.02]
§ 83(c) . . . . 6[2.02]
§ 83(c)(1) . . . . 6[1.02]; 6[4.02(b)]
§ 83(c)(3) . . . . 6[2.02]
§ 83(d) . . . . 6[2.02]
§ 83(e) . . . . 6[3.02]
§ 83(e)(1) . . . . 6[4.01]; 6[4.02(b)]
§ 83(e)(3) . . . . . 6[3]; 6[3.02]; 6[3.03]; 6[3.04(a)]; 6[4.02(b)]
§ 83(e)(4) . . . . 6[3.02]; 6[3.03]; 6[3.04(a)]
§ 83(f) . . . . 3[4.03]
§ 83(h) . . . 6; 6[1.01]; 6[2.02]; 6[2.03]; 6[3.04(a)]
§ 102 . . . 1[2.03]; 1[2.04]; 5[3.03]; 6[1.01]; 7[2.02]
§ 103(a) . . . . 6[4.02(a)]
§ 104(a)(2) . . . . 1[2.02]
§ 107(b) . . . . 7[3.03(a)]
§ 108 . . . . 3; 3[2.01]; 3[2.02]; 3[2.03]; 3[3.01(b)]; 3[3.04]; 3[4]; 3[5]; 3[5.01]; 3[5.03]; 4[4.02]
§ 108(a) . . . . 2[6.01]; 3[5]
§ 108(a)(1)(A) . . . . 3[5]
§ 108(a)(1)(B) . . . . 3[5]; 3[5.01]
§ 108(a)(1)(C) . . . . 3[5]
§ 108(a)(1)(D) . . . . 3[3.04]; 3[5]
§ 108(a)(1)(E) . . . . 3[3.04]; 3[5]
§ 108(a)(2) . . . . 3[5]
§ 108(a)(2)(A) . . . . 3[5]
§ 108(a)(2)(B) . . . . 3[5]
§ 108(a)(3) . . . . 3[5.01]
§ 108(b) . . . . 2[6.01]; 3[1.02]; 3[5]
§ 108(b)(2) . . . . 3[5]
§ 108(b)(2)(A) . . . . 3[5.02]
§ 108(b)(3)(A) . . . . 3[5.02]
§ 108(b)(3)(B) . . . . 3[5.02]
§ 108(b)(4)(A) . . . . 3[5.02]
§ 108(b)(4)(B) . . . . 3[5.02]
§ 108(b)(5) . . . . 3[5]; 3[5.03]
§ 108(c) . . . . 3[3.04]; 3[5]
§ 108(c)(1) . . . . 3[5.03]
§ 108(c)(3) . . . . 3[5.03]

[*References are to chapter numbers followed by section/subsection numbers in brackets.*]

§ 108(c)(4) . . . . 3[5.03]
§ 108(d) . . . . 3[5]
§ 108(d)(1) . . . . 3[2.03]
§ 108(d)(1)(A) . . . . 3[2.03]
§ 108(d)(1)(B) . . . . 3[2.03]
§ 108(d)(3) . . . . 3[2.03]; 3[5.01]
§ 108(d)(5) . . . . 3[5.03]
§ 108(e) . . . . 3[2.03]; 3[5]
§ 108(e)(1) . . . . 3[2.03]; 3[5.01]
§ 108(e)(2) . . . . 3[2.01]; 3[2.02]; 3[2.03]; 3[4.02]; 3[4.03]; 3[5]
§ 108(e)(3) . . . . 3[2.01]
§ 108(e)(4) . . . . 3[5]
§ 108(e)(5) . 3[2.02]; 3[2.03]; 3[3.04]; 3[5]; 3[5.03]; 4[3.06(c)]
§ 108(e)(6) . . . . 3[5]
§ 108(e)(7) . . . . 3[5]
§ 108(e)(8) . . . . 3[2.01]; 3[5]
§ 108(e)(10) . . . . 3[2.01]; 3[5]
§ 108(f) . . . . 3[5]
§ 108(g) . . . . 3[5]
§ 108(g)(3)(B) . . . . 3[5.03]
§ 108(g)(3)(C) . . . . 3[5.03]
§ 108(h) . . . . 3[3.04]; 3[5]; 3[5.03]
§ 108(h)(1) . . . . 3[5.03]
§ 108(h)(2) . . . . 3[5.03]
§ 108(h)(3) . . . . 3[5.03]
§ 108(h)(4) . . . . 3[5.03]
§ 111 . . . . 1[2.06]; 5[1.01]; 5[2.05]
§ 112 . . . . 1[2.06]; 5[1.01]
§ 112(a) . . . . 1[2.06]; 5[1.01]
§ 112(b) . . . . 1[2.06]; 5[1.01]
§ 112(b)(1) . . . . 5[1.01]
§ 112(b)(2) . . . . 5[1.01]
§ 112(b)(3) . . . . 5[1.01]
§ 112(b)(5) . . . . 5[1.01]
§ 112(c) . . . . 5[1.01]
§ 112(c)(1) . . . . 5[1.01]
§ 112(e) . . . . 5[1.01]
§ 112(f) . . . . 5[2.03]
§ 113 . . . . 1[2.06]
§ 113(a) . . . . 1[2.06]
§ 113(a)(6) . . . . 5[1.01]
§ 114 . . . . 1[2.06]
§ 117 . . . . 7[3.03(a)]
§ 117(a) . . . . 2[3.03(a)]
§ 117(a)(1) . . . . 2[3.02]
§ 121 . . . . 5; 5[3]; 5[3.02]
§ 121(a) . . . . 5[3.02]
§ 121(b) . . . . 5[3.02]
§ 121(b)(3) . . . . 5[3.02]
§ 121(b)(4) . . . . 5[3.02]
§ 121(c) . . . . 5[3.02]
§ 121(d) . . . . 5[3.02]
§ 121(d)(5) . . . . 5[3.02]
§ 121(d)(5)(B) . . . . 5[3.02]
§ 121(d)(6) . . . . 5[3.02]
§ 121(d)(8)(A) . . . . 5[3.02]
§ 121(d)(8)(B) . . . . 5[3.02]
§ 121(d)(9) . . . . 5[3.02]
§ 122(b) . . . . 1[2.06]
§ 122(b)(1) . . . . 5[1.01]
§ 130A . . . . 6[3.02]
§ 131(b)(3)(B) . . . . 2[6.03(c)]
§ 139(g) . . . . 5[2.01]
§ 139(g)(3) . . . . 5[2.01]
§ 141(e)(1)(B) . . . . 6[4.02(a)]
§ 151 . . . . 2[2.01(d)]; 6[4.02(b)]
§ 161 . . . . 4[2.01]; 4[3.02]
§ 162 . . 3[1.02]; 3[4.03]; 4[1.01]; 4[2.01]; 4[2.03]; 4[2.05]; 4[3.02]; 4[3.04(a)]; 4[3.04(b)]; 4[3.04(c)]; 4[3.07]; 6[1.01]; 6[2.03]; 6[3.04(a)]; 6[3.04(b)]; 6[4.02(a)]; 7[3.02]; 8[5.02]
§ 162(a) . . . . . 1[4.03]; 4[2.01]; 4[2.03]; 4[3.02]; 4[3.04(b)]; 7[1.04]
§ 162(a)(1) . . . . 4[2.01]; 7[4.01]
§ 162(a)(3) . . . . 7[1.04]
§ 162(m) . . . . 6[1.02]
§ 163 . . . . 3[1.02]; 3[4.03]
§ 163(a) . . . . 3[1.02]; 4[3.02]; 7[1.05]
§ 163(d) . . . . 7[4.01]
§ 163(d)(4)(B)(iii) . . . . 2[2.01(b)]
§ 164 . . . . 4[3.02]
§ 165 . 1[3.06]; 2[4.02]; 2[4.04(b)]; 4[2.03]; 4[3.02]; 4[3.04(c)]; 7[2.02]; 8[1]; 8[4.01]
§ 165(a) . 1[2.06]; 1[3.02]; 2[1]; 2[4.02]; 8[1]; 8[2]
§ 165(c) . . . . 1[2.07]; 2[1]
§ 165(c)(1) . . . . 2[6.02(b)]; 2[6.02(c)]; 8[1]
§ 165(c)(2) . . . . . . 1[3.03(a)]; 2[4.02]; 8[1]; 8[2]
§ 165(c)(3) . . . . 2[6.02(b)]; 8[1]
§ 165(f) . . . . 2[1]; 2[4.02]; 8[1]
§ 165(g) . . . . 2[4.02]; 2[4.04(a)]
§ 165(h) . . . . 1[3.03(a)]; 2[6.02(b)]; 8[1]
§ 166(d) . . . . 2[4.04(a)]
§ 166(d)(1)(B) . . . . 2[4.02]

[*References are to chapter numbers followed by section/subsection numbers in brackets.*]

§ 167 . . . . 1[2.01]; 2[3.03(b)]; 2[6.01]; 2[6.02(a)]; 2[6.03]; 2[6.03(a)]; 2[6.03(b)]; 3[3.01(a)]; 3[3.02]; 4[1.01]; 4[2.01]; 4[3.01]; 4[3.03]; 4[3.05]; 4[3.06(a)]; 4[3.06(b)]; 4[3.07]; 4[3.07(a)]; 4[3.07(b)]; 4[4.02]; 7[1.04]; 7[1.05]
§ 167(a) . . . . . 3[3.02]; 4[2.01]; 4[3.05]; 4[3.06]; 4[3.06(a)]; 4[3.06(b)]; 4[3.07]; 4[3.07(b)]
§ 167(a)(1) . . . . 4[2.01]
§ 167(b) . . . . 4[3.06]; 4[3.06(a)]; 4[3.07(b)]
§ 167(c) . . . . 3[3.01(a)]; 3[3.02]
§ 167(c)(2) . . . . 1[2.01]; 7[3.02]
§ 167(e) . . . . 5[1.01]; 7[1.03]
§ 167(f) . . . . 4[3.07(b)]
§ 167(f)(1) . . . . 4[3.04(a)]; 4[3.07(b)]
§ 167(f)(1)(B) . . . . 4[3.05]
§ 167(f)(2) . . . . 4[3.07(b)]
§ 167(g) . . . . 4[3.07(b)]
§ 167(g)(1)(A) . . . . 4[3.07(b)]
§ 167(g)(1)(C) . . . . 4[3.07(b)]
§ 167(g)(1)(D) . . . . 4[3.07(b)]
§ 167(g)(2) . . . . 4[3.07(b)]
§ 167(g)(3) . . . . 4[3.07(b)]
§ 167(g)(4) . . . . 4[3.07(b)]
§ 167(g)(6) . . . . 4[3.07(b)]
§ 167(m) . . . . 4[3.06(b)]
§ 168 . . . . 2[2.01(a)]; 2[3.03(b)]; 4[1.01]; 4[2.03]; 4[3.01]; 4[3.03]; 4[3.04(b)]; 4[3.05]; 4[3.06(a)]; 4[3.06(b)]; 4[3.06(c)]; 4[3.07(a)]; 4[4]; 4[4.01]; 4[4.02]; 7[1.04]; 8[4.01]; 8[4.04]
§ 168(a) . . . . 4[3.06]; 4[3.06(a)]; 4[3.06(b)]
§ 168(b) . . . . 4[3.06]; 4[3.06(b)]
§ 168(b)(1) . . . . 4[3.06(a)]; 4[3.06(b)]
§ 168(b)(1)(B) . . . . 4[3.06(b)]
§ 168(b)(2) . . . . 4[3.06(b)]
§ 168(b)(2)(C) . . . . 4[3.06(b)]
§ 168(b)(3) . . . . 2[6.01]; 4[3.06(b)]
§ 168(b)(3)(G) . . . . 4[3.06(c)]
§ 168(b)(3)(H) . . . . 4[3.06(b)]
§ 168(b)(4) . . . . 4[3.06(b)]
§ 168(b)(5) . . . . 4[3.06(b)]
§ 168(c) . 4[3.06]; 4[3.06(a)]; 4[3.06(b)]; 4[3.06(c)]
§ 168(c)(1) . . . . 4[3.06(a)]
§ 168(c)(3) . . . . 4[3.06(b)]
§ 168(d) . . . . 4[3.06]; 4[3.06(b)]
§ 168(d)(2) . . . . 4[3.06(b)]
§ 168(d)(3) . . . . 4[3.06(b)]
§ 168(d)(3)(B) . . . . 4[3.06(b)]
§ 168(d)(4) . . . . 4[3.06(b)]
§ 168(e) . . . . 4[3.06]
§ 168(e)(1) . . . . 4[3.06(b)]
§ 168(e)(2) . . . . 4[3.06(b)]
§ 168(e)(2)(A) . . . . 4[3.06(b)]; 4[3.06(c)]
§ 168(e)(2)(A)(ii)(I) . . . . 4[3.06(b)]
§ 168(e)(2)(B) . . . . 4[3.06(c)]
§ 168(e)(3) . . . . 4[3.06(b)]
§ 168(e)(3)(B) . . . . 4[3.06(b)]
§ 168(e)(3)(B)(i) . . . . 4[3.06(b)]
§ 168(e)(3)(B)(iv) . . . . 4[3.06(b)]
§ 168(e)(3)(B)(vi) . . . . 4[3.06(b)]
§ 168(e)(3)(E)(iv) . . . . 4[3.06(c)]
§ 168(e)(3)(E)(v) . . . . 4[3.06(b)]
§ 168(e)(6) . . . . 4[3.06(c)]
§ 168(e)(6)(A) . . . . 4[3.06(c)]
§ 168(e)(6)(B) . . . . 4[3.06(c)]
§ 168(e)(7) . . . . 4[3.06(b)]
§ 168(f) . . . . 4[3.06]; 4[3.06(b)]
§ 168(f)(1) . . . . 4[3.06(b)]; 4[3.06(c)]
§ 168(f)(2) . . . . 4[3.06(b)]
§ 168(f)(3) . . . . 4[3.06(b)]
§ 168(f)(4) . . . . 4[3.06(b)]
§ 168(f)(5) . . . . 4[3.06(b)]
§ 168(g) . . . . 4[3.06(b)]; 4[3.06(c)]
§ 168(g)(1) . . . . 4[3.06(c)]
§ 168(g)(1)(2) . . . . 8[6]
§§ 168(g)(1)–(3) . . . . 8[6]
§ 168(g)(1)(A) . . . . 8[6]
§ 168(g)(2) . . . . 4[3.06(b)]; 4[3.06(c)]
§ 168(g)(2)(C) . . . . 4[3.06(b)]
§ 168(g)(3) . . . . 4[3.06(b)]
§ 168(g)(3)(A) . . . . 8[6]
§ 168(g)(3)(B) . . . . 4[3.06(b)]; 4[3.06(c)]
§ 168(g)(3)(C) . . . . 4[3.06(b)]; 8[6]
§ 168(g)(3)(D) . . . . 4[3.06(b)]
§ 168(g)(3)(E) . . . . 4[3.06(b)]
§ 168(g)(4) . . . . 4[3.06(b)]
§ 168(g)(7) . . . . 4[3.06(b)]; 4[3.06(c)]
§ 168(h) . . . . 4[3.06(b)]; 8[6]
§ 168(h)(1) . . . . 8[6]
§§ 168(h)(1)–(4) . . . . 8[6]
§ 168(h)(1)(C) . . . . 8[6]
§ 168(h)(2) . . . . 8[6]
§ 168(h)(3) . . . . 8[6]
§ 168(i)(1) . . . . 4[3.06(b)]; 8[6]
§ 168(i)(1)(B) . . . . 4[3.06(b)]
§ 168(i)(1)(E) . . . . 4[3.06(b)]
§ 168(i)(2) . . . . 4[3.06(b)]; 8[6]
§ 168(i)(4) . . . . 4[3.06(c)]
§ 168(i)(6) . . . . 4[3.06(c)]
§ 168(i)(8) . . . . 4[3.06(c)]

[*References are to chapter numbers followed by section/subsection numbers in brackets.*]

§ 168(i)(9)(C) . . . . 4[3.06(b)]
§ 168(k) . . . . 4[3.05]; 4[3.06(b)]; 4[3.06(c)]; 4[4]; 8[4.01]; 8[4.04]
§ 168(k)(1) . . . . 4[3.05]
§ 168(k)(1)(A) . . . . 4[3.05]
§ 168(k)(1)(B) . . . . 4[3.05]
§ 168(k)(2)(A) . . . . 4[3.05]
§ 168(k)(2)(E)(i) . . . . 4[3.05]
§ 168(k)(2)(F)(i) . . . . 4[3.06(c)]
§ 168(k)(3) . . . . 4[3.06(c)]
§ 168(k)(3)(A) . . . . 4[3.06(c)]
§ 168(k)(3)(B) . . . . 4[3.06(c)]
§ 168(m) . . . . 4[3.06(b)]
§ 170 . . . . 2[3.03(e)]; 5[3.03]; 7[2.01(c)]
§ 170(b)(1) . . . . 6[4.02(a)]
§ 170(e) . . . . 5[3.03]
§ 170(e)(1)(A) . . . . 2[3.03(c)]; 2[3.03(e)]
§ 171(b) . . . . 3[1.02]
§ 172 . . . . 6[4.02(b)]; 6[4.02(c)]
§ 172(a) . . . . 6[4.02(c)]
§ 172(b) . . . . 6[4.02(c)]
§ 172(b)(3) . . . . 6[4.02(c)]
§ 172(b)(3)(C) . . . . 6[4.02(c)]
§ 172(c) . . . . 6[4.02(b)]; 6[4.02(c)]
§ 172(d) . . . . 6[4.02(c)]
§ 172(d)(2)(A) . . . . 6[4.02(b)]
§ 172(d)(4) . . . . 6[4.02(b)]
§ 174 . . . . 4[3.02]; 4[3.04(a)]; 4[3.07]
§ 174(a) . . . . 4[3.04(a)]
§ 174(a)(3) . . . . 4[3.04(a)]
§ 174(b) . . . . 4[3.04(a)]
§ 174(c) . . . . 4[3.04(a)]
§ 177 . . . . 2[3.03]
§ 179 . 2[6.01]; 2[6.03(c)]; 4[3.01]; 4[3.03]; 4[3.05]; 4[3.06(b)]; 4[3.06(c)]; 4[3.07]; 4[4]; 4[4.01]; 8[4.01]; 8[4.04]
§ 179A . . . . 2[6.01]
§ 179(a) . . . . 4[3.03]
§ 179(b)(1) . . . . 4[3.03]
§ 179(b)(2) . . . . 4[3.03]
§ 179(b)(3)(A) . . . . 4[3.03]
§ 179(b)(3)(B) . . . . 4[3.03]
§ 179(b)(6) . . . . 4[3.06(c)]
§ 179(d)(1) . . . . 4[3.03]
§ 179(d)(8) . . . . 4[3.03]
§ 179(d)(10) . . . . 4[3.03]
§ 179(f) . . . . 4[3.03]
§ 183 . . . . 5[3.02]
§ 190 . . . . 2[6.01]
§ 193 . . . . 2[6.01]
§ 195 . . . . 4[3.02]; 4[3.04(a)]
§ 195(a) . . . . 4[3.02]
§ 195(b) . . . . 4[3.02]
§ 195(b)(3) . . . . 4[3.02]
§ 195(c)(1) . . . . 4[3.02]
§ 195(c)(1)(A) . . . . 4[3.02]
§ 195(c)(1)(B) . . . . 4[3.02]
§ 197 . . . . . 1[2.01]; 1[4.02]; 2[6.01]; 2[6.02(c)]; 2[6.03(a)]; 4[1.01]; 4[2.04]; 4[3.01]; 4[3.02]; 4[3.07]; 4[3.07(a)]; 4[3.07(b)]; 4[4.01]; 5[1.06]; 5[1.07]; 7[3.01]; 7[3.02]; 7[3.03(c)]
§ 197(a) . 1[4.02]; 4[3.07(a)]; 7[3.03(a)]; 7[3.03(b)]; 7[3.03(c)]
§§ 197(a)–(e) . . . . 4[3.07(a)]
§ 197(c)(1) . 1[4.02]; 4[2.04]; 4[3.07(a)]; 7[3.03(a)]; 7[3.03(b)]; 7[3.03(c)]
§ 197(c)(2) . . . . 4[3.07(a)]; 7[3.03(a)]; 7[3.03(b)]; 7[3.03(c)]
§ 197(d)(1) . . . . 4[3.07(a)]
§ 197(d)(1)(A) . . . . 1[4.02]
§ 197(d)(1)(B) . . . . 1[4.02]
§ 197(d)(1)(C)(iii) . . . . 7[3.03(a)]; 7[3.03(b)]
§ 197(d)(1)(E) . . . . 1[4.02]
§ 197(d)(1)(F) . . . . 7[3.03(c)]
§ 197(d)(2)(A) . . . . 4[3.07(a)]
§ 197(e) . . . . 4[3.07(a)]
§ 197(e)(3)(A)(i) . . . . 4[3.03]
§ 197(e)(4)(C) . . . . 7[3.03(a)]; 7[3.03(b)]
§ 197(f)(1)(A) . . . . 4[3.07(a)]
§ 197(f)(1)(B) . . . . 4[3.07(a)]
§§ 197(f)(1)–(f)(3) . . . . 4[3.07(a)]
§ 197(f)(4) . . . . 7[3.03(c)]
§ 197(f)(7) . 2[6.01]; 2[6.03(a)]; 4[3.07(a)]; 4[4.01]
§ 198 . . . . 4[3.01]; 4[3.04(b)]
§ 198(a) . . . . 4[3.04(b)]
§ 198(b)(1) . . . . 4[3.04(b)]
§ 198(b)(2) . . . . 4[3.04(b)]
§ 198(c)(1) . . . . 4[3.04(b)]
§ 198(c)(3) . . . . 4[3.04(b)]
§ 198(e) . . . . 4[3.04(b)]
§ 212 . . 3[1.02]; 4[1.01]; 4[2.01]; 4[2.03]; 4[2.05]; 4[3.07(a)]; 6[1.01]; 6[2.03]; 8[5.02]
§ 261 . . . . 4[2.01]; 4[3.02]
§ 263 . . 4[1.01]; 4[2.01]; 4[2.03]; 4[2.04]; 4[2.05]; 4[3.01]; 4[3.02]; 4[3.04(b)]; 4[3.06(c)]; 4[3.07]; 4[3.07(b)]
§ 263A . 4[1.01]; 4[2.01]; 4[2.02]; 4[2.03]; 4[3.01]; 4[3.04(b)]; 4[3.06(b)]; 4[3.06(c)]; 4[3.07]; 4[3.07(b)]
§ 263(a) . . . . . 4[2.01]; 4[2.02]; 4[2.03]; 4[3.02]; 4[3.04(b)]

[*References are to chapter numbers followed by section/subsection numbers in brackets.*]

§ 263(a)(1) . . . . 4[2.01]; 4[3.04(b)]
§ 263(a)(2) . . . . 4[3.04(b)]
§ 263(c) . . . . 3[3.03]; 4[3.04(c)]; 4[4.03]
§ 263(f) . . . . 4[2.02]
§ 267 . . . . 5[1.08]; 8[1]; 8[3]
§ 267(a) . . . . 8[3]
§ 267(a)(1) . . . . 1[3.06]; 8[3]
§ 267(b) . . . 4[2.04]; 5[1.03]; 5[1.04]; 8[3]; 8[4.02]
§ 267(b)(1) . . . . 8[3]
§ 267(b)(2) . . . . 8[3]
§ 267(b)(11) . . . . 8[3]
§ 267(b)(12) . . . . 8[3]
§ 267(c) . . . . 8[3]
§ 263A(b) . . . . 4[2.02]
§ 263A(b)(1) . . . . 4[2.02]
§ 263A(b)(2) . . . . 4[2.02]
§ 263A(b)(2)(B) . . . . 4[2.02]
§ 263A(d)(3) . . . . 4[3.06(b)]
§ 263A(e)(2)(A) . . . . 4[3.06(b)]
§ 263A(f) . . . . 4[2.02]
§ 263A(f)(1) . . . . 4[2.02]
§ 263A(f)(4)(B) . . . . 4[2.02]
§ 263A(g)(1) . . . . 4[2.02]; 4[3.04(b)]
§ 267(c)(4) . . . . 8[3]
§ 267(d) . . . . 8[3]
§ 267(g) . . . . 8[3]
§ 268(a)(1)(B) . . . . 4[2.04]
§ 268(f) . . . . 4[3.06(b)]
§ 269A . . . . 7[4.01]
§ 280A(f)(1) . . . . 5[3.02]
§ 280C . . . . 6[4.02(a)]
§ 280F . . . . 4[3.06(b)]; 4[3.06(c)]
§ 280F(a) . . . . 4[3.06(c)]
§ 280F(a)(1) . . . . 4[3.06(c)]
§ 280F(a)(1)(B) . . . . 4[3.06(c)]
§ 280F(a)(2) . . . . 4[3.06(c)]
§ 280F(b) . . . . 4[3.06(c)]
§ 280F(b)(1) . . . . 4[3.06(c)]
§ 280F(b)(2) . . . . 4[3.06(c)]
§ 280F(d)(1) . . . . 4[3.06(c)]
§ 280F(d)(5)(A) . . . . 4[3.06(c)]
§ 280F(d)(5)(B) . . . . 4[3.06(c)]
§ 280F(d)(7) . . . . 4[3.06(c)]
§ 280G . . . . 6[3.04(b)]
§ 291(a)(1) . . . . 2[6.01]
§ 291(b) . . . . 4[3.04(c)]
§ 291(b)(1) . . . . 4[3.04(c)]; 4[3.04(d)]
§ 291(b)(2) . . . . 4[3.04(c)]; 4[3.04(d)]
§ 291(b)(4) . . . . 4[3.04(c)]
§ 301 . . . . 6[3.03]
§ 301(c)(3) . . . . 2[4.04(e)]
§ 301(d) . . . . 1[2.02]
§ 302(b) . . . . 6[2.01]
§ 305 . . . . 1[3.01]
§ 311(b)(1) . . . . 6[3.03]
§ 312(k)(3) . . . . 4[3.06(b)]
§ 316 . . . . 6[3.03]
§ 317 . . . . 6[3.03]
§ 331 . . . . 2[4.03]
§ 331(a)(2) . . . . 6[4.01]
§ 333 . . . . 5[1.07]
§ 334(a) . . . . 3[3.01(b)]
§ 334(b) . . . . 2[5.05(b)]
§ 337 . . . . 3[4.03]; 7[2.01(c)]; 7[3.02]
§ 337(a) . . . . 3[4.03]
§ 338 . . . . 1[4.03]; 6[3.03]; 6[3.04(a)]
§ 338(h)(10) . . . . 3[4.03]
§ 351 . . . . 1[2.01]; 1[2.05]; 1[3.03(c)]; 2[5.05(a)]; 2[6.01]; 3[1.01]; 3[1.02]; 3[2.01]; 3[2.03]; 3[3.02]; 3[4.01]; 4[2.01]; 4[3.06(c)]; 4[4.01]; 4[4.02]; 5; 5[1.01]; 5[1.07]; 7[4.02]
§ 351(a) . . . . 1[2.05]; 3[1.02]
§ 351(b) . . . . 1[2.05]
§ 354 . . . . 2[5.05(a)]; 5
§ 355 . . . . 1[4.02]; 2[5.05(a)]; 5; 6[3.03]
§ 356(a) . . . . 5[1.02(b)]
§ 356(a)(1) . . . . 5[1.02(b)]
§ 357 . . . . 3[4.01]
§ 357(a) . . . . 3[4.01]
§ 357(a)(1) . . . . 3[4]
§ 357(c) . . . . 3[1.02]; 3[4]; 3[4.01]
§ 357(c)(1) . . . . 3[1.02]; 3[3.01(a)]; 3[4.01]
§ 357(c)(3) . . . . 3[1.02]; 3[2.03]; 3[4.01]
§ 357(c)(3)(B) . . . . 3[1.02]
§ 357(d) . . . . 3[4.01]
§ 358 . . . . 2[5.05(a)]; 3[1.02]
§ 358(a) . . . . 1[2.05]
§ 358(a)(1) . . . . 3[1.02]
§ 358(a)(1)(A)(ii) . . . . 3[1.02]
§ 358(d) . . . . 3[1.02]; 3[4]
§ 358(d)(1) . . . . 3[1.02]
§ 358(d)(2) . . . . 3[1.02]
§ 358(h) . . . . 3[1.02]
§ 361 . . . . 2[3.03(c)]; 5
§ 362 . . . . 1[3.03(c)]; 2[5.05(b)]; 3[1.02]; 3[4.01]
§ 362(a) . . . . 1[2.01]; 1[2.05]; 3[4.01]
§ 368 5
§ 368(a)(1)(A) . . . . 4[2.04]

[*References are to chapter numbers followed by section/subsection numbers in brackets.*]

§ 368(a)(1)(C) . . . 4[2.04]
§ 368(a)(1)(D) . . . 4[2.04]
§ 368(c) . . . 6[2.03]
§ 401(a) . . . 3[1.02]
§ 401(a)(2) . . . 3[1.02]
§ 401(a)(4) . . . 3[1.02]
§ 401(a)(5) . . . 3[1.02]
§ 401(a)(13) . . . 1[3.03(b)]
§ 401(a)(17) . . . 3[1.02]
§ 401(a)(26) . . . 3[1.02]
§ 402(a) . . . 6[4.02]
§ 402(b) . . . 6[1.01]
§ 402(e)(1)(A) . . . 1[3.03(b)]
§ 404 . . . 3[1.02]
§ 404(a) . . . 6[1.01]
§ 404(a)(5) . . . 3[1.02]; 3[4.03]; 6; 6[1.01]; 6[2.01]
§ 404(b) . . . 6[2.01]
§ 404(d) . . . 3[1.02]; 6[1.01]; 6[1.02]
§ 408(m) . . . 2[2.01(a)]
§ 409(a)(2) . . . 6[1.02]
§ 409(b) . . . 6[1.02]
§ 409(e)(3) . . . 6[1.02]
§ 409A . 6[1.01]; 6[1.02]; 6[2.01]; 6[2.02]; 6[3.02]; 6[3.03]; 6[3.04(a)]; 6[4.01]
§ 409A(4)(b) . . . 6[1.02]
§ 409A(a) . . . 6[1.02]
§ 409A(a)(1) . . . 6[1.02]
§ 409A(a)(1)(A) . . . 6[2.01]; 6[4.01]
§ 409A(a)(1)(B) . . . 6[1.02]
§ 409A(a)(1)(i)(II) . . . 6[2.02]
§ 409A(a)(2)(A) . . . 6[2.01]; 6[4.01]
§ 409A(a)(3) . . . 6[1.02]
§ 409A(a)(4)(A) . . . 6[2.01]; 6[4.01]
§ 409A(a)(4)(B) . . . 6[1.02]; 6[2.01]; 6[4.01]
§ 409A(a)(4)(B)(iii) . . . 6[1.02]
§ 409A(a)(4)(C) . . . 6[1.02]
§ 409A(a)(B) . . . 6[1.02]
§ 409A(b)(1) . . . 6[1.02]
§ 409A(b)(2) . . . 6[1.02]
§ 409A(d)(1) . . . 6[1.02]; 6[2.01]; 6[4.01]
§ 409A(d)(2) . . . 6[1.02]
§ 409A(d)(3) . . . 6[1.02]
§ 409A(d)(4) . . . 6[1.02]
§ 410 . . . 3[1.02]
§ 414(p) . . . 1[3.03(b)]
§ 415 . . . 3[1.02]
§ 421 . . 6[3.02]; 6[3.03]; 6[4]; 6[4.01]; 6[4.02(a)]; 6[4.02(b)]; 6[4.02(c)]
§§ 421–424 . . . 6[4]
§ 421(a) . . . 6[4.02(b)]; 6[4.02(c)]
§ 421(a)(1) . . . 6[4]
§ 421(a)(2) . . . 6[4]
§ 421(a)(3) . . . 6[4]
§ 422 . . . 6[3]; 6[3.03]; 6[4]; 6[4.02(b)]
§ 422(a) . . . 6[4.02(c)]
§ 422(a)(1) . . . 6[4.01]; 6[4.02(c)]
§ 422(a)(2) . . . 6[4.01]
§ 422(b) . . . 6[3.03]; 6[4.01]
§ 422(b)(5) . . . 6[4.01]
§ 422(c)(1) . . . 6[4.01]
§ 422(c)(2) . . . 6[4.02(c)]
§ 423 . . . 6; 6[3]; 6[4]; 6[4.01]; 6[4.02(b)]
§ 423(b) . . . 6[4.01]
§ 423(b)(9) . . . 6[4.01]
§ 423(c) . . . 6[4.01]
§ 424 . . . 6[3.03]
§ 424(a) . . . 6[4.01]
§ 424(a)(3)(ii) . . . 6[4.01]
§ 424(b) . . . 6[4.02(b)]
§ 424(c)(4) . . . 6[4.01]
§ 424(h)(1) . . . 6[4.01]
§ 424(h)(3) . . . 6[4.01]
§ 424(h)(3)(A) . . . 6[4.01]
§ 425(c) . . . 6[4.01]
§ 441(b)(3) . . . 3[4.03]
§ 443(a)(2) . . . 3[4.03]
§ 446 . . . 3[4.03]
§ 446(e) . . . 3[4.03]
§ 453 . . . 1[4.03]; 2[6.01]; 2[6.02(a)]; 4[4.01]; 5[1.02(b)]; 5[3.01]; 8[5.06]
§ 453(a) . . . 5[1.02(b)]; 5[3.01]
§ 453(b) . . . 5[3.01]
§ 453(b)(1) . . . 5[1.02(b)]
§ 453(c) . . . 5[1.02(b)]; 5[3.01]
§ 453(f) . . . 5[1.02(b)]; 5[3.01]
§ 453(f)(6) . . . 5[1.02(b)]
§ 453(f)(7) . . . 5[1.02(b)]
§ 453(i) . . . 2[6.01]; 4[4.01]; 4[4.02]
§ 453B(a) . . . 5[3.01]
§ 453B(g) . . . 1[3.03(b)]
§ 457A . . . 6[1.02]
§ 461(h) . . . 3[4.03]; 4[3.04(b)]
§ 461(h)(2)(C) . . . 3[2.03]
§ 465 . . . 1[2.08]; 3[3.03]; 8[4]; 8[4.01]; 8[4.02]; 8[4.03]; 8[4.04]; 8[5.01]; 8[5.06]; 8[6]
§ 465(a) . . . 3[3.01(b)]; 8[4.02]; 8[4.03]
§ 465(a)(1) . . . 8[4.01]; 8[4.02]; 8[4.03]
§ 465(a)(1)(A) . . . 8[4.01]
§ 465(a)(1)(B) . . . 8[4.01]
§ 465(a)(2) . . . 8[4.01]; 8[4.03]

[*References are to chapter numbers followed by section/subsection numbers in brackets.*]

§ 465(a)(3) . . . . 8[4.01]
§ 465(b) . . . . 8[4.02]
§ 465(b)(1) . . . . 8[4.03]
§ 465(b)(1)(A) . . . . 8[4.02]
§ 465(b)(1)(B) . . . . 8[4.02]
§ 465(b)(2) . . . . 8[4.02]; 8[4.03]
§ 465(b)(2)(A) . . . . 8[4.02]
§ 465(b)(3) . . . . 8[4.02]
§ 465(b)(3)(A) . . . . 8[4.03]
§ 465(b)(3)(C) . . . . 8[4.02]
§ 465(b)(4) . . . . 8[4.02]; 8[4.03]
§ 465(b)(5) . . . . 8[4.02]
§ 465(b)(6) . . . . 8[4.04]
§ 465(b)(6)(A) . . . . 8[4.04]
§ 465(b)(6)(B) . . . . 8[4.04]
§ 465(b)(6)(C) . . . . 8[4.04]
§ 465(b)(6)(D)(i) . . . . 8[4.04]
§ 465(b)(6)(D)(ii) . . . . 8[4.04]
§ 465(c)(1) . . . . 8[4.01]; 8[4.04]
§ 465(c)(1)(C) . . . . 8[4.02]; 8[4.03]
§ 465(c)(2)(A) . . . . 8[4.01]
§ 465(c)(2)(B) . . . . 8[4.01]
§ 465(c)(3) . . . . 8[4.01]; 8[4.04]
§ 465(c)(3)(B) . . . . 8[4.01]
§ 465(c)(4) . . . . 8[4.01]
§ 465(d) . . . . 8[4.01]
§ 465(e) . . . . 8[4.02]
§ 465(e)(1)(A) . . . . 8[4.02]
§ 465(e)(1)(B) . . . . 8[4.02]
§ 465(e)(2) . . . . 8[4.02]
§ 467 . . . . 7[1.05]; 8[6]
§ 468B . . . . 5[1.04]; 7[2.01(d)]
§ 468B(g) . . . . 7[2.01(d)]
§ 468B(g)(1) . . . . 5[1.04]
§ 469 . 1[2.08]; 8[1]; 8[4.01]; 8[4.04]; 8[5]; 8[5.01]; 8[5.02]; 8[5.03]; 8[5.04]; 8[5.05]; 8[5.06]; 8[6]
§ 469(a) . . . . 8[5.04]; 8[5.05]
§ 469(a)(1) . . . . 8[5.03]
§ 469(a)(2) . . . . 8[5.02]
§ 469(b) . . . . 8[5.02]; 8[5.05]
§ 469(c)(1) . . . . 8[5.03]; 8[5.04]; 8[5.05]
§ 469(c)(1)(A) . . . . 8[5.02]
§ 469(c)(1)(B) . . . . 8[5.03]; 8[5.04]
§ 469(c)(2) . . . . 8[5.01]; 8[5.04]; 8[5.05]
§ 469(c)(4) . . . . 8[5.01]; 8[5.04]
§ 469(c)(6) . . . . 8[5.02]; 8[5.04]
§ 469(c)(7) . . . . 8[5.04]; 8[5.05]
§ 469(c)(7)(A) . . . . 8[5.04]
§ 469(c)(7)(A)(ii) . . . . 8[5.04]
§ 469(c)(7)(B) . . . . 8[5.04]
§ 469(c)(7)(C) . . . . 8[5.04]
§ 469(d)(1) . . . . 8[5.02]; 8[5.03]; 8[5.04]; 8[5.05]
§ 469(e)(1) . . . . 8[5.02]
§ 469(g) . . . . 8[6]
§ 469(g)(1) . . . . 8[5.06]
§ 469(g)(2)(A) . . . . 8[5.06]
§ 469(g)(2)(B) . . . . 8[5.06]
§ 469(g)(3) . . . . 8[5.06]
§ 469(h)(1) . . . . 8[5.01]; 8[5.03]; 8[5.04]
§ 469(h)(2) . . . . 8[5.01]; 8[5.03]
§ 469(h)(5) . . . . 8[5.03]; 8[5.04]
§ 469(i)(1) . . . . 8[5.04]
§ 469(i)(2) . . . . 8[5.04]
§ 469(i)(3) . . . . 8[5.04]
§ 469(i)(6)(A) . . . . 8[5.04]
§ 469(i)(6)(C) . . . . 8[5.04]
§ 469(i)(6)(D) . . . . 8[5.04]
§ 469(j)(1) . . . . 8[5.02]
§ 469(j)(2) . . . . 8[5.02]
§ 469(j)(6) . . . . 8[5.06]
§ 469(j)(8) . . . . 8[5.04]
§ 469(l)(1) . . . . 8[5.03]; 8[5.05]
§ 469(l)(2) . . . . 8[5.05]
§ 470 . . . . 8[6]
§ 470(a) . . . . 8[6]
§ 470(b) . . . . 8[6]
§ 470(c)(1) . . . . 8[6]
§ 470(d)(1) . . . . 8[6]
§ 470(d)(2) . . . . 8[6]
§ 470(d)(3) . . . . 8[6]
§ 471 . 2[3.03(a)]; 2[3.03(d)]; 2[3.03(h)]; 2[6.03(b)]; 4[3.01]
§ 475 . . . . 1[3.01]
§ 482 . . . . 7[4.01]; 7[4.02]
§ 483 . . . . 7[1.01]
§ 501(a) . . . . 6[1.01]
§ 501(c)(3) . . . . 3[1.02]; 5[1.07]
§ 512(b)(4) . . . . 7[1.01]
§ 514 . . . . 7[1.01]
§§ 531–537 . . . . 7[4.01]
§ 542(a)(2) . . . . 8[4.01]
§ 611 . . . . 4[3.06(b)]; 4[3.08]
§ 611(a) . . . . 4[3.08]
§ 611(b)(1) . . . . 4[3.08]
§ 612 . . . . 4[3.08]
§ 613 . . . . 4[3.08]
§ 613A . . . . 4[3.08]
§ 613(a) . . . . 4[3.08]
§ 613A(b)(1) . . . . 4[3.08]
§ 613(b) . . . . 4[3.08]

[*References are to chapter numbers followed by section/subsection numbers in brackets.*]

§ 613(c) . . . . . 4[3.08]
§ 613(d) . . . . . 4[3.08]
§ 613(e)(2) . . . . . 4[3.04(c)]
§ 614 . . . . . 4[3.08]
§ 616 . . . . . 4[3.04(d)]; 4[4.03]
§ 616(a) . . . . . 4[3.04(d)]
§ 616(b) . . . . . 4[3.04(d)]
§ 617 . . . . . 4[3.04(d)]; 4[4.03]
§ 617(a)(1) . . . . . 4[3.04(d)]
§ 617(b)(1)(A) . . . . . 4[3.04(d)]
§ 617(b)(1)(B) . . . . . 4[3.04(d)]
§ 631 . . . . . 2[6.03]; 2[6.03(c)]; 7[2.02]
§ 631(a) . . . . . 2[6.03(c)]
§ 631(c) . . . . . 2[6.03(c)]
§ 636 . . . . . 3[3.03]; 7[2.02]
§ 636(a) . . . . . 3[3.03]
§ 636(b) . . . . . 3[3.03]
§ 641(b) . . . . . 8[4.01]
§ 671 . . . . . 6[1.01]
§§ 671–678 . . . . . 6[3.03]
§ 674 . . . . . 6[1.01]
§ 691 . . . . . 5[1.04]
§ 702 . . . . . 2[1]; 4[3.03]
§ 704 . . . . . 3[3.03]; 8[4.02]
§ 704(b) . . . . . 8[4.02]
§ 704(b)(2) . . . . . 8[4.02]
§ 704(c) . . . . . 3[1.02]
§ 704(c)(3) . . . . . 3[1.02]
§ 704(d) . . . . . 3[3.03]
§ 704(e) . . . . . 7[4.01]
§ 705 . . . . . 3[3.03]
§ 707(b) . . . . . 4[2.04]; 5[1.03]; 5[1.04]; 7[4.02]
§ 707(b)(1) . . . . . 1[3.06]; 8[3]; 8[4.02]
§ 707(b)(1)(B) . . . . . 8[3]
§ 707(e) . . . . . 7[4.01]
§ 721 . 1[2.05]; 2[5.05(a)]; 2[6.01]; 4[4.01]; 4[4.02]; 5; 5[1.07]
§ 721(a) . . . . . 1[2.05]
§ 722 . . . . . 1[2.05]; 2[5.05(a)]; 3[3.03]
§ 723 . . . . . 1[2.05]; 2[3.03(c)]; 2[5.05(b)]
§ 731 . . . . . 4[4.01]; 4[4.02]; 5
§ 731(a) . . . . . 2[4.04(e)]; 2[5.05(a)]
§ 731(a)(1) . . . . . 1[2.05]
§ 732(a) . . . . . 1[2.05]; 2[5.05(b)]
§ 732(b) . . . . . 2[5.05(a)]
§ 736(a) . . . . . 3[1.02]
§ 741 . . . . . 2[5.03]; 3[3.01(b)]
§ 751 . . . . . 2[5.03]
§ 751(a) . . . . . 2[2.01(c)]
§ 752 . . . . . 3; 3[1]; 3[1.02]; 8[4.04]
§ 752(a) . . . . . 3[3.03]
§ 752(c) . . . . . 3[4]; 3[4.01]
§ 752(d) . . . . . 3[3.01(b)]
§ 761(a) . . . . . 6[1.01]
§ 861 . . . . . 6[3.04(a)]
§ 862 . . . . . 6[3.04(a)]
§ 901 . . . . . 6[3.04(a)]
§ 1001 . . 1[1]; 1[2.01]; 1[2.06]; 1[3.02]; 1[3.03(a)]; 1[3.03(b)]; 1[3.03(c)]; 2[1]; 2[4.01]; 2[4.02]; 3[3.01(a)]; 3[3.01(b)]; 3[5.01]; 4[1.01]; 5[1.01]; 5[1.02(a)]
§ 1001(a) . . . . . 1[2.01]; 1[2.09]; 1[3.01]; 1[3.02]; 2[4.01]; 3[3.01(a)]; 3[3.01(b)]; 3[4.02]; 4[3.06(c)]; 5[1.01]; 5[1.02(a)]
§ 1001(b) . . 1[3.01]; 3[3.01(a)]; 3[3.01(b)]; 7[1.03]
§ 1001(c) . . . 1[3.02]; 1[3.06]; 2[4.01]; 2[6.02(a)]; 3[3.01(b)]; 3[5.01]; 5; 8[3]
§ 1001(e) . . . . . 7[2.02]
§ 1011 . . . . . 1[2.01]; 1[2.09]; 1[3.03(b)]; 3[1.02]; 3[3.01(a)]; 3[3.01(b)]; 3[3.02]; 4[3.06(a)]; 4[3.07(a)]; 4[3.07(b)]; 4[3.08]
§ 1011(a) . . . . . 3[3.01(a)]
§ 1011(b) . . . . . 1[3.04]; 3[3.01(b)]
§ 1012 . . 1[2.01]; 1[2.02]; 1[2.03]; 1[2.06]; 1[2.08]; 1[2.09]; 1[3.03(b)]; 3[3.01(a)]; 3[3.01(b)]; 3[4.01]; 4[1.01]; 5[3.02]; 6[4.02(c)]
§ 1014 . . . 1[2.04]; 2[3.03(c)]; 3[3.01(a)]; 4[3.03]; 8[5.06]
§ 1014(a) . . . . . 1[2.04]
§ 1014(c) . . . . . 2[5.04]
§ 1014(e) . . . . . 1[2.04]
§ 1014(f) . . . . . 1[2.04]
§ 1015 . . . 1[2.03]; 1[2.04]; 2[3.03(c)]; 2[5.05(b)]; 3[3.01(b)]; 8[3]
§ 1015(a) . . . . . 1[2.03]; 2[5.05(b)]
§ 1015(d) . . . . . 2[5.05(b)]; 6[3.03]
§ 1015(d)(2) . . . . . 1[2.03]
§ 1015(d)(6) . . . . . 1[2.03]
§ 1016 . . . 1[2.01]; 1[2.09]; 3[3.01(a)]; 4[3.06(b)]; 8[4.02]
§ 1016(a) . . . . . 1[2.09]
§ 1016(a)(2) . . . . . 3[3.01(a)]; 4[3.08]
§ 1017 . . 3[2.01]; 3[3.01(b)]; 3[5]; 3[5.03]; 4[4.01]; 4[4.02]
§ 1017(a) . . . . . 3[5.03]
§ 1017(b) . . . . . 2[6.01]
§ 1017(b)(1) . . . . . 3[5]; 3[5.03]
§ 1017(b)(2) . . . . . 3[5.03]
§ 1017(b)(3)(A) . . . . . 3[5.03]
§ 1017(b)(3)(B) . . . . . 3[5.03]
§ 1017(b)(3)(C) . . . . . 3[5.03]

[*References are to chapter numbers followed by section/subsection numbers in brackets.*]

§ 1017(b)(3)(D) . . . . 3[5.03]
§ 1017(b)(3)(F) . . . . 3[5.03]
§ 1017(c)(2) . . . . 3[5.03]
§ 1017(d) . . . . 2[6.01]; 3[5.03]; 4[4.01]
§ 1017(d)(2) . . . . 3[5.03]; 4[4.02]
§ 1022 . . . . 1[2.04]; 2[3.03(c)]
§ 1022(a) . . . . 1[2.04]
§ 1022(b) . . . . 1[2.04]
§ 1022(c) . . . . 1[2.04]
§ 1022(d) . . . . 1[2.04]
§ 1022(d)(2) . . . . 1[2.04]
§ 1022(d)(3) . . . . 1[2.04]
§ 1022(d)(4) . . . . 1[2.04]
§ 1023 . . . . 3[1.02]
§ 1031 . . . . . . 1[2.05]; 1[3.02]; 1[3.06]; 1[4.02]; 2[5.05(a)]; 2[6.01]; 3[5.03]; 4[4.01]; 4[4.02]; 5; 5[1]; 5[1.01]; 5[1.02]; 5[1.02(a)]; 5[1.02(b)]; 5[1.03]; 5[1.04]; 5[1.05]; 5[1.06]; 5[1.07]; 5[1.08]; 5[2]; 5[2.02]; 5[2.04]; 5[2.05]; 5[3.02]; 8[6]
§ 1031(a) . . . . . 5[1]; 5[1.01]; 5[1.02]; 5[1.02(a)]; 5[1.03]; 5[1.04]; 5[1.06]; 5[1.07]; 5[1.08]; 5[2.04]; 5[3.02]; 7[2.02]
§ 1031(a)(1) . . . . 5[1.05]; 5[1.08]
§ 1031(a)(2) . . . . 5[1]; 5[1.02(a)]
§ 1031(a)(2)(A) . . . . 5[1]
§ 1031(a)(2)(D) . . . . 5[1.06]; 5[1.07]
§ 1031(a)(2)(F) . . . . 5[1]
§ 1031(a)(3) . . . . 5[1.04]; 5[1.05]; 5[1.08]
§ 1031(a)(3)(B) . . . . 5[1.07]
§ 1031(b) . . . . . 2[5.05(a)]; 5[1]; 5[1.01]; 5[1.02]; 5[1.02(a)]; 5[1.02(b)]; 5[1.03]; 5[1.04]; 5[3.02]
§ 1031(c) . . . . 5[1]; 5[1.01]; 5[1.02]; 5[1.04]
§ 1031(d) . . . 2[5.05(a)]; 3[1.02]; 5[1.01]; 5[1.02]; 5[1.02(a)]; 5[1.02(b)]; 5[1.08]; 5[2]; 5[3.02]
§ 1031(f) . . . . 5[1]; 5[1.08]; 5[2.05]
§ 1031(f)(1) . . . . 5[1.08]
§ 1031(f)(1)(B) . . . . 5[1.08]
§ 1031(f)(2)(C) . . . . 5[1.08]
§ 1031(f)(4) . . . . 5[1.08]
§ 1031(g) . . . . 5[2.04]
§ 1031(h)(1) . . . . 5[1.06]
§ 1031(h)(2)(A) . . . . 5[1.06]
§ 1032 . . . . 5; 6[3.03]; 6[3.04(a)]; 6[3.04(b)]
§ 1032(a)(2)(B) . . . . 5[1]
§ 1032(a)(2)(C) . . . . 5[1]
§ 1032(a)(2)(D) . . . . 5[1]
§ 1032(a)(2)(E) . . . . 5[1]
§ 1033 . . . . . 1[3.06]; 2[5.05(a)]; 5; 5[2]; 5[2.01]; 5[2.03]; 5[2.04]; 5[2.05]; 5[3]; 5[3.02]; 7[1.03]; 8[6]
§ 1033(a) . . . . 5[2]; 5[2.02]; 5[2.03]; 5[2.04]
§ 1033(a)(1) . . . . 5[2.02]
§ 1033(a)(2) . . . . 5[2.05]
§ 1033(a)(2)(A) . . . . 5[2.02]
§ 1033(a)(2)(B) . . . . 5[2]
§ 1033(a)(2)(B)(i) . . . . 5[2]
§ 1033(a)(2)(B)(ii) . . . . 5[2]
§ 1033(a)(3)(A) . . . . 5[2.02]; 5[2.04]
§§ 1033(a)–(d) . . . . 5[2.01]
§ 1033(b) . . . . 5[2]
§ 1033(d) . . . . 5[2.01]
§ 1033(e) . . . . 5[2.01]
§ 1033(f) . . . . 5[2.02]
§ 1033(g) . . . . 5[2.04]
§ 1033(h) . . . . 5[2.01]
§ 1033(i) . . . . 5[2.05]
§ 1034 . . . . 5; 5[1.04]; 5[3]; 5[3.02]
§ 1035 . . . . 5[1.02(b)]
§ 1036 . . . . 5[1.02(b)]; 6[4.01]
§ 1037 . . . . 5[1.02(b)]
§ 1038 . . . . 2[5.05(c)]; 5; 5[3]; 5[3.01]
§ 1038(a) . . . . 5[3.01]
§ 1038(b) . . . . 5[3.01]
§ 1038(b)(1) . . . . 5[3.01]
§ 1038(b)(2) . . . . 5[3.01]
§ 1038(c) . . . . 5[3.01]
§ 1038(d) . . . . 5[3.01]
§ 1041 . . . . 1[3.03(b)]; 5; 6[3.03]; 8[3]
§ 1060 . . . . . . 1[2.01]; 1[2.06]; 1[4.01]; 1[4.02]; 4[3.07(a)]
§ 1060(e) . . . . 1[4.02]
§ 1091 . . . . . 1[3.06]; 2[5.05(c)]; 8[1]; 8[2]; 8[3]
§ 1091(a) . . . . 8[2]
§ 1091(d) . . . . 8[2]
§ 1141 . . . . 4[2.01]
§ 1201 . . . . 2[2.02]; 7[2.02]
§ 1201(a) . . . . 2[2.02]
§ 1201(a)(1) . . . . 7[2.02]
§ 1202 . . . 2[1]; 2[2.01(a)]; 2[6.03(c)]; 3[3.01(b)]; 4[4.02]
§ 1202(a) . . . . 2[2.01(a)]
§ 1202(a)(1) . . . . 2[2.01(a)]
§ 1202(a)(2)(A) . . . . 2[2.01(a)]
§ 1202(a)(3) . . . . 2[2.01(a)]
§ 1202(a)(4) . . . . 2[2.01(a)]
§ 1202(a)(4)(C) . . . . 2[2.01(a)]
§ 1202(b)(1) . . . . 2[2.01(a)]
§ 1211 . . . 1[3.06]; 2[2.01(b)]; 2[2.01(d)]; 2[2.02]; 2[3.03]; 2[3.03(f)]; 2[4.02]; 2[4.04(a)]; 6[4.02(c)]; 8[1]; 8[5.02]

[*References are to chapter numbers followed by section/subsection numbers in brackets.*]

§ 1211(a) . . . . 2[1]; 2[2.02]; 2[4.02]
§ 1211(b) . . . 2[1]; 2[2.01(d)]; 2[4.02]; 6[4.02(c)]; 8[5.02]
§ 1211(b)(1) . . . . 2[4.02]
§ 1211(b)(2) . . . . 2[2.01(d)]
§ 1212 . . . . . 2[2.01(d)]; 2[2.02]; 2[4.02]; 8[5.02]
§ 1212(a)(1) . . . . 2[1]; 2[2.02]
§ 1212(a)(1)(A) . . . . 2[2.02]
§ 1212(a)(1)(A)(ii) . . . . 2[2.02]
§ 1212(a)(1)(B) . . . . 2[2.02]
§ 1212(b) . . . . 2[1]; 2[2.01(d)]; 6[4.02(c)]
§ 1212(b)(1) . . . . 2[2.01(d)]
§ 1212(b)(1)(A) . . . . 2[2.01(d)]
§ 1212(b)(1)(B) . . . . 2[2.01(d)]
§ 1212(b)(2)(A) . . . . 2[2.01(d)]
§ 1212(b)(2)(B) . . . . 2[2.01(d)]
§ 1221 . . 1[4.01]; 2[1]; 2[2.01(b)]; 2[3.01]; 2[3.02]; 2[3.03]; 2[3.03(a)]; 2[3.03(b)]; 2[3.03(c)]; 2[3.03(f)]; 2[6.01]; 2[6.03(b)]; 3[3.01(b)]; 4[1.01]; 4[4]; 6[4.02(c)]; 7[2.02]; 7[3.01]; 7[3.02]; 7[3.03(a)]
§ 1221(1) . . . . 2[3.03(a)]; 4[2.02]; 7[3.01]
§ 1221(3) . . . . 7[3.01]
§ 1221(3)(A) . . . . 7[3.01]
§ 1221(a) . . . 2[3.01]; 2[3.02]; 2[3.03]; 2[3.03(c)]; 2[6.03(b)]; 7[3.03(b)]
§ 1221(a)(1) . . . . . 2[3.03]; 2[3.03(a)]; 2[3.03(c)]; 2[3.03(d)]; 2[3.03(g)]; 2[3.03(h)]; 2[6.03]; 2[6.03(a)]; 2[6.03(b)]
§ 1221(a)(2) . . . . . . 2[3.01]; 2[3.03]; 2[3.03(a)]; 2[3.03(b)]; 2[6.01]; 2[6.03]; 2[6.03(a)]
§ 1221(a)(3) . . 2[3.03]; 2[3.03(c)]; 2[6.03]; 7[3.03]; 7[3.03(a)]; 7[3.03(c)]
§ 1221(a)(3)(A) . . . . 2[3.03(c)]
§ 1221(a)(3)(B) . . . . 2[3.03(c)]
§ 1221(a)(3)(C) . . . . 2[3.03(c)]
§ 1221(a)(4) . . . . 2[3.03]; 2[3.03(d)]
§ 1221(a)(5) . . . . 2[3.03]; 2[3.03(e)]; 2[6.03]
§ 1221(a)(6) . . . . 2[3.03]; 2[3.03(g)]
§ 1221(a)(6)(A) . . . . 2[3.03(g)]
§ 1221(a)(6)(B) . . . . 2[3.03(g)]
§ 1221(a)(7) . . . . . 2[3.03]; 2[3.03(a)]; 2[3.03(f)]; 2[3.03(h)]; 2[6.03(b)]
§ 1221(a)(8) . . . . 2[3.03]; 2[3.03(h)]
§ 1221(b) . . . . 2[3.03(c)]
§ 1221(b)(1)(B) . . . . 2[3.03(g)]
§ 1221(b)(1)(B)(i) . . . . 2[3.03(g)]
§ 1221(b)(1)(B)(ii) . . . . 2[3.03(g)]
§ 1221(b)(2)(A)(i) . . . . 2[3.03(f)]
§ 1221(b)(2)(A)(ii) . . . . 2[3.03(f)]
§ 1221(b)(2)(B) . . . . 2[3.03(f)]
§ 1221(b)(3) . . . . . 2[3.03(c)]; 7[3.03]; 7[3.03(a)]
§ 1222 . . 2[1]; 2[2.01(b)]; 2[3.01]; 2[4.01]; 2[4.02]; 2[4.03]; 2[4.04(b)]; 2[4.04(d)]; 2[5.01]; 2[6.02(a)]; 6[3.01]; 6[4.02(c)]; 7[1.01]; 8[3]
§ 1222(1) . . . . 2[1]
§§ 1222(1)–(4) . . . . 2[2.01(b)]; 2[3.01]
§ 1222(2) . . . . 2[1]
§ 1222(3) . . . . 2[1]; 2[3.02]; 2[5.01]; 7[1.01]
§ 1222(4) . . . . 2[1]; 2[5.01]
§ 1222(5) . . . . 2[2.01(b)]
§ 1222(6) . . . . 2[2.01(b)]
§ 1222(7) . . . . 2[2.01(b)]
§ 1222(8) . . . . 2[2.01(b)]
§ 1222(10) . . . . 2[2.01(d)]
§ 1222(11) . . . . 2[1]; 2[2.01(b)]; 2[5.01]
§ 1223 . . . . . 2[3.01]; 2[3.03(a)]; 2[5]; 2[5.05(a)]; 2[5.05(c)]; 5
§ 1223(1) . . . . 2[5.03]; 2[5.05(a)]
§ 1223(1)(A) . . . . 2[5.05(a)]
§ 1223(1)(B) . . . . 2[5.05(a)]
§ 1223(2) . . . . 2[5.05(b)]
§ 1223(3) . . . . 2[5.05(c)]; 8[2]
§ 1223(4) . . . . 2[5.05(c)]
§ 1223(5) . . . . 2[5.05(c)]
§ 1223(6) . . . . 2[5.05(c)]
§ 1223(7) . . . . 2[5.05(c)]
§ 1223(9) . . . . 2[5.04]
§ 1223(9)(A) . . . . 2[5.04]
§ 1223(9)(B) . . . . 2[5.04]
§ 1223(14) . . . . 2[5.05(c)]
§ 1231 . . . . . 1[4.01]; 2[1]; 2[2.01(b)]; 2[2.01(c)]; 2[3.03(b)]; 2[4.01]; 2[4.04(d)]; 2[5.05(a)]; 2[6.01]; 2[6.02]; 2[6.02(a)]; 2[6.02(b)]; 2[6.02(c)]; 2[6.02(d)]; 2[6.03]; 2[6.03(a)]; 2[6.03(b)]; 2[6.03(c)]; 3[4.03]; 3[5.01]; 3[5.03]; 4[1.01]; 4[4]; 4[4.01]; 4[4.02]; 5; 5[1]; 5[1.01]; 5[1.02]; 5[1.06]; 5[3.01]; 5[3.02]; 7; 7[2]; 7[2.02]; 7[3.02]; 7[3.03]; 8[5.02]
§ 1231(a)(1) . . . . 2[6.01]; 2[6.02(c)]
§ 1231(a)(2) . . . . 2[6.01]; 2[6.02(c)]
§ 1231(a)(3)(A)(i) . . . . 2[6.02(a)]; 2[6.02(c)]
§ 1231(a)(3)(A)(ii) . . . . 2[6.02(a)]; 2[6.02(c)]
§ 1231(a)(3)(B) . . . . 2[6.02(a)]
§ 1231(a)(4)(A) . . . . 2[6.02(a)]
§ 1231(a)(4)(B) . . . . 2[6.02(a)]
§ 1231(a)(4)(B)(ii) . . . . 2[6.02(a)]
§ 1231(a)(4)(C) . . . . 2[6.01]; 2[6.02(b)]
§ 1231(a)(4)(C)(ii) . . . . 2[6.02(a)]
§ 1231(b) . . . . 7[2.02]
§ 1231(b)(1) . . . . . 2[3.03(b)]; 2[6.02(a)]; 2[6.03]; 2[6.03(a)]; 2[6.03(b)]

[*References are to chapter numbers followed by section/subsection numbers in brackets.*]

§ 1231(b)(1)(A) . . . . 2[6.03]; 2[6.03(b)]
§ 1231(b)(1)(B) . . . . 2[6.03]; 2[6.03(b)]
§ 1231(b)(1)(C) . . . . 2[6.03]
§ 1231(b)(1)(D) . . . . 2[6.03]
§ 1231(b)(2) . . . . 2[6.03]; 2[6.03(c)]
§ 1231(b)(3) . . . . 2[6.03]; 2[6.03(c)]
§ 1231(b)(4) . . . . 2[6.03]; 2[6.03(c)]
§ 1231(c) . 2[6.01]; 2[6.02(c)]; 2[6.02(d)]; 2[6.03(c)]
§ 1231(c)(1) . . . . 2[6.02(d)]
§ 1231(c)(2) . . . . 2[6.02(d)]
§ 1231(c)(3) . . . . 2[6.02(d)]
§ 1231(c)(4) . . . . 2[6.02(d)]
§ 1233 . . . . 6[3.01]
§ 1233(b) . . . . 6[3.01]
§ 1233(c) . . . . 6[3.01]
§ 1234 . . . . 2[4.04(b)]; 6[3.01]; 6[3.04(b)]
§ 1234A . . . . 2[4.03]; 2[4.04(d)]; 7[3.01]; 7[3.02]
§ 1234(a) . . . . 2[3.01]
§ 1234(a)(1) . . . . 2[4.04(b)]; 6[3.01]
§ 1234(a)(2) . . . . 2[4.04(b)]; 6[3.01]
§ 1234(b) . . . . 2[3.01]
§ 1234(b)(1) . . . . . 2[4.04(b)]; 6[3.01]; 6[3.04(a)]
§ 1234(b)(2)(A) . . . . 6[3.01]
§ 1234(b)(2)(B) . . . . 2[4.04(b)]
§ 1235 . . . . . 2[3.01]; 2[4.02]; 2[4.04(e)]; 7[1.01]; 7[3.03]; 7[3.03(b)]; 7[3.03(c)]
§ 1235(a) . . . . 7[3.03(b)]
§ 1235(a)(2) . . . . 2[4.04(e)]
§ 1235(d) . . . . 7[3.03(b)]
§ 1236 . . . . 2[3.03(g)]
§ 1237 . . . . 2[3.03(a)]
§ 1237(a)(1) . . . . 2[3.03(a)]
§ 1237(a)(2) . . . . 2[3.03(a)]
§ 1237(a)(3) . . . . 2[3.03(a)]
§ 1237(b)(1) . . . . 2[3.03(a)]
§ 1237(b)(2) . . . . 2[3.03(a)]
§ 1239 . . . . 7[4.02]
§ 1241 . . . 2[4.03]; 2[4.04(c)]; 2[4.04(d)]; 7[2.02]; 7[3.01]
§ 1245 . . . 2[3.03(b)]; 2[6.01]; 2[6.02(c)]; 3[5.03]; 4[2.03]; 4[3.03]; 4[3.04(b)]; 4[3.06(a)]; 4[3.06(b)]; 4[3.06(c)]; 4[4]; 4[4.01]; 4[4.02]; 4[4.03]; 7[3.01]; 8[4.01]
§ 1245(a) . . . . 4[4.01]
§ 1245(a)(1) . . . . 2[6.01]
§ 1245(a)(2)(A) . . . . 2[6.01]
§ 1245(a)(2)(B) . . . . 4[4.01]
§ 1245(a)(2)(C) . . . . 4[4.01]
§ 1245(a)(3) . . . . 2[6.01]; 4[4.01]
§ 1245(b)(1) . . . . 4[4.01]
§§ 1245(b)(1)–(5) . . . . 2[6.01]
§ 1245(b)(2) . . . . 4[4.01]
§ 1245(b)(3) . . . . 4[4.01]
§ 1245(b)(4) . . . . 4[4.01]
§ 1245(b)(8)(A) . . . . 2[6.01]; 4[4.01]
§ 1245(b)(8)(B) . . . . 2[6.01]
§ 1245(c) . . . . 4[4.03]
§ 1250 . . . . . 1[4.02]; 2[1]; 2[2.01(a)]; 2[2.01(b)]; 2[2.01(c)]; 2[3.03(b)]; 2[6.01]; 2[6.02(c)]; 2[6.02(d)]; 3[3.01(b)]; 3[5.03]; 4[3.06(b)]; 4[3.06(c)]; 4[4]; 4[4.02]; 4[4.03]; 5[1.02]; 8[4.01]
§ 1250(a)(1) . . . . 2[6.01]
§ 1250(a)(1)(A) . . . . 2[2.01(a)]; 4[4.02]
§ 1250(a)(1)(B) . . . . 4[4.02]
§ 1250(a)(1)(B)(ii) . . . . 2[6.01]
§ 1250(b)(1) . . . . 2[2.01(a)]; 2[6.01]; 4[4.02]
§ 1250(b)(3) . . . . 5[3.02]
§ 1250(c) . . . . 4[4.02]
§ 1250(d) . . . . 4[4.02]
§§ 1250(d)(1)–(5) . . . . 2[6.01]
§ 1250(d)(4) . . . . 5[1.03]
§ 1253 . . . . 2[4.02]; 2[4.04(e)]; 7[3.03(c)]
§ 1253(a) . . . . 2[4.04(e)]; 7[3.03(c)]
§ 1253(b)(2) . . . . 7[3.03(c)]
§ 1253(b)(2)(A) . . . . 7[3.03(c)]
§ 1253(b)(3) . . . . 7[3.03(c)]
§ 1253(c) . . . . 7[3.03(c)]
§ 1253(d)(1) . . . . 7[3.03(c)]
§ 1253(d)(2) . . . . 7[3.03(c)]
§ 1253(d)(2)(A) . . . . 7[3.03(c)]
§ 1253(d)(2)(B) . . . . 7[3.03(c)]
§ 1254 . . . . 4[3.04(d)]; 4[4.03]
§ 1254(a) . . . . 4[3.04(c)]; 4[3.04(d)]; 4[4.03]
§ 1254(b)(1) . . . . 4[4.03]
§ 1256 . . . . 1[3.01]
§ 1271 . . . . 2[4.04(e)]
§ 1271(a) . . . . 2[4.01]
§ 1271(a)(1) . . . . 2[4.03]
§ 1272 . . . . 7[4.02]
§ 1272(a)(1) . . . . 2[4.03]
§ 1272(a)(4) . . . . 3[1.02]; 3[2.01]
§ 1273(a) . . . . 2[3.03(a)]
§ 1273(b) . . . . 3[1.02]
§ 1273(b)(2) . . . . 3[2.01]
§ 1273(b)(4) . . . . 3[2.01]
§ 1274 . . . . 1[4.03]; 7[1.01]
§ 1274(c)(2) . . . . 3[3.04]
§ 1275 . . . . 1[4.03]
§ 1286 . . . . 7[2.01(b)]; 7[3.02]

[*References are to chapter numbers followed by section/subsection numbers in brackets.*]

§ 1286(a) . . . . 7[2.01(b)]
§ 1286(b) . . . . 7[2.01(b)]
§ 1303 . . . . 3[2.01]
§ 1366 . . . . 2[1]; 4[3.03]
§ 1366(a)(1) . . . . 2[2.02]
§ 1366(e) . . . . 7[4.01]
§ 1397C(b) . . . . 2[2.01(a)]
§§ 1501–04 . . . . 7[4.02]
§ 1551 . . . . 7[4.02]
§ 1552 . . . . 7[4.02]
§ 1561 . . . . 7[4.02]
§ 1563 . . . . 7[4.02]
§ 1703 . . . . 5[3.03]
§ 1962 . . . . 4[3.06(a)]
§ 2032 . . . . 1[2.04]
§§ 2687(b)(3)–(b)(7) . . . . 8[3]
§ 3121(v)(2) . . . . 6[2.02]
§ 3402 . . . . 6[2.03]
§ 6031 . . . . 6[1.01]
§ 6039 . . . . 6[4]
§ 6041(g) . . . . 6[1.02]
§ 6050P . . . . 3[5]
§ 6051(a)(13) . . . . 6[1.02]
§ 6662 . . . . 6[4.02(c)]
§ 6662(a) . . . . 4[3.06(a)]
§ 7122 . . . . 3[2.02]
§ 7701(a)(42) . . . . 1[2.05]; 5
§ 7701(a)(43) . . . . 1[2.03]; 1[2.05]; 5
§ 7701(a)(44) . . . . 1[2.05]; 5
§ 7701(e) . . . . 8[6]
§ 7701(g) . . . . 3[3.01(b)]; 3[4.01]
§ 7872(c)(1)(B) . . . . 6[2.02]
§ 12221(a)(3)(C) . . . . 2[3.03(c)]
§ 15025(2)(a) . . . . 5[1.07]

JOB CREATION AND WORKER ASSISTANCE ACT OF 2002

Pub. L. No. 107-147, § 101 . . . . 4[3.05]

JOBS AND GROWTH TAX RELIEF RECONCILIATION ACT OF 2003

Pub. L. No. 108-27, § 201 . . . . 4[3.05]

REVENUE ACTS

Revenue Act of 1918

generally . . . . 7[2.01(a)]

Revenue Act of 1921

generally . . . . 3[2.01]; 7[2.01(a)]
§ 202(c) . . . . 5[1.01]
Article 545(1)(c) . . . . 3[2.01]

Revenue Act of 1924

§ 202(a) . . . . 1[3.02]

Revenue Act of 1932

generally . . . . 7[2.02]

Revenue Act of 1934

generally . . . . 7[2.01(b)]
§ 117(d) . . . . 2[4.02]

Revenue Act of 1936

§ 111(a) . . . . 1[3.03(b)]
§ 111(b) . . . . 1[3.03(b)]
§ 113(a) . . . . 1[3.03(b)]
§ 113(b) . . . . 1[3.03(b)]

Revenue Act of 1938

§ 111(a) . . . . 3[3.01(a)]
Reg.101, Art. 113(a) . . . . 3[3.01(a)]

SECURITIES ACT OF 1933

Generally . . . . 7[2.01(d)]

SECURITIES AND EXCHANGE ACT OF 1934

§ 10(b) . . . . 2[3.02]
§ 16(b) . . . . 6[2.02]; 6[4.02(b)]

SMALL BUSINESS JOBS ACT OF 2010

Generally . . . . 2[2.01(a)]
§ 2022(a) . . . . 4[3.05]
§ 2031(a) . . . . 4[3.02]

STATE ACTS

Colorado River Basin Project Act

Pub. L. No. 90-537 . . . . 1[2.01]

[*References are to chapter numbers followed by section/subsection numbers in brackets.*]

Ga. Ann. Code

§ 11-8-319(a) . . . . 8[2]
§ 11-8-319(b) . . . . 8[2]

Iowa Code

§ 491.25 . . . . 4[2.05]

Wyo. Stat. Ann.

§ 17-15-113 . . . . 8[4.02]
§ 17-15-121(a) . . . . 8[4.02]
§ 17-15-121(c) . . . . 8[4.02]
§ 17-15-123(a) . . . . 8[4.02]

TAX REFORM ACT OF 1969

Generally . . . . 6[4.02(b)]

TAX REFORM ACT OF 1976

Generally . . . . 8[4.02]

TAX REFORM ACT OF 1984

§ 555 . . . . 6[4.02(b)]

TAX REFORM ACT OF 1986

Generally . . 4[3.06(a)]; 6[4.02(c)]; 8[5.01]; 8[5.03]; 8[5.05]
§ 1855(b) . . . . 6[2.02]

TAX RELIEF RECONCILIATION ACT OF 2005

H.R. Rep. No. 109-304, 109th Cong., 1st Sess. 51-52 . . . . 4[3.03]

TREASURY REGULATIONS

§ 1.1(h)-1 . . . . 2[1]; 2[2.01(c)]
§ 1.1(h)-1(b)(2)(ii) . . . . 2[2.01(c)]
§ 1.1(h)-1(b)(3)(ii) . . . . 2[2.01(c)]
§ 1.1(h)-1(b)(3)(iii) . . . . 2[2.01(c)]
§ 1.1(h)-1(d) . . . . 2[2.01(c)]
§ 1.1(h)-1(e) . . . . 2[2.01(c)]
§ 1.16-15(c) . . . . 6[3.04(a)]
§ 1.48-1(3)(1) . . . . 4[3.06(c)]
§ 1.48-1(c) . . . . 4[3.06(c)]
§ 1.48-1(d) . . . . 4[3.06(b)]
§ 1.48-1(e) . . . . 4[3.06(b)]
§ 1.48-1(e)(1) . . . . 4[3.06(c)]
§ 1.48-1(e)(2) . . . . 4[3.06(c)]
§ 1.57-1(f)(3) . . . . 6[4.02(b)]
§ 1.61-2(c) . . . . 7[2.01(a)]
§ 1.61-2(d) . . . . 1[2.02]; 6[3.03]
§ 1.61-2(d)(1) . . . . 1[2.02]; 6[3.03]
§ 1.61-2(d)(2) . . . . 1[2.02]
§ 1.61-2(d)(4) . . . . 6[2.01]
§ 1.61-2(d)(6)(i) . . . . 6[3.04(a)]
§ 1.61-6 . . . . 1[3.01]
§ 1.61-6(a) . . . . 1[2.01]
§ 1.61-12(a) . . . . 3[2.01]
§ 1.61-15 . . 6[3.03]; 6[3.04]; 6[3.04(a)]; 6[3.04(b)]
§ 1.61-15(a) . . . . 6[3.04(a)]
§ 1.61-15(b) . . . . 6[3.03]
§ 1.61-15(b)(1)(ii) . . . . 6[3.04(a)]
§ 1.61-15(b)(2) . . . . 6[3.03]
§ 1.62-11(b) . . . . 7[1.03]
§§ 1.83-1–6 . . . . 6[2.02]
§ 1.83-1(a) . . . . 3[1.02]; 6[2.02]; 6[3.03]
§ 1.83-1(a)(1) . . . . 6[2.02]
§ 1.83-1(b) . . . . 6[2.02]; 6[3.03]
§ 1.83-1(c) . . . . 6[2.02]; 6[3.03]
§ 1.83-1(e) . . . . 6[2.02]
§ 1.83-2 . . . . 6[2.02]
§ 1.83-2(a) . . . . 6[2.02]
§ 1.83.2(a) . . . . 6[2.02]
§ 1.83-2(a)(2) . . . . 6[3.02]
§ 1.83-3(a)(1) . . . . 6[2.02]
§ 1.83-3(a)(2) . . . . 6[2.02]; 6[3.02]
§ 1.83-3(c) . . . . 6[1.02]
§ 1.83-3(c)(1) . . . . 6[2.02]; 6[4.02(b)]
§ 1.83-3(c)(3) . . . . 6[1.02]
§ 1.83-3(e) . . . . 6[2.02]; 6[3.04(a)]
§ 1.83-3(h) . . . . 6[2.02]; 6[4.02(b)]
§ 1.83-3(i) . . . . 6[2.02]
§ 1.83-3(j) . . . . 6[2.02]
§ 1.83-4(c) . . . . 3[2.02]
§ 1.83-5(a) . . . . 6[2.02]
§ 1.83-5(b) . . . . 6[2.02]
§ 1.83-6 . . . . 6[2.02]
§ 1.83-6(a)(1) . . . . 6[2.02]; 6[2.03]
§ 1.83-6(a)(2) . . . . 6[2.02]; 6[2.03]
§ 1.83-6(a)(3) . . . . 6[3.03]
§ 1.83-6(a)(4) . . . . 6[2.02]
§ 1.83-6(b) . . . . 6[3.03]
§ 1.83-6(c) . . . . 6[2.02]
§ 1.83-6(d) . . . . 6[2.03]
§ 1.83-6(d)(2) . . . . 6[2.02]
§ 1.83-7 . . . . 6[3.02]; 6[3.03]; 6[3.04]; 6[3.04(a)]
§ 1.83-7(a) . . . . 6[3.03]; 6[4.02(b)]

[References are to chapter numbers followed by section/subsection numbers in brackets.]

§ -7(b) . . . . 6[3.02]; 6[3.03]; 6[3.04(a)]
3-7(b)(2) . . . . 6[3.02]; 6[3.03]
.83-7(b)(3) . . . . 6[3.03]
1.83-8 . . . . 6[2.02]; 6[3.04(a)]
§ 1.83.8(b)(1) . . . . 6[2.02]
§ 1.97-2(b)(5) . . . . 7[3.03(a)]
§ 1.108-4 . . . . 3[5.02]; 3[5.03]
§ 1.108-5 . . . . 3[5.03]
§ 1.108-6 . . . . 3[5.03]
§ 1.108-7 . . . . 3[5.02]
§ 1.108-7(a)(1)(i) . . . . 3[5.02]
§ 1.108-7(b) . . . . 3[5.02]
§ 1.108-7(b), ex. 1 . . . . 3[5.02]
§ 1.108-7(b), ex. 2 . . . . 3[5.02]
§ 1.108(a)-1 . . . . 3[2.01]
§ 1.111-1(a) . . . . 5[2.05]
§ 1.111-1(a)(2) . . . . 5[2.05]
§ 1.121-1 . . . . 5[3.02]
§§ 1.121-1–4 . . . . 5[3.02]
§ 1.121-1(b) . . . . 5[3.02]
§ 1.121-1(c) . . . . 5[3.02]
§ 1.121-1(c)(3)(i) . . . . 5[3.02]
§ 1.121-1(d) . . . . 5[3.02]
§ 1.121-1(d)(1) . . . . 5[3.02]
§ 1.121-1(e) . . . . 5[3.02]
§ 1.121-1(e)(2) . . . . 5[3.02]
§ 1.121-1(e)(3) . . . . 5[3.02]
§ 1.121-2 . . . . 5[3.02]
§ 1.121-3 . . . . 5[3.02]
§ 1.121-4 . . . . 5[3.02]
§ 1.121-4(d) . . . . 5[3.02]
§ 1.121-4(e)(1) . . . . 5[3.02]
§ 1.121-4(e)(2) . . . . 5[3.02]
§ 1.121-4(e)(2)(B) . . . . 5[3.02]
§ 1.121-5 . . . . 5[3.02]
§ 1.162-1(a) . . . . 4[2.01]; 4[3.02]
§ 1.162-3 . . . . 4[2.03]
§ 1.162-4 . . . . 4[2.01]; 4[2.03]
§ 1.162-7(a) . . . . 6[3.04(a)]
§ 1.162-14 . . . . 4[2.04]
§ 1.162-20(a)(2) . . . . 4[2.01]; 4[2.04]
§ 1.162-27 . . . . 6[1.02]
§ 1.162-27(e) . . . . 6[1.02]
§ 1.162-27(e)(2)(v) . . . . 6[1.02]
§ 1.165-1(b) . . . . 1[3.03(a)]
§ 1.165-1(d)(1) . . . . 1[3.03(a)]
§ 1.165-8(d) . . . . 1[3.03(a)]
§ 1.167(a) . . . . 1[4.03]; 4[2.01]
§ 1.167(a)-2 . . . . 4[3.06]; 4[3.06(a)]
§ 1.167(a)-3 . . . . 4[3.07]; 4[3.07(b)]
§ 1.167(a)-3(a) . . . . 4[3.07(b)]
§ 1.167(a)-3(b) . . . . 4[3.07(b)]
§ 1.167(a)-4(a) . . . . 7[1.03]
§ 1.167(a)-5 . . . . 4[3.06]
§ 1.167(a)-6(a) . . . . 4[3.07]; 4[3.07(b)]
§ 1.167(a)-8(a)(4) . . . . 1[3.03(a)]
§ 1.167(a)-9 . . . . 4[3.06]
§ 1.167(a)-14 . . . . 4[3.07(b)]
§ 1.167(a)-14(b)(1) . . . . 4[3.05]; 4[3.07(b)]
§ 1.167(a)-14(b)(2) . . . . 4[3.07(b)]
§ 1.167(a)-14(c) . . . . 4[3.07(b)]
§ 1.167(a)-14(c)(1)(ii) . . . . 4[3.07(b)]
§ 1.167(a)-14(c)(4) . . . . 4[3.07(b)]
§ 1.167(a)-14(c)(a)(i) . . . . 4[3.07(b)]
§ 1.167(g)-1 . . . . 4[3.06]
§ 1.167(k)-1(d)(3), ex. 2 . . . . 4[3.05]
§ 1.168(d)-1(a) . . . . 4[3.06]
§ 1.168(d)-1(b)(2) . . . . 4[3.06]
§ 1.168(d)-1(b)(4) . . . . 4[3.06]
§ 1.168(i)-1 . . . . 4[3.06(c)]
§ 1.168(i)-1(c)(1) . . . . 4[3.06(c)]
§ 1.168(i)-1(c)(2) . . . . 4[3.06(c)]
§ 1.168(i)-1(e)(1) . . . . 4[3.06(c)]
§ 1.168(i)-1(e)(2) . . . . 4[3.06(c)]
§ 1.168(i)-1(e)(2)(v), *examples* . . . . . . 4[3.06(c)]
§ 1.168(i)-1(e)(3)(ii) . . . . 4[3.06(c)]
§ 1.168(i)-1(e)(3)(iii) . . . . 4[3.06(c)]
§ 1.168(i)-2 . . . . 8[6]
§ 1.168(i)-6(c) . . . . 5[1.02]
§ 1.168(i)-6(c)(2) . . . . 5[1.02]
§ 1.168(i)-6(c)(4) . . . . 5[1.02]
§ 1.168(i)-6(c)(i) . . . . 5[1.02]
§ 1.168(i)-6(d) . . . . 5[1.02]
§ 1.168(i)-6(i) . . . . 5[1.02]
§ 1.168(i)-6(i)(1) . . . . 5[1.02]
§ 1.168(k)-1 . . . . 4[3.05]
§ 1.168(k)-1(b)(3)(i) . . . . 4[3.05]
§ 1.170-4A(a) . . . . 5[3.03]
§ 1.170-4A(b)(1) . . . . 5[3.03]
§ 1.170-4A(b)(2) . . . . 5[3.03]
§ 1.170-4A(d), ex. 1 . . . . 5[3.03]
§ 1.170A-1(b) . . . . 7[2.01(c)]
§ 1.170A-1(c)(2) . . . . 5[3.03]
§ 1.174-1 . . . . 4[3.04(a)]
§ 1.174-2 . . . . 4[3.04(a)]
§ 1.174-2(a)(1) . . . . 4[3.04(a)]
§ 1.174-2(a)(2) . . . . 4[3.04(a)]
§ 1.174-2(a)(3) . . . . 4[3.04(a)]

[References are to chapter numbers followed by section/subsection numbers in brackets[illegible]

§ 1.174-2(b)(1) . . . 4[3.04(a)]
§ 1.174-2(b)(4) . . . 4[3.04(a)]
§ 1.174-3 . . . 4[3.04(a)]
§ 1.174-3(a) . . . 4[3.04(a)]
§ 1.174-4 . . . 4[3.04(a)]
§ 1.179-1 . . . 4[3.03]
§ 1.179-1(a) . . . 4[3.03]
§ 1.179-1(e) . . . 4[3.03]
§ 1.179-2 . . . 4[3.03]
§ 1.179-2(b)(3) . . . 4[3.03]
§ 1.179-2(b)(4) . . . 4[3.03]
§ 1.179-2(c) . . . 4[3.03]
§ 1.179-3 . . . 4[3.03]
§ 1.179-4 . . . 4[3.03]
§ 1.179-4(a) . . . 4[3.03]
§ 1.179-4(c) . . . 4[3.03]
§ 1.179-5 . . . 4[3.03]
§ 1.195-1 . . . 4[3.02]
§§ 1.197-2(a)–(f) . . . 4[3.07(a)]
§ 1.197-2(b)(1) . . . 1[4.02]
§ 1.197-2(b)(2) . . . 1[4.02]
§§ 1.197-2(b)(3)–(5) . . . 1[4.02]
§ 1.197-2(b)(5) . . . 7[3.03(b)]
§ 1.197-2(b)(10) . . . 7[3.03(c)]
§ 1.197-2(c)(7) . . . 7[3.03(b)]
§ 1.197-2(d)(1) . . . 1[4.02]
§ 1.197-2(d)(2)(iii) . . . 7[3.03(c)]
§ 1.197-2(e)(1) . . . 1[4.02]; 4[3.07(a)]
§ 1.197-2(e)(2) . . . 7[3.03(c)]
§ 1.197-2(f)(1) . . . 4[3.07(a)]
§ 1.197-2(f)(3)(ii) . . . 4[3.07(a)]
§ 1.197-2(f)(3)(iv)(A) . . . 7[3.03(c)]
§ 1.197-2(f)(4)(i) . . . 7[3.03(c)]
§§ 1.197-2(g)(1)–(g)(2) . . . 4[3.07(a)]
§ 1.197-2(g)(1)(i) . . . 4[3.07(a)]
§ 1.197-2(g)(1)(iii) . . . 4[3.07(a)]
§ 1.197-2(g)(6) . . . 7[3.03(c)]
§ 1.197-2(g)(7) . . . 4[3.07(b)]
§ 1.197-2(g)(8) . . . 2[6.01]
§ 1.197-2(k), ex. 5 . . . 7[3.03(c)]
§ 1.197-2(k), ex. 7 . . . 7[3.03(b)]
§ 1.197-2(k), ex. 8 . . . 7[3.03(c)]
§ 1.197-2(k), ex.10 . . . 7[3.03(b)]
§§ 1.197-2(k), exs. 1–10 . . . 4[3.07(a)]
§ 1.212-1(a) . . . 4[2.01]
§ 1.212-1(k) . . . 4[2.01]; 4[2.05]
§ 1.212-1(n) . . . 4[2.01]
§ 1.233-1(d) . . . 8[2]
§ 1.263(a)-1 . . . 4[2.01]; 4[2.03]
§ 1.263(a)-1(a) . . . 4[2.03]; [illegible]3.02]
§ 1.263(a)-1(b) . . . 4[2.03]; 4[3.[illegible]b)]
§ 1.263(a)-2 . . . 4[2.01]; 4[[illegible]]
§ 1.263(a)-2(a) . 4[2.01]; 4[2.05]; 4[3.02]; 4[3.04[illegible]
§ 1.263(a)-2(c) . . . 4[2.0[illegible]
§ 1.263(a)-2(d)(1) . . . 4[2.03]
§ 1.263(a)-2(d)(4) . . . 4[2.03]
§ 1.263(a)-2(e) . . . 4[2.05]
§ 1.263(a)-3 . . . 4[2.03]
§ 1.263(a)-4 . . . 4[2.04]; 4[2.05]; 4[3.02]
§ 1.263(a)-4(b)(1) . . . 4[2.04]
§ 1.263(a)-4(b)(1)(iv) . . . 4[2.04]
§ 1.263(a)-4(b)(2) . . . 4[2.04]
§ 1.263(a)-4(b)(3) . . . 4[2.04]
§ 1.263(a)-4(c)(1) . . . 4[2.04]
§ 1.263(a)-4(d)(2) . . . 4[2.04]
§ 1.263(a)-4(d)(3) . . . 4[2.04]
§ 1.263(a)-4(d)(4) . . . 4[2.04]
§ 1.263(a)-4(d)(5) . . . 4[2.04]
§ 1.263(a)-4(d)(6) . . . 4[2.04]
§ 1.263(a)-4(d)(7) . . . 4[2.04]
§ 1.263(a)-4(d)(8) . . . 4[2.04]
§ 1.263(a)-4(d)(9) . . . 4[2.04]
§ 1.263(a)-4(e)(1) . . . 4[2.04]
§ 1.263(a)-4(e)(3) . . . 4[2.04]
§ 1.263(a)-4(e)(4)(i) . . . 4[2.04]
§ 1.263(a)-4(e)(4)(ii) . . . 4[2.04]
§ 1.263(a)-4(e)(4)(iii) . . . 4[2.04]
§ 1.263(a)-4(f)(1) . . . 4[2.04]
§ 1.263(a)-4(f)(8), ex. 5 . . . 4[2.04]
§ 1.263(a)-4(g)(1) . . . 4[2.04]
§ 1.263(a)-5 . . . 4[2.04]; 4[2.05]; 4[3.02]
§ 1.263(a)-5(b)(1) . . . 4[2.04]
§ 1.263(a)-5(c)(8) . . . 4[2.04]
§ 1.263(a)-5(d) . . . 4[2.04]
§ 1.263(a)-5(e)(1) . . . 4[2.04]
§ 1.263(a)-5(e)(2) . . . 4[2.04]
§ 1.263(a)-5(e)(3) . . . 4[2.04]
§ 1.263(c)-1 . . . 4[3.04(c)]
§ 1.263A-1(a)(1) . . . 4[2.02]
§ 1.263A-1(a)(3) . . . 4[2.02]
§ 1.263A-1(b)(1) . . . 4[2.02]
§ 1.263A-1(b)(5) . . . 4[2.02]
§ 1.263A-1(b)(9) . . . 4[2.02]
§ 1.263A-1(b)(11) . . . 4[2.02]
§ 1.263A-1(c) . . . 4[2.02]
§ 1.263A-1(c)(1) . . . 3[1.02]
§ 1.263A-1(c)(2) . . . 3[1.02]
§ 1.263A-1(e) . . . 4[2.02]

[*References are to chapter numbers followed by section/subsection numbers in brackets.*]

§ 1.263A-1(e)(2)(i)*(A)* . . . . 4[2.02]
§ 1.263A-1(e)(2)(i)*(B)* . . . . 4[2.02]
§ 1.263A-1(e)(3)(i) . . . . 4[2.02]
§ 1.263A-1(e)(3)(ii) . . . . 4[2.02]
§ 1.263A-1(e)(3)(iii) . . . . 4[2.02]
§ 1.263A-1(f) . . . . 4[2.02]
§ 1.263A-1(g) . . . . 4[2.02]
§ 1.263A-1(g)(3) . . . . 4[2.02]
§ 1.263A-2(a)(1) . . . . 4[2.02]
§ 1.263A-2(a)(1)(i) . . . . 4[2.02]
§ 1.263A-2(a)(2) . . . . 4[2.02]
§ 1.263A-2(a)(2)(ii)*(B)(2)* . . . . 4[2.02]
§ 1.263A-2(a)(3) . . . . 4[2.02]
§ 1.263A-2(a)(3)(ii) . . . . 4[2.02]
§ 1.263A-2(a)(3)(iii) . . . . 4[2.02]
§ 1.263A-3(a)(1) . . . . 4[2.02]
§ 1.263A-3(b) . . . . 4[2.02]
§ 1.263A-8(a) . . . . 4[2.02]
§ 1.263A-9(a)(1) . . . . 4[2.02]
§ 1.263A-9(b) . . . . 4[2.02]
§ 1.263A-9(c)(1) . . . . 4[2.02]
§ 1.263A-9(c)(5)(i) . . . . 4[2.02]
§ 1.263A-9(c)(5)(ii) . . . . 4[2.02]
§ 1.263A-9(c)(5)(iii) . . . . 4[2.02]
§ 1.263A-12(c)(2) . . . . 4[2.02]
§ 1.263A-12(c)(3) . . . . 4[2.02]
§ 1.263A-12(e) . . . . 4[2.02]
§ 1.267(b)-1 . . . . 8[3]
§ 1.267(c)-1 . . . . 8[3]
§ 1.267(d)-1 . . . . 8[3]
§ 1.301-1(b) . . . . 6[3.03]
§ 1.338-6 . . . . 1[4.02]
§§ 1.338-6(a)–(c)(2) . . . . 1[4.02]
§ 1.338-6(b) . . . . 1[4.02]
§ 1.338-6(b)(1) . . . . 1[4.02]
§ 1.338-6(b)(2) . . . . 1[4.02]
§ 1.338-7 . . . . 1[4.02]
§ 1.338-7(b)(1) . . . . 1[4.03]
§ 1.338-7(d)(1) . . . . 1[4.03]
§ 1.338-7(e) Example 1 . . . . 1[4.03]
§ 1.338-7(e) Example 2 . . . . 1[4.03]
§ 1.402(b)-1(a)(1) . . . . 6[1.01]
§ 1.404(a)-12 . . . . 6[1.01]
§ 1.409-1(c)(1) . . . . 6[1.02]
§ 1.409-2(a)(6) . . . . 6[1.02]
§ 1.409A . . . . 6[3.04(a)]
§ 1.409A-1 . . . . 6[1.02]
§§ 1.409A-1–3 . . . . 6[1.02]
§ 1.409A-1(a) . . . . 6[1.02]
§ 1.409A-1(a)(1) . . . . 6[1.02]
§ 1.409A-1(a)(2) . . . . 6[1.02]
§ 1.409A-1(a)(3) . . . . 6[1.02]
§ 1.409A-1(b) . . . . 6[1.02]
§ 1.409A-1(b)(1) . . . . 6[1.02]
§ 1.409A-1(b)(2) . . . . 6[1.02]
§ 1.409A-1(b)(4) . . . . 6[1.02]
§ 1.409A-1(b)(5)(i) . . . . 6[1.02]; 6[4.01]
§ 1.409A-1(b)(5)(i)(A) . . . . 6[3.02]
§ 1.409A-1(b)(5)(i)(B) . . . . 6[2.01]
§ 1.409A-1(b)(5)(i)(C) . . . . 6[2.01]
§ 1.409A-1(b)(5)(i)(D) . . . . 6[2.01]
§ 1.409A-1(b)(5)(i)(E) . . . . 6[2.01]
§ 1.409A-1(b)(5)(ii) . . . . 6[1.02]; 6[4.01]
§ 1.409A-1(b)(5)(ii)(A) . . . . 6[3.02]; 6[3.03]
§ 1.409A-1(b)(5)(iv) . . . . 6[3.02]; 6[3.03]
§ 1.409A-1(b)(5)(iv)(A) . . . . 6[2.01]
§ 1.409A-1(b)(5)(iv)(B) . . . . 6[2.01]
§ 1.409A-1(b)(5)(iv)(B)(1) . . . . 6[2.01]
§ 1.409A-1(b)(5)(iv)(B)(2) . . . . 6[2.01]
§ 1.409A-1(b)(5)(iv)(B)(3) . . . . 6[2.01]
§ 1.409A-1(b)(6) . . . . 6[1.02]; 6[2.02]
§ 1.409A-1(c) . . . . 6[1.02]
§ 1.409A-1(d)(1) . . . . 6[1.02]
§ 1.409A-1(d)(2) . . . . 6[1.02]
§ 1.409A-1(e) . . . . 6[1.02]
§ 1.409A-2(a)(1) . . . . 6[1.02]
§ 1.409A-2(a)(5) . . . . 6[1.02]
§ 1.409A-2(a)(7) . . . . 6[1.02]
§ 1.409A-2(a)(8) . . . . 6[1.02]
§ 1.409A-2(a)(9), ex. 4 . . . . 6[1.02]
§ 1.409A-2(b)(1) . . . . 6[1.02]
§ 1.409A-2(b)(2)(ii) . . . . 6[1.02]
§ 1.409A-2(b)(2)(iii) . . . . 6[1.02]
§ 1.409A-2(b)(i) . . . . 6[1.02]
§ 1.409A-3(a) . . . . 6[1.02]
§ 1.409A-3(h)(1) . . . . 6[1.02]
§ 1.409A-3(j) . . . . 6[1.02]
§ 1.409A-5(b)(i) . . . . 6[4.01]
§ 1.409A-5(b)(ii) . . . . 6[4.01]
§ 1.409A-6 . . . . 6[1.02]
§ 1.421-1 . . . . 6[4]
§ 1.421-1b(2) . . . . 6[4.01]
§ 1.421-1(b)(3) . . . . 6[4.01]
§ 1.421-1(h)(2) . . . . 6[4.01]
§ 1.421-2 . . . . 6[4]
§ 1.421-6 . . . . 6[3.03]; 6[3.04]; 6[3.04(a)]
§§ 1.422-1–5 . . . . 6[4]
§ 1.422-1(a)(1)(i)(B) . . . . 6[4.01]

[*References are to chapter numbers followed by section/subsection numbers in brackets.*]

§ 1.422-2 . . . . . 6[4.01]
§ 1.422-2(b)(1) . . . . . 6[4.01]
§ 1.422-2(b)(3) . . . . . 6[4.01]
§ 1.422-2(e)(2)(i) . . . . . 6[4.01]
§ 1.422-2(e)(2)(ii) . . . . . 6[4.01]
§ 1.422-2(e)(2)(iii) . . . . . 6[4.01]
§ 1.422-2(e)(2)(iv) . . . . . 6[4.01]
§ 1.422-4(a) . . . . . 6[4.01]
§ 1.422-4(b)(2) . . . . . 6[4.01]
§ 1.422-4(b)(3) . . . . . 6[4.01]
§ 1.422-4(b)(5) . . . . . 6[4.01]
§ 1.422-4(c)(2) . . . . . 6[4.01]
§ 1.422-4(d), ex.1 . . . . . 6[4.01]
§ 1.422-4(d), ex. 6 . . . . . 6[4.01]
§§ 1.422-4(d), exs. 2–5 . . . . . 6[4.01]
§§ 1.422-5(b)(1)–(3) . . . . . 6[4.01]
§ 1.422-5(b)(2) . . . . . 6[4.01]
§ 1.422-5(b)(3) . . . . . 6[4.01]
§ 1.422-5(d) . . . . . 6[4.01]
§ 1.422-5(d)(2) . . . . . 6[4.01]
§ 1.422-5(d)(3) . . . . . 6[4.01]
§ 1.422-5(e), ex. 1 . . . . . 6[4.01]
§ 1.422-5(e), ex. 2 . . . . . 6[4.01]
§ 1.422-5(e), ex. 3 . . . . . 6[4.01]
§ 1.422-(e)(2) . . . . . 6[4.01]
§ 1.422-(f) . . . . . 6[4.01]
§ 1.423-1 . . . . . 6[4.01]
§ 1.423-1(k) . . . . . 6[4.01]
§ 1.424-1 . . . . . 6[4]
§ 1.424-1(a) . . . . . 6[3.03]; 6[4.01]
§ 1.424-1(a)(3)(ii) . . . . . 6[4.01]
§ 1.424-1(c)(3) . . . . . 6[4.01]
§ 1.424-1(e)(2) . . . . . 6[4.01]
§ 1.425-1(a)(1)(ii) . . . . . 6[4.01]
§ 1.446-1(c)(1)(i) . . . . . 3[4.03]
§ 1.446-1(c)(1)(ii) . . . . . 3[4.03]
§ 1.453-9(a) . . . . . 5[3.01]
§ 1.453-12 . . . . . 4[4.02]
§ 1.461-1(a)(1) . . . . . 3[4.03]
§ 1.461-1(a)(3) . . . . . 3[2.02]
§ 1.461-1(c)(3) . . . . . 3[2.02]
§ 1.461-4(d)(5) . . . . . 3[4.03]
§ 1.461-4(g)(1)(C) . . . . . 3[4.03]
§ 1.465-8 . . . . . 8[4]
§ 1.465-8(a) . . . . . 8[4.02]
§ 1.465-8(b)(1) . . . . . 8[4.02]
§ 1.465-8(b)(2) . . . . . 8[4.02]
§ 1.465-8(b)(3) . . . . . 8[4.02]
§ 1.465-20 . . . . . 8[4]
§ 1.465-27 . . . . . 8[4]
§ 1.465-27(a) . . . . . 8[4.04]
§ 1.465-27(b)(1) . . . . . 8[4.04]
§ 1.467-3(c)(4) . . . . . 7[1.05]
§ 1.468-6 . . . . . 5[1.04]
§ 1.468-6(c)(2) . . . . . 5[1.04]
§ 1.468-6(e), ex. 2 . . . . . 5[1.04]
§ 1.468-6(e), ex. 3 . . . . . 5[1.04]
§ 1.468B-1 . . . . . 7[2.01(d)]
§§ 1.468B-1–4 . . . . . 7[2.01(d)]
§ 1.468B-2 . . . . . 7[2.01(d)]
§ 1.468B-6 . . . . . 5[1.04]; 5[1.05]
§ 1.468B-7 . . . . . 7[2.01(d)]
§ 1.468B-8 . . . . . 7[2.01(d)]
§ 1.468B-9 . . . . . 7[2.01(d)]
§ 1.469-2(e)(3)(iii) . . . . . 8[5.04]
§ 1.469-4 . . . . . 8[5]
§ 1.469-4(c)(1) . . . . . 8[5.02]
§ 1.469-4(c)(2) . . . . . 8[5.02]
§ 1.469-4(c)(3) . . . . . 8[5.02]
§ 1.469-4(d)(1) . . . . . 8[5.02]
§ 1.469-4(d)(2) . . . . . 8[5.02]
§ 1.469-4(d)(3) . . . . . 8[5.02]
§ 1.469-4(e)(1) . . . . . 8[5.02]
§ 1.469-4(e)(2) . . . . . 8[5.02]
§ 1.469-4(f)(1) . . . . . 8[5.02]
§ 1.469-9(b)(3) . . . . . 8[5.04]
§ 1.469-9(e)(1) . . . . . 8[5.04]
§§ 1.469-9–ex. 3 . . . . . 8[5]
§ 1.469-9(g)(1) . . . . . 8[5.04]
§ 1.471-1 . . . . . 2[3.03(a)]
§ 1.482-1(a) . . . . . 7[4.02]
§ 1.482-1(a)(1) . . . . . 7[4.01]
§ 1.482-1(d)(4) . . . . . 7[4.02]
§§ 1.482-2–8 . . . . . 7[4.02]
§ 1.482-2(a)(1) . . . . . 7[4.02]
§ 1.568B-6(c)(1) . . . . . 5[1.04]
§ 1.568B-6(e), ex. 8 . . . . . 5[1.04]
§ 1.611-1 . . . . . 4[3.08]
§ 1.611-1(a) . . . . . 4[3.08]
§ 1.611-1(b)(1) . . . . . 4[3.08]; 7[1.02]
§ 1.611-2(a) . . . . . 4[3.08]
§§ 1.611-2(a)–(c) . . . . . 4[3.08]
§ 1.611-2(b) . . . . . 4[3.08]
§ 1.611-2(c)(2) . . . . . 4[3.08]
§ 1.611-3(b) . . . . . 4[3.08]
§ 1.611-3(d)(3) . . . . . 4[3.08]
§ 1.611-3(e) . . . . . 4[3.08]
§ 1.612-1 . . . . . 4[3.08]

[*References are to chapter numbers followed by section/subsection numbers in brackets.*]

§ 1.612-1(a) . . . . 4[3.08]
§ 1.612-1(b) . . . . 4[3.08]
§ 1.612-4 . . . . 4[3.04(c)]
§ 1.612-4(a) . . . . 3[3.03]; 4[3.04(c)]
§ 1.612-4(b)(1) . . . . 4[3.04(c)]
§ 1.612-4(b)(2) . . . . 4[3.04(c)]
§ 1.612-4(c)(1) . . . . 4[3.04(c)]
§ 1.613-1 . . . . 4[3.08]
§ 1.613-1(a) . . . . 4[3.08]
§ 1.613-2 . . . . 4[3.08]
§ 1.613-3 . . . . 4[3.08]
§ 1.613-4 . . . . 4[3.08]
§ 1.613-4(c)(1) . . . . 4[3.08]
§ 1.613-5 . . . . 4[3.08]
§ 1.613-5(a) . . . . 4[3.08]
§ 1.614-1(a) . . . . 4[3.08]
§ 1.616-1 . . . . 4[3.04(d)]
§ 1.616-1(a) . . . . 4[3.04(d)]
§ 1.616-1(b)(1) . . . . 4[3.04(d)]
§ 1.616-1(b)(2) . . . . 4[3.04(d)]
§ 1.616-2 . . . . 4[3.04(d)]
§ 1.617-1 . . . . 4[3.04(d)]
§ 1.617-1(a) . . . . 4[3.04(d)]
§ 1.617-1(b)(2) . . . . 4[3.04(d)]
§ 1.617-1(b)(4) . . . . 4[3.04(d)]
§ 1.617-2 . . . . 4[3.04(d)]
§ 1.617-3 . . . . 4[3.04(d)]
§ 1.617-3(a)(1) . . . . 4[3.04(d)]
§ 1.617-3(a)(2) . . . . 4[3.04(d)]
§ 1.617-4 . . . . 4[3.04(d)]
§ 1.704-1(b) . . . . 8[4.02]
§ 1.704-1(b)(2)(ii)*(b)(3)* . . . . 8[4.02]
§ 1.752-1 . . . . 3[1]
§ 1.752-1(a)(4) . . . . 3[1]; 3[1.02]
§ 1.752-1(a)(4)(A) . . . . 3[1.01]; 3[3.01]
§ 1.752-1(a)(4)(i) . . . . 3[2.03]
§ 1.752-1(a)(4)(i)(A) . . . . 3[1.01]
§ 1.752-1(a)(4)(i)(B) . . . . 3[1.02]
§ 1.752-1(a)(4)(i)(C) . . . . 3[2.03]
§ 1.752-1(a)(4)(ii) . . . . 3[1.01]
§ 1.752-1(d) . . . . 3[4]; 3[4.01]
§ 1.752-1(e) . . . . 3[4]; 3[4.01]
§ 1.1001-1 . . . . 1[2.09]; 1[3.02]
§ 1.1001-1(a) . . . . 1[3.01]; 1[3.02]
§ 1.1001-1(e) . . . . 1[3.04]
§ 1.1001-1(e)(2), ex. (1) . . . . 1[3.04]
§ 1.1001-1(g) . . . . 3[4.03]
§ 1.1001-1(g)(2) . . . . 1[4.03]
§ 1.1001-1(g)(3) . . . . 3[4.03]
§ 1.1001-2 . . . . 1[3.06]; 3[3.01(b)]; 3[4]; 3[4.01]
§ 1.1001-2(a) . . . . 3[3.01(b)]; 3[4.01]; 5[1.02(a)]
§ 1.1001-2(a)(1) . . . 2[4.02]; 3[4]; 3[4.02]; 3[5.01]
§ 1.1001-2(a)(2) . 2[4.02]; 3[3.01(b)]; 3[4]; 3[4.01]; 3[4.02]; 3[5.01]
§ 1.1001-2(a)(3) . . . . 3[4.01]
§ 1.1001-2(a)(4)(i) . . . 2[4.02]; 3[3.01(b)]; 3[3.04]; 3[4.01]
§ 1.1001-2(a)(4)(ii) . . . . 2[4.02]; 3[4.01]
§ 1.1001-2(a)(4)(iii) . . . . 3[3.01(b)]
§ 1.1001-2(a)(a) . . . . 3[4.03]
§ 1.1001-2(b) . . . . 3[3.01(b)]; 3[4.01]
§ 1.1001-2(c), ex. 2 . . . . 3[3.01(b)]
§ 1.1001-2(c), ex. 8 . . . 3[3.01(b)]; 3[4.02]; 3[5.01]
§ 1.1001-2(e), ex. 5 . . . . 3[3.01(b)]
§ 1.1001-3 . . . . 1[3.02]
§ 1.1001-3(b) . . . . 1[3.02]
§ 1.1001-3(c)(1)(i) . . . . 1[3.02]
§ 1.1001-3(c)(1)(ii) . . . . 1[3.02]
§ 1.1001-3(c)(2) . . . . 1[3.02]
§ 1.1001-3(d) . . . . 1[3.02]
§ 1.1001-3(d), ex. (1) . . . . 1[3.02]
§ 1.1001-3(d), ex. (2) . . . . 1[3.02]
§ 1.1001-3(d), ex. (4) . . . . 1[3.02]
§ 1.1001-3(d), ex. (5) . . . . 1[3.02]
§ 1.1001-3(d), ex. (7) . . . . 1[3.02]
§ 1.1001-3(d), ex. (8) . . . . 1[3.02]
§ 1.1001-3(d), ex. (11) . . . . 1[3.02]
§ 1.1001-3(e) . . . . 1[3.02]
§ 1.1001-3(g) . . . . 1[3.02]
§ 1.1002-1 . . . . 5[1.04]
§ 1.1002-1(b) . . . . 5[1.04]; 5[1.07]
§ 1.1002-1(c) . . . . 1[3.02]; 5; 5[1.07]; 7[2.02]
§ 1.1011-1 . . . . 1[2.09]
§ 1.1011-2 . . . . 1[3.03(c)]; 1[3.04]
§ 1.1012-1 . . . . 1[2.01]; 1[2.09]; 3[3.02]
§ 1.1012-1(a) . . . . 1[2.01]; 3[3.01(a)]
§ 1.1012-1(c) . . . . 2[5.03]
§ 1.1012-1(f) . . . . 3[4.03]
§ 1.1012-1(g) . . . . 3[3.02]; 3[4.03]
§ 1.1014-1 . . . . 1[2.04]
§ 1.1014-4 . . . . 1[2.04]; 7[2.02]
§ 1.1014-5 . . . . 7[2.02]
§ 1.1015-1 . . . . 1[2.03]
§ 1.1015-4 . . . . 1[3.04]
§ 1.1015-5 . . . . 1[2.03]
§ 1.1015-5(b)(1)(ii) . . . . 1[2.03]
§ 1.1016-1 . . . . 1[2.09]
§ 1.1016-3 . . . . 1[2.09]

[*References are to chapter numbers followed by section/subsection numbers in brackets.*]

§ 1.1017 . . . . 3[5.03]
§ 1.1017-1 . . . . 3[5.03]
§ 1.1017-1(a) . . . . 3[5.03]
§ 1.1017-1(a)(2) . . . . 3[5]
§§ 1.1017-1(a)–(d) . . . . 3[2.01]
§ 1.1017-1(b)(1) . . . . 3[5.03]
§ 1.1017-1(b)(2) . . . . 3[5.03]
§ 1.1017-1(b)(3) . . . . 3[5.03]
§ 1.1017-1(c) . . . . 3[5.03]
§ 1.1017-1(c)(1) . . . . 3[5.03]
§ 1.1017-1(c)(2) . . . . 3[5.03]
§ 1.1017-1(c)(3) . . . . 3[5.03]
§ 1.1017-1(e) . . . . 3[5.03]
§ 1.1017-1(f) . . . . 3[5.03]
§ 1.1031-1(d) . . . . 3[4]
§ 1.1031-1(f)(1)(iii) . . . . 5[1.02(b)]
§ 1.1031-1(f)(1)(iv), ex. 3 . . . . 5[1.02(b)]
§ 1.1031-1(k) . . . . 5[1.08]
§ 1.1031(a)-1(a) . . . . 5[1.01]
§ 1.1031(a)-1(a)(2) . . . . 5[1.02]
§ 1.1031(a)-1(b) . . . . . . 5[1.06]; 5[2.04]; 7[2.02]
§ 1.1031(a)-1(c) . . . . . . 5[1.01]; 5[1.04]; 5[1.06]
§ 1.1031(a)-1(c)(2) . . . . 5[2.04]
§ 1.1031(a)-1(d) . . . . 5[1.06]
§ 1.1031(a)-2 . . . . 5[1.06]
§ 1.1031(a)-2(b)(1) . . . . 5[1.06]
§ 1.1031(a)-2(b)(2) . . . . 5[1.06]
§ 1.1031(a)-2(b)(2)(a) . . . . 5[1.06]
§ 1.1031(a)-2(b)(3) . . . . 5[1.06]
§ 1.1031(a)-2(c)(1) . . . . 5[1.06]
§ 1.1031(a)-2(c)(2) . . . . 5[1.06]
§ 1.1031(a)-2(c)(3) . . . . 5[1.06]
§ 1.1031(b)-1 . 5[1.02]; 5[1.02(b)]; 5[1.03]; 5[1.04]; 5[1.05]; 5[3.01]
§ 1.1031(b)-1(2) . . . . 5[1.03]
§ 1.1031(b)-1(c) . . . . 5[1.02(a)]; 5[1.03]
§ 1.1031(c)-1 . 5[1.02]; 5[1.02(b)]; 5[1.04]; 5[1.05]; 5[3.01]
§ 1.1031(d)-1 . 5[1.02]; 5[1.02(b)]; 5[1.04]; 5[1.05]; 5[3.01]
§ 1.1031(d)-2 . 3[4]; 5[1.02(a)]; 5[1.02(b)]; 5[1.04]; 5[1.05]; 5[3.01]
§ 1.1031(d)-2, ex. 1 . . . . 5[1.03]
§ 1.1031(d)-2, ex. 2 . . . . 5[1.03]
§ 1.1031(j)-1 . . . . 5[1.06]
§ 1.1031(j)-1(a)(2) . . . . 5[1.06]
§ 1.1031(j)-1(b)(1) . . . . 5[1.06]
§ 1.1031(j)-1(b)(2)(i) . . . . 5[1.06]
§ 1.1031(j)-1(b)(2)(ii) . . . . 5[1.06]
§ 1.1031(j)-1(b)(2)(iv) . . . . 5[1.06]
§ 1.1031(j)-1(b)(3) . . . . 5[1.06]
§ 1.1031(j)-1(c) . . . . 5[1.06]
§ 1.1031(j)-1(d) . . . . 5[1.06]
§ 1.1031(k)-1 . . . 5[1.04]; 5[1.05]; 5[1.07]; 5[1.08]
§ 1.1031(k)-1(a) . . . . 5[1.05]
§ 1.1031(k)-1(c) . . . . 5[1.04]; 5[1.05]
§ 1.1031(k)-1(c)(4) . . . . 5[1.05]
§ 1.1031(k)-1(d) . . . . 5[1.04]
§ 1.1031(k)-1(e) . . . . 5[1.04]
§ 1.1031(k)-1(f) . . . . 5[1.04]
§ 1.1031(k)-1(g) . . . . 5[1.03]; 5[1.04]
§ 1.1031(k)-1(g)(3) . . . . 5[1.03]; 5[1.04]
§ 1.1031(k)-1(g)(4) . . . . 5[1.04]; 5[1.05]
§ 1.1031(k)-1(g)(4)(i) . . . . 5[1.08]
§ 1.1031(k)-1(g)(5) . . . . 5[1.04]
§ 1.1031(k)-1(g)(6) . . . . 5[1.04]
§ 1.1031(k)-1(h) . . . . 5[1.04]
§ 1.1031(k)-1(h)(2) . . . . 5[1.04]
§ 1.1031(k)-1(j) . . . . 5[1.04]
§ 1.1031(k)-1(k) . . . . . . 5[1.03]; 5[1.04]; 5[1.05]
§ 1.1031(k)-1(k)(1) . . . . 5[1.03]
§ 1.1031(k)-1(k)(2) . . . . 5[1.03]
§ 1.1031(k)-1(k)(3) . . . . 5[1.03]
§ 1.1031(k)-1(k)(4) . . . . 5[1.03]
§ 1.1032-3 . . . . 6[3.03]
§ 1.1032-3(c) . . . . 6[3.03]
§ 1.1032-3(d) . . . . 6[3.03]
§§ 1.1032-3(e), exs. 6–9 . . . . 6[3.03]
§ 1.1033-1(g) . . . . 5[2.04]
§ 1.1033-2(c)(10) . . . . 5[2.05]
§ 1.1033-2(c)(11) . . . . 5[2.05]
§ 1.1033-2(e)(11) . . . . 5[2.05]
§§ 1.1033(a)1–3 . . . . 5[2.01]
§§ 1.1033(a)-1–3 . . . . 5[2]
§ 1.1033(a)-1(a) . . . . 5[2.02]
§ 1.1033(a)-2(b)(9) . . . . 5[2.02]
§ 1.1033(a)-2(c)(3) . . . . 5[2]
§ 1.1033(a)-2(c)(9) . . . . 5[2.02]; 5[2.03]
§ 1.1033(b)-1 . . . . 5[2]; 5[2.01]
§ 1.1033-(c)(11) . . . . 5[2.05]
§ 1.1033(d)-1 . . . . 5[2.01]
§ 1.1033(e)-1 . . . . 5[2.01]
§ 1.1033(g)-1(a) . . . . 5[2]
§ 1.1038-1 . . . . 5[3.01]
§ 1.1038-1(b) . . . . 5[3.01]
§ 1.1038-1(d) . . . . 5[3.01]
§ 1.1038-1(g) . . . . 5[3.01]
§ 1.1038-1(g)(3) . . . . 2[5.05(c)]
§ 1.1060-1(a) . . . . 1[4.02]

[*References are to chapter numbers followed by section/subsection numbers in brackets.*]

§ 1.1060-1(a)(1) . . . . 1[4.02]
§ 1.1060-1(b)(1) . . . . 1[4.02]
§§ 1.1060-1(b)(1)–(7) . . . . 1[4.02]
§ 1.1060-1(b)(2) . . . . 1[4.02]; 4[3.07(a)]
§§ 1.1060-1(c)(1)–(4) . . . . 1[4.02]
§ 1.1060-1(c)(2) . . . . 1[4.02]
§ 1.1060-1(c)(3) . . . . 1[4.02]
§ 1.1060-1(c)(4) . . . . 1[4.02]
§ 1.1060-1(d) Example 2 . . . . 1[4.02]
§ 1.1060-1(e) . . . . 1[4.02]
§ 1.1091-1 . . . . 8[2]
§ 1.1091-1(a) . . . . 8[2]
§ 1.1091-1(b) . . . . 8[2]
§ 1.1091-2 . . . . 8[2]
§ 1.1091-2(a), ex. 1 . . . . 8[2]
§ 1.1221-1(a) . . . . 2[3.02]
§ 1.1221-1(b) . . . . 2[3.03(b)]
§ 1.1221-1(c) . . . . 2[3.03(c)]; 7[3.03(a)]
§ 1.1221-1(c)(1) . . . . 2[3.03(c)]
§ 1.1221-1(c)(1)(4)(ii) . . . . 2[3.03(f)]
§ 1.1221-1(c)(2) . . . . 2[3.03(c)]
§ 1.1221-1(c)(3) . . . . 2[3.03(c)]
§ 1.1221-1(c)(4)(i) . . . . 2[3.03(f)]
§ 1.1221-1(d) . . . . 2[3.03(d)]
§ 1.1221-1(d)(1)(i) . . . . 2[3.03(f)]
§ 1.1221-1(d)(1)(ii) . . . . 2[3.03(f)]
§ 1.1221-1(d)(1)(iii) . . . . 2[3.03(f)]
§ 1.1221-1(d)(1)(iv) . . . . 2[3.03(f)]
§ 1.1221-1(d)(2) . . . . 2[3.03(f)]
§ 1.1221-1(d)(3) . . . . 2[3.03(f)]
§ 1.1221-1(d)(4) . . . . 2[3.03(f)]
§ 1.1221-1(d)(5)(i) . . . . 2[3.03(f)]
§ 1.1221-1(d)(5)(ii), ex. 1 . . . . 2[3.03(f)]
§ 1.1221-1(d)(5)(ii), ex. 2 . . . . 2[3.03(f)]
§ 1.1221-1(d)(5)(ii), ex. 3 . . . . 2[3.03(f)]
§ 1.1221-2 . . . . 2[3.03(f)]
§ 1.1221-2(a)(1) . . . . 2[3.03(f)]
§ 1.1221-2(a)(3) . . . . 2[3.03(a)]
§ 1.1221-2(b)(1) . . . . 2[3.03(f)]
§ 1.1221-2(b)(2) . . . . 2[3.03(f)]
§ 1.1221-2(c)(1) . . . . 2[3.03(f)]
§ 1.1221-2(c)(2) . . . . 2[3.03(f)]
§ 1.1221-2(e) . . . . 2[3.03(f)]
§ 1.1221-2(e)(1) . . . . 2[3.03(f)]
§ 1.1221-2(e)(2) . . . . 2[3.03(f)]
§ 1.1221-2(e)(2)(ii) . . . . 2[3.03(f)]
§ 1.1221-2(e)(2)(iii) . . . . 2[3.03(f)]
§ 1.1221-2(f)(1) . . . . 2[3.03(f)]
§ 1.1221-2(f)(2) . . . . 2[3.03(f)]
§ 1.1221-2(f)(2)(i) . . . . 2[3.03(f)]
§ 1.1221-2(f)(2)(ii) . . . . 2[3.03(f)]
§ 1.1221-2(f)(4) . . . . 2[3.03(f)]
§ 1.1221-2(g) . . . . 2[3.03(f)]
§ 1.1223-1(a) . . . . 2[5]
§ 1.1223-1(b) . . . . 2[5]; 2[5.05(b)]
§ 1.1223-1(f) . . . . 2[5]; 2[5.05(c)]
§ 1.1223-1(i) . . . . 2[5.03]
§ 1.1223-3 . . . . 2[5.03]
§ 1.1223-3(b)(1) . . . . 2[5.03]
§ 1.1223-3(c) . . . . 2[5.03]
§ 1.1223-3(f), ex. (1) . . . . 2[5.05(a)]
§ 1.1223-3(f), ex. 7 . . . . 2[5.03]
§ 1.1231-1(a) . . . . 2[6.01]; 2[6.02(a)]
§ 1.1231-1(b) . . . . 2[6.01]
§ 1.1231-1(c)(1) . . . 2[6.02(a)]; 2[6.03]; 2[6.03(a)]
§ 1.1231-1(c)(1)(i) . . . . 2[6.03]
§ 1.1231-1(c)(1)(ii) . . . . 2[6.03]
§ 1.1231-1(c)(2) . . . . 2[6.02(a)]
§ 1.1231-1(c)(3) . . . . 2[6.03]
§ 1.1231-1(c)(4) . . . . 2[6.03]
§ 1.1231-1(c)(5) . . . . 2[6.03]
§ 1.1231-1(d) . . . . 2[6.02(a)]
§ 1.1231-1(e)(1) . . . . 2[6.02(a)]
§ 1.1231-1(e)(3) . . . . 2[6.02(a)]; 2[6.02(b)]
§ 1.1231-1(f) . . . . 2[6.03(c)]
§ 1.1231-2(a)(3) . . . . 2[6.03(c)]
§ 1.1231-2(b)(1) . . . . 2[6.03(c)]
§ 1.1234-1 . . . . 2[4.04(b)]
§ 1.1234-1(a)(1) . . . . 2[4.04(b)]; 6[3.01]
§ 1.1234-1(b) . . . . . . 2[4.04(b)]; 5[3.01]; 6[3.01]
§ 1.1234-1(f) . . . . 2[4.04(b)]
§ 1.1234-1(g), ex. 2 . . . . 2[4.04(b)]
§ 1.1235-1 . . . . 7[3.03(b)]
§ 1.1235-1(b) . . . . 7[3.03(b)]
§ 1.1235-2(a) . . . . 7[3.03(b)]
§ 1.1235-2(b) . . . . 7[3.03(b)]
§ 1.1235-2(b)(i) . . . . 7[3.03(b)]
§ 1.1235-2(c) . . . . 7[3.03(b)]
§ 1.1235-2(f)(1) . . . . 7[3.03(b)]
§ 1.1235-2(f)(3) . . . . 7[3.03(b)]
§ 1.1235-2(f)(4) . . . . 7[3.03(b)]
§ 1.1237-1 . . . . 2[3.03(a)]
§ 1.1237-1(a)(2) . . . . 2[3.03(a)]
§ 1.1237-1(a)(5) . . . . 2[3.03(a)]
§ 1.1237-1(b)(1) . . . . 2[3.03(a)]
§ 1.1237-1(b)(3) . . . . 2[3.03(a)]
§ 1.1237-1(c)(1) . . . . 2[3.03(a)]
§ 1.1237-1(c)(3)(ii) . . . . 2[3.03(a)]

[*References are to chapter numbers followed by section/subsection numbers in brackets.*]

§ 1.1237-1(d) . . . . 2[3.03(a)]
§ 1.1237-1(e)(2)(i) . . . . 2[3.03(a)]
§ 1.1237-1(e)(2)(ii) . . . . 2[3.03(a)]
§ 1.1237-1(e)(2)(ii), ex. (1) . . . . 2[3.03(a)]
§ 1.1237-1(e)(2)(ii), ex. (2) . . . . 2[3.03(a)]
§ 1.1241-1(a) . . . . 2[4.04(c)]
§ 1.1241-1(b) . . . . 2[4.04(c)]
§ 1.1241-1(c) . . . . 2[4.04(c)]
§§ 1.1245-1(a)–(d) . . . . 4[4.01]
§§ 1.1245-2(a)(1)–(4) . . . . 4[4.01]
§ 1.1245-3 . . . . 4[4.01]
§§ 1.1245-4(a)–(d) . . . . 4[4.01]
§ 1.1245-5(a) . . . . 4[4.01]
§ 1.1245-6(a) . . . . 4[4.01]
§ 1.1253-2(d) . . . . 7[3.03(c)]
§ 1.1253-2(d)(9) . . . . 7[3.03(c)]
§ 1.1254-1 . . . . 4[4.03]
§ 1.1254-2 . . . . 4[4.03]
§ 1.1273-1(d)(2) . . . . 6[3.04(a)]
§ 1.1273-2(d) . . . . 3[2.01]
§ 1.1273-2(h) . . . . 6[3.04(a)]
§ 1.1275-4(c) . . . . 1[4.03]; 3[3.02]
§ 1.1361-1(b)(4) . . . . 6[2.01]
§ 1.1398-3 . . . . 5[3.02]
§ 1.6039-1(a) . . . . 6[4]
§ 1.6039-1(b) . . . . 6[4]
§ 1.6039-2(a) . . . . 6[4]
§ 1.6039-2(b) . . . . 6[4]
§ 1.6050P . . . . 3[5]
§ 1.6050P-1 . . . . 3[5]
§ 1.6050P-2 . . . . 3[5]
§ 15A.453-1(b)(2) . . . . 5[1.02(b)]
§ 15A.453-1(b)(2)(iii) . . . . 5[1.02(b)]
§ 15A.453-1(b)(2)(iv) . . . . 5[1.02(b)]
§ 15A.453-1(c) . . . . 1[4.03]
§ 29.112(b)(1)-1 . . . . 5[1.01]
§ 31.3121(v)(2)-1 . . . . 6[2.02]
§ 31.3121(v)(2)-1(b)(4)(ii) . . . . . 6[2.01]; 6[3.02]
§ 31.3121(v)(2)-1(b)(5), ex. 7 . . . . 6[3.02]
§ 31.3121(v)(2)-1(b)(5), ex. 8 . . . . 6[2.01]
§ 167 . . . . 4[4.01]
§ 301.7701-2(a) . . . . 8[5.03]
§ 301.7701-3(b)(1)(i) . . . . 8[5.03]
§ 301.7701-3(b)(1)(ii) . . . . 2[3.03(a)]
§ 301.7701-3(b)(2)(C) . . . . 2[3.03(a)]

Proposed Regulations (Prop. Reg.)

§ 1.167(n)-1(a) . . . . 4[3.07(b)]
§ 1.167(n)-1(b) . . . . 4[3.07(b)]
§ 1.167(n)-2 . . . . 4[3.07(b)]
§ 1.167(n)-2(a)(1) . . . . 4[3.07(b)]
§ 1.167(n)-2(a)(2) . . . . 4[3.07(b)]
§ 1.167(n)-2(b) . . . . 4[3.07(b)]
§ 1.167(n)-3 . . . . 4[3.07(b)]
§ 1.167(n)-3(a)(1) . . . . 4[3.07(b)]
§ 1.167(n)-3(b) . . . . 4[3.07(b)]
§ 1.167(n)-3(c) . . . . 4[3.07(b)]
§ 1.167(n)-4 . . . . 4[3.07(b)]
§ 1.167(n)-4(a) . . . . 4[3.07(b)]
§ 1.167(n)-4(b)(1) . . . . 4[3.07(b)]
§ 1.167(n)-4(c)(1) . . . . 4[3.07(b)]
§ 1.167(n)-4(c)(2) . . . . 4[3.07(b)]
§ 1.167(n)-4(d)(1) . . . . 4[3.07(b)]
§ 1.167(n)-5 . . . . 4[3.07(b)]
§ 1.167(n)-6 . . . . 4[3.07(b)]
§ 1.167(n)-6(a) . . . . 4[3.07(b)]
§ 1.167(n)-6(c) . . . . 4[3.07(b)]
§ 1.167(n)-6(d) . . . . 4[3.07(b)]
§ 1.167(n)-6(d)(2)(ii) . . . . 4[3.07(b)]
§ 1.167(n)-6(d)(3)(iii) . . . . 4[3.07(b)]
§ 1.167(n)-6(e)(1) . . . . 4[3.07(b)]
§ 1.167(n)-6(e)(2)(i) . . . . 4[3.07(b)]
§ 1.167(n)-6(f) . . . . 4[3.07(b)]
§ 1.168-1 . . . . 4[3.06]
§ 1.168-2(d) . . . . 4[3.06(c)]
§ 1.168-2(d)(3) . . . . 4[3.06]
§ 1.168-2(d)(3)(i) . . . . 4[3.06(c)]
§ 1.168-2(d)(3)(ii) . . . . 4[3.06(c)]
§ 1.168-2(e)(1) . . . . 4[3.06(c)]
§ 1.168-4(b) . . . . 4[3.06]
§§ 1.168-5(b)(1)–(7) . . . . 4[3.06]
§ 1.168-5(f)(3) . . . . 4[3.06]
§ 1.168-5(f)(4) . . . . 4[3.06]
§ 1.263(a)-1(c)(1) . . . . 4[2.03]
§ 1.263(a)-2 . . . . 4[2.01]; 4[2.05]
§ 1.263(a)-2(c)(2) . . . . 4[2.03]
§ 1.263(a)-2(d)(1) . . . . 4[2.03]
§ 1.263(a)-2(d)(2) . . . . 4[2.03]
§ 1.263(a)-2(d)(2)(iii) . . . . 4[2.03]
§ 1.263(a)-2(d)(2)(iv) . . . . 4[2.03]
§ 1.263(a)-2(d)(2)(v) . . . . 4[2.03]
§ 1.263(a)-2(d)(2)(vi) . . . . 4[2.03]
§§ 1.263(a)-2(d)(2)(vii), exs. 1–15 . . . . . . 4[2.03]
§ 1.263(a)-2(d)(3) . . . . 4[2.03]
§ 1.263(a)-2(e) . . . . 4[2.03]
§§ 1.263(a)-2(e)(4), exs. 1– 17 . . . . 4[2.03]
§ 1.263(a)-2(f) . . . . 4[2.03]
§ 1.263(a)-3 . . . . 4[2.01]; 4[3.04(b)]

[*References are to chapter numbers followed by section/subsection numbers in brackets.*]

§ 1.263(a)-3(d)(1) . . . . 4[2.03]
§ 1.263(a)-3(d)(2) . . . . 4[2.03]
§ 1.263(a)-3(d)(2)(ii) . . . . 4[2.03]
§ 1.263(a)-3(d)(2)(vii) . . . . 4[2.03]
§ 1.263(a)-3(e)(1) . . . . 4[2.03]
§ 1.263(a)-3(e)(2) . . . . 4[2.03]
§ 1.263(a)-3(e)(3) . . . . 4[2.03]
§ 1.263(a)-3(f)(1) . . . . 4[2.03]
§ 1.263(a)-3(f)(2)(i) . . . . 4[2.03]
§ 1.263(a)-3(f)(2)(ii) . . . . 4[2.03]
§ 1.263(a)-3(f)(2)(iii) . . . . 4[2.03]
§ 1.263(a)-3(f)(3) . . . . 4[2.03]
§ 1.263(a)-3(f)(3)(i) . . . . 4[2.03]
§ 1.263(a)-3(f)(3)(ii) . . . . 4[2.03]
§ 1.263(a)-3(f)(3)(iii) . . . . 4[2.03]
§ 1.263(a)-3(f)(3)(iv) . . . . 4[2.03]
§§ 1.263(a)-3(f)(4), exs. 1–18 . . . . 4[2.03]
§ 1.263(a)-3(h) . . . . 4[2.03]
§ 1.263(a)-3(i) . . . . 4[2.03]
§ 1.263(a)-4 . . . . 4[2.01]
§ 1.269A-1(b)(6) . . . . 7[4.01]
§ 1.409-4(a)(1) . . . . 6[1.02]
§ 1.409-4(a)(1)(ii) . . . . 6[1.02]
§ 1.409-4(a)(2) . . . . 6[1.02]
§ 1.409-4(a)(3) . . . . 6[1.02]
§ 1.409-4(b) . . . . 6[1.02]
§ 1.409-4(c) . . . . 6[1.02]
§ 1.409-4(d) . . . . 6[1.02]
§ 1.409-4(e) . . . . 6[1.02]
§ 1.409-4(f) . . . . 6[1.02]
§ 1.409-4(g) . . . . 6[1.02]
§ 1.409-4(h) . . . . 6[1.02]
§ 1.409A-4 . . . . 6[1.02]
§ 1.453-1(f) . . . . 5[1.02(b)]; 5[3.01]
§ 1.453-1(f)(1) . . . . 5[1.02(b)]
§ 1.465-1 . . . . 8[4]
§ 1.465-1(a) . . . . 8[4.01]
§ 1.465-2 . . . . 8[4]
§ 1.465-2(a) . . . . 8[4.01]
§ 1.465-2(b) . . . . 8[4.01]
§ 1.465-3 . . . . 8[4]; 8[4.02]
§ 1.465-4 . . . . 8[4]
§ 1.465-5 . . . . 8[4]; 8[4.02]
§ 1.465-6 . . . . 8[4]
§ 1.465-6(a) . . . . 8[4.02]
§ 1.465-6(b) . . . . 8[4.02]
§ 1.465-6(c) . . . . 8[4.02]
§ 1.465-7 . . . . 8[4]
§ 1.465-9 . . . . 8[4]
§ 1.465-11 . . . . 8[4]
§ 1.465-11(a) . . . . 8[4.01]
§ 1.465-12 . . . . 8[4]
§ 1.465-13 . . . . 8[4]
§ 1.465-22 . . . . 8[4]
§ 1.465-22(a) . . . . 8[4.02]
§ 1.465-22(b) . . . . 8[4.02]
§ 1.465-22(c)(1) . . . . 8[4.02]
§ 1.465-22(c)(2) . . . . 8[4.02]
§ 1.465-23 . . . . 8[4]
§ 1.465-23(a) . . . . 8[4.02]
§ 1.465-23(c) . . . . 8[4.02]
§ 1.465-24 . . . . 8[4]
§ 1.465-24(a)(1) . . . . 8[4.02]
§ 1.465-24(a)(2) . . . . 8[4.02]
§ 1.465-25 . . . . 8[4]
§ 1.465-25(a)(1) . . . . 8[4.02]
§ 1.465-38 . . . . 8[4]
§ 1.465-41 . . . . 8[4]
§ 1.465-66 . . . . 8[4]
§§ 1.468B-7–9 . . . . 7[2.01(d)]
§ 1.469-7 . . . . 8[5.05]
§ 1.6039-1(a) . . . . 6[4]
§ 1.6039-1(b) . . . . 6[4]
§ 1.6039-2(a) . . . . 6[4]
§ 1.6039-2(b) . . . . 6[4]

Temporary Regulations (Temp. Reg.)

§ 1.167(a)-1T . . . . 4[3.06]
§ 1.168(b)-1T . . . . 4[3.06]
§ 1.168(d)-1T(b)(3) . . . . 4[3.06]
§ 1.280F-2T . . . . 4[3.06(c)]
§ 1.280F-2T(i)(1) . . . . 4[3.06(c)]
§ 1.404(b)-1T Q&A-2 . . . . 6[2.01]
§ 1.465-1T . . . . 8[4.01]
§§ 1.469-1T(a)–(e)(3) . . . . 8[5]
§ 1.469-1T(d)(1) . . . . 8[5.02]
§ 1.469-1T(d)(1), example . . . . 8[5.02]
§ 1.469-1T(d)(2) . . . . 8[5.02]
§ 1.469-1T(e)(3) . . . . 8[5.04]
§ 1.469-1T(e)(3)(i) . . . . 8[5.04]
§ 1.469-1T(e)(3)(ii)(A) . . . . 8[5.04]
§§ 1.469-1T(e)(3)(ii)–(viii) . . . . 8[5.04]
§ 1.469-1T(e)(6) . . . . 8[5]
§ 1.469-1T(f) . . . . 8[5]
§ 1.469-1T(f)(2)(i) . . . . 8[5.02]
§ 1.469-1T(f)(2)(ii) . . . . 8[5.02]
§ 1.469-1T(f)(2)(iii) . . . . 8[5.02]

[*References are to chapter numbers followed by section/subsection numbers in brackets.*]

§§ 1.469-1T(g)(1)–(4) . . . . 8[5]
§§ 1.469-2T(a)–(c)(4) . . . . 8[5]
§ 1.469-2T(c)(3) . . . . 8[5.02]
§ 1.469-2T(c)(7) . . . . 8[5]
§§ 1.469-2T(d)(1)–(d)(6) . . . . 8[5]
§ 1.469-2T(d)(8) . . . . 8[5]
§ 1.469-2T(e)(1) . . . . 8[5]
§§ 1.469-2T(f)(1)–(f)(3) . . . . 8[5]
§ 1.469-2T(f)(7) . . . . 8[5]
§ 1.469-5T . . . . 8[5]; 8[5.03]
§ 1.469-5T(a) . . . . 8[5.03]; 8[5.04]
§ 1.469-5T(a)(1) . . . . 8[5.03]
§§ 1.469-5T(a)(1)–(7) . . . . 8[5.03]
§ 1.469-5T(a)(4) . . . . 8[5.03]
§ 1.469-5T(a)(5) . . . . 8[5.03]
§ 1.469-5T(a)(6) . . . . 8[5.03]
§ 1.469-5T(b)(2)(iii) . . . . 8[5.03]
§ 1.469-5T(c) . . . . 8[5.03]
§ 1.469-5T(e)(1) . . . . 8[5.03]
§ 1.469-5T(e)(2) . . . . 8[5.03]
§ 1.469-5T(e)(3) . . . . 8[5.03]
§ 1.469-5T(e)(3)(i) . . . . 8[5.03]
§ 1.469-5T(e)(3)(i)(B) . . . . 8[5.03]
§ 1.469-5T(e)(3)(ii) . . . . 8[5.03]
§ 1.469-5T(f) . . . . 8[5.04]
§ 1.469-5T(f)(2) . . . . 8[5.03]
§ 1.469-5T(f)(2)(i) . . . . 8[5.03]; 8[5.04]
§ 1.469-5T(f)(2)(ii) . . . . 8[5.03]
§ 1.469-5T(f)(2)(ii)(A) . . . . 8[5.04]
§ 1.469-5T(f)(4) . . . . 8[5.03]; 8[5.04]
§ 5h.5(a)(2) . . . . 4[3.06(b)]
§ 14a.422A-1, Q&A-1 . . . . 6[4.02(c)]
§ 14a.422A-1, Q&A-2 . . . . 6[4.02(c)]
.1469-5T(f)(3) . . . . 8[5.03]

UNIFORM ACTS

Revised Uniform Limited Partnership Act

generally . . . . 5[1.07]
§ 303(a) . . . . 8[5.03]

Uniform Limited Partnership Act

§ 7 . . . . 8[5.03]

Uniform Partnership Act

generally . . . . 1[4.01]

UNITED STATES CODE (U.S.C.)

Title 11

§ 101(32)(A) . . . . 3[5.01]

Title 17

generally . . . . 7[3.03(a)]

Title 26

§ 61(a)(12) . . . . 3[2.02]; 3[3.01(b)]
§§ 101–124 . . . . 5[3.03]
§ 108 . . . . 3[2.02]
§ 108(a)(1) . . . . 3[2.02]
§ 108(a)(1)(B) . . . . 3[5.01]
§ 108(d)(3) . . . . 3[5.01]
§ 161 . . . . 4[2.01]
§ 162(a) . . . . 1[4.03]; 4[2.01]
§ 162(a)(1) . . . . 4[2.01]
§ 167(a) . . . . 1[4.03]; 4[2.01]
§ 261 . . . . 4[2.01]
§ 263(a)(1) . . . . 1[4.03]; 4[2.01]
§ 336(a) . . . . 1[4.03]; 4[2.01]
§ 351 . . . . 4[2.01]
§ 465 . . . . 8[4.03]
§ 465(b)(1)(B) . . . . 8[4.03]
§ 465(b)(2)(A) . . . . 8[4.03]
§ 465(b)(4) . . . . 8[4.03]
§ 469 . . . . 8[5.03]
§ 469(a) . . . . 8[5.05]
§ 469(l)(2) . . . . 8[5.05]
§ 482 . . . . 7[4.01]
§§ 701–04 . . . . 8[5.05]
§ 761(a) . . . . 8[5.05]
§ 1017 . . . . 3[2.02]
§ 1031(a)(1) . . . . 1[3.02]
§ 1366(a)(1)(A) . . . . 8[5.05]
§ 7482(a)(1) . . . . 8[5.05]
§ 7805(a) . . . . 1[3.02]
§ 7805(b) . . . . 6[2.02]

Title 28

§ 1291 . . . . 8[4.03]

TABLE OF SECONDARY AUTHORITIES

[References are to chapter numbers followed by section/subsection numbers in brackets.]

ACTIONS ON DECISIONS

A.O.D.

1991-09 (Mar. 29, 1991) . . . . 3[3.04]

BOOKS

Configurations of Gross Income, The, J. Sneed (1967) . . . . 3[3.01(b)]

Familiar Quotations, Bartlett (12th ed. 1951) . . . . 4[3.06(a)]

Federal Income Taxation, Cases and Materials, Surrey, Warren, McDaniel and Ault (1972) . 5[1.03]

Federal Income Taxation, Marvin A. Chirelstein (9th ed. 2002) . . . . 2[3.02]

Federal Income Taxation, William A. Klein, et al. (12th ed. 2000) . . . . 2[3.02]

Federal Tax Accounting, Lang, Manning, & Willis (LexisNexis, Graduate Tax Series, 2006) . . . . 1[4.03]

Federal Taxation of Income, Estates and Gifts 2, Bittker & Lokken (3d ed. 2000) . . . . 2[3.02]

Tax Treatment of Securities Compensation: Problems of Underwriters, Fleischer & Meyer (1960) . . . . 6[3.03]

Webster's New World Dictionary (3d Coll. Ed. 1988) . . . . 4[3.06(a)]

CHIEF COUNSEL ADVICE

Chief Couns. Adv.

2000-39-037 . . . . 3[2.03]

2004-02-004 . . . . 3[2.01]

2008-36-025 . . . . 3[1.02]

2009-11-006 . . . . 5[1.06]

FEDERAL HOME LOAN BANK BOARD (FHLBB) MEMORANDA

Memorandum

R-49 . . . . 1[3.02]

FIELD ATTORNEY ADVICE

20040302F . . . . 4[3.02]

FIELD SERVICE ADVICE

Field Serv. Adv.

1999-41-018 . . . . 6[3.04(b)]

1999-51-006 . . . . 5[1.06]

1999-492 . . . . 4[3.02]

1999 TNT 110-39 . . . . 6[3.04(b)]

2000-11-006 . . . . 6[3.04(a)]; 6[3.04(b)]

2000-48-006 . . . . 3[4.03]

200125019 . . . . 4[3.04(a)]

FINANCIAL ACCOUNTING STANDARDS BOARD STATEMENTS

FAS

No. 123 . . . . 6[3.05]

GENERAL COUNSEL MEMORANDA

G.C.M.

24849 . . . . 2[4.03]; 7[2.02]

33256 . . . . 5[2.04]

34284 . . . . 5[2.04]

39606 . . . . 2[3.02]

HOUSE REPORTS

H.R. Rep. No. 97-201 . . . . 4[3.06(a)]

H.R. Rep. No. 99-841 . . . . 8[5.05]

H.R. Rep. No. 101-247 . . . . 5[1.08]

H.R. Rep. No. 103-111 . . . . 8[5.04]

H.R. Rep. No. 107-251 . . . . 4[3.05]

H.R. Rep. No. 108-548 . . . 4[3.06(b)]; 4[3.06(c)]

H.R. Rep. No. 108-755 . . . . 6[1.02]; 8[6]

H.R. Rep. No. 109-304 . . . . 2[3.03(c)]; 4[3.03]

H.R. Rep. No. 148 . . . . 2[4.04(d)]

H.R. Rep. No. 220 . . . . 4[3.04(b)]

H.R. Rep. No. 426 . . . . 4[2.02]; 8[4.04]

H.R. Rep. No. 658 . . . . 2[5.01]

H.R. Rep. No. 855 . . . . 3[2.02]

H.R. Rep. No. 1278 . . . . 4[3.02]

H.R. Rep. No. 1337 . . . . 4[2.01]

H.R. Rep. No. 2794 . . . . 6[4.02(b)]

I.R.S. ANNOUNCEMENTS

Announcement

2003-37, 2003-1 C.B. 1025 . . . . 3[4.01]

I.R.S. FORMS

Form

1040X . . . . 6[4.02(b)]

1099-C . . . . 3[2.02]; 3[4.02]; 3[5]

6251 . . . . 6[4.02(b)]

8275-R . . . . 6[4.02(b)]

W-2 . . . . 6[2.02]

I.R.S. NOTICES

Notice

97-59, 1997-2 C.B. 309 . . . . 2[6.02(d)]

2001-17, 2001-1 C.B. 730 . . . . 3[1.02]

2005-1, 2005-1 C.B. 274 . . . . 6[1.02]

2005-13, 2005-1 C.B. 630 . . . . 8[6]

LAW REVIEW/TAX JOURNAL ARTICLES

Advance Notice of Proposed Rulemaking, Liabilities Assumed in Certain Transactions, 68 Fed. Reg. 23,931 (May 6, 2003) . . . . 3[4.01]

[*References are to chapter numbers followed by section/subsection numbers in brackets.*]

APB Accounting Principles, Accounting Terminology Bulletin No. 1-Review and Resume 2 (1973) . . . . 4[2.01]

Assignment of Income: Fruit and Tree as Irrigated by the P. G. Lake Case, Lyon & Eustice, 17 Tax L. Rev. 295 (1962) . . . . 7[3.02]

Confusion Over Tax Ownership, The, Charles I. Kingson, 93 Tax Notes 409 (2001) . . 7[1.05]

Cost Segregation, IRS, Audit Techniques (Jan. 14, 2005) . . . . 4[3.06(c)]

Description and Technical Explanation of the Conference Agreement of H.R. 6, Title XIII, The "Energy Tax Incentives Act of 2005," Staff of the Joint Committee on Taxation, 80-81 (JCX-60-05) . . . . 2[6.01]; 4[4.01]

Further Guidance on the Application of Section 409A to Nonqualified Deferred Compensation Plans, 73 Fed. Reg. 74,380, 74,392 (12/9/2008) . . . . 6[1.02]

General Explanation of Tax Legislation Enacted in the 105th Congress 48, Staff of the Joint Committee on Taxation (1997) . . . . 2[1]

General Explanation of the Tax Reform Act of 1976, Staff of Joint Comm. on Taxation, 1976-3 (Vol. 2) 51 . . . . 8[4.02]

General Explanation of the Tax Reform Act of 1986, Staff of J. Comm. of Taxation, 209 . . 8[5.03]

General Explanation of the Tax Reform Act of 1986, Staff of Joint Comm. on Taxation, 438 . . . . 6[4.02(c)]

General Explanations of the Administration's Fiscal Year 2005 Revenue Proposals 124-126, U.S. Treasury Department (February 2004) . . 8[6]

Is Compromise of a Tax Liability Itself Taxable? A Problem of Circularity in the Logic of Taxation, Richard C.E. Beck, 14 Va. Tax Rev. 153 (1994) . . . . 3[2.02]

Limiting the Substitute-for-Ordinary Income Doctrine: An Analysis Through Its Most Recent Application Involving the Sale of Future Lottery Rights, Comment, Thomas G. Sinclair, 56 S.C. L. Rev. 387, 421-22 (2004) . . . . 2[3.02]

Lottery Winnings as Capital Gains, Case Comment, Matthew S. Levine, 114 Yale L.J. 195, 197-202 (2004) . . . . 2[3.02]

Note, 82 Colum. L. Rev., at 1526-1529 . 3[3.01(b)]

Notice of Proposed Rulemaking, 71 Fed. Reg. 48,590 (2006) . . . . 4[2.03]

Realization of Income Through Cancellations, Modifications, and Bargain Purchases of Indebtedness: I, Wright, 49 Mich. L. Rev. 459, 477, 492 (1951) . . . . 3[2.02]

Sales and Other Dispositions of Property Under Section 1001: The Taxable Event, Amount Realized and Related Problems of Basis, Del Cotto, 26 Buffalo L. Rev. 219, 323-324 (1977) . . . . 3[3.01(b)]

Tax Efficiency of Stock-Based Compensation, The, Knoll, 103 Tax Notes 203 (Apr. 12, 2004) . . . . 6[4.01]

Tax Reform Proposals: Tax Shelters and Minimum Tax 2, Staff of J. Comm. on Taxation (Com.. Print 1985) . . . . 8[5.03]

Tax Shelters, Nonrecourse Debt, and the Crane Case, Bittker, 33 Tax L. Rev. 277, 283 (1978) . . . . 3[3.01(b)]

2009-10 Priority Guidance Plan (2009 TNT 225-28) . . . . 3[4.01]

PRIVATE LETTER RULINGS

P.L.R.

20-04-11-023 . . . . 1[3.02]
78-11-037 . . . . 5[1.06]
78-11-056 . . . . 5[1.06]
81-13-107 . . . . 6[1.01]
81-19-029 . . . . 5[2.04]
82-40-009 . . . . 2[3.03(e)]
84-06-012 . . . . 6[1.01]
91-23-004 . . . . 7[3.02]
93-17-002 . . . . 6[4.02(c)]
93-21-063 . . . . 6[4.02(a)]
93-41-019 . . . . 6[2.01]
93-44-038 . . . . 6[1.01]
94-13-006 . . . . 5[1.04]
94-13-023 . . . . 6[2.01]
94-13-024 . . . . 5[1.03]
95-14-008 . . . . 7[2.01(a)]
96-16-035 . . . . 6[3.03]; 6[3.05]
96-19-028 . . . . 5[2.02]; 5[2.03]; 5[2.04]
96-20-010 . . . . 5[2.04]
97-22-022 . . . . 6[3.03]; 6[3.05]
97-23-032 . . . . 5[2.03]; 5[2.04]
97-51-012 . . . . 5[1.06]
98-03-008 . . . . 6[2.01]
98-03-023 . . . . 6[2.01]
98-10-005 . . . . 6[1.01]
98-14-019 . . . . 5[1.05]
98-22-012 . . . . 6[3.02]
98-23-045 . . . . 5[1.05]
98-29-025 . . . . 5[1.04]
1999-49-014 . . . . 6[1.02]
2000-07-033 . . . . 6[4.01]

[*References are to chapter numbers followed by section/subsection numbers in brackets.*]

2000-09-013 . . . . 6[2.01]
2000-13-044 . . . . 3[1.02]; 3[2.01]; 3[2.03]
2000-45-019 . . . . 7[2.02]
2001-11-025 . . . . 5[1.05]
2001-18-023 . . . . 5[1.01]
2002-04-005 . . . . 6[2.02]
2002-19-016 . . . . 6[2.03]
2002-36-026 . . . . 5[1.04]
2002-51-008 . . . . 5[1.08]
2004-08-027 . . . . 5[2.01]
2004-11-001 . . . . 5[2.05]
2004-27-025 . . . . 2[4.03]
2004-40-002 . . . . 5[1.08]
2005-04-012 . . . . 5[3.02]
2005-13-010 . . . . 5[1.06]
2005-19-011 . . . . 6[4.01]
2005-21-002 . . . . 5[1.07]
2005-41-037 . . . . 5[1.06]; 5[1.08]
2006-13-012 . . . . 6[1.02]
2007-12-013 . . . . 5[1.08]
2007-18-028 . . . . 5[1.05]
2007-28-034 . . . . 6[3.03]
2008-04-004 . . . . 6[1.02]
2008-28-016 . . . . 6[2.02]
2008-50-010 . . . . 7[2]
2009-12-004 . . . . 5[1.06]
2010-30-020 . . . . 5[1.03]

REVENUE PROCEDURES

Rev. Proc.

71-19, 1971-1 C.B. 698 . . . . 6[1.01]
75-21 . . . . 7[1.05]
80-11, 1980-1 C.B. 616 . . . . 6[2.02]
83-35, 1983-1 C.B. 745 . . . . 4[3.06(b)]
87-56, 1987-2 C.B.
674 . . . . 4[3.06(b)]; 4[3.06(c)]; 5[1.06]
87-57, 1987-2 C.B. 687 . . . . 4[3.06(b)]
92-64, 1992-2 C.B. 422 . . . . 6[1.01]
92-65, 1992-2 C.B. 428 . . . . 6[1.01]
98-34, 1998-1 C.B. 983 . . . . 6[3.05]
2000-37, 2000-2 C.B. 308 . . . . 5[1.05]; 5[1.08]
2000-46, 2000-2 C.B. 438 . . . . 5[1.06]
2000-50, 2000-1 C.B. 601 . . . . 4[3.04(a)]
2001-28, 2001-1 C.B. 1156 . . . . . 7[1.05]; 8[6]
2001-28, 2001-2 C.B. 1156 . . . . 8[6]
2002-13, 2002-8 I.R.B. 549 . . . . 6[3.05]
2002-22, 2002-1 C.B.
733 . . . . 5[1.06]; 5[2.02]; 5[2.04]
2003-39, 2003-1 C.B. 971 . . . . 5[1.04]
2004-51, 2004-2 C.B. 294 . . . . 5[1.05]
2005-14, 2005-7 I.R.B. 528 . . . . 5[3.02]
2007-3 . . . . 6[3.02]
2008-22, 2008-12 I.R.B. 658 . . . . . . 4[3.06(c)]
2010-3, 2010-1 I.R.B. 110 . . . . 6[3.02]
2010-13, 2010-4 I.R.B. 329 . . . . 8[5.02]
2010-14, 2010-14 I.R.B. 456 . . . . 5[1.03]

REVENUE RULINGS

Rev. Rul.

54-409, 1954-2 C.B. 174 . . . . 7[3.03(a)]
54-581, 1954-2 C.B. 112 . . . . 1[3.03(a)]
54-599, 1954-2 C.B. 52 . . . . 7[3.03(a)]
55-252, 1955-1 C.B. 319 . . . . 4[2.01]
55-410, 1955-2 C.B. 297 . . . . 5[3.03]
55-540, 1955-2 C.B. 39 . . . . . . 7[1.04]; 7[1.05]
55-541, 1955-2 C.B. 19 . . . . 7[1.05]
55-706, 1955-2 C.B. 300 . . . . 2[3.03(c)]
55-727, 1955-2 C.B. 25 . . . . 6[1.01]
55-749, 1955-2 C.B. 295 . . . . 5[1.06]
56-406, 1956-2 C.B. 523 . . . . 8[2]
56-437, 1956-2 C.B. 507 . . . . 1[3.02]
56-452, 1956-2 C.B. 525 . . . . 8[2]
56-531, 1956-2 C.B 983 . . . . 2[4.03]
56-602, 1956-2 C.B. 527 . . . . 8[2]
57-37, 1957-1 C.B. 18 . . . . 6[1.01]
57-528, 1957-2 C.B. 263 . . . . 6[1.01]
58-210, 1958-1 C.B. 523 . . . . 8[2]
58-211, 1958-1 C.B. 529 . . . . 8[2]
58-230, 1958-1 C.B. 204 . . . . 6[2.01]
58-234, 1958-1 C.B. 279 . . . . 6[3.01]
58-353, 1958-2 C.B. 408 . . . 7[1.01]; 7[3.03(a)]
59-72, 59-1 C.B. 203 . . . . 5[3.02]
59-121, 1959-1, C.B. 212 . . . . 1[2.01]
59-121, 1959-1 C.B. 212 . . . . 7[2]
59-380, 1959-2 C.B. 87 . . . . 4[2.01]
60-31, 1960-1 C.B. 174 . . . . . . 6[1.01]; 6[1.02]
60-195, 1960-1 C.B. 300 . . . . 8[2]
60-226, 1960-1 C.B. 26 . . . . 7[1.01]; 7[3.03(a)]
60-345, 1960-2 C.B. 311 . . . . 3[1.02]
60-358, 1960-2 C.B. 68 . . . . 4[3.07(b)]
61-119, 1961-1 C.B. 395 . . . . . 5[1.01]; 5[1.03]
61-119, 1961-1 C.B. 396 . . . . 5[1.01]
61-216, 1961-2 C.B. 134 . . . . 2[6.03(c)]
62-140, 1962-2 C.B. 181 . . . . 2[5.05(c)]
62-141, 1962-2 C.B. 182 . . . . 2[3.03(c)]
63-221, 1963-2 C.B. 332 . . . . 5[2.01]
64-90, 1964-1 C.B. 226 . . . . 7[2.01(a)]
64-235, 1964-2 C.B. 18 . . . . 7[3.02]
64-237 . . . . 5[2.02]; 5[2.04]
64-237, 1964-2 C.B. 319 . . . . 5[2.03]
64-273, 1964-2 C.B. 62 . . . . 4[3.07(b)]
64-279, 1964-2 C.B. 121 . . . . 6[1.01]
65-155 . . . . 5[1.02(b)]

[*References are to chapter numbers followed by section/subsection numbers in brackets.*]

66-7, 1966-1 C.B. 188 . . . . 2[5.02]
66-58, 1966-1 C.B. 186 . . . . 1[2.01]
66-167, 1966-1 C.B. 20 . . . . 7[2.01(a)]
67-136, 1967-1 C.B. 58 . . . . 7[3.03(b)]
67-169, 1967-1 C.B. 159 . . . . 4[3.04(d)]
67-254, 1967-2 C.B. 269 . . . . . 5[2.02]; 5[2.04]
67-255, 1967-2 C.B. 270 . . . . 5[2.04]
67-380, 1967-2 C.B. 291 . . . . 5[1.06]
68-226, 1968-1 C.B. 362 . . . . 7[2]
68-291, 1968-1 C.B. 351 . . . . 1[2.01]
68-331, 1968-1 C.B. 352 . . . . 5[1.06]
68-394, 1968-2 C.B. 338 . . . . 5[2.04]
68-503, 1968-2 C.B. 44 . . . . 7[2.01(a)]
68-602, 1968-2 C.B. 135 . . . . 3[2.02]
68-642, 1968-2 C.B. 337 . . . . 5[2.05]
69-50, 1969-1 C.B. 140 . . . . 6[1.01]
69-77, 1969-1 C.B. 59 . . . . 3[3.02]
69-77, 1969-1 C.B. 69 . . . . 3[3.02]
69-135, 1969-1 C.B. 198 . . . . 1[3.02]
69-303, 1969-1 C.B. 201 . . . . 5[2.01]
69-352, 1969-1 C.B. 34 . . . . . . 7[1.02]; 7[1.03]
69-474, 1969-2 C.B. 105 . . . . 6[1.01]
69-482, 1969-2 C.B. 164 . . . . 7[3.03(b)]
69-511, 1969-2 C.B. 24 . . . . 7[3.02]
69-643, 1969-2 C.B. 10 . . . . 1[4.02]
69-654, 1969-2 C.B. 162 . . . . 5[2.01]
70-45, 1970-1 C.B. 17 . . . . 7[3.02]
70-287, 1970-1 C.B. 146 . . . . 4[3.04(d)]
70-288, 1970-1 C.B. 146 . . . . 4[3.04(d)]
70-289, 1970-1 C.B. 147 . . . . 4[3.04(d)]
70-330, 1970-1 C.B. 14 . . . . 5[3.03]
70-392, 1970-2 C.B. 33 . . . . 4[2.01]
70-399, 1970-2 C.B. 164 . . . . . 5[2.03]; 5[2.04]
70-414, 1970-2 C.B. 132 . . . . 4[3.04(c)]
70-435, 1970-2 C.B. 100 . . . . 6[1.01]
70-466, 1970-2 C.B. 165 . . . . 5[2.03]
70-498, 1970-2 C.B. 6 . . . . 5[3.03]
70-510, 1970-2 C.B. 159 . . . . 1[2.01]
70-567, 1970-2 C.B. 133 . . . . 7[2.01(d)]
70-596, 1970-2 C.B. 68 . . . . 4[3.04(c)]
70-598, 1970-2 C.B. 168 . . . . 2[5.02]
71-33, 1971-1 C.B. 30 . . . . 7[2.01(a)]
71-41 . . . . 5[2.03]; 5[2.04]
71-63, 1971-1 C.B. 143 . . . . 3[2.02]
71-119, 1971-1 C.B. 163 . . . . 7[2.01(d)]
71-137, 1971-1 C.B. 104 . . . . 5[1.06]
71-141, 1971-1 C.B. 311 . . . . 5[2.03]
71-160 . . . . 3[2.02]
71-166, 1971-1 C.B. 135 . . . . 6[4.01]
71-283, 1971-2 C.B. 168 . . . . 7[3.02]
71-521, 1971-2 C.B. 313 . . . . 6[3.01]
71-568, 1971-2 C.B. 312 . . . . 8[2]
72-25, 1972-1 C.B. 127 . . . . 6[1.01]
72-85, 1972-1 C.B. 234 . . . . 2[6.03(a)]
72-95, 1972-1 C.B. 429 . . . . 7[2]
72-265, 1972-1 C.B. 222 . . . . 1[3.02]
72-350, 1972-2 C.B. 394 . . . . 3[3.03]
72-372, 1972-2 C.B. 471 . . . . 5[2.01]
72-403, 1972-2 C.B. 102 . . . . 4[3.06(b)]
72-451, 1972-2 C.B. 480 . . . . 2[5.05(a)]
72-542, 1972-2 C.B. 37 . . . . 7[2.01(a)]
72-549, 1972-2 C.B. 472 . . . . 5[1.05]
72-601, 1972-2 C.B. 467 . . . . 5[1.06]
73-160, 1973-1 C.B. 365 . . . . 1[3.02]
73-235, 1973-1 C.B. 519 . . . . 5[2.05]
73-341, 1973-2 C.B. 306 . . . . 7[2]
73-476, 1973-2 C.B. 300 . . . 1[3.02]; 5[1.02(a)]
73-580, 1973-2 C.B. 86 . . . . 4[3.02]
74-206, 1974-1 C.B. 198 . . . . 5[2.05]
74-218, 1974-1 C.B. 202 . . . . 5[1.06]; 8[2]
74-347, 1974-2 C.B. 26 . . . . 1[3.03(b)]
74-503, 1974-2 C.B. 117 . . . . . 3[4.01]; 6[3.03]
74-532, 1974-2 C.B. 270 . . . . 5[2.01]
74-581, 1974-2 C.B. 25 . . . . 7[2.01(a)]
75-291, 1975-2 C.B. 332 . . . . . 5[1.03]; 5[1.07]
75-292, 1975-2 C.B. 333 . . . . 5[1.07]
75-524, 1975-2 C.B. 342 . . . . 2[5.03]
75-527, 1975-2 C.B. 30 . . . . 2[4.03]
75-563, 1975-2 C.B. 199 . . . . 2[5.03]
76-214, 1976-1 C.B. 218 . . . . 5[1.06]
76-249, 1976-2 C.B. 21 . . . . 5[1.06]
76-308, 1976-2 C.B. 133 . . . . 3[2.02]
76-319, 1976-2 C.B. 242 . . . . . 5[2.02]; 5[2.04]
76-346, 1976-2 C.B. 247 . . . . 8[2]
76-377, 1976-2 C.B. 89 . . . . 8[3]
76-390, 72-2 C.B. 242 . . . . 5[2.02]
76-390 1976-2 C.B. 243 . . . . 5[2.04]
76-391, 1976-2 C.B. 243 . . . . . 5[2.03]; 5[2.04]
76-479, 1976-2 C.B. 20 . . . . 7[2.01(a)]
77-110, 1977-1 C.B. 58 . . . . 3[3.03]
77-121, 1977-1 C.B. 17 . . . . 7[2.01(a)]
77-125, 1977-1 C.B. 130 . . . . 3[3.03]
77-188, 1977-1 C.B. 76 . . . . 4[3.04(c)]
77-190, 1977-1 C.B. 88 . . . . 7[3.02]
77-201, 1977-1 C.B. 250 . . . . 8[2]
77-254, 1977-2 C.B. 63 . . . . 4[3.02]
77-297, 1977-2 C.B. 304 . . . . . 5[1.03]; 5[1.07]
77-308, 1977-2 C.B. 208 . . . . 4[3.04(d)]
77-337, 1977-2 C.B. 305 . . . . 5[1.07]
77-402, 1977-2 C.B. 222 . . . . 3[3.01(b)]
77-414, 1977-2 C.B. 299 . . . . 7[2]
77-420, 1977-2 C.B. 172 . . . . 6[1.01]

[References are to chapter numbers followed by section/subsection numbers in brackets.]

77-437, 1977-2 C.B. 28 . . . . 3[2.01]
78-4, 1978-1 C.B. 256 . . . . 5[1.06]
78-28, 1978-1 C.B. 51 . . . . 4[3.07(b)]
78-29, 1978-1 C.B. 62 . . . . 3[3.03]
78-125 . . . . 3[3.03]
78-146, 78-1 C.B. 260 . . . . 5[3.02]
78-182, 1978-1 C.B. 265 . . . . 3[1.01]; 6[3.01]; 6[3.04(a)]
78-197, 1978-1 C.B. 83 . . . . 7[2.01(c)]
78-330, 1978-2 C.B. 147 . . . . 3[2.02]
78-377, 1978-2 C.B. 208 . . . . 5[2.01]
79-44, 1979-1 C.B. 265 . . . . 1[3.02]; 5[1.02(a)]; 5[1.02(b)]; 5[1.03]; 5[1.04]; 5[1.05]; 5[3.01]
79-143, 1979-1 C.B. 264 . . . . 5[1.06]
79-155, 1979-1 C.B. 153 . . . . 1[3.02]
79-261, 1979-2 C.B. 295 . . . . . 5[2.03]; 5[2.04]
79-285, 1979-2 C.B. 91 . . . . 4[3.07(b)]
80-76, 1980-1 C.B. 15 . . . . 6[2.03]
80-175, 1980-2 C.B. 230 . . . . 5[2.01]
80-184, 1980-2 C.B. 232 . 5[2.03]; 5[2.04]; 5[2.05]
80-196, 1980-2 C.B. 32 . . . . 6[2.03]
80-198, 1980-2 C.B. 113 . 3[1.02]; 3[2.01]; 3[2.03]; 3[4.03]; 7[4.02]
80-199, 1980-2 C.B. 122 . 3[1.02]; 3[2.01]; 3[2.03]; 3[4.03]; 7[4.02]
80-235, 1980-2 C.B. 229 . . . . 3[3.03]
80-244, 1980-2 C.B. 234 . . . . 6[4.01]
80-300, 1980-2 C.B. 165 . . . . . 6[2.01]; 6[2.02]
80-338, 1980-2 C.B. 30 . . . . 7[2.01(a)]
81-163, 1981-1 C.B. 433 . . . 3[3.01(b)]; 3[4.01]
81-180, 1981-2 C.B. 161 . . . . 5[2.01]
81-181, 1981-2 C.B. 162 . . . . 5[2.01]
81-204, 1981-2 C.B. 157 . . . . 1[3.02]
81-283, 1981-2 C.B. 115 . . . . 8[4.02]
81-292, 1981-2 C.B. 152 . . . . 1[3.03(b)]
82-26 . . . . 5[3.02]
82-74, 1982-1 C.B. 110 . . . . 5[2.01]
82-96, 1982-1 C.B. 113 . . . . 5[1.06]
82-121, 1982-1 C.B. 79 . . . . 6[4.01]
82-144, 1982-2 C.B. 34 . . . . 5[1.05]
82-166, 1982-2 C.B. 190 . . . . 5[1.06]
82-202, 1982-2 C.B. 35 . . . . . . 3[3.04]; 3[5.03]
82-225, 1982-2 C.B. 100 . . . . 8[4.02]
83-22, 1983-1 C.B. 17 . . . . . . 3[1.02]; 6[2.02]
83-70, 1983-1 C.B. 189 . . . . 5[2.02]
83-105, 1983-2 C.B. 51 . . . . 4[3.04(c)]
83-127, 1983-2 C.B. 25 . . . . 7[2.01(a)]
83-160, 1983-2 C.B. 99 . . . . 4[3.08]
84-1, 1984-1 C.B. 39 . . . . 5[3.03]
84-5 . . . . 3[3.03]
84-43, 1984-1 C.B. 27 . . . . 5[3.02]
84-52, 1984-1 C.B. 157 . . . . 5[1.07]
84-68, 1984-1 C.B. 31 . . . . 6[2.03]
84-88, 1984-1 C.B. 141 . . . . 4[3.08]
84-121, 1984-2 C.B. 168 . . . . 5[1.07]
84-176, 1984-2 C.B. 34 . . . . 3[2.02]
85-87, 1985-1 C.B. 268 . . . . 8[2]
85-125, 1985-2 C.B. 180 . . . . 1[3.02]
86-12, 1986-1 C.B. 290 . . . . 5[2.05]
86-24, 1986-1 C.B. 80 . . . . 1[2.01]
86-83, 1986-1 C.B. 251 . . . . 4[3.04(d)]
86-149, 1986-2 C.B. 67 . . . . 2[6.03(b)]
87-44, 1987-1 C.B. 3 . . . . 6[4.02(c)]
87-112, 1987-2 C.B. 207 . . . . 1[3.03(b)]
88-38, 1988-1 C.B. 246 . . . . 7[4.01]
88-57, 1988-2 C.B. 36 . . . . 4[2.01]
88-68, 1988-2 C.B. 117 . . . . 6[1.02]
88-77, 1988-2 C.B. 128 . . . . 3[4.03]
88-77, 1988-2 C.B. 129 . 3[1.02]; 3[2.01]; 3[2.03]
89-56, 1989-1 C.B. 83 . . . . 4[3.04(c)]
90-16, 1990-1 C.B. 12 . . . . . . 3[5.01]; 3[5.03]
90-34, 1990-1 C.B. 154 . . . . . . 5[1.03]; 5[1.07]
90-109, 1990-2 C.B. 191 . . . . 1[3.02]
91-31, 1991-1 C.B. 19 . . . . . . 3[3.04]; 3[5.03]
91-46, 1991-2 C.B. 358 . . . . 7[3.02]
92-51, 1992-2 C.B. 102 . . . . 7[2.01(d)]
92-53, 1992-2 C.B. 48 . . . . . . 3[5.01]; 3[5.03]
92-80, 1992-2 C.B. 57 . . . . . 4[2.01]; 6[3.04(b)]
92-99, 1992-2 C.B. 35 . . . . . . 3[3.04]; 3[5.03]
93-26, 1993-1 C.B. 50 . . . . 4[3.04(c)]
93-80, 1993-2 C.B. 239 . . . . 2[4.02]; 3[3.01(b)]
94-12, 1994-1 C.B. 36 . . . . 4[2.01]
94-38, 1994-1 C.B. 35 . . . . . 4[2.01]; 4[3.04(b)]
94-38, 1998-1 C.B. 998 . . . . 4[3.04(b)]
94-77, 1994-2 C.B. 19 . . . . 4[2.01]
95-22, 1995-1 C.B. 145 . . . . 5[2.02]
95-26, 1995-1 C.B. 131 . 3[1.01]; 3[2.01]; 3[2.03]
95-32, 1995-1 C.B. 8 . . . . 4[2.01]
95-45, 1995-1 C.B. 53 . 3[1.01]; 3[2.01]; 3[2.03]
95-71, 1995-2 C.B. 323 . . . . 7[3.02]
95-74, 1995-2 C.B. 36 . 3[1.02]; 3[2.01]; 3[2.03]; 3[3.02]; 3[4.03]
96-32, 1996-1 C.B. 177 . . . . 5[2]; 5[2.01]
98-21, 1998-1 C.B. 975 . . . . 6[3.05]
98-25 . . . . 4[3.04(b)]
99-23, 1999-1 C.B. 998 . . . . 4[3.02]
99-57, 1999-2 C.B. 678 . . . . 6[3.03]
286, 1953-2 C.B. 20 . . . . 1[2.07]
2001-4, 2001-1 C.B. 295 . . . . . 4[2.01]; 4[2.03]
2002-1, 2002-1 C.B. 268 . . . . 6[3.03]
2002-9, 2002-1 C.B. 614 . . . . 4[2.02]

[References are to chapter numbers followed by section/subsection numbers in brackets.]

2002-22, 2002-1 C.B. 849 . . . 1[3.03(b)]; 6[3.03]
2002-83, 2002-2 C.B. 927 . . . 5[1.08]
2003-56, 2003-1 C.B. 985 . . . 5[1.04]
2003-98, 2003-2 C.B. 378 . . . 6[3.03]; 6[3.04(a)]
2004-18, 2004-1 C.B. 509 . . . 4[3.04(b)]
2004-37, 2004-1 C.B. 583 . . . 3[2.02]
2004-60, 2004-1 C.B. 1051 . . . 6[3.03]
2004-86, 2004-2 C.B. 191 . . . 5[1.01]; 5[1.06]
2005-42, 2005-2 C.B. 67 . . . 3[1.02]; 4[3.04(b)]
2005-46, 2005-2 C.B. 120 . . . 5[2.05]
2005-48, 2005-2 C.B. 259 . . . 6[2.02]; 6[3.02]
2006-2, 2006-1 C.B. 261 . . . 3[4.01]; 6[3.03]
2007-37, 2007-1 C.B. 1390 . . . 7[3.01]
2007-49, 2007-2 C.B. 237 . . . 6[2.02]
2008-13, 2008-10 C.B. 518 . . . 6[1.02]
2008-34, 2008-28 I.R.B. 76 . . . 3[5]

SENATE REPORTS

S. Rep. No. 33 . . . 2[4.03]; 4[3.04(b)]
S. Rep. No. 94-938 . . . 8[4.03]
S. Rep. No. 96-498 . . . 8[4.02]
S. Rep. No. 96-1035 . . . 3[5.01]
S. Rep. No. 97-144 . . . 4[3.06(a)]
S. Rep. No. 99-313 . . . 8[5.01]; 8[5.03]; 8[5.06]
S. Rep. No. 108-192 . . . 4[3.06(c)]
S. Rep. No. 120 . . . 2[3.03(g)]
S. Rep. No. 201 . . . 2[3.03(a)]
S. Rep. No. 313 . . . 4[2.02]; 4[3.06(a)]
S. Rep. No. 558 . . . 8[3]
S. Rep. No. 938 . . . 8[4.03]
S. Rep. No. 1000 . . . 5[1.02(b)]; 5[3.01]
S. Rep. No. 1036 . . . 4[3.02]
S. Rep. No. 1263 . . . 4[3.06(c)]
S. Rep. No. 1631 . . . 3[2.02]

SERVICE CENTER ADVICE

Serv. Cent. Adv.

1998-039 . . . 3[2.02]

TECHNICAL ADVICE MEMORANDA

T.A.M.

80-03-004 . . . 5[1.02(a)]; 5[1.02(b)]; 5[1.03]; 5[1.04]; 5[1.05]
81-32-017 . . . 5[3.02]
83-07-007 . . . 5[2.02]; 5[2.03]; 5[2.04]
85-47-001 . . . 3[3.04]
87-06-009 . . . 6[2.02]
89-39-002 . . . 3[4.03]
90-27-002 . . . 4[3.02]
90-37-001 . . . 2[3.03(c)]
92-06-004 . . . 6[3.03]; 6[3.04(a)]; 6[3.04(b)]
92-40-004 . . . 4[3.04(b)]
93-15-004 . . . 4[3.04(b)]
93-36-001 . . . 6[1.01]
94-11-002 . . . 4[2.01]; 4[3.04(b)]
94-38-001 . . . 3[4.03]; 6[3.03]
94-48-001 . . . 5[1.06]
95-25-002 . . . 5[1.06]
95-27-005 . . . 6[4.01]
96-40-001 . . . 3[4.01]
97-21-002 . . . 3[4.03]; 6[3.03]; 6[3.04(b)]
97-31-001 . . . 3[4.03]; 6[3.03]; 6[3.04(b)]
97-44-001 . . . 6[2.02]
98-22-005 . . . 3[2.02]
2000-35-004 . . . 5[1.06]
2000-39-005 . . . 5[1.05]
2000-40-004 . . . 3[1.01]
2000-43-013 . . . 6[3.04(a)]; 6[3.04(b)]
2000-49-009 . . . 7[3.02]
2001-30-001 . . . 5[1.04]
2002-24-004 . . . 5[1.06]
2003-38-010 . . . 6[4.02(b)]
2005-12-021 . . . 4[2.04]
2005-21-032 . . . 4[2.04]
2005-48-022 . . . 4[3.02]
2006-02-034 . . . 5[1.06]
2006-22-046 . . . 6[3.04(b)]

TREASURY DEPARTMENT MEMORANDA

T.D.

8346, 1991-1 C.B. 150 . . . 5[1.05]
8346, 1991-1 C.B. 151 . . . 5[1.05]

INDEX

[References are to **chapters**: sections, e.g., **2**:3.03(b).]

A

ABANDONMENT
Realization event . . . **1**:3.03(a)

ACCELERATED COST RECOVERY SYSTEM
General principals . . . **4**:3.06(a)
Depreciation, mechanics of . . . **4**:3.06(b)
Special provisions . . . **4**:3.06(c)

ACCOUNTS RECEIVABLE
Capital asset . . . **2**:3.03(d)

ADJUSTMENTS
Basis, to . . . **1**:2.09

ADVANCED CHARACTERIZATION PROBLEMS
Artists . . . **7**:3.03
Contract rights . . . **7**:3; **7**:3.01
Copyrights . . . **7**:3.03(a)
Franchises . . . **7**:3.03; **7**:3.03(c)
Goodwill
    Generally . . . **7**:3
    Future services versus . . . **7**:3.02
Gratuitous transfers of partial interests
    Generally . . . **7**:2.01
    Appreciated property versus realized income . . . **7**:2.01(c)
    Escrows . . . **7**:2.01(d)
    Property, income from . . . **7**:2.01(b)
    Realized income, appreciated property versus . . . **7**:2.01(c)
    Services, income from . . . **7**:2.01(a)
Intangible assets . . . **7**:3
Inventors . . . **7**:3.03
Patents . . . **7**:3.03(b)
Reality of sale (See REALITY OF SALE)
Related taxpayers
    Generally . . . **7**:4
    Applicability . . . **7**:4.01
    Applied . . . **7**:4.02
    § 482 . . . **7**:4.01; **7**:4.02
Self-created property . . . **7**:3
Trade names . . . **7**:3.03(c)
Transfers of partial interests
    Generally . . . **7**:2
    Gratuitous transfers of partial interests (See subhead: Gratuitous transfers of partial interests)
    Sales of partial interests . . . **7**:2.02

ALTERNATIVE MINIMUM TAX (AMT)
Generally . . . **6**:4.02; **6**:4.02(b)
Computation of . . . **6**:4.02(a)
Net operating loss carryovers under . . . **6**:4.02(c)

AMORTIZATION OF INTANGIBLE ASSETS (See INTANGIBLE ASSETS, subhead: Amortization)

AMOUNT REALIZED
Debt inclusion . . . **1**:3.05
Mortgaged property . . . **3**:3.01(b)
Retained interest versus . . . **7**:1.03

AMT (See ALTERNATIVE MINIMUM TAX (AMT))

ARTISTS
Generally . . . **7**:3.03
Property, capital asset . . . **2**:3.03(c)

AT-RISK RULES
Generally . . . **8**:4; **8**:4.01
Amount, at-risk . . . **8**:4.02
Qualified nonrecourse financing . . . **8**:4.04
Stop loss agreements . . . **8**:4.03

B

BASIS
Generally . . . **1**:1; **1**:2.01
Adjustments to . . . **1**:2.09
Carryover basis transactions, tacking permitted in . . . **2**:5.05(b)
Debt inclusion . . . **1**:2.08
Discharge of indebtedness income and § 108 . . . **3**:5.03
Gifts, of . . . **1**:2.03
Inherited property, of . . . **1**:2.04
Like-kind exchanges . . . **5**:1.02
Mortgaged property . . . **3**:3.01(a)
Property received in taxable exchange . . . **1**:2.06
§ 108, discharge of indebtedness income and . . . **3**:5.03
Split basis . . . **1**:2.07
Substituted basis
    Generally . . . **1**:2.05
    Tacking permitted . . . **2**:5.05(a)
Tacking permitted
    Carryover basis transactions . . . **2**:5.05(b)
    Substituted basis transactions . . . **2**:5.05(a)
Tax cost . . . **1**:2.02

BOOT
Like-kind exchanges . . . **5**:1.02; **5**:1.02(b)

BUSINESS (See TRADE OR BUSINESS)

C

CAPITAL ASSET
Overview . . . **2**:3.01
Accounts receivable . . . **2**:3.03(d)
Artistic property . . . **2**:3.03(c)
Business or trade
    Property . . . **2**:3.03(b)

[References are to **chapters**: sections, e.g., **2**:3.03(b).]

CAPITAL ASSET—Cont.
Business or trade—Cont.
Supplies . . . **2**:3.03(h)
Commodities derivative financial instruments . . . **2**:3.03(g)
Dealer property . . . **2**:3.03(a)
Defined . . . **2**:3.03
Government publications . . . **2**:3.03(e)
Hedging transactions . . . **2**:3.03(f)
Intellectual property . . . **2**:3.03(c)
Notes receivable . . . **2**:3.03(d)
Property, definition of . . . **2**:3.02
Trade or business
Property . . . **2**:3.03(b)
Supplies . . . **2**:3.03(h)

CAPITAL GAINS AND LOSSES
Generally . . . **2**:1
Capital asset (See CAPITAL ASSET)
Exchange (See subhead: Sale or exchange)
Holding period (See HOLDING PERIOD)
Net capital gain, determination
Corporate taxpayers . . . **2**:2.02
Non-corporate taxpayer
Capital loss limitations . . . **2**:2.01(d)
Look-through rules applicable to pass-thru entities . . . **2**:2.01(c)
Netting capital gains and losses . . . **2**:2.01(b)
Tax rate applicable . . . **2**:2.01(a)
Sale or exchange
Overview . . . **2**:4.01
Extinguishment doctrine . . . **2**:4.03
Judicial interpretation . . . **2**:4.02
Statutory sales (See subhead: Statutory sales)
§ 1231
Overview . . . **2**:6.01
Business or trade (See TRADE OR BUSINESS, subhead: § 1231)
Mechanics of
Generally . . . **2**:6.02
Non-recaptured net § 1231 losses . . . **2**:6.02(d)
Preliminary hotchpot . . . **2**:6.02(b)
Primary hotchpot . . . **2**:6.02(c)
Types of property . . . **2**:6.02(a)
Trade or business (See TRADE OR BUSINESS, subhead: § 1231)
Statutory sales
Generally . . . **2**:4.04
Amounts received on cancellation
Lease, of . . . **2**:4.04(c)
Property rights, of . . . **2**:4.04(d)
Lease, amounts received on cancellation of . . . **2**:4.04(c)
Loss on option lapse . . . **2**:4.04(b)
Miscellaneous . . . **2**:4.04(e)
Nonbusiness bad debts . . . **2**:4.04(a)
Option lapse, loss on . . . **2**:4.04(b)
Property rights, amounts received on cancellation of . . . **2**:4.04(d)
Worthless securities . . . **2**:4.04(a)

CAPITALIZATION
Generally . . . **4**:1.01; **4**:2.01
Claim, origin of . . . **4**:2.05
Disputes . . . **4**:2.05
Economics of . . . **4**:1.02
Intangible assets . . . **4**:2.04
Litigation . . . **4**:2.05
Origin of claim . . . **4**:2.05
Tangible assets . . . **4**:2.03
Uniform capitalization rules . . . **4**:2.02

CARRYOVERS
Basis transactions, tacking permitted in . . . **2**:5.05(b)
Net operating loss carryovers under alternative minimum tax . . . **6**:4.02(c)
Tacking permitted in basis transactions . . . **2**:5.05(b)

CASUALTIES
Realization event . . . **1**:3.03(a)

CHARITABLE CONTRIBUTIONS
Nonrecognition provisions . . . **5**:3.03

CLAIMS
Origin of . . . **4**:2.05
Transfer in satisfaction of . . . **1**:3.03(b)

COMMODITIES DERIVATIVE FINANCIAL INSTRUMENTS
Capital asset . . . **2**:3.03(g)

CONTRACT RIGHTS
Generally . . . **7**:3; **7**:3.01

COPYRIGHTS
Generally . . . **7**:3.03(a)

COST RECOVERY
Generally . . . **4**:1.01; **4**:3.01
Accelerated cost recovery system, modification (See ACCELERATED COST RECOVERY SYSTEM)
Amortization of intangible assets (See INTANGIBLE ASSETS, subhead: Amortization)
Bonus depreciation . . . **4**:3.05
Capital expenditures, expensing of
Development, mining exploration and . . . **4**:3.04(d)
Environmental remediation costs . . . **4**:3.04(b)
Experimental expenses, research and . . . **4**:3.04(a)
Intangible drilling costs . . . **4**:3.04(c)
Mining exploration and development . . . **4**:3.04(d)
Research and experimental expenses . . . **4**:3.04(a)
Depletion . . . **4**:3.08
Development expenditures, exploration and . . . **4**:3.04(d)
Economics of . . . **4**:1.02
Election to expense certain business assets . . . **4**:3.03
Environmental remediation costs . . . **4**:3.04(b)
Experimental expenses, research and . . . **4**:3.04(a)

[References are to **chapters**: sections, e.g., **2**:3.03(b).]

COST RECOVERY—Cont.
Exploration and development expenditures . . . **4**:3.04(d)
Intangible drilling costs . . . **4**:3.04(c)
Research and experimental expenses . . . **4**:3.04(a)
Start-up expenditures . . . **4**:3.02

D

DEALER PROPERTY
Capital asset . . . **2**:3.03(a)

DEBT INCLUSION
Amount realized . . . **1**:3.05
Basis . . . **1**:2.08

DEDUCTIONS AND LOSSES
Generally . . . **8**:1
At-risk rules (See AT-RISK RULES)
Leasing transactions, from . . . **8**:6
Passive losses (See PASSIVE LOSSES)
Related parties, between . . . **8**:3
Securities, wash sales of . . . **8**:2
Wash sales of securities . . . **8**:2

DEFERRED COMPENSATION
Generally . . . **6**:1
§ 409A . . . **6**:1.02
Traditional deferred compensation principles . . . **6**:1.01
2004 limitations . . . **6**:1.02

DEFERRED EXCHANGES
Like-kind exchanges . . . **5**:1.04

DEPLETION
Cost recovery . . . **4**:3.08

DEPRECIATION
Bonus depreciation . . . **4**:3.05
Mechanics of . . . **4**:3.06(b)
Recapture
  Generally . . . **4**:4
  Mining interests and timber . . . **4**:4.03
  Personal property . . . **4**:4.01
  Real property . . . **4**:4.02
  Timber, mining interests and . . . **4**:4.03

DISCHARGE OF INDEBTEDNESS (DOI)
Generally . . . **3**:2
Contingent liability . . . **3**:2.03
Disputed liability . . . **3**:2.03
Income
  Defined . . . **3**:2.01
  § 108 and (See subhead: § 108)
Medium of payment . . . **3**:2.02
Payment, medium of . . . **3**:2.02
§ 108
  Generally . . . **3**:5
  Attribute reduction . . . **3**:5.02
  Basis reduction . . . **3**:5.03
  Insolvency . . . **3**:5.01
  § 1017 . . . **3**:5.03

DOI (See DISCHARGE OF INDEBTEDNESS (DOI))

E

EXCHANGE (See SALE OR EXCHANGE)

EXECUTIVE COMPENSATION AND STOCK OPTIONS
Deferred compensation (See DEFERRED COMPENSATION)
Incentive stock options (See INCENTIVE STOCK OPTIONS (ISOs))
Nonstatutory stock options (See NONSTATUTORY STOCK OPTIONS (NSOs))
Restricted property (See RESTRICTED PROPERTY)

EXTINGUISHMENT DOCTRINE
Sale or exchange requirement . . . **2**:4.03

F

FRANCHISES
Generally . . . **7**:3.03; **7**:3.03(c)

FUTURE SERVICES VERSUS GOODWILL
Generally . . . **7**:3.02

G

GAINS
Capital gains and losses (See CAPITAL GAINS AND LOSSES)
Realization (See REALIZATION OF GAIN OR LOSS)

GIFTS
Basis of . . . **1**:2.03
Part as . . . **1**:3.04

GOODWILL
Generally . . . **7**:3
Future services versus . . . **7**:3.02

GOVERNMENT PUBLICATIONS
Capital asset . . . **2**:3.03(e)

H

HEDGING TRANSACTIONS
Capital asset . . . **2**:3.03(f)

HOLDING PERIOD
Overview . . . **2**:5.01
Basic rules for . . . **2**:5.02
Inherited property, for . . . **2**:5.04
Split . . . **2**:5.03
Tacked holding periods
  Generally . . . **2**:5.05
  Carryover basis transactions, tacking permitted in . . . **2**:5.05(b)
  Miscellaneous tacking provisions . . . **2**:5.05(c)

[References are to **chapters**: sections, e.g., **2**:3.03(b).]

HOLDING PERIOD—Cont.
Tacked holding periods—Cont.
Substituted basis transactions, tacking permitted in . . . **2**:5.05(a)

I

INCENTIVE STOCK OPTIONS (ISOS)
Generally . . . **6**:4
Alternative minimum tax and (See ALTERNATIVE MINIMUM TAX (AMT))
Effects . . . **6**:4.01
Requirements . . . **6**:4.01

INHERITED PROPERTY
Basis of . . . **1**:2.04
Holding period for . . . **2**:5.04

INSOLVENCY
Discharge of indebtedness income and § 108 . . . **3**:5.01
§ 108, discharge of indebtedness income and . . . **3**:5.01

INSTALLMENT SALES
Like-kind exchanges . . . **5**:1.02(b)
Nonrecognition provisions . . . **5**:3.01

INTANGIBLE ASSETS
Generally . . . **7**:3
Amortization
Generally . . . **4**:3.07
Non-Section 197 intangible assets . . . **4**:3.07(b)
Section 197 intangible assets . . . **4**:3.07(a)
Capitalization . . . **4**:2.04

INTELLECTUAL PROPERTY
Capital asset . . . **2**:3.03(c)

INVENTORS
Generally . . . **7**:3.03
Lessors and, Involuntary conversion . . . **5**:2.03

INVOLUNTARY CONVERSION
Generally . . . **5**:2; **5**:2.01
Investor-lessor . . . **5**:2.03
Lessor-investor . . . **5**:2.03
Like kind revisited . . . **5**:2.04
Proceeds . . . **5**:2.05
Similar in service or use . . . **5**:2.02

ISOS (See INCENTIVE STOCK OPTIONS (ISOs))

J

JUDICIAL INTERPRETATION
Sale or exchange requirement . . . **2**:4.02

L

LEASES
Amounts received on cancellation of . . . **2**:4.04(c)
Leveraged leasing . . . **7**:1.05

LEASES—Cont.
Losses from leasing transactions, limitations on . . . **8**:6
Sale versus . . . **7**:1.04

LESSOR-INVESTOR
Involuntary conversion . . . **5**:2.03

LIABILITIES
Conditions . . . **3**:1.01
Contingencies . . . **1**:4.03; **3**:1.01; **3**:2.03
Defined . . . **3**:1
Disputed liability . . . **3**:2.03
Like-kind exchanges . . . **5**:1.02; **5**:1.02(a)
Obligations versus . . . **3**:1.02
Transfer of
Generally . . . **3**:4
Deductible items . . . **3**:4.03
Deficiency . . . **3**:4.02
Primary liability . . . **3**:4.01
Secondary liability . . . **3**:4.01

LIKE-KIND EXCHANGES
Generally . . . **5**:1; **5**:1.01; **5**:1.06
Basis . . . **5**:1.02
Boot . . . **5**:1.02; **5**:1.02(b)
Deferred exchanges . . . **5**:1.04
Held . . . **5**:1.07
Installment sales . . . **5**:1.02(b)
Involuntary conversion . . . **5**:2.04
Liabilities . . . **5**:1.02; **5**:1.02(a)
Multiparty exchanges . . . **5**:1.03
Related parties . . . **5**:1.08
Reverse *Starker* exchanges . . . **5**:1.05

LOSSES
Capital gains and losses (See CAPITAL GAINS AND LOSSES)
Deductions and, limitations on (See DEDUCTIONS AND LOSSES)
Non-recaptured net § 1231 losses . . . **2**:6.02(d)
Option lapse, on . . . **2**:4.04(b)
Passive losses (See PASSIVE LOSSES)
Realization (See REALIZATION OF GAIN OR LOSS)

M

MORTGAGED PROPERTY
Generally . . . **3**:3.01
Amount realized . . . **3**:3.01(b)
Basis . . . **3**:3.01(a)
Contingencies . . . **3**:3.02
Realization event, as . . . **1**:3.03(c)
§ 108(e)(5), *Tufts* and . . . **3**:3.04
Speculative security . . . **3**:3.03
Tufts and § 108(e)(5) . . . **3**:3.04

MULTIPARTY EXCHANGES
Like-kind exchanges . . . **5**:1.03

[References are to **chapters**: sections, e.g., **2**:3.03(b).]

N

NET OPERATING LOSS (NOL)
Carryovers under alternative minimum tax . . . **6**:4.02(c)

NOL (See NET OPERATING LOSS (NOL))

NONRECOGNITION TRANSACTIONS
Involuntary conversion (See INVOLUNTARY CONVERSION)
Like-kind exchanges (See LIKE-KIND EXCHANGES)
Other nonrecognition provisions
  Generally . . . **5**:3
  Charitable contributions . . . **5**:3.03
  Installment sales . . . **5**:3.01
  Principal residences . . . **5**:3.02
  Repossessions . . . **5**:3.01

NONSTATUTORY STOCK OPTIONS (NSOS)
Generally . . . **6**:3
Exercise . . . **6**:3.02
Grant . . . **6**:3.02
Lapse . . . **6**:3.02
Noncompensatory nonstatutory stock options
  Generally . . . **6**:3.04
  Compensatory or, determination . . . **6**:3.04(a)
  Options taxed on exercise . . . **6**:3.04(b)
Purchased options . . . **6**:3.01
Transfers . . . **6**:3.03
Valuation . . . **6**:3.05

NOTES RECEIVABLE
Capital asset . . . **2**:3.03(d)

NSOS (See NONSTATUTORY STOCK OPTIONS (NSOs))

O

OBLIGATIONS VERSUS LIABILITIES
Generally . . . **3**:1.02

P

PASSIVE LOSSES
Generally . . . **8**:5; **8**:5.01
Investment activity . . . **8**:5.02
Material and significant participation . . . **8**:5.03
Non-passive activity . . . **8**:5.02
Passive activity
  Generally . . . **8**:5.02
  Disposition of . . . **8**:5.06
Rental activities . . . **8**:5.04
Self-charged items . . . **8**:5.05
Significant participation, material and . . . **8**:5.03

PATENTS
Generally . . . **7**:3.03(b)

PAYMENTS
Contingent payments . . . **1**:4.03
Medium of . . . **3**:2.02

R

REALITY OF SALE
Generally . . . **7**:1
Amount realized, retained interest versus . . . **7**:1.03
Bootstrap sales . . . **7**:1.01
Lease
  Leveraged leasing . . . **7**:1.05
  Sale versus . . . **7**:1.04
Natural resource interests . . . **7**:1.02
Retained interest versus amount realized . . . **7**:1.03

REALIZATION OF GAIN OR LOSS
Generally . . . **1**:1; **1**:3.01
Abandonment . . . **1**:3.03(a)
Allowance . . . **1**:3.06
Casualties . . . **1**:3.03(a)
Claim, transfer in satisfaction of . . . **1**:3.03(b)
Debt inclusion in amount realized . . . **1**:3.05
Exchange or sale . . . **1**:3.02
Mortgaging property . . . **1**:3.03(c)
Part
  Gift, as . . . **1**:3.04
  Sale, as . . . **1**:3.04
Recognition . . . **1**:3.06
Sale or exchange . . . **1**:3.02
Transfer in satisfaction of claim . . . **1**:3.03(b)

RELATED PARTIES
Like-kind exchanges . . . **5**:1.08
Losses between . . . **8**:3

RESTRICTED PROPERTY
Generally . . . **6**:2
§ 83 . . . **6**:2.02
Shareholder grants . . . **6**:2.03
Stock Appreciation Rights . . . **6**:2.01

REVERSE *STARKER* EXCHANGES
Like-kind exchanges . . . **5**:1.05

S

SALE OR EXCHANGE
Business sale
  Overview . . . **1**:4.01
  Contingent payments and liabilities . . . **1**:4.03
  Liabilities, contingent payments and . . . **1**:4.03
  Residual allocation method, § 1060 and . . . **1**:4.02
  § 1060 and residual allocation method . . . **1**:4.02
Capital gains and losses (See CAPITAL GAINS AND LOSSES, subhead: Sale or exchange)
Like-kind exchanges (See LIKE-KIND EXCHANGES)
Part sale . . . **1**:3.04
Reality of (See REALITY OF SALE)
Realization of gain or loss . . . **1**:3.02
Securities, wash sales of . . . **8**:2
Wash sales of securities . . . **8**:2

[References are to **chapters**: sections, e.g., **2**:3.03(b).]

SARS (See STOCK APPRECIATION RIGHTS (SARs))

SIMILAR IN SERVICE OR USE
Involuntary conversion . . . **5**:2.02

SPLITS
Basis . . . **1**:2.07
Holding period . . . **2**:5.03

STOCK APPRECIATION RIGHTS (SARS)
Restricted property . . . **6**:2.01

STOCK OPTIONS (See EXECUTIVE COMPENSATION AND STOCK OPTIONS)

SUBSTITUTED BASIS
Generally . . . **1**:2.05
Tacking permitted . . . **2**:5.05(a)

T

TANGIBLE ASSETS
Capitalization . . . **4**:2.03

TANGIBLE ASSETS—Cont.
Cost recovery for (See COST RECOVERY)

TRADE NAMES
Generally . . . **7**:3.03(c)

TRADE OR BUSINESS
Capital asset
  Property . . . **2**:3.03(b)
  Supplies . . . **2**:3.03(h)
Election to expense certain business assets . . . **4**:3.03
Nonbusiness bad debts . . . **2**:4.04(a)
Property
  Capital asset . . . **2**:3.03(b)
  § 1231 (See subhead: § 1231)
Sale of business (See SALE OR EXCHANGE, subhead: Business sale)
§ 1231
  Generally . . . **2**:6.03; **2**:6.03(a)
  Inventory exclusion . . . **2**:6.03(b)
  Miscellaneous property under . . . **2**:6.03(c)
Supplies . . . **2**:3.03(h)